THE BROADVIEW ANTHOLOGY OF EXPOSITORY PROSE

A Note to Students

Included in the price of each new copy of *The Broadview Anthology of Expository Prose, Third Canadian Edition* is access to a companion website that features additional readings and interactive writing exercises.

A set of notes that go beyond the footnotes in the bound book is also provided on the anthology's companion website. These notes are designed to be of particular help to students who have limited familiarity with Canadian culture, and/or students who have learned English as an additional language—though the extra notes may offer support to any student. Words and phrases for which additional notes are provided on the website are marked with a small asterisk in these pages. The notes themselves may either be consulted online or be printed out and kept handy as you read.

A passcode to the companion site is provided with each new copy purchased; those who have purchased a used copy may obtain access through the Broadview website for a modest fee.

THE BROADVIEW ANTHOLOGY OF EXPOSITORY PROSE

Third Canadian Edition

Editors
Laura Buzzard
Don LePan
Nora Ruddock
Alexandria Stuart

broadview press

BROADVIEW PRESS – www.broadviewpress.com
Peterborough, Ontario, Canada

Founded in 1985, Broadview Press remains a wholly independent publishing house. Broadview's focus is on academic publishing; our titles are accessible to university and college students as well as scholars and general readers. With over 600 titles in print, Broadview has become a leading international publisher in the humanities, with world-wide distribution. Broadview is committed to environmentally responsible publishing and fair business practices.

Library and Archives Canada Cataloguing in Publication

The Broadview anthology of expository prose / editors, Laura Buzzard, Don LePan, Nora Ruddock, Alexandria Stuart. — Third Canadian edition.

Includes bibliographical references and index.
ISBN 978-1-55481-346-9 (softcover)

1. Essays. 2. Exposition (Rhetoric). 3. College readers.
I. LePan, Don, 1954-, editor II. Buzzard, Laura, editor
III. Ruddock, Nora, editor IV. Stuart, Alexandria, editor

PN6142.B76 2017 808.84 C2017-904194-0

Broadview Press handles its own distribution in North America
PO Box 1243, Peterborough, Ontario K9J 7H5, Canada
555 Riverwalk Parkway, Tonawanda, NY 14150, USA
Tel: (705) 743-8990; Fax: (705) 743-8353
email: customerservice@broadviewpress.com

Distribution is handled by Eurospan Group in the UK, Europe, Central Asia, Middle East, Africa, India, Southeast Asia, Central America, South America, and the Caribbean. Distribution is handled by Footprint Books in Australia and New Zealand.

Broadview Press acknowledges the financial support of
the Government of Canada
for our publishing activities.

Canada

Editorial Assistants: Laura-Lee Bowers, Emily Farrell, John Geddert, and Helena Snopek.
Design and typeset by Eileen Eckert.
Cover design by Lisa Brawn.

PRINTED IN CANADA

Contents

PREFACE

The first edition of this anthology had its origin in the space between books. For many years, the Broadview list had included two very different anthologies, both intended for use in first-year composition and literature courses. One was an anthology that brought together virtually every sort of nonfiction prose *except* scholarly writing; the other brought together an excellent selection of *purely* scholarly writing. Another attractive approach, it seemed to us, would be an anthology that combined a wide range of literary and non-academic essays with a good selection of scholarly writing.

Central to the idea of this anthology, then, was the inclusion of a substantial selection of academic writing. Very frequently, anthologies which make a stab at including academic writing end up selecting journalistic pieces that are written by academics, rather than truly scholarly writing. Granted, it is not easy to find examples of purely academic discourse that are at all accessible to a first- or second-year student who is unlikely to be familiar with the conventions of academic disciplines. But it is not impossible. One guideline we have followed in searching out such selections has been to look for academic pieces which have exerted considerable influence beyond their discipline. Selections such as those by Milgram on obedience and conformity, or Card and Krueger on the effect of raising the minimum wage, are examples of research that has been widely discussed and widely influential outside academia. Also included here are numerous pieces which, while they might not have reached the general public in any form, have been widely influential in their discipline.

A second central principle of the book is variety. At the heart of the anthology are a wide range of essays that attempt in one way or another to persuade the reader of something. But a variety of other modes of prose writing are also included. The reader will find personal essays, occasional pieces, speeches, letters, and humorous sketches. For the new edition a number of op-ed pieces have been added, as have been examples of blog posts, articles from online media, and book reviews. Also new for this edition are several pieces written in a lyric mode. Selections range from more than twenty pages in length to less than a single page; for this edition the number of short essays has been substantially increased.

There is variety in level of difficulty, in type of audience, and in subject matter as well. In some selections the writing is almost transparent in its simplicity; in others the reader may be challenged by complex syntax as well as by the inherent difficulty of the material. In many cases the intended audience is clearly the general reader, but some selections aim at a much narrower readership. And the anthology includes writing on an extraordinarily wide range of topics—though, as in any anthology, certain themes receive more emphasis than others. For this edition, in response to requests from a great many instructors, we have placed special emphasis on contemporary issues such as climate change, the lives of Aboriginal Canadians, and the rise of populism in Europe and the United States. In pursuing these themes, we have shifted the anthology's balance slightly in favour of the contemporary; while the anthology continues to offer classics such as "A Modest Proposal," "Politics and the English Language," and "Letter from Birmingham Jail," we now offer a substantially larger selection of articles from the past few years.

Most of the selections are of course written in English, but we have also included a handful of pieces that were first written in other languages, either because (as in the case of Montaigne) they have been extraordinarily influential in shaping the history of the essay, or because of the central position of their authors in shaping intellectual discourse (as in the cases of Barthes, Foucault, and Ai Weiwei).

One feature of previous editions that has been particularly well received has been the inclusion of paired articles; this edition includes an increased number of these. In some cases the pairings are of pieces that take opposing points of view on the same topic. In others, they are of similar material treated for different anticipated audiences, such as a scholarly paper and a newspaper op-ed piece presenting the same research in simplified form for lay readers. Finally, a number of the pairings involve essays that are in conversation with each other. Darryl Whetter's "The Kids Are Alright," for example, is a direct response to Ron Srigley's condemnation of Canadian universities in "Pass, Fail," while in "Is There a Moral Case for Meat?" Nathanel Johnson attempts to refute Peter Singer's famous argument against speciesism in *Animal Liberation*.

We have attempted in this volume's contents to feature a substantial proportion of material specifically relevant to Canadians, from important historical speeches by figures such as Sir Wilfrid Laurier and Tommy Douglas to essays on recent events in Canada, such as the fentanyl crisis in Vancouver's Downtown Eastside, the Truth and Reconciliation Commission, and the trial of Jian Ghomeshi. We have endeavoured to provide as well a rich sense of cultural and geographical diversity through the selections. A selection of the most celebrated Canadian writers of the modern era—from Anne Carson to Naomi Klein—appears alongside a diverse selection of non-Canadian writers, from bell hooks and David Foster Wallace to Nelson Mandela and Jacqueline Rose. We have also included almost twice as many women authors as appeared in the second Canadian edition, and more than three times the number of writers of colour as appeared in that edition.

With all these additions, the anthology has inevitably become larger. To some extent we have been able to balance the addition of many new selections by excisions. Many selections that instructors told us they were teaching only rarely, if at all, are gone from this edition. (Where copyright permissions costs have not been prohibitive, selections previously included in the bound book anthology may be found on the anthology's companion website.)

One issue in assembling almost any anthology is whether or not to excerpt. If the book is to be essentially an anthology of essays, does the integrity of the form demand that all essays selected for inclusion be included in their entirety? Should selections taken from full-length books be excluded on the grounds of their provenance? To both these questions we have answered in the negative. If an anthology such as this is to do the best possible job of presenting the widest possible range within a manageable compass, practical and pedagogical concerns seem to us to justify the occasional decision to excerpt a very long essay, or to select a discreet section from a full-length book. We have, however, included a considerable number of longer essays in their entirety.

Most essay anthologies designed for university use are arranged either by broad subject category ("nature," "science," and so on) or by rhetorical category ("descriptive essays," "persuasive essays," etc.). On the good advice of the majority of academics we consulted on this matter prior to the publication of the first edition, we decided instead to use a loosely chronological arrangement, in the interests both of simplicity and flexibility. In an anthology where the grouping is by subject or by rhetorical category, each essay must of necessity appear as part of only one grouping—whereas in reality, of course, many of the finest and most interesting essays will have more than one subject, many of the best persuasive essays also employ description or narration, and so on. The chronological approach allows the instructor to group the essays in whatever combinations seem most interesting or appropriate, and to change those groupings as desired each time a course is taught. (Tables of contents by subject category and rhetorical category—in both of which a given essay is quite likely to appear many times—appear following this preface.) A chronological organization is flexible in another respect too; it lends itself to use in courses on the history of the essay or on nonfiction prose as a genre as well as in courses on composition and rhetoric.

We have made improvements to the book's apparatus for the new edition. The headnotes for each selection have been substantially expanded with a view to providing contextual background for the student. As before, each selection is accompanied by discussion questions. Further questions can be found in the online instructor's guide, which has also been expanded to include classroom exercises that can aid in teaching some of the book's most popular selections. Biographical notes still appear at the back of the anthology, as they did in previous editions, and explanatory notes are still provided at the bottom of the page.

For this edition we have also provided a set of additional notes on the anthology's companion website—notes designed to be of particular help to EAL students and/or students who have little familiarity with Canadian culture. Phrases such as "X factor" or "tar and feather" require no glossing for the student who has just graduated from a high school in Red Deer or Halifax, but may seem obscure or confusing to a student who has recently arrived in Canada for the first time. And of course some students will always arrive at university with a larger vocabulary than others. These notes, then, offer additional support to any student who may wish to consult them. Words and phrases for which additional notes are provided are marked with a small asterisk in these pages. Students wishing to consult the notes may find them on the anthology's companion website; these additional notes may be read online or printed out and kept handy as the student reads the relevant selections.

We should say something, finally, about the book's title. There may be no satisfactory solution to naming a book of this sort. "Anthology of Prose" is obviously inappropriate, since prose fiction is excluded. "Anthology of Essays" becomes unsuitable once the decision has been made to include selections from longer works as well. "Anthology of Non-Fiction Prose" is clunky and would argue for the inclusion of a much wider variety of forms of non-fiction prose than are presented here (among them business memos, advertising copy, and car maintenance manuals); conversely, it would argue for the exclusion of pieces such as the "essays" in this collection by Daniel Heath Justice and Sherman Alexie, both of which hover on the border of fiction and non-fiction.

In the end we settled on "Anthology of Expository Prose." That too is a title that if taken narrowly might argue for the exclusion of certain of the selections in the anthology. Defined according to traditional rhetorical categories, expository writing is an umbrella category of writing that involves explanation. It has traditionally been taken to include writing engaged in comparison or contrast, definition, analysis, and persuasion or argument—but not to include purely descriptive or narrative forms of non-fiction prose. More broadly, though, "expository prose" has come to be frequently used nowadays as a short form for "non-fiction prose that aims to set something forth for a public readership." There are good grounds on which to base this more inclusive meaning; "exposition" may refer simply to "setting forth," and that is certainly what descriptive and even some narrative prose may fairly be said to do, quite as much as prose that attempts to argue or persuade sets something forth. (Though much argument attempts to explain, often the line between explanation and assertion is exceedingly thin—a good deal thinner in many cases than the line separating, say, description from explanation.) In any case, writing that falls within the traditional criteria of expository prose constitutes the overwhelming majority of the prose that appears of these pages; we beg the indulgence of the purist who would have it approach more nearly to one hundred percent.

• • •

Broadview Developmental Editor Nora Ruddock has been instrumental in putting together this volume, as has Editorial Assistant Alexandria Stuart. Assistant English Editor Tara Bodie did great work canvassing academics who had used the second edition to ask their advice, and we also received editorial assistance from several people on a freelance basis—notable among them Emily Farrell, Helena Snopek, John Geddert, and Laura-Lee Bowers. Catherine Nelson-McDermott of the University of British Columbia kindly allowed her discussion questions from a related Broadview anthology, *Science and Society*, to be repurposed for this book for the article "'Torture at Yale.'" As he has done for so many Broadview publications, Joe Davies did excellent work proofreading. Eileen Eckert is once again to be thanked for her superb work in book design and typesetting. Rights and Permissions Manager Merilee Atos did an excellent job of clearing copyright permissions on a tight schedule, and artist and cover designer Lisa Brawn has given a much brighter look to the book's cover.

The first edition of the anthology is now far in the past, but the contributions of those who helped to put together that volume deserve to be acknowledged; particularly helpful was the work of then-Broadview staff members Julia Gaunce, Mical Moser, Tammy Roberts, and Craig Lawson.

• • •

We would like to thank the following academics for the advice they have provided to us along the way: at California State University, East Bay, Alison Wariner; at Camosun College, Candace Fertile; at Dalhousie University, David McNeil; at Framingham State University, Emma Katherine Atwood; at George Washington University, Susan Willens; at Humber College, Lisa Salem-Wiseman; at Mount Royal University, Richard Harrison and Natalie Meisner; at The New School, Fiore Sireci; at New York University, Victoria Anderson, Lane Anderson, Taylor Black, Bruce Bromley, Katherine Carlson, Courtney Chatellier, Lorraine Doran, Alexandra Falek, Elisabeth Fay, Andrei Guruianu, Jonathan Hamrick, Michele Hanks, Robert Huddleston, Abigail Joseph, Amanda Kotch, Alexander Landfair, Denice Martone, David Markus, Victoria Olsen, Gerard O'Donoghue, Amira Pierce, Benjamin Pollak, Rebecca Porte, Jackie Reitzes, Dara Rossman Regaignon, Raymond Ricketts, Christopher Stahl, Benjamin Stewart, Emily Stone, Kirin Wachter-Grene, Justin Warner,

Laura Wellnert, Michelle Wilson, and Jenny Xie; at NorQuest College, Leigh Dyrda, Brooklin Schneider, and Dana Wight; at Okanagan University College, Kenneth Phillips; at Red Deer College, Heather Marcovitch; at San Francisco State University, Michael John Martin; at Simon Fraser University, Orion Ussner Kidder; at the University of Michigan, Randall Tessier; at the Université de Moncton, Laurie Cooper; at the University of British Columbia, Gisele M. Baxter and Suzanne James; at the University of Northern British Columbia, Linda MacKinley-Hay; at Vancouver Island University, Terri Doughty, Gwyneth Evans, Farah Moosa, Melissa Stephens, Craig Tapping, and Deborah Torkko; and at West Virginia University, Beth Staley.

• • •

We welcome the comments and suggestions of all readers—instructors or students—about any and all aspects of this book, from the selections themselves to the book's organization and ancillary material (both within these pages and on the companion website). Please feel free to email us at <broadview@broadviewpress.com>. We hope you will enjoy this book as it stands—but we never stop thinking of possible improvements for future editions.

Don LePan and Laura Buzzard

Contents by Subject

Aboriginal North Americans / Black Lives in North America / Canadian Politics / Childhood and Education / Colonization, Postcolonialism, and Global Politics / Communication and Language / Death and Dying / Nature and Climate Change / Gender / History, and Other Ways of Looking at the Past / The Human Psyche / Humans and Other Animals / The Law and the State / LGBTQ / Literature, Photography, and Other Arts / Love and Sex / Mental and Physical Health / Personal Ethics and the Good Life / Populism and Authoritarianism / Race(s) and Culture(s) / Science and Technology / Social Class and Economic Inequality / Sport / War and Peace / Work and Business

Note: Many selections deal with more than one of these subjects.

Aboriginal North Americans

Black Lives in North America

Canadian Politics

Childhood and Education

Colonization, Postcolonialism, and Global Politics

Communication and Language

Death and Dying

Nature and Climate Change

Note: See also "Humans and Other Animals" below.

Gender

History, and Other Ways of Looking at the Past

The Human Psyche

Humans and Other Animals

The Law and the State

LGBTQ

Literature, Photography, and Other Arts

Love and Sex

Mental and Physical Health

Personal Ethics and the Good Life

Populism and Authoritarianism

Race(s) and Culture(s)

Science and Technology

Social Class and Economic Inequality

Sport

War and Peace

Work and Business

Contents by Rhetorical Category and Medium

Academic Writing / Analysis / Cause and Effect / Classification / Comparison and Contrast / Definition / Description / Epistolary Writing / Humour and Satire / Journalism / Lyric and Other Creative Forms / Memoir and Personal Experience / Narration / Online Media / Persuasion and Argument / Speeches and Lectures

Note: Many selections occupy more than one of these categories.

Academic Writing

Analysis

Cause and Effect

Classification

Comparison and Contrast

Definition

Description

Epistolary Writing

Humour and Satire

Journalism

Lyric and Other Creative Forms

Memoir and Personal Experience

Narration

Online Media

Note: This section does not include numerous articles that were published in both print and online versions of newspapers or journals.

Persuasion and Argument

Speeches and Lectures

MICHEL DE MONTAIGNE

from ON CANNIBALS[1]

Michel de Montaigne, frequently credited with creating the modern essay, was the first to use the word "essai" (meaning "attempt" in French) in its modern sense, applying the term to his efforts to arrive through writing at a deeper understanding of himself and of the world. The attempts were often repeated; Montaigne published three different versions of the following piece on the inhabitants of the "new world."

Though Montaigne does not name them, and we can expect his second-hand account of them to be distorted, the group on which he based his descriptions was in all probability the Tupinambás, inhabitants of an island off the northeastern coast of Brazil. By 1580 (when the first version of Montaigne's essay appeared), their society had already been described in several works—perhaps most notably an account by the German explorer Hans Staden, who had spent several years as a captive of the Tupinambás in the 1550s.

... For a long time I had with me a man who had lived ten or twelve years in that other world which was discovered in our century, in the place where Villegaignon[2] landed, which he called Antarctic France. This discovery of [such an] enormous country seems [to merit] serious consideration. I do not know if I can affirm that another such discovery will not occur in the future, given that so many people more important than we have been wrong about this one. I fear that our eyes are larger than our stomachs, that we have more curiosity than comprehension. We embrace everything, yet catch nothing but wind....

Modern navigators have almost certainly already established that the new world is not an island but a mainland, connected on one side with the East Indies and on the other with the lands under the two poles. Or else, if it is

---

1 *On Cannibals* This translation, prepared for Broadview Press by Ian Johnston of Vancouver Island University, is based upon the final (1595) version of the essay. Montaigne's frequent quotations in Latin have also been translated into English.

2 *Villegaignon* In 1555 Nicolas Durand Villegaignon landed in the Bay of Rio de Janeiro, Brazil, and set up a French colony on a nearby island.

divided off from them, what separates it a narrow strait, a distance that does not entitle it to be called an island....

The man I had [with me] was a plain, rough fellow, the sort likely to provide a true account. For intelligent people notice more and are much more curious, but they [also] provide their own gloss* on things and, to strengthen their own interpretation and make it persuasive, they cannot help changing their story a little. They never give you a pure picture of things, but bend and disguise them to fit the view they had of them. To lend credit to their judgment and attract you to it, they willingly add to the material, stretching it out and amplifying it. We need either a very honest man or one so simple that he lacks what it takes to build up inventive falsehoods and make them plausible, someone not wedded to anything. My man was like that, and, in addition, at various times he brought some sailors and merchants he had known on that voyage to see me. Thus, I am happy with [his] information, without enquiring into what the cosmographers* [may] say about it....

Now, to return to my subject, I find, from what I have been told about these people, that there is nothing barbarous and savage about them, except that everyone calls things which he does not practice himself barbaric. For, in fact, we have no test of truth and of reason other than examples and ideas of the opinions and habits in the country where we live. There we always have the perfect religion, the perfect political arrangements, the perfect and [most] accomplished ways of dealing with everything. Those [natives] are wild in the same way we call wild the fruits which nature has produced on her own in her normal manner; whereas, in fact, the ones we should really call wild are those we have altered artificially and whose ordinary behaviour we have modified. The former contain vital and vigorous virtues and properties, genuinely beneficial and natural, [qualities] which we have bastardized in the latter, by adapting them to gratify our corrupt taste....

5 These nations therefore seem to me barbarous in the sense that they have received very little molding from the human mind and are still very close to their original naive condition. Natural laws* still govern them, hardly corrupted at all by our own. They live in such purity that I sometimes regret we did not learn about them earlier, at a time when there were men more capable of assessing them than we are. I am sad that Lycurgus[3] and Plato* did not know them. For it seems to me that what our experience enables us to see in those nations there surpasses not only all the pictures with which poetry has embellished the Golden Age,* as well as all its inventiveness in portraying a happy human condition, but also the conceptions and even the desires of

---

3 *Lycurgus* Political thinker who, according to legend, established the laws of Sparta in the eighth century BCE. It is not known whether he actually existed.

philosophy. They have scarcely imagined such a pure and simple innocence as the one our experience reveals to us, and they would hardly have believed that our society could survive with so little artifice and social bonding among people. It is a nation, I would tell Plato, in which there is no form of commerce, no knowledge of letters, no science of numbers, no name for magistrate or political superior, no customs of servitude, no wealth or poverty, no contracts, no inheritance, no division [of property], no occupations, other than leisure ones, no respect for family kinship, except for common ties, no clothing, no agriculture, no metal, no use of wine or wheat. The very words which signify lying, treason, dissimulation, avarice, envy, slander, and forgiveness are unknown. How distant from this perfection would [Plato] find the republic he imagined—"men freshly come from the gods."[4]

These are the habits nature first ordained.[5]

As for the rest, they live in a very pleasant and temperate country, so that, according to what my witnesses have told me, it is rare to see a sick person there. They have assured me that in this land one does not notice any [of the inhabitants] doddering, with rheumy eyes, toothless, or bowed down with old age. They have settled along the sea [coast], closed off on the landward side by large, high mountains, with a stretch of territory about one hundred leagues wide in between. They have a great abundance of fish and meat, which has no resemblances to ours and which they simply cook and eat, without any other preparation. The first man who rode a horse there, although he had had dealings with them on several other voyages, so horrified them by his [riding] posture, that they killed him with arrows before they could recognize him....

They spend the entire day dancing. Younger men go off to hunt [wild] animals with bows. Meanwhile, some of the women keep busy warming the drinks, which is their main responsibility. In the morning, before they begin their meal, one of the old men preaches to everyone in the whole barn, walking from one end to the other and repeating the same sentence several times until he has completed his tour of the building, which is easily one hundred paces long. He recommends only two things to them: courage against their enemies and affection for their wives. And [these old men] never fail to mention this obligation, [adding] as a refrain that their wives are the ones who keep their drinks warm and seasoned for them.

In several places, including my own home, there are examples of their beds, their ropes, their swords, their wooden bracelets, which they use to cover their wrists in combat, and their large canes open at one end, with whose sound they keep time in their dances. They are close shaven all over, and remove the

4 *"men freshly ... the gods"* From Seneca, *Letters* 90.
5 *These are ... first ordained* From Virgil, *Georgics* 2.20.

hair much more cleanly than we do, using only wood or stone as a razor. They believe that the soul is immortal and that those who have deserved well of the gods are lodged in that part of the sky where the sun rises, [while] the damned [are] in regions to the west.

They have some sort of priests or prophets, who appear before the people relatively seldom, for they live in the mountains. When they arrive, there is a grand celebration and a solemn assembly of several villages (each barn, as I have described it, makes up a village, and the distance between them is approximately one French league[6]). This prophet speaks to them in public, urging them to be virtuous and to do their duty. But their entire ethical knowledge contains only the two following articles, courage in warfare and affection for their wives. He prophesies to them about things to come and about the results they should expect from their endeavours and encourages them to go to war or to refrain from it. But [he does this] on the condition, that he must prophesy correctly, and if what happens to them is different from what he has predicted, he is cut up into a thousand pieces, if they catch him, and condemned as a false prophet. For this reason, a prophet who has been wrong once is never seen again.

Divination is a gift of God. For that reason, abusing it should be punished as fraud. Among the Scythians,[7] when the divines failed with their [predictions], they were chained by their hands and feet, laid out on carts full of kindling and pulled by oxen, and burned there. Those who deal with matters in which the outcome depends on what human beings are capable of may be excused if they do their best. But surely the others, [those] who come to us with deluding assurances of an extraordinary faculty beyond our understanding, should be punished for not keeping their promises and for the recklessness of their deceit.

These [natives] have wars with the nations living on the other side of their mountains, further inland. They go out [against] them completely naked with no weapons except bows or wooden swords with a point at one end, like the tips of our hunting spears. What is astonishing is their resolution in combat, which never ends except in slaughter and bloodshed, for they have no idea of terror or flight. Each man brings back as a trophy the head of the enemy he has killed and attaches it to the entrance of his dwelling. After treating their prisoners well for a long time with every consideration they can possibly think of, the man who has a prisoner summons a grand meeting of his acquaintances. He ties a rope to one of the prisoner's arms and holds him there, gripping the other end, some paces away for fear of being injured, and he gives his dearest friend

6 *French league* Unit of measurement equal to approximately 3 miles.

7 *Scythians* Nomadic people who flourished in parts of Eastern Europe and Central Asia in the first millennium BCE.

the prisoner's other arm to hold in the same way. [Then] the two of them, in the presence of the entire assembly, stab the prisoner to death with their swords. After that, they roast him. [Then] they all eat him together and send portions to their absent friends. They do this not, as people think, to nourish themselves, the way the Scythians did in ancient times, but as an act manifesting extreme vengeance. We see evidence for this from the following: having noticed that the Portuguese, who were allied with their enemies, used a different method of killing them when they took them prisoner—which was to bury them up to the waist, shoot the rest of their body full of arrows, and then hang them—they thought that this people who had come there from another world (and who had already spread the knowledge of many vicious practices throughout the neighbouring region and were much greater masters of all sorts of evil than they were) did not select this sort of vengeance for no reason and that therefore [this method] must be harsher than their own. And so they began to abandon their old practice and to follow this one.

I am not so much concerned that we call attention to the barbarous horror of this action as I am that, in judging their faults correctly, we should be so blind to our own. I believe that there is more barbarity in eating a man when he is alive than in eating him when he is dead, more in tearing apart by tortures and the rack a body still full of feeling, roasting it piece by piece, having it mauled and eaten by dogs and pigs (things I have not only read about but witnessed a short time ago, not among ancient enemies but among neighbours and fellow citizens, and, what is worse, under the pretext of piety and religion*) than there is in roasting and eating a man once he has died….

Thus, we can indeed call these [natives] barbarians, as far as the laws of reason are concerned, but not in comparison with ourselves, who surpass them in barbarity of every kind. Their warfare is entirely noble and generous, as excusable and beautiful as this human malady can possibly be. With them it is based only on one thing, a jealous rivalry in courage. They do not argue about conquering new lands, for they still enjoy that natural fecundity which furnishes them without toil and trouble everything necessary and in such abundance that they do not need to expand their borders. They are still at that fortunate stage where they do not desire anything more than their natural demands prescribe. Everything over and above that is for them superfluous.

Those among them of the same age generally call each other brothers, those who are younger they call children, and the old men are fathers to all the others. These leave the full possession of their goods undivided to their heirs in common, without [any] other title, except the completely simple one which nature gives to [all] her creatures by bringing them into the world.

If their neighbours cross the mountains to attack them and defeat them in battle, what the victors acquire is glory and the advantage of having proved themselves more courageous and valiant. For they have no further interest in the possessions of the conquered. They return to their [own] country, where they have no lack of anything they need, just as they do not lack that great benefit of knowing how to enjoy their condition in happiness and how to remain content with it. And [the natives we are talking about], when their turn comes, do the same. They demand no ransom of their prisoners, other than a confession and a recognition that they have been beaten. But in an entire century there has not been one [prisoner] who did not prefer to die [rather] than to yield, either by his expression or by his words, a single bit of the grandeur of [his] invincible courage. Not one of them has been observed who did not prefer to be killed and eaten than merely to ask that he be spared....

Truly we have here really savage men in comparison to us. For that is what they must be beyond all doubt—either that, or we must be, [for] there is an amazing distance between their ways and ours.

The men there have several wives, and the higher their reputation for valour the greater the number. In their marriages there is something remarkably beautiful: with our wives jealousy deprives us of the friendship and kindness of other women, [but with them] a very similar jealousy leads their wives to acquire these relationships [for their men]. Since they care more for the honour of their husbands than for anything else, they go to great lengths to seek out and obtain as many companions [for them] as they can, since that is a testimony to their husbands' merit.

Our wives will cry out that this is a miracle. It is not. It is a proper marital virtue, but of the highest order. In the Bible, Leah, Rachel, Sarah, and Jacob's wives gave their beautiful servants to their husbands.[8] ...

And so that people do not think that they do all this out of a simple and servile duty to habit and under pressure from the authority of their ancient customs, without reflection and judgment, because they have such stupid souls that they cannot choose any other way, I must cite some features of their capabilities. Apart from what I have just recited from one of their warrior songs, I have another, a love song which begins as follows: "Adder, stay, stay, adder, so that from the coloured markings on your skin my sister may take down the style and workmanship for a rich belt which I can give the woman I love—and in this way your beauty and your patterning will be preferred forever above all other snakes." This first couplet is the refrain of the song. Now, I am sufficiently familiar with poetry to judge this one: not only is there nothing barbaric in the imagination

8 *Leah, Rachel ... their husbands* Cf. Genesis 30. Jacob had children with his wives Rachel and Leah, as well as with their slaves Bilhah and Zilpah. Sarah, Abraham's wife, was unable to conceive children, and offered her servant to Abraham as a surrogate.

here, but it captures the spirit of Anacreon[9] throughout. Their language, too, is soft, with a pleasing sound, not unlike Greek in its word endings.

Three of these men, not knowing how much it will cost them one day in a loss of repose and happiness to learn about the corruptions among us and how interacting [with us] will lead to their ruin, which I assume is already well advanced (poor miserable creatures to let themselves be seduced by the desire for novelty and to have left the softness of their sky to come and see ours) were at Rouen when the late King Charles IX was there.[10] The king talked to them for a long time. They were shown our way of life, our splendour, and the layout of a beautiful city. After that, someone asked them their opinion, wishing to learn from them what they had found most astonishing. They answered that there were three things. I regret to say that I have forgotten the third, but I still remember two. They said, first of all, that they found it very strange that so many large, strong men with beards and weapons, who were around the king (they were probably talking about the Swiss soldiers in his guard) would agree to obey a child and that one of them was not chosen to command instead; and secondly (in their language they have a way of speaking of men as halves of one another) that they had noticed there were among us men completely gorged with all sorts of commodities while their other halves were beggars at their doors, emaciated by hunger and poverty. They found it strange that these needy halves could tolerate such an injustice and did not seize the others by the throat or set fire to their dwellings.

(1580, revised 1595)

Questions

1. What does Montaigne suggest is "wild" and what "barbaric"?
2. Why does Montaigne think that the man he knew who had lived in "Antarctic France" (Brazil) was a reliable witness? Does his information about the people in Brazil seem to you to be reliable?
3. How does Montaigne view nature? How does that view influence his opinion about "barbarians"?
4. Is the structure of the essay effective? Why or why not?

---

9 *Anacreon* Greek poet (c. 572–c. 488 BCE) known for his love lyrics.

10 *Three of ... was there* About fifty native Brazilians were brought to Rouen in 1550, and some were presented to King Charles IX of France (then twelve years old) when he visited Rouen in 1562.

5. How would you characterize the tone of the essay? How does it shape your thoughts about the writer?
6. What seems worse to Montaigne than cannibalism? Why?
7. To what extent (if any) is this article prejudiced? To what extent (if any) does it oppose prejudice?

Margaret Cavendish

from Sociable Letters [On Social Class and Happiness]

A prolific writer who flouted seventeenth-century English gender roles by publishing under her own name, Margaret Cavendish wrote in a remarkable range of forms including scientific treatises, drama, poetry, and prose fiction. In Sociable Letters, *Cavendish turns to the epistolary form to address a similarly diverse array of subjects, from marriage and medical science to politics and literary criticism. In her preface to the volume, Cavendish writes that she has "endeavoured under the cover of letters to express the humours of mankind ... by the correspondence of two ladies, living at some short distance from each other, which make it not only their chief delight and pastime, but their tie in friendship, to discourse by letters, as they would do if they were personally together." The following is one of those letters.*

Madam,

You were pleased in your last letter to tell me, that you had been in the country, and that you did almost envy the peasants for living so merrily; it is a sign, Madam, they live happily, for mirth seldom dwells with troubles and discontents, neither doth riches nor grandeur live so easily, as that unconcerned freedom that is in low and mean[1] fortunes and persons, for the ceremony of grandeur is constrained and bound with forms and rules, and a great estate and high fortune is not so easily managed as a less, a little is easily ordered,[2] where much doth require time, care, wisdom and study as considerations; but poor, mean peasants that live by their labour, are for the most part happier and pleasanter than great rich persons, that live in luxury and idleness, for idle time is tedious, and luxury is unwholesome, whereas labour is healthful and recreative, and surely country housewives take more pleasure in milking their cows,

1 *mean* Poor.

2 *ordered* Put into order.

making their butter and cheese, and feeding their poultry, than great ladies do in painting, curling, and adorning themselves, also they have more quiet and peaceable minds and thoughts, for they never, or seldom, look in a glass to view their faces, they regard not their complexions, nor observe their decays, they defy time's ruins of their beauties, they are not peevish and froward if they look not as well one day as another, a pimple or spot in their skin tortures not their minds, they fear not the sun's heat, but out-face the sun's power, they break not their sleeps to think of fashions, but work hard to sleep soundly, they lie not in sweats to clear their complexions, but rise to sweat to get them food, their appetites are not queasy with surfeits, but sharpened with fasting, they relish with more savour their ordinary coarse fare, than those who are pampered do their delicious rarities; and for their mirth and pastimes, they take more delight and true pleasure, and are more inwardly pleased and outwardly merry at their wakes,[3] than the great ladies at their balls, and though they dance not with such art and measure, yet they dance with more pleasure and delight, they cast not envious, spiteful eyes at each other, but meet friendly and lovingly. But great ladies at public meetings take not such true pleasures, for their envy at each other's beauty and bravery disturbs their pastimes; and obstructs their mirth, they rather grow peevish and froward through envy, than loving and kind through society, so that whereas the country peasants meet with such kind hearts and unconcerned freedom as they unite in friendly jollity, and depart with neighbourly love, the greater sort of persons meet with constrained ceremony, converse with formality, and for the most part depart with enmity; and this is not only amongst women, but amongst men, for there is amongst the better sort a greater strife[4] for bravery than for courtesy, for place[5] than friendship, and in their societies there is more vainglory than pleasure, more pride than mirth, and more vanity than true content; yet in one thing the better sort of men, as the nobles and gentry, are to be commended, which is, that though they are oftener drunken and more debauched than peasants, having more means to maintain their debaucheries, yet at such times as at great assemblies, they keep themselves more sober and temperate than peasants do, which are for the most part drunk at their departing; but to judge between the peasantry and nobles for happiness, I believe where there's one noble that is truly happy, there are a hundred peasants; not that there be more peasants than nobles, but that they are more happy, number for number, as having not the envy, ambition, pride, vainglory, to cross, trouble, [and] vex them, as nobles have; when I say nobles, I mean those that have been ennobled by time as well as title, as the gentry.

3 *wakes* Traditional English festivals thrown in celebration of a church's patron saint.

4 *strife* Striving.

5 *place* Social position.

But, Madam, I am not a fit judge for the several sorts or degrees, or courses of lives, or actions of mankind, as to judge which is happiest, for happiness lives not in outward show or concourse, but inwardly in the mind, and the minds of men are too obscure to be known, and too various and inconstant to fix a belief in them, and since we cannot know ourselves, how should we know others? Besides, pleasure and true delight lives in everyone's own delectation; but let me tell you, my delectation is, to prove myself,

Madam,

Your Faithful Fr. and S.
I, M.N. (1664)

Questions

1. Looked at from one angle, this letter might be seen as an essay on wealth and privilege being no guarantee of happiness—but from another angle it is possible to see Cavendish's arguments as providing a rationalization for the continuance of injustice. Form an argument supporting one or the other of these two approaches to Cavendish's letter.
2. It was common when Cavendish wrote to use expressions such as "the greater sort of persons" and "the better sort" to refer to the nobility, contrasted with the "lower orders." Comment on this hierarchy as expressed in language, and on the implications of the terms we use nowadays with which to discuss social class (middle class, working class, etc.).
3. Comment on the way in which Cavendish structures her sentences.
4. Write a short essay about the way in which you perceive the relationship between wealth and happiness.

SAMUEL JOHNSON

THE RAMBLER NO. 114 [ON CAPITAL PUNISHMENT]

Samuel Johnson is considered one of the most distinguished English prose writers. His remarkably prolific body of work includes moral essays, biographies, satires, criticism, letters, a diary, and his famous and influential Dictionary of the English Language. *While compiling his Dictionary, Johnson took breaks to write two weekly essays for* The Rambler *(1750–52), a periodical in which he discussed literature, politics, and social issues. While most periodicals of the period aimed to be witty and accessible in tone,* The Rambler *displays a more elevated style.*

The following example from The Rambler *examines capital punishment. It was written at a time when the number of capital crimes in English law was increasing rapidly. In 1688 there were 50 crimes that could incur the death penalty under English law; by 1765 there were more than three times that many. It became a capital offence not only to commit murder or treason but also to shoplift, to cut down trees in a garden, or to pickpocket more than a shilling. However, not everyone who committed such crimes was killed. Judges and juries were reluctant to convict minor criminals of capital crimes—even when they were obviously guilty—and many of those who were sentenced to death received royal pardons before the sentence was carried out.*

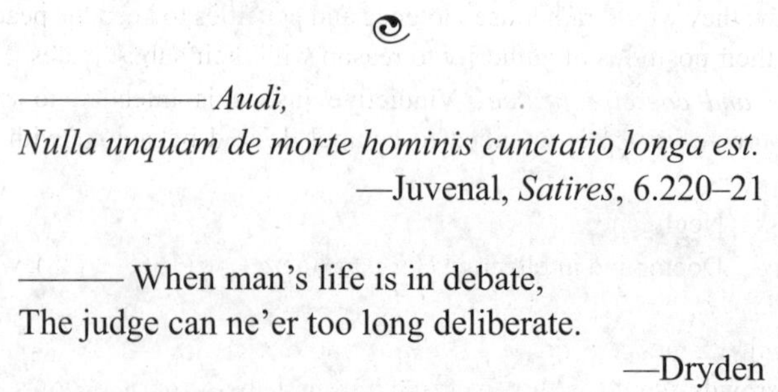

————— *Audi,*
Nulla unquam de morte hominis cunctatio longa est.
—Juvenal, *Satires*, 6.220–21

——— When man's life is in debate,
The judge can ne'er too long deliberate.
—Dryden

Power and superiority are so flattering and delightful that, fraught with temptation and exposed to danger as they are, scarcely any virtue is so cautious, or any prudence so timorous, as to decline them.* Even those that have most reverence for the laws of right are pleased with showing that not fear, but choice, regulates their behaviour; and would be thought to comply, rather than obey.* We love to overlook the boundaries which we do not wish to pass; and, as the Roman satirist[1] remarks, he that has no design to take the life of another, is yet glad to have it in his hands.

From the same principle, tending yet more to degeneracy and corruption, proceeds the desire of investing lawful authority with terror, and governing by force rather than persuasion. Pride is unwilling to believe the necessity of assigning any other reason than her own will, and would rather maintain the most equitable claims by violence and penalties than descend from the dignity of command to dispute and expostulation.[2]

It may, I think, be suspected that this political arrogance has sometimes found its way into legislative assemblies and mingled with deliberations upon property and life. A slight perusal of the laws by which the measures of vindictive and coercive justice[3] are established will discover so many disproportions between crimes and punishments, such capricious distinctions of guilt, and such confusion of remissness[4] and severity, as can scarcely be believed to have been produced by public wisdom, sincerely and calmly studious of public happiness.

The learned, the judicious, the pious Boerhaave[5] relates that he never saw a criminal dragged to execution without asking himself, "Who knows whether this man is not less culpable than me?" On the days when the prisons of this city are emptied into the grave,[6] let every spectator of the dreadful procession put the same question to his own heart. Few among those that crowd

1 *Roman satirist* Juvenal, in his *Satires* 10.96–97.

2 *Pride ... expostulation* The pride of those in authority leads them to give no justification for the punishment of a given crime beyond the fact that it is the punishment assigned by law; they would rather use violence and penalties to keep the peace rather than descend from their positions of authority to reason with their subordinates.

3 *vindictive and coercive justice* Vindictive justice is intended to exact revenge for crimes; coercive justice is intended to compel desired behaviour with the threat of punishment.

4 *remissness* Negligence.

5 *Boerhaave* Doctor and intellectual Herman Boerhaave (1668–1738), whom Johnson greatly admired.

6 *On the days ... into the grave* Days of public execution in London were treated as holidays; crowds would gather in stands around the Tyburn gallows to watch the executions.

in thousands to the legal massacre and look with carelessness, perhaps with triumph, on the utmost exacerbations of human misery, would then be able to return without horror and dejection. For who can congratulate himself upon a life passed without some act more mischievous to the peace or prosperity of others than the theft of a piece of money?[7]

It has been always the practice, when any particular species of robbery becomes prevalent and common, to endeavour its suppression by capital denunciations.[8] Thus, one generation of malefactors[9] is commonly cut off, and their successors are frighted into new expedients;[10] the art of thievery is augmented with greater variety of fraud, and subtilized to higher degrees of dexterity and more occult methods of conveyance.[11] The law then renews the pursuit in the heat of anger, and overtakes the offender again with death. By this practice, capital inflictions are multiplied, and crimes very different in their degrees of enormity are equally subjected to the severest punishment that man has the power of exercising upon man.

The lawgiver is undoubtedly allowed to estimate the malignity[12] of an offence not merely by the loss or pain which single acts may produce, but by the general alarm and anxiety arising from the fear of mischief and insecurity of possession. He therefore exercises the right which societies are supposed to have over the lives of those that compose them, not simply to punish a transgression, but to maintain order and preserve quiet; he enforces those laws with severity that are most in danger of violation, as the commander of a garrison[13] doubles the guard on that side which is threatened by the enemy.

This method has been long tried, but tried with so little success that rapine[14] and violence are hourly increasing. Yet few seem willing to despair of its efficacy, and of those who employ their speculations upon the present corruption of the people, some propose the introduction of more horrid, lingering and terrific[15] punishments;* some are inclined to accelerate the executions; some to discourage pardons; and all seem to think that lenity[16] has given confidence

---

7 *The learned ... of money* Cf. John 8.7, when Christ says to those gathered to stone a woman for adultery: "He that is without sin among you, let him first cast a stone at her."

8 *by capital denunciations* I.e., by trying criminals for capital offenses.

9 *malefactors* Criminals.

10 *expedients* Ways (here, of thieving).

11 *occult* Secret; *conveyance* Stealing.

12 *malignity* Evil nature.

13 *garrison* Fortress.

14 *rapine* Plunder.

15 *terrific* Terrifying.

16 *lenity* Mercifulness.

to wickedness, and that we can only be rescued from the talons of robbery by inflexible rigour and sanguinary[17] justice.

Yet since the right of setting an uncertain and arbitrary value upon life has been disputed,* and since experience of past times gives us little reason to hope that any reformation will be effected by a periodical havoc[18] of our fellow beings, perhaps it will not be useless to consider what consequences might arise from relaxations of the law and a more rational and equitable adaptation of penalties to offences.*

Death is, as one of the ancients observes, *τὸ τ ν φοβερ ν φοβερώτατον*, "of dreadful things the most dreadful";[19] an evil beyond which nothing can be threatened by sublunary[20] power, or feared from human enmity or vengeance. This terror should, therefore, be reserved as the last resort of authority, as the strongest and most operative of prohibitory sanctions, and placed before the treasure of life, to guard from invasion what cannot be restored.* To equal robbery with murder is to reduce murder to robbery, to confound in common minds the gradations of iniquity, and incite the commission of a greater crime to prevent the detection of a less.* If only murder were punished with death, very few robbers would stain their hands in blood; but when by the last act of cruelty no new danger is incurred, and greater security may be obtained, upon what principle shall we bid them forbear?*

It may be urged that the sentence is often mitigated to simple robbery;[21] but surely this is to confess that our laws are unreasonable in our own opinion; and, indeed, it may be observed that all but murderers have, at their last hour, the common sensations[22] of mankind pleading in their favour.

From this conviction of the inequality of the punishment to the offence* proceeds the frequent solicitation of pardons.[23] They who would rejoice at the correction of a thief are yet shocked at the thought of destroying him. His crime shrinks to nothing, compared with his misery; and severity defeats itself by exciting pity.

---

17 *sanguinary* Bloody.

18 *havoc* Devastation.

19 *of dreadful ... dreadful* The quotation is from Aristotle, *Nicomachean Ethics* 3.

20 *sublunary* Earthly, or human, power (as opposed to spiritual power).

21 *simple robbery* I.e., petty larceny. Grand larceny (theft of anything with a value over one shilling) was punishable by death, while petty larceny (under one shilling) incurred lesser punishments; judges often deliberately underestimated the cost of stolen goods for this reason.

22 *common sensations* Common feelings.

23 *pardons* Government decisions to free people from their convictions (as though the convictions had never happened).

The gibbet,[24] indeed, certainly disables those who die upon it from infesting the community; but their death seems not to contribute more to the reformation of their associates than any other method of separation.* A thief seldom passes much of his time in recollection or anticipation, but from robbery hastens to riot, and from riot to robbery; nor, when the grave closes upon his companion, has any other care than to find another.

The frequency of capital punishments therefore rarely hinders the commission of a crime, but naturally and commonly prevents its detection, and is, if we proceed only upon prudential principles, chiefly for that reason to be avoided. Whatever may be urged by casuists[25] or politicians, the greater part of mankind, as they can never think that to pick the pocket and to pierce the heart is equally criminal, will scarcely believe that two malefactors so different in guilt can be justly doomed to the same punishment; nor is the necessity of submitting the conscience to human laws so plainly evinced, so clearly stated, or so generally allowed, but that the pious, the tender, and the just, will always scruple to concur with the community in an act which their private judgment cannot approve.*

He who knows not how often rigorous laws produce total impunity, and how many crimes are concealed and forgotten for fear of hurrying the offender to that state in which there is no repentance, has conversed very little with mankind.* And whatever epithets of reproach or contempt this compassion may incur from those who confound cruelty with firmness, I know not whether any wise man would wish it less powerful, or less extensive.

If those whom the wisdom of our laws has condemned to die had been detected in their rudiments[26] of robbery, they might by proper discipline and useful labour have been disentangled from their habits; they might have escaped all the temptations to subsequent crimes, and passed their days in reparation and penitence; and detected they might all have been, had the prosecutors been certain that their lives would have been spared. I believe every thief will confess that he has been more than once seized and dismissed; and that he has sometimes ventured upon capital crimes because he knew that those whom he injured would rather connive at his escape than cloud their minds with the horrors of his death.

All laws against wickedness are ineffectual unless some will inform, and some will prosecute; but till we mitigate the penalties for mere violations of property, information will always be hated, and prosecution dreaded.* The heart of a good man cannot but recoil at the thought of punishing a slight

24 *gibbet* Gallows. Hanging was the most common method of execution.

25 *casuists* People who reason cleverly but misleadingly.

26 *rudiments* Beginnings.

injury with death; especially when he remembers that the thief might have procured safety by another crime,[27] from which he was restrained only by his remaining virtue.

The obligations to assist the exercise of public justice are indeed strong; but they will certainly be overpowered by tenderness for life. What is punished with severity contrary to our ideas of adequate retribution will be seldom discovered;[28] and multitudes will be suffered to advance from crime to crime till they deserve death, because if they had been sooner prosecuted, they would have suffered death before they deserved it.

This scheme of invigorating the laws by relaxation, and extirpating[29] wickedness by lenity, is so remote from common practice that I might reasonably fear to expose it to the public, could it be supported only by my own observations: I shall, therefore, by ascribing it to its author, Sir Thomas More,[30] endeavour to procure it that attention which I wish always paid to prudence, to justice, and to mercy.

(1751)

Questions

1. What does Johnson say about power and people in powerful positions? Why (according to Johnson) do they tend to support an unyielding and harsh justice system?
2. What does Johnson report was the dominant response to the increase in robberies experienced in London? What does Johnson suggest should be society's response to an increase in crime? Could any of Johnson's arguments apply to aspects of Canada's criminal justice system today? Explain.
3. While Johnson's arguments don't extend to questioning the justice of capital punishment for cases of murder, can a modern reader look to them for support in arguing against capital punishment? Why or why not?

---

27 *another crime* I.e. murder.

28 *discovered* Revealed.

29 *extirpating* Eliminating.

30 *Sir Thomas More* In the fictional society of More's *Utopia* (1516), capital punishment is used in very few circumstances.

Jonathan Swift

A Modest Proposal

For Preventing the Children of Poor People in Ireland from Being a Burden to Their Parents or the Country, and for Making Them Beneficial to the Public

The Penal Laws in early eighteenth-century Ireland excluded most Irish people from land ownership and political power; land was for the most part owned by English landlords and farmed by Irish peasants. Much of the resulting produce and meat was shipped to England, leaving the Irish impoverished and hungry. In the following essay (first published anonymously, as a pamphlet), Swift offered a solution to Ireland's economic crisis—a solution at once "innocent, cheap, easy, and effectual."

"A Modest Proposal" is the last of a series of passionate writings Swift produced on Irish affairs. It remains the most widely reprinted essay in the English language.

It is a melancholy object to those who walk through this great town,[1] or travel in the country, when they see the streets, the roads, and cabin doors crowded with beggars of the female sex, followed by three, four, or six children, all in rags and importuning every passenger[2] for an alms. These mothers, instead of being able to work for their honest livelihood, are forced to employ all their time in strolling[3] to beg sustenance for their helpless infants, who, as they grow up, either turn thieves for want of work, or leave their dear native country to fight for the Pretender in Spain, or sell themselves to the Barbados.[4]

1 *this great town* I.e., Dublin.

2 *passenger* Passerby.

3 *strolling* Wandering, roving.

4 *the Pretender* James Francis Edward Stuart, son of James II who was deposed from the throne in the Glorious Revolution due to his overt Catholicism. Catholic Ireland was loyal

I think it is agreed by all parties that this prodigious number of children in the arms, or on the backs, or at the heels of their mothers, and frequently of their fathers, is, in the present deplorable state of the kingdom, a very great additional grievance; and therefore, whoever could find out a fair, cheap, and easy method of making these children sound and useful members of the commonwealth would deserve so well of the public as to have his statue set up for a preserver of the nation.

But my intention is very far from being confined to provide only for the children of professed beggars; it is of a much greater extent, and shall take in the whole number of infants at a certain age who are born of parents in effect as little able to support them as those who demand our charity in the streets.

As to my own part, having turned my thoughts for many years upon this important subject and maturely weighed the several schemes of other projectors,[5] I have always found them grossly mistaken in their computation. 'Tis true, a child just dropped from its dam* may be supported by her milk for a solar year with little other nourishment, at most not above the value of two shillings, which the mother may certainly get, or the value in scraps, by her lawful occupation of begging; and it is exactly at one year old that I propose to provide for them in such a manner as, instead of being a charge upon their parents or the parish, or wanting food and raiment for the rest of their lives, they shall on the contrary contribute to the feeding, and partly to the clothing, of many thousands.

There is likewise another great advantage in my scheme, that it will pre- 5
vent those abortions, and that horrid practice of women murdering their bastard children, alas, too frequent among us, sacrificing the poor innocent babes, I doubt,[6] more to avoid the expense than the shame, which would move tears and pity in the most savage and inhuman breast.

The number of souls in this kingdom being usually reckoned one million and a half, of these I calculate there may be about two hundred thousand couple whose wives are breeders, from which number I subtract thirty thousand couples who are able to maintain children, although I apprehend there cannot be as many under the present distresses of the kingdom; but this being granted, there will remain one hundred and seventy thousand breeders.

---

to Stuart, and the Irish were often recruited by France and Spain to fight against England; *Barbados* Because of the extreme poverty in Ireland, many Irish people emigrated to the West Indies, selling their labour to sugar plantations in advance to pay for the voyage.

5 *projectors* Those who design or propose experiments or projects.

6 *doubt* Think.

I again subtract fifty thousand for those women who miscarry, or whose children die by accident or disease within the year. There only remain one hundred and twenty thousand children of poor parents annually born. The question therefore is how this number shall be reared and provided for, which, as I have already said, under the present situation of affairs is utterly impossible by all the methods hitherto proposed. For we can neither employ them in handicraft or agriculture; we neither build houses (I mean in the country) nor cultivate land.[7] They can very seldom pick up a livelihood by stealing till they arrive at six years old, except where they are of towardly parts,[8] although I confess they learn the rudiments much earlier, during which time they can however be properly looked upon only as probationers,[9] as I have been informed by a principal gentleman in the county of Cavan, who protested to me that he never knew above one or two instances under the age of six, even in a part of the kingdom so renowned for the quickest proficiency in that art.

I am assured by our merchants that a boy or a girl before twelve years old is no saleable commodity; and even when they come to this age, they will not yield above three pounds, or three pounds and half a crown at most, on the Exchange, which cannot turn to account[10] either to the parents or the kingdom, the charge of nutriment and rags having been at least four times that value.

I shall now therefore humbly propose my own thoughts, which I hope will not be liable to the least objection.

I have been assured by a very knowing American[11] of my acquaintance in London that a young healthy child well nursed is at a year old a most delicious, nourishing, and wholesome food, whether stewed, roasted, baked, or boiled; and I make no doubt that it will equally serve in a fricassee or a ragout.[12]

I do therefore humbly offer it to public consideration that of the hundred and twenty thousand children already computed, twenty thousand may be reserved for breed, whereof only one fourth part to be males, which is more than we allow to sheep, black cattle, or swine, and my reason is that these children are seldom the fruits of marriage, a circumstance not much regarded by our savages; therefore, one male will be sufficient to serve four females. That the remaining hundred thousand may at a year old be offered in sale to the persons of quality and fortune through the kingdom, always advising the mother to let

---

7 *neither build ... land* The British placed numerous restrictions on the Irish agricultural industry, retaining the majority of land for the grazing of sheep. The vast estates of British absentee landlords further contributed to Ireland's poverty.

8 *of towardly parts* Exceptionally able.

9 *probationers* Novices.

10 *on the Exchange* At the market; *turn to account* Result in profit.

11 *American* I.e., Native American.

12 *fricassee or a ragout* Stews.

them suck plentifully of the last month, so as to render them plump and fat for a good table. A child will make two dishes at an entertainment for friends, and when the family dines alone, the fore or hind quarter will make a reasonable dish, and seasoned with a little pepper or salt will be very good boiled on the fourth day, especially in winter.

I have reckoned upon a medium that a child just born will weigh twelve pounds, and in a solar year if tolerably nursed increase to twenty-eight pounds.

I grant this food will be somewhat dear,[13] and therefore very proper for landlords, who, as they have already devoured most of the parents, seem to have the best title* to the children.

Infants' flesh will be in season throughout the year, but more plentiful in March, and a little before and after. For we are told by a grave author, an eminent French physician, that, fish being a prolific[14] diet, there are more children born in Roman Catholic countries about nine months after Lent* than at any other season; therefore, reckoning a year after Lent, the markets will be more glutted than usual because the number of popish[15] infants is at least three to one in this kingdom, and therefore it will have one other collateral advantage by lessening the number of papists* among us.

I have already computed the charge of nursing a beggar's child (in which list I reckon all cottagers,[16] labourers, and four fifths of the farmers) to be about two shillings per annum, rags included, and I believe no gentleman would repine to give ten shillings for the carcass of a good fat child, which, as I have said, will make four dishes of excellent nutritive meat when he hath only some particular friend or his own family to dine with him. Thus the squire[17] will learn to be a good landlord and grow popular among his tenants; the mother will have eight shillings net profit and be fit for work till she produces another child.

Those who are more thrifty (as I must confess the times require) may flay the carcass, the skin of which, artificially[18] dressed, will make admirable gloves for ladies and summer boots for fine gentlemen.

As to our city of Dublin, shambles[19] may be appointed for this purpose in the most convenient parts of it, and butchers we may be assured will not be

---

13 *dear* Expensive.

14 *grave author* Sixteenth-century satirist François Rabelais. See his *Gargantua and Pantagruel*; *prolific* I.e., causing increased fertility.

15 *popish* Derogatory term meaning "Catholic."

16 *cottagers* Country dwellers.

17 *squire* Owner of a country estate.

18 *artificially* Artfully, skillfully.

19 *shambles* Slaughterhouses.

wanting, although I rather recommend buying the children alive and dressing them hot from the knife, as we do roasting pigs.

A very worthy person, a true lover of his country, and whose virtues I highly esteem, was lately pleased, in discoursing on this matter, to offer a refinement upon my scheme. He said that, many gentlemen of this kingdom having of late destroyed their deer, he conceived that the want of venison might be well supplied by the bodies of young lads and maidens, not exceeding fourteen years of age nor under twelve, so great a number of both sexes in every county being now ready to starve for want of work and service; and these to be disposed of by their parents if alive, or otherwise by their nearest relations. But with due deference to so excellent a friend and so deserving a patriot, I cannot be altogether in his sentiments; for as to the males, my American acquaintance assured me from frequent experience that their flesh was generally tough and lean, like that of our schoolboys, by continual exercise, and their taste disagreeable, and to fatten them would not answer the charge. Then as to the females, it would, I think with humble submission, be a loss to the public because they soon would become breeders themselves. And besides, it is not improbable that some scrupulous people might be apt to censure such a practice (although indeed very unjustly) as a little bordering upon cruelty, which, I confess, hath always been with me the strongest objection against any project, however well intended.

But in order to justify my friend, he confessed that this expedient was put into his head by the famous Psalmanazar,[20] a native of the island of Formosa, who came from thence to London above twenty years ago, and in conversation told my friend that in his country, when any young person happened to be put to death the executioner sold the carcass to persons of quality as a prime dainty, and that in his time the body of a plump girl of fifteen, who was crucified for an attempt to poison the emperor, was sold to his Imperial Majesty's Prime Minister of State and other great Mandarins* of the court, in joints from the gibbet,[21] at four hundred crowns. Neither indeed can I deny that if the same use were made of several plump young girls in this town who, without one single groat to their fortunes, cannot stir abroad without a chair,[22] and appear at the

20 *Psalmanazar* George Psalmanazar, a French adventurer who pretended to be from Formosa (now Taiwan) and published an account of Formosan customs, *Historical and Geographical Description of Formosa* (1704), which was later exposed as fraudulent. The story Swift recounts here is found in the second edition of Psalmanazar's work.

21 *gibbet* Gallows.

22 *groat* Silver coin equal in value to four pence. It was removed from circulation in 1662, and thereafter "a groat" was used metaphorically to signify any very small sum; *chair* Sedan chair, which seated one person and was carried on poles by two men.

playhouse and assemblies in foreign fineries which they never will pay for, the kingdom would not be the worse.

Some persons of a desponding spirit are in great concern about that vast 20
number of poor people who are aged, diseased, or maimed, and I have been desired to employ my thoughts what course may be taken to ease the nation of so grievous an encumbrance. But I am not in the least pain upon that matter because it is very well known that they are every day dying and rotting by cold and famine, and filth and vermin, as fast as can be reasonably expected. And as to the younger labourers, they are now in almost as hopeful a condition. They cannot get work, and consequently pine away* for want of nourishment to a degree that if at any time they are accidentally hired to common labour, they have not strength to perform it; and thus the country and themselves are happily delivered from the evils to come.

I have too long digressed, and therefore shall return to my subject. I think the advantages by the proposal which I have made are obvious and many, as well as of the highest importance.

For first, as I have already observed, it would greatly lessen the number of papists, with whom we are yearly overrun, being the principal breeders of the nation as well as our most dangerous enemies, and who stay at home on purpose with a design to deliver the kingdom to the Pretender, hoping to take their advantage by the absence of so many good Protestants, who have chosen rather to leave their country than stay at home and pay tithes against their conscience to an Episcopal curate.[23]

Secondly, the poorer tenants will have something valuable of their own, which by law may be made liable to distress[24] and help to pay their landlord's rent, their corn and cattle being already seized, and money a thing unknown.

Thirdly, whereas the maintenance of an hundred thousand children from two years old and upwards cannot be computed at less than ten shillings apiece per annum, the nation's stock will be thereby increased fifty thousand pounds per annum, besides the profit of a new dish introduced to the tables of all gentlemen of fortune in the kingdom who have any refinement in taste, and the money will circulate among ourselves, the goods being entirely of our own growth and manufacture.

Fourthly, the constant breeders, besides the gain of eight shillings sterling 25
per annum by the sale of their children, will be rid of the charge of maintaining them after the first year.

---

23 *Episcopal curate* I.e., Anglican church official.

24 *distress* Seizure of property for the payment of debt.

Fifthly, this food would likewise bring great customs* to taverns, where the vintners* will certainly be so prudent as to procure the best receipts[25] for dressing it to perfection, and consequently have their houses frequented by all the fine gentlemen who justly value themselves upon their knowledge in good eating. And a skillful cook who understands how to oblige his guests will contrive to make it as expensive as they please.

Sixthly, this would be a great inducement to marriage, which all wise nations have either encouraged by rewards or enforced by laws and penalties. It would increase the care and tenderness of mothers toward their children, when they were sure of a settlement for life to the poor babes, provided in some sort by the public, to their annual profit instead of expense. We should soon see an honest emulation[26] among the married women, which of them could bring the fattest child to market. Men would become as fond of their wives during the time of their pregnancy as they are now of their mares in foal, their cows in calf, or sows when they are ready to farrow, nor offer to beat or kick them (as it is too frequent a practice) for fear of a miscarriage.

Many other advantages might be enumerated: for instance, the addition of some thousand carcasses in our exportation of barreled beef; the propagation of swine's flesh and improvement in the art of making good bacon, so much wanted among us by the great destruction of pigs, too frequent at our tables, which are no way comparable in taste or magnificence to a well-grown, fat yearling* child, which, roasted whole, will make a considerable figure at a Lord Mayor's feast or any other public entertainment. But this and many others I omit, being studious of* brevity.

Supposing that one thousand families in this city would be constant customers for infants' flesh, besides others who might have it at merry-meetings, particularly weddings and christenings, I compute that Dublin would take off annually about twenty thousand carcasses, and the rest of the kingdom (where probably they will be sold somewhat cheaper) the remaining eighty thousand.

I can think of no one objection that will possibly be raised against this proposal, unless it should be urged that the number of people will be thereby much lessened in the kingdom. This I freely own, and it was indeed one principal design in offering it to the world. I desire the reader will observe that I calculate my remedy for this one individual kingdom of Ireland, and for no other that ever was, is, or, I think, ever can be upon earth. Therefore let no man talk to me of other expedients:[27] of taxing our absentees* at five shillings a pound;

---

25 *receipts* Recipes.

26 *emulation* Rivalry.

27 *other expedients* All of which Swift had already proposed in earnest attempts to remedy Ireland's poverty. See, for example, his *Proposal for the Universal Use of Irish*

of using neither clothes nor household furniture, except what is of our own growth and manufacture; of utterly rejecting the materials and instruments that promote foreign luxury; of curing the expensiveness of pride, vanity, idleness, and gaming[28] in our women; of introducing a vein of parsimony, prudence, and temperance; of learning to love our country, wherein we differ even from Laplanders* and the inhabitants of Topinamboo; of quitting our animosities and factions, nor act any longer like the Jews, who were murdering one another at the very moment their city was taken;[29] of being a little cautious not to sell our country and consciences for nothing; of teaching landlords to have at least one degree of mercy toward their tenants; lastly, of putting a spirit of honesty, industry, and skill into our shopkeepers, who, if a resolution could now be taken to buy only our native goods, would immediately unite to cheat and exact upon us in the price, the measure, and the goodness, nor could ever yet be brought to make one fair proposal of just dealing, though often in earnest invited to it.

Therefore I repeat, let no man talk to me of these and the like expedients till he hath at least some glimpse of hope that there will ever be some hearty and sincere attempt to put them in practice.

But as to myself, having been wearied out for many years with offering vain, idle, visionary thoughts, and at length utterly despairing of success, I fortunately fell upon this proposal, which, as it is wholly new, so it hath something solid and real, of no expense and little trouble, full in our own power, and whereby we can incur no danger in disobliging* England. For this kind of commodity will not bear exportation, the flesh being of too tender a consistence to admit a long continuance in salt, although perhaps I could name a country[30] which would be glad to eat up our whole nation without it.

After all, I am not so violently bent upon my own opinion as to reject any offer, proposed by wise men, which shall be found equally innocent, cheap, easy, and effectual. But before something of that kind shall be advanced in contradiction to my scheme, and offering a better, I desire the author or authors will be pleased maturely to consider two points.

First, as things now stand, how they will be able to find food and raiment for one hundred thousand useless mouths and backs.

And secondly, there being a round million of creatures in human figure throughout this kingdom whose whole subsistence, put into a common stock,

---

Manufactures. In early editions the following proposals were italicized to show the suspension of Swift's ironic tone.

28 *gaming* Gambling.

29 *Topinamboo* District in Brazil; *Jews ... was taken* According to the history of Flavius Joseph, Roman Emperor Titus's invasion and capture of Jerusalem in 70 BCE was aided by the fact that factional fighting had divided the city.

30 *a country* I.e., England.

would leave them in debt two million of pounds sterling, adding those who are beggars by profession to the bulk of farmers, cottagers, and labourers with their wives and children, who are beggars in effect.

I desire those politicians who dislike my overture, and may perhaps be so bold to attempt an answer, that they will first ask the parents of these mortals whether they would not at this day think it a great happiness to have been sold for food at a year old in the manner I prescribe, and thereby have avoided such a perpetual scene of misfortunes as they have since gone through by the oppression of landlords, the impossibility of paying rent without money or trade, the want of common sustenance, with neither house nor clothes to cover them from the inclemencies of the weather, and the most inevitable prospect of entailing[31] the like or greater miseries upon their breed forever.

I profess in the sincerity of my heart that I have not the least personal interest in endeavouring to promote this necessary work, having no other motive than the public good of my country by advancing our trade, providing for infants, relieving the poor, and giving some pleasure to the rich. I have no children by which I can propose to get a single penny, the youngest being nine years old, and my wife past childbearing.

(1729)

Questions

1. At what point does the reader realize that this is a satire? What effect does this delay have?
2. What is it possible to infer about the character of this essay's speaker?
3. What is the purpose of the long list of other "expedients" provided in paragraph 30?
4. Comment on Swift's diction, and in particular on the use of such terms as "dam," "breeders," and "yearling child." Can you think of parallels in the way in which humans refer to the animals they eat?

31 *entailing* Bestowing, conferring.

Mary Wollstonecraft

Dedication to *A Vindication of the Rights of Woman*

The following dedication appears at the beginning of A Vindication of the Rights of Woman, *Mary Wollstonecraft's groundbreaking essay on women's rights and the importance of equal education for men and women. She addresses M. Talleyrand-Périgord, the former Bishop of Autun, who was then minister of finance in the French revolutionary government and had been a member of the Committee that drafted the French Constitution of 1791. In that same year, he had also authored a pamphlet concerning public education that was presented to the National Assembly. Wollstonecraft was disappointed that Revolutionary France—founded on the ideals of liberty, equality, and fraternity—had not claimed for women the rights it had claimed for men. In the Dedication she asserts the injustice of this omission and summarizes many of her book's main arguments.*

Sir,

Having read with great pleasure a pamphlet which you have lately published, I dedicate this volume to you; to induce you to reconsider the subject, and maturely weigh what I have advanced respecting the rights of woman and national education: and I call with the firm tone of humanity; for my arguments, Sir, are dictated by a disinterested* spirit—I plead for my sex—not for myself. Independence I have long considered as the grand blessing of life, the basis of every virtue—and independence I will ever secure by contracting my wants, though I were to live on a barren heath.

It is then an affection for the whole human race that makes my pen dart rapidly along to support what I believe to be the cause of virtue: and the same motive leads me earnestly to wish to see woman placed in a station in which she would advance, instead of retarding, the progress of those glorious principles that give a substance to morality. My opinion, indeed, respecting the rights and duties of woman, seems to flow so naturally from these simple principles, that

I think it scarcely possible, but that some of the enlarged minds who formed your admirable constitution, will coincide with me.

In France there is undoubtedly a more general diffusion of knowledge than in any part of the European world, and I attribute it, in a great measure, to the social intercourse* which has long subsisted between the sexes. It is true, I utter my sentiments with freedom, that in France the very essence of sensuality has been extracted to regale the voluptuary,* and a kind of sentimental lust has prevailed, which, together with the system of duplicity that the whole tenor of their political and civil government taught, have given a sinister sort of sagacity to the French character, properly termed finesse; from which naturally flow a polish of manners that injures the substance, by hunting sincerity out of society.—And, modesty, the fairest garb of virtue!* has been more grossly insulted in France than even in England, till their women have treated as *prudish* that attention to decency, which brutes instinctively observe.

Manners and morals are so nearly allied that they have often been confounded; but, though the former should only be the natural reflection of the latter, yet, when various causes have produced factitious and corrupt manners, which are very early caught, morality becomes an empty name. The personal reserve, and sacred respect for cleanliness and delicacy in domestic life, which French women almost despise, are the graceful pillars of modesty; but, far from despising them, if the pure flame of patriotism have reached their bosoms, they should labour to improve the morals of their fellow-citizens, by teaching men, not only to respect modesty in women, but to acquire it themselves, as the only way to merit their esteem.

5 Contending for the rights of woman, my main argument is built on this simple principle, that if she be not prepared by education to become the companion of man, she will stop the progress of knowledge and virtue; for truth must be common to all, or it will be inefficacious with respect to its influence on general practice. And how can woman be expected to co-operate unless she know why she ought to be virtuous? unless freedom strengthen her reason till she comprehend her duty, and see in what manner it is connected with her real good? If children are to be educated to understand the true principle of patriotism, their mother must be a patriot; and the love of mankind, from which an orderly train of virtues spring, can only be produced by considering the moral and civil interest of mankind; but the education and situation of woman, at present, shuts her out from such investigations.

In this work I have produced many arguments, which to me were conclusive, to prove that the prevailing notion respecting a sexual character[1] was

---

1 *prevailing notion respecting a sexual character* I.e., prevailing notion regarding what is natural and appropriate for the two sexes.

subversive of morality, and I have contended, that to render the human body and mind more perfect, chastity must more universally prevail, and that chastity will never be respected in the male world till the person of a woman is not, as it were, idolized, when little virtue or sense embellish it with the grand traces of mental beauty, or the interesting simplicity of affection.

Consider, Sir, dispassionately,* these observations—for a glimpse of this truth seemed to open before you when you observed, "that to see one half of the human race excluded by the other from all participation of government, was a political phenomenon that, according to abstract principles, it was impossible to explain." If so, on what does your constitution rest? If the abstract rights of man will bear discussion and explanation, those of woman, by a parity of reasoning, will not shrink from the same test: though a different opinion prevails in this country, built on the very arguments which you use to justify the oppression of woman—prescription.*

Consider, I address you as a legislator, whether, when men contend for their freedom, and to be allowed to judge for themselves respecting their own happiness, it be not inconsistent and unjust to subjugate women, even though you firmly believe that you are acting in the manner best calculated to promote their happiness? Who made man the exclusive judge, if woman partake with him the gift of reason?

In this style, argue tyrants of every denomination, from the weak king to the weak father of a family; they are all eager to crush reason; yet always assert that they usurp its throne only to be useful. Do you not act a similar part, when you *force* all women, by denying them civil and political rights, to remain immured in their families groping in the dark? for surely, Sir, you will not assert, that a duty can be binding which is not founded on reason? If indeed this be their destination, arguments may be drawn from reason: and thus augustly supported, the more understanding women acquire, the more they will be attached to their duty—comprehending it—for unless they comprehend it, unless their morals be fixed on the same immutable principle as those of man, no authority can make them discharge it in a virtuous manner. They may be convenient slaves, but slavery will have its constant effect, degrading the master and the abject dependent.

But, if women are to be excluded, without having a voice, from a par- 10
ticipation of the natural rights of mankind, prove first, to ward off the charge of injustice and inconsistency, that they want[2] reason—else this flaw in your NEW CONSTITUTION will ever show that man must, in some shape, act like a tyrant, and tyranny, in whatever part of society it rears its brazen front, will ever undermine morality.

---

2 *want* Lack.

I have repeatedly asserted, and produced what appeared to me irrefragable* arguments drawn from matters of fact, to prove my assertion, that women cannot, by force, be confined to domestic concerns; for they will, however ignorant, intermeddle with more weighty affairs, neglecting private duties only to disturb, by cunning tricks, the orderly plans of reason which rise above their comprehension.

Besides, whilst they are only made to acquire personal accomplishments, men will seek for pleasure in variety, and faithless husbands will make faithless wives; such ignorant beings, indeed, will be very excusable when, not taught to respect public good, nor allowed any civil rights, they attempt to do themselves justice by retaliation.

The box of mischief thus opened in society, what is to preserve private virtue, the only security of public freedom and universal happiness?

Let there be then no coercion *established* in society, and the common law of gravity prevailing, the sexes will fall into their proper places. And, now that more equitable laws are forming your citizens, marriage may become more sacred: your young men may choose wives from motives of affection, and your maidens allow love to root out vanity.

The father of a family will not then weaken his constitution and debase his sentiments, by visiting the harlot, nor forget, in obeying the call of appetite, the purpose for which it was implanted. And, the mother will not neglect her children to practice the arts of coquetry,* when sense and modesty secure her the friendship of her husband.

But, till men become attentive to the duty of a father, it is vain to expect women to spend that time in their nursery which they, "wise in their generation," choose to spend at their glass;[3] for this exertion of cunning is only an instinct of nature to enable them to obtain indirectly a little of that power of which they are unjustly denied a share: for, if women are not permitted to enjoy legitimate rights, they will render both men and themselves vicious, to obtain illicit privileges.

I wish, Sir, to set some investigations of this kind afloat in France; and should they lead to a confirmation of my principles, when your constitution is revised the Rights of Woman may be respected, if it be fully proved that reason calls for this respect, and loudly demands JUSTICE for one half of the human race.

I am, SIR,

Your's respectfully,

M.W.

(1792)

---

3 *glass* Mirror.

Questions

1. In no more than three paragraphs, summarize the main points of the argument Wollstonecraft makes here.
2. What in Wollstonecraft's style of writing do you think might have helped make her work influential?
3. Can you think of additional arguments in support of Wollstonecraft's position?

HARRIET MARTINEAU

from A RETROSPECT OF WESTERN TRAVEL

In 1834, Harriet Martineau, an English writer known for her work on political, social, and economic subjects, travelled to New York to begin a two-year tour of the United States. She visited hospitals, prisons, government houses, and scientific and literary institutions, paying particular attention to the status of women and to the abolitionist movement. Upon her return to England, she published her experiences in two travel narratives, Society in America *(1837) and* A Retrospect of Western Travel *(1838). The following passages from the latter narrative offer some of her observations of slavery, which had been abolished in most of the British Empire in 1833 but was still practiced in parts of the United States. Further selections from* A Retrospect of Western Travel, *on Martineau's visit to Niagara Falls and her views on the American prison system, are included in the online portion of this anthology.*

from FIRST SIGHT OF SLAVERY

... From the day of my entering the States till that of my leaving Philadelphia I had seen society basking in one bright sunshine of good-will. The sweet temper and kindly manners of the Americans are so striking to foreigners, that it is some time before the dazzled stranger perceives that, genuine as is all this good, evils as black as night exist along with it. I had been received with such hearty hospitality everywhere, and had lived among friends so conscientious in their regard for human rights, that, though I had heard of abolition riots,[1] and had observed somewhat of the degradation of the blacks, my mind had not yet been really troubled about the enmity of the races. The time of awakening must come. It began just before I left Philadelphia.

1 *abolition riots* Pro-slavery riots, which occurred in cities such as New York, Philadelphia, and Boston in response to anti-slavery movements.

I was calling on a lady[2] whom I had heard speak with strong horror of the abolitionists* (with whom I had then no acquaintance), and she turned round upon me with the question whether I would not prevent, if I could, the marriage of a white person with a person of colour. I saw at once the beginning of endless troubles in this inquiry, and was very sorry it had been made; but my determination had been adopted long before, never to evade the great question of colour; never to provoke it; but always to meet it plainly in whatever form it should be presented. I replied that I would never, under any circumstances, try to separate persons who really loved, believing such to be truly those whom God had joined; but I observed that the case she put was one not likely to happen, as I believed the blacks were no more disposed to marry the whites than the whites to marry the blacks. "You are an amalgamationist!" cried she. I told her that the party term was new to me; but that she must give what name she pleased to the principle I had declared in answer to her question. This lady is an eminent religionist, and denunciations spread rapidly from her. The day before I left Philadelphia my old shipmate, the Prussian physician,[3] arrived there, and lost no time in calling to tell me, with much agitation, that I must not go a step farther south; that he had heard on all hands, within two hours of his arrival, that I was an amalgamationist, and that my having published a story against slavery would be fatal to me in the slave states. I did not give much credit to the latter part of this news, and saw plainly that all I had to do was to go straight on. I really desired to see the working of the slave system, and was glad that my having published against its principles[4] divested me altogether of the character of a spy, and gave me an unquestioned liberty to publish the results of what I might observe. In order to see things as they were, it was necessary that people's minds should not be prepossessed by my friends as to my opinions and conduct; and therefore forbade my Philadelphia friends to publish in the newspapers, as they wished, an antidote to the charges already current against me.

The next day I first set foot in a slave state, arriving in the evening at Baltimore. I dreaded inexpressibly the first sight of a slave, and could not help speculating on the lot of every person of colour I saw from the windows the first few days. The servants in the house where I was were free blacks.

---

2 *a lady* Probably Deborah Norris Logan (1761–1839), diarist, memoirist, and historian. Her diary includes accounts of Martineau's visits.

3 *Prussian physician* Nicolaus Heinrich Julius (1783–1862). Martineau describes him in her Autobiography as "a philanthropist going to America ... to inquire into the state of prison discipline there" and notes that there was "something mysterious and doubtful about him."

4 *my having ... its principles* In the story "Demerara" (1832), Martineau critiques slavery, primarily on economic grounds. Martineau also wrote two antislavery articles that appeared in the *Monthly Repository* in 1830 and 1831.

Before a week was over I perceived that all that is said in England of the hatred of the whites to the blacks in America is short of the truth. The slanders that I heard of the free blacks were too gross to injure my estimation of any but those who spoke them. In Baltimore the bodies of coloured people exclusively are taken for dissection, "because the whites do not like it, and the coloured people cannot resist." It is wonderful that the bodily structure can be (with the exception of the colouring of the skin) thus assumed to be the pattern of that of the whites; that the exquisite nervous system, the instrument of moral as well as physical pleasures and pains, can be nicely[5] investigated, on the ground of its being analogous with that of the whites; that not only the mechanism, but the sensibilities of the degraded race should be argued from to those of the exalted order, and that men come from such a study with contempt for these brethren in their countenances, hatred in their hearts, and insult on their tongues. These students are the men who cannot say that the coloured people have not nerves that quiver under moral injury, nor a brain that is on fire with insult, nor pulses that throb under oppression. These are the men who should stay the hand of the rash and ignorant possessors of power, who crush the being of creatures, like themselves, "fearfully and wonderfully made."[6] But to speak the right word, to hold out the helping hand, these searchers into man have not light nor strength.

5 It was in Baltimore that I heard Miss Edgeworth[7] denounced as a woman of no intelligence or delicacy, whose works could never be cared for again, because, in *Belinda*, poor Juba was married, at length, to an English farmer's daughter! The incident is so subordinate that I had entirely forgotten it; but a clergyman's lady threw the volume to the opposite corner of the floor when she came to the page. As I have said elsewhere, Miss Edgeworth is worshipped throughout the United States; but it is in spite of this terrible passage, this clause of a sentence in *Belinda*, which nobody in America can tolerate, while no one elsewhere ever, I should think, dreamed of finding fault with it.

A lady from New England, staying in Baltimore, was one day talking over slavery with me, her detestation of it being great, when I told her I dreaded seeing a slave. "You have seen one," said she. "You were waited on by a slave yesterday evening." She told me of a gentleman who let out and lent out his slaves to wait at gentlemen's houses, and that the tall handsome mulatto[8] who handed the tea at a party the evening before was one of these. I was glad it

---

5 *nicely* Precisely.

6 *fearfully and wonderfully made* See Psalm 139.14.

7 *Miss Edgeworth* Maria Edgeworth (1768–1849), one of the most popular and prolific early nineteenth-century British writers. Her second novel, Belinda, includes an interracial marriage.

8 *mulatto* Person of combined white and black lineage.

was over for once; but I never lost the painful feeling caused to a stranger by intercourse with slaves. No familiarity with them, no mirth and contentment on their part, ever soothed the miserable restlessness caused by the presence of a deeply-injured fellow-being. No wonder or ridicule on the spot avails anything to the stranger. He suffers, and must suffer from this, deeply and long, as surely as he is human and hates oppression.

The next slave that I saw, knowing that it was a slave, was at Washington, where a little negro child took hold of my gown in the passage of our boarding-house, and entered our drawing-room with me. She shut the door softly, as asking leave to stay. I took up a newspaper. She sat at my feet, and began amusing herself with my shoestrings. Finding herself not discouraged, she presently begged play by peeping at me above and on each side the newspaper. She was a bright-eyed, merry-hearted child; confiding, like other children, and dreading no evil, but doomed, hopelessly doomed, to ignorance, privation, and moral degradation. When I looked at her, and thought of the fearful disobedience to the first of moral laws, the cowardly treachery, the cruel abuse of power involved in thus dooming to blight a being so helpless, so confiding, and so full of promise, a horror came over me which sickened my very soul. To see slaves is not to be reconciled to slavery....

from City Life in the South

... I made it a rule to allow others to introduce the subject of slavery, knowing that they would not fail to do so, and that I might learn as much from their method of approaching the topic as from anything they could say upon it. Before half an hour had passed, every man, woman, or child I might be conversing with had entered upon the question. As it was likewise a rule with me never to conceal or soften my own opinions, and never to allow myself to be irritated by what I heard (for it is too serious a subject to indulge frailties with), the best understanding existed between slaveholders and myself. We never quarrelled, while, I believe, we never failed to perceive the extent of the difference of opinion and feeling between us. I met with much more cause for admiration in their frankness than reason to complain of illiberality....

Charleston[9] is the place in which to see those contrasting scenes of human life brought under the eye which moralists gather together for the purpose of impressing the imagination. The stranger has but to pass from street to street, to live from hour to hour in this city, to see in conjunction the extremes between which there is everywhere else a wide interval. The sights of one morning I should remember if every other particular of my travels were forgotten. I was

9 *Charleston* City in South Carolina.

driven round the city by a friend[10] whose conversation was delightful all the way. Though I did not agree in all his views of society, the thoughtfulness of his mind and the benevolence of his exertions betokened a healthy state of feeling, and gave value to all he said. He had been a friend of the lamented Grimké;[11] and he showed me the house where Grimké lived and died, and told me much of him; of the nobleness of his character, the extent of his attainments, and how, dying at fifty-four, he had lived by industry a long life.* My mind was full of the contemplation of the heights which human beings are destined to reach, when I was plunged into a new scene; one which it was my own conscientious choice to visit, but for which the preceding conversation had ill-prepared me. I went into the slave market, a place which the traveller ought not to avoid to spare his feelings. There was a table on which stood two auctioneers, one with a hammer, the other to exhibit "the article" and count the bids. The slaves for sale were some of them in groups below, and some in a long row behind the auctioneers. The sale of a man was just concluding when we entered the market. A woman, with two children, one at the breast, and another holding by her apron, composed the next lot. The restless, jocose zeal of the auctioneer who counted the bids was the most infernal sight I ever beheld. The woman was a mulatto; she was neatly dressed, with a clean apron and a yellow head-handkerchief. The elder child clung to her. She hung her head low, lower, and still lower on her breast, yet turning her eyes incessantly from side to side, with an intensity of expectation which showed that she had not reached the last stage of despair. I should have thought that her agony of shame and dread would have silenced the tongue of every spectator; but it was not so. A lady[12] chose this moment to turn to me and say, with a cheerful air of complacency, "You know my theory, that one race must be subservient to the other. I do not care which; and if the blacks should ever have the upper hand, I should not mind standing on that table, and being sold with two of my children." Who could help saying within himself, "Would you were! so that that mother were released!" Who could help seeing in vision the blacks driving the whites into the field, and preaching from the pulpits of Christian churches the doctrines

---

10 *a friend* Samuel Gilman (1791–1858), a Unitarian minister who hosted Martineau during her stay in the city.

11 *Grimké* Thomas Smith Grimké (1786–1834), a lawyer, politician, and native of Charleston. His political and social beliefs were reflected in his service on the boards of the American Institute of Education and the American Peace Society, as well as his involvement in the temperance movement in South Carolina.

12 *a lady* In her Autobiography, Martineau ascribes this comment to Caroline Howard Gilman (1794–1888), an author of poetry, children's books, housekeeping manuals, and a memoir.

now given out there, that God has respect of persons;[13] that men are to hold each other as property, instead of regarding each other as brethren; and that the right interpretation of the golden rule* by the slaveholder is, "Do unto your slaves as you would wish your master to do unto you if you were a slave!" A little boy of eight or nine years old apparently, was next put up alone. There was no bearing the child's look of helplessness and shame. It seemed like an outrage to be among the starers from whom he shrunk, and we went away before he was disposed of....

(1838)

Questions

1. What rules does Martineau give herself for interactions with supporters of slavery? When it comes to moral issues you feel strongly about, how do you choose to interact with people who hold opposing views? Would it work for you to follow Martineau's rules?
2. How do you think these passages would have been received by a British reader in 1838? How do you think they would have been received by an American reader of the same period?
3. What attitudes toward slavery does Martineau observe among white Americans? What reasons do pro-slavery Americans give to justify the practice?
4. Although it had many defenders in the 1840s, from a present-day perspective slavery is clearly unjust. What (if any) present-day practices do you think will be seen as obviously immoral a century or two from now? How do people living today justify those practices?

13 *respect of persons* In Acts 10.34, Peter claims that "God is no respecter of persons," i.e., that he does not favour people of higher status.

Elizabeth Cady Stanton

Seneca Falls Keynote Address[1]

The struggle for women's rights and the struggle to overthrow slavery—and then to achieve full citizenship rights for black people—have often been intertwined, and sometimes in tension with each other. When the young anti-slavery activist Elizabeth Cady married Henry Brewster Stanton in May 1840, the two travelled to London on their honeymoon, planning to attend the World Anti-Slavery Convention. When that Convention decided not to allow women to be full participants, Stanton and Lucretia Mott, a delegate from Philadelphia, resolved to organize a convention of their own. The eventual result was the Seneca Falls Women's Rights Convention in 1848, the first such gathering in America; it attracted some 300 attendees, notable among them Mott, Mary Ann McClintock (who, with Stanton, took the lead in drafting the convention's Declaration of Sentiments)—and pre-eminent abolitionist Frederick Douglass.

We have met here today to discuss our rights and wrongs, civil and political, and not, as some have supposed, to go into the detail of social life alone. We do not propose to petition the legislature to make our husbands just, generous, and courteous, to seat every man at the head of a cradle, and to clothe every woman in male attire.

None of these points, however important they may be considered by leading men, will be touched in this convention. As to their costume,* the gentlemen need feel no fear of our imitating that, for we think it in violation of every principle of taste, beauty, and dignity; notwithstanding all the contempt cast upon our loose, flowing garments, we still admire the graceful folds, and consider our costume far more artistic than theirs. Many of the nobler sex[2] seem to agree with us in this opinion, for the bishops, priests, judges, barristers,

1 *Keynote Address* Stanton's speech was delivered 19 July 1848 at the Women's Rights Convention, Seneca Falls, New York.

2 *nobler sex* The sex possessing higher social and political status—i.e., men.

and lord mayors of the first nation on the globe,* and the Pope of Rome, with his cardinals, too, all wear the loose flowing robes, thus tacitly acknowledging that the male attire is neither dignified nor imposing.

No, we shall not molest you in your philosophical experiments with stocks,[3] pants, high-heeled boots, and Russian belts. Yours be the glory to discover, by personal experience, how long the kneepan[4] can resist the terrible strapping down which you impose, in how short time the well-developed muscles of the throat can be reduced to mere threads by the constant pressure of the stock,[5] how high the heel of a boot must be to make a short man tall, and how tight the Russian belt may be drawn and yet have wind enough left to sustain life.

But we are assembled to protest against a form of government existing without the consent of the governed—to declare our right to be free as man is free, to be represented in the government which we are taxed to support, to have such graceful laws as give man the power to chastise and imprison his wife, to take the wages which she earns, the property which she inherits, and, in case of separation, the children of her love;* laws which make her the mere dependent on his bounty. It is to protest against such unjust laws as these that we are assembled today, and to have them, if possible, forever erased from our statute books, deeming them a shame and a disgrace to a Christian republic in the nineteenth century. We have met to uplift woman's fallen divinity upon an even pedestal with man's. And, strange as it may seem to many, we now demand our right to vote according to the declaration of the government under which we live.

5 This right no one pretends to deny. We need not prove ourselves equal to Daniel Webster to enjoy this privilege, for the ignorant Irishman in the ditch[6] has all the civil rights he has. We need not prove our muscular power equal to this same Irishman to enjoy this privilege, for the most tiny, weak, ill-shaped stripling[7] of twenty-one has all the civil rights of the Irishman. We have no objection to discuss the question of equality, for we feel that the weight of

---

3 *molest* Cause trouble to; *stocks* Neckties.

4 *kneepan* Kneecap.

5 *well-developed ... stock* Sometimes the stock tie was stiffened with starch to give the wearer a more formal appearance by forcing the chin up.

6 *Daniel Webster* American Secretary of State, senator, and presidential candidate (1782–1852); *Irishman in the ditch* The Irish peasantry had suffered for centuries under English rule; during the 1840s the potato famine brought millions of them to the brink of starvation. Hundreds of thousands—the vast majority of them poor and uneducated—emigrated to the United States, where few starved, but where anti-Irish feeling was widespread.

7 *stripling* Young man.

argument lies wholly with us, but we wish the question of equality kept distinct from the question of rights, for the proof of the one does not determine the truth of the other. All white men in this country have the same rights, however they may differ in mind, body, or estate.

The right is ours. The question now is: how shall we get possession of what rightfully belongs to us? We should not feel so sorely grieved if no man who had not attained the full stature of a Webster, Clay, Van Buren, or Gerrit Smith[8] could claim the right of the elective franchise. But to have drunkards, idiots, horse-racing, rum-selling rowdies, ignorant foreigners, and silly boys fully recognized, while we ourselves are thrust out from all the rights that belong to citizens, it is too grossly insulting to the dignity of woman to be longer quietly submitted to.

The right is ours. Have it, we must. Use it, we will. The pens, the tongues, the fortunes, the indomitable wills of many women are already pledged to secure this right. The great truth that no just government can be formed without the consent of the governed* we shall echo and re-echo in the ears of the unjust judge, until by continual coming we shall weary him.

There seems now to be a kind of moral stagnation in our midst. Philanthropists have done their utmost to rouse the nation to a sense of its sins. War, slavery, drunkenness, licentiousness, gluttony, have been dragged naked before the people, and all their abominations and deformities fully brought to light, yet with idiotic laugh we hug those monsters to our breasts and rush on to destruction. Our churches are multiplying on all sides, our missionary societies, Sunday schools, and prayer meetings and innumerable charitable and reform organizations are all in operation, but still the tide of vice is swelling, and threatens the destruction of everything, and the battlements of righteousness are weak against the raging elements of sin and death.

Verily,* the world waits the coming of some new element, some purifying power, some spirit of mercy and love. The voice of woman has been silenced in the state, the church, and the home, but man cannot fulfill his destiny alone, he cannot redeem his race unaided. There are deep and tender chords of sympathy and love in the hearts of the downfallen and oppressed that woman can touch more skillfully than man.

10 The world has never yet seen a truly great and virtuous nation, because in the degradation of woman the very fountains of life are poisoned at their source. It is vain to look for silver and gold from mines of copper and lead.

It is the wise mother that has the wise son. So long as your women are slaves you may throw your colleges and churches to the winds. You can't have

8 *Webster ... Smith* Here, Webster, Henry Clay, Martin Van Buren, and Gerrit Smith serve as examples of prominent, respectable American men.

scholars and saints so long as your mothers are ground to powder between the upper and nether millstone of tyranny and lust. How seldom, now, is a father's pride gratified, his fond hopes realized, in the budding genius of his son!

The wife is degraded, made the mere creature of caprice,* and the foolish son is heaviness to his heart. Truly are the sins of the fathers visited upon the children to the third and fourth generation.* God, in His wisdom, has so linked the whole human family together that any violence done at one end of the chain is felt throughout its length, and here, too, is the law of restoration, as in woman all have fallen, so in her elevation shall the race be recreated.

"Voices" were the visitors and advisers of Joan of Arc.[9] Do not "voices" come to us daily from the haunts of poverty, sorrow, degradation, and despair, already too long unheeded? Now is the time for the women of this country, if they would save our free institutions, to defend the right, to buckle on the armour that can best resist the keenest weapons of the enemy—contempt and ridicule. The same religious enthusiasm that nerved[10] Joan of Arc to her work nerves us to ours. In every generation God calls some men and women for the utterance of truth, a heroic action, and our work today is the fulfilling of what has long since been foretold by the Prophet—Joel 2.28:

> "And it shall come to pass afterward, that I will pour out my spirit upon all flesh; and your sons and your daughters shall prophesy."

We do not expect our path will be strewn with the flowers of popular applause, but over the thorns of bigotry and prejudice will be our way, and on our banners will beat the dark storm clouds of opposition from those who have entrenched themselves behind the stormy bulwarks of custom and authority, and who have fortified their position by every means, holy and unholy. But we will steadfastly abide the result. Unmoved we will bear it aloft. Undauntedly we will unfurl it to the gale, for we know that the storm cannot rend from it a shred, that the electric flash will but more clearly show to us the glorious words inscribed upon it, "Equality of Rights."

(1848)

---

9 *Joan of Arc* Jeanne D'Arc (1412–31), young peasant woman who was persuaded by the "voices" she heard to become involved in military affairs. Her visionary leadership led the French to several victories over English forces during the Hundred Years' War; distrusted by Church authorities, she was burnt at the stake but later canonized as a saint.

10 *nerved* Mentally strengthened and prepared.

Questions

1. What possible objections to women's rights does Stanton anticipate in this speech? How does she answer them?
2. Paragraphs 2 and 3 of this speech are about men's clothing. What is the tone of these paragraphs? What is the effect of their inclusion in the opening of this speech?
3. What distinction does Stanton draw between "the question of equality" and "the question of rights"?
4. Stanton makes several arguments in support of her claim that women's rights should be equal to those of men. Which arguments appeal to you most as a twenty-first-century reader? Do any of the arguments seem dated?

FREDERICK DOUGLASS

from FOURTH OF JULY ORATION[1]

By the early 1850s Douglass was among the best-known figures in the abolitionist movement. Now living as a free man in Rochester, New York, he had become a newspaper publisher and editor, founding the North Star *to further the cause of abolition (and to promote the cause of freedom more generally). He had also become very involved in the local community (working, for example, to end segregation in Rochester's public schools), and in 1852 he was invited by the Rochester Ladies' Anti-Slavery Society to deliver a speech to the citizenry of Rochester, as part of the local Independence Day celebrations. A substantial excerpt from the address appears here; the full speech is over 10,000 words long.*

The papers and placards say that I am to deliver a 4th of July oration....

This, for the purpose of this celebration, is the 4th of July.[2] It is the birthday of your National Independence, and of your political freedom.... This celebration also marks the beginning of another year of your national life; and reminds you that the Republic of America is now 76 years old....

Fellow Citizens, I am not wanting in respect for the fathers of this republic. The signers of the Declaration of Independence were brave men. They were great men too—great enough to give fame to a great age.... The point from which I am compelled to view them is not, certainly, the most favourable; and yet I cannot contemplate their great deeds with less than admiration. They were statesmen, patriots and heroes, and for the good they did, and the principles they contended for, I will unite with you to honour their memory....

1 *Fourth of July Oration* Douglass did not give the speech a title; it is often referred to as "What to the Slave Is the Fourth of July," and often, in excerpted form, given the title "The Hypocrisy of American Slavery."

2 *for the purpose of this celebration, is the 4th of July* Though the address was part of the Independence Day festivities, it was delivered on the 5th of July rather than the 4th.

They were peace men; but they preferred revolution to peaceful submission to bondage. They were quiet men; but they did not shrink from agitating against oppression. They showed forbearance; but that they knew its limits. They believed in order; but not in the order of tyranny. With them, nothing was "settled" that was not right. With them, justice, liberty and humanity were "final"; not slavery and oppression. You may well cherish the memory of such men. They were great in their day and generation....

5 Friends and citizens, I need not enter further into the causes which led to this anniversary. Many of you understand them better than I do.... The causes which led to the separation of the colonies from the British crown* have never lacked for a tongue. They have all been taught in your common schools, narrated at your firesides, unfolded from your pulpits, and thundered from your legislative halls, and are as familiar to you as household words. They form the staple of your national poetry and eloquence.

I remember, also, that, as a people, Americans are remarkably familiar with all facts which make in their own favour. This is esteemed by some as a national trait—perhaps a national weakness. It is a fact, that whatever makes for the wealth or for the reputation of Americans (and can be had cheap!) will be found by Americans. I shall not be charged with slandering Americans, if I say I think the American side of any question may be safely left in American hands.

I leave, therefore, the great deeds of your fathers to other gentlemen whose claim to have been regularly descended will be less likely to be disputed than mine!

My business, if I have any here to-day, is with the present. The accepted time with God and his cause is the ever-living now….

Fellow-citizens, pardon me, allow me to ask, why am I called upon to speak here to-day? What have I, or those I represent, to do with your national independence? Are the great principles of political freedom and of natural justice, embodied in that Declaration of Independence, extended to us? And am I, therefore, called upon to bring our humble offering to the national altar, and to confess the benefits and express devout gratitude for the blessings resulting from your independence to us?

10 Would to God, both for your sakes and ours, that an affirmative answer could be truthfully returned to these questions! Then would my task be light, and my burden easy and delightful....

But, such is not the state of the case. I say it with a sad sense of the disparity between us. I am not included within the pale* of this glorious anniversary! Your high independence only reveals the immeasurable distance between us. The blessings in which you, this day, rejoice, are not enjoyed in common.—The rich inheritance of justice, liberty, prosperity and independence, bequeathed by your fathers, is shared by you, not by me. The sunlight that brought life and healing to you, has brought stripes and death to me. This Fourth [of] July is yours, not mine. You may rejoice, I must mourn. To drag a man in fetters into the grand illuminated temple of liberty, and call upon him to join you in joyous anthems, were inhuman mockery and sacrilegious irony. Do you mean, citizens, to mock me, by asking me to speak to-day? …

Fellow-citizens; above your national, tumultuous joy, I hear the mournful wail of millions! whose chains, heavy and grievous yesterday, are, to-day, rendered more intolerable by the jubilee shouts that reach them.... My subject, then fellow-citizens, is American slavery. I shall see, this day, and its popular characteristics, from the slave's point of view. Standing, there, identified with the American bondman, making his wrongs mine, I do not hesitate to declare, with all my soul, that the character and conduct of this nation never looked blacker to me than on this 4th of July! Whether we turn to the declarations of the past, or to the professions of the present, the conduct of the nation seems equally hideous and revolting. America is false to the past, false to the present, and solemnly binds herself to be false to the future....

But I fancy I hear some one of my audience say, it is just in this circumstance that you and your brother abolitionists fail to make a favourable impression on the public mind. Would you argue more, and denounce less, would you persuade more, and rebuke less, your cause would be much more likely to succeed. But, I submit, where all is plain there is nothing to be argued. What point in the anti-slavery creed would you have me argue? On what branch of the subject do the people of this country need light? Must I undertake to prove that the slave is a man? That point is conceded already. Nobody doubts it. The slaveholders themselves acknowledge it in the enactment of laws for their government. They acknowledge it when they punish disobedience on the part of the slave. There are seventy-two crimes in the State of Virginia, which, if committed by a black man, (no matter how ignorant he be), subject him to the punishment of death; while only two of the same crimes will subject a white man to the like punishment. What is this but the acknowledgment that the slave is a moral, intellectual and responsible being? The manhood of the slave is conceded. It is admitted in the fact that Southern statute books are covered with enactments forbidding, under severe fines and penalties, the teaching of the slave to read or to write. When you can point to any such laws, in reference to the beasts of the field, then I may consent to argue the manhood of the slave. When the dogs in your streets, when the fowls of the air, when the cattle on your hills, when the fish of the sea, and the reptiles that crawl, shall be unable to distinguish the slave from a brute, then will I argue with you that the slave is a man!...

Would you have me argue that man is entitled to liberty? That he is the rightful owner of his own body? You have already declared it.... What, am I to argue that it is wrong to make men brutes, to rob them of their liberty, to work them without wages, to keep them ignorant of their relations to their fellow men, to beat them with sticks, to flay their flesh with the lash, to load their limbs with irons, to hunt them with dogs, to sell them at auction, to sunder their families, to knock out their teeth, to burn their flesh, to starve them into obedience and submission to their masters? Must I argue that a system thus marked with blood, and stained with pollution, is wrong? No! I will not. I have better employments for my time and strength than such arguments would imply.

What, then, remains to be argued? Is it that slavery is not divine; that God did not establish it; that our doctors of divinity are mistaken? … The time for such argument is passed.

At a time like this, scorching irony, not convincing argument, is needed. O! had I the ability, and could I reach the nation's ear, I would, to-day, pour out a fiery stream of biting ridicule, blasting reproach, withering sarcasm, and stern rebuke. For it is not light that is needed, but fire; it is not the gentle shower, but thunder. We need the storm, the whirlwind, and the earthquake. The feeling of the nation must be quickened; the conscience of the nation must be roused; the propriety of the nation must be startled; the hypocrisy of the nation must be exposed; and its crimes against God and man must be proclaimed and denounced.

What, to the American slave, is your 4th of July? I answer: a day that reveals to him, more than all other days in the year, the gross injustice and cruelty to which he is the constant victim. To him, your celebration is a sham; your boasted liberty, an unholy license; your national greatness, swelling vanity; your sounds of rejoicing are empty and heartless; your denunciations of tyrants, brass fronted impudence; your shouts of liberty and equality, hollow mockery; your prayers and hymns, your sermons and thanksgivings, with all your religious parade, and solemnity, are, to him, mere bombast, fraud, deception, impiety, and hypocrisy—a thin veil to cover up crimes which would disgrace a nation of savages. There is not a nation on the earth guilty of practices, more shocking and bloody, than are the people of these United States, at this very hour.

Go where you may, search where you will, roam through all the monarchies and despotisms of the old world, travel through South America, search out every abuse, and when you have found the last, lay your facts by the side of the everyday practices of this nation, and you will say with me, that, for revolting barbarity and shameless hypocrisy, America reigns without a rival.

Take the American slave-trade, which, we are told by the papers, is especially prosperous just now.... This trade is one of the peculiarities of American institutions. It is carried on in all the large towns and cities in one-half of this confederacy; and millions are pocketed every year, by dealers in this horrid traffic. In several states, this trade is a chief source of wealth. It is called (in contradistinction to the foreign slave-trade) "the internal slave trade." It is, probably, called so, too, in order to divert from it the horror with which the foreign slave-trade is contemplated. That trade has long since been denounced by this government, as piracy.... Everywhere, in this country, it is safe to speak of this foreign slave-trade, as a most inhuman traffic, opposed alike to the laws of God and of man.... It is, however, a notable fact that, while so much execration is poured out by Americans upon those engaged in the foreign slave-trade, the men engaged in the slave-trade between the states pass without condemnation, and their business is deemed honourable.

Behold the practical operation of this internal slave-trade, the American 20
slave-trade, sustained by American politics and American religion. Here you will see men and women reared like swine for the market. You know what is a swine-drover? I will show you a man-drover. They inhabit all our Southern States. They perambulate the country, and crowd the highways of the nation, with droves of human stock. You will see one of these human flesh-jobbers, armed with pistol, whip and bowie-knife, driving a company of a hundred men, women, and children, from the Potomac* to the slave market at New Orleans. These wretched people are to be sold singly, or in lots, to suit purchasers. They are food for the cotton-field, and the deadly sugar-mill. Mark the sad procession, as it moves wearily along, and the inhuman wretch who drives them. Hear his savage yells and his blood-chilling oaths, as he hurries on his affrighted captives! There, see the old man, with locks thinned and grey. Cast one glance, if you please, upon that young mother, whose shoulders are bare to the scorching sun, her briny tears falling on the brow of the babe in her arms. See, too, that girl of thirteen, weeping, yes! weeping, as she thinks of the mother from whom she has been torn! The drove moves tardily. Heat and sorrow have nearly consumed their strength; suddenly you hear a quick snap, like the discharge of a rifle; the fetters clank, and the chain rattles simultaneously; your ears are saluted with a scream, that seems to have torn its way to the centre of your soul! The crack you heard, was the sound of the slave-whip; the scream you heard, was from the woman you saw with the babe. Her speed had faltered under the weight of her child and her chains! that gash on her shoulder tells her to move on. Follow the drove to New Orleans. Attend the auction; see men examined like horses; see the forms of women rudely and brutally exposed to the shocking gaze of American slave-buyers. See this drove sold and separated forever; and never forget the deep, sad sobs that arose from that scattered multitude. Tell me citizens, *where*, under the sun, you can witness a spectacle more fiendish and shocking. Yet this is but a glance at the American slave-trade, as it exists, at this moment, in the ruling part of the United States....

But the church of this country is not only indifferent to the wrongs of the slave, it actually takes sides with the oppressors.... Many of its most eloquent Divines, who stand as the very lights of the church, have shamelessly given the sanction of religion and the Bible to the whole slave system. They have taught that man may, properly, be a slave; that the relation of master and slave is ordained of God; that to send back an escaped bondman to his master is clearly the duty of all the followers of the Lord Jesus Christ; and this horrible blasphemy is palmed off upon the world for Christianity.

For my part, I would say, welcome infidelity! welcome atheism! welcome anything! in preference to the gospel, as preached by those Divines! … [It is] a religion which favours the rich against the poor; which exalts the proud above the humble; which divides mankind into two classes, tyrants and slaves; which says to the man in chains, stay there; and to the oppressor, oppress on; it is a religion which may be professed and enjoyed by all the robbers and enslavers of mankind; it makes God a respecter of persons,[3] denies his fatherhood of the race, and tramples in the dust the great truth of the brotherhood of man….

I have detained my audience entirely too long already. At some future period I will gladly avail myself of an opportunity to give this subject a full and fair discussion.

Allow me to say, in conclusion, notwithstanding the dark picture I have this day presented of the state of the nation, I do not despair of this country. There are forces in operation, which must inevitably work the downfall of slavery. "The arm of the Lord is not shortened,"* and the doom of slavery is certain. I, therefore, leave off where I began, with hope. While drawing encouragement from the Declaration of Independence, the great principles it contains, and the genius of American Institutions, my spirit is also cheered by the obvious tendencies of the age. Nations do not now stand in the same relation to each other that they did ages ago. No nation can now shut itself up from the surrounding world, and trot round in the same old path of its fathers without interference. The time was when such could be done. Long established customs of hurtful character could formerly fence themselves in, and do their evil work with social impunity. Knowledge was then confined and enjoyed by the privileged few, and the multitude walked on in mental darkness. But a change has now come over the affairs of mankind. Walled cities and empires have become unfashionable. The arm of commerce has borne away the gates of the strong city. Intelligence is penetrating the darkest corners of the globe. It makes its pathway over and under the sea, as well as on the earth. Wind, steam, and lightning are its chartered agents. Oceans no longer divide, but link nations together. From Boston to London is now a holiday excursion. Space is comparatively annihilated. Thoughts expressed on one side of the Atlantic, are distinctly heard on the other. The far off and almost fabulous Pacific rolls in grandeur at our feet….

(1852)

---

3 *respecter of persons* In Acts 10.34, Peter claims that "God is no respecter of persons," i.e., that he does not favour people of higher status.

Questions

1. Douglass was invited by a women's anti-slavery society to deliver this speech, and his audience was composed primarily of white women abolitionists. How (if at all) is Douglass's speech tailored to this initial audience? What kind of response do you think Douglass's speech would have evoked in this audience?
2. Find a point in the speech where Douglass uses repetition for rhetorical effect. How effective is this use of repetition? What does it accomplish?
3. Douglass claims that "[a]t a time like this, scorching irony, not convincing argument, is needed" (paragraph 16). What does this mean? How much of the speech excerpted here is devoted to rational argument, and how much is devoted to alternative appeals of the sort Douglass describes?
4. To what extent (if at all) do the criticisms of America advanced by Douglass still apply in the present?

Mary Ann Shadd

from Relations of Canada to American Slavery

In the United States, the Fugitive Slave Act (1850) imposed fines and jail time on anyone who assisted a fugitive slave and made it nearly impossible for accused fugitives to defend themselves in court. This not only increased the already considerable hazards faced by escaped slaves but also effectively allowed for the enslavement of free black people, who could be captured and condemned as fugitives without being allowed to testify in their own defence. Among the many blacks who fled America after the passage of this act was Mary Ann Shadd, an abolitionist, women's rights activist, and teacher born to free parents in the slave state of Delaware. Once in Canada, Shadd co-founded* The Provincial Freeman and Daily Advertiser, *a paper addressing issues such as abolition, women's rights, education, and temperance; she thus became the first woman to start a newspaper in Canada, as well as the first black woman newspaper editor in North America. The following piece, published in the 24 March 1854 edition of* The Provincial Freeman, *is unsigned but was almost certainly written by Shadd.*

The fact that this is a British Province, and that slavery has no existence on British soil, the fact that this soil never was polluted by slaver, and the fact that (since the ever memorable Somerset decision[1]) the slave of another country became a freeman by touching our soil, place us in relations of antagonism to slavery. This was early seen and felt by the slave, and as early seen and felt by the slaveholder. Accordingly, so early as 1825, the attention of the U.S. Government was directed to this point. In the month of May, of that year, the House of Representatives passed a resolution calling upon the President to enter into correspondence with the British Government, for the recovery of slaves

1 *Somerset decision* Landmark 1772 legal ruling that was popularly interpreted to mean that slavery was illegal in Britain, though not in its colonies—and that a slave automatically became free upon entering Britain.

who had escaped into Canada.... From that time to 1842, the number of slaves escaping to Canada constantly and rapidly increased. Then, when a treaty was made between the two Governments, called the Ashburton Treaty, it was most earnestly sought, on the part of the United States Government ... to have an article inserted which should authorize slave catching in Canada; ... but the Court of St. James[2] promptly refused ... to allow the American slaveholder to use Canada as a park to chase human game in.... Canada, therefore, from her connection with the British Crown, is legally and constitutionally in an attitude of antagonism to American slavery. She offers and secures to the American slave, the moment he arrives here, Freedom—British Freedom—impartial Freedom. And when he has stood his seven years' probation, and taken the oath of allegiance, Canada secures to him, at home and abroad, in law and in equity, all the rights and immunities of a British subject.

But there is another view of our relations to this subject. It is painful to admit it ... but disgraceful as it is, it is useless to conceal it. Friendliness to slavery is to be found in this Province in more forms than one.

1. There are some parties here who practised slave-driving in the South. They love slavery as they love the gain they derived from wielding the whip over its victims. A sprinkling of such customers is to be found here and there, the Province over.

2. There are others, too, who have married heiresses to slave estates. Having received their wives and slaves by the same act of matrimony, they are strongly tempted to regard slavery to be as sacred as marriage itself.

3. Then there are persons resident in Canada who were once slaveholders 5
in the West Indies. The glorious people of Great Britain, determined to have the great principle of British freedom applied practically to the enslaved, as well as to all others, like Job, they, through the Government, "broke the jaws of the wicked, and delivered the spoiled out of their teeth."[3] But these ex-slaveholders were never convinced of the sin of slave-holding—or, if convinced of it, they then were converted from it. Hence they are in spirit now, what they were in practice before the act of '32.[4] The influence of these parties is as deeply and wickedly pro-slavery as that of the vilest slaveocrats[5] of New York, Boston, Philadelphia or Baltimore.

---

2 *Court of St. James* Court of the British sovereign, concerned primarily with foreign affairs.

3 *broke the ... their teeth* See Job 29.17.

4 *act of '32* The Act for the Abolition of Slavery throughout the British Colonies was in fact passed by Parliament in August 1833, and began to take effect in August 1834.

5 *slaveocrats* Members of the "slaveocracy," a term abolitionists used to refer to slave-owning elites who used their wealth and power in support of the legality of slavery.

4. As a born Yankee,[6] we are ashamed of it, but it is true that too many of the natives of the United States have brought their pro-slaveryism with them, from the other side. Like the refugee slaves, they come here to enjoy an improvement of their condition, and like them, too, they enjoy the protecting care of this good British realm; but they turn scornfully upon the black man, and do what [they can] to rob him of his rights—to which the latter is as fully entitled as themselves. From sympathy with their native country, and from their own negro-hate, they maintain a constant and growing pro-slavery influence wherever they are settled. There are but very few exceptions to this rule, for it is a rule; and most safely may it be said, that while the Yankees are far from being the only negro-haters, or pro-slavery parties, whose principles disgrace our country, it is nevertheless true that the mass of them are the most decided slaveocrats in the land; and what is more, they most industriously spread and promulgate their sentiments, and seek to make them prevalent and controlling, even to the violation of Her Majesty's laws. We could give abundant illustrations of this.

5. It remains to be said, that the prejudice against negroes, so prevalent in various parts of the Province, as maintained by many persons of all nations, including, of course, native Canadians, is one of the strongest pro-slavery influences that disgraces and degrades our fair county; it does more to place us side by side with American oppressors than any other thing. Everybody knows that it is the North and not the South that supplies the power of public opinion, of the pulpit, the press, commerce, manufactures, literature, religion, politics, everything that keeps slavery alive. Now the sentiment—the controlling sentiment of the people of the North, that renders them the volunteer bodyguard of slavery—is their negro-hate. The maintenance of a like negro-hate here, of course, encourages the same feeling there, and aids it in doing its very worst work. Every Canadian negro-hater is a volunteer British slaveocrat. Every such one is a strengthener of the slave system, and we repeat, that there should be such, is one of the worst facts—the foulest disgrace, the deepest degradation—in all our history.

So long as these facts exist, we shall want anti-slavery labours, organizations, agitation, and newspapers in Canada. Our humble life shall be devoted to the counteracting of the pro-slaveryism of our adopted country. It is for this reason that we leave our own hearthstone, and expose ourselves to so many disagreeables,* as a lecturing agent of the Canadian Anti-Slavery Society.

6 *Yankee* Used within the United Sates, this nickname refers to a native of New England or more generally to those from northern states and Union troops during the Civil War. Used outside the US, the nickname refers more broadly to any resident of the United States. Shadd invokes both usages, for she refers to those in the northern states who abhor slavery while acknowledging that "slaveocrats" reside in northern cities.

Hence it is we consent, without pay, to scribble for the *Provincial Freeman*. And we do believe that the education and improvement of our own people will lay this enmity to liberty and humanity—this friendship for despotism—low, in a death and burial that shall know no resurrection, and that at no very distant day. At any rate we shall labour on in hope.

Let the pro-slaveryism of Canada be overcome, and let the anti-slavery influence of our laws, constitution, and position be fully and freely exerted, and there is no portion of the British Empire whose influence against slavery would be so healthful and so potent as that of Canada.

(1854)

Questions

1. What can you gather from this article about how Canadians in the 1850s conceived of their relationship to Britain? How does Shadd appeal to this relationship?According to Shadd, to what extent could Canadians' actions affect the lives of enslaved people in the United States? In your view, to what extent (if at all) were Canadians obligated to take action regarding slavery in America?
2. In this article, Shadd links slavery both to the corrupting effects of wealth and to sin in general. How does she do this? How persuasive is this strategy?

SIR JOHN A. MACDONALD

from SPEECH DELIVERED ON 6 FEBRUARY 1865 [ON CONFEDERATION]

In 1864, leaders from the Province of Canada (now Ontario and Quebec) persuaded the leaders of Nova Scotia, New Brunswick, Prince Edward Island, and Newfoundland[1] *that all five colonies should form one nation that would be to some degree independent from the British Empire. In October of that year, the leaders met at the Quebec Conference to discuss the mechanisms that would govern the new country. The resulting 72 resolutions—the Quebec Resolutions—would become the basis for the Canadian constitution adopted in 1867.*

Though he was a latecomer to the cause, Sir John A. Macdonald, then serving as "Attorney General West" for the Province of Canada, was a key figure in the proposal to unite the country under a single federal government. In the speech excerpted here, a contribution to the 1865 confederation debates held by the Province of Canada's legislative assembly, Macdonald defends a resolution to petition the British government to unify the British North American Provinces under the terms of the Quebec Resolutions.

Mr. Speaker, in fulfilment of the promise made by the Government to Parliament at its last session, I have moved this resolution. I have had the honour of being charged, on behalf of the Government, to submit a scheme for the Confederation of all the British North American Provinces—a scheme which has been received, I am glad to say, with general, if not universal, approbation in Canada. The scheme, as propounded through the press, has received almost no opposition. While there may be occasionally, here and there, expressions of dissent from some of the details, yet the scheme as a whole has met with

1 Newfoundland did not end up joining Canada at the time of confederation, and did not become a province until 1949.

almost universal approval, and the Government has the greatest satisfaction in presenting it to this House.

This subject, which now absorbs the attention of the people of Canada, and of the whole of British North America, is not a new one. For years it has more or less attracted the attention of every statesman and politician in these provinces, and has been looked upon by many far-seeing politicians as being eventually the means of deciding and settling very many of the vexed questions which have retarded* the prosperity of the colonies as a whole, and particularly the prosperity of Canada.…

The whole scheme of Confederation, as propounded by the Conference,[2] as agreed to and sanctioned by the Canadian Government, and as now presented for the consideration of the people, and the Legislature, bears upon its face the marks of compromise. Of necessity there must have been a great deal of mutual concession. When we think of the representatives of five colonies, all supposed to have different interests, meeting together, charged with the duty of protecting those interests and of pressing the views of their own localities and sections, it must be admitted that had we not met in a spirit of conciliation, and with an anxious desire to promote this union; if we had not been impressed with the idea contained in the words of the resolution—"That the best interests and present and future prosperity of British North America would be promoted by a Federal Union under the Crown of Great Britain"[3]—all our efforts might have proved to be of no avail. If we had not felt that, after coming to this conclusion, we were bound to set aside our private opinions on matters of detail, if we had not felt ourselves bound to look at what was practicable, not obstinately rejecting the opinions of others nor adhering to our own; if we had not met, I say, in a spirit of conciliation, and with an anxious overruling desire to form one people under one government, we never would have succeeded. With these views, we press the question on this House and the country.

I say to this House, if you do not believe that the union of the colonies is for the advantage of the country, that the joining of these five peoples into one nation, under one sovereign, is for the benefit of all, then reject the scheme. Reject it if you do not believe it to be for the present advantage and future prosperity of yourselves and your children. But if, after a calm and full consideration of this scheme, it is believed, as a whole, to be for the advantage of this province—if the House and the country believe this union to be one which

---

2 *the Conference* The Quebec Conference.

3 *"That the ... Great Britain"* The full text of this, the first of the 72 Quebec Resolutions, is as follows: "The best interests and present and future prosperity of British North America will be promoted by a Federal Union under the Crown of Great Britain, provided such Union can be effected on principles just to the several Provinces."

will ensure for us British laws, British connection, and British freedom—and increase and develop the social, political and material prosperity of the country, then I implore this House and the country to lay aside all prejudices, and accept the scheme which we offer. I ask this House to meet the question in the same spirit in which the delegates met it. I ask each member of this House to lay aside his own opinions as to particular details, and to accept the scheme as a whole if he think it beneficial as a whole.…

I hope the House will not adopt any such a course as will postpone, perhaps for ever, or at all events for a long period, all chances of union. All the statesmen and public men who have written or spoken on the subject admit the advantages of a union, if it were practicable: and now when it is proved to be practicable, if we do not embrace this opportunity the present favourable time will pass away, and we may never have it again. Because, just so surely as this scheme is defeated, will be revived the original proposition for a union of the Maritime Provinces, irrespective of Canada;[4] they will not remain as they are now, powerless, scattered, helpless communities; they will form themselves into a power, which, though not so strong as if united with Canada, will nevertheless, be a powerful and considerable community, and it will be then too late for us to attempt to strengthen ourselves by this scheme, which, in the words of the resolution, "is for the best interests, and present and future prosperity of British North America."

If we are not blind to our present position, we must see the hazardous situation in which all the great interests of Canada stand in respect to the United States. I am no alarmist. I do not believe in the prospect of immediate war. I believe that the common sense of the two nations will prevent a war; still we cannot trust to probabilities. The Government and Legislature would be wanting in their duty to the people if they ran any risk. We know that the United States at this moment are engaged in a war of enormous dimensions[5]—that the occasion of a war with Great Britain has again and again arisen, and may at any time in the future again arise.[6] We cannot foresee what may be the result; we cannot say but that the two nations may drift into a war as other nations have done before. It would then be too late when war had commenced to think of measures for strengthening ourselves, or to begin negotiations for a union with the sister provinces.…

---

4 *proposition ... Canada* The leaders of New Brunswick, Nova Scotia, and Prince Edward Island had expressed interest in joining together in a Maritime union, but their negotiations were halted in favour of pursuing the larger confederation scheme.

5 *a war of enormous dimensions* The American Civil War (1861–65).

6 *may ... arise* Tensions between the United States and the United Kingdom over the Trent Affair—a diplomatic incident in 1861 that could have resulted in a war—were fresh in the minds of the government.

The Conference having come to the conclusion that a legislative union, pure and simple, was impracticable, our next attempt was to form a government upon federal principles,[7] which would give to the General Government the strength of a legislative and administrative union, while at the same time it preserved that liberty of action for the different sections which is allowed by the Federal Union. And I am strong in the belief—that we have hit upon the happy medium in those resolutions, and that we have formed a scheme of government which unites the advantages of both, giving us the strength of a legislative union and the sectional freedom of a federal union, with protection to local interests.

In doing so we had the advantage of the experience of the United States. It is the fashion now to enlarge on the defects of the Constitution of the United States, but I am not one of those who look upon it as a failure. [Hear, hear.][8] I think and believe that it is one of the most skillful works which human intelligence ever created; is one of the most perfect organizations that ever governed a free people. To say that it has some defects is but to say that it is not the work of Omniscience,* but of human intellects. We are happily situated in having had the opportunity of watching its operation, seeing its working from its infancy till now. It was in the main formed on the model of the Constitution of Great Britain, adapted to the circumstances of a new country, and was perhaps the only practicable system that could have been adopted under the circumstances existing at the time of its formation. We can now take advantage of the experience of the last seventy-eight years, during which that Constitution has existed, and I am strongly of the belief that we have, in a great measure, avoided in this system which we propose for the adoption of the people of Canada, the defects which time and events have shown to exist in the American Constitution....

In the Constitution we propose to continue the system of Responsible Government, which has existed in this province since 1841, and which has long obtained in the Mother Country. This is a feature of our Constitution as we have it now, and as we shall have it in the Federation, in which, I think, we avoid one of the great defects in the Constitution of the United States. There the President, during his term of office, is in a great measure a despot, a one-man power, with the command of the naval and military forces—with an immense amount of patronage as head of the Executive,[9] and with the veto power as a

---

7 *legislative union ... federal principles* A legislative union would unite all the provinces under a single legislative body with one set of laws; a federal union would allow provinces to maintain separate legislatures with autonomy in specific areas of governance.

8 *[Hear, hear.]* Interjections made by the audience are recorded in square brackets.

9 *Executive* The American government is made of up three branches: The Executive (the office of the President), the Legislative (Congress), and the Judicial (the courts).

branch of the legislature, perfectly uncontrolled by responsible advisers, his cabinet being departmental officers merely, whom he is not obliged by the Constitution to consult with, unless he chooses to do so. With us the Sovereign, or in this country the Representative of the Sovereign, can act only on the advice of his ministers, those ministers being responsible to the people through Parliament.

Prior to the formation of the American Union, as we all know, the different states which entered into it were separate colonies. They had no connection with each other further than that of having a common sovereign, just as with us at present. Their constitutions and their laws were different. They might and did legislate against each other, and when they revolted against the Mother Country they acted as separate sovereignties, and carried on the war by a kind of treaty of alliance against the common enemy. Ever since the union was formed the difficulty of what is called "State Rights" has existed, and this had much to do in bringing on the present unhappy war in the United States.

They commenced, in fact, at the wrong end. They declared by their Constitution that each state was a sovereignty in itself, and that all the powers incident to a sovereignty belonged to each state, except those powers which by the Constitution, were conferred upon the General Government and Congress.

Here we have adopted a different system. We have strengthened the General Government. We have given the General Legislature all the great subjects of legislation. We have conferred on them, not only specifically and in detail, all the powers which are incident to sovereignty, but we have expressly declared that all subjects of general interest not distinctly and exclusively conferred upon the local governments and local legislatures, shall be conferred upon the General Government and Legislature. We have thus avoided that great source of weakness which has been the cause of the disruption of the United States. We have avoided all conflict of jurisdiction and authority, and if this Constitution is carried out, as it will be in full detail in the Imperial Act[10] to be passed if the colonies adopt the scheme, we will have in fact, as I said before, all the advantages of a legislative union under one administration, with, at the same time the guarantees for local institutions and for local laws, which are insisted upon by so many in the provinces now, I hope, to be united....

It is true that we stand in danger, as we have stood in danger again and again in Canada, of being plunged into war and suffering all its dreadful consequences, as the result of causes over which we have no control, by reason of [our] connection [to the British Empire]. This, however, did not intimidate us. At the very mention of the prospect of a war some time ago, how were the

10 *Imperial Act* Enacted by the Imperial Parliament in London, the British North America Act creating the Dominion of Canada came into effect on 1 July 1867.

feelings of the people aroused from one extremity of British America to the other, and preparations made for meeting its worst consequences. Although the people of this country are fully aware of the horrors of war—should a war arise, unfortunately, between the United States and England, and we all pray it never may—they are still ready to encounter all perils of that kind, for the sake of the connection with England. There is not one adverse voice, not one adverse opinion on that point.

We all feel the advantages we derive from our connection with England. So long as that alliance is maintained, we enjoy, under her protection, the privileges of constitutional liberty according to the British system. We will enjoy here that which is the great test of constitutional freedom—we will have the rights of the minority respected. [Hear, hear.] In all countries the rights of the majority take care of themselves, but it is only in countries like England, enjoying constitutional liberty, and safe from the tyranny of a single despot or of an unbridled democracy, that the rights of minorities are regarded. So long, too, as we form a portion of the British Empire, we shall have the example of her free institutions, of the high standard of the character of her statesmen and public men, of the purity of her legislation, and the upright administration of her laws. In this younger country one great advantage of our connection with Great Britain will be, that, under her auspices, inspired by her example, a portion of her empire, our public men will be actuated[11] by principles similar to those which actuate the statesmen at home. These although not material physical benefits, of which you can make an arithmetical calculation, are of such overwhelming advantage to our future interests and standing as a nation, that to obtain them is well worthy of any sacrifices we may be called upon to make, and the people of this country are ready to make them. [Cheers.]

We should feel, also, sincerely grateful to beneficent Providence that we have had the opportunity vouchsafed us of calmly considering this great constitutional change, this peaceful revolution—that we have not been hurried into it, like the United States, by the exigencies of war—that we have not had a violent revolutionary period forced on us, as in other nations, by hostile action from without, or by domestic dissensions within. Here we are in peace and prosperity, under the fostering government of Great Britain—a dependent people, with a government having only a limited and delegated authority, and yet allowed, without restriction, and without jealousy on the part of the Mother Country, to legislate for ourselves, and peacefully and deliberately to consider and to determine the future of Canada and of British North America. It is our happiness to know the expression of the will of our Gracious Sovereign, through Her Ministers, that we have her full sanction for our deliberations, that

11 *actuated* Motivated.

Her only solicitude is that we shall adopt a system which shall be really for our advantage, and that She promises to sanction whatever conclusion after full deliberation we may arrive at as to the best mode of securing the well-being—the present and future prosperity of British America. [Cheers.] It is our privilege and happiness to be in such a position, and we cannot be too grateful for the blessings thus conferred upon us. [Hear, hear.]

I must apologize for having detained you so long—for having gone perhaps too much into tedious details with reference to the questions bearing on the Constitution now submitted to this House. [Cries of "no, no" and "go on."] In conclusion, I would again implore the House not to let this opportunity to pass. It is an opportunity that may never recur. At the risk of repeating myself, I would say, it was only by a happy concurrence of circumstances, that we were enabled to bring this great question to its present position. If we do not take advantage of the time, if we show ourselves unequal to the occasion, it may never return, and we shall hereafter bitterly and unavailingly regret having failed to embrace the happy opportunity now offered of founding a great nation under the fostering care of Great Britain, and our Sovereign Lady, Queen Victoria. [Loud cheers, amidst which the honourable gentleman resumed his seat.]

(1865)

Questions

1. According to Macdonald, how is Canada's governmental structure like America's? How is it different?
2. Consider the province or territory you are in. How would you characterize this province or territory's relationship to the federal government? In your experience, has the country's constitution fostered a smooth relationship between levels of government?
3. What, according to Macdonald, were the advantages of maintaining a connection with the United Kingdom? Given these arguments, do you think Canada was right to preserve its connection to the UK?
4. From this speech, what can you surmise about what objections had been raised in opposition to confederation? How effectively does Macdonald's speech address these objections?

Charles Darwin

from On the Origin of Species by Means of Natural Selection

The 1859 publication of Darwin's On the Origin of Species *is a landmark in the history of ideas as it is in the history of science. From ancient Greece to the early nineteenth century, many had suggested that life as we know it had evolved over time (though others denied that there had been any change in species since their creation). The theory of natural selection, however, was the first detailed, cogent, and plausible theory as to how the mechanism of evolution operates. Its impact on many aspects of Western thought—from belief in divine creation to views regarding the relationship between humans and other living beings—was tremendous. In the excerpts included here, Darwin outlines some of the background to the development of his theory, and some of its key precepts.*

Introduction

When on board H.M.S. *Beagle*, as naturalist,[1] I was much struck with certain facts in the distribution of the inhabitants of South America, and in the geological relations of the present to the past inhabitants of that continent. These facts seemed to me to throw some light on the origin of species—that mystery of mysteries, as it has been called by one of our greatest philosophers. On my return home, it occurred to me, in 1837, that something might perhaps be made out on this question by patiently accumulating and reflecting on all sorts of facts which could possibly have any bearing on it. After five years' work I allowed myself to speculate on the subject, and drew up some short notes; these I enlarged in 1844 into a sketch of the conclusions, which then seemed to me probable: from that period to the present day I have steadily pursued the same object. I hope that I may be excused for entering on these personal details, as I give them to show that I have not been hasty in coming to a decision.

---

1 *When on board ... naturalist* Darwin travelled on the *Beagle* between 1831 and 1836.

My work is now nearly finished; but as it will take me two or three more years to complete it, and as my health is far from strong, I have been urged to publish this abstract. I have more especially been induced to do this, as Mr. Wallace,[2] who is now studying the natural history of the Malay archipelago, has arrived at almost exactly the same general conclusions that I have on the origin of species. Last year he sent to me a memoir* on this subject, with a request that I would forward it to Sir Charles Lyell,[3] who sent it to the Linnean Society,[4] and it is published in the third volume of the Journal of that Society. Sir C. Lyell and Dr. Hooker,[5] who both knew of my work—the latter having read my sketch of 1844—honoured me by thinking it advisable to publish, with Mr. Wallace's excellent memoir, some brief extracts from my manuscripts....

In considering the origin of species, it is quite conceivable that a naturalist, reflecting on the mutual affinities of organic beings, on their embryological relations, their geographical distribution, geological succession, and other such facts, might come to the conclusion that each species had not been independently created, but had descended, like varieties,[6] from other species. Nevertheless, such a conclusion, even if well founded, would be unsatisfactory, until it could be shown how the innumerable species inhabiting this world have been modified, so as to acquire that perfection of structure and coadaptation which most justly excites our admiration. Naturalists continually refer to external conditions, such as climate, food, *et cetera*, as the only possible cause of variation. In one very limited sense, as we shall hereafter see, this may be true; but it is preposterous to attribute to mere external conditions, the structure, for instance, of the woodpecker, with its feet, tail, beak, and tongue, so admirably adapted to catch insects under the bark of trees. In the case of the mistletoe, which draws its nourishment from certain trees, which has seeds that must be transported by certain birds, and which has flowers with separate sexes absolutely requiring the agency of certain insects to bring pollen from one flower to the other, it is equally preposterous to account for the structure

---

2 *Mr. Wallace* Alfred Russel Wallace (1823–1913), English naturalist and social critic. Though it was Darwin who developed the theory at length and in detail, Wallace is credited as a co-discoverer of the theory of natural selection.

3 *Sir Charles Lyell* British geologist (1797–1875).

4 *Linnean Society* Prominent London scientific society.

5 *Dr. Hooker* Joseph Dalton Hooker (1817–1911), botanist and friend of Darwin.

6 *varieties* In biology, a "variety" is a smaller category than a species or subspecies. While the members of two different species cannot normally interbreed, and the members of two different subspecies can interbreed but usually do not in practice, the members of two varieties can and do interbreed.

of this parasite, with its relations to several distinct organic beings, by the effects of external conditions, or of habit, or of the volition of the plant itself.

The author of the *Vestiges of Creation*[7] would, I presume, say that, after a certain unknown number of generations, some bird had given birth to a woodpecker, and some plant to the mistletoe, and that these had been produced perfect as we now see them; but this assumption seems to me to be no explanation, for it leaves the case of the co-adaptations of organic beings to each other and to their physical conditions of life, untouched and unexplained.

It is, therefore, of the highest importance to gain a clear insight into the means of modification and coadaptation. At the commencement of my observations it seemed to me probable that a careful study of domesticated animals and of cultivated plants would offer the best chance of making out this obscure problem. Nor have I been disappointed; in this and in all other perplexing cases I have invariably found that our knowledge, imperfect though it be, of variation under domestication, afforded the best and safest clue. I may venture to express my conviction of the high value of such studies, although they have been very commonly neglected by naturalists.

From these considerations, I shall devote the first chapter of this abstract to variation under domestication. We shall thus see that a large amount of hereditary modification is at least possible, and, what is equally or more important, we shall see how great is the power of man in accumulating by his selection successive slight variations. I will then pass on to the variability of species in a state of nature; but I shall, unfortunately, be compelled to treat this subject far too briefly, as it can be treated properly only by giving long catalogues of facts. We shall, however, be enabled to discuss what circumstances are most favourable to variation. In the next chapter the struggle for existence amongst all organic beings throughout the world, which inevitably follows from their high geometrical ratio[8] of increase, will be treated of. This is the doctrine of Malthus,[9] applied to the whole animal and vegetable kingdoms. As many more individuals of each species are born than can possibly survive; and as, consequently, there is a frequently recurring struggle for existence, it follows that any being, if it vary however slightly in any manner profitable to itself, under the complex and sometimes varying conditions of life, will have a better

---

7 *Vestiges of Creation* 1844 book, published anonymously but written by Robert Chambers, which suggests that progressive evolution is God's act of creation through geological time.

8 *geometrical ratio* Each number in a geometric sequence is produced by multiplying the previous number by a fixed number called the "geometric ratio."

9 *Malthus* Thomas Robert Malthus (1766–1834), who theorized in his 1798 work *An Essay on the Principle of Population* that the human population would eventually outstrip its food resources.

chance of surviving, and thus be *naturally selected.* From the strong principle of inheritance, any selected variety will tend to propagate its new and modified form.

This fundamental subject of natural selection will be treated at some length in the fourth chapter; and we shall then see how natural selection almost inevitably causes much extinction of the less improved forms of life and induces what I have called divergence of character. In the next chapter I shall discuss the complex and little known laws of variation and of correlation of growth. In the four succeeding chapters, the most apparent and gravest difficulties on the theory will be given: namely, first, the difficulties of transitions, or in understanding how a simple being or a simple organ can be changed and perfected into a highly developed being or elaborately constructed organ; secondly the subject of instinct, or the mental powers of animals, thirdly, hybridism, or the infertility of species and the fertility of varieties when intercrossed; and fourthly, the imperfection of the geological record. In the next chapter I shall consider the geological succession of organic beings throughout time; in the eleventh and twelfth, their geographical distribution throughout space; in the thirteenth, their classification or mutual affinities, both when mature and in an embryonic condition. In the last chapter I shall give a brief recapitulation of the whole work, and a few concluding remarks.

No one ought to feel surprise at much remaining as yet unexplained in regard to the origin of species and varieties, if he makes due allowance for our profound ignorance in regard to the mutual relations of all the beings which live around us. Who can explain why one species ranges widely and is very numerous, and why another allied species has a narrow range and is rare? Yet these relations are of the highest importance, for they determine the present welfare, and, as I believe, the future success and modification of every inhabitant of this world. Still less do we know of the mutual relations of the innumerable inhabitants of the world during the many past geological epochs in its history. Although much remains obscure, and will long remain obscure, I can entertain no doubt, after the most deliberate study and dispassionate judgment of which I am capable, that the view which most naturalists entertain, and which I formerly entertained—namely, that each species has been independently created—is erroneous. I am fully convinced that species are not immutable; but that those belonging to what are called the same genera[10] are lineal descendants of some other and generally extinct species, in the same manner as the acknowledged varieties of any one species are the descendants of that species. Furthermore, I am convinced that natural selection has been the main but not exclusive means of modification....

---

10 *genera* Latin: groupings of species. Plural of "genus."

CHAPTER 3: STRUGGLE FOR EXISTENCE

Before entering on the subject of this chapter, I must make a few preliminary remarks, to show how the struggle for existence bears on natural selection. It has been seen in the last chapter that amongst organic beings in a state of nature there is some individual variability; indeed I am not aware that this has ever been disputed. It is immaterial for us whether a multitude of doubtful forms be called species or sub-species or varieties; what rank, for instance, the two or three hundred doubtful forms of British plants are entitled to hold, if the existence of any well-marked varieties be admitted. But the mere existence of individual variability and of some few well-marked varieties, though necessary as the foundation for the work, helps us but little in understanding how species arise in nature. How have all those exquisite adaptations of one part of the organization to another part, and to the conditions of life, and of one distinct organic being to another being, been perfected? We see these beautiful co-adaptations most plainly in the woodpecker and mistletoe; and only a little less plainly in the humblest parasite which clings to the hairs of a quadruped or feathers of a bird; in the structure of the beetle which dives through the water; in the plumed seed which is wafted by the gentlest breeze; in short, we see beautiful adaptations everywhere and in every part of the organic world.

Again, it may be asked, how is it that varieties, which I have called incipi- 10
ent species, become ultimately converted into good and distinct species, which in most cases obviously differ from each other far more than do the varieties of the same species? How do those groups of species, which constitute what are called distinct genera, and which differ from each other more than do the species of the same genus, arise? All these results, as we shall more fully see in the next chapter, follow inevitably from the struggle for life. Owing to this struggle for life, any variation, however slight and from whatever cause proceeding, if it be in any degree profitable to an individual of any species, in its infinitely complex relations to other organic beings and to external nature, will tend to the preservation of that individual, and will generally be inherited by its offspring. The offspring, also, will thus have a better chance of surviving, for, of the many individuals of any species which are periodically born, but a small number can survive. I have called this principle, by which each slight variation, if useful, is preserved, by the term of natural selection, in order to mark its relation to man's power of selection. We have seen that man by selection can certainly produce great results, and can adapt organic beings to his own uses, through the accumulation of slight but useful variations, given to him by the hand of nature. But natural selection, as we shall hereafter see, is a power incessantly ready for action, and is as immeasurably superior to man's feeble efforts, as the works of nature are to those of art.

We will now discuss in a little more detail the struggle for existence. In my future work this subject shall be treated, as it well deserves, at much greater length. The elder De Candolle[11] and Lyell have largely and philosophically shown that all organic beings are exposed to severe competition. In regard to plants, no one has treated this subject with more spirit and ability than W. Herbert,[12] Dean of Manchester, evidently the result of his great horticultural knowledge. Nothing is easier than to admit in words the truth of the universal struggle for life, or more difficult—at least I have found it so—than constantly to bear this conclusion in mind. Yet unless it be thoroughly engrained in the mind, I am convinced that the whole economy of nature, with every fact on distribution, rarity, abundance, extinction, and variation, will be dimly seen or quite misunderstood. We behold the face of nature bright with gladness, we often see superabundance of food; we do not see, or we forget, that the birds which are idly singing round us mostly live on insects or seeds, and are thus constantly destroying life; or we forget how largely these songsters, or their eggs, or their nestlings, are destroyed by birds and beasts of prey; we do not always bear in mind, that though food may be now superabundant, it is not so at all seasons of each recurring year.

I should premise that I use the term struggle for existence in a large and metaphorical sense, including dependence of one being on another, and including (which is more important) not only the life of the individual, but success in leaving progeny. Two canine animals in a time of dearth, may be truly said to struggle with each other which shall get food and live. But a plant on the edge of a desert is said to struggle for life against the drought, though more properly it should be said to be dependent on the moisture. A plant which annually produces a thousand seeds, of which on an average only one comes to maturity, may be more truly said to struggle with the plants of the same and other kinds which already clothe the ground. The mistletoe is dependent on the apple and a few other trees, but can only in a far-fetched sense be said to struggle with these trees, for if too many of these parasites grow on the same tree, it will languish and die. But several seedling mistletoes, growing close together on the same branch, may more truly be said to struggle with each other. As the mistletoe is disseminated by birds, its existence depends on birds; and it may metaphorically be said to struggle with other fruit-bearing plants, in order to tempt birds to devour and thus disseminate its seeds rather than those of other plants. In these several senses, which pass into each other, I use for convenience' sake the general term of struggle for existence.

---

11 *The elder De Candolle* Augustin-Pyramus de Candolle (1778–1841), Swiss botanist.

12 *W. Herbert* William Herbert (1778–1847).

A struggle for existence inevitably follows from the high rate at which all organic beings tend to increase. Every being, which during its natural lifetime produces several eggs or seeds, must suffer destruction during some period of its life, and during some season or occasional year, otherwise, on the principle of geometrical increase, its numbers would quickly become so inordinately great that no country could support the product. Hence, as more individuals are produced than can possibly survive, there must in every case be a struggle for existence, either one individual with another of the same species, or with the individuals of distinct species, or with the physical conditions of life. It is the doctrine of Malthus applied with manifold force to the whole animal and vegetable kingdoms; for in this case there can be no artificial increase of food, and no prudential restraint from marriage. Although some species may be now increasing, more or less rapidly, in numbers, all cannot do so, for the world would not hold them.

There is no exception to the rule that every organic being naturally increases at so high a rate, that if not destroyed, the earth would soon be covered by the progeny of a single pair. Even slow-breeding man has doubled in twenty-five years, and at this rate, in a few thousand years, there would literally not be standing room for his progeny. Linnaeus[13] has calculated that if an annual plant produced only two seeds—and there is no plant so unproductive as this—and their seedlings next year produced two, and so on, then in twenty years there would be a million plants. The elephant is reckoned to be the slowest breeder of all known animals, and I have taken some pains to estimate its probable minimum rate of natural increase: it will be under the mark to assume that it breeds when thirty years old, and goes on breeding till ninety years old, bringing forth three pair of young in this interval; if this be so, at the end of the fifth century there would be alive fifteen million elephants, descended from the first pair.

But we have better evidence on this subject than mere theoretical calculations, namely, the numerous recorded cases of the astonishingly rapid increase of various animals in a state of nature, when circumstances have been favourable to them during two or three following seasons. Still more striking is the evidence from our domestic animals of many kinds which have run wild in several parts of the world: if the statements of the rate of increase of slow-breeding cattle and horses in South America, and latterly in Australia, had not been well authenticated, they would have been quite incredible. So it is with plants: cases could be given of introduced plants which have become common throughout whole islands in a period of less than ten years. Several of the plants

13 *Linnaeus* Carolus Linnaeus (1707–78), Swedish scientist who laid the foundations of modern taxonomy.

now most numerous over the wide plains of La Plata,[14] clothing square leagues of surface almost to the exclusion of all other plants, have been introduced from Europe; and there are plants which now range in India, as I hear from Dr. Falconer,[15] from Cape Comorin[16] to the Himalaya, which have been imported from America since its discovery. In such cases, and endless instances could be given, no one supposes that the fertility of these animals or plants has been suddenly and temporarily increased in any sensible degree. The obvious explanation is that the conditions of life have been very favourable, and that there has consequently been less destruction of the old and young, and that nearly all the young have been enabled to breed. In such cases the geometrical ratio of increase, the result of which never fails to be surprising, simply explains the extraordinarily rapid increase and wide diffusion of naturalized productions in their new homes....

Many cases are on record showing how complex and unexpected are the checks and relations between organic beings, which have to struggle together in the same country. I will give only a single instance, which, though a simple one, has interested me. In Staffordshire, on the estate of a relation where I had ample means of investigation, there was a large and extremely barren heath, which had never been touched by the hand of man; but several hundred acres of exactly the same nature had been enclosed twenty-five years previously and planted with Scotch fir. The change in the native vegetation of the planted part of the heath was most remarkable, more than is generally seen in passing from one quite different soil to another: not only the proportional numbers of the heath-plants were wholly changed, but twelve species of plants (not counting grasses and carices[17]) flourished in the plantations, which could not be found on the heath. The effect on the insects must have been still greater, for six insectivorous birds were very common in the plantations, which were not to be seen on the heath; and the heath was frequented by two or three distinct insectivorous birds. Here we see how potent has been the effect of the introduction of a single tree, nothing whatever else having been done, with the exception that the land had been enclosed, so that cattle could not enter. But how important an element enclosure is, I plainly saw near Farnham, in Surrey. Here there are extensive heaths, with a few clumps of old Scotch firs on the distant hill-tops: within the last ten years large spaces have been enclosed, and self-sown firs are now springing up in multitudes, so close together that all cannot live. When I

---

14 *La Plata* Region of Argentina.

15 *Dr. Falconer* Hugh Falconer (1808–65), one of the pre-eminent British paleontologists of the time.

16 *Cape Comorin* Southernmost point of the Indian subcontinent.

17 *carices* Sedges.

ascertained that these young trees had not been sown or planted, I was so much surprised at their numbers that I went to several points of view, whence I could examine hundreds of acres of the unenclosed heath, and literally I could not see a single Scotch fir, except the old planted clumps. But on looking closely between the stems of the heath, I found a multitude of seedlings and little trees, which had been perpetually browsed down by the cattle. In one square yard, at a point some hundreds yards distant from one of the old clumps, I counted thirty-two little trees; and one of them, judging from the rings of growth, had during twenty-six years tried to raise its head above the stems of the heath, and had failed. No wonder that, as soon as the land was enclosed, it became thickly clothed with vigorously growing young firs. Yet the heath was so extremely barren and so extensive that no one would ever have imagined that cattle would have so closely and effectually searched it for food.

Here we see that cattle absolutely determine the existence of the Scotch fir; but in several parts of the world insects determine the existence of cattle. Perhaps Paraguay offers the most curious instance of this; for here neither cattle nor horses nor dogs have ever run wild, though they swarm southward and northward in a feral state; and Azara and Rengger[18] have shown that this is caused by the greater number in Paraguay of a certain fly, which lays its eggs in the navels of these animals when first born. The increase of these flies, numerous as they are, must be habitually checked by some means, probably by birds. Hence, if certain insectivorous birds (whose numbers are probably regulated by hawks or beasts of prey) were to increase in Paraguay, the flies would decrease—then cattle and horses would become feral, and this would certainly greatly alter (as indeed I have observed in parts of South America) the vegetation: this again would largely affect the insects; and this, as we just have seen in Staffordshire, the insectivorous birds, and so onwards in ever-increasing circles of complexity. We began this series by insectivorous birds, and we have ended with them. Not that in nature the relations can ever be as simple as this. Battle within battle must ever be recurring with varying success; and yet in the long-run the forces are so nicely balanced, that the face of nature remains uniform for long periods of time, though assuredly the merest trifle would often give the victory to one organic being over another. Nevertheless so profound is our ignorance, and so high our presumption, that we marvel when we hear of the extinction of an organic being; and as we do not see the cause, we invoke cataclysms to desolate the world, or invent laws on the duration of the forms of life!

---

18 *Azara and Rengger* Félix de Azara (1746–1821), Spanish explorer and naturalist, and Johann Rudolph Rengger (1795–1832), German naturalist. In the early part of the nineteenth century, both published influential studies on Paraguayan fauna.

I am tempted to give one more instance showing how plants and animals, most remote in the scale of nature, are bound together by a web of complex relations. I shall hereafter have occasion to show that the exotic *Lobelia fulgens*,[19] in this part of England, is never visited by insects, and consequently, from its peculiar structure, never can set a seed. Many of our orchidaceous plants absolutely require the visits of moths to remove their pollen-masses and thus to fertilize them. I have, also, reason to believe that humble-bees* are indispensable to the fertilization of the heartsease (*Viola tricolor*), for other bees do not visit this flower. From experiments which I have tried, I have found that the visits of bees, if not indispensable, are at least highly beneficial to the fertilization of our clovers; but humble-bees alone visit the common red clover (*Trifolium pratense*), as other bees cannot reach the nectar. Hence I have very little doubt, that if the whole genus of humble-bees became extinct or very rare in England, the heartsease and red clover would become very rare, or wholly disappear. The number of humble-bees in any district depends in a great degree on the number of field-mice, which destroy their combs and nests; and Mr. H. Newman,[20] who has long attended to the habits of humble-bees, believes that "more than two thirds of them are thus destroyed all over England." Now the number of mice is largely dependent, as every one knows, on the number of cats; and Mr. Newman says, "Near villages and small towns I have found the nests of humble-bees more numerous than elsewhere, which I attribute to the number of cats that destroy the mice." Hence it is quite credible that the presence of a feline animal in large numbers in a district might determine, through the intervention first of mice and then of bees, the frequency of certain flowers in that district! …

(1859)

Questions

1. In your own words, define natural selection as it is described in this passage.
2. Consider the description of the "struggle for existence" Darwin offers in chapter 3. Choose any living species; what are the major factors in its struggle for existence?
3. Can the concepts of natural selection and the struggle for existence tell us anything about how human society should function? If so, what do they tell us? If not, why not?
4. What vision of nature does this selection put forward?

---

19 *Lobelia fulgens* Cardinal flower.

20 *Mr. H. Newman* Unidentified.

Oscar Wilde

from The Decay of Lying

Oscar Wilde embodied late nineteenth-century aestheticism in his life, in his prose fiction, and in his plays; he also explored the principles behind it. In "The Decay of Lying," a Platonic dialogue, Wilde sets out a theory of aesthetics through the conversation of two characters, Vivian and Cyril (named after Wilde's two sons). Vivian, prompted by Cyril's questioning, has been reading aloud from his essay-in-progress, also entitled "The Decay of Lying"—an essay supporting Plato's claim that art is falsehood, yet challenging Plato's assertions that art is a mere imitation of life, and that the lies of art are morally repugnant.*

CYRIL. ... The spirit of an age may be best expressed in the abstract ideal arts,[1] for the spirit itself is abstract and ideal. Upon the other hand, for the visible aspect of an age, for its look, as the phrase goes, we must of course go to the arts of imitation.

VIVIAN. I don't think so. After all, what the imitative arts really give us are merely the various styles of particular artists, or of certain schools of artists. Surely you don't imagine that the people of the Middle Ages bore any resemblance at all to the figures on medieval stained glass, or in medieval stone and wood carving, or on medieval metal-work, or tapestries, or illuminated manuscripts. They were probably very ordinary-looking people, with nothing grotesque, or remarkable, or fantastic in their appearance.... Take an example from our own day. I know that you are fond of Japanese things. Now, do you really imagine that the Japanese people, as they are presented to us in art, have any existence? If you do, you have never understood Japanese art at all. The Japanese people are the deliberate self-conscious creation of certain individual artists. If you set a picture by Hokusai, or Hokkei,[2] or any of the great native

---

1 *abstract ideal arts* Forms of art (such as music) that do not attempt to imitate nature.

2 *Hokusai, or Hokkei* Katsushika Hokusai (1760–1849) and Totoya Hokkei (c.1780–1850) were both artists known for works in the highly stylized representational form known as ukiyo-e.

painters, beside a real Japanese gentleman or lady, you will see that there is not the slightest resemblance between them.... The actual people who live in Japan are not unlike the general run of English people; that is to say, they are extremely commonplace, and have nothing curious or extraordinary about them. In fact the whole of Japan is a pure invention. There is no such country, there are no such people.... Or, to return again to the past, take as another instance the ancient Greeks. Do you think that Greek art ever tells us what the Greek people were like? ... The fact is that we look back on the ages entirely through the medium of art, and art, very fortunately, has never once told us the truth.

CYRIL. But modern portraits by English painters, what of them? Surely they are like the people they pretend to represent?

VIVIAN. Quite so. They are so like them that a hundred years from now no one will believe in them. The only portraits in which one believes are portraits where there is very little of the sitter, and a very great deal of the artist. Holbein's drawings[3] of the men and women of his time impress us with a sense of their absolute reality. But this is simply because Holbein compelled life to accept his conditions, to restrain itself within his limitations, to reproduce his type, and to appear as he wished it to appear. It is style that makes us believe in a thing—nothing but style. Most of our modern portrait painters are doomed to absolute oblivion. They never paint what they see. They paint what the public sees, and the public never sees anything.

5 CYRIL. Well, after that I think I should like to hear the end of your article.

VIVIAN. With pleasure. Whether it will do any good I really cannot say. Ours is certainly the dullest and most prosaic century possible.... As for the Church, I cannot conceive anything better for the culture of a country than the presence in it of a body of men whose duty it is to believe in the supernatural, to perform daily miracles, and to keep alive that mythopoeic faculty which is so essential for the imagination. But in the English Church a man succeeds, not through his capacity for belief, but through his capacity for disbelief.... The growth of common sense in the English Church is a thing very much to be regretted. It is really a degrading concession to a low form of realism. It is silly, too. It springs from an entire ignorance of psychology. Man can believe the impossible, but man can never believe the improbable. However, I must read the end of my article:

---

3 *Holbein's drawings* The German-Swiss artist Hans Holbein (1497–1543) lived for some years in England and became well-known for his portraits of such figures as Sir Thomas More and King Henry VIII.

> What we have to do, what at any rate it is our duty to do, is to revive this old art of lying. Much of course may be done, in the way of educating the public, by amateurs in the domestic circle, at literary lunches, and at afternoon teas. But this is merely the light and graceful side of lying.... There are many other forms. Lying for the sake of gaining some immediate personal advantage, for instance—lying with a moral purpose, as it is usually called—though of late it has been rather looked down upon, was extremely popular with the antique world.... Lying for the sake of the improvement of the young, which is the basis of home education, still lingers amongst us, and its advantages are so admirably set forth in the early books of Plato's *Republic** that it is unnecessary to dwell upon them here. It is a mode of lying for which all good mothers have peculiar capabilities, but it is capable of still further development, and has been sadly overlooked by the School Board. Lying for the sake of a monthly salary is of course well known in Fleet Street, and the profession of a political leader-writer[4] is not without its advantages. But it is said to be a somewhat dull occupation, and it certainly does not lead to much beyond a kind of ostentatious obscurity. The only form of lying that is absolutely beyond reproach is lying for its own sake, and the highest development of this is, as we have already pointed out, Lying in Art. Just as those who do not love Plato more than Truth cannot pass beyond the threshold of the Academy, so those who do not love Beauty more than Truth never know the inmost shrine of Art.... [W]e must cultivate the lost art of Lying.

CYRIL. Then we must certainly cultivate it at once. But in order to avoid making any error I want you to tell me briefly the doctrines of the new aesthetics.

VIVIAN. Briefly, then, they are these. Art never expresses anything but itself. It has an independent life, just as Thought has, and develops purely on its own lines. It is not necessarily realistic in an age of realism, nor spiritual in an age of faith. So far from being the creation of its time, it is usually in direct opposition to it, and the only history that it preserves for us is the history of its own progress. Sometimes it returns upon its footsteps, and revives some antique form, as happened in the archaistic movement of late Greek Art, and in the pre-Raphaelite movement[5] of our own day. At other times it entirely

---

4 *Fleet Street ... leader-writer* Fleet Street was long the centre of the English newspaper business. A "leader" in an English newspaper is an editorial.

5 *archaistic ... Greek Art* Reference to a claim made by the critic Walter Pater that Greek art of the fourth century BCE drew on a style that had been employed several

anticipates its age, and produces in one century work that it takes another century to understand, to appreciate and to enjoy. In no case does it reproduce its age. To pass from the art of a time to the time itself is the great mistake that all historians commit.

The second doctrine is this. All bad art comes from returning to Life and Nature, and elevating them into ideals. Life and Nature may sometimes be used as part of Art's rough material, but before they are of any real service to art they must be translated into artistic conventions. The moment Art surrenders its imaginative medium it surrenders everything. As a method Realism is a complete failure, and the two things that every artist should avoid are modernity of form and modernity of subject-matter. To us, who live in the nineteenth century, any century is a suitable subject for art except our own. The only beautiful things are the things that do not concern us. It is, to have the pleasure of quoting myself, exactly because Hecuba is nothing to us that her sorrows are so suitable a motive for a tragedy.[6] Besides, it is only the modern that ever becomes old-fashioned. M. Zola sits down to give us a picture of the Second Empire.[7] Who cares for the Second Empire now? It is out of date. Life goes faster than Realism, but Romanticism is always in front of Life.

The third doctrine is that Life imitates Art far more than Art imitates Life. This results not merely from Life's imitative instinct, but from the fact that the self-conscious aim of Life is to find expression, and that Art offers it certain beautiful forms through which it may realize that energy. It is a theory that has never been put forward before, but it is extremely fruitful, and throws an entirely new light upon the history of Art.

It follows, as a corollary from this, that external Nature also imitates Art. The only effects that she can show us are effects that we have already seen through poetry, or in paintings. This is the secret of Nature's charm, as well as the explanation of Nature's weakness.

---

centuries earlier; *pre-Raphaelite movement* Mid-nineteenth-century English artistic movement that revived aspects of late medieval and early Renaissance style.

6 *exactly because Hecuba ... tragedy* Hecuba, Queen of Troy when that city was conquered by the Greeks, saw her husband and sons murdered. In Shakespeare's Hamlet, one of the players performing for Hamlet recites an emotional monologue on the terrible fate of Hecuba, prompting Hamlet to wonder, "What's Hecuba to him, or he to Hecuba, / That he should weep for her?" (2.2).

7 *M. Zola ... the Second Empire* Louis Napoleon, nephew of Napoleon 1st, and heir to the Napoleonic title, was elected president of France in 1848, and in 1852 dismissed Parliament and declared himself emperor. The Second Empire ended when he was forced from power after France's defeat at the hands of Prussia in 1871. Emile Zola, a leading novelist of the period, coined the term naturalisme (naturalism) to describe his approach to realistic fiction.

The final revelation is that Lying, the telling of beautiful untrue things, is the proper aim of Art. But of this I think I have spoken at sufficient length. And now let us go out on the terrace, where "droops the milk-white peacock like a ghost," while the evening star "washes the dusk with silver."[8] At twilight nature becomes a wonderfully suggestive effect, and is not without loveliness, though perhaps its chief use is to illustrate quotations from the poets. Come! We have talked long enough.

(1889)

Questions

1. Wilde uses the pre-Raphaelite movement as an example of the way in which successful art need not be "the creation of its time," but rather "is usually in direct opposition to it." Ironically, the pre-Raphaelite paintings of Rossetti, Hunt, and others, are now perceived as embodying a good many of the values that were central to Victorian England. In contrast to Wilde, many have claimed that it is impossible for art to escape its own time. With reference to specific works, argue one side of this issue in two or three paragraphs.
2. What are the advantages and disadvantages of putting forward ideas in the form of a dialogue? Discuss whether or not this approach suits Wilde's subject matter here.
3. Victor Cousin first advocated "art for art's sake" ("l'art pour l'art") in a lecture at the Sorbonne in the 1860s. By the late 1880s the aesthetic movement, which took "art for art's sake" as its central principle, had become widely influential. Wilde became one of the leading exponents in the English-speaking world of this movement (variously known as "the aesthetic movement," "the decadents," or simply "fin de siècle" after the time in which the movement flourished). Are there any parallels in the twenty-first century to this movement? What are some of the attractions to the retreat from social involvement that is inherent in the aesthetic movement, and in the valuing of the beautiful for its own sake rather than for any presumed social benefit?

8 *droops the ... ghost* See "Now Sleeps the Crimson Petal," a poem by Alfred, Lord Tennyson; *washes the ... silver* Paraphrased from William Blake's poem "To the Evening Star."

Sir Wilfrid Laurier

from Speech Delivered on 14 October 1904 [The Twentieth Century Shall Be the Century of Canada]

Perhaps the most famous quotation attributed to Canada's seventh prime minister, Sir Wilfrid Laurier, is the pronouncement that "the twentieth century belongs to Canada." In fact Laurier seems not to have said exactly those words on any occasion, but he did say similar things several times during the election campaign of 1904. In a speech given that year to the Canadian Club in Ottawa, for example, he is quoted as having delivered this rather more wordy version of the same sentiment: "the nineteenth century was the century of the United States; I think we can claim that it is Canada that shall fill the 20th century." More succinctly, he declared in the speech included here that "the twentieth century shall be the century of Canada." The immediate context of the remark was a discussion of the Liberal government's plans to assist in the building of a second national railway—one that, unlike the Canadian Pacific Railway, would run entirely on Canadian soil and not connect Quebec and Atlantic Canada by cutting through the American state of Maine.

The Liberals' 14 October campaign event in Toronto, held in Massey Hall, was a major event, featuring several other speeches before the main address by Laurier. Accounts of the evening take up virtually all of the front page of the 15 October issue of the Toronto Star, as well as a good deal of space in interior pages. As was common practice at the time, one of the newspaper's reporters transcribed every word and noted when the crowd interrupted with cheering; the entire speech was reprinted as part of the newspaper's coverage of the event, which a headline described as the "grandest meeting Toronto ever had." The excerpts reprinted here constitute approximately one third of the full speech.

Mr. Chairman, ladies and gentlemen,

Yet once more it is my privilege to appear before an audience of my fellow-citizens of this, the banner city of the banner province of the Dominion.[1] …

Sir, we have been in office now for eight years—our record is before the people of Canada. It is open for search, always open for search, and search under the most glaring light that can be found. To this I have no objections. This I rather welcome. I do not claim that we have been infallible. I do not claim that we may not have made mistakes.

On the contrary, I am prepared to admit that in some things purely departmental[2] we may have been led into errors. But this I may tell you at once, gentlemen of the Province of Ontario, electors of the Dominion of Canada: we have given you a pure and honest government. We are assailed with all the bitterness of the Tory party[3] when they are in opposition; but … the charges which are brought against us [are], after all, very small, very minute, and very trivial. There are no serious charges against us. If those made are to be compared with the offences proved and charged against those who are now our traducers, when they were in office—they are simply as the weight of a feather against a mountain of iniquity. [Loud cheers.] Gentlemen, it is easy to criticize, it is always easy to find fault.

The problem is, the difficulty is, to construct and to build, and I submit again to the judgment of friend and foe, that after eight years in office[4] there is not here, there is not in the country, a man, a citizen, who does not feel prouder in his heart to call himself a Canadian than he was eight years ago. [Loud cheers.] I do not claim credit for the prosperity which this country has witnessed, but I assert that as a result of the policy followed by this government the name of Canada has obtained a prominence which it had not eight years ago. [Applause.] I assert that the name of Canada during these eight years has travelled far and wide, and whether a man be a friend or be a foe, he knows he must admit that there are today in Europe thousands and thousands of men who had never heard the name of Canada eight years ago, and who to-day, every

1 *Dominion* From the time of Confederation in 1867 until the second half of the twentieth century Canada was known as the Dominion of Canada; though the term is now virtually never used, the country still officially maintains the status of a "dominion."

2 *departmental* I.e., administrative. The suggestion is that the party may have made mistakes, but is not guilty of any corruption.

3 *Tory party* Both in Britain and in colonies such as Canada, the Tory Party was the nineteenth century precursor of the Conservative Party; Conservatives are still informally referred to as "Tories."

4 *eight years in office* The Liberal Party took office on 11 July 1896; Laurier and the Liberals would remain in power until 6 October 1911.

day, turn their eyes toward this new star which has appeared in the western sky. [Applause.] …

[D]uring those eight years we have helped the people of Canada. We did not spend our time disputing, quarrelling, or fault finding. We did not spend our time disputing with one another or conspiring one against the other. We spent our time in action, trying to improve for the Canadian people the benefits of Providence, the benefits which Providence had showered upon us.… [I]f Canada has obtained the position it has today it is due altogether to measures which have been advised and enacted by the present government. And the first of these measures, gentlemen, has been the British preference.[5] [Cheers.] … The press commented upon it, the trade commented upon it, indeed, it inspired the poets, and the greatest of all the living poets, of all the English-speaking poets, Rudyard Kipling, made it the subject of one of those noble productions when he said in that famous poem in which he characterized Canada speaking to the Mother Land, "Daughter am I in my mother's house, but mistress in my own." [Applause.] From that day, I say, Canada came before the British public, from that day Canada took the position which it has had ever since. [Applause.] …

But, sir, that is not all. There is another measure which has been undertaken by the Canadian government and which has caused the admiration—the word is not too strong—not only of every right-thinking citizen of this country but of every nation of Europe, and it is that we have undertaken to grapple with the new transportation problem which confronts us and to build a real way from the Pacific Ocean to the Atlantic Ocean on the other side of the continent. [Applause.] I appear before you under no false pretence. I appear before you, I appear before the Canadian people, as the exponent of the Canadian Government upon the subject, upon this position, that at this time of our national development the construction of a railway from a Canadian port upon the Pacific Ocean to a Canadian port upon the Atlantic Ocean—and every inch of it upon Canadian soil—is a political and commercial necessity. Sir, I need not enter upon a lengthy exposition of the project. You understand it and approve it. We are just at the beginning of the twentieth century; we are in the year 1904. We are a nation of six million people already; we expect soon to be twenty-five—yes, forty millions. There are men living in this audience, men over there [pointing to the top gallery], the hope of the country—[applause]—who before they die, if they live to old age, will see this country with at least sixty millions of people. [Renewed applause.]

---

5 *British preference* The Canadian policy of giving preferential treatment in trade policy to Britain was known as British preference; imports were taxed (or taxed more) if they came to Canada from countries other than Britain.

Under such circumstances are we not to provide for the future? Shall we be content to grow up in the gutter and not take steps towards our higher destiny? It is often the mistake of nations that they do not apprehend fully the necessities of the situation. They fail in boldness. That is not and never shall be the case with the government which I represent before you today. [Applause.] We shall not, whatever our errors are otherwise, we shall not err because of want of boldness. [Renewed applause.] We want to grapple with the problems that are before us, and I am free to say, gentlemen, without undue boast, that during the last eight years we have never failed to grapple with any difficulty which has risen before us. [Applause.] …

It … has been asked in the House of Commons, "What is the use of this new railway? You have … communication over the C.P.R., and over American territory." Yes, and this is one of the very reasons why I want this new railway. Our relations with our American neighbours are good at the present time and friendly, and, for my own part, I make no hesitation in saying that I am an admirer of the American people. I admire their energy, I admire their enterprise, and many other qualities. But I have learned in the eight short years that I have been in office that if you want to keep the best possible relations with our neighbours the best way is to be independent of them at every point. [Loud and prolonged cheers.] …

It took a long time for the Conservative party to come to the conclusion upon [whether and how a railway should be built]. They made many and many soundings before they at last found their moorings. They wobbled, and they wobbled, and they wobbled.… I have no right to speak for the Conservative party, but in this new policy[6] I do not find, I do not recognize, the grand old Conservative party which at one time was strong in this country, and to which men were not afraid to belong. It is no longer the party of Sir John MacDonald, or Sir Charles Tupper; it is the party of populism, which found its birth on the other side of the line.[7] [Applause.] It is a party which is cutting away from

---

6 *this new policy* Though the Conservative Party had indeed vacillated in its railway policy under various leaders since the death of Sir John A. Macdonald, it was at this time advocating a second national railway be built under government ownership. The Liberals, on the other hand, insisted that private companies could do the job, provided they were given enough assistance in the form of government loans, loan guarantees, etc. A second national railway was eventually patched together out of the Grand Trunk Pacific Railway, the Canadian Northern Railway, and others; ironically, however, both the Grand Trunk and the Canadian Northern went bankrupt, and the Canadian government had to step in and nationalize both. The resulting railway, the Canadian National, remained under government ownership from 1918 until 1995.

7 *on ... the line* On the other side of the border (i.e., in the United States). In America the People's Party or Populist Party played a significant role in politics from 1892 until

the principles it advocated at one time [and] drifting into the prodigal policy of Government ownership and Government operation of railways. [Renewed applause.] The common sense of the people will not have that, will not listen to them. They understand that we are opposed utterly and wholly to the Government operation.… [Y]ou cannot have a railway operated by the Government with the same efficiency, with the same economy, as by a company. This railway is, my fellow-countrymen, to be built, and in six or seven years it shall be built—[cheers]—and operated by a company.

Gentlemen, I hope to live long enough to see it in operation. I hope to live to see the fertile west, into which thousands and thousands of men are crowding every year—I hope to see the goods of Ontario and Quebec carried into the new territory for the use of the settlers who are pouring in there—nay, I hope also to see the goods of Asia, Japan, the new nation, and of China, the old nation, passing over that railway *en route* to the harbours of Great Britain. [Cheers.] I hope to see that, and it is not a vain hope; if God spares me some years yet, I shall have the satisfaction of seeing it. [Cheers.] …

Sir, I tell you nothing but what you know when I tell you that the nineteenth century has been the century of United States development. The past 100 years has been filled with the pages of their history. Let me tell you, my fellow-countrymen, that all the signs point this way, that the twentieth century shall be the century of Canada and of Canadian development. [Cheers.] For the next 70 years—nay, for the next 100 years—Canada shall be the star towards which all men who love progress and freedom shall come.

Men of Toronto, I have no right to speak to you; I am simply a Canadian like yourselves, coming from another province, but trying the best I can to unite our common people. [Applause.] Men of Toronto, I ask you, and this is the prayer I want to convey to you—I simply ask you to forever sink the petty differences which have divided you in the past, and unite with us and take your share of the grand future which lies before us. [Cheers.] … But if there is one class to which above all others I would convey the appeal it is not to you older men, not to you middle-aged men, but to the young boys in the gallery, the hope of the country. [Cheers.] To those, sir, who have life before them, let my prayer be this: "Remember from this day forth never to look simply at the horizon as it may be limited by the limits of the Province, but look abroad all over the continent, wherever the British flag floats,[8] and let your motto be

---

early in the twentieth century (finally disbanding in 1908). It defended the interests of small farmers against big business—notably including the companies that ran American railroads.

8 *wherever the British flag floats* The British Union Jack retained official status as the flag of Canada until 1946 (although the red Ensign was widely flown from 1868 onwards).

"Canada first, Canada last, and Canada always." [Applause, lasting several minutes.]

(1904)

Questions

1. What vision of Canada's role in the world does Laurier articulate? How does this compare with how you see Canada's role in the world today?
2. Find examples of some of the different ways in which Laurier employs parallel structures in his writing; what effect do these structures have on the reader/listener?
3. As was conventional for many speakers during this era, Laurier sometimes addresses his remarks to "Sir"—in other words, to the person chairing the meeting. He also sometimes addresses his remarks to "gentlemen" or to "men of Toronto." Comment on these styles of address.
4. Write a short speech in an inspirational style on either one of these themes: "Canada and Trade in the Twenty-First Century"; "The Twenty-First Century Shall Be the Century of Canada."

W.E.B. Du Bois

A Mild Suggestion

In the early decades of the twentieth century two sets of ideas held particular importance in African American intellectual life. On the one hand, Booker T. Washington, who was accepted by much of the white establishment as a representative of black Americans, advocated compromise and cooperation with white America, even in the face of Jim Crow laws and other forms of discrimination. On the other, the Harvard-educated academic W.E.B. Du Bois was a much sharper critic of the status quo, and advocated struggle on an ongoing basis for full equality.*

"A Mild Suggestion" was first published in the January 1912 issue of The Crisis, *the NAACP's* monthly magazine, of which Du Bois was the founding editor.*

They were sitting on the leeward deck of the vessel and the coloured man was there with his usual look of unconcern. Before the seasickness his presence aboard had caused some upheaval. The Woman, for instance, glancing at the Southerner, had refused point blank to sit beside him at meals, so she had changed places with the Little Old Lady. The Westerner, who sat opposite, said he did not care a ——, then he looked at the Little Old Lady, and added in a lower voice to the New Yorker that there was no accounting for tastes. The Southerner from the other table broadened his back and tried to express with his shoulders both ancestors and hauteur. All this, however was half forgotten during the seasickness, and the Woman sat beside the coloured man for a full half hour before she noticed it, and then was glad to realize that the Southerner was too sick to see. Now again with sunshine and smiling weather, they all quite naturally reverted (did the Southerner suggest it?) to the Negro problem. The usual solutions had been suggested: education, work, emigration, etc.

They had not noticed the back of the coloured man, until the thoughtless Westerner turned toward him and said breezily: "Well, now, what do you say? I guess you are rather interested." The coloured man was leaning over the rail and about to light his cigarette—he had several such bad habits, as the Little Old Lady noticed. The Southerner simply stared. Over the face of the coloured man went the shadow of several expressions; some the New Yorker could interpret, others he could not.

"I have," said the coloured man, with deliberation, "a perfect solution." The Southerner selected a look of disdain from his repertoire, and assumed it. The Woman moved nearer, but partly turned her back. The Westerner and the Little Old Lady sat down. "Yes," repeated the coloured man, "I have a perfect solution. The trouble with most of the solutions which are generally suggested is that they aggravate the disease." The Southerner could not help looking interested. "For instance," proceeded the coloured man, airily waving his hand, "take education; education means ambition, dissatisfaction and revolt. You cannot both educate people and hold them down."

"Then stop educating them," growled the Southerner aside.

"Or," continued the coloured man, "if the black man works, he must come into competition with whites——"

"He sure will, and it ought to be stopped," returned the Westerner. "It brings down wages."

"Precisely," said the speaker, "and if by underselling the labour market he develops a few millionaires, how now would you protect your residential districts or your select social circles or—your daughters?"

The Southerner started angrily, but the coloured man was continuing placidly with a far-off look in his eyes. "Now, migration is both costly and inhuman; the transportation would be the smallest matter. You must buy up perhaps a thousand millions' worth of Negro property; you must furnish some capital for the masses of poor; you must get some place for them to go; you must protect them there, and here you must pay not only higher wages to white men, but still higher on account of the labour scarcity. Meantime, the Negroes suddenly removed from one climate and social system to another climate and utterly new conditions would die in droves—it would be simply prolonged murder at enormous cost.

"Very well," continued the coloured man, seating himself and throwing away his cigarette, "listen to my plan," looking almost quizzically at the Little Old Lady; "you must not be alarmed at its severity—it may seem radical, but really it is—it is—well, it is quite the only practical thing and it has surely one advantage: it settles the problem once, suddenly, and forever. My plan is this: You now outnumber us nearly ten to one. I propose that on a certain date, shall we say next Christmas, or possibly Easter, 1912? No, come to think of it, the first of January, 1913, would, for historical reasons, probably be best. Well, then, on the first of January, 1913, let each person who has a coloured friend invite him to dinner. This would take care of a few; among such friends might be included the black mammies and faithful old servants of the South; in this way we could get together quite a number. Then those who have not the pleasure of black friends might arrange for meetings, especially in 'white' churches and Young Men's and Young Women's Christian Associations, where Negroes are not expected. At such meetings, contrary to custom, the black people should not be seated by themselves, but distributed very carefully among the whites. The remaining Negroes who could not be flattered or attracted by these invitations should be induced to assemble among themselves at their own churches or at little parties and house warmings.

"The few stragglers, vagrants and wanderers could be put under careful watch and ward. Now, then, we have the thing in shape. First, the hosts of those invited to dine should provide themselves with a sufficient quantity of cyanide of potassium, placing it carefully in the proper cups, and being careful not to mix the cups. Those at church and prayer meeting could choose between long sharp stilettoes and pistols—I should recommend the former as less noisy. Those who guard the coloured assemblies and the stragglers without should carefully surround the groups and use Winchesters. Then, at a given signal, let the coloured folk of the United States be quietly dispatched; the signal might be a church bell or the singing of the national hymn; probably the bell would be best, for the diners would be eating."

By this time the auditors of the coloured man were staring; the Southerner had forgotten to pose; the Woman had forgotten to watch the Southerner; the Westerner was staring with admiration; there were tears in the eyes of the Little Old Lady, while the New Yorker was smiling; but the coloured man held up a deprecating hand: "Now don't prejudge my plan," he urged. "The next morning there would be ten million funerals, and therefore no Negro problem. Think how quietly the thing would be settled; no more bother, no more argument; the whole country united and happy. Even the Negroes would be a great deal happier than they are at present. Instead of being made heirs to hope by education, or ambitious by wealth, or exiled invalids on the fever coast, they would all be happily ensconced in Heaven. Of course, I admit that at first the plan may seem a little abrupt and cruel, and yet is it more cruel than present conditions, and would it not be well to be a little more abrupt in our social solutions? At any rate think it over," and the coloured man dropped lazily into his steamer chair and felt for another cigarette.

The crowd slowly dispersed; the Southerner chose the Woman, but was heard to say something about fools. The Westerner turned to the New Yorker and said: "Now, what in hell do you suppose that darky meant?" But the Little Old Lady went silently to her cabin.

(1912)

Questions

1. This essay is similar in several respects to "A Modest Proposal" by Jonathan Swift. What are some of these similarities? Are there also significant differences between the two essays in tone and approach?
2. "A Mild Suggestion" was published almost 50 years after "emancipation"; in what ways were African Americans evidently still not fully free in 1912?
3. Comment on the tone and diction of Du Bois's prose in this piece. What can you say about the choice of verbs when the crucial part of the proposal is set out ("provide themselves with," "choose between," "carefully surround the groups," "be quietly dispatched")?

Zora Neale Hurston

How It Feels to Be Coloured Me

Among leading figures of the Renaissance in African American literature and culture in the 1920s and 30s, there were often differences of opinion over the degree to which literature and the other arts should be political. Notables such as Langston Hughes and Richard Wright thought black writers and artists had a responsibility to assist the African American struggle against oppression by celebrating African American identity and culture; in his essay "The Negro Artist and the Racial Mountain," Hughes condemns any African American poet who says "I want to be a poet—not a Negro poet," arguing that such a desire to escape race in art is tantamount to a desire to be white. Some others—among them Hurston and Nella Larsen—resisted the sorts of identity politics that Hughes, Wright, and political figures such as W.E.B. Du Bois advocated.*

"How It Feels to Be Coloured Me" was first published in The World Tomorrow, *a magazine devoted to the causes of pacifism and Christian socialism.*

I am coloured but I offer nothing in the way of extenuating circumstances except the fact that I am the only Negro in the United States whose grandfather on the mother's side was *not* an Indian chief.[1]

I remember the very day that I became coloured. Up to my thirteenth year I lived in the little Negro town of Eatonville, Florida. It is exclusively a coloured town. The only white people I knew passed through the town going to or coming from Orlando.* The native whites rode dusty horses, the Northern* tourists chugged down the sandy village road in automobiles. The town knew the Southerners and never stopped cane chewing when they passed. But the Northerners were something else again. They were peered at cautiously from

1 *I am ... Indian chief* An improbably high number of African Americans claimed to have Native American heritage (considered prestigious in African American communities at this time).

behind curtains by the timid. The more venturesome would come out on the porch to watch them go past and got just as much pleasure out of the tourists as the tourists got out of the village.

The front porch might seem a daring place for the rest of the town, but it was a gallery[2] seat for me. My favourite place was atop the gate-post. Proscenium box for a born first-nighter.[3] Not only did I enjoy the show, but I didn't mind the actors knowing that I liked it. I usually spoke to them in passing. I'd wave at them and when they returned my salute, I would say something like this: "Howdy-do-well-I-thank-you-where-you-goin'?" Usually automobile or the horse paused at this, and after a queer exchange of compliments, I would probably "go a piece of the way" with them, as we say in farthest Florida. If one of my family happened to come to the front in time to see me, of course negotiations would be rudely broken off. But even so, it is clear that I was the first "welcome-to-our-state" Floridian, and I hope the Miami Chamber of Commerce* will please take notice.

During this period, white people differed from coloured to me only in that they rode through town and never lived there. They liked to hear me "speak pieces" and sing and wanted to see me dance the parse-me-la,[4] and gave me generously of their small silver for doing these things, which seemed strange to me for I wanted to do them so much that I needed bribing to stop. Only they didn't know it. The coloured people gave no dimes. They deplored any joyful tendencies in me, but I was their Zora nevertheless. I belonged to them, to the nearby hotels, to the county—everybody's Zora.

5 But changes came in the family when I was thirteen, and I was sent to school in Jacksonville. I left Eatonville, the town of the oleanders,* as Zora. When I disembarked from the river-boat at Jacksonville, she was no more. It seemed that I had suffered a sea change.* I was not Zora of Orange County* any more, I was now a little coloured girl. I found it out in certain ways. In my heart as well as in the mirror, I became a fast[5] brown—warranted not to rub nor run.

But I am not tragically coloured. There is no great sorrow dammed up in my soul, nor lurking behind my eyes. I do not mind at all. I do not belong to the sobbing school of Negrohood who hold that nature somehow has given

---

2 *gallery* Theatre seating area situated in an elevated balcony.

3 *Proscenium box* Theatre seating area near the proscenium, the frame of the stage; *first-nighter* Person who frequently appears in the audience of opening night performances.

4 *parse-me-la* Dance common in African American communities in the American South in the early twentieth century.

5 *fast* Adjective applied to dyes that will not run or change colour.

them a lowdown dirty deal and whose feelings are all hurt about it. Even in the helter-skelter skirmish that is my life, I have seen that the world is to the strong regardless of a little pigmentation more or less. No, I do not weep at the world—I am too busy sharpening my oyster knife.*

Someone is always at my elbow reminding me that I am the granddaughter of slaves. It fails to register depression with me. Slavery is sixty years in the past.[6] The operation was successful and the patient is doing well, thank you. The terrible struggle that made me an American out of a potential slave said "On the line!" The Reconstruction[7] said "Get set!"; and the generation before said "Go!"* I am off to a flying start and I must not halt in the stretch to look behind and weep. Slavery is the price I paid for civilization, and the choice was not with me. It is a bully[8] adventure and worth all that I have paid through my ancestors for it. No one on earth ever had a greater chance for glory. The world to be won and nothing to be lost. It is thrilling to think—to know that for any act of mine, I shall get twice as much praise or twice as much blame. It is quite exciting to hold the centre of the national stage, with the spectators not knowing whether to laugh or to weep.

The position of my white neighbour is much more difficult. No brown spectre pulls up a chair beside me when I sit down to eat. No dark ghost thrusts its leg against mine in bed. The game of keeping what one has is never so exciting as the game of getting.

I do not always feel coloured. Even now I often achieve the unconscious Zora of Eatonville before the Hegira.[9] I feel most coloured when I am thrown against a sharp white background.

10 For instance at Barnard.[10] "Beside the waters of the Hudson"[11] I feel my race. Among the thousand white persons, I am a dark rock surged upon, and overswept, but through it all, I remain myself. When covered by the waters, I am; and the ebb but reveals me again.

---

6 *Slavery is ... the past* In 1863, the Emancipation Proclamation legally ended slavery in America.

7 *Reconstruction* Period (1865–77) after the Civil War during which federal troops occupied the former Confederacy and enforced federal laws, as the South tried to build a society without slavery. (With the withdrawal of those troops following the "compromise of 1877," conditions for African Americans in many Southern jurisdictions reverted for many decades to a state little better than slavery.)

8 *bully* Merry, splendid.

9 *Hegira* I.e., journey; refers to Mohammed's journey from Mecca to Medina, which marks the beginning of the current era in the Islamic calendar.

10 *Barnard* Women's liberal arts college in New York City, affiliated with Columbia University.

11 *"Beside ... Hudson"* Barnard school song.

Sometimes it is the other way around. A white person is set down in our midst, but the contrast is just as sharp for me. For instance, when I sit in the drafty basement that is The New World Cabaret with a white person, my colour comes. We enter chatting about any little nothing that we have in common and are seated by the jazz waiters. In the abrupt way that jazz orchestras have, this one plunges into a number. It loses no time in circumlocutions, but gets right down to business. It constricts the thorax and splits the heart with its tempo and narcotic harmonies. This orchestra grows rambunctious, rears on its hind legs and attacks the tonal veil with primitive fury, rending it, clawing it until it breaks through to the jungle beyond. I follow those heathen—follow them exultingly. I dance wildly inside myself; I yell within, I whoop; I shake my assegai[12] above my head, I hurl it true to the mark *yeeeeooww!* I am in the jungle and living in the jungle way. My face is painted red and yellow and my body is painted blue. My pulse is throbbing like a war drum. I want to slaughter something—give pain, give death to what, I do not know. But the piece ends. The men of the orchestra wipe their lips and rest their fingers. I creep back slowly to the veneer we call civilization with the last tone and find the white friend sitting motionless in his seat smoking calmly.

"Good music they have here," he remarks, drumming the table with his fingertips.

Music. The great blobs of purple and red emotion have not touched him. He has only heard what I felt. He is far away and I see him but dimly across the ocean and the continent that have fallen between us. He is so pale with his whiteness then and I am *so* coloured.

At certain times I have no race, I am *me*. When I set my hat at a certain angle and saunter down Seventh Avenue, Harlem City,* feeling as snooty as the lions in front of the Forty-Second Street Library, for instance. So far as my feelings are concerned, Peggy Hopkins Joyce on the Boule Mich[13] with her gorgeous raiment, stately carriage, knees knocking together in a most aristocratic manner, has nothing on me. The cosmic Zora emerges. I belong to no race nor time. I am the eternal feminine with its string of beads.

I have no separate feeling about being an American citizen and coloured. I 15
am merely a fragment of the Great Soul that surges within the boundaries. My country, right or wrong.*

---

12 *assegai* Spear made of a tree of the same name, used by people of southern Africa.

13 *Peggy Hopkins Joyce* White American actress (1893–1957) known for her extravagant lifestyle; *Boule Mich* Boulevard Saint-Michel, a major street in Paris.

Sometimes, I feel discriminated against, but it does not make me angry. It merely astonishes me. How *can* any deny themselves the pleasure of my company? It's beyond me.

But in the main, I feel like a brown bag of miscellany propped against a wall. Against a wall in company with other bags, white, red and yellow. Pour out the contents, and there is discovered a jumble of small things priceless and worthless. A first-water[14] diamond, an empty spool, bits of broken glass, lengths of string, a key to a door long since crumbled away, a rusty knife-blade, old shoes saved for a road that never was and never will be, a nail bent under the weight of things too heavy for any nail, a dried flower or two still a little fragrant. In your hand is the brown bag. On the ground before you is the jumble it held—so much like the jumble in the bags, could they be emptied, that all might be dumped in a single heap and the bags refilled without altering the content of any greatly. A bit of coloured glass more or less would not matter. Perhaps that is how the Great Stuffer of Bags filled them in the first place—who knows?

(1928)

Questions

1. What was the young Zora Neale Hurston like? What was her experience of race and racism in Eatonville as a girl?
2. What does Hurston mean when she says she is "too busy sharpening [her] oyster knife" to "weep at the world"?
3. What metaphor does Hurston use at the close of this essay to describe a human being? What does the metaphor suggest about race?
4. How does Hurston see her own generation in relation to the generations of African Americans before her? How does she see her position in comparison to that of white Americans of her own time?
5. When does Hurston feel most "coloured"? Are the feelings empowering or disempowering?

---

14 *first-water* Best quality of diamond or other gem.

Janet Flanner

Mme. Marie Curie

(1866–1934)

Janet Flanner was the Paris correspondent for The New Yorker *for 50 years, beginning in 1925 when the magazine was founded. She wrote a bi-monthly "Paris Letter" relating the news of Paris, where she was part of an expatriate community that included such important literary figures as Gertrude Stein, Ernest Hemingway, James Joyce, and the many artists associated with them. Flanner's witty, elegant prose helped shape* The New Yorker *house style. She contributed various reviews, journalistic articles, and focus pieces to the magazine over her career, but her many years of writing were distinguished not least of all by her brief biographical obituaries, one of which is printed here. "Marie Curie" was published in the 4 August 1934 issue of* The New Yorker.

The death of Mme. Curie here was an international death. A native of Poland, a worker in France, with radium donated by America, she was a terrifying example of strict scientific fidelity to each of those lands, to all civilized lands. During the early years of her marriage, "I did the housework," she said, "for we had to pay for our scientific research out of our own pockets. We worked in an abandoned shed. It was only a wooden shack with a skylight roof which didn't always keep the rain out." In winter, the poor Curies worked in their overcoats to keep warm; they were then, as always, very much in love with each other and with chemistry.

Today, in America, radium is characteristically supposed to have been found by Mme. Curie, and in France, naturally, the discovery is accredited to Monsieur. Probably both discovered it together, since they were never apart until he was killed in 1906 on a Paris street by a truck. Certainly the husband's first work was with crystals. And no Curie at all, but a friend of theirs, Henri Becquerel, discovered uranium rays. Still, it was Mme. Curie, intrigued and alone, who devised a method of measuring this radioactivity, as she named it; her proving that it contained essential atomic properties instituted a new method of chemical research, altered the conceptions of the nineteenth century, and for the twentieth gave the base for all modern theories concerning matter and energy. Eventually her husband deserted crystals to work with her on the discovery of polonium (which they named after her native land; Madame, *née* Sklodowska, was always a patriotic Pole); then she or he or they discovered radium. Madame thereupon determined the atomic weight of radium and obtained radium in metallic form. For this she was crowned with the Nobel Chemistry Prize. She was the only woman ever permitted to hold the post of university professor in France.

She called fame a burden, was busy, sensible, shy, had no time for polite palaver, was a good mother to her two girls. The younger, Éve, is beautiful and a professional pianist. The older daughter, Irène, carried on her mother's tradition by also marrying a scientist, Fred Joliot; they are the most promising laboratory couple here today, and have already made extremely important discoveries concerning the neutron.

When the Curies were first wed, Madame put her wedding money into a tandem bicycle; later they got around, financially, to two bicycles. Early snapshots show her young, fetching, in short skirt, mutton-leg sleeves, and an incredible hat, flat as a laboratory saucepan. Later in life, her husband said, "No matter what it does to one, even if it makes of one a body without a soul, one must go on with one's work."

5 Mme. Curie had long since been in that zealous condition before she finally died.

(1934)

Questions

1. What does the word "naturally" (paragraph 2) imply about the attitudes Flanner believed to be common in France when she was writing?
2. Much of the effectiveness of brief biographical profiles rests on the degree to which the author is able to select telling details. What can you say about the way in which the details given here about Curie serve to suggest a fully rounded person?
3. Write a brief description of someone who has died—either someone you knew yourself or a public figure who you have not known personally.
4. What effect does the lack of adjectives in Flanner's style have on the reader? Would the impression created of Curie be stronger or weaker if Flanner employed more adjectives to describe her for us?

Virginia Woolf

Professions for Women

Today, Virginia Woolf is admired and studied primarily as the author of such masterpieces as Mrs. Dalloway *(1925),* To the Lighthouse *(1927), and* The Waves *(1931), novels that attempt to capture the rhythms of consciousness by rendering the subjective interplay of perception, recollection, emotion, and understanding. But in her own lifetime Woolf was best known for her non-fiction—in much of which she employed "the democratic art of prose" to communicate with a broad readership on fundamental ethical and political questions. In "Professions for Women," Woolf considers her own history as a writer and the obstacles women face as they pursue work in the professional world. This piece was first delivered as a lecture to the National Society for Women's Service in January 1931; it was later developed into the book-length essay* Three Guineas *(1938), which is excerpted in this anthology's online component.*

When your secretary invited me to come here, she told me that your Society is concerned with the employment of women and she suggested that I might tell you something about my own professional experiences. It is true that I am a woman; it is true I am employed; but what professional experiences have I had? It is difficult to say. My profession is literature; and in that profession there are fewer experiences for women than in any other, with the exception of the stage—fewer, I mean, that are peculiar to women. For the road was cut many years ago—by Fanny Burney, by Aphra Behn, by Harriet Martineau, by Jane Austen, by George Eliot—many famous women, and many more unknown and forgotten, have been before me, making the path smooth, and regulating my steps. Thus, when I came to write, there were very few material obstacles in my way. Writing was a reputable and harmless occupation. The family peace was not broken by the scratching of a pen. No demand was made upon the family purse. For ten and sixpence one can buy paper enough to write all the plays of Shakespeare—if one has a mind that way. Pianos and models, Paris, Vienna, and Berlin,[1] masters and mistresses, are not needed by a writer. The cheapness of writing paper is, of course, the reason why women have succeeded as writers before they have succeeded in the other professions.

But to tell you my story—it is a simple one. You have only got to figure to yourselves a girl in a bedroom with a pen in her hand. She had only to move that pen from left to right—from ten o'clock to one. Then it occurred to her to do what is simple and cheap enough after all—to slip a few of those pages into an envelope, fix a penny stamp in the corner, and drop the envelope into the red box at the corner. It was thus that I became a journalist; and my effort was rewarded on the first day of the following month—a very glorious day it was for me—by a letter from an editor containing a check for one pound ten shillings and sixpence. But to show you how little I deserve to be called a professional woman, how little I know of the struggles and difficulties of such lives, I have to admit that instead of spending that sum upon bread and butter, rent, shoes and stockings, or butcher's bills, I went out and bought a cat—a beautiful cat, a Persian cat, which very soon involved me in bitter disputes with my neighbours.

What could be easier than to write articles and to buy Persian cats with the profits? But wait a moment. Articles have to be about something. Mine, I seem to remember, was about a novel by a famous man. And while I was writing this review, I discovered that if I were going to review books I should need to do battle with a certain phantom. And the phantom was a woman, and when I came to know her better I called her after the heroine of a famous poem, *The Angel in the House*.[2] It was she who used to come between me and my paper when I was writing reviews. It was she who bothered me and wasted my time and so tormented me that at last I killed her. You who come of a younger and happier generation may not have heard of her—you may not know what I mean by the Angel in the House. I will describe her as shortly as I can. She was intensely sympathetic. She was immensely charming. She was utterly unselfish. She excelled in the difficult arts of family life. She sacrificed herself daily. If there was chicken, she took the leg; if there was a draft she sat in it—in short she was so constituted that she never had a mind or a wish of her own, but preferred to sympathize always with the minds and wishes of others. Above all—I need not say it—she was pure. Her purity was supposed to be her chief beauty—her blushes, her great grace. In those days—the last

---

1 *Paris, Vienna, and Berlin* All three are cities that Britons frequently travelled to for training in art and music.

2 *The Angel in the House* Title of an 1854 poem by Coventry Patmore depicting the Victorian ideal of the selfless, domestic wife and mother; the phrase "angel in the house" became a shorthand for this ideal.

of Queen Victoria—every house had its Angel. And when I came to write I encountered her with the very first words. The shadow of her wings fell on my page; I heard the rustling of her skirts in the room. Directly, that is to say, I took my pen in my hand to review that novel by a famous man, she slipped behind me and whispered: "My dear, you are a young woman. You are writing about a book that has been written by a man. Be sympathetic; be tender; flatter; deceive; use all the arts and wiles of our sex. Never let anybody guess that you have a mind of your own. Above all, be pure." And she made as if to guide my pen. I now record the one act for which I take some credit to myself, though the credit rightly belongs to some excellent ancestors of mine who left me a certain sum of money—shall we say five hundred pounds a year?—so that it was not necessary for me to depend solely on charm for my living. I turned upon her and caught her by the throat. I did my best to kill her. My excuse if I were to be had up at a court of law, would be that I acted in self-defense. Had I not killed her she would have killed me. She would have plucked the heart out of my writing. For as I found directly* I put pen to paper, you cannot review even a novel without having a mind of your own, without expressing what you think to be the truth about human relations, morality, sex. And all these questions, according to the Angel of the House cannot be dealt with freely and openly by women; they must charm, they must conciliate, they must—to put it bluntly—tell lies if they are to succeed. Thus, whenever I felt the shadow of her wing or the radiance of her halo upon my page, I took up the inkpot and flung it at her. She died hard.* Her fictitious nature was of great assistance to her. It is far harder to kill a phantom than a reality. She was always creeping back when I thought I had dispatched her. Though I flatter myself that I killed her in the end, the struggle was severe; it took much time that had better have been spent upon learning Greek grammar; or in roaming the world in search of adventures. But it was a real experience; it was an experience that was bound to befall all writers at that time. Killing the Angel in the House was part of the occupation of a woman writer.

But to continue my story. The Angel was dead; what then remained? You may say that what remained was a simple and common object—a young woman in a bedroom with an inkpot. In other words, now that she had rid herself of falsehood, that young woman had only to be herself. Ah, but what is "herself"? I mean, what is a woman? I assure you, I do not know. I do not believe that you know. I do not believe that anybody can know until she has expressed herself in all the arts and professions open to human skill. That indeed is one of the reasons why I have come here—out of respect for you, who are in process of showing us by your experiments what a woman is, who are in process of providing us, by your failures and successes, with that extremely important piece of information.

But to continue the story of my professional experiences. I made one pound ten and six by my first review; and I bought a Persian cat with the proceeds. Then I grew ambitious. A Persian cat is all very well, I said; but a Persian cat is not enough. I must have a motor-car. And it was thus that I became a novelist—for it is a very strange thing that people will give you a motor-car if you will tell them a story. It is a still stranger thing that there is nothing so delightful in the world as telling stories. It is far pleasanter than writing reviews of famous novels. And yet, if I am to obey your secretary and tell you my professional experiences as a novelist, I must tell you about a very strange experience that befell me as a novelist. And to understand it you must try first to imagine a novelist's state of mind. I hope I am not giving away professional secrets if I say that a novelist's chief desire is to be as unconscious as possible. He has to induce in himself a state of perpetual lethargy. He wants life to proceed with the utmost quiet and regularity. He wants to see the same faces, to read the same books, to do the same things day after day, month after month, while he is writing, so that nothing may break the illusion in which he is living—so that nothing may disturb or disquiet the mysterious nosings about, feelings round, darts, dashes, and sudden discoveries of that very shy and illusive spirit, the imagination. I suspect that this state is the same both for men and women. Be that as it may, I want you to imagine me writing a novel in a state of trance. I want you to figure to yourselves a girl sitting with a pen in her hand, which for minutes, and indeed for hours, she never dips into the inkpot. The image that comes to my mind when I think of this girl is the image of a fisherman lying sunk in dreams on the verge of a deep lake with a rod held out over the water. She was letting her imagination sweep unchecked round every rock and cranny of the world that lies submerged in the depths of our unconscious being. Now came the experience that I believe to be far commoner with women writers than with men. The line raced through the girl's fingers. Her imagination had rushed away. It had sought the pools, the depths, the dark places where the largest fish slumber. And then there was a smash. There was an explosion. There was foam and confusion. The imagination had dashed itself against something hard. The girl was roused from her dream. She was indeed in a state of the most acute and difficult distress. To speak without figure, she had thought of something, something about the body, about the passion, which it was unfitting for her as a woman to say. Men, her reason told her, would be shocked. The consciousness of what men will say of a woman who speaks the truth about her passions had roused her from her artist's state of consciousness. She could write no more. The trance was over. Her imagination could work no longer. This I believe to be a very common experience with women writers—they are impeded by the extreme conventionality of the other sex. For though men sensibly allow themselves great freedom in these respects,

I doubt that they realize or can control the extreme severity with which they condemn such freedom in women.

These then were two very genuine experiences of my own. These were two of the adventures of my professional life. The first—killing the Angel in the House—I think I solved. She died. But the second, telling the truth about my own experiences as a body, I do not think I solved. I doubt that any woman has solved it yet. The obstacles against her are still immensely powerful—and yet they are very difficult to define. Outwardly, what is simpler than to write books? Outwardly, what obstacles are there for a woman rather than for a man? Inwardly, I think the case is very different; she has still many ghosts to fight, many prejudices to overcome. Indeed it will be a long time still, I think, before a woman can sit down to write a book without finding a phantom to be slain, a rock to be dashed against. And if this is so in literature, the freest of all professions for women, how is it in the new professions which you are now for the first time entering?

Those are the questions that I should like, had I time, to ask you. And indeed, if I have laid stress upon these professional experiences of mine, it is because I believe that they are, though in different forms, yours also. Even when the path is nominally open—when there is nothing to prevent a woman from being a doctor, a lawyer, a civil servant—there are many phantoms and obstacles, as I believe, looming in her way. To discuss and define them is I think of great value and importance; for thus only can the labour be shared, the difficulties be solved. But besides this, it is necessary also to discuss the ends and the aims for which we are fighting, for which we are doing battle with these formidable obstacles. Those aims cannot be taken for granted; they must be perpetually questioned and examined. The whole position, as I see it—here in this hall surrounded by women practicing for the first time in history I know not how many different professions—is one of extraordinary interest and importance. You have won rooms of your own in the house hitherto exclusively owned by men. You are able, though not without great labour and effort, to pay the rent. You are earning your five hundred pounds a year. But this freedom is only a beginning; the room is your own, but it is still bare. It has to be furnished; it has to be decorated; it has to be shared. How are you going to furnish it, how are you going to decorate it? With whom are you going to share it, and upon what terms? These, I think are questions of the utmost importance and interest. For the first time in history you are able to ask them; for the first time you are able to decide for yourselves what the answers should be. Willingly would I stay and discuss those questions and answers—but not tonight. My time is up; and I must cease.

(1931)

Questions

1. The title of this essay suggests a focus on the economic and the practical. How relevant do Woolf's reflections seem to you to be to the stated topic? To what extent do you feel it appropriate to surprise one's audience in a public address by approaching the stated topic from unexpected angles?
2. Comment on the tone with which Woolf describes her own situation in paragraphs 2 and 3 of "Professions for Women." What is the effect of this tone on the reader? Would the effect be altered in a public speech?
3. What do you think Woolf means when she refers in "Professions for Women" to "telling the truth about my own experiences as a body" (paragraph 6)?
4. To what extent is "the Angel in the House" still alive for women today?
5. In paragraph 6 of "Professions for Women" Woolf employs a variety of sentence structures. Comment on the structures of individual sentences—and on structural connections between the various sentences in the paragraph.

THE DEATH OF THE MOTH

This essay was first published in Woolf's posthumous 1942 collection The Death of the Moth and Other Stories.

Moths that fly by day are not properly to be called moths; they do not excite that pleasant sense of dark autumn nights and ivy-blossom which the commonest yellow-underwing asleep in the shadow of the curtain never fails to rouse in us. They are hybrid creatures, neither gay like butterflies nor sombre like their own species. Nevertheless the present specimen, with his narrow hay-coloured wings, fringed with a tassel of the same colour, seemed to be content with life. It was a pleasant morning, mid-September, mild, benignant, yet with a keener breath than that of the summer months. The plough was already scoring the field opposite the window, and where the share[1] had been, the earth

1 *share* Blade of a plow.

was pressed flat and gleamed with moisture. Such vigour came rolling in from the fields and down beyond that it was difficult to keep the eyes strictly turned upon the book. The rooks too were keeping one of their annual festivities; soaring round the tree tops until it looked as if a vast net with thousands of black knots in it had been cast up into the air; which, after a few moments sank slowly down upon the trees until every twig seemed to have a knot at the end of it. Then, suddenly, the net would be thrown into the air again in a wider circle this time, with the utmost clamour and vociferation, as though to be thrown into the air and settle slowly down upon the tree tops were a tremendously exciting experience.

The same energy which inspired the rooks, the ploughmen, the horses, and even, it seemed, the lean bare-backed downs, sent the moth fluttering from side to side of his square of the window pane. One could not help watching him. One was, indeed, conscious of a queer feeling of pity for him. The possibilities of pleasure seemed that morning so enormous and so various that to have only a moth's part in life, and a day moth's at that, appeared a hard fate, and his zest in enjoying his meagre opportunities to the full, pathetic. He flew vigorously to one corner of his compartment, and, after waiting there for a second, flew across to the other. What remained for him but to fly to a third corner and then to a fourth? That was all he could do, in spite of the size of the downs, the width of the sky, the far-off smoke of houses, and the romantic voice, now and then, of a steamer out at sea. What he could do he did. Watching him, it seemed as if a fibre, very thin but pure, of the enormous energy of the world had been thrust into his frail and diminutive body. As often as he crossed the pane, I could fancy that a thread of vital light became visible. He was little or nothing but life.

Yet, because he was so small, and so simple a form of the energy that was rolling in at the open window and driving its way through so many narrow and intricate corridors in my own brain and in those of other human beings, there was something marvellous as well as pathetic about him. It was as if someone had taken a tiny bead of pure life and decking it as lightly as possible with down and feathers, had set it dancing and zig-zagging to show us the true nature of life. Thus displayed one could not get over the strangeness of it. One is apt to forget all about life, seeing it humped and bossed and garnished and cumbered so that it has to move with the greatest circumspection and dignity. Again, the thought of all that life might have been had he been born in any other shape caused one to view his simple activities with a kind of pity.

After a time, tired by his dancing apparently, he settled on the window ledge in the sun, and, the queer spectacle being at an end, I forgot about him. Then, looking up, my eye was caught by him. He was trying to resume his dancing, but seemed either so stiff or so awkward that he could only flutter to the bottom of the window-pane; and when he tried to fly across it he failed. Being intent on other matters I watched these futile attempts for a time without thinking, unconsciously waiting for him to resume his flight, as one waits for a machine, that has stopped momentarily, to start again without considering the reason of its failure. After perhaps a seventh attempt he slipped from the wooden ledge and fell, fluttering his wings, on to his back on the window sill. The helplessness of his attitude roused me. It flashed upon me that he was in difficulties; he could no longer raise himself; his legs struggled vainly. But, as I stretched out a pencil, meaning to help him to right himself, it came over me that the failure and awkwardness were the approach of death. I laid the pencil down again.

5 The legs agitated themselves once more. I looked as if for the enemy against which he struggled. I looked out of doors. What had happened there? Presumably it was midday, and work in the fields had stopped. Stillness and quiet had replaced the previous animation. The birds had taken themselves off to feed in the brooks. The horses stood still. Yet the power was there all the same, massed outside indifferent, impersonal, not attending to anything in particular. Somehow it was opposed to the little hay-coloured moth. It was useless to try to do anything. One could only watch the extraordinary efforts made by those tiny legs against an oncoming doom which could, had it chosen, have submerged an entire city, not merely a city, but masses of human beings; nothing, I knew, had any chance against death. Nevertheless after a pause of exhaustion the legs fluttered again. It was superb this last protest, and so frantic that he succeeded at last in righting himself. One's sympathies, of course, were all on the side of life. Also, when there was nobody to care or to know, this gigantic effort on the part of an insignificant little moth, against a power of such magnitude, to retain what no one else valued or desired to keep, moved one strangely. Again, somehow, one saw life, a pure bead. I lifted the pencil again, useless though I knew it to be. But even as I did so, the unmistakable tokens of death showed themselves. The body relaxed, and instantly grew stiff. The struggle was over. The insignificant little creature now knew death. As I looked at the dead moth, this minute wayside triumph of so great a force over so mean an antagonist filled me with wonder. Just as life had been strange a few minutes before, so death was now as strange. The moth having righted himself now lay most decently and uncomplainingly composed. O yes, he seemed to say, death is stronger than I am.

(1942)

Questions

1. Explain the phrase, "He was little or nothing but life," in paragraph 2 of this essay.
2. What is Woolf's attitude toward the moth? How does she inform the reader of this attitude?
3. What are the stages of the moth's life, according to this essay?
4. Describe Woolf's use of irony in this essay.
5. Explain the use of juxtaposition in "The Death of the Moth." What effect does this have on the reader?
6. Have you ever had an experience similar to Woolf's in watching an insect die? What were your feelings and observations?

George Orwell

Shooting an Elephant

George Orwell is best known to modern readers for two novels—the anti-Stalinist allegory Animal Farm *(1945) and the dystopian nightmare* 1984 *(1949). The imprint he left on English literary non-fiction may be even deeper than that which he left on English fiction; the scholar Leo Rockas is not alone in suggesting that Orwell's style, with its "no-nonsense approach," is more often "pointed to as a model than any other modern prose style."*

In 1922 (at the age of nineteen), Orwell left England to begin service with the Indian Imperial Police in Burma. As a province of British India, Burma was part of the British Empire, and the Indian Imperial Police were predominantly white (entrance was not open to Indians until 1920). Orwell remained with the Imperial Police for six years. "Shooting an Elephant" was first published in the British magazine New Writing *in 1936; the following decade would see the end of British rule in India.*

In Moulmein, in Lower Burma, I was hated by large numbers of people—the only time in my life that I have been important enough for this to happen to me. I was sub-divisional police officer of the town, and in an aimless, petty kind of way anti-European feeling was very bitter. No one had the guts to raise a riot, but if a European woman went through the bazaars alone somebody would probably spit betel[1] juice over her dress. As a police officer I was an obvious target and was baited whenever it seemed safe to do so. When a nimble Burman tripped me up on the football field and the referee (another Burman) looked the other way, the crowd yelled with hideous laughter. This happened more than once. In the end the sneering yellow faces of young men that met me everywhere, the insults hooted after me when I was at a safe distance, got badly on my nerves. The young Buddhist priests were the worst of all. There

1 *betel* Leaf and nut mixture that is chewed as a stimulant, common in Southeast Asia.

were several thousands of them in the town and none of them seemed to have anything to do except stand on street corners and jeer at Europeans.

All this was perplexing and upsetting. For at that time I had already made up my mind that imperialism was an evil thing and the sooner I chucked up my job and got out of it the better. Theoretically—and secretly, of course—I was all for the Burmese and all against their oppressors, the British. As for the job I was doing, I hated it more bitterly than I can perhaps make clear. In a job like that you see the dirty work of Empire at close quarters. The wretched prisoners huddling in the stinking cages of the lock-ups, the grey, cowed faces of the long-term convicts, the scarred buttocks of the men who had been flogged with bamboos—all these oppressed me with an intolerable sense of guilt. But I could get nothing into perspective. I was young and ill-educated and I had had to think out my problems in the utter silence that is imposed on every Englishman in the East. I did not even know that the British Empire is dying, still less did I know that it is a great deal better than the younger empires that are going to supplant it. All I knew was that I was stuck between my hatred of the empire I served and my rage against the evil-spirited little beasts who tried to make my job impossible. With one part of my mind I thought of the British Raj* as an unbreakable tyranny, as something clamped down, *in saecula saeculorum*,[2] upon the will of prostrate peoples; with another part I thought that the greatest joy in the world would be to drive a bayonet into a Buddhist priest's guts. Feelings like these are the normal by-products of imperialism; ask any Anglo-Indian official, if you can catch him off duty.

One day something happened which in a roundabout way was enlightening. It was a tiny incident in itself, but it gave me a better glimpse than I had had before of the real nature of imperialism—the real motives for which despotic governments act. Early one morning the sub-inspector at a police station the other end of the town rang me up on the phone and said that an elephant was ravaging the bazaar. Would I please come and do something about it? I did not know what I could do, but I wanted to see what was happening and I got on to a pony and started out. I took my rifle, an old .44 Winchester and much too small to kill an elephant, but I thought the noise might be useful *in terrorem*.[3] Various Burmans stopped me on the way and told me about the elephant's doings. It was not, of course, a wild elephant, but a tame one which had gone "must."[4]

---

2 *in saecula saeculorum* Latin: for centuries upon centuries; forever. This phrase appears frequently in the New Testament.

3 *in terrorem* Legal term for a warning; literally, Latin phrase meaning "in fear or alarm."

4 *"must"* Condition characterized by aggressive behaviour brought on by a surge in testosterone.

It had been chained up, as tame elephants always are when their attack of "must" is due, but on the previous night it had broken its chain and escaped. Its mahout,[5] the only person who could manage it when it was in that state, had set out in pursuit, but had taken the wrong direction and was now twelve hours' journey away, and in the morning the elephant had suddenly reappeared in the town. The Burmese population had no weapons and were quite helpless against it. It had already destroyed somebody's bamboo hut, killed a cow and raided some fruit-stalls and devoured the stock; also it had met the municipal rubbish van and, when the driver jumped out and took to his heels, had turned the van over and inflicted violences upon it.

The Burmese sub-inspector and some Indian constables were waiting for me in the quarter where the elephant had been seen. It was a very poor quarter, a labyrinth of squalid bamboo huts, thatched with palmleaf, winding all over a steep hillside. I remember that it was a cloudy, stuffy morning at the beginning of the rains. We began questioning the people as to where the elephant had gone and, as usual, failed to get any definite information. That is invariably the case in the East; a story always sounds clear enough at a distance, but the nearer you get to the scene of events the vaguer it becomes. Some of the people said that the elephant had gone in one direction, some said that he had gone in another, some professed not even to have heard of any elephant. I had almost made up my mind that the whole story was a pack of lies, when we heard yells a little distance away. There was a loud, scandalized cry of "Go away, child! Go away this instant!" and an old woman with a switch in her hand came round the corner of a hut, violently shooing away a crowd of naked children. Some more women followed, clicking their tongues and exclaiming; evidently there was something that the children ought not to have seen. I rounded the hut and saw a man's dead body sprawling in the mud. He was an Indian, a black Dravidian coolie,[6] almost naked, and he could not have been dead many minutes. The people said that the elephant had come suddenly upon him round the corner of the hut, caught him with its trunk, put its foot on his back and ground him into the earth. This was the rainy season and the ground was soft, and his face had scored a trench a foot deep and a couple of yards long. He was lying on his belly with arms crucified and head sharply twisted to one side. His face was coated with mud, the eyes wide open, the teeth bared and grinning with an expression of unendurable agony. (Never tell me, by the way, that the dead look peaceful. Most of the corpses I have seen looked devilish.) The friction of the great beast's foot had stripped the skin from his back as neatly as one skins a rabbit. As soon as I saw the dead man I sent an orderly to a friend's

---

5 *mahout* Elephant trainer or keeper.

6 *Dravidian coolie* I.e., southern Indian manual labourer.

house nearby to borrow an elephant rifle. I had already sent back the pony, not wanting it to go mad with fright and throw me if it smelt the elephant.

The orderly came back in a few minutes with a rifle and five cartridges, and meanwhile some Burmans had arrived and told us that the elephant was in the paddy fields below, only a few hundred yards away. As I started forward practically the whole population of the quarter flocked out of the houses and followed me. They had seen the rifle and were all shouting excitedly that I was going to shoot the elephant. They had not shown much interest in the elephant when he was merely ravaging their homes, but it was different now that he was going to be shot. It was a bit of fun to them, as it would be to an English crowd; besides they wanted the meat. It made me vaguely uneasy. I had no intention of shooting the elephant—I had merely sent for the rifle to defend myself if necessary—and it is always unnerving to have a crowd following you. I marched down the hill, looking and feeling a fool, with the rifle over my shoulder and an ever-growing army of people jostling at my heels. At the bottom, when you got away from the huts, there was a metaled road and beyond that a miry waste of paddy fields a thousand yards across, not yet ploughed but soggy from the first rains and dotted with coarse grass. The elephant was standing eight yards from the road, his left side towards us. He took not the slightest notice of the crowd's approach. He was tearing up bunches of grass, beating them against his knees to clean them and stuffing them into his mouth.

I had halted on the road. As soon as I saw the elephant I knew with perfect certainty that I ought not to shoot him. It is a serious matter to shoot a working elephant—it is comparable to destroying a huge and costly piece of machinery—and obviously one ought not to do it if it can possibly be avoided. And at that distance, peacefully eating, the elephant looked no more dangerous than a cow. I thought then and I think now that his attack of "must" was already passing off; in which case he would merely wander harmlessly about until the mahout came back and caught him. Moreover, I did not in the least want to shoot him. I decided that I would watch him for a little while to make sure that he did not turn savage again, and then go home.

But at that moment I glanced round at the crowd that had followed me. It was an immense crowd, two thousand at the least and growing every minute. It blocked the road for a long distance on either side. I looked at the sea of yellow faces above the garish clothes—faces all happy and excited over this bit of fun, all certain that the elephant was going to be shot. They were watching me as they would watch a conjurer about to perform a trick. They did not like me, but with the magical rifle in my hands I was momentarily worth watching. And suddenly I realized that I should have to shoot the elephant after all. The people expected it of me and I had got to do it; I could feel their two thousand wills pressing me forward, irresistibly. And it was at this moment, as I stood there with the rifle in my hands, that I first grasped the hollowness, the futility of the white man's dominion in the East. Here was I, the white man with his gun, standing in front of the unarmed native crowd—seemingly the leading actor of the piece; but in reality I was only an absurd puppet pushed to and fro by the will of those yellow faces behind. I perceived in this moment that when the white man turns tyrant it is his own freedom that he destroys. He becomes a sort of hollow, posing dummy, the conventionalized figure of a sahib.[7] For it is the condition of his rule that he shall spend his life in trying to impress the "natives," and so in every crisis he has got to do what the "natives" expect of him. He wears a mask, and his face grows to fit it. I had got to shoot the elephant. I had committed myself to doing it when I sent for the rifle. A sahib has got to act like a sahib; he has got to appear resolute, to know his own mind and do definite things. To come all that way, rifle in hand, with two thousand people marching at my heels, and then to trail feebly away, having done nothing—no, that was impossible. The crowd would laugh at me. And my whole life, every white man's life in the East, was one long struggle not to be laughed at.

But I did not want to shoot the elephant. I watched him beating his bunch of grass against his knees, with that preoccupied grandmotherly air that elephants have. It seemed to me that it would be murder to shoot him. At that age I was not squeamish about killing animals, but I had never shot an elephant and never wanted to. (Somehow it always seems worse to kill a *large* animal.) Besides, there was the beast's owner to be considered. Alive, the elephant was worth at least a hundred pounds; dead, he would only be worth the value of his tusks, five pounds, possibly. But I had got to act quickly. I turned to some experienced-looking Burmans who had been there when we arrived, and asked them how the elephant had been behaving. They all said the same thing: he took no notice of you if you left him alone, but he might charge if you went too close to him.

It was perfectly clear to me what I ought to do. I ought to walk up to within, say, twenty-five yards of the elephant and test his behaviour. If he charged, I could shoot; if he took no notice of me, it would be safe to leave him until the mahout came back. But also I knew that I was going to do no such thing. I was a poor shot with a rifle and the ground was soft mud into which one would sink at every step. If the elephant charged and I missed him, I should have about as much chance as a toad under a steam-roller. But even then I was not thinking particularly of my own skin, only of the watchful yellow faces behind. For at that moment, with the crowd watching me, I was not afraid in the ordinary sense, as I would have been if I had been alone. A white man mustn't

---

7 *sahib* I.e., colonial Englishman; this title of respect was used to address European men in colonial India.

be frightened in front of "natives"; and so, in general, he isn't frightened. The sole thought in my mind was that if anything went wrong those two thousand Burmans would see me pursued, caught, trampled on and reduced to a grinning corpse like that Indian up the hill. And if that happened it was quite probable that some of them would laugh. That would never do.

There was only one alternative. I shoved the cartridges into the magazine and lay down on the road to get a better aim. The crowd grew very still, and a deep, low, happy sigh, as of people who see the theatre curtain go up at last, breathed from innumerable throats. They were going to have their bit of fun after all. The rifle was a beautiful German thing with cross-hair sights. I did not then know that in shooting an elephant one would shoot to cut an imaginary bar running from ear-hole to ear-hole. I ought, therefore, as the elephant was sideways on, to have aimed straight at his ear-hole, actually I aimed several inches in front of this, thinking the brain would be further forward.

When I pulled the trigger I did not hear the bang or feel the kick—one never does when a shot goes home—but I heard the devilish roar of glee that went up from the crowd. In that instant, in too short a time, one would have thought, even for the bullet to get there, a mysterious, terrible change had come over the elephant. He neither stirred nor fell, but every line of his body had altered. He looked suddenly stricken, shrunken, immensely old, as though the frightful impact of the bullet had paralyzed him without knocking him down. At last, after what seemed a long time—it might have been five seconds, I dare say—he sagged flabbily to his knees. His mouth slobbered. An enormous senility seemed to have settled upon him. One could have imagined him thousands of years old. I fired again into the same spot. At the second shot he did not collapse but climbed with desperate slowness to his feet and stood weakly upright, with legs sagging and head drooping. I fired a third time. That was the shot that did for him. You could see the agony of it jolt his whole body and knock the last remnant of strength from his legs. But in falling he seemed for a moment to rise, for as his hind legs collapsed beneath him he seemed to tower upward like a huge rock toppling, his trunk reaching skyward like a tree. He trumpeted, for the first and only time. And then down he came, his belly towards me, with a crash that seemed to shake the ground even where I lay.

I got up. The Burmans were already racing past me across the mud. It was obvious that the elephant would never rise again, but he was not dead. He was breathing very rhythmically with long rattling gasps, his great mound of a side painfully rising and falling. His mouth was wide open—I could see far down into caverns of pale pink throat. I waited a long time for him to die, but his breathing did not weaken. Finally I fired my two remaining shots into the spot where I thought his heart must be. The thick blood welled out of him like red velvet, but still he did not die. His body did not even jerk when the shots hit him, the tortured breathing continued without a pause. He was dying, very slowly and in great agony, but in some world remote from me where not even a bullet could damage him further. I felt that I had got to put an end to that dreadful noise. It seemed dreadful to see the great beast lying there, powerless to move and yet powerless to die, and not even to be able to finish him. I sent back for my small rifle and poured shot after shot into his heart and down his throat. They seemed to make no impression. The tortured gasps continued as steadily as the ticking of a clock.

In the end I could not stand it any longer and went away. I heard later that it took him half an hour to die. Burmans were bringing dahs[8] and baskets even before I left, and I was told they had stripped his body almost to the bones by the afternoon.

Afterwards, of course, there were endless discussions about the shooting of the elephant. The owner was furious, but he was only an Indian and could do nothing. Besides, legally I had done the right thing, for a mad elephant has to be killed, like a mad dog, if its owner fails to control it. Among the Europeans opinion was divided. The older men said I was right, the younger men said it was a damn shame to shoot an elephant for killing a coolie, because an elephant was worth more than any damn Coringhee[9] coolie. And afterwards I was very glad that the coolie had been killed; it put me legally in the right and it gave me a sufficient pretext for shooting the elephant. I often wondered whether any of the others grasped that I had done it solely to avoid looking a fool.

(1950)

Questions

1. What is Orwell arguing about the nature of imperialism?
2. Orwell uses an autobiographical story in order to make a political claim. How does he accomplish this? Find places in the text where he signals the connection between his personal experience and his political argument.
3. What might the elephant symbolize?
4. Orwell describes the dead Indian man and the death of the elephant in vivid detail. How do these graphic descriptions of violence affect the impact of the essay?

---

8 *dahs* Short swords or knives.

9 *Coringhee* From Coringha, a town on the coast of India.

5. What does Orwell mean when he says, "All I knew was that I was stuck between my hatred of the empire I served and my rage against the evil-spirited little beasts who tried to make my job impossible"?
6. Find examples of racist language in the essay. Do you think such language was used intentionally or unconsciously? What effect does it have in the context of the essay?
7. Read Jamaica Kincaid's essay "On Seeing England for the First Time," elsewhere in this anthology. How does Orwell's experience of colonialism compare with Kincaid's?

POLITICS AND THE ENGLISH LANGUAGE

The word "Orwellian" entered the English language with reference to Orwell's novels Animal Farm *and* 1984, *as a signifier for oppressive, invasive, and manipulative practices—especially those having to do with language—that seem to threaten the freedom of a society. Orwell's non-fiction writing also often focuses on ways in which "Orwellian" practices can infect our linguistic habits. His essay "Politics and the English Language" was first published in the British literary magazine* Horizon *in 1946; it has been reprinted thousands of times in the decades since.*

① Most people who bother with the matter at all would admit that the English language is in a bad way, but it is generally assumed that we cannot by conscious action do anything about it. Our civilization is decadent* and our language—so the argument runs—must inevitably share in the general collapse. It follows that any struggle against the abuse of language is a sentimental archaism, like preferring candles to electric light or hansom cabs* to airplanes. Underneath this lies the half-conscious belief that language is a natural growth and not an instrument which we shape for our own purposes.

② Now, it is clear that the decline of a language must ultimately have political and economic causes: it is not due simply to the bad influence of this or that individual writer. But an effect can become a cause, reinforcing the original cause and producing the same effect in an intensified form, and so on indefinitely. A man may take to drink because he feels himself to be a failure, and then fail all the more completely because he drinks. It is rather the same thing that is happening to the English language. It becomes ugly and inaccurate because our thoughts are foolish, but the slovenliness of our language makes it easier for us to have foolish thoughts. The point is that the process is reversible. Modern English, especially written English, is full of bad habits which spread by imitation and which can be avoided if one is willing to take the necessary trouble. If one gets rid of these habits one can think more clearly, and to think clearly is a necessary first step towards political regeneration: so that the fight against bad English is not frivolous and is not the exclusive concern of professional writers. I will come back to this presently, and I hope that by that time the meaning of what I have said here will have become clearer. Meanwhile, here are five specimens of the English language as it is now habitually written.

These five passages have not been picked out because they are especially bad—I could have quoted far worse if I had chosen—but because they illustrate various of the mental vices from which we now suffer. They are a little below the average, but are fairly representative samples. I number them so that I can refer back to them when necessary:

> (1) I am not, indeed, sure whether it is not true to say that the Milton who once seemed not unlike a seventeenth-century Shelley* had not become, out of an experience ever more bitter in each year, more alien [*sic*] to the founder of that Jesuit* sect which nothing could induce him to tolerate.
>
> Professor Harold Laski (Essay in *Freedom of Expression*).
>
> (2) Above all, we cannot play ducks and drakes* with a native battery of idioms which prescribes such egregious collocations of vocables as the Basic *put up with* for *tolerate* or *put at a loss* for *bewilder*.
>
> Professor Lancelot Hogben (*Interglossa*).
>
> (3) On the one side we have the free personality: by definition it is not neurotic, for it has neither conflict nor dream. Its desires, such as they are, are transparent, for they are just what institutional approval keeps in the forefront of consciousness; another institutional pattern would alter their number and intensity; there is little in them that is natural, irreducible, or culturally dangerous. But *on the other side*, the social bond itself is nothing but the mutual reflection of these self-secure integrities. Recall the definition of love. Is not this the very picture of a small academic? Where is there a place in this hall of mirrors for either personality or fraternity?
>
> Essay on psychology in *Politics* (New York).

(4) All the "best people" from the gentlemen's clubs, and all the frantic fascist captains, united in common hatred of Socialism and bestial horror of the rising tide of the mass revolutionary movement, have turned to acts of provocation, to foul incendiarism, to medieval legends of poisoned wells, to legalize their own destruction of proletarian organizations, and rouse the agitated petty-bourgeoisie to chauvinistic fervour on behalf of the fight against the revolutionary way out of the crisis.

Communist pamphlet.

(5) If a new spirit *is* to be infused into this old country, there is one thorny and contentious reform which must be tackled, and that is the humanization and galvanization of the B.B.C.* Timidity here will bespeak canker and atrophy of the soul. The heart of Britain may be sound and of strong beat, for instance, but the British lion's* roar at present is like that of Bottom in Shakespeare's *Midsummer Night's Dream**—as gentle as any sucking dove. A virile new Britain cannot continue indefinitely to be traduced in the eyes or rather ears, of the world by the effete languors of Langham Place, brazenly masquerading as 'standard English.' When the Voice of Britain is heard at nine o'clock, better far and infinitely less ludicrous to hear aitches honestly dropped than the present priggish, inflated, inhibited, school-ma'amish arch braying of blameless bashful mewing maidens!

Letter in *Tribune*.

Each of these passages has faults of its own, but, quite apart from avoidable ugliness, two qualities are common to all of them. The first is staleness of imagery: the other is lack of precision. The writer either has a meaning and cannot express it, or he inadvertently says something else, or he is almost indifferent as to whether his words mean anything or not. This mixture of vagueness and sheer incompetence is the most marked characteristic of modern English prose, and especially of any kind of political writing. As soon as certain topics are raised, the concrete melts into the abstract and no one seems able to think of turns of speech that are not hackneyed: prose consists less and less of *words* chosen for the sake of their meaning, and more and more of *phrases* tacked together like the sections of a prefabricated hen-house. I list below, with notes and examples, various of the tricks by means of which the work of prose-construction is habitually dodged:

Dying Metaphors. A newly invented metaphor assists thought by evoking 5
a visual image, while on the other hand a metaphor which is technically "dead" (e.g., *iron resolution*) has in effect reverted to being an ordinary word and can generally be used without loss of vividness. But in between these two classes

there is a huge dump of worn-out metaphors which have lost all evocative power and are merely used because they save people the trouble of inventing phrases for themselves. Examples are: *Ring the changes on, take up the cudgels for, toe the line, ride roughshod over, stand shoulder to shoulder with, play into the hands of, no axe to grind, grist to the mill, fishing in troubled waters, on the order of the day, Achilles' heel, swan song, hotbed.* Many of these are used without knowledge of their meaning (what is a "rift," for instance?), and incompatible metaphors are frequently mixed, a sure sign that the writer is not interested in what he is saying. Some metaphors now current have been twisted out of their original meaning without those who use them even being aware of the fact. For example, *toe the line* is sometimes written *tow the line*. Another example is *the hammer and the anvil*, now always used with the implication that the anvil gets the worst of it. In real life it is always the anvil that breaks the hammer, never the other way about: a writer who stopped to think what he was saying would be aware of this, and would avoid perverting the original phrase.

Operators or *verbal false limbs.* These save the trouble of picking out appropriate verbs and nouns, and at the same time pad each sentence with extra syllables which give it an appearance of symmetry. Characteristic phrases are: *render inoperative, militate against, make contact with, be subjected to, give rise to, give grounds for, have the effect of, play a leading part (role) in, make itself felt, take effect, exhibit a tendency to, serve the purpose of, etc., etc.* The keynote is the elimination of simple verbs. Instead of being a single word, such as *break, stop, spoil, mend, kill*, a verb becomes a *phrase*, made up of a noun or adjective tacked on to some general-purpose verb such as *prove, serve, form, play, render.* In addition, the passive voice* is wherever possible used in preference to the active, and noun constructions are used instead of gerunds* (*by examination of* instead of *by examining*). The range of verbs is further cut down by means of the *-ize* and *de-* formations, and the banal statements are given an appearance of profundity by means of the *not un-* formation. Simple conjunctions and prepositions are replaced by such phrases as *with respect to, having regard to, the fact that, by dint of, in view of, in the interests of, on the hypothesis that*; and the ends of sentences are saved from anti-climax by such resounding commonplaces as *greatly to be desired, cannot be left out of account, a development to be expected in the near future, deserving of serious consideration, brought to a satisfactory conclusion*, and so on and so forth.

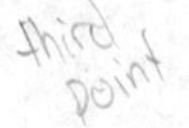

Pretentious diction. Words like *phenomenon, element, individual* (as noun), *objective, categorical, effective, virtual, basic, primary, promote, constitute, exhibit, exploit, utilize, eliminate, liquidate*, are used to dress up simple statements and give an air of scientific impartiality to biased judgments.

Adjectives like *epoch-making*, *epic*, *historic*, *unforgettable*, *triumphant*, *age-old*, *inevitable*, *inexorable*, *veritable*, are used to dignify the sordid processes of international politics, while writing that aims at glorifying war usually takes on an archaic colour, its characteristic words being: *realm*, *throne*, *chariot*, *mailed fist*, *trident*, *sword*, *shield*, *buckler*, *banner*, *jackboot*, *clarion*. Foreign words and expressions such as *cul de sac*, *ancien régime*, *deus ex machina*, *mutatis mutandis*, *status quo*, *Gleichschaltung*, *Weltanschauung*, are used to give an air of culture and elegance. Except for the useful abbreviations *i.e.*, *e.g.*, and *etc.*, there is no real need for any of the hundreds of foreign phrases now current in English. Bad writers, and especially scientific, political and sociological writers, are nearly always haunted by the notion that Latin or Greek words are grander than Saxon* ones, and unnecessary words like *expedite*, *ameliorate*, *predict*, *extraneous*, *deracinated*, *clandestine*, *subaqueous* and hundreds of others constantly gain ground from their Anglo-Saxon opposite numbers.[1] The jargon peculiar to Marxist writing (*hyena*, *hangman*, *cannibal*, *petty bourgeois*, *these gentry*, *lacquey*, *flunkey*, *mad dog*, *White Guard*, etc.) consists largely of words and phrases translated from Russian, German or French; but the normal way of coining a new word is to use a Latin or Greek root with the appropriate affix and, where necessary, the *-ize* formation. It is often easier to make up words of this kind (*deregionalize*, *impermissible*, *extramarital*, *non-fragmentatory* and so forth) than to think up the English words that will cover one's meaning. The result, in general, is an increase in slovenliness and vagueness.

Meaningless words. In certain kinds of writing, particularly in art criticism and literary criticism, it is normal to come across long passages which are almost completely lacking in meaning.[2] Words like *romantic*, *plastic*, *values*, *human*, *dead*, *sentimental*, *natural*, *vitality*, as used in art criticism, are strictly meaningless, in the sense that they not only do not point to any discoverable object, but are hardly ever expected to do so by the reader. When one critic writes, "The outstanding feature of Mr. X's work is its living quality," while another writes, "The immediately striking thing about Mr. X's work is its

---

1 [Orwell's note] An interesting illustration of this is the way in which the English flower names which were in use till very recently are being ousted by Greek ones, snapdragon becoming antirrhinum, forget-me-not becoming myosotis, etc. It is hard to see any practical reason for this change of fashion; it is probably due to an instinctive turning-away from the more homely word and a vague feeling that the Greek word is scientific.

2 [Orwell's note] Example: "Comfort's catholicity of perception and image, strangely Whitmanesque in range, almost the exact opposite in aesthetic compulsion, continues to evoke that trembling atmospheric hinting at a cruel, an inexorably serene timelessness.... Wrey Gardiner scores by aiming at simple bull's-eyes with precision. Only they are not so simple, and through this contented sadness runs more than the surface bitter-sweet of resignation" (*Poetry Quarterly*).

peculiar deadness," the reader accepts this as a simple difference of opinion. If words like *black* and *white* were involved, instead of the jargon words *dead* and *living*, he would see at once that language was being used in an improper way. Many political words are similarly abused. The word *Fascism* has now no meaning except in so far as it signifies "something not desirable." The words *democracy*, *socialism*, *freedom*, *patriotic*, *realistic*, *justice*, have each of them several different meanings which cannot be reconciled with one another. In the case of a word like *democracy*, not only is there no agreed definition, but the attempt to make one is resisted from all sides. It is almost universally felt that when we call a country democratic we are praising it: consequently the defenders of every kind of régime claim that it is a democracy, and fear that they might have to stop using the word if it were tied down to any one meaning. Words of this kind are often used in a consciously dishonest way. That is, the person who uses them has his own private definition, but allows his hearer to think he means something quite different. Statements like *Marshal Pétain was a true patriot*, *The Soviet Press is the freest in the world*, *The Catholic Church is opposed to persecution*,* are almost always made with intent to deceive. Other words used in variable meanings, in most cases more or less dishonestly, are: *class*, *totalitarian*, *science*, *progressive*, *reactionary*, *bourgeois*, *equality*.

Now that I have made this catalogue of swindles and perversions, let me give another example of the kind of writing that they lead to. This time it must of its nature be an imaginary one. I am going to translate a passage of good English into modern English of the worst sort. Here is a well-known verse from *Ecclesiastes*:*

> I returned and saw under the sun, that the race is not to the swift, nor the battle to the strong, neither yet bread to the wise, nor yet riches to men of understanding, nor yet favour to men of skill; but time and chance happeneth to them all.

Here it is in modern English:

> Objective consideration of contemporary phenomena compels the conclusion that success or failure in competitive activities exhibits no tendency to be commensurate with innate capacity, but that a considerable element of the unpredictable must invariably be taken into account.

This is a parody, but not a very gross one. Exhibit (3), above, for instance, contains several patches of the same kind of English. It will be seen that I have not made a full translation. The beginning and ending of the sentence follow the original meaning fairly closely, but in the middle the concrete illustrations—race, battle, bread—dissolve into the vague phrase "success or failure in competitive activities." This had to be so, because no modern writer of the kind I am discussing—no one capable of using phrases like "objective consideration of contemporary phenomena"—would ever tabulate his thoughts in that precise and detailed way. The whole tendency of modern prose is away from concreteness. Now analyze these two sentences a little more closely. The first contains forty-nine words but only sixty syllables, and all its words are those of everyday life. The second contains thirty-eight words of ninety syllables: eighteen of its words are from Latin roots, and one from Greek. The first sentence contains six vivid images, and only one phrase ("time and chance") that could be called vague. The second contains not a single fresh, arresting phrase, and in spite of its ninety syllables it gives only a shortened version of the meaning contained in the first. Yet without a doubt it is the second kind of sentence that is gaining ground in modern English. I do not want to exaggerate. This kind of writing is not yet universal, and outcrops of simplicity will occur here and there in the worst-written page. Still, if you or I were told to write a few lines on the uncertainty of human fortunes, we should probably come much nearer to my imaginary sentence than to the one from *Ecclesiastes*.

As I have tried to show, modern writing at its worst does not consist in picking out words for the sake of their meaning and inventing images in order to make the meaning clearer. It consists in gumming together long strips of words which have already been set in order by someone else, and making the results presentable by sheer humbug.* The attraction of this way of writing is that it is easy. It is easier—even quicker, once you have the habit—to say *In my opinion it is a not unjustifiable assumption that* than to say *I think*. If you use ready-made phrases, you not only don't have to hunt about for words; you also don't have to bother with the rhythms of your sentences, since these phrases are generally so arranged as to be more or less euphonious. When you are composing in a hurry—when you are dictating to a stenographer, for instance, or making a public speech—it is natural to fall into a pretentious, Latinized style. Tags like *a consideration which we should do well to bear in mind* or *a conclusion to which all of us would readily assent* will save many a sentence from coming down with a bump. By using stale metaphors, similes and idioms, you save much mental effort, at the cost of leaving your meaning vague, not only for your reader but for yourself. This is the significance of mixed metaphors. The sole aim of a metaphor is to call up a visual image. When these images clash—as in *The Fascist octopus has sung its swan song, the jackboot is thrown into the melting pot*—it can be taken as certain that the writer is not seeing a mental image of the objects he is naming; in other words he is not really thinking. Look again at the examples I gave at the beginning of this essay. Professor Laski (1) uses five negatives in fifty-three words. One of these is superfluous, making nonsense of the whole passage, and in addition there is the slip *alien* for akin, making further nonsense, and several avoidable pieces of clumsiness which increase the general vagueness. Professor Hogben (2) plays ducks and drakes with a battery which is able to write prescriptions, and, while disapproving of the everyday phrase *put up with*, is unwilling to look *egregious* up in the dictionary and see what it means. (3), if one takes an uncharitable attitude towards it, is simply meaningless: probably one could work out its intended meaning by reading the whole of the article in which it occurs. In (4), the writer knows more or less what he wants to say, but an accumulation of stale phrases chokes him like tea leaves blocking a sink. In (5), words and meaning have almost parted company. People who write in this manner usually have a general emotional meaning—they dislike one thing and want to express solidarity with another—but they are not interested in the detail of what they are saying. A scrupulous writer, in every sentence that he writes, will ask himself at least four questions, thus: What am I trying to say? What words will express it? What image or idiom will make it clearer? Is this image fresh enough to have an effect? And he will probably ask himself two more: Could I put it more shortly? Have I said anything that is avoidably ugly? But you are not obliged to go to all this trouble. You can shirk it by simply throwing your mind open and letting the ready-made phrases come crowding in. They will construct your sentences for you—even think your thoughts for you, to a certain extent—and at need they will perform the important service of partially concealing your meaning even from yourself. It is at this point that the special connection between politics and the debasement of language becomes clear.

In our time it is broadly true that political writing is bad writing. Where it is not true, it will generally be found that the writer is some kind of rebel, expressing his private opinions and not a "party line." Orthodoxy, of whatever colour, seems to demand a lifeless, imitative style. The political dialects to be found in pamphlets, leading articles, manifestos, White Papers* and the speeches of under-secretaries do, of course, vary from party to party, but they are all alike in that one almost never finds in them a fresh, vivid, homemade turn of speech. When one watches some tired hack on the platform mechanically repeating the familiar phrases—*bestial atrocities*, *iron heel*, *bloodstained tyranny*, *free peoples of the world*, *stand shoulder to shoulder*—one often has a curious feeling that one is not watching a live human being but some kind of dummy: a feeling which suddenly becomes stronger at moments when the light catches the speaker's spectacles and turns them into blank discs which seem to have no eyes behind them. And this is not altogether fanciful. A speaker who uses that kind of phraseology has gone some distance towards turning himself into a machine. The appropriate noises are coming out of his larynx, but his brain is not involved as it would be if he were choosing his words for himself. If the speech he is making is one that he is accustomed to make over and over again, he may be almost unconscious of what he is saying, as one is when one utters the responses in church. And this reduced state of consciousness, if not indispensable, is at any rate favourable to political conformity.

In our time, political speech and writing are largely the defense of the indefensible. Things like the continuance of British rule in India, the Russian purges* and deportations, the dropping of the atom bombs on Japan, can indeed be defended, but only by arguments which are too brutal for most people to face, and which do not square with the professed aims of political parties. Thus political language has to consist largely of euphemism, question-begging* and sheer cloudy vagueness. Defenseless villages are bombarded from the air, the inhabitants driven out into the countryside, the cattle machine-gunned, the huts set on fire with incendiary bullets: this is called *pacification*. Millions of peasants are robbed of their farms and sent trudging along the roads with no more than they can carry: this is called *transfer of population* or *rectification of frontiers*. People are imprisoned for years without trial, or shot in the back of the neck or sent to die of scurvy in Arctic lumber camps: this is called *elimination of unreliable elements*. Such phraseology is needed if one wants to name things without calling up mental pictures of them. Consider for instance some comfortable English professor defending Russian totalitarianism. He cannot say outright, "I believe in killing off your opponents when you can get good results by doing so." Probably, therefore, he will say something like this:

> "While freely conceding that the Soviet regime exhibits certain features which the humanitarian may be inclined to deplore, we must, I think, agree that a certain curtailment of the right to political opposition is an unavoidable concomitant of transitional periods, and that the rigours which the Russian people have been called upon to undergo have been amply justified in the sphere of concrete achievement."

The inflated style is itself a kind of euphemism. A mass of Latin words 15
falls upon the facts like soft snow, blurring the outlines and covering up all the details. The great enemy of clear language is insincerity. When there is a gap between one's real and one's declared aims, one turns as it were instinctively to long words and exhausted idioms, like a cuttlefish squirting out ink.* In our age there is no such thing as "keeping out of politics." All issues are political issues, and politics itself is a mass of lies, evasions, folly, hatred and schizophrenia. When the general atmosphere is bad, language must suffer. I should expect to find—this is a guess which I have not sufficient knowledge to verify—that the German, Russian and Italian languages have all deteriorated in the last ten or fifteen years, as a result of dictatorship.

But if thought corrupts language, language can also corrupt thought. A bad usage can spread by tradition and imitation, even among people who should and do know better. The debased language that I have been discussing is in some ways very convenient. Phrases like *a not unjustifiable assumption, leave much to be desired, would serve no good purpose, a consideration which we should do well to bear in mind*, are a continuous temptation, a packet of aspirins always at one's elbow. Look back through this essay, and for certain you will find that I have again and again committed the very faults I am protesting against. By this morning's post I have received a pamphlet dealing with conditions in Germany.* The author tells me that he "felt impelled" to write it. I open it at random, and here is almost the first sentence that I see: "(The Allies) have an opportunity not only of achieving a radical transformation of Germany's social and political structure in such a way as to avoid a nationalistic reaction in Germany itself, but at the same time of laying the foundations of a co-operative and unified Europe." You see, he "feels impelled" to write—feels, presumably, that he has something new to say—and yet his words, like cavalry horses answering the bugle,* group themselves automatically into the familiar dreary pattern. This invasion of one's mind by ready-made phrases (*lay the foundations*, *achieve a radical transformation*) can only be prevented if one is constantly on guard against them, and every such phrase anaesthetizes a portion of one's brain.

I said earlier that the decadence of our language is probably curable. Those who deny this would argue, if they produced an argument at all, that language merely reflects existing social conditions, and that we cannot influence its development by any direct tinkering with words and constructions. So far as the general tone or spirit of a language goes, this may be true, but it is not true in detail. Silly words and expressions have often disappeared, not through any evolutionary process but owing to the conscious action of a minority. Two recent examples were *explore every avenue* and *leave no stone unturned*, which were killed by the jeers of a few journalists. There is a long list of flyblown metaphors which could similarly be got rid of if enough people would interest themselves in the job; and it should also be possible to laugh the *not un-* formation out of existence,[3] to reduce the amount of Latin and Greek in the average sentence, to drive out foreign phrases and strayed scientific words, and, in general, to make pretentiousness unfashionable. But all these are minor points. The defense of the English language implies more than this, and perhaps it is best to start by saying what it does *not* imply.

To begin with it has nothing to do with archaism, with the salvaging of obsolete words and turns of speech, or with the setting up of a "standard

3 [Orwell's note] One can cure oneself of the not un- formation by memorizing this sentence: *A not unblack dog was chasing a not unsmall rabbit across a not ungreen field.*

English" which must never be departed from. On the contrary, it is especially concerned with the scrapping of every word or idiom which has outworn its usefulness. It has nothing to do with correct grammar and syntax, which are of no importance so long as one makes one's meaning clear, or with the avoidance of Americanisms, or with having what is called a "good prose style." On the other hand it is not concerned with fake simplicity and the attempt to make written English colloquial. Nor does it even imply in every case preferring the Saxon word to the Latin one, though it does imply using the fewest and shortest words that will cover one's meaning. What is above all needed is to let the meaning choose the word, and not the other way about. In prose, the worst thing one can do with words is to surrender to them. When you think of a concrete object, you think wordlessly, and then, if you want to describe the thing you have been visualizing you probably hunt about till you find the exact words that seem to fit it. When you think of something abstract you are more inclined to use words from the start, and unless you make a conscious effort to prevent it, the existing dialect will come rushing in and do the job for you, at the expense of blurring or even changing your meaning. Probably it is better to put off using words as long as possible and get one's meaning as clear as one can through pictures or sensations. Afterwards one can choose—not simply *accept*—the phrases that will best cover the meaning, and then switch round and decide what impression one's words are likely to make on another person. This last effort of the mind cuts out all stale or mixed images, all prefabricated phrases, needless repetitions, and humbug and vagueness generally. But one can often be in doubt about the effect of a word or a phrase, and one needs rules that one can rely on when instinct fails. I think the following rules will cover most cases:

(i) Never use a metaphor, simile or other figure of speech which you are used to seeing in print.
(ii) Never use a long word where a short one will do.
(iii) If it is possible to cut a word out, always cut it out.
(iv) Never use the passive where you can use the active.
(v) Never use a foreign phrase, a scientific word or a jargon word if you can think of an everyday English equivalent.
(vi) Break any of these rules sooner than say anything outright barbarous.

These rules sound elementary, and so they are, but they demand a deep change of attitude in anyone who has grown used to writing in the style now fashionable. One could keep all of them and still write bad English, but one could not write the kind of stuff that I quoted in those five specimens at the beginning of this article.

20 I have not here been considering the literary use of language, but merely language as an instrument for expressing and not for concealing or preventing thought. Stuart Chase and others have come near to claiming that all abstract words are meaningless, and have used this as a pretext for advocating a kind of political quietism. Since you don't know what Fascism is, how can you struggle against Fascism? One need not swallow such absurdities as this, but one ought to recognize that the present political chaos is connected with the decay of language, and that one can probably bring about some improvement by starting at the verbal end. If you simplify your English, you are freed from the worst follies of orthodoxy. You cannot speak any of the necessary dialects, and when you make a stupid remark its stupidity will be obvious, even to yourself. Political language—and with variations this is true of all political parties, from Conservatives to Anarchists—is designed to make lies sound truthful and murder respectable, and to give an appearance of solidity to pure wind. One cannot change this all in a moment, but one can at least change one's own habits, and from time to time one can even, if one jeers loudly enough, send some worn-out and useless phrase—some *jackboot*, *Achilles' heel*, *hotbed*, *melting pot*, *acid test*, *veritable inferno* or other lump of verbal refuse—into the dustbin where it belongs.

(1946)

Questions

1. As Orwell sees it, why does it matter how political material is presented verbally?
2. What examples can you give of euphemisms being used to disguise unpleasant aspects of political actions?
3. Aside from implications for political discourse, what arguments does Orwell put forward for "the defense of the English language"?
4. What are the principles underlying the six rules that Orwell presents in paragraph 18?
5. Orwell and many others have argued for simplicity of expression, shorter words over longer ones, and so on. The contrary argument, however, has also been often made: that the extraordinarily large vocabulary of the English language, including many long and complex words of Latin origin, allows for greater precision in expressing one's meaning than do languages with much smaller vocabularies. Write one paragraph arguing each side of this argument, in each case referring to passages from other essays in this anthology.

6. At several points Orwell distinguishes between words of Anglo-Saxon origin and words of Latin origin. What are some of the characteristics of the two? Why does Orwell prefer one to the other?
7. Aside from the examples Orwell gives, think of some "ready-made phrases" (paragraph 12) that "construct your sentences for you" aside from the examples Orwell gives.
8. Describe the tone of Orwell's writing in this essay.
9. Orwell advises using concrete words or phrases whenever possible. Write two or three sentences expressing abstract principles, and then re-write so as to express the same principles in more concrete language, or using concrete examples.
10. Express in your own words the difference between live metaphors and those that are stale, dead, or dying. Think of three dead metaphors not mentioned by Orwell, and think up three fresh metaphors in sentences of your own. (See for reference paragraphs 5 and 12.)
11. Explain how the confusion between "toe the line" and "tow the line" would have arisen.

Hannah Arendt

from The Origins of Totalitarianism

In The Origins of Totalitarianism *(1951) German-Jewish political theorist Hannah Arendt analyzes the emergence of the genocidal regimes of Nazi Germany (1933–45) and Stalinist Russia (1924–53). Both of these regimes, though differing in their ideologies, were characterized by the subordination of all state institutions and individuals to the will of a charismatic leader (Adolf Hitler and Joseph Stalin, respectively). These leaders and their parties had "total" power, wielding not only political power but also power over the personal lives, thoughts, and beliefs of citizens. In their efforts to gain control and to fulfill their ideological ambitions, both Hitler and Stalin murdered millions of people.*

Arendt is particularly incisive about how a population comes to accept a totalitarian leader: "The ideal subject of totalitarian rule is not the convinced Nazi or the dedicated communist, but people for whom the distinction between fact and fiction, true and false, no longer exists." In the excerpts below, she discusses the conditions in which a democracy is vulnerable to totalitarian ideology, as well as the kinds of propaganda that are used to consolidate authoritarian power. The Origins of Totalitarianism *is widely considered to be one of the most important books of the twentieth century.*

from Chapter 10: A Classless Society

Totalitarian movements are possible wherever there are masses who for one reason or another have acquired the appetite for political organization. Masses are not held together by a consciousness of common interest and they lack that specific class articulateness which is expressed in determined, limited, and obtainable goals. The term masses applies only where we deal with people who either because of sheer numbers, or indifference, or a combination of both, cannot be integrated into any organization based on common interest, into political parties or municipal governments or professional organizations or trade unions. Potentially, they exist in every country and form the majority of those large numbers of neutral, politically indifferent people who never join a party and hardly ever go to the polls.

It was characteristic of the rise of the Nazi movement in Germany and of the Communist movements in Europe after 1930 that they recruited their members from this mass of apparently indifferent people whom all other parties had given up as too apathetic or too stupid for their attention. The result was that the majority of their membership consisted of people who never before had appeared on the political scene. This permitted the introduction of entirely new methods into political propaganda, and indifference to the arguments of political opponents; these movements not only placed themselves outside and against the party system as a whole, they found a membership that had never been reached, never been "spoiled" by the party system. Therefore they did not need to refute opposing arguments and consistently preferred methods which ended in death rather than persuasion, which spelled terror rather than conviction. They presented disagreements as invariably originating in deep natural, social, or psychological sources beyond the control of the individual and therefore beyond the power of reason. This would have been a shortcoming only if they had sincerely entered into competition with other parties; it was not if they were sure of dealing with people who had reason to be equally hostile to all parties.

The success of totalitarian movements among the masses meant the end of two illusions of democratically ruled countries in general and of European nation-states and their party system in particular. The first [illusion] was that the people in its majority had taken an active part in government and that each individual was in sympathy with one's own or somebody else's party. On the contrary, the movements showed that the politically neutral and indifferent masses could easily be the majority in a democratically ruled country, that therefore a democracy could function according to rules which are actively recognized by only a minority. The second democratic illusion exploded by the totalitarian movements was that these politically indifferent masses did not matter, that they were truly neutral and constituted no more than the inarticulate backward setting for the political life of the nation. Now they made apparent what no other organ of public opinion had ever been able to show, namely, that democratic government had rested as much on the silent approbation and tolerance of the indifferent and inarticulate sections of the people as on the articulate and visible institutions and organizations of the country. Thus when the totalitarian movements invaded Parliament with their contempt for parliamentary government, they merely appeared inconsistent: actually, they succeeded in convincing the people at large that parliamentary majorities were spurious and did not necessarily correspond to the realities of the country, thereby undermining the self-respect and the confidence of governments which also believed in majority rule rather than in their constitutions....

[The] apolitical character of the nation-state's populations came to light only when the class system broke down and carried with it the whole fabric of visible and invisible threads which bound the people to the body politic.

The breakdown of the class system meant automatically the breakdown of the party system, chiefly because these parties, being interest parties, could no longer represent class interests. Their continuance was of some importance to the members of former classes who hoped against hope to regain their old social status and who stuck together not because they had common interests any longer but because they hoped to restore them. The parties, consequently, became more and more psychological and ideological in their propaganda, more and more apologetic and nostalgic in their political approach. They had lost, moreover, without being aware of it, those neutral supporters who had never been interested in politics because they felt that parties existed to take care of their interests. So that the first signs of the breakdown of the Continental party system[1] were not the desertion of old party members, but the failure to recruit members from the younger generation, and the loss of the silent consent and support of the unorganized masses who suddenly shed their apathy and went wherever they saw an opportunity to voice their new violent opposition.

The fall of protecting class walls transformed the slumbering majorities behind all parties into one great unorganized, structureless mass of furious individuals who had nothing in common except their vague apprehension that the hopes of party members were doomed, that, consequently, the most respected, articulate and representative members of the community were fools and that all the powers that be were not so much evil as they were equally stupid and fraudulent. It was of no great consequence for the birth of this new terrifying negative solidarity that the unemployed worker hated the status quo and the powers that be in the form of the Social Democratic Party, the expropriated small property owner in the form of a centrist or rightist party, and former members of the middle and upper classes in the form of the traditional extreme right. The number of this mass of generally dissatisfied and desperate men increased rapidly in Germany and Austria after the first World War, when inflation and unemployment added to the disrupting consequences of military defeat; they existed in great proportion in all the succession states,[2] and they

1 *Continental party system* According to Arendt, this system is composed of parties that define themselves consciously as part of the whole, rather than identifying themselves with the people; while parties in this system may argue with other parties, they do not seek to destroy them, and they do not wish to be the only party.

2 *succession states* New states that are created in territory once administered by another state, as a result of decolonization, unification, or separation. Arendt refers here to the states created after the fall of the Austro-Hungarian empire (1867–1918): Austria, Hungary, First Czechoslovak Republic, Second Polish Republic, Yugoslavia, and Romania.

have supported the extreme movements in France and Italy since the second World War.

… [T]he leaders of totalitarian movements have in common with their intellectual sympathizers the fact that both had been outside the class and national system of respectable European society even before this system broke down.

This breakdown, when the smugness of spurious respectability gave way to anarchic despair, seemed the first great opportunity for the elite as well as the mob.[3] This is obvious for the new mass leaders whose careers reproduce the features of earlier mob leaders: failure in professional and social life, perversion and disaster in private life. The fact that their lives prior to their political careers had been failures, naively held against them by the more respectable leaders of the old parties, was the strongest factor in their mass appeal. It seemed to prove that individually they embodied the mass destiny of the time and that their desire to sacrifice everything for the movement, their assurance of devotion to those who had been struck by catastrophe, their determination never to be tempted back into the security of normal life, and their contempt for respectability were quite sincere and not just inspired by passing ambitions.…

from CHAPTER 11: THE TOTALITARIAN MOVEMENT

i: Totalitarian Propaganda

Only the mob and the elite can be attracted by the momentum of totalitarianism itself; the masses have to be won by propaganda. Under conditions of constitutional government and freedom of opinion, totalitarian movements struggling for power can use terror to a limited extent only and share with other parties the necessity of winning adherents and of appearing plausible to a public which is not yet rigorously isolated from all other sources of information.

It was recognized early and has frequently been asserted that in totalitarian countries propaganda and terror present two sides of the same coin.[4] This,

---

3 *the mob* In *The Origins of Totalitarianism* 1.4.4, Arendt defines the mob as "a group in which the residue of all classes are represented." The mob, she writes, "hates society from which it is excluded, as well as Parliament where it is not represented."

4 [Arendt's note] See, for instance, E. Kohn-Bramstedt, *Dictatorship and Political Police: The Technique of Control by Fear*, London, 1945, p. 164 ff. The explanation is that "terror without propaganda would lose most of its psychological effect, whereas propaganda without terror does not contain its full punch" (p. 175). What is overlooked in these and similar statements, which mostly go around in circles, is the fact that not only political propaganda but the whole of modern mass publicity contains an element of threat; that terror, on the other hand, can be fully effective without propaganda, so long as it is only a question of conventional political terror of tyranny. Only when terror is intended

however, is only partly true. Wherever totalitarianism possesses absolute control, it replaces propaganda with indoctrination and uses violence not so much to frighten people (this is done only in the initial stages when political opposition still exists) as to realize constantly its ideological doctrines and its practical lies. Totalitarianism will not be satisfied to assert, in the face of contrary facts, that unemployment does not exist; it will abolish unemployment benefits as part of its propaganda.[5] Equally important is the fact that the refusal to acknowledge unemployment realized—albeit in a rather unexpected way—the old socialist doctrine: He who does not work shall not eat....

Similarly, the Nazis in the Eastern occupied territories[6] at first used chiefly antisemitic propaganda to win firmer control of the population. They neither needed nor used terror to support this propaganda. When they liquidated the greater part of the Polish intelligentsia, they did it not because of its opposition, but because according to their doctrine Poles had no intellect, and when they planned to kidnap blue-eyed and blond-haired children, they did not intend to frighten the population but to save "Germanic blood."[7] ...

Totalitarian movements use socialism and racism by emptying them of their utilitarian content, the interests of a class or nation. The form of

---

to coerce not merely from without but, as it were, from within, when the political regime wants more than power, is terror in need of propaganda....

5 [Arendt's note] "At that time, it was officially announced that unemployment was 'liquidated' in Soviet Russia. The result of the announcement was that all unemployment benefits were equally 'liquidated'" (Anton Ciliga, *The Russian Enigma*, London, 1940, p. 109).

6 *Eastern occupied territories* Areas of Western Poland annexed by Nazi Germany in 1939 and referred to as "the incorporated Eastern territories." Hitler had long planned to incorporate this part of Poland into the "Greater Germany" and to kill, starve, or enslave the local population and settle Germans in their stead.

7 [Arendt's note] The so-called "Operation Hay" began with a decree dated February 16, 1942, by Himmler [leading member of the Nazi party] "concerning [individuals] of German stock in Poland," stipulating that their children should be sent to families "that are willing [to accept them] without reservations, out of love for the good blood in them" (Nuremberg Document R 135, photostated by the Centre de Documentation Juive, Paris). It seems that in June, 1944, the Ninth Army actually kidnapped 40,000 to 50,000 children and subsequently transported them to Germany.... How the selection of these children was arrived at can be gathered from medical certificates made out by Medical Section II at Minsk on August 10, 1942: "The racial examination of Natalie Harpf, born August 14, 1922, showed a normally developed girl of predominantly East Baltic type with Nordic features."—"Examination of Arnold Cornies, born February 19, 1930, showed a normally developed boy, twelve years old, of predominantly Eastern type with Nordic features." Signed: N. Wc. (Document in the archives of the Yiddish Scientific Institute, New York. No. Occ E 3a-17).

For the extermination of the Polish intelligentsia, which, in Hitler's opinion, could be "wiped out without qualms," see [Léon] Poliakov, [*Bréviaire de la Haine*, Paris, 1951], p. 321, and Document NO 2472.

infallible prediction in which these concepts were presented has become more important than their content.[8] The chief qualification of a mass leader has become unending infallibility; he can never admit an error.[9] The assumption of infallibility, moreover, is based not so much on superior intelligence as on the correct interpretation of the essentially reliable forces in history or nature, forces which neither defeat nor ruin can prove wrong because they are bound to assert themselves in the long run.... Mass leaders in power have one concern which overrules all utilitarian considerations: to make their predictions come true. The Nazis did not hesitate to use, at the end of the war, the concentrated force of their still intact organization to bring about as complete a destruction of Germany as possible, in order to make true their prediction that the German people would be ruined in case of defeat.

The propaganda effect of infallibility, the striking success of posing as a mere interpreting agent of predictable forces, has encouraged in totalitarian dictators the habit of announcing their political intentions in the form of prophecy. The most famous example is Hitler's announcement to the German Reichstag[10] in January, 1939: "I want today once again to make a prophecy: In case the Jewish financiers … succeed once more in hurling the peoples into a world war, the result will be … the annihilation of the Jewish race in Europe."[11] Translated into nontotalitarian language, this meant: I intend to make war and I intend to kill the Jews of Europe. Similarly Stalin, in the great speech before the Central Committee of the Communist Party in 1930 in which he prepared the physical liquidation of intraparty right and left deviationists,[12] described

---

8 [Arendt's note] Hitler based the superiority of ideological movements over political parties on the fact that ideologies (*Weltanschauungen*) always "proclaim their infallibility" (*Mein Kampf*, Book II, chapter v. "*Weltanschauungen* and Organization"). The first pages of the official handbook for the Hitler Youth, *The Nazi Primer*, New York, 1938, consequently emphasize that all questions of Weltanschauungen, formerly deemed "unrealistic" and "ununderstandable," "have become so clear, simple and *definite* [my italics] that every comrade can understand them and co-operate in their solution."

9 [Arendt's note] The first among the "pledges of the Party member," as enumerated in the *Organisationsbuch der NSDAP*, reads: "The Führer is always right." Edition published in 1936, p. 8. But the *Dienstvorschrift für die P.O. der NSDAP*, 1932, p. 38, puts it this way: "Hitler's decision is final!" Note the remarkable difference in phraseology....

10 *Reichstag* German Parliament. Under the Nazis (1933–45), Parliament was a façade; members gathered to listen to Hitler's speeches and unanimously approve his proposals.

11 [Arendt's note] Quoted from Goebbels [Hitler's Minister of Propaganda]: *The Goebbels Diaries (1942-1943)*, ed. by Louis Lochner, New York, 1948, p. 148.

12 *intraparty ... deviationists* Those within the Communist party who held beliefs outside official party doctrine (whether their views were to the left or the right of that doctrine on the political spectrum).

them as representatives of "dying classes."[13] This definition not only gave the argument its specific sharpness but also announced, in totalitarian style, the physical destruction of those whose "dying out" had just been prophesied. In both instances the same objective is accomplished: the liquidation is fitted into a historical process in which man only does or suffers what, according to immutable laws, is bound to happen anyway. As soon as the execution of the victims has been carried out, the "prophecy" becomes a retrospective alibi: nothing happened but what had already been predicted.[14] It does not matter whether the "laws of history" spell the "doom" of the classes and their representatives, or whether the "laws of nature … exterminate" all those elements—democracies, Jews, Eastern subhumans (*Untermenschen*),[15] or the incurably sick—that are not "fit to live" anyway. Incidentally, Hitler too spoke of "dying classes" that ought to be "eliminated without much ado."[16]

This method, like other totalitarian propaganda methods, is foolproof only after the movements have seized power. Then all debate about the truth or falsity of a totalitarian dictator's prediction is as weird as arguing with a potential murderer about whether his future victim is dead or alive—since by killing the person in question the murderer can promptly provide proof of the correctness of his statement. The only valid argument under such conditions is promptly to rescue the person whose death is predicted. Before mass leaders seize the power to fit reality to their lies, their propaganda is marked by its extreme contempt for facts as such,[17] for in their opinion fact depends entirely on the power of man who can fabricate it. The assertion that the Moscow subway is the only

---

13 [Arendt's note] Stalin, [*Leninism* (1933), Vol. II, chapter iii.]

14 [Arendt's note] In a speech he made in September, 1942, when the extermination of the Jews was in full swing, Hitler explicitly referred to his speech of January 30, 1939 (published as a booklet titled *Der Führer vor dem ersten Reichstag Grossdeutschlands*, 1939), and to the Reichstag session of September 1, 1939, when he had announced that "if Jewry should instigate an international world war to exterminate the Aryan peoples of Europe, not the Aryan peoples but Jewry will [rest of sentence drowned by applause]" (see *Der Führer zum Kriegswinterhilfswerk*, Schriften NSV, No. 14, p. 33).

15 *Eastern subhumans (Untermenschen)* In Nazi racist ideology, untermenschen (subhumans) were any peoples who were not "ethnic Germans." Arendt is here referring to the categorization of non-Nordic Europeans (particularly Slavic peoples) as *untermenschen*.

16 [Arendt's note] In the speech of January 30, 1939, p. 19, as quoted above.

17 [Arendt's note] Konrad Heiden, *Der Fuehrer: Hitler's Rise to Power*, Boston, 1944, underlines Hitler's "phenomenal untruthfulness," "the lack of demonstrable reality in nearly all his utterances," his "indifference to facts which he does not regard as vitally important" (pp. 368, 374). In almost identical terms, Khrushchev describes "Stalin's reluctance to consider life's realities" and his indifference to "the real state of affairs," ["Speech on Stalin," New York *Times*, June 5, 1956]. Stalin's opinion of the importance of facts is best expressed in his periodic revisions of Russian history.

one in the world is a lie only so long as the Bolsheviks[18] have not the power to destroy all the others. In other words, the method of infallible prediction, more than any other totalitarian propaganda device, betrays its ultimate goal of world conquest, since only in a world completely under his control could the totalitarian ruler possibly realize all his lies and make true all his prophecies.

The language of prophetic scientificality corresponded to the needs of masses who had lost their home in the world and now were prepared to be reintegrated into eternal, all-dominating forces which by themselves would bear man, the swimmer on the waves of adversity, to the shores of safety. "We shape the life of our people and our legislation according to the verdicts of genetics,"[19] said the Nazis, just as the Bolsheviks assure their followers that economic forces have the power of a verdict of history. They thereby promise a victory which is independent of "temporary" defeats and failures in specific enterprises. For masses, in contrast to classes, want victory and success as such, in their most abstract form; they are not bound together by those special collective interests which they feel to be essential to their survival as a group and which they therefore may assert even in the face of overwhelming odds. More important to them than the cause that may be victorious, or the particular enterprise that may be a success, is the victory of no matter what cause, and success in no matter what enterprise.

Totalitarian propaganda perfects the techniques of mass propaganda, but it neither invents them nor originates their themes.... Like the earlier mob leaders, the spokesmen for totalitarian movements possessed an unerring instinct for anything that ordinary party propaganda or public opinion did not care or dare to touch. Everything hidden, everything passed over in silence, became of major significance, regardless of its own intrinsic importance. The mob really believed that truth was whatever respectable society had hypocritically passed over, or covered up with corruption.

Mysteriousness as such became the first criterion for the choice of topics. The origin of mystery did not matter; it could lie in a reasonable, politically comprehensible desire for secrecy, as in the case of the British Secret Services or the French Deuxième Bureau;[20] or in the conspiratory need of revolutionary

---

18 *Bolsheviks* Members of the Russian Democratic-Workers' Party. Led by Lenin (1870–1924), the party seized control of the government in 1917 and took power. They became the Russian Communist Party of Bolsheviks in 1918, the All-Union Communist Party in 1925, and the Communist Party of the Soviet Union in 1952. Stalin took control of the party after Lenin's death in 1924.

19 [Arendt's note] *Nazi Primer*.

20 *French Deuxième Bureau* France's military intelligence agency (1871–1940); it was replaced by the Service de documentation extérieure et de contre-espionnage (SDECE) in 1945.

groups, as in the case of anarchist and other terrorist sects … or in age-old superstitions which had woven legends around certain groups, as in the case of the Jesuits[21] and the Jews....

The effectiveness of this kind of propaganda demonstrates one of the chief characteristics of modern masses. They do not believe in anything visible, in the reality of their own experience; they do not trust their eyes and ears but only their imaginations, which may be caught by anything that is at once universal and consistent in itself. What convinces masses are not facts, and not even invented facts, but only the consistency of the system of which they are presumably part. Repetition, somewhat overrated in importance because of the common belief in the masses' inferior capacity to grasp and remember, is important only because it convinces them of consistency in time.

What the masses refuse to recognize is the fortuitousness that pervades reality. They are predisposed to all ideologies because they explain facts as mere examples of laws and eliminate coincidences by inventing an all-embracing omnipotence which is supposed to be at the root of every accident. Totalitarian propaganda thrives on this escape from reality into fiction, from coincidence into consistency.

The chief disability of totalitarian propaganda is that it cannot fulfill this longing of the masses for a completely consistent, comprehensible, and predictable world without seriously conflicting with common sense….

Before they seize power and establish a world according to their doctrines, totalitarian movements conjure up a lying world of consistency which is more adequate to the needs of the human mind than reality itself; in which, through sheer imagination, uprooted masses can feel at home and are spared the never-ending shocks which real life and real experiences deal to human beings and their expectations. The force possessed by totalitarian propaganda—before the movements have the power to drop iron curtains to prevent anyone's disturbing, by the slightest reality, the gruesome quiet of an entirely imaginary world—lies in its ability to shut the masses off from the real world. The only signs which the real world still offers to the understanding of the unintegrated and disintegrating masses—whom every new stroke of ill luck makes more gullible—are, so to speak, its lacunae, the questions it does not care to discuss publicly, or the rumours it does not dare to contradict because they hit, although in an exaggerated and deformed way, some sore spot.

---

21 *Jesuits* Members of the Society of Jesus, a Catholic male religious organization. Known for their educational work, Jesuits have historically been viewed with suspicion, as being too clever, practical, and powerful. Hitler persecuted the Jesuits and considered them a dangerous ideological enemy; many priests were killed in occupied territories and in concentration camps.

From these sore spots the lies of totalitarian propaganda derive the element of truthfulness and real experience they need to bridge the gulf between reality and fiction.... They succeed best where the official authorities have surrounded themselves with an atmosphere of secrecy. In the eyes of the masses, they then acquire the reputation of superior "realism" because they touch upon real conditions whose existence is being hidden. Revelations of scandals in high society, of corruption of politicians, every thing that belongs to yellow journalism,[22] becomes in their hands a weapon of more than sensational importance....

(1951)

Questions

1. In paragraph 13 of this selection, Arendt translates a line from one of Hitler's speeches into "nontotalitarian language." What, according to Arendt, distinguishes the language of totalitarian leaders?
2. Why, according to Arendt, do totalitarian leaders disdain facts?
3. What, according to Arendt, are the two "illusions" held by democratically ruled countries that the success of totalitarian movements deconstructed? Do we still hold these illusions?
4. Arendt writes that the masses "do not believe in anything visible, in the reality of their own experience; they do not trust their eyes and ears but only their imaginations, which may be caught by anything that is at once universal and consistent in itself." To what extent could this description be applied to "the masses" today in Canada? In America?
5. Why is a consistent fiction so appealing to masses of people? How can producing this consistency become a problem for totalitarian propaganda?
6. *The Origins of Totalitarianism* sold out online in January 2017, when Donald Trump became President of the United States.
   a. Do the Trump campaign and administration share any common ground with the totalitarian governments described in these excerpts? If so, in what ways? In what ways do the situations differ?
   b. Does Arendt's text offer you insight into current political events? Why or why not?

---

22 *yellow journalism* Sensationalist, over-dramatic journalism (especially that which is exaggerated and not well-substantiated).

TOMMY DOUGLAS

MEDICARE: THE TIME TO TAKE A STAND

As leader of the provincial CCF[1] and premier of Saskatchewan from 1944 to 1961, Tommy Douglas laid the groundwork for Canada's universal government-funded health care system. Douglas faced significant opposition; Medicare was an extremely politically divisive issue in Canada in the 1950s and 60s, much as it is today in the United States. The following speech was delivered in the Saskatchewan legislature in 1961, during Douglas's tenure as premier. Saskatchewan adopted universal medical care in 1962, and the federal government launched a national version of the program in 1966.

I think it is significant that in his address yesterday the Leader of the Opposition[2] said nothing about the basic principles of medical care. His only references to a medical care program were those which were designed to throw cold water on the idea. First he said, "Why don't we wait for a national plan?" Well, Mr. Speaker, I am sure there were a lot of people in Saskatchewan who heard that and who said to themselves, "How long are we supposed to wait?" The Liberal party at its national convention in 1919 promised a national comprehensive health insurance program. They were in office from 1921 to 1930 and from 1935 to 1957....

There was one statement made by the Leader of the Opposition about medical care which astonished me. He said, "There's not a shred of evidence to show that any person in the province has been unable to get medical attention." Surely if ever a comment indicated that an individual was out of touch with

---

1 *CCF* Co-operative Commonwealth Federation, a progressive social-democratic political coalition. In 1961, it united with other groups to form Canada's New Democratic Party.

2 *Leader of the Opposition* Wilbert Ross Thatcher (1917–71). Thatcher became leader of the Saskatchewan Liberal Party in 1959; he served as Leader of the Opposition until the 1964 election when the CCF party was defeated and he became premier.

people, it is that remark. It is like Marie Antoinette* at the time of the French Revolution when the people were crying for bread saying, "Why don't they eat cake?" To say that there is no evidence to show that any person in the province has been unable to get medical attention, is to fly in the face of all the facts.

The Canadian Sickness Report, 1951, conducted by the Government of Canada, shows clearly that the lower income groups in the period under study had more illness and more days of disability than did the higher income groups. It shows, conversely, that the volume of medical care received is much less than that received by higher income groups. The low income groups, because of poor diet, poor housing conditions, and harder working conditions, have more illness and more disability. Yet the records show that they are the people who get the least medical care. The Canadian Sickness Report shows that the low income groups spent on an average $58.10 per family, whereas the higher income groups spent on an average $158.70 per family. The higher income groups spent almost three times as much per family on medical care as did the low income groups despite the fact that the low income groups had more sickness and more disability....

Now I readily grant that no doctor has turned patients away. No doctor could do so without violating his Hippocratic oath.* But what happens? First of all, patients are reluctant to go to the doctor if they know they can't pay. People fail to seek medical counsel and medical advice when they should get it and they often time[s] leave it until the situation is serious and even dangerous. The second fact is that many people who do go to the doctors incur bills and debts which cripple them for years to come, and this does not just apply to poor people. There are thousands of people in Saskatchewan and across Canada living on reasonably comfortable incomes who are able to make the payments on their houses and their cars and on their television sets and who can get by providing two things: firstly, they don't lose their jobs; and secondly, that the breadwinner doesn't get seriously ill. For such people, doctor bills amounting to large sums of money can put that family in a serious financial predicament for years to come.

The Leader of the Opposition yesterday spent a good deal of time talking 5
about the terrible costs which this would place upon the taxpayers of this province. I thought some of his sentences were gems. He said, "The Liberals believe in a medical care plan if it can be done without hardship to the taxpayer." Now, which taxpayer is he worried about—the ones that are going to be paying less under the plan than they pay now, or the ones that are going to be paying more? Which is he worried about? ...

I want to point out, Mr. Speaker, that the cost of a medical care plan is not a new cost to the people of Saskatchewan. The people of this province now are spending $18 million to $20 million a year for medical care. This is not a new cost. It is a different distribution of the cost—that is all. This money had to be paid before. Doctors of this province had to be paid. Everything has had to be paid for—their staff, x-ray technicians, lab technicians, these things all had to be paid for. But they have been paid for by those who were unfortunate enough to be ill. We are now saying they should be paid for by spreading the cost over all the people. We propose that the family tax, which we admit is a regressive tax, since there is a flat rate on every family, and therefore bears no relationship to ability to pay, should be kept as small as possible. We propose that the balance of the cost—probably two-thirds of the cost—ought to be raised by factors which have a measure of ability to pay....

It seems to me to be begging the question[3] to be talking about whether or not the people of this province, or the people of Canada can afford a plan to spread the cost of sickness over the entire population. This is not a new principle. This has existed in nearly all the countries of western Europe—many of them for a quarter of a century. It has been in Great Britain since 1948; it has been in New Zealand since 1935; it has been in Australia. The little state of Israel that only came into existence in 1948 has today the most comprehensive health insurance plan in the world. It has more doctors, and nurses and dentists per thousand of its population than any other industrialized country or any country for which we can get statistics.

It is not a new principle. To me it seems to be sheer nonsense to suggest that medical care is something which ought to be measured just in dollars. When we're talking about medical care we're talking about our sense of values. Do we think human life is important? Do we think that the best medical care which is available is something to which people are entitled, by virtue of belonging to a civilized community? I looked up the figures, and I found that, in 1959, the people of Canada spent $1,555 million, or eight percent of their personal expenditures on alcohol and tobacco. I would be the last person to argue that people do not have the right, if they want to, to spend part of their income for either alcohol or tobacco or entertainment, or anything else. But in the same period of time, the people of Canada spent $944 million for medical and dental care, or four and one-half percent of their income expenses. In other words, in the year 1959 we spent almost twice as much on luxuries such as tobacco and alcohol as we spent on providing ourselves and our families with the medical and dental care which they require.

If we can afford large sums of money for other such things as horse-racing, and many other things, and we do—I'm not arguing against them—then I say we ought to have sufficient sense of values to say that health is more important

3 *begging the question* Fallacy in which the premises of an argument include an assumption that the conclusion is true.

than these things, and if we can find money for relatively non-essential things, we can find the money to give our people good health.

The Liberal press in this province has been running editorials regularly for 10
months now against the welfare state, particularly attacking the welfare state in United Kingdom. The other day they pointed out that the British government was spending more on the welfare state than they were spending on national defence. Well, this to me is not a crushing criticism....

Mr. Speaker, 50 dollars per capita gives every man, woman and child in Great Britain security from the cradle to the grave. It takes care of their doctor bills, dental bills, hospital bills, optometric care and appliances. The only thing for which there is a deterrent fee is drugs, and that is very small. It gives them unemployment insurance, baby bonuses, and pensions when they are physically disabled. It provides benefits in the event of death, and it provides adequate pensions for widows and their children. I say that if any government, of any country, can give its people that kind of security for less than $50 per capita, then it is worth the price, and many times over....

There are two basic weaknesses in the proposals which were put forward by those who wanted a limited coverage for medical care. The first is the private plans bear no relationship to ability to pay....

The other weakness in the proposal of a partial coverage medical care program is that a great many groups in the province would only get coverage if they could prove need. This means imposing a means test; this means probing into people's affairs, and this is a pretty serious thing to do.

I want to say that the time is surely past when people should have to depend on proving need in order to get services that should be the inalienable right of every citizen of a good society.

It is all very well for some people to say that there is no stigma or humili- 15
ation connected with having to prove need. This is always said by people who know that they are in no danger of having to prove need. I am very glad that the committee recommended and the government decided that there will be no such stigma and that there will be no means test. Every person in the province who is self-supporting and able to pay a relatively small per capita tax, will be eligible for care and those who are not self-supporting will be covered by other programs.

I want to say that I think there is a value in having every family and every individual make some individual contribution. I think it has psychological value. I think it keeps the public aware of the cost and gives the people a sense of personal responsibility. I would say to the members of this House that even if we could finance the plan without a per capita tax, I personally would strongly advise against it. I would like to see the per capita tax so low that it is merely a nominal tax, but I think there is a psychological value in people paying something for their cards. It is something which they have bought; it entitles them to certain services. We should have a constant realization that if those services are abused and costs get out of hand, then of course the cost of the medical care is bound to go up.

I believe, Mr. Speaker, that if this medical care insurance program is successful, and I think it will be, it will prove to be the forerunner of a national medical care insurance plan. It will become the nucleus around which Canada will ultimately build a comprehensive health insurance program which will cover all health services—not just hospital and medical care—but eventually dental care, optometric care, drugs and all the other health services which people require. I believe such a plan operated by the federal and provincial governments jointly will ultimately come in Canada. But I don't think it will come unless we lead the way. I want to say that when the history of our time is written, it may well be recorded that in October 1961, the Saskatchewan legislature and the Saskatchewan people pioneered in this field and took a first step towards ultimately establishing a system of medical care insurance for all the people of Canada....

The government believes that health is too important to be left to the chance that the average family will have the necessary money to buy health services.... I am convinced that inside two or three years both the doctors who provide the service and the people who receive the service will be so completely satisfied with it that no government will dare to take it away.

(1961)

Questions

1. Evaluate the rhetorical effectiveness of this speech.
2. What does Douglas present as the values underlying the health care system he proposes? To what extent do you share these values?
3. Douglas predicts that "the people who receive the service will be so completely satisfied with it that no government will dare to take it away." To what extent are you satisfied with Canada's health care system? How, if at all, do you think it should be changed?
4. Canada's public health care system currently covers 70 percent of Canadians' medical expenses; though coverage varies, many provinces' universal health plans do not include prescription drugs, vision care, dental care, long-term home care, and many mental health services. Should publicly funded health care be expanded to include any of these (or any other) uncovered expenses? Why or why not?
5. Who is the intended audience of this speech? How can you tell?

Stanley Milgram

from Behavioural Study of Obedience

The 1961 public trial of Adolf Eichmann, a high-ranking Nazi war criminal, brought the Holocaust to the forefront of public consciousness and raised questions regarding the capacity of ordinary human beings to act unethically, especially when prompted by authority to do so. In the same year, Stanley Milgram—a recent Harvard graduate and an assistant professor at Yale—conducted a series of related experiments that together would become famous as the "Milgram experiment." His studies, one of which is described in the following paper, are often taken to demonstrate the likelihood that human beings will obey authority even when ordered to perform unethical acts. The experiment has been a subject of immense controversy since its publication, with many psychologists arguing for its continuing relevance (and, for the most part, accepting its central conclusions), and others questioning both the validity of its surprising findings and the ethics of its treatment of the research participants.

Obedience is as basic an element in the structure of social life as one can point to. Some system of authority is a requirement of all communal living, and it is only the man dwelling in isolation who is not forced to respond, through defiance or submission, to the commands of others. Obedience, as a determinant of behaviour, is of particular relevance to our time. It has been reliably established that from 1933–45 millions of innocent persons were systematically slaughtered on command. Gas chambers were built, death camps were guarded, daily quotas of corpses were produced with the same efficiency as the manufacture of appliances. These inhumane policies may have originated in the mind of a single person, but they could only be carried out on a massive scale if a very large number of persons obeyed orders....

General Procedure

A procedure was devised which seems useful as a tool for studying obedience (Milgram, 1961). It consists of ordering a naive subject* to administer electric shock to a victim. A simulated shock generator is used, with 30 clearly marked voltage levels that range from 15 to 450 volts. The instrument bears verbal designations that range from Slight Shock to Danger: Severe Shock. The responses of the victim, who is a trained confederate of the experimenter, are standardized. The orders to administer shocks are given to the naive subject in the context of a "learning experiment" ostensibly set up to study the effects of punishment on memory. As the experiment proceeds the naive subject is commanded to administer increasingly more intense shocks to the victim, even to a point of reaching the level marked Danger: Severe Shock. Internal resistances become stronger, and at a certain point the subject refuses to go on with the experiment. Behaviour prior to this rupture is considered "obedience," in that the subject complies with the commands of the experimenter. The point of rupture is the act of disobedience. A quantitative value is assigned to the subject's performance based on the maximum intensity shock he is willing to administer before he refuses to participate further. Thus for any particular subject and for any particular experimental condition the degree of obedience may be specified with a numerical value. The crux of the study is to systematically vary the factors believed to alter the degree of obedience to the experimental commands....

METHOD

Subjects

The subjects were 40 males between the ages of 20 and 50, drawn from New Haven and surrounding communities. Subjects were obtained by a newspaper advertisement and direct mail solicitations. Those who responded to the appeal believed they were to participate in a study of memory and learning at Yale University. A wide range of occupations is represented in the sample. Typical subjects were postal clerks, high school teachers, salesmen, engineers, and labourers. Subjects ranged in educational level from one who had not finished elementary school, to those who had doctorate and other professional degrees. They were paid $4.50 for their participation in the experiment. However, subjects were told that payment was simply for coming to the laboratory, and that the money was theirs no matter what happened after they arrived....

Personnel and Locale

The experiment was conducted on the grounds of Yale University in the elegant interaction laboratory. (This detail is relevant to the perceived legitimacy of the experiment. In further variations, the experiment was dissociated from the university, with consequences for performance.) The role of experimenter was played by a 31-year-old high school teacher of biology. His manner was impassive, and his appearance somewhat stern throughout the experiment. He was dressed in a grey technician's coat. The victim was played by a 47-year-old accountant, trained for the role; he was of Irish-American stock, whom most observers found mild-mannered and likeable.

Procedure

One naive subject and one victim (an accomplice) performed in each ex- 5
periment. A pretext had to be devised that would justify the administration of electric shock by the naive subject. This was effectively accomplished by the cover story. After a general introduction on the presumed relation between punishment and learning, subjects were told:

> But actually, we know *very little* about the effect of punishment on learning, because almost no truly scientific studies have been made of it in human beings.
>
> For instance, we don't know how *much* punishment is best for learning—and we don't know how much difference it makes as to who is giving the punishment, whether an adult learns best from a younger or an older person than himself—or many things of that sort.
>
> So in this study we are bringing together a number of adults of different occupations and ages. And we're asking some of them to be teachers and some of them to be learners.
>
> We want to find out just what effect different people have on each other as teachers and learners, and also what effect *punishment* will have on learning in this situation.
>
> Therefore, I'm going to ask one of you to be the teacher here tonight and the other one to be the learner.
>
> Does either of you have a preference?

Subjects then drew slips of paper from a hat to determine who would be the teacher and who would be the learner in the experiment. The drawing was rigged so that the naive subject was always the teacher and the accomplice always the learner. (Both slips contained the word "Teacher.") Immediately after the drawing, the teacher and learner were taken to an adjacent room and the learner was strapped into an "electric chair" apparatus.

The experimenter explained that the straps were to prevent excessive movement while the learner was being shocked. The effect was to make it impossible for him to escape from the situation. An electrode was attached to the learner's wrist, and electrode paste was applied "to avoid blisters and burns." Subjects were told that the electrode was attached to the shock generator in the adjoining room.

In order to improve credibility the experimenter declared, in response to a question by the learner: "Although shocks can be extremely painful, they cause no permanent tissue damage."

Learning task. The lesson administered by the subject was a paired-associate learning task. The subject read a series of word pairs to the learner, and then read the first word of the pair along with four terms. The learner was to indicate which of the four terms had originally been paired with the first word. He communicated his answer by pressing one of four switches in front of him, which in turn lit up one of four numbered quadrants in a answer-box located atop the shock generator.

10 *Shock generator.* The instrument panel consists of 30 lever switches set in a horizontal line. Each switch is clearly labelled with a voltage designation that ranges from 15 to 450 volts. There is a 15-volt increment from one switch to the next going from left to right. In addition, the following verbal designations are clearly indicated for groups of four switches going from left to right: Slight Shock, Moderate Shock, Strong Shock, Intense Shock, Extremely Intense Shock, Danger: Severe Shock. (Two switches after this last designation are simply marked XXX.)

Upon depressing a switch: a pilot light corresponding to each switch is illuminated in bright red; an electric buzzing is heard; an electric blue light, labelled "voltage energizer," flashes; the dial on the voltage meter swings to the right; various relay clicks are sounded.

The upper left-hand corner of the generator is labelled Shock generator, Type ZLB, Dyson Instrument Company, Waltham, Mass. Output 15 volts–450 volts.

Details of the instrument were carefully handled to ensure an appearance of authenticity. The panel was engraved by precision industrial engravers, and all components were of high quality. No subject in the experiment suspected that the instrument was merely a simulated shock generator.

Sample shock. Each naive subject is given a sample shock on the shock generator, prior to beginning his run as teacher. This shock is always 45 volts, and is applied by pressing the third switch of the generator. The shock is applied to the wrist of the naive subject, and has its source in a 45-volt battery wired to the generator. This further convinces the subject of the authenticity of the generator.

Shock instructions. The subject is told to administer a shock to the learner each time he gives a wrong response. Moreover—and this is the key command—the subject is instructed to "move one level higher on the shock generator each time the learner flashes a wrong answer." He is also instructed to announce the voltage level before administering a shock. This serves to continually remind subjects of the increasing intensity of shocks administered to the learner.

Preliminary and regular run. Pretests revealed that the procedure of reading words and administering shocks requires some practice before it can be handled smoothly. Therefore, immediately preceding the regular run, the teacher is given a preliminary series of 10 words to read to the learner. There are 3 neutral words in the practice series (i.e., words that the learner answers correctly), so that the shocks are administered for 7 of the words, with the maximum shock of 105 volts (moderate shock). Almost all subjects master the procedure by the time the preliminary run is over.

Subjects are then presented with a second list, and are told that the procedure is the same as for the first list; the experimenter adds however:

> When you get to the bottom of the list, repeat it over again, and continue giving shocks, until the learner has learned all the pairs correctly.

The experimenter instructs the subject to,

> start from 15 volts and increase the shock level one step each time the learner gives a wrong answer.

Feedback from the victim. In all conditions the learner gives a predetermined set of responses to the word pair test, based on a schedule of approximately three wrong answers to one correct answer. In the present experimental condition no vocal response or other sign of protest is heard from the learner until Shock Level 300 is reached. When the 300-volt shock is administered, the learner pounds on the wall of the room in which he is bound to the electric chair. The pounding can be heard by the subject. From this point on, the learner's answers no longer appear on the four-way panel.

At this juncture, subjects ordinarily turn to the experimenter for guidance. The experimenter instructs the subject to treat absence of a response as a wrong answer, and to shock the subject according to the usual schedule. He advises the subject to allow 5–10 seconds before considering no response as a wrong answer, and to increase the shock level one step each time the learner fails to respond correctly. The learner's pounding is repeated after the 315-volt shock is administered; afterwards he is not heard from, nor do his answers reappear on the four-way signal box.

20 *Experimenter feedback.* At various points in the experiment the subject may turn to the experimenter for advice on whether he should continue to administer shocks. Or he may indicate that he does not wish to go on. It was important to standardize the experimenter's responses to these inquiries and reactions.

If the subject indicated his unwillingness to go on, the experimenter responded with a sequence of "prods," using as many as necessary to bring the subject into line.

Prod 1: Please continue. *or* Please go on.

Prod 2: The experiment requires that you continue.

Prod 3: It is absolutely essential that you continue.

Prod 4: You have no other choice, you *must* go on.

The prods were always made in sequence: Only if Prod 1 had been unsuccessful, could Prod 2 be used. If the subject still refused to obey the experimenter after Prod 4, the experiment was terminated. The experimenter's tone of voice was at all times firm, but not impolite. The sequence was begun anew on each occasion that the subject balked or showed reluctance to follow orders.

Special prods. If the subject asked if the learner was liable to suffer permanent physical injury, the experimenter said:

> Although the shocks may be painful, there is no permanent tissue damage, so please go on. [Followed by Prods 2, 3, and 4 if necessary.]

If the subject said that the learner did not want to go on, the experimenter replied:

> Whether the learner likes it or not, you must go on until he has learned all the word pairs correctly. So please go on. [Followed by Prods 2, 3, and 4 if necessary.]

Dependent Measures

The primary dependent measure for any subject is the maximum shock he ad- 25
ministers before he refuses to go any further. In principle this may vary from 0 (for a subject who refuses to administer even the first shock) to 30 (for a subject who administers the highest shock on the generator). A subject who breaks off the experiment at any point prior to administering the thirtieth shock level is termed a *defiant subject*. One who complies with experimental command fully, and proceeds to administer all shock levels commanded, is termed an *obedient* subject....

Interview and dehoax. Following the experiment, subjects were interviewed; open-ended questions, projective measures, and attitude scales were employed. After the interview, procedures were undertaken to assure that the subject would leave the laboratory in a state of well being. A friendly reconciliation was arranged between the subject and the victim, and an effort was made to reduce any tensions that arose as a result of the experiment.

RESULTS

Preliminary Notions

Before giving an account of the experimental results, it is instructive to consider how persons predict others will perform when commanded to administer powerful shocks to another person. Fourteen Yale seniors, all psychology majors, were provided with a detailed description of the experimental situation. They were asked to reflect carefully on it, and to predict the behaviour of 100 hypothetical subjects. More specifically, they were instructed to plot the distribution of obedience of "100 Americans of diverse occupations, and ranging in age from 20 to 50 years," who were placed in the experimental situation.

There was considerable agreement among the respondents on the expected behaviour or hypothetical subjects. All respondents predicted that only an insignificant minority would go through to the end of the shock series. (The estimates ranged from 0 to 3%; i.e., the most "pessimistic" member of the class predicted that of 100 persons, 3 would continue through to the most potent shock available on the shock generator—450 volts.) The class mean was 1.2%. The question was also posed informally to colleagues of the author, and the most general feeling was that few if any subjects would go beyond the designation Very Strong Shock.

Result of Experiment 1

Subjects accept situation. With few exceptions subjects were convinced of the reality of the experimental situation, that they were administering shocks to another person, and the most potent shocks were extremely painful. In the post-experimental interview subjects were asked: "How painful to the learner were the last few shocks that you administered to him?" Subjects were instructed to indicate their answers on a printed 14-point scale ranging from "Not at all painful" to "Extremely painful." The modal response* was 14 (Extremely painful) with the mean at 13.42.

30 *Signs of extreme tension.* Many subjects showed signs of nervousness in the experimental situation, and especially upon administering the more powerful shocks. In a large number of cases the degree of tension reached extremes that are rarely seen in sociopsychological laboratory studies. Subjects were observed to sweat, tremble, stutter, bite their lips, groan, and dig their fingernails into their flesh. These were characteristic rather than exceptional responses to the experiment.

One sign of tension was the regular occurrence of nervous laughing fits. Fourteen of the 40 subjects showed definite signs of nervous laughter and smiling. The laughter seemed entirely out of place, even bizarre. Full-blown, uncontrollable seizures were observed for 3 subjects. On one occasion we observed a seizure so violently convulsive that it was necessary to call a halt to the experiment. The subject, a 46-year-old encyclopedia salesman, was seriously embarrassed by his untoward and uncontrollable behaviour. In the post-experimental interviews subjects took such pains to point out that they were not sadistic types, and that the laughter did not mean they enjoyed shocking the victim.

Distribution of scores. It had been conjectured that persons would not, in general, agree to administer shocks beyond the level designated Very Strong Shock. The distribution of maximum shocks for this experiment is shown in Table 1. The obtained distribution of scores deviates radically from the prediction.

Upon command of the experimenter, each of the 40 subjects went beyond the expected breakoff point. No subject stopped prior to administering Shock Level 20. (At this level—300 volts—the victim kicks on the wall and no longer provides answers to the teacher's multiple-choice questions.)

Of the 40 subjects, 5 refused to obey the experimental commands beyond the 300-volt level. Four more subjects administered one further shock, and then refused to go on. Two broke off at the 330-volt level, and 1 each at 345, 360,

TABLE 1
Distribution of Breakoff Points

Verbal designation and voltage indication	*Number of subjects for whom this was maximum shock*
Slight Shock	
15	0
30	0
45	0
60	0
Moderate Shock	
75	0
90	0
105	0
120	0
Strong Shock	
135	0
150	0
165	0
180	0
Very Strong Shock	
195	0
210	0
225	0
240	0
Intense Shock	
255	0
270	0
285	0
300	5
Extreme Intensity Shock	
315	4
330	2
345	1
360	1
Danger: Severe Shock	
375	1
390	0
405	0
420	0
XXX	
435	0
450	26

and 375 volts. Thus a total of 14 subjects defied the experimenter. It is instructive to reprint their remarks at the point of defiance, as transcribed from the tape recordings:

> [0124] I think he's trying to communicate, he's knocking.... Well it's not fair to shock the guy ... these are terrific volts. I don't think this is very humane.... Oh, I can't go on with this; no this isn't right. It's a hell of an experiment. The guy is suffering in there. No, I don't want to go on. This is crazy. [Subject refused to administer more shocks.]

> [0123] He's banging in there. I'm gonna chicken out. I'd like to continue, but I can't do that to a man.... I'm sorry I can't do that to a man. I'll hurt his heart. You take your cheque.... No really, I couldn't do it.

These subjects were frequently in a highly agitated and even angered state. Sometimes, verbal protest was at a minimum, and the subject simply got up from his chair in front of the shock generator, and indicated that he wished to leave the laboratory.

Of the 40 subjects, 26 obeyed the orders of the experimenter to the end, proceeding to punish the victim until they reached the most potent shock available on the shock generator. At that point, the experimenter called a halt to the sessions. (The maximum shock is labelled 450 volts, and is two steps beyond the designation: Danger: Severe Shock.) Although obedient subjects continued to administer shocks, they often did so under extreme stress. Some expressed reluctance to administer shocks beyond the 300-volt level, and displayed fears similar to those who defied the experimenter; yet they obeyed.

After the maximum shocks had been delivered, and the experimenter called a halt to the proceedings, many obedient subjects heaved sighs of relief, mopped their brows, rubbed their fingers over their eyes, or nervously fumbled cigarettes. Some shook their heads, apparently in regret. Some subjects had remained calm throughout the experiment, and displayed only minimal signs of tension from beginning to end.

Discussion

The experiment yielded two findings that were surprising. The first finding concerns the sheer strength of obedient tendencies manifested in this situation. Subjects have learned from childhood that it is a fundamental breach of moral conduct to hurt another person against his will. Yet, 26 subjects abandon this tenet in following the instructions of an authority who has no special powers to enforce his commands. To disobey would bring no material loss to the subject;

no punishment would ensue. It is clear from the remarks and outward behaviour of many participants that in punishing the victim they are often acting against their own values. Subjects often expressed deep disapproval of shocking a man in the face of his objections, and others denounced it as stupid and senseless. Yet the majority complied with the experimental commands. This outcome was surprising from two perspectives: first, from the standpoint of predictions made in the questionnaire described earlier. (Here, however, it is possible that the remoteness of the respondents from the actual situation, and the difficulty of conveying to them the concrete details of the experiment, could account for the serious underestimation of obedience.)

But the results were also unexpected to persons who observed the experiment in progress, through one-way mirrors. Observers often uttered expressions of disbelief upon seeing a subject administrate more powerful shocks to the victim. These persons had a full acquaintance with the details of the situation, and yet systematically underestimated the amount of obedience that subjects would display.

The second unanticipated effect was the extraordinary tension generated by the procedures. One might suppose that a subject would simply break off or continue as his conscience dictated. Yet, this is very far from what happened. There were striking reactions of tension and emotional strain.

(1961)

Questions

1. What was the purpose of the experiment conducted at Yale?
2. What elements were included to make the experiment seem authentic? How did the experimenters signify authority to the naive subjects?
3. What is the effect of the very scientific style in which this paper is written?
4. What does the term "naive subject" refer to, literally? What does it seem to imply figuratively?
5. What effect does the contrast between the subjects' nervous laughter and the seriousness of their situation have? What is Milgram implying about human behaviour under stress?
6. How did the experiment's actual outcome compare to your own expectations? Were you as surprised as the Yale academics? What do you think might account for the discrepancy between the expected outcome and the actual one? How do you feel you would have performed? Can you honestly predict whether you would have been as obedient or less so?

RAYMOND WILLIAMS

from THE LONG REVOLUTION

With his studies of the relationships between socioeconomics, politics, the arts, and the history of ideas, Raymond Williams contributed significantly to the formation of the discipline of cultural studies. This short piece is excerpted from Williams's second major scholarly work, The Long Revolution, *which argues that Western society is in the midst of a "cultural revolution" involving the extension of "the skills of literacy and other advanced communication ... to all people rather than to limited groups." Such a revolution, Williams argues, is "comparable in importance to the growth of democracy" and to the industrial revolution, and is inextricable from them. In the course of his argument, Williams offers a history of English language and communications; the following passage appears in his chapter on "The Growth of 'Standard English.'"*

The late seventeenth and eighteenth centuries saw a strenuous effort to rationalize English, by a number of differently motivated groups. The Royal Society's Committee "for improving the English tongue" (1664) represents the effort of a new scientific philosophy to clarify the language for the purposes of its own kind of discourse. A different group, running from Addison and Swift to Pope and Johnson,[1] were concerned with the absence of a "polite standard" in the new society. Yet behind these intellectual groups there was the practical pressure of a newly powerful and self-conscious middle class which, like most groups which find themselves suddenly possessed of social standing but deficient in social tradition, thought "correctness" a systematic thing which had simply to be acquired. Eighteenth-century London abounded in spelling-masters and pronunciation-coaches: many of them, as it happened, ignorant men. Yet if they had all been scholars, within the concepts of their period, the result might not have been greatly different. The scholarly teaching of grammar was locked in the illusion that Latin grammatical rules

1 *Addison ... Johnson* Joseph Addison (1672–1719), Jonathan Swift (1667–1745), Alexander Pope (1688–1744), and Samuel Johnson (1709–84) belonged to a London circle of important writers and intellectuals.

were the best possible guide to correctness in English. And Johnson himself emphatically expounded a doctrine equally false: that the spelling of a word is the best guide to its pronunciation, "the most elegant speakers ... [those] who deviate least from the written words." The new "standard," therefore, was not, as the earlier common language had been, the result mainly of growth through contact and actual relationships, but to a considerable extent an artificial creation based on false premises. The habits of a language are too strong to be wholly altered by determined yet relatively ignorant teachers, but the mark of their effort is still on us, and the tension they created is still high.

Common pronunciation (as distinct from regional variations) changed considerably during this period: partly through ordinary change, partly through the teaching of "correctness." English spelling, as is now well known, is in fact extremely unreliable as a guide to pronunciation, for not only, at best, does it frequently record sounds that have become obsolete, but in fact many of these were obsolete when the spellings were fixed, and moreover certain plain blunders have become embedded by time. *Iland*, *sissors*, *sithe*, *coud*, and *ancor* were altered, by men ignorant of their origins, confident of false origins, to *island*, *scissors*, *scythe*, *could*, and *anchor*, but in these cases, fortunately, pronunciation has not been affected. Similar false alterations, however, such as *fault*, *vault*, *assault* (which need no l's), or *advantage* and *advance* (which need no d's) have perpetuated their errors not only into spelling but into sound. The principle of following the spelling changed the sound *offen* into *often*, *forrid* into *forehead*, *summat* into *somewhat*, *lanskip* into *landscape*, *yumer* into *humour*, *at ome* into *at home*, *weskit* into *waistcoat*, and so on, in a list that could be tediously prolonged. Words like these are among the pressure points* of distinction between "educated" and "uneducated" speech, yet the case is simply that the uneducated, less exposed to the doctrines of "correctness," have preserved the traditional pronunciation.

(1961)

Questions

1. List examples of words that have been added to the English language, or whose spelling or meaning have changed, in your lifetime. How do you think these changes occur?
2. In your opinion, what is the difference between "educated" and "uneducated" speech? Do you feel there is a value in this distinction?
3. How would you describe Williams's writing style? Who do you think is his intended audience?
4. Express in your own words some of the irony inherent in the history of "correct" pronunciation, according to Williams.

Martin Luther King Jr.

Letter from Birmingham Jail

In the spring of 1963, Martin Luther King Jr. was among the civil rights activists leading protests against segregation in Birmingham, Alabama—where racial tensions were higher than almost anywhere else in the American South. In response to the civil rights demonstrators' activities, the city obtained an injunction making "parading, demonstrating, boycotting," and other nonviolent forms of protest illegal. When King continued undeterred, he was arrested two days later. The following essay, written during the eight days he spent in prison, is a response to "A Call for Unity," a condemnation of the American Civil Rights Movement by a group of white clergy that had been published in the Birmingham News. *King's letter became perhaps the best known exposition of the principles of the movement.*

King's "Letter from Birmingham Jail" was published in 1963 in several newspapers and periodicals (including The New York Post, Christianity Today, *and* Ebony*); it was also included in King's 1964 book* Why We Can't Wait.

My Dear Fellow Clergymen:

While confined here in the Birmingham city jail, I came across your recent statement calling my present activities "unwise and untimely." Seldom do I pause to answer criticism of my work and ideas. If I sought to answer all the criticisms that cross my desk, my secretaries would have little time for anything other than such correspondence in the course of the day, and I would have no time for constructive work. But since I feel that you are men of genuine good will and that your criticisms are sincerely set forth, I want to try to answer your statement in what I hope will be patient and reasonable terms.

I think I should indicate why I am here in Birmingham, since you have been influenced by the view which argues against "outsiders coming in." I have the honour of serving as president of the Southern Christian Leadership Conference, an organization operating in every southern state, with headquarters in Atlanta, Georgia. We have some eighty-five affiliated organizations across the South, and one of them is the Alabama Christian Movement for Human Rights. Frequently we share staff, educational, and financial resources with our affiliates. Several months ago the affiliate here in Birmingham asked us to be on call to engage in a nonviolent direct-action program if such were deemed necessary. We readily consented, and when the hour came we lived up to our promise. So I, along with several members of my staff, am here because I was invited here. I am here because I have organizational ties here.

But more basically, I am in Birmingham because injustice is here. Just as the prophets of the eighth century BC left their villages and carried their "thus saith the Lord" far beyond the boundaries of their home towns, and just as the Apostle Paul left his village of Tarsus and carried the gospel of Jesus Christ to the far corners of the Greco-Roman world, so am I compelled to carry the gospel of freedom beyond my own home town. Like Paul, I must constantly respond to the Macedonian call for aid.

Moreover, I am cognizant of the interrelatedness of all communities and states. I cannot sit idly by in Atlanta and not be concerned about what happens in Birmingham. Injustice anywhere is a threat to justice everywhere. We are caught in an inescapable network of mutuality, tied in a single garment of destiny. Whatever affects one directly, affects all indirectly. Never again can we afford to live with the narrow, provincial "outside agitator" idea. Anyone who lives inside the United States can never be considered an outsider anywhere within its bounds.

You deplore the demonstrations taking place in Birmingham. But your 5
statement, I am sorry to say, fails to express a similar concern for the conditions that brought about the demonstrations. I am sure that none of you would want to rest content with the superficial kind of social analysis that deals merely with effects and does not grapple with underlying causes. It is unfortunate that demonstrations are taking place in Birmingham, but it is even more unfortunate that the city's white power structure left the Negro community with no alternative.

In any nonviolent campaign there are four basic steps: collection of the facts to determine whether injustices exist; negotiation; self-purification; and direct action. We have gone through all these steps in Birmingham. There can be no gainsaying the fact that racial injustice engulfs this community. Birmingham is probably the most thoroughly segregated city* in the United States. Its ugly record of brutality is widely known. Negroes have experienced grossly unjust treatment in the courts. There have been more unsolved bombings of Negro homes and churches in Birmingham than in any other city in the nation. These are the hard, brutal facts of the case. On the basis of these conditions, Negro leaders sought to negotiate with the city fathers. But the latter consistently refused to engage in good-faith negotiation.

Then, last September, came the opportunity to talk with leaders of Birmingham's economic community. In the course of the negotiations, certain promises were made by the merchants—for example, to remove the stores' humiliating racial signs. On the basis of these promises, the Reverend Fred Shuttlesworth and the leaders of the Alabama Christian Movement for Human Rights agreed to a moratorium on all demonstrations. As the weeks and months went by, we realized that we were the victims of a broken promise. A few signs, briefly removed, returned; the others remained.

As in so many past experiences, our hopes had been blasted, and the shadow of deep disappointment settled upon us. We had no alternative except to prepare for direct action, whereby we could present our very bodies as a means of laying our case before the conscience of the local and the national community. Mindful of the difficulties involved, we decided to undertake a process of self-purification. We began a series of workshops on nonviolence, and we repeatedly asked ourselves: "Are you able to accept blows without retaliating?" "Are you able to endure the ordeal of jail?" We decided to schedule our direct-action program for the Easter season, realizing that except for Christmas, this is the main shopping period of the year. Knowing that a strong economic-withdrawal program would be the by-product of direct action, we felt that this would be the best time to bring pressure to bear on the merchants for the needed change.

Then it occurred to us that Birmingham's mayoral election was coming up in March, and we speedily decided to postpone action until after election day. When we discovered that the Commissioner of Public Safety, Eugene "Bull" Connor, had piled up enough votes to be in the run-off, we decided again to postpone action until the day after the run-off so that the demonstrations could not be used to cloud the issues. Like many others, we wanted to see Mr. Connor defeated, and to this end we endured postponement after postponement. Having aided in this community need, we felt that our direct-action program could be delayed no longer.

10 You may well ask, "Why direct action? Why sit-ins, marches, and so forth? Isn't negotiation a better path?" You are quite right in calling for negotiation. Indeed, this is the very purpose of direct action. Nonviolent direct action seeks so to create such a crisis and foster such tension that a community which has constantly refused to negotiate is forced to confront the issue. It seeks to dramatize the issue that it can no longer be ignored. My citing the creation of tension as part of the work of the nonviolent-resister may sound rather shocking. But I must confess that I am not afraid of the word "tension." I have earnestly opposed violent tension, but there is a type of constructive, nonviolent tension which is necessary for growth. Just as Socrates felt that it was necessary to create a tension in the mind so that individuals could rise

from the bondage of myths and half-truths to the unfettered realm of creative analysis and objective appraisal, so must we see the need for nonviolent gadflies* to create the kind of tension in society that will help men rise from the dark depths of prejudice and racism to the majestic heights of understanding and brotherhood.

The purpose of our direct-action program is to create a situation so crisis-packed that it will inevitably open the door to negotiation. I therefore concur with you in your call for negotiation. Too long has our beloved Southland been bogged down in a tragic effort to live in monologue rather than dialogue.

One of the basic points in your statement is that the action that I and my associates have taken in Birmingham is untimely. Some have asked: "Why didn't you give the new city administration time to act?" The only answer that I can give to this query is that the new Birmingham administration must be prodded about as much as the outgoing one, before it will act. We are sadly mistaken if we feel that the election of Albert Boutwell as mayor will bring the millennium to Birmingham. While Mr. Boutwell is a much more gentle person than Mr. Connor, they are both segregationists, dedicated to maintenance of the status quo. I have hoped that Mr. Boutwell will be reasonable enough to see the futility of massive resistance to desegregation. But he will not see this without pressure from devotees of civil rights. My friends, I must say to you that we have not made a single gain in civil rights without determined legal and nonviolent pressure. Lamentably, it is an historical fact that privileged groups seldom give up their privileges voluntarily. Individuals may see the moral light and voluntarily give up their unjust posture; but, as Reinhold Niebuhr has reminded us, groups tend to be more immoral than individuals.

We know through painful experience that freedom is never voluntarily given by the oppressor; it must be demanded by the oppressed. Frankly, I have yet to engage in a direct-action campaign that was "well timed" in the view of those who have not suffered unduly from the disease of segregation. For years now I have heard the word "Wait!" It rings in the ear of every Negro with piercing familiarity. This "Wait" has almost always meant "Never." We must come to see, with one of our distinguished jurists, that "justice too long delayed is justice denied."

We have waited for more than 340 years for our constitutional and God-given rights. The nations of Asia and Africa are moving with jetlike speed toward gaining political independence, but we still creep at horse-and-buggy pace toward gaining a cup of coffee at a lunch counter. Perhaps it is easy for those who have never felt the stinging darts of segregation to say, "Wait." But when you have seen vicious mobs lynch your mothers and fathers at will and drown your sisters and brothers at whim; when you have seen hate-filled policemen curse, kick, and even kill your black brothers and sisters; when you see the vast majority of your twenty million Negro brothers smothering in an airtight cage of poverty in the midst of an affluent society; when you suddenly find your tongue twisted and your speech stammering as you seek to explain to your six-year-old daughter why she can't go to the public amusement park that has just been advertised on television, and see tears welling up in her eyes when she is told that Funtown is closed to coloured children, and see ominous clouds of inferiority beginning to form in her little mental sky, and see her beginning to distort her personality by developing an unconscious bitterness toward white people; when you have to concoct an answer for a five-year-old son who is asking, "Daddy, why do white people treat coloured people so mean?"; when you take a cross-country drive and find it necessary to sleep night after night in the uncomfortable corners of your automobile because no motel will accept you; when you are humiliated day in and day out by nagging signs reading "white" and "coloured"; when your first name becomes "nigger," your middle name becomes "boy" (however old you are) and your last name becomes "John," and your wife and mother are never given the respected title "Mrs."; when you are harried by day and haunted by night by the fact that you are a Negro, living constantly at tiptoe stance, never quite knowing what to expect next, and are plagued with inner fears and outer resentments; when you are forever fighting a degenerating sense of "nobodiness"—then you will understand why we find it difficult to wait. There comes a time when the cup of endurance runs over, and men are no longer willing to be plunged into the abyss of despair. I hope, sirs, you can understand our legitimate and unavoidable impatience.

15 You express a great deal of anxiety over our willingness to break laws. This is certainly a legitimate concern. Since we so diligently urge people to obey the Supreme Court's decision of 1954[1] outlawing segregation in the public schools, at first glance it may seem rather paradoxical for us consciously to break laws. One may well ask: "How can you advocate breaking some laws and obeying others?" The answer lies in the fact that there are two types of laws: just and unjust. I would be the first to advocate obeying just laws. One has not only a legal but a moral responsibility to obey just laws. Conversely, one has a moral responsibility to disobey unjust laws. I would agree with St. Augustine* that "an unjust law is no law at all."

Now, what is the difference between the two? How does one determine whether a law is just or unjust? A just law is a man-made code that squares with the moral law or the law of God. An unjust law is a code that is out of

1 *Supreme Court's decision of 1954* Brown v. Board of Education, a landmark 1954 Supreme Court case that declared the segregation of schoolchildren on the basis of race to be unconstitutional.

harmony with the moral law. To put it in the terms of St. Thomas Aquinas:* An unjust law is a human law that is not rooted in eternal law and natural law. Any law that uplifts human personality is just. Any law that degrades human personality is unjust. All segregation statutes are unjust because segregation distorts the soul and damages the personality. It gives the segregator a false sense of superiority and the segregated a false sense of inferiority. Segregation, to use the terminology of the Jewish philosopher Martin Buber, substitutes an "I-it" relationship for an "I-thou" relationship and ends up relegating persons to the status of things. Hence segregation is not only politically, economically, and sociologically unsound, it is morally wrong and sinful. Paul Tillich* has said that sin is separation. Is not segregation an existential expression of man's tragic separation, his awful estrangement, his terrible sinfulness? Thus it is that I can urge men to obey the 1954 decision of the Supreme Court, for it is morally right; and I can urge them to disobey segregation ordinances, for they are morally wrong.

Let us consider a more concrete example of just and unjust laws. An unjust law is a code that a numerical or power majority group compels a minority group to obey but does not make binding on itself. This is *difference* made legal. By the same token, a just law is a code that a majority compels a minority to follow and that it is willing to follow itself. This is *sameness* made legal.

Let me give another explanation. A law is unjust if it is inflicted on a minority that, as a result of being denied the right to vote, had no part in enacting or devising the law. Who can say that the legislature of Alabama which set up that state's segregation laws was democratically elected? Throughout Alabama all sorts of devious methods are used to prevent Negroes from becoming registered voters, and there are some counties in which, even though Negroes constitute a majority of the population, not a single Negro is registered. Can any law enacted under such circumstances be considered democratically structured?

Sometimes a law is just on its face and unjust in its application. For instance, I have been arrested on a charge of parading without a permit. Now, there is nothing wrong in having an ordinance which requires a permit for a parade. But such an ordinance becomes unjust when it is used to maintain segregation and to deny citizens the First-Amendment privilege of peaceful assembly and protest.

I hope you are able to see the distinction I am trying to point out. In no sense 20
do I advocate evading or defying the law, as would the rabid segregationist. That would lead to anarchy. One who breaks an unjust law must do so openly, lovingly, and with a willingness to accept the penalty. I submit that an individual who breaks a law that conscience tells him is unjust, and who willingly accepts the penalty of imprisonment in order to arouse the conscience of the community over its injustice, is in reality expressing the highest respect for law.

Of course, there is nothing new about this kind of civil disobedience. It was evidenced sublimely in the refusal of Shadrach, Meshach, and Abednego* to obey the laws of Nebuchadnezzar, on the ground that a higher moral law was at stake. It was practised superbly by the early Christians, who were willing to face hungry lions and the excruciating pain of chopping blocks rather than submit to certain unjust laws of the Roman Empire.* To a degree, academic freedom is a reality today because Socrates practiced civil disobedience. In our own nation, the Boston Tea Party* represented a massive act of civil disobedience.

We should never forget that everything Adolf Hitler did in Germany was "legal" and everything the Hungarian freedom fighters[2] did in Hungary was "illegal." It was "illegal" to aid and comfort a Jew in Hitler's Germany. Even so, I am sure that, had I lived in Germany at the time, I would have aided and comforted my Jewish brothers. If today I lived in a Communist country where certain principles dear to the Christian faith are suppressed, I would openly advocate disobeying that country's anti-religious laws.

I must make two honest confessions to you, my Christian and Jewish brothers. First, I must confess that over the past few years I have been gravely disappointed with the white moderate. I have almost reached the regrettable conclusion that the Negro's great stumbling block in his stride toward freedom is not the White Citizen's Counciler or the Ku Klux Klanner,* but the white moderate, who is more devoted to "order" than to justice; who prefers a negative peace which is the absence of tension to a positive peace which is the presence of justice; who constantly says, "I agree with you in the goal you seek, but I cannot agree with your methods of direct action"; who paternalistically believes he can set the timetable for another man's freedom; who lives by a mythical concept of time and who constantly advises the Negro to wait for a "more convenient season." Shallow understanding from people of good will is more frustrating than absolute misunderstanding from people of ill will. Lukewarm acceptance is much more bewildering than outright rejection.

I had hoped that the white moderate would understand that law and order exist for the purpose of establishing justice and that when they fail in this purpose they become the dangerously structured dams that block the flow of social progress. I had hoped that the white moderate would understand that the present tension in the South is a necessary phase of the transition from an obnoxious negative peace, in which the Negro passively accepted his unjust plight, to a substantive and positive peace, in which all men will respect the dignity and worth of human personality. Actually, we who engage in nonviolent direct action are not the creators of tension. We merely bring

---

2 *Hungarian freedom fighters* The Hungarian Rebellion in 1956 against an oppressive government was brutally suppressed with the help of the Soviet army.

to the surface the hidden tension that is already alive. We bring it out in the open, where it can be seen and dealt with. Like a boil that can never be cured so long as it is covered up but must be opened with all its ugliness to the natural medicines of air and light, injustice must be exposed, with all the tension its exposure creates, to the light of human conscience and the air of national opinion, before it can be cured.

In your statement you assert that our actions, even though peaceful, must 25
be condemned because they precipitate violence. But is this a logical assertion? Isn't this like condemning a robbed man because his possession of money precipitated the evil act of robbery? Isn't this like condemning Socrates because his unswerving commitment to truth and his philosophical inquiries precipitated the act by the misguided populace in which they made him drink hemlock? Isn't this like condemning Jesus because his unique God-consciousness and never-ceasing devotion to God's will precipitated the evil act of crucifixion? We must come to see that, as the federal courts have consistently affirmed, it is wrong to urge an individual to cease his efforts to gain his basic constitutional rights because the quest may precipitate violence. Society must protect the robbed and punish the robber.

I had also hoped that the white moderate would reject the myth concerning time in relation to the struggle for freedom. I have just received a letter from a white brother in Texas. He writes: "All Christians know that the coloured people will receive equal rights eventually, but it is possible that you are in too great a religious hurry. It has taken Christianity almost two thousand years to accomplish what it has. The teachings of Christ take time to come to earth." Such an attitude stems from a tragic misconception of time, from the strangely irrational notion that there is something in the very flow of time that will inevitably cure all ills. Actually, time itself is neutral; it can be used either destructively or constructively. More and more I feel that the people of ill will have used time much more effectively than have the people of good will. We will have to repent in this generation not merely for the hateful words and actions of the bad people, but for the appalling silence of the good people. Human progress never rolls in on wheels of inevitability; it comes through the tireless efforts of men willing to be co-workers with God, and without this hard work, time itself becomes an ally of the forces of social stagnation. We must use time creatively, in the knowledge that the time is always ripe to do right. Now is the time to make real the promise of democracy and transform our pending national elegy into a creative psalm of brotherhood. Now is the time to lift our national policy from the quicksand of racial injustice to the solid rock of human dignity.

You speak of our activity in Birmingham as extreme. At first I was rather disappointed that fellow clergymen would see my nonviolent efforts as those of an extremist. I began thinking about the fact that I stand in the middle of two opposing forces in the Negro community. One is a force of complacency, made up in part of Negroes who, as a result of long years of oppression, are so drained of self-respect and a sense of "somebodiness" that they have adjusted to segregation; and in part of a few middle-class Negroes who, because of a degree of academic and economic security and because in some ways they profit by segregation, have become insensitive to the problems of the masses. The other force is one of bitterness and hatred, and it comes perilously close to advocating violence. It is expressed in the various black nationalist groups that are springing up across the nation, the largest and best-known being Elijah Muhammad's Muslim movement.* Nourished by the Negro's frustration over the continued existence of racial discrimination, this movement is made up of people who have lost faith in America, who have absolutely repudiated Christianity, and who have concluded that the white man is an incorrigible "devil."

I have tried to stand between these two forces, saying that we need emulate neither the "do-nothingism" of the complacent nor the hatred and despair of the black nationalist. For there is the more excellent way of love and nonviolent protest. I am grateful to God that, through the influence of the Negro church, the way of nonviolence became an integral part of our struggle.

If this philosophy had not emerged, by now many streets of the South would, I am convinced, be flowing with blood. And I am further convinced that if our white brothers dismiss as "rabblerousers" and "outside agitators" those of us who employ nonviolent direct action, and if they refuse to support our nonviolent efforts, millions of Negroes will, out of frustration and despair, seek solace and security in black-nationalist ideologies—a development that would inevitably lead to a frightening racial nightmare.

30 Oppressed people cannot remain oppressed forever. The yearning for freedom eventually manifests itself, and that is what has happened to the American Negro. Something within has reminded him of his birthright of freedom, and something without has reminded him that it can be gained. Consciously or unconsciously, he has been caught up by the *Zeitgeist*,* and with his black brothers of Africa and his brown and yellow brothers of Asia, South America, and the Caribbean, the United States Negro is moving with a sense of great urgency toward the promised land of racial justice. If one recognizes this vital urge that has engulfed the Negro community, one should readily understand why public demonstrations are taking place. The Negro has many pent-up resentments and latent frustrations, and he must release them. So let him march; let him make prayer pilgrimages to the city hall; let him go on freedom rides—and try to understand why he must do so. If his repressed emotions are not released in nonviolent ways, they will seek expression through violence; this is not a threat but a fact of history. So I have not said to my people, "Get rid of your discontent." Rather, I have tried to say that this normal and healthy discontent

can be channelled into the creative outlet of nonviolent direct action. And now this approach is being termed extremist.

But though I was initially disappointed at being categorized as an extremist, as I continued to think about the matter I gradually gained a measure of satisfaction from the label. Was not Jesus an extremist for love: "Love your enemies, bless them that curse you, do good to them that hate you, and pray for them which despitefully use you, and persecute you." Was not Amos an extremist for justice: "Let justice roll down like waters and righteousness like an ever-flowing stream." Was not Paul an extremist for the Christian gospel: "I bear in my body the marks of the Lord Jesus." Was not Martin Luther an extremist: "Here I stand; I cannot do otherwise, so help me God." And John Bunyan: "I will stay in jail to the end of my days before I make a butchery of my conscience." And Abraham Lincoln: "This nation cannot survive half slave and half free." And Thomas Jefferson: "We hold these truths to be self-evident, that all men are created equal...."* So the question is not whether we will be extremists, but what kind of extremists we will be. Will we be extremists for hate or for love? Will we be extremists for the preservation of injustice or for the extension of justice? In that dramatic scene on Calvary's hill three men were crucified. We must never forget that all three were crucified for the same crime—the crime of extremism. Two were extremists for immorality, and thus fell below their environment. The other, Jesus Christ, was an extremist for love, truth, and goodness, and thereby rose above his environment. Perhaps the South, the nation, and the world are in dire need of creative extremists.

I had hoped that the white moderate would see this need. Perhaps I was too optimistic; perhaps I expected too much. I suppose I should have realized that few members of the oppressor race can understand the deep groans and passionate yearnings of the oppressed race, and still fewer have the vision to see that injustice must be rooted out by strong, persistent, and determined action. I am thankful, however, that some of our white brothers in the South have grasped the meaning of this social revolution and committed themselves to it. They are still all too few in quantity, but they are big in quality. Some—such as Ralph McGill, Lillian Smith, Harry Golden, James McBridge Dabbs, Ann Braden, and Sarah Patton Boyle—have written about our struggle in eloquent and prophetic terms. Others have marched with us down nameless streets of the South. They have languished in filthy, roach-infested jails, suffering the abuse and brutality of policemen who view them as "dirty nigger-lovers." Unlike so many of their moderate brothers and sisters, they have recognized the urgency of the moment and sensed the need for powerful "action" antidotes to combat the disease of segregation.

Let me take note of my other major disappointment. I have been so greatly disappointed with the white church and its leadership. Of course, there are some notable exceptions. I am not unmindful of the fact that each of you has taken some significant stands on this issue. I commend you, Reverend Stallings, for your Christian stand on this past Sunday, in welcoming Negroes to your worship service on a nonsegregated basis. I commend the Catholic leaders of this state for integrating Spring Hill College several years ago.

But despite these notable exceptions, I must honestly reiterate that I have been disappointed with the church. I do not say this as one of those negative critics who can always find something wrong with the church. I say this as a minister of the gospel, who loves the church; who was nurtured in its bosom; who has been sustained by its spiritual blessings and who will remain true to it as long as the cord of life shall lengthen.

When I was suddenly catapulted into the leadership of the bus protest in Montgomery, Alabama,[3] a few years ago, I felt we would be supported by the white church. I felt that the white ministers, priests, and rabbis of the South would be among our strongest allies. Instead, some have been outright opponents, refusing to understand the freedom movement and misrepresenting its leaders; all too many others have been more cautious than courageous and have remained silent behind the anesthetizing security of stained glass windows.

In spite of my shattered dreams, I came to Birmingham with the hope that the white religious leadership of this community would see the justice of our cause and, with deep moral concern, would serve as the channel through which our just grievances could reach the power structure. I had hoped that each of you would understand. But again I have been disappointed.

I have heard numerous southern religious leaders admonish their worshippers to comply with a desegregation decision because it is the law, but I have longed to hear white ministers declare: "Follow this decree because integration is morally right and because the Negro is your brother." In the midst of blatant injustices inflicted upon the Negro, I have watched white churchmen stand on the sideline and mouth pious irrelevancies and sanctimonious trivialities. In the midst of a mighty struggle to rid our nation of racial and economic injustice, I have heard many ministers say: "Those are social issues, with which the gospel has no real concern." And I have watched many churches commit themselves to a completely otherworldly religion which makes a strange un-Biblical distinction between the body and soul, between the sacred and the secular.

I have travelled the length and breadth of Alabama, Mississippi, and all the other southern states. On sweltering summer days and crisp autumn mornings I have looked at the South's beautiful churches with their lofty spires

---

3 *bus protest in Montgomery, Alabama* In December 1955, Rosa Lee Parks, a 42-year-old Civil Rights activist, refused to give her seat on a local bus to a white man, sparking a year-long boycott by African Americans of the Montgomery buses.

pointing heavenward. I have beheld the impressive outlines of her massive religious-education buildings. Over and over I have found myself asking: "What kind of people worship here? Who is their God? Where were their voices when the lips of Governor Barnett dripped with words of interposition and nullification? Where were they when Governor Wallace gave a clarion call for defiance and hatred? Where were their voices of support when bruised and weary Negro men and women decided to rise from the dark dungeons of complacency to the bright hills of creative protest?"

Yes, these questions are still in my mind. In deep disappointment I have wept over the laxity of the church. But be assured that my tears have been tears of love. There can be no deep disappointment where there is not deep love. Yes, I love the church. How could I do otherwise? I am in the rather unique position of being the son, the grandson, and the great-grandson of preachers. Yes, I see the church as the body of Christ. But, oh! How we have blemished and scarred that body through social neglect and through fear of being nonconformists.

There was a time when the church was very powerful—in the time when 40
the early Christians rejoiced at being deemed worthy to suffer for what they believed. In those days the church was not merely a thermometer that recorded the ideas and principles of popular opinion; it was a thermostat that transformed the mores of society. Whenever the early Christians entered a town, the people in power became disturbed and immediately sought to convict the Christians of being "disturbers of the peace" and "outside agitators." But the Christians pressed on, in the conviction that they were "a colony of heaven," called to obey God rather than man. Small in number, they were big in commitment. They were too God-intoxicated to be "astronomically intimidated." By their effort and example they brought an end to such ancient evils as infanticide and gladiatorial contests.

Things are different now. So often the contemporary church is a weak, ineffectual voice with an uncertain sound. So often it is an arch-defender of the status quo. Far from being disturbed by the presence of the church, the power structure of the average community is consoled by the church's silent—and often even vocal—sanction of things as they are.

But the judgment of God is upon the church as never before. If today's church does not recapture the sacrificial spirit of the early church, it will lose its authenticity, forfeit the loyalty of millions, and be dismissed as an irrelevant social club with no meaning for the twentieth century. Every day I meet young people whose disappointment with the church has turned into outright disgust.

Perhaps I have once again been too optimistic. Is organized religion too inextricably bound to the status quo to save our nation and the world? Perhaps I must turn my faith to the inner spiritual church, the church within the church, as the true *ekklesia*[4] and the hope of the world. But again I am thankful to God that some noble souls from the ranks of organized religion have broken loose from the paralyzing chains of conformity and joined us as active partners in the struggle for freedom. They have left their secure congregations and walked the streets of Albany, Georgia, with us. They have gone down the highways of the South on tortuous rides for freedom. Yes, they have gone to jail with us. Some have been dismissed from their churches, have lost the support of their bishops and fellow ministers. But they have acted in the faith that right defeated is stronger than evil triumphant. Their witness has been the spiritual salt that has preserved the true meaning of the gospel in these troubled times. They have carved a tunnel of hope through the dark mountain of disappointment.

I hope the church as a whole will meet the challenge of this decisive hour. But even if the church does not come to the aid of justice, I have no despair about the future. I have no fear about the outcome of our struggle in Birmingham, even if our motives are at present misunderstood. We will reach the goal of freedom in Birmingham and all over the nation, because the goal of America is freedom. Abused and scorned though we may be, our destiny is tied up with America's destiny. Before the pilgrims landed at Plymouth,* we were here. Before the pen of Jefferson etched the majestic words of the Declaration of Independence across the pages of history, we were here. For more than two centuries our forebears laboured in this country without wages; they made cotton king;* they built the homes of their masters while suffering gross injustice and shameful humiliation—and yet out of a bottomless vitality they continued to thrive and develop. If the inexpressible cruelties of slavery could not stop us, the opposition we now face will surely fail. We will win our freedom because the sacred heritage of our nation and the eternal will of God are embodied in our echoing demands.

45 Before closing I feel impelled to mention one other point in your statement that has troubled me profoundly. You warmly commended the Birmingham police for keeping "order" and "preventing violence." I doubt that you would have so warmly commended the police force if you had seen its dogs sinking their teeth into unarmed, nonviolent Negroes. I doubt that you would so quickly commend the policemen if you were to observe their ugly and inhumane treatment of Negroes here in the city jail; if you were to watch them push and curse old Negro women and young Negro girls; if you were to see them slap and kick old Negro men and young boys; if you were to observe them, as they did on two occasions, refuse to give us food because we wanted to sing our grace together. I cannot join you in your praise of the Birmingham police department.

---

4 *ekklesia* Latin: Christian church, especially when understood as an abstract entity made up of all Christians throughout time, rather than as a specific worldly organization.

It is true that the police have exercised a degree of discipline in handling the demonstrators. In this sense they have conducted themselves rather "nonviolently" in public. But for what purpose? To preserve the evil system of segregation. Over the past few years I have consistently preached that nonviolence demands that the means we use must be as pure as the ends we seek. I have tried to make clear that it is wrong to use immoral means to attain moral ends. But now I must affirm that it is just as wrong, or perhaps even more so, to use moral means to preserve immoral ends. Perhaps Mr. Connor and his policemen have been rather nonviolent in public, as was Chief Pritchett in Albany, Georgia, but they have used moral means of nonviolence to maintain the immoral end of racial injustice. As T.S. Eliot has said, "The last temptation is the greatest treason: To do the right deed for the wrong reason."[5]

I wish you had commended the Negro sit-inners and demonstrators of Birmingham for their sublime courage, their willingness to suffer, and their amazing discipline in the midst of great provocation. One day the South will recognize its real heroes. They will be the James Merediths,[6] with the noble sense of purpose that enables them to face jeering and hostile mobs, and with the agonizing loneliness that characterizes the life of the pioneer. They will be old, oppressed, battered Negro women, symbolized in a seventy-two-year-old woman in Montgomery, Alabama, who rose up with a sense of dignity and with her people decided not to ride segregated buses,* and who responded with ungrammatical profundity to one who inquired about her weariness: "My feets is tired, but my soul is at rest." They will be the young high school and college students, the young ministers of the gospel and a host of their elders, courageously and nonviolently sitting in at lunch counters and willingly going to jail for conscience' sake. One day the South will know that when these disinherited children of God sat down at lunch counters, they were in reality standing up for what is best in the American dream and for the most sacred values in our Judaeo-Christian heritage, thereby bringing our nation back to those great wells of democracy which were dug deep by the founding fathers in their formulation of the Constitution and the Declaration of Independence.

Never before have I written such a long letter. I'm afraid it is much too long to take your precious time. I can assure you that it would have been much shorter if I had been writing from a comfortable desk, but what else can one do when he is alone in a narrow jail cell, other than write long letters, think long thoughts, and pray long prayers?

---

5 *The last ... wrong reason* These lines are part of the response of St. Thomas à Becket to the fourth tempter in T.S. Eliot's play *Murder in the Cathedral*.

6 *James Merediths* In 1962 James H. Meredith became the first African American student at the University of Mississippi.

If I have said anything in this letter that overstates the truth and indicates an unreasonable impatience, I beg you to forgive me. If I have said anything that understates the truth and indicates my having a patience that allows me to settle for anything less than brotherhood, I beg God to forgive me.

I hope this letter finds you strong in the faith. I also hope that circumstances will soon make it possible for me to meet each of you, not as an integrationist or a civil-rights leader but as a fellow clergyman and a Christian brother. Let us all hope that the dark clouds of racial prejudice will soon pass away and the deep fog of misunderstanding will be lifted from our fear-drenched communities, and in some not too distant tomorrow the radiant stars of love and brotherhood will shine over our great nation with all their scintillating beauty.

Yours for the cause of Peace and Brotherhood,

MARTIN LUTHER KING JR.

(1963)

Questions

1. Summarize the various reasons King gives, first of all for the Birmingham protest, and second for the means through which the protest is pursued.
2. To what extent is it ever desirable—or possible—to separate ethical from political questions?
3. Find at least three examples of parallel structure in King's writing, involving words, phrases, or clauses.

Nelson Mandela

from An Ideal for Which I Am Prepared to Die

Black Africans had been ill-treated under the British colonial regime in South Africa, and their situation deteriorated further with the 1948 institution by the new National Party government of a system of apartheid—rigid segregation, with non-whites assigned an inferior status and accorded virtually no rights. Mandela, one of the leaders of the resistance movement against this system (and, from 1994 to 1999, the first president of a democratic South Africa), was arrested on 5 August 1962; he was convicted of relatively minor charges and sentenced to five years imprisonment. After other rebel leaders were captured on 11 July 1963, Mandela was again put on trial with them. The speech excerpted below was made 20 April 1964 from the dock at the rebels' trial on charges of sabotage and "conspiracy to overthrow the government." The full speech runs to well over 10,000 words and took about three hours to deliver.

Mandela was convicted, but was sentenced not to death (as the prosecution had asked) but to life imprisonment; he had spent 27 years in prison by the time he was released in 1990.

I am the first accused. I hold a bachelor's degree in arts and practised as an attorney in Johannesburg for a number of years in partnership with Oliver Tambo. I am a convicted prisoner serving five years for leaving the country without a permit and for inciting people to go on strike at the end of May 1961.

At the outset, I want to say that the suggestion made by the state in its opening that the struggle in South Africa is under the influence of foreigners or communists is wholly incorrect. I have done whatever I did, both as an individual and as a leader of my people, because of my experience in South Africa and my own proudly felt African background, and not because of what any outsider might have said.

In my youth in the Transkei* I listened to the elders of my tribe telling stories of the old days. Amongst the tales they related to me were those of wars fought by our ancestors in defense of the fatherland. The names of Dingane and Bambata, Hintsa and Makana, Squngthi and Dalasile, Moshoeshoe and Sekhukhuni,* were praised as the glory of the entire African nation. I hoped then that life might offer me the opportunity to serve my people and make my own humble contribution to their freedom struggle. This is what has motivated me in all that I have done in relation to the charges made against me in this case.

Having said this, I must deal immediately and at some length with the question of violence. Some of the things so far told to the court are true and some are untrue. I do not, however, deny that I planned sabotage. I did not plan it in a spirit of recklessness, nor because I have any love of violence. I planned it as a result of a calm and sober assessment of the political situation that had arisen after many years of tyranny, exploitation, and oppression of my people by the whites.

5 I admit immediately that I was one of the persons who helped to form Umkhonto we Sizwe,[1] and that I played a prominent role in its affairs until I was arrested in August 1962....

I, and the others who started the organization, did so for two reasons. Firstly, we believed that as a result of Government policy, violence by the African people had become inevitable, and that unless responsible leadership was given to canalize and control the feelings of our people, there would be outbreaks of terrorism which would produce an intensity of bitterness and hostility between the various races of this country which is not produced even by war. Secondly, we felt that without violence there would be no way open to the African people to succeed in their struggle against the principle of white supremacy. All lawful modes of expressing opposition to this principle had been closed by legislation, and we were placed in a position in which we had either to accept a permanent state of inferiority, or to defy the government. We chose to defy the law. We first broke the law in a way which avoided any recourse to violence; when this form was legislated against, and then the government resorted to a show of force to crush opposition to its policies, only then did we decide to answer violence with violence.

But the violence which we chose to adopt was not terrorism. We who formed Umkhonto were all members of the African National Congress,* and had behind us the ANC tradition of non-violence and negotiation as a means of solving political disputes. We believe that South Africa belongs to all the people who live in it, and not to one group, be it black or white. We did not want an interracial war, and tried to avoid it to the last minute. If the court is in doubt about this, it will be seen that the whole history of our organization bears out what I have said....

---

1 *Umkhonto we Sizwe* Zulu: Spear of the Nation. Military wing of the African National Congress.

In 1960 there was the shooting at Sharpeville,[2] which resulted in the proclamation of a state of emergency and the declaration of the ANC as an unlawful organization. My colleagues and I, after careful consideration, decided that we would not obey this decree. The African people were not part of the government and did not make the laws by which they were governed. We believed in the words of the Universal Declaration of Human Rights, that "the will of the people shall be the basis of authority of the government," and for us to accept the banning was equivalent to accepting the silencing of the Africans for all time. The ANC refused to dissolve, but instead went underground. We believed it was our duty to preserve this organization which had been built up with almost fifty years of unremitting toil. I have no doubt that no self-respecting white political organization would disband itself if declared illegal by a government in which it had no say....

What were we, the leaders of our people, to do? Were we to give in to the show of force and the implied threat against future action, or were we to fight it and, if so, how?

We had no doubt that we had to continue the fight. Anything else would 10
have been abject surrender. Our problem was not whether to fight, but was how to continue the fight. We of the ANC had always stood for a non-racial democracy, and we shrank from any action which might drive the races further apart than they already were. But the hard facts were that fifty years of non-violence had brought the African people nothing but more and more repressive legislation, and fewer and fewer rights. It may not be easy for this court to understand, but it is a fact that for a long time the people had been talking of violence—of the day when they would fight the white man and win back their country—and we, the leaders of the ANC, had nevertheless always prevailed upon them to avoid violence and to pursue peaceful methods. When some of us discussed this in May and June of 1961, it could not be denied that our policy to achieve a non-racial state by non-violence had achieved nothing, and that our followers were beginning to lose confidence in this policy and were developing disturbing ideas of terrorism.

It must not be forgotten that by this time violence had, in fact, become a feature of the South African political scene. There had been violence in 1957 when the women of Zeerust were ordered to carry passes; there was violence in 1958 with the enforcement of cattle culling in Sekhukhuniland; there was violence in 1959 when the people of Cato Manor protested against pass raids;

2 *shooting at Sharpeville* The incident now known as the Sharpeville Massacre took place on 21 March 1960; police fired repeatedly into a crowd of several thousand who were protesting the government's "pass laws," which placed severe restrictions on the free movement of black people. The police killed at least 69 people (including 10 children) and injured at least 170.

there was violence in 1960 when the government attempted to impose Bantu authorities in Pondoland.* Thirty-nine Africans died in these disturbances. In 1961 there had been riots in Warmbaths, and all this time the Transkei had been a seething mass of unrest. Each disturbance pointed clearly to the inevitable growth among Africans[3] of the belief that violence was the only way out—it showed that a government which uses force to maintain its rule teaches the oppressed to use force to oppose it. Already small groups had arisen in the urban areas and were spontaneously making plans for violent forms of political struggle. There now arose a danger that these groups would adopt terrorism against Africans, as well as whites, if not properly directed....

[I]n view of the situation I have described, the ANC was prepared to depart from its fifty-year-old policy of non-violence to this extent that it would no longer disapprove of properly controlled violence. Hence members who undertook such activity would not be subject to disciplinary action by the ANC.

I say "properly controlled violence" because I made it clear that if I formed the organization I would at all times subject it to the political guidance of the ANC and would not undertake any different form of activity from that contemplated without the consent of the ANC. And I shall now tell the court how that form of violence came to be determined.

As a result of this decision, Umkhonto was formed in November 1961. When we took this decision, and subsequently formulated our plans, the ANC heritage of non-violence and racial harmony was very much with us. We felt that the country was drifting towards a civil war in which blacks and whites would fight each other. We viewed the situation with alarm. Civil war could mean the destruction of what the ANC stood for; with civil war, racial peace would be more difficult than ever to achieve....

[In such situations] four forms of violence are possible. There is sabotage, there is guerrilla warfare, there is terrorism, and there is open revolution. We chose to adopt the first method and to exhaust it before taking any other decision.

In the light of our political background the choice was a logical one. Sabotage did not involve loss of life, and it offered the best hope for future race relations. Bitterness would be kept to a minimum and, if the policy bore fruit, democratic government could become a reality. This is what we felt at the time, and this is what we said in our manifesto:

> We of Umkhonto we Sizwe have always sought to achieve liberation without bloodshed and civil clash. We hope, even at this late hour, that

---

3 *Africans* I.e., Black Africans. At this time white South Africans were classed as "Europeans"; there were also separate categories for people of mixed race ("Coloureds") and people of Asian descent.

> our first actions will awaken everyone to a realization of the disastrous situation to which the nationalist policy is leading. We hope that we will bring the government and its supporters to their senses before it is too late, so that both the government and its policies can be changed before matters reach the desperate state of civil war.

The initial plan was based on a careful analysis of the political and economic situation of our country. We believed that South Africa depended to a large extent on foreign capital and foreign trade. We felt that planned destruction of power plants, and interference with rail and telephone communications, would tend to scare away capital from the country, make it more difficult for goods from the industrial areas to reach the seaports on schedule, and would in the long run be a heavy drain on the economic life of the country, thus compelling the voters of the country to reconsider their position.

Attacks on the economic life-lines of the country were to be linked with sabotage on government buildings and other symbols of apartheid. These attacks would serve as a source of inspiration to our people. In addition, they would provide an outlet for those people who were urging the adoption of violent methods and would enable us to give concrete proof to our followers that we had adopted a stronger line and were fighting back against government violence....

I turn now to my own position. I have denied that I am a communist, and I think that in the circumstances I am obliged to state exactly what my political beliefs are.

I have always regarded myself, in the first place, as an African patriot. After all, I was born in Umtata, forty-six years ago. My guardian was my cousin, who was the acting paramount chief of Tembuland, and I am related both to the present paramount chief of Tembuland, Sabata Dalindyebo, and to Kaizer Matanzima, the Chief Minister of the Transkei.

Today I am attracted by the idea of a classless society, an attraction which 20
springs in part from Marxist reading[4] and, in part, from my admiration of the structure and organization of early African societies in this country. The land, then the main means of production, belonged to the tribe. There were no rich or poor and there was no exploitation.

It is true, as I have already stated, that I have been influenced by Marxist thought. But this is also true of many of the leaders of the new independent states. Such widely different persons as Gandhi, Nehru, Nkrumah, and Nasser*

---

4 *Marxist reading* Reading of the works of Karl Marx and his followers. Among white South Africans at this time (as among most Americans in the 1950s and 1960s, during the height of the Cold War) Marxism, socialism, and communism were all viewed with great suspicion, and those suspected of Marxist or communist sympathies were often persecuted.

all acknowledge this fact. We all accept the need for some form of socialism to enable our people to catch up with the advanced countries of this world and to overcome their legacy of extreme poverty. But this does not mean we are Marxists.

Indeed, for my own part, I believe that it is open to debate whether the Communist party has any specific role to play at this particular stage of our political struggle. The basic task at the present moment is the removal of race discrimination and the attainment of democratic rights on the basis of the Freedom Charter. In so far as that party furthers this task, I welcome its assistance. I realize that it is one of the means by which people of all races can be drawn into our struggle.

From my reading of Marxist literature and from conversations with Marxists, I have gained the impression that communists regard the parliamentary system of the west as undemocratic and reactionary. But, on the contrary, I am an admirer of such a system.

The Magna Carta, the Petition of Right, and the Bill of Rights[5] are documents which are held in veneration by democrats throughout the world. I have great respect for British political institutions, and for the country's system of justice. I regard the British Parliament as the most democratic institution in the world, and the independence and impartiality of its judiciary never fails to arouse my admiration.

The American Congress, that country's doctrine of separation of powers,* as well as the independence of its judiciary, arouses in me similar sentiments.

I have been influenced in my thinking by both west and east. All this has led me to feel that in my search for a political formula, I should be absolutely impartial and objective. I should tie myself to no particular system of society other than of socialism. I must leave myself free to borrow the best from the west and from the east....

Our fight is against real, and not imaginary, hardships or, to use the language of the state prosecutor, "so-called hardships." Basically, we fight against two features which are the hallmarks of African life in South Africa and which are entrenched by legislation which we seek to have repealed. These features are poverty and lack of human dignity, and we do not need communists or so-called "agitators" to teach us about these things.

South Africa is the richest country in Africa, and could be one of the richest countries in the world. But it is a land of extremes and remarkable contrasts. The whites enjoy what may well be the highest standard of living in the world,

---

5 *Magna Carta, the Petition of Right, and the Bill of Rights* British legal documents dating respectively from 1215, 1628, and 1689—all of which set out various limits on the arbitrary exercise of power by the monarch or government.

whilst Africans live in poverty and misery. Forty per cent of the Africans live in hopelessly overcrowded and, in some cases, drought-stricken Reserves,[6] where soil erosion and the overworking of the soil makes it impossible for them to live properly off the land. Thirty per cent are labourers, labour tenants, and squatters on white farms and work and live under conditions similar to those of the serfs of the Middle Ages. The other 30 per cent live in towns where they have developed economic and social habits which bring them closer in many respects to white standards. Yet most Africans, even in this group, are impoverished by low incomes and high cost of living.

The highest-paid and the most prosperous section of urban African life is in Johannesburg. Yet their actual position is desperate. The latest figures were given on 25 March 1964 by Mr. Carr, Manager of the Johannesburg non-European affairs department. The poverty datum line for the average African family in Johannesburg (according to Mr. Carr's department) is 42.84 rand[7] per month. He showed that the average monthly wage is 32.24 rand and that 46 per cent of all African families in Johannesburg do not earn enough to keep them going.

Poverty goes hand in hand with malnutrition and disease. The incidence of malnutrition and deficiency diseases is very high amongst Africans. Tuberculosis, pellagra, kwashiorkor, gastro-enteritis, and scurvy bring death and destruction of health. The incidence of infant mortality is one of the highest in the world. According to the medical officer of health for Pretoria, tuberculosis kills forty people a day (almost all Africans), and in 1961 there were 58,491 new cases reported. These diseases not only destroy the vital organs of the body, but they result in retarded mental conditions and lack of initiative, and reduce powers of concentration. The secondary results of such conditions affect the whole community and the standard of work performed by African labourers.

The complaint of Africans, however, is not only that they are poor and the whites are rich, but that the laws which are made by the whites are designed to preserve this situation. There are two ways to break out of poverty. The first is by formal education, and the second is by the worker acquiring a greater skill at his work and thus higher wages. As far as Africans are concerned, both these avenues of advancement are deliberately curtailed by legislation....

---

6 *Reserves* Under the apartheid system, black Africans were required to live on land designated as Reserves (typically, areas with poor soil and few facilities), unless they had obtained a pass to visit or work in white areas. In many cases families were divided by these rules, with one family member working in a white area while the rest of the family had to stay on the Reserve.

7 *rand* South African currency unit; a rough equivalent to 42.84 rand in current US dollars would be less than $3.

The government often answers its critics by saying that Africans in South Africa are economically better off than the inhabitants of the other countries in Africa. I do not know whether this statement is true and doubt whether any comparison can be made without having regard to the cost-of-living index in such countries. But even if it is true, as far as the African people are concerned it is irrelevant. Our complaint is not that we are poor by comparison with people in other countries, but that we are poor by comparison with the white people in our own country, and that we are prevented by legislation from altering this imbalance.

The lack of human dignity experienced by Africans is the direct result of the policy of white supremacy. White supremacy implies black inferiority. Legislation designed to preserve white supremacy entrenches this notion. Menial tasks in South Africa are invariably performed by Africans. When anything has to be carried or cleaned the white man will look around for an African to do it for him, whether the African is employed by him or not. Because of this sort of attitude, whites tend to regard Africans as a separate breed. They do not look upon them as people with families of their own; they do not realize that they have emotions—that they fall in love like white people do; that they want to be with their wives and children like white people want to be with theirs; that they want to earn enough money to support their families properly, to feed and clothe them and send them to school. And what "house-boy" or "garden-boy" or labourer can ever hope to do this?

Pass laws, which to the Africans are among the most hated bits of legislation in South Africa, render any African liable to police surveillance at any time. I doubt whether there is a single African male in South Africa who has not at some stage had a brush with the police over his pass. Hundreds and thousands of Africans are thrown into jail each year under pass laws. Even worse than this is the fact that pass laws keep husband and wife apart and lead to the breakdown of family life.

Poverty and the breakdown of family life have secondary effects. Children wander about the streets of the townships because they have no schools to go to, or no money to enable them to go to school, or no parents at home to see that they go to school, because both parents (if there be two) have to work to keep the family alive. This leads to a breakdown in moral standards, to an alarming rise in illegitimacy, and to growing violence which erupts not only politically, but everywhere. Life in the townships is dangerous. There is not a day that goes by without somebody being stabbed or assaulted. And violence is carried out of the townships in to the white living areas. People are afraid to walk alone in the streets after dark. Housebreakings and robberies are increasing, despite the fact that the death sentence can now be imposed for such offences. Death sentences cannot cure the festering sore.

Africans want to be paid a living wage. Africans want to perform work which they are capable of doing, and not work which the government declares them to be capable of. Africans want to be allowed to live where they obtain work, and not be endorsed out of an area because they were not born there. Africans want to be allowed to own land in places where they work, and not to be obliged to live in rented houses which they can never call their own. Africans want to be part of the general population, and not confined to living in their own ghettoes. African men want to have their wives and children to live with them where they work, and not be forced into an unnatural existence in men's hostels. African women want to be with their menfolk and not be left permanently widowed in the Reserves. Africans want to be allowed out after eleven o'clock at night and not to be confined to their rooms like little children. Africans want to be allowed to travel in their own country and to seek work where they want to and not where the labour bureau tells them to. Africans want a just share in the whole of South Africa; they want security and a stake in society.

Above all, we want equal political rights, because without them our disabilities will be permanent. I know this sounds revolutionary to the whites in this country, because the majority of voters will be Africans. This makes the white man fear democracy.

But this fear cannot be allowed to stand in the way of the only solution which will guarantee racial harmony and freedom for all. It is not true that the enfranchisement of all will result in racial domination. Political division, based on colour, is entirely artificial and, when it disappears, so will the domination of one colour group by another. The ANC has spent half a century fighting against racialism. When it triumphs it will not change that policy.

This then is what the ANC is fighting. Their struggle is a truly national one. It is a struggle of the African people, inspired by their own suffering and their own experience. It is a struggle for the right to live.

During my lifetime I have dedicated myself to this struggle of the African people. I have fought against white domination, and I have fought against black domination. I have cherished the ideal of a democratic and free society in which all persons live together in harmony and with equal opportunities. It is an ideal which I hope to live for and to achieve. But if needs be, it is an ideal for which I am prepared to die.

(1964)

Questions

1. How does the opening statement, "I am the first accused," set the speech's tone?
2. According to Mandela, why did Umkhonto we Sizwe choose to "answer violence with violence"? How does "sabotage" differ ethically from "terrorism"?
3. Mandela states that "[t]he complaint of Africans ... is not only that they are poor and the whites are rich, but that the laws which are made by the whites are designed to preserve this situation." Make a list of the oppressive laws referenced in Mandela's speech (often, Mandela does not explicitly say what laws exist, but readers can deduce them from the "wants" he describes). How do these laws work to preserve African poverty?
4. Mandela explains that "Death sentences cannot cure the festering sore": the policing of Africans does nothing to alleviate the pain of violence caused by poverty and a lack of education. How do police surveillance and harsh punishment not only fail to help black Africans, but actually worsen the situation?
5. Describe the intended audience or audiences of this speech. How is the speech constructed to be persuasive to that audience or audiences?

ROLAND BARTHES

from MYTHOLOGIES[1]

Roland Barthes was a pioneer in semiology, the study of signs. For him, a sign is any unit that communicates meaning, such as a word, gesture, or image; by treating its components as signs, an interpreter can examine any work of art or advertising, any event or behaviour, much as one might analyze a written or spoken work. In his book Mythologies *(1957) he writes that "a photograph will be a kind of speech for us in the same way as a newspaper article; even objects will become speech, if they mean something." Barthes considers how cultural artifacts and practices—wine, Einstein's brain, a cruise, wrestling—reveal the way society constructs meaning, how its ideologies and power structures are sustained and created. "Soap-powders and Detergents" and "Toys" are two essays from* Mythologies.

SOAP-POWDERS AND DETERGENTS[2]

The first World Detergent Congress (Paris, September 1954) had the effect of authorizing the world to yield to *Omo*[3] euphoria: not only do detergents have no harmful effect on the skin, but they can even perhaps save miners from silicosis.[4] These products have been in the last few years the object of such massive advertising that they now belong to a region of French daily

1 *Mythologies* Translated by Annette Lavers, 1972.

2 *Soap-Powders and Detergents* Soaps are made of mainly natural ingredients (fats mixed with sodium or potassium salts), whereas detergents are mainly synthetic. Detergents are generally preferred for laundry, as they don't react to the minerals found in water, but they can also be toxic and damaging to the environment.

3 *Omo* One of the Unilever brands of laundry detergent.

4 *silicosis* Also called "black lung," silicosis is a potentially fatal lung disease that afflicts miners. The lungs are scarred by the inhalation of silica dust in the mines; silicosis also leads to increased risk of tuberculosis and lung cancer. It was thought to be helpful to wash the silica dust off the miners' clothes so they would not bring it home with them.

life which the various types of psychoanalysis would do well to pay some attention to if they wish to keep up to date. One could then usefully contrast the psycho-analysis of purifying fluids (chlorinated, for example) with that of soap-powders (*Lux, Persil*[5]) or that of detergents (*Omo*). The relations between the evil and the cure, between dirt and a given product, are very different in each case.

Chlorinated fluids, for instance, have always been experienced as a sort of liquid fire, the action of which must be carefully estimated, otherwise the object itself would be affected, "burnt." The implicit legend of this type of product rests on the idea of a violent, abrasive modification of matter: the connotations are of a chemical or mutilating type: the product "kills" the dirt. Powders, on the contrary, are separating agents: their ideal role is to liberate the object from its circumstantial imperfection: dirt is "forced out" and no longer killed; in the *Omo* imagery, dirt is a diminutive enemy, stunted and black, which takes to its heels from the fine immaculate linen at the sole threat of the judgment of *Omo*. Products based on chlorine and ammonia are without doubt the representatives of a kind of absolute fire, a saviour but a blind one. Powders, on the contrary, are selective, they push, they drive dirt through the texture of the object, their function is keeping public order not making war. This distinction has ethnographic correlatives: the chemical fluid is an extension of the washerwoman's movements when she beats the clothes, while powders rather replace those of the housewife pressing and rolling the washing against a sloping board.

But even in the category of powders, one must in addition oppose against advertisements based on psychology those based on psychoanalysis[6] (I use this word without reference to any specific school). "Persil Whiteness" for instance, bases its prestige on the evidence of a result; it calls into play vanity, a social concern with appearances, by offering for comparison two objects, one of which is whiter than the other. Advertisements for *Omo* also indicate the effect of the product (and in superlative fashion, incidentally), but they chiefly reveal its mode of action; in doing so, they involve the consumer in a kind of direct experience of the substance, make him the accomplice of a liberation rather than the mere beneficiary of a result; matter here is endowed with value-bearing states.

Omo uses two of these, which are rather novel in the category of detergents: the deep and the foamy. To say that *Omo* cleans in depth (see the

5 *Lux, Persil* Brands of laundry soap. Persil was the first "self-activated" soap that combined bleach with the soap flakes, rendering sun-drying unnecessary.

6 *psychology* Scientific study of the human mind; *psychoanalysis* Method of psychiatric therapy, originated by Sigmund Freud; treatment involves analysis of conscious and unconscious elements in the patient's mind, using techniques of association and dream interpretation.

Cinéma-Publicité advertisement[7]) is to assume that linen is deep, which no one had previously thought, and this unquestionably results in exalting it, by establishing it as an object favourable to those obscure tendencies to enfold and caress which are found in every human body. As for foam, it is well known that it signifies luxury. To begin with, it appears to lack any usefulness; then, its abundant, easy, almost infinite proliferation allows one to suppose there is in the substance from which it issues a vigorous germ, a healthy and powerful essence, a great wealth of active elements in a small original volume. Finally, it gratifies in the consumer a tendency to imagine matter as something airy, with which contact is effected in a mode both light and vertical, which is sought after like that of happiness either in the gustatory category (foie gras, entremets,[8] wines), in that of clothing (muslin, tulle), or that of soaps (filmstar in her bath). Foam can even be the sign of a certain spirituality, inasmuch as the spirit has the reputation of being able to make something out of nothing, a large surface of effects out of a small volume of causes (creams have a very different "psychoanalytical" meaning, of a soothing kind: they suppress wrinkles, pain, smarting, etc.). What matters is the art of having disguised the abrasive function of the detergent under the delicious image of a substance at once deep and airy which can govern the molecular order of the material without damaging it. A euphoria, incidentally, which must not make us forget that there is one plane on which *Persil* and *Omo* are one and the same: the plane of the Anglo-Dutch trust Unilever.[9]

(1957)

Questions

1. What, according to Barthes, is the "psychoanalysis" of bleach ("chlorinated fluids")? What kind of language surrounds these products? How does it differ from the language surrounding soap-powders? How do advertisers use this language to appeal to buyers?

2. Barthes cautions that we must not "forget that there is one plane on which *Persil* and *Omo* are one and the same: the plane of the

---

7 *Cinéma-Publicité advertisement* Advertisement placed in advance of a film shown in the movie theatre.

8 *foie gras* Creamy spread made of fattened duck livers, considered a delicacy in France; *entremets* Dish served between courses, most often a dessert; modern entremets are usually layered mousse cakes.

9 *Unilever* Large multinational corporation that sells food, cleaning agents, and personal care products.

Anglo-Dutch trust Unilever." What is the significance of this statement?

3. How does Barthes deconstruct the appeal of "foamy" products? Why do they appeal to us?
4. Barthes describes the effects of soap and detergent advertising on the mind (and on society in general) as euphoric. Do you agree that a kind of intoxicating pleasure can be found in products and in the advertisement of products? Why or why not? What might be the social consequences of such euphoric states?
5. Find a present-day advertisement that markets a soap or detergent to a North American audience. What (if any) aspects of Barthes's analysis can be applied to this advertisement?

TOYS

French toys: one could not find a better illustration of the fact that the adult Frenchman sees the child as another self. All the toys one commonly sees are essentially a microcosm of the adult world; they are all reduced copies of human objects, as if in the eyes of the public the child was, all told, nothing but a smaller man, a homunculus[1] to whom must be supplied objects of his own size.

Invented forms are very rare: a few sets of blocks, which appeal to the spirit of do-it-yourself, are the only ones which offer dynamic forms. As for the others, French toys *always mean something*, and this something is always entirely socialized, constituted by the myths or the techniques of modern adult life: the Army, Broadcasting, the Post Office, Medicine (miniature instrument-cases, operating theatres for dolls), School, Hair-Styling (driers for permanent-waving), the Air Force (Parachutists), Transport (trains, Citroens, Vedettes, Vespas,[2] petrol-stations), Science (Martian toys).

The fact that French toys *literally* prefigure the world of adult functions obviously cannot but prepare the child to accept them all, by constituting for him, even before he can think about it, the alibi of a Nature which has at all times created soldiers, postmen and Vespas. Toys here reveal the list of all the things the adult does not find unusual: war, bureaucracy, ugliness, Martians, etc. It is not so much, in fact, the imitation which is the sign of an abdication,

---

1 *homunculus* Little or miniature man.

2 *Citroens, Vedettes, Vespas* European cars and scooters.

as its literalness: French toys are like a Jivaro head,[3] in which one recognizes, shrunken to the size of an apple, the wrinkles and hair of an adult. There exist, for instance, dolls which urinate; they have an esophagus, one gives them a bottle, they wet their nappies;[4] soon, no doubt, milk will turn to water in their stomachs. This is meant to prepare the little girl for the causality of housekeeping, to "condition" her to her future role as mother. However, faced with this world of faithful and complicated objects, the child can only identify himself as owner, as user, never as creator; he does not invent the world, he uses it: there are, prepared for him, actions without adventure, without wonder, without joy. He is turned into a little stay-at-home householder who does not even have to invent the mainsprings of adult causality;* they are supplied to him readymade: he has only to help himself, he is never allowed to discover anything from start to finish. The merest set of blocks, provided it is not too refined, implies a very different learning of the world: then, the child does not in any way create meaningful objects, it matters little to him whether they have an adult name; the actions he performs are not those of a user but those of a demiurge.[5] He creates forms which walk, which roll, he creates life, not property: objects now act by themselves, they are no longer an inert and complicated material in the palm of his hand. But such toys are rather rare: French toys are usually based on imitation, they are meant to produce children who are users, not creators.

The bourgeois* status of toys can be recognized not only in their forms, which are all functional, but also in their substances. Current toys are made of a graceless material, the product of chemistry, not of nature. Many are now moulded from complicated mixtures; the plastic material of which they are made has an appearance at once gross and hygienic, it destroys all the pleasure, the sweetness, the humanity of touch. A sign which fills one with consternation is the gradual disappearance of wood, in spite of its being an ideal material because of its firmness and its softness, and the natural warmth of its touch. Wood removes, from all the forms which it supports, the wounding quality of angles which are too sharp, the chemical coldness of metal. When the child handles it and knocks it, it neither vibrates nor grates, it has a sound at once muffled and sharp. It is a familiar and poetic substance, which does not sever the child from close contact with the tree, the table, the floor. Wood does not wound or break down; it does not shatter, it wears out, it can last a long time, live with the child, alter little by little the relations between the object and the

3 *Jivaro head* The Jivaroan people of northern Peru and eastern Ecuador are known for shrinking the heads severed on annual head-hunting expeditions. The heads are shrunk to about the size of a large apple.

4 *nappies* Diapers.

5 *demiurge* Maker or creator of worlds.

hand. If it dies, it is in dwindling, not in swelling out like those mechanical toys which disappear behind the hernia of a broken spring. Wood makes essential objects, objects for all time. Yet there hardly remain any of these wooden toys from the Vosges, these fretwork[6] farms with their animals, which were only possible, it is true, in the days of the craftsman. Henceforth, toys are chemical in substance and colour; their very material introduces one to a coenaesthesis[7] of use, not pleasure. These toys die in fact very quickly, and once dead, they have no posthumous life for the child.

(1957)

Questions

1. What, according to Barthes, is wrong with the materials used to make children's toys today? Why would he rather see wood used instead? Do you agree with his suggestion that wood is a better material for toys?
2. According to Barthes, what kinds of toys make children into "users"? How do they do this? What are the social repercussions of giving children these toys? How do they preserve the status quo, particularly in regard to class?
3. In both "Soap-Powders and Detergents" and "Toys," Barthes looks closely at cultural artifacts and interprets them as signs, showing how these artifacts perpetuate social ideologies and hierarchies. Choose a contemporary artifact and interpret it in a similar way (what values does it represent? How is it advertised? How does using it affect you? Does it perpetuate or challenge the status quo? How?).

6 *Vosges* Mountainous area of eastern France with a thriving wood industry; *fretwork* Type of intricate woodworking.

7 *coenaesthesis* Feeling of existence that arises from sensory information.

JOHN BERGER

PHOTOGRAPHS OF AGONY

John Berger is perhaps best known for his 1972 Ways of Seeing, *a short book adapted from the script for a BBC television series. That volume has played a hugely influential role in leading critics and students of art in the decades since to see art in relation to politics and ideology rather than in "purely" aesthetic terms. Writing in the essay form, Berger is equally adept at helping us to see the connections between art and politics; "Photographs of Agony" is a notable example. This essay is also included in Berger's 1980 collection* About Looking.

The news from Vietnam did not make big headlines in the papers this morning. It was simply reported that the American air force is systematically pursuing its policy of bombing the north.[1] Yesterday there were 270 raids.

Behind this report there is an accumulation of other information. The day before yesterday the American air force launched the heaviest raids of this month. So far more bombs have dropped this month than during any other comparable period. Among the bombs being dropped are the seven-ton superbombs, each of which flattens an area of approximately 8,000 square metres. Along with the large bombs, various kinds of small antipersonnel bombs are being dropped. One kind is full of plastic barbs which, having ripped through the flesh and embedded themselves in the body, cannot be located by x-ray. Another is called the Spider: a small bomb like a grenade with almost invisible 30-centimetre-long antennae, which, if touched, act as detonators. These bombs, distributed over the ground where larger explosions have taken place, are designed to blow up survivors who run to put out the fires already burning, or go to help those already wounded.

---

1 *American ... the north* During the Vietnam War (1955–75) the American forces (allied with those of South Vietnam) fought against those of North Vietnam and its allies.

There are no pictures from Vietnam in the papers today. But there is a photograph taken by Donald McCullin in Hue[2] in 1968 which could have been printed with the reports this morning. (See *The Destruction Business* by Donald McCullin, London, 1972.) It shows an old man squatting with a child in his arms, both of them are bleeding profusely with the black blood of black-and-white photographs.

In the last year or so, it has become normal for certain mass circulation newspapers to publish war photographs which earlier would have been suppressed as being too shocking. One might explain this development by arguing that these newspapers have come to realize that a large section of their readers are now aware of the horrors of war and want to be shown the truth. Alternatively, one might argue that these newspapers believe that their readers have become inured to violent images and so now compete in terms of ever more violent sensationalism.[3]

5 The first argument is too idealistic and the second too transparently cynical. Newspapers now carry violent war photographs because their effect, except in rare cases, is not what it was once presumed to be. A paper like the *Sunday Times* continues to publish shocking photographs about Vietnam or Northern Ireland[4] whilst politically supporting the policies responsible for the violence. This is why we have to ask: What effect do such photographs have?

Many people would argue that such photographs remind us shockingly of the reality, the lived reality, behind the abstractions of political theory, casualty statistics or news bulletins. Such photographs, they might go on to say, are printed on the black curtain which is drawn across what we choose to forget and refuse to know. According to them, McCullin serves as an eye we cannot shut. Yet what is it that they make us see?

They bring us up short. The most literal adjective that could be applied to them is *arresting*. We are seized by them. (I am aware that there are people who pass them over, but about them there is nothing to say.) As we look at them, the moment of the other's suffering engulfs us. We are filled with either

---

2 *Hue* Major city in central Vietnam. In 1968 it was heavily bombed by American forces, and North Vietnamese forces carried out a mass killing known as the Huế Massacre.

3 *a large section ... violent sensationalism* Here, and throughout the essay, Berger focuses on newspaper coverage in discussing images of violence; although the Vietnam War is often referred to as the first televised war, and television networks did indeed run coverage of the war daily, the networks (in the UK as well as the US) were for the most part much more reticent about showing gruesome or horrific images than were major newspapers.

4 *Northern Ireland* Reference to The Troubles, a violent conflict over Northern Ireland's political status that lasted much of the latter half of the twentieth century.

despair or indignation. Despair takes on some of the other's suffering to no purpose. Indignation demands action. We try to emerge from the moment of the photograph back into our lives. As we do so, the contrast is such that the resumption of our lives appears to be a hopelessly inadequate response to what we have just seen.

McCullin's most typical photographs record sudden moments of agony—a terror, a wounding, a death, a cry of grief. These moments are in reality utterly discontinuous with normal time. It is the knowledge that such moments are probable and the anticipation of them that makes "time" in the front line unlike all other experiences of time. The camera which isolates a moment of agony isolates no more violently than the experience of that moment isolates itself. The word *trigger*, applied to rifle and camera, reflects a correspondence which does not stop at the purely mechanical. The image seized by the camera is doubly violent and both violences reinforce the same contrast: the contrast between the photographed moment and all others.

As we emerge from the photographed moment back into our lives, we do not realize this; we assume that the discontinuity is our responsibility. The truth is that any response to that photographed moment is bound to be felt as inadequate. Those who are there in the situation being photographed, those who hold the hand of the dying or staunch a wound, are not seeing the moment as we have and their responses are of an altogether different order. It is not possible for anyone to look pensively at such a moment and to emerge stronger. McCullin, whose "contemplation" is both dangerous and active, writes bitterly underneath a photograph: "I only use the camera like I use a toothbrush. It does the job."

The possible contradictions of the war photograph now become apparent. 10
It is generally assumed that its purpose is to awaken concern. The most extreme examples—as in most of McCullin's work—show moments of agony in order to extort the maximum concern. Such moments, whether photographed or not, are discontinuous with all other moments. They exist by themselves. But the reader who has been arrested by the photograph may tend to feel this discontinuity as his own personal moral inadequacy. *And as soon as this happens even his sense of shock is dispersed*: his own moral inadequacy may now shock him as much as the crimes being committed in the war. Either he shrugs off this sense of inadequacy as being only too familiar, or else he thinks performing a kind of penance—of which the purest example would be to make a contribution to OXFAM or to UNICEF.*

In both cases, the issue of the war which has caused that moment is effectively depoliticised. The picture becomes evidence of the general human condition. It accuses nobody and everybody.

Confrontation with photographed moments of agony can mask a far more extensive and urgent confrontation. Usually the wars which we are shown are being fought directly or indirectly in "our" name. What we are shown horrifies us. The next step should be for us to confront our own lack of political freedom. In the political systems as they exist, we have no legal opportunity of effectively influencing the conduct of wars waged in our name. To realize this and to act accordingly is the only effective way of responding to what the photograph shows. Yet the double violence of the photographed moment actually works against this realization. That is why they can be published with impunity.

(1972)

Questions

1. Berger notes that in the early 70s major newspapers began to publish increasing numbers of graphic war photographs. What are two possible reasons he initially gives for this change? What does Berger think of these explanations?
2. Berger writes that "The word *trigger*, applied to rifle and camera, reflects a correspondence which does not stop at the purely mechanical." What, according to Berger, is this "correspondence"? Do you agree with his assessment?
3. Do you agree with Berger's claim that photographs of agony necessarily "effectively depoliticize" their subjects?

Marvin Harris

from Pig Lovers and Pig Haters

In Cows, Pigs, Wars, and Witches: The Riddles of a Culture, *anthropologist Marvin Harris examines "the causes of apparently irrational and inexplicable lifestyles" and finds that, when one considers human societies rationally, "even the most bizarre-seeming beliefs and practices turn out on closer inspection to be based on ordinary ... conditions, needs, and activities." Attending to a wide range of historical and contemporary cultures, Harris considers such "riddles" as religious food prohibitions, warfare, and belief in witches; the following selection discusses different cultures' varying attitudes toward eating pigs.*

Everyone knows examples of apparently irrational food habits. Chinese like dog meat but despise cow milk; we like cow milk but we won't eat dogs; some tribes in Brazil relish ants but despise venison. And so it goes around the world.

The riddle of the pig strikes me as a good follow-up to mother cow.[1] It presents the challenge of having to explain why certain people should hate, while others love, the very same animal.

The half of the riddle that pertains to pig haters is well known to Jews, Moslems, and Christians. The god of the ancient Hebrews went out of His way (once in the Book of Genesis and again in Leviticus*) to denounce the pig as unclean, a beast that pollutes if it is tasted or touched. About 1,500 years later, Allah told His prophet Mohammed that the status of swine was to be the same for the followers of Islam. Among millions of Jews and hundreds of millions of Moslems, the pig remains an abomination, despite the fact that it can convert grains and tubers into high-grade fats and protein more efficiently than any other animal.

Less commonly known are the traditions of the fanatic pig lovers. The pig-loving centre of the world is located in New Guinea and the South Pacific

1 *follow-up to mother cow* This essay occurs as the second in a volume which begins with a piece on why cows are regarded as sacred in some cultures.

Melanesian islands. To the village-dwelling horticultural tribes of this region, swine are holy animals that must be sacrificed to the ancestors and eaten on all important occasions, such as marriages and funerals. In many tribes, pigs must be sacrificed to declare war and to make peace. The tribesmen believe that their departed ancestors crave pork. So overwhelming is the hunger for pig flesh among both the living and the dead that from time to time huge feasts are organized and almost all of a tribe's pigs are eaten at once. For several days in a row, the villagers and their guests gorge on great quantities of pork, vomiting what they cannot digest in order to make room for more. When it is all over, the pig herd is so reduced in size that years of painstaking husbandry are needed to rebuild it. No sooner is this accomplished than preparations are made for another gluttonous orgy. And so the bizarre cycle of apparent mismanagement goes on.

5 I shall begin with the problem of the Jewish and Islamic pig haters. Why should gods so exalted as Jahweh and Allah have bothered to condemn a harmless and even laughable beast whose flesh is relished by the greater part of mankind? Scholars who accept the biblical and Koranic condemnation of swine have offered a number of explanations. Before the Renaissance, the most popular was that the pig is literally a dirty animal—dirtier than others because it wallows in its own urine and eats excrement. But linking physical uncleanliness to religious abhorrence leads to inconsistencies. Cows that are kept in a confined space also splash about in their own urine and feces. And hungry cows will eat human excrement with gusto. Dogs and chickens do the same thing without getting anyone very upset, and the ancients must have known that pigs raised in clean pens make fastidious house pets. Finally, if we invoke purely aesthetic standards of "cleanliness," there is the formidable inconsistency that the Bible classifies locusts and grasshoppers as "clean." The argument that insects are aesthetically more wholesome than pigs will not advance the cause of the faithful.

These inconsistencies were recognized by the Jewish rabbinate at the beginning of the Renaissance. To Moses Maimonides, court physician to Saladin during the twelfth century in Cairo, Egypt, we owe the first naturalistic explanation of the Jewish and Moslem rejection of pork. Maimonides said that God had intended the ban on pork as a public health measure. Swine's flesh "has a bad and damaging effect upon the body," wrote the rabbi. Maimonides was none too specific about the medical reasons for this opinion, but he was the emperor's physician, and his judgment was widely respected.

In the middle of the nineteenth century, the discovery that trichinosis was caused by eating undercooked pork was interpreted as a precise verification of the wisdom of Maimonides. Reform-minded Jews rejoiced in the rational substratum of the biblical codes and promptly renounced the taboo on pork. If properly cooked, pork is not a menace to public health, and so its consumption cannot be offensive to God. This provoked rabbis of more fundamentalist persuasion to launch a counter-attack against the entire naturalistic tradition. If Jahweh had merely wanted to protect the health of His people, He would have instructed them to eat only well-cooked pork rather than no pork at all. Clearly, it is argued, Jahweh had something else in mind—something more important than mere physical well-being.

In addition to this theological inconsistency, Maimonides' explanation suffers from medical and epidemiological contradictions. The pig is a vector for human disease, but so are other domestic animals freely consumed by Moslems and Jews. For example, under-cooked beef is a source of parasites, notably tapeworms, which can grow to a length of sixteen to twenty feet within a man's intestines, induce severe anemia, and lower resistance to other infectious diseases. Cattle, goats, and sheep are also vectors for brucellosis, a common bacterial infection in underdeveloped countries that is accompanied by fever, chills, sweats, weakness, pain, and aches. The most dangerous form is *Brucellosis melitensis*, transmitted by goats and sheep. Its symptoms are lethargy, fatigue, nervousness, and mental depression often mistaken for psychoneurosis. Finally, there is anthrax, a disease transmitted by cattle, sheep, goats, horses, and mules, but not by pigs. Unlike trichinosis, which seldom has fatal consequences and which does not even produce symptoms in the majority of infected individuals, anthrax often runs a rapid course that begins with body boils and terminates in death through blood poisoning. The great epidemics of anthrax that formerly swept across Europe and Asia were not brought under control until the development of the anthrax vaccine by Louis Pasteur in 1881.

Jahweh's failure to interdict contact with the domesticated vectors* of anthrax is especially damaging to Maimonides' explanation, since the relationship between this disease in animals and man was known during biblical times. As described in the Book of Exodus,* one of the plagues sent against the Egyptians clearly relates the symptomology of animal anthrax to a human disease:

> ... and it became a boil breaking forth with blains upon man and beast.
> And the magicians could not stand before Moses because of the boils,
> for the boils were upon the magicians, and upon all the Egyptians.

Faced with these contradictions, most Jewish and Moslem theologians 10
have abandoned the search for a naturalistic basis of pig hatred. A frankly mystical stance has recently gained favour, in which the grace afforded by conformity to dietary taboos is said to depend upon not knowing exactly what Jahweh had in mind and in not trying to find out.

Modern anthropological scholarship has reached a similar impasse. For example, with all his faults, Moses Maimonides was closer to an explanation than Sir James Frazer, renowned author of *The Golden Bough*. Frazer declared that pigs, like "all so-called unclean animals, were originally sacred; the reason for not eating them was that many were originally divine." This is of no help whatsoever, since sheep, goats, and cows were also once worshiped in the Middle East, and yet their meat is much enjoyed by all ethnic and religious groups in the region. In particular, the cow, whose golden calf was worshiped at the foot of Mt. Sinai, would seem by Frazer's logic to make a more logical unclean animal for the Hebrews than the pig....

I prefer Maimonides' approach. At least the rabbi tried to understand the taboo by placing it in a natural context of health and disease where definite mundane and practical forces were at work. The only trouble was that his view of the relevant conditions of pig hate was constrained by a physician's typical narrow concern with bodily pathology.

The solution to the riddle of the pig requires us to adopt a much broader definition of public health, one that includes the essential processes by which animals, plants, and people manage to coexist in viable natural and cultural communities. I think that the Bible and the Koran condemned the pig because pig farming was a threat to the integrity of the basic cultural and natural ecosystems of the Middle East.

To begin with, we must take into account the fact that the protohistoric Hebrews—the children of Abraham,* at the turn of the second millennium BC—were culturally adapted to life in the rugged, sparsely inhabited arid areas between the river valleys of Mesopotamia and Egypt. Until their conquest of the Jordan Valley in Palestine, beginning in the thirteenth century BC, the Hebrews were nomadic pastoralists, living almost entirely from herds of sheep, goats, and cattle. Like all pastoral peoples they maintained close relationships with the sedentary farmers who held the oases and the great rivers. From time to time these relationships matured into a more sedentary, agriculturally oriented lifestyle. This appears to have been the case with Abraham's descendants in Mesopotamia, Joseph's* followers in Egypt, and Isaac's* followers in the western Negev. But even during the climax of urban and village life under King David and King Solomon,* the herding of sheep, goats, and cattle continued to be a very important economic activity.

15 Within the overall pattern of this mixed farming and pastoral complex, the divine prohibition against pork constituted a sound ecological strategy. The nomadic Israelites could not raise pigs in their arid habitats, while for the semi-sedentary and village farming populations, pigs were more of a threat than an asset.

The basic reason for this is that the world zones of pastoral nomadism correspond to unforested plains and hills that are too arid for rainfall agriculture and that cannot easily be irrigated. The domestic animals best adapted to these zones are the ruminants—cattle, sheep, and goats. Ruminants have sacks anterior to their stomachs which enable them to digest grass, leaves, and other foods consisting mainly of cellulose more efficiently than any other mammals.

The pig, however, is primarily a creature of forests and shaded riverbanks. Although it is omnivorous, its best weight gain is from food low in cellulose—nuts, fruits, tubers, and especially grains, making it a direct competitor of man. It cannot subsist on grass alone, and nowhere in the world do fully nomadic pastoralists raise significant numbers of pigs. The pig has the further disadvantage of not being a practical source of milk and of being notoriously difficult to herd over long distances.

Above all, the pig is thermodynamically ill-adapted to the hot, dry climate of the Negev, the Jordan Valley, and the other lands of the Bible and the Koran. Compared to cattle, goats and sheep, the pig has an inefficient system for regulating body temperature. Despite the expression "To sweat like a pig," it has recently been proved that pigs can't sweat at all. Human beings, the sweatiest of all mammals, cool themselves by evaporating as much as 1,000 grams of body liquid per hour from each square metre of body surface. The best the pig can manage is 30 grams per square metre. Even sheep evaporate twice as much body liquid through their skins as pigs. Sheep also have the advantage of thick white wool that both reflects the sun's rays and provides insulation when the temperature of the air rises above that of the body. According to L.E. Mount of the Agricultural Research Council Institute of Animal Physiology in Cambridge, England, adult pigs will die if exposed to direct sunlight and air temperatures over 98°F. In the Jordan Valley, air temperatures of 110°F occur almost every summer, and there is intense sunshine throughout the year.

To compensate for its lack of protective hair and its inability to sweat, the pig must dampen its skin with external moisture. It prefers to do this by wallowing in fresh clean mud, but it will cover its skin with its own urine and feces if nothing else is available. Below 84°F, pigs kept in pens deposit their excreta away from their sleeping and feeding areas, while above 84°F they begin to excrete indiscriminately throughout the pen. The higher the temperature, the "dirtier" they become. So there is some truth to the theory that the religious uncleanliness of the pig rests upon actual physical dirtiness. Only it is not in the nature of the pig to be dirty everywhere; rather it is in the nature of the hot, arid habitat of the Middle East to make the pig maximally dependent upon the cooling effect of its own excrement.

20 Sheep and goats were the first animals to be domesticated in the Middle East, possibly as early as 9,000 BC. Pigs were domesticated in the same general region about 2,000 years later. Bone counts conducted by archeologists at early prehistoric village farming sites show that the domesticated pig was almost always a relatively minor part of the village fauna, constituting only about 5 per cent of the food animal remains. This is what one would expect of a creature which had to be provided with shade and mudholes, couldn't be milked, and ate the same food as man.

... Under preindustrial conditions, any animal that is raised primarily for its meat is a luxury. This generalization applies as well to preindustrial pastoralists, who seldom exploit their herds primarily for meat.

Among the ancient mixed farming and pastoralist communities of the Middle East, domestic animals were valued primarily as sources of milk, cheese, hides, dung, fibre, and traction for plowing. Goats, sheep, and cattle provided ample amounts of these items plus an occasional supplement of lean meat. From the beginning, therefore, pork must have been a luxury food, esteemed for its succulent, tender, and fatty qualities.

Between 7,000 and 2,000 BC pork became still more of a luxury. During this period there was a sixtyfold increase in the human population of the Middle East. Extensive deforestation accompanied the rise in population, especially as a result of permanent damage caused by the large herds of sheep and goats. Shade and water, the natural conditions appropriate for pig raising, became progressively more scarce, and pork became even more of an ecological and economical luxury.

As in the case of the beef-eating taboo, the greater the temptation, the greater the need for divine interdiction. This relationship is generally accepted as suitable for explaining why the gods are always so interested in combating sexual temptations such as incest and adultery. Here I merely apply it to a tempting food. The Middle East is the wrong place to raise pigs, but pork remains a succulent treat. People always find it difficult to resist such temptations on their own. Hence Jahweh was heard to say that swine were unclean, not only as food, but to the touch as well. Allah was heard to repeat the same message for the same reason: It was ecologically maladaptive to try to raise pigs in substantial numbers. Small-scale production would only increase the temptation. Better then, to interdict the consumption of pork entirely, and to concentrate on raising goats, sheep, and cattle. Pigs tasted good but it was too expensive to feed them and keep them cool.

25 Many questions remain, especially why each of the other creatures interdicted by the Bible—vultures, hawks, snakes, snails, shellfish, fish without scales, and so forth—came under the same divine taboo. And why Jews and Moslems, no longer living in the Middle East, continue—with varying degrees

of exactitude and zeal—to observe the ancient dietary laws. In general, it appears to me that most of the interdicted birds and animals fall squarely into one of two categories. Some, like ospreys, vultures, and hawks, are not even potentially significant sources of food. Others, like shellfish, are obviously unavailable to mixed pastoral-farming populations. Neither of these categories of tabooed creatures raises the kind of question I have set out to answer—namely, how to account for an apparently bizarre and wasteful taboo. There is obviously nothing irrational about not spending one's time chasing vultures for dinner, or not hiking fifty miles across the desert for a plate of clams on the half shell.

This is an appropriate moment to deny the claim that all religiously sanctioned food practices have ecological explanations. Taboos also have social functions, such as helping people to think of themselves as a distinctive community. This function is well served by the modern observance of dietary rules among Moslems and Jews outside of their Middle Eastern homelands. The question to be put to these practices is whether they diminish in some significant degree the practical and mundane welfare of Jews and Moslems by depriving them of nutritional factors for which there are no readily available substitutes. I think the answer is almost certainly negative. But now permit me to resist another kind of temptation—the temptation to explain everything. I think more will be learned about pig haters if we turn to the other half of the riddle, to the pig lovers.

Pig love is the soulful opposite of the divine opprobrium that Moslems and Jews heap on swine. This condition is not reached through mere gustatory enthusiasm for pork cookery. Many culinary traditions, including the Euro-American and Chinese, esteem the flesh and fat of pigs. Pig love is something else. It is a state of total community between man and pig. While the presence of pigs threatens the human status of Moslems and Jews, in the ambience of pig love one cannot truly be human except in the company of pigs.

Pig love includes raising pigs to be a member of the family, sleeping next to them, talking to them, stroking and fondling them, calling them by name, leading them on a leash to the fields, weeping when they fall sick or are injured, and feeding them with choice morsels from the family table. But unlike Hindu love of cow, pig love also includes obligatory sacrificing and eating of pigs on special occasions. Because of ritual slaughter and sacred feasting, pig love provides a broader prospect for communion between man and beast than is true of the Hindu farmer and his cow. The climax of pig love is the incorporation of the pig as flesh into the flesh of the human host and of the pig as spirit into the spirit of the ancestors. . . .

Professor Roy Rappaport of the University of Michigan has made a detailed study of the relationship between pigs and pig-loving Maring, a remote group of tribesmen living in the Bismarck Mountains of New Guinea. In his book *Pigs for the Ancestors: Ritual in the Ecology of a New Guinea People*, Rappaport describes how pig love contributes to the solution of basic human problems. Under the given circumstances of Maring life, there are few viable alternatives.

30 Each local Maring subgroup or clan holds a pig festival on the average about once every twelve years. The entire festival—including various preparations, small-scale sacrifices, and the final massive slaughter—lasts about a year and is known in the Maring language as a *kaiko*. In the first two or three months immediately following the completion of its *kaiko*, the clan engages in armed combat with enemy clans, leading to many casualties and eventual loss or gain of territory. Additional pigs are sacrificed during the fighting, and both the victors and the vanquished soon find themselves entirely bereft of adult pigs with which to curry favour from their respective ancestors. Fighting ceases abruptly, and the belligerents repair to sacred spots to plant small trees known as *rumbim*....

The war magician addresses the ancestors, explaining that they have run out of pigs and are thankful to be alive. He assures the ancestors that the fighting is now over and that there will be no resumption of hostilities as long as the *rumbim* remains in the ground. From now on, the thoughts and efforts of the living will be directed toward raising pigs; only when a new herd of pigs has been raised, enough for a mighty *kaiko* with which to thank the ancestors properly, will the warriors think of uprooting the *rumbim* and returning to the battlefield.

By a detailed study of one clan called the Tsembaga, Rappaport has been able to show that the entire cycle ... is no mere psychodrama of pig farmers gone berserk. Every part of this cycle is integrated within a complex, self-regulating ecosystem, that effectively adjusts the size and distribution of the Tsembaga's human and animal population to conform to available resources and production opportunities.

The one question that is central to the understanding of pig love among the Maring is: How do the people decide when they have enough pigs to thank the ancestors properly? The Maring themselves were unable to state how many years should elapse or how many pigs are needed to stage a proper *kaiko*. Possibility of agreement on the basis of a fixed number of animals or years is virtually eliminated because the Maring have no calendar and their language lacks words for numbers larger than three.

The *kaiko* of 1963 observed by Rappaport began when there were 169 pigs and about 200 members of the Tsembaga clan. It is the meaning of these numbers in terms of daily work routines and settlement patterns that provides the key to the length of the cycle.

The task of raising pigs, as well as that of cultivating yams, taro, and sweet 35
potatoes, depends primarily upon the labour of the Maring women. Baby pigs are carried along with human infants to the gardens. After they are weaned, their mistresses train them to trot along behind like dogs. At the age of four or five months, the pigs are turned loose in the forests to scrounge for themselves until their mistresses call them home at night to be fed a daily ration of leftover or substandard sweet potatoes and yams. As each woman's pigs mature and as their numbers increase, she must work harder to provide them with their evening meal.

While the *rumbim* remained in the ground, Rappaport found that the Tsembaga women were under considerable pressure to increase the size of their gardens, to plant more sweet potatoes and yams, and to raise more pigs as quickly as possible in order to have "enough" pigs to hold the next *kaiko* before the enemy did. Mature pigs, weighing about 135 pounds, are heavier than the average adult Maring, and even with their daily scrounging, they cost each woman about as much effort to feed as an adult human. At the time of the uprooting of the *rumbim* in 1963, the more ambitious Tsembaga women were taking care of the equivalent of six 135-pounders in addition to gardening for themselves and their families, cooking, nursing, carrying infants about, and manufacturing household items such as net bags, string aprons, and loincloths. Rappaport calculates that taking care of six pigs alone uses up over 50 per cent of the total daily energy which a healthy, well-fed Maring woman is capable of expending.

The increase in the pig population is normally also accompanied by an increase in the human population, especially among groups that have been victorious in the previous war. Pigs and people must be fed from the gardens which are hacked and burned out of the tropical forest that covers the slopes of the Bismarck Mountains. Like similar horticultural systems in other tropical areas, the fertility of the Maring gardens depends upon the nitrogen that is put into the soil by the ashes left from burning off the trees. These gardens cannot be planted for more than two or three years consecutively, since once the trees are gone, the heavy rains quickly wash away the nitrogen and other soil nutrients. The only remedy is to choose another site and burn off another segment of the forest. After a decade or so, the old gardens get covered over with enough secondary growth so that they can be burned again and re-planted. These old garden sites are preferred because they are easier to clear than virgin forest.* But as the pig and human populations spurt upward during the *rumbim* truce, the maturation of the old garden sites lags behind and new gardens must be established in the virgin tracts. While there is plenty of virgin forest available, the new garden sites place an extra strain on everybody and lower the typical rate of return for every unit of labour the Maring invest in feeding themselves and their pigs.

The men whose task it is to clear and burn the new gardens must work harder because of the greater thickness and height of the virgin trees. But it is the women who suffer most, since the new gardens are necessarily located at a greater distance from the centre of the village. Not only must the women plant larger gardens to feed their families and pigs, but they must consume more and more of their time just walking to work and more and more of their energy hauling piglets and babies up to and down from the garden and the heavy loads of harvested yams and sweet potatoes back to their houses.

A further source of tension arises from the increased effort involved in protecting the gardens from being eaten up by the mature pigs that are let loose to scrounge for themselves. Every garden must be surrounded by a stout fence to keep the pigs out. A hungry 150-pound sow, however, is a formidable adversary. Fences are breached and gardens invaded more frequently as the pig herd multiplies. If caught by an irate gardener, the offending pig may be killed. These disagreeable incidents set neighbour against neighbour and heighten the general sense of dissatisfaction. As Rappaport points out, incidents involving pigs necessarily increase more rapidly than the pigs themselves.

40 In order to avoid such incidents and to get closer to their gardens, the Maring begin to move their houses farther apart over a wider area. This dispersion lowers the security of the group in case of renewed hostilities. So everyone becomes more jittery. The women begin to complain about being overworked. They bicker with their husbands and snap at their children. Soon the men begin to wonder if perhaps there are "enough pigs." They go down to inspect the *rumbim* to see how tall it has grown. The women complain more loudly, and finally the men, with considerable unanimity and without counting the pigs, agree that the moment has come to begin the *kaiko*.

During the *kaiko* year of 1963, the Tsembaga killed off three-fourths of their pigs by number and seven-eighths by weight. Much of this meat was distributed to in-laws and military allies who were invited to participate in the yearlong festivities. At the climactic rituals held on November 7 and 8, 1963, 96 pigs were killed and their meat and fat were distributed directly or indirectly to an estimated two or three thousand people. The Tsembaga kept about 2,500 pounds of pork and fat for themselves, or 12 pounds for each man, woman, and child, a quantity which they consumed in five consecutive days of unrestrained gluttony....

Over a thousand people crowded into the Tsembaga dance ground to participate in the rituals that followed the great pig slaughter witnessed by Rappaport in 1963. Special reward packages of salted pig fat were heaped high behind the window of a three-sided ceremonial building that adjoined the dance grounds. In Rappaport's words:

> ... The mouth of the honoured man was stuffed with cold salted belly-fat by the Tsembaga whom he had come to help in the last fight and who now also passed out to him through the window a package containing additional salted belly for his followers. With the belly fat hanging from his mouth the hero now retired, his supporters close behind him, shouting, singing, beating their drums, dancing....

Within limits set by the basic technological and environmental conditions of the Maring, all of this has a practical explanation. First of all, the craving for pig meat is a perfectly rational feature of Maring life in view of the general scarcity of meat in their diet. While they can supplement their staple vegetables with occasional frogs, rats, and a few hunted marsupials, domesticated pork is their best potential source of high-quality animal fat and protein. This does not mean that the Maring suffer from an acute form of protein deficiency. On the contrary, their diet of yams, sweet potatoes, taro, and other plant foods provides them with a broad variety of vegetable proteins that satisfies but does not far exceed minimum nutritional standards. Getting proteins from pigs is something else, however. Animal protein in general is more concentrated and metabolically more effective than vegetable protein, so for human populations that are mainly restricted to vegetable foods (no cheese, milk, eggs, or fish), meat is always an irresistible temptation.

Moreover, up to a point, it makes good ecological sense for the Maring to raise pigs. The temperature and humidity are ideal. Pigs thrive in the damp, shady environment of the mountain slopes and obtain a substantial portion of their food by roaming freely over the forest floor. The complete interdiction of pork—the Middle Eastern solution—would be a most irrational and uneconomic practice under these conditions.

On the other hand, unlimited growth of the pig population can only lead 45
to competition between man and pig. If permitted to go too far, pig farming overburdens the women and endangers the gardens upon which the Maring depend for survival. As the pig population increases, the Maring women must work harder and harder. Eventually they find themselves working to feed pigs rather than to feed people. As virgin lands are brought into use, the efficiency of the entire agricultural system plummets. It is at this point that the *kaiko* takes place, the role of the ancestors being to encourage a maximum effort at pig raising but at the same time to see to it that the pigs do not destroy the women and the gardens. Their task is admittedly more difficult than Jahweh's or Allah's, since a total taboo is always easier to administer than a partial one. Nonetheless, the belief that a kaiko must be held as soon as possible, in order to keep the ancestors happy, effectively rids the Maring of animals that have grown parasitic and helps keep the pig population from becoming "too much of a good thing."

If ancestors are so clever, why don't they simply set a limit on the number of pigs that each Maring woman can raise? Would it not be better to keep a constant number of pigs than to permit the pig population to cycle through extremes of scarcity and abundance?

This alternative would be preferable only if each Maring clan had zero growth, no enemies, a wholly different form of agriculture, powerful rulers, and written laws—in short, if they weren't the Maring. No one, not even the ancestors can predict how many pigs are "too much of a good thing." The point at which the pigs become burdensome does not depend upon any set of constants, but rather on a set of variables which changes from year to year. It depends on how many people there are in the whole region and in each clan, on their state of physical and psychological vigour, on the size of their territory, on the amount of secondary forest they have, and on the condition and intentions of the enemy groups in neighbouring territories....

To satisfy the ancestors, a maximum effort must be made not only to produce as much food as possible, but to accumulate it in the form of the pig herd. This effort, even though it results in cyclical surpluses of pork, enhances the ability of the group to survive and to defend its territory.

It does this in several ways. First, the extra effort called forth by the pig lust of the ancestors raises the levels of protein intake for the entire group during the *rumbim* truce, resulting in a taller, healthier, and more vigorous population. Furthermore, by linking the *kaiko* to the end of the truce, the ancestors guarantee that massive doses of high-quality fats and proteins are consumed at the period of greatest social stress—in the months immediately prior to the outbreak of intergroup fighting. Finally, by banking large amounts of extra food in the form of nutritionally valuable pig meat, the Maring clans are able to attract and reward allies when they are most needed, again just before the outbreak of war.

50 The Tsembaga and their neighbours are conscious of the relationship between success in raising pigs and military power. The number of pigs slaughtered at the *kaiko* provides the guests with an accurate basis for judging the health, energy, and determination of the feast givers. A group that cannot manage to accumulate pigs is not likely to put up a good defense of its territory, and will not attract strong allies. No mere irrational premonition of defeat hangs over the battlefield when one's ancestors aren't given enough pork at the *kaiko*. Rappaport insists—correctly, I believe—that in a fundamental ecological sense, the size of a group's pig surplus does indicate its productive and military strength and does validate or invalidate its territorial claims. In other words, the entire system results in an efficient distribution of plants, animals, and people in the region, from a human ecological point of view.

I am sure that many readers will now want to insist that the pig love is maladaptive and terribly inefficient because it is geared to periodic outbreaks of warfare. If warfare is irrational, then so is the *kaiko*.... In the next chapter I will discuss the mundane causes of Maring warfare. But for the moment, let me point out that warfare is not caused by pig love. Millions of people who have never even seen a pig wage war; nor does pig hatred (ancient and modern) discernibly enhance the peacefulness of the intergroup relations in the Middle East. Given the prevalence of warfare in human history and prehistory, we can only marvel at the ingenious system devised by New Guinea "savages" for maintaining extensive periods of truce. After all, as long as their neighbour's *rumbim* remains in the ground, the Tsembaga don't have to worry about being attacked. One can perhaps say as much, but not more, about nations that plant missiles instead of *rumbim*.

(1974)

Questions

1. Harris is unusual among academics in aiming his writing both at other academics and at students and general readers with no prior specialized knowledge. Comment on the ways in which the diction, syntax, and organization of ideas in this essay are appropriate to an audience with no prior familiarity with the topic or with the discipline of anthropology.
2. Express in your own words the logical problem with the argument that pig-eating became taboo in the cultures Harris is discussing because pigs had been regarded as sacred (paragraph 11).
3. What are the key facts about the physiology of the pig so far as Harris's argument is concerned?
4. In two paragraphs, summarize the practices of the miring of pigs and Harris's explanation as to why these seemingly bizarre practices make sense.
5. Does it "make sense," either from the sort of angle of approach that Harris uses or from other angles, for North American society to consume as much beef and pork as it does?
6. Does the sort of discussion that Harris engages in undermine the foundations of the religions he is discussing in any way?

MICHEL FOUCAULT

THE PERVERSE IMPLANTATION[1] [from *THE HISTORY OF SEXUALITY*]

Philosopher and historian Michel Foucault's work is primarily concerned with the way power creates knowledge and identity by shaping discourses—systems of language, practices, and cultural meanings. His engagement with these ideas has been influential across the humanities and social sciences. The History of Sexuality, *in which the following chapter appeared, became a foundational work in the development of queer theory, a branch of critical theory focused on the relationship between sexuality and culture. In the book's opening chapters, Foucault argues against what he calls "the repressive hypothesis": the widespread belief that between the seventeenth and mid-twentieth centuries western society repressed sexuality and its discussion. In fact, he suggests, this period saw a "proliferation of discourses" surrounding sexuality.*

A possible objection: it would be a mistake to see in this proliferation of discourses merely a quantitative phenomenon, something like a pure increase, as if what was said in them were immaterial, as if the fact of speaking about sex were of itself more important than the forms of imperatives that were imposed on it by speaking about it. For was this transformation of sex into discourse not governed by the endeavour to expel from reality the forms of sexuality that were not amenable to the strict economy of reproduction: to say no to unproductive activities, to banish casual pleasures, to reduce or exclude practices whose object was not procreation? Through the various discourses, legal sanctions against minor perversions were multiplied; sexual irregularity was annexed to mental illness; from childhood to old age, a norm of sexual development was defined and all the possible deviations were carefully described; pedagogical controls and medical treatments were organized; around the least fantasies, moralists, but especially doctors, brandished the whole emphatic vocabulary of abomination.* Were these anything more than means

1 *The Perverse Implantation* Translated by Robert Hurley, 1978.

employed to absorb, for the benefit of a genitally centred sexuality, all the fruitless pleasures?* All this garrulous attention which has us in a stew over sexuality, is it not motivated by one basic concern: to ensure population, to reproduce labour capacity, to perpetuate the form of social relations: in short, to constitute a sexuality that is economically useful and politically conservative?

I still do not know whether this is the ultimate objective. But this much is certain: reduction has not been the means employed for trying to achieve it. The nineteenth century and our own have been rather the age of multiplication: a dispersion of sexualities, a strengthening of their disparate forms, a multiple implantation of "perversions." Our epoch has initiated sexual heterogeneities.

Up to the end of the eighteenth century, three major explicit codes—apart from the customary regularities and constraints of opinion—governed sexual practices: canonical law, the Christian pastoral,[2] and civil law. They determined, each in its own way, the division between licit and illicit. They were all centred on matrimonial relations: the marital obligation, the ability to fulfill it, the manner in which one complied with it, the requirements and violences that accompanied it, the useless or unwarranted caresses for which it was a pretext, its fecundity or the way one went about making it sterile, the moments when one demanded it (dangerous periods of pregnancy or breast-feeding, forbidden times of Lent* or abstinence), its frequency or infrequency, and so on. It was this domain that was especially saturated with prescriptions. The sex of husband and wife was beset by rules and recommendations. The marriage relation was the most intense focus of constraints; it was spoken of more than anything else; more than any other relation, it was required to give a detailed accounting of itself. It was under constant surveillance: if it was found to be lacking, it had to come forward and plead its case before a witness. The "rest" remained a good deal more confused: one only has to think of the uncertain status of "sodomy,"[3] or the indifference regarding the sexuality of children.

Moreover, these different codes did not make a clear distinction between violations of the rules of marriage and deviations with respect to genitality.* Breaking the rules of marriage or seeking strange pleasures brought an equal measure of condemnation. On the list of grave sins, and separated only by their relative importance, there appeared debauchery (extramarital relations),

---

2 *canonical law* Law imposed by the Church (here, the Catholic Church); *Christian pastoral* Care for a congregation by a priest, pastor, or other member of a church; in Catholicism, this includes giving sacraments, providing spiritual counselling, and nursing the ill and dying.

3 *uncertain status of "sodomy"* In the Middle Ages, for example, definitions of sodomy could incorporate not only anal sex (its present-day definition), but also any type of sex between men, bestiality, and any number of other acts deemed unnatural between men and women.

adultery, rape, spiritual or carnal incest, but also sodomy, or the mutual "caress." As to the courts, they could condemn homosexuality as well as infidelity, marriage without parental consent, or bestiality. What was taken into account in the civil and religious jurisdictions alike was a general unlawfulness. Doubtless acts "contrary to nature" were stamped as especially abominable, but they were perceived simply as an extreme form of acts "against the law"; they were infringements of decrees which were just as sacred as those of marriage, and which had been established for governing the order of things and the plan of beings. Prohibitions bearing on sex were essentially of a juridical nature. The "nature" on which they were based was still a kind of law. For a long time hermaphrodites were criminals, or crime's offspring, since their anatomical disposition, their very being, confounded the law that distinguished the sexes and prescribed their union.

5 The discursive explosion of the eighteenth and nineteenth centuries caused this system centred on legitimate alliance to undergo two modifications. First, a centrifugal movement with respect to heterosexual monogamy.* Of course, the array of practices and pleasures continued to be referred to it as their internal standard; but it was spoken of less and less, or in any case with a growing moderation. Efforts to find out its secrets were abandoned; nothing further was demanded of it than to define itself from day to day. The legitimate couple, with its regular sexuality, had a right to more discretion. It tended to function as a norm, one that was stricter, perhaps, but quieter. On the other hand, what came under scrutiny was the sexuality of children, mad men and women, and criminals; the sensuality of those who did not like the opposite sex; reveries, obsessions, petty manias, or great transports of rage. It was time for all these figures, scarcely noticed in the past, to step forward and speak, to make the difficult confession of what they were. No doubt they were condemned all the same; but they were listened to; and if regular sexuality happened to be questioned once again, it was through a reflux movement, originating in these peripheral sexualities.

Whence the setting apart of the "unnatural" as a specific dimension in the field of sexuality. This kind of activity assumed an autonomy with regard to the other condemned forms such as adultery or rape (and the latter were condemned less and less): to marry a close relative or practise sodomy, to seduce a nun or engage in sadism, to deceive one's wife or violate cadavers, became things that were essentially different. The area covered by the Sixth Commandment[4] began to fragment. Similarly, in the civil order, the confused category of "debauchery," which for more than a century had been one of the

4 *Sixth Commandment* In Catholic and many other Christian interpretations of the Bible, the sixth commandment is "Thou shalt not commit adultery."

most frequent reasons for administrative confinement, came apart. From the debris, there appeared on the one hand infractions against the legislation (or morality) pertaining to marriage and the family, and on the other, offenses against the regularity of a natural function (offenses which, it must be added, the law was apt to punish). Here we have a likely reason, among others, for the prestige of Don Juan,[5] which three centuries have not erased. Underneath the great violator of the rules of marriage—stealer of wives, seducer of virgins, the shame of families, and an insult to husbands and fathers—another personage can be glimpsed: the individual driven, in spite of himself, by the sombre madness of sex. Underneath the libertine, the pervert.* He deliberately breaks the law, but at the same time, something like a nature gone awry transports him far from all nature; his death is the moment when the supernatural return of the crime and its retribution thwarts the flight into counternature. There were two great systems conceived by the West for governing sex: the law of marriage and the order of desires—and the life of Don Juan overturned them both. We shall leave it to psychoanalysts to speculate whether he was homosexual, narcissistic, or impotent.

Although not without delay and equivocation, the natural laws of matrimony and the immanent rules of sexuality began to be recorded on two separate registers. There emerged a world of perversion which partook of that of legal or moral infraction, yet was not simply a variety of the latter. An entire sub-race race was born, different—despite certain kinship ties—from the libertines of the past. From the end of the eighteenth century to our own, they circulated through the pores of society; they were always hounded, but not always by laws; were often locked up, but not always in prisons; were sick perhaps, but scandalous, dangerous victims, prey to a strange evil that also bore the name of vice and sometimes crime. They were children wise beyond their years, precocious little girls, ambiguous schoolboys, dubious servants and educators, cruel or maniacal husbands, solitary collectors, ramblers with bizarre impulses; they haunted the houses of correction, the penal colonies, the tribunals, and the asylums; they carried their infamy to the doctors and their sickness to the judges. This was the numberless family of perverts who were on friendly terms with delinquents and akin to madmen. In the course of the century they successively bore the stamp of "moral folly," "genital neurosis," "aberration of the genetic instinct," "degenerescence," or "physical imbalance."

What does the appearance of all these peripheral sexualities signify? Is the fact that they could appear in broad daylight a sign that the code had become more lax? Or does the fact that they were given so much attention testify to a stricter regime and to its concern to bring them under close supervision? In

---

5 *Don Juan* Legendary character who seduced large numbers of women.

terms of repression, things are unclear. There was permissiveness, if one bears in mind that the severity of the codes relating to sexual offenses diminished considerably in the nineteenth century and that law itself often deferred to medicine. But an additional ruse of severity, if one thinks of all the agencies of control and all the mechanisms of surveillance that were put into operation by pedagogy or therapeutics. It may be the case that the intervention of the Church in conjugal sexuality and its rejection of "frauds" against procreation had lost much of their insistence over the previous two hundred years. But medicine made a forceful entry into the pleasures of the couple: it created an entire organic, functional, or mental pathology arising out of "incomplete" sexual practices; it carefully classified all forms of related pleasures; it incorporated them into the notions of "development" and instinctual "disturbances"; and it undertook to manage them.

Perhaps the point to consider is not the level of indulgence or the quantity of repression but the form of power that was exercised. When this whole thicket of disparate sexualities was labelled, as if to disentangle them from one another, was the object to exclude them from reality? It appears, in fact, that the function of the power exerted in this instance was not that of interdiction, and that it involved four operations quite different from simple prohibition.

10 1. Take the ancient prohibitions of consanguine marriages[6] (as numerous and complex as they were) or the condemnation of adultery, with its inevitable frequency of occurrence; or on the other hand, the recent controls through which, since the nineteenth century, the sexuality of children has been subordinated and their "solitary habits" interfered with. It is clear that we are not dealing with one and the same power mechanism. Not only because in the one case it is a question of law and penality, and in the other, medicine and regimentation; but also because the tactics employed is not the same. On the surface, what appears in both cases is an effort at elimination that was always destined to fail and always constrained to begin again. But the prohibition of "incests" attempted to reach its objective through an asymptotic decrease in the thing it condemned, whereas the control of infantile sexuality hoped to reach it through a simultaneous propagation of its own power and of the object on which it was brought to bear. It proceeded in accordance with a twofold increase extended indefinitely. Educators and doctors combatted children's onanism[7] like an epidemic that needed to be eradicated. What this actually entailed, throughout this whole secular campaign that mobilized the adult world around the sex of children, was using these tenuous pleasures as a prop, constituting them as secrets (that is, forcing them into hiding so as

6 *consanguine marriages* Marriages between relatives.

7 *onanism* I.e., masturbation.

to make possible their discovery), tracing them back to their source, tracking them from their origins to their effects, searching out everything that might cause them or simply enable them to exist. Wherever there was the chance they might appear, devices of surveillance were installed; traps were laid for compelling admissions; inexhaustible and corrective discourses were imposed; parents and teachers were alerted, and left with the suspicion that all children were guilty, and with the fear of being themselves at fault if their suspicions were not sufficiently strong; they were kept in readiness in the face of this recurrent danger; their conduct was prescribed and their pedagogy recodified; an entire medico-sexual regime took hold of the family milieu. The child's "vice" was not so much an enemy as a support; it may have been designated as the evil to be eliminated, but the extraordinary effort that went into the task that was bound to fail leads one to suspect that what was demanded of it was to persevere, to proliferate to the limits of the visible and the invisible, rather than to disappear for good. Always relying on this support, power advanced, multiplied its relays and its effects, while its target expanded, subdivided, and branched out, penetrating further into reality at the same pace. In appearance, we are dealing with a barrier system; but in fact, all around the child, indefinite lines of penetration were disposed.

2. This new persecution of the peripheral sexualities entailed an *incorporation* of perversions* and a new *specification of individuals*. As defined by the ancient civil or canonical codes, sodomy was a category of forbidden acts; their perpetrator was nothing more than the juridical subject of them. The nineteenth-century homosexual became a personage, a past, a case history, and a childhood, in addition to being a type of life, a life form, and a morphology,[8] with an indiscreet anatomy and possibly a mysterious physiology. Nothing that went into his total composition was unaffected by his sexuality. It was everywhere present in him: at the root of all his actions because it was their insidious and indefinitely active principle; written immodestly on his face and body because it was a secret that always gave itself away. It was consubstantial with him, less as a habitual sin than as a singular nature. We must not forget that the psychological, psychiatric, medical category of homosexuality was constituted from the moment it was characterized—Westphal's[9] famous article of 1870 on "contrary sexual sensations" can stand as its date of birth[10]—less by a type of

8 *morphology* Here, form according to which something (especially a biological organism) is classified.

9 *Westphal* Carl Friedrich Otto Westphal (1833–90), German psychiatrist. In the article referenced here, Westphal provides short case histories of several men and women who experience same-sex attraction.

10 [Foucault's note] Carl Westphal, *Archiv für Neurologie*, 1870.

sexual relations than by a certain quality of sexual sensibility, a certain way of inverting the masculine and the feminine in oneself. Homosexuality appeared as one of the forms of sexuality when it was transposed from the practice of sodomy onto a kind of interior androgyny, a hermaphrodism of the soul. The sodomite had been a temporary aberration; the homosexual was now a species.

So too were all those minor perverts whom nineteenth-century psychiatrists entomologized* by giving them strange baptismal names: there were Krafft-Ebing's zoophiles and zooerasts, Rohleder's auto-monosexualists; and later, mixoscopophiles, gynecomasts, presbyophiles, sexoesthetic inverts, and dyspareunist women.[11] These fine names for heresies referred to a nature that was overlooked by the law, but not so neglectful of itself that it did not go on producing more species, even where there was no order to fit them into. The machinery of power that focused on this whole alien strain did not aim to suppress it, but rather to give it an analytical, visible, and permanent reality: it was implanted in bodies, slipped in beneath modes of conduct, made into a principle of classification and intelligibility, established as a *raison d'être** and a natural order of disorder. Not the exclusion of these thousand aberrant sexualities, but the specification, the regional solidification of each one of them. The strategy behind this dissemination was to strew reality with them and incorporate them into the individual.

3. More than the old taboos, this form of power demanded constant, attentive, and curious presences for its exercise; it presupposed proximities; it proceeded through examination and insistent observation; it required an exchange of discourses, through questions that extorted admissions, and confidences that went beyond the questions that were asked. It implied a physical proximity and an interplay of intense sensations. The medicalization of the sexually peculiar was both the effect and the instrument of this. Imbedded in bodies, becoming deeply characteristic of individuals, the oddities of sex relied on a technology of health and pathology. And conversely, since sexuality was a medical and medicalizable object, one had to try and detect it—as a lesion, a dysfunction,

11 *Krafft-Ebing* Author of *Psychopathia Sexualis* (1886), a reference book outlining a wide range of sexual behaviours he classifies as perversities; *zoophiles* People who experience sexual pleasure from petting animals; *zooerasts* People who have or desire to have sex with animals; *Rohleder* Hermann Rohleder, author of *Masturbation: A Monograph for Physicians, Educators and Educated Parents* (1899); *auto-monosexualists* People who only experience sexual satisfaction from masturbation; *mixoscopophiles* People who experience sexual satisfaction from watching others have sex; *gynecomasts* People who experience excessive attraction to women; *presbyophiles* People who are attracted to elderly men; *sexoesthetic inverts* People who dress and act like members of the opposite sex; *dyspareunist women* Women who experience pain or insufficient pleasure during sex.

or a symptom—in the depths of the organism, or on the surface of the skin, or among all the signs of behaviour. The power which thus took charge of sexuality set about contacting bodies, caressing them with its eyes, intensifying areas, electrifying surfaces, dramatizing troubled moments. It wrapped the sexual body in its embrace. There was undoubtedly an increase in effectiveness and an extension of the domain controlled; but also a sensualization of power and a gain of pleasure. This produced a twofold effect: an impetus was given to power through its very exercise; an emotion rewarded the overseeing control and carried it further; the intensity of the confession renewed the questioner's curiosity; the pleasure discovered fed back to the power that encircled it. But so many pressing questions singularized the pleasures felt by the one who had to reply. They were fixed by a gaze, isolated and animated by the attention they received. Power operated as a mechanism of attraction; it drew out those peculiarities over which it kept watch. Pleasure spread to the power that harried it; power anchored the pleasure it uncovered.

The medical examination, the psychiatric investigation, the pedagogical report, and family controls may have the over-all and apparent objective of saying no to all wayward or unproductive sexualities, but the fact is that they function as mechanisms with a double impetus: pleasure and power. The pleasure that comes of exercising a power that questions, monitors, watches, spies, searches out, palpates, brings to light; and on the other hand, the pleasure that kindles at having to evade this power, flee from it, fool it, or travesty it. The power that lets itself be invaded by the pleasure it is pursuing; and opposite it, power asserting itself in the pleasure of showing off, scandalizing, or resisting. Capture and seduction, confrontation and mutual reinforcement: parents and children, adults and adolescents, educator and students, doctors and patients, the psychiatrist with his hysteric and his perverts, all have played this game continually since the nineteenth century. These attractions, these evasions, these circular incitements have traced around bodies and sexes, not boundaries not to be crossed, but *perpetual spirals of power and pleasure*.

4. Whence those *devices of sexual saturation* so characteristic of the space 15
and the social rituals of the nineteenth century. People often say that modern society has attempted to reduce sexuality to the couple—the heterosexual and, insofar as possible, legitimate couple. There are equal grounds for saying that it has, if not created, at least outfitted and made to proliferate, groups with multiple elements and a circulating sexuality: a distribution of points of power, hierarchized and placed opposite to one another; "pursued" pleasures, that is, both sought after and searched out; compartmental sexualities that are tolerated or encouraged; proximities that serve as surveillance procedures, and function as mechanisms of intensification; contacts that operate as inductors. This is the way things worked in the case of the family, or rather the household, with

parents, children, and in some instances, servants. Was the nineteenth-century family really a monogamic[12] and conjugal cell? Perhaps to a certain extent. But it was also a network of pleasures and powers linked together at multiple points and according to transformable relationships. The separation of grown-ups and children, the polarity established between the parents' bedroom and that of the children (it became routine in the course of the century when working-class housing construction was undertaken), the relative segregation of boys and girls, the strict instructions as to the care of nursing infants (maternal breast-feeding, hygiene), the attention focused on infantile sexuality, the supposed dangers of masturbation, the importance attached to puberty, the methods of surveillance suggested to parents, the exhortations, secrets, and fears, the presence—both valued and feared—of servants: all this made the family, even when brought down to its smallest dimensions, a complicated network, saturated with multiple, fragmentary, and mobile sexualities. To reduce them to the conjugal relationship, and then to project the latter, in the form of a forbidden desire, onto the children, cannot account for this apparatus which, in relation to these sexualities, was less a principle of inhibition than an inciting and multiplying mechanism. Educational or psychiatric institutions, with their large populations, their hierarchies, their spatial arrangements, their surveillance systems, constituted, alongside the family, another way of distributing the interplay of powers and pleasures; but they too delineated areas of extreme sexual saturation, with privileged spaces or rituals such as the classroom, the dormitory, the visit, and the consultation. The forms of a nonconjugal, nonmonogamous sexuality were drawn there and established.

Nineteenth-century "bourgeois" society—and it is doubtless still with us—was a society of blatant and fragmented perversion. And this was not by way of hypocrisy, for nothing was more manifest and more prolix, or more manifestly taken over by discourses and institutions. Not because, having tried to erect too rigid or too general a barrier against sexuality, society succeeded only in giving rise to a whole perverse outbreak and a long pathology of the sexual instinct. At issue, rather, is the type of power it brought to bear on the body and on sex. In point of fact, this power had neither the form of the law, nor the effects of the taboo. On the contrary, it acted by multiplication of singular sexualities. It did not set boundaries for sexuality; it extended the various forms of sexuality, pursuing them according to lines of indefinite penetration. It did not exclude sexuality, but included it in the body as a mode of specification of individuals. It did not seek to avoid it; it attracted its varieties by means of spirals in which pleasure and power reinforced one another. It did not set up a barrier; it provided places of maximum saturation. It produced and

12 *monogamic* Monogamous.

determined the sexual mosaic. Modern society is perverse, not in spite of its puritanism or as if from a backlash provoked by its hypocrisy; it is in actual fact, and directly, perverse.

In actual fact. The manifold sexualities—those which appear with the different ages (sexualities of the infant or the child), those which become fixated on particular tastes or practices (the sexuality of the invert, the gerontophile,[13] the fetishist), those which, in a diffuse manner, invest relationships (the sexuality of doctor and patient, teacher and student, psychiatrist and mental patient), those which haunt spaces (the sexuality of the home, the school, the prison)—all form the correlate[14] of exact procedures of power. We must not imagine that all these things that were formerly tolerated attracted notice and received a pejorative designation when the time came to give a regulative role to the one type of sexuality that was capable of reproducing labour power and the form of the family. These polymorphous[15] conducts were actually extracted from people's bodies and from their pleasures; or rather, they were solidified in them; they were drawn out, revealed, isolated, intensified, incorporated, by multifarious power devices. The growth of perversions is not a moralizing theme that obsessed the scrupulous minds of the Victorians. It is the real product of the encroachment of a type of power on bodies and their pleasures. It is possible that the West has not been capable of inventing any new pleasures, and it has doubtless not discovered any original vices. But it has defined new rules for the game of powers and pleasures. The frozen countenance[16] of the perversions is a fixture of this game.

Directly. This implantation of multiple perversions is not a mockery of sexuality taking revenge on a power that has thrust on it an excessively repressive law. Neither are we dealing with paradoxical forms of pleasure that turn back on power and invest it in the form of a "pleasure to be endured." The implantation of perversions is an instrument-effect:[17] it is through the isolation, intensification, and consolidation of peripheral sexualities that the relations of power to sex and pleasure branched out and multiplied, measured the body, and penetrated modes of conduct. And accompanying this encroachment of powers, scattered sexualities rigidified, became stuck to an age, a place, a type of practice. A proliferation of sexualities through the extension of power; an

---

13 *invert* Person of same-sex sexual orientation; *gerontophile* Person who is primarily attracted to elderly people.

14 *correlate* Related elements.

15 *polymorphous* Of many forms.

16 *countenance* Appearance.

17 *instrument-effect* Literally, in scientific experiments, a change in measurements caused by a change in the instruments used for measuring.

optimization of the power to which each of these local sexualities gave a surface of intervention: this concatenation,* particularly since the nineteenth century, has been ensured and relayed by the countless economic interests which, with the help of medicine, psychiatry, prostitution, and pornography, have tapped into both this analytical multiplication of pleasure and this optimization of the power that controls it. Pleasure and power do not cancel or turn back against one another; they seek out, overlap, and reinforce one another. They are linked together by complex mechanisms and devices of excitation and incitement.

We must therefore abandon the hypothesis that modern industrial societies ushered in an age of increased sexual repression. We have not only witnessed a visible explosion of unorthodox sexualities; but—and this is the important point—a deployment quite different from the law, even if it is locally dependent on procedures of prohibition, has ensured, through a network of interconnecting mechanisms, the proliferation of specific pleasures and the multiplication of disparate sexualities. It is said that no society has been more prudish; never have the agencies of power taken such care to feign ignorance of the thing they prohibited, as if they were determined to have nothing to do with it. But it is the opposite that has become apparent, at least after a general review of the facts: never have there existed more centres of power; never more attention manifested and verbalized; never more circular contacts and linkages; never more sites where the intensity of pleasures and the persistency of power catch hold, only to spread elsewhere.

(1976)

Questions

1. What "possible objection" (paragraph 1) does Foucault raise at the beginning of the chapter? How does he respond to this objection?
2. What does Foucault mean by the statement that "[t]he sodomite had been a temporary aberration; the homosexual was now a species" (paragraph 11)? Is this still an accurate description of Western society's perception of sexuality and identity?
3. What are the "four operations" (paragraph 9) of the power exercised over sexuality that Foucault proposes? Can you identify an example of each of these "operations" in present-day Canadian society?
4. Foucault's writing style is more difficult to read than the styles of most writers in this anthology. How does this style affect the experience of the reader? What—if anything—is Foucault able to communicate through this style that might not be communicated as effectively in a simpler style?

Peter Singer

from Animal Liberation

Now long established as one of the world's most prominent philosophers, Peter Singer was a 26-year old lecturer in 1973 when The New York Review of Books *published his long review article discussing an essay collection called* Animals, Men and Morals*—and discussing more generally the ways in which humans treat other animals. Singer's review article was entitled "Animal Liberation"; the article was the germ of Singer's 1975 book* Animal Liberation, *which may well have done more to change human behaviour than any other book of the past fifty years. The selection excerpted here is from the 2009 revised edition of* Animal Liberation, *appropriately subtitled "The Definitive Classic of the Animal Movement."*

All Animals Are Equal

... Speciesism—the word is not an attractive one, but I can think of no better term—is a prejudice or attitude of bias in favour of the interests of members of one's own species and against those of members of other species. It should be obvious that the fundamental objections to racism and sexism made by Thomas Jefferson and Sojourner Truth[1] apply equally to speciesism. If possessing a higher degree of intelligence does not entitle one human to use another for his

1 *Thomas Jefferson* 3rd President of the United States, as well as one of the nation's founders (1743–1826). Jefferson opposed slavery despite viewing black people as generally inferior to white people. In an earlier portion of the chapter not excerpted here, Singer quotes an 1809 letter in which Jefferson says of black Americans, "whatever be their degree of talent it is no measure of their rights"; *Sojourner Truth* African-American women's rights activist and abolitionist (1797–1883). In an earlier portion of the chapter not excerpted here, Singer quotes a record of her speech "Ain't I a Woman?" (1851), in which she responds to the claim that gender inequality is justified because women are intellectually inferior: "What's that got to do with women's rights or negroes' rights? If my cup won't hold but a pint, and yours holds a quart, wouldn't you be mean not to let me have my little half measure full?"

or her own ends, how can it entitle humans to exploit nonhumans for the same purpose?[2]

Many philosophers and other writers have proposed the principle of equal consideration of interests, in some form or other, as a basic moral principle; but not many of them have recognized that this principle applies to members of other species as well as to our own. Jeremy Bentham[3] was one of the few who did realize this. In a forward-looking passage written at a time when black slaves had been freed by the French but in the British dominions were still being treated in the way we now treat animals, Bentham wrote:

> The day *may* come when the rest of the animal creation may acquire those rights which never could have been withholden from them but by the hand of tyranny. The French have already discovered that the blackness of the skin is no reason why a human being should be abandoned without redress to the caprice of a tormentor. It may one day come to be recognized that the number of the legs, the villosity of the skin, or the termination of the *os sacrum* are reasons equally insufficient for abandoning a sensitive being to the same fate. What else is it that should trace the insuperable line? Is it the faculty of reason, or perhaps the faculty of discourse? But a full-grown horse or dog is beyond comparison a more rational, as well as a more conversable animal, than an infant of a day or a week or even a month, old. But suppose they were otherwise, what would it avail? The question is not, Can they *reason*? nor Can they *talk*? but, Can they *suffer*?[4]

In this passage Bentham points to the capacity for suffering as the vital characteristic that gives a being the right to equal consideration. The capacity for suffering—or more strictly, for suffering and/or enjoyment or happiness—is not just another characteristic like the capacity for language or higher mathematics. Bentham is not saying that those who try to mark "the insuperable line" that determines whether the interests of a being should be considered happen to have chosen the wrong characteristic. By saying that we must consider the interests of all beings with the capacity for suffering or enjoyment Bentham does not arbitrarily exclude from consideration any interests at all—as those who draw the line with reference to the possession of reason or language do.

---

2 [Singer's note] I owe the term "speciesism" to Richard Ryder. It has become accepted in general use since the first edition of this book, and now appears in *The Oxford English Dictionary*, second edition (Oxford: Clarendon Press, 1989).

3 *Jeremy Bentham* English philosopher (1748–1832) known for his philosophy of utilitarianism, which suggests that the most moral actions are those which produce the most happiness for the greatest number of people.

4 [Singer's note] *Introduction to the Principles of Morals and Legislation*, chapter 17.

The capacity for suffering and enjoyment is *a prerequisite for having interests at all*, a condition that must be satisfied before we can speak of interests in a meaningful way. It would be nonsense to say that it was not in the interests of a stone to be kicked along the road by a schoolboy. A stone does not have interests because it cannot suffer. Nothing that we can do to it could possibly make any difference to its welfare. The capacity for suffering and enjoyment is, however, not only necessary, but also sufficient for us to say that a being has interests—at an absolute minimum, an interest in not suffering. A mouse, for example, does have an interest in not being kicked along the road, because it will suffer if it is.

Although Bentham speaks of "rights" in the passage I have quoted, the argument is really about equality rather than about rights. Indeed, in a different passage, Bentham famously described "natural rights" as "nonsense" and "natural and imprescriptable rights" as "nonsense upon stilts." He talked of moral rights as a shorthand way of referring to protections that people and animals morally ought to have; but the real weight of the moral argument does not rest on the assertion of the existence of the right, for this in turn has to be justified on the basis of the possibilities for suffering and happiness. In this way we can argue for equality for animals without getting embroiled in philosophical controversies about the ultimate nature of rights.

In misguided attempts to refute the arguments of this book, some philosophers have gone to much trouble developing arguments to show that animals do not have rights.[5] They have claimed that to have rights a being must be autonomous, or must be a member of a community, or must have the ability to respect the rights of others, or must possess a sense of justice. These claims are irrelevant to the case for Animal Liberation. The language of rights is a convenient political shorthand. It is even more valuable in the era of thirty-second TV news clips than it was in Bentham's day; but in the argument for a radical change in our attitude to animals, it is in no way necessary.

If a being suffers there can be no moral justification for refusing to take 5
that suffering into consideration. No matter what the nature of the being, the principle of equality requires that its suffering be counted equally with the like suffering—insofar as rough comparisons can be made—of any other being. If a being is not capable of suffering, or of experiencing enjoyment or happiness, there is nothing to be taken into account. So the limit of sentience (using the term as a convenient if not strictly accurate shorthand for the capacity to suffer and/or experience enjoyment) is the only defensible boundary of concern for

5 [Singer's note] See M. Levin, "Animal Rights Evaluated," *Humanist* 37: 14–15 (July/August 1977); M.A. Fox, "Animal Liberation: A Critique," *Ethics* 88: 134–138 (1978); C. Perry and G.E. Jones, "On Animal Rights," *International Journal of Applied Philosophy* 1: 39–57 (1982).

the interests of others. To mark this boundary by some other characteristic like intelligence or rationality would be to mark it in an arbitrary manner. Why not choose some other characteristic, like skin colour?

Racists violate the principle of equality by giving greater weight to the interests of members of their own race when there is a clash between their interests and the interests of those of another race. Sexists violate the principle of equality by favouring the interests of their own sex. Similarly, speciesists allow the interests of their own species to override the greater interests of members of other species. The pattern is identical in each case.

Most human beings are speciesists.... [O]rdinary human beings—not a few exceptionally cruel or heartless humans, but the overwhelming majority of humans—take an active part in, acquiesce in, and allow their taxes to pay for practices that require the sacrifice of the most important interests of members of other species in order to promote the most trivial interests of our own species....

DOWN ON THE FACTORY FARM

For most human beings, especially those in modern urban and suburban communities, the most direct form of contact with nonhuman animals is at mealtime: we eat them. This simple fact is the key to our attitudes to other animals, and also the key to what each one of us can do about changing these attitudes. The use and abuse of animals raised for food far exceeds, in sheer numbers of animals affected, any other kind of mistreatment. Over 100 million cows, pigs, and sheep are raised and slaughtered in the United States alone each year; and for poultry the figure is a staggering 5 billion. (That means that about eight thousand birds—mostly chickens—will have been slaughtered in the time it takes you to read this page.) It is here, on our dinner table and in our neighbourhood supermarket or butcher's shop, that we are brought into direct touch with the most extensive exploitation of other species that has ever existed.

In general, we are ignorant of the abuse of living creatures that lies behind the food we eat. Buying food in a store or restaurant is the culmination of a long process, of which all but the end product is delicately screened from our eyes. We buy our meat and poultry in neat plastic packages. It hardly bleeds. There is no reason to associate this package with a living, breathing, walking, suffering animal. The very words we use conceal its origins: we eat beef, not bull, steer, or cow, and pork, not pig—although for some reason we seem to find it easier to face the true nature of a leg of lamb. The term "meat" is itself deceptive. It originally meant any solid food, not necessarily the flesh of animals. This usage still lingers in an expression like "nut meat," which seems to imply a substitute for "flesh meat" but actually has an equally good claim to be called "meat" in its own right. By using the more general "meat" we avoid facing the fact that what we are eating is really flesh.

These verbal disguises are merely the top layer of a much deeper ignorance 10
of the origin of our food. Consider the images conjured up by the word "farm": a house; a barn; a flock of hens, overseen by a strutting rooster, scratching around the farmyard; a herd of cows being brought in from the fields for milking; and perhaps a sow rooting around in the orchard with a litter of squealing piglets running excitedly behind her.

Very few farms were ever as idyllic as that traditional image would have us believe. Yet we still think of a farm as a pleasant place, far removed from our own industrial, profit-conscious city life. Of those few who think about the lives of animals on farms, not many know much about modern methods of animal raising. Some people wonder whether animals are slaughtered painlessly, and anyone who has followed a truckload of cattle on the road will probably know that farm animals are transported in extremely crowded conditions; but not many suspect that transportation and slaughter are anything more than the brief and inevitable conclusion of a life of ease and contentment, a life that contains the natural pleasures of animal existence without the hardships that wild animals must endure in their struggle for survival.

These comfortable assumptions bear little relation to the realities of modern farming. For a start, farming is no longer controlled by simple country folk. During the last fifty years, large corporations and assembly-line methods of production have turned agriculture into agribusiness....

Broiler chickens are killed when they are seven weeks old (the natural lifespan of a chicken is about seven years). At the end of this brief period, the birds weigh between four and five pounds; yet they still may have as little as half a square foot of space per chicken—or less than the area of a sheet of standard typing paper. (In metric terms, this is 450 square centimetres for a hen weighing more than two kilos.) Under these conditions, when there is normal lighting, the stress of crowding and the absence of natural outlets for the birds' energies lead to outbreaks of fighting, with birds pecking at each other's feathers and sometimes killing and eating one another. Very dim lighting has been found to reduce such behaviour and so the birds are likely to live out their last weeks in near-darkness....

The sufferings of laying chickens begin early in life. The newly hatched chicks are sorted into males and females by a "chick-puller." Since the male chicks have no commercial value, they are discarded. Some companies gas the little birds, but often they are dumped alive into a plastic sack and allowed to suffocate under the weight of other chicks dumped on top of them. Others are ground up, while still alive, to be turned into feed for their sisters. At least 160 million birds are gassed, suffocated, or die this way every year in the United

States alone.[6] Just how many suffer each particular fate is impossible to tell, because no records are kept: the growers think of getting rid of male chicks as we think of putting out the trash.

Life for the female laying birds is longer, but this is scarcely a benefit....

In most egg factories the cages are stacked in tiers, with food and water troughs running along the rows filled automatically from a central supply. The cages have sloping wire floors. The slope—usually a gradient of one in five—makes it more difficult for the birds to stand comfortably, but it causes the eggs to roll to the front of the cage where they can easily be collected by hand or, in the more modern plants, carried by conveyor belt to a packing plant.

The wire floor also has an economic justification. The excrement drops through and can be allowed to pile up for many months until it is all removed in a single operation....

In the pig industry, in contrast to the broiler and egg industry, total confinement is not yet universal. But the trend is in that direction. A University of Missouri survey revealed that as long ago as 1979, 54 percent of all medium-sized producers and 63 percent of all large producers had total confinement facilities.[7] Increasingly, it is the large producers that dominate the industry. In 1987 William Haw, president of National Farms, Inc., said that "within ten years the hog business will be the same as the broiler chicken industry is now, with fewer than 100 operators of any significance."[8] It is the old story: small family farms are being pushed out of business by large factories, each "manufacturing" between 50,000 and 300,000 pigs a year. Tyson Foods, the largest broiler company in the world, slaughtering more than 8.5 million birds a week, has now entered the pig market. The company runs sixty-nine farrowing and nursery complexes and sends to slaughter more than 600,000 pigs per year.[9]

So most pigs now spend their entire lives indoors. They are born and suckled in a farrowing unit, raised initially in a nursery, and brought to slaughter weight in a growing-feeding unit. Unless they are to be used as breeders, they are sent to market at between five and six months of age weighing about 220 pounds.

The desire to cut labour costs has been one major reason for the shift to confinement. With an intensive system, one man is said to be able to handle

---

6 [Singer's note] USDA statistics indicate that in 1986 the population of commercial layers was 246 million. Assuming that the male/female hatching ratio is roughly 50 percent, and that each bird is replaced approximately every eighteen months, the above estimate is a minimum one.

7 [Singer's note] "Swine Production Management," Hubbard Milling Company, Mankato, Minnesota, 1984.

8 [Singer's note] William Robbins, "Down on the Superfarm: Bigger Share of Profits," *The New York Times*, August 4, 1987.

9 [Singer's note] *Feedstuffs*, January 6, 1986, p. 6.

the entire operation, thanks to automated feeding and slatted floors that allow the manure to drop through for easy disposal. Another saving, with this as with all other confinement systems, is that with less room to move about, the pig will burn up less of its food in "useless" exercise, and so can be expected to put on more weight for each pound of food consumed. In all of this, as one pig producer said, "What we are really trying to do is modify the animal's environment for maximum profit."[10] ...

The dairy cow, once seen peacefully, even idyllically, roaming the hills, is now a carefully monitored, fine-tuned milk machine. The bucolic picture of the dairy cow playing with her calf in the pasture is no part of commercial milk production. Many dairy cows are reared indoors. Some are kept in individual pens with only enough room to stand up and lie down. Their environment is completely controlled: they are fed calculated amounts of feed, temperatures are adjusted to maximize milk yield, and lighting is artificially set. Some farmers have found that a cycle of sixteen hours of light with only eight hours of darkness is conducive to greater output.

After her first calf is taken away, the cow's production cycle begins. She is milked twice, sometimes three times a day, for ten months. After the third month she will be made pregnant again. She will be milked until about six or eight weeks before her next calf is due, and then again as soon as the calf is removed. Usually this intense cycle of pregnancy and hyperlactation can last only about five years, after which the "spent" cow is sent to slaughter to become hamburger or dog food....

By comparison with chickens, pigs, veal calves, and dairy cows, beef cattle still see more of the great outdoors, but the time they have to do so has been diminished. Twenty years ago, cattle would have roamed for about two years. Now, the lucky ones who get to roam at all are rounded up after about six months to be "finished"—that is, to be brought to market weight and condition by being fed a richer diet than grass. For this purpose they are shipped long distances to feedlots. Here for six to eight months they eat corn and other cereals. Then they are sent for slaughter.

The growth of large feedlots has been the dominant trend in the cattle industry. Of the 34 million cattle slaughtered in 1987 in the U.S., 70 percent were sent for slaughter from feedlots. Large feedlots are now responsible for one third of the nation's beef. They are substantial commercial undertakings, often financed by oil companies or Wall Street money looking for tax concessions. Feedlots are profitable because cattle fatten more quickly on grain than on grass. Yet, like dairy cows, beef cattle do not have stomachs suited for the concentrated diet that they receive in feedlots. Often, in an effort to obtain more fibre than their feedlot diets provide, the cattle lick their own and

---

10 [Singer's note] *Hog Farm Management*, December 1975, p. 16.

each other's coats. The large amount of hair taken into the rumen may cause abscesses.[11] Diluting the grain with the roughage that cattle need and crave, however, would slow down their weight gain....

I have been concentrating on conditions in the United States and Britain. Readers in other countries may be inclined to believe that conditions in their own country are not so bad; but if they live in one of the industrialized nations (other than Sweden) they have no grounds for complacency. In most countries, conditions are much closer to those in the United States than to those recommended above.[12] ...

[Even where reforms have occurred, t]hey represent, to varying degrees, an enlightened and more humane form of speciesism, but speciesism nonetheless. In no country yet has a government body questioned the idea that the interests of animals count less than similar human interests. The issue is always whether there is "avoidable" suffering, and this means suffering that can be avoided while the same animal products are produced, at a cost that is not significantly higher than before. The unchallenged assumption is that humans may use animals for their own purposes, and they may raise and kill them to satisfy their preference for a diet containing animal flesh....

(1975, revised 2009)

Questions

1. Summarize the argument Singer makes in the first six paragraphs here. What are the strengths of the argument? Does it have any weaknesses?
2. What can you say about Singer's recitation of facts concerning the ways in which animals are treated under factory-farming conditions, and the effect these facts have on the reader? How might this information have been presented differently, and how would that alter the effect?
3. Why do you think Singer devotes considerably more space to the issue of animal suffering than to the issue of whether or not humans should eat other animals at all?
4. Singer bases his argument against speciesism on parallel arguments made against racism and sexism. Is this offensive to women and people of colour? Why or why not?

---

11 [Singer's note] "Is Pain the Price of Farm Efficiency?" *New Scientist*, October 13, 1973, p. 171.

12 *above* This paragraph follows a series of recommendations for reforms, which are not included in this excerpt.

AUDRE LORDE

POETRY IS NOT A LUXURY

Much of Black lesbian feminist poet, writer, and activist Audre Lorde's work combats patriarchy, racism, heterosexism, and classism, insisting upon the acknowledgment of differences among women and among people of colour. "[M]y poetry," she said, "comes from the intersection of me and my worlds." The following essay appeared in Chrysalis: A Magazine of Women's Culture, *which published the work of a large number of influential feminist writers and artists between 1977 and 1980. When the following essay was published, Lorde was the poetry editor for* Chrysalis; *she would later leave the magazine over disagreements regarding its treatment of the work of women of colour.*

The quality of light by which we scrutinize our lives has direct bearing upon the product which we live, and upon the changes which we hope to bring about through those lives. It is within this light that we form those ideas by which we pursue our magic and make it realized. This is poetry as illumination, for it is through poetry that we give name to those ideas which are—until the poem—nameless and formless, about to be birthed, but already felt. That distillation of experience from which true poetry springs births thought as dream births concept, as feeling births idea, as knowledge births (precedes) understanding.

As we learn to bear the intimacy of scrutiny and to flourish within it, as we learn to use the products of that scrutiny for power within our living, those fears which rule our lives and form our silences begin to lose their control over us.

For each of us as women, there is a dark place within, where hidden and growing our true spirit rises, "beautiful/and tough as chestnut/stanchions against (y)our nightmare of weakness/"[1] and of impotence.

1 [Lorde's note] From "Black Mother Woman," first published in *From a Land Where Other People Live* (Broadside Press, Detroit, 1973), and collected in *Chosen Poems: Old and New* (W.W. Norton and Company, New York, 1982) p. 53.

These places of possibility within ourselves are dark because they are ancient and hidden; they have survived and grown strong through that darkness. Within these deep places, each one of us holds an incredible reserve of creativity and power, of unexamined and unrecorded emotion and feeling. The woman's place of power within each of us is neither white nor surface; it is dark, it is ancient, and it is deep.

5 When we view living in the european mode only as a problem to be solved, we rely solely upon our ideas to make us free, for these were what the white fathers told us were precious.

But as we come more into touch with our own ancient, noneuropean consciousness of living as a situation to be experienced and interacted with, we learn more and more to cherish our feelings, and to respect those hidden sources of our power from where true knowledge and, therefore, lasting action comes.

At this point in time, I believe that women carry within ourselves the possibility for fusion of these two approaches so necessary for survival, and we come closest to this combination in our poetry. I speak here of poetry as a revelatory distillation of experience, not the sterile word play that, too often, the white fathers distorted the word *poetry* to mean—in order to cover their desperate wish for imagination without insight.

For women, then, poetry is not a luxury. It is a vital necessity of our existence. It forms the quality of the light within which we predicate our hopes and dreams toward survival and change, first made into language, then into idea, then into more tangible action. Poetry is the way we help give name to the nameless so it can be thought. The farthest horizons of our hopes and fears are cobbled by our poems, carved from the rock experiences of our daily lives.

As they become known to and accepted by us, our feelings and the honest exploration of them become sanctuaries and fortresses and spawning grounds for the most radical and daring of ideas. They become a safe-house for that difference so necessary to change and the conceptualization of any meaningful action. Right now, I could name at least ten ideas I would have found intolerable or incomprehensible and frightening, except as they came after dreams and poems. This is not idle fantasy, but a disciplined attention to the true meaning of "it feels right to me." We can train ourselves to respect our feelings and to transpose them into a language so they can be shared. And where that language does not yet exist, it is our poetry which helps to fashion it. Poetry is not only dream and vision; it is the skeleton architecture of our lives. It lays the foundations for a future of change, a bridge across our fears of what has never been before.

10 Possibility is neither forever nor instant. It is not easy to sustain belief in its efficacy. We can sometimes work long and hard to establish one beachhead*

of real resistance to the deaths we are expected to live, only to have that beachhead assaulted or threatened by those canards* we have been socialized to fear, or by the withdrawal of those approvals that we have been warned to seek for safety. Women see ourselves diminished or softened by the falsely benign accusations of childishness, of nonuniversality, of changeability, of sensuality. And who asks the question: Am I altering your aura, your ideas, your dreams, or am I merely moving you to temporary and reactive action? And even though the latter is no mean task, it is one that must be seen within the context of a need for true alteration of the very foundations of our lives.

The white fathers told us: I think, therefore I am.[2] The Black mother within each of us—the poet—whispers in our dreams: I feel, therefore I can be free. Poetry coins the language to express and charter this revolutionary demand, the implementation of that freedom. However, experience has taught us that the action in the now is also necessary, always. Our children cannot dream unless they live, they cannot live unless they are nourished, and who else will feed them the real food without which their dreams will be no different from ours? "If you want us to change the world someday, we at least have to live long enough to grow up!" shouts the child.

Sometimes we drug ourselves with dreams of new ideas. The head will save us. The brain alone will set us free. But there are no new ideas still waiting in the wings to save us as women, as human. There are only old and forgotten ones, new combinations, extrapolations and recognitions from within ourselves—along with the renewed courage to try them out. And we must constantly encourage ourselves and each other to attempt the heretical actions that our dreams imply, and so many of our old ideas disparage. In the forefront of our move toward change, there is only poetry to hint at possibility made real. Our poems formulate the implications of ourselves, what we feel within and dare make real (or bring action into accordance with), our fears, our hopes, our most cherished terrors.

For within living structures defined by profit, by linear power, by institutional dehumanization, our feelings were not meant to survive. Kept around as unavoidable adjuncts or pleasant pastimes, feelings were expected to kneel to thought as women were expected to kneel to men. But women have survived. As poets. And there are no new pains. We have felt them all already. We have hidden that fact in the same place where we have hidden our power. They surface in our dreams, and it is our dreams that point the way to freedom. Those

2 *I think, therefore I am* English translation of "je pense, donc je suis" (also often expressed in Latin as "cogito, ergo sum"), a statement made by the French philosopher René Descartes in his 1637 *Discourse on Method*. Descartes viewed this argument as foundational to the construction of all human knowledge— and his view became highly influential among subsequent Western philosophers.

dreams are made realizable through our poems that give us the strength and courage to see, to feel, to speak, and to dare.

If what we need to dream, to move our spirits most deeply and directly toward and through promise, is discounted as a luxury, then we give up the core—the fountain—of our power, our womanness; we give up the future of our worlds.

15 For there are no new ideas. There are only new ways of making them felt—of examining what those ideas feel like being lived on Sunday morning at 7 A.M., after brunch, during wild love, making war, giving birth, mourning our dead—while we suffer the old longings, battle the old warnings and fears of being silent and impotent and alone, while we taste new possibilities and strengths.

(1977, revised 1984)

Questions

1. According to Lorde, what is poetry's relationship to thinking? To feeling?
2. In this essay Lorde capitalizes "Black" but not "european." What effect does this have?
3. Of the claims Lorde makes in this essay, which (if any) apply only to women, and which (if any) apply more broadly?
4. What is meant, in the context of this essay, by the claim "there are no new ideas" (paragraphs 12 and 15)? Argue for or against this claim.
5. Lorde was a poet as well as a theorist. Identify a place in this essay where the writing displays characteristics of poetry.

THE USES OF ANGER: WOMEN RESPONDING TO RACISM

The theme of the 1981 National Women's Studies Association Conference, where Lorde delivered the following keynote address, was "Women Respond to Racism." The conference, which was predominantly white—about 300 women of colour attended, out of about 1400 participants—offered a series of consciousness-raising groups for people of shared background: an extensive range of choices for white women, from "white/immigrant" to "white/working-class," and only one group for all women of colour. There was a great deal of tension regarding the failure both of the conference and of mainstream feminism in general to adequately address racial differences and the relationship between racial and patriarchal oppression.

Racism. The belief in the inherent superiority of one race over all others and thereby the right to dominance, manifest and implied.

Women respond to racism. My response to racism is anger. I have lived with that anger, on that anger, ignoring it, feeding upon it, learning to use it before it laid my visions to waste, for most of my life. Once I did it in silence, afraid of the weight. My fear of that anger taught me nothing. Your fear of that anger will teach you nothing, also.

Women responding to racism means women responding to anger, the anger of exclusion, of unquestioned privilege, of racial distortions, of silence, ill-use, stereotyping, defensiveness, misnaming, betrayal, and co-optation.*

My anger is a response to racist attitudes and to the actions and presumptions that arise out of those attitudes. If your dealings with other women reflect those attitudes, then my anger and your attendant fears are spotlights that can be used for growth in the same way I have used learning to express anger for my growth. But for corrective surgery, not guilt. Guilt and defensiveness are bricks in a wall against which we all flounder; they serve none of our futures.

Because I do not want this to become a theoretical discussion, I am going 5
to give a few examples of interchanges between women that illustrate these points. In the interest of time, I am going to cut them short. I want you to know that there were many more.

For example:

• I speak out of a direct and particular anger at a particular academic conference, and a white woman says, "Tell me how you feel but don't say it too harshly or I cannot hear you." But is it my manner that keeps her from hearing, or the threat of a message that her life may change?

• The Women's Studies Program of a southern university invites a Black woman to read following a week-long forum on Black and white women. "What has this week given to you?" I ask. The most vocal white woman says, "I think I've gotten a lot. I feel Black women really understand me a lot better now; they have a better idea of where I'm coming from." As if understanding her lay at the core of the racist problem.

• After fifteen years of a women's movement which professes to address the life concerns and possible futures of all women, I still hear, on campus after campus, "How can we address the issues of racism? No women of Colour attended." Or, the other side of that statement, "We have no one in our department equipped to teach their work." In other words, racism is a Black women's problem, a problem of women of Colour, and only we can discuss it.

• After I have read from my work entitled "Poems for Women in Rage"[1] a white woman asks me, "Are you going to do anything with how we can deal directly with *our* anger? I feel it's so important." I ask, "How do you use *your* rage?" And then I have to turn away from the blank look in her eyes, before she can invite me to participate in her own annihilation. I do not exist to feel her anger for her.

• White women are beginning to examine their relationships to Black women, yet often I hear them wanting only to deal with the little coloured children across the roads of childhood, the beloved nursemaid, the occasional second-grade classmate—those tender memories of what was once mysterious and intriguing or neutral. You avoid the childhood assumptions formed by the raucous laughter at Rastus and Alfalfa,[2] the acute message of your mommy's handkerchief spread upon the park bench because I had just been sitting there, the indelible and dehumanizing portraits of Amos 'n Andy[3] and your daddy's humorous bedtime stories.

---

1 [Lorde's note] One poem from this series is included in *Chosen Poems: Old and New* (W.W. Norton and Company, New York, 1982), pp. 105–108.

2 *Rastus* Stock character of a cheerful African American man that appeared in minstrel shows and other racist works of popular culture in the late nineteenth and early twentieth centuries; *Alfalfa* Character in the series of films *Our Gang* (1922–44), which were later shown as the television series *Little Rascals*. Alfalfa was white, but the show was groundbreaking in its portrayal of African American and white children playing together. It has also, however, been heavily criticized for stereotypical treatment of its African American characters.

3 *Amos 'n Andy* Mid-twentieth-century radio show that also became a television series. On the radio, the show's white creators, Freeman Gosden and Charles Correll, voiced most of the characters, including the two African American main characters.

I wheel my two-year-old daughter in a shopping cart through a supermarket in Eastchester[4] in 1967, and a little white girl riding past in her mother's cart calls out excitedly, "Oh look, Mommy, a baby maid!" And your mother shushes you, but she does not correct you. And so fifteen years later, at a conference on racism, you can still find that story humorous. But I hear your laughter is full of terror and dis-ease.

• A white academic welcomes the appearance of a collection by non-Black women of Colour.[5] "It allows me to deal with racism without dealing with the harshness of Black women," she says to me.

• At an international cultural gathering of women, a well-known white american woman poet interrupts the reading of the work of women of Colour to read her own poem, and then dashes off to an "important panel."

If women in the academy truly want a dialogue about racism, it will require recognizing the needs and the living contexts of other women. When an academic woman says, "I can't afford it," she may mean she is making a choice about how to spend her available money. But when a woman on welfare says, "I can't afford it," she means she is surviving on an amount of money that was barely subsistence in 1972, and she often does not have enough to eat. Yet the National Women's Studies Association here in 1981 holds a conference in which it commits itself to responding to racism, yet refuses to waive the registration fee for poor women and women of Colour who wished to present and conduct workshops. This has made it impossible for many women of Colour—for instance, Wilmette Brown, of Black Women for Wages for Housework—to participate in this conference. Is this to be merely another case of the academy discussing life within the closed circuits of the academy?

To the white women present who recognize these attitudes as familiar, but most of all, to all my sisters of Colour who live and survive thousands of such encounters—to my sisters of Colour who like me still tremble their rage under harness, or who sometimes question the expression of our rage as useless and disruptive (the two most popular accusations)—I want to speak about anger, my anger, and what I have learned from my travels through its dominions.

Everything can be used / except what is wasteful / (you will need / to remember this when you are accused of destruction.)[6]

4 *Eastchester* Town in Westchester County on Long Island in the state of New York.

5 [Lorde's note] *This Bridge Called My Back: Writings by Radical Women of Color* edited by Cherríe Moraga and Gloria E. Anzaldúa (Kitchen Table: Women of Color Press, New York, 1984), first published in 1981.

6 [Lorde's note] From "For Each of You," first published in *From A Land Where Other People Live* (Broadside Press, Detroit, 1973), and collected in *Chosen Poems: Old and New* (W.W. Norton and Company, New York, 1982), p. 42.

Every woman has a well-stocked arsenal of anger potentially useful against those oppressions, personal and institutional, which brought that anger into being. Focused with precision it can become a powerful source of energy serving progress and change. And when I speak of change, I do not mean a simple switch of positions or a temporary lessening of tensions, nor the ability to smile or feel good. I am speaking of a basic and radical alteration in all those assumptions underlining our lives.

I have seen situations where white women hear a racist remark, resent what has been said, become filled with fury, and remain silent because they are afraid. That unexpressed anger lies within them like an undetonated device, usually to be hurled at the first woman of Colour who talks about racism.

But anger expressed and translated into action in the service of our vision and our future is a liberating and strengthening act of clarification, for it is in the painful process of this translation that we identify who are our allies with whom we have grave differences, and who are our genuine enemies.

Anger is loaded with information and energy. When I speak of women of Colour, I do not only mean Black women. The woman of Colour who is not Black and who charges me with rendering her invisible by assuming that her struggles with racism are identical with my own has something to tell me that I had better learn from, lest we both waste ourselves fighting the truths between us. If I participate, knowingly or otherwise, in my sister's oppression and she calls me on it, to answer her anger with my own only blankets the substance of our exchange with reaction. It wastes energy. And yes, it is very difficult to stand still and to listen to another woman's voice delineate an agony I do not share, or even one to which I myself have participated.

In this place we speak removed from the more blatant reminders of our embattlement as women. This need not blind us to the size and complexities of the forces mounting against us and all that is most human within our environment. We are not here as women examining racism in a political and social vacuum. We operate in the teeth of a system for which racism and sexism are primary, established, and necessary props of profit. Women responding to racism is a topic so dangerous that when the local media attempt to discredit this conference they choose to focus upon the provision of lesbian housing as a diversionary device[7]—as if the Hartford *Courant* dare not mention the topic chosen for discussion here, racism, lest it become apparent that women are in fact attempting to examine and to alter all the repressive conditions of our lives.

---

7 *the provision ... device* A 19 May 1981 article in the *Hartford Courant* discussed the conference; its headline was "Lesbian Housing Available for Women's Conference at UConn."

Mainstream communication does not want women, particularly white women, responding to racism. It wants racism to be accepted as an immutable given in the fabric of your existence, like eveningtime or the common cold.

So we are working in a context of opposition and threat, the cause of which is certainly not the angers which lie between us, but rather that virulent hatred levelled against all women, people of Colour, lesbians and gay men, poor people—against all of us who are seeking to examine the particulars of our lives as we resist our oppressions, moving toward coalition and effective action.

Any discussion among women about racism must include the recognition 25
and the use of anger. It must be direct and creative because it is crucial. We cannot allow our fear of anger to deflect us nor seduce us into settling for anything less than the hard work of excavating honesty; we must be quite serious about the choice of this topic and the angers entwined within it because, rest assured, our opponents are quite serious about their hatred of us and of what we are trying to do here.

And while we scrutinize the often painful face of each other's anger, please remember that it is not our anger which makes me caution you to lock your doors at night and not to wander the streets of Hartford alone. It is the hatred which lurks in those streets, that urge to destroy us all if we truly work for change rather than merely indulge in our academic rhetoric.

This hatred and our anger are very different. Hatred is the fury of those who do not share our goals, and its object is death and destruction. Anger is the grief of distortions between peers, and its object is change. But our time is getting shorter. We have been raised to view any difference other than sex as a reason for destruction, and for Black women and white women to face each other's angers without denial or immobility or silence or guilt is in itself a heretical and generative* idea. It implies peers meeting upon a common basis to examine difference, and to alter those distortions which history has created around our difference. For it is those distortions which separate us. And we must ask ourselves: Who profits from all this?

Women of Colour in america have grown up within a symphony of anger, at being silenced, at being unchosen, at knowing that when we survive, it is in spite of a world that takes for granted our lack of humanness, and which hates our very existence outside of its service. And I say *symphony* rather than *cacophony* because we have had to learn to orchestrate those furies so that they do not tear us apart. We have had to learn to move through them and use them for strength and force and insight within our daily lives. Those of us who did not learn this difficult lesson did not survive. And part of my anger is always libation* for my fallen sisters.

Anger is an appropriate reaction to racist attitudes, as is fury when the actions arising from those attitudes do not change. To those women here who fear the anger of women of Colour more than their own unscrutinized racist attitudes, I ask: Is the anger of women of Colour more threatening than the woman-hatred that tinges all aspects of our lives?

30 It is not the anger of other women that will destroy us but our refusals to stand still, to listen to its rhythms, to learn within it, to move beyond the manner of presentation to the substance, to tap that anger as an important source of empowerment.

I cannot hide my anger to spare you guilt, nor hurt feelings, nor answering anger; for to do so insults and trivializes all our efforts. Guilt is not a response to anger; it is a response to one's own actions or lack of action. If it leads to change then it can be useful, since it is then no longer guilt but the beginning of knowledge. Yet all too often, guilt is just another name for impotence, for defensiveness destructive of communication; it becomes a device to protect ignorance and the continuation of things the way they are, the ultimate protection for changelessness.

Most women have not developed tools for facing anger constructively. CR[8] groups in the past, largely white, dealt with how to express anger, usually at the world of men. And these groups were made up of white women who shared the terms of their oppressions. There was usually little attempt to articulate the genuine differences between women, such as those of race, colour, age, class, and sexual identity. There was no apparent need at that time to examine the contradictions of self, woman as oppressor. There was work on expressing anger, but very little on anger directed against each other. No tools were developed to deal with other women's anger except to avoid it, deflect it, or flee from it under a blanket of guilt.

I have no creative use for guilt, yours or my own. Guilt is only another way of avoiding informed action, of buying time out of the pressing need to make clear choices, out of the approaching storm that can feed the earth as well as bend the trees. If I speak to you in anger, at least I have spoken to you: I have not put a gun to your head and shot you down in the street; I have not looked at your bleeding sister's body and asked, "What did she do to deserve it?" This was the reaction of two white women to Mary Church Terrell's[9] telling of the lynching of a pregnant Black woman whose baby was then torn from her body. That was in 1921, and Alice Paul had just refused to publicly endorse

---

8 *CR* Consciousness-raising.

9 *Mary Church Terrell* Journalist, educator, and activist for civil rights and women's rights (1863–1954). She was a founding member of the National Association for the Advancement of Colored People and the first African American woman to serve on a city schoolboard.

the enforcement of the Nineteenth Amendment for all women—by refusing to endorse the inclusion of women of Colour, although we had worked to help bring about that amendment.[10]

The angers between women will not kill us if we can articulate them with precision, if we listen to the content of what is said with at least as much intensity as we defend ourselves from the manner of saying. When we turn from anger we turn from insight, saying we will accept only the designs already known, those deadly and safely familiar. I have tried to learn my anger's usefulness to me, as well as its limitations.

For women raised to fear, too often anger threatens annihilation. In the male construct of brute force, we were taught that our lives depended upon the good will of patriarchal power. The anger of others was to be avoided at all costs because there was nothing to be learned from it but pain, a judgment that we had been bad girls, come up lacking, not done what we were supposed to do. And if we accept our powerlessness, then of course any anger can destroy us.

But the strength of women lies in recognizing differences between us as creative, and in standing to those distortions which we inherited without blame, but which are now ours to alter. The angers of women can transform difference through insight into power. For anger between peers births change, not destruction, and the discomfort and sense of loss it often causes is not fatal, but a sign of growth.

My response to racism is anger. That anger has eaten clefts into my living only when it remained unspoken, useless to anyone. It has also served me in classrooms without light or learning, where the work and history of Black women was less than a vapour. It has served me as fire in the ice zone of uncomprehending eyes of white women who see in my experience and the experience of my people only new reasons for fear or guilt. And my anger is no excuse for not dealing with your blindness, no reason to withdraw from the results of your own actions.

When women of Colour speak out of the anger that laces so many of our contacts with white women, we are often told that we are "creating a mood of hopelessness," "preventing white women from getting past guilt," or "standing

---

10 *Alice Paul* Women's rights activist (1885–1977) and leader of the campaign that resulted in the Nineteenth Amendment (1920), which gave women the right to vote; *I have not ... amendment* Terrell asked Paul to make a statement in favour of enforcing the Nineteenth Amendment universally; many measures had been taken in Southern states to make it more difficult for African American women to vote. Paul refused to do so, and Terrell then made a speech to the Resolutions Committee of the Woman's Party requesting backing; in the course of this speech she described the lynching of a pregnant woman. When one white woman asked why the lynching had occurred, another added "She [the victim] did something, of course."

in the way of trusting communication and action." All these quotes come directly from letters to me from members of this organization within the last two years. One woman wrote, "Because you are Black and Lesbian, you seem to speak with the moral authority of suffering."[11] Yes, I am Black and Lesbian, and what you hear in my voice is fury, not suffering. Anger, not moral authority. There is a difference.

To turn aside from the anger of Black women with excuses or the pretexts of intimidation is to award no one power—it is merely another way of preserving racial blindness, the power of unaddressed privilege, unbreached, intact. Guilt is only another form of objectification. Oppressed peoples are always being asked to stretch a little more, to bridge the gap between blindness and humanity. Black women are expected to use our anger only in the service of other people's salvation or learning. But that time is over. My anger has meant pain to me but it has also meant survival, and before I give it up I'm going to be sure that there is something at least as powerful to replace it on the road to clarity.

What woman here is so enamoured of her own oppression that she cannot see her heelprint upon another woman's face? What woman's terms of oppression have become precious and necessary to her as a ticket into the fold of the righteous, away from the cold winds of self-scrutiny?

I am a lesbian woman of Colour whose children eat regularly because I work in a university. If their full bellies make me fail to recognize my commonality with a woman of Colour whose children do not eat because she cannot find work, or who has no children because her insides are rotted from home abortions and sterilization; if I fail to recognize the lesbian who chooses not to have children, the woman who remains closeted because her homophobic community is her only life support, the woman who chooses silence instead of another death, the woman who is terrified lest my anger trigger the explosion of hers; if I fail to recognize them as other faces of myself, then I am contributing not only to each of their oppressions but also to my own, and the anger which stands between us then must be used for clarity and mutual empowerment, not for evasion by guilt or for further separation. I am not free while any woman is unfree, even when her shackles are very different from my own. And I am not free as long as one person of Colour remains chained. Nor is any one of you.

I speak here as a woman of Colour who is not bent upon destruction, but upon survival. No woman is responsible for altering the psyche of her oppressor,

---

11 *Because ... suffering* Lorde quotes from a letter she received from the organizers of a 1979 conference in which she had participated. In Lorde's view, the conference had failed to adequately address matters of race, class, and sexual orientation, and she had pointed this out in a now-famous speech, "The Master's Tools Will Never Dismantle the Master's House," made during the conference.

even when that psyche is embodied in another woman. I have suckled the wolf's lip of anger and I have used it for illumination, laughter, protection, fire in places where there was no light, no food, no sisters, no quarter.* We are not goddesses or matriarchs or edifices of divine forgiveness; we are not fiery fingers of judgment or instruments of flagellation; we are women forced back always upon our woman's power. We have learned to use anger as we have learned to use the dead flesh of animals, and bruised, battered, and changing, we have survived and grown and, in Angela Wilson's words, we *are* moving on. With or without uncoloured women. We use whatever strengths we have fought for, including anger, to help define and fashion a world where all our sisters can grow, where our children can love, and where the power of touching and meeting another woman's difference and wonder will eventually transcend the need for destruction.

For it is not the anger of Black women which is dripping down over this globe like a diseased liquid. It is not my anger that launches rockets, spends over sixty thousand dollars a second on missiles and other agents of war and death, slaughters children in cities, stockpiles nerve gas and chemical bombs, sodomizes our daughters and our earth. It is not the anger of Black women which corrodes into blind, dehumanizing power, bent upon the annihilation of us all unless we meet it with what we have, our power to examine and to redefine the terms upon which we will live and work; our power to envision and to reconstruct, anger by painful anger, stone upon heavy stone, a future of pollinating difference and the earth to support our choices.

We welcome all women who can meet us, face to face, beyond objectification and beyond guilt.

(1981, revised 1984)

Questions

1. How, according to Lorde, can anger be useful?
2. Lorde's speech includes a listing of examples of racism she encountered within academia and/or the feminist movement. Give an example of racism in your own academic experience.
3. What issues of injustice cause you to experience the most anger? To what extent do you find this anger productive?

ADRIENNE RICH

from COMPULSORY HETEROSEXUALITY AND LESBIAN EXISTENCE

Lesbian feminism emerged in the late 1960s and 70s, as lesbians critiqued mainstream feminism for disregarding their concerns, many arguing that lesbian relationships posed an important challenge to patriarchal norms that would help to liberate all women regardless of sexual orientation. Some mainstream feminists responded negatively to the movement—in 1969 Betty Friedan, president of the National Organization for Women, famously referred to it as the "lavender menace"—and some lesbian feminists advocated separating from mainstream feminism altogether and forming fully woman-identified communities. Despite heterosexism within mainstream feminism, lesbian feminism exerted a strong influence on feminist thought in general in the 1970s and 80s. "Compulsory Heterosexuality and Lesbian Existence," by poet, critic, and theorist Adrienne Rich, was a particularly influential contribution to the movement. In her foreword to the 50-page article, Rich writes that "[i]t was written in part to challenge the erasure of lesbian existence from so much of scholarly feminist literature ... and to sketch, at least, some bridge over the gap between lesbian and feminist."

I

Biologically men have only one innate orientation—a sexual one that draws them to women,—while women have two innate orientations, sexual toward men and reproductive toward their young.[1]

I was a woman terribly vulnerable, critical, using femaleness as a sort of standard or yardstick to measure and discard men. Yes—something

1 [Rich's note] Alice Rossi, "Children and Work in the Lives of Women," paper delivered at the University of Arizona, Tucson, February 1976.

> like that. I was an Anna who invited defeat from men without ever being conscious of it. (But I am conscious of it. And being conscious of it means I shall leave it all behind me and become—but what?) I was stuck fast in an emotion common to women of our time, that can turn them bitter, or Lesbian, or solitary. Yes, that Anna during that time was ...
>
> [Another blank line across the page:][2]

The bias of compulsory heterosexuality, through which lesbian experience is perceived on a scale ranging from deviant to abhorrent or simply rendered invisible, could be illustrated from many texts other than the two just preceding. The assumption made by Rossi, that women are "innately" sexually oriented only toward men, and that made by Lessing, that the lesbian is simply acting out of her bitterness toward men, are by no means theirs alone; these assumptions are widely current in literature and in the social sciences.

I am concerned here with two other matters as well: first, how and why women's choice of women as passionate comrades, life partners, co-workers, lovers, community has been crushed, invalidated, forced into hiding and disguise; and second, the virtual or total neglect of lesbian existence in a wide range of writings, including feminist scholarship. Obviously there is a connection here. I believe that much feminist theory and criticism is stranded on this shoal.

My organizing impulse is the belief that it is not enough for feminist thought that specifically lesbian texts exist. Any theory or cultural/political creation that treats lesbian existence as a marginal or less "natural" phenomenon, as mere "sexual preference,"* or as the mirror image of either heterosexual or male homosexual relations is profoundly weakened thereby, whatever its other contributions. Feminist theory can no longer afford merely to voice a toleration of "lesbianism" as an "alternative life style"* or make token allusion to lesbians. A feminist critique of compulsory heterosexual orientation for women is long overdue. In this exploratory paper, I shall try to show why....

... In *The Mermaid and the Minotaur: Sexual Arrangements and the Human Malaise*, Dorothy Dinnerstein makes an impassioned argument for the sharing of parenting between women and men and for an end to what she perceives as the male/female symbiosis of "gender arrangements," which she feels are leading the species further and further into violence and self-extinction. Apart from other problems that I have with this book ... I find Dinnerstein's view of the relations between women and men as "a collaboration to keep history mad" utterly

---

2 [Rich's note] Doris Lessing, *The Golden Notebook*, 1962 (New York: Bantam, 1977), p. 480.

ahistorical.* She means by this a collaboration to perpetuate social relations which are hostile, exploitative, and destructive to life itself. She sees women and men as equal partners in the making of "sexual arrangements," seemingly unaware of the repeated struggles of women to resist oppression (their own and that of others) and to change their condition. She ignores, specifically, the history of women who—as witches, *femmes seules*,[3] marriage resisters, spinsters, autonomous widows, and/or lesbians—have managed on varying levels *not* to collaborate. It is this history, precisely, from which feminists have so much to learn and on which there is overall such blanketing silence. Dinnerstein acknowledges at the end of her book that "female separatism," though "on a large scale and in the long run widely impractical," has something to teach us: "Separate, women could in principle set out to learn from scratch—undeflected by the opportunities to evade this task that men's presence has so far offered—what intact self-creative humanness is."[4] Phrases like "intact self-creative humanness" obscure the question of what the many forms of female separatism have actually been addressing. The fact is that women in every culture and throughout history *have* undertaken the task of independent, nonheterosexual, woman-connected existence, to the extent made possible by their context, often in the belief that they were the "only ones" ever to have done so. They have undertaken it even though few women have been in an economic position to resist marriage altogether, and even though attacks against unmarried women have ranged from aspersion* and mockery to deliberate gynocide,[5] including the burning and torturing of millions of widows and spinsters during the witch persecutions of the fifteenth, sixteenth, and seventeenth centuries in Europe.

5 Nancy Chodorow does come close to the edge of an acknowledgment of lesbian existence. Like Dinnerstein, Chodorow believes that the fact that women, and women only, are responsible for child care in the sexual division of labour has led to an entire social organization of gender inequality, and that men as well as women must become primary carers for children if that inequality is to change. In the process of examining, from a psychoanalytic perspective, how mothering by women affects the psychological development of girl and boy children, she offers documentation that men are "emotionally secondary" in women's lives, that "women have a richer, ongoing inner world to fall back on ... men do not become as emotionally important to women as

---

3 *femmes seules* In contrast to a married woman—defined in English common law as "feme covert"—a feme sole (single woman) could own property, keep her own money, and enter into legal agreements on her own.

4 [Rich's note] [Dorothy Dinnerstein, *The Mermaid and the Minotaur: Sexual Arrangements and the Human Malaise* (New York: Harper & Row, 1976)], p. 272.

5 *gynocide* Killing of women, especially with a political or cultural motivation.

women do to men."[6] ... Chodorow concludes that because many women have women as mothers, "the mother remains a primary internal object [*sic*] to the girl, so that heterosexual relationships are on the model of the nonexclusive, second relationship for her, whereas for the boy they re-create an exclusive, primary relationship." According to Chodorow, women "have learned to deny the limitations of masculine lovers for both psychological and practical reasons."[7]

But the practical reasons (like witch burnings, male control of law, theology, and science, or economic nonviablity within the sexual division of labour) are glossed over. Chodorow's account barely glances at the constraints and sanctions which historically have enforced or ensured the coupling of women with men and obstructed or penalized women's coupling or allying in independent groups with other women. She dismisses lesbian existence with the comment that "lesbian relationships do tend to re-create mother-daughter emotions and connections, but most women are heterosexual" (implied: more mature, having developed beyond the mother-daughter connection?). She then adds: "This heterosexual preference and taboos on homosexuality, in addition to objective economic dependence on men, make the option of primary sexual bonds with other women unlikely—though more prevalent in recent years."[8] The significance of that qualification seems irresistible, but Chodorow does not explore it further. Is she saying that lesbian existence has become more *visible* in recent years (in certain groups), that economic and other pressures have changed (under capitalism, socialism, or both), and that consequently more women are rejecting the heterosexual "choice"? She argues that women want children because their heterosexual relationships lack richness and intensity, that in having a child a woman seeks to re-create her own intense relationship with her mother. It seems to me that on the basis of her own findings, Chodorow leads us implicitly to conclude that heterosexuality is *not* a "preference" for women, that, for one thing, it fragments the erotic from the emotional in a way that women find impoverishing and painful. Yet her book participates in mandating it. Neglecting the covert socializations and the overt forces which have channelled women into marriage and heterosexual romance, pressures ranging from the selling of daughters to the silences of literature to the images of the television screen, she, like Dinnerstein, is stuck with trying to reform a man-made institution—compulsory heterosexuality—as if, despite profound emotional impulses and complementarities drawing women toward

6 [Rich's note] [Nancy Chodorow, *The Reproduction of Mothering* (Berkeley: University of California Press, 1978)], pp. 197–198.

7 [Rich's note] *Ibid.*, pp. 198–199.

8 [Rich's note] *Ibid.*., p. 200.

women, there is a mystical/biological heterosexual inclination, a "preference" or "choice" which draws women toward men.

Moreover, it is understood that this "preference" does not need to be explained unless through the tortuous theory of the female Oedipus complex[9] or the necessity for species reproduction. It is lesbian sexuality which (usually, and incorrectly, "included" under male homosexuality) is seen as requiring explanation. This assumption of female heterosexuality seems to me in itself remarkable: it is an enormous assumption to have glided so silently into the foundations of our thought....

... I am suggesting that heterosexuality, like motherhood, needs to be recognized and studied as a *political institution*—even, or especially, by those individuals who feel they are, in their personal experience, the precursors of a new social relation between the sexes.

II

If women are the earliest sources of emotional caring and physical nurture for both female and male children, it would seem logical, from a feminist perspective at least, to pose the following questions: whether the search for love and tenderness in both sexes does not originally lead toward women; *why in fact women would ever redirect that search*; why species survival, the means of impregnation, and emotional/erotic relationships should ever have become so rigidly identified with each other; and why such violent strictures should be found necessary to enforce women's total emotional, erotic loyalty and subservience to men. I doubt that enough feminist scholars and theorists have taken the pains to acknowledge the societal forces which wrench women's emotional and erotic energies away from themselves and other women and from woman-identified values. These forces, as I shall try to show, range from literal physical enslavement to disguising and distorting of possible options....

10 In her essay "The Origin of the Family," Kathleen Gough lists eight characteristics of male power in archaic and contemporary societies which I would

---

9 *female Oedipus complex* Stage of psychological development posited by Sigmund Freud and named for the title character of the ancient Greek tragedy *Oedipus the King*, who learns that he has unknowingly murdered his father and married his mother. Freud claimed that young boys desire their mothers and want to kill their fathers, whom they view as sexual rivals; the resolution of this complex of desires is, he argued, an important stage in a child's maturation. Freud later claimed that girls experience a "feminine" or "negative" version of the complex in which they desire their mothers but realize that, without a penis, they are unable to possess their mothers sexually; in a healthy resolution of this complex, according to Freud, desire is then redirected toward the father, and then toward men in general.

like to use as a framework: "men's ability to deny women sexuality or to force it upon them; to command or exploit their labour to control their produce; to control or rob them of their children; to confine them physically and prevent their movement; to use them as objects in male transactions; to cramp their creativeness; or to withhold from them large areas of the society's knowledge and cultural attainments."[10] (Gough does not perceive these power characteristics as specifically enforcing heterosexuality, only as producing sexual inequality.) Below, Gough's words appear in italics; the elaboration of each of her categories, in brackets, is my own.

Characteristics of male power include *the power of men*

1. *to deny women* [their own] *sexuality*—[by means of clitoridectomy and infibulation;[11] chastity belts; punishment, including death, for female adultery; punishment, including death, for lesbian sexuality; psychoanalytic denial of the clitoris;[12] strictures against masturbation; denial of maternal and postmenopausal sensuality; unnecessary hysterectomy; pseudolesbian images in the media and literature;* closing of archives and destruction of documents relating to lesbian existence]
2. *or to force it* [male sexuality] *upon them*—[by means of rape (including marital rape*) and wife beating; father-daughter, brother-sister incest; the socialization of women to feel that male sexual "drive" amounts to a right;[13] idealization of heterosexual romance in art, literature, the media, advertising, etc.; child marriage; arranged marriage; prostitution; the harem; psychoanalytic doctrines of frigidity and vaginal orgasm;[14] pornographic depictions of women responding pleasurably to sexual violence and humiliation (a subliminal message being that sadistic heterosexuality is more "normal" than sensuality between women)]

---

10 [Rich's note] Kathleen Gough, "The Origin of the Family," in *Toward an Anthropology of Women*, ed. Rayna [Rapp] Reiter (New York: Monthly Review Press, 1975), pp. 69–70.

11 *clitoridectomy* Removal of the clitoris, a type of female genital mutilation; *infibulation* Form of female genital mutilation in which, in addition to removal of the clitoris, external genitalia are cut off and the vaginal opening is partially closed with either stitching or intentional scarring.

12 *psychoanalytic ... clitoris* Freud and his followers tended to view the clitoris as inferior to the penis, and Freud described focus on clitoral pleasure as an immature stage of sexual development.

13 [Rich's note] [Kathleen Barry, *Female Sexual Slavery* (Englewood Cliffs, N.J.: Prentice-Hall, Inc., 1979)], pp. 216–219.

14 *psychoanalytic ... orgasm* Freud claimed that a sexually mature woman should experience "vaginal orgasm"—achieved through penetration by a penis—as opposed to the "immature" orgasm achieved through stimulation of the clitoris. Women who could not orgasm from penetration alone were described as "frigid."

3. *to command or exploit their labour to control their produce*—[by means of the institutions of marriage and motherhood as unpaid production; the horizontal segregation of women in paid employment; the decoy of the upwardly mobile token woman;* male control of abortion, contraception, sterilization, and childbirth; pimping; female infanticide, which robs mothers of daughters and contributes to generalized devaluation of women]
4. *to control or rob them of their children*—[by means of father right and "legal kidnapping";[15] enforced sterilization; systematized infanticide; seizure of children from lesbian mothers by the courts; the malpractice of male obstetrics; use of the mother as the "token torturer"[16] in genital mutilation or in binding the daughter's feet (or mind) to fit her for marriage]
5. *to confine them physically and prevent their movement*—[by means of rape as terrorism, keeping women off the streets; purdah;[17] foot binding; atrophying of women's athletic capabilities; high heels and "feminine" dress codes in fashion; the veil; sexual harassment on the streets; horizontal segregation of women in employment; prescriptions for "full-time" mothering at home; enforced economic dependence of wives]
6. *to use them as objects in male transactions*—[use of women as "gifts"; bride price; pimping; arranged marriage; use of women as entertainers to facilitate male deals—e.g., wife-hostess, cocktail waitress required to dress for male sexual titillation, call girls, "bunnies,"* geisha, *kisaeng* prostitutes,[18] secretaries]
7. *to cramp their creativeness*—[witch persecutions as campaigns against midwives and female healers, and as pogrom* against independent, "unassimilated" women;[19] definition of male pursuits as more valuable than female within any culture, so that cultural values become the embodiment of male subjectivity; restriction of female self-fulfilment to marriage and

15 [Rich's note] Anna Demeter, *Legal Kidnapping* (Boston: Beacon, 1977), pp. xx, 126–128.

16 [Rich's note] [Mary Daly, *Gyn/Ecology: The Metaethics of Radical Feminism* (Boston: Beacon Press, 1978)], pp. 139–141, 163–165.

17 *purdah* Custom of preventing women from being seen by men, either through the use of clothing that fully conceals women's bodies and faces or by keeping women in segregated and private spaces.

18 *kisaeng prostitutes* Korean women entertainers, artists, medical practitioners, and providers of paid sex, often highly educated but belonging to a slave caste. Though the enslavement of kisaeng ended in the late nineteenth century, some aspects of the practice remain in the twenty-first century.

19 [Rich's note] Barbara Ehrenreich and Deirdre English, *Witches, Midwives, and Nurses: A History of Women Healers* (Old Westbury, N.Y.: Feminist Press, 1973); Andrea Dworkin, *Woman Hating* (New York: Dutton, 1974), pp. 118–154; Daly, pp. 178–222.

motherhood; sexual exploitation of women by male artists and teachers; the social and economic disruption of women's creative aspirations;[20] erasure of female tradition][21]

8. *to withhold from them large areas of the society's knowledge and cultural attainments*—[by means of noneducation of females; the "Great Silence" regarding women and particularly lesbian existence in history and culture;[22] sex-role tracking which deflects women from science, technology, and other "masculine" pursuits; male social/professional bonding which excludes women; discrimination against women in the professions]

These are some of the methods by which male power is manifested and maintained. Looking at the schema, what surely impresses itself is the fact that we are confronting not a simple maintenance of inequality and property possession, but a pervasive cluster of forces, ranging from physical brutality to control of consciousness, which suggests that an enormous potential counter-force is having to be restrained.

Some of the forms by which male power manifests itself are more easily recognizable as enforcing heterosexuality on women than are others. Yet each one I have listed adds to the cluster of forces within which women have been convinced that marriage and sexual orientation toward men are inevitable—even if unsatisfying or oppressive—components of their lives. The chastity belt;* child marriage; erasure of lesbian existence (except as exotic and perverse) in art, literature, film; idealization of heterosexual romance and marriage—these are some fairly obvious forms of compulsion, the first two exemplifying physical force, the second two control of consciousness. While clitoridectomy has been assailed by feminists as a form of woman torture, Kathleen Barry first pointed out that it is not simply a way of turning the young girl into a "marriageable" woman through brutal surgery. It intends that women in the intimate proximity of polygynous marriage will not form sexual relationships with each other, that—from a male, genital-fetishist perspective—female erotic connections, even in a sex-segregated situation, will be literally excised.[23]

The function of pornography as an influence on consciousness is a major public issue of our time, when a multibillion-dollar industry has the power to

---

20 [Rich's note] See Virginia Woolf, *A Room of One's Own* (London: Hogarth 1929), and *id.*, *Three Guineas* (New York: Harcourt Brace, [1938] 1966); Tillie Olsen, *Silences* (Boston: Delacorte, 1978); Michelle Cliff, "The Resonance of Interruption," *Chrysalis: A Magazine of Women's Culture* 8 (1979): 29–37.

21 [Rich's note] Mary Daly, *Beyond God the Father* (Boston: Beacon, 1973), pp. 347–351; Olsen, pp. 22–46.

22 [Rich's note] Daly, *Beyond God the Father*, p. 93.

23 [Rich's note] Barry, pp. 163–164.

disseminate increasingly sadistic, women-degrading visual images. But even so-called soft-core pornography and advertising depict women as objects of sexual appetite devoid of emotional context, without individual meaning or personality—essentially as a sexual commodity to be consumed by males. (So-called lesbian pornography, created for the male voyeuristic eye, is equally devoid of emotional context or individual personality.) The most pernicious message relayed by pornography is that women are natural sexual prey to men and love it, that sexuality and violence are congruent, and that for women sex is essentially masochistic, humiliation pleasurable, physical abuse erotic. But along with this message comes another, not always recognized: that enforced submission and the use of cruelty, if played out in heterosexual pairing, is sexually "normal," while sensuality between women, including erotic mutuality and respect, is "queer," "sick," and either pornographic in itself or not very exciting compared with the sexuality of whips and bondage.[24] Pornography does not simply create a climate in which sex and violence are interchangeable; *it widens the range of behaviour considered acceptable from men in heterosexual intercourse*—behaviour which reiteratively strips women of their autonomy, dignity, and sexual potential, including the potential of loving and being loved by women in mutuality and integrity.

In her brilliant study *Sexual Harassment of Working Women: A Case of Sex Discrimination*, Catharine A. MacKinnon delineates the intersection of compulsory heterosexuality and economics. Under capitalism, women are horizontally segregated by gender and occupy a structurally inferior position in the workplace. This is hardly news, but MacKinnon raises the question why, even if capitalism "requires some collection of individuals to occupy low-status, low-paying positions ... such persons must be biologically female," and goes on to point out that "the fact that male employers often do not hire qualified women, *even when they could pay them less than men* suggests that more than the profit motive is implicated" [emphasis added].[25] She cites a wealth of material documenting the fact that women are not only segregated in low-paying service jobs (as secretaries, domestics, nurses, typists, telephone operators, child-care workers, waitresses), but that "sexualization of the woman" is part of the job. Central and intrinsic to the economic realities of women's lives is the requirement that women will "market sexual attractiveness to men, who tend to hold the economic power and position to enforce their predilections." And

24 [Rich's note] The issue of "lesbian sadomasochism" needs to be examined in terms of dominant cultures' teachings about the relation of sex and violence. I believe this to be another example of the "double life" of women.

25 [Rich's note] Catharine A. MacKinnon, *Sexual Harassment of Working Women: A Case of Sex Discrimination* (New Haven, Conn.: Yale University Press, 1979), pp. 15–16.

MacKinnon documents that "sexual harassment perpetuates the interlocked structure by which women have been kept sexually in thrall to men at the bottom of the labour market. Two forces of American society converge: men's control over women's sexuality and capital's control over employees' work lives."[26] Thus, women in the workplace are at the mercy of sex as power in a vicious circle.* Economically disadvantaged, women—whether waitresses or professors—endure sexual harassment to keep their jobs and learn to behave in a complaisantly and ingratiatingly heterosexual manner because they discover this is their true qualification for employment, whatever the job description. And, MacKinnon notes, the woman who too decisively resists sexual overtures in the workplace is accused of being "dried up" and sexless, or lesbian. This raises a specific difference between the experiences of lesbians and homosexual men. A lesbian, closeted on her job because of heterosexual prejudice, is not simply forced into denying the truth of her outside relationships or private life. Her job depends on her pretending to be not merely heterosexual, but a heterosexual *woman* in terms of dressing and playing the feminine, deferential role required of "real" women.

MacKinnon raises radical questions as to the qualitative differences between sexual harassment, rape, and ordinary heterosexual intercourse. ("As one accused rapist put it, he hadn't used 'any more force than is usual for males during the preliminaries.'") She criticizes Susan Brownmiller[27] for separating rape from the mainstream of daily life and for her unexamined premise that "rape is violence, intercourse is sexuality," removing rape from the sexual sphere altogether. More crucially she argues that "taking rape from the realm of 'the sexual,' placing it in the realm of 'the violent,' allows one to be against it without raising any questions about the extent to which the institution of heterosexuality has defined force as a normal part of 'the preliminaries.'"[28] "Never is it asked whether, under conditions of male supremacy, the notion of 'consent' has any meaning."[29]

The fact is that the workplace, among other social institutions, is a place where women have learned to accept male violation of their psychic and physical boundaries as the price of survival....

The means of assuring male sexual access to women have recently received searching investigation by Kathleen Barry.[30] She documents extensive

26 [Rich's note] *Ibid.*, p. 174.

27 [Rich's note] [Susan Brownmiller, *Against Our Will: Men, Women, and Rape* (New York: Simon & Schuster, 1975)], *op. cit.*

28 [Rich's note] MacKinnon, p. 219....

29 [Rich's note] MacKinnon, p. 298.

30 [Rich's note] Barry, *op. cit.*

and appalling evidence for the existence, on a very large scale, of international female slavery, the institution once known as "white slavery" but which in fact has involved, and at this very moment involves, women of every race and class. In the theoretical analysis derived from her research, Barry makes the connection between all enforced conditions under which women live subject to men: prostitution, marital rape, father-daughter and brother-sister incest, wife beating, pornography, bride price, the selling of daughters, purdah, and genital mutilation. She sees the rape paradigm—where the victim of sexual assault is held responsible for her own victimization—as leading to the rationalization and acceptance of other forms of enslavement where the woman is presumed to have "chosen" her fate, to embrace it passively, or to have courted it perversely through rash or unchaste behaviour. On the contrary, Barry maintains, "female sexual slavery is present in ALL situations where women or girls cannot change the conditions of their existence; where regardless of how they got into those conditions, e.g., social pressure, economic hardship, misplaced trust or the longing for affection, they cannot get out; and where they are subject to sexual violence and exploitation."[31] ...

... [W]omen are all, in different ways and to different degrees, ... victims [of sexual slavery]; and part of the problem with naming and conceptualizing female sexual slavery is, as Barry clearly sees, compulsory heterosexuality.[32] Compulsory heterosexuality simplifies the task of the procurer and pimp in world-wide prostitution rings and "eros centres,"[33] while, in the privacy of the home, it leads the daughter to "accept" incest/rape by her father, the mother to deny that it is happening, the battered wife to stay on with an abusive husband. "Befriending or love" is a major tactic of the procurer, whose job it is to turn the runaway or the confused young girl over to the pimp for seasoning. The ideology of heterosexual romance, beamed at her from childhood out of fairy tales, television, films, advertising, popular songs, wedding pageantry, is a tool ready to the procurer's hand and one which he does not hesitate to use, as Barry documents. Early female indoctrination in "love" as an emotion may be largely a Western concept; but a more universal ideology concerns the primacy and controllability of the male sexual drive....

... The adolescent male sex drive, which, as both young women and men are taught, once triggered cannot take responsibility for itself or take no for an answer, becomes, according to Barry, the norm and rationale for adult male sexual behaviour: a condition of *arrested sexual development*. Women learn to accept as natural the inevitability of this "drive" because they receive it as

31 [Rich's note] Barry, p. 33.

32 [Rich's note] *Ibid.*, p. 100.

33 *eros centres* Buildings or streets where prostitution is conducted in European cities.

dogma. Hence, marital rape; hence, the Japanese wife resignedly packing her husband's suitcase for a weekend in the *kisaeng* brothels of Taiwan; hence, the psychological as well as economic imbalance of power between husband and wife, male employer and female worker, father and daughter, male professor and female student.

The effect of male identification means

> internalizing the values of the colonizer and actively participating in carrying out the colonization of one's self and one's sex.... Male identification is the act whereby women place men above women, including themselves, in credibility, status, and importance in most situations, regardless of the comparative quality the women may bring to the situation.... Interaction with women is seen as a lesser form of relating on every level.[34]

What deserves further exploration is the doublethink* many women engage in and from which no woman is permanently and utterly free: However woman-to-woman relationships, female support networks, a female and feminist value system are relied on and cherished, indoctrination in male credibility and status can still create synapses in thought, denials of feeling, wishful thinking, a profound sexual and intellectual confusion.... I quote here from a letter I received the day I was writing this passage: "I have had very bad relationships with men—I am now in the midst of a very painful separation. I am trying to find my strength through women—without my friends, I could not survive." How many times a day do women speak words like these or think them or write them, and how often does the synapse reassert itself? ...

The assumption that "most women are innately heterosexual" stands as a theoretical and political stumbling block for feminism. It remains a tenable assumption partly because lesbian existence has been written out of history or catalogued under disease, partly because it has been treated as exceptional rather than intrinsic, partly because to acknowledge that for women heterosexuality may not be a "preference" at all but something that has had to be imposed, managed, organized, propagandized, and maintained by force is an immense step to take if you consider yourself freely and "innately" heterosexual. Yet the failure to examine heterosexuality as an institution is like failing to admit that the economic system called capitalism or the caste system of racism is maintained by a variety of forces, including both physical violence and false consciousness. To take the step of questioning heterosexuality as a "preference" or "choice" for women—and to do the intellectual and emotional work that follows—will call for a special quality of courage in heterosexually

---

34 [Rich's note] *Ibid.*, p. 172.

identified feminists, but I think the rewards will be great: a freeing-up of thinking, the exploring of new paths, the shattering of another great silence, new clarity in personal relationships.

III

I have chosen to use the terms *lesbian existence* and *lesbian continuum* because the word *lesbianism* has a clinical and limiting ring. *Lesbian existence* suggests both the fact of the historical presence of lesbians and our continuing creation of the meaning of that existence. I mean the term *lesbian continuum* to include a range—through each woman's life and throughout history—of woman-identified experience, not simply the fact that a woman has had or consciously desired genital sexual experience with another woman. If we expand it to embrace many more forms of primary intensity between and among women, including the sharing of a rich inner life, the bonding against male tyranny, the giving and receiving of practical and political support, if we can also hear it in such associations as *marriage resistance* and the "haggard" behaviour identified by Mary Daly (obsolete meanings: "intractable," "willful," "wanton," and "unchaste," "a woman reluctant to yield to wooing"),[35] we begin to grasp breadths of female history and psychology which have lain out of reach as a consequence of limited, mostly clinical, definitions of *lesbianism*.

Lesbian existence comprises both the breaking of a taboo and the rejection of a compulsory way of life. It is also a direct or indirect attack on male right of access to women. But it is more than these, although we may first begin to perceive it as a form of naysaying to patriarchy, an act of resistance. It has, of course, included isolation, self-hatred, breakdown, alcoholism, suicide, and intrawoman violence; we romanticize at our peril what it means to love and act against the grain, and under heavy penalties; and lesbian existence has been lived (unlike, say, Jewish or Catholic existence*) without access to any knowledge of a tradition, a continuity, a social underpinning. The destruction of records and memorabilia and letters documenting the realities of lesbian existence must be taken very seriously as a means of keeping heterosexuality compulsory for women, since what has been kept from our knowledge is joy, sensuality, courage, and community, as well as guilt, self-betrayal, and pain....

As the term *lesbian* has been held to limiting, clinical associations in its patriarchal definition, female friendship and comradeship have been set apart from the erotic, thus limiting the erotic itself. But as we deepen and broaden the range of what we define as lesbian existence, as we delineate a lesbian continuum, we begin to discover the erotic in female terms: as that which is

35 [Rich's note] Daly, *Gyn/Ecology*, p. 15.

unconfined to any single part of the body or solely to the body itself; as an energy not only diffuse but, as Audre Lorde has described it, omnipresent in "the sharing of joy, whether physical, emotional, psychic," and in the sharing of work; as the empowering joy which "makes us less willing to accept powerlessness, or those other supplied states of being which are not native to me, such as resignation, despair, self-effacement, depression, self-denial."[36] ...

If we consider the possibility that all women—from the infant suckling at her mother's breast, to the grown woman experiencing orgasmic sensations while suckling her own child, perhaps recalling her mother's milk smell in her own, to two women, like Virginia Woolf's Chloe and Olivia, who share a laboratory,[37] to the woman dying at ninety, touched and handled by women—exist on a lesbian continuum, we can see ourselves as moving in and out of this continuum, whether we identify ourselves as lesbian or not.

We can then connect aspects of woman identification as diverse as the impudent, intimate girl friendships of eight or nine year olds and the banding together of those women of the twelfth and fifteenth centuries known as the Beguines who "shared houses, rented to one another, bequeathed houses to their room-mates ... in cheap subdivided houses in the artisans' area of town," who "practised Christian virtue on their own, dressing and living simply and not associating with men," who earned their livings as spinsters, bakers, nurses, or ran schools for young girls, and who managed—until the Church forced them to disperse—to live independent both of marriage and of conventual[38] restrictions.[39] It allows us to connect these women with the more celebrated "Lesbians" of the women's school around Sappho[40] of the seventh century B.C., with the secret sororities and economic networks reported among African women, and with the Chinese marriage-resistance sisterhoods—communities of women who refused marriage or who, if married, often refused to consummate their marriages and soon left their husbands, the only women in China who were not

---

36 [Rich's note] Audre Lorde, "Uses of the Erotic: The Erotic as Power," in *Sister Outsider* (Trumansburg, N.Y.: Crossing Press, 1984).

37 [Rich's note] Woolf, *A Room of One's Own*, p. 126. [In *A Room of One's Own*, Woolf quotes from a recent book a passage beginning "Chloe liked Olivia. They shared a laboratory together...." and discusses the failure of literature to represent complex relationships between women.]

38 *conventual* Of convents.

39 [Rich's note] Gracia Clark, "The Beguines: A Mediaeval Women's Community," *Quest: A Feminist Quarterly* 1, no. 4 (1975): 73–80.

40 *Sappho* Ancient Greek poet (seventh–sixth century BCE); many of her poems express passion toward women, and the word "lesbian" originated as a reference to her place of birth, the island of Lesbos. She is often described as having run a school for girls, but this is unlikely to be true.

footbound[41] and who, Agnes Smedley tells us, welcomed the births of daughters and organized successful women's strikes in the silk mills.[42] It allows us to connect and compare disparate individual instances of marriage resistance: for example, the strategies available to Emily Dickinson,[43] a nineteenth-century white woman genius, with the strategies available to Zora Neale Hurston,[44] a twentieth-century Black woman genius. Dickinson never married, had tenuous intellectual friendships with men, lived self-convented in her genteel father's house in Amherst, and wrote a lifetime of passionate letters to her sister-in-law Sue Gilbert and a smaller group of such letters to her friend Kate Scott Anthon. Hurston married twice but soon left each husband, scrambled her way from Florida to Harlem to Columbia University* to Haiti and finally back to Florida, moved in and out of white patronage and poverty, professional success, and failure; her survival relationships were all with women, beginning with her mother. Both of these women in their vastly different circumstances were marriage resisters, committed to their own work and selfhood, and were later characterized as "apolitical." Both were drawn to men of intellectual quality; for both of them women provided the ongoing fascination and sustenance of life.

If we think of heterosexuality as *the* natural emotional and sensual inclination for women, lives as these are seen as deviant, as pathological, or as emotionally and sensually deprived. Or, in more recent and permissive jargon, they are banalized* as "life styles." And the work of such women, whether merely the daily work of individual or collective survival and resistance or the work of the writer, the activist, the reformer, the anthropologist, or the artist—the work of self-creation—is undervalued, or seen as the bitter fruit of "penis

---

41 *footbound* From the tenth century into the early twentieth century, bound feet were considered an enhancement of female beauty in China. The process of foot binding involved breaking bones in a child's feet, then bandaging them tightly, to create a smaller, "lotus" shaped foot.

42 [Rich's note] See Denise Paulmé, ed., *Women of Tropical Africa* (Berkeley: University of California Press, 1963), pp. 7, 266–267. Some of these sororities are described as "a kind of defensive syndicate against the male element," their aims being "to offer concerted resistance to an oppressive patriarchate," "independence in relation to one's husband and with regard to motherhood, mutual aid, satisfaction of personal revenge." See also Audre Lorde, "Scratching the Surface: Some Notes on Barriers to Women and Loving," in *Sister Outsider*, pp. 45–52; Marjorie Topley, "Marriage Resistance in Rural Kwangtung," in *Women in Chinese Society*, ed. M. Wolf and R. Witke (Stanford, Calif.: Stanford University Press, 1978), pp. 67–89; Agnes Smedley, *Portraits of Chinese Women in Revolution*, ed. J. MacKinnon and S. MacKinnon (Old Westbury, N.Y.: Feminist Press, 1976), pp. 103–110.

43 *Emily Dickinson* American poet (1830–86).

44 *Zora Neale Hurston* American writer of fiction and non-fiction (1891–1960).

envy"[45] or the sublimation of repressed eroticism or the meaningless rant of a "man-hater." But when we turn the lens of vision and consider the degree to which and the methods whereby heterosexual "preference" has actually been imposed on women, not only can we understand differently the meaning of individual lives and work, but we can begin to recognize a central fact of women's history: that women have always resisted male tyranny.... And we can connect these rebellions and the necessity for them with the physical passion of woman for woman which is central to lesbian existence: the erotic sensuality which has been, precisely, the most violently erased fact of female experience.

Heterosexuality has been both forcibly and subliminally imposed on women. Yet everywhere women have resisted it, often at the cost of physical torture, imprisonment, psychosurgery,[46] social ostracism, and extreme poverty. "Compulsory heterosexuality" was named as one of the "crimes against women" by the Brussels International Tribunal on Crimes against Women in 1976. Two pieces of testimony from two very different cultures reflect the degree to which persecution of lesbians is a global practice here and now. A report from Norway relates:

> A lesbian in Oslo was in a heterosexual marriage that didn't work, so she started taking tranquillizers and ended up at the health sanatorium for treatment and rehabilitation.... The moment she said in family group therapy that she believed she was a lesbian, the doctor told her she was not. He knew from "looking into her eyes," he said. She had the eyes of a woman who wanted sexual intercourse with her husband. So she was subjected to so-called "couch therapy." She was put into a comfortably heated room, naked, on a bed, and for an hour her husband was to ... try to excite her sexually.... The idea was that the touching was always to end with sexual intercourse. She felt stronger and stronger aversion. She threw up and sometimes ran out of the room to avoid this "treatment." The more strongly she asserted that she was a lesbian, the more violent the forced heterosexual intercourse became. This treatment went on for about six months. She escaped from the hospital, but she was brought back. Again she escaped. She has not been there since. In the end she realized that she had been subjected to forcible rape for six months.

45 *"penis envy"* Psychoanalytic term coined by Freud, who claimed that jealousy over lack of a penis was a normal component of women's psychological development.

46 *psychosurgery* Surgery (lobotomy, for example) intended as psychological treatment.

30 And from Mozambique:

> I am condemned to a life of exile because I will not deny that I am a lesbian, that my primary commitments are, and will always be to other women. In the new Mozambique, lesbianism is considered a left-over from colonialism and decadent Western civilization. Lesbians are sent to rehabilitation camps to learn through self-criticism the correct line about themselves.... If I am forced to denounce my own love for women, if I therefore denounce myself, I could go back to Mozambique and join forces in the exciting and hard struggle of rebuilding a nation, including the struggle for the emancipation of Mozambiquan women. As it is, I either risk the rehabilitation camps, or remain in exile.[47]

Nor can it be assumed that women like those in Carroll Smith-Rosenberg's study,[48] who married, stayed married, yet dwelt in a profoundly female emotional and passional world, "preferred" or "chose" heterosexuality. Women have married because it was necessary, in order to survive economically, in order to have children who would not suffer economic deprivation or social ostracism, in order to remain respectable, in order to do what was expected of women, because coming out of "abnormal" childhoods they wanted to feel "normal" and because heterosexual romance has been represented as the great female adventure, duty, and fulfillment. We may faithfully or ambivalently have obeyed the institution, but our feelings—and our sensuality—have not been tamed or contained within it. There is no statistical documentation of the numbers of lesbians who have remained in heterosexual marriages for most of their lives....

This *double life*—this apparent acquiescence to an institution founded on male interest and prerogative—has been characteristic of female experience: in motherhood and in many kinds of heterosexual behaviour, including the rituals of courtship; the pretense of asexuality by the nineteenth-century wife; the simulation of orgasm by the prostitute, the courtesan, the twentieth-century "sexually liberated" woman....

47 [Rich's note] [Diana Russell and Nicole van de Ven, eds., *Proceedings of the International Tribunal on Crimes against Women* (Millbrae, Calif.: Les Femmes, 1976)], pp. 42–43, 56–57.

48 *Carroll Smith-Rosenberg's study* See "The Female World of Love and Ritual: Relations between Women in Nineteenth-Century America" in *Signs* (Autumn 1975), referenced in an earlier portion of Rich's essay that is omitted here.

IV

Woman identification is a source of energy, a potential springhead of female power, curtailed and contained under the institution of heterosexuality. The denial of reality and invisibility to women's passion for women, women's choice of women as allies, life companions, and community, the forcing of such relationships into dissimulation and their disintegration under intense pressure have meant an incalculable loss to the power of all women *to change the social relations of the sexes, to liberate ourselves and each other*. The lie of compulsory female heterosexuality today afflicts not just feminist scholarship, but every profession, every reference work, every curriculum, every organizing attempt, every relationship or conversation over which it hovers. It creates, specifically, a profound falseness, hypocrisy, and hysteria in the heterosexual dialogue, for every heterosexual relationship is lived in the queasy strobe light of that lie. However we choose to identify ourselves, however we find ourselves labelled, it flickers across and distorts our lives.[49]

The lie keeps numberless women psychologically trapped, trying to fit mind, spirit, and sexuality into a prescribed script because they cannot look beyond the parameters of the acceptable. It pulls on the energy of such women even as it drains the energy of "closeted" lesbians—the energy exhausted in the double life. The lesbian trapped in the "closet," the woman imprisoned in prescriptive ideas of the "normal" share the pain of blocked options, broken connections, lost access to self-definition freely and powerfully assumed....

... [W]e can say that there is a *nascent** feminist political content in the act of choosing a woman lover or life partner in the face of institutionalized heterosexuality.... But for lesbian existence to realize this political content in an ultimately liberating form, the erotic choice must deepen and expand into conscious woman identification—into lesbian feminism.

The work that lies ahead, of unearthing and describing what I call here "lesbian existence," is potentially liberating for all women. It is work that must assuredly move beyond the limits of white and middle-class Western Women's Studies to examine women's lives, work, and groupings within every racial, ethnic, and political structure. There are differences, moreover, between "lesbian existence" and the "lesbian continuum," differences we can discern even in the movement of our own lives. The lesbian continuum, I suggest, needs delineation in light of the "double life" of women, not only women self-described as heterosexual but also of self-described lesbians. We need a far

---

49 [Rich's note] See Russell and van de Ven, p. 40: "Few heterosexual women realize their lack of free choice about their sexuality, and few realize how and why compulsory sexuality is also a crime against them."

more exhaustive account of the forms the double life has assumed. Historians need to ask at every point how heterosexuality as institution has been organized and maintained through the female wage scale, the enforcement of middle-class women's "leisure," the glamorization of so-called sexual liberation, the withholding of education from women, the imagery of "high art" and popular culture, the mystification of the "personal" sphere, and much else. We need an economics which comprehends the institution of heterosexuality, with its doubled workload for women and its sexual divisions of labour, as the most idealized of economic relations.

The question inevitably will arise: Are we then to condemn all heterosexual relationships, including those which are least oppressive? I believe this question, though often heartfelt, is the wrong question here. We have been stalled in a maze of false dichotomies which prevents our apprehending the institution as a whole: "good" versus "bad" marriages; "marriage for love" versus arranged marriage; "liberated" sex versus prostitution; heterosexual intercourse versus rape; *Liebeschmerz*[50] versus humiliation and dependency. Within the institution exist, of course, qualitative differences of experience; but the absence of choice remains the great unacknowledged reality, and in the absence of choice, women will remain dependent upon the chance or luck of particular relationships and will have no collective power to determine the meaning and place of sexuality in their lives. As we address the institution itself, moreover, we begin to perceive a history of female resistance which has never fully understood itself because it has been so fragmented, miscalled, erased. It will require a courageous grasp of the politics and economics, as well as the cultural propaganda, of heterosexuality to carry us beyond individual cases or diversified group situations into the complex kind of overview needed to undo the power men everywhere wield over women, power which has become a model for every other form of exploitation and illegitimate control.

(1980)

Questions

1. In this essay, Rich both critiques and builds on the work of other feminist scholars. Choose one of the following scholars: Dorothy Dinnerstein, Nancy Chodorow, Kathleen Gough, Catherine MacKinnon, Kathleen Barry, or Mary Daly. How does Rich position her own argument in relation to this scholar's work? What (if any) aspects of the scholar's work does she accept, and what (if anything) does she

50 *Liebeschmerz* German: love pain.

argue against? What does the incorporation of your chosen scholar's work add to Rich's argument?

2. Rich lists seven "characteristics of male power" (paragraph 10). Does this list describe gender relations in the twenty-first century? If you feel that it does, give a present-day example of each of the listed characteristics. If you feel that it does not, explain how things have changed and offer evidence in support of your view.
3. What roles do sexual desire and sexual intercourse between women play in Rich's understanding of lesbian existence and of the lesbian continuum?
4. How, if at all, does compulsory heterosexuality impact your own romantic relationships?

Elaine Showalter

Representing Ophelia: Women, Madness, and the Responsibilities of Feminist Criticism

Elaine Showalter is a feminist critic particularly well-known for her work on hysteria and madness in literature. Her book A Literature of Their Own *(1977) founded gynocritics, a discourse dedicated to examining from a female perspective women's writing and the treatment of female characters. In this essay, Showalter discusses the character of Ophelia in Shakespeare's* Hamlet, *with particular attention to the history of her representation.*

"As a sort of a come-on, I announced that I would speak today about that piece of bait named Ophelia, and I'll be as good as my word." These are the words which begin the psychoanalytic seminar on *Hamlet* presented in Paris in 1959 by Jacques Lacan. But despite his promising come-on, Lacan was *not* as good as his word. He goes on for some 41 pages to speak about Hamlet, and when he does mention Ophelia, she is merely what Lacan calls "the object Ophelia"—that is, the object of Hamlet's male desire. The etymology of Ophelia, Lacan asserts, is "O-phallus," and her role in the drama can only be to function as the exteriorized figuration of what Lacan predictably and, in view of his own early work with psychotic women, disappointingly suggests is the phallus as transcendental signifier.[1] To play such a part obviously makes

1 Jacques Lacan, "Desire and the interpretation of desire in *Hamlet*," in *Literature and Psychoanalysis: The Question of Reading: Otherwise*, ed. Shoshana Felman (Baltimore, 1982), 11, 20, 23. Lacan is also wrong about the etymology of Ophelia, which probably derives from the Greek for "help" or "succor." Charlotte M. Yonge suggested a derivation from "ophis," "serpent." See her *History of Christian Names* (1884, republished Chicago, 1966), 346–7. I am indebted to Walter Jackson Bate for this reference. [Unless otherwise noted, all notes to this essay are from the author.]

Ophelia "essential," as Lacan admits; but only because, in his words, "she is linked forever, for centuries, to the figure of Hamlet."[2]

The bait-and-switch game* that Lacan plays with Ophelia is a cynical but not unusual instance of her deployment in psychiatric and critical texts. For most critics of Shakespeare, Ophelia has been an insignificant minor character in the play, touching in her weakness and madness but chiefly interesting, of course, in what she tells us about Hamlet. And while female readers of Shakespeare have often attempted to champion Ophelia, even feminist critics have done so with a certain embarrassment. As Annette Kolodny ruefully admits: "it is after all, an imposition of high order to ask the viewer to attend to Ophelia's sufferings in a scene where, before, he's always so comfortably kept his eye fixed on Hamlet."

Yet when feminist criticism allows Ophelia to upstage Hamlet, it also brings to the foreground the issues in an ongoing theoretical debate about the cultural links between femininity, female sexuality, insanity, and representation. Though she is neglected in criticism, Ophelia is probably the most frequently illustrated and cited of Shakespeare's heroines. Her visibility as a subject in literature, popular culture, and painting, from Redon who paints her drowning, to Bob Dylan, who places her on Desolation Row, to Cannon Mills,* which has named a flowery sheet pattern after her, is in inverse relation to her invisibility in Shakespearean critical texts. Why has she been such a potent and obsessive figure in our cultural mythology? Insofar as Hamlet names Ophelia as "woman" and "frailty," substituting an ideological view of femininity for a personal one, is she indeed representative of Woman, and does her madness stand for the oppression of women in society as well as in tragedy? Furthermore, since Laertes calls Ophelia a "document in madness," does she represent the textual archetype of woman *as* madness, or madness *as* woman? And finally, how should feminist criticism represent Ophelia in its own discourse? What is our responsibility towards her as character and as woman?

Feminist critics have offered a variety of responses to these questions. Some have maintained that we should represent Ophelia as a lawyer represents a client, that we should become her Horatia,* in this harsh world reporting her and her cause aright to the unsatisfied. Carol Neely, for example, describes advocacy—speaking *for* Ophelia—as our proper role: "As a feminist critic," she writes, "I must 'tell' Ophelia's story."[3] But what can we mean by Ophelia's story? The story of her life? The story of her betrayal at the hands of her father,

---

2 Annette Kolodny, "Dancing through the minefield: some observations on the theory, practice, and politics of feminist literary criticism" (*Feminist Studies*, 6 (1980)), 7.

3 Carol Neely, "Feminist modes of Shakespearean criticism" (*Women's Studies*, 9 (1981)), 11.

brother, lover, court, society? The story of her rejection and marginalization by male critics of Shakespeare? Shakespeare gives us very little information from which to imagine a past for Ophelia. She appears in only five of the play's twenty scenes; the pre-play course of her love story with Hamlet is known only by a few ambiguous flashbacks. Her tragedy is subordinated in the play; unlike Hamlet, she does not struggle with moral choices or alternatives. Thus another feminist critic, Lee Edwards, concludes that it is impossible to reconstruct Ophelia's biography from the text: "We can imagine Hamlet's story without Ophelia, but Ophelia literally has no story without Hamlet."[4]

5 If we turn from American to French feminist theory, Ophelia might confirm the impossibility of representing the feminine in patriarchal discourse as other than madness, incoherence, fluidity, or silence. In French theoretical criticism, the feminine or "Woman" is that which escapes representation in patriarchal language and symbolism; it remains on the side of negativity, absence, and lack. In comparison to Hamlet, Ophelia is certainly a creature of lack. "I think nothing, my lord," she tells him in the Mousetrap scene, and he cruelly twists her words:

> *Hamlet:* That's a fair thought to lie between maids' legs.
> *Ophelia:* What is, my lord?
> *Hamlet:* Nothing.
>
> (III.ii.117–19)

In Elizabethan slang, "nothing" was a term for the female genitalia, as in *Much Ado About Nothing*. To Hamlet, then, "nothing" is what lies between maids' legs, for, in the male visual system of representation and desire, women's sexual organs, in the words of the French psychoanalyst Luce Irigaray, "represent the horror of having nothing to see."[5] When Ophelia is mad, Gertrude says that "Her speech is nothing," mere "unshaped use." Ophelia's speech represents the horror of having nothing to say in the public terms defined by the court. Deprived of thought, sexuality, language, Ophelia's story becomes the story of O—the zero, the empty circle or mystery of feminine difference, the cipher of female sexuality to be deciphered by feminist interpretation.[6]

---

4 Lee Edwards, "The labors of Psyche" (*Critical Inquiry*, 6 (1979)), 36.

5 Luce Irigaray: see *New French Feminisms*, ed. Elaine Marks and Isabelle de Courtivron (New York, 1982), 101. The quotation above, from III.ii, is taken from the Arden Shakespeare, *Hamlet*, ed. Harold Jenkins (London and New York, 1982), 295. All quotations from *Hamlet* are from this text.

6 On images of negation and feminine enclosure, see David Wilbern, "Shakespeare's 'nothing,'" in *Representing Shakespeare: New Psychoanalytic Essays*, ed. Murray M. Schwartz and Coppélia Kahn (Baltimore, 1981).

A third approach would be to read Ophelia's story as the female subtext of the tragedy, the repressed story of Hamlet. In this reading, Ophelia represents the strong emotions that the Elizabethans as well as the Freudians thought womanish and unmanly. When Laertes weeps for his dead sister he says of his tears that "When these are gone, / The woman will be out"—that is to say, that the feminine and shameful part of his nature will be purged. According to David Leverenz, in an important essay called "The Woman in *Hamlet*," Hamlet's disgust at the feminine passivity in himself is translated into violent revulsion against women, and into his brutal behaviour towards Ophelia. Ophelia's suicide, Leverenz argues, then becomes "a microcosm of the male world's banishment of the female, because 'woman' represents everything denied by reasonable men."[7]

It is perhaps because Hamlet's emotional vulnerability can so readily be conceptualized as feminine that this is the only heroic male role in Shakespeare which has been regularly acted by women, in a tradition from Sarah Bernhardt to, most recently, Diane Venora, in a production directed by Joseph Papp. Leopold Bloom speculates on this tradition in *Ulysses*,* musing on the Hamlet of the actress Mrs. Bandman Palmer: "Male impersonator. Perhaps he was a woman? Why Ophelia committed suicide?"[8]

While all of these approaches have much to recommend them, each also presents critical problems. To liberate Ophelia from the text, or to make her its tragic centre, is to re-appropriate her for our own ends; to dissolve her into a female symbolism of absence is to endorse our own marginality; to make her Hamlet's anima* is to reduce her to a metaphor of male experience. I would like to propose instead that Ophelia *does* have a story of her own that feminist criticism can tell; it is neither her life story, nor her love story, nor Lacan's story, but rather the *history* of her representation. This essay tries to bring together some of the categories of French feminist thought about the "feminine" with the empirical energies of American historical and critical research: to yoke French theory and Yankee* knowhow.

10 Tracing the iconography of Ophelia in English and French painting, photography, psychiatry, and literature, as well as in theatrical production, I will be showing first of all the representational bonds between female insanity and female sexuality. Secondly, I want to demonstrate the two-way transaction between psychiatric theory and cultural representation. As one medical historian has observed, we could provide a manual of female insanity by chronicling the illustrations of Ophelia; this is so because the illustrations of Ophelia have

---

7 David Leverenz, "The woman in *Hamlet*: an interpersonal view" (*Signs*, 4 (1978)), 303.

8 James Joyce, *Ulysses* (New York, 1961), 76.

played a major role in the theoretical construction of female insanity.[9] Finally, I want to suggest that the feminist revision of Ophelia comes as much from the actress's freedom as from the critic's interpretation.[10] When Shakespeare's heroines began to be played by women instead of boys,* the presence of the female body and female voice, quite apart from details of interpretation, created new meanings and subversive tensions in these roles, and perhaps most importantly with Ophelia. Looking at Ophelia's history on and off the stage, I will point out the contest between male and female representations of Ophelia, cycles of critical repression and feminist reclamation of which contemporary feminist criticism is only the most recent phase. By beginning with these data from cultural history, instead of moving from the grid of literary theory, I hope to conclude with a fuller sense of the responsibilities of feminist criticism, as well as a new perspective on Ophelia.

"Of all the characters in *Hamlet*," Bridget Lyons has pointed out, "Ophelia is most persistently presented in terms of symbolic meanings."[11] Her behaviour, her appearance, her gestures, her costume, her props, are freighted with emblematic significance, and for many generations of Shakespearean critics her part in the play has seemed to be primarily iconographic.* Ophelia's symbolic meanings, moreover, are specifically feminine. Whereas for Hamlet madness is metaphysical, linked with culture, for Ophelia it is a product of the female body and female nature, perhaps that nature's purest form. On the Elizabethan stage, the conventions of female insanity were sharply defined. Ophelia dresses in white, decks herself with "fantastical garlands" of wild flowers, and enters, according to the stage directions of the "Bad" Quarto, "distracted" playing on a lute with her "hair down singing." Her speeches are marked by extravagant metaphors, lyrical free associations, and "explosive sexual imagery."[12] She sings wistful and bawdy ballads, and ends her life by drowning.

All of these conventions carry specific messages about femininity and sexuality. Ophelia's virginal and vacant white is contrasted with Hamlet's scholar's garb, his "suits of solemn black." Her flowers suggest the discordant double images of female sexuality as both innocent blossoming and whorish contamination; she is the "green girl" of pastoral, the virginal "Rose of May"

9 Sander L. Gilman, *Seeing the Insane* (New York, 1981), 126.

10 See Michael Goldman, *The Actor's Freedom: Toward a Theory of Drama* (New York, 1975), for a stimulating discussion of the interpretative interaction between actor and audience.

11 Bridget Lyons, "The iconography of Ophelia" (*English Literary History*, 44 (1977)), 61.

12 See Maurice and Hanna Charney, "The language of Shakespeare's madwomen" (*Signs*, 3 (1977)), 451, 457; and Carroll Camden, "On Ophelia's madness" (*Shakespeare Quarterly* (1964)), 254.

and the sexually explicit madwoman who, in giving away her wild flowers and herbs, is symbolically deflowering herself. The "weedy trophies" and phallic "long purples" which she wears to her death intimate an improper and discordant sexuality that Gertrude's lovely elegy cannot quite obscure.[13] In Elizabethan and Jacobean drama, the stage direction that a woman enters with dishevelled hair indicates that she might either be mad or the victim of a rape; the disordered hair, her offense against decorum, suggests sensuality in each case.[14] The mad Ophelia's bawdy songs and verbal license, while they give her access to "an entirely different range of experience" from what she is allowed as the dutiful daughter, seem to be her one sanctioned form of self-assertion as a woman, quickly followed, as if in retribution, by her death.[15]

Drowning too was associated with the feminine, with female fluidity as opposed to masculine aridity. In his discussion of the "Ophelia complex," the phenomenologist Gaston Bachelard traces the symbolic connections between women, water, and death. Drowning, he suggests, becomes the truly feminine death in the dramas of literature and life, one which is a beautiful immersion and submersion in the female element. Water is the profound and organic symbol of the liquid woman whose eyes are so easily drowned in tears, as her body is the repository of blood, amniotic fluid, and milk. A man contemplating this feminine suicide understands it by reaching for what is feminine in himself, like Laertes, by a temporary surrender to his own fluidity—that is, his tears; and he becomes a man again in becoming once more dry—when his tears are stopped.[16]

Clinically speaking, Ophelia's behaviour and appearance are characteristic of the malady the Elizabethans would have diagnosed as female love-melancholy, or erotomania. From about 1580, melancholy* had become a fashionable disease among young men, especially in London, and Hamlet himself is a prototype of the melancholy hero. Yet the epidemic of melancholy associated with intellectual and imaginative genius "curiously bypassed women." Women's melancholy was seen instead as biological, and emotional in origins.[17]

---

13 See Margery Garber, *Coming of Age in Shakespeare* (London, 1981), 155–7; and Lyons, op. cit., 65, 70–2.

14 On dishevelled hair as a signifier of madness or rape, see Charney and Charney, op. cit., 452–3, 457; and Allan Dessen, *Elizabethan Stage Conventions and Modern Interpreters* (Cambridge, 1984), 36–8. Thanks to Allan Dessen for letting me see advance proofs of his book.

15 Charney and Charney, op. cit., 456.

16 Gaston Bachelard, *L'Eau et les rêves* (Paris, 1942), 109–25. See also Brigitte Peucker, "Dröste-Hulshof's Ophelia and the recovery of voice" (*The Journal of English and Germanic Philology* (1983)), 374–91.

17 Vieda Skultans, *English Madness: Ideas on Insanity 1580–1890* (London, 1977), 79–81. On historical cases of love-melancholy, see Michael MacDonald, *Mystical Bedlam* (Cambridge, 1982).

15 On the stage, Ophelia's madness was presented as the predicable outcome of erotomania. From 1660, when women first appeared on the public stage, to the beginnings of the eighteenth century, the most celebrated of the actresses who played Ophelia were those whom rumour credited with disappointments in love. The greatest triumph was reserved for Susan Mountfort, a former actress at Lincoln's Inn Fields who had gone mad after her lover's betrayal. One night in 1720 she escaped from her keeper, rushed to the theatre, and just as the Ophelia of the evening was to enter for her mad scene, "sprang forward in her place ... with wild eyes and wavering motion."[18] As a contemporary reported, "she was in truth *Ophelia herself*, to the amazement of the performers as well as of the audience—nature having made this last effort, her vital powers failed her and she died soon after."[19] These theatrical legends reinforced the belief of the age that female madness was a part of female nature, less to be imitated by an actress than demonstrated by a deranged woman in a performance of her emotions.

The subversive or violent possibilities of the mad scene were nearly eliminated, however, on the eighteenth-century stage. Late Augustan* stereotypes of female love-melancholy were sentimentalized versions which minimized the force of female sexuality, and made female insanity a pretty stimulant to male sensibility. Actresses such as Mrs. Lessingham in 1772, and Mary Bolton in 1811, played Ophelia in this decorous style, relying on the familiar images of the white dress, loose hair, and wild flowers to convey a polite feminine distraction, highly suitable for pictorial reproduction, and appropriate for Samuel Johnson's description of Ophelia as young, beautiful, harmless, and pious. Even Mrs. Siddons in 1785 played the mad scene with stately and classical dignity. For much of the period, in fact, Augustan objections to the levity and indecency of Ophelia's language and behaviour led to censorship of the part. Her lines were frequently cut, and the role was often assigned to a singer instead of an actress, making the mode of representation musical rather than visual or verbal.

But whereas the Augustan response to madness was a denial, the romantic* response was an embrace.[20] The figure of the madwoman permeates romantic literature, from the gothic novelists to Wordsworth and Scott in such texts as "The Thorn" and *The Heart of Midlothian*, where she stands for sexual victimization, bereavement, and thrilling emotional extremity. Romantic artists

---

18 C.E.L. Wingate, *Shakespeare's Heroines on the Stage* (New York, 1895), 283–4, 288–9.

19 Charles Hiatt, *Ellen Terry* (London, 1898), 11.

20 Max Byrd, *Visits to Bedlam: Madness and Literature in the Eighteenth Century* (Columbia, 1971), xiv.

such as Thomas Barker and George Shepheard painted pathetically abandoned Crazy Kates and Crazy Anns, while Henry Fuseli's "Mad Kate" is almost demonically possessed, an orphan of the romantic storm.

In the Shakespearean theatre, Ophelia's romantic revival began in France rather than England. When Charles Kemble made his Paris debut as Hamlet with an English troupe in 1827, his Ophelia was a young Irish ingénue named Harriet Smithson. Smithson used "her extensive command of mime to depict in precise gesture the state of Ophelia's confused mind."[21] In the mad scene, she entered in a long black veil, suggesting the standard imagery of female sexual mystery in the gothic novel, with scattered bedlamish wisps of straw in her hair. Spreading the veil on the ground as she sang, she spread flowers upon it in the shape of a cross, as if to make her father's grave, and mimed a burial, a piece of stage business which remained in vogue for the rest of the century.

The French audiences were stunned. Dumas recalled that "it was the first time I saw in the theatre real passions, giving life to men and women of flesh and blood."[22] The 23-year-old Hector Berlioz, who was in the audience on the first night, fell madly in love, and eventually married Harriet Smithson despite his family's frantic opposition. Her image as the mad Ophelia was represented in popular lithographs and exhibited in bookshop and printshop windows. Her costume was imitated by the fashionable, and a coiffure "à la folle," consisting of a "black veil with wisps of straw tastefully interwoven" in the hair, was widely copied by the Parisian beau monde,* always on the lookout for something new.[23]

Although Smithson never acted Ophelia on the English stage, her intense- 20
ly visual performance quickly influenced English productions as well; and indeed the romantic Ophelia—a young girl passionately and visibly driven to picturesque madness—became the dominant international acting style for the next 150 years, from Helena Modjeska in Poland in 1871, to the 18-year-old Jean Simmons in the Laurence Olivier film of 1948.

Whereas the romantic Hamlet, in Coleridge's famous dictum, thinks too much, has an "overbalance of the contemplative faculty" and an over-active intellect, the romantic Ophelia is a girl who *feels* too much, who drowns in feelings. The romantic critics seem to have felt that the less said about Ophelia the better; the point was to *look* at her. Hazlitt, for one, is speechless before her, calling her "a character almost too exquisitely touching to be dwelt upon."[24] While the Augustans represent Ophelia as music, the romantics transform her

21 Peter Raby, *Fair Ophelia: Harriet Smithson Berlioz* (Cambridge, 1982), 63.

22 Ibid., 68.

23 Ibid., 72, 75.

24 Quoted in Camden, op. cit., 217.

into an *objet d'art*, as if to take literally Claudius's lament, "poor Ophelia / Divided from herself and her fair judgment, / Without the which we are pictures."

Smithson's performance is best recaptured in a series of pictures done by Delacroix from 1830 to 1850, which show a strong romantic interest in the relation of female sexuality and insanity.[25] The most innovative and influential of Delacroix's lithographs is *La Mort d'Ophélie* of 1843, the first of three studies. Its sensual languor, with Ophelia half-suspended in the stream as her dress slips from her body, anticipated the fascination with the erotic trance of the hysteric as it would be studied by Jean-Martin Charcot and his students, including Janet and Freud. Delacroix's interest in the drowning Ophelia is also reproduced to the point of obsession in later nineteenth-century painting. The English Pre-Raphaelites* painted her again and again, choosing the drowning which is only described in the play, and where no actress's image had preceded them or interfered with their imaginative supremacy.

In the Royal Academy show of 1852, Arthur Hughes's entry shows a tiny waif-like creature—a sort of Tinker Bell* Ophelia—in a filmy white gown, perched on a tree trunk by the stream. The overall effect is softened, sexless, and hazy, although the straw in her hair resembles a crown of thorns. Hughes's juxtaposition of childlike femininity and Christian martyrdom was overpowered, however, by John Everett Millais's great painting of Ophelia in the same show. While Millais's Ophelia is sensuous siren as well as victim, the artist rather than the subject dominates the scene. The division of space between Ophelia and the natural details Millais had so painstakingly pursued reduces her to one more visual object; and the painting has such a hard surface, strangely flattened perspective, and brilliant light that it seems cruelly indifferent to the woman's death.

• • •

These Pre-Raphaelite images were part of a new and intricate traffic between images of women and madness in late nineteenth-century literature, psychiatry, drama, and art. First of all, superintendents of Victorian lunatic asylums were also enthusiasts of Shakespeare, who turned to his dramas for models of mental aberration that could be applied to their clinical practice. The case study of Ophelia was one that seemed particularly useful as an account of hysteria or mental breakdown in adolescence, a period of sexual instability which the Victorians regarded as risky for women's mental health. As Dr. John Charles Bucknill, president of the Medico-Psychological Association, remarked in 1859, "Ophelia is the very type of a class of cases by no means uncommon. Every mental physician of moderately extensive experience must have seen

25 Raby, op. cit., 182.

many Ophelias. It is a copy from nature, after the fashion of the Pre-Raphaelite school."[26] Dr. John Conolly, the celebrated superintendent of the Hanwell Asylum, and founder of the committee to make Stratford a national trust, concurred. In his *Study of Hamlet* in 1863 he noted that even casual visitors to mental institutions could recognize an Ophelia in the wards: "the same young years, the same faded beauty, the same fantastic dress and interrupted song."[27] Medical textbooks illustrated their discussions of female patients with sketches of Ophelia-like maidens.

But Conolly also pointed out that the graceful Ophelias who dominated the Victorian stage were quite unlike the women who had become the majority of the inmate population in Victorian public asylums. "It seems to be supposed," he protested, "that it is an easy task to play the part of a crazy girl, and that it is chiefly composed of singing and prettiness. The habitual courtesy, the partial rudeness of mental disorder, are things to be witnessed.... An actress, ambitious of something beyond cold imitation, might find the contemplation of such cases a not unprofitable study."[28]

Yet when Ellen Terry took up Conolly's challenge, and went to an asylum to observe real madwomen, she found them "too *theatrical*" to teach her anything.[29] This was because the iconography of the romantic Ophelia had begun to infiltrate reality, to define a style for mad young women seeking to express and communicate their distress. And where the women themselves did not willingly throw themselves into Ophelia-like postures, asylum superintendents, armed with the new technology of photography, imposed the costume, gesture, props, and expression of Ophelia upon them. In England, the camera was introduced to asylum work in the 1850s by Dr. Hugh Welch Diamond, who photographed his female patients at the Surrey Asylum and at Bethlem. Diamond was heavily influenced by literary and visual models in his posing of the female subjects. His pictures of madwomen, posed in prayer, or decked with Ophelia-like garlands, were copied for Victorian consumption as touched-up lithographs in professional journals.[30]

Reality, psychiatry, and representational convention were even more confused in the photographic records of hysteria produced in the 1870s by

---

26 J.C. Bucknill, *The Psychology of Shakespeare* (London, 1859, reprinted New York, 1979), 110. For more extensive discussions of Victorian psychiatry and Ophelia figures, see Elaine Showalter, *The Female Malady: Women, Madness and English Culture* (New York, 1986).

27 John Conolly, *Study of Hamlet* (London, 1863), 177.

28 Ibid., 177–8, 180.

29 Ellen Terry, *The Story of My Life* (London, 1908), 154.

30 Diamond's photographs are reproduced in Sander L. Gilman, *The Face of Madness: Hugh W. Diamond and the Origin of Psychiatric Photography* (New York, 1976).

Jean-Martin Charcot. Charcot was the first clinician to install a fully equipped photographic atelier in his Paris hospital, La Salpêtrière, to record the performances of his hysterical stars. Charcot's clinic became, as he said, a "living theatre" of female pathology; his women patients were coached in their performances for the camera, and, under hypnosis, were sometimes instructed to play heroines from Shakespeare. Among them, a 15-year-old girl named Augustine was featured in the published volumes called *Iconographies* in every posture of *la grande hystérie*.* With her white hospital gown and flowing locks, Augustine frequently resembles the reproductions of Ophelia as icon and actress which had been in wide circulation.[31]

But if the Victorian madwoman looks mutely out from men's pictures, and acts a part men had staged and directed, she is very differently represented in the feminist revision of Ophelia initiated by newly powerful and respectable Victorian actresses, and by women critics of Shakespeare. In their efforts to defend Ophelia, they invent a story for her drawn from their own experiences, grievances, and desires.

Probably the most famous of the Victorian feminist revisions of the Ophelia story was Mary Cowden Clarke's *The Girlhood of Shakespeare's Heroines*, published in 1852. Unlike other Victorian moralizing and didactic studies of the female characters of Shakespeare's plays, Clarke's was specifically addressed to the wrongs of women, and especially to the sexual double standard. In a chapter on Ophelia called "The rose of Elsinore," Clarke tells how the child Ophelia was left behind in the care of a peasant couple when Polonius was called to the court at Paris, and raised in a cottage with a foster-sister and brother, Jutha and Ulf. Jutha is seduced and betrayed by a deceitful knight, and Ophelia discovers the bodies of Jutha and her still-born child, lying "white, frigid, and still" in the deserted parlour of the cottage in the middle of the night. Ulf, a "hairy loutish boy," likes to torture flies, to eat songbirds, and to rip the petals off roses, and he is also very eager to give little Ophelia what he calls a bear-hug. Both repelled and masochistically attracted by Ulf, Ophelia is repeatedly cornered by him as she grows up; once she escapes the hug by hitting him with a branch of wild roses; another time, he sneaks into her bedroom "in his brutish pertinacity to obtain the hug he had promised himself," but just as he bends over to her trembling body, Ophelia is saved by the reappearance of her real mother.

A few years later, back at the court, she discovers the hanged body of another friend, who has killed herself after being "victimized and deserted by the

31 See Georges Didi-Huberman, *L'Invention de l'hystérie* (Paris, 1982), and Stephen Heath, *The Sexual Fix* (London, 1983), 36.

same evil seducer." Not surprisingly, Ophelia breaks down with brain fever—a staple mental illness of Victorian fiction—and has prophetic hallucinations of a brook beneath willow trees where something bad will happen to her. The warnings of Polonius and Laertes have little to add to this history of female sexual trauma.[32]

On the Victorian stage, it was Ellen Terry, daring and unconventional in her own life, who led the way in acting Ophelia in feminist terms as a consistent psychological study in sexual intimidation, a girl terrified of her father, of her lover, and of life itself. Terry's debut as Ophelia in Henry Irving's production in 1878 was a landmark. According to one reviewer, her Ophelia was "the terrible spectacle of a normal girl becoming hopelessly imbecile as the result of overwhelming mental agony. Hers was an insanity without wrath or rage, without exaltation or paroxysms."[33] Her "poetic and intellectual performance" also inspired other actresses to rebel against the conventions of invisibility and negation associated with the part.

Terry was the first to challenge the tradition of Ophelia's dressing in emblematic white. For the French poets, such as Rimbaud, Hugo, Musset, Mallarmé and Laforgue, whiteness was part of Ophelia's essential feminine symbolism; they call her "blanche Ophélia" and compare her to a lily, a cloud, or snow. Yet whiteness also made her a transparency, an absence that took on the colours of Hamlet's moods, and that, for the symbolists like Mallarmé, made her a blank page to be written over or on by the male imagination. Although Irving was able to prevent Terry from wearing black in the mad scene, exclaiming "My God, Madam, there must be only *one* black figure in this play, and that's Hamlet!" (Irving, of course, was playing Hamlet), nonetheless actresses such as Gertrude Eliot, Helen Maude, Nora de Silva, and in Russia Vera Komisarjevskaya, gradually won the right to intensify Ophelia's presence by clothing her in Hamlet's black.[34]

By the turn of the century, there was both a male and female discourse on Ophelia. A.C. Bradley spoke for the Victorian male tradition when he noted in *Shakespearean Tragedy* (1906) that "a large number of readers feel a kind of personal irritation against Ophelia; they seem unable to forgive her for not having been a heroine."[35] The feminist counterview was represented by actresses in such works as Helena Faucit's study of Shakespeare's female

32 Mary Cowden Clarke, *The Girlhood of Shakespeare's Heroines* (London, 1852). See also George C. Gross, "Mary Cowden Clarke, *The Girlhood of Shakespeare's Heroines*, and the sex education of Victorian women" (*Victorian Studies*, 16 (1972)), 37–58, and Nina Auerbach, *Woman and the Demon* (Cambridge, Mass., 1983), 210–15.

33 Hiatt, op. cit., 114. See also Wingate, op. cit., 304–5.

34 Terry, op. cit., 155–6.

35 Andrew C. Bradley, *Shakespearean Tragedy* (London, 1906), 160.

characters, and *The True Ophelia*, written by an anonymous actress in 1914, which protested against the "insipid little creature" of criticism, and advocated a strong and intelligent woman destroyed by the heartlessness of men.[36] In women's paintings of the *fin de siècle** as well, Ophelia is depicted as an inspiring, even sanctified emblem of righteousness.[37]

While the widely read and influential essays of Mary Cowden Clarke are now mocked as the epitome of naive criticism, these Victorian studies of the girlhood of Shakespeare's heroines are of course alive and well as psychoanalytic criticism, which has imagined its own prehistories of oedipal conflict and neurotic fixation;* and I say this not to mock psychoanalytic criticism, but to suggest that Clarke's musings on Ophelia are a pre-Freudian* speculation on the traumatic sources of a female sexual identity. The Freudian interpretation of *Hamlet* concentrated on the hero, but also had much to do with the re-sexualization of Ophelia. As early as 1900, Freud had traced Hamlet's irresolution to an Oedipus complex, and Ernest Jones, his leading British disciple, developed this view, influencing the performances of John Gielgud and Alec Guinness in the 1930s. In his final version of the study, *Hamlet and Oedipus*, published in 1949, Jones argued that "Ophelia should be unmistakably sensual, as she seldom is on stage. She may be 'innocent' and docile, but she is very aware of her body."[38]

35 In the theatre and in criticism, this Freudian edict has produced such extreme readings as that Shakespeare intends us to see Ophelia as a loose woman, and that she has been sleeping with Hamlet. Rebecca West has argued that Ophelia is not "a correct and timid virgin of exquisite sensibilities," a view she attributes to the popularity of the Millais painting; but rather "a disreputable young woman."[39] In his delightful autobiography, Laurence Olivier, who made a special pilgrimage to Ernest Jones when he was preparing his *Hamlet* in the 1930s, recalls that one of his predecessors as actor-manager had said in response to the earnest question, "Did Hamlet sleep with Ophelia?"—"In my company, always."[40]

The most extreme Freudian interpretation reads *Hamlet* as two parallel male and female psychodramas, the counterpointed stories of the incestuous attachments of Hamlet and Ophelia. As Theodor Lidz presents this view, while

---

36 Helena Faucit Martin, *On Some of Shakespeare's Female Characters* (Edinburgh and London, 1891), 4, 18; and *The True Ophelia* (New York, 1914), 15.

37 Among these paintings are the Ophelias of Henrietta Rae and Mrs. F. Littler. Sarah Bernhardt sculpted a bas relief of Ophelia for the Women's Pavilion at the Chicago World's Fair in 1893.

38 Ernest Jones, *Hamlet and Oedipus* (New York, 1949), 139.

39 Rebecca West, *The Count and the Castle* (New Haven, 1958), 18.

40 Laurence Olivier, *Confessions of an Actor* (Harmondsworth, 1982), 102, 152.

Hamlet is neurotically attached to his mother, Ophelia has an unresolved oedipal attachment to her father. She has fantasies of a lover who will abduct her from or even kill her father, and when this actually happens, her reason is destroyed by guilt as well as by lingering incestuous feelings. According to Lidz, Ophelia breaks down because she fails in the female developmental task of shifting her sexual attachment from her father "to a man who can bring her fulfillment as a woman."[41] We see the effects of this Freudian Ophelia on stage productions since the 1950s, where directors have hinted at an incestuous link between Ophelia and her father, or more recently, because this staging conflicts with the usual ironic treatment of Polonius, between Ophelia and Laertes. Trevor Nunn's production with Helen Mirren in 1970, for example, made Ophelia and Laertes flirtatious doubles, almost twins in their matching fur-trimmed doublets, playing duets on the lute with Polonius looking on, like Peter, Paul, and Mary.* In other productions of the same period, Marianne Faithfull was a haggard Ophelia equally attracted to Hamlet and Laertes, and, in one of the few performances directed by a woman, Yvonne Nicholson sat on Laertes' lap in the advice scene, and played the part with "rough sexual bravado."[42]

Since the 1960s, the Freudian representation of Ophelia has been supplemented by an antipsychiatry that represents Ophelia's madness in more contemporary terms. In contrast to the psychoanalytic representation of Ophelia's sexual unconscious that connected her essential femininity to Freud's essays on female sexuality and hysteria, her madness is now seen in medical and biochemical terms, as schizophrenia. This is so in part because the schizophrenic woman has become the cultural icon of dualistic femininity in the mid-twentieth century as the erotomaniac was in the seventeenth and the hysteric in the nineteenth. It might also be traced to the work of R.D. Laing on female schizophrenia in the 1960s. Laing argued that schizophrenia was an intelligible response to the experience of invalidation within the family network, especially to the conflicting emotional messages and mystifying double binds experienced by daughters. Ophelia, he noted in *The Divided Self*, is an empty space. "In her madness there is no one there.... There is no integral selfhood expressed through her actions or utterances. Incomprehensible statements are said by nothing. She has already died. There is now only a vacuum where there was once a person."[43]

---

41 Theodor Lidz, *Hamlet's Enemy: Madness and Myth in Hamlet* (New York, 1975), 88, 113.

42 Richard David, *Shakespeare in the Theatre* (Cambridge, 1978), 75. This was the production directed by Buzz Goodbody, a brilliant young feminist radical who killed herself that year. See Colin Chambers, *Other Spaces: New Theatre and the RSC* (London, 1980), especially 63–7.

43 R.D. Laing, *The Divided Self* (Harmondsworth, 1965), 195n.

Despite his sympathy for Ophelia, Laing's readings silence her, equate her with "nothing," more completely than any since the Augustans; and they have been translated into performances which only make Ophelia a graphic study of mental pathology. The sickest Ophelias on the contemporary stage have been those in the productions of the pathologist-director Jonathan Miller. In 1974 at the Greenwich Theatre his Ophelia sucked her thumb; by 1981, at the Warehouse in London, she was played by an actress much taller and heavier than the Hamlet (perhaps punningly cast as the young actor Anton Lesser). She began the play with a set of nervous tics and tuggings of hair which by the mad scene had become a full set of schizophrenic routines—head banging, twitching, wincing, grimacing, and drooling.[44]

But since the 1970s too we have had a feminist discourse which has offered a new perspective on Ophelia's madness as protest and rebellion. For many feminist theorists, the madwoman is a heroine, a powerful figure who rebels against the family and the social order; and the hysteric who refuses to speak the language of the patriarchal order, who speaks otherwise, is a sister.[45] In terms of effect on the theatre, the most radical application of these ideas was probably realized in Melissa Murray's agit-prop play *Ophelia*, written in 1979 for the English women's theatre group "Hormone Imbalance." In this blank verse retelling of the Hamlet story, Ophelia becomes a lesbian and runs off with a woman servant to join a guerilla commune.[46]

While I've always regretted that I missed this production, I can't proclaim that this defiant ideological gesture, however effective politically or theatrically, is all that feminist criticism desires, or all to which it should aspire. When feminist criticism chooses to deal with representation, rather than with women's writing, it must aim for a maximum interdisciplinary contextualism, in which the complexity of attitudes towards the feminine can be analyzed in their fullest cultural and historical frame. The alternation of strong and weak Ophelias on the stage, virginal and seductive Ophelias in art, inadequate or oppressed Ophelias in criticism, tells us how these representations have overflowed the text, and how they have reflected the ideological character of their times, erupting as debates between dominant and feminist views in periods of gender crisis and redefinition. The representation of Ophelia changes independently of theories of the meaning of the play or the Prince, for it depends on attitudes towards women and madness. The decorous and pious Ophelia of the Augustan age

44 David, op. cit., 82–3; thanks to Marianne DeKoven, Rutgers University, for the description of the 1981 Warehouse production.

45 See, for example, Hélène Cixous and Catherine Clément, *La Jeune Née* (Paris, 1975).

46 For an account of this production, see Micheline Wandor, *Understudies: Theatre and Sexual Politics* (London, 1981), 47.

and the postmodern schizophrenic heroine who might have stepped from the pages of Laing can be derived from the same figure; they are both contradictory and complementary images of female sexuality in which madness seems to act as the "switching-point, the concept which allows the co-existence of both sides of the representation."[47] There is no "true" Ophelia for whom feminist criticism must unambiguously speak, but perhaps only a Cubist* Ophelia of multiple perspectives, more than the sum of all her parts.

But in exposing the ideology of representation, feminist critics have also the responsibility to acknowledge and to examine the boundaries of our own ideological positions as products of our gender and our time. A degree of humility in an age of critical hubris* can be our greatest strength, for it is by occupying this position of historical self-consciousness in both feminism and criticism that we maintain our credibility in representing Ophelia, and that unlike Lacan, when we promise to speak about her, we make good on our word.

(1985)

Questions

1. According to Showalter's essay, what approach should feminist critics use in order to give the character of Ophelia "a story of her own"?
2. What are the component parts of Showalter's analysis? How does she organize her argument?
3. What is Showalter's thesis in this essay? Is there a thesis statement?
4. Describe Showalter's use of language in this essay. How does the language indicate the intended audience?
5. If you were directing a version of *Hamlet* for film or stage production, how would you represent Ophelia? Explain your choices.

47 I am indebted for this formulation to a critique of my earlier draft of this paper by Carl Friedman, at the Wesleyan Center for the Humanities, April 1981.

Ngũgĩ wa Thiong'o

from Decolonizing the Mind

Early on in Decolonizing the Mind, *the pre-eminent Kenyan novelist Ngũgĩ wa Thiong'o quotes his Nigerian counterpart Chinua Achebe questioning whether it is right for a writer to "abandon his mother tongue for someone else's." Achebe concluded that he had "no other choice" in an English-dominated world than to write in English rather than his native tongue, and for many years Ngũgĩ followed the same path, writing his novels in English. In the late 1970s, however, after he had been imprisoned by the Kenyan authorities for writing a play critical of the capitalist exploitation of a peasant farmer, Ngũgĩ began to write a novel in his native Gĩkũyũ, and since then virtually all his writing has been in that language.* Decolonizing the Mind, *a collection of four long essays, explores these issues at length: it is very largely through language, Ngũgĩ insists, that the power of colonialism has "fascinated and held the soul prisoner."*

The excerpt included here is from the first essay in the book, "The Language of African Literature."

III

I was born into a large peasant family: father, four wives and about twenty-eight children. I also belonged, as we all did in those days, to a wider extended family and to the community as a whole.

We spoke Gĩkũyũ as we worked in the fields. We spoke Gĩkũyũ in and outside the home. I can vividly recall those evenings of storytelling around the fireside. It was mostly the grown-ups telling the children but everybody was interested and involved. We children would re-tell the stories the following day to other children who worked in the fields picking the pyrethrum flowers, tea-leaves or coffee beans of our European and African landlords.

The stories, with mostly animals as the main characters, were all told in Gĩkũyũ. Hare, being small, weak but full of innovative wit and cunning, was our hero. We identified with him as he struggled against the brutes of prey like lion, leopard, hyena. His victories were our victories and we learnt that the apparently weak can outwit the strong. We followed the animals in their struggle against hostile nature—drought, rain, sun, wind—a confrontation often forcing them to search for forms of co-operation. But we were also interested in their struggles amongst themselves, and particularly between the beasts and the victims of prey. These twin struggles, against nature and other animals, reflected real-life struggles in the human world.

Not that we neglected stories with human beings as the main characters. There were two types of characters in such human-centred narratives: the species of truly human beings with qualities of courage, kindness, mercy, hatred of evil, concern for others; and a man-eat-man two-mouthed species with qualities of greed, selfishness, individualism and hatred of what was good for the larger co-operative community. Co-operation as the ultimate good in a community was a constant theme. It could unite human beings with animals against ogres and beasts of prey, as in the story of how dove, after being fed with castor-oil seeds, was sent to fetch a smith working far away from home and whose pregnant wife was being threatened by these man-eating two-mouthed ogres.

There were good and bad story-tellers. A good one could tell the same 5
story over and over again, and it would always be fresh to us, the listeners. He or she could tell a story told by someone else and make it more alive and dramatic. The differences really were in the use of words and images and the inflexion of voices to effect different tones.

We therefore learnt to value words for their meaning and nuances. Language was not a mere string of words. It had a suggestive power well beyond the immediate and lexical meaning. Our appreciation of the suggestive magical power of language was reinforced by the games we played with words through riddles, proverbs, transpositions of syllables, or through nonsensical but musically arranged words. So we learnt the music of our language on top of the content. The language, through images and symbols, gave us a view of the world, but it had a beauty of its own. The home and the field were then our pre-primary school but what is important, for this discussion, is that the language of our evening teach-ins, and the language of our immediate and wider community, and the language of our work in the fields were one.

And then I went to school, a colonial school, and this harmony was broken. The language of my education was no longer the language of my culture. I first went to Kamaandura, missionary run, and then to another called Maanguuũ run by nationalists grouped around the Gĩkũyũ Independent and Karinga Schools Association. Our language of education was still Gĩkũyũ. The very first time I was ever given an ovation for my writing was over a composition in Gĩkũyũ. So for my first four years there was still harmony between the language of my formal education and that of the Limuru peasant community.

It was after the declaration of a state of emergency over Kenya in 1952 that all the schools run by patriotic nationalists were taken over by the colonial regime and were placed under District Education Boards chaired by Englishmen. English became the language of my formal education. In Kenya, English became more than a language: it was *the* language, and all the others had to bow before it in deference.

Thus one of the most humiliating experiences was to be caught speaking Gĩkũyũ in the vicinity of the school. The culprit was given corporal punishment—three to five strokes of the cane on bare buttocks—or was made to carry a metal plate around the neck with inscriptions such as I AM STUPID or I AM A DONKEY. Sometimes the culprits were fined money they could hardly afford. And how did the teachers catch the culprits? A button was initially given to one pupil who was supposed to hand it over to whoever was caught speaking his mother tongue. Whoever had the button at the end of the day would sing who had given it to him and the ensuing process would bring out all the culprits of the day. Thus children were turned into witch-hunters and in the process were being taught the lucrative value of being a traitor to one's immediate community.

The attitude to English was the exact opposite: any achievement in spoken or written English was highly rewarded; prizes, prestige, applause; the ticket to higher realms. English became the measure of intelligence and ability in the arts, the sciences, and all the other branches of learning. English became *the* main determinant of a child's progress up the ladder of formal education.

As you may know, the colonial system of education in addition to its apartheid racial demarcation* had the structure of a pyramid: a broad primary base, a narrowing secondary middle, and an even narrower university apex. Selections from primary into secondary were through an examination, in my time called Kenya African Preliminary Examination, in which one had to pass six subjects ranging from Maths to Nature Study and Kiswahili. All the papers were written in English. Nobody could pass the exam who failed the English language paper no matter how brilliantly he had done in the other subjects. I remember one boy in my class of 1954 who had distinctions in all subjects except English, which he had failed. He was made to fail the entire exam. He went on to become a turn boy in a bus company. I who had only passes but a credit in English got a place at the Alliance High School, one of the most elitist institutions for Africans in colonial Kenya. The requirements for a place at the University, Makerere University College, were broadly the same: nobody could go on to wear the undergraduate red gown, no matter how brilliantly they had performed in all the other subjects unless they had a credit—not even a simple pass!—in English. Thus the most coveted place in the pyramid and in the system was only available to the holder of an English language credit card. English was the official vehicle and the magic formula to colonial elitedom.

Literary education was now determined by the dominant language while also reinforcing that dominance. Orature (oral literature) in Kenyan languages stopped. In primary school I now read simplified Dickens and Stevenson alongside Rider Haggard. Jim Hawkins, Oliver Twist, Tom Brown—not Hare, Leopard and Lion—were now my daily companions in the world of imagination. In secondary school, Scott and G.B. Shaw vied with more Rider Haggard, John Buchan, Alan Paton, Captain W.E. Johns. At Makerere I read English: from Chaucer to T.S. Eliot with a touch of Grahame Greene.*

Thus language and literature were taking us further and further from ourselves to other selves, from our world to other worlds.

What was the colonial system doing to us Kenyan children? What were the consequences of, on the one hand, this systematic suppression of our languages and the literature they carried, and on the other the elevation of English and the literature it carried? To answer those questions, let me first examine the relationship of language to human experience, human culture, and the human perception of reality.

IV

15 Language, any language, has a dual character: it is both a means of communication and a carrier of culture. Take English. It is spoken in Britain and in Sweden and Denmark. But for Swedish and Danish people English is only a means of communication with non-Scandinavians. It is not a carrier of their culture. For the British, and particularly the English, it is additionally, and inseparably from its use as a tool of communication, a carrier of their culture and history. Or take Swahili in East and Central Africa. It is widely used as a means of communication across many nationalities. But it is not the carrier of a culture and history of many of those nationalities. However in parts of Kenya and Tanzania, and particularly in Zanzibar, Swahili is inseparably both a means of communication and a carrier of the culture of those people to whom it is a mother-tongue.

Language as communication has three aspects or elements. There is first what Karl Marx once called the language of real life, the element basic to the whole notion of language, its origins and development: that is, the relations people enter into with one another in the labour process, the links they necessarily establish among themselves in the act of a people, a community of human beings, producing wealth or means of life like food, clothing, houses. A human community really starts its historical being as a community of co-operation in production through the division of labour; the simplest is between man, woman and child within a household; the more complex divisions are between branches of production such as those who are sole hunters, sole gatherers of fruits or sole workers in metal. Then there are the most complex divisions such as those in modern factories where a single product, say a shirt or a shoe, is the result of many hands and minds. Production is co-operation, is communication, is language, is expression of a relation between human beings and it is specifically human.

The second aspect of language as communication is speech and it imitates the language of real life, that is communication in production. The verbal signposts both reflect and aid communication or the relation established between human beings in the production of their means of life. Language as a system of verbal signposts makes that production possible. The spoken word is to relations between human beings what the hand is to the relations between human beings and nature. The hand through tools mediates between human beings and nature and forms the language of real life: spoken words mediate between human beings and form the language of speech.

The third aspect is the written signs. The written word imitates the spoken. Where the first two aspects of language as communication through the hand and the spoken word historically evolved more or less simultaneously, the written aspect is a much later historical development. Writing is representation of sounds with visual symbols, from the simplest knot among shepherds to tell the number in a herd or the hieroglyphics among the Agĩkũyũ gicaandi singers and poets of Kenya, to the most complicated and different letter and picture writing systems of the world today.

In most societies the written and the spoken languages are the same, in that they represent each other: what is on paper can be read to another person and be received as that language, which the recipient has grown up speaking. In such a society there is broad harmony for a child between the three aspects of language as communication. His interaction with nature and with other men is expressed in written and spoken symbols or signs which are both a result of that double interaction and a reflection of it. The association of the child's sensibility is with the language of his experience of life.

20 But there is more to it: communication between human beings is also the basis and process of evolving culture. In doing similar kinds of things and actions over and over again under similar circumstances, similar even in their mutability, certain patterns, moves, rhythms, habits, attitudes, experiences and knowledge emerge. Those experiences are handed over to the next generation and become the inherited basis for their further actions on nature and on themselves. There is a gradual accumulation of values which in time become almost self-evident truths governing their conception of what is right and wrong, good and bad, beautiful and ugly, courageous and cowardly, generous and mean in

their internal and external relations. Over a time this becomes a way of life distinguishable from other ways of life. They develop a distinctive culture and history. Culture embodies those moral, ethical and aesthetic values, the set of spiritual eyeglasses, through which they come to view themselves and their place in the universe. Values are the basis of a people's identity, their sense of particularity as members of the human race. All this is carried by language. Language as culture is the collective memory bank of a people's experience in history. Culture is almost indistinguishable from the language that makes possible its genesis, growth, banking, articulation and indeed its transmission from one generation to the next.

Language as culture also has three important aspects. Culture is a product of the history which it in turn reflects. Culture in other words is a product and a reflection of human beings communicating with one another in the very struggle to create wealth and to control it. But culture does not merely reflect that history, or rather it does so by actually forming images or pictures of the world of nature and nurture. Thus the second aspect of language as culture is as an image-forming agent in the mind of a child. Our whole conception of ourselves as a people, individually and collectively, is based on those pictures and images which may or may not correctly correspond to the actual reality of the struggles with nature and nurture which produced them in the first place. But our capacity to confront the world creatively is dependent on how those images correspond or not to that reality, how they distort or clarify the reality of our struggles. Language as culture is thus mediating between me and my own self; between my own self and other selves; between me and nature. Language is mediating in my very being. And this brings us to the third aspect of language as culture. Culture transmits or imparts those images of the world and reality through the spoken and the written language, that is through a specific language. In other words, the capacity to speak, the capacity to order sounds in a manner that makes for mutual comprehension between human beings is universal. This is the universality of language, a quality specific to human beings. It corresponds to the universality of the struggle against nature and that between human beings. But the particularity of the sounds, the words, the word order into phrases and sentences, and the specific manner, or laws, of their ordering is what distinguishes one language from another. Thus a specific culture is not transmitted through language in its universality but in its particularity as the language of a specific community with a specific history. Written literature and orature are the main means by which a particular language transmits the images of the world contained in the culture it carries.

Language as communication and as culture are then products of each other. Communication creates culture: culture is a means of communication. Language carries culture, and culture carries, particularly through orature and literature, the entire body of values by which we come to perceive ourselves and our place in the world. How people perceive themselves affects how they look at their culture, at their politics and at the social production of wealth, at their entire relationship to nature and to other beings. Language is thus inseparable from ourselves as a community of human beings with a specific form and character, a specific history, a specific relationship to the world.

V

So what was the colonialist imposition of a foreign language doing to us children?

The real aim of colonialism was to control the people's wealth: what they produced, how they produced it, and how it was distributed; to control, in other words, the entire realm of the language of real life. Colonialism imposed its control of the social production of wealth through military conquest and subsequent political dictatorship. But its most important area of domination was the mental universe of the colonized, the control, through culture, of how people perceived themselves and their relationship to the world. Economic and political control can never be complete or effective without mental control. To control a people's culture is to control their tools of self-definition in relationship to others.

For colonialism this involved two aspects of the same process: the destruction or the deliberate undervaluing of a people's culture, their art, dances, religions, history, geography, education, orature and literature, and the conscious elevation of the language of the colonizer. The domination of a people's language by the languages of the colonizing nations was crucial to the domination of the mental universe of the colonized.

Take language as communication. Imposing a foreign language, and suppressing the native languages as spoken and written, were already breaking the harmony previously existing between the African child and the three aspects of language. Since the new language as a means of communication was a product of and was reflecting the "real language of life" elsewhere, it could never as spoken or written properly reflect or imitate the real life of that community. This may in part explain why technology always appears to us as slightly external, *their* product and not *ours*. The word "missile" used to hold an alien far-away sound until I recently learnt its equivalent in Gĩkũyũ, *ngurukuhĩ* and it made me apprehend it differently. Learning, for a colonial child, became a cerebral activity* and not an emotionally felt experience.

But since the new, imposed languages could never completely break the native languages as spoken, their most effective area of domination was the third aspect of language as communication, the written. The language of an

African child's formal education was foreign. The language of the books he read was foreign. The language of his conceptualization was foreign. Thought, in him, took the visible form of a foreign language. So the written language of a child's upbringing in the school (even his spoken language within the school compound) became divorced from his spoken language at home. There was often not the slightest relationship between the child's written world, which was also the language of his schooling, and the world of his immediate environment in the family and the community. For a colonial child, the harmony existing between the three aspects of language as communication was irrevocably broken. This resulted in the disassociation of the sensibility of that child from his natural and social environment, what we might call colonial alienation. The alienation became reinforced in the teaching of history, geography, music, where bourgeois Europe was always the centre of the universe.

This disassociation, divorce, or alienation from the immediate environment becomes clearer when you look at colonial language as a carrier of culture.

Since culture is a product of the history of a people which it in turn reflects, the child was now being exposed exclusively to a culture that was a product of a world external to himself. He was being made to stand outside himself to look at himself. *Catching Them Young* is the title of a book on racism, class, sex, and politics in children's literature by Bob Dixon. "Catching them young" as an aim was even more true of a colonial child. The images of his world and his place in it implanted in a child take years to eradicate, if they ever can be.

Since culture does not just reflect the world in images but actually, through those images, conditions a child to see that world a certain way, the colonial child was made to see the world and where he stands in it as seen and defined by or reflected in the culture of the language of imposition.

And since those images are mostly passed on through orature and literature it meant the child would now only see the world as seen in the literature of his language of adoption. From the point of view of alienation, that is of seeing oneself from outside oneself as if one was another self, it does not matter that the imported literature carried the great humanist tradition of the best in Shakespeare, Goethe, Balzac, Tolstoy, Gorky, Brecht, Sholokhov, Dickens. The location of this great mirror of imagination was necessarily Europe and its history and culture and the rest of the universe was seen from that centre.

But obviously it was worse when the colonial child was exposed to images of his world as mirrored in the written languages of his colonizer. Where his own native languages were associated in his impressionable mind with low status, humiliation, corporal punishment, slow-footed intelligence and ability or downright stupidity, non-intelligibility and barbarism, this was reinforced by the world he met in the works of such geniuses of racism as a Rider Haggard or a Nicholas Monsarrat; not to mention the pronouncement of some of the giants of western intellectual and political establishment, such as Hume ("... The negro is naturally inferior to the whites ..."), Thomas Jefferson ("... The blacks ... are inferior to the whites on the endowments of both body and mind ..."), or Hegel* with his Africa comparable to a land of childhood still enveloped in the dark mantle of the night as far as the development of self-conscious history was concerned. Hegel's statement that there was nothing harmonious with humanity to be found in the African character is representative of the racist images of Africans and Africa such a colonial child was bound to encounter in the literature of the colonial languages. The results could be disastrous.

(1986)

Questions

1. What is the rhetorical purpose of paragraph 14? Is it effective?
2. In paragraph 15, Ngũgĩ argues that a language has a communication function for all people who speak that language, but that it also serves as a carrier of culture for all those for whom that language is the mother-tongue. If you speak two or more languages, does this assertion meet with your own experience?
3. Discuss how the imposition of a foreign language breaks "the harmony previously existing between the African child and the three aspects of language" (paragraph 26).
4. Toward the end of this selection, Ngũgĩ makes reference to the European-based writers of literature he was forced to study as a child, and how these stories did not match his own experiences. How well do the texts you are being asked to read in this course reflect your experiences? If you were the instructor of this course, how would you go about selecting a reading list?

Drew Hayden Taylor

Pretty Like a White Boy: The Adventures of a Blue-Eyed Ojibway[1]

Drew Hayden Taylor is a writer from the Curve Lake First Nation in southern Ontario. This piece first appeared in Funny, You Don't Look Like One: Observations from a Blue-Eyed Ojibway *(1996), the first of several collections of his humorous non-fiction writing.*

In this big, huge world, with all its billions and billions of people, it's safe to say that everybody will eventually come across personalities and individuals that will touch them in some peculiar yet poignant way. Individuals that in some way represent and help define who you are. I'm no different, mine was Kermit the Frog.* Not just because Natives have a long tradition of savouring frogs' legs, but because of his music. If you all may remember, Kermit is quite famous for his rendition of "It's Not Easy Being Green" I can relate. If I could sing, my song would be "It's Not Easy Having Blue Eyes in a Brown Eyed Village."

Yes, I'm afraid it's true. The author happens to be a card-carrying Indian.* Once you get past the aforementioned eyes, the fair skin, light brown hair, and noticeable lack of cheekbones, there lies the heart and spirit of an Ojibway storyteller. Honest Injun, or as the more politically correct term may be, honest aboriginal.

You see, I'm the product of a white father I never knew, and an Ojibway woman who evidently couldn't run fast enough. As a kid I knew I looked a bit different. But, then again, all kids are paranoid when it comes to their peers. I had a fairly happy childhood, frolicking through the bullrushes. But there were certain things that, even then, made me notice my unusual appearance. Whenever we played cowboys and Indians,* guess who had to be the bad guy, the cowboy.

---

1 *Ojibway* Aboriginal peoples belonging to the Anishinaabeg, a wider cultural group from the North American Great Lakes region.

It wasn't until I left the Reserve* for the big bad city, that I became more aware of the role people expected me to play, and the fact that physically I didn't fit in. Everybody seemed to have this preconceived idea of how every Indian looked and acted. One guy, on my first day of college, asked me what kind of horse I preferred. I didn't have the heart to tell him "hobby."

5 I've often tried to be philosophical about the whole thing. I have both white and red blood in me, I guess that makes me pink. I am a "Pink" man. Try to imagine this, I'm walking around on any typical Reserve in Canada, my head held high, proudly announcing to everyone "I am a Pink Man." It's a good thing I ran track in school.

My pinkness is constantly being pointed out to me over and over and over again. "You don't look Indian?" "You're not Indian, are you?" "Really?!?" I got questions like that from both white and Native people, for a while I debated having my status card tattooed on my forehead.

And like most insecure people and specially a blue-eyed Native writer, I went through a particularly severe identity crisis at one point. In fact, I admit it, one depressing spring evening, I died my hair black. Pitch black.

The reason for such a dramatic act, you may ask? Show Business. You see, for the last eight years or so, I've worked in various capacities in the performing arts, and as a result I'd always get calls to be an extra or even try out for an important role in some Native oriented movie. This anonymous voice would phone, having been given my number, and ask if I would be interested in trying out for a movie. Being a naturally ambitious, curious, and greedy young man, I would always readily agree, stardom flashing in my eyes and hunger pains from my wallet.

A few days later I would show up for the audition, and that was always an experience. What kind of experience you may ask? Picture this, the picture calls for the casting of seventeenth-century Mohawk* warriors living in a traditional longhouse.* The casting director calls the name "Drew Hayden Taylor" and I enter.

10 The casting director, the producer, and the film's director look up from the table and see my face, blue eyes flashing in anticipation. I once was described as a slightly chubby beachboy. But even beachboys have tans. Anyway, there would be a quick flush of confusion, a recheck of the papers, and a hesitant "Mr. Taylor?" Then they would ask if I was at the right audition. It was always the same. By the way, I never got any of the parts I tried for, except for a few anonymous crowd shots. Politics tells me it's because of the way I look, reality tells me it's probably because I can't act. I'm not sure which is better.

It's not just film people either. Recently I've become quite involved in Theatre, Native theatre to be exact. And one cold October day I was happily attending the Toronto leg of a province-wide tour of my first play, *Toronto at*

Dreamer's Rock. The place was sold out, the audience very receptive and the performance was wonderful. Ironically one of the actors was also half white.

The director later told me he had been talking with the actor's father, an older non-Native type chap. Evidently he had asked a few questions about me, and how I did my research. This made the director curious and he asked about the father's interest. He replied, "He's got an amazing grasp of the Native situation for a white person."

Not all these incidents are work-related either. One time a friend and I were coming out of a rather upscale bar (we were out YUPPIE[2] watching) and managed to catch a cab. We thanked the cab driver for being so comfortably close on such a cold night, he shrugged and nonchalantly talked about knowing what bars to drive around. "If you're not careful, all you'll get is drunk Indians." I hiccuped.

Another time this cab driver droned on and on about the government. He started out by criticizing Mulroney, and eventually to his handling of the Oka crisis.[3] This perked up my ears, until he said "If it were me, I'd have teargassed the place by the second day. No more problem." He got a dime tip. A few incidents like this and I'm convinced I'd make a great undercover agent for one of the Native political organizations.

But then again, even Native people have been known to look at me with a fair amount of suspicion. Many years ago when I was a young man, I was working on a documentary on Native culture up in the wilds of Northern Ontario. We were at an isolated cabin filming a trapper woman* and her kids. This one particular nine-year-old girl seemed to take a shine to me. She followed me around for two days both annoying me and endearing herself to me. But she absolutely refused to believe that I was Indian. The whole film crew tried to tell her but to no avail. She was certain I was white.

Then one day as I was loading up the car with film equipment, she asked me if I wanted some tea. Being in a hurry I declined the tea. She immediately smiled with victory crying out, "See, you're not Indian, all Indians drink tea!"

Frustrated and a little hurt I whipped out my Status card and thrust it at her. Now there I was, standing in a Northern Ontario winter, showing my Status card to a nine-year-old non-status Indian girl who had no idea what one was. Looking back, this may not have been one of my brighter moves.

---

2 *YUPPIE* Young urban or upwardly-mobile professional. The term was first used to refer to city-dwelling fashionable young business professionals in the 1980s.

3 *Mulroney* Brian Mulroney, Canadian Prime Minister (1984–93); *Oka crisis* Violent conflict between Mohawk protesters and government military and police forces. Protesters occupied the disputed land—which the town of Oka, Quebec, wanted to use for a golf course—from July to September in 1990.

But I must admit, it was a Native woman that boiled everything down in one simple sentence. You may know that woman, Marianne Jones from *The Beachcombers*[4] television series. We were working on a film together out west and we got to gossiping. Eventually we got around to talking about our respective villages. Hers on the Queen Charlotte Islands, or Haida Gwaii as the Haida call them, and mine in central Ontario.

Eventually childhood on the Reserve was being discussed and I made a comment about the way I look. She studied me for a moment, smiled, and said "Do you know what the old women in my village would call you?" Hesitant but curious, I shook my head. "They'd say you were pretty like a white boy." To this day I'm still not sure if I like that.

Now some may argue that I am simply a Métis* with a Status card. I disagree, I failed French in grade 11. And the Métis as everyone knows have their own separate and honourable culture, particularly in western Canada. And of course I am well aware that I am not the only person with my physical characteristics.

I remember once looking at a video tape of a drum group, shot on a Reserve up near Manitoulin Island.* I noticed one of the drummers seemed quite fairhaired, almost blond. I mentioned this to my girlfriend of the time and she shrugged saying, "Well, that's to be expected. The highway runs right through the Reserve."

Perhaps I'm being too critical. There's a lot to be said for both cultures. For example, on the left hand, you have the Native respect for Elders. They understand the concept of wisdom and insight coming with age.

On the white hand, there's Italian food. I mean I really love my mother and family but seriously, does anything really beat good Veal Scallopini? Most of my aboriginal friends share my fondness for this particular brand of food. Wasn't there a warrior at Oka named Lasagna? I found it ironic, though curiously logical, that Columbus was Italian. A connection I wonder?

Also Native people have this wonderful respect and love for the land. They believe they are part of it, a mere chain in the cycle of existence. Now as many of you know, this conflicts with the accepted Judeo-Christian, i.e., western view of land management. I even believe somewhere in the first chapters of the Bible it says something about God giving man dominion over Nature. Check it out, Genesis 4:? "Thou shalt clear cut." So I grew up understanding that everything around me is important and alive. My Native heritage gave me that.

And again, on the white hand, there's breast implants. Darn clever them white people. That's something Indians would never have invented, seriously.

---

4 *The Beachcombers* Canadian series set on the BC coast that aired from 1972 to 1990.

We're not ambitious enough. We just take what the Creator decides to give us, but no, not the white man. Just imagine it, some serious looking white man, and let's face it people, we know it was a man who invented them, don't we? So just imagine some serious looking white doctor sitting around in his laboratory muttering to himself, "Big tits, big tits, hmmm, how do I make big tits?" If it was an Indian, it would be "Big tits, big tits, white women sure got big tits" and leave it at that.

So where does that leave me on the big philosophical scoreboard, what exactly are my choices again; Indian—respect for elders, love of the land. White people—food and big tits. In order to live in both cultures I guess I'd have to find an Indian woman with big tits who lives with her grandmother in a cabin out in the woods and can make Fettuccini Alfredo on a wood stove.

Now let me make this clear, I'm not writing this for sympathy, or out of anger, or even some need for self-glorification. I am just setting the facts straight. For as you read this, a new Nation is born. This is a declaration of independence, my declaration of independence.

I've spent too many years explaining who and what I am repeatedly, so as of this moment, I officially secede from both races. I plan to start my own separate nation. Because I am half Ojibway, and half Caucasian, we will be called the Occasions. And I, of course, since I'm founding the new nation, will be a Special Occasion.

(1996)

Questions

1. To what extent do you think this piece is intended to appeal to Native audiences? To non-Native Canadian audiences? To white non-Native Canadians specifically? How can you tell?
2. How would you characterize the author's relationship to white Canadian culture? What criticisms of white Canadian culture does he advance?
3. What purpose or purposes does humour serve in this essay?
4. Taylor has written extensively for film, television, and stage. How (if at all) is his background in writing for performance reflected in the style of this piece?
5. In discussing his work, Taylor has said "I hope that I have provided a window of understanding between Native and non-Native cultures by demystifying Native life." To what extent does "Pretty Like a White Boy" accomplish this goal?

Sherman Alexie

Indian Education

Novelist, essayist, and short fiction writer Sherman Alexie has described the following essay as "a true (and truer) account of my public school days." A Spokane/Coeur D'Alene Indian, Alexie was raised in Wellpinit, Washington, and chose not to attend high school on his reservation, opting for the greater educational resources offered at a white-dominated school in nearby Reardan. That experience, fictionalized to some extent, is reflected in "Indian Education," which first appeared in Alexie's 1993 collection* The Lone Ranger and Tonto Fistfight in Heaven. *In the interconnected pieces that make up the book, Alexie draws upon his memories and observations of life on the Spokane Reservation, creating a text he calls "not an autobiography of details but an autobiography of the soul."* The Lone Ranger and Tonto Fistfight in Heaven *was awarded a PEN/Hemingway citation for first fiction.*

First Grade

My hair was too short and my US Government glasses were horn-rimmed, ugly, and all that first winter in school, the other Indian boys chased me from one corner of the playground to the other. They pushed me down, buried me in the snow until I couldn't breathe, thought I'd never breathe again.

They stole my glasses and threw them over my head, around my outstretched hands, just beyond my reach, until someone tripped me and sent me falling again, facedown in the snow.

I was always falling down; my Indian name* was Junior Falls Down. Sometimes it was Bloody Nose or Steal-His-Lunch. Once, it was Cries-Like-a-White-Boy, even though none of us had seen a white boy cry.

Then it was Friday morning recess and Frenchy SiJohn threw snowballs at me while the rest of the Indian boys tortured some other *top-yogh-yaught* kid, another weakling. But Frenchy was confident enough to torment me all by himself, and most days I would have let him.

5 But the little warrior in me roared to life that day and knocked Frenchy to the ground, held his head against the snow, and punched him so hard that

my knuckles and the snow made symmetrical bruises on his face. He almost looked like he was wearing war paint.

But he wasn't the warrior. I was. And I chanted *It's a good day to die, it's a good day to die*,[1] all the way down to the principal's office.

SECOND GRADE

Betty Towle, missionary teacher,* redheaded and so ugly that no one ever had a puppy crush* on her, made me stay in for recess fourteen days straight.

"Tell me you're sorry," she said.

"Sorry for what?" I asked.

"Everything," she said and made me stand straight for fifteen minutes, eagle-armed with books in each hand. One was a math book; the other was English. But all I learned was that gravity can be painful.

For Halloween I drew a picture of her riding a broom with a scrawny cat on the back. She said that her God would never forgive me for that.

Once, she gave the class a spelling test but set me aside and gave me a test designed for junior high students. When I spelled all the words right, she crumpled up the paper and made me eat it.

"You'll learn respect," she said.

She sent a letter home with me that told my parents to either cut my braids or keep me home from class. My parents came in the next day and dragged their braids across Betty Towle's desk.

"Indians, indians, indians." She said it without capitalization. She called me "indian, indian, indian."

And I said, *Yes, I am. I am Indian. Indian, I am.*

THIRD GRADE

My traditional Native American art career began and ended with my very first portrait: *Stick Indian Taking a Piss in My Backyard.*

As I circulated the original print around the classroom, Mrs. Schluter intercepted and confiscated my art.

Censorship, I might cry now. *Freedom of expression*, I would write in editorials to the tribal newspaper.

In third grade, though, I stood alone in the corner, faced the wall, and waited for the punishment to end.

I'm still waiting.

---

1 *it's a good day to die* Battle cry attributed to Ta-sunko-witko (c. 1842–77), Sioux chief and war leader also known as Crazy Horse. According to popular legend, he shouted "It's a good day to die!" before the Sioux victory against United States forces at the Battle of the Little Bighorn (1876).

FOURTH GRADE

"You should be a doctor when you grow up," Mr. Schluter told me, even though his wife, the third grade teacher, thought I was crazy beyond my years. My eyes always looked like I had just hit-and-run someone.

"Guilty," she said. "You always look guilty."

"Why should I be a doctor?" I asked Mr. Schluter.

"So you can come back and help the tribe. So you can heal people."

That was the year my father drank a gallon of vodka a day and the same year that my mother started two hundred different quilts but never finished any. They sat in separate, dark places in our HUD[2] house and wept savagely.

I ran home after school, heard their Indian tears, and looked in the mirror. *Doctor Victor*, I called myself, invented an education, talked to my reflection. *Doctor Victor to the emergency room.*

FIFTH GRADE

I picked up a basketball for the first time and made my first shot. No. I missed my first shot, missed the basket completely, and the ball landed in the dirt and sawdust, sat there just like I had sat there only minutes before.

But it felt good, that ball in my hands, all those possibilities and angles. It was mathematics, geometry. It was beautiful.

At that same moment, my cousin Steven Ford sniffed rubber cement from a paper bag and leaned back on the merry-go-round. His ears rang, his mouth was dry, and everyone seemed so far away.

But it felt good, that buzz in his head, all those colours and noises. It was chemistry, biology. It was beautiful.

Oh, do you remember those sweet, almost innocent choices that the Indian boys were forced to make?

SIXTH GRADE

Randy, the new Indian kid from the white town of Springdale, got into a fight an hour after he first walked into the reservation school.

Stevie Flett called him out, called him a squawman,[3] called him a pussy, and called him a punk.

---

2 *HUD* Housing and Urban Development, a department of the United States federal government responsible for facilitating access to affordable housing.

3 *squawman* Offensive term usually referring to a white man who marries a Native American woman.

Randy and Stevie, and the rest of the Indian boys, walked out into the 35
playground.

"Throw the first punch," Stevie said as they squared off.

"No," Randy said.

"Throw the first punch," Stevie said again.

"No," Randy said again.

"Throw the first punch!" Stevie said for the third time, and Randy reared 40
back and pitched a knuckle fastball that broke Stevie's nose.

We all stood there in silence, in awe.

That was Randy, my soon-to-be first and best friend, who taught me the most valuable lesson about living in the white world: *Always throw the first punch.*

SEVENTH GRADE

I leaned through the basement window of the HUD house and kissed the white girl who would later be raped by her foster-parent father, who was also white. They both lived on the reservation, though, and when the headlines and stories filled the papers later, not one word was made of their colour.

Just Indians being Indians, someone must have said somewhere and they were wrong.

But on the day I leaned through the basement window of the HUD house 45
and kissed the white girl, I felt the good-byes I was saying to my entire tribe. I held my lips tight against her lips, a dry, clumsy, and ultimately stupid kiss.

But I was saying good-bye to my tribe, to all the Indian girls and women I might have loved, to all the Indian men who might have called me cousin, even brother.

I kissed that white girl and when I opened my eyes, she was gone from the reservation, and when I opened my eyes, I was gone from the reservation, living in a farm town where a beautiful white girl asked my name.

"Junior Polatkin," I said, and she laughed.

After that, no one spoke to me for another five hundred years.

EIGHTH GRADE

At the farm town junior high, in the boys' bathroom, I could hear voices from 50
the girls' bathroom, nervous whispers of anorexia and bulimia.* I could hear the white girls' forced vomiting, a sound so familiar and natural to me after years of listening to my father's hangovers.

"Give me your lunch if you're just going to throw it up," I said to one of those girls once.

I sat back and watched them grow skinny from self pity.

Back on the reservation, my mother stood in line to get us commodities. We carried them home, happy to have food, and opened the canned beef that even the dogs wouldn't eat.

But we ate it day after day and grew skinny from self pity.

There is more than one way to starve.

NINTH GRADE

At the farm town high school dance, after a basketball game in an overheated gym where I had scored twenty-seven points and pulled down thirteen rebounds, I passed out during a slow song.

As my white friends revived me and prepared to take me to the emergency room where doctors would later diagnose my diabetes, the Chicano* teacher ran up to us.

"Hey," he said. "What's that boy been drinking? I know all about these Indian kids. They start drinking real young."

Sharing dark skin doesn't necessarily make two men brothers.

TENTH GRADE

I passed the written test easily and nearly flunked the driving, but still received my Washington State driver's license on the same day that Wally Jim killed himself by driving his car into a pine tree.

No traces of alcohol in his blood, good job, wife and two kids.

"Why'd he do it?" asked a white Washington State trooper.

All the Indians shrugged their shoulders, looked down at the ground.

"Don't know," we all said, but when we look in the mirror, see the history of our tribe in our eyes, taste failure in the tap water, and shake with old tears, we understand completely.

Believe me, everything looks like a noose if you stare at it long enough.

ELEVENTH GRADE

Last night I missed two free throws which would have won the game against the best team in the state. The farm town high school I play for is nicknamed the "Indians," and I'm probably the only actual Indian ever to play for a team with such a mascot.

This morning I pick up the sports page and read the headline: INDIANS LOSE AGAIN.

Go ahead and tell me none of this is supposed to hurt me very much.

TWELFTH GRADE

I walk down the aisle, valedictorian of this farm town high school, and my cap doesn't fit because I've grown my hair longer than it's ever been. Later, I stand as the school-board chairman recites my awards, accomplishments, and scholarships.

I try to remain stoic for the photographers as I look toward the future.

Back home on the reservation, my former classmates graduate: a few can't read, one or two are just given attendance diplomas, most look forward to the parties. The bright students are shaken, frightened, because they don't know what comes next.

They smile for the photographer as they look back toward tradition.

The tribal newspaper runs my photograph and the photograph of my former classmates side by side.

POSTSCRIPT: CLASS REUNION

Victor said, "Why should we organize a reservation high school reunion? My graduating class has a reunion every weekend at the Powwow Tavern."

(1993)

Questions

1. In "Indian Education," does education function as a tool of colonization? Does it function as a means of resisting colonization?
2. This narrative has been called a personal essay, but it also contains fictional characters that appear in some of Alexie's other stories. What do you think Alexie means when he calls it "a true (and truer) account" of his own school days?
3. Alexie is known for his use of humour. What effects does he create with humour in "Indian Education"?
4. Explain the significance of this essay's postscript.

ANNE CARSON

from SHORT TALKS

Poet, prose writer, translator, and classicist Anne Carson is known for works that blur the boundaries of genre—from her verse essay The Idea of the Husband *(2001), told in "twenty-nine tangos," to her* Autobiography of Red *(1998), subtitled* A Novel in Verse. *Her "short talks," some of which appear below, have been variously described by critics as "poetic meditations," "prose poems," "miniature essays," and "micro truths."*

INTRODUCTION

Early one morning words were missing. Before that, words were not. Facts were, faces were. In a good story, Aristotle tells us, everything that happens is pushed by something else.[1] Three old women were bending in the fields. What use is it to question us? they said. Well it shortly became clear that they knew everything there is to know about the snowy fields and the blue-green shoots and the plant called "audacity," which poets mistake for violets. I began to copy out everything that was said. The marks construct an instant of nature gradually, without the boredom of a story. I emphasize this. I will do anything to avoid boredom. It is the task of a lifetime. You can never know enough, never work enough, never use the infinitives and participles oddly enough, never impede the movement harshly enough, never leave the mind quickly enough.

---

1 *In a ... else* In his *Poetics*, Aristotle claims that the middle and concluding events of a plot should follow logically from the events that come before. (In his *Physics*, he also argues that motion occurs when one object is acted on by another, a "mover," that is already in motion; that mover must in turn be moved by another mover, and so on. Since this chain cannot carry on forever, Aristotle thought, this necessitates the existence of at least one "unmoved mover" that moves itself. According to later Christian theologians, the "unmoved mover" is God.)

ON PARMENIDES[2]

We pride ourselves on being civilized people. Yet what if the names for things were utterly different? Italy, for example. I have a friend named Andreas, an Italian. He has lived in Argentina as well as in England, and also in Costa Rica for some time. Everywhere he lives, he invites people over for supper. It is a lot of work. Artichoke pasta. Peaches. His deep smile never fades. What if the proper name for Italy turns out to be Brzoy—will Andreas continue to travel the world like the wandering moon with her borrowed light? I fear we failed to understand what he was saying or his reasons. What if every time he said *cities*, he meant *delusion*, for example?

ON SLEEP STONES

Camille Claudel[3] lived the last thirty years of her life in an asylum, wondering why, writing letters to her brother the poet, who had signed the papers. Come visit me, she says. Remember, I am living here with madwomen; days are long. She did not smoke or stroll. She refused to sculpt. Although they gave her sleep stones—marble and granite and porphyry—she broke them, then collected the pieces and buried these outside the walls at night. Night was when her hands grew, huger and huger until in the photograph they are like two parts of someone else loaded onto her knees.

ON WALKING BACKWARDS

My mother forbad us to walk backwards. That is how the dead walk, she would say. Where did she get this idea? Perhaps from a bad translation. The dead, after all, do not walk backwards but they do walk behind us. They have no lungs and cannot call out but would love for us to turn around. They are victims of love, many of them.

ON THE TOTAL COLLECTION

From childhood he dreamed of being able to keep with him all the objects in 5
the world lined up on his shelves and bookcase. He denied lack, oblivion or even the likelihood of a missing piece. Order streamed from Noah* in blue triangles and as the pure fury of his classifications rose around him, engulfing his life, they came to be called waves by others, who drowned, a world of them.

---

2 *Parmenides* Greek poet-philosopher of the early fifth century BCE who claimed that our experience of change and variety in the world is an illusion, and that the universe is in reality pure, undifferentiated "Being."

3 *Camille Claudel* French sculptor (1864–1943). Though she was a successful artist in her own right, she is also remembered for a tumultuous romance and working relationship with the more famous sculptor Auguste Rodin (1840–1917).

ON SUNDAY DINNER WITH FATHER

Are you going to put that chair back where it belongs or just leave it there looking like a uterus? (Our balcony is a breezy June balcony.) Are you going to let your face distorted by warring desires pour down on us all through the meal or tidy yourself so we can at least enjoy dessert? (We weight down the corners of everything on the table with little solid-silver laws.) Are you going to nick your throat open on those woodpecker scalps as you do every Sunday night or just sit quietly while Laetitia plays her clarinet for us? (My father, who smokes a brand of cigar called Dimanche Eternel,[4] uses them as ashtrays.)

(1992, revised 1995)

Questions

1. In an interview,[5] Anne Carson said "My first book of poems, *Short Talks*, was initially a set of drawings with just titles. Then I expanded the titles a bit and then gradually realized nobody was interested in the drawings, so I just took the titles off and then they were pellets of a lecture." In what ways (if any) are these pieces ekphrastic? Do you think "pellets of a lecture" is a good way to describe them? Why or why not?
2. What does the title of this series of poems suggest about them?
3. The speaker of "Introduction" lays out a series of maxims in the last sentence. What are they? What do they say about the practice of writing (or of living)? To what extent do they describe the approach to writing taken in these "short talks"?
4. In "On Parmenides," is it important that Andreas is Italian? Why or why not? What is the speaker saying about words and the meaning we attach to them?
5. Who was Camille Claudel? Research her life and work. Does knowing her story change your experience of "On Sleep Stones"?
6. Consider the last sentence of "On Sleep Stones." Why would Claudel's hands "grow," and in whose perception? In "On Sunday Dinner with Father," how do the statements in parentheses work in the piece? How do they relate to the preceding questions?

---

4 *Dimanche Eternel* French: Eternal Sunday.

5 Carson, Anne. "The Art of Poetry, No. 88." Interview by Will Aitken, *The Paris Review*, Issue 171, Fall 2004, www.theparisreview.org/interviews/5420/anne-carson-the-art-of-poetry-no-88-anne-carson.

EMILY MARTIN

THE EGG AND THE SPERM:

HOW SCIENCE HAS CONSTRUCTED A ROMANCE BASED ON STEREOTYPICAL MALE-FEMALE ROLES

Anthropologist Emily Martin is best known for her work on American science and medicine—and especially for her analysis of scientific metaphors surrounding women's bodies and human reproductive processes. The following article, one of her most famous pieces, appeared in the major feminist journal Signs *in 1991.*

The theory of the human body is always a part of a world-picture ...
The theory of the human body is always a part of a fantasy.

[James Hillman, *The Myth of Analysis*][1]

As an anthropologist, I am intrigued by the possibility that culture shapes how biological scientists describe what they discover about the natural world. If this were so, we would be learning about more than the natural world in high school biology class; we would be learning about cultural beliefs and practices as if they were part of nature. In the course of my research I realized that the picture of egg and sperm drawn in popular as well as scientific accounts of reproductive biology relies on stereotypes central to our cultural definitions of male and female. The stereotypes imply not only that female biological processes are less worthy than their male counterparts but also that women are less worthy than men. Part of my goal in writing this article is to shine a bright light on the gender stereotypes hidden within the scientific language of biology. Exposed in such a light, I hope they will lose much of their power to harm us.

1 James Hillman, *The Myth of Analysis* (Evanston, Ill.: Northwestern University Press, 1972), 220. [Unless otherwise noted, all notes to this essay are from the author.]

EGG AND SPERM: A SCIENTIFIC FAIRY TALE

At a fundamental level, all major scientific textbooks depict male and female reproductive organs as systems for the production of valuable substances, such as eggs and sperm.[2] In the case of women, the monthly cycle is described as being designed to produce eggs and prepare a suitable place for them to be fertilized and grown—all to the end of making babies. But the enthusiasm ends there. By extolling the female cycle as a productive enterprise, menstruation must necessarily be viewed as a failure. Medical texts describe menstruation as the "debris" of the uterine lining, the result of necrosis, or death of tissue. The descriptions imply that a system has gone awry, making products of no use, not to specification, unsalable, wasted, scrap. An illustration in a widely used medical text shows menstruation as a chaotic disintegration of form, complementing the many texts that describe it as "ceasing," "dying," "losing," "denuding," "expelling."[3]

Male reproductive physiology is evaluated quite differently. One of the texts that sees menstruation as failed production employs a sort of breathless prose when it describes the maturation of sperm: "The mechanisms which guide the remarkable cellular transformation from spermatid to mature sperm remain uncertain.... Perhaps the most amazing characteristic of spermatogenesis is its sheer magnitude: the normal human male may manufacture several hundred million sperm per day."[4] In the classic text *Medical Physiology*, edited by Vernon Mountcastle, the male/female, productive/destructive comparison is more explicit: "Whereas the female *sheds* only a single gamete each month, the seminiferous tubules *produce* hundreds of millions of sperm each day" (emphasis mine).[5] The female author of another text marvels at the length of the microscopic seminiferous tubules, which, if uncoiled and placed end to end, "would span almost one-third of a mile!" She writes, "In an adult male these structures produce millions of sperm cells each day." Later she asks, "How is this feat accomplished?"[6] None of these texts expresses such intense

---

2 The textbooks I consulted are the main ones used in classes for undergraduate premedical students or medical students (or those held on reserve in the library for these classes) during the past few years at Johns Hopkins University. These texts are widely used at other universities in the country as well.

3 Arthur C. Guyton, *Physiology of the Human Body*, 6th ed. (Philadelphia: Saunders College Publishing, 1984), 624.

4 Arthur J. Vander, James H. Sherman, and Dorothy S. Luciano, *Human Physiology: The Mechanisms of Body Function*, 3rd ed. (New York: McGraw Hill, 1980), 483–84.

5 Vernon B. Mountcastle, *Medical Physiology*, 14th ed. (London: Mosby, 1980), 2:1624.

6 Eldra Pearl Solomon, *Human Anatomy and Physiology* (New York: CBS College Publishing, 1983), 678.

enthusiasm for any female processes. It is surely no accident that the "remarkable" process of making sperm involves precisely what, in the medical view, menstruation does not: production of something deemed valuable.[7]

One could argue that menstruation and spermatogenesis are not analogous processes and, therefore, should not be expected to elicit the same kind of response. The proper female analogy to spermatogenesis, biologically, is ovulation. Yet ovulation does not merit enthusiasm in these texts either. Textbook descriptions stress that all of the ovarian follicles containing ova are already present at birth. Far from being *produced*, as sperm are, they merely sit on the shelf, slowly degenerating and aging like overstocked inventory: "At birth, normal human ovaries contain an estimated one million follicles [each], and no new ones appear after birth. Thus, in marked contrast to the male, the newborn female already has all the germ cells she will ever have. Only a few, perhaps 400, are destined to reach full maturity during her active productive life. All the others degenerate at some point in their development so that few, if any remain by the time she reaches menopause at approximately 50 years of age."[8] Note the "marked contrast" that this description sets up between male and female, who has stockpiled germ cells by birth and is faced with their degeneration.

Nor are the female organs spared such vivid descriptions. One scientist 5
writes in a newspaper article that a woman's ovaries become old and worn out from ripening eggs every month, even though the woman herself is still relatively young: "When you look through a laparoscope ... at an ovary that has been through hundreds of cycles, even in a superbly healthy American female, you see a scarred, battered organ."[9]

To avoid the negative connotations that some people associate with the female reproductive system, scientists could begin to describe male and female processes as homologous.* They might credit females with "producing" mature ova one at a time, as they're needed each month, and describe males as having to face problems of degenerating germ cells. This degeneration would occur throughout life among spermatogonia, the undifferentiated germ cells in the testes that are the long-lived, dormant precursors of sperm.

But the texts have an almost dogged insistence on casting female processes in a negative light. The texts celebrate sperm production because it is continuous from puberty to senescence, while they portray egg production as inferior because it is finished at birth. This makes the female seem unproductive, but

---

7 For elaboration, see Emily Martin, *The Woman in the Body: A Cultural Analysis of Reproduction* (Boston: Beacon, 1987), 27–53.

8 Vander, Sherman, and Luciano, 568.

9 Melvin Konner, "Childbearing and Age," *New York Times Magazine* (December 27, 1987), 22–23, esp. 22.

some texts will also insist that it is she who is wasteful.[10] In a section heading for *Molecular Biology of the Cell*, a best-selling text, we are told that "Oogenesis is wasteful." The text goes on to emphasize that of the seven million oogonia, or egg germ cells, in the female embryo, most degenerate in the ovary. Of those that do go on to become oocytes, or eggs, many also degenerate, so that at birth only two million eggs remain in the ovaries. Degeneration continues throughout a woman's life: by puberty 300,000 eggs remain, and only a few are present by menopause. "During the 40 or so years of a woman's reproductive life only 400 to 500 eggs will have been released," the authors write. "All the rest will have degenerated. It is still a mystery why so many eggs are formed only to die in the ovaries."[11]

The real mystery is why the male's vast production of sperm is not seen as wasteful.[12] Assuming that a man "produces" 100 million (10^8) sperm per day (a conservative estimate) during an average reproductive life of sixty years, he would produce well over two trillion sperm in his lifetime. Assuming that a woman "ripens" one egg per lunar month, or thirteen per year, over the course of her forty-year reproductive life, she would total five hundred eggs in her lifetime. But the word "waste" implies an excess, too much produced. Assuming two or three offspring, for every baby a woman produces, she wastes only around two hundred eggs. For every baby a man produces, he wastes more than one trillion (10^{12}) sperm.

---

10 I have found but one exception to the opinion that the female is wasteful: "Smallpox being the nasty disease it is, one might expect nature to have designed antibody molecules with combining sites that specifically recognize the epitopes on smallpox virus. Nature differs from technology, however: it thinks nothing of wastefulness. (For example, rather than improving the chance that a spermatozoon will meet an egg cell, nature finds it easier to produce millions of spermatozoa.)" (Niels Kaj Jerne, "The Immune System," *Scientific American* 229, no. 1 [July 1973]: 53). Thanks to a *Signs* reviewer for bringing this reference to my attention.

11 Bruce Alberts et al., *Molecular Biology of the Cell* (New York: Garland, 1983), 795.

12 In her essay "Have Only Men Evolved?" (in *Discovering Reality: Feminist Perspectives on Epistemology, Metaphysics, Methodology, and Philosophy of Science*, ed. Sandra Harding and Merrill B. Hintikka [Dordrecht: Reidel, 1983], 45–69, esp. 60–61), Ruth Hubbard points out that sociobiologists have said the female invests more energy than the male in the production of her large gametes, claiming that this explains why the female provides parental care. Hubbard questions whether it "really takes more 'energy' to generate the one or relatively few eggs than the large excess of sperms required to achieve fertilization." For further critique of how the greater size of eggs is interpreted in sociobiology, see Donna Haraway, "Investment Strategies for the Evolving Portfolio of Primate Females," in *Body/Politics*, ed. Mary Jacobus, Evelyn Fox Keller, and Sally Shuttleworth (New York: Routledge, 1990), 155–56.

How is it that positive images are denied to the bodies of women? A look at language—in this case, scientific language—provides the first clue. Take the egg and the sperm.[13] It is remarkable how "femininely" the egg behaves and how "masculinely" the sperm.[14] The egg is seen as large and passive.[15] It does not *move* or *journey*, but passively "is transported," "is swept,"[16] or even "drifts"[17] along the fallopian tube. In utter contrast, sperm are small, "streamlined,"[18] and invariably active. They "deliver" their genes to the egg, "activate the developmental program of the egg,"[19] and have a "velocity" that is often remarked upon.[20] Their tails are "strong" and efficiently powered.[21] Together with the forces of ejaculation, they can "propel the semen into the deepest recesses of the vagina."[22] For this they need "energy," "fuel,"[23] so that with a "whiplashlike motion and strong lurches"[24] they can "burrow through the egg coat"[25] and "penetrate" it.[26]

At its extreme, the age-old relationship of the egg and the sperm takes on a royal or religious patina. The egg coat, its protective barrier, is sometimes

---

13 The sources I used for this article provide compelling information on interactions among sperm. Lack of space prevents me from taking up this theme here, but the elements include competition, hierarchy, and sacrifice. For a newspaper report, see Malcolm W. Browne, "Some Thoughts on Self Sacrifice," *New York Times* (July 5, 1988), C6. For a literary rendition, see John Barth, "Night-Sea Journey," in his *Lost in the Funhouse* (Garden City, NY: Doubleday, 1968), 3–13.

14 See Carol Delaney, "The Meaning of Paternity and the Virgin Birth Debate," *Man* 21, no. 3 (September 1986): 494–513. She discusses the difference between this scientific view that women contribute genetic material to the fetus and the claim of long-standing Western folk theories that the origin and identity of the fetus comes from the male, as in the metaphor of planting a seed in soil.

15 For a suggested direct link between human behaviour and purportedly passive eggs and active sperm, see Erik H. Erikson, "Inner and Outer Space: Reflections on Womanhood," *Daedalus* 93, no. 2 (Spring 1964): 582–606, esp. 591.

16 Guyton (n. 3 above), 619; and Mountcastle (n. 5 above), 1609.

17 Jonathan Miller and David Pelham, *The Facts of Life* (New York: Viking Penguin, 1984), 5.

18 Alberts et al., 796.

19 Ibid., 796.

20 See, e.g., William F. Ganong, *Review of Medical Physiology*, 7th ed. (Los Altos, Calif.: Lange Medical Publications, 1975), 322.

21 Alberts et al. (n. 11 above), 796.

22 Guyton, 615.

23 Solomon (n. 6 above), 683.

24 Vander, Sherman, and Luciano (n. 4 above), 4th ed. (1985), 580.

25 Alberts et al., 796.

26 All biology texts quoted above use the word "penetrate."

called its "vestments,"* a term usually reserved for sacred, religious dress. The egg is said to have a "corona,"[27] a crown, and to be accompanied by "attendant cells."[28] It is holy, set apart and above, the queen to the sperm's king. The egg is also passive, which means it must depend on sperm for rescue. Gerald Schatten and Helen Schatten liken the egg's role to that of Sleeping Beauty: "a dormant bride awaiting her mate's magic kiss, which instills the spirit that brings her to life."[29] Sperm, by contrast, have a "mission,"[30] which is to "move through the female genital tract in quest of the ovum."[31] One popular account has it that the sperm carry out a "perilous journey" into the "warm darkness," where some fall away "exhausted." "Survivors" "assault" the egg, the successful candidates "surrounding the prize."[32] Part of the urgency of this journey, in more scientific terms, is that "once released from the supportive environment of the ovary, an egg will die within hours unless rescued by a sperm."[33] The wording stresses the fragility and dependency of the egg, even though the same text acknowledges elsewhere that sperm also live for only a few hours.[34]

In 1948, in a book remarkable for its early insights into these matters, Ruth Herschberger argued that female reproductive organs are seen as biologically interdependent, while male organs are viewed as autonomous, operating independently and in isolation:

> At present the functional is stressed only in connection with women: it is in them that ovaries, tubes, uterus, and vagina have endless interdependence. In the male, reproduction would seem to involve "organs" only.
>
> Yet the sperm, just as much as the egg, is dependent on a great many related processes. There are secretions which mitigate the urine in the urethra before ejaculation, to protect the sperm. There is the reflex shutting off of the bladder connection, the provision of prostatic secretions, and various types of muscular propulsion. The sperm is no more independent of its milieu than the egg, and yet from a wish that it were, biologists have lent their support to the notion that the human

27 Solomon, 700.

28 A. Beldecos et al., "The Importance of Feminist Critique for Contemporary Cell Biology," *Hypatia* 3, no. 1 (Spring 1988): 61–76.

29 Gerald Schatten and Helen Schatten, "The Energetic Egg," *Medical World News* 23 (January 23, 1984): 51–53, esp. 51.

30 Alberts et al., 796.

31 Guyton (n. 3 above), 613.

32 Miller and Pelham (n. 17 above), 7.

33 Alberts et al. (n. 11 above), 804.

34 Ibid., 801.

female, beginning with the egg, is congenitally more dependent than the male.[35]

Bringing out another aspect of the sperm's autonomy, an article in the journal *Cell* has the sperm making an "existential decision" to penetrate the egg: "Sperm are cells with a limited behavioural repertoire, one that is directed toward fertilizing eggs. To execute the decision to abandon the haploid state, sperm swim to an egg and there acquire the ability to effect membrane fusion."[36] Is this a corporate manager's version of the sperm's activities—"executing decisions" while fraught with dismay over difficult options that bring with them very high risk?

There is another way that sperm, despite their small size, can be made to loom in importance over the egg. In a collection of scientific papers, an electron micrograph of an enormous egg and tiny sperm is titled "A Portrait of the Sperm."[37] This is a little like showing a photo of a dog and calling it a picture of the fleas. Granted, microscopic sperm are harder to photograph than eggs, which are just large enough to see with the naked eye. But surely the use of the term "portrait," a word associated with the powerful and wealthy, is significant. Eggs have only micrographs or pictures, not portraits.

One depiction of sperm as weak and timid, instead of strong and powerful—the only such representation in western civilization, so far as I know—occurs in Woody Allen's movie *Everything You Always Wanted to Know about Sex* (*But Were Afraid to Ask)*. Allen, playing the part of an apprehensive sperm inside a man's testicles, is scared of the man's approaching orgasm. He is reluctant to launch himself into the darkness, afraid of contraceptive devices, afraid of winding up on the ceiling if the man masturbates.

The more common picture—egg as damsel in distress, shielded only by 15
her sacred garments; sperm as heroic warrior to the rescue—cannot be proved to be dictated by the biology of these events. While the "facts" of biology may not *always* be constructed in cultural terms, I would argue that in this case they are. The degree of metaphorical content in these descriptions, the extent to which differences between egg and sperm are emphasized, and the parallels between cultural stereotypes of male and female behaviour and the character of egg and sperm all point to this conclusion.

35 Ruth Herschberger, *Adam's Rib* (New York: Pelligrini & Cudaby, 1948), esp. 84. I am indebted to Ruth Hubbard for telling me about Herschberger's work, although at a point when this paper was already in draft form.

36 Bennett M. Shapiro. "The Existential Decision of a Sperm," *Cell* 49, no. 3 (May 1987): 293–94, esp. 293.

37 Lennart Nilsson, "A Portrait of the Sperm," in *The Functional Anatomy of the Spermatozoan*, ed. Bjorn A. Afzelius (New York: Pergamon, 1975), 79–82.

New Research, Old Imagery

As new understandings of egg and sperm emerge, textbook gender imagery is being revised. But the new research, far from escaping the stereotypical representations of egg and sperm, simply replicates elements of textbook gender imagery in a different form. The persistence of this imagery calls to mind what Ludwig Fleck termed "the self-contained" nature of scientific thought. As he described it, "the interaction between what is already known, what remains to be learned, and those who are to apprehend it, go to ensure harmony within the system. But at the same time they also preserve the harmony of illusions, which is quite secure within the confines of a given thought style."[38] We need to understand the way in which the cultural content in scientific descriptions changes as biological discoveries unfold, and whether that cultural content is solidly entrenched or easily changed.

In all of the texts quoted above, sperm are described as penetrating the egg, and specific substances on a sperm's head are described as binding to the egg. Recently, this description of events was rewritten in a biophysics lab at Johns Hopkins University—transforming the egg from the passive to the active party.[39]

Prior to this research, it was thought that the zona, the inner vestments of the egg, formed an impenetrable barrier. Sperm overcame the barrier by mechanically burrowing through, thrashing their tails and slowly working their way along. Later research showed that the sperm released digestive enzymes that chemically broke down the zona; thus, scientists presumed that the sperm used mechanical and chemical means to get through to the egg.

In this recent investigation, the researchers began to ask questions about the mechanical force of the sperm's tail. (The lab's goal was to develop a contraceptive that worked topically on sperm.) They discovered, to their great surprise, that the forward thrust of sperm is extremely weak, which contradicts the assumption that sperm are forceful penetrators.[40] Rather than thrusting forward, the sperm's head was now seen to move mostly back and forth. The sideways motion of the sperm's tail makes the head move sideways with a force

38 Ludwig Fleck, *Genesis and Development of a Scientific Fact*, ed. Thaddeus J. Trenn and Robert K. Merton (Chicago: University of Chicago Press, 1979), 38.

39 Jay M. Baltz carried out the research I describe when he was a graduate student in the Thomas C. Jenkins Department of Biophysics at Johns Hopkins University.

40 Far less is known about the physiology of sperm than comparable female substances, which some feminists claim is no accident. Greater scientific scrutiny of female reproduction has long enabled the burden of birth control to be placed on women. In this case, the researchers' discovery did not depend on development of any new technology: The experiments made use of glass pipettes, a manometer, and a simple microscope, all of which have been available for more than one hundred years.

that is ten times stronger than its forward movement. So even if the overall force of the sperm were strong enough to mechanically break the zona, most of its force would be directed sideways rather than forward. In fact, its strongest tendency, by tenfold, is to *escape* by attempting to pry itself off the egg. Sperm, then, must be exceptionally efficient at escaping from any cell surface they contact. And the surface of the egg must be designed to trap the sperm and prevent their escape. Otherwise, few if any sperm would reach the egg.

The researchers at Johns Hopkins concluded that the sperm and egg stick 20
together because of adhesive molecules on the surfaces of each. The egg traps the sperm and adheres to it so tightly that the sperm's head is forced to lie flat against the surface of the zona, a little bit, they told me, "like Br'er Rabbit getting more and more stuck to tar baby the more he wriggles."* The trapped sperm continues to wiggle ineffectually side to side. The mechanical force of its tail is so weak that a sperm cannot break even one chemical bond. This is where the digestive enzymes released by the sperm come in. If they start to soften the zona just at the tip of the sperm and the sides remain stuck, then the weak, flailing sperm can get oriented in the right direction and make it through the zona—provided that its bonds to the zona dissolve as it moves in.

Although this new version of the saga of the egg and the sperm broke through cultural expectations, the researchers who made the discovery continued to write papers and abstracts as if the sperm were the active party who attacks, binds, penetrates, and enters the egg. The only difference was that the sperm were now seen as performing these actions weakly.[41] Not until August 1987, more than three years after the findings described above, did these researchers reconceptualize the process to give the egg a more active role. They began to describe the zona as an aggressive sperm catcher, covered with adhesive molecules that can capture a sperm with a single bond and clasp it to the zona's surface.[42] In the words of their published account: "The innermost

---

41 Jay Baltz and Richard A. Cone, "What Force Is Needed to Tether a Sperm?" (abstract for Society for the Study of Reproduction, 1985), and "Flagellar Torque on the Head Determines the Force Needed to Tether a Sperm" (abstract for Biophysical Society, 1986).

42 Jay M. Baltz, David F. Katz, and Richard A. Cone, "The Mechanics of the Sperm-Egg Interaction at the Zona Pellucida," *Biophysical Journal* 54, no. 4 (October 1988): 643–54. Lab members were somewhat familiar with work on metaphors in the biology of female reproduction. Richard Cone, who runs the lab, is my husband, and he talked with them about my earlier research on the subject from time to time. Even though my current research focuses on biological imagery and I heard about the lab's work from my husband every day, I myself did not recognize the role of imagery in the sperm research until many weeks after the period of research and writing I describe. Therefore, I assume that any awareness the lab members may have had about how underlying metaphor might be guiding this particular research was fairly inchoate.

vestment, the *zona pellucida*, is a glycoprotein shell, which captures and tethers the sperm before they penetrate it.... The sperm is captured at the initial contact between the sperm tip and the *zona*.... Since the thrust [of the sperm] is much smaller than the force needed to break a single affinity bond, the first bond made upon the tip-first meeting of the sperm and *zona* can result in the capture of the sperm."[43]

Experiments in another lab reveal similar patterns of data interpretation. Gerald Schatten and Helen Schatten set out to show that, contrary to conventional wisdom, the "egg is not merely a large, yolk-filled sphere into which the sperm burrows to endow new life. Rather, recent research suggests the almost heretical* view that sperm and egg are mutually active partners."[44] This sounds like a departure from the stereotypical textbook view, but further reading reveals Schatten and Schatten's conformity to the aggressive-sperm metaphor. They describe how "the sperm and egg first touch when, from the tip of the sperm's triangular head, a long, thin filament shoots out and harpoons the egg." Then we learn that "remarkably, the harpoon is not so much fired as assembled at great speed, molecule by molecule, from a pool of protein stored in a specialized region called the acrosome. The filament may grow as much as twenty times longer than the sperm head itself before its tip reaches the egg and sticks."[45] Why not call this "making a bridge" or "throwing out a line" rather than firing a harpoon? Harpoons pierce prey and injure or kill them, while this filament only sticks. And why not focus, as the Hopkins lab did, on the stickiness of the egg, rather than the stickiness of the sperm?[46] Later in the article, the Schattens replicate the common view of the sperm's perilous journey into the warm darkness of the vagina, this time for the purpose of explaining its journey into the egg itself: "[The sperm] still has an arduous journey ahead. It must penetrate farther into the egg's huge sphere of cytoplasm and somehow locate the nucleus, so that the two cells' chromosomes can fuse. The sperm dives down into the cytoplasm, its tail beating. But it is soon interrupted by the sudden and swift migration of the egg nucleus, which rushes toward the sperm with a velocity triple that of the movement of chromosomes during cell division, crossing the entire egg in about a minute."[47]

Like Schatten and Schatten and the biophysicists at Johns Hopkins, another researcher has recently made discoveries that seem to point to a more

43 Ibid., 643, 650.

44 Schatten and Schatten (n. 29 above), 51.

45 Ibid., 52.

46 Surprisingly, in an article intended for a general audience, the authors do not point out that these are sea urchin sperm and note that human sperm do not shoot out filaments at all.

47 Schatten and Schatten, 53.

interactive view of the relationship of egg and sperm. This work, which Paul Wassarman conducted on the sperm and eggs of mice, focuses on identifying the specific molecules in the egg coat (the zona pellucida) that are involved in egg-sperm interaction. At first glance, his descriptions seem to fit the model of an egalitarian relationship. Male and female gametes "recognize one another," and "interactions ... take place between sperm and egg."[48] But the article in *Scientific American* in which those descriptions appear begins with a vignette that presages the dominant motif of their presentation: "It has been more than a century since Hermann Fol, a Swiss zoologist, peered into his microscope and became the first person to see a sperm penetrate an egg, fertilize it and form the first cell of a new embryo."[49] This portrayal of the sperm as the active party—the one that *penetrates* and *fertilizes* the egg and *produces* the embryo—is not cited as an example of an earlier, now outmoded view. In fact, the author reiterates the point later in the article: "Many sperm can bind to and penetrate the zona pellucida, or outer coat, of an unfertilized mouse egg, but only one sperm will eventually fuse with the thin plasma membrane surrounding the egg proper (*inner sphere*), *fertilizing the egg and giving rise to a new embryo*."[50]

The imagery of sperm as aggressor is particularly startling in this case: the main discovery being reported is isolation of a particular molecule *on the egg coat* that plays an important role in fertilization! Wassarman's choice of language sustains the picture. He calls the molecule that has been isolated, ZP3, a "sperm receptor." By allocating the passive, waiting role to the egg, Wassarman can continue to describe the sperm as the actor, the one that makes it all happen: "The basic process begins when many sperm first attach loosely and then bind tenaciously to receptors on the surface of the egg's thick outer coat, the zona pellucida. Each sperm, which has a large number of egg-binding proteins on its surface, binds to many sperm receptors on the egg. More specifically, a site on each of the egg-binding proteins fits a complementary site on a sperm receptor, much as a key fits a lock."[51] With the sperm designated as the "key" and the egg the "lock," it is obvious which one acts and which one is acted upon. Could this imagery not be reversed, letting the sperm (the lock) wait until the egg produces the key? Or could we speak of two halves of a locket matching, and regard the matching itself as the action that initiates the fertilization?

---

48 Paul M. Wassarman, "Fertilization in Mammals," *Scientific American* 259, no. 6 (December 1988): 78–84, esp. 78, 84.

49 Ibid., 78.

50 Ibid., 79.

51 Ibid., 78.

25 It is as if Wassarman were determined to make the egg the receiving partner. Usually in biological research, the protein member of the pair of binding molecules is called the receptor, and physically it has a pocket in it rather like a lock. As the diagrams that illustrate Wassarman's article show, the molecules on the sperm are proteins and have "pockets." The small, mobile molecules that fit into these pockets are called ligands. As shown in the diagrams, ZP3 on the egg is a polymer of "keys"; many small knobs stick out. Typically, molecules in the sperm would be called receptors and molecules on the egg would be called ligands. But Wassarman chose to name ZP3 on the egg the receptor and to create a new term, "the egg-binding protein," for the molecule on the sperm that otherwise would have been called the receptor.[52]

Wassarman does credit the egg coat with having more functions than those of a sperm receptor. While he notes that "the zona pellucida has at times been viewed by investigators as a nuisance, a barrier to sperm and hence an impediment to fertilization," his new research reveals that the egg coat "serves as a sophisticated biological security system that screens incoming sperm, selects only those compatible with fertilization and development, prepares sperm for fusion with the egg and later protects the resulting embryo from polyspermy [a lethal condition caused by fusion of more than one sperm with a single egg]."[53] Although this description gives the egg an active role, that role is drawn in stereotypically feminine terms. The egg *selects* an appropriate mate, *prepares* him for fusion, and then *protects* the resulting offspring from harm. This is courtship and mating behaviour as seen through the eyes of a sociobiologist: woman as the hard-to-get prize, who, following union with the chosen one, becomes woman as servant and mother.

And Wassarman does not quit there. In a review article for *Science*, he outlines the "chronology of fertilization."[54] Near the end of the article are two subject headings. One is "Sperm Penetration," in which Wassarman describes how the chemical dissolving of the zona pellucida combines with the "substantial propulsive force generated by sperm." The next heading is "Sperm-Egg Fusion." This section details what happens inside the zona after a sperm "penetrates" it. Sperm "can make contact with, adhere to, and fuse with (that is, fertilize) an egg."[55] Wassarman's word choice, again, is astonishingly

---

52 Since receptor molecules are relatively *immotile* and the ligands that bind to them relatively *motile*, one might imagine the egg being called the receptor and the sperm the ligand. But the molecules in question on egg and sperm are immotile molecules. It is the sperm as a *cell* that has motility, and the egg as a cell that has relative immotility.

53 Wassarman, 78–79.

54 Paul M. Wassarman, "The Biology and Chemistry of Fertilization," *Science* 235, no. 4788 (January 30, 1987): 553–60, esp. 554.

55 Ibid., 557.

skewed in favour of the sperm's activity, for in the next breath he says that sperm *lose* all motility upon fusion with the egg's surface. In mouse and sea urchin eggs, the sperm enters at the *egg's* volition, according to Wassarman's description: "Once fused with egg plasma membrane [the surface of the egg], how does a sperm enter the egg? The surface of both mouse and sea urchin eggs is covered with thousands of plasma membrane-bound projections, called microvilli [tiny 'hairs']. Evidence in sea urchins suggests that, after membrane fusion, a group of elongated microvilli cluster tightly around and interdigitate over the sperm head. As these microvilli are resorbed, the sperm is drawn into the egg. Therefore, sperm motility, which ceases at the time of fusion in both sea urchins and mice, is not required for sperm entry."[56] The section called "Sperm Penetration" more logically would be followed by a section called "The Egg Envelopes," rather than "Sperm-Egg Fusion." This would give a parallel—and more accurate—sense that both the egg and the sperm initiate action.

Another way that Wassarman makes less of the egg's activity is by describing components of the egg but referring to the sperm as a whole entity. Deborah Gordon has described such an approach as "atomism" ("the part is independent of and primordial to the whole") and identified it as one of the "tenacious assumptions" of Western science and medicine.[57] Wassarman employs atomism to his advantage. When he refers to processes going on within sperm, he consistently returns to descriptions that remind us from whence these activities came: they are part of sperm that penetrate an egg or generate propulsive force. When he refers to processes going on within eggs, he stops there. As a result, any active role he grants them appears to be assigned to the parts of the egg, and not to the egg itself. In the quote above, it is the microvilli that actively cluster around the sperm. In another example, "the driving force for engulfment of a fused sperm comes from a region of cytoplasm just beneath an egg's plasma membrane."[58]

SOCIAL IMPLICATIONS

All three of these revisionist accounts of egg and sperm cannot seem to escape the hierarchical imagery of older accounts. Even though each new account gives the egg a larger and more active role, taken together they bring into play another

---

56 Ibid., 557–58. This finding throws into question Schatten and Schatten's description (n. 29 above) of the sperm, its tail beating, diving down into the egg.

57 Deborah R. Gordon, "Tenacious Assumptions in Western Medicine," in *Bio-medicine Examined*, ed. Margaret Lock and Deborah Gordon (Dordrecht: Kluwer, 1988), 19–56, esp. 26.

58 Wassarman, "The Biology and Chemistry of Fertilization," 558.

cultural stereotype: woman as a dangerous and aggressive threat. In the Johns Hopkins lab's revised model, the egg ends up as the female aggressor who "captures and tethers" the sperm with her sticky zona, rather like a spider lying in wait in her web.[59] The Schatten lab has the egg's nucleus "interrupt" the sperm's dive with a "sudden and swift" rush by which she "clasps the sperm and guides its nucleus to the centre."[60] Wassarman's description of the surface of the egg "covered with thousands of plasma membrane-bound projections, called microvilli" that reach out and clasp the sperm adds to the spiderlike imagery.[61]

These images grant the egg an active role but at the cost of appearing disturbingly aggressive. Images of woman as dangerous and aggressive, the femme fatale* who victimizes men, are widespread in Western literature and culture.[62] More specific is the connection of spider imagery with the idea of an engulfing, devouring mother.[63] New data did not lead scientists to eliminate gender stereotypes in their descriptions of egg and sperm. Instead, scientists simply began to describe egg and sperm in different, but no less damaging, terms.

Can we envision a less stereotypical view? Biology itself provides another model that could be applied to the egg and the sperm. The cybernetic model—with its feedback loops, flexible adaptation to change, coordination of the parts within a whole, evolution over time, and changing response to the environment—is common in genetics, endocrinology, and ecology and has a growing influence in medicine in general.[64] This model has the potential to shift our imagery from the negative, in which the female reproductive system is castigated both for not producing eggs after birth and for producing (and thus wasting) too many eggs overall, to something more positive. The female reproductive system could be seen as responding to the environment (pregnancy or menopause), adjusting to monthly changes (menstruation), and flexibly changing from reproductivity after puberty to nonreproductivity later in life. The sperm and egg's interaction could also be described in cybernetic terms. J.F. Hartman's research in reproductive biology demonstrated fifteen years ago that if an egg is killed by being pricked with a needle, live sperm cannot get

59 Baltz, Katz, and Cone (n. 42 above), 643, 650.

60 Schatten and Schatten, 53.

61 Wassarman, "The Biology and Chemistry of Fertilization," 557.

62 Mary Ellman, *Thinking about Women* (New York: Harcourt Brace Jovanovich, 1968), 140; Nina Auerbach, *Woman and the Demon* (Cambridge, Mass.: Harvard University Press, 1982), esp. 186.

63 Kenneth Alan Adams, "Arachnophobia: Love American Style," *Journal of Psychoanalytic Anthropology* 4, no. 2 (1981): 157–97.

64 William Ray Arney and Bernard Bergen, *Medicine and the Management of Living* (Chicago: University of Chicago Press, 1984).

through the zona.[65] Clearly, this evidence shows that the egg and sperm do interact on more mutual terms, making biology's refusal to portray them that way all the more disturbing.

We would do well to be aware, however, that cybernetic imagery is hardly neutral. In the past, cybernetic models have played an important part in the imposition of social control. These models inherently provide a way of thinking about a "field" of interacting components. Once the field can be seen, it can become the object of new forms of knowledge, which in turn can allow new forms of social control to be exerted over the components of the field. During the 1950s, for example, medicine began to recognize the psychosocial *environment* of the patient: the patient's family and its psychodynamics. Professions such as social work began to focus on this new environment, and the resulting knowledge became one way to further control the patient. Patients began to be seen not as isolated, individual bodies, but as psychosocial entities located in an "ecological" system: management of "the patient's psychology was a new entrée to patient control."[66]

The models that biologists use to describe their data can have important social effects. During the nineteenth century, the social and natural sciences strongly influenced each other: the social ideas of Malthus about how to avoid the natural increase of the poor inspired Darwin's *Origin of Species*.[67] Once the *Origin* stood as a description of the natural world, complete with competition and market struggles, it could be reimported into social science as social Darwinism,* in order to justify the social order of the time. What we are seeing now is similar: the importation of cultural ideas about passive females and heroic males into the "personalities" of gametes. This amounts to the "implanting of social imagery on representations of nature so as to lay a firm basis for reimporting exactly that same imagery as natural explanations of social phenomena."[68]

Further research would show us exactly what social effects are being wrought from the biological imagery of egg and sperm. At the very least, the imagery keeps alive some of the hoariest old stereotypes about weak damsels in distress and their strong male rescuers. That these stereotypes are now being written in at the level of the cell constitutes a powerful move to make them seem so natural as to be beyond alteration.

---

65 J.F. Hartman, R.B. Gwatkin, and C.F. Hutchison, "Early Contact Interactions between Mammalian Gametes In Vitro," *Proceedings of the National Academy of Sciences* (US) 69, no. 10 (1972): 2767–69.

66 Arney and Bergen, 68.

67 Ruth Hubbard, "Have Only Men Evolved?" (n. 12 above), 51–52.

68 David Harvey, personal communication, November 1989.

35 The stereotypical imagery might also encourage people to imagine that what results from the interaction of egg and sperm—a fertilized egg—is the result of deliberate "human" action at the cellular level. Whatever the intentions of the human couple, in this microscopic "culture" a cellular "bride" (or femme fatale) and a cellular "groom" (her victim) make a cellular baby. Rosalind Petchesky points out that through visual representations such as sonograms, we are given "*images* of younger and younger, and tinier and tinier, fetuses being 'saved.'" This leads to "the point of visibility being 'pushed back' *indefinitely*."[69] Endowing egg and sperm with intentional action, a key aspect of personhood in our culture, lays the foundation for the point of viability being pushed back to the moment of fertilization. This will likely lead to greater acceptance of technological developments and new forms of scrutiny and manipulation, for the benefit of these inner "persons": court-ordered restrictions on a pregnant woman's activities in order to protect her fetus, fetal surgery, amniocentesis, and rescinding of abortion rights, to name but a few examples.[70]

Even if we succeed in substituting more egalitarian, interactive metaphors to describe the activities of egg and sperm, and manage to avoid the pitfalls of cybernetic models, we would still be guilty of endowing cellular entities with personhood. More crucial, then, than what *kinds* of personalities we bestow on cells is the very fact that we are doing it at all. This process could ultimately have the most disturbing social consequences.

One clear feminist challenge is to wake up sleeping metaphors in science, particularly those involved in descriptions of the egg and the sperm. Although the literary convention is to call such metaphors "dead," they are not so much dead as sleeping, hidden within the scientific content of texts—and all the more powerful for it.[71] Waking up such metaphors, by becoming aware of when we are projecting cultural imagery onto what we study, will improve our ability to investigate and understand nature. Waking up such metaphors, by becoming aware of their implications, will rob them of their power to naturalize our social conventions about gender.

(1991)

---

69 Rosalind Petchesky, "Fetal Images: The Power of Visual Culture in the Politics of Reproduction," *Feminist Studies* 13, no. 2 (Summer 1987): 263–92, esp. 272.

70 Rita Arditti, Renate Klein, and Shelley Minden, *Test-Tube Women* (London: Pandora, 1984); Ellen Goodman, "Whose Right to Life?" *Baltimore Sun* (November 17, 1987); Tamar Lewin, "Courts Acting to Force Care of the Unborn," *New York Times* (November 23, 1987), A1 and B10; Susan Irwin and Brigitte Jordon, "Knowledge, Practice, and Power: Court Ordered Cesarean Sections," *Medical Anthropology Quarterly* 1, no. 3 (September 1987): 319–34.

71 Thanks to Elizabeth Fee and David Spain, who in February 1989 and April 1989, respectively, made points related to this.

Questions

1. We tend to think of metaphor as the province of literary writing; by contrast, we think of scientific writing as purely descriptive. Is metaphor in fact a useful mode of description for scientific matters? Is it to some extent necessary to resort to metaphor in order to explain scientific processes adequately?
2. Why in Martin's view are the Johns Hopkins researchers who carried out the work she discusses in paragraphs 17–21 not more deserving of praise for their ground-breaking research? (The researchers in question are not named in the body of the article but identified in the references as J.M. Baltz, David F. Catz, and Richard A. Cone.)
3. What effect might the use of the active or the passive voice have when used in scientific research to describe gendered processes or behaviours? Select (or make up) a sentence on this sort of topic written in the active voice, and then re-write the sentence in the passive voice.
4. Discuss the organization of Martin's essay. Is there an overall progression in the ideas she presents?

JAMAICA KINCAID

ON SEEING ENGLAND FOR THE FIRST TIME

Novelist, memoirist, and essayist Jamaica Kincaid often writes unflinchingly about the oppression, erasure, and power imbalances created by colonialism. In the following piece, she references her childhood in Antigua in the mid-twentieth century. Antigua, an island in the eastern Caribbean, was colonized by Britain in the seventeenth century, and until the 1830s sugarcane and other export crops were produced there by western African slaves. In 1949, when Kincaid was born, Antigua was still a colony; it became self-governing in 1967 and gained complete political independence in 1981. "On Seeing England for the First Time" was first published in 1991, in Transition: The Magazine of Africa and the Diaspora.

When I saw England for the first time, I was a child in school sitting at a desk. The England I was looking at was laid out on a map gently, beautifully, delicately, a very special jewel; it lay on a bed of sky blue—the background of the map—its yellow form mysterious, because though it looked like a leg of mutton, it could not really look like anything so familiar as a leg of mutton because it was England—with shadings of pink and green, unlike any shadings of pink and green I had seen before, squiggly veins of red running in every direction. England was a special jewel all right, and only special people got to wear it. The people who got to wear England were English people. They wore it well and they wore it everywhere: in jungles, in deserts, on plains, on top of the highest mountains, on all the oceans, on all the seas, in places where they were not welcome, in places they should not have been. When my teacher had pinned this map up on the blackboard, she said, "This is England"—and she said it with authority, seriousness, and adoration, and we all sat up. It was as if she had said, "This is Jerusalem,* the place you will go to when you die but only if you have been good." We understood then—we were meant to understand then—that England was to be our source of myth and the source from which we got our sense of reality, our sense of what was meaningful, our sense of what was meaningless—and much about our own lives and much about the very idea of us headed that last list.

At the time I was a child sitting at my desk seeing England for the first time, I was already very familiar with the greatness of it. Each morning before I left for school, I ate a breakfast of half a grapefruit, an egg, bread and butter and a slice of cheese, and a cup of cocoa; or half a grapefruit, a bowl of oat porridge, bread and butter and a slice of cheese, and a cup of cocoa. The can of cocoa was often left on the table in front of me. It had written on it the name of the company, the year the company was established, and the words, "Made in England." Those words, "Made in England," were written on the box the oats came in too. They would also have been written on the box the shoes I was wearing came in; a bolt of grey linen cloth lying on the shelf of a store from which my mother had bought three yards to make the uniform that I was wearing had written along its edge those three words. The shoes I wore were made in England; so were my socks and cotton undergarments and the satin ribbons I wore tied at the end of two plaits of my hair. My father, who might have sat next to me at breakfast, was a carpenter and cabinet maker. The shoes he wore to work would have been made in England, as were his khaki shirt and trousers, his underpants and undershirt, his socks and brown felt hat. Felt was not the proper material from which a hat that was expected to provide shade from the hot sun should be made, but my father must have seen and admired a picture of an Englishman wearing such a hat in England, and this picture that he saw must have been so compelling that it caused him to wear the wrong hat for a hot climate most of his long life. And this hat—a brown felt hat—became so central to his character that it was the first thing he put on in the morning as he stepped out of bed and the last thing he took off before he stepped back into bed at night. As we sat at breakfast a car might go by. The car, a Hillman or a Zephyr, was made in England. The very idea of the meal itself, breakfast, and its substantial quality and quantity was an idea from England; we somehow knew that in England they began the day with this meal called breakfast and a proper breakfast was a big breakfast. No one I knew liked eating so much food so early in the day; it made us feel sleepy, tired. But this breakfast business was Made in England like almost everything else that surrounded us, the exceptions being the sea, the sky, and the air we breathed.

At the time I saw this map—seeing England for the first time—I did not say to myself, "Ah, so that's what it looks like," because there was no longing in me to put a shape to those three words that ran through every part of my life no matter how small; for me to have had such a longing would have meant that I lived in a certain atmosphere, an atmosphere in which those three words were felt as a burden. But I did not live in such an atmosphere. My father's brown felt hat would develop a hole in its crown, the lining would separate from the hat itself, and six weeks before he thought that he could not be seen wearing it—he was a very vain man—he would order another hat from England. And my mother taught me to eat my food in the English way: the knife in the right hand, the fork in the left, my elbows held still close to my side, the food carefully balanced on my fork and then brought up to my mouth. When I had finally mastered it, I overheard her saying to a friend, "Did you see how nicely she can eat?" But I knew then that I enjoyed my food more when I ate it with my bare hands, and I continued to do so when she wasn't looking. And when my teacher showed us the map, she asked us to study it carefully, because no test we would ever take would be complete without this statement: "Draw a map of England."

I did not know then that the statement, "Draw a map of England" was something far worse than a declaration of war, for in fact a flatout declaration of war would have put me on alert, and again in fact, there was no need for war—I had long ago been conquered. I did not know then that this statement was part of a process that would result in my erasure, not my physical erasure, but my erasure all the same. I did not know then that this statement was meant to make me feel in awe and small whenever I heard the word England: awe at its existence, small because I was not from it. I did not know very much of anything then—certainly not what a blessing it was that I was unable to draw a map of England correctly.

5 After that there were many times of seeing England for the first time. I saw England in history. I knew the names of all the kings of England. I knew the names of their children, their wives, their disappointments, their triumphs, the names of people who betrayed them, I knew the dates on which they were born and the dates they died. I knew their conquests and was made to feel glad if I figured in them; I knew their defeats. I knew the details of the year 1066 (The Battle of Hastings, the end of the reign of the Anglo-Saxon kings*) before I knew the details of the year 1832 (the year slavery was abolished).[1] It wasn't as bad as I make it sound now; it was worse. I did like so much hearing again and again how Alfred the Great,[2] travelling in disguise, had been left to watch cakes, and because he wasn't used to this the cakes got burned, and Alfred burned his hands pulling them out of the fire, and the woman who had left him to watch the cakes screamed at him. I loved King Alfred. My grandfather was named after him; his son, my uncle, was named after King Alfred; my brother is named after King Alfred. And so there are three people in my family named after a man they have never met, a man who died over ten centuries ago. The first view I got of

---

1 *1832 ... abolished* The Slavery Abolition Act, signed in 1833 and put into practice in 1834, marked the end of slavery in Britain and its colonies.

2 *Alfred the Great* Anglo-Saxon ruler of the kingdom of Wessex from 871 to 899.

England then was not unlike the first view received by the person who named my grandfather.

This view though—the naming of the kings, their deeds, their disappointments—was the vivid view, the forceful view. There were other views, subtler ones, softer, almost not there—but these were the ones that made the most lasting impression on me, these were the ones that made me really feel like nothing. "When morning touched the sky" was one phrase, for no morning touched the sky where I lived. The morning where I lived came on abruptly, with a shock of heat and loud noises. "Evening approaches" was another, but the evenings where I lived did not approach; in fact, I had no evening—I had night and I had day and they came and went in a mechanical way: on, off; on, off. And then there were gentle mountains and low blue skies and moors over which people took walks for nothing but pleasure, when where I lived a walk was an act of labour, a burden, something only death or the automobile could relieve. And there were things that a small turn of a head could convey—entire worlds, whole lives would depend on this thing, a certain turn of a head. Everyday life could be quite tiring, more tiring than anything I was told not to do. I was told not to gossip, but they did that all the time. And they ate so much food, violating another of those rules they taught me: do not indulge in gluttony. And the foods they ate actually: if only sometime I could eat cold cuts after theatre, cold cuts of lamb and mint sauce, and Yorkshire pudding and scones, and clotted cream, and sausages that came from up-country (imagine, "up-country").* And having troubling thoughts at twilight, a good time to have troubling thoughts, apparently; and servants who stole and left in the middle of a crisis, who were born with a limp or some other kind of deformity, not nourished properly in their mother's womb (that last part I figured out for myself; the point was, oh to have an untrustworthy servant); and wonderful cobbled streets onto which solid front doors opened; and people whose eyes were blue and who had fair skins and who smelled only of lavender, or sometimes sweet pea or primrose. And those flowers with those names: delphiniums, foxgloves, tulips, daffodils, floribunda, peonies; in bloom, a striking display, being cut and placed in large glass bowls, crystal, decorating rooms so large twenty families the size of mine could fit in comfortably but used only for passing through. And the weather was so remarkable because the rain fell gently always, only occasionally in deep gusts, and it coloured the air various shades of grey, each an appealing shade for a dress to be worn when a portrait was being painted; and when it rained at twilight, wonderful things happened: people bumped into each other unexpectedly and that would lead to all sorts of turns of events—a plot, the mere weather caused plots. I saw that people rushed: they rushed to catch trains, they rushed toward each other and away from each other; they rushed and rushed and rushed. That word: Rushed! I did not know what it was to do that. It was too hot to do that, and so I came to envy people who would rush, even though it had no meaning to me to do such a thing. But there they are again. They loved their children; their children were sent to their own rooms as a punishment, rooms larger than my entire house. They were special, everything about them said so, even their clothes; their clothes rustled, swished, soothed. The world was theirs, not mine; everything told me so.

If now as I speak of all this I give the impression of someone on the outside looking in, nose pressed up against a glass window, that is wrong. My nose was pressed up against a glass window all right, but there was an iron vise at the back of my neck forcing my head to stay in place. To avert my gaze was to fall back into something from which I had been rescued, a hole filled with nothing, and that was the word for everything about me, nothing. The reality of my life was conquests, subjugation, humiliation, enforced amnesia. I was forced to forget. Just for instance, this: I lived in a part of St. John's, Antigua, called Ovals. Ovals was made up of five streets, each of them named after a famous English seaman—to be quite frank, an officially sanctioned criminal: Rodney Street (after George Rodney), Nelson Street (after Horatio Nelson), Drake Street (after Francis Drake), Hood Street, and Hawkins Street (after John Hawkins).[3] But John Hawkins was knighted after a trip he made to Africa, opening up a new trade, the slave trade. He was then entitled to wear as his crest a negro bound with a cord. Every single person living on Hawkins street was descended from a slave. John Hawkins' ship, the one in which he transported the people he had bought and kidnapped, was called *The Jesus*. He later became the Treasurer of the Royal Navy and Rear Admiral.

Again, the reality of my life, the life I led at the time I was being shown these views of England for the first time, for the second time, for the one-hundred-millionth time, was this: the sun shone with what sometimes seemed to be a deliberate cruelty; we must have done something to deserve that. My dresses did not rustle in the evening air as I strolled to the theatre (I had no evening, I had no theatre; my dresses were made of a cheap cotton, the weave of which would give way after not too many washings). I got up in the morning, I did my chores (fetched water from the public pipe for my mother, swept the yard), I washed myself, I went to a woman to have my hair combed freshly every day (because before we were allowed into our classroom our teachers would inspect us, and

3 *George Rodney* Admiral (1718–92) known for capturing French, Dutch, and Spanish ships in the Caribbean; *Horatio Nelson* Naval commander (1758–1805) who used the Navigation Act to confiscate goods from ships sailing through the West Indies; *Francis Drake* Admiral (c.1540–96) famed for his piracy against enemy ships in the Caribbean and cousin of John Hawkins, with whom he collaborated in slave-trading ventures; *Hood* Samuel Hood (1724–1816), English admiral who served as Rodney's second in command in the Caribbean; *John Hawkins* Naval commander (1532–95) who rose to success as the first English slave trader.

children who had not bathed that day, or had dirt under their fingernails, or whose hair had not been combed anew that day might not be allowed to attend class). I ate that breakfast. I walked to school. At school we gathered in an auditorium and sang a hymn, "All Things Bright and Beautiful,"[4] and looking down on us as we sang were portraits of the queen of England and her husband; they wore jewels and medals and they smiled. I was a Brownie.[5] At each meeting we would form a little group around a flagpole, and after raising the union jack, we would say, "I promise to do my best, to do my duty to God and the Queen, to help other people every day and obey the scouts' law."

Who were these people and why had I never seen them, I mean, really seen them, in the place where they lived. I had never been to England. No one I knew had ever been to England, or should I say, no one I knew had ever been and returned to tell me about it. All the people I knew who had gone to England had stayed there. Sometimes they left behind their small children, never to see them again. England! I had seen England's representatives. I had seen the governor general at the public grounds at a ceremony celebrating the queen's birthday. I had seen an old princess and I had seen a young princess. They had both been extremely not beautiful, but who of us would have told them that? I had never seen England, really seen it, I had only met a representative, seen a picture, read books, memorized its history. I had never set foot, my own foot, in it.

The space between the idea of something and its reality is always wide and 10
deep and dark. The longer they are kept apart—idea of thing, reality of thing—the wider the width, the deeper the depth, the thicker and darker the darkness. This space starts out empty, there is nothing in it, but it rapidly becomes filled up with obsession or desire or hatred or love—sometimes all of these things, sometimes some of these things, sometimes only one of these things. The existence of the world as I came to know it was a result of this: idea of thing over here, reality of thing way, way over there. There was Christopher Columbus, an unlikable man, an unpleasant man, a liar (and so of course, a thief) surrounded by maps and schemes and plans, and there was the reality on the other side of that width, that depth, that darkness. He became obsessed, he became filled with desire, the hatred came later, love was never a part of it. Eventually, his idea met the longed-for reality. That the idea of something and its reality are often two completely different things is something no one ever remembers; and so when they meet and find that they are not compatible, the weaker of the two, idea or reality, dies. That

---

4 *All Things Bright and Beautiful* Anglican hymn (1848) by Irish poet Cecil Frances Alexander; the lyrics reference English geography, seasons, and social classes.

5 *Brownie* Member of the Brownies, a scouting organization for girls founded in England in 1914; the name "Brownie" and the narratives associated with the group's activities are based on fairy-like creatures from English folklore.

idea Christopher Columbus had was more powerful than the reality he met and so the reality he met died.

And so finally, when I was a grownup woman, the mother of two children, the wife of someone, a person who resides in a powerful country that takes up more than its fair share of a continent, the owner of a house with many rooms in it and of two automobiles, with the desire and will (which I very much act upon) to take from the world more than I give back to it, more than I deserve, more than I need, finally then, I saw England, the real England, not a picture, not a painting, not through a story in a book, but England, for the first time. In me, the space between the idea of it and its reality had become filled with hatred, and so when at last I saw it I wanted to take it into my hands and tear it into little pieces and then crumble it up as if it were clay, child's clay. That was impossible, and so I could only indulge in not-favourable opinions.

There were monuments everywhere; they commemorated victories, battles fought between them and the people who lived across the sea from them, all vile people, fought over which of them would have dominion over the people who looked like me. The monuments were useless to them now, people sat on them and ate their lunch. They were like markers on an old useless trail, like a piece of old string tied to a finger to jog the memory, like old decoration in an old house, dirty, useless, in the way. Their skins were so pale, it made them look so fragile, so weak, so ugly. What if I had the power to simply banish them from their land, send boat after boatload of them on a voyage that in fact had no destination, force them to live in a place where the sun's presence was a constant. This would rid them of their pale complexion and make them look more like me, make them look more like the people I love and treasure and hold dear, and more like the people who occupy the near and far reaches of my imagination, my history, my geography, and reduce them and everything they have ever known to figurines as evidence that I was in divine favour, what if all this was in my power? Could I resist it? No one ever has.

And they were rude, they were rude to each other. They didn't like each other very much. They didn't like each other in the way they didn't like me, and it occurred to me that their dislike for me was one of the few things they agreed on.

I was on a train in England with a friend, an English woman. Before we were in England she liked me very much. In England she didn't like me at all. She didn't like the claim I said I had on England, she didn't like the views I had of England. I didn't like England, she didn't like England, but she didn't like me not liking it too. She said, "I want to show you my England, I want to show you the England that I know and love." I had told her many times before that I knew England and I didn't want to love it anyway. She no longer lived in England; it was her own country, but it had not been kind to her, so she left. On the train, the conductor was rude to her; she asked something, and he responded in a rude way. She became ashamed. She was ashamed at the way he treated her; she was ashamed at the way he behaved. "This is the new England," she said. But I liked the conductor being rude; his behaviour seemed quite appropriate. Earlier this had happened: We had gone to a store to buy a shirt for my husband; it was meant to be a special present, a special shirt to wear on special occasions. This was a store where the Prince of Wales has his shirts made but the shirts sold in this store are beautiful all the same. I found a shirt I thought my husband would like and I wanted to buy him a tie to go with it. When I couldn't decide which one to choose, the salesman showed me a new set. He was very pleased with these, he said, because they bore the crest of the Prince of Wales, and the Prince of Wales had never allowed his crest to decorate an article of clothing before. There was something in the way he said it; his tone was slavish, reverential, awed. It made me feel angry; I wanted to hit him. I didn't do that. I said, my husband and I hate princes, my husband would never wear anything that had a prince's anything on it. My friend stiffened. The salesman stiffened. They both drew themselves in, away from me. My friend told me that the prince was a symbol of her Englishness and I could see that I had caused offense. I looked at her. She was an English person, the sort of English person I used to know at home, the sort who was nobody in England but somebody when they came to live among the people like me. There were many people I could have seen England with; that I was seeing it with this particular person, a person who reminded me of the people who showed me England long ago as I sat in church or at my desk, made me feel silent and afraid, for I wondered if, all these years of our friendship, I had had a friend or had been in the thrall of a racial memory.

I went to Bath[6]—we, my friend and I, did this, but though we were together, I was no longer with her. The landscape was almost as familiar as my own hand, but I had never been in this place before, so how could that be again? And the streets of Bath were familiar, too, but I had never walked on them before. It was all those years of reading, starting with Roman Britain. Why did I have to know about Roman Britain? It was of no real use to me, a person living on a hot, drought-ridden island, and it is of no use to me now, and yet my head is filled with this nonsense, Roman Britain. In Bath, I drank tea in a room I had read about in a novel written in the eighteenth century. In this very same room, young women wearing those dresses that rustled and so on danced and flirted and sometimes disgraced themselves with young men, soldiers, sailors, who

6 *Bath* English city located on the site of hot springs, where the ancient Romans had built baths; it became a popular tourist destination in the eighteenth century and is used as a setting by many classic English novelists, including Jane Austen and Charles Dickens.

were on their way to Bristol[7] or someplace like that, so many places like that where so many adventures, the outcome of which was not good for me, began. Bristol, England. A sentence that began "That night the ship sailed from Bristol, England" would end not so good for me. And then I was driving through the countryside in an English motor car, on narrow winding roads, and they were so familiar, though I had never been on them before; and through little villages the names of which I somehow knew so well though I had never been there before. And the countryside did have all those hedges and hedges, fields hedged in. I was marvelling at all the toil of it, the planting of the hedges to begin with and then the care of it, all that clipping, year after year of clipping, and I wondered at the lives of the people who would have to do this, because wherever I see and feel the hands that hold up the world, I see and feel myself and all the people who look like me. And I said, "Those hedges" and my friend said that someone, a woman named Mrs. Rothchild, worried that the hedges weren't being taken care of properly; the farmers couldn't afford or find the help to keep up the hedges, and often they replaced them with wire fencing. I might have said to that, well if Mrs. Rothchild doesn't like the wire fencing, why doesn't she take care of the hedges herself, but I didn't. And then in those fields that were now hemmed in by wire fencing that a privileged woman didn't like was planted a vile yellow flowering bush that produced an oil, and my friend said that Mrs. Rothchild didn't like this either; it ruined the English countryside, it ruined the traditional look of the English countryside.

It was not at that moment that I wished every sentence, everything I knew, that began with England, would end with "and then it all died; we don't know how, it just all died." At that moment, I was thinking, who are these people who forced me to think of them all the time, who forced me to think that the world I knew was incomplete, or without substance, or did not measure up because it was not England; that I was incomplete, or without substance, and did not measure up because I was not English. Who were these people? The person sitting next to me couldn't give me a clue; no one person could. In any case, if I had said to her, I find England ugly, I hate England; the weather is like a jail sentence, the English are a very ugly people, the food in England is like a jail sentence, the hair of English people is so straight, so deadlooking, the English have an unbearable smell so different from the smell of people I know, real people of course, she would have said that I was a person full of prejudice. Apart from the fact that it is I—that is, the people who look like me—who made her aware of the unpleasantness of such a thing, the idea of such a thing, prejudice, she would have been only partly right, sort of right: I may be capable of prejudice, but my

---

7 *Bristol* English port city that played a major role in seventeenth- to nineteenth-century British marine trade, including the slave trade.

prejudices have no weight to them, my prejudices have no force behind them, my prejudices remain opinions, my prejudices remain my personal opinion. And a great feeling of rage and disappointment came over me as I looked at England, my head full of personal opinions that could not have public, my public, approval. The people I come from are powerless to do evil on a grand scale.

The moment I wished every sentence, everything I knew, that began with England would end with "and then it all died, we don't know how, it just all died" was when I saw the white cliffs of Dover.[8] I had sung hymns and recited poems that were about a longing to see the white cliffs of Dover again. At the time I sang the hymns and recited the poems, I could really long to see them again because I had never seen them at all, nor had anyone around me at the time. But there we were, groups of people longing for something we had never seen. And so there they were, the white cliffs, but they were not that pearly majestic thing I used to sing about, that thing that created such a feeling in these people that when they died in the place where I lived they had themselves buried facing a direction that would allow them to see the white cliffs of Dover when they were resurrected, as surely they would be. The white cliffs of Dover, when finally I saw them, were cliffs, but they were not white; you would only call them that if the word "white" meant something special to you; they were dirty and they were steep; they were so steep, the correct height from which all my views of England, starting with the map before me in my classroom and ending with the trip I had just taken, should jump and die and disappear forever.

(1991)

Questions

1. Define the following rhetorical devices and find an example from Kincaid's essay: anaphora, litotes, paradox, synecdoche, and metaphor. Explain the effect of the rhetorical device in each example.
2. Explain the significance of the felt hat that Kincaid's father wears.
3. Why do the cliffs of Dover in particular inspire such hatred for Kincaid?
4. How would you describe the emotional tone of this piece? How is it achieved? How does it affect your response to the ideas in the essay?

---

8 *white cliffs of Dover* Geographical landmark on England's southeastern coast; the cliffs are frequently referenced in music and literature expressing pride, affection, or nostalgia with regard to England.

5. Kincaid often constructs sentences with words or phrases placed in apposition. Discuss this stylistic trait with particular reference to paragraph 9.
6. By the end of the narrative, to what extent has Kincaid freed herself from colonialism's hold on her mind?
7. Read George Orwell's essay "Shooting an Elephant" (elsewhere in this anthology). How does Kincaid's experience of colonialism compare with Orwell's?

David Card and Alan B. Krueger

from Minimum Wages and Employment: A Case Study of the Fast-Food Industry in New Jersey and Pennsylvania

Until the early 1990s it was accepted almost universally among economists that, all else being equal, raising the minimum wage would increase unemployment; employers who were forced to pay workers more would, according to the economic models, respond by laying off some of those workers. It was thus often argued that keeping the minimum wage low benefitted not just companies and their shareholders, but also the minimum wage workers themselves.

The article below, now considered a classic in its discipline, challenged that conventional wisdom. Card and Krueger first published the essay in October 1993 through the National Bureau of Economic Research as Working Paper No. 4509. It was published in a slightly revised form the following year in The American Economic Review. *In 1995 the authors presented broader evidence along the same lines in their book* Myth and Measurement: The New Economics of the Minimum Wage.

[Abstract]

On April 1, 1992, New Jersey's minimum wage rose from $4.25 to $5.05 per hour. To evaluate the impact of the law we surveyed 410 fast-food restaurants in New Jersey and eastern Pennsylvania before and after the rise. Comparisons of employment growth at stores in New Jersey and Pennsylvania (where the minimum wage was constant) provide simple estimates of the effect of the higher minimum wage. We also compare employment changes at stores in New Jersey that were initially paying high wages (above $5) to the changes at lower-wage stores. We find no indication that the rise in the minimum wage reduced employment.

How do employers in a low-wage labour market respond to an increase in the minimum wage?

The prediction from conventional economic theory is unambiguous: a rise in the minimum wage leads perfectly competitive employers to cut employment (George J. Stigler, 1946). Although studies in the 1970's based on aggregate[1] teenage employment rates usually confirmed this prediction,[2] earlier studies based on comparisons of employment at affected and unaffected establishments often did not (e.g., Richard A. Lester, 1960, 1964). Several recent studies that rely on a similar comparative methodology have failed to detect a negative employment effect of higher minimum wages. Analyses of the 1990–1991 increases in the federal minimum wage (Lawrence F. Katz and Krueger, 1992; Card, 1992a) and of an earlier increase in the minimum wage in California (Card, 1992b) find no adverse employment impact. A study of minimum-wage floors[3] in Britain (Stephen Machin and Alan Manning, 1993) reaches a similar conclusion.

This paper presents new evidence on the effect of minimum wages on establishment-level[4] employment outcomes. We analyze the experiences of 410 fast-food restaurants in New Jersey and Pennsylvania following the increase in New Jersey's minimum wage from $4.25 to $5.05 per hour. Comparisons of employment, wages, and prices at stores in New Jersey and Pennsylvania before and after the rise offer a simple method for evaluating the effects of the minimum wage. Comparisons within New Jersey between initially high-wage stores (those paying more than the new minimum rate prior to its effective date) and other stores provide an alternative estimate of the impact of the new law.

5 In addition to the simplicity of our empirical methodology, several other features of the New Jersey law and our data set are also significant. First, the rise in the minimum wage occurred during a recession. The increase had been legislated two years earlier when the state economy was relatively healthy. By the time of the actual increase, the unemployment rate in New Jersey had risen substantially and last-minute political action almost succeeded in reducing the

---

1 *aggregate* Combined; calculated by combining data.

2 [Card and Krueger's note] See Charles Brown et al. (1982, 1983) for surveys of this literature. A recent update (Allison J. Wellington, 1991) concludes that the employment effects of the minimum wage are negative but small: a 10-percent increase in the minimum is estimated to lower teenage employment rates by 0.06 percentage points.

3 *minimum-wage floors* Minimums (set by government) which dictate a rate that wages must not fall below.

4 *establishment-level* Concerning individual operational establishments (as opposed to "firm-level," which concerns businesses that may have many establishments operating as extensions).

minimum-wage increase. It is unlikely that the effects of the higher minimum wage were obscured by a rising tide of general economic conditions.

Second, New Jersey is a relatively small state with an economy that is closely linked to nearby states. We believe that a control group[5] of fast-food stores in eastern Pennsylvania forms a natural basis for comparison with the experiences of restaurants in New Jersey. Wage variation across stores in New Jersey, however, allows us to compare the experiences of high-wage and low-wage stores in New Jersey and *test* the validity of the Pennsylvania control group. Moreover, since seasonal patterns of employment are similar in New Jersey and eastern Pennsylvania, as well as across high- and low-wage stores within New Jersey, our comparative methodology effectively "differences out" any seasonal employment effects.

Third, we successfully followed nearly 100 percent of stores from a first wave of interviews conducted just before the rise in the minimum wage (in February and March 1992) to a second wave conducted 7–8 months after (in November and December 1992). We have complete information on store closings and take account of employment changes at the closed stores in our analyses. We therefore measure the overall effect of the minimum wage on average employment, and not simply its effect on surviving establishments.

Our analysis of employment trends at stores that were open for business before the increase in the minimum wage ignores any potential effect of minimum wages on the rate of new store openings. To assess the likely magnitude of this effect we relate state-specific growth rates in the number of McDonald's fast food outlets between 1986 and 1991 to measures of the relative minimum wage in each state.

1. THE NEW JERSEY LAW

A bill signed into law in November 1989 raised the Federal minimum wage from $3.35 per hour to $3.80 effective April 1, 1990, with a further increase to $4.25 per hour on April 1, 1991. In early 1990 the New Jersey legislature went one step further, enacting parallel increases in the state minimum wage for 1990 and 1991 and an increase to $5.05 per hour effective April 1, 1992. The scheduled 1992 increase gave New Jersey the highest state minimum wage rate in the country and was strongly opposed by business leaders in the state (see Bureau of National Affairs, *Daily Labor Report*, 5 May 1990).

In the two years between passage of the $5.05 minimum wage and its ef- 10
fective date, New Jersey's economy slipped into recession. Concerned with

---

5 *control group* Group that, ideally, is like the group being studied in every way except for the variable under consideration.

the potentially adverse impact of a higher minimum wage, the state legislature voted in March 1992 to phase in the 80-cent increase over two years. The vote fell just short of the margin required to override a gubernatorial veto,[6] and the Governor allowed the $5.05 rate to go into effect on April 1 before vetoing the two-step legislation. Faced with the prospect of having to roll back wages for minimum-wage earners, the legislature dropped the issue. Despite a strong last-minute challenge, the $5.05 minimum rate took effect as originally planned.

2. SAMPLE DESIGN AND EVALUATION

Early in 1992 we decided to evaluate the impending increase in the New Jersey minimum wage by surveying fast-food restaurants in New Jersey and eastern Pennsylvania.[7] Our choice of the fast-food industry was driven by several factors. First, fast-food stores are a leading employer of low-wage workers: in 1987, franchised restaurants employed 25 percent of all workers in the restaurant industry (see U.S. Department of Commerce, 1990 table 13). Second, fast-food restaurants comply with minimum-wage regulations and would be expected to raise wages in response to a rise in the minimum wage. Third, the job requirements and products of fast-food restaurants are relatively homogeneous,* making it easier to obtain reliable measures of employment, wages, and product prices. The absence of tips greatly simplifies the measurement of wages in the industry. Fourth, it is relatively easy to construct a sample frame[8] of franchised restaurants. Finally, past experience (Katz and Krueger, 1992) suggested that fast-food restaurants have high response rates to telephone surveys.[9]

Based on these considerations we constructed a sample frame of fast-food restaurants in New Jersey and eastern Pennsylvania from the Burger King, KFC, Wendy's, and Roy Rogers chains. The first wave of the survey was conducted by telephone in late February and early March 1992, a little over a month before the scheduled increase in New Jersey's minimum wage. The survey included questions on employment, starting wages, prices, and other store characteristics....

---

6 *gubernatorial veto* Legally binding rejection of a state bill by the governor.

7 [Card and Krueger's note] At the time we were uncertain whether the $5.05 rate would go into effect or be overridden.

8 *sample frame* Exhaustive list of all the members of a population being studied. To create a sample for the study, individuals are randomly selected from the list.

9 [Card and Krueger's note] In a pilot survey Katz and Krueger (1992) obtained very low response rates from McDonald's restaurants. For this reason, McDonald's restaurants were excluded from Katz and Krueger's and our sample frames.

The average starting wage at fast-food restaurants in New Jersey increased by 10 percent following the rise in the minimum wage.... In wave 1 [before the wage increase] the wage distributions in New Jersey and Pennsylvania were very similar. By wave 2 [after the increase] virtually all restaurants in New Jersey that had been paying below $5.05 per hour reported a starting wage equal to the new rate. Interestingly, the minimum-wage increase had no apparent "spillover" on higher-wage restaurants in the state: the mean percentage wage change for these stores was -3.1 percent.

Despite the increase in wages, full-time equivalent employment *increased* in New Jersey relative to Pennsylvania. Whereas New Jersey stores were initially smaller, employment gains in New Jersey coupled with losses in Pennsylvania led to a small and statistically significant interstate difference in wave 2. Only two other variables show a relative change between waves 1 and 2: the fraction of full-time employees and the price of a meal. Both variables increased in New Jersey relative to Pennsylvania....

3. EMPLOYMENT EFFECTS OF THE MINIMUM-WAGE INCREASE

A. Differences-in-Differences

... New Jersey stores were initially smaller than their Pennsylvania counterparts but grew relative to Pennsylvania stores after the rise in the minimum wage. The relative gain (the "difference in differences" of the changes in employment) is 2.76 FTE[10] employees (or 13 percent), with a *t* statistic[11] of 2.03....

Within New Jersey, employment expanded at the low-wage stores (those paying $4.25 per hour in wave 1) and contracted at the high-wage stores (those paying $5.00 or more per hour). Indeed, the average change in employment at the high-wage stores (-2.16 FTE employees) is almost identical to the change among Pennsylvania stores (-2.28 FTE employees). Since high-wage stores in New Jersey should have been largely unaffected by the new minimum wage, this comparison provides a specification test of the validity of the Pennsylvania control group. The test is clearly passed. Regardless of whether the affected stores are compared to stores in Pennsylvania or high-wage stores in New Jersey, the estimated employment effect of the minimum wage is similar.

The results ... suggest that employment contracted between February and November of 1992 at fast-food stores that were unaffected by the rise in the minimum wage (stores in Pennsylvania and stores in New Jersey paying $5.00

---

10 *FTE* Full time equivalent, a term used in reference to the number of working hours per week that add up to a full time job (if two people each work one half-time job, for example, this would add up to one FTE).

11 *t statistic* Number used to determine if a finding is statistically significant.

per hour or more in wave 1). We suspect that the reason for this contraction was the continued worsening of the economies of the middle-Atlantic states during 1992.[12] Unemployment rates in New Jersey, Pennsylvania, and New York all trended upward between 1991 and 1993, with a larger increase in New Jersey than Pennsylvania during 1992. Since sales of franchised fast-food restaurants are pro-cyclical,[13] the rise in unemployment would be expected to lower fast-food employment in the absence of other factors....

4. NONWAGE OFFSETS

One explanation of our finding that a rise in the minimum wage does not lower employment is that restaurants can offset the effect of the minimum wage by reducing nonwage compensation. For example, if workers value fringe benefits* and wages equally, employers can simply reduce the level of fringe benefits by the amount of the minimum-wage increase, leaving their employment costs unchanged. The main fringe benefits for fast-food employees are free and reduced-price meals. In the first wave of our survey about 19 percent of fast-food restaurants offered workers free meals, 72 percent offered reduced-price meals, and 9 percent offered a combination of both free and reduced-price meals. Low-price meals are an obvious fringe benefit to cut if the minimum-wage increase forces restaurants to pay higher wages.

... The proportion of restaurants offering reduced-price meals fell in both New Jersey and Pennsylvania after the minimum wage increased, with a somewhat greater decline in New Jersey. Contrary to an offset story, however, the reduction in reduced-price meal programs was accompanied by an *increase* in the fraction of stores offering free meals. Relative to stores in Pennsylvania, New Jersey employers actually shifted toward more generous fringe benefits (i.e., free meals rather than reduced-price meals). However, the relative shift is not statistically significant....

5. PRICE EFFECTS OF THE MINIMUM-WAGE INCREASE

20 A final issue we examine is the effect of the minimum wage on the prices of meals at fast-food restaurants. A competitive model[14] of the fast-food industry

12 An alternative possibility is that seasonal factors produce higher employment at fast-food restaurants in February and March than in November and December. An analysis of national employment data for food preparation and service workers, however, shows higher average employment in the fourth quarter than in the first quarter. [authors' note]

13 *pro-cyclical* Directly correlated with changes in the overall economy.

14 *competitive model* Economic model according to which prices, wages, and so on are determined by market forces; in a perfectly competitive market, no employer would pay a worker wages that were greater than the amount of revenue the worker produced.

implies that an increase in the minimum wage will lead to an increase in product prices. If we assume constant returns to scale in the industry, the increase in price should be proportional to the share of minimum-wage labour in total factor cost.[15] The average restaurant in New Jersey initially paid about half its workers less than the new minimum wage. If wages rose by roughly 15 percent for these workers, and if labour's share of total costs is 30 percent, we would expect prices to rise by about 2.2 percent (= 0.15 x 0.5 x 0.3) due to the minimum-wage rise.[16]

In each wave of our survey we asked managers for the prices of three standard items: a medium soda, a small order of french fries, and a main course. The main course was a basic hamburger at Burger King, Roy Rogers, and Wendy's restaurants, and two pieces of chicken at KFC stores. We define "full meal" price as the after-tax price of a medium soda, a small order of french fries, and a main course....

... [A]fter-tax meal prices rose 3.2-percent faster in New Jersey than in Pennsylvania between February and November 1992.[17] The effect is slightly larger controlling for chain and company-ownership.... Since the New Jersey sales tax rate fell by 1 percentage point between the waves of our survey, these estimates suggest that pretax prices rose 4-percent faster as a result of the minimum-wage increase in New Jersey—slightly more than the increase needed to pass through the cost increase caused by the minimum-wage hike.

The pattern of price changes *within* New Jersey is less consistent with a simple "pass-through" view of minimum-wage cost increases. In fact, meal prices rose at approximately the same rate at stores in New Jersey with differing levels of initial wages....

In sum, these results provide mixed evidence that higher minimum wages result in higher fast-food prices. The strongest evidence emerges from a comparison of New Jersey and Pennsylvania stores. The magnitude of the price increase is consistent with predictions from a conventional model of a competitive industry. On the other hand, we find no evidence that prices rose

---

15 *constant returns to scale* Pattern in which increases or decreases in input produce the same increase or decrease in output; *total factor cost* Amount paid for one facet of an operation.

16 [Card and Krueger's note] According to the McDonald's Corporation 1991 Annual Report, payroll and benefits are 31.3 percent of operating costs at company-owned stores. This calculation is only approximate because minimum-wage workers make up less than half of payroll even though they are about half of workers, and because a rise in the minimum wage causes some employers to increase the pay of other higher-wage workers in order to maintain relative pay differentials.

17 [Card and Krueger's note] The effect is attributable to a 2.0-percent increase in prices in New Jersey and a 1.0-percent decrease in prices in Pennsylvania.

faster among stores in New Jersey that were most affected by the rise in the minimum wage….

7. BROADER EVIDENCE ON EMPLOYMENT CHANGES IN NEW JERSEY

Our establishment-level analysis suggests that the rise in the minimum wage in New Jersey may have increased employment in the fast-food industry. Is this just an anomaly associated with our particular sample, or a phenomenon unique to the fast-food industry? Data from the monthly Current Population Survey (CPS) allow us to compare state-wide employment trends in New Jersey and the surrounding states, providing a check on the interpretation of our findings. Using monthly CPS files for 1991 and 1992, we computed employment-population rates for teenagers and adults (age 25 and older) for New Jersey, Pennsylvania, New York, and the entire United States. Since the New Jersey minimum wage rose on April 1, 1992, we computed the employment rates for April-December of both 1991 and 1992. The relative changes in employment in New Jersey and the surrounding states then give an indication of the effect of the new law.

A comparison of changes in adult employment rates show that the New Jersey labour market fared slightly worse over the 1991–1992 period than either the U.S. labour market as a whole or labour markets in Pennsylvania or New York (see Card and Krueger, 1993 table 9).[18] Among teenagers, however, the situation was reversed. In New Jersey, teenage employment rates fell by 0.7 percent from 1991 to 1992. In New York, Pennsylvania, and the United States as a whole, teenage employment rates dropped faster. Relative to teenagers in Pennsylvania, for example, the teenage employment rate in New Jersey rose by 2.0 percentage points. While this point estimate is consistent with our findings for the fast-food industry, the standard error is too large (3.2 percent) to allow any confident assessment.

8. INTERPRETATION

... [O]ur empirical findings on the effects of the New Jersey minimum wage are inconsistent with the predictions of a conventional competitive model of the fast-food industry. Our employment results are consistent with several alternative models, although none of these models can also explain the apparent rise in fast-food prices in New Jersey….

---

18 [Card and Krueger's note] The employment rate of individuals age 25 and older fell by 2.6 percent in New Jersey between 1991 and 1992, while it rose by 0.3 percent in Pennsylvania, and fell by 0.2 percent in the United States as a whole.

9. CONCLUSIONS

Contrary to the central prediction of the textbook model of the minimum wage, but consistent with a number of recent studies based on cross-sectional time-series comparisons of affected and unaffected markets or employers, we find no evidence that the rise in New Jersey's minimum wage reduced employment at fast-food restaurants in the state. Regardless of whether we compare stores in New Jersey that were affected by the $5.05 minimum to stores in eastern Pennsylvania (where the minimum wage was constant at $4.25 per hour) or to stores in New Jersey that were initially paying $5.00 per hour or more (and were largely unaffected by the new law), we find that the increase in the minimum wage increased employment. We present a wide variety of alternative specifications to probe the robustness of this conclusion. None of the alternatives shows a negative employment effect. We also check our findings for the fast-food industry by comparing changes in teenage employment rates in New Jersey, Pennsylvania, and New York in the year following the increase in the minimum wage. Again, these results point toward a relative *increase* in employment of low-wage workers in New Jersey. We also find no evidence that minimum-wage increases negatively affect the number of McDonald's outlets opened in a state.

Finally, we find that prices of fast-food meals increased in New Jersey relative to Pennsylvania, suggesting that much of the burden of the minimum-wage rise was passed on to consumers. Within New Jersey, however, we find *no* evidence that prices increased more in stores that were most affected by the minimum-wage rise. Taken as a whole, these findings are difficult to explain with the standard competitive model or with models in which employers face supply constraints….

(1994)

REFERENCES

Brown, Charles; Gilroy, Curtis and Kohen, Andrew. "The Effect of the Minimum Wage on Employment and Unemployment." *Journal of Economic Literature*, June 1982, *20*(2), pp. 487–528.

——. "Time Series Evidence on the Effect of the Minimum Wage on Youth Employment and Unemployment." *Journal of Human Resources*, Winter 1983, *18*(1), pp. 3–31....

Bureau of National Affairs. *Daily Labor Report.* Washington, DC: Bureau of National Affairs, 5 May 1990....

Card, David. "Using Regional Variation in Wages to Measure the Effects of the Federal Minimum Wage." *Industrial and Labor Relations Review*, October 1992a, *46*(1), pp. 22–37.

——. "Do Minimum Wages Reduce Employment? A Case Study of California, 1987–89." *Industrial and Labor Relations Review*, October 1992b, *46*(1), pp. 38–54.

Card, David and Krueger, Alan B. "Minimum Wages and Employment: A Case Study of the Fast Food Industry in New Jersey and Pennsylvania." National Bureau of Economic Research (Cambridge, MA) Working Paper No. 4509, October 1993.
Katz, Lawrence F. and Krueger, Alan B. "The Effect of the Minimum Wage on the Fast Food Industry." *Industrial and Labor Relations Review*, October 1992, *46*(1), pp. 6–21.
Lester, Richard A. "Employment Effects of Minimum Wages." *Industrial and Labor Relations Review*, January 1960, *13*, pp. 254–64.
——. *The economics of labor*, 2nd Ed. New York: Macmillan, 1964.
Machin, Stephen and Manning, Alan. "The Effects of Minimum Wages on Wage Dispersion and Employment: Evidence from the U.K. Wage Councils." *Industrial and Labor Relations Review*, January 1994, *47*(2), pp. 319–29.
McDonald's Corporation. *1991 Annual report.* Chicago, 1991....
Stigler, George J. "The Economics of Minimum Wage Legislation." *American Economic Review*, June 1946, *36*(3), pp. 358–65....
U.S. Department of Commerce. *1987 Census of retail trade: Miscellaneous subjects*. Washington, DC: U.S. Government Printing Office, October 1990.
Wellington, Alison J. "Effects of the Minimum Wage on the Employment Status of Youths: An Update." *Journal of Human Resources*, Winter 1991, *26*(1), pp. 27–46.

Questions

1. Does this study lead you to think that the minimum wage should be raised where you live? Why or why not?
2. How do Card and Krueger attempt to ensure that their conclusions are not compromised by factors unrelated to the minimum wage that might have affected the number of jobs (such as larger changes in the overall economy and seasonal changes in employment)? In your view, how effectively have the authors controlled for such factors?
3. Despite the existence of studies such as Card and Krueger's, it is still often presented as self-evidently true that an increase in the minimum wage will lead to a decrease in available jobs. Why do you think that is?

URSULA FRANKLIN

SILENCE AND THE NOTION OF THE COMMONS

Ursula Franklin was a leading physicist and activist whose work explores the social ramifications of science and technology. In this essay, first published in the experimental music magazine Musicworks, *she discusses the implications of two changes wrought by acoustic technology: separating sound from its source, and making the sound permanent.*

In a technological world, where the acoustic environment is largely artificial, silence takes on new dimensions, be it in terms of the human need for silence (perhaps a person's right to be free from acoustic assault), of communication, or of intentional modification of the environment.

This article is based on the text of a lecture given at the Banff Centre in August of 1993 as part of "The Tuning of the World" conference on acoustic ecology. It consists of two separate but interrelated parts: silence as spiritual experience (drawing largely, but not exclusively, on the Quaker tradition of religious worship) and silence as a common good. Silence is examined in terms of the general patterns of the social impact of modern technology. Silence possesses striking similarities with such aspects of life and community as unpolluted water, air, or soil, which once were taken for granted, but which have become special and precious in technologically mediated environments. The threat of a privatization of the soundscape is discussed and some immediate measures suggested.

I would like to thank everyone involved in this conference, and the organizers in particular, for inviting me to deliver this talk. I am very obviously an outsider and wish to come to this group to talk about something that is central to all the work that you people are doing. And so I come in a way as a friend and colleague, in a field where I am fully aware that silence has been the subject of many publications. It is the subject of more than a chapter in R. Murray Schafer's *The Tuning of the World* and John Cage and others have written books on it. I would like to examine how our concept—as well as our practice—of silence has been influenced by all the other things that have changed as our world has become what Jacques Ellul calls a "technological milieu," a world that is, in all its facets, increasingly mediated by technology.

Before we had a technologically mediated society, before we had electronics and electro-magnetic devices, sound was rightly seen as being ephemeral, sound was coupled to its source, and lasted only a very short time. This is very different from what we see in a landscape: however much we feel that the landscape might be modified, however much we feel that there is a horrible building somewhere in front of a beautiful mountain, on the scale of the soundscape, the landscape is permanent. What is put up is there. That's very different from the traditional soundscape. What modern technology has brought to sound is the possibility of doing two things: to separate the sound from the source and to make the sound permanent. In addition, modern devices make it possible to decompose, recompose, analyze and mix sounds, to change the initial magnitude and sustainability of sound, as well as to change all the characteristics that link the sound with its source. R. Murray Schafer called this "schizophonia," separating the sound from the source. We now have easy access to the multitude of opportunities that result from overcoming that coupling.

5 The social impact of this technology is significant. Prior to these developments there was a limitation to sound and sound penetration. If you heard a bagpipe band there was a limit to the amount of time it would play; if you found it displeasing you could patiently wait until the players got exhausted. But with a recording of a bagpipe band, you are out of luck. It's never going to be exhausted. Electronics, then, have altered the modern soundscape. While modern technology is a source of joy in modern composition, through the opening of many doors for expression, it is also the source of a good number of problems related to the soundscape, problems which society as a whole must adjust to, cope with, and possibly ameliorate.

But then there is not only sound, there is silence. Silence is affected by these same technological developments, the same means of separating sound from source and overcoming the ephemeral nature of a soundscape. I have attempted to define silence and to analyze the attributes that make it valuable. Defining silence as the absence of external or artificially generated sound is fine, but it's a little bit shallow, because silence in many ways is very much more than the absence of sound. Absence of sound is a condition necessary to silence but it is not sufficient in itself to define what we mean by silence. When one thinks about the concept of silence, one notices that there has to be somebody who listens before you can say there is silence. Silence, in addition to being an absence of sound, is defined by a listener, by hearing.

A further attribute, or parameter of silence, from my point of view, comes out of the question: *why is it that we worry about silence?* I feel that one comes to the root of the meaning and practice of silence only when one asks; *why is it that we value and try to establish silence?* Because silence is an enabling environment. This is the domain that we have traditionally associated with silence, the enabling condition in which unprogrammed and unprogrammable events can take place. That is the silence of contemplation; it is the silence when people get in touch with themselves; it is the silence of meditation and worship. The distinctive character of this domain of silence is that it is an enabling condition that opens up the possibility of unprogrammed, unplanned and unprogrammable happenings.

In this light we understand why, as Christians, traditional Quakers found it necessary in the seventeenth century, when they were surrounded by all the pomp and circumstance of the church of England, to reject it. We understand why they felt any ritual, in the sense of its programmed nature and predictability, to be a straitjacket rather than a comfort, and why they said to the amazement of their contemporaries: *we worship God in silence*. Their justification for the practice of silence was that they required it to hear God's voice. Beyond the individual's centring, beyond the individual effort of meditation, there was the need for *collective* silence. Collective silence is an enormously powerful event. There are contemporaneous accounts of Quaker meetings under heavy persecution in England, when thousands of people met silently on a hillside. Then out of the silence, one person—unappointed, unordained, unexpected, and unprogrammed—might speak, to say: *Out of the silence there can come a ministry*. The message is not essentially within that person, constructed in their intellect, but comes out of the silence to them. This isn't just history and theory. I think that if any one of you attended Quaker meetings, particularly on a regular basis, you would find that, suddenly, out of the silence, somebody speaks about something that had just entered *your* mind. It's an uncanny thing. The strength of collective silence is probably one of the most powerful spiritual forces.

Now, in order for something like this to happen, a lot of things are required. There is what Quakers call: *to be with heart and mind prepared*. But there is also the collective decision to be silent. And to be silent in order to let unforeseen, unforeseeable, and unprogrammed things happen. Such silence, I repeat, is the environment that enables the unprogrammed. I feel it is very much at risk.

I will elaborate on this, but first I want to say: there is another silence. 10
There is the silence that enables a programmed, a planned, event to take place. There is the silence in which you courteously engage so that I might be heard: in order for one to be heard all the others have to be silent. But in many cases silence is not taken on voluntarily and it is this false silence of which I am afraid. It is not the silence only of the padded cell, or of solitary confinement; it is the silence that is enforced by the megaphone, the boom box, the PA system,

and any other device that stifles other sounds and voices in order that a planned event can take place.

There is a critical juncture between the planned and the unplanned, the programmed and the unplannable that must be kept in mind. I feel very strongly that our present technological trends drive us toward a decrease in the space—be it in the soundscape, the landscape, or the mindscape—in which the unplanned and unplannable can happen. Yet silence has to remain available in the soundscape, the landscape, and the mindscape. Allowing openness to the unplannable, to the unprogrammed, is the core of the strength of silence. It is also the core of our individual and collective sanity. I extend that to the collectivity because, as a community, as a people, we are threatened just as much, if not more, by the impingement of the programmed over the silent, over that which enables the unprogrammed. Much of the impingement goes unnoticed, uncommented upon, since it is much less obvious than the intrusion of a structure into the landscape. While we may not win all the battles at City Hall to preserve our trees, at least there is now a semi-consciousness that this type of struggle is important.

Where can one go to get away from the dangers of even the gentle presence of programmed music, or Muzak,* in our public buildings? Where do I protest that upon entering any place, from the shoe store to the restaurant, I am deprived of the opportunity to be quiet? Who has asked my permission to put that slop into the elevator I may have to use umpteen times every day? Many such "background" activities are intentionally manipulative. This is not merely "noise" that can be dealt with in terms of noise abatement. There are two aspects to be stressed in this context. One is that the elimination of silence is being done without anybody's consent. The other is that one really has to stop and think and analyze in order to see just how manipulative these interventions can be.

For instance, in the Toronto Skydome, friends tell me that the sound environment is coupled and geared to the game: if the home team misses, there are mournful and distressing sounds over the PA; when the home team scores there is a sort of athletic equivalent of the Hallelujah Chorus.* Again, the visitor has no choice; the programmed soundscape is part of the event. You cannot be present at the game without being subjected to that mood manipulation. I wonder if music will soon be piped into the voter's booth, maybe an upbeat, slightly military tune: "*Get on with it. Get the votes in*." Joking aside, soundscape manipulation is a serious issue. Who on earth has given anybody the right to manipulate the sound environment?

Now, I want to come back to the definition of silence and introduce the notion of the commons, because the soundscape essentially doesn't belong to anyone in particular. What we are hearing, I feel, is very much the privatization of the soundscape, in the same manner in which the enclosure laws in Britain destroyed the commons of old.* There was a time when in fact every community had what was called "the commons," an area that belonged to everybody and where sheep could graze—a place important to all, belonging to all. The notion of the commons is deeply embedded in our social mind as something that all share. There are many "commons" that we take for granted and for millennia, clean air and clean water were the norm. Because of the ephemeral nature of sound in the past, silence was not considered part of the commons. Today, the technology to preserve and multiply sound and separate it from its source has resulted in our sudden awareness that silence, too, is a common good. Silence, which we need in order that unprogrammed and unprogrammable things can take place, is being removed from common access without much fuss and civic bother. It is being privatized.

This is another illustration of an often-observed occurrence related to the impact of technology: that things considered in the past to be normal or ordinary become rare or extraordinary, while those things once considered rare and unusual become normal and routine. Flying is no longer a big deal, but a handmade dress or a home-cooked meal may well be special. We essentially consider polluted water as normal now, and people who can afford it drink bottled water. It is hard to have bottled silence. But money still can buy distance from sound. Today, when there is civic anger, it is with respect to "noise"—like airport noise, etc. There is not yet such anger with respect to the manipulative elimination of silence from the soundscape.

There are those of us who have acknowledged and seen the deterioration of the commons as far as silence is concerned, who have seen that the soundscape is not only polluted by noise—so that one has to look for laws related to noise abatement—but also that the soundscape has become increasingly polluted through the private use of sound in the manipulative dimension of setting and programming moods and conditions. There is a desperate need for awareness of this, and for awareness of it in terms of the collectivity, rather than just individual needs. I feel very much that this is a time for civic anger. This is a time when one has to say: *town planning is constrained by by-laws on height, density, and other features; what are town planning's constraints in relation to silence?*

You may ask, what would I suggest? First of all, we must insist that, as human beings in a society, we have a right to silence. Just as we feel we have the right to walk down the street without being physically assaulted by people and preferably without being visually assaulted by ugly outdoor advertising, we also have the right not to be assaulted by sound, and in particular, not to be assaulted by sound that is there solely for the purpose of profit. Now is the time for civic rage, as well as civic education, but also for some action.

Think of the amount of care that goes into the regulation of parking, so that our good, precious, and necessary cars have a place to be well and safe. That's very important to society. I have yet to see, beyond hospitals, a public building that has a quiet room. Is not our sanity at least as important as the safety of our cars? One should begin to think: are there places, even in conferences like this, that are hassle-free, quiet spaces, where people can go? There were times when one could say to a kid: *"Where did you go?"—"Out."—"What did you do?"—"Nothing."* That sort of blessed time is past. The kid is programmed. We are programmed. And we don't even ask for a quiet space anymore.

One possible measure, relatively close at hand, is to set aside, as a normal matter of human rights, in those buildings over which we have some influence, a quiet room. Further, I highly recommend starting committee meetings with two minutes of silence, and ending them with a few minutes of silence, too. I sit on committees that have this practice, and find that it not only can expedite the business before the committee, but also contributes to a certain amount of peacefulness and sanity. One can start a lecture with a few minutes of silence, and can close it the same way. There can be a few minutes of silence before a shared meal. Such things help, even if they help only in small ways. I do think even small initiatives make silence "visible" as an ever-present part of life. I now invite you to have two minutes of silence before we go on into the question period. Let us be quiet together.

(1994)

Questions

1. This article appeared in a journal (*Musicworks: The Journal of Sound Exploration*) that might appropriately be described as semi-scholarly; its audience consists primarily of academics in music departments and of other people who are well-versed in the technical aspects of music and sound. How does Franklin position herself in paragraph 3 in relationship to this audience? In the remainder of the article, does Franklin invite a wider audience?
2. Using paragraph 6 of this essay as an example, explain why it is often necessary to go beyond dictionary definitions in defining a term for technical or academic purposes.
3. How strong are the connections between silence and religion? Discuss with relation both to Franklin's argument in paragraph 8 and to whatever evidence you are able to assemble from outside this article about religious attitudes and practices.

4. How in Franklin's view is silence often "enforced" (paragraph 10)?
5. Explain in your own words the notion of "the commons" (paragraph 14).
6. Write up a plan of Franklin's argument, with a phrase or two summarizing each paragraph, and using headings and/or connector arrows as you feel appropriate.
7. Do technological developments inevitably tend towards a reduction in the level of silence in society?
8. Write a brief essay arguing for or against increased regulation of the soundscape in your community.

BELL HOOKS

Coming to Class Consciousness [from *Where We Stand*]

An important critical theorist known for her writing on the intersections of race, sex, and class, bell hooks in this essay considers her journey through college and university as a working-class black woman. "Coming to Class Consciousness" first appeared as the second chapter in hooks's Where We Stand: Class Matters, *published in 2000; the book as a whole takes class in America as its primary focus, combining autobiographical essays with more general critiques of systemic inequality.*

As a child I often wanted things money could buy that my parents could not afford and would not get. Rather than tell us we did not get some material thing because money was lacking, mama would frequently manipulate us in an effort to make the desire go away. Sometimes she would belittle and shame us about the object of our desire. That's what I remember most. That lovely yellow dress I wanted would become in her storytelling mouth a really ugly mammy-made* thing that no girl who cared about her looks would desire. My desires were often made to seem worthless and stupid. I learned to mistrust and silence them. I learned that the more clearly I named my desires, the more unlikely those desires would ever be fulfilled.

I learned that my inner life was more peaceful if I did not think about money, or allow myself to indulge in any fantasy of desire. I learned the art of sublimation and repression.[1] I learned it was better to make do with acceptable material desires than to articulate the unacceptable. Before I knew money mattered, I had often chosen objects to desire that were costly, things a girl of my class would not ordinarily desire. But then I was still a girl who was unaware of

1 *sublimation* According to early twentieth-century psychoanalyst Sigmund Freud, sublimation transforms an instinctual impulse into a more socially acceptable interest; *repression* In psychoanalysis, the action of keeping unacceptable ideas out of the conscious mind.

class, who did not think my desires were stupid and wrong. And when I found they were I let them go. I concentrated on survival, on making do.

When I was choosing a college to attend, the issue of money surfaced and had to be talked about. While I would seek loans and scholarships, even if everything related to school was paid for, there would still be transportation to pay for, books, and a host of other hidden costs. Letting me know that there was no extra money to be had, mama urged me to attend any college nearby that would offer financial aid. My first year of college I went to a school close to home. A plain-looking white woman recruiter had sat in our living room and explained to my parents that everything would be taken care of, that I would be awarded a full academic scholarship, that they would have to pay nothing. They knew better. They knew there was still transportation, clothes, all the hidden costs. Still they found this school acceptable. They could drive me there and pick me up. I would not need to come home for holidays. I could make do.

After my parents dropped me at the predominately white women's college, I saw the terror in my roommate's face that she was going to be housed with someone black, and I requested a change. She had no doubt also voiced her concern. I was given a tiny single room by the stairs—a room usually denied a first-year student—but I was a first-year black student, a scholarship girl who could never in a million years have afforded to pay her way or absorb the cost of a single room. My fellow students kept their distance from me. I ate in the cafeteria and did not have to worry about who would pay for pizza and drinks in the world outside. I kept my desires to myself, my lacks and my loneliness; I made do.

I rarely shopped. Boxes came from home with brand-new clothes mama 5
had purchased. Even though it was never spoken she did not want me to feel ashamed among privileged white girls. I was the only black girl in my dorm. There was no room in me for shame. I felt contempt and disinterest. With their giggles and their obsession to marry, the white girls at the women's college were aliens. We did not reside on the same planet. I lived in the world of books. The one white woman who became my close friend found me there reading. I was hiding under the shadows of a tree with huge branches, the kinds of trees that just seemed to grow effortlessly on well-to-do college campuses. I sat on the "perfect" grass reading poetry, wondering how the grass around me could be so lovely and yet when daddy had tried to grow grass in the front yard of Mr. Porter's house it always turned yellow or brown and then died. Endlessly, the yard defeated him, until finally he gave up. The outside of the house looked good but the yard always hinted at the possibility of endless neglect. The yard looked poor.

Foliage and trees on the college grounds flourished. Greens were lush and deep. From my place in the shadows I saw a fellow student sitting alone weeping. Her sadness had to do with all the trivia that haunted our day's classwork, the fear of not being smart enough, of losing financial aid (like me she had loans and scholarships, though her family paid some), and boys. Coming from an Illinois family of Czechoslovakian immigrants she understood class.

When she talked about the other girls who flaunted their wealth and family background there was a hard edge of contempt, anger, and envy in her voice. Envy was always something I pushed away from my psyche. Kept too close for comfort envy could lead to infatuation and on to desire. I desired nothing that they had. She desired everything, speaking her desires openly without shame. Growing up in the kind of community where there was constant competition to see who could buy the bigger better whatever, in a world of organized labour, of unions and strikes, she understood a world of bosses and workers, of haves and have-nots.

White friends I had known in high school wore their class privilege modestly. Raised, like myself, in church traditions that taught us to identify only with the poor, we knew that there was evil in excess. We knew rich people were rarely allowed into heaven.[2] God had given them a paradise of bounty on earth and they had not shared. The rare ones, the rich people who shared, were the only ones able to meet the divine in paradise, and even then it was harder for them to find their way. According to the high school friends we knew, flaunting wealth was frowned upon in our world, frowned upon by God and community.

The few women I befriended my first year in college were not wealthy. They were the ones who shared with me stories of the other girls flaunting the fact that they could buy anything expensive—clothes, food, vacations. There were not many of us from working class backgrounds; we knew who we were. Most girls from poor backgrounds tried to blend in, or fought back by triumphing over wealth with beauty or style or some combination of the above. Being black made me an automatic outsider. Holding their world in contempt pushed me further to the edge. One of the fun* things the "in" girls did was choose someone and trash their room. Like so much else deemed cute by insiders, I dreaded the thought of strangers entering my space and going through my things. Being outside the in crowd made me an unlikely target. Being contemptuous made me first on the list. I did not understand. And when my room was trashed it unleashed my rage and deep grief over not being able to protect my space from violation and invasion. I hated that girls who had so much, took so much for granted, never considered that those of us who did not have mad money would not be able to replace broken things, perfume poured

---

2 *We knew ... into heaven* See Matthew 19.24: "And again I say unto you, it is easier for a camel to go through the eye of a needle, than for a rich man to enter into the kingdom of God."

out, or talcum powder spread everywhere—that we did not know everything could be taken care of at the dry cleaner's because we never took our clothes there. My rage fuelled by contempt was deep, strong, and long lasting. Daily it stood as a challenge to their fun, to their habits of being.

Nothing they did to win me over worked. It came as a great surprise. They had always believed black girls wanted to be white girls, wanted to possess their world. My stoney gaze, silence, and absolute refusal to cross the threshold of their world was total mystery; it was for them a violation they needed to avenge. After trashing my room, they tried to win me over with apologies and urges to talk and understand. There was nothing about me I wanted them to understand. Everything about their world was overexposed, on the surface.

One of my English professors had attended Stanford University. She felt that was the place for me to go—a place where intellect was valued over foolish fun and games and dress up, and finding a husband did not overshadow academic work. She had gone to Stanford. I had never thought about the state of California. Getting my parents to agree to my leaving Kentucky to attend a college in a nearby state had been hard enough. They had accepted a college they could reach by car, but a college thousands of miles away was beyond their imagination. Even I had difficulty grasping going that far away from home. The lure for me was the promise of journeying and arriving at a destination where I would be accepted and understood.

All the barely articulated understandings of class privilege that I had learned my first year of college had not hipped me[3] to the reality of class shame. It still had not dawned on me that my parents, especially mama, resolutely refused to acknowledge any difficulties with money because her sense of shame around class was deep and intense. And when this shame was coupled with her need to feel that she had risen above the low-class backwoods culture of her family, it was impossible for her to talk in a straightforward manner about the strains it would put on the family for me to attend Stanford.

All I knew then was that, as with all my desires, I was told that this desire was impossible to fulfill. At first it was not talked about in relation to money, it was talked about in relation to sin. California was an evil place, a modern-day Babylon[4] where souls were easily seduced away from the path of righteousness. It was not a place for an innocent young girl to go on her own. Mama brought the message back that my father had absolutely refused to give permission.

I expressed my disappointment through ongoing unrelenting grief. I explained to mama that other parents wanted their children to go to good schools. It still had not dawned on me that my parents knew nothing about "good"

---

3 *hipped me* Made me "hip," that is, well-informed.

4 *Babylon* Proverbially decadent or sinful large city.

schools. Even though I knew mama had not graduated from high school I still held her in awe. Mama and daddy were awesome authority figures—family fascists[5] of a very high order. As children we knew that it was better not to doubt their word or their knowledge. We blindly trusted them.

A crucial aspect of our family fascism was that we were not allowed much contact with other families. We were rarely allowed to go to someone's house. We knew better than to speak about our family in other people's homes. While we caught glimpses of different habits of being, different ways of doing things in other families, we knew that to speak of those ways at our home, to try to use them to influence or change our parents, was to risk further confinement.

Our dad had travelled to foreign countries as a soldier but he did not speak of these experiences. Safety, we had been religiously taught in our household, was always to be found close to home. We were not a family who went on vacations, who went exploring. When relatives from large cities would encourage mama to let us children go back with them, their overtures were almost always politely refused. Once mama agreed that I could go to Chicago to visit an elderly cousin, Schuyler[6]—a name strange and beautiful on our lips.

Retired Cousin Schuyler lived a solitary life in a basement flat of the brownstone he shared with Lovie, his wife of many years. Vocationally a painter, he did still lifes and nudes. When they came to visit us, Mama had shown them the painting I had done that won a school prize. It was a portrait of a poor lonely boy with sad eyes. Despite our class background all of us took art classes in school. By high school the disinterested had forgotten about art and only those of us who were committed to doing art, to staying close to an artistic environment, remained. For some that closeness was just a kindly voyeurism. They had talent but were simply not sufficiently interested to use it. Then there were folks like me, full of passion and talent, but without the material resources to do art. Making art was for people with money.

I understood this when my parents adamantly refused to have my painting framed. Only framed work could be in the show. My art teacher, an Italian immigrant who always wore black, showed me how to make a frame from pieces of wood found in the trash. Like my granddaddy he was a lover of found objects. Both of them were men without resources who managed to love beauty and survive. In high school art classes we talked about beauty—about

5 *fascists* Fascism is a nationalistic, totalitarian form of government that enforces conformity and oppresses those who disagree. The term is most frequently used in reference to political movements in Italy, Germany, and other European countries after World War I.

6 *Schuyler* Often pronounced "sky-lar" by American speakers, this Dutch name for "shelter" or "hiding place" also means "scholar" in German.

aesthetics. But it was after class that I told the teacher how I had learned these things already from my grandmother.

Each year students would choose an artist and study their work and then do work in that same tradition. I chose abstract expressionism[7] and the work of Willem de Kooning. Choosing to paint a house in autumn, the kind of house I imagined living in, with swirls of colour—red, yellow, brown—I worked for hours after class, trying to give this house the loneliness I felt inside. This painting was my favourite. I showed it to Cousin Schuyler along with the image of the lonely boy.

It remains a mystery how Schuyler and Lovie convinced mama that it 20
would be fine to let me spend some time with them in Chicago—my first big city. Travelling to Chicago was my first sojourn out of the apartheid south.* It was my first time in a world where I saw black people working at all types of jobs. They worked at the post office delivering mail, in factories, driving buses, collecting garbage—black people with good jobs. This new world was awesome. It was a world where black people had power. I worked in a little store owned by a black male friend of my aunt. The wife of this friend had her own beauty parlour but no children. They had money.

Lovie talked to me about class. There were low-class folks one should not bother with. She insisted one should aim high. These were big city ideas. In our small town community we had been taught to see everyone as worthy. Mama especially preached that you should never see yourself as better than anyone, that no matter anyone's lot in life they deserved respect. Mama preached this even though she aimed high. These messages confused me. The big city was too awesome[8] and left me afraid.

Yet it also changed my perspective, for it had shown me a world where black people could be artists. And what I saw was that artists barely survived. No one in my family wanted me to pursue art; they wanted me to get a good job, to be a teacher. Painting was something to do when real work was done. Once, maybe twice even, I expressed my desire to be an artist. That became an occasion for dire warning and laughter, since like so many desires it was foolish, hence the laughter. Since foolish girls are likely to do foolish things dire warnings had to come after the laughter. Black folks could not make a living as artists. They pointed to the one example—the only grown-up black artist they knew, Cousin Schuyler, living in a dark basement like some kind of mole or rat.

---

7 *abstract expressionism* Fine art form using abstraction to convey powerful feeling. First used to describe the painting style of Wassily Kandinsky, the term also applies to a mid-century American art movement including painters such as Jackson Pollock, Mark Rothko, and Willem de Kooning.

8 *awesome* Awe-inspiring.

Like everything else the choice to be an artist was talked about in terms of race, not class. The substance of the warnings was always to do with the untalked-about reality of class in America. I did not think about being an artist anymore. I struggled with the more immediate question of where to continue college, of how to find a place where I would not feel like such an alien.

When my parents refused to permit me to attend Stanford, I accepted the verdict for awhile. Overwhelmed by grief, I could barely speak for weeks. Mama intervened and tried to change my father's mind as folks she respected in the outside world told her what a privilege it was for me to have this opportunity, that Stanford University was a good school for a smart girl. Without their permission I decided I would go. And even though she did not give her approval mama was willing to help.

My decision made conversations about money necessary. Mama explained that California was too far away, that it would always "cost" to get there, that if something went wrong they would not be able to come and rescue me, that I would not be able to come home for holidays. I heard all this but its meaning did not sink in. I was just relieved I would not be returning to the women's college, to the place where I had truly been an outsider.

There were other black students at Stanford. There was even a dormitory where many black students lived. I did not know I could choose to live there. I went where I was assigned. Going to Stanford was the first time I flew somewhere. Only mama stood and waved farewell as I left to take the bus to the airport. I left with a heavy heart, feeling both excitement and dread. I knew nothing about the world I was journeying to. Not knowing made me afraid but my fear of staying in place was greater.

Since we do not talk about class in this society and since information is never shared or talked about freely in a fascist family, I had no idea what was ahead of me. In small ways I was ignorant. I had never been on an escalator, a city bus, an airplane, or a subway. I arrived in San Francisco with no understanding that Palo Alto was a long drive away—that it would take money to find transportation there. I decided to take the city bus. With all my cheap overpacked bags I must have seemed like just another innocent immigrant when I struggled to board the bus.

This was a city bus with no racks for luggage. It was filled with immigrants. English was not spoken. I felt lost and afraid. Without words the strangers surrounding me understood the universal language of need and distress. They reached for my bags, holding and helping. In return I told them my story—that I had left my village in the South to come to Stanford University, that like them my family were workers, they worked the land—they worked in the world. They were workers. They understood workers. I would go to college and learn how to make a world where they would not have to work so hard.

When I arrived at my destination, the grown-ups in charge cautioned me about trusting strangers, telling me what I already knew, that I was no longer in my town, that nothing was the same. On arriving I called home. Before I could speak, I began to weep as I heard the far-away sound of mama's voice. I tried to find the words, to slow down, to tell her how it felt to be a stranger, to speak my uncertainty and longing. She told me this is the lot I had chosen. I must live with it. After her words there was only silence. She had hung up on me—let me go into this world where I am a stranger still.

Stanford University was a place where one could learn about class from the ground up. Built by a man who believed in hard work, it was to have been a place where students of all classes would come, women and men, to work together and learn. It was to be a place of equality and communalism. His vision was seen by many as almost communist.[9] The fact that he was rich made it all less threatening. Perhaps no one really believed the vision could be realized. The university was named after his son who had died young, a son who had carried his name but who had no future money could buy. No amount of money can keep death away. But it could keep memory alive. And so we work and learn in buildings that remind us of a young son carried away by death too soon, of a father's unrelenting grief remembered.

Everything in the landscape of my new world fascinated me, the plants brought from a rich man's travels all over the world back to this place of water and clay. At Stanford University adobe buildings blend with Japanese plum trees and leaves of kumquat.[10] On my way to study medieval literature, I ate my first kumquat. Surrounded by flowering cactus and a South American shrub bougainvillea[11] of such trailing beauty it took my breath away, I was in a landscape of dreams, full of hope and possibility. If nothing else would hold me, I would not remain a stranger to the earth. The ground I stood on would know me.

Class was talked about behind the scenes. The sons and daughters from rich, famous, or notorious families were identified. The grownups in charge of us were always looking out for a family who might give their millions to the college. At Stanford my classmates wanted to know me, thought it hip, cute, and downright exciting to have a black friend. They invited me on the expensive vacations and ski trips I could not afford. They offered to pay. I never went. Along with other students who were not from privileged families,

---

9 *communist* Embodying the ideals of communism, a political doctrine advocating collective ownership, revolution to end capitalism, and the establishment of a classless society.

10 *kumquat* Small orange citrus fruit originating in southern China and Malaysia.

11 *bougainvillea* Tropical plants with large leaves that nearly cover their flowers.

I searched for places to go during the holiday times when the dormitory was closed. We got together and talked about the assumption that everyone had money to travel and would necessarily be leaving. The staff would be on holiday as well, so all students had to leave. Now and then the staff did not leave and we were allowed to stick around. Once, I went home with one of the women who cleaned for the college.

Now and then when she wanted to make extra money mama would work as a maid. Her decision to work outside the home was seen as an act of treason by our father. At Stanford I was stunned to find that there were maids who came by regularly to vacuum and tidy our rooms. No one had ever cleaned up behind me and I did not want them to. At first I roomed with another girl from a working-class background—a beautiful white girl from Orange County who looked like pictures I had seen on the cover of *Seventeen*[12] magazine. Her mother had died of cancer during her high school years and she had since been raised by her father. She had been asked by the college officials if she would find it problematic to have a black roommate. A scholarship student like myself, she knew her preferences did not matter and as she kept telling me, she did not really care.

Like my friend during freshman year she shared the understanding of what it was like to be a have-not in a world of haves. But unlike me she was determined to become one of them. If it meant she had to steal nice clothes to look the same as they did, she had no problem taking these risks. If it meant having a privileged boyfriend who left bruises on her body now and then, it was worth the risk. Cheating was worth it. She believed the world the privileged had created was all unfair—all one big cheat; to get ahead one had to play the game. To her I was truly an innocent, a lamb being led to the slaughter. It did not surprise her one bit when I began to crack under the pressure of contradictory values and longings.

35 Like all students who did not have seniority, I had to see the school psychiatrists to be given permission to live off campus. Unaccustomed to being around strangers, especially strangers who did not share or understand my values, I found the experience of living in the dorms difficult. Indeed, almost everyone around me believed working-class folks had no values. At the university where the founder, Leland Stanford, had imagined different classes meeting on common ground, I learned how deeply individuals with class privilege feared and hated the working classes. Hearing classmates express contempt and hatred toward people who did not come from the right backgrounds shocked me. Naively, I believed them to be so young to hold those views, so devoid of life experiences that would serve to uphold or make sense

12 *Seventeen* Magazine for teenage girls; beauty and fashion tips are its primary focus.

of these thoughts. I had always worked. Working-class people had always encouraged and supported me.

To survive in this new world of divided classes, this world where I was also encountering for the first time a black bourgeois elite that was as contemptuous of working people as their white counterparts were, I had to take a stand, to get clear my own class affiliations. This was the most difficult truth to face. Having been taught all my life to believe that black people were inextricably bound in solidarity by our struggles to end racism, I did not know how to respond to elitist black people who were full of contempt for anyone who did not share their class, their way of life.

At Stanford I encountered for the first time a black diaspora.[13] Of the few black professors present, the vast majority were from African or Caribbean backgrounds. Elites themselves, they were only interested in teaching other elites. Poor folks like myself, with no background to speak of, were invisible. We were not seen by them or anyone else. Initially, I went to all meetings welcoming black students, but when I found no one to connect with I retreated. In the shadows I had time and books to teach me about the nature of class—about the ways black people were divided from themselves.

Despite this rude awakening, my disappointment at finding myself estranged from the group of students I thought would understand, I still looked for connections. I met an older black male graduate student who also came from a working-class background. Even though he had gone to the right high school, a California school for gifted students, and then to Princeton as an undergraduate, he understood intimately the intersections of race and class. Good in sports and in the classroom, he had been slotted early on to go far, to go where other black males had not gone. He understood the system. Academically, he fit. Had he wanted to, he could have been among the elite but he chose to be on the margins, to hang with an intellectual artistic avant garde.[14] He wanted to live in a world of the mind where there was no race or class. He wanted to worship at the throne of art and knowledge. He became my mentor, comrade, and companion.

When we were not devoting ourselves to books and to poetry we confronted a real world where we were in need of jobs. Even though I taught an occasional class, I worked in the world of the mundane. I worked at a bookstore, cooked at a club, worked for the telephone company. My way out of being a

---

13 *diaspora* Group of people who have dispersed from their original or traditional homeland. The term "African diaspora" or "black diaspora" refers to the movement of African people out of Africa over the past centuries—with a particular emphasis on enforced movement via the slave trade.

14 *avant garde* Literally, the front line of an advancing army, though the term is most often used to describe intellectual innovators.

maid, of doing the dirty work of cleaning someone else's house, was to become a schoolteacher. The thought terrified me. From grade school on I feared and hated the classroom. In my imagination it was still the ultimate place of inclusion and exclusion, discipline and punishment—worse than the fascist family because there was no connection of blood to keep in check impulses to search and destroy.

Now and then a committed college professor opened my mind to the reality that the classroom could be a place of passion and possibility, but, in general, at the various colleges I attended it was the place where the social order was kept in place. Throughout my graduate student years, I was told again and again that I lacked the proper decorum of a graduate student, that I did not understand my place. Slowly I began to understand fully that there was no place in academe for folks from working-class backgrounds who did not wish to leave the past behind. That was the price of the ticket. Poor students would be welcome at the best institutions of higher learning only if they were willing to surrender memory, to forget the past and claim the assimilated present as the only worthwhile and meaningful reality.

Students from nonprivileged backgrounds who did not want to forget often had nervous breakdowns. They could not bear the weight of all the contradictions they had to confront. They were crushed. More often than not they dropped out with no trace of their inner anguish recorded, no institutional record of the myriad ways their take on the world was assaulted by an elite vision of class and privilege. The records merely indicated that even after receiving financial aid and other support, these students simply could not make it, simply were not good enough.

At no time in my years as a student did I march in a graduation ceremony. I was not proud to hold degrees from institutions where I had been constantly scorned and shamed. I wanted to forget these experiences, to erase them from my consciousness. Like a prisoner set free I did not want to remember my years on the inside. When I finished my doctorate I felt too much uncertainty about who I had become. Uncertain about whether I had managed to make it through without giving up the best of myself, the best of the values I had been raised to believe in—hard work, honesty, and respect for everyone no matter their class—I finished my education with my allegiance to the working class intact. Even so, I had planted my feet on the path leading in the direction of class privilege. There would always be contradictions to face. There would always be confrontations around the issue of class. I would always have to reexamine where I stand.

(2000)

Questions

1. What is hooks's attitude towards formal education? What does she hope to gain from it, and what are its limitations and risks?
2. The author recounts an incident in which her room is "trashed" by fellow students. Why does the incident impact her so profoundly? Why does she respond contemptuously to her classmates' attempts to apologize?
3. What are some of the contradictions between the values with which hooks was raised and the values she encounters in her classmates?
4. The author transferred from a women's college to Stanford, which is co-ed. Though she does not discuss gender explicitly, how have gender expectations affected her educational experience?
5. Topics often change quickly without extensive transitions in this essay. For example, hooks describes her parents with love and awe before abruptly calling the family fascist. Find at least one other example of abrupt transition in this essay. What effects do these abrupt transitions have on the reader?
6. Consider hooks's critique of postsecondary institutions, especially that advanced in the final paragraphs. To what extent does this critique apply to your institution? What can your institution learn from hooks's critique?

RICHARD RODRIGUEZ

from CROSSING BORDERS [SAN DIEGO AND TIJUANA]

An unconventional and sometimes controversial figure in American letters, Rodriguez first attracted attention with his 1982 book, Hunger of Memory, *an account of his upbringing that also touches on large cultural issues such as bilingualism and assimilation. As someone steeped both in Mexican and in American culture, Rodriguez has been well-placed to comment on the differences, similarities, and connections between the two.*

The commentary on San Diego and Tijuana included here is an excerpt from the adapted text of a 1997 interview with Scott London that was originally aired on the public radio series "Insight & Outlook." The written version of the interview has appeared either in full or in abridged form under various titles, including "Crossing Borders: An Interview with Richard Rodriguez" and "A View from the Melting Pot: An Interview with Richard Rodriguez." Rodriguez is responding here to London's suggestion that the combination of Tijuana and San Diego "offers a glimpse of what America might look like in another generation or two."*

Talk about alter ego: Tijuana was created by the lust of San Diego. Everything that was illegal in San Diego was permitted in Tijuana. When boxing was illegal in San Diego, there were boxing matches in Tijuana; when gambling was illegal, there was always Tijuana. Mexicans would say, "We're not responsible for Tijuana; it's the Americans who created it." And there was some justification for that. But, in fact, the whore was a Mexican, the bartender a Mexican. Tijuana was this lovely meeting of Protestant hypocrisy with Catholic cynicism: the two cities went to bed and both denied it in the morning.

To this day, you will see American teenagers going to Mexico on Saturday nights to get drunk. Mexico gives them permission. The old Southern Catholic tradition gives permission to the Northern Protestant culture to misbehave. But what has happened in the last generation is that Tijuana has become a new Third

World capital—much to the chagrin of Mexico City, which is more and more aware of how little it controls Tijuana politically and culturally. In addition to whorehouses and discos, Tijuana now has Korean factories and Japanese industrialists and Central American refugees, and a new Mexican bourgeoisie that takes its lessons from cable television.

And then there is San Diego—this retirement village, with its prim petticoat, that doesn't want to get too near the water. San Diego worries about all the turds washing up on the lovely, pristine beaches of La Jolla.[1] San Diego wishes Mexico would have fewer babies. And San Diego, like the rest of America, is growing middle-aged. The average age in the U.S. is now thirty-three, whereas Mexico gets younger and younger, retreats deeper and deeper into adolescence. Mexico is fifteen. Mexico is wearing a Hard Rock Cafe T-shirt* and wandering around Tijuana looking for a job, for a date, for something to put on her face to take care of the acne.

It is not simply that these two cities are perched side by side at the edge of the Pacific; it is that adolescence sits next to middle age, and they don't know how to relate to each other. In a way, these two cities exist in different centuries. San Diego is a post-industrial city talking about settling down, slowing down, building clean industry. Tijuana is a preindustrial city talking about changing, moving forward, growing. Yet they form a single metropolitan area.

(1997)

Questions

1. In what ways is Tijuana the "alter ego" of San Diego?
2. How does Rodriguez personify the two cities discussed in this selection?

---

1 *La Jolla* Fashionable coastal area of San Diego.

Philip Gourevitch

from We Wish to Inform You That Tomorrow We Will Be Killed with Our Families

In the central African country of Rwanda, the majority Hutu and the minority Tutsi have a long history of conflict. In April 1994, the country's Hutu president was killed when rocket fire shot down his plane. Extremists in the Rwandan government blamed Tutsi dissidents, provided machetes to the citizenry, and encouraged Hutu citizens to form militias and to (as the radio broadcasts put it) "kill the Tutsis; they are cockroaches." The killing went on for more than six weeks, leaving some 800,000 Tutsi dead; it remains one of the worst instances of genocide since the Holocaust.

Gourevitch published a series of magazine articles on the genocide starting in the spring of 1995; his 1999 book on the subject, from which the following excerpt is taken, is widely regarded as a non-fiction classic.

In the Province of Kibungo, in eastern Rwanda, in the swamp- and pastureland near the Tanzanian border, there's a rocky hill called Nyarubuye with a church where many Tutsis were slaughtered in mid-April of 1994. A year after the killing I went to Nyarubuye with two Canadian military officers. We flew in a United Nations helicopter, travelling low over the hills in the morning mists, with the banana trees like green starbursts dense over the slopes. The uncut grass blew back as we dropped into the centre of the parish schoolyard. A lone soldier materialized with his Kalashnikov,* and shook our hands with stiff, shy formality. The Canadians presented the paperwork for our visit, and I stepped up into the open doorway of a classroom.

At least fifty mostly decomposed cadavers covered the floor, wadded in clothing, their belongings strewn about and smashed. Macheted skulls had rolled here and there.

The dead looked like pictures of the dead. They did not smell. They did not buzz with flies. They had been killed thirteen months earlier, and they hadn't been moved. Skin stuck here and there over the bones, many of which lay scattered away from the bodies, dismembered by the killers, or by scavengers—birds, dogs, bugs. The more complete figures looked a lot like people, which they were once. A woman in a cloth wrap printed with flowers lay near the door. Her fleshless hip bones were high and her legs slightly spread, and a child's skeleton extended between them. Her torso was hollowed out. Her ribs and spinal column poked through the rotting cloth. Her head was tipped back and her mouth was open: a strange image—half agony, half repose.

I had never been among the dead before. What to do? Look? Yes. I wanted to see them, I suppose; I had come to see them—the dead had been left unburied at Nyarubuye for memorial purposes—and there they were, so intimately exposed. I didn't need to see them. I already knew, and believed, what had happened in Rwanda. Yet looking at the buildings and the bodies, and hearing the silence of the place, with the grand Italianate basilica standing there deserted, and beds of exquisite, decadent, death-fertilized flowers blooming over the corpses, it was still strangely unimaginable. I mean one still had to imagine it.

Those dead Rwandans will be with me forever, I expect. That was why 5
I had felt compelled to come to Nyarubuye: to be stuck with them—not with their experience, but with the experience of looking at them. They had been killed there, and they were dead there. What else could you really see at first? The Bible bloated with rain lying on top of one corpse or, littered about, the little woven wreaths of thatch which Rwandan women wear as crowns to balance the enormous loads they carry on their heads, and the water gourds, and the Converse tennis sneaker stuck somehow in a pelvis.

The soldier with the Kalashnikov—Sergeant Francis of the Rwandese Patriotic Army, a Tutsi whose parents had fled to Uganda with him when he was a boy, after similar but less extensive massacres in the early 1960s, and who had fought his way home in 1994 and found it like this—said that the dead in this room were mostly women who had been raped before being murdered. Sergeant Francis had high, rolling girlish hips, and he walked and stood with his butt stuck out behind him, an oddly purposeful posture, tipped forward, driven. He was, at once, candid and briskly official. His English had the punctilious clip of military drill, and after he told me what I was looking at I looked instead at my feet. The rusty head of a hatchet lay beside them in the dirt.

A few weeks earlier, in Bukavu, Zaire, in the giant market of a refugee camp that was home to many Rwandan Hutu militiamen, I had watched a man butchering a cow with a machete. He was quite expert at his work, taking big precise strokes that made a sharp hacking noise. The rallying cry to the killers during the genocide was "Do your work!" And I saw that it *was* work, this butchery; hard work. It took many hacks—two, three, four, five hard hacks—to chop through the cow's leg. How many hacks to dismember a person?

Considering the enormity of the task, it is tempting to play with theories of collective madness, mob mania, a fever of hatred erupted into a mass crime of passion, and to imagine the blind orgy of the mob, with each member killing one or two people. But at Nyarubuye, and at thousands of other sites in this tiny country, on the same days of a few months in 1994, hundreds of thousands of Hutus had worked as killers in regular shifts. There was always the next victim, and the next. What sustained them, beyond the frenzy of the first attack, through the plain physical exhaustion and mess of it?

The pygmy in Gikongoro* said that humanity is part of nature and that we must go against nature to get along and have peace. But mass violence, too, must be organized; it does not occur aimlessly. Even mobs and riots have a design, and great and sustained destruction requires great ambition. It must be conceived as the means toward achieving a new order, and although the idea behind that new order may be criminal and objectively very stupid, it must also be compellingly simple and at the same time absolute. The ideology of genocide is all of those things, and in Rwanda it went by the bald name of Hutu Power. For those who set about systematically exterminating an entire people—even a fairly small and unresisting subpopulation of perhaps a million and a quarter men, women, and children, like the Tutsis in Rwanda—blood lust surely helps. But the engineers and perpetrators of a slaughter like the one just inside the door where I stood need not enjoy killing, and they may even find it unpleasant. What is required above all is that they want their victims dead. They have to want it so badly that they consider it a necessity.

10 So I still had much to imagine as I entered the classroom and stepped carefully between the remains. These dead and their killers had been neighbours, schoolmates, colleagues, sometimes friends, even in-laws. The dead had seen their killers training as militias in the weeks before the end, and it was well known that they were training to kill Tutsis; it was announced on the radio, it was in the newspapers, people spoke of it openly. The week before the massacre at Nyarubuye, the killing began in Rwanda's capital, Kigali. Hutus who opposed the Hutu Power ideology were publicly denounced as "accomplices" of the Tutsis and were among the first to be killed as the extermination got under way. In Nyarubuye, when Tutsis asked the Hutu Power mayor how they might be spared, he suggested that they seek sanctuary at the church. They did, and a few days later the mayor came to kill them. He came at the head of a pack of soldiers, policemen, militiamen, and villagers; he gave out arms and orders to complete the job well. No more was required of the mayor, but he was also said to have killed a few Tutsis himself.

The killers killed all day at Nyarubuye. At night they cut the Achilles tendons of survivors and went off to feast behind the church, roasting cattle looted from their victims in big fires, and drinking beer. (Bottled beer, banana beer—Rwandans may not drink more beer than other Africans, but they drink prodigious quantities of it around the clock.) And, in the morning, still drunk after whatever sleep they could find beneath the cries of their prey, the killers at Nyarubuye went back and killed again. Day after day, minute to minute, Tutsi by Tutsi: all across Rwanda, they worked like that. "It was a process," Sergeant Francis said. I can see that it happened, I can be told how, and after nearly three years of looking around Rwanda and listening to Rwandans, I can tell you how, and I will. But the horror of it—the idiocy, the waste, the sheer wrongness—remains uncircumscribable.

Like Leontius, the young Athenian in Plato,* I presume that you are reading this because you desire a closer look, and that you, too, are properly disturbed by your curiosity. Perhaps, in examining this extremity with me, you hope for some understanding, some insight, some flicker of self-knowledge—a moral, or a lesson, or a clue about how to behave in this world: some such information. I don't discount the possibility, but when it comes to genocide, you already know right from wrong. The best reason I have come up with for looking closely into Rwanda's stories is that ignoring them makes me even more uncomfortable about existence and my place in it. The horror, as horror, interests me only insofar as a precise memory of the offense is necessary to understand its legacy.

The dead at Nyarubuye were, I'm afraid, beautiful. There was no getting around it. The skeleton is a beautiful thing. The randomness of the fallen forms, the strange tranquility of their rude exposure, the skull here, the arm bent in some uninterpretable gesture there—these things were beautiful, and their beauty only added to the affront of the place. I couldn't settle on any meaningful response: revulsion, alarm, sorrow, grief, shame, incomprehension, sure, but nothing truly meaningful. I just looked, and I took photographs, because I wondered whether I could really see what I was seeing while I saw it, and I wanted also an excuse to look a bit more closely.

We went on through the first room and out the far side. There was another room and another and another and another. They were all full of bodies, and more bodies were scattered in the grass and there were stray skulls in the grass, which was thick and wonderfully green. Standing outside, I heard a crunch. The old Canadian colonel stumbled in front of me, and I saw, though he did not notice, that his foot had rolled on a skull and broken it. For the first time at Nyarubuye my feelings focused, and what I felt was a small but keen anger at this man. Then I heard another crunch, and felt a vibration underfoot. I had stepped on one, too.

Rwanda is spectacular to behold. Throughout its centre, a winding succession 15
of steep, tightly terraced slopes radiates out from small roadside settlements and solitary compounds. Gashes of red clay and black loam mark fresh hoe work;

eucalyptus trees flash silver against brilliant green tea plantations; banana trees are everywhere. On the theme of hills, Rwanda produces countless variations: jagged rain forests, round-shouldered buttes, undulating moors, broad swells of savanna, volcanic peaks sharp as filed teeth. During the rainy season, the clouds are huge and low and fast, mists cling in highland hollows, lightning flickers through the nights, and by day the land is lustrous. After the rains, the skies lift, the terrain takes on a ragged look beneath the flat unvarying haze of the dry season, and in the savannas of the Akagera Park wildlife blackens the hills.

One day, when I was returning to Kigali from the south, the car mounted a rise between two winding valleys, the windshield filled with purple-bellied clouds, and I asked Joseph, the man who was giving me a ride, whether Rwandans realize what a beautiful country they have. "Beautiful?" he said. "You think so? After the things that happened here? The people aren't good. If the people were good, the country might be OK." Joseph told me that his brother and sister had been killed, and he made a soft hissing click with his tongue against his teeth. "The country is empty," he said. "Empty!"

It was not just the dead who were missing. The genocide had been brought to a halt by the Rwandese Patriotic Front, a rebel army led by Tutsi refugees from past persecutions, and as the RPF advanced through the country in the summer of 1994, some two million Hutus had fled into exile at the behest of the same leaders who had urged them to kill. Yet except in some rural areas in the south, where the desertion of Hutus had left nothing but bush to reclaim the fields around crumbling adobe houses, I, as a newcomer, could not see the emptiness that blinded Joseph to Rwanda's beauty. Yes, there were grenade-flattened buildings, burnt homesteads, shot-up facades, and mortar-pitted roads. But these were the ravages of war, not of genocide, and by the summer of 1995, most of the dead had been buried. Fifteen months earlier, Rwanda had been the most densely populated country in Africa. Now the work of the killers looked just as they had intended: invisible.

From time to time, mass graves were discovered and excavated, and the remains would be transferred to new, properly consecrated mass graves. Yet even the occasionally exposed bones, the conspicuous number of amputees and people with deforming scars, and the superabundance of packed orphanages could not be taken as evidence that what had happened to Rwanda was an attempt to eliminate a people. There were only people's stories.

"Every survivor wonders why he is alive," Abbé Modeste, a priest at the cathedral in Butare, Rwanda's second-largest city, told me. Abbé Modeste had hidden for weeks in his sacristy, eating communion wafers, before moving under the desk in his study, and finally into the rafters at the home of some neighbouring nuns. The obvious explanation of his survival was that the RPF had come to the rescue. But the RPF didn’t reach Butare till early July, and roughly seventy-five percent of the Tutsis in Rwanda had been killed by early May. In this regard, at least, the genocide had been entirely successful: to those who were targeted, it was not death but life that seemed an accident of fate.

“I had eighteen people killed at my house,” said Etienne Niyonzima, a 20
former businessman who had become a deputy in the National Assembly. “Everything was totally destroyed—a place of fifty-five metres by fifty metres. In my neighbourhood they killed six hundred and forty-seven people. They tortured them, too. You had to see how they killed them. They had the number of everyone’s house, and they went through with red paint and marked the homes of all the Tutsis and of the Hutu moderates. My wife was at a friend’s, shot with two bullets. She is still alive, only”—he fell quiet for a moment—“she has no arms. The others with her were killed. The militia left her for dead. Her whole family of sixty-five in Gitarama were killed.” Niyonzima was in hiding at the time. Only after he had been separated from his wife for three months did he learn that she and four of their children had survived. “Well,” he said, “one son was cut in the head with a machete. I don’t know where he went.” His voice weakened, and caught. “He disappeared.” Niyonzima clicked his tongue, and said, “But the others are still alive. Quite honestly, I don’t understand at all how I was saved.”

Laurent Nkongoli attributed his survival to “Providence, and also good neighbours, an old woman who said, ‘Run away, we don’t want to see your corpse.’” Nkongoli, a lawyer, who had become the vice president of the National Assembly after the genocide, was a robust man, with a taste for double-breasted suit jackets and lively ties, and he moved, as he spoke, with a brisk determination. But before taking his neighbour’s advice, and fleeing Kigali in late April of 1994, he said, “I had accepted death. At a certain moment this happens. One hopes not to die cruelly, but one expects to die anyway. Not death by machete, one hopes, but with a bullet. If you were willing to pay for it, you could often ask for a bullet. Death was more or less normal, a resignation. You lose the will to fight. There were four thousand Tutsis killed here at Kacyiru”—a neighbourhood of Kigali. “The soldiers brought them here, and told them to sit down because they were going to throw grenades. And they sat.

“Rwandan culture is a culture of fear,” Nkongoli went on. “I remember what people said.” He adopted a pipey voice, and his face took on a look of disgust: “‘Just let us pray, then kill us,’ or ‘I don’t want to die in the street, I want to die at home.’” He resumed his normal voice. “When you’re that resigned and oppressed you’re already dead. It shows the genocide was prepared for too long. I detest this fear. These victims of genocide had been psychologically prepared to expect death just for being Tutsi. They were being killed for so long that they were already dead.”

I reminded Nkongoli that, for all his hatred of fear, he had himself accepted death before his neighbour urged him to run away. "Yes," he said. "I got tired in the genocide. You struggle so long, then you get tired."

Every Rwandan I spoke with seemed to have a favourite, unanswerable question. For Nkongoli, it was how so many Tutsis had allowed themselves to be killed. For François Xavier Nkurunziza, a Kigali lawyer, whose father was Hutu and whose mother and wife were Tutsi, the question was how so many Hutus had allowed themselves to kill. Nkurunziza had escaped death only by chance as he moved around the country from one hiding place to another, and he had lost many family members. "Conformity is very deep, very developed here," he told me. "In Rwandan history, everyone obeys authority. People revere power, and there isn't enough education. You take a poor, ignorant population, and give them arms, and say, 'It's yours. Kill.' They'll obey. The peasants, who were paid or forced to kill, were looking up to people of higher socio-economic standing to see how to behave. So the people of influence, or the big financiers, are often the big men in the genocide. They may think they didn't kill because they didn't take life with their own hands, but the people were looking to them for their orders. And, in Rwanda, an order can be given very quietly."

As I travelled around the country, collecting accounts of the killing, it almost seemed as if, with the machete, the *masu*—a club studded with nails—a few well-placed grenades, and a few bursts of automatic-rifle fire, the quiet orders of Hutu Power had made the neutron bomb obsolete.

"Everyone was called to hunt the enemy," said Theodore Nyilinkwaya, a survivor of the massacres in his home village of Kimbogo, in the southwestern province of Cyangugu. "But let's say someone is reluctant. Say that guy comes with a stick. They tell him, 'No, get a *masu*.' So, OK, he does, and he runs along with the rest, but he doesn't kill. They say, 'Hey, he might denounce us later. He must kill. Everyone must help to kill at least one person.' So this person who is not a killer is made to do it. And the next day it's become a game for him. You don't need to keep pushing him."

At Nyarubuye, even the little terracotta votive statues in the sacristy had been methodically decapitated. "They were associated with Tutsis," Sergeant Francis explained.

(1999)

Questions

1. What is the author's conclusion at the end of his journey? What message is Gourevitch trying to convey to us about Rwanda's experience, and how it may relate to us?
2. How does Gourevitch communicate the horror of the scene of the corpses in the schoolroom?
3. How can you explain Gourevitch's use of the word "beautiful" in reference to the massacred bodies he sees? What effect does it have on the reader?
4. The first part of this selection deals with how Gourevitch dealt personally with confronting the facts of the massacre. The second part deals in a more objective way with the politics underlying the massacre. How does the first part of the selection affect the reading of the second part?

LARISSA LAI

POLITICAL ANIMALS AND THE BODY OF HISTORY[1]

Novelist, poet, and scholar Larissa Lai's first novel, When Fox Is a Thousand *(1995), combines elements drawn from Chinese folklore, ninth-century Chinese history, and life in twentieth-century Vancouver. The novel was widely acclaimed and has been the focus of substantial academic and critical attention in Canada—as have Lai's subsequent works. Lai, a Chinese Canadian, offers her views on race and writing in the following paper. Originally delivered at a conference on* Making History, Constructing Race *at the University of Victoria in 1998, it was subsequently published in the journal* Canadian Literature *the following year.*

Entranceways are the most difficult because you have to pass through them alone. I wanted to bring someone with me, someone who in this moment might function as a translator, not from some other language into English but from one English to another. Because I already know this entranceway is not where I come from, and yet I must say I do, in order for you to understand me.

Ashok Mathur, a writer, critic and activist, but mostly a trusted friend was here first, keeping watch over the literary/academic entranceway, asking the leading question. I did not want to come in the door like that. And yet it seemed to be the main entrance. He thought it was important that I enter the dialogue, and so asked the question—a door-opening kind of question, a come-right-this-way sort of question to lead the sniff-sniffing fox out of her lair onto the green. Not to assume she'd be hunted, but no sense denying the possibility.

The question was this: How could you or would you describe your writing as coming from a racialized* space?[2]

1 [Lai's note] This piece was originally produced for the conference Making History, Constructing Race at the University of Victoria, October 23–25, 1998.

2 [Lai's note] E-mail interview with Ashok Mathur, July 1998. Available at http://www.acs.ucalgary.ca/~amathur/.

A question from the middle of a conversation, begun in some other place, long ago and far away. Which is to say right here and now, but of another root, another wellspring. An awkward question because it demands a starting point apart from the self. A question that assumes one already knows how she is looked at from someplace that is by definition outside of her, and yet familiar at the same time.

It took me a long time to answer. I kept turning the question around in my 5
head, asking myself what he meant when he asked it, and how he perceived his own work in that regard. We'd talked about the question before, so I knew he understood my ambivalence. How can a person write from a place constructed for her, pejoratively, by someone else? Why would she want to? But then, does she have a choice? My racialization is a historical fact, begun in Europe centuries before I was born, and perpetuated in a sometimes friendly Canadian sort of way through the social, bureaucratic and corporate structures of this society. I still live with the hope that the body exists prior to race, that experience exists prior to race. Living in a country that could not and does not exist without the concept of race, and for that matter, why be polite, white superiority, it is often hard to maintain this hope. When I say pejorative, I mean, you know, I didn't ask for this. And when Ashok asks me how I see my work coming from a racialized space, he is implicitly acknowledging that we both know this. He is asking me, faced with this recognition, what I intend to do about the injustice of it. He is asking me whether I see this othering of my body and my work by the mainstream as my responsibility to undo. If it is not my responsibility, are there reasons why I would choose to do it? He is asking me whether or not I think I have a choice. He is asking me because he faces similar questions.

These questions rise from the context this country has handed me. They are not the centre of my world. What I mean to say is, I didn't want to come in the door like this, nor dressed in these clothes, these shackles. But would you, white or brown, content or discontent, have recognized me otherwise? Perhaps. But I am not yet a creature of great faith.

My work comes from many places at once. There is an aspect in recent years that has been about trying, Houdini-like* to break from the box which allows only two possibilities—to understand and work from the racialized position this society allots to the likes of us, or to work from a "colour-blind" liberal position which actively denies the way we have been racialized even as it perpetuates the very racial interests it claims not to see.

Growing up in Canada in the seventies, and eighties, I was very much crammed inside the racism-was-terrible-but-now-it's-over box—a quick-fix product of official Multiculturalism that did precious little materially except sweep the problem of white racism under the carpet. This liberal position, so seemingly loaded with good intentions, had a pale, clammy underside that merely masked existing power imbalances while doing little to rectify them. For those of us who grew up in that era, it meant knowing something was wrong but never being able to put your finger on it.

In the late eighties/early nineties, I was drawn to the anti-oppression movements, which, though they had been growing for years, were currently flowering on the West Coast and in other parts of the country. It was and continues to be incredibly empowering to embrace a confrontative politic that refuses to accept the historically rooted racism of this country and to call it into question wherever it rears its ugly head. I was and am very interested in questions of strategy—How can people of colour and First Nations people empower ourselves and one another given the colonial and neo-colonial contexts we live with? In a collective sense, this means taking particular stands on issues such as appropriation and affirmative action as a means of pushing white liberals to look at the hypocrisies of colourblindness, multiculturalism and other stances that seemed so liberal in the seventies. It means forcing the hand of those who would like credit for a belief in equality without having to put that belief into practice by giving up the ill-gotten gains of racially endowed power.

10 I took a particular interest in questions of history for a number of reasons. I think part of what is so aggravating about the reactionary racism that is so often the knee-jerk response to an anti-racist critique is the way in which it denies this country's ugly histories—the histories of the residential schools, the Japanese Internment, the Chinese Exclusion Act, the Komagata Maru[3] incident as well as larger international histories of colonialism and exploitation which shaped and continue to shape the globe. It was particularly empowering to be introduced to works by marginalized people that addressed these histories from our own points of view. There was an urgency around their production and reading which I still feel. Gloria Anzaldua and Cherie Moraga's *This Bridge Called My Back* was seminal, as much as a presence as a test. I remember being thrilled by the publication of *Piece of My Heart: A Lesbian of Colour Anthology* put out by Sister Vision Press in 1990.

---

3 *Japanese Internment* During the Second World War, the Canadian government forced Japanese Canadians to leave their homes and businesses and live in overcrowded camps with inadequate amenities. This was ostensibly done to prevent Japanese Canadians from assisting an invasion of Canada by Japan, but it is now generally acknowledged that no such threat existed; *Chinese Exclusion Act* 1923 Act that specifically forbade the immigration of Chinese people to Canada. It was not repealed until 1947; *Komagata Maru* Ship on which, in 1914, several hundred Punjabi people attempted to immigrate to Canada despite racist laws that were calculated to prevent such immigration from India. The Canadian government turned almost all of the passengers away, and most were imprisoned (or, in some cases, killed by police) after their return to India.

Trinh's *Woman, Native, Other* was also important, as was bell hooks' *Ain't I a Woman*. There were also numerous cultural projects and special issues of periodicals that while problematic in their tokenized status were, nonetheless, affirming and thought-provoking. Although very few of these things became institutionalized or regularized, each served as a form to move dialogue forward. In some ways the ad hoc* nature of these projects was liberating in that they allowed various communities different ways of entering the discussions and validated a variety of voices in a variety of media.

I began to take note, however, of how certain texts became rapidly fetishized by critics, academics and the general public in ways comparable to the way anthropologists and missionaries address field notes. I attended many readings and I can't count the number of times audience members have asked writers of colour, referring to the main character of any particular writer's text: "Is that you?" Or of my own work, which at moments actively resists that question: "Did you get these stories from your grandmother?" The suggestion is, of course, that we are not creative agents capable of constructing nuanced fictions which address historical situations, but rather mere native informants reconstructing, as accurately as our second-rate minds allow, what actually happened. Not, I might add, that I am trying to create a hierarchy of genres that inadvertently favours narrative fiction—I think it is very important that those who remember "what actually happened" write about it, and I have faith that they have written and will continue to write it well. It is rather the reception of the work, and the assumptions around that reception, that I wish to critique.

I understand that these questions may well be addressed to novel writers across race, class, gender and sexuality lines; however, their anthropological resonance with regard to marginalized peoples can not be denied. (I betcha no one ever asked Dickens if he was really Tiny Tim.[4]) I feel a certain ambivalence here. My authority as an author is of no great importance or interest to me. My one great wish for readers is that they understand writing as a practice rather than as the production of an inert, consumable text. In some ways, the question "Is that you?" affirms this wish.

There are other genres that have a tradition of foregrounding within the body of their texts questions about how we read, that have a history of resisting readings that would consume them. These are the same texts that within many circles, both progressive and conservative, get labelled as too intellectual, too academic, incomprehensible. They are circulated within certain small if thoughtful circles, but do not reach the audiences which novels reach. I do not wish to address the question of whether their "elitism"* is inherent or

---

4 *Tiny Tim* Young boy in Charles Dickens's *A Christmas Carol* (1843); for much of the novella, he is dying of a debilitating disease that his family cannot afford to cure.

constructed. I am conscious of my choice to write fiction as a strategy chosen because it reaches people. On the other hand, in this age of steroid-enhanced capitalism,* the tension between engaging those technologies which enable one to reach large numbers of people, and opening oneself and one's work to quick fix consumption, is no easy thing to resolve. Indeed, the quick fix consumptive scrutiny itself is all too easily transmuted into a kind of surveillance which generates new stereotypes, dangerous ones if their sources can be traced to a semblance of native reportage. This is the editorial power of capital.

And yet the fact remains that narrative compels me. What is history, after all, but narrative? And she who inhabits that narrative truly has ground to stand on. That grounding is necessary when her belonging to the land she lives on is so contested.

My second interest in the question of history is a more personal one, tied to my own historical situation. It is also very much caught up in questions of strategy: How do we diasporized* types make a homespace for ourselves given all the disjunctures and discontinuities of our histories, and for that matter, the co-temporalities of some of them? It is also about the second box, if you were following my Houdini metaphor. The paradox of claiming a racialized space as a space from which to work is an uncomfortable one. To claim a racialized space is empowering in that it demands acknowledgment of a history of racism to which the mainstream does not want to admit. It demands acknowledgment of the continued perpetuation of that racism often, though not always, in new forms in the present. On the other hand, to claim that space also confirms and validates that eurocentric racist stance by placing ourselves in opposition to it, enforcing a binarism which itself is a Western social construct. So how to break from the second box without falling back into the first one, the one which denies a history or race and racialization as shaping our lives?

My strategy in recent years has been to make a project of constructing a consciously artificial history for myself and others like me—a history with women identified women of Chinese descent living in the West at its centre. (I eschew the term "lesbian" because of its eurocentric roots, and because it does not necessarily connote community or social interdependence.) It must be artificial because our history is so disparate, and also because it has been so historically rare for women to have control over the means of recording and dissemination. The writing and rewriting of history has always been the prerogative of men and of the upper classes. I have the added disadvantage—the result of an unfortunate combination of my own childhood foolishness and the pressures of assimilation—of not being able to read Chinese. So my readings of history are bleached not only by the ideological interests of gender and class but also of race and culture.

As a quick example, my research into the life of Yu Hsuan-chi, the courtesan and poet on whom the "Poetess" character in *When Fox Is a Thousand* is based, turned up two records of her. One described her as a woman with many lovers, hence lascivious, hence immoral, hence capable of murder. The second suggested she might have been framed for the murder of a young maidservant by an official who did not like her strong ideas about the role of women in Chinese society. Although she is supposed to have left a sizable body of poetry, very little of it appears in anthologies of Chinese poetry in translation, which tend to favour sanctioned male heavyweights.

The history I'm going to write, I told myself, may be ideologically interested, but no more so than what's already out there.

Several queer Asian theorists caution against projecting the needs and contexts of the present onto the past (see Shah, Lee). How can we understand, for instance, temple images in South Asia in the same terms that the makers of those images understood them, regardless of what we think we see? At the same time, without claiming those histories what are we? Shah suggests that the fact that we are here now in the present should be enough. But it isn't. In the everyday discussions of politically active people of colour, lesbian, gay or straight, I hear this nostalgic referring back to a homeland that no longer exists, indeed, one that never did. I don't think this practice originates so much with naiveté as with a burning desire for that past; that it should have form, that it should have a body. Sometimes I feel our very survival in this country depends on the articulation of this form, the construction and affirmation of this body.

Animals at last. The myth and the tall tale. The secret and the subterranean. 20
The dark, the feminine, the yin. All allies in this task. For, if diaspora cultures in the West are to be living breathing things they must change. We must have the power of construction, as long, of course, as we behave as responsibly as we know how in the act of construction. (By "responsibly" I mean that the ideas I have discussed above do matter. I do not hold the ideal of freedom of speech, or freedom of the imagination above other freedoms and other ideals, especially at a historical moment when these freedoms are regularly invoked in order to justify the reproduction of tired stereotypes and the perpetuation of historically unjust power imbalances. I do not believe in censorship, because I think it solves nothing. I do believe in integrity, and expect it of myself and of other writers.) This project obviously can not be one of creating a totalizing history; it is rather one of uninhibited, zany invention for the sheer joy of it.

My interest in the archetype of the fox began with my stumbling across Pu Songling's *Strange Tales of Liaozhai*, a well-known text of the sixteenth century. Pu is supposed to have collected these various tales of the supernatural from ordinary people and compiled them into this anthology. The preface to one translation (which comes out of the PRC[5]) talks about these tales as proto-socialist in their critiques of class structure, corruption and abuse of power. A reason to love them—or is this merely a pretext to circulate an old text that has been such a pleasurable read for so many years? There are stories in the compilation which are obviously allegorical in their intentions. And then there are the fox stories, which certainly have their allegorical aspects, but I like to think that there is more to them than that. Some are not so politically palatable at all, such as the one about a wily supernatural fox woman who leads an innocent man from his pious life into debauchery, sickness and death. There is another about an unsavoury young man who leers at a beautiful woman; the woman turns out to be a fox, and the fox trounces him. There is yet another about how a fox and a young man fall in love—star-crossed love, of course, because the human and the divine are not supposed to have carnal dealings with one another. I suppose this one could be read as a comment on class or a critique of the repression of romantic love.

But what is more compelling in many ways is the figure of the fox herself, as a creature of darkness, death, germination and sexuality. The fox has the power to travel both above the earth and below it. In order to work her mischief she needs human form, which she achieves by entering the graveyard late at night and finding the corpse of some poor young girl who has died before her time. She breathes life into it. In this form, her power over men (and perhaps women too?) is the power of seduction. I find these stories very rich and very visceral. They are also politically compelling for a number of reasons. The first is contemporary feminism's struggle with questions of sexual representation. What does it mean for a feminist to embrace the power of seduction? And am I a feminist, or is that also a colonized space? The second is the question of how to deal with sexual representations of Asians in the West where we have been so much exoticized and/or de-sexualized in a society which insists on pathologizing the sexuality of the other. I was compelled to find out what kind of warrior the fox could be in that battle. The third is the possibility of employing the fox as a new trope of lesbian representation, or, if that term and its history reeks too much of its Western origins, then as a trope of Asian women's community and power.

I have been much influenced by the work of the Vancouver collective Kiss and Tell, and by much of the sex-positive work that has come out of Canada and the United States in recent years. The work is valuable in that it makes sex a site of resistance as well as a site of pleasure. I can't help thinking, however, that much as using one's racialization as a point of entry into political and philosophical discussions shapes what one can say and learn, so using sex as a point of departure shapes the way one thinks about women's community,

5 *PRC* People's Republic of China.

and how one goes about looking for echoes of it in the past. My concern here, I hope, is not one of prudery or reaction, but one of wanting a little more give in the technologies we use to tap history. Elsewhere I have spoken about my interest in a tradition of spinsterhood, which became radicalized in Shundak (my father's long-ago county of origin, in Guandong Province) at the turn of the last century. Although my sources on this tradition are entirely and problematically anthropological, I was struck by the argument (see Sankar) that the act that clinched this practice for women was not sex but the acceptance of the idea that younger generations of spinsters could feed, through ancestral worship, the souls of the older generation. This practice is normally reserved for the members of patriarchal families only.

That said, I must also add that it is extremely difficult to find historical materials on Chinese lesbians. I suspect this is not because they did not exist, but because for a long time sexual practice was not considered as a focal point for identity. It could be argued, in fact, that the notion of identity arose from Western philosophical traditions, and from the needs of Western colonial practices. Later, the absence of such texts could be ascribed to the fact that women's lives were not deemed important enough to write about, or if worthy of writing, not deemed worthy of translation. The only scholarship on lesbian history in China that I could find in English was an appendix to a book called *Passions of the Cut Sleeve*, which dealt in its main body with the history of gay men. That appendix, perhaps ten pages long, focused exclusively on the question of sexual practice, which felt empty and unsatisfying in its narrowness.

Insofar as *When Fox Is a Thousand* concerns anti-racism—and it does, although I think it also goes much further than that—I think issues of the body are primary. There are the obvious metaphors—the Fox breathing life into the bodies of the dead is like an Asian woman trying to breathe life into the assimilated almost-white self required by the social pressures of liberalism. She can never do it perfectly. There are always moments where the synapses don't connect, where there are understandings missing. But for the Fox, these moments of breathing life into the dead are also moments of passion. This is something she is compelled to do. It is her nature. The work of Calgary writer Yasmin Ladha is compelling in that it talks about colonialism and its effect in terms of romance. A very messy and dangerous romance, rife with the abuse of power, but also tinged with hope. I think in doing so she takes a great risk, particularly as the spectres of Pocahontas,* Suzy Wong, Madame Butterfly[6] and their ilk

6 *Suzy Wong* The subject of the popular 1957 novel *The World of Suzie Wong* is a love affair between a white artist and a Chinese prostitute; *Madame Butterfly* Title character of a 1904 opera about a Japanese woman who commits suicide after she is abandoned by her husband, a white lieutenant in the American navy.

loom above us. But to engage in this way also opens up possibilities for living here that might not otherwise exist.

It did not occur to me until well after completing the book that the notion of transformation through breath is both a Taoist and a Buddhist notion. Or perhaps, indeed, it is a remnant of some earlier indigenous religion that has since disappeared or become subsumed by these more organized forms. Breath, like writing, is stilling and insistent. It moves and it sustains life. To engage the breath is to disrupt the binary opposition of Houdini's two boxes, to break from what Judith Butler refers to as "the discursive site of injury." What happens for me in the process of writing, at certain electric moments, is a contacting of the past that resonates with something akin to truth and belonging. A bit metaphysical perhaps but in a country built on denial, I am used to ghosts and not frightened of things that are only half apparent. These are not moments that sing of hurt but rather compel my interest in Taoist and pre-Taoist cosmologies. Here again, there are dangers. My compunction towards home-making belongs to the realm of the feminine in a way of which some branches of feminism might not approve. I think it is important to remember, to get back to the question of racialization, that there are entire knowledge systems and ways of living in our historical pasts that pre-date white racist modes of identification and their reclamations. How to touch those systems and practices may not be obvious, and the dangers of naïve idealization are far from negligible. For me, the consciously artificial narrative construction of history that acknowledges the desires of the present but also resonates with the past, seems a very useful possibility.

(1999)

Thanks to Rita Wong, Ashok Mathur and Debora O for their support and feedback on this piece.

WORKS CITED

Butler, Judith. "Subjection, Resistance, Resignification: Between Freud and Foucault." *Psychic Life of Power: Theories on Subjection*. Stanford: Stanford UP, 1997. 83-105.

Eng, David L. and Alice Y. Hom, ed. *Q&A: Queer in Asian America*. Philadelphia: Temple UP, 1998.

Hinsch, Bret. *Passions of the Cut Sleeve: The Male Homosexual Tradition in China*. Los Angeles: U of California P, 1992.

Ladha, Yasmin. *Lion's Granddaughter and Other Stories*. Edmonton: NeWest Press, 1992.

Lai, Larissa. "The Heart of the Matter: Interview with Yasmin Ladha," *Kinesis*. Vancouver, February 1993. 15.

——. *When Fox Is a Thousand*. Vancouver: Press Gang, 1995.

Lee, JeeYeun. "Toward a Queer Korean American Diasporic History." *Eng and Hom*. 185-209.

Pu, Songling, *Selected Tales of Liaozhai*. Trans. Yang Xianyi and Gladys Yang. Beijing: Panda Books, 1981.

——. *Strange Tales of Liaozhai*. Trans. Lu Yunzhong et al. Hong Kong: The Commercial Press, 1988.

P'u Sung-ling. *Strange Stories from a Chinese Studio*. Trans. Herbert A. Giles. Hong Kong: Kelly and Walsh, 1968.

Sankar, Andrea. "Sisters and brothers, lovers and enemies: marriage resistance in southern Kwangtung." *Journal of Homosexuality*. 11.3/4 (1985): 69-81.

Shah, Nayan. "Sexuality, Identity and the Uses of History." *Eng and Hom*. 141-56.

Questions

1. What does Lai mean in paragraph 5 when she writes, "I still live with the hope that the body exists prior to race, that experience exists prior to race"?
2. Why does Lai wish to construct a "consciously artificial" history in her writing?
3. In paragraph 9, Lai refers to "pushing white liberals to look at the hypocrisies of colour-blindness." According to Lai, how has racism in Canada changed over the decades?
4. The article was originally published in *Canadian Literature*, a scholarly journal. Discuss the ways in which Lai has geared her article toward this particular audience.
5. In what ways is publishing an essay such as this one effective in the fight against racism? Compare the effect of such an essay with that of writing an article in a popular magazine, demonstrating in an anti-racism rally, or standing up to racism when you see it in practice.

MARGARET ATWOOD

FIRST JOB

Set in Toronto's Yorkville neighbourhood in the early 1960s, this piece by poet and novelist Margaret Atwood relates her experience working as a server in a hotel coffee shop. "First Job" was first published in The New Yorker *in 2001.*

I'll pass over the mini-jobs of adolescence—the summer-camp stints that were more like getting paid for having fun. I'll pass over, too, the self-created pin-money* generators—the puppet shows put on for kids at office parties, the serigraph[1] posters turned out on the Ping-Pong table—and turn to my first real job. By "real job," I mean one that had nothing to do with friends of my parents or parents of my friends but was obtained in the adult manner, by looking through the ads in newspapers and going in to be interviewed—one for which I was entirely unsuited, and that I wouldn't have done except for the money. I was surprised when I got it, underpaid while doing it, and frustrated in the performance of it, and these qualities have remained linked, for me, to the ominous word "job."

The year was 1962, the place was Toronto. It was summer, and I was faced with the necessity of earning the difference between my scholarship for the next year and what it would cost me to live. The job was in the coffee shop of a small hotel on Avenue Road; it is now in the process of being torn down, but at that time it was a clean, well-lighted place,[2] with booths along one side and a counter—possibly marble—down the other. The booths were served by a waitressing pro who lipsticked outside the lines,* and who thought I was a mutant. My job would be serving things at the counter—coffee I would pour, toast I would create from bread, milkshakes I would whip up in the obstetrical stainless-steel device provided. ("Easy as pie," I was told.) I would also be running the customers' money through the cash register—an opaque machine

1 *serigraph* Printed using a silkscreen technique.

2 *a clean, well-lighted place* Reference to "A Clean, Well-Lighted Place" (1933), an Ernest Hemingway short story set in a café.

with buttons to be pushed, little drawers that shot in and out, and a neurotic system of locks.

I said I had never worked a cash register before. This delighted the manager, a plump, unctuous character out of some novel I hadn't yet read. He said the cash register, too, was easy as pie, and I would catch on to it in no time, as I was a smart girl with an MA. He said I should go and get myself a white dress.

I didn't know what he meant by "white dress." I bought the first thing I could find on sale, a nylon afternoon number with daisies appliquéd onto the bodice. The waitress told me this would not do: I needed a dress like hers, a *uniform*. ("How dense can you be?" I overheard her saying.) I got the uniform, but I had to go through the first day in my nylon daisies.

This first humiliation set the tone. The coffee was easy enough—I just had 5
to keep the Bunn filled—and the milkshakes were possible; few people wanted them anyway. The sandwiches and deep-fried shrimp were made at the back: all I had to do was order them over the intercom and bin the leftovers.

But the cash register was perverse. Its drawers would pop open for no reason, or it would ring eerily when I swore I was nowhere near it; or it would lock itself shut, and the queue of customers waiting to pay would lengthen and scowl as I wrestled and sweated. I kept expecting to be fired for incompetence, but the manager chortled more than ever. Occasionally, he would bring some man in a suit to view me. "She's got an MA," he would say, in a proud but pitying voice, and the two of them would stare at me and shake their heads.

An ex-boyfriend discovered my place of employment, and would also come to stare and shake his head, ordering a single coffee, taking an hour to drink it, leaving me a sardonic nickel* tip. The Greek short-order cook decided I would be the perfect up-front woman for the restaurant he wanted to open: he would marry me and do the cooking, I would speak English to the clientele and work—was he mad?—the cash register. He divulged his bank balance, and demanded to meet my father so the two of them could close the deal. When I declined, he took to phoning me over the intercom to whisper blandishments, and to plying me with deep-fried shrimp. A girl as scrawny as myself, he pointed out, was unlikely to get such a good offer again.

Then the Shriners* hit town, took over the hotel, and began calling for buckets of ice, or for doctors because they'd had heart attacks: too much tricycle-riding in the hot sun was felling them in herds. I couldn't handle the responsibility, the cash register had betrayed me once too often, and the short-order cook was beginning to sing Frank Sinatra* songs to me. I gave notice.

Only when I'd quit did the manager reveal his true stratagem: they'd wanted someone inept as me because they suspected their real cashier of skimming the accounts, a procedure I was obviously too ignorant to ever figure out. "Too stunned," as the waitress put it. She was on the cashier's side, and had me fingered as a stoolie* all along.

(2001)

Questions

1. Describe as concisely as you can Atwood's tone in this essay.
2. What are some of the sources of humour in this piece? To what extent do you think the humour holds appeal for readers unfamiliar with North American culture?
3. Say as much as you can about the unusual use of words in the following phrases in paragraph 2; what is going on in each case, and what effect does it have on the reader?

   "lipsticked outside the lines"

   "toast I would create from bread"

   "an opaque machine"
4. Comment on the choice of the verb "pointed out" in the last sentence of paragraph 7.
5. Write a short and light-hearted essay about a job you have worked at; in writing it try out some of the same stylistic devices that Atwood employs.

MIRIAM TOEWS

A FATHER'S FAITH

Much of Toews's work draws upon her experience growing up in a Mennonite community. Her best-known novel,* A Complicated Kindness *(2004), is set in a fictionalized version of her hometown; she also revisits her past in* Swing Low: A Life *(2000), a memoir written in the voice of her father, who committed suicide after a long struggle with bipolar disorder. She addresses the same subject in her earlier essay "A Father's Faith," which was first published in* Saturday Night Magazine *in 1999, a year after his death.*

On the morning on May 13, 1998, my father woke up, had breakfast, got dressed and walked away from the Steinbach Bethesda Hospital, where he had been a patient for two and a half weeks. He walked through his beloved hometown, along Hespeler Road, past the old farmhouse where his mother had lived with her second husband, past the water tower, greeting folks in his loud, friendly voice, wishing them well. He passed the site on First Street where the house in which my sister and I grew up once stood. He walked down Main Street, past the Mennonite church where, throughout his life, he had received countless certificates for perfect attendance, past Elmdale School where he had taught grade six for forty years.

As he walked by his home on Brandt Road, he saw his old neighbour Bill sitting in his lawn chair. He waved and smiled again, then he continued on past the cemetery where his parents were buried, and the high school his daughters had attended, and down Highway 52, out of town, past the Frantz Motor Inn, which is just outside the town limits because it serves alcohol and Steinbach is a dry town. He kept walking until he got too tired, so he hitched a ride with a couple of guys who were on their way to buy a fishing licence in the small village of Woodridge on the edge of the Sandilands Forest.

The sun would have been very warm by the time they dropped him off, and he would have taken off his stylish cap and wiped his brow with the back of his hand. I'm sure he thanked them profusely, perhaps offering them ten dollars for their trouble, and then he walked the short distance to the café near the railroad tracks, the place he and my mom would sometimes go for a quiet coffee and a change of scenery. He would have been able to smell the clover growing in the ditches beside the tracks and between the ties. He may have looked down the line and remembered that the train would be coming from Ontario, through Warroad, Minnesota, on its way to Winnipeg.

A beautiful young woman named Stephanie was just beginning her shift and she spoke to him through the screen door at the side of the restaurant. Yes, she said, the train will be here soon. And my dad smiled and thanked her, and mentioned that he could hear the whistle. Moments later, he was dead.

5 Steinbach is an easy forty-minute drive from Winnipeg, east on the Trans-Canada, then south on Highway 12. On the way into town there's a sign proclaiming "Jesus Saves." On the way back to the city just off Highway 12 there's another that says, "Satan is Real. You Can't Be Neutral. Choose Now." The town has recently become a city of 8,500 people, two-thirds of whom are Mennonite, so it's not surprising that about half of the twenty-four churches are Mennonite and conservative. There is a Catholic church too, but it's new and I'm not sure exactly where it is. A little way down from the bowling alley I can still make out my name on the sidewalk, carved in big bold letters when I was ten and marking my territory.

My town made sense to me then. For me it was a giant playground where my friends and I roamed freely, using the entire town in a game of arrows—something like hide-and-seek—for which my dad, the teacher, provided boxes and boxes of fresh new chalk and invaluable tips. He had, after all, played the same game in the same town many years before.

At six p.m. the siren would go off at the firehall, reminding all the kids to go home for supper, and at nine p.m. it was set off again, reminding us to go home to bed. I had no worries, and no desire ever to leave this place where everyone knew me. If they couldn't remember my name, they knew I was the younger daughter of Mel and Elvira Toews, granddaughter of C.T. Loewen and Henry Toews, from the Kleine Gemeinde congregation, and so on and so on. All the kids in town, other than the church-sponsored Laotians who came over in the seventies, could be traced all the way back to the precise Russian veldt their great-grandparents had emigrated from. They were some of the thousands of Mennonites who came to Manitoba in the late 1800s to escape religious persecution. They were given free land and a promise that they could, essentially, do their own thing without interference. They wanted to keep the world away from their children and their children away from the world. Naturally it was an impossible ideal.

As I grew older, I became suspicious and critical and restless and angry. Every night I plotted my escape. I imagined that Barkman's giant feed mill on Main Street, partially visible from my bedroom window, was a tall ship that would take me away some day. I looked up places like Hollywood and

Manhattan and Venice and Montreal in my Childcraft encyclopedias. I begged my sister to play, over and over, the sad songs from her Jacques Brel piano book, and I'd light candles and sing along, wearing a Pioneer Girls tam[1] on my head, using a chopstick as a cigarette holder, pretending I was Jackie Brel, Jacques's long-lost but just as world-weary Mennonite twin. I couldn't believe that I was stuck in a town like Steinbach, where dancing was a sin and serving beer a felony.

There were other things I became aware of as well. That my grandmother was a vanilla alcoholic who believed she was a teetotaller.* That seventy-five-year-old women who had borne thirteen children weren't allowed to speak to the church congregation, but that fifteen-year-old boys were. That every family had a secret. And I learned that my dad had been depressed all his life.

I had wondered, when I was a kid, why he spent so much of the weekend in bed and why he didn't talk much at home. Occasionally he'd tell me, sometimes in tears, that he loved me very much and that he wished he were a better father, that he were more involved in my life. But I never felt the need for an apology. It made me happy and a bit envious to know that my dad's students were able to witness his humour and intelligence firsthand, to hear him expound on his favourite subjects: Canadian history, Canadian politics and Canadian newspapers. I remember watching him at work and marvelling at his energy and enthusiasm. I thought he looked very handsome when he rolled up his sleeves and tucked his tie in between the buttons of his shirt, his hands on his hips, all ready for business and hard work.

Teaching school—helping others make sense of the world—was a good profession for a man who was continuously struggling to find meaning in life. I think he needed his students as much as they needed him. By fulfilling his duties, he was also shoring up a psyche at risk of erosion.

Four years before his death he was forced to retire from teaching because of a heart attack and some small strokes. He managed to finish the book he was writing on Canada's prime ministers, but then he seemed to fade away. He spent more and more of his time in bed, in the dark, not getting up even to eat or wash, not interested in watching TV or listening to the radio. Despite our pleading and cajoling, despite the medication and visits to various doctors' offices, appointments he dutifully kept, and despite my mother's unwavering love, we felt we were losing him.

I know about brain chemistry and depression, but there's still a part of me that blames my dad's death on being Mennonite and living in that freaky, austere place where this world isn't good enough and admission into the next

---

1 *Jacques Brel* Belgian singer-songwriter (1929–78) who became famous performing his poetic ballads in Paris clubs; *tam* Scottish soft hat similar to a beret.

one, the perfect one, means everything, where every word and deed gets you closer to or farther away from eternal life. If you don't believe that then nothing Steinbach stands for will make sense. And if life doesn't make sense you lose yourself in it, your spirit decays. That's what I believed had happened to my dad, and that's why I hated my town.

In the weeks and months after his death, my mom and my sister and I tried to piece things together. William Ashdown, the executive director of the Mood Disorders Association of Manitoba, told us the number of mentally ill Mennonites is abnormally high. "We don't know if it's genetic or cultural," he said, "but the Steinbach area is one that we're vitally concerned about."

"It's the way the church delivers the message," says a Mennonite friend of mine, "the message of sin and accountability. To be human, basically, is to be a sinner. So a person, a real believer, starts to get down on himself, and where does it end? They say self-loathing is the cornerstone of depression, right?"

Years ago, the Mennonite Church practised something called "shunning," whereby if you were to leave your husband, or marry outside the Church, or elope, or drink, or in some way contravene the Church's laws or act "out of faith," you could be expelled from the Church and ignored, shunned by the entire community, including your own family. Depression or despair, as it would have been referred to then, was considered to be the result of a lack of faith and therefore could be another reason for shunning.

These days most Mennonites don't officially practise shunning, although William Ashdown claims there are still Mennonites from extreme conservative sects who are being shunned and shamed into silence within their communities for being mentally ill. Certainly Arden Thiessen, the minister of my dad's church, and a long-time friend of his, is aware of the causes of depression and the pain experienced by those who suffer from it. He doesn't see it as a lack of faith, but as an awful sickness.

But I can't help thinking that that history had just a little to do with my alcoholic grandmother's insisting that she was a non-drinker, and my dad's telling his doctors, smiling that beautiful smile of his, that he was fine, just fine.

Not long before he died my dad told me about the time he was five and was having his tonsils out. Just before the operation began he was knocked out with ether and he had a dream that he was somersaulting through the hospital walls, right through, easily, he said, moving his hands in circles through the air. It was wonderful. He told me he would never forget that feeling.

But mostly, the world was a sad and unsafe place for him, and his town provided shelter from it. Maybe he saw this as a gift, while I came to see it as oppression. He could peel back the layers of hypocrisy and intolerance and see what was good, and I couldn't. He believed that it mattered what he did in life, and he believed in the next world, one that's better. He kept the faith of his

Mennonite forebears to the very end, or what he might call the beginning, and removed himself from this world entirely.

Stephanie, the waitress in the café in Woodridge, told my mother that my dad was calm and polite when he spoke to her, as if he were about to sit down to a cup of tea. She told her that he hadn't seemed at all afraid. But why would you be if you believed you were going to a place where there is no more sadness?

My dad never talked to us about God or religion. We didn't have family devotion like everybody else. He never quoted out loud from the Bible or lectured us about not going to church. In fact his only two pieces of advice to me were "Be yourself" and "You can do anything."

But he still went to church. It didn't matter how low he felt, or how cold it was outside. He would put on his suit and tie and stylish cap and walk the seven or eight blocks to church. He always walked, through searing heat or sub-arctic chill. If he was away on holidays he would find a church and go to it. At the lake he drove forty miles down gravel roads to attend an outdoor church in the bush. I think he needed church like a junkie needs a fix: to get him through another day in a world of pain.

What I love about my town is that it gave my dad the faith that stopped him from being afraid in those last violent seconds he spent on earth. And the place in my mind where we meet is on the front steps of my dad's church, the big one on Main Street across from Don's Bakery and the Goodwill store. We smile and talk for a few minutes outside, basking in the warmth of the summer sun he loved so much. Then he goes in and I stay outside, and we're both happy where we are.

(1999)

Questions

1. Discuss how this essay might come across differently to the following readers: a Mennonite from Manitoba, a non-Mennonite Canadian from elsewhere in the country, and a reader from outside Canada. Do you think the essay would resonate with any one of these readers more than the others?
2. To what extent was religion a positive force in Toews' father's life? To what extent was it a negative force?
3. How effective is the final paragraph of this essay? Why?
4. What attitude (or attitudes) toward mental illness does Toews describe as predominant in Steinbach's Mennonite community? Compare it (or them) with the attitudes in your community.

SUSAN SONTAG

from REGARDING THE PAIN OF OTHERS

Since they began to be published in the 1970s, Susan Sontag's essays have remained among the most widely read—and widely debated—works of American non-fiction. The excerpt below is from the first chapter of her 2003 book Regarding the Pain of Others*—a work that is often considered a follow-up to her famous 1980 book-length essay* On Photography. Regarding the Pain of Others *explores the effects on viewers of images of wartime suffering, and asks if we are justified in hoping that such images can help to end or to prevent wars.*

In June 1938 Virginia Woolf[1] published *Three Guineas*,[2] her brave, unwelcomed reflections on the roots of war. Written during the preceding two years, while she and most of her intimates and fellow writers were rapt by the advancing fascist insurrection in Spain,[3] the book was couched as the very tardy reply to a letter from an eminent lawyer in London who had asked, "How in your opinion are we to prevent war?" Woolf begins by observing tartly that a truthful dialogue between them may not be possible. For though they belong to the same class, "the educated class," a vast gulf separates them: the lawyer is a man and she is a woman. Men make war. Men (most men) like war, since for men there is "some glory, some necessity, some satisfaction in fighting" that woman (most women) do not feel or enjoy. What does an educated—read: privileged, well-off—woman like her know of war? Can her recoil from its allure be like his?

Let us test this "difficulty of communication," Woolf proposes, by looking together at images of war. The images are some of the photographs the

1 *Virginia Woolf* English modernist author (1882–1941), feminist, and pacifist.

2 *Three Guineas* Excerpts from *Three Guineas* are included in this anthology's web component.

3 *fascist insurrection in Spain* The Spanish Civil War (1936–39), in which nationalist and fascist forces revolted against the democratic Second Spanish Republic, established eight years earlier. The eventual Nationalist victory led to the decades-long dictatorship of Francisco Franco.

beleaguered Spanish government has been sending out twice a week; she footnotes: "Written in the winter of 1936-37." Let's see, Woolf writes, "whether when we look at the same photographs we feel the same things." She continues:

> This morning's collection contains the photograph of what might be a man's body, or a woman's; it is so mutilated that it might, on the other hand, be the body of a pig. But those certainly are dead children, and that undoubtedly is the section of a house. A bomb has torn open the side; there is still a bird-cage hanging in what was presumably the sitting room …

The quickest, driest way to convey the inner commotion caused by these photographs is by noting that one can't always make out the subject, so thorough is the ruin of flesh and stone they depict. And from there Woolf speeds to her conclusion. We do have the same responses, "however different the education, the traditions behind us," she says to the lawyer. Her evidence: both "we"—here women are the "we"—and you might well respond in the same words.

> You, Sir, call them "horror and disgust." We also called them horror and disgust … War, you say, is an abomination; a barbarity; war must be stopped at whatever cost.
>
> And we echo your words. War is an abomination; a barbarity; war must be stopped.

Who believes today that war can be abolished? No one, not even pacifists. We hope only (so far in vain) to stop genocide and to bring to justice those who commit gross violations of the laws of war (for there are laws of war, to which combatants should be held), and to be able to stop specific wars by imposing negotiated alternatives to armed conflict. It may be hard to credit the desperate resolve produced by the aftershock of the First World War, when the realization of the ruin Europe had brought on itself took hold. Condemning war as such did not seem so futile or irrelevant in the wake of the paper fantasies of the Kellogg-Briand Pact[4] of 1928, in which fifteen leading nations, including the United States, France, Great Britain, Germany, Italy, and Japan, solemnly renounced war as an instrument of national policy; even Freud and Einstein* were drawn into the debate with a public exchange of letters in 1932 titled "Why War?" Woolf's *Three Guineas*, appearing toward the close of nearly two decades of plangent denunciations of war, offered the originality (which made this the least well received of all her books) of focusing on what was

---

4 *Kellogg-Briand Pact* Written by US Secretary of State Frank B. Kellogg (1856–1937) and French Prime Minister and Foreign Minister Aristide Briand (1862–1932), the pact stated that the signatory nations "condemn recourse to war for the solution of international controversies, and renounce it, as an instrument of national policy in their relations with one another," and that settlement of disputes "shall never be sought except by pacific means."

regarded as too obvious or inapposite[5] to be mentioned, much less brooded over: that war is a man's game—that the killing machine has a gender, and it is male. Nevertheless, the temerity* of Woolf's version of "Why War?" does not make her revulsion against war any less conventional in its rhetoric, in its summations, rich in repeated phrases. And photographs of the victims of war are themselves a species of rhetoric. They reiterate. They simplify. They agitate. They create the illusion of consensus.

Invoking this hypothetical shared experience ("we are seeing with you the same dead bodies, the same ruined houses"), Woolf professes to believe that the shock of such pictures cannot fail to unite people of good will. Does it? To be sure, Woolf and the unnamed addressee of this book-length letter are not any two people. Although they are separated by the age-old affinities of feeling and practice of their respective sexes, as Woolf has reminded him, the lawyer is hardly a standard-issue bellicose* male. His anti-war opinions are no more in doubt than are hers. After all, his question was not, What are *your* thoughts about preventing war? It was, How in your opinion are *we* to prevent war?

It is this "we" that Woolf challenges at the start of her book: she refuses to allow her interlocutor to take a "we" for granted. But into this "we," after pages devoted to the feminist point, she then subsides.

5 No "we" should be taken for granted when the subject is looking at other people's pain.

Who are the "we" at whom such shock-pictures are aimed? That "we" would include not just the sympathizers of a smallish nation or a stateless people fighting for its life, but—a far larger constituency—those only nominally concerned about some nasty war taking place in another country. The photographs are a means of making "real" (or "more real") matters that the privileged and the merely safe might prefer to ignore.

"Here then on the table before us are photographs," Woolf writes of the thought experiment she is proposing to the reader as well as to the spectral lawyer, who is eminent enough, as she mentions, to have K.C., King's Counsel, after his name—and may or may not be a real person. Imagine then a spread of loose photographs extracted from an envelope that arrived in the morning post. They show the mangled bodies of adults and children. They show how war evacuates, shatters, breaks apart, levels the built world. "A bomb has torn open the side," Woolf writes of the house in one of the pictures. To be sure, a cityscape is not made of flesh. Still, sheared-off buildings are almost as eloquent as bodies in the street. (Kabul,[6] Sarajevo,[7]

---

5 *plangent* Loud, emotional; *inapposite* Beside the point; inappropriate.

6 *Kabul* Capital of Afghanistan. The 1992–96 Afghan Civil War damaged much of the city's infrastructure and caused thousands of civilian deaths.

7 *Sarajevo* Capital of Bosnia and Herzegovina, which was under siege by Bosnian Serbs of Republic of Srpska for almost four years during the Bosnian War (1992–96).

East Mostar,[8] Grozny,[9] sixteen acres of lower Manhattan after September 11, 2001, the refugee camp in Jenin[10] …) Look, the photographs say, *this* is what it's like. This is what war *does*. And *that*, that is what it does too. War tears, rends. War rips open, eviscerates. War scorches. War dismembers. War *ruins*.

Not to be pained by these pictures, not to recoil from them, not to strive to abolish what causes this havoc, this carnage—these, for Woolf, would be the reactions of a moral monster. And, she is saying, we are not monsters, we members of the educated class. Our failure is one of imagination, of empathy: we have failed to hold this reality in mind.

But is it true that these photographs, documenting the slaughter of non-combatants rather than the clash of armies, could only stimulate the repudiation of war? Surely they could also foster greater militancy on behalf of the Republic. Isn't this what they were meant to do? The agreement between Woolf and the lawyer seems entirely presumptive, with the grisly photographs confirming an opinion already held in common. Had the question been, How can we best contribute to the defense of the Spanish Republic against the forces of militarist and clerical fascism?, the photographs might instead have reinforced their belief in the justness of that struggle.

The pictures Woolf has conjured up do not in fact show what war, war as such, does. They show a particular way of waging war, a way at that time routinely described as "barbaric," in which civilians are the target. General Franco[11] was using the same tactics of bombardment, massacre, torture, and the killing and mutilation of prisoners that he had perfected as a commanding officer in Morocco in the 1920s.[12] Then, more acceptably to ruling powers, his victims had been Spain's colonial subjects, darker-hued and infidels to boot; now his victims were compatriots. To read in the pictures, as Woolf does, only what confirms a general abhorrence of war is to stand back from an engagement with Spain as a country with a history. It is to dismiss politics.

---

8 *East Mostar* The side of Mostar, Bosnia and Herzegovina that was occupied by Bosniak soldiers; the West side was occupied by Croat soldiers. Croatian forces beseiged East Mostar in 1993–94.

9 *Grozny* Capital city of Chechnya, a Republic and federal subject of Russia, which was assaulted and heavily damaged by Russian forces in 2000. The city, which had been the capital of the separatist Chechen Republic of Ichkeria, was captured by Russia in a decisive victory.

10 *Jenin* Palestinian city and location of a refugee camp that was attacked by Israeli defense forces in 2002. A large portion of the camp was bulldozed and hundreds of homes rendered uninhabitable.

11 *General Franco* Francisco Franco (1892–1975), fascist military leader during the Spanish Civil War, and thereafter long time dictator.

12 *Morocco in the 1920s* The Second Moroccan War, or Rif War, was the last in a series of conflicts between Spanish colonial forces and the native Riffian Berbers of northern Morocco.

10 For Woolf, as for many antiwar polemicists, war is generic, and the images she describes are of anonymous generic victims. The pictures sent out by the government in Madrid seem, improbably, not to have been labelled. (Or perhaps Woolf is simply assuming that a photograph should speak for itself.) But the case against war does not rely on information about who and when and where; the arbitrariness of the relentless slaughter is evidence enough. To those who are sure that right is on one side, oppression and injustice on the other, and that the fighting must go on, what matters is precisely who is killed and by whom. To an Israeli Jew, a photograph of a child torn apart in the attack on the Sbarro pizzeria[13] in downtown Jerusalem is first of all a photograph of a Jewish child killed by a Palestinian suicide-bomber. To a Palestinian, a photograph of a child torn apart by a tank round in Gaza[14] is first of all a photograph of a Palestinian child killed by Israeli ordnance. To the militant, identity is everything. And all photographs wait to be explained or falsified by their captions. During the fighting between Serbs and Croats at the beginning of the recent Balkan wars,[15] the same photographs of children killed in the shelling of a village were passed around at both Serb and Croat propaganda briefings. Alter the caption, and the children's deaths could be used and reused.

Images of dead civilians and smashed houses may serve to quicken hatred of the foe, as did the hourly reruns by Al Jazeera, the Arab satellite television network based in Qatar, of the destruction in the Jenin refugee camp in April 2002. Incendiary as that footage was to the many who watch Al Jazeera throughout the world, it did not tell them anything about the Israeli army they were not already primed to believe. In contrast, images offering evidence that contradicts cherished pieties are invariably dismissed as having been staged for the camera. To photographic corroboration of the atrocities committed by one's own side, the standard response is that the pictures are a fabrication, that no such atrocity ever took place, those were bodies the other side had brought in trucks from the city morgue and placed about the street, or that, yes, it happened and it was the other side who did it, to themselves. Thus the chief of propaganda for Franco's Nationalist rebellion maintained that it was the Basques[16] who

---

13 *Sbarro pizzeria* American chain restaurant which was the site of a 2001 bombing that killed fifteen civilians, including seven children.

14 *Gaza* Geographically independent strip of Palestinian territory along the Mediterranean sea. Despite Israeli military withdrawal from Gaza in 2005 the territory remains externally controlled by Israel.

15 *Balkan wars* The Croatian War of Independence (1991–95), which began before and was concurrent with the Bosnian war; the conflict involved Croats who sought independence from Yugoslavia and Croatian Serbs who sought unity with Serbia and the Republic of Srpska.

16 *Basques* Indigenous ethnic group of the western Pyrenees, who now live in the autonomous regions of Basque Country and Navarre in Spain.

had destroyed their own ancient town and former capital, Guernica,[17] on April 26, 1937, by placing dynamite in the sewers (in a later version, by dropping bombs manufactured in Basque territory) in order to inspire indignation abroad and reinforce the Republican resistance. And thus a majority of Serbs living in Serbia or abroad maintained right to the end of the Serb siege of Sarajevo, and even after, that the Bosnians themselves perpetrated the horrific "breadline massacre" in May 1992 and "market massacre"[18] in February 1994, lobbing large-calibre shells into the centre of their capital or planting mines in order to create some exceptionally gruesome sights for the foreign journalists' cameras and rally more international support for the Bosnian side.

Photographs of mutilated bodies certainly can be used the way Woolf does, to vivify the condemnation of war, and may bring home, for a spell, a portion of its reality to those who have no experience of war at all. However, someone who accepts that in the world as currently divided war can become inevitable, and even just, might reply that the photographs supply no evidence, none at all, for renouncing war—except to those for whom the notions of valour and sacrifice have been emptied of meaning and credibility. The destructiveness of war—short of total destruction, which is not war but suicide—is not in itself an argument against waging war unless one thinks (as few people actually do think) that violence is always unjustifiable, that force is always and in all circumstances wrong—wrong because, as Simone Weil affirms in her sublime essay on war, "The Iliad, or The Poem of Force" (1940), violence turns anybody subjected to it into a thing.[19] No, retort those who in a given situation see no alternative to armed struggle, violence can exalt someone subjected to it into a martyr or a hero.

In fact, there are many uses of the innumerable opportunities a modern life supplies for regarding—at a distance, through the medium of photography—other people's pain. Photographs of an atrocity may give rise to opposing

---

17 *Guernica* The town of Gernika was in fact bombed by German and Italian air forces. The bombings famously inspired Pablo Picasso's painting of the horrors of war, titled *Guernica*.

18 *breadline massacre ... market massacre* Both bombings are generally accepted to have been perpetrated by Serbian forces under the leadership of Radovan Karadžić (b. 1945), though there was much uncertainty at the time they occurred; no official investigation of the "breadline massacre" was carried out.

19 [Sontag's note] Her condemnation of war notwithstanding, Weil sought to participate in the defense of the Spanish Republic and in the fight against Hitler's Germany. In 1936 she went to Spain as a non-combatant volunteer in an international brigade; in 1942 and early 1943, a refugee in London and already ill, she worked at the office of the Free French and hoped to be sent on a mission in Occupied France. (She died in an English sanatorium in August 1943).

responses. A call for peace. A cry for revenge. Or simply the bemused awareness, continually restocked by photographic information, that terrible things happen. Who can forget the three colour pictures by Tyler Hicks that *The New York Times* ran across the upper half of the first page of its daily section devoted to America's new war, "A Nation Challenged,"[20] on November 13, 2001? The triptych* depicted the fate of a wounded Taliban soldier in uniform who had been found in a ditch by Northern Alliance[21] soldiers advancing toward Kabul. First panel: being dragged on his back by two of his captors—one has grabbed an arm, the other a leg—along a rocky road. Second panel (the camera is very near): surrounded, gazing up in terror as he is being pulled to his feet. Third panel: at the moment of death, supine with arms outstretched and knees bent, naked and bloodied from the waist down, being finished off by the military mob that has gathered to butcher him. An ample reservoir of stoicism is needed to get through the great newspaper record each morning, given the likelihood of seeing photographs that could make you cry. And the pity and disgust that pictures like Hick's inspire should not distract you from asking what pictures, whose cruelties, whose deaths are *not* being shown.

• • •

For a long time some people believed that if the horror could be made vivid enough, most people would finally take in the outrageousness, the insanity of war.

Fourteen years before Woolf published *Three Guineas*—in 1924, on the tenth anniversary of the national mobilization against Germany for the First World War—the conscientious objector Ernst Friedrich[22] published his *Krieg dem Krieg!* (*War Against War!*). This is photography as shock therapy: an album of more than one hundred and eighty photographs mostly drawn from German military and medical archives, many of which were deemed unpublishable by government censors while the war was on. The book starts with pictures of toy soldiers, toy cannons, and other delights of male children everywhere, and

---

20 *A Nation Challenged* Newspaper section that ran daily from September 18 through to the last day of 2001; it focused on the September 11 attacks and the ensuing "War on Terror."

21 *Taliban* Islamic fundamentalist militant movement and governing body of Afghanistan from 1996 to 2001. As an ally of Al-Qaeda and other terrorist groups, the Taliban government was targeted and overthrown by Coalition forces of the US and other NATO nations; *Northern Alliance* The United Islamic Front for the Salvation of Afghanistan, a group allied with the US-led forces that invaded.

22 *Ernst Friedrich* Pacifist and anarchist (1894–1967) accused of sabotage during the First World War. He also resisted the Nazi regime and refused to fight in the Second World War.

concludes with pictures taken in military cemeteries. Between the toys and the graves, the reader has an excruciating photo-tour of four years of ruin, slaughter, and degradation: pages of wrecked and plundered churches and castles, obliterated villages, ravaged forests, torpedoed passenger steamers, shattered vehicles, hanged conscientious objectors, half-naked prostitutes in military brothels, soldiers in death agonies after poison-gas attack, skeletal Armenian children.[23] Almost all the sequences in *War Against War!* are difficult to look at, notably the pictures of dead soldiers belonging to the various armies putrefying in heaps on fields and roads and in the front-line trenches. But surely the most unbearable pages in this book, the whole of which was designed to horrify and demoralize, are in the section titled "The Face of War," twenty-four close-ups of soldiers with huge facial wounds. And Friedrich did not make the mistake of supposing that that heartrending, stomach-turning pictures would simply speak for themselves. Each photograph has an impassioned caption in four languages (German, French, Dutch, and English), and the wickedness of militarist ideology is excoriated and mocked on every page. Immediately denounced by the government and by veterans' and other patriotic organizations—in some cities the police raided bookstores, and lawsuits were brought against the public display of the photographs—Friedrich's declaration of war against war was acclaimed by left-wing writers, artists, and intellectuals, as well as by the constituencies of the numerous antiwar leagues, who predicted that the book would have a decisive influence on public opinion. By 1930, *War Against War!* had gone through ten editions in Germany and been translated into many languages.

In 1938, the year of Woolf's *Three Guineas*, the great French director Abel Gance featured in close-up some of the mostly hidden population of hideously disfigured ex-combatants—*les gueules cassées* ("the broken mugs") they were nicknamed in French—at the climax of his new *J'accuse*.[24] (Gance had made an earlier, primitive version of the incomparable antiwar film, with the same hallowed title, in 1918-19.) As in the final section of Friedrich's book, Gance's film ends in a new military cemetery, not just to remind us of how many millions of young men were sacrificed to militarism and ineptitude between 1914 and 1918 in the war cheered on as "the war to end all wars," but to advance the sacred judgment these dead would surely bring against Europe's

23 *Armenian children* Approximately one and a half million people are estimated to have been killed during the Armenian Genocide, which was perpetrated starting in 1915 by the Ottoman Empire against the ethnic minority of Armenians who lived within what is now Turkey.

24 *J'accuse* French: I accuse. The phrase comes from an 1898 newspaper letter by Émile Zola, with the heading "*J'accuse…!*,"; the letter accuses the French government of anti-Semitism.

politicians and generals could they know that, twenty years later, another war was imminent. *"Morts de Verdun, levez-vous!"* (Rise, dead of Verdun!), cries the deranged veteran who is the protagonist of the film, and he repeats his summons in German and in English: "Your sacrifices were in vain!" And the vast mortuary plain disgorges its multitudes, an army of shambling ghosts in rotted uniforms with mutilated faces, who rise from their graves and set out in all directions, causing mass panic among the populace already mobilized for a new pan-European war. "Fill your eyes with this horror! It is the only thing that can stop you!" the madman cries to the fleeing multitudes of the living, who reward him with a martyr's death, after which he joins his dead comrades: a sea of impassive ghosts overrunning the cowering future combatants and victims of *la guerre de demain*.[25] War beaten back by apocalypse.

And the following year the war came.

(2003)

Questions

1. What does Sontag mean when she says "No 'we' should be taken for granted when the subject is looking at other people's pain" (paragraph 5)? What reasons does she give for this? Make your own argument for or against her claim.
2. Consider the final line of this selection. What does it imply?
3. Sontag writes that "Photographs of an atrocity may give rise to opposing responses. A call for peace. A cry for revenge. Or simply the bemused awareness … that terrible things happen." Look through recent newspapers or online news sources until you find a recent photograph of a war or other violent political event. How do you respond to this photograph? Is there something about the photograph itself that you think would cause most viewers to respond similarly—or is viewer response to the photograph, as Sontag suggests, dependent on the information provided with the photograph and the beliefs the photograph's viewer already holds?

---

25 *la guerre de demain* French: the war of tomorrow.

DAVID FOSTER WALLACE

CONSIDER THE LOBSTER

David Foster Wallace was an American writer of novels, essays, and short stories. Seeking to avoid what he called "pre-formed positions, rigid filters, the 'moral clarity' of the immature," Wallace's texts are often wildly discursive—peppered with asides, qualifications, and tangential discussions. Infinite Jest *(1996), his most successful novel, has hundreds of endnotes, many of which are themselves annotated. The essay collected here, "Consider the Lobster," also employs extensive notes. It was first published in* Gourmet Magazine *(2004) and then reissued in* Consider the Lobster and Other Essays *(2005).*

The enormous, pungent, and extremely well-marketed Maine Lobster Festival is held every late July in the state's midcoast region, meaning the western side of Penobscot Bay, the nerve stem of Maine's lobster industry. What's called the midcoast runs from Owl's Head and Thomaston in the south to Belfast in the north. (Actually, it might extend all the way up to Bucksport, but we were never able to get farther north than Belfast on Route 1, whose summer traffic is, as you can imagine, unimaginable.) The region's two main communities are Camden, with its very old money and yachty harbour and five-star restaurants and phenomenal B&Bs, and Rockland, a serious old fishing town that hosts the festival every summer in historic Harbor Park, right along the water.[1]

Tourism and lobster are the midcoast region's two main industries, and they're both warm-weather enterprises, and the Maine Lobster Festival represents less an intersection of the industries than a deliberate collision, joyful and lucrative and loud. The assigned subject of this *Gourmet* article is the 56th Annual MLF, 30 July–3 August, 2003, whose official theme this year was "Lighthouses, Laughter, and Lobster." Total paid attendance was over 100,000, due partly to a national CNN spot in June during which a senior editor

1 [Wallace's note] There's a comprehensive native apothegm: "Camden by the sea, Rockland by the smell."

of *Food & Wine* magazine hailed the MLF as one of the best food-themed galas in the world. 2003 festival highlights: concerts by Lee Ann Womack and Orleans,[2] annual Maine Sea Goddess beauty pageant, Saturday's big parade, Sunday's William G. Atwood Memorial Crate Race, annual Amateur Cooking Competition, carnival rides and midway attractions and food booths, and the MLF's Main Eating Tent, where something over 25,000 pounds of fresh-caught Maine lobster is consumed after preparation in the World's Largest Lobster Cooker near the grounds' north entrance. Also available are lobster rolls, lobster turnovers, lobster sauté, Down East lobster salad, lobster bisque, lobster ravioli, and deep-fried lobster dumplings. Lobster thermidor[3] is obtainable at a sit-down restaurant called the Black Pearl on Harbor Park's northwest wharf. A large all-pine booth sponsored by the Maine Lobster Promotion Council has free pamphlets with recipes, eating tips, and Lobster Fun Facts. The winner of Friday's Amateur Cooking Competition prepares Saffron Lobster Ramekins, the recipe for which is now available for public downloading at www.mainelobsterfestival.com. There are lobster T-shirts and lobster bobblehead dolls and inflatable lobster pool toys and clamp-on lobster hats with big scarlet claws that wobble on springs. Your assigned correspondent saw it all, accompanied by one girlfriend and both his own parents—one of which parents was actually born and raised in Maine, albeit in the extreme northern inland part, which is potato country and a world away from the touristic midcoast.[4]

For practical purposes, everyone knows what a lobster is. As usual, though, there's much more to know than most of us care about—it's all a matter of what your interests are. Taxonomically speaking, a lobster is a marine crustacean of the family Homaridae, characterized by five pairs of jointed legs, the first pair terminating in large pincerish claws used for subduing prey. Like many other species of benthic[5] carnivore, lobsters are both hunters and scavengers. They have stalked eyes, gills on their legs, and antennae. There are a dozen or so different kinds worldwide, of which the relevant species here is the Maine lobster, *Homarus americanus*. The name "lobster" comes from the Old English *loppestre*, which is thought to be a corrupt form of the Latin word for locust combined with the Old English *loppe*, which meant spider.

Moreover, a crustacean is an aquatic arthropod of the class Crustacea, which comprises crabs, shrimp, barnacles, lobsters, and freshwater crayfish.

---

2 *Lee Ann Womack* American pop-country musician; *Orleans* American pop-rock band.

3 *Lobster thermidor* French lobster in cream sauce dish requiring extensive preparation.

4 [Wallace's note] N.B. All personally connected parties have made it clear from the start that they do not want to be talked about in this article.

5 *benthic* Bottom-dwelling.

All this is right there in the encyclopedia. And arthropods are members of the phylum Arthropoda, which phylum covers insects, spiders, crustaceans, and centipedes/millipedes, all of whose main commonality, besides the absence of a centralized brain-spine assembly, is a chitinous exoskeleton composed of segments, to which appendages are articulated in pairs.

The point is that lobsters are basically giant sea insects.[6] Like most ar- 5
thropods, they date from the Jurassic period, biologically so much older than mammalia that they might as well be from another planet. And they are—particularly in their natural brown-green state, brandishing their claws like weapons and with thick antennae awhip—not nice to look at. And it's true that they are garbagemen of the sea, eaters of dead stuff,[7] although they'll also eat some live shellfish, certain kinds of injured fish, and sometimes one another.

But they are themselves good eating. Or so we think now. Up until sometime in the 1800s, though, lobster was literally low-class food, eaten only by the poor and institutionalized. Even in the harsh penal environment of early America, some colonies had laws against feeding lobsters to inmates more than once a week because it was thought to be cruel and unusual, like making people eat rats. One reason for their low status was how plentiful lobsters were in old New England. "Unbelievable abundance" is how one source describes the situation, including accounts of Plymouth Pilgrims* wading out and capturing all they wanted by hand, and of early Boston's seashore being littered with lobsters after hard storms—these latter were treated as a smelly nuisance and ground up for fertilizer. There is also the fact that premodern lobster was cooked dead and then preserved, usually packed in salt or crude hermetic containers. Maine's earliest lobster industry was based around a dozen such seaside canneries in the 1840s, from which lobster was shipped as far away as California, in demand only because it was cheap and high in protein, basically chewable fuel.

Now, of course, lobster is posh, a delicacy, only a step or two down from caviar. The meat is richer and more substantial than most fish, its taste subtle compared to the marine-gaminess of mussels and clams. In the US pop-food imagination, lobster is now the seafood analogue to steak, with which it's so often twinned as Surf 'n' Turf* on the really expensive part of the chain steakhouse menu.

In fact, one obvious project of the MLF, and of its omnipresently sponsorial Maine Lobster Promotion Council, is to counter the idea that lobster is unusually luxe or unhealthy or expensive, suitable only for effete palates or the occasional blow-the-diet treat. It is emphasized over and over in presentations

6 [Wallace's note] Midcoasters' native term for a lobster is, in fact, "bug," as in "Come around on Sunday and we'll cook up some bugs."

7 [Wallace's note] Factoid: Lobster traps are usually baited with dead herring.

and pamphlets at the festival that lobster meat has fewer calories, less cholesterol, and less saturated fat than chicken.[8] And in the Main Eating Tent, you can get a "quarter" (industry shorthand for a 1¼-pound lobster), a four-ounce cup of melted butter, a bag of chips, and a soft roll w/ butter-pat for around $12.00, which is only slightly more expensive than supper at McDonald's.

Be apprised, though, that the Main Lobster Festival's democratization of lobster comes with all the massed inconvenience and aesthetic compromise of real democracy. See, for example, the aforementioned Main Eating Tent, for which there is a constant Disneyland-grade queue,* and which turns out to be a square quarter mile of awning-shaded cafeteria lines and rows of long institutional tables at which friend and stranger alike sit cheek by jowl, cracking and chewing and dribbling. It's hot, and the sagged roof traps the steam and the smells, which latter are strong and only partly food-related. It is also loud, and a good percentage of the total noise is masticatory. The suppers come in styrofoam trays, and the soft drinks are iceless and flat, and the coffee is convenience-store coffee in more styrofoam, and the utensils are plastic (there are none of the special long skinny forks for pushing out the tail meat, though a few savvy diners bring their own). Nor do they give you near enough napkins considering how messy lobster is to eat, especially when you're squeezed onto benches alongside children of various ages and vastly different levels of fine-motor development—not to mention the people who've somehow smuggled in their own beer in enormous aisle-blocking coolers, or who all of a sudden produce their own plastic tablecloths and spread them over large portions of tables to try to reserve them (the tables) for their little groups. And so on. Any one example is no more than a petty inconvenience, of course, but the MLF turns out to be full of irksome little downers like this—see for instance the Main Stage's headliner shows, where it turns out you have to pay $20 extra for a folding chair if you want to sit down; or the North Tent's mad scramble for the Nyquil-cup-sized samples of finalists' entries handed out after the Cooking Competition; or the much-touted Maine Sea Goddess pageant finals, which turn out to be excruciatingly long and to consist mainly of endless thanks and tributes to local sponsors. Let's not even talk about the grossly inadequate Port-A-San facilities* or the fact that there's nowhere to wash your hands before or after eating. What the Maine Lobster Festival really is is a midlevel county fair with a culinary hook, and in this respect it's not unlike Tidewater crab festivals, Midwest corn festivals, Texas chili festivals, etc., and shares with these

8 [Wallace's note] Of course, the common practice of dipping the lobster meat in melted butter torpedoes all these happy fat-specs, which none of the council's promotional stuff ever mentions, any more than potato industry PR talks about sour cream and bacon bits.

venues the core paradox of all teeming commercial demotic[9] events: It's not for everyone.[10] Nothing against the euphoric senior editor of *Food & Wine*, but I'd be surprised if she'd ever actually been here in Harbor Park, amid crowds of people slapping canal-zone mosquitoes as they eat deep-fried Twinkies* and watch Professor Paddywhack, on six-foot stilts in a raincoat with plastic lobsters protruding from all directions on springs, terrify their children.

Lobster is essentially a summer food. This is because we now prefer our lob- 10
sters fresh, which means they have to be recently caught, which for both tactical and economic reasons takes place at depths less than 25 fathoms. Lobsters tend to be hungriest and most active (i.e., most trappable) at summer water temperatures of 45–50 degrees. In the autumn, most Maine lobsters migrate out

---

9 *demotic* Popular; for the masses.

10 [Wallace's note] In truth, there's a great deal to be said about the differences between working-class Rockland and the heavily populist flavour of its festival versus comfortable and elitist Camden with its expensive view and shops given entirely over to $200 sweaters and great rows of Victorian homes converted to upscale B&Bs. And about these differences as two sides of the great coin that is US tourism. Very little of which will be said here, except to amplify the above-mentioned paradox and to reveal your assigned correspondent's own preferences. I confess that I have never understood why so many people's idea of a fun vacation is to don flip-flops and sunglasses and crawl through maddening traffic to loud, hot, crowded tourist venues in order to sample a "local flavour" that is by definition ruined by the presence of tourists. This may (as my festival companions keep pointing out) all be a matter of personality and hardwired taste: the fact that I do not like tourist venues means that I'll never understand their appeal and so am probably not the one to talk about it (the supposed appeal). But, since this FN will almost surely not survive magazine-editing anyway, here goes:

As I see it, it probably really is good for the soul to be a tourist, even if it's only once in a while. Not good for the soul in a refreshing or enlivening way, though, but rather in a grim, steely-eyed, let's-look-honestly-at-the-facts-and-find-some-way-to-deal-with-them way. My personal experience has not been that travelling around the country is broadening or relaxing, or that radical changes in place and context have a salutary effect, but rather that intranational tourism is radically constricting, and humbling in the hardest way—hostile to my fantasy of being a true individual, of living somehow outside and above it all. (Coming up is the part that my companions find especially unhappy and repellent, a sure way to spoil the fun of vacation travel:) To be a mass tourist, for me, is to become a pure late-date American: alien, ignorant, greedy for something you cannot ever have, disappointed in a way you can never admit. It is to spoil, by way of sheer ontology, the very unspoiledness you are there to experience. It is to impose yourself on places that in all non-economic ways would be better, realer, without you. It is, in lines and gridlock and transaction after transaction, to confront a dimension of yourself that is as inescapable as it is painful: As a tourist, you become economically significant but existentially loathsome, an insect on a dead thing.

into deeper water, either for warmth or to avoid the heavy waves that pound New England's coast all winter. Some burrow into the bottom. They might hibernate; nobody's sure. Summer is also lobsters' molting season—specifically early- to mid-July. Chitinous arthropods grow by molting, rather the way people have to buy bigger clothes as they age and gain weight. Since lobsters can live to be over 100, they can also get to be quite large, as in 30 pounds or more—though truly senior lobsters are rare now, because New England's waters are so heavily trapped.[11] Anyway, hence the culinary distinction between hard- and soft-shell lobsters, the latter sometimes a.k.a.* shedders. A soft-shell lobster is one that has recently molted. In midcoast restaurants, the summer menu often offers both kinds, with shedders being slightly cheaper even though they're easier to dismantle and the meat is allegedly sweeter. The reason for the discount is that a molting lobster uses a layer of seawater for insulation while its new shell is hardening, so there's slightly less actual meat when you crack open a shedder, plus a redolent gout of water that gets all over everything and can sometimes jet out lemonlike and catch a tablemate right in the eye. If it's winter or you're buying lobster someplace far from New England, on the other hand, you can almost bet that the lobster is a hard-shell, which for obvious reasons travel better.

As an à la carte entrée,* lobster can be baked, broiled, steamed, grilled, sautéed, stir-fried, or microwaved. The most common method, though, is boiling. If you're someone who enjoys having lobster at home, this is probably the way you do it, since boiling is so easy. You need a large kettle w/ cover, which you fill about half full with water (the standard advice is that you want 2.5 quarts of water per lobster). Seawater is optimal, or you can add two tbsp salt per quart from the tap. It also helps to know how much your lobsters weigh. You get the water boiling, put in the lobsters one at a time, cover the kettle, and bring it back up to a boil. Then you bank the heat and let the kettle simmer—ten minutes for the first pound of lobster, then three minutes for each pound after that. (This is assuming you've got hard-shell lobsters, which, again, if you don't live between Boston and Halifax is probably what you've got. For shedders, you're supposed to subtract three minutes from the total.) The reason the kettle's lobsters turn scarlet is that boiling somehow suppresses every pigment in their chitin but one. If you want an easy test of whether the lobsters are done, you try pulling on one of their antennae—if it comes out of the head with minimal effort, you're ready to eat.

A detail so obvious that most recipes don't even bother to mention it is that each lobster is supposed to be alive when you put it in the kettle. This

11 [Wallace's note] Datum: In a good year, the US industry produces around 80,000,000 pounds of lobster, and Maine accounts for more than half that total.

is part of lobster's modern appeal—it's the freshest food there is. There's no decomposition between harvesting and eating. And not only do lobsters require no cleaning or dressing or plucking, they're relatively easy for vendors to keep alive. They come up alive in the traps, are placed in containers of seawater, and can—so long as the water's aerated and the animals' claws are pegged or banded to keep them from tearing one another up under the stresses of captivity[12]—survive right up until they're boiled. Most of us have been in supermarkets or restaurants that feature tanks of live lobsters, from which you can pick out your supper while it watches you point. And part of the overall spectacle of the Maine Lobster Festival is that you can see actual lobstermen's vessels docking at the wharves along the northeast grounds and unloading fresh-caught product, which is transferred by hand or cart 150 yards to the great clear tanks stacked up around the festival's cooker—which is, as mentioned, billed as the World's Largest Lobster Cooker and can process over 100 lobsters at a time for the Main Eating Tent.

So then here is a question that's all but unavoidable at the World's Largest Lobster Cooker, and may arise in kitchens across the US: Is it all right to boil a sentient creature alive just for our gustatory[13] pleasure? A related set of concerns: Is the previous question irksomely PC* or sentimental? What does "all right" even mean in this context? Is the whole thing just a matter of personal choice?

As you may or may not know, a certain well-known group called People for the Ethical Treatment of Animals* thinks that the morality of lobster-boiling is not just a matter of individual conscience. In fact, one of the very first things we hear about the MLF … well, to set the scene: We're coming in by cab from the almost indescribably odd and rustic Knox County Airport[14] very late on the night before the festival opens, sharing the cab with a wealthy political

---

12 [Wallace's note] N.B. Similar reasoning underlies the practice of what's termed "debeaking" broiler chickens and brood hens in modern factory farms. Maximum commercial efficiency requires that enormous poultry populations be confined in unnaturally close quarters, under which conditions many birds go crazy and peck one another to death. As a purely observational side-note, be apprised that debeaking is usually an automated process and that the chickens receive no anesthetic. It's not clear to me whether most *Gourmet* readers know about debeaking, or about related practices like dehorning cattle in commercial feed lots, cropping swine's tails in factory hog farms to keep psychotically bored neighbours from chewing them off, and so forth. It so happens that your assigned correspondent knew almost nothing about standard meat-industry operations before starting work on this article.

13 *gustatory* Taste-related.

14 [Wallace's note] The terminal used to be somebody's house, for example, and the lost-luggage-reporting room was clearly once a pantry.

consultant who lives on Vinalhaven Island in the bay half the year (he's headed for the island ferry in Rockland). The consultant and cabdriver are responding to informal journalistic probes about how people who live in the midcoast region actually view the MLF, as in is the festival just a big-dollar tourist thing or is it something local residents look forward to attending, take genuine civic pride in, etc. The cabdriver (who's in his seventies, one of apparently a whole platoon of retirees the cab company puts on to help with the summer rush, and wears a US-flag lapel pin, and drives in what can only be called a very *deliberate* way) assures us that locals do endorse and enjoy the MLF, although he himself hasn't gone in years, and now come to think of it no one he and his wife know has, either. However, the demilocal consultant's been to recent festivals a couple times (one gets the impression it was at his wife's behest), of which his most vivid impression was that "you have to line up for an ungodly long time to get your lobsters, and meanwhile there are all these ex–flower children coming up and down along the line handing out pamphlets that say the lobsters die in terrible pain and you shouldn't eat them."

And it turns out that the post-hippies of the consultant's recollection were activists from PETA.* There were no PETA people in obvious view at the 2003 MLF,[15] but they've been conspicuous at many of the recent festivals. Since at least the mid-1990s, articles in everything from *The Camden Herald* to *The New York Time*s have described PETA urging boycotts of the Maine Lobster Festival, often deploying celebrity spokesmen like Mary Tyler Moore* for open letters and ads saying stuff like "Lobsters are extraordinarily sensitive" and "To me, eating a lobster is out of the question." More concrete is the oral

15 [Wallace's note] It turned out that one Mr. William R. Rivas-Rivas, a high-ranking PETA official out of the group's Virginia headquarters, was indeed there this year, albeit solo, working the festival's main and side entrances on Saturday, 2 August, handing out pamphlets and adhesive stickers emblazoned with "Being Boiled Hurts," which is the tagline in most of PETA's published material about lobsters. I learned that he'd been there only later, when speaking with Mr. Rivas-Rivas on the phone. I'm not sure how we missed seeing him *in situ* at the festival, and I can't see much to do except apologize for the oversight—although it's also true that Saturday was the day of the big MLF parade through Rockland, which basic journalistic responsibility seemed to require going to (and which, with all due respect, meant that Saturday was maybe not the best day for PETA to work the Harbor Park grounds, especially if it was going to be just one person for one day, since a lot of diehard MLF partisans were off-site watching the parade (which, again with no offense intended, was in truth kind of cheesy and boring, consisting mostly of slow homemade floats and various midcoast people waving at one another, and with an extremely annoying man dressed as Blackbeard* ranging up and down the length of the crowd saying "Arrr" over and over and brandishing a plastic sword at people, etc.; plus it rained)).

testimony of Dick, our florid and extremely gregarious rental-car liason,[16] to the effect that PETA's been around so much during recent years that a kind of brittlely tolerant homeostasis[17] now obtains between the activists and the festival's locals, e.g.: "We had some incidents a couple years ago. One lady took most of her clothes off and painted herself like a lobster, almost got herself arrested. But for the most part they're let alone. [Rapid series of small ambiguous laughs, which with Dick happens a lot.] They do their thing and we do our thing."

This whole interchange takes place on Route 1, 30 July, during a four-mile, 50-minute ride from the airport[18] to the dealership to sign car-rental papers. Several irreproducible segues down the road from the PETA anecdotes, Dick—whose son-in-law happens to be a professional lobsterman and one of the Main Eating Tent's regular suppliers—explains what he and his family feel is the crucial mitigating factor in the whole morality-of-boiling-lobsters-alive issue: "There's a part of the brain in people and animals that lets us feel pain, and lobsters' brains don't have this part."

Besides the fact that it's incorrect in about nine different ways, the main reason Dick's statement is interesting is that its thesis is more or less echoed by the festival's own pronouncement on lobsters and pain, which is part of a Test Your Lobster IQ quiz that appears in the 2003 MLF program courtesy of the Maine Lobster Promotion Council:

> The nervous system of a lobster is very simple, and is in fact most similar to the nervous system of the grasshopper. It is decentralized with no brain. There is no cerebral cortex, which in humans is the area of the brain that gives the experience of pain.

Though it sounds more sophisticated, a lot of the neurology in this latter claim is still either false or fuzzy. The human cerebral cortex is the brain-part that deals with higher faculties like reason, metaphysical self-awareness, language, etc. Pain reception is known to be part of a much older and more primitive system of nociceptors and prostaglandins that are managed by the brain stem and

16 [Wallace's note] By profession, Dick is actually a car salesman; the midcoast region's National Car Rental franchise operates out of a Chevy dealership in Thomaston.

17 *homeostasis* I.e., balance.

18 [Wallace's note] The short version regarding why we were back at the airport after already arriving the previous night involves lost luggage and a miscommunication about where and what the midcoast's National franchise was—Dick came out personally to the airport and got us, out of no evident motive but kindness. (He also talked nonstop the entire way, with a very distinctive speaking style that can be described only as manically laconic; the truth is that I now know more about this man than I do about some members of my own family.)

thalamus.[19] [20] On the other hand, it is true that the cerebral cortex is involved in what's variously called suffering, distress, or the emotional experience of pain—i.e., experiencing painful stimuli as unpleasant, very unpleasant, unbearable, and so on.

Before we go any further, let's acknowledge that the questions of whether and how different kinds of animals feel pain, and of whether and why it might be justifiable to inflict pain on them in order to eat them, turn out to be extremely complex and difficult. And comparative neuroanatomy is only part of the problem. Since pain is a totally subjective mental experience, we do not have direct access to anyone or anything's pain but our own; and even just the principles by which we can infer that other human beings experience pain and have a legitimate interest in not feeling pain involve hard-core philosophy—metaphysics, epistemology, value theory, ethics. The fact that even the most highly evolved nonhuman mammals can't use language to communicate with us about their subjective mental experience is only the first layer of additional complication in trying to extend our reasoning about pain and morality to animals. And everything gets progressively more abstract and convolved as we move farther and farther out from the higher-type mammals into cattle and swine and dogs and cats and rodents, and then birds and fish, and finally invertebrates like lobsters.

The more important point here, though, is that the whole animal-cruelty-and-eating issue is not just complex, it's also uncomfortable. It is, at any rate, uncomfortable for me, and for just about everyone I know who enjoys a variety of foods and yet does not want to see herself as cruel or unfeeling. As far as I can tell, my own main way of dealing with this conflict has been to avoid thinking about the whole unpleasant thing. I should add that it appears to me unlikely that many readers of *Gourmet* wish to think about it, either, or to be queried about the morality of their eating habits in the pages of a culinary monthly. Since, however, the assigned subject of this article is what it was like to attend the 2003 MLF, and thus to spend several days in the midst of a great mass of Americans all eating lobster, and thus to be more or less impelled to think hard about lobster and the experience of buying and eating lobster, it turns out that there is no honest way to avoid certain moral questions.

---

19 *prostaglandins* Chemicals similar to hormones; *thalamus* Part of the brain that transmits sensory input to the cerebral cortex.

20 [Wallace's note] To elaborate by way of example: The common experience of accidentally touching a hot stove and yanking your hand back before you're even aware that anything's going on is explained by the fact that many of the processes by which we detect and avoid painful stimuli do not involve the cortex. In the case of the hand and stove, the brain is bypassed altogether; all the important neurochemical action takes place in the spine.

There are several reasons for this. For one thing, it's not just that lobsters 20
get boiled alive, it's that you do it yourself—or at least it's done specifically for you, on-site.[21] As mentioned, the World's Largest Lobster Cooker, which is highlighted as an attraction in the festival's program, is right out there on the MLF's north grounds for everyone to see. Try to imagine a Nebraska Beef Festival[22] at which part of the festivities is watching trucks pull up and the live cattle get driven down the ramp and slaughtered right there on the World's Largest Killing Floor or something—there's no way.

The intimacy of the whole thing is maximized at home, which of course is where most lobster gets prepared and eaten (although note already the semi-conscious euphemism "prepared," which in the case of lobsters really means killing them right there in our kitchens). The basic scenario is that we come in from the store and make our little preparations like getting the kettle filled and boiling, and then we lift the lobsters out of the bag or whatever retail container they came home in … whereupon some uncomfortable things start to happen. However stuporous a lobster is from the trip home, for instance, it tends to come alarmingly to life when placed in boiling water. If you're tilting it from a container into the steaming kettle, the lobster will sometimes try to cling to the container's sides or even to hook its claws over the kettle's rim like a person trying to keep from going over the edge of a roof. And worse is when the lobster's fully immersed. Even if you cover the kettle and turn away, you can usually hear the cover rattling and clanking as the lobster tries to push it off. Or the creature's claws scraping the sides of the kettle as it thrashes around.

---

21 [Wallace's note] Morality-wise, let's concede that this cuts both ways. Lobster-eating is at least not abetted by the system of corporate factory farms that produces most beef, pork, and chicken. Because, if nothing else, of the way they're marketed and packaged for sale, we eat these latter meats without having to consider that they were once conscious, sentient creatures to whom horrible things were done. (N.B. "Horrible" here meaning really, really horrible. Write off to PETA or peta.org for their free "Meet Your Meat" video, narrated by Mr. Alec Baldwin, if you want to see just about everything meat-related you don't want to see or think about. (N.B.$_2$ Not that PETA's any sort of font of unspun truth. Like many partisans in complex moral disputes, the PETA people are fanatics, and a lot of their rhetoric seems simplistic and self-righteous. But this particular video, replete with actual factory-farm and corporate-slaughterhouse footage, is both credible and traumatizing.))

22 [Wallace's note] Is it significant that "lobster," "fish," and "chicken" are our culture's words for both the animal and the meat, whereas most mammals seem to require euphemisms like "beef" and "pork" that help us separate the meat we eat from the living creature the meat once was? Is this evidence that some kind of deep unease about eating higher animals is endemic enough to show up in English usage, but that the unease diminishes as we move out of the mammalian order? (And is "lamb"/"lamb" the counterexample that sinks the whole theory, or are there special, biblico-historical reasons for that equivalence?)

The lobster, in other words, behaves very much as you or I would behave if we were plunged into boiling water (with the obvious exception of screaming).[23] A blunter way to say this is that the lobster acts as if it's in terrible pain, causing some cooks to leave the kitchen altogether and to take one of those little lightweight plastic oven-timers with them into another room and wait until the whole process is over.

There happen to be two main criteria that most ethicists agree on for determining whether a living creature has the capacity to suffer and so has genuine interests that it may or may not be our moral duty to consider.[24] One is how much of the neurological hardware required for pain-experience the animal comes equipped with—nociceptors, prostaglandins, neuronal opioid receptors, etc. The other criterion is whether the animal demonstrates behaviour associated with pain. And it takes a lot of intellectual gymnastics and behaviourist hairsplitting not to see struggling, thrashing, and lid-clattering as just such pain-behaviour. According to marine zoologists, it usually takes lobsters between 35 and 45 seconds to die in boiling water. (No source I could find talked about how long it takes them to die in superheated steam; one rather hopes it's faster.)

There are, of course, other fairly common ways to kill your lobster on-site and so achieve maximum freshness. Some cooks' practice is to drive a sharp heavy knife point-first into a spot just above the midpoint between the lobster's eyestalks (more or less where the Third Eye is in human foreheads). This is alleged either to kill the lobster instantly or to render it insensate, and is said at least to eliminate some of the cowardice involved in throwing a creature into boiling water and then fleeing the room. As far as I can tell from talking to proponents of

---

23 [Wallace's note] There's a relevant populist myth about the high-pitched whistling sound that sometimes issues from a pot of boiling lobster. The sound is really vented steam from the layer of seawater between the lobster's flesh and its carapace (this is why shedders whistle more than hard-shells), but the pop version has it that the sound is the lobster's rabbit-like death-scream. Lobsters communicate via pheromones in their urine and don't have anything close to the vocal equipment for screaming, but the myth's very persistent—which might, once again, point to a low-level cultural unease about the boiling thing.

24 [Wallace's note] "Interests" basically means strong and legitimate preferences, which obviously require some degree of consciousness, responsiveness to stimuli, etc. See, for instance, the utilitarian philosopher Peter Singer, whose 1974 *Animal Liberation* is more or less the bible of the modern animal-rights movement:

> It would be nonsense to say that it was not in the interests of a stone to be kicked along the road by a schoolboy. A stone does not have interests because it cannot suffer. Nothing that we can do to it could possibly make any difference to its welfare. A mouse, on the other hand, does have an interest in not being kicked along the road, because it will suffer if it is.

the knife-in-the-head method, the idea is that it's more violent but ultimately more merciful, plus that a willingness to exert personal agency and accept responsibility for stabbing the lobster's head honours the lobster somehow and entitles one to eat it (there's often a vague sort of Native American spirituality-of-the-hunt flavour to pro-knife arguments). But the problem with the knife method is basic biology: Lobsters' nervous systems operate off not one but several ganglia, a.k.a. nerve bundles, which are sort of wired in series and distributed all along the lobster's underside, from stem to stern. And disabling only the frontal ganglion does not normally result in quick death or unconsciousness.

Another alternative is to put the lobster in cold saltwater and then very slowly bring it up to a full boil. Cooks who advocate this method are going on the analogy to a frog, which can supposedly be kept from jumping out of a boiling pot by heating the water incrementally. In order to save a lot of research-summarizing, I'll simply assure you that the analogy between frogs and lobsters turns out not to hold—plus, if the kettle's water isn't aerated seawater, the immersed lobster suffers from slow suffocation, although usually not decisive enough suffocation to keep it from still thrashing and clattering when the water gets hot enough to kill it. In fact, lobsters boiled incrementally often display a whole bonus set of gruesome, convulsionlike reactions that you don't see in regular boiling.

Ultimately, the only certain virtues of the home-lobotomy and slow-heating 25
methods are comparative, because there are even worse/crueler ways people prepare lobster. Time-thrifty cooks sometimes microwave them alive (usually after poking several extra vent-holes in the carapace, which is a precaution most shellfish-microwavers learn about the hard way). Live dismemberment, on the other hand, is big in Europe—some chefs cut the lobster in half before cooking; others like to tear off the claws and tail and toss only these parts in the pot.

And there's more unhappy news respecting suffering-criterion number one. Lobsters don't have much in the way of eyesight or hearing, but they do have an exquisite tactile sense, one facilitated by hundreds of thousands of tiny hairs that protrude through their carapace. "Thus it is," in the words of T.M. Prudden's industry classic *About Lobster*, "that although encased in what seems a solid, impenetrable armour, the lobster can receive stimuli and impressions from without as readily as if it possessed a soft and delicate skin." And lobsters do have nociceptors,[25] as well as invertebrate versions of the prostaglandins and major neurotransmitters via which our own brains register pain.

---

25 [Wallace's note] This is the neurological term for special pain-receptors that are "sensitive to potentially damaging extremes of temperature, to mechanical forces, and to chemical substances which are released when body tissues are damaged."

Lobsters do not, on the other hand, appear to have the equipment for making or absorbing natural opioids like endorphins and enkephalins, which are what more advanced nervous systems use to try to handle intense pain. From this fact, though, one could conclude either that lobsters are maybe even *more* vulnerable to pain, since they lack mammalian nervous systems' built-in analgesia,[26] or, instead, that the absence of natural opioids implies an absence of the really intense pain-sensations that natural opioids are designed to mitigate. I for one can detect a marked upswing in mood as I contemplate this latter possibility. It could be that their lack of endorphin/enkephalin hardware means that lobsters' raw subjective experience of pain is so radically different from mammals' that it may not even deserve the term "pain." Perhaps lobsters are more like those frontal-lobotomy patients one reads about who report experiencing pain in a totally different way than you and I. These patients evidently do feel physical pain, neurologically speaking, but don't dislike it—though neither do they like it; it's more that they feel it but don't feel anything *about* it—the point being that the pain is not distressing to them or something they want to get away from. Maybe lobsters, who are also without frontal lobes, are detached from the neurological-registration-of-injury-or-hazard we call pain in just the same way. There is, after all, a difference between (1) pain as a purely neurological event, and (2) actual suffering, which seems crucially to involve an emotional component, an awareness of pain as unpleasant, as something to fear/dislike/want to avoid.

Still, after all the abstract intellection, there remain the facts of the frantically clanking lid, the pathetic clinging to the edge of the pot. Standing at the stove, it is hard to deny in any meaningful way that this is a living creature experiencing pain and wishing to avoid/escape the painful experience. To my lay mind, the lobster's behaviour in the kettle appears to be the expression of a *preference*; and it may well be that an ability to form preferences is the decisive criterion for real suffering.[27] The logic of this (preference → suffering) relation may be easiest to see in the negative case. If you cut certain kinds of worms in half, the halves will often keep crawling around and going about their vermiform business as if nothing had happened. When we assert, based on their post-op behaviour, that these worms appear not to be suffering, what we're really saying is that there's no sign that the worms know anything bad has happened or would *prefer* not to have gotten cut in half.

---

26 *analgesia* Pain reduction.

27 [Wallace's note] "Preference" is maybe roughly synonymous with "interests," but it is a better term for our purposes because it's less abstractly philosophical—"preference" seems more personal, and it's the whole idea of a living creature's personal experience that's at issue.

Lobsters, though, are known to exhibit preferences. Experiments have shown that they can detect changes of only a degree or two in water temperature; one reason for their complex migratory cycles (which can often cover 100-plus miles a year) is to pursue the temperatures they like best.[28] And, as mentioned, they're bottom-dwellers and do not like bright light—if a tank of food lobsters is out in the sunlight or a store's fluorescence, the lobsters will always congregate in whatever part is darkest. Fairly solitary in the ocean, they also clearly dislike the crowding that's part of their captivity in tanks, since (as also mentioned) one reason why lobsters' claws are banded on capture is to keep them from attacking one another under the stress of close-quarter storage.

In any event, at the MLF, standing by the bubbling tanks outside the World's 30
Largest Lobster Cooker, watching the fresh-caught lobsters pile over one another, wave their hobbled claws impotently, huddle in the rear corners, or scrabble frantically back from the glass as you approach, it is difficult not to sense that they're unhappy, or frightened, even if it's some rudimentary version of these feelings … and, again, why does rudimentariness even enter into it? Why is a primitive, inarticulate form of suffering less urgent or uncomfortable for the person who's helping to inflict it by paying for the food it results in? I'm not trying to give you a PETA-like screed here—at least I don't think so. I'm trying, rather, to work out and articulate some of the troubling questions that

---

28 [Wallace's note] Of course, the most common sort of counterargument here would begin by objecting that "like best" is really just a metaphor, and a misleadingly anthropomorphic* one at that. The counterarguer would posit that the lobster seeks to maintain a certain optimal ambient temperature out of nothing but unconscious instinct (with a similar explanation for the low-light affinities upcoming in the main text). The thrust of such a counterargument will be that the lobster's thrashings and clankings in the kettle express not unpreferred pain but involuntary reflexes, like your leg shooting out when the doctor hits your knee. Be advised that there are professional scientists, including many researchers who use animals in experiments, who hold to the view that nonhuman creatures have no real feelings at all, merely "behaviours." Be further advised that this view has a long history that goes all the way back to Descartes, although its modern support comes mostly from behaviourist psychology. [René Descartes (1596–1650) was an influential French philosopher; behaviourist psychology interprets psychology exclusively in terms of behaviour as opposed to internal mental states.]

To these what-looks-like-pain-is-really-just-reflexes counterarguments, however, there happen to be all sorts of scientific and pro-animal-rights counter-counterarguments. And then further attempted rebuttals and redirects, and so on. Suffice to say that both the scientific and the philosophical arguments on either side of the animal-suffering issue are involved, abstruse, technical, often informed by self-interest or ideology, and in the end so totally inconclusive that as a practical matter, in the kitchen or restaurant, it all still seems to come down to individual conscience, going with (no pun) your gut.

arise amid all the laughter and saltation[29] and community pride of the Maine Lobster Festival. The truth is that if you, the festival attendee, permit yourself to think that lobsters can suffer and would rather not, the MLF begins to take on the aspect of something like a Roman circus[30] or medieval torture-fest.

Does that comparison seem a bit much? If so, exactly why? Or what about this one: Is it possible that future generations will regard our own present agribusiness and eating practices in much the same way we now view Nero's entertainments or Mengele's experiments?[31] My own immediate reaction is that such a comparison is hysterical, extreme—and yet the reason it seems extreme to me appears to be that I believe animals are less morally important than human beings;[32] and when it comes to defending such a belief, even to myself, I have to acknowledge that (a) I have an obvious selfish interest in this belief, since I like to eat certain kinds of animals and want to be able to keep doing it, and (b) I haven't succeeded in working out any sort of personal ethical system in which the belief is truly defensible instead of just selfishly convenient.

Given this article's venue and my own lack of culinary sophistication, I'm curious about whether the reader can identify with any of these reactions and acknowledgments and discomforts. I am also concerned not to come off as shrill or preachy when what I really am is more like confused. For those *Gourmet* readers who enjoy well-prepared and -presented meals involving beef, veal, lamb, pork, chicken, lobster, etc.: Do you think much about the (possible) moral status and (probable) suffering of the animals involved? If you do, what ethical convictions have you worked out that permit you not just to eat but to savour and enjoy flesh-based viands[33] (since of course refined *enjoyment*, rather than mere ingestion, is the whole point of gastronomy)? If, on the other hand, you'll have no truck with confusions or convictions and regard stuff like the previous paragraph as just so much fatuous navel-gazing, what makes it feel truly okay, inside, to just dismiss the whole issue out of hand? That is,

---

29 *saltation* I.e., dancing, jumping around.

30 *circus* Mass entertainment, which in ancient Rome could include the killing of humans by animals, of animals by humans, or of humans by each other.

31 *Nero's entertainments* Among the spectacles that Roman Emperor Nero (37–68 CE) staged for his people's enjoyment were gladiator battles and the brutal public execution of Christians; *Mengele's experiments* Nazi doctor Josef Mengele (1911–79) conducted cruel medical experiments on inmates at the Auschwitz concentration camp.

32 [Wallace's note] Meaning a *lot* less important, apparently, since the moral comparison here is not the value of one human's life vs. the value of one animal's life, but rather the value of one animal's life vs. the value of one human's taste for a particular kind of protein. Even the most diehard carniphile* will acknowledge that it's possible to live and eat well without consuming animals.

33 *viands* Foods.

is your refusal to think about any of this the product of actual thought, or is it just that you don't want to think about it? And if the latter, then why not? Do you ever think, even idly, about the possible reasons for your reluctance to think about it? I am not trying to bait anyone here—I'm genuinely curious. After all, isn't being extra aware and attentive and thoughtful about one's food and its overall context part of what distinguishes a real gourmet? Or is all the gourmet's extra attention and sensibility just supposed to be sensuous? Is it really all just a matter of taste and presentation?

These last few queries, though, while sincere, obviously involve much larger and more abstract questions about the connections (if any) between aesthetics and morality—about what the adjective in a phrase like "The Magazine of Good Living"[34] is really supposed to mean—and these questions lead straightaway into such deep and treacherous waters that it's probably best to stop the public discussion right here. There are limits to what even interested persons can ask of each other.

(2004)

Questions

1. In Wallace's description of the Lobster Festival, what sensory details does he give that reveal his own dislike for it? Would the same details cause you to dislike the festival?
2. In footnote 28, Wallace suggests that the question of whether or not a lobster has "preferences" and feels pain is not answered conclusively by science, and that in the end it comes down to "individual conscience" whether to consider them sentient beings. Do you agree? What does Wallace seem to think?
3. This article is extremely funny in parts. How does the humour affect our experience of the argument? Our feeling toward the narrator?

---

34 *The Magazine ... Living* Slogan of *Gourmet* magazine.

Jan Wong

from Coming Clean

In Canada, debate regarding the minimum wage has long generated strong opinions: some argue that the minimum wage is woefully inadequate to cover living expenses, while others argue that a higher minimum wage harms the economy. In a five-part series for The Globe and Mail *entitled "Maid for a Month," journalist Jan Wong chronicles a month spent working undercover as a domestic housecleaner and reflects on the quality of life for those working minimum (and less than minimum) wage jobs in Ontario. The selection included here is excerpted from the first installment in the series, which was published in the spring of 2006.*

My partner takes the kitchen and I tackle the bathroom. Big mistake. When I ask the client, a sexy twentysomething in tight jeans and top, if she wants to use the washroom before I get started, she looks horrified. "I never use the toilet here," she says.

And then I see why. Frisbee-sized stains of ochre urine encircle the base of the toilet. Feces splatter its rim and underside. The seat is streaked with old urine. Solidified toothpaste, spit, phlegm, beard stubble and pubic hairs—how did they get there?—coat the sink. The floor is thick with dust balls and more hair.

It turns out the young woman doesn't actually live here. This 12th-floor condominium at trendy Queens Quay, off Lake Ontario, belongs to her boyfriend. They're professionals, in finance. His condo is closer to their offices. But she refuses to move in until he has had the condo professionally cleaned.

By us, a crack team from a company I'll call Metro Maids. My partner and I have been sent here at a one-time, first-clean rate of $28 per hour, per maid, plus GST. At least, that's what the company gets. For workdays that stretch to 11 or 12 hours, I will earn less than minimum wage.

But I don't know that yet. One of the many bad things about working at low-wage jobs is, incredibly, it's not always clear what you are getting paid. Right now, I'm concentrating on the toilet, which apparently hasn't been cleaned in a year, possibly two.

I spray it all over with Fantastik Original. Then I use Fantastik With Bleach, Vim Oxy-Gel, Mr. Clean, old-fashioned soap and water, scouring brushes, paper towels. I let the poisons marinate, while I attack the sink.

Meanwhile, Mr. Filth and his paramour are necking on the dusty couch. She's in his lap, giggling. He's feeling her up. My middle-aged partner has a clear view from the galley kitchen, which opens onto the living room. I see them every time I step into the hall for more paper towels.

I am working undercover—though I applied for this job using my real name—but this is ridiculous. I'm practically under the covers with them. Then I understand. We are maids, and therefore we are invisible, subhuman, beneath notice. We are the untouchables of the Western world.

Every other lousy job has a euphemistic title. Garbage men are sanitation workers. Undertakers are funeral directors. Whores became prostitutes and then sex workers. Gender-specific professions have neutered their titles too. Stewardess has become flight attendant. Waitress has become server. But maids! The companies that employ us—and try to entice you—revel in the feudal grovelling and female subservience the word implies.

10 And so there are dozens of companies in North America that invoke the name: Maid Brigade, Maid for You, Maids to the Rescue, Maid to Sparkle, Magic Maids, Maid Marian Cleaning Service, Maids-R-Us, Sunshine Maids, Maid to Clean, Merry Maids and, of course, Molly Maid.

And so the client behaves as if we're not there. He's a tall, pale blond man in his late 20s or early 30s. By his accent, I surmise he's from northern Europe. She appears to be from India. Mercifully, they finally stop necking and go out on an errand.

"Aren't they a lovely couple?" my fellow maid calls sweetly from the kitchen, where she is sweeping up the pistachio shells and used bamboo skewers that litter the floor.

"They're doomed," I mutter. "The relationship is doomed."

"Why do you say that?" she asks reproachfully.

15 "Because neither of them will clean a toilet."

On Feb. 1, Ontario's minimum hourly wage rose to $7.75 from $7.45.[1] For reasons that now escape me, I thought the best way to tell the story of that 30-cent raise was to work—and live—at the bottom of the food chain. I would find a low-paying job, a low-rent apartment and, single-mom-like, take my boys with me for the month and see how we survived.

In real life, we live close to the top of the chain. Our riding, which includes the Bridle Path, has the highest average income in the country, according to

1 *$7.75 from $7.45* In 2016 dollars, $9.18 from $8.82.

the Elections Canada's website. We vacation abroad. We have a part-time housekeeper. My boys go to a private school, where they wear grey flannels and speak French all day. Ben has two violin lessons a week. Sam's hockey gear costs more than his cello (yes, he's a goalie).

But to my surprise, both they and my husband, Norman, readily agreed. (Norman was thrilled with the prospect of having the house to himself.) "Cool, what are we going to eat? KD?" said Sam, 12, who prizes Kraft Dinner because he's sick of triple crème French brie. His brother, Ben, 15, was the embodiment of teen irony. "So I'll have a urine-soaked mattress?" he said. "Is the floor going to be, like, concrete?"

Before I set out on this assignment, I assumed $7.75 an hour, at 40 hours a week, was a living wage. I began crunching numbers. My monthly pre-tax income would be $1,240, or $14,880 a year. To my horror, I realized I wouldn't even reach halfway to the so-called "low-income cut-off line" of $31,126 set by Statistics Canada for an urban family of three.

I also assumed an increase in the minimum wage meant that the minimum wage had actually increased. Wrong again. Over the past 30 years, the minimum wage declined 13 per cent in real terms. In 1976, Ontario's minimum wage was $2.65 an hour, or $8.93 in today's dollars. In the meantime, Canada's standard of living soared 43 per cent, in real terms, from 1981 to 2003. In other words, the rich got richer. And Metro Maids? I was about to find out.

I had never considered Canada to be a poor country. But it turns out that despite ever-higher educational levels and productivity, we have one of the biggest proportions of low-paid workers in the world, defined as those earning less than two-thirds of a country's median annual earnings. In Canada, … about 21 per cent of the work force is low-paid, versus 26 per cent in the United States, the world's richest country. In European countries, the proportion ranges from 7 per cent in Finland to 13 per cent in Germany….

Maid work, it turns out, is surprisingly compatible with investigative reporting. Aside from rummaging through people's dirty laundry, I get to manhandle their garbage, eyeball the paperwork on their desks, inspect the size of their underwear and peek inside their refrigerators.

Many clients are *Globe and Mail* subscribers—I know because I stack the recycling. At first, I worry someone will recognize me. What airs I give myself! Everyone looks straight through me, even when I say, "Hi, I'm Jan from Metro Maids." If clients speak to us at all, it's to alert us to cobwebs, dirty grouting and window mould.

About one-third of our clients leave keys. We never see them. Yet we know the most intimate things about them. We know if they're menopausal, or if it's that time of the month. And we know that you—yes, you—are the vice-president of a financial services company and make $175,000 a year. (You left your paycheque lying on the desk we wipe clean.)

We know the colour of your hair, and how long it is. It's all over the bathtub 25
and your sheets, and, yuck, even on the kitchen counter. We know if it's curly, and whether you have a problem with that. That's your bottle of no-frizz oil on the bathroom vanity. Or if you have straight hair and prefer otherwise. Yes, we see the plastic curlers, tossed in a basket under the sink.

We know if you're plus-sized and care. Tsk, tsk. You haven't been exercising. The stationary bike beside your bed is covered in dust. And isn't that a Size 16 label from Laura clothing that you left lying on the bedroom floor for us to pick up? (We can't vacuum plastic tags; they wreck our equipment.)

We know the date you got married, and what you wore. You framed the wedding invitation, and the photos—sometimes the same one three times. Your dried-out bouquet is displayed in your living room. But we know when the bloom is off the rose. The day after Valentine's Day, we know who got flowers—and who didn't.

We even know what you will do before you do it. Tonight, you'll dine on beef stew. It's simmering in the Crock Pot while we wash your kitchen floor. And don't kid yourself. Of course we know if you drink a lot. The empties are there, and we can track them from week to week....

If I earned $1,200 to $1,400 a month, and spent no more than one-third of my income on rent—the limit financial planners advise—my housing budget would be $400 to $470. An editor mentioned that an artist friend was subletting a small studio on Queen Street West. The price was $500 a month. I e-mailed in a nanosecond, but someone had already snapped it up. Another friend mentioned a one-bedroom somewhere on Kingston Road. It wouldn't be available for six weeks. A cousin's friend had a basement studio for $650. That was high, but alas, it also had been rented out.

A poverty analyst at Toronto's City Hall suggested that I try deepest Scar- 30
borough. "It has a lot of working poor," he said. So I headed there and, for moral support, brought along a friend. Fifteen minutes into our search, I passed a favourite sushi restaurant. I was starving. "It's 10:45 a.m.," said my friend disapprovingly. "You're supposed to be a single mom."

In a coffee shop, where my friend would not let me buy a muffin, I picked up a free newspaper listing rentals. After phoning several leads and getting nowhere, we drove to the address in one ad, a seedy high-rise at Ellesmere and Markham.

"Right now, it's renter's choice," said the building manager. He took me up in an elevator redolent of cumin and garlic to see a one-bedroom apartment on the 14th floor. It cost $795 a month and had a view of the CN Tower.

The kitchen was still grimy. Someone had dumped a bucket of urethane on top of the scarred parquet floors, leaving a thick, clear and solid puddle in the centre. Three holes in the bedroom door had been clumsily patched.

"Husband and wife fight," said the building manager, in Chinese-accented English. He seemed much more interested in hitting on my friend, but I managed to elicit bits of information. Parking was extra. The building's laundromat cost $1.25 per load. Roaches were possibly in residence. I would have to pass a credit check and fork over two months' deposit in advance.

35 I had almost decided on the first apartment when I explained my project to a social worker who specializes in Scarborough. "Not that building. It's full of gangs and drugs," she said, steering me, instead, to the Scarborough Housing Help Centre.

I told the receptionist there that my budget was tight. I was willing to sleep in the same room with my boys.

"That's not a good thing," she said kindly. "Your children are supposed to have their own bedroom, or family services might get involved."

Two days later, I pored over the centre's new listings and made seven phone calls. Happily, the only one I got through to was for the cheapest apartment on the list, described as a one-bedroom basement unit, for $590. I rushed over.

The 1980s pink-brick monster home looked respectable. The owner, a Bangladeshi immigrant, met me on the frozen driveway in flip-flops. He told me that, alas, with my "share of utilities," the rent would actually be $670. He asked how many people would be moving in. When I told him, he said, "How will you sleep? How will your boys study?"

40 I said I would sleep in the living room. He shrugged, then led me down a flight of stairs and pounded on a door. After a few moments, a sleepy young Bangladeshi opened it and let us in. The room was a mess. It smelled so bad I needed to mouth-breathe. Then I saw why. There were no windows. There was no living room either. The basement consisted of a small, filthy kitchen and a narrow room, also windowless, which masqueraded as a bedroom, but was really a storage room enclosing the electrical box. Every time a fuse blew upstairs, the landlord would be in my children's bedroom.

Aside from windowless housing, I was also worried about signing a 12-month lease—a lawyer who specializes in tenants' rights warned me that with current high vacancy rates, landlords are suing renters who try to leave early. So I called an agent who settles newly arrived students from mainland China. She introduced me to Chen (all names have been changed), who was willing to rent me the basement of his tiny Scarborough bungalow for a month—just as soon as he got rid of two spoiled brats from China.

The students—both male—hadn't cleaned the place in a year. The white linoleum floor in the kitchen was so dirty it looked black. And at $750 a month, it would devastate my budget. But I didn't hesitate. It was the cheapest place I had found with windows. Besides, Chen, a cleaner at the Four Seasons Hotel, promised that once the students moved out, he would scrub it clean for me.

In the meantime, I hunted for work. Armed with a doctored résumé, I walked down Yonge Street, from College to King, resolving to answer every single "Help Wanted" sign I found. My résumé claimed I had a university degree—true—no recent experience and was entering the work force after raising my children. I dropped the CVs* at Pizza Pizza, Money Mart, a clothing store (that was offering $7 per hour, cash) and Grand & Toy.

At Mamma's Pizza, I lined up behind three mid-afternoon customers. "Can I help you?" asked the burly counter man, smiling. I pointed to the "Help Wanted" sign. The smile faded. "It's not for you," he said. "We need a driver."

"I can drive," I said, feeling embarrassed and, somehow, poor. "How much does it pay?"

"Depends on how fast you work," he said, turning away.

The woman ahead of me said gently, "I think it's by the pizza."

I asked the counter man one last question: How much per pizza?

"$1.50," he said. "Plus tips. And you need your own car."

During the Industrial Revolution, those in power cared little about living conditions as peasants flocked to cities to work in factories. But when they declared war on one another, they noticed the soldiers they conscripted were puny, sickly. Suddenly, governments began paying attention to sanitation, malnutrition, clean air—and labour laws.

In 1894, New Zealand became the first country to pass a minimum-wage law. The Australian state of Victoria soon followed. Great Britain introduced similar legislation in 1909. In 1900, Canada imposed a minimum wage for government contracts and public works. But it was up to the provinces to enact comprehensive legislation. British Columbia and Manitoba passed the first laws, in 1918. Ontario, Nova Scotia, Quebec and Saskatchewan soon followed. Initially, they protected only female workers. In 1925, B.C. passed the first law for male workers. Prince Edward Island was the last to pass minimum-wage laws: for women in 1959 and men in 1960.

For decades, provincial minimum-wage laws set higher pay for men than for women. The last gender-based difference disappeared in 1974. Today, the problem seems to be getting hired as a female driver at a pizza franchise.

A few days after getting rejected there, I flipped through Employment News, a freebie paper. One company wanted 20 experienced sewing-machine operators, but I don't know how to sew. But I do know how to interview someone. An ad from Ipsos-ASI, an advertising research company, seemed tailor-made for me. It needed telephone interviewers with "strong reading and keyboarding skills" for "market research." I e-mailed a résumé, emphasizing I don't have a foreign accent.

I also e-mailed a résumé to Kentucky Fried Chicken, which needed full-time kitchen help in its Fairview Mall location. I downloaded an application from Wal-Mart's website, and dropped it off. "We're not hiring," the clerk said. "We'll keep it on file for 60 days."

55 I had applied for eight minimum-wage jobs. No one called me back.

Then I remembered once lunching with a businesswoman who told me that Molly Maid always needed staff. I called the headquarters, which directed me to a franchise in the outskirts of the city. They were hiring!

Daulat, the franchise owner, was a pretty woman from India with a plummy British accent.* She wore high-heeled boots and slim pants and had long dark hair. She ran the franchise out of her apartment. She escorted me into her small office and asked why I was so desperate that I would clean houses.

"Marriage issues," I said.

She nodded sympathetically. She had bought the franchise 15 months ago when her own marriage collapsed. She cleaned for two days, to familiarize herself with the business. "I was absolutely exhausted."

60 Daulat already had three teams and was looking for a fourth.

"You get 18-per-cent commission on every clean," she said. When I looked puzzled, she explained. A client typically paid $75 for a clean by two maids that lasted an hour and a half. I got 18 per cent of the clean, or $40 to $50 a day for cleaning four houses.

Travel time was unpaid. That meant for a workday of 10 or 11 hours, I would be getting paid for only five or six. Apparently, calling it a "commission" gets around the minimum wage.

When I looked unimpressed, she asked, "Can you drive?" A "route manager" gets two extra percentage points commission. I would get a pink and purple Molly Maid car. But I would have to drive, figure out the schedule, the route, keep time sheets and handle all the cash, cheques and, ominously, "non-payments." I'd work the longest hours because I'd have to pick up and drop off my teammate. On Friday nights, I would have to go to the office to cash out, and return all the keys.

"Oh, and you have to wash the rags. We pay 35 cents per house. We don't use paper towels because it's too costly."

65 I told her that I could start the following week. But when I called back, she said she was now interviewing others.

So I called my last hope, Metro Maids. The owner, Nariman, a soft-spoken man from India, met me at a Coffee Time in Scarborough. His deal wasn't much different from Molly Maid's: a long day, starting at 7 a.m. and finishing by 5. Or 6. Or 7 p.m.

"Are you mentally prepared for cleaning?" When I nodded, Nariman said he would pay me $9 an hour until I gained experience. After a few weeks, he would put me on salary—$600 every two weeks. To earn that, I would have to work Saturdays, but I would get one weekday off every other week.

"How are you with dogs and cats?" he asked.

I hesitated, and he quickly added, "We're not looking at pit bulls or anything."

I took the job. In fact, I'm allergic to cats.

Did I mention I'm also allergic to dust? But I didn't tell Nariman that, either.

Two days later, I start working. It seems every house I clean has pets, several of them, and all of them shed. At a high-rise condo, with two cats in residence, the floors are adrift with hair and dust. The fur balls are so thick and tufty they look like grey snowdrifts.

I begin to sneeze. My eyes turn red and itchy. I look, and feel, like I have the flu. At the next home, thankfully, the absentee owner has locked the dog in a room.

The third and final clean is an elegant townhouse in a Cabbagetown alleyway. The owner works in film and has exquisite taste in art. His adult daughter works in advertising. They are both out, but have left the television on for their small dog, tuned to Animal Planet.

I'm almost finished mopping the pale oak floor when I spot a little pile of turds at the entrance to the den. Gingerly, I pick them up. The turds are light and dry. They do not smell. They must be at least two days old. My partner says the owners knew we were coming, and left them for us....

(2006)

Questions

1. Find out what the current minimum wage is where you live. What standard of living does that wage provide? Are there loopholes that allow certain jobs or certain types of people to receive less than the minimum wage? Given this information, would you recommend any changes to the local minimum wage and/or how it is implemented?
2. Read the articles "Guarantee a Minimum Income, Not a Minimum Wage" and "'Basic Income' Is Tempting—But It Could Backfire," also included in this anthology. Does anything in Wong's article incline you toward minimum income or toward minimum wage—or toward something else—as the best approach to the problem of poverty in Canada?
3. Wong is open about her own affluence. How (if at all) does the fact that she is actually wealthy affect the way you read this article?

Binyavanga Wainaina

How to Write about Africa

In this biting piece, a leading Kenyan writer provides a series of instructions to foreigners aspiring to write about his home continent. The essay first appeared in a special issue of the British literary periodical Granta *in 2005; the volume was entitled* The View from Africa.

The tendencies Wainaina draws attention to here have centuries-old roots in Western culture; arguably they became even more pronounced in America in the early years of the twenty-first century, as George W. Bush focused considerable attention on the African continent (and increased medical assistance to many African nations), declaring in 2001 that "Africa is a nation that suffers from incredible disease."

Always use the word "Africa" or "Darkness" or "Safari" in your title. Subtitles may include the words "Zanzibar," "Masai," "Zulu," "Zambezi," "Congo," "Nile," "Big," "Sky," "Shadow," "Drum," "Sun" or "Bygone." Also useful are words such as "Guerrillas," "Timeless," "Primordial" and "Tribal." Note that "People" means Africans who are not black, while "The People" means black Africans.

Never have a picture of a well-adjusted African on the cover of your book, or in it, unless that African has won the Nobel Prize. An AK-47, prominent ribs, naked breasts: use these. If you must include an African, make sure you get one in Masai or Zulu or Dogon dress.

In your text, treat Africa as if it were one country. It is hot and dusty with rolling grasslands and huge herds of animals and tall, thin people who are starving. Or it is hot and steamy with very short people who eat primates. Don't get bogged down with precise descriptions. Africa is big: fifty-four countries, 900 million people who are too busy starving and dying and warring and emigrating to read your book. The continent is full of deserts, jungles, highlands, savannahs and many other things, but your reader doesn't care about all that, so keep your descriptions romantic and evocative and unparticular.

Make sure you show how Africans have music and rhythm deep in their souls, and eat things no other humans eat. Do not mention rice and beef and wheat; monkey-brain is an African's cuisine of choice, along with goat, snake, worms and grubs and all manner of game meat. Make sure you show that you are able to eat such food without flinching, and describe how you learn to enjoy it—because you care.

Taboo subjects: ordinary domestic scenes, love between Africans (unless 5
a death is involved), references to African writers or intellectuals, mention of school-going children who are not suffering from yaws or Ebola fever or female genital mutilation.

Throughout the book, adopt a *sotto** voice, in conspiracy with the reader, and a sad *I-expected-so-much* tone. Establish early on that your liberalism is impeccable, and mention near the beginning how much you love Africa, how you fell in love with the place and can't live without her. Africa is the only continent you can love—take advantage of this. If you are a man, thrust yourself into her warm virgin forests. If you are a woman, treat Africa as a man who wears a bush jacket and disappears off into the sunset. Africa is to be pitied, worshipped or dominated. Whichever angle you take, be sure to leave the strong impression that without your intervention and your important book, Africa is doomed.

Your African characters may include naked warriors, loyal servants, diviners and seers, ancient wise men living in hermitic splendour. Or corrupt politicians, inept polygamous travel-guides, and prostitutes you have slept with. The Loyal Servant always behaves like a seven-year-old and needs a firm hand; he is scared of snakes, good with children, and always involving you in his complex domestic dramas. The Ancient Wise Man always comes from a noble tribe (not the money-grubbing tribes like the Gikuyu, the Igbo or the Shona). He has rheumy eyes and is close to the Earth. The Modern African is a fat man who steals and works in the visa office, refusing to give work permits to qualified Westerners who really care about Africa. He is an enemy of development, always using his government job to make it difficult for pragmatic and good-hearted expats to set up NGOs* or Legal Conservation Areas. Or he is an Oxford-educated intellectual turned serial-killing politician in a Savile Row suit. He is a cannibal who likes Cristal champagne, and his mother is a rich witch-doctor who really runs the country.

Among your characters you must always include The Starving African, who wanders the refugee camp nearly naked, and waits for the benevolence of the West. Her children have flies on their eyelids and pot bellies, and her breasts are flat and empty. She must look utterly helpless. She can have no past, no history; such diversions ruin the dramatic moment. Moans are good. She must never say anything about herself in the dialogue except to speak of her (unspeakable) suffering. Also be sure to include a warm and motherly woman who has a rolling laugh and who is concerned for your well-being. Just call her Mama. Her children are all delinquent. These characters should buzz around your main hero, making him look good. Your hero can teach them, bathe them, feed them; he carries lots of babies and has seen Death. Your hero is you (if reportage), or a beautiful, tragic international celebrity/aristocrat who now cares for animals (if fiction).

Bad Western characters may include children of Tory* cabinet ministers, Afrikaners, employees of the World Bank.* When talking about exploitation by foreigners mention the Chinese and Indian traders. Blame the West for Africa's situation. But do not be too specific.

Broad brushstrokes throughout are good. Avoid having the African characters laugh, or struggle to educate their kids, or just make do in mundane circumstances. Have them illuminate something about Europe or America in Africa. African characters should be colourful, exotic, larger than life—but empty inside, with no dialogue, no conflicts or resolutions in their stories, no depth or quirks to confuse the cause.

Describe, in detail, naked breasts (young, old, conservative, recently raped, big, small) or mutilated genitals, or enhanced genitals. Or any kind of genitals. And dead bodies. Or, better, naked dead bodies. And especially rotting naked dead bodies. Remember, any work you submit in which people look filthy and miserable will be referred to as the "real Africa," and you want that on your dust jacket. Do not feel queasy about this: you are trying to help them to get aid from the West. The biggest taboo in writing about Africa is to describe or show dead or suffering white people.

Animals, on the other hand, must be treated as well rounded, complex characters. They speak (or grunt while tossing their manes proudly) and have names, ambitions and desires. They also have family values: *see how lions teach their children?* Elephants are caring, and are good feminists or dignified patriarchs. So are gorillas. Never, ever say anything negative about an elephant or a gorilla. Elephants may attack people's property, destroy their crops, and even kill them. Always take the side of the elephant. Big cats have public-school accents. Hyenas are fair game and have vaguely Middle Eastern accents. Any short Africans who live in the jungle or desert may be portrayed with good humour (unless they are in conflict with an elephant or chimpanzee or gorilla, in which case they are pure evil).

After celebrity activists and aid workers, conservationists are Africa's most important people. Do not offend them. You need them to invite you to their 30,000-acre game ranch or "conservation area," and this is the only way you will get to interview the celebrity activist. Often a book cover with a heroic-looking conservationist on it works magic for sales. Anybody white, tanned and wearing khaki who once had a pet antelope or a farm is a conservationist, one who is preserving Africa's rich heritage. When interviewing him or her, do not ask how much funding they have; do not ask how much money they make off their game. Never ask how much they pay their employees.

Readers will be put off if you don't mention the light in Africa. And sunsets, the African sunset is a must. It is always big and red. There is always a big sky. Wide empty spaces and game are critical—Africa is the Land of Wide Empty Spaces. When writing about the plight of flora and fauna, make sure you mention that Africa is overpopulated. When your main character is in a desert or jungle living with indigenous peoples (anybody short) it is okay to mention that Africa has been severely depopulated by Aids and War (use caps).

You'll also need a nightclub called Tropicana, where mercenaries, evil nouveau riche Africans and prostitutes and guerrillas and expats hang out.

Always end your book with Nelson Mandela* saying something about rainbows or renaissances. Because you care.

(2005)

Questions

1. Summarize in your own words what mistakes Wainaina observes Western writers making when they write about Africa. Are his accusations fair?
2. Comment on Wainaina's use of satire. How else might he have written this piece? Would other ways have been more effective, or less?
3. Choose a group that you feel is widely misrepresented in the media (e.g. youth, protesters, people on welfare, people with disabilities) and write a piece on "How to Write about" that group in the style of this article.
4. Look in your library or on the Internet and find some examples of recent writing about Africa. To what extent does "How to Write about Africa" describe the writing you find?
5. In this piece, Wainaina gives us a clear picture of what bad writing about Africa looks like. How much can we learn from the essay about what good writing about Africa should look like?

MALCOLM GLADWELL

NONE OF THE ABOVE: WHAT I.Q. DOESN'T TELL YOU ABOUT RACE

Malcolm Gladwell is a journalist and staff writer at The New Yorker. *His work often examines research findings in the social sciences and interprets them for a broader audience. In the following article Gladwell reviews* What Is Intelligence? *(2007), by the scholar James Flynn, delving into the debate among psychologists and geneticists surrounding IQ and its relationship to race, class, and culture. "None of the Above" was first published in* The New Yorker *in 2007.*

One Saturday in November of 1984, James Flynn, a social scientist at the University of Otago, in New Zealand, received a large package in the mail. It was from a colleague in Utrecht, and it contained the results of I.Q. tests* given to two generations of Dutch eighteen-year-olds. When Flynn looked through the data, he found something puzzling. The Dutch eighteen-year-olds from the nineteen-eighties scored better than those who took the same tests in the nineteen-fifties—and not just slightly better, *much* better.

Curious, Flynn sent out some letters. He collected intelligence-test results from Europe, from North America, from Asia, and from the developing world, until he had data for almost thirty countries. In every case, the story was pretty much the same. I.Q.s around the world appeared to be rising by 0.3 points per year, or three points per decade, for as far back as the tests had been administered. For some reason, human beings seemed to be getting smarter.

Flynn has been writing about the implications of his findings—now known as the Flynn effect—for almost twenty-five years. His books consist of a series of plainly stated statistical observations, in support of deceptively modest conclusions, and the evidence in support of his original observation is now so overwhelming that the Flynn effect has moved from theory to fact. What remains uncertain is how to make sense of the Flynn effect. If an American born in the nineteen-thirties has an I.Q. of 100, the Flynn effect says that his children will have I.Q.s of 108, and his grandchildren I.Q.s of close to 120—more than a standard deviation higher. If we work in the opposite direction, the typical teen-ager of today, with an I.Q. of 100, would have had grandparents with average I.Q.s of 82—seemingly below the threshold necessary to graduate from high school. And, if we go back even farther, the Flynn effect puts the average I.Q.s of the schoolchildren of 1900 at around 70, which is to suggest, bizarrely, that a century ago the United States was populated largely by people who today would be considered mentally retarded.

For almost as long as there have been I.Q. tests, there have been I.Q. fundamentalists. H.H. Goddard, in the early years of the past century, established the idea that intelligence could be measured along a single, linear scale. One of his particular contributions was to coin the word "moron." "The people who are doing the drudgery are, as a rule, in their proper places," he wrote. Goddard was followed by Lewis Terman, in the nineteen-twenties, who rounded up the California children with the highest I.Q.s, and confidently predicted that they would sit at the top of every profession. In 1969, the psychometrician Arthur Jensen argued that programs like Head Start, which tried to boost the academic performance of minority children, were doomed to failure, because I.Q. was so heavily genetic; and in 1994 Richard Herrnstein and Charles Murray, in "The Bell Curve," notoriously proposed that Americans with the lowest I.Q.s be sequestered in a "high-tech" version of an Indian reservation,* "while the rest of America tries to go about its business."[1] To the I.Q. fundamentalist, two things are beyond dispute: first, that I.Q. tests measure some hard and identifiable trait that predicts the quality of our thinking; and, second, that this trait is stable—that is, it is determined by our genes and largely impervious to environmental influences.

This is what James Watson, the co-discoverer of DNA, meant when he 5
told an English newspaper recently that he was "inherently gloomy" about the prospects for Africa. From the perspective of an I.Q. fundamentalist, the fact that Africans score lower than Europeans on I.Q. tests suggests an ineradicable cognitive disability. In the controversy that followed, Watson was defended by the journalist William Saletan, in a three-part series for the online magazine *Slate*. Drawing heavily on the work of J. Philippe Rushton—a psychologist who specializes in comparing the circumference of what he calls the Negroid brain with the length of the Negroid penis—Saletan took the fundamentalist position to its logical conclusion. To erase the difference between blacks and whites, Saletan wrote, would probably require vigorous interbreeding between the races, or some kind of corrective genetic engineering aimed at upgrading

---

1 *in 1994 ... business* *The New Yorker* posted the following correction to this statement: "In fact, Herrnstein and Murray deplored the prospect of such 'custodialism' and recommended that steps be taken to avert it. We regret the error."

African stock.* "Economic and cultural theories have failed to explain most of the pattern," Saletan declared, claiming to have been "soaking [his] head in each side's computations and arguments." One argument that Saletan never soaked his head in, however, was Flynn's, because what Flynn discovered in his mailbox upsets the certainties upon which I.Q. fundamentalism rests. If whatever the thing is that I.Q. tests measure can jump so much in a generation, it can't be all that immutable and it doesn't look all that innate.

The very fact that average I.Q.s shift over time ought to create a "crisis of confidence," Flynn writes in "What Is Intelligence?," his latest attempt to puzzle through the implications of his discovery. "How could such huge gains be intelligence gains? Either the children of today were far brighter than their parents or, at least in some circumstances, I.Q. tests were not good measures of intelligence."

The best way to understand why I.Q.s rise, Flynn argues, is to look at one of the most widely used I.Q. tests, the so-called WISC (for Wechsler Intelligence Scale for Children). The WISC is composed of ten subtests, each of which measures a different aspect of I.Q. Flynn points out that scores in some of the categories—those measuring general knowledge, say, or vocabulary or the ability to do basic arithmetic—have risen only modestly over time. The big gains on the WISC are largely in the category known as "similarities," where you get questions such as "In what way are 'dogs' and 'rabbits' alike?" Today, we tend to give what, for the purposes of I.Q. tests, is the right answer: dogs and rabbits are both mammals. A nineteenth-century American would have said that "you use dogs to hunt rabbits."

"If the everyday world is your cognitive home, it is not natural to detach abstractions and logic and the hypothetical from their concrete referents," Flynn writes. Our great-grandparents may have been perfectly intelligent. But they would have done poorly on I.Q. tests because they did not participate in the twentieth century's great cognitive revolution, in which we learned to sort experience according to a new set of abstract categories. In Flynn's phrase, we have now had to put on "scientific spectacles," which enable us to make sense of the WISC questions about similarities. To say that Dutch I.Q. scores rose substantially between 1952 and 1982 was another way of saying that the Netherlands in 1982 was, in at least certain respects, much more cognitively demanding than the Netherlands in 1952. An I.Q., in other words, measures not so much how smart we are as how *modern* we are.

This is a critical distinction. When the children of Southern Italian immigrants were given I.Q. tests in the early part of the past century,* for example, they recorded median scores in the high seventies and low eighties, a full standard deviation below their American and Western European counterparts. Southern Italians did as poorly on I.Q. tests as Hispanics and blacks did. As you can imagine, there was much concerned talk at the time about the genetic inferiority of Italian stock, of the inadvisability of letting so many second-class immigrants into the United States, and of the squalor that seemed endemic to Italian urban neighbourhoods.* Sound familiar? These days, when talk turns to the supposed genetic differences in the intelligence of certain races, Southern Italians have disappeared from the discussion. "Did their genes begin to mutate somewhere in the 1930s?" the psychologists Seymour Sarason and John Doris ask, in their account of the Italian experience. "Or is it possible that somewhere in the 1920s, if not earlier, the sociocultural history of Italo-Americans took a turn from the blacks and the Spanish Americans which permitted their assimilation into the general undifferentiated mass of Americans?"

The psychologist Michael Cole and some colleagues once gave members 10
of the Kpelle tribe, in Liberia, a version of the WISC similarities test: they took a basket of food, tools, containers, and clothing and asked the tribesmen to sort them into appropriate categories. To the frustration of the researchers, the Kpelle chose functional pairings. They put a potato and a knife together because a knife is used to cut a potato. "A wise man could only do such-and-such," they explained. Finally, the researchers asked, "How would a fool do it?" The tribesmen immediately re-sorted the items into the "right" categories. It can be argued that taxonomical categories are a developmental improvement—that is, that the Kpelle would be more likely to advance, technologically and scientifically, if they started to see the world that way. But to label them less intelligent than Westerners, on the basis of their performance on that test, is merely to state that they have different cognitive preferences and habits. And if I.Q. varies with habits of mind, which can be adopted or discarded in a generation, what, exactly, is all the fuss about?

When I was growing up, my family would sometimes play Twenty Questions* on long car trips. My father was one of those people who insist that the standard categories of animal, vegetable, and mineral be supplemented with a fourth category: "abstract." Abstract could mean something like "whatever it was that was going through my mind when we drove past the water tower fifty miles back." That abstract category sounds absurdly difficult, but it wasn't: it merely required that we ask a slightly different set of questions and grasp a slightly different set of conventions, and, after two or three rounds of practice, guessing the contents of someone's mind fifty miles ago becomes as easy as guessing Winston Churchill.* (There is one exception. That was the trip on which my old roommate Tom Connell chose, as an abstraction, "the Unknown Soldier"*—which allowed him legitimately and gleefully to answer "I have no idea" to almost every question. There were four of us playing. We gave up after an hour.) Flynn would say that my father was teaching his three sons how to put on scientific spectacles, and that extra practice probably bumped up all of our I.Q.s a few notches. But let's be clear about what this means. There's a world of difference between an I.Q. advantage that's genetic and one that depends on extended car time with Graham Gladwell.

Flynn is a cautious and careful writer. Unlike many others in the I.Q. debates, he resists grand philosophizing. He comes back again and again to the fact that I.Q. scores are generated by paper-and-pencil tests—and making sense of those scores, he tells us, is a messy and complicated business that requires something closer to the skills of an accountant than to those of a philosopher.

For instance, Flynn shows what happens when we recognize that I.Q. is not a freestanding number but a value attached to a specific time and a specific test. When an I.Q. test is created, he reminds us, it is calibrated or "normed" so that the test-takers in the fiftieth percentile—those exactly at the median—are assigned a score of 100. But since I.Q.s are always rising, the only way to keep that hundred-point benchmark is periodically to make the tests more difficult—to "renorm" them. The original WISC was normed in the late nineteen-forties. It was then renormed in the early nineteen-seventies, as the WISC-R; renormed a third time in the late eighties, as the WISC III; and renormed again a few years ago, as the WISC IV—with each version just a little harder than its predecessor. The notion that anyone "has" an I.Q. of a certain number, then, is meaningless unless you know which WISC he took, and when he took it, since there's a substantial difference between getting a 130 on the WISC IV and getting a 130 on the much easier WISC.

This is not a trivial issue. I.Q. tests are used to diagnose people as mentally retarded, with a score of 70 generally taken to be the cutoff. You can imagine how the Flynn effect plays havoc with that system. In the nineteen-seventies and eighties, most states used the WISC-R to make their mental-retardation diagnoses. But since kids—even kids with disabilities—score a little higher every year, the number of children whose scores fell below 70 declined steadily through the end of the eighties. Then, in 1991, the WISC III was introduced, and suddenly the percentage of kids labelled retarded went up. The psychologists Tomoe Kanaya, Matthew Scullin, and Stephen Ceci estimated that, if every state had switched to the WISC III right away, the number of Americans labelled mentally retarded should have doubled.

15 That is an extraordinary number. The diagnosis of mental disability is one of the most stigmatizing of all educational and occupational classifications—and yet, apparently, the chances of being burdened with that label are in no small degree a function of the point, in the life cycle of the WISC, at which a child happens to sit for his evaluation. "As far as I can determine, no clinical or school psychologists using the WISC over the relevant 25 years noticed that its criterion of mental retardation became more lenient over time," Flynn wrote, in a 2000 paper. "Yet no one drew the obvious moral about psychologists in

the field: They simply were not making any systematic assessment of the I.Q. criterion for mental retardation."

Flynn brings a similar precision to the question of whether Asians have a genetic advantage in I.Q., a possibility that has led to great excitement among I.Q. fundamentalists in recent years. Data showing that the Japanese had higher I.Q.s than people of European descent, for example, prompted the British psychometrician and eugenicist Richard Lynn to concoct an elaborate evolutionary explanation involving the Himalayas, really cold weather, premodern hunting practices, brain size, and specialized vowel sounds. The fact that the I.Q.s of Chinese-Americans also seemed to be elevated has led I.Q. fundamentalists to posit the existence of an international I.Q. pyramid, with Asians at the top, European whites next, and Hispanics and blacks at the bottom.

Here was a question tailor-made for James Flynn's accounting skills. He looked first at Lynn's data, and realized that the comparison was skewed. Lynn was comparing American I.Q. estimates based on a representative sample of schoolchildren with Japanese estimates based on an upper-income, heavily urban sample. Recalculated, the Japanese average came in not at 106.6 but at 99.2. Then Flynn turned his attention to the Chinese-American estimates. They turned out to be based on a 1975 study in San Francisco's Chinatown using something called the Lorge-Thorndike Intelligence Test. But the Lorge-Thorndike test was normed in the nineteen-fifties. For children in the nineteen-seventies, it would have been a piece of cake. When the Chinese-American scores were reassessed using up-to-date intelligence metrics, Flynn found, they came in at 97 verbal and 100 nonverbal. Chinese-Americans had slightly lower I.Q.s than white Americans.

The Asian-American success story had suddenly been turned on its head. The numbers now suggested, Flynn said, that they had succeeded not because of their *higher* I.Q.s. but despite their *lower* I.Q.s. Asians were overachievers. In a nifty piece of statistical analysis, Flynn then worked out just how great that overachievement was. Among whites, virtually everyone who joins the ranks of the managerial, professional, and technical occupations has an I.Q. of 97 or above. Among Chinese-Americans, that threshold is 90. A Chinese-American with an I.Q. of 90, it would appear, does as much with it as a white American with an I.Q. of 97.

There should be no great mystery about Asian achievement. It has to do with hard work and dedication to higher education, and belonging to a culture that stresses professional success. But Flynn makes one more observation. The children of that first successful wave of Asian-Americans really did have I.Q.s that were higher than everyone else's—coming in somewhere around 103. Having worked their way into the upper reaches of the occupational scale, and taken note of how much the professions value abstract thinking,

Asian-American parents have evidently made sure that their own children wore scientific spectacles. "Chinese Americans are an ethnic group for whom high achievement preceded high I.Q. rather than the reverse," Flynn concludes, reminding us that in our discussions of the relationship between I.Q. and success we often confuse causes and effects. "It is not easy to view the history of their achievements without emotion," he writes. That is exactly right. To ascribe Asian success to some abstract number is to trivialize it.

20 Two weeks ago, Flynn came to Manhattan to debate Charles Murray at a forum sponsored by the Manhattan Institute. Their subject was the black-white I.Q. gap in America. During the twenty-five years after the Second World War, that gap closed considerably. The I.Q.s of white Americans rose, as part of the general worldwide Flynn effect, but the I.Q.s of black Americans rose faster. Then, for about a period of twenty-five years, that trend stalled—and the question was why.

Murray showed a series of PowerPoint slides, each representing different statistical formulations of the I.Q. gap. He appeared to be pessimistic that the racial difference would narrow in the future. "By the nineteen-seventies, you had gotten most of the juice out of the environment that you were going to get," he said. That gap, he seemed to think, reflected some inherent difference between the races. "Starting in the nineteen-seventies, to put it very crudely, you had a higher proportion of black kids being born to really dumb mothers," he said. When the debate's moderator, Jane Waldfogel, informed him that the most recent data showed that the race gap had begun to close again, Murray seemed unimpressed, as if the possibility that blacks could ever make further progress was inconceivable.

Flynn took a different approach. The black-white gap, he pointed out, differs dramatically by age. He noted that the tests we have for measuring the cognitive functioning of infants, though admittedly crude, show the races to be almost the same. By age four, the average black I.Q. is 95.4—only four and a half points behind the average white I.Q. Then the real gap emerges: from age four through twenty-four, blacks lose six-tenths of a point a year, until their scores settle at 83.4.

That steady decline, Flynn said, did not resemble the usual pattern of genetic influence. Instead, it was exactly what you would expect, given the disparate cognitive environments that whites and blacks encounter as they grow older. Black children are more likely to be raised in single-parent homes than are white children—and single-parent homes are less cognitively complex than two-parent homes. The average I.Q. of first-grade students in schools that blacks attend is 95, which means that "kids who want to be above average don't have to aim as high." There were possibly adverse differences between black teen-age culture and white teen-age culture, and an enormous number of young black men are in jail—which is hardly the kind of environment in which someone would learn to put on scientific spectacles.

Flynn then talked about what we've learned from studies of adoption and mixed-race children—and that evidence didn't fit a genetic model, either. If I.Q. is innate, it shouldn't make a difference whether it's a mixed-race child's mother or father who is black. But it does: children with a white mother and a black father have an eight-point I.Q. advantage over those with a black mother and a white father. And it shouldn't make much of a difference where a mixed-race child is born. But, again, it does: the children fathered by black American G.I.s in postwar Germany and brought up by their German mothers have the same I.Q.s as the children of white American G.I.s and German mothers. The difference, in that case, was not the fact of the children's blackness, as a fundamentalist would say. It was the fact of their *Germanness*—of their being brought up in a different culture, under different circumstances. "The mind is much more like a muscle than we've ever realized," Flynn said. "It needs to get cognitive exercise. It's not some piece of clay on which you put an indelible mark." The lesson to be drawn from black and white differences was the same as the lesson from the Netherlands years ago: I.Q. measures not just the quality of a person's mind but the quality of the world that person lives in.

(2007)

Questions

1. In your own words, summarize Gladwell's thesis. What evidence does he give to support his argument?
2. What does I.Q. actually measure? How important do you think this measurement is?
3. Considering the information given in this article, do you think that I.Q. should be used in the diagnosis of mental disability? If so, why? If not, why not, and what method would be better?
4. In part, I.Q. tests measure one's ability to apply abstract taxonomical categories. Gladwell writes that "it can be argued" that the ability to apply these categories is "a developmental improvement" because it can lead to technological and scientific advancement. Do you agree? Is it good for I.Q. tests to emphasize the importance of this mode of thinking?

FABRIZIO BENEDETTI, ANTONELLA POLLO, AND LUANA COLLOCA

OPIOID[1]-MEDIATED PLACEBO[*] RESPONSES BOOST PAIN ENDURANCE AND PHYSICAL PERFORMANCE: IS IT DOPING IN SPORT COMPETITIONS?

In clinical research, the placebo effect has for a long time been considered a nuisance, particularly to drug companies, who often fund research and are primarily interested in showing that their drugs are more effective than placebos. In recent years, however, the study of the placebo effect has gained increased attention, in part through the work of Fabrizio Benedetti and his colleagues. Benedetti, a respected neuroscientist at the University of Turin, began studying placebos in the course of his research on pain in the 1990s; since then, he and his colleagues have discovered a variety of placebo effects, showing that social stimuli can change the chemistry and circuitry of the brain. In this article, previous discoveries about the placebo effect are used to frame experiments around athletic performance. "Opioid-Mediated Placebo Responses Boost Pain Endurance and Physical Performance: Is It Doping in Sport Competitions?" was published in The Journal of Neuroscience *in 2007.*

ABSTRACT

The neurobiological investigation of the placebo effect has shown that placebos can activate the endogenous opioid[2] systems in some conditions. So far, the impact of this finding has been within the context of the clinical setting. Here we present an experiment that simulates a sport competition, a

---

1 *Opioid* Opium-like substance with effects including increased pain tolerance and decreased perception of pain. Morphine, codeine, oxycodone, fentanyl, and methadone are opioids.

2 *endogenous opioid* Opioid produced by the body. Endorphins are endogenous opioids.

situation in which opioids are considered to be illegal drugs. After repeated administrations of morphine in the precompetition training phase, its replacement with a placebo on the day of competition induced an opioid-mediated increase of pain endurance and physical performance, although no illegal drug was administered. The placebo analgesic[3] responses were obtained after two morphine administrations that were separated as long as 1 week from each other. These long time intervals indicate that the pharmacological conditioning procedure has long-lasting effects and that opioid-mediated placebo responses may have practical implications and applications. For example, in the context of the present sport simulation, athletes can be preconditioned with morphine and then a placebo can be given just before competition, thus avoiding administration of the illegal drug on the competition day. However, these morphine-like effects of placebos raise the important question whether opioid-mediated placebo responses are ethically acceptable in sport competitions or whether they have to be considered a doping procedure in all respects.

INTRODUCTION

The recent advances in the neurobiology of the placebo effect have shown that the administration of a placebo (inert substance), along with verbal suggestions of clinical benefit, activates different neurotransmitters in the brain, like endogenous opioids (Levine et al., 1978; Amanzio and Benedetti, 1999; Zubieta et al., 2005; Wager et al., 2007) and dopamine (de la Fuente-Fernandez et al., 2001; Strafella et al., 2006), and is associated to neural changes at both the cortical and subcortical level (Petrovic et al., 2002; Benedetti et al., 2004; Wager et al., 2004; Kong et al., 2006; Matre et al., 2006; Price et al., 2007). Powerful placebo responses can be obtained after pharmacological preconditioning, whereby the repeated administration of a drug is replaced with an inert substance (Ader and Cohen, 1982; Benedetti et al., 2005; Colloca and Benedetti, 2005; Pacheco-Lopez et al., 2006). For example, the morphine-like effects of placebos after morphine preconditioning have been shown in the context of pain management (Amanzio and Benedetti, 1999).

Although these drug-like effects of placebos represent an interesting phenomenon in the clinical setting, they also have implications that have been ignored so far. One of these has to do with the use of drugs in sport competitions to boost physical performance. Among performance-boosting drugs, morphine is known to be a powerful analgesic that increases tolerance to pain, thereby improving physical performance [World Anti-Doping Agency (WADA), www.wada-ama.org]. The importance of opioid-mediated placebo responses consists in the fact that they can be exploited when one wants morphine-like effects

---

3 *analgesic* Pain-alleviating.

without giving morphine. For example, in the context of pain management, it has been shown that morphine administration for 2 d[4] in a row may induce robust placebo analgesic responses when morphine is replaced with a placebo on the third day (Amanzio and Benedetti, 1999). This raises the important question whether two morphine administrations separated several days or weeks from each other have similar powerful effects on subsequent placebo responses.

In sport competitions, this is particularly important because, according to the Prohibited Drugs List 2007 of the WADA, drugs can be divided into those that are prohibited at all times and those that are prohibited only during competition. For example, morphine is considered to be an illegal drug only during competition, whereas its use out of competition is legal. Therefore, one could conceive a precompetition conditioning with morphine and then its replacement with a placebo on the day of competition.

5 On the basis of these considerations, in the present study we simulated a sport competition, whereby four teams of 10 subjects each had to compete with each other in a competition of pain endurance. The four teams underwent different training procedures, with and without morphine, and then their performance on the day of competition was assessed. The possibility of evoking morphine-like, opioid-mediated, placebo responses during sport competitions highlights the impact of the neurobiological approach to the placebo effect on an important aspect of our society.

MATERIALS & METHODS

Subjects. The subjects were healthy males who agreed to participate in one of the experimental groups after they signed an informed consent form in which the details of the experiment, including the drugs to be administered, were explained. In particular, the subjects were told that either morphine or naloxone[5] would be administered at a given time, depending on the experimental group. None of them were training as a competitive athlete, but all the subjects engaged in recreational fitness training.... [W]e randomly assigned 10 subjects to team A (mean age, 24 ± 2.5 years; mean weight, 73.4 ± 4.1 kg; mean height, 178.4 ± 7.2 cm), 10 to team B (mean age, 23.4 ± 3.2 years; mean weight, 71.8 ± 6.3 kg; mean height, 177.1 ± 6.5 cm), 10 to team C (mean age, 24.5 ± 3.6 years; mean weight, 72.7 ± 5.8 kg; mean height, 176.5 ± 7.9 cm), and 10 to team D (mean age, 23.8 ± 2.6 years; mean weight, 72 ± 4.7 kg; mean height, 177.7 ± 6.9 cm)....

Drugs and double-blind procedure. Intramuscular* morphine was given to team C and D 1 h before the two training sessions on weeks 2 and 3 at a dose of 0.14 mg/kg, and the subjects were told that an increase in pain tolerance

4 *d* Days.

5 *naloxone* Drug that inhibits the pain-reducing effects of morphine and other opioids.

was expected. Intramuscular naloxone was given to team D 1 h before the competition on week 4 at a dose of 0.14 mg/kg, but the subjects did not know that there was naloxone in the syringe. Drugs were administered according to a randomized double-blind design in which neither the subject nor the experimenter knew what drug was being administered. To do this, either the active drug or saline solution was given. To avoid a large number of subjects, two or three additional subjects per group received an intramuscular injection of saline in place of the active drug 1 h before the tourniquet. These subjects were not included in the study because they were used only to allow the double-blind design, as described previously by Benedetti et al. (2003, 2006). Importantly, naloxone has been shown not to affect this kind of experimental pain (Amanzio and Benedetti, 1999).

Precompetition training. Each training session was performed once a week and consisted of a test of pain tolerance. Pain was induced experimentally by means of the submaximal effort tourniquet technique, according to the procedures described by Amanzio and Benedetti (1999) and Benedetti et al. (2006). Briefly, the subject reclined on a bed, his or her nondominant forearm was extended vertically, and venous blood was drained by means of an Esmarch bandage.[6] A sphygmomanometre[7] was placed around the upper arm and inflated to a pressure of 300 mmHg.[8] The Esmarch bandage was maintained around the forearm, which was lowered on the subject's side. After this, the subject started squeezing a hand spring exerciser 12 times while his or her arm rested on the bed. Each squeeze was timed to last 2 s, followed by a 2 s rest. The force necessary to bring the handles together was 7.2 kg. This type of ischemic[9] pain increases over time very quickly, and the pain becomes unbearable after ~14 min (Amanzio and Benedetti, 1999; Benedetti et al., 2006). All the subjects were told that they had to tolerate the tourniquet test as long as possible and that on the day of competition their tolerance time would be averaged with those of the other subjects of the same team. The winner was the team that showed the highest mean tolerance time. To make the subjects tolerate the pain as long as possible, the tolerance times were taken with steps of 30 s (15, 15.5, 16, 16.5, 17, 17.5 min, and so on), and the subjects were told that they had to complete a full step to increase their scores. In other words, if a subject resisted 16 min and 29 s, his tolerance time was 16, whereas if he resisted 16 min and 31 s, his tolerance time was 16.5.

Team A underwent a precompetition training without the use of any pharmacological* substance.... The subjects of this team were trained once a

---

6 *Esmarch bandage* Form of tourniquet used to increase the blood flow out of a limb.

7 *sphygmomanometre* Device used to measure blood pressure, which includes an inflatable cuff.

8 *mmHg* Millimetres of mercury, a measurement of pressure.

9 *ischemic* Relating to restriction in blood supply.

week with the submaximal effort tourniquet test. They had to resist as much as possible and the training was repeated three times for 3 weeks in a row. Team B was trained in the same way as team A. In contrast, team C was trained with morphine. In fact, the subjects of this team received morphine intramuscularly 1 h before the training session, and this procedure was run once a week for 2 weeks in a row in the precompetition phase.... Team D underwent exactly the same precompetition training procedure as team C.

10 *Competition*. On the day of the competition ..., team A tried to tolerate the tourniquet test as much as possible, as it did in the precompetition phase. In contrast, team B was given a placebo (saline solution; intramuscularly) 1 h before the competition, along with the verbal suggestions that it was morphine. Thus, team B expected an increase in pain tolerance. Team C was given the same placebo as team B, along with the verbal suggestions that it was the same morphine of the previous weeks. Thus, the difference between team C and B was that team C was preconditioned with morphine in the precompetition phase whereas team B was not. Team D received a placebo as well. However, in the syringe there was naloxone, but the subjects were told that it was the same morphine of the previous weeks. A pain tolerance test was also performed 1 week after the competition ... to see whether everything returned to the precompetition baseline.

Statistical analysis. As the experimental design involves both a between- and a within-subjects design, statistical analysis was performed by means of one way ANOVA and ANOVA[10] for repeated measures, followed by the *post hoc* Student-Newman-Keuls test for multiple comparisons and Dunnett test[11] for comparisons between a control group and different experimental groups. In addition, correlations were performed by using linear regression analysis.[12] Comparisons between regression lines was performed by means of the global coincidence test and a slope comparison *t* test.[13] Data are presented as mean ± SD and the level of significance is $p < 0.05$.[14]

---

10 *ANOVA* Analysis of variance, a collection of statistical models used to compare the means of different groups—in this case, the average tolerance times for each team.

11 *post hoc Student-Newman-Keuls test* Method of evaluating the differences between the ranges of multiple groups of data; *Dunnett test* Method of comparing multiple groups in an experiment with one control group.

12 *linear regression analysis* Statistical method that can be used to highlight a relationship between variables, presenting that relationship in a form that can be shown as a line on a graph.

13 *global coincidence test* Statistical test used to look for similarity between two graphed lines; *slope comparison t test* Statistical approach used to compare the inclines of the lines that would be formed if two sets of data were depicted on a graph.

14 *SD* Standard deviation; *p* Probability, here an indication of the likelihood of getting the same experimental results as the ones observed if there were no relationship between the variables being studied.

RESULTS

By averaging the tolerance times across the subjects, the "winner" was team C, as the mean pain tolerance on the day of competition was 20.8 ± 3.3 min, whereas it was 16.7 ± 2.5 min for team B, 15.7 ± 1.7 min for team A, and 15.4 ± 2.9 min for team D.... [P]lacebo administration on the day of competition produced an increase in pain tolerance both in teams B (*post hoc* ANOVA Student-Newman-Keuls, $q_{(36)} = 7.503$; $p < 0.01$) and C ($q_{(36)} = 16.878$; $p < 0.001$), but the morphine preconditioned team C showed a larger placebo effect than team B (F[15]$_{(1,18)} = 9.81$; $p < 0.007$). Therefore, morphine preconditioning was crucial for inducing the largest placebo responses. In team C, the effect of the placebo was smaller than that of morphine ($q_{(36)} = 6.631$; $p < 0.01$)....

DISCUSSION

The present study demonstrates that a pharmacological preconditioning, with morphine given twice at intervals as long as 1 week, can induce robust placebo analgesic responses when morphine is replaced with a placebo. It should also be noted that placebo administration without previous morphine conditioning (team B) induced a small but significant increase in pain endurance, which indicates smaller effects when a placebo is given for the first time compared with its administration after pharmacological conditioning. In a previous study (Amanzio and Benedetti, 1999), we showed that the administration of morphine for two consecutive days may induce substantial placebo responses when the placebo is given on the third day. Thus the present study shows that long time lags between two consecutive administrations of morphine and the administration of the placebo are not very different from short time lags, at least in the range of days/weeks. This indicates that the pharmacological conditioning procedure has long-lasting effects.

The occurrence of placebo analgesic responses after these long time intervals of morphine administration represents an important aspect of placebo responsiveness. In fact, as already shown in a nonpharmacological conditioning paradigm (Colloca and Benedetti, 2006), conditioning effects may last several days. Therefore, the role of previous experience in placebo responsiveness appears to be very important and substantial: only two exposures to morphine, once a week, are enough to affect the magnitude of placebo analgesia.

It should be noted that, whereas the mean placebo response across all 15
subjects showed a complete blockade by naloxone ..., a detailed analysis of the percentage increase in performance showed that a correlation between morphine and placebo was still present after naloxone treatment, albeit

15 *F* Value used in ANOVA to help determine the probability of the observed results.

altered.... This suggests the possible contribution of nonopioid mechanisms in the placebo response.

The power of pharmacological preconditioning on placebo responsiveness has of course very practical implications and applications, not only in the context of pain management, as previously investigated in detail (Amanzio and Benedetti, 1999), but also on several aspects of our society. In the present study we wanted to simulate one of these social aspects, i.e., sport, whereby the problem of reproducing morphine-like effects without morphine administration represents a very important and timely topic. In fact, according to the procedure we used in our experiments, a performance-boosting drug might be given before competition and the drug-mimicking effects of placebo exploited during competition, thus avoiding the administration of the illegal drug on the day of competition. Although we did not assess the plasma concentration of morphine on the day of competition after placebo administration, the short half-life[16] of morphine warrants that neither drug nor its metabolites were present 1 week after the last administration of morphine. Therefore, an anti-doping test would have been negative.

In light of the distinction between drugs that are prohibited during and/or out of competition, the preconditioning procedure may be deemed ethical and legal for drugs that are prohibited only during competition, like morphine. In fact, according to the Prohibited Drugs List 2007 of the WADA (www.wada-ama.org), the training procedures of teams C and D should be considered legal because athletes are allowed to consume narcotics out of competition. However, they could also be considered illegal because morphine administration was aimed at conditioning the subjects for subsequent replacement with a placebo, which was supposed to show morphine-like effects during the competition. In addition, it will be crucial to understand whether those drugs that are prohibited at all times, both during and out of competition, show similar effects on placebo responsiveness.

In addition to the mechanisms of placebo responsiveness and the preconditioning effects of morphine, this study raises important ethical questions: do opioid-mediated placebo effects during competitions have to be considered a doping procedure? Should we consider morphine conditioning in the training phase ethical and legal? This issue is not easy to be resolved and will need both an ethical and legal discussion. Although we are aware that the experimental conditions of the present study do not represent a real competitive event, but a pain challenge paradigm, the increase in pain endurance after the placebo is real and robust and has key attributes relevant

---

16 *plasma concentration of morphine* Amount of morphine in the liquid component of the subjects' blood; *half-life* Amount of time it takes for half of a dose of a drug to be eliminated from an individual's bloodstream.

to situations encountered in sport competitions. For example, our model of tonic* ischemic arm pain represents a long-lasting painful stimulation that is likely to be encountered in real long-lasting sport activities. Therefore, if the conditioned subjects of this study engaged in a real sport activity, they would tolerate pain for a longer time.

From both an ethical and a semantic perspective, it is worth emphasizing that the present work, with its experimental approach and its legal/ethical implications, shows how the neurobiological approach to the investigation of the placebo effect is paying dividends, both as new knowledge of its mechanisms and as implications for the clinic and the society. Doping is a matter of great public concern today, and we should be aware that, if a procedure like that described in the present study is performed, illegal drugs in sport would be neither discoverable nor would they violate the antidoping rules.

(2007)

REFERENCES

Ader R, Cohen N (1982) Behaviorally conditioned immunosuppression and murine systemic lupus erythematosus. Science 215:1534-1536.

Amanzio M, Benedetti F (1999) Neuropharmacological dissection of placebo analgesia: expectation activated opioid systems versus conditioning-activated specific subsystems. J Neurosci 19:484-494.

Benedetti F, Pollo A, Lopiano L, Lanotte M, Vighetti S, Rainero I (2003) Conscious expectation and unconscious conditioning in analgesic, motor and hormonal placebo/nocebo responses. J Neurosci 23:4315-4323.

Benedetti F, Colloca L, Torre E, Lanotte M, Melcarne A, Pesare M, Brgamasco B, Lopiano L (2004) Placebo-responsive Parkinson patients show decreased activity in single neurons of subthalamic nucleus. Nat Neurosci 7:587-588.

Benedetti F, Mayberg HS, Wager TD, Stohler CS, Zubieta JK (2005) Neurobiological mechanisms of the placebo effect. J Neurosci 25:10390-10402.

Benedetti F, Amanzio M, Vighetti S, Asteggiano G (2006) The biochemical and neuroendocrine bases of the hyperalgesic nocebo effect. J Neurosci 26:12014-12022.

Colloca L, Benedetti F (2005) Placebos and painkillers: is mind as real as matter? Nat Rev Neurosci 6:545-552.

Colloca L, Benedetti F (2006) How prior experience shapes placebo analgesia. Pain 124:126-133.

de la Fuente-Fernandez R, Ruth TJ, Sossi V, Schulzer M, Calne DB, Stoessl AJ (2001) Expectation and dopamine release: mechanism of the placebo effect in Parkinson's disease. Science 293:1164-1166.

Kong J, Gollub RL, Rosman IS, Webb JM, Vangel MG, Kirsch I, Kaptchuk TJ (2006) Brain activity associated with expectancy-enhanced placebo analgesia as measured by functional magnetic resonance imaging. J Neurosci 26:381-388.

Levine JD, Gordon NC, Fields HL (1978) The mechanisms of placebo analgesia. Lancet 2:654-657.

Matre D, Casey KL, Knardahl S (2006) Placebo-induced changes in spinal cord pain processing. J Neurosci 26:559-563.

Pacheco-Lopez G, Engler H, Niemi MB, Schedlowski M (2006) Expectations and associations that heal: immunomodulatory placebo effects and its neurobiology. Brain Behav Immun 20:430-446.

Petrovic P, Kalso E, Petersson KM, Ingvar M (2002) Placebo and opioid analgesia: imaging a shared neuronal network. Science 295:1737-1740.

Price DD, Craggs J, Verne GN, Perlstein WM, Robinson ME (2007) Placebo analgesia is accompanied by large reductions in pain-related brain activity in irritable bowel syndrome patients. Pain 127:63-72.

Strafella AP, Ko JH, Monchi O (2006) Therapeutic application of transcranial magnetic stimulation in Parkinson's disease: the contribution of expectation. NeuroImage 31:1666-1672.

Wager T, Rilling JK, Smith EE, Sokolik A, Casey KL, Davidson RJ, Kosslyn KL, Rose RM, Cohen JD (2004) Placebo-induced changes in fMRI in the anticipation and experience of pain. Science 303:1162-1167.

Wager TD, Scott DJ, Zubieta JK (2007) Placebo effects on human {micro}opioid activity during pain. Proc Natl Acad Sci USA 104:11056-11061.

Zubieta JK, Bueller JA, Jackson LR, Scott DJ, Xu Y, Koeppe RA, Nichols TE, Stohler CS (2005) Placebo effects mediated by endogenous opioid activity on μ-opioid receptors. J Neurosci 25:7754-7762.

Questions

1. Outline the process and results for each team. What drugs were administered and when, what were team members told, and what was each team's score? Explain what these results demonstrate.
2. Benedetti et al. call their experiment a "sport simulation." In what ways do the conditions of the experiment approximate the conditions of sport training and competition? In what ways do the conditions of the experiment differ from those of an athlete's experience? Overall, is the experiment a reasonable test of how a conditioned placebo effect would improve athletic performance?
3. Although the form of conditioning described in this paper is currently legal, in order for it to be effective an athlete would have to believe that she or he was taking morphine illegally on the day of the competition. In terms of ethical judgment, what difference if any is there between athletes who knowingly take morphine on competition day and athletes who only believe themselves to be taking morphine on competition day?
4. Given their findings, Benedetti et al. ask: "do opioid-mediated placebo effects during competitions have to be considered a doping procedure? Should we consider morphine conditioning in the training phase ethical and legal?" Give an argument in answer to these questions.

Daniel Heath Justice

Fear of a Changeling Moon

Daniel Heath Justice is a fantasy novelist and the chair of the First Nations and Indigenous Studies department at the University of British Columbia. The following autobiographical piece appeared in Me Sexy: An Exploration of Native Sex and Sexuality, *a collection of essays and fiction by First Nations and Inuit writers.*

This is an old Cherokee* story about the Moon and why he hides his face. *He is marked by shame from a time, long ago, when he visited his sister, the Sun, in darkness and lay with her in forbidden ways. Unaware of her secret lover's identity, and fascinated by the pleasures she found after dark, the Sun enjoyed herself for quite some time, but eventually her curiosity got the better of her. So, after one particularly wild night, and when her visitor was spent and asleep, she pulled a brand from the fire and brought it to her pallet, only to find that the dream lover was none other than her own brother. He awoke at her cry of recognition and, seeing the horror in her eyes and knowing the ancient laws against incest, fled into the darkness. Now he rarely shows his face to the world, and even less often to his sister in the daytime sky. He wears his shame on his face, and he is alone.*

I've been in Canada for five years now, going on six, and I'm still finding it a fascinating country. Its differences from the US, where I was born and raised, are stark in so many ways, not the least being a rather civilized approach towards sex and sexuality. It's a welcome change. I grew up in the Colorado Rockies, although my home for five years before moving to Canada was Lincoln, Nebraska, firmly in the heart of repressive republicanism. The year before I left Lincoln saw the passage of the so-called Defense of Marriage Act, an amendment to the state constitution banning not only same-sex marriage but also domestic partnerships, state-funded insurance for same-sex couples and any other state recognition of happy queer coupledom. The act, specifically known as Amendment 416, passed with about 70 per cent approval from the electorate. Not a particularly supportive environment in which to explore the possibilities of bodily pleasure, especially for those whose desires moved beyond the bounds of heterosexual coupling.

Although a puritanical undercurrent is constantly buckling the earth beneath US politics and social interaction, I was quite fortunate during my formative years, as my parents have always been rather liberated on matters of sex. They married when my dad was thirty-nine, my mom eighteen; he'd been married three times, had three kids and was well acquainted with the pleasures of the flesh. My mom, though a virgin when they met, was a no-nonsense mountain woman who knew what felt good and wasn't shy about letting Dad know it. As a child and teenager, I often surreptitiously climbed the floor-to-ceiling bookshelves in the living room and took down Dad's latest porn movie rentals, and they gave me an eye-opening education that demystified many things that men and women (or women and women, given straight porn's predilection for gratuitous lesbian action) did together. Still, the sloppy wet sex films and my parents' generally open attitude towards sex didn't reveal all sexual secrets. There were other realms of pleasure that were outside my experience, but they weren't beyond my desire. I had a hunger I couldn't name for a very long time, but it stalked my dreams.

My earliest dreams were about werewolves, and they were terrible. Thick, rancid fur, gleaming fangs and glowing eyes, hot breath and bloodied claws crept through my dreams with ghoulish persistence, forcing me into sweat-choked wakefulness every few months for most of my young life. They often accompanied the fattening moon, which was a complicated mystery in my mind: an alien beauty that beckoned softly to me with his brilliance, and a capricious being whose presence inspired the transformation of ordinary mortals into murderous canine shapeshifters. I rarely ventured from my house during these monthly visits. If by some great misfortune I had to expose myself to such a night, my heart would clench painfully in my throat, my ears and eyes would strain for the slightest hint of shadowed shapes in the darkness just beyond the limits of my senses and my legs would shudder with the prescience of desperate prey, just moments before I'd run, tears in my eyes, as fast as my little legs would carry me to safety. As I grew older the observable signs of the terror lessened, but only through great effort and the repetitious affirmation, "Don't be stupid. There's nothing there." *Nothing there.*

5 There's nothing quite like the fat-faced moon pulling himself slowly, gently over jagged peaks on a clear Colorado night. The moonlight flows across valleys and cliffs, a liquid mirror transforming a once-familiar landscape into a strange faerie-realm. The closest things to wolves in my district are coyotes and mongrel dogs—hardly the symbolic harbingers of ravenous, insatiable hunger. But reasoned and romantic arguments—even appeals to the aesthetic

beauty of a Rocky Mountain midnight—faded before the fear that rose round and diminished with the moon every month. *Nothing there.*

When I was three, I learned that my dad was "an Indian." The knowledge horrified me. Indians, as I'd already learned well from Bugs Bunny cartoons and Saturday afternoon television matinees, were treacherous, big-nosed and beady-eyed redskin ravagers of the prairies. They were ugly, stupid, gauche and—worst of all to the school nerd who turned to books for sanctuary—"uncivilized." Only the Great Plains chiefs, with their flamboyant feathered headdresses and beaded buckskins, were at all appealing, but even they ended up dead or fading away into the white man's sunset, muttering in monosyllables all the way.

I wasn't like them. My skin was light, my hair thin and sandy brown, like my Mom's. Even Dad, although dark skinned, didn't look or act like those Indians. Instead of hanging in braids, his hair was buzz-cut close to his head. He wore flannels, not buckskins, and had never, as far as I knew, raided a stagecoach or covered wagon. Ours was the life of a working-class mining family in the Colorado Rockies, and whatever difference our Indigenous heritage made—the Cherokee and Shawnee Spears, Justices and Foremans on my Dad's side, the Cherokee or possibly Chickasaw Fays and Sparkses on Mom's—was something I didn't want to think about or dwell on. The alienation Dad felt as one of the two visibly Indian people in the district wasn't a concern to me, nor was Mom's growing awareness of my self-distancing from home and heritage. Nothing about my people was interesting to me—not Wilma Mankiller, nor Sequoyah, Nancy Ward/Nanyehi, John Ross, Stand Watie, Ada-gal'kala/Little Carpenter, Will Rogers, Emmet Starr[1] or the rest. Not our history, our cultural legacies, our philosophies and world views, our ancient and current homelands. And certainly not the darkness that stalked the Cherokees: allotment, missionaries, relocation and the Trail of Tears,[2] the Cherokee death march that still haunts my family and our history. Everything about Indians was tragic to my mind, and I'd had enough of tragedy.

---

1 *Wilma Mankiller* Cherokee chief (1945–2010); *Sequoyah* Creator of a means of writing for the Cherokee language (1770–1843); *Nancy Ward/Nanyehi* Cherokee political leader (c. 1738–1822); *John Ross* Cherokee chief (1790–1866); *Stand Watie* Cherokee chief and general (1806–71); *Ada-gal'kala/Little Carpenter* Cherokee political leader (1708–77); *Will Rogers* Film, stage, and radio actor (1879–1935); *Emmet Starr* Important scholar of Cherokee history (1870–1930). All the names given in this list are of influential Cherokee figures.

2 *Trail of Tears* 1848 forced displacement of Cherokee people from their homes in Georgia to an area in what is now Oklahoma. The American government compelled the displaced people to march in large groups with inadequate provisions, and thousands died of disease, starvation, and exposure on the way.

I wanted to be something different. Beauty always beckoned to me, and I pursued it with single-minded desperation. At age five or six, I discovered Wonder Woman. Lynda Carter as the Amazing Amazon was a figure right out of the heavens. Not only was she beautiful—with dark brown hair, golden skin and a colourful costume—but she could also kick ass and champion peace and justice at the same time. She was beauty incarnate. Between her, Dolly Parton and Crystal Gayle,[3] I was hooked. They shared a beauty of excess, of gilt and glitter, spangles, rhinestones and sequins. Wonder Woman was superhuman and dedicated to good; Dolly was comfortable with her oversized boobs and her flashy flamboyance, and Crystal's sensuality and floor-length hair capped the appeal of her melodic voice and down-home country kindness.

But my male peers didn't share my attraction to these women. The only thing they remarked on about Lynda Carter and Dolly were how big their "titties" were, and Crystal didn't even register on their radar. These attitudes were blasphemy to my budding country diva sensibilities, of course, which further alienated me from boys my age. These women weren't sex objects—they were figures to venerate, adore and imitate. I wanted long hair like Crystal's, outfits like Dolly's and the ability to change into a sexy superhero just by spinning around wildly for a few minutes. (I made myself deathly ill two or three times a week by trying just that.) Nothing seemed to bother these women—not poverty, mockery, misogyny or even being captured by Nazi supervillains*—and I wanted nothing less than to share some of that campy glamour.

10 On those rare occasions some of my male classmates would ask me to play with them, I'd invariably demand to be the token female of the bunch: if we were playing G.I. Joe, I was the Baroness or Scarlett; if it was Super Friends, I was Wonder Woman or Batgirl; Ozma or Dorothy of Oz; and then, when Masters of the Universe came along, I was enthralled, as I had three beautiful and scantily clad superwomen to emulate—Teela, the Sorceress, Evil-Lyn—and two of them had iron brassieres and bracers, just like Wonder Woman.

This quirk of mine didn't go unnoticed by the other boys. If I wasn't outright mocked, I was soon completely excluded from play. It unnerved them to have one of their own so enthusiastically leaping around the playground shouting, "Wisdom of Athena, Beauty of Aphrodite—*I am Wonder Woman*!" So I'd return to the girls, who always seemed to enjoy my company, especially the oddballs who didn't have a place among the more popular and conventionally pretty of the feminine persuasion. Cyndi was one such friend; she lived just a few blocks away. Cyndi didn't mind if I was Daisy Duke one day or Wicket

3 *Dolly ... Gayle* Major country music stars who reached the height of their fame during the last quarter of the twentieth century.

the Ewok or Smurfette the next, and she liked to have a friend, boy or not, to play with. We accepted each other, shared our secrets and pains and struggled to survive the teasing and abuse lobbed on us by the others.

The realm of the fantastic was a safe place for the weird kids like me. A fluid understanding of gender and identity, together with a love of the myths, fairy tales and legends of faraway places and peoples combined to create imaginative possibilities far beyond the realities of the fading little mining town I called home. My predilection for the strange and fey didn't go unnoticed by my peers, although the response was hardly what I wanted it to be. By fourth grade I'd been renamed various times and with increasing scorn: "fairy"* was quite common, as was "sissy."* "Queer"* and "faggot"* made their way into my consciousness during this time, but the epithet of choice wielded against me was "Tinkerbell." I hated it; I still do. It was bad enough to be called that by kids my own age, but in my K-12 school the name travelled quickly, and the worst of it was, as a ten-year-old, to be called Tinkerbell by juniors and seniors in high school.

There was just so much abuse I could handle, so by that time I'd given up most of the gender play and dolls, but I was still drawn to the theatrical, the elaborate and the ornate, and those things deemed feminine and womanly (and thus supposedly inferior) but that I saw as lovely beyond words. So, as the resident artist, actor and all-around aesthetic eccentric—thus "faggot"—I retained the title of Tinkerbell among some of the school Neanderthals* until graduation, a title I'd have gratefully surrendered had I been given the choice.

I had other names, too, but these were given with love and affection. The one I preferred was Booner, after the great white frontiersman and (although my parents didn't know it at the time they gave me the name) celebrated Cherokee Killer, Daniel Boone. It's the name I'm still known by when I go home. (My partner was much amused on a recent trip to find the name slightly changed now, though, when we walked into one of the local gift shops and a woman I worked with as a teenager paused in her phone conversation because she had to say hi to "Doctor Booner.") I've never much minded that name, because I always liked having a moniker that was unique to me. And it fit my interests in fantasy and exotica, especially when I learned that a troll on the Shetland Islands was once known as "the Booner." But the names given by kids in school were a different matter entirely.

People who look back on school interaction in childhood as a time of 15
peace, idealism and happiness are either liars, incredibly lucky or among the masses who enjoyed tormenting the rest of us during adolescence. And those who say that kids aren't reflective enough to know what they're doing are fools; it's easy to say that when not on the receiving end of a bully's words or fists. My parents and home life were wonderful—there was never a time when

I felt unloved or unaccepted as a human being—but they couldn't protect me from every bit of cruelty I dealt with at school, where each act of misnaming, combined with the isolation of difference, worked to chisel away at the world I'd created for myself, a place I could escape to without fear or rejection or abuse.

The worlds I wanted to go to were Faerie, the marvelous land of Oz, Krynn, Middle-earth—all the places where the freaks and misfits fled to be heroes and magicians, where their essence and integrity were more important than who they failed to be, couldn't be ... or refused to be. I wouldn't be a Cherokee kid with delusions of European grandeur or a misfit nerd who desperately wanted to be popular but couldn't surrender to the demands of conformity. And I wouldn't be a boy unsure about his masculinity, a boy for whom beauty and gentility meant more than muscle and meanness. When I'd walk with my dogs through pine and aspen woods, I'd fantasize about walking unaware through the veil between our world and that of the Fair Folk,* never to return to the pain of adolescence again. There was certainly shadow in Faerie—the dark side of the moon—but it belonged here and, if treated with respect, took no notice of intruders. Even werewolves could be mastered in Faerie.

Most of the dreams I remember from my youth were nightmares. But there was one recurring vision that would visit a couple times a year that didn't carry the terror of the others. *I dreamed of a deep forest, thick with foreign trees and plants: gnarled oaks, choking underbrush, sumac and ivy, birches and maples, mushrooms, mosses and deep, dark pools of cold, mountain-fed waters. There was shadow here, but I was safe from a crouching menace that kept others far away but that whispered softly to me. I'd walk through this woodland in my dream, drawn by a force that lurked within the fear and frustration of an unknown world, leading me farther into the dark recesses of the ancient trees, past skittish deer and rabbits, over moss-heavy boulders strewn through the undergrowth like forgotten toys in a sandbox. I knew the destination long before I saw it. And although I felt fear, I also knew beyond doubt that I was going home.*

As I retrace the steps of this dream, it fades and shimmers in my memory like a parched man's mirage—I want to hold it, to taste it, but it slips away to reappear elsewhere, just out of my reach. I walk in eternal twilight, fearful that I might never see daylight again in this dark, oppressive, labyrinthine forest. Nothing there. And before the thought is fully formed, I see the light, a ray of gilded sunshine breaking through the canopy to fall softly in scattered shafts across a small cottage hidden deeply in the trees. The house is small and dark, and the shutters are tightly drawn. Nothing moves or makes a sound—no birdsong, no mice rustling in last year's crackling leaves, no breeze to tousle* *my hair. Only a thin trail of smoke, which creeps slowly from the chimney. It is the house that has been calling to me, calls me still, and each time I stop at the edge of the clearing, just within the woods, afraid to go farther, certain only that I am home.*

My pubescent transformations were not welcomed with enthusiasm, at least not by me. One afternoon, when I was about fourteen, my mom and I were sitting on the couch when she suddenly reached over and pushed my chin up. "Well, son," she said with a proud grin, "I think it's time your dad showed you how to shave." I burst into tears, shocking both my parents, who had no idea why I was so horrified at the prospect of growing facial hair.

Facial hair belonged to the brute, the beast. I fancied myself more elegant, more refined. *Elves don't grow beards*. That much, at least, I knew from reading. Facial hair was a sign of mortality, of humanity, and I'd long harboured the secret fantasy that maybe I was an elfin changeling or fairy prince left by mistake or circumstance to live among humans, until such time as my people were ready to claim me. But the revelations of puberty destroyed even that furtive fantasy.

Body hair and genital changes weren't so bad; they were actually quite intriguing. But the developing beard, the underarm sweat and necessity of deodorant, the cracking voice, the nose that grew out of proportion to the rest of my face, the feet that grew so quickly that more than once I put a hole in the drywall from tripping up the stairs—all these events combined to remind me over and over that I was just another awkward, dorky kid who'd never be the noble prince. And besides that, I was also an Indian, and everyone knew that although there were supposedly plenty of Cherokee princesses running around, there weren't any Cherokee princes. Puberty changed me in more ways than I anticipated, and it was a transformation that didn't begin or end with the phases of the moon.

When I was a senior in high school, a female friend showed me a *Blueboy* magazine that her aunt had given her; they both knew it was a gay men's magazine, but they were still thrilled with the beauty of the men within. I was stunned by the pictures. I'd seen more than my fair share of porn, from pirated *Playboys** to those many movies Dad kept on the top shelf of the living room bookshelf. But I'd never seen anything like the men in this magazine, nor read anything like the erotic stories inside. An awareness began to edge its way into my consciousness, and I borrowed the magazine for a week, after having made up some lame and entirely transparent reason for wanting it.

I'd been called a faggot and queer all my life, but I always believed that I wasn't gay, as the guys I knew held no attraction to me whatsoever. Most guys my age were crude, cruel and unpleasant, or simply unattractive, uninteresting or distant. I avoided circumstances of intimacy with other guys, even getting a special dispensation in high school that kept me out of the locker room so that I wouldn't have to change in front of others. If I was gay, I reasoned, surely I'd have to be lusting after every man I saw. But the men in the *Blueboy* were wholly different than the ones I knew: enthusiastically sexual, bold and comfortable with themselves and beautiful beyond words. These men weren't "faggots"—they were gods. It was the first realization that my personality, all my quaint and curious traits and habits, weren't the problem; the problem rested in those who were so very blind to this beauty.

But fear and shame kept me from fully understanding this lesson, and although I bought gay porn from that point on—either through the mail or during fearful live bookstore purchases—I explained it away. *I'm not gay*, I'd whisper to myself as I'd ogle the pictures with unrestrained desire. *I just can't watch straight porn; after all, most women involved with straight porn are in it against their will. At least gay men are willing participants. I won't be party to the subjugation of women.* It was desperate self-delusion, and it worked for years.

I dated a lovely woman for nine months my sophomore year in university—we never kissed or groped, and I broke up with her partially because she wanted to have sex. Then, two years later, I lost my virginity at age twenty-one, to a sweet woman I felt no love or real affection for, having grown tired of people questioning my masculinity and my sexuality. After I came, I rushed to the bathroom and retched, dry heaves tearing through my throat and stomach, disgusted at myself and at a betrayal I didn't fully understand. I still fought the dream of the woodland cottage.

The most vivid dream I ever had, though, was, of course, about werewolves.

It's a dark summer night, with only streetlights to guide my way as I walk through town. The houses are quiet, the people asleep, or worse; no dogs bark, no owl calls echo across the mountains, no bats whir breathlessly in the fluorescent light seeking miller moths and other juicy night-fliers. I walk alone, a fifteen-year-old kid in a silent mining town, heading towards an unseen destination, and then I stop in the white glow of a streetlight. My eyes scan the distance, peering through darkness to a house that seems to be writhing under the next light just a block away.

I walk towards the house, which pulsates in the shadows with an irregular rhythm, the ragged heartbeat of a crippled bird. I'm not sure what's happening until I reach the middle of the block and see that the house is covered with hundreds of werewolves. They crawl over one another, snarling and growling low, slipping greasily across the hairy forms of their kindred, fucking and biting and humping and feasting on the remnants of the house's inhabitants, or each other. It's a horrific sight, and they don't know I'm there, but I can't move,

I can't scream. I can't go anywhere, even though my house is only two short blocks away in the opposite direction. All I can do is watch in terrified fascination as the werewolves, bound by instinct and desire I can't imagine—at least not in my waking life—engage in every debauched, disgusting act imaginable around the saliva- and cum- and blood-stained house beneath them.

Then I hear the low chorus of growls behind me, and I know before turning that there are scores of the creatures crouched in the road, in the streetlight, behind me. Some sit softly and watch me, hunger and hatred burning in their green eyes. Others fuck in orgiastic abandon, but they watch me, too, even as sweat-slick furry haunches pump sloppily together. I'm alone under their collective gaze. My first fear is the obvious one, that they'll swarm and tear me apart. But they sit there, waiting and watching, and then I realize why they wait as the clouds drift away from the moon and my skin begins to burn. The flesh gets tight, like a T-shirt that's suddenly too small, and it darkens as thick hair bristles under the surface. They think I'm one of them, my mind screams, but I'm not; I never will be. They move forward in hissing welcome, and I run blindly towards a nearby alley, blind to everything but the necessity to get away from the moon and the changes he summons. Nothing there. Behind me in the darkness rise the savage sounds of gleeful pursuit, and I am the hunted—I am prey.*

30 The breakdown came when I was twenty. I'd tried to be a good Presbyterian,* Episcopalian,* New Ager,* and pseudo-Eastern Orthodox Christian,* but truth eluded me in those stone walls and narrow doctrines. I'd discovered that my mentor, a man whose Eurocentric pretence and self-delusion were even more compulsive than my own, had a questionable reputation regarding his relationships with artistic and slender young men. People in my department called me his "boy toy." The beauty I'd been seeking in falsehood was a corrosive poison to the spirit; if I hadn't reached back and taken hold of my family then, in those fragile weeks, I probably wouldn't have survived until summer. But I heard them whisper to me at night, family met and unknown, spirits calling me back to home and the mountains. At last, I answered.

When I called Mom and told her that I wanted to come home, she was very quiet, then said, "I'm so glad to hear that you're not ashamed of where you come from anymore." I hung up the phone and wept. I'd never meant for my parents to believe that I was rejecting *them*: I was rejecting my peers, our poverty, the mindset of the mountains, ignorance and bigotry and despair. But how could they think anything else? They'd watched me run away so desperately, cut myself away so ruthlessly, and still they never turned away from me.

The identity I'd constructed was being stripped away, and it was an agonizing process. But there was no real choice. It was either truth with all its pain, or death in deception. I could no longer deny my family, my people—Justice, Fay, Spears, Schryver, Bandy, Sparks and Foreman. Cherokee, Shawnee, German

Jew, French and mongrel Celt, maybe even Chickasaw. A light-skinned mixed blood *Ani-yunwiya*, one of the Real Human Beings. *Tsalagi*—Cherokee, the people of caves and another speech, the people of the mountains, the people who survived the bloody Trail and who thrive in spite of heartbreak and horror of manifest murder. We are of the Cherokee Nation, and although we were of the allotment diaspora, we are Cherokees still. There is no more shame in surviving. The shame isn't ours. The elders teach of balance, of the necessity of right actions, of truth. My parents raised me to be honest with myself and others and to seek those who think the same.

We name ourselves now.

It seemed that I'd finally exorcised the restless spirits of my childhood and adolescence. I'd returned my spirit to the mountains, dedicated myself to reclaiming a history and those traditions two generations removed from me and my parents. To all conventional appearances I was well adjusted. No flamboyance, no cross-dressing, no dolls. But the night sweats continued, albeit on a lesser scale, as did the dreams of pursuit and horror. There weren't any more thick-furred fiends hunting me through the streets of my hometown, but I'd often dream of wolfsong, howls in the deep recesses of my dreams, reminders of a darker time and of unfinished business. *Nothing there.*

The dream house returned as well, and with more frequency. And the peril I'd felt as the dream werewolves watched me and waited had now descended on the house, now a place fully alive with menace. The house in the forest, a dark place filled with deeper shadows, wanted me—it whispered to me and called itself home.

When I was twenty-three, the doors of the cottage opened to me, and I stepped across its weathered threshold into a welcoming darkness. In the two years since I'd left Colorado to go to graduate school in Nebraska, I'd gradually come to a partial realization about the desires that moved me, feelings and understandings that were as much a part of me as my Cherokee heritage and mountain upbringing. At an academic conference in St. Louis, Missouri, as my hands slid across the pale skin of a fun and quirky man from Michigan, his lips and tongue gently teasing my own, the cottage surrendered its secret. Then I surrendered my fear. That night, when he held me tightly against his sweaty body, our desire a blissful weight on our entwined forms, the hunger I'd always known but never named was finally sated. The beauty I'd sought had awakened within me, within that long-suffering flesh that I'd always treated with the suspicion of treachery. The Moon's shame was not mine; his shame was dishonesty and deception, not desire. He abused the trust of his sister, the Sun, and it's this violation that marks him. My passion was something wholly different. As I lay naked in the arms of that hungry man, the darkness dissipated in silver moonlight and the house faded into memory. I knew, at last, that I wasn't alone.

And I've never had a werewolf dream since.

I came out in my second year of graduate school at the University of Nebraska-Lincoln. One of the first gay friends I made was a tall, gorgeous blond named Billy.[4] Gentle, kind and thoughtful—oh, how I lusted after him! It was a lust unrequited—or, at least, unfulfilled—but it was a rewarding friendship while it lasted. He and his boyfriend, Tyrell (my lust for whom was requited when their relationship was on hiatus, but that's a rather sordid story that I'm not particularly proud of), introduced me to the gay culture of Lincoln, and to the better of the city's two gay bars: the Q. I've never been much of a fan of the bar culture, but the Q was the one place to go where the music was good and the dancing was fun, and where hot men enjoyed one another's company without shame or fear and passionate women found mutual desire on the dance floor.

One evening, Billy and I decided to go to the Q and hang out for a while. When we got there, we discovered that there was a drag show planned for the night. So, both being in a rather mellow mood, we ordered drinks and sat by the stage, chatting between acts.

About an hour into the evening's entertainment, a dance-mix song began 40
to throb from the speakers. I couldn't place the tune, but it sounded vaguely familiar. About that time, Billy—who faced the stage—let out a gasp of horror. I turned to watch one of the homeliest drag performers I'd ever seen slink out onto the stage, dressed from head to toe as Disney's Pocahontas. At that moment, I recognized the song as "Colours of the Wind" from the cartoon's soundtrack. I sat there in stunned silence as the queen began to jump up and down, singing an old-time Hollywood war whoop, channelling the spirits of all the savage squaws* in bad TV Westerns.

And then, from the audience, came the all-too-familiar sound of "whoo-whoo-whoo," as men throughout the room began to slap their hands to their open mouths and laugh uproariously at the white drag queen in redface on the stage.

The Q should have been a safe place that night, and it was—for racist white people. But not for us. Billy and I left very soon after the Pocahontas performance was finished. He went home to Tyrell, and I went home to take a shower, suddenly feeling very sick and very unclean. It was one of my last visits to the Q.

In all the time I've been in Toronto, I've never once been to a gay bar. I like thinking of this city as a place removed from such experiences, that the

---

4 [Justice's note] *The names of people in this essay have been changed.*

anti-Aboriginal racism that permeates Canadian politics, media and mainstream opinion wouldn't make its way to a queer club if my partner and I decided to go dancing one night, or if a friend and I just wanted to sit at a table and talk. I like to think that I could just enjoy myself in a place where queerness is the norm, where I wouldn't have to be assaulted by another drag queen in a corset playing Indian to a bunch of jeering white folks.

And if I'm wrong, which I probably am, I'd rather not know it.

45 The first graduate course I ever taught was burdened with the rather awkward title of "First Nations Literatures: Lesbian, Gay, Bisexual, Transgendered, and Two-Spirited* Native Writers." There were eight students, all non-Native—six ostensibly straight women, one queer woman and one gay man—and we studied works by openly queer writers from both sides of the border, such as Chrystos, Tomson Highway, Greg Sarris, Craig Womack, Joy Harjo, Gregory Scofield and Beth Brant. It was a powerful experience. The male student, when presenting on Womack's coming out/coming-of-age novel *Drowning in Fire*, began to sob uncontrollably as he talked about one passage out of the novel, where the protagonist, Josh Henneha, looks out over an expanse of water at sunset and comes to a point of acceptance of himself and his desires. The student found release in that scene of the book, words that named something of his own struggle to name and embrace his sexuality—and all the fears, hopes, pleasures and sacrifices that such acceptance necessitates.

Such moments are all too rare in teaching, and they're a gift when they arrive. Yet not all the course was as powerful. A student mentioned how interesting it was that although we were reading all these amazing texts by queer Native writers, we never actually talked about sex. I was taken aback by the statement, but not because it was inaccurate. What shocked me was that, in a city with a thriving queer community and a country with some of the most progressive attitudes toward sexuality in the hemisphere, we'd gone half the term reading books that had some of the most eloquent, profoundly moving scenes of sexuality and physical pleasure in contemporary literature, and yet we'd never discussed these scenes. We'd never said fun, festive and troubling words from the texts like *fuck*, *suck*, *cunt* or *cock*, or even used the rather more clinical *vagina* or *penis*.

In short, we'd never dealt with one of the substantive issues the literature itself was expressing. For these writers, embracing their desire for others of the same gender wasn't something separate from—but was fundamentally a part of—their struggle to express their dignity as Native people. Just as indigenousness itself has long been a colonialist target, so too has our joy, our desire, our sense of ourselves as beings able to both give and receive pleasure. To take joy in sex isn't just about enjoying the bump and grind, suck and squirt, lick and quiver of hot moist flesh on flesh. It's about being beautiful to ourselves and others. And such loving self-awareness is a hard thing to come by in a world that sees Aboriginal peoples as historical artifacts, degraded vagrants or grieving ghosts. To take joy in our bodies—and those bodies in relation to others—is to strike out against five-hundred-plus years of disregard, disrespect and dismissal.

So, we talked about it in class, even when it was difficult. We spoke about the things we hadn't discussed until that point. I addressed my own discomfort in talking about sexual matters in the classroom, a stand-offish-ness that I'd developed as an openly gay teaching assistant in a homophobic state, where just being out was a political act with the very real danger of aggressive reaction by students. Some of the straight students talked about finding an unfamiliar beauty in the works they'd read and were far more comfortable with reading across that experiential gap than I'd anticipated. The queer students found something of themselves in these writers' work but in a way that acknowledged both connections and differences without collapsing the two together.

And I was reminded again that I wasn't in Nebraska anymore. In Canada, as a gay man, I wasn't a second-class citizen. (As a Native man, however, the jury is still out. But I digress ...) And queer sexuality, although not treated with universal acceptance, isn't a realm of inquiry alienated from the critical work of the academy. Teaching about sex and sexuality was both a liberating experience and a frightening jump into the realm of some of the most emotionally reactive social fears, phobias and dysfunctions. Friends who have taught queer lit courses in the US have encountered blustering criticism from aggressively politicized students (and, sometimes, administrators) who believe that there's nothing worthwhile to be learned from talking about sex, especially sex and desire they consider deviant because of the archaic administrations of an arrogant and hostile god with cosmic delusions of grandeur.

I was fearful of this reaction but was both surprised and pleased to dis- 50
cover no such anti-intellectualism among these students in this place. There's a broader public consciousness in Canada, and it's one of the reasons why I will never return to the US to live. This is home for me now. It's not a perfect country, by any means, but to my admittedly limited experience it's a place where difference doesn't demand attack; you can ask questions, even difficult ones, and anticipate a respectful response, even from those who disagree. The two-spirit lit class, although small, was mixed in political orientation, background, comfort level, but all involved were committed to the intellectual questions elicited by our readings. We differed on a number of points and discussed our disagreements, coming away with a stronger sense of what was at stake in sex. I've been thankful that this attitude toward discussing sexuality has been the case with all of my classes and the vast majority of my students since that

time. It's not a constant point of discussion, but we don't ignore or minimize it when the issue emerges from course readings. When the atmosphere is one of committed intellectual analysis of texts and their ideas, with mutually respectful interaction with one another, *everyone* has a place in the conversation, and whether conservative or progressive, queer or straight, avowedly religious or affirmatively agnostic or atheist, we can all learn something from the willingness to engage some of these basic questions of life, love and belonging. Because, like it or not, we share a world as well as a classroom, and if we can't talk about the larger implications of sex in the intellectual arena of the academy—implications both positive and negative—we can hardly expect to deal with them in any thoughtful way in the larger public and political sphere.

The discussion in class that day was a good one, and it opened my eyes to some of my own fears and repressions. And I've thought a lot about it since. Queer desire is a reality of life for hundreds of millions of people the world over, and the expression of that desire is an intimate fuel for the cause of liberation among many dominated and oppressed peoples. As a scholar, and as a queer Native man, I have responsibilities to truth—both cerebral and bodily—and to understand how those truths can serve our dignity and survival in respectful, affirming and constructive ways. To ignore sex and embodied pleasure in the cause of Indigenous liberation is to ignore one of our greatest resources. It is to deny us one of our most precious gifts.

Every orgasm can be an act of decolonization.

I came to Canada almost six years ago, and a lot has changed in that time. The boyfriend I came here with became my husband, and then my ex, as his own desires took him elsewhere. I've met a lot of wonderful people, including a number of fabulous and well-adjusted two-spirit folks who find strength in the knowledge that we weren't always perceived as strange, deviant or disposable. In the traditions of many Indigenous nations, queer folks had—and continue to have—special gifts granted by the Creator for the benefit of our families and the world at large. In this understanding, our sexuality isn't just a part of our Nativeness—it's fuel for the healing of our nations. And although my own nation isn't quite as progressive in this regard—being predominantly Southern Baptist, the Cherokee Nation in Oklahoma has the dubious and sadly retrograde distinction of being one of (if not *the*) first Native nation to pass a same-sex marriage ban—the fact that there's still significant debate in the Nation on this issue gives me hope for the future. It may take us a while to come around, but it'll happen. The sacred fire doesn't burn only for straight folks. We queer folks dance around the fire, too, our voices strong, our hearts full, our spirits shining. We have gifts of healing to bring, too.

Rollie Lynn Riggs was a queer mixed-blood Cherokee, a poet and a playwright. His play *Green Grow the Lilacs* became the musical *Oklahoma!** and is still regarded as one of the finest studies of the mindset of the people of that state. It's also devoid of Indians. Their absence is palpable, a visible erasure from a man who proudly claimed his Cherokee heritage but left the land of his people because of his sexuality. Oklahoma lingered in his mind, wandering through the red dusk of his imagination until he died of cancer in a New York City hospital. Throughout his life he explored in the shadows what it was to be Indian and gay in a world that had no use for either. And he died alone.

Riggs and I share much in our love of language, our connection to the land and the people and our struggles with understanding our desires. But his rich and artistically inspiring life is also an object lesson in the corrosive consequences of accepting the world's bigotry as a measure of your own worth. He's a much-honoured queer Cherokee forefather, but I don't want to be like him. I want to continue to live the life and celebrate the love he couldn't. And if the spirits are willing, I will.

It's been over eleven years now since I began the long walk back to Cherokee pride and wholeness, and about nine since I came out. I'm now with a beautiful, blue-eyed, big-hearted Scots-Canadian man who has taught me more about love, passion and tenderness that I'd ever thought to know in all the years of self-hatred and shame that came before. In his gentle eyes I am lovely and desired, not for what I can give to him alone but for what we can give one another. It helps that he's also more than happy to help me make a horizontal stand against colonization whenever I'm in the mood—and, being the committed and passionate activist that I am, I am often in the mood.

I think back on this continuing journey, all the unexpected twists and double-backs along the trail, where fragile flesh has hungered for human touch and all too often come away unfulfilled. Would awkward and insecure eighteen-year-old Booner recognize the relatively confident and self-assured thirty-two-year-old Daniel? In those days I thought I'd be a perfectly "civilized," tweed-bound Oxford don and High Church Christian apologist by this point, not a balding, goateed Cherokee nationalist and proud son of the Rockies with multiple tattoos and piercings, a queer Native lit professor living and loving in the semi-socialist wilds of Canada. Booner had expected to have a wife and children, although he had no physical desire for women, nor any significant need to be a father. Although he had furtive dreams of sex with men, he certainly never imagined finding a deep and abiding love with a same-sex partner. Would that shy, scared and ashamed young man have faced all the mingled fears of the flesh earlier if he'd known that surrendering to the wolfsong and the moonlit shadows of the night would have brought such a healing balm to the spirit of his older self?

I'm not at all sure that he'd have understood or approved if he could see the man who would one day type these words. But maybe, when walking his dogs on a cold, clear winter's night, as he stood looking to the lonely moon's scarred face in the Colorado darkness, he might have known that his hunger was anything but a curse, that his desire was fundamentally different from that of the shame-marked Moon, that the howls in the dark dreams were a kinship cry drawing him towards all the primal power and beauty that passion could offer. Wolves aren't monsters; the monsters abide in deception, fear and self-loathing, not in truthful joy. We all hunger; we long to be loved and to love in return. That, at least, he might have found comforting as he trudged through the moonlit snow towards the warming lights of home.

(2008)

Questions

1. Describing how he felt about being Native when he was a child, Justice writes, "Nothing about my people was interesting to me." What does he mean, and why did he feel this way? How does he later reinterpret his heritage?
2. Trace the appearance through this essay of one of the following images: werewolves, the moon, or the land of Faerie. What is the significance of this image? Does Justice's orientation to the image change in the course of the narrative?
3. Comment on the significance of names and naming in this essay.
4. How does Justice's Native identity affect his experience of being gay? How does being gay affect his experience of Nativeness?
5. What does Justice argue about the political importance of sex? Do you agree?
6. How does Justice describe the difference between the political environments in Canada and in the US? In your experience, how accurate is his description of the country you are in?

Eula Biss

Time and Distance Overcome

"Time and Distance Overcome" first appeared in The Iowa Review *in 2008; the following year it appeared in Biss's collection* Notes from No Man's Land: American Essays.

"Of what use is such an invention?" the *New York World* asked shortly after Alexander Graham Bell[1] first demonstrated his telephone in 1876. The world was not waiting for the telephone.

Bell's financial backers asked him not to work on his new invention because it seemed too dubious an investment. The idea on which the telephone depended—the idea that every home in the country could be connected with a vast network of wires suspended from poles set an average of one hundred feet apart—seemed far more unlikely than the idea that the human voice could be transmitted through a wire.

Even now it is an impossible idea, that we are all connected, all of us.

"At the present time we have a perfect network of gas pipes and water pipes throughout our large cities," Bell wrote to his business partners in defense of his idea. "We have main pipes laid under the streets communicating by side pipes with the various dwellings.... In a similar manner it is conceivable that cables of telephone wires could be laid under ground, or suspended overhead, communicating by branch wires with private dwellings, counting houses, shops, manufactories, etc., uniting them through the main cable."

5 Imagine the mind that could imagine this. That could see us joined by one branching cable. This was the mind of a man who wanted to invent, more than the telephone, a machine that would allow the deaf to hear.

For a short time the telephone was little more than a novelty. For twenty-five cents you could see it demonstrated by Bell himself, in a church, along with singing and recitations by local talent. From some distance away, Bell would

---

1 *New York World* Daily newspaper (1860–1931) known for sensational stories meant to attract readership; *Alexander Graham Bell* Scottish-born inventor (1847–1922) best known for the invention of the telephone. He is also credited with several other inventions, many of them also related to sound, and was an influential educator of deaf children.

receive a call from "the invisible Mr. Watson." Then the telephone became a plaything of the rich. A Boston banker paid for a private line between his office and his home so that he could let his family know exactly when he would be home for dinner.

Mark Twain* was among the first Americans to own a telephone, but he wasn't completely taken with the device. "The human voice carries entirely too far as it is," he remarked.

By 1889, the *New York Times* was reporting a "War on Telephone Poles." Wherever telephone companies were erecting poles, homeowners and business owners were sawing them down, or defending their sidewalks with rifles.

Property owners in Red Bank, New Jersey, threatened to tar and feather* the workers putting up telephone poles. A judge granted a group of homeowners an injunction to prevent the telephone company from erecting any new poles. Another judge found that a man who had cut down a pole because it was "obnoxious" was not guilty of malicious mischief.

10 Telephone poles, newspaper editorials complained, were an urban blight. The poles carried a wire for each telephone—sometimes hundreds of wires. And in some places there were also telegraph wires, power lines, and trolley cables. The sky was netted with wires.

The war on telephone poles was fuelled, in part, by that terribly American concern for private property, and a reluctance to surrender it for a shared utility. And then there was a fierce sense of aesthetics, an obsession with purity, a dislike for the way the poles and wires marred a landscape that those other new inventions, skyscrapers and barbed wire, were just beginning to complicate. And then perhaps there was also a fear that distance, as it had always been known and measured, was collapsing.

The city council in Sioux Falls, South Dakota, ordered policemen to cut down all the telephone poles in town. And the mayor of Oshkosh, Wisconsin, ordered the police chief and the fire department to chop down the telephone poles there. Only one pole was chopped down before the telephone men climbed all the poles along the line, preventing any more chopping. Soon, Bell Telephone Company began stationing a man at the top of each pole as soon as it had been set, until enough poles had been set to string a wire between them, at which point it became a misdemeanour to interfere with the poles. Even so, a constable cut down two poles holding forty or fifty wires. And a homeowner sawed down a recently wired pole, then fled from police. The owner of a cannery ordered his workers to throw dirt back into the hole the telephone company was digging in front of his building. His men threw the dirt back in as fast as the telephone workers could dig it out. Then he sent out a team with a load of stones to dump into the hole. Eventually, the pole was erected on the other side of the street.

Despite the war on telephone poles, it would take only four years after Bell's first public demonstration of the telephone for every town of more than ten thousand people to be wired, although many towns were wired only to themselves. By the turn of the century, there were more telephones than bathtubs in America.

"Time and dist. overcome," read an early advertisement for the telephone. Rutherford B. Hayes[2] pronounced the installation of a telephone in the White House "one of the greatest events since creation." The telephone, Thomas Edison* declared, "annihilated time and space, and brought the human family in closer touch."

In 1898, in Lake Cormorant, Mississippi, a black man was hanged from a telephone pole. And in Weir City, Kansas. And in Brook Haven, Mississippi. And in Tulsa, Oklahoma, where the hanged man was riddled with bullets. In Danville, Illinois, a black man's throat was slit, and his dead body was strung up on a telephone pole. Two black men were hanged from a telephone pole in Lewisburg, West Virginia. And two in Hempstead, Texas, where one man was dragged out of the courtroom by a mob, and another was dragged out of jail.

A black man was hanged from a telephone pole in Belleville, Illinois, where a fire was set at the base of the pole and the man was cut down half-alive, covered in coal oil, and burned. While his body was burning the mob beat it with clubs and nearly cut it to pieces.

Lynching, the first scholar of the subject determined, is an American invention.[3] Lynching from bridges, from arches, from trees standing alone in fields, from trees in front of the county courthouse, from trees used as public billboards, from trees barely able to support the weight of a man, from telephone poles, from street lamps, and from poles erected solely for that purpose. From the middle of the nineteenth century to the middle of the twentieth century black men were lynched for crimes real and imagined, for whistles, for rumours, for "disputing with a white man," for "unpopularity," for "asking a white woman in marriage," for "peeping in a window."

---

2 *Rutherford B. Hayes* President of the United States from 1877 to 1881.

3 *Lynching ... invention* In 1905 James E. Cutler wrote *Lynch-Law: An Investigation into the History of Lynching in the United States*, considered to be the first academic account of the practice. While lynching has not been entirely confined to the United States, it became a very prominent form of violence in America especially in the late nineteenth to mid-twentieth centuries—the era of Jim Crow, a legal system that maintained racial inequality and was often reinforced by vigilante mob violence. The term "lynch" is believed to have originated with Charles Lynch, a Virginia farmer and Revolutionary War colonel.

The children's game of telephone depends on the fact that a message passed quietly from one ear to another to another will get distorted at some point along the line.

More than two hundred antilynching bills were introduced in the U.S. Congress during the twentieth century, but none were passed. Seven presidents lobbied for antilynching legislation, and the House of Representatives passed three separate measures, each of which was blocked by the Senate.

20 In Pine Bluff, Arkansas, a black man charged with kicking a white girl was hanged from a telephone pole. In Long View, Texas, a black man accused of attacking a white woman was hanged from a telephone pole. In Greenville, Mississippi, a black man accused of attacking a white telephone operator was hanged from a telephone pole. "The negro only asked time to pray." In Purcell, Oklahoma, a black man accused of attacking a white woman was tied to a telephone pole and burned. "Men and women in automobiles stood up to watch him die."

The poles, of course, were not to blame. It was only coincidence that they became convenient as gallows, because they were tall and straight, with a crossbar, and because they stood in public places. And it was only coincidence that the telephone poles so closely resembled crucifixes.

Early telephone calls were full of noise. "Such a jangle of meaningless noises had never been heard by human ears," Herbert Casson wrote in his 1910 *History of the Telephone*. "There were spluttering and bubbling, jerking and rasping, whistling and screaming."

In Shreveport, Louisiana, a black man charged with attacking a white girl was hanged from a telephone pole. "A knife was left sticking in the body." In Cumming, Georgia, a black man accused of assaulting a white girl was shot repeatedly, then hanged from a telephone pole. In Waco, Texas, a black man convicted of killing a white woman was taken from the courtroom by a mob and burned, then his charred body was hanged from a telephone pole.

A postcard was made from the photo of a burned man hanging from a telephone pole in Texas, his legs broken off below the knee and his arms curled up and blackened. Postcards of lynchings were sent out as greetings and warnings until 1908, when the postmaster general declared them unmailable. "This is the barbecue we had last night," reads one.

25 "If we are to die," W.E.B. Du Bois[4] wrote in 1911, "in God's name let us not perish like bales of hay." And "if we must die," Claude McKay[5] wrote ten years later, "let it not be like hogs."

4 *W.E.B. Du Bois* African American writer and activist (1868–1963) who championed equal rights and promoted the social and political advancement of African Americans.

5 *Claude McKay* Jamaican-born poet and novelist (1889–1948); as a key figure of the Harlem Renaissance, he helped to establish a distinct African American literary and cultural movement.

In Pittsburg, Kansas, a black man was hanged from a telephone pole, cut down, burned, shot, and stoned with bricks. "At first the negro was defiant," the *New York Times* reported, "but just before he was hanged he begged hard for his life."

In the photographs, the bodies of the men lynched from telephone poles are silhouetted against the sky. Sometimes two men to a pole, hanging above the buildings of a town. Sometimes three. They hung like flags in still air.

In Cumberland, Maryland, a mob used a telephone pole as a battering ram to break into the jail where a black man charged with the murder of a policeman was being held. They kicked him to death, then fired twenty shots into his head. They wanted to burn his body, but a minister asked them not to.

The lynchings happened everywhere, in all but four states. From shortly before the invention of the telephone to long after the first trans-Atlantic call. More in the South, and more in rural areas. In the cities and in the North, there were race riots.*

Riots in Cincinnati, New Orleans, Memphis, New York, Atlanta, Philadelphia, Houston ...

During the race riots that destroyed the black section of Springfield, Ohio,[6] a black man was shot and hanged from a telephone pole.

During the race riots that set fire to East St. Louis[7] and forced five hundred black people to flee their homes, a black man was hanged from a telephone pole. The rope broke and his body fell into the gutter. "Negros are lying in the gutters every few feet in some places," read the newspaper account.

In 1921, the year before Bell died, four companies of the National Guard were called out to end a race war in Tulsa[8] that began when a white woman accused a black man of rape. Bell had lived to complete the first call from New York to San Francisco, which required 14,000 miles of copper wire and 130,000 telephone poles.

---

6 *Springfield, Ohio* In 1904, the lynching of African American local Richard Dixon escalated into a full riot in Springfield, Ohio, with hundreds of white men inflicting destruction on the black neighbourhood known as the Levee.

7 *East St. Louis* Riots erupted in East St. Louis, Illinois, in 1917 as tensions escalated between the white population and a number of black workers who had migrated to find employment in factories. After a series of isolated violent incidents, a mob of thousands burned homes and killed more than one hundred African Americans.

8 *race war in Tulsa* The riot that broke out in Tulsa, Oklahoma, after Dick Rowland was arrested based on a false accusation led to sixteen hours of violent clashes between large groups of white and black residents, and to the destruction of the Deep Greenwood district, a vibrant black neighbourhood. The National Guard brought martial law to the city and placed black rioters in internment centres, while no white rioters were penalized.

My grandfather was a lineman.[9] He broke his back when a telephone pole fell. "Smashed him onto the road," my father says.

When I was young, I believed that the arc and swoop of telephone wires along the roadways was beautiful. I believed that the telephone poles, with their transformers catching the evening sun, were glorious. I believed my father when he said, "My dad could raise a pole by himself." And I believed that the telephone itself was a miracle.

Now, I tell my sister, these poles, these wires, do not look the same to me. Nothing is innocent, my sister reminds me. But nothing, I would like to think, remains unrepentant.

One summer, heavy rains fell in Nebraska and some green telephone poles grew small leafy branches.

(2009)

Questions

1. This essay incorporates two seemingly disparate topics: the history of lynching and the rise of the telephone. What kind of connection (if any) does this essay suggest exists between these subjects?
2. How does the telephone "annihilate time and space"? What fears might the telephone evoke, and how were these fears enacted by Americans as the telephone poles went up?
3. To what extent does this essay follow the conventions of a personal essay? What, if any, other forms does Biss make use of?
4. Biss ends the essay with the symbol of the sprouting telephone pole. What does this symbol connote, given the context of the essay?

---

9 *lineman* Person tasked with installing or maintaining telephone lines.

MARILYN WANN

from FAT STUDIES: AN INVITATION TO REVOLUTION

The Fat Studies Reader, *published by NYU Press in November 2009, is considered to be the first book of its kind, amassing a variety of writing in the emergent field of "fat studies." Articles in the collection span the disciplines of women's studies, psychology, medicine, cultural studies, and more. The collection, edited by Esther D. Rothblum and Sondra Solovay, received the 2010 Distinguished Publication Award from the Association for Women in Psychology, as well as the 2010 Susan Koppelman Award for the Best Edited Volume in Women's Studies from the Popular Culture Association. The following selection is from the foreword to the volume.*

... As a new, interdisciplinary* field of intellectual inquiry, fat studies is defined in part by what it is not.

For example, if you believe that fat people could (and should) lose weight, then you are not doing fat studies—you are part of the $58.6 billion-per-year weight-loss industry or its vast customer base (Marketdata Enterprises, 2007).

If you believe that being fat is a disease and that fat people cannot possibly enjoy good health or long life, then you are not doing fat studies. Instead, your approach is aligned with "obesity" researchers, bariatric surgeons,[1] public health officials who declare "war on obesity" (Koop, 1997), and the medico-pharmaceutical industrial complex that profits from dangerous attempts to "cure" people of bodily difference (more on "obesity" later).

If you believe that thin is inherently beautiful and fat is obviously ugly, then you are not doing fat studies work either. You are instead in the realm of advertising, popular media, or the more derivative types of visual art—in other words, propaganda.

---

1 *bariatric surgeons* Medical professionals who perform surgery on the digestive system to cause weight loss.

5 Fat studies is a radical field, in the sense that it goes to the root of weight-related belief systems.

The contrasting endeavours mentioned above are prescriptive in nature. They assume that human weight is mutable and negotiable, assumptions that are informed by current social bias and stigma against fatness and fat people. On this point, fat studies is—in strong contrast—descriptive.* Weight, like height, is a human characteristic that varies across any population in a bell curve (Flegal, 2006). An individual person's weight also varies over the course of a lifetime, influenced largely by inherited predisposition and only marginally by environmental factors like eating and exercise patterns (Hainer, Stunkard, Kunesova, Parizkova, Stich, & Allison, 2001). Most people naturally occupy a middle range of weights (and heights), whereas some people naturally weigh less and some people naturally weigh more (just as some people are naturally tall or short). Heights and weights also vary between populations and time periods, due in large part to levels of economic development, access to food, advances in medicine and immunization, and other large-scale factors (Kolata, 2006). There have always been and will always be people of different heights. There have also always been and there will also always be people of different weights. Unlike traditional approaches to weight, a fat studies approach offers no opposition to the simple fact of human weight diversity, but instead looks at what people and societies make of this reality.

The field of fat studies requires scepticism about weight-related beliefs that are popular, powerful, and prejudicial. This scepticism is currently rare, even taboo. Questioning the received knowledge on weight is socially risky. American culture is engaged in a pervasive witch hunt targeting fatness and fat people (a project that is rapidly being exported worldwide). Whenever members of a society have recourse to only one opinion on a basic human experience, that is precisely the discourse and the experience that should attract intellectual curiosity....

WHAT DO YOU SAY?

Word choice is a good place to begin to examine assumptions. How do you refer to people at the heavier-than-average end of the weight bell curve? Currently, in mainstream U.S. society, the O-words, "overweight" and "obese," are considered more acceptable, even more polite, than the F-word, "fat." In the field of fat studies, there is agreement that the O-words are neither neutral nor benign. (The editors and contributors of this *Reader* have chosen to surround the O-words with scare quotes* to indicate their compromised status.) In fat studies, there is respect for the political project of reclaiming the word *fat*, both as the preferred neutral adjective (i.e., short/tall, young/old, fat/thin) and also as a preferred term of political identity. There is nothing negative or rude in the word *fat* unless someone makes the effort to put it there; using the word *fat* as a descriptor (not a discriminator) can help dispel prejudice. Seemingly well-meaning euphemisms like “heavy,” “plump,” “husky,” and so forth put a falsely positive spin on a negative view of fatness.

OVER WHAT WEIGHT?

“Overweight” is inherently anti-fat. It implies an extreme goal: instead of a bell curve distribution of human weights, it calls for a lone, towering, unlikely bar graph with everyone occupying the same (thin) weights. If a word like “overweight” is acceptable and even preferable, then weight prejudice becomes accepted and preferred. (The population is getting taller, but we do not bemoan *overheight* or warn people to keep below, say, five feet eight. Being tall is valued. For an important introduction to height prejudice, see Ellen Frankel’s book *Beyond Measure: A Memoir About Short Stature and Inner Growth*, 2006.)

In related terminology, it is not meaningful to call weights “normal” or 10
“abnormal.” (Although mathematically, “average” weights certainly exist in any population.) The body shape that is normal for tall and thin Broadway choreographer Tommy Tune is not the weight that is normal for short and fat movie and television actor/producer Danny DeVito. Expecting either of these entertainers to look like the other would not be healthy, nor would it increase their box-office value. There would also be no benefit if Olympic weightlifter Cheryl Haworth and tennis champion Maria Sharapova were expected to trade weights.

Similarly, health is a problematic concept when linked with weight. Health is not a number, but rather a subjective experience with many influences. Stepping onto a scale cannot prove a person healthy or unhealthy. In Health at Every Size (HAES),[2] people discuss weight in health-neutral ways and discuss health in weight-neutral ways. (... As a field, Health at Every Size joins fat studies and fat pride community in creating a sturdy tripod of support for the larger project of questioning and undoing weight prejudice.) Weight is an inaccurate basis for predicting individual health or longevity, much less someone’s eating or exercise habits. For example, the majority of people categorized as “obese”—seven out of eight—are not diabetic (National Center for Health Statistics, 2006). “Health” can be used to police body conformity and can be code for weight-related judgments that are socially, not scientifically, driven. “Health” can also cover a

---

2 *Health at Every Size (HAES)* Movement that aims to decrease medical and social stigma against fat people and promote the idea that health can be attained at a wide variety of body sizes and weights.

whole range of beliefs and behaviours (eating disorders, moralizing about food or fitness, alienation from one's own body) that reinforce social control around weight and can be very damaging to well-being. Like the F-word, health is a term that calls for a conscious project of reclamation.

THE EPIDEMIC OF THE WORD "OBESITY"

... Calling fat people "obese" medicalizes* human diversity. Medicalizing diversity inspires a misplaced search for a "cure" for naturally occurring difference. Far from generating sympathy for fat people, medicalization of weight fuels anti-fat prejudice and discrimination in all areas of society. People think: If fat people need to be cured, there must be something wrong with them. Cures should work; if they do not, it is the fat person's fault and a license not to employ, date, educate, rent to, sell clothes to, give a medical exam to, see on television, respect, or welcome such fat people in society. Such hateful attitudes are acceptable because no one really believes that being fat is any kind of disease. If fat people suffered from a real illness, our detractors' attitudes would be unacceptably cruel. The pretense of concern for fat people's health wards anti-fat attitudes against exposure as a simple hatred. Belief in a "cure" also masks that hatred. It is not possible to hate a group of people for our own good. Medicalization actually helps categorize fat people as social untouchables. It is little surprise, then, that when fat people do fall ill, we get blame, not compassion. We receive punishment, not help. Medical cures are inappropriate when applied to social ills. Such a misdiagnosis can be very dangerous. Ascribing illness to everyone whose weight falls above an arbitrary cutoff inevitably yields mistakes—when I give weight diversity talks, I say, "The only thing that anyone can diagnose, with any certainty, by looking at a fat person, is their own level of stereotype and prejudice toward fat people."

WHO IS FAT?

In the United States, any number of self-appointed authorities are eager to designate who is fat and who is not. The federal government, health insurers, medical doctors, school nurses, popular media, advertising, the fashion industry, strangers, acquaintances, friends, family members, romantic partners, and, of course, the bathroom scale—each alleged authority draws its own line between fat and thin, does so at different weights, and may redraw the line at any time. For example, a Blue Cross of California health insurance underwriter admitted to me in 2003 that the company's weight limit for people it deems "morbidly obese" (and thus uninsurable) had changed six times in the preceding decade.

I replied, "Those lines sure are infallible!" Such intermittent feedback can be very disorienting. When being thin or fat in our society confers privilege or oppression, the stakes are high.

The federal government has used a variety of "ideal" weight charts, most recently switching to Body Mass Index[3] (BMI, a way to collapse height and weight into one number). (It is no more meaningful to know that I have a BMI of 49 than it is to know that I'm five feet four inches and weigh 285 pounds.) In 1998, the BMI cutoff points that define "overweight" and "obese" categories were lowered; with that change, millions of people became fat overnight. The "obesity" researchers who lobbied for this redefinition argued that the new lines were evidence-based: the "overweight" line was supposed to indicate the weight at which people face increased risk of disease (morbidity), and the "obese" line was supposed to indicate the weight at which people face increased risk of death (mortality). Morbidity/mortality correlations with weight are often contradictory. Sometimes being fat protects against disease. Sometimes fatter people live longer (Andres, 1980; Flegal, Graubard, Williamson, & Gail, 2005). The federal government stills draws lines at the conveniently memorable BMIs of 25 and 30. People with a BMI under 18.5 are labelled "underweight." People with a BMI of 25 and up are labelled "overweight." And people with a BMI of 30 and up are labelled "obese." (The term "morbidly obese" refers to BMI 40 and up, but is not used as a major reporting category; mostly it is used to sell stomach amputations.) In *Health, United States, 2006* (National Center for Health Statistics, 2006), a publication of the National Center for Health Statistics, part of the Centers for Disease Control, results from the National Health and Nutrition Examination Survey for 2001 to 2004 indicate that 1.7 percent of Americans between the ages of 20 and 74 fell into the "underweight" category, 32.2 percent fell into the "healthy" weight category, 34 percent fell into the "overweight" category, and 32.1 percent fell into the "obese" category.

The weight divide is not just a fat/thin binary. In *The Culture of Conformism:* 15
Understanding Social Consent, Patrick Colm Hogan (2001) describes micro-hierarchization,* a process that certainly applies to weight-based attitudes. People feel superiority or self-loathing based on each calorie or gram of food consumed or not consumed, in each belt notch, pound, or inch gained or lost, in each clothing size smaller or larger. Each micro-rung on the weight-based hierarchy exerts pressure to covet the next increment thinner and regret the next increment fatter, leaving little room for people to recognize and revolt against the overall system that alienates us from our own bodies.

---

3 *Body Mass Index* One's BMI is calculated by dividing one's body weight by the square of one's height.

Power lies both in naming and in rejecting naming. The federal government categorizes me as "morbidly obese"; I identify as fat. Is it self-contradictory to claim membership in the fat club when I seek to disrupt belief in the meaningfulness or usefulness of weight categories? No, it's just ironic. Claiming one's embodiment (whatever one weighs) is a form of political resistance, a way to undo alienation. A fat-hating society asks fearfully, "Do I look fat?" I respond, "I am Fatacus!"[4] Just as Kurt Cobain of Nirvana (1993) sang, "Everyone is gay,"[5] in a fat-hating society everyone is fat. Fat functions as a floating signifier,[6] attaching to individuals based on a power relationship, not a physical measurement. People all along the weight spectrum may experience fat oppression. A young woman who weighs eighty-seven pounds because of her anorexia knows something about fat oppression. So does a fat person who is expected to pay double for the privilege of sitting down during an airplane flight. Each person brings useful leverage to help shift attitudes. I welcome thin people not as allies but as colleagues. If we imagine that the conflict is between fat and thin, weight prejudice continues. Instead, the conflict is between all of us against a system that would weigh our value as people. If we cannot feel at home in our own skins, where else are we supposed to go?

The field of fat studies is not concerned with a small subgroup of people. U.S. government health officials designate two-thirds of people as over the line for "ideal," "healthy," or "normal" weight. The remaining third are encouraged to live in fear of getting fat. Frustrated by a failed, forty-year effort to cut adults down to cookie-cutter* size, hysteria mongers have shifted their aim to children. One scare tactic involves schools alerting parents their children have fallen into the nonsensical category "at risk of becoming overweight." Yet Americans are fatter and taller and healthier and longer-lived than ever before in human history (Kolata, 2006). Nonetheless, it's public policy to aggressively export fear of the fat menace—"globesity"—even to places where people go hungry (World Health Organization, 2006). Fat or not, everybody has a stake in the findings of scholars who advance the new field of fat studies.

---

4 *I am Fatacus!* Allusion to a well-known and much-parodied line from Stanley Kubrick's 1960 film *Spartacus*, in which a group of slaves who have revolted against their Roman masters refuse to turn over their leader, Spartacus, to the authorities. Each slave claims "I am Spartacus!" to confuse the Romans.

5 *Just as ... "Everyone is gay"* Reference to lyrics from the Nirvana song "All Apologies."

6 *floating signifier* Word or symbol that doesn't have a fully defined, specific meaning and so can be used in a wide range of contexts.

THREE HUNDRED THOUSAND FAT DEATHS? DO I HEAR FOUR HUNDRED THOUSAND?

For a decade, fat people have been hearing more frequent and more insistent death threats. The threats first became popular when Interneuron Pharmaceuticals and Wyeth-Ayerst sought FDA approval for Redux[7] in 1997. (Redux produced six pounds of weight loss compared to placebo. It was recalled when users developed serious illness and even died.) "Obesity" researchers who testified in support of Redux claimed that three hundred thousand people die annually from being fat. University of California, Davis, nutrition professor Judith Stern testified that things were dire, and that anyone who did not vote to approve Redux should be shot (McAfee, 1994). The three hundred thousand claim was based on an estimate of extra deaths due to poor nutrition and lack of exercise. The original study, by McGinnis and Foege (1998), included no weight data. Its authors took the unusual step of publishing an open letter in the *New England Journal of Medicine* in April 1998 asking people to stop misusing their results. By that point, however, the FDA had already responded to the threats by approving Redux.

Although journalists continue to cite the debunked three hundred thousand figure, "obesity" researchers invented a new, improved version—four hundred thousand fat deaths per year. They developed this number by applying estimates of how many fat people *should* be dying to the current number of fat people and the current number of deaths. In comparison, Katherine Flegal, PhD, a researcher for the National Center for Health Statistics at the Centers for Disease Control, published a methodologically unassailable study of actual deaths in various weight categories and found a much lower figure—111,900 more deaths—among the alleged "obese" than in the "normal" weight category (Flegal, 2006; Flegal et al., 2005). She also found 86,000 *fewer* deaths among people whom the government labels "overweight," and 33,746 *more* deaths among "underweight" people. In an editorial, she admonished, "We thought it important to clarify in our article that any associations of weight with mortality were not necessarily causal but might be due, wholly or in part, to other factors, such as activity, diet, body composition or fat distribution, that were associated both with weight and with mortality" (Flegal, 2006, p. 1171).

One need not quote Mark Twain regarding exaggerated predictions of our 20
demise[8] to note that most of the experts who influence federal "obesity" policy fantasize about fat people dying in droves. To put these fantasies in harsh

7 *Redux* Drug meant to reduce appetite in consumers, thereby promoting weight loss.

8 *quote Mark Twain ... our demise* Allusion to a frequently quoted and misquoted statement by American novelist and satirist Mark Twain, who wrote in a letter in 1897, in

perspective, consider that in the twenty-five-year history of the HIV/AIDS epidemic in the United States,[9] more than 529,000 people have died from AIDS. At its worst, in 1995, more than 50,000 people died from this infectious disease (Centers for Disease Control, 2004). If fat deaths truly were sixfold or eightfold compared to AIDS deaths, I think we would have noticed. There'd be an outcry. Lynn McAfee, the medical liaison for the Council on Size and Weight Discrimination, would not be the only self-identified fat person to attend CDC and FDA meetings to ask the government to check its facts on "obesity." With no giant pile of dead fat bodies, death threats about fatness sound like wishful thinking. During the last quarter century, while Americans have gained on average twenty or so pounds, the mainstream media has gone from mentioning the term "obesity" only sixty times per year in the early 1980s to five hundred times per year in 1990, to one thousand mentions in 1995, three thousand mentions in 2000, and seven thousand panic-stricken mentions of "obesity" in 2003 (Saguy & Riley, 2005). When Flegal significantly lowered estimates of fat deaths, none of the "obesity" researchers were glad.

Only sturdy people could endure the kind of neglect and endangerment that fat people often experience at the hands of the medical establishment and continue to live as long as we do....

REASONS FOR REVOLUTION

In the hope of offering a partial indication of what may be at stake when we confront attitudes about weight, here is a review of some of the data documenting the impact of weight-based prejudice and discrimination in the United States.

Weight-based discrimination is a cradle-to-grave phenomenon.* Fat people are officially barred from adopting babies from China. In Britain, health clinics may refuse in vitro fertilization[10] to fat women, and the British Fertility Society has recommended a general ban (BBC News, 2006). In the United States, public health departments advertise that parents should prevent childhood "obesity." ...

---

response to rumours of his being gravely ill and even dead, "The report of my death was an exaggeration."

9 *twenty-five-year history ... United States* The discovery of AIDS, the syndrome caused by the human immunodeficiency virus (HIV), in 1981 was followed by a severe epidemic throughout the 1980s and 90s.

10 *in vitro fertilization* Procedure designed to assist those with fertility problems by fertilizing eggs in a laboratory, then implanting the resulting embryos into the patient's uterus.

The National Education Association reports, "For fat students the school experience is one of ongoing prejudice, unnoticed discrimination, and almost constant harassment. From nursery school through college, fat students experience ostracism, discouragement, sometimes violence. Often ridiculed by their peers and discouraged by even well-meaning education employees, fat students develop low self-esteem and have limited horizons. They are deprived of places on honour rolls, sports teams, and cheerleading squads and are denied letters of recommendation" (1994, p. 1).

Fatter children are sadder, lonelier, more worried about school and their 25
futures, and face greater ridicule from gym teachers (Rimm & Rimm, 2004). Average-weight children who fear becoming fat may eat too little, thereby slowing growth and delaying puberty (Pugliese, Lifshitz, Grad, Ford, & Marks-Katz, 1983). Fatter teens are more likely to face humiliating or shaming experiences that can lead to depression (Sjöberg, Nilsson, & Leppert, 2005). Teens who think that they're not the "right" weight are more likely to contemplate or attempt suicide (Eaton, Lowry, Brener, Galuska, & Crosby, 2005). A disordered relationship with food is standard among young women (Polivy & Herman, 1987). Boys are not immune. After playing with GI Joe* dolls, they are more likely to starve themselves, lift weights compulsively, or take steroids (Pope, Olivardia, Gruber, & Borowiecki, 1999).

High school counsellors are less likely to encourage fat students to apply for college, colleges are less likely to admit equally qualified fat applicants, and parents are less likely to pay a fat daughter's college tuition (Crandall, 1995). Colleges are typically unaware of fat students' seating needs.

Adulthood is no escape from mistreatment. In the workplace, 93 percent of human resources professionals said that they would hire a "normal weight" applicant over a fat applicant with the same qualifications. Fifteen percent would not promote a fat employee. One in ten think it is acceptable to fire an employee for being fat (Fattism Rife in Business, 2005). There is little stigma attached to discriminating against fat people (Crandall, 1994). Fat women earn nearly seven thousand dollars less in annual household income than thinner women (Gortmaker, Must, Perrin, Sobol, & Dietz, 1993). Fat workers are paid less, for no other documentable reason than weight; over a forty-year career, the disparity can total one hundred thousand dollars less in pre-tax earnings (Ford & Baum, 2004). In a review of twenty-nine weight discrimination studies, the fattest women earned one-fourth less than thinner workers. Women who weighed sixty-five pounds more than average-weight women received 7 percent less in salary. Employers admitted routinely turning down promising fat applicants for not "fitting the corporate image" (Cawley, 2000; Roehling, 1999, p. 969). Weight may outweigh other characteristics in influencing hiring and other employment decisions (Larkin & Pines, 1979). Fat employees are denied health insurance benefits and are pressured to resign or are fired for being fat (Rothblum, Brand, Miller, & Oetjen, 1990)....

Fat prejudice has a profound impact on social life. Fat men are 11 percent less likely to be married, and fat women are 20 percent less likely to be married (Gortmaker et al., 1993). Just being seen with a fat person can affect the social status of an average-weight person (Gallagher, Tate, McCologan, Dovey, & Halford, 2003).... Social isolation is a serious concern, not just because it is emotionally painful, but also because it can affect health. Men who have numerous friends and close friendships are half as likely to develop heart disease (Rosengren, Wilhelmsena, & Orth-Gomérb, 2004)....

The biased attitudes of health-care providers also put fat patients at risk (O'Neil & Rogers, 1998). Physicians view fat patients negatively and avoid spending time with us (Hebl & Xu, 2001). Even doctors and researchers who specialize in "obesity" harbour stereotypes of fat people as lazy, stupid, and worthless (Schwartz, Chambliss, Brownell, Blair, & Billington, 2003; Teachman & Brownell, 2001) (the Rudd Center scholars who authored these studies also specialize in "obesity," but do not disclose their own levels of weight bias). Nurses hold negative views of fat patients (Brown, 2006; Maroney & Golub, 1992). Students of exercise science see fat people as bad and lazy (Chambliss, Finley, & Blair, 2004). Mental health professionals are more likely to evaluate fat people negatively (Agell & Rothblum, 1991; Young & Powell, 1985). Fat people who need organ transplants may be told to lose weight to be eligible (Hasse, 1997).

30 Fat women are a third less likely to receive breast exams, Pap smears,* or gynecologic exams, but are no less likely to receive mammograms,* which may indicate obstetric/gynecology physicians' hesitation to touch fat patients. Researchers admitted that weight-based barriers to care "may exacerbate or even account for some of the increased health risks correlated with higher weights" (Fontaine, Faith, Allison, & Cheskin, 1998, p. 383). Twelve percent of well-educated women reported delaying or cancelling physician appointments because they knew they would be weighed. Olson, Schumaker, and Yawn (1994, p. 891) wrote, "If we are to reach our goal of health maintenance, we must work to remove the barriers that keep obese patients out of their physicians' offices." Even when fat women have health insurance, we avoid doctors because of "disrespectful treatment, embarrassment at being weighed, negative attitudes of providers, unsolicited advice to lose weight, and medical equipment that was too small to be functional" (Amy, Aalborg, Lyons, & Keranen, 2006, p. 147). Given the intensity of fat stigma, especially in the medical setting, it is no surprise that a third of "obese" people would risk death or trade five years of life to lose even 10 percent of their weight. The more we weigh, the more willing we are to risk our lives to lose weight (Wee, Hamel, Davis, & Phillips,

2004; these findings explain, to some extent, why fat people consent to life-threatening stomach amputations). If fat people believe the lie that our lives are not worth living, we are unlikely to hold our health-care providers to a high standard of safety or efficacy for our care.

The anti-fat bias of health-care providers leads to improper diagnoses. For example, physicians told a fat man in London for an entire decade that his abdominal pain was due to his "obesity." Finally, he received a scan and surgeons removed a fifty-five-pound malignant tumour ("Overweight" Man, 2005).

Anti-fat attitudes are rigged to be impervious. Anti-fat attitudes increase when weight is explained by overeating and lack of exercise, but do not decrease with a genetic explanation. Stories of weight discrimination (like the above litany*) reduce anti-fat attitudes only in people who are fat (Teachman, Gapinski, Brownell, Rawlings, & Jeyaram, 2003). Fat studies can challenge this ingrown thinking.

(2009)

REFERENCES

Agell, G., & Rothblum, E.D. (1991). Effects of Clients' Obesity and Gender on the Therapy Judgments of Psychologists, *Professional Psychology: Theory and Practice*, 22, 223-229.

Amy, N.K., Aalborg, A., Lyons, P., & Keranen, L. (2006). Barriers to Routine Gynecological Cancer Screening for White and African-American Obese Women, *International Journal of Obesity, 30(1)*, 147-155.

Andres, R. (1980). Effect of Obesity on Total Mortality, *International Journal of Obesity, 4(4)*, 381-386.

Baum, C.L., & Ford, F.F. (2004). The Wage Effects of Obesity: A Longitudinal Study, *Health Economics*, 13(9), 885-899.

BBC News (2006, August 30). Call for Fertility Ban for Obese. Retrieved February 28, 2007, from http://news.bbc.co.uk/2/hi/health/5296200.stm....

Brown, I. (2006). Nurses' Attitudes Towards Adult Patients Who Are Obese, *Journal of Advanced Nursing, 53(2)*, 221-232....

Cawley, J. (2000, August). Body Weight and Women's Labor Market Outcomes, National Bureau of Economic Research, Working Paper W7841.

Centers for Disease Control and Prevention (2004). *HIV/AIDS Surveillance Report*, 16. Retrieved April 3, 2009, from http://www.cdc.gov/hiv/topics/surveillance/resources/reports/2004report/pdf/2004SurveillanceReport.pdf.

Chambliss, H.O., Finley, C.E., & Blair, S.N. (2004). Attitudes Toward Obese Individuals Among Exercise Science Students, *Medical Science of Sports Exercise, 36(3)*, 468-474.

Crandall, C.S. (1994). Prejudice Against Fat People: Ideology and Self-Interest, *Journal of Personality and Social Psychology, 66(5)*, 882-894.

Crandall, C.S. (1995). Do Parents Discriminate Against Their Heavyweight Daughters? *Personality and Social Psychology Bulletin, 21(7)*, 724-735....

Eaton, D.K., Lowry, R., Brener, N.D., Galuska, D.A., & Crosby, A.E. (2005). Associations of Body Mass Index and Perceived Weight with Suicide Ideation and Suicide Attempts

Among US High School Students, *Archives of Pediatric Adolescent Medicine, 159*, 513-519.

Fattism Rife in Business (2005, October 25). Retrieved January 26, 2009, from http://www.personneltoday.com/articles/2005/10/25/32212/fattism-rife-in-business.html.

Flegal, K.M., Graubard, B.I., Williamson, D.F., & Gail, M.H. (2005). Excess Deaths Associated with Underweight, Overweight, and Obesity, *Journal of the American Medical Association, 293*, 1861-1867.

Flegal, K. (2006). Excess Deaths Associated with Obesity: Cause and Effect, *International Journal of Obesity, 30*, 1171-1172.

Fontaine K.R., Faith, M.S., Allison, D.B., & Cheskin, L.J. (1998, July-August). Body Weight and Health Care Among Women in the General Population, *Archives of Family Medicine, 7*, 381-384.

Frankel, E. (2006). *Beyond Measure: A Memoir About Short Stature and Inner Growth.* Nashville, TN: Pearlsong Press.

Gallagher, S., Tate, T.J., McColgan, B., Dovey, T.M., & Halford, J.C.G. (2003). Negative Judgments About Male Associates of Obese Females, *Obesity Research, 11(5)*, A118-119....

Gortmaker, S.L., Must, A., Perrin, J.M., Sobol, A.M., & Dietz, W.H. (1993). Social and Economic Consequences of Overweight in Adolescence and Young Adulthood, *New England Journal of Medicine, 329(14)*, 1008-1012.

Hainer, V., Stunkard, A., Kunesova, M., Parizkova, J., Stich, V., & Allison, D.B. (2001). A Twin Study of Weight Loss and Metabolic Efficiency, *International Journal of Obesity Related Metabolic Disorders, 25(4)*, 533-537....

Hasse, J. (1997). Is Obesity an Independent Risk Factor for Transplantation? *New Developments in Transplantation Medicine, 4*, 1.

Hebl, M.R., & Xu, J. (2001, August). Weighing the Care: Physicians' Reactions to the Size of a Patient. *International Journal of Obesity, 25(8)*, 1246-1252.

Hogan, P.C. (2001). *The Culture of Conformism: Understanding Social Consent.* Durham, NC: Duke University Press. ...

Kolata, G. (2006, July 30). The New Age: So Big and Healthy Grandpa Wouldn't Even Know You, *New York Times*. Retrieved April 3, 2009, from http://www.nytimes.com/2006/07/30/health/30age.html.

Koop, C.E. (1997, September). In Spite of Diet Drug Withdrawal, the War on Obesity Must Continue Says Dr. C. Everett Koop, Shape Up America! press release. Retrieved September 30, 2006, from http://www.shapeup.org/about/arch_pr/091997.php....

Larkin, J.C., & Pines, H.A. (1979). No Fat Persons Need Apply. *Sociology of Work and Occupations, 6*, 312-327....

Marketdata Enterprises (2007, April 19). U.S. Weight Loss Market to Reach $58 Billion in 2007. Retrieved January 26, 2009, from http://www.prwebdirect.com/releases/2007/4/prweb520127.php.

Maroney, D., & Golub, S. (1992). Nurses' Attitudes Toward Obese Persons and Certain Ethnic Groups, *Perceptual and Motor Skills, 75(2)*, 387-391.

McAfee, Lynn (1994, April). Personal communication to author by McAfee, who attended FDA hearings on approval of Redux.

McGinnis, J.M., & Foege, W.H. (1998). The Obesity Problem, *New England Journal of Medicine, 338(16)*, 1157-1158.

National Center for Health Statistics (2006). *Health, United States, 2006: With Chartbook on Trends in the Health of Americans*. Retrieved November 27, 2006, from http://www.cdc.gov/nchs/hus.htm.

National Education Association (1994, October 7). Report on Discrimination Due to Physical Size. Retrieved September 30, 2006, from http://www.lectlaw.com/files/con28.htm.

Nirvana (1993). All Apologies, *In Utero*, Geffen Records.

Olson, C.L., Schumaker, H.D., & Yawn, B.P. (1994). Overweight Women Delay Medical Care, *Archives of Family Medicine, 3(10)*, 888-892.

O'Neil, P.M., & Rogers, R. (1998). Health Care Providers' Unhealthy Attitudes Towards Obese People, *Weight Control Digest, 8*, 765-767.

"Overweight" Man Had 55lb Tumour. (2005, March 14). *The Evening Standard*. Retrieved September 30, 2006, from http://www.thisislondon.co.uk.news/articles/17257602?source=PA.

Polivy, J, & Herman, C.P. (1987). Diagnosis and Treatment of Normal Eating, *Journal of Consulting and Clinical Psychology, 5(1)*, 635-644.

Pope, H.G., Olivardia, R., Gruber, A., & Borowiecki, J. (1999). Evolving Ideals of Male Body Image as Seen Through Action Toys, *International Journal of Eating Disorders, 26(1)*, 65-72.

Pugliese M.T., Lifshitz F., Grad G., Fort P., & Marks-Katz M. (1983). Fear of Obesity. A Cause of Short Stature and Delayed Puberty, *New England Journal of Medicine, 309(9)*, 513-518....

Rimm, S., & Rimm, E. (2004). *Rescuing the Emotional Lives of Overweight Children*. New York: Rodale.

Roehling, M. (1999). Weight-Based Discrimination in Employment: Psychological and Legal Aspects, *Personnel Psychology, 52*, 969-1016.

Rosengren, A., Wilhelmsena, L., & Orth-Gomérb, K. (2004). Coronary Disease in Relation to Social Support and Social Class in Swedish Men, *European Heart Journal, 25(1)*, 56-63.

Rothblum, E.D., Brand, P.A., Miller, C.T., & Oetjen, H.A. (1990). The Relationship Between Obesity, Employment Discrimination, and Employment-Related Victimization, *Journal of Vocational Behavior, 37*, 251-266.

Rudd Center on Food Policy and Obesity (2006). Who We Are: Rudd Center Mission. Retrieved September 30, 2006, from http://www.yaleruddcenter.org/default.aspx?id=29.

Saguy, A.C., & Riley, K.W. (2005). Weighing Both Sides: Morality, Mortality, and Framing Contests over Obesity, *Journal of Health Politics, Policy, and Law, 30(5)*, 869-921.

Schwartz M.B., Chambliss, H.O., Brownell, K.D., Blair, S.N., & Billington, C. (2003). Weight Bias Among Health Professionals Specializing in Obesity, *Obesity Research, 11(9)*, 1033-1039.

Sjöberg, R.L., Nilsson, K.W., & Leppert, J. (2005). Obesity, Shame, and Depression in School-Age Children: A Population-Based Study, *Pediatrics, 116(3)*, e389-e393....

Teachman, B.A., & Brownell, K.D. (2002). Implicit Anti-fat Bias Among Health Professionals: Is Anyone Immune? *International Journal of Obesity, 25(10)*, 1525-1531.

Teachman, B.A., Gapinski, K.D., Brownell, K.D., Rawlins, M., & Jeyaram, S. (2003). Demonstrations of Implicit Anti-fat Bias: The Impact of Providing Causal Information and Evoking Empathy, *Health Psychology, 22(1)*, 68-78.

Wee, C.C., Hamel, M.B., Davis, R.B., & Phillips, R.S. (2004). Assessing the Value of Weight

Loss Among Primary Care Patients, *Journal of General Internal Medicine, 19*, 1206-1211.

World Health Organization (2006). Controlling the Global Obesity Epidemic. Retrieved November 27, 2006, from http://www.who.int/nutrition/topics/obesity/en/index.html.

Young, L., & Powell, B. (1985). The Effects of Obesity on the Clinical Judgments of Mental Health Professionals, *Journal of Health and Social Behavior, 26(3)*, 233-246.

Questions

1. Does the field of fat studies by its nature necessitate that scholars hold certain views on the topic of weight and bodily diversity? To what degree are those views that Wann opposes in her article valuable or worth considering?
2. Discuss Wann's frequent association of weight diversity with height diversity. Do you find this comparison convincing? Why or why not?
3. How do you feel about Wann's project of reclaiming the word "fat," and her criticism of euphemisms such as "heavy"? Examine your own response to the word "fat." Does the word make you uncomfortable? Why or why not?
4. Does Wann's foreword challenge any assumptions or beliefs you hold regarding weight? Discuss.
5. Wann states that "in a fat-hating society everyone is fat." What does she mean by this?
6. Compare the fat acceptance movement to other historical and contemporary social justice movements. How are they similar or different? In your opinion, should fat acceptance receive the same degree of attention that other issues, such as LGBTQ rights, have gained in media and popular discussion?

AI WEIWEI

HEARTLESS[1]

The artist and activist Ai Weiwei played a major role in the formation of China's contemporary art scene. His own work—which ranges from documentary film to sculpture to architecture—often engages critically with Chinese history and politics. Censorship of mainstream media in China has prompted increased interest in blogs, which now play a major role in Chinese political and intellectual life. For several years beginning in 2005 Ai began to post almost daily on the blog from which the following selections are taken, amassing more than 2,700 posts. In 2009, when the blog was deleted by government censors, Ai shifted his online presence to Twitter. Ai's relationship with the government remained tense, and he was arrested and held for almost three months in 2011; since his arrest, he has continued to speak openly about political issues in China.

Decades ago, "Dr. Bethunes"[2] fighting on the medical front lines sold human organs for transplant; now China has become the world's most active market for human organs. It's not because the Chinese people are cheap; even though you live cheaply doesn't mean you'll become cheap after you die. As to why a human might be cheap, that is a philosophical question not addressed in this essay.

Here, we will be discussing purely technical issues.

To put it most accurately, harvesting organs from the bodies of executed criminals is stealing. This is a public secret. Even though they want you dead, your remains should naturally be addressed to you, even in death. This includes

1 *Heartless* Translated by Lee Ambrozy, 2011.

2 *Dr. Bethunes* Reference to Norman Bethune (1890–1939), a Canadian doctor known for medical innovations including the invention of mobile blood transfusion units, and for playing a major role in the provision of medical services to Chinese troops and rural civilians during the Sino-Japanese War (1937–45). He is a celebrated historical figure in China.

the bullet you consumed, and this is probably the reason why it is paid for by the family of the executed.[3]

Not too long ago, "counterrevolutionaries" were paraded through the streets and people flocked in throngs to their execution grounds. You would often hear people talking about who "had a lucky fate," because if one bullet didn't do the trick, they would be forced to use leather shoes to finish the job, "saving a bullet" for the nation.

5 There's not much difference between that era and this one. In this "Spring Tale,"[4] public appreciation of executions is no longer encouraged, and taking into account the excess value that the deceased will produce, the bullet's point of entry requires a much more exacting skill, so that it kills but does not wound. An ambulance is parked where the executed can plainly see it, and as soon as the gun sounds, the whiteclothed angels lunge toward the still-warm corpse with organ transplant coolers in hand.

As a key nation enforcing the death penalty, China executes one-half of the world's population of death row criminals, with a bloodcurdling yearly average of more than four thousand people.[5] All thanks should go to twenty years of "strike hard"[6] and "heavy fist" remediation campaigns. Even before execution, one's fundamental rights and human dignity are forfeited. In the high-profile Yang Jia[7] case, neither he nor his family was notified the day before his execution, and when his mother, who had been secretly incarcerated in a mental hospital, was released to see her son, she had no idea it was to be what we often call their "final moment."

Mr. Wang Jianrong, deputy director of policy and regulations at the Ministry of Health, confirmed that more than 600 hospitals in China are developing

---

3 *the bullet ... executed* In 2010, the Chinese government announced its intention of making lethal injection its standard method of execution, but in 2009 firing squad was still the most common method. The practice of charging the deceased's family for bullets was probably discontinued in the 1980s.

4 *Spring Tale* 1992 song praising the reforms instituted by prominent government leader Deng Xiaoping (1904–97).

5 *China executes ... thousand people* The Chinese government does not keep accurate public records of executions, so the number of annual executions is not known; many human rights organizations estimate that it exceeds the number in all the other countries of the world combined.

6 *"strike hard"* The Strike Hard campaigns, first instituted by Deng, are periodic crackdowns on crime during which the number of arrests is increased and sentences are made more severe.

7 *Yang Jia* In 2008, Yang Jia, who had been beaten and otherwise mistreated by police the previous year, attacked a police station and killed six officers. Many believe that Yang was not given a fair trial, and that the police covered up information concerning events that had provoked the attack; he is widely considered to be a hero.

the technology for organ transplant, and more than 160 among them already possess the necessary qualifications. That figure doesn't include military hospitals and illegal organizations.

You will discover that, as an average person, once you are disassembled and sold, you will become very expensive. If someone opens you and sells your spare parts once you've departed, you become much more valuable than you were as a complete living and breathing organism. On the Chinese mainland, a single kidney, liver, or heart transplant can cost from RMB[8] 140,000–150,000, often surpassing RMB 400,000. Sales to foreign nationals could be many more times than that.

Looking at the global market, prices for human components in Turkey range around US $5,000, in India US $3,000, in Baghdad, Iraq, costs range from US $700 to 1,000, and the average price in the Philippines is US $1,500. You can see that the price is directly related to the harmoniousness and nonharmoniousness of the nation, and whether or not there was suffering.

In China, the phrase "everyone is born equal" is true mostly after death; there's no difference in price between the innards of Deputy Governor Mr. Hu Changqing and People's Congress Vice Chairman Mr. Cheng Kejie from those of murderers Qiu Xinghua or Ma Jiajue.

When melamine destroyed infant kidneys with stones,[9] sufferers with severe damage were compensated at most 30,000 yuan, and those with mild damage were accorded 2,000—that's an awful lot of stir-fried kidneys. Families of those killed in the Beichuan earthquake[10] have been notified that they ought to "be considerate of the government's difficulty," and 60,000 sent them packing. If they refuse to sign for their compensation, they won't get a single penny and they still face potential detention. Price is such a devil.

The market price for Chinese hearts, livers, and lungs isn't the lowest, so why is there an international market? Because China is a nation of harmony, it has a strong army and the state guarantees stability—the supply is abundant,

---

8 *RMB* Renminbi, Chinese currency.

9 *When melamine ... stones* Reference to the 2008 Chinese milk scandal, in which it was discovered that the toxic chemical melamine had been added to baby formula and other dairy products to make the protein content appear higher. More than three hundred thousand children became sick, and it is not yet known how many will face long-term health consequences; at least six children died. It was widely believed that the Chinese government delayed recalling the contaminated products so as not to cause alarm during the Olympics, which were held in Beijing that summer.

10 *Beichuan earthquake* Major 2008 natural disaster, also called the Sichuan earthquake, in which more than 69,000 people died. Much of Ai's activism during this period surrounded the deaths of a large number of children who had been attending poorly constructed schools that collapsed during the earthquake.

fresh, and boasts a high potential for a match. Recently, the Japanese Kyodo News Agency reported that seventeen Japanese citizens exchanged kidneys and livers in China, spending a per capita average of 8 million yen, equivalent to 500,000 yuan. Each operation was stimulating national demand.

Ashamed to admit to the sale of human organs, Chinese officials always respond to the Western media's reports by saying these are "vicious accusations," that such reporting is "anti-Chinese" or "reflects ulterior motives."[11] However, people are often caught red-handed. The "Regulations for Human Organ Transplant" were published in 2007, although this document only exists as a printed pamphlet.

That heartless process of reform and opening has sold off basically everything that can, and can't, be sold. Development is hard logic; if you don't sell, that's your own problem. In the near future the Chinese might wander anywhere, either in our homeland or overseas, and gaze proudly at those people in the distance—it's possible they have a Chinese heart.

Those clever Shanghainese knew they shouldn't sell Yang Jia's organs to the Japanese. If the Japanese were to have even an ounce of his courage, it would take countless warriors to take one of them down.

(11 FEBRUARY 2009)

Questions

1. In this blog post, Ai frequently uses the pronoun "you" when discussing prisoner execution and organ harvesting. What effect does this have?
2. This article was originally published in Chinese on Ai's political blog, which was deleted by government censors later in the same year. How (if at all) is this context reflected in the article's content and style? How (if at all) does its context affect the way you read the article?
3. Describe Ai's tone as he lists the prices of various body parts (paragraphs 8–10). What is the effect of this tone?
4. What connections does this article suggest between the Chinese government's role in organ harvesting and its role other scandals, such as the Chinese milk scandal and the Beichuan earthquake?

---

11 *Chinese ... ulterior motives* The Chinese government deviated from this policy later in 2009 with a public statement acknowledging that two-thirds of transplant organs in China were taken from executed prisoners. Despite repeated official statements that the organ donation system will be or has been reformed, executed prisoners appear to remain a major source of organs in China as of 2016.

5. "In the near future the Chinese might wander anywhere, either in our homeland or overseas, and gaze proudly at those people in the distance—it's possible they have a Chinese heart." Explain the significance of this sentence in the context of the article, taking into consideration the article's title.

LET US FORGET[1]

The following post appeared on Ai's blog on 3 June 2009, the day before the anniversary of the Tiananmen Square massacre (more commonly referred to in China as the "June Fourth Incident"). In 1989, as part of a movement in cities throughout China, protesters demanding democracy and other reforms gathered in Tiananmen Square, Beijing. The Chinese government sent military forces with tanks to clear the square, and an attack on protesters began late in the evening on 3 June; official reports claim that 241 people were killed, but the actual numbers were much higher. The Chinese government instituted more repressive policies following the protest, and as of 2016, public discussion of the massacre is still censored in China.

Let us forget June Fourth, forget that day with no special significance. Life has taught us that every day under totalitarianism is the same day, all totalitarian days are one day, there is no day two, there was no yesterday and is no tomorrow.

Likewise, we no longer need segments of reality, and we no longer need fragmented justice or equality.

People with no freedom of speech, no freedom of the press, and no right to vote aren't human, and they don't need memory. With no right to memory, we choose to forget.

Let us forget every persecution, every humiliation, every massacre, every coverup, every lie, every collapse, and every death. Forget everything that could be a painful memory and forget every time we forget. Everything is just so they might laugh at us like fair and upstanding gentlemen.

Forget those soldiers firing on civilians, the tank wheels crushing the bod- 5
ies of students, the bullets whistling down streets and the bloodshed, the city

1 *Let Us Forget* Translated by Lee Ambrozy, 2011.

and the square that didn't shed tears. Forget the endless lies, the leaders in power who insist that everyone must forget, forget their weaknesses, wickedness, and ineptitude. You surely will forget, they must be forgotten, they can exist only when they are forgotten. For our own survival, let us forget.

(3 June 2009)

Questions

1. Explain the role of irony in this article.
2. Why does Ai say we must forget "[f]or our own survival"? How (if at all) might remembering also be a matter of survival?
3. What connection does this blog post draw between freedom and memory?
4. Comment on the use of repetition in this piece. Is it an effective rhetorical strategy?

ELIZABETH KOLBERT

THE SIXTH EXTINCTION?

In this 2009 article for The New Yorker*, an environmentalist journalist investigates the worldwide reduction in natural diversity—and its disturbing resemblance to the mass extinctions of our planet's past.*

Kolbert later expanded the ideas she had put forward in the article into a full-length book; The Sixth Extinction: An Unnatural History*, published in 2014, was awarded the Pulitzer Prize for General Non-fiction.*

The town of El Valle de Antón, in central Panama, sits in the middle of a volcanic crater formed about a million years ago. The crater is almost four miles across, but when the weather is clear you can see the jagged hills that surround the town, like the walls of a ruined tower. El Valle has one main street, a police station, and an open-air market that offers, in addition to the usual hats and embroidery, what must be the world's largest selection of golden-frog figurines. There are golden frogs sitting on leaves and—more difficult to understand—golden frogs holding cell phones. There are golden frogs wearing frilly skirts, and golden frogs striking dance poses, and ashtrays featuring golden frogs smoking cigarettes through a holder, after the fashion of F.D.R.* The golden frog, which is bright yellow with dark brown splotches, is endemic to the area around El Valle. It is considered a lucky symbol in Panama—its image is often printed on lottery tickets—though it could just as easily serve as an emblem of disaster.

In the early nineteen-nineties, an American graduate student named Karen Lips established a research site about two hundred miles west of El Valle, in the Talamanca Mountains, just over the border in Costa Rica. Lips was planning to study the local frogs, some of which, she later discovered, had never been identified. In order to get to the site, she had to drive two hours from the nearest town—the last part of the trip required tire chains—and then hike for an hour in the rain forest.

Lips spent two years living in the mountains. "It was a wonderland," she recalled recently. Once she had collected enough data, she left to work on her dissertation. She returned a few months later, and though nothing seemed to have changed, she could hardly find any frogs. Lips couldn't figure out what was happening. She collected all the dead frogs that she came across—there were only a half dozen or so—and sent their bodies to a veterinary pathologist in the United States. The pathologist was also baffled: the specimens, she told Lips, showed no signs of any known disease.

A few years went by. Lips finished her dissertation and got a teaching job. Since the frogs at her old site had pretty much disappeared, she decided that she needed to find a new location to do research. She picked another isolated spot in the rain forest, this time in western Panama. Initially, the frogs there seemed healthy. But, before long, Lips began to find corpses lying in the streams and moribund animals sitting on the banks. Sometimes she would pick up a frog and it would die in her hands. She sent some specimens to a second pathologist in the US, and, once again, the pathologist had no idea what was wrong.

5 Whatever was killing Lips's frogs continued to move, like a wave, east across Panama. By 2002, most frogs in the streams around Santa Fé, a town in the province of Veraguas, had been wiped out. By 2004, the frogs in the national park of El Copé, in the province of Coclé, had all but disappeared. At that point, golden frogs were still relatively common around El Valle; a creek not far from the town was nicknamed Thousand Frog Stream. Then, in 2006, the wave hit.

Of the many species that have existed on earth—estimates run as high as fifty billion—more than ninety-nine per cent have disappeared. In the light of this, it is sometimes joked that all of life today amounts to little more than a rounding error.

Records of the missing can be found everywhere in the world, often in forms that are difficult to overlook. And yet extinction has been a much contested concept. Throughout the eighteenth century, even as extraordinary fossils were being unearthed and put on exhibit, the prevailing view was that species were fixed, created by God for all eternity. If the bones of a strange creature were found, it must mean that the creature was out there somewhere.

"Such is the economy of nature," Thomas Jefferson* wrote, "that no instance can be produced, of her having permitted any one race of her animals to become extinct; of her having formed any link in her great work so weak as to be broken." When, as President, he dispatched Meriwether Lewis and William Clark to the Northwest,* Jefferson hoped that they would come upon live mastodons roaming the region.

The French naturalist Georges Cuvier was more sceptical. In 1812, he published an essay on the "Revolutions of the Surface of the Globe," in which he asked, "How can we believe that the immense mastodons, the gigantic megatheriums, whose bones have been found in the earth in the two Americas, still live on this continent?" Cuvier had conducted studies of the fossils found in gypsum mines in Paris, and was convinced that many organisms once common to the area no longer existed. These he referred to as *espèces perdues*, or lost species. Cuvier had no way of knowing how much time had elapsed in forming the fossil record. But, as the record indicated that Paris had, at various points, been under water, he concluded that the *espèces perdues* had been swept away by sudden cataclysms.

"Life on this earth has often been disturbed by dreadful events," he wrote. "Innumerable living creatures have been victims of these catastrophes." Cuvier's essay was translated into English in 1813 and published with an introduction by the Scottish naturalist Robert Jameson, who interpreted it as proof of Noah's flood.* It went through five editions in English and six in French before Cuvier's death, in 1832.

Charles Darwin was well acquainted with Cuvier's ideas and the theological spin they had been given. (He had studied natural history with Jameson at the University of Edinburgh.) In his theory of natural selection, Darwin embraced extinction; it was, he realized, essential that some species should die out as new ones were created. But he believed that this happened only slowly. Indeed, he claimed that it took place even more gradually than speciation: "The complete extinction of the species of a group is generally a slower process than their production." In "On the Origin of Species," published in the fall of 1859, Darwin heaped scorn on the catastrophist approach:

> So profound is our ignorance, and so high our presumption, that we marvel when we hear of the extinction of an organic being; and as we do not see the cause, we invoke cataclysms to desolate the world.

By the start of the twentieth century, this view had become dominant, and to be a scientist meant to see extinction as Darwin did. But Darwin, it turns out, was wrong.

Over the past half-billion years, there have been at least twenty mass extinctions, when the diversity of life on earth has suddenly and dramatically contracted. Five of these—the so-called Big Five—were so devastating that they are usually put in their own category. The first took place during the late Ordovican period, nearly four hundred and fifty million years ago, when life was still confined mainly to water. Geological records indicate that more than eighty per cent of marine species died out. The fifth occurred at the end of the Cretaceous period, sixty-five million years ago. The end-Cretaceous event exterminated not just the dinosaurs but seventy-five per cent of all species on earth.

The significance of mass extinctions goes beyond the sheer number of organisms involved. In contrast to ordinary, or so-called background, extinctions, which claim species that, for one reason or another, have become unfit, mass extinctions strike down the fit and the unfit at once. For example, brachiopods, which look like clams but have an entirely different anatomy, dominated the ocean floor for hundreds of millions of years. In the third of the Big Five extinctions—the end-Permian—the hugely successful brachiopods were nearly wiped out, along with trilobites, blastoids, and eurypterids. (In the end-Permian event, more than ninety per cent of marine species and seventy per cent of terrestrial species vanished; the event is sometimes referred to as "the mother of mass extinctions" or "the great dying.")

Once a mass extinction occurs, it takes millions of years for life to recover, and when it does it generally has a new cast of characters; following the end-Cretaceous event, mammals rose up (or crept out) to replace the departed dinosaurs. In this way, mass extinctions, though missing from the original theory of evolution, have played a determining role in evolution's course; as Richard Leakey has put it, such events "restructure the biosphere" and so "create the pattern of life." It is now generally agreed among biologists that another mass extinction is under way. Though it's difficult to put a precise figure on the losses, it is estimated that, if current trends continue, by the end of this century as many as half of earth's species will be gone.

The El Valle Amphibian Conservation Center, known by the acronym EVACC (pronounced "e-vac"), is a short walk from the market where the golden-frog figurines are sold. It consists of a single building about the size of an average suburban house. The place is filled, floor to ceiling, with tanks. There are tall tanks for species that, like the Rabb's fringe-limbed tree frog, live in the forest canopy, and short tanks for species that, like the big-headed robber frog, live on the forest floor. Tanks of horned marsupial frogs, which carry their eggs in a pouch, sit next to tanks of casque-headed frogs, which carry their eggs on their backs.

The director of EVACC is a herpetologist named Edgardo Griffith. Griffith is tall and broad-shouldered, with a round face and a wide smile. He wears a silver ring in each ear and has a large tattoo of a toad's skeleton on his left shin. Griffith grew up in Panama City, and fell in love with amphibians one day in college when a friend invited him to go frog hunting. He collected most of the frogs at EVACC—there are nearly six hundred—in a rush, just as corpses were beginning to show up around El Valle. At that point, the centre was little more than a hole in the ground, and so the frogs had to spend several months in temporary tanks at a local hotel. "We got a very good rate," Griffith assured me. While the amphibians were living in rented rooms, Griffith and his wife, a former Peace Corps volunteer, would go out into a nearby field to catch crickets for their dinner. Now EVACC raises bugs for the frogs in what looks like an oversized rabbit hutch.

EVACC is financed largely by the Houston Zoo, which initially pledged twenty thousand dollars to the project and has ended up spending ten times that amount. The tiny centre, though, is not an outpost of the zoo. It might be thought of as a preserve, except that, instead of protecting the amphibians in their natural habitat, the centre's aim is to isolate them from it. In this way, EVACC represents an ark built for a modern-day deluge. Its goal is to maintain twenty-five males and twenty-five females of each species—just enough for a breeding population.

The first time I visited, Griffith pointed out various tanks containing frogs that have essentially disappeared from the wild. These include the Panamanian golden frog, which, in addition to its extraordinary colouring, is known for its unusual method of communication; the frogs signal to one another using a kind of semaphore.* Griffith said that he expected between a third and a half of all Panama's amphibians to be gone within the next five years. Some species, he said, will probably vanish without anyone's realizing it: "Unfortunately, we are losing all these amphibians before we even know that they exist."

Griffith still goes out collecting for EVACC. Since there are hardly any frogs 20
to be found around El Valle, he has to travel farther afield, across the Panama Canal, to the eastern half of the country.

One day this winter, I set out with him on one of his expeditions, along with two American zookeepers who were also visiting EVACC. The four of us spent a night in a town called Cerro Azul and, at dawn the next morning, drove in a truck to the ranger station at the entrance to Chagres National Park. Griffith was hoping to find females of two species that EVACC is short of. He pulled out his collecting permit and presented it to the sleepy officials manning the station. Some underfed dogs came out to sniff around.

Beyond the ranger station, the road turned into a series of craters connected by ruts. Griffith put Jimi Hendrix on the truck's CD player, and we bounced along to the throbbing beat. (When the driving got particularly gruesome, he would turn down the volume.) Frog collecting requires a lot of supplies, so Griffith had hired two men to help with the carrying. At the very last cluster of houses, in the village of Los Ángeles, they materialized out of the mist. We bounced on until the truck couldn't go any farther; then we all got out and started walking.

The trail wound its way through the rain forest in a slather of red mud. Every few hundred yards, the main path was crossed by a narrower one; these paths had been made by leaf-cutter ants, making millions—perhaps billions—of trips to bring bits of greenery back to their colonies. (The colonies, which look like mounds of sawdust, can cover an area the size of a suburban back yard.) One of the Americans, Chris Bednarski, from the Houston Zoo, warned me to avoid the soldier ants, which will leave their jaws in your shin even after they're dead. "Those'll really mess you up," he observed. The other American, John Chastain, from the Toledo Zoo, was carrying a long hook, for use against venomous snakes. "Fortunately, the ones that can really mess you up are pretty rare," Bednarski said. Howler monkeys screamed in the distance. Someone pointed out jaguar prints in the soft ground.

After about five hours, we emerged into a small clearing. While we were setting up camp, a blue morpho butterfly flitted by, its wings the colour of the sky.

That evening, after the sun set, we strapped on headlamps and clambered down to a nearby stream. Many amphibians are nocturnal, and the only way to see them is to go looking in the dark, an exercise that's as tricky as it sounds. I kept slipping, and violating Rule No. 1 of rain-forest safety: never grab on to something if you don't know what it is. After one of my falls, Bednarski showed me a tarantula the size of my fist that he had found on a nearby tree.

One technique for finding amphibians at night is to shine a light into the forest and look for the reflecting glow of their eyes. The first amphibian sighted this way was a San José Cochran frog, perched on top of a leaf. San José Cochran frogs are part of a larger family known as "glass frogs," so named because their translucent skin reveals the outline of their internal organs. This particular glass frog was green, with tiny yellow dots. Griffith pulled a pair of surgical gloves out of his pack. He stood entirely still and then, with a heronlike gesture, darted to scoop up the frog. With his free hand, he took what looked like the end of a Q-tip and swabbed the frog's belly. Finally, he put the Q-tip in a little plastic vial, placed the frog back on the leaf, and pulled out his camera. The frog stared into the lens impassively.

We continued to grope through the blackness. Someone spotted a La Loma robber frog, which is an orangey-red, like the forest floor; someone else spotted a Warzewitsch frog, which is bright green and shaped like a leaf. With every frog, Griffith went through the same routine—snatching it up, swabbing its belly, photographing it. Finally, we came upon a pair of Panamanian robber frogs locked in amplexus—the amphibian version of sex. Griffith left those two alone.

One of the frogs that Griffith was hoping to catch, the horned marsupial frog, has a distinctive call that's been likened to the sound of a champagne bottle being uncorked. As we sloshed along, the call seemed to be emanating from several directions at once. Sometimes it sounded as if we were right nearby, but then, as we approached, it would fall silent. Griffith began imitating the call, making a cork-popping sound with his lips. Eventually, he decided that the rest of us were scaring the frogs with our splashing. He waded ahead, while we stood in the middle of the stream, trying not to move. When Griffith gestured us over, we found him standing in front of a large yellow frog with long toes and an owlish face. It was sitting on a tree limb, just above eye level. Griffith grabbed the frog and turned it over. Where a female marsupial frog would have a pouch, this one had none. Griffith swabbed it, photographed it, and put it back in the tree.

"You are a beautiful boy," he told the frog.

Amphibians are among the planet's greatest survivors. The ancestors of today's 30
frogs and toads crawled out of the water some four hundred million years ago, and by two hundred and fifty million years ago the earliest representatives of what became the modern amphibian clades*—one includes frogs and toads, a second newts and salamanders—had evolved. This means that amphibians have been around not just longer than mammals, say, or birds; they have been around since before there were dinosaurs. Most amphibians—the word comes from the Greek meaning "double life"—are still closely tied to the aquatic realm from which they emerged. (The ancient Egyptians thought that frogs were produced by the coupling of land and water during the annual flooding of the Nile.) Their eggs, which have no shells, must be kept moist in order to develop. There are frogs that lay their eggs in streams, frogs that lay them in temporary pools, frogs that lay them underground, and frogs that lay them in nests that they construct out of foam. In addition to frogs that carry their eggs on their backs and in pouches, there are frogs that carry them in their vocal sacs, and, until recently at least, there were frogs that carried their eggs in their stomachs and gave birth through their mouths. Amphibians emerged at a time when all the land on earth was part of one large mass; they have since adapted to conditions on every continent except Antarctica. Worldwide, more than six thousand species have been identified, and while the greatest number are found in the tropical rain forests, there are amphibians that, like the sandhill frog of Australia, can live in the desert, and also amphibians that, like the wood frog, can live above the Arctic Circle. Several common North American frogs, including spring peepers, are able to survive the winter frozen solid.

When, about two decades ago, researchers first noticed that something odd was happening to amphibians, the evidence didn't seem to make sense. David Wake is a biologist at the University of California at Berkeley. In the early nineteen-eighties, his students began returning from frog-collecting trips in the Sierra Nevadas empty-handed. Wake remembered from his own student days that frogs in the Sierras had been difficult to avoid. "You'd be walking through meadows, and you'd inadvertently step on them," he told me. "They were just everywhere." Wake assumed that his students were just going to the wrong spots, or that they just didn't know how to look. Then a postdoc* with several years of experience told him that he couldn't find any, either. "I said, 'OK, I'll go up with you and we'll go out to some proven places,'" Wake recalled. "And I took him out to this proven place and we found, like, two toads."

Around the same time, other researchers, in other parts of the world, reported similar difficulties. In the late nineteen-eighties, a herpetologist named Marty Crump went to Costa Rica to study golden toads; she was forced to change her project because, from one year to the next, the toad essentially vanished. (The golden toad, now regarded as extinct, was actually orange; it is not to be confused with the Panamanian golden frog, which is technically also a toad.) Probably simultaneously, in central Costa Rica the populations of twenty species of frogs and toads suddenly crashed. In Ecuador, the jambato toad, a familiar visitor to back-yard gardens, disappeared in a matter of years. And in northeastern Australia biologists noticed that more than a dozen amphibian species, including the southern day frog, one of the more common in the region, were experiencing drastic declines.

But, as the number of examples increased, the evidence only seemed to grow more confounding. Though amphibians in some remote and—relatively speaking—pristine spots seemed to be collapsing, those in other, more obviously disturbed habitats seemed to be doing fine. Meanwhile, in many parts of the world there weren't good data on amphibian populations to begin with, so it was hard to determine what represented terminal descent and what might be just a temporary dip.

"It was very controversial to say that amphibians were disappearing," Andrew Blaustein, a zoology professor at Oregon State University, recalls. Blaustein, who was studying the mating behaviour of frogs and toads in the Cascade Mountains, had observed that some long-standing populations simply weren't there anymore. "The debate was whether or not there really was an amphibian population problem, because some people were saying it was just natural variation." At the point that Karen Lips went to look for her first research site, she purposefully tried to steer clear of the controversy.

"I didn't want to work on amphibian decline," she told me. "There were endless debates about whether this was a function of randomness or a true pattern. And the last thing you want to do is get involved when you don't know what's going on."

But the debate was not to be avoided. Even amphibians that had never seen a pond or a forest started dying. Blue poison-dart frogs, which are native to Suriname, had been raised at the National Zoo, in Washington, DC, for several generations. Then, suddenly, the zoo's tank-bred frogs were wiped out.

It is difficult to say when, exactly, the current extinction event—sometimes called the sixth extinction—began. What might be thought of as its opening phase appears to have started about fifty thousand years ago. At that time, Australia was home to a fantastic assortment of enormous animals; these included a wombatlike creature the size of a hippo, a land tortoise nearly as big as a VW Beetle, and the giant short-faced kangaroo, which grew to be ten feet tall. Then all of the continent's largest animals disappeared. Every species of marsupial weighing more than two hundred pounds—there were nineteen of them—vanished, as did three species of giant reptiles and a flightless bird with stumpy legs known as *Genyornis newtoni*.

This die-off roughly coincided with the arrival of the first people on the continent, probably from Southeast Asia. Australia is a big place, and there couldn't have been very many early settlers. For a long time, the coincidence was discounted. Yet, thanks to recent work by geologists and paleontologists, a clear global pattern has emerged. About eleven thousand years ago, three-quarters of North America's largest animals—among them mastodons, mammoths, giant beavers, short-faced bears, and sabre-toothed tigers—began to go extinct. This is right around the time the first humans are believed to have wandered across the Bering land bridge. In relatively short order, the first humans settled South America as well. Subsequently, more than thirty species of South American "megamammals," including elephant-size ground sloths and rhino-like creatures known as toxodons, died out.

And what goes for Australia and the Americas also goes for many other parts of the world. Humans settled Madagascar around two thousand years ago; the island subsequently lost all mammals weighing more than twenty pounds, including pygmy hippos and giant lemurs. "Substantial losses have occurred throughout near time," Ross MacPhee, a curator at the American Museum of Natural History, in New York, and an expert on extinctions of the recent geological past, has written. "In the majority of cases, these losses occurred when, and only when, people began to expand across areas that had never before experienced their presence." The Maori arrived in New Zealand around eight hundred years ago. They encountered eleven species of moas—huge ostrichlike creatures without wings. Within a few centuries—and possibly within a single century—all eleven moa species were gone. While these "first contact" extinctions were most pronounced among large animals, they were not confined to them. Humans discovered the Hawaiian Islands around fifteen hundred years ago; soon afterward, ninety per cent of Hawaii's native bird species disappeared.

"We expect extinction when people arrive on an island," David Steadman, the curator of ornithology at the Florida Museum of Natural History, has written. "Survival is the exception."

Why was the first contact with humans so catastrophic? Some of the animals may have been hunted to death; thousands of moa bones have been found at Maori archaeological sites, and man-made artifacts have been uncovered near mammoth and mastodon remains at more than a dozen sites in North America. Hunting, however, seems insufficient to account for so many losses across so many different taxa in so many parts of the globe. A few years ago, researchers analyzed hundreds of bits of emu and *Genyornis newtoni* eggshell, some dating from long before the first people arrived in Australia and some from after. They found that around forty-five thousand years ago, rather abruptly, emus went from eating all sorts of plants to relying mainly on shrubs. The researchers hypothesized that Australia's early settlers periodically set the countryside on fire—perhaps to flush out prey—a practice that would have reduced the variety of plant life. Those animals which, like emus, could cope with a changed landscape survived, while those which, like *Genyornis*, could not died out.

When Australia was first settled, there were maybe half a million people on earth. There are now more than six and a half billion, and it is expected that within the next three years the number will reach seven billion.

Human impacts on the planet have increased proportionately. Farming, logging, and building have transformed between a third and a half of the world's land surface, and even these figures probably understate the effect, since land not being actively exploited may still be fragmented. Most of the world's major waterways have been diverted or dammed or otherwise manipulated—in the United States, only two per cent of rivers run unimpeded—and people now use half the world's readily accessible freshwater runoff. Chemical plants fix more atmospheric nitrogen than all natural terrestrial processes combined, and fisheries remove more than a third of the primary production of the temperate coastal waters of the oceans. Through global trade and international travel, humans have transported countless species into ecosystems that are not prepared for them. We have pumped enough carbon dioxide into the air to alter the climate and to change the chemistry of the oceans.

Amphibians are affected by many—perhaps most—of these disruptions. Habitat destruction is a major factor in their decline, and agricultural chemicals seem to be causing a rash of frog deformities. But the main culprit in the wave-like series of crashes, it's now believed, is a fungus. Ironically, this fungus, which belongs to a group known as chytrids (pronounced "kit-rids"), appears to have been spread by doctors.

Chytrid fungi are older even than amphibians—the first species evolved more than six hundred million years ago—and even more widespread. In a manner of speaking, they can be found—they are microscopic—just about everywhere, from the tops of trees to deep underground. Generally, chytrid fungi feed off dead plants; there are also species that live on algae, species that live on roots, and species that live in the guts of cows, where they help break down cellulose. Until two pathologists, Don Nichols and Allan Pessier, identified a weird microorganism growing on dead frogs from the National Zoo, chytrids had never been known to attack vertebrates. Indeed, the new chytrid was so unusual that an entire genus had to be created to accommodate it. It was named *Batrachochytrium dendrobatidis*—*batrachos* is Greek for "frog"—or Bd for short.

Nichols and Pessier sent samples from the infected frogs to a mycologist at the University of Maine, Joyce Longcore, who managed to culture the Bd fungus. Then they exposed healthy blue poison-dart frogs to it. Within three weeks, the animals had sickened and died.

The discovery of Bd explained many of the data that had previously seemed so puzzling. Chytrid fungi generate microscopic spores that disperse in water; these could have been carried along by streams, or in the runoff after a rainstorm, producing what in Central America showed up as an eastward-moving scourge. In the case of zoos, the spores could have been brought in on other frogs or on tracked-in soil. Bd seemed to be able to live on just about any frog or toad, but not all amphibians are as susceptible to it, which would account for why some populations succumbed while others appeared to be unaffected.

Rick Speare is an Australian pathologist who identified Bd right around the same time that the National Zoo team did. From the pattern of decline, Speare suspected that Bd had been spread by an amphibian that had been moved around the globe. One of the few species that met this condition was *Xenopus laevis*, commonly known as the African clawed frog. In the early nineteen-thirties, a British zoologist named Lancelot Hogben discovered that female *Xenopus laevis*, when injected with certain types of human hormones, laid eggs. His discovery became the basis for a new kind of pregnancy test and, starting in the late nineteen-thirties, thousands of African clawed frogs were exported out of Cape Town. In the nineteen-forties and fifties, it was not uncommon for obstetricians to keep tanks full of the frogs in their offices.

To test his hypothesis, Speare began collecting samples from live African clawed frogs and also from specimens preserved in museums. He found that specimens dating back to the nineteen-thirties were indeed already carrying the fungus. He also found that live African clawed frogs were widely infected with Bd, but seemed to suffer no ill effects from it. In 2004, he co-authored an influential paper that argued that the transmission route for the fungus began in southern Africa and ran through clinics and hospitals around the world.

"Let's say people were raising African clawed frogs in aquariums, and 50
they just popped the water out," Speare told me. "In most cases when they did that, no frogs got infected, but then on that hundredth time, one local frog

might have been infected. Or people might have said, 'I'm sick of this frog. I'm going to let it go.' And certainly there are populations of African clawed frogs established in a number of countries around the world, to illustrate that that actually did occur."

At this point, Bd appears to be, for all intents and purposes, unstoppable. It can be killed by bleach—Clorox is among the donors to EVACC—but it is impossible to disinfect an entire rain forest. Sometime in the last year or so, the fungus jumped the Panama Canal. (When Edgardo Griffith swabbed the frogs on our trip, he was collecting samples that would eventually be analyzed for it.) It also seems to be heading into Panama from the opposite direction, out of Colombia. It has spread through the highlands of South America, down the eastern coast of Australia, and into New Zealand, and has been detected in Italy, Spain, and France. In the US, it appears to have radiated from several points, not so much in a wavelike pattern as in a series of ripples.

In the fossil record, mass extinctions stand out, so sharply that the very language scientists use to describe the earth's history derives from them. In 1840, the British geologist John Phillips divided life into three chapters: the Paleozoic (from the Greek for "ancient life"), the Mesozoic ("middle life"), and the Cenozoic ("new life"). Phillips fixed as the dividing point between the first and second eras what would now be called the end-Permian extinction, and between the second and the third the end-Cretaceous event. The fossils from these eras were so different that Phillips thought they represented three distinct episodes of creation.

Darwin's resistance to catastrophism meant that he couldn't accept what the fossils seemed to be saying. Drawing on the work of the eminent geologist Charles Lyell, a good friend of his, Darwin maintained that the apparent discontinuities in the history of life were really just gaps in the archive. In "On the Origin of Species," he argued:

> With respect to the apparently sudden extermination of whole families or orders, as of Trilobites at the close of the palaeozoic period and of Ammonites at the close of the secondary period, we must remember what has been already said on the probable wide intervals of time between our consecutive formations; and in these intervals there may have been much slow extermination.

All the way into the nineteen-sixties, paleontologists continued to give talks with titles like "The Incompleteness of the Fossil Record." And this view might have persisted even longer had it not been for a remarkable, largely inadvertent discovery made in the following decade.

In the mid-nineteen-seventies, Walter Alvarez, a geologist at the Lamont 55
Doherty Earth Observatory, in New York, was studying the earth's polarity. It had recently been learned that the orientation of the planet's magnetic field reverses, so that every so often, in effect, south becomes north and then vice versa. Alvarez and some colleagues had found that a certain formation of pinkish limestone in Italy, known as the *scaglia rossa*, recorded these occasional reversals. The limestone also contained the fossilized remains of millions of tiny sea creatures called foraminifera. In the course of several trips to Italy, Alvarez became interested in a thin layer of clay in the limestone that seemed to have been laid down around the end of the Cretaceous. Below the layer, certain species of foraminifera—or forams, for short—were preserved. In the clay layer there were no forams. Above the layer, the earlier species disappeared and new forams appeared. Having been taught the uniformitarian view, Alvarez wasn't sure what to make of what he was seeing, because the change, he later recalled, certainly "looked very abrupt."

Alvarez decided to try to find out how long it had taken for the clay layer to be deposited. In 1977, he took a post at the University of California at Berkeley, where his father, the Nobel prize-winning physicist Luis Alvarez, was also teaching. The older Alvarez suggested using the element iridium to answer the question.

Iridium is extremely rare on the surface of the earth, but more plentiful in meteorites, which, in the form of microscopic grains of cosmic dust, are constantly raining down on the planet. The Alvarezes reasoned that, if the clay layer had taken a significant amount of time to deposit, it would contain detectable levels of iridium, and if it had been deposited in a short time it wouldn't. They enlisted two other scientists, Frank Asaro and Helen Michel, to run the tests, and gave them samples of the clay. Nine months later, they got a phone call. There was something seriously wrong. Much too much iridium was showing up in the samples. Walter Alvarez flew to Denmark to take samples of another layer of exposed clay from the end of the Cretaceous. When they were tested, these samples, too, were way out of line.

The Alvarez hypothesis, as it became known, was that everything—the clay layer from the *scaglia rossa*, the clay from Denmark, the spike in iridium, the shift in the fossils—could be explained by a single event. In 1980, the Alvarezes and their colleagues proposed that a six-mile-wide asteroid had slammed into the earth, killing off not only the forams but the dinosaurs and all the other organisms that went extinct at the end of the Cretaceous. "I can remember working very hard to make that 1980 paper just as solid as it could possibly be," Walter Alvarez recalled recently. Nevertheless, the idea was greeted with incredulity.

"The arrogance of these people is simply unbelievable," one paleontologist told the *Times*.

60 "Unseen bodies dropping into an unseen sea are not for me," another declared.

Over the next decade, evidence in favour of an enormous impact kept accumulating. Geologists looking at rocks from the end of the Cretaceous in Montana found tiny mineral grains that seemed to have suffered a violent shock. (Such "shocked quartz" is typically found in the immediate vicinity of meteorite craters.) Other geologists, looking in other parts of the world, found small, glasslike spheres of the sort believed to form when molten-rock droplets splash up into the atmosphere. In 1990, a crater large enough to have been formed by the enormous asteroid that the Alvarezes were proposing was found, buried underneath the Yucatán.* In 1991, that crater was dated, and discovered to have been formed at precisely the time the dinosaurs died off.

"Those eleven years seemed long at the time, but looking back they seem very brief," Walter Alvarez told me. "Just think about it for a moment. Here you have a challenge to a uniformitarian viewpoint that basically every geologist and paleontologist had been trained in, as had their professors and their professors' professors, all the way back to Lyell. And what you saw was people looking at the evidence. And they gradually did come to change their minds."

Today, it's generally accepted that the asteroid that plowed into the Yucatán led, in very short order, to a mass extinction, but scientists are still uncertain exactly how the process unfolded. One theory holds that the impact raised a cloud of dust that blocked the sun, preventing photosynthesis and causing widespread starvation. According to another theory, the impact kicked up a plume of vaporized rock travelling with so much force that it broke through the atmosphere. The particles in the plume then recondensed, generating, as they fell back to earth, enough thermal energy to, in effect, broil the surface of the planet.

Whatever the mechanism, the Alvarezes' discovery wreaked havoc with the uniformitarian idea of extinction. The fossil record, it turned out, was marked by discontinuities because the history of life was marked by discontinuities.

65 In the nineteenth century, and then again during the Second World War, the Adirondacks were a major source of iron ore. As a result, the mountains are now riddled with abandoned mines. On a grey day this winter, I went to visit one of the mines (I was asked not to say which) with a wildlife biologist named Al Hicks. Hicks, who is fifty-four, is tall and outgoing, with a barrel chest and ruddy cheeks. He works at the headquarters of the New York State Department of Environmental Conservation, in Albany, and we met in a parking lot not far from his office. From there, we drove almost due north.

Along the way, Hicks explained how, in early 2007, he started to get a lot of strange calls about bats. Sometimes the call would be about a dead bat that had been brought inside by somebody's dog. Sometimes it was about a live—or half-alive—bat flapping around on the driveway. This was in the middle of winter, when any bat in the Northeast should have been hanging by its feet in a state of torpor. Hicks found the calls bizarre, but, beyond that, he didn't know what to make of them. Then, in March 2007, some colleagues went to do a routine census of hibernating bats in a cave west of Albany. After the survey, they, too, phoned in.

"They said, 'Holy shit, there's dead bats everywhere,'" Hicks recalled. He instructed them to bring some carcasses back to the office, which they did. They also shot photographs of live bats hanging from the cave's ceiling. When Hicks examined the photographs, he saw that the animals looked as if they had been dunked, nose first, in talcum powder. This was something he had never run across before, and he began sending the bat photographs to all the bat specialists he could think of. None of them could explain it, either.

"We were thinking, Oh boy, we hope this just goes away," he told me. "It was like the Bush Administration.* And, like the Bush Administration, it just wouldn't go away." In the winter of 2008, bats with the white powdery substance were found in thirty-three hibernating spots. Meanwhile, bats kept dying. In some hibernacula, populations plunged by as much as ninety-seven per cent.

That winter, officials at the National Wildlife Health Center, in Madison, Wisconsin, began to look into the situation. They were able to culture the white substance, which was found to be a never before identified fungus that grows only at cold temperatures. The condition became known as white-nose syndrome, or W.N.S. White nose seemed to be spreading fast; by March, 2008, it had been found on bats in three more states—Vermont, Massachusetts, and Connecticut—and the mortality rate was running above seventy-five per cent. This past winter, white nose was found to have spread to bats in five more states: New Jersey, New Hampshire, Virginia, West Virginia, and Pennsylvania.

In a paper published recently in *Science*, Hicks and several co-authors 70
observed that "parallels can be drawn between the threat posed by W.N.S. and that from chytridiomycosis, a lethal fungal skin infection that has recently caused precipitous global amphibian population declines."

When we arrived at the base of a mountain not far from Lake Champlain, more than a dozen people were standing around in the cold, waiting for us. Most, like Hicks, were from the D.E.C., and had come to help conduct a bat census. In addition, there was a pair of biologists from the US Fish and Wildlife Service and a local novelist who was thinking of incorporating a subplot about white nose into his next book. Everyone put on snowshoes, except for the novelist, who hadn't brought any, and began tromping up the slope toward the mine entrance.

The snow was icy and the going slow, so it took almost half an hour to reach an outlook over the Champlain Valley. While we were waiting for the novelist to catch up—apparently, he was having trouble hiking through the three-foot-deep drifts—the conversation turned to the potential dangers of entering an abandoned mine. These, I was told, included getting crushed by falling rocks, being poisoned by a gas leak, and plunging over a sheer drop of a hundred feet or more.

After another fifteen minutes or so, we reached the mine entrance—essentially, a large hole cut into the hillside. The stones in front of the entrance were white with bird droppings, and the snow was covered with paw prints. Evidently, ravens and coyotes had discovered that the spot was an easy place to pick up dinner.

"Well, shit," Hicks said. Bats were fluttering in and out of the mine, and in some cases crawling on the ground. Hicks went to catch one; it was so lethargic that he grabbed it on the first try. He held it between his thumb and his forefinger, snapped its neck, and placed it in a ziplock bag.

"Short survey today," he announced.

At this point, it's not known exactly how the syndrome kills bats. What is known is that bats with the syndrome often wake up from their torpor and fly around, which leads them to die either of starvation or of the cold or to get picked off by predators.

We unstrapped our snowshoes and put on helmets. Hicks handed out headlamps—we were supposed to carry at least one extra—and packages of batteries; then we filed into the mine, down a long, sloping tunnel. Shattered beams littered the ground, and bats flew up at us through the gloom. Hicks cautioned everyone to stay alert. "There's places that if you take a step you won't be stepping back," he warned. The tunnel twisted along, sometimes opening up into concert-hall-size chambers with side tunnels leading out of them. Over the years, the various sections of the mine had acquired names; when we reached something called the Don Thomas section, we split up into groups to start the survey. The process consisted of photographing as many bats as possible. (Later on, back in Albany, someone would have to count all the bats in the pictures.) I went with Hicks, who was carrying an enormous camera, and one of the biologists from the Fish and Wildlife Service, who had a laser pointer. The biologist would aim the pointer at a cluster of bats hanging from the ceiling. Hicks would then snap a photograph. Most of the bats were little brown bats; these are the most common bats in the US, and the ones you are most likely to see flying around on a summer night. There were also Indiana bats, which are on the federal endangered-species list, and small-footed bats, which, at the rate things are going, are likely to end up there. As we moved along, we kept disturbing the bats, which squeaked and started to rustle around, like half-asleep children.

Since white nose grows only in the cold, it's odd to find it living on mammals, which, except when they're hibernating (or dead), maintain a high body temperature. It has been hypothesized that the fungus normally subsists by breaking down organic matter in a chilly place, and that it was transported to bat hibernacula, where it began to break down bats. When news of white nose began to get around, a spelunker sent Hicks photographs that he had shot in Howe's Cave, in central New York. The photographs, which had been taken in 2006, showed bats with clear signs of white nose and are the earliest known record of the syndrome. Howe's Cave is connected to Howe's Caverns, a popular tourist destination.

"It's kind of interesting that the first record we have of this fungus is photographs from a commercial cave in New York that gets about two hundred thousand visits a year," Hicks told me.

Despite the name, white nose is not confined to bats' noses; as we worked 80
our way along, people kept finding bats with freckles of fungus on their wings and ears. Several of these were dispatched, for study purposes, with a thumb and forefinger. Each dead bat was sexed—males can be identified by their tiny penises—and placed in a ziplock bag.

At about 7 pm, we came to a huge, rusty winch, which, when the mine was operational, had been used to haul ore to the surface. By this point, we were almost down at the bottom of the mountain, except that we were on the inside of it. Below, the path disappeared into a pool of water, like the River Styx.* It was impossible to go any further, and we began working our way back up.

Bats, like virtually all other creatures alive today, are masters of adaptation descended from lucky survivors. The earliest bat fossil that has been found dates from fifty-three million years ago, which is to say twelve million years after the impact that ended the Cretaceous. It belongs to an animal that had wings and could fly but had not yet developed the specialized inner ear that, in modern bats, allows for echolocation. Worldwide, there are now more than a thousand bat species, which together make up nearly a fifth of all species of mammals. Most feed on insects; there are also bats that live off fruit, bats that eat fish—they use echolocation to detect minute ripples in the water—and a small but highly celebrated group that consumes blood. Bats are great colonizers—Darwin noted that even New Zealand, which has no other native mammals, has its own bats—and they can be found as far north as Alaska and as far south as Tierra del Fuego.

In the time that bats have evolved and spread, the world has changed a great deal. Fifty-three million years ago, at the start of the Eocene, the planet was very warm, and tropical palms grew at the latitude of London. The climate cooled, the Antarctic ice sheet began to form, and, eventually, about two million years ago, a period of recurring glaciations began. As recently as fifteen thousand years ago, the Adirondacks were buried under ice.

One of the puzzles of mass extinction is why, at certain junctures, the resourcefulness of life seems to falter. Powerful as the Alvarez hypothesis proved to be, it explains only a single mass extinction.

85 "I think that, after the evidence became pretty strong for the impact at the end of the Cretaceous, those of us who were working on this naïvely expected that we would go out and find evidence of impacts coinciding with the other events," Walter Alvarez told me. "And, of course, it's turned out to be much more complicated. We're seeing right now that a mass extinction can be caused by human beings. So it's clear that we do not have a general theory of mass extinction."

Andrew Knoll, a paleontologist at Harvard, has spent most of his career studying the evolution of early life. (Among the many samples he keeps in his office are fossils of microorganisms that lived 2.8 billion years ago.) He has also written about more recent events, like the end-Permian extinction, which took place two hundred and fifty million years ago, and the current extinction event.

Knoll noted that the world can change a lot without producing huge losses; ice ages, for instance, come and go. "What the geological record tells us is that it's time to worry when the rate of change is fast," he told me. In the case of the end-Permian extinction, Knoll and many other researchers believe that the trigger was a sudden burst of volcanic activity; a plume of hot mantle rock from deep in the earth sent nearly a million cubic miles' worth of flood basalts streaming over what is now Siberia. The eruption released enormous quantities of carbon dioxide, which presumably led—then as now—to global warming, and to significant changes in ocean chemistry.

"CO_2 is a paleontologist's dream," Knoll told me. "It can kill things directly, by physiological effects, of which ocean acidification is the best known, and it can kill things by changing the climate. If it gets warmer faster than you can migrate, then you're in trouble."

In the end, the most deadly aspect of human activity may simply be the pace of it. Just in the past century, CO_2 levels in the atmosphere have changed by as much—a hundred parts per million—as they normally do in a hundred-thousand year glacial cycle. Meanwhile, the drop in ocean pH levels that has occurred over the past fifty years may well exceed anything that happened in the seas during the previous fifty million. In a single afternoon, a pathogen like

Bd can move, via United or American Airlines, halfway around the world. Before man entered the picture, such a migration would have required hundreds, if not thousands, of years—if, indeed, it could have been completed at all.

Currently, a third of all amphibian species, nearly a third of reef-building 90
corals, a quarter of all mammals, and an eighth of all birds are classified as "threatened with extinction." These estimates do not include the species that humans have already wiped out or the species for which there are insufficient data. Nor do the figures take into account the projected effects of global warming or ocean acidification. Nor, of course, can they anticipate the kinds of sudden, terrible collapses that are becoming almost routine.

I asked Knoll to compare the current situation with past extinction events. He told me that he didn't want to exaggerate recent losses, or to suggest that an extinction on the order of the end-Cretaceous or end-Permian was imminent. At the same time, he noted, when the asteroid hit the Yucatán, "it was one terrible afternoon." He went on, "But it was a short-term event, and then things started getting better. Today, it's not like you have a stress and the stress is relieved and recovery starts. It gets bad and then it keeps being bad, because the stress doesn't go away. Because the stress is us."

Aeolus Cave, in Dorset, Vermont, is believed to be the largest bat hibernaculum in New England; it is estimated that, before white nose hit, more than two hundred thousand bats—some from as far away as Ontario and Rhode Island—came to spend the winter here. In late February, I went with Hicks to visit Aeolus. In the parking lot of the local general store, we met up with officials from the Vermont Fish and Wildlife Department, who had organized the trip. The entrance to Aeolus is about a mile and a half from the nearest road, up a steep, wooded hillside. This time, we approached by snowmobile. The temperature outside was about twenty-five degrees—far too low for bats to be active—but when we got near the entrance we could, once again, see bats fluttering around. The most senior of the Vermont officials, Scott Darling, announced that we'd have to put on latex gloves and Tyvek suits before proceeding. At first, this seemed to me to be paranoid; soon, however, I came to see the sense of it.

Aeolus is a marble cave that was created by water flow over the course of thousands of years. The entrance is a large, horizontal tunnel at the bottom of a small hollow. To keep people out, the Nature Conservancy, which owns the cave, has blocked off the opening with huge iron slats, so that it looks like the gate of a medieval fortress. With a key, one of the slats can be removed; this creates a narrow gap that can be crawled (or slithered) through. Despite the cold, there was an awful smell emanating from the cave—half game farm, half garbage dump. When it was my turn, I squeezed through the gap and immediately slid on the ice, into a pile of dead bats. The scene, in the dimness, was horrific. There were giant icicles hanging from the ceiling, and from the floor large knobs of ice rose up, like polyps. The ground was covered with dead bats; some of the ice knobs, I noticed, had bats frozen into them. There were torpid bats roosting on the ceiling, and also wide-awake ones, which would take off and fly by or, sometimes, right into us.

Why bat corpses pile up in some places, while in others they get eaten or in some other way disappear, is unclear. Hicks speculated that the weather conditions at Aeolus were so harsh that the bats didn't even make it out of the cave before dropping dead. He and Darling had planned to do a count of the bats in the first chamber of the cave, known as Guano Hall, but this plan was soon abandoned, and it was decided just to collect specimens. Darling explained that the specimens would be going to the American Museum of Natural History, so that there would at least be a record of the bats that had once lived in Aeolus. "This may be one of the last opportunities," he said. In contrast to a mine, which has been around at most for centuries, Aeolus, he pointed out, has existed for millennia. It's likely that bats have been hibernating there, generation after generation, since the end of the last ice age.

"That's what makes this so dramatic—it's breaking the evolutionary chain," Darling said.

He and Hicks began picking dead bats off the ground. Those which were too badly decomposed were tossed back; those which were more or less intact were sexed and placed in two-quart plastic bags. I helped out by holding open the bag for females. Soon, it was full and another one was started. It struck me, as I stood there holding a bag filled with several dozen stiff, almost weightless bats, that I was watching mass extinction in action.

Several more bags were collected. When the specimen count hit somewhere around five hundred, Darling decided that it was time to go. Hicks hung back, saying that he wanted to take some pictures. In the hours we had been slipping around the cave, the carnage had grown even more grotesque; many of the dead bats had been crushed and now there was blood oozing out of them. As I made my way up toward the entrance, Hicks called after me: "Don't step on any dead bats." It took me a moment to realize that he was joking.

(2009)

Questions

1. What is “the sixth extinction”? Is this an appropriate name?
2. Comment on how Kolbert uses imagery to provoke an emotional response to the deaths of animals.
3. Rather than structure her article as one continuous, flowing piece, Kolbert has divided it into sections. Outline the structure of the article in terms of these divisions. How effective is this structure?
4. Kolbert quotes Hicks, who says of white nose syndrome, “‘It’s kind of interesting that the first record we have of this fungus is photographs from a commercial cave in New York that gets about two hundred thousand visits a year.’” What is he implying? To what extent does the information in the article support this implication?
5. Kolbert focuses on frogs and bats as illustrative examples of the current extinctions. Find and research another example, and write about it in the style of Kolbert.
6. Does reading this article make you in any way reconsider the impact you have on the environment? Why or why not?

Irene Pepperberg

from Alex & Me: How a Scientist and a Parrot Uncovered a Hidden World of Animal Intelligence—and Formed a Deep Bond in the Process

In Alex & Me, *Irene Pepperberg recounts the thirty years she spent as a researcher conducting experiments with Alex, an African grey parrot. Alex could communicate with a vocabulary of over one hundred words, apply concepts, and count and add as well as a young child. This memoir records Pepperberg's experiences as she worked to scientifically prove Alex's exceptional linguistic and cognitive abilities. In the excerpt printed here, Pepperberg had just taken an appointment teaching in the anthropology department at Northwestern University; she and Alex had just arrived to their new lab.*

A few months after we moved in, a student volunteered to help in the lab. In exchange, I offered to train his parrot, who at that point was wordless. The parrot's favourite thing in the world was apple, so we decided to train her to produce the label "apple." Alex would take part, too. We had never before used food items as training objects with Alex, so this was going to be an exception. Alex had acquired "grape," "banana," and "cherry" on his own, because we named everything we fed him. "Apple" was therefore going to be his fourth fruit label. Or so we thought. Alex apparently had other ideas.

By the end of the season for fresh apples, Alex had learned to produce a puny little "puh" sound, a pathetic fragment of "apple." Nothing more. And he entirely refused to eat apple. We decided to try again the next spring, when fresh apples would arrive from the Southern Hemisphere. Months later Alex did condescend unenthusiastically to eat some apple when offered, but still only produced "puh."

Then suddenly, in the second week of training in mid-March 1985, he looked at the apple quite intently, looked at me, and said "Banerry … I want banerry." He snatched a bite of the apple and ate it happily. He looked as if he had suddenly achieved something he had been searching for.

I had no idea what he was talking about. So I said, "No, Alex, apple."

"Banerry," Alex replied, quickly but quite patiently.

"Apple," I said again.

"Banerry," Alex said again.

OK, buddy, I thought. *I'll make it a bit easier for you.* "Ap-*ple*," I said, emphasizing the second syllable.

Alex paused a second or two, looked at me more intently, and said, "Ban-*erry*," exactly mimicking my cadence.

We went through this double act several times: "Ap-*ple*." "Ban-*erry*." "Ap-*ple*." "Ban-*erry*." I was a little ticked off. I thought Alex was being deliberately obtuse. In retrospect, it was quite hysterical. When I told one of my students, Jennifer Newton, about it later, she literally fell off her chair laughing. But Alex hadn't quite finished with me just yet. At the end of that session he said, very slowly and deliberately, "Ban-*err*-eeee," just as I might do with him when I was trying to teach him a new label. Maybe he was thinking, *Listen carefully, lady. I'm trying to make this easy for you.* I wrote in my journal that Alex seemed "almost angry with us."

I still had no idea what Alex was talking about, even though he obviously thought he did. Try as we might, he wouldn't budge from "banerry." No matter how hard we worked to get him to say "apple," he stuck with his label. As far as Alex was concerned, "banerry" it was and "banerry" it was going to stay.

A few days later I was talking to a linguist friend about all this. He said, "It sounds like lexical elision." It's a fancy term for putting parts of two different words together to form a new word. Alex might have thought the apple tasted a bit like a banana. Certainly it looked like a very large cherry (it was a red apple). "Banana" + "cherry" = "banerry."

Had Alex done this intentionally? It certainly seemed so, but intentionality is a hot-button issue in animal behaviour circles, and proving it is very difficult. Alex often played with sounds, particularly when learning new labels, and especially when he was by himself in the evening. In contrast, these novel sounds typically were nonsensical. And until this point Alex had not said "banerry" in any session with an apple, nor in any informal setting. It really did look like some bird brain creativity of a sort never previously seen. Of course I can't document that scientifically. I can't report that he'd actually gone and decided that that's what he was going to call an apple, and that he was not going to change his mind. It had to remain something remarkable just between Alex and me.…

As the list of scientific publications grew—and as our work garnered more and more public attention—I found a slowly growing acceptance that I wasn't just "that woman who talks to a parrot." I was beginning to be taken seriously in scientific circles. But the chorus of "Oh, he's just mimicking" or "He's just following her cues" still sounded loudly in my ears. At least that is how I perceived it. I found myself having to prove over and over that Alex had more going on in his bird brain than some mechanical trickery or other. One such challenge was, "Oh, he can produce labels all right, and he *sounds* convincing, but does he really understand what he's saying? Does he comprehend the noises coming from his beak?"

It seemed quite clear to me from my hundreds and hundreds of hours watching and listening to Alex that he did indeed know what he was saying. A simple example: if Alex said "Want grape" and you gave him banana, he'd spit it right back at you and repeat insistently, "Want grape." He wouldn't stop until you gave him a grape. If you were dealing with a child, you would accept without question that he or she really wanted a grape, and that banana simply wouldn't do. But that's not science. Science needs numbers. Science needs tests to be done over and over again—actually, sometimes sixty times or more—before the answer has statistical legitimacy, and before scientists will take you seriously. Poor Alex.

A few years into our Northwestern period—my initial, temporary job ultimately stretched out to six and a half years—we embarked on a rigorous series of tests of Alex's comprehension ability. Scientifically I can report that he passed each test, and move on to the next part of our story. But *how* he did it gives us insights into his mind that are striking, if not always quite so easily classified as scientific.

The tests involved putting various of his "toys" on a tray and asking questions such as "What object is green?" "What matter is blue and three-corner?" "What shape is purple?" "How many four-corner wood?" At first, Alex answered correctly most of the time: "key" or "wood" or "wool" or "three," et cetera. But before too long, he started to act up. He would say "green" and then pull at the green felt lining of the tray, hard enough that all the objects would fall off. Or he would say "tray" and bite the tray. Sometimes he'd say nothing and suddenly start preening. Or he'd turn around and lift his butt in my direction, a gesture too obvious to need translation. Once he grabbed the tray out of my hand and flung it on the floor, saying, "Wanna go back," which meant, *I'm done with this. Take me back to my cage.*

Who can blame him? None of the objects were new to him. He'd answered these kinds of questions dozens of times, and yet we still kept asking them, because we needed our statistical sample. You could imagine him thinking, *I've already told you that, stupid*, or simply, *This is getting very boring*. He was like the bright little kid at school who finds none of the work challenging and so passes the time by making trouble.

Sometimes, however, Alex chose to show his opinion of the boring task at hand by playing with our heads. For instance, we would ask him, "What colour key?" and he would give every colour in his repertoire, skipping only the correct colour. Eventually, he became quite ingenious with this game, having more fun getting us agitated rather than giving us the answers we wanted and he surely knew. We were pretty certain he wasn't making mistakes, because it was statistically near to impossible that he could list all but the correct answer. These observations are not science, but they tell you a lot about what was going on in his head; they tell you a lot about how sophisticated his cognitive processes really were. Whether you would describe what he did as something to amuse himself or as making a joke at our expense, I cannot say. But he was definitely doing something other than routinely answering questions.

We became ever more ingenious in presenting our questions, to keep a 20
step ahead of his boredom. Sometimes we succeeded, sometimes we didn't. In the end we did arrive at a statistically valid answer to the question "Does Alex know what he's saying?" Yes, he did. His level of comprehension was equal to that of chimpanzees and dolphins, no small achievement for so small a brain.

Alex faced the same boredom with the next major challenge we gave him: namely, would he understand the concept of "same" and "different"? It might seem like common sense that in order to survive in the wild, birds would, for example, have to identify the songs of individuals and distinguish among species. Surely this involves some grasp of "same" and "different." Yet when I embarked on the "same/different" project with Alex, the scientists who test such things thought that apes were at par or slightly below humans in this conceptual ability, monkeys were below apes, and birds ... well, they hardly counted at all.

The concept of "same/different" is fairly sophisticated cognitively. We trained Alex to use colour and shape as categories with which to determine same or different. When presented with a pair of objects, such as green four-corner wood and blue four-corner wood, Alex's correct response to "What's same?" and "What's different?" would be "shape" and "colour," respectively, not the specific colour or shape. To answer the question correctly, Alex would have to take note of the various attributes of the two objects, understand exactly what I was asking him to compare, make that judgment, and then vocally tell me the answer. No small order for a bird brain.

It took many months to train him, but eventually he was ready to be tested. Because many of the objects we used were familiar, boredom again became an issue. We tried to keep his interest by interspersing "same/different" tests with teaching him new numbers, new labels, and other novel tasks. He was a trouper. Overall, he got the right answer—"shape" or "colour"—about three-quarters of the time. (We also included a third category, "matter," or material.) When we gave him pairs of objects that were novel to him, colours he could not label, for instance, he was right 85 percent of the time, which is actually a better measure of his ability. The novelty obviously held his attention better.

Now, when David Premack had tested chimps on this kind of test, all the animal had to do was indicate whether two objects were the same or different. Alex went a step further in our tests. He was able to tell me exactly what was the same or different: colour, shape, or material. When I reported our results at the International Primatological Congress in Göttingen, Germany in 1986, a senior primatology professor—we called them "silverbacks," referring to the markings of older gorillas—lumbered to his feet and said, "You mean to tell me that your parrot can do what Premack's chimps can do, only in a more sophisticated manner?"

I said, "Yes, that's right," wondering what onslaught might follow. Nothing. He simply said, "Oh," and sat down. I might have burst into song, with "Anything chimps can do, Alex can do better,"* but I restrained myself. Besides, my voice isn't up to it. Nevertheless, this was a moment of triumph for Alex. Pity he wasn't there to witness it.

From the "same/different" challenge, it was natural to go on to relative concepts, such as size difference. Alex got that, too. I could show him two different-sized keys, each a different colour, for instance, and ask him, "Alex, what colour bigger?" and he could tell me. These various achievements attracted a lot of public attention. Bob Bazell, of NBC television, came to film Alex, as did crews from ABC and CBS. Alex was even on the front page of the *Wall Street Journal*. Very smart bird! ...

(2008)

Questions

1. Is Pepperberg's treatment of Alex ethical? Why or why not?
2. Why is intentionality a "hot-button issue in animal behaviour circles"? From reading this excerpt, does it seem to you that Alex displays intentionality?
3. What is Pepperberg's explanation for Alex's label "banerry" for "apple"? Do you think this explanation makes sense? Why or why not?

Marina Keegan

Why We Care about Whales

Marina Keegan was a sophomore at Yale University's Saybrook College when this essay was published in the 11 September 2009 issue of the Yale Daily News. *The essay—which returns repeatedly to the question of how we should ration our caring as we try to help other humans and non-human animals—was republished in Keegan's only book, the posthumous collection* The Opposite of Loneliness *(2014).*

When the moon gets bored, it kills whales. Blue whales and fin whales and humpback, sperm and orca whales; centrifugal forces don't discriminate.

With a hushed retreat, the moon pulls waters out from under fins and flippers, oscillating them backward and forward before they slip outward. At nighttime, the moon watches its work. Silver light traces the strips of lingering water, the jittery crabs, the lumps of tangled seaweed.

Slowly, awkwardly, the whales find their footing. They try to fight the waves, but they can't fight the moon. They can't fight the world's rotation or the bathymetry of oceans or the inevitability that sometimes things just don't work out.

Over 2,000 cetaceans die from beaching every year. Occasionally they trap themselves in solitude, but whales are often beached in groups, huddled together in clusters and rows. Whales feel cohesion, a sense of community, of loyalty. The distress call of a lone whale is enough to prompt its entire pod to rush to its side—a gesture that lands them nose-to-nose in the same sand. It's a fatal symphony of echolocation; a siren call to the sympathetic.

The death is slow. As mammals of the Artiodactyla order, whales are 5
conscious breathers. Inhalation is a choice, an occasional rise to the ocean's surface. Although their ancestors lived on land, constant oxygen exposure overwhelms today's creatures.

Beached whales become frantic, captives to their hyperventilation. Most die from dehydration. The salty air shrinks their oily pores, capturing their moisture. Deprived of the buoyancy water provides, whales can literally crush themselves to death. Some collapse before they dry out—their lungs suffocating under their massive bodies—or drown when high tides cover their blowholes, filling them slowly while they're too weak to move. The average whale can't last more than 24 hours on land.

In their final moments, they begin belching and erupting in violent thrashing. Finally, their jaws open slightly—not all the way, but just enough that the characteristic illusion of a perpetual smile disappears. This means it's over. I know this because I watched as 23 whale mouths unhinged. As 23 pairs of whale eyes glazed over.

I had woken up that morning to a triage centre* outside my window. Fifty or so pilot whales were lying along the stretch of beach in front of my house, surrounded by frenzied neighbours and animal activists. The Coast Guard had arrived while I was still sleeping, and guardsmen were already using boats with giant nets in an attempt to pull the massive bodies back into the water. Volunteers hurried about in groups, digging trenches around the whales' heads to cool them off, placing wet towels on their skin, and forming assembly lines to pour buckets of water on them. The energy was nervous, confused and palpably urgent.

Pilot whales are among the most populous of the marine mammals in the cetacean order. Fully-grown males can measure up to 20 feet and weigh three tons, while females usually reach 16 feet and 1.5 tons.

Their enormity was their problem. Unlike the three dolphins that had managed to strand themselves near our house the previous summer, fifty pilot whales were nearly impossible to manoeuvre. If a combination of unfavourable tidal currents and topography unites, the larger species may be trapped. Sandbars sneak up on them, and the tides tie them back.

People are strange about animals. Especially large ones. Daily, on the docks of Wellfleet Harbor, thousands of fish are scaled, gutted and seasoned with thyme and lemon. No one strokes their sides with water. No one cries when their jaws slip open.

Pilot whales are not an endangered species, and yet people spend tens of thousands of dollars in rescue efforts, trucking the wounded to aquariums and in some places even airlifting them off of beaches. Perhaps the whales' sheer immensity fosters sympathy. Perhaps the stories of Jonah or Moby Dick* do the same. Or maybe it's that article we read last week about that whale in Australia understanding hand signals. Intelligence matters, doesn't it? Brain size is important, right? Those whales knew they were dying. They have some sort of language, some sort of emotion. They give birth, for God's sake! There aren't any pregnant fish in the Wellfleet nets. No communal understanding of their imminent fatality.

I worry sometimes that humans are afraid of helping humans. There's less risk associated with animals, less fear of failure, fear of getting too involved. In war movies, a thousand soldiers can die gruesomely, but when the horse is shot, the audience is heartbroken. It's the *My Dog Skip* effect. The *Homeward Bound** syndrome.

When we hear that the lady on the next street over has cancer, we don't see the entire town flock to her house. We push and shove and wet whales all day, then walk home through town past homeless men curled up on benches—washed up like whales on the curb sides. Pulled outside by the moon and struggling for air among the sewers. They're suffocating too, but there's no town assembly line of food. No palpable urgency, no airlifting plane.

Fifty stranded whales is a tangible crisis with a visible solution. There's 15
camaraderie in the process, a *Free Willy* fantasy, an image of Flipper in everyone's mind.* There's nothing romantic about waking up a man on a park bench and making him walk to a shelter. Little self-righteous fulfillment comes from sending a cheque to Oxfam International.*

Would there be such a commotion if a man washed up on the beach? Yes. But stranded humans don't roll in with the tide—they hide in the corners and the concrete houses and the plains of exotic countries we've never heard of, dying of diseases we can't pronounce.

In theory I can say that our resources should be concentrated on saving human lives, that our "Save the Whales" T-shirts should read "Save the Starving Ethiopians." Logically, it's an easy argument to make. Why do we spend so much time caring about animals? Yes, their welfare is important, but surely that of humans is more so.

Last year a non-profit spent $10,000 transporting a whale to an aquarium in Florida, where it died only three days after arriving. That same $10,000 could have purchased hundreds of thousands of food rations. In theory, this is easy to say.

But looking in the eye of a dying pilot whale at four in the morning, my thoughts were not so philosophical. Four hours until high tide. Keep his skin moist. Just three hours now. There wasn't time for logic. My rationality had slipped away with the ebbing dance of the waves.

I had helped all day. We had managed to save 27 of the 50 whales, but 23 20
others were deemed too far up shore, too old or already too close to death. That night, after most of the volunteers had gone home, I went back outside my bedroom to check on the whales.

It was mid-tide, and the up-shore seaweed still crunched under my bare feet. The water was rising. The moonlight drifted down on the salt-caked battlefield, reflected in the tiny pools of water and half-shell oysters.

It was easy to spot the living whales. Their bodies, still moist, shined in the moonlight. I weaved between carcasses, kneeling down beside an old whale that was breathing deeply and far too rapidly for a healthy pilot.

I put my hands on his nose and placed my face in front of his visible eye. I knew he was going to die, and he knew he was going to die, and we both understood that there was nothing either of us could do about it.

Beached whales die on their sides, one eye pressed into the sand, the other facing up and forced to look at the moon, at the orb that pulled the water out from under its fins.

There's no echolocation on land. I imagined dying slowly next to my mother or a lover, helplessly unable to relay my parting message. I remember trying to convince myself that everything would be fine. But he wouldn't be fine. Just like the homeless man and the Ethiopian aren't fine.

Perhaps I should have been comforting one of them, placing my hands on one of their shoulders. Spending my time and my money and my life saving those who walked on two legs and spoke without echoes.

The moon pulled the waters forward and backward, then inward and around my ankles. Before I could find an answer, the whale's jaw unclenched, opening slightly around the edges.

(2009)

Questions

1. What is the tone of Keegan's opening paragraph?
2. According to this essay, why are humans more motivated to help whales than to help other humans? Why are humans more motivated to help whales than to help fish?
3. To what extent does Keegan personify whales? To what extent does she emphasize their difference from humans?
4. What might the moon symbolize in this piece? How does the symbolism of the moon help structure the essay?
5. When confronted with the suffering of so many humans and other animals worldwide, how should we decide where to put our own limited resources? To what extent should we be guided by reason, and to what extent should we be guided by our own emotions?

Jonathan Safran Foer
from Eating Animals

Foer was already famous as a novelist when he published Eating Animals, *his first non-fiction work, at the age of thirty-two. Moved by the impending arrival of his first child to re-consider the ethics of eating, Foer ended up writing a book that combines anecdote and personal reflection with rigorous argumentation.*

Throughout the book Foer touches on cultural and family traditions relating to the eating of animals; he inquires repeatedly into how it may be possible to square a decision not to eat animals with the seemingly very different values of his grandmother. The excerpt included here is from the book's last chapter, in which he returns to this vexed issue.

The Last Thanksgiving of My Childhood

Throughout my childhood, we celebrated Thanksgiving at my uncle and my aunt's house. My uncle, my mother's younger brother, was the first person on that side of the family to be born on this side of the Atlantic. My aunt can trace her lineage back to the *Mayflower*.* That unlikely pairing of histories was no small part of what made those Thanksgivings so special, and memorable, and, in the very best sense of the word, American.

We would arrive around two o'clock. The cousins would play football on the sloping sliver of a front yard until my little brother got hurt, at which point we would head up to the attic to play football on the various video game systems. Two floors beneath us, Maverick salivated at the stove's window, my father talked politics and cholesterol, the Detroit Lions played their hearts out on an unwatched TV, and my grandmother, surrounded by her family, thought in the language of her dead relatives.

Two dozen or so mismatched chairs circumscribed four tables of slightly different heights and widths, pushed together and covered in matching cloths. No one was fooled into thinking this setup was perfect, but it was. My aunt placed a small pile of popcorn kernels on each plate, which, in the course of the meal, we were supposed to transfer to the table as symbols of things we were thankful for. Dishes came out continuously; some went clockwise, some counter, some zigzagged down the length of the table: sweet potato casserole, homemade rolls, green beans with almonds, cranberry concoctions, yams, buttery mashed potatoes, my grandmother's wildly incongruous kugel,[1] trays of gherkins and olives and marinated mushrooms, and a cartoonishly large turkey that had been put in the oven when last year's was taken out. We talked and talked: about the Orioles and Redskins,* changes in the neighbourhood, our accomplishments, and the anguish of others (our own anguish was off-limits), and all the while, my grandmother would go from grandchild to grandchild, making sure no one was starving....

Thanksgiving is the meal we aspire for other meals to resemble. Of course most of us can't (and wouldn't want to) cook all day every day, and of course such food would be fatal if consumed with regularity, and how many of us really want to be surrounded by our extended families every single night? (It can be challenge enough to have to eat with myself.) But it's nice to imagine all meals being so deliberate. Of the thousand-or-so meals we eat every year, Thanksgiving dinner is the one that we try most earnestly to get right. It holds the hope of being a *good* meal, whose ingredients, efforts, setting, and consuming are expressions of the best in us. More than any other meal, it is about good eating and good thinking.

5 And more than any other food, the Thanksgiving turkey embodies the paradoxes of eating animals: what we do to living turkeys is just about as bad as anything humans have ever done to any animal in the history of the world. Yet what we do with their dead bodies can feel so powerfully good and right. The Thanksgiving turkey is the flesh of competing instincts—of remembering and forgetting.

I'm writing these final words a few days before Thanksgiving. I live in New York now and only rarely—at least according to my grandmother—get back to DC. No one who was young is young anymore. Some of those who transferred kernels to the table are gone. And there are new family members. (I am now we.) As if the musical chairs I played at birthday parties were preparation for all of this ending and beginning.

This will be the first year we celebrate in my home, the first time I will prepare the food, and the first Thanksgiving meal at which my son will be old enough to eat the food the rest of us eat. If this entire book could be decanted into a single question—not something easy, loaded, or asked in bad faith, but a question that fully captured the problem of eating and not eating animals—it might be this: Should we serve turkey at Thanksgiving?

WHAT DO TURKEYS HAVE TO DO WITH THANKSGIVING?

What is added by having a turkey on the Thanksgiving table? Maybe it tastes good, but taste isn't the reason it's there—most people don't eat very much

---

1 *kugel* Traditional Jewish casserole.

turkey throughout the year. (Thanksgiving Day accounts for 18 percent of annual turkey consumption.) And despite the pleasure we take in eating vast amounts, Thanksgiving is not about being gluttonous—it is about the opposite.

Perhaps the turkey is there because it is fundamental to the ritual—it is how we celebrate Thanksgiving. Why? Because Pilgrims might have eaten it at their first Thanksgiving?* It's more likely that they didn't. We know that they didn't have corn, apples, potatoes, or cranberries, and the only two written reports from the legendary Thanksgiving at Plymouth mention venison and wildfowl. Though it's conceivable that they ate wild turkey, we know that the turkey wasn't made part of the ritual until the nineteenth century. And historians have now discovered an even earlier Thanksgiving than the 1621 Plymouth celebration that English-American historians made famous. Half a century before Plymouth, early American settlers celebrated Thanksgiving with the Timucua Indians in what is now Florida—the best evidence suggests that the settlers were Catholic rather than Protestant, and spoke Spanish rather than English. They dined on bean soup.

But let's just make believe that the Pilgrims invented Thanksgiving and 10
were eating turkey. Putting aside the obvious fact that the Pilgrims did many things that we wouldn't want to do now (and that we want to do many things they didn't), the turkeys *we* eat have about as much in common with the turkeys the Pilgrims might have eaten as does the ever-punch-lined tofurkey.* At the centre of *our* Thanksgiving tables is an animal that never breathed fresh air or saw the sky until it was packed away for slaughter. At the end of *our* forks is an animal that was incapable of reproducing sexually. In *our* bellies is an animal with antibiotics in its belly. The very genetics of our birds are radically different. If the Pilgrims could have seen into the future, what would they have thought of the turkey on our table? Without exaggeration, it's unlikely that they would have recognized it as a turkey.

And what would happen if there were no turkey? Would the tradition be broken, or injured, if instead of a bird we simply had the sweet potato casserole, homemade rolls, green beans with almonds, cranberry concoctions, yams, buttery mashed potatoes, pumpkin and pecan pies? Maybe we could add some Timucuan bean soup.[2] It's not so hard to imagine it. See your loved ones around the table. Hear the sounds, smell the smells. There is no turkey. Is the holiday undermined? Is Thanksgiving no longer Thanksgiving?

Or would Thanksgiving be enhanced? Would the choice not to eat turkey be a more active way of celebrating how thankful we feel? Try to imagine the conversation that would take place. *This is why our family celebrates this way.*

---

2 *Timucuan bean soup* Traditional soup from Timucua First Nation which was present at what is now considered the first Thanksgiving.

Would such a conversation feel disappointing or inspiring? Would fewer or more values be transmitted? Would the joy be lessened by the hunger to eat that particular animal? Imagine your family's Thanksgivings after you are gone, when the question is no longer "Why don't we eat this?" but the more obvious one: "Why did they ever?" Can the imagined gaze of future generations shame us, in Kafka's sense of the word,[3] into remembering?

The secrecy that has enabled the factory farm is breaking down. The three years I spent writing this book, for example, saw the first documentation that livestock contribute more to global warming than anything else; saw the first major research institution (the Pew Commission) recommend the total phaseout of multiple dominant intensive-confinement practices (gestation and veal crates) as a result of negotiations with industry (rather than campaigns against industry); saw the first supermarket chain of any kind (Whole Foods) commit to a systematic and extensive program of animal welfare labelling; and saw the first major national newspaper (the *New York Times*) editorialize against factory farming as a whole, arguing that "animal husbandry has been turned into animal abuse," and "manure ... has been turned into toxic waste."

We can't plead ignorance, only indifference. Those alive today are the generations that came to know better. We have the burden and the opportunity of living in the moment when the critique of factory farming broke into the popular consciousness. We are the ones of whom it will be fairly asked, *What did you do when you learned the truth about eating animals?*

THE TRUTH ABOUT EATING ANIMALS

5 Since 2000—*after* Temple Grandin reported improvement in slaughterhouse conditions—workers have been documented using poles like baseball bats to hit baby turkeys, stomping on chickens to watch them "pop," beating lame pigs with metal pipes, and knowingly dismembering fully conscious cattle. One needn't rely on undercover videos by animal right organizations to know of these atrocities—although they are plentiful and sufficient. I could have filled several books—an encyclopedia of cruelty—with worker testimonials.

Gail Eisnitz comes close to creating such an encyclopedia in her book *Slaughterhouse*. Researched over a ten-year period, it is filled with interviews with workers who, combined, represent more than two million hours of slaughterhouse experience; no work of investigative journalism on the topic is as comprehensive.

---

3 *shame ... word* Earlier in *Eating Animals*, Foer examines the claim that in Kafka's work shame is presented as "the core experience of the ethical."

> One time the knocking gun[4] was broke all day, they were taking a knife and cutting the back of the cow's neck open while he's still standing up. They would just fall down and be ashaking. And they stab cows in the butt to make 'em move. Break their tails. They beat them so bad.... And the cow be crying with its tongue stuck out.
>
> This is hard to talk about. You're under all this stress, all this pressure. And it really sounds mean, but I've taken [electric] prods and stuck them in their eyes. And held them there.
>
> Down in the blood pit[5] they say that the smell of blood makes you aggressive. And it does. You get an attitude that if that hog kicks at me, I'm going to get even. You're already going to kill the hog, but that's not enough. It has to suffer.... You go in hard, push hard, blow the windpipe, make it drown in its own blood. Split its nose. ... I wasn't the only guy doing this kind of stuff. One guy I work with actually chases hogs into the scalding tank. And everybody—hog drivers, shacklers, utility men—uses lead pipes on hogs. Everybody knows it, all of it.

These statements are disturbingly representative of what Eisnitz discovered in interviews. The events described are not sanctioned by industry, but they should not be regarded as uncommon.

Undercover investigations have consistently revealed that farmworkers, labouring under what Human Rights Watch describes as "systematic human rights violations," have often let their frustrations loose on farmed animals or simply succumbed to the demands of supervisors to keep slaughter lines moving at all costs and without second thoughts. Some workers clearly are sadistic in the literal sense of that term. But I never met such a person. The several dozen workers I met were good people, smart and honest people doing their best in an impossible situation. The responsibility lies with the mentality of the meat industry that treats both animals and "human capital" like machines....

Just how common do such savageries have to be for a decent person to be unable to overlook them? ...

When Temple Grandin first began to quantify the scale of abuse in slaughterhouses, she reported witnessing "deliberate acts of cruelty occurring on a regular basis" at 32 percent of the plants she surveyed during announced visits in the United States. It's such a shocking statistic I had to read it three times. *Deliberate* acts, occurring on a *regular* basis, witnessed by an *auditor*—witnessed

---

4 *knocking gun* Captive bolt pistol used to stun livestock before slaughter.

5 *blood pit* Area allocated to slaughter.

during *announced* audits that gave the slaughterhouse time to clean up the worst problems. … In recent surveys, Grandin witnessed a worker dismembering a fully conscious cow, cows waking up on the bleed rail, and workers "poking cows in the anus area with an electric prod." What went on when she was not looking? And what about the vast majority of plants that don't open their doors to audits in the first place?

Farmers have lost—have had taken from them—a direct, human relationship with their work. Increasingly, they don't own the animals, can't determine their methods, aren't allowed to apply their wisdom, and have no alternative to high-speed industrial slaughter. The factory model has estranged them not only from how they labour (hack, chop, saw, stick, lop, cut), but what they produce (disgusting, unhealthy food) and how the product is sold (anonymously and cheaply). Human beings cannot be human (much less humane) under the conditions of a factory farm or slaughterhouse. It's the most perfect workplace alienation in the world right now. Unless you consider what the animals experience.

THE AMERICAN TABLE

We shouldn't kid ourselves about the number of ethical eating options available to most of us. There isn't enough nonfactory chicken produced in America to feed the population of Staten Island and not enough nonfactory pork to serve New York City, let alone the country. Ethical meat is a promissory note, not a reality. Any ethical-meat advocate who is serious is going to be eating a lot of vegetarian fare.

A good number of people seem to be tempted to continue supporting factory farms while also buying meat outside that system when it is available. That's nice. But if it is as far as our moral imaginations can stretch, then it's hard to be optimistic about the future. Any plan that involves funnelling money to the factory farm won't end factory farming. How effective would the Montgomery bus boycott* have been if the protesters had used the bus when it became inconvenient not to? How effective would a strike be if workers announced they would go back to work as soon as it became difficult to strike? If anyone finds in this book encouragement to buy some meat from alternative sources while buying factory farm meat as well, they have found something that isn't here.

If we are at all serious about ending factory farming, then the absolute least we can do is stop sending cheques to the absolute worst abusers. For some, the decision to eschew factory-farmed products will be easy. For others, the decision will be a hard one. To those for whom it sounds like a hard decision (I would have counted myself in this group), the ultimate question is whether it is worth the inconvenience. We *know*, at least, that this decision will help prevent deforestation, curb global warming, reduce pollution, save oil reserves, lessen the burden on rural America, decrease human rights abuses, improve public health, and help eliminate the most systematic animal abuse in world history. What we don't know, though, may be just as important. How would making such a decision change *us?*

Setting aside the direct material changes initiated by opting out of the factory farm system, the decision to eat with such deliberateness would itself be a force with enormous potential. What kind of world would we create if three times a day we activated our compassion and reason as we sat down to eat, if we had the moral imagination and the pragmatic will to change our most fundamental act of consumption? Tolstoy famously argued that the existence of slaughterhouses and battlefields is linked. Okay, we don't fight wars because we eat meat, and some wars should be fought—which is not to mention that Hitler was a vegetarian. But compassion is a muscle that gets stronger with use, and the regular exercise of choosing kindness over cruelty would change us.

It might sound naive to suggest that whether you order a chicken patty or a 25
veggie burger is a profoundly important decision. Then again, it certainly would have sounded fantastic if in the 1950s you were told that where you sat in a restaurant or on a bus[6] could begin to uproot racism. It would have sounded equally fantastic if you were told in the early 1970s, before Cesar Chavez's workers' rights campaigns,* that refusing to eat grapes could begin to free farmworkers from slave-like conditions. It might sound fantastic, but when we bother to look, it's hard to deny that our day-to-day choices shape the world. When America's early settlers decided to throw a tea party in Boston,* forces powerful enough to create a nation were released. Deciding what to eat (and what to toss overboard) is the founding act of production and consumption that shapes all others. Choosing leaf or flesh, factory farm or family farm, does not in itself change the world, but teaching ourselves, our children, our local communities, and our nation to choose conscience over ease can. One of the greatest opportunities to live our values—or betray them—lies in the food we put on our plates. And we will live or betray our values not only as individuals, but as nations.

We have grander legacies than the quest for cheap products. Martin Luther King Jr. wrote passionately about the time when "one must take a position that is neither safe, nor politic, nor popular. Sometimes we simply have to make a decision because one's conscience tells one that it is right." These famous words of King's, and the efforts of Chavez's United Farm Workers, are also our legacy. We might want to say that these social-justice movements have

---

6 *where you sat ... on a bus* Reference to means of protesting segregation laws by passively disobeying them (such as the Woolworth Sit-In or Rosa Parks' refusal to obey a bus driver).

nothing to do with the situation of the factory farm. Human oppression is not animal abuse. King and Chavez were moved by a concern for suffering humanity, not suffering chickens or global warming. Fair enough. One can certainly quibble with, or even become enraged by, the comparison implicit in invoking them here, but it is worth noting that Cesar Chavez and King's wife, Coretta Scot King, were vegans, as is King's son Dexter. We interpret the Chavez and King legacies—we interpret America's legacy—too narrowly if we assume in advance that they cannot speak against the oppression of the factory farm.

THE GLOBAL TABLE

... Rationally, factory farming is so obviously wrong, in so many ways. In all of my reading and conversations, I've yet to find a credible defense of it. But food is not rational. Food is culture, habit, and identity. For some, that irrationality leads to a kind of resignation. Food choices are likened to fashion choices or lifestyle preferences—they do not respond to judgments about how we should live. And I would agree that the messiness of food, the almost infinite meanings it proliferates, does make the question of eating—and eating animals especially—surprisingly fraught. Activists I spoke with were endlessly puzzled and frustrated by the disconnect between clear thinking and people's food choices. I sympathize but I also wonder if it is precisely the irrationality of food that holds the most promise.

Food is never simply a calculation about which diet uses the least water or causes the least suffering. And it is in this, perhaps, that our greatest hope for actually motivating ourselves to change lies. In part, the factory farm requires us to suppress conscience in favour of craving. But at another level, the ability to reject the factory farm can be exactly what we most desire.

The debacle of the factory farm is not, I've come to feel, just a problem about ignorance—it's not, as activists often say, a problem that arose because "people don't know the facts." Clearly that is one cause. I've filled this book with an awful lot of facts because they are a necessary starting point. And I've presented what we know scientifically about the legacy we are creating with our daily food choices because that also matters a great deal. I'm not suggesting our reason should not guide us in many important ways, but simply that being human, being humane, is more than an exercise of reason. Responding to the factory farm calls for a capacity to care that dwells beyond information, and beyond the oppositions of desire and reason, fact and myth, and even human and animal.

The factory farm will come to an end because of its absurd economics someday. It is radically unsustainable. The earth will eventually shake off factory farming like a dog shakes off fleas; the only question is whether we will get shaken off along with it.

Thinking about eating animals, especially publicly, releases unexpected forces into the world. The questions are charged like few others. From one angle of vision, meat is just another thing we consume, and matters in the same way as the consumption of paper napkins or SUVs—if to a greater degree. Try changing napkins at Thanksgiving, though—even do it bombastically, with a lecture on the immorality of such and such a napkin maker—and you will have a hard time getting anyone worked up. Raise the question of a vegetarian Thanksgiving, though, and you'll have no problem eliciting strong opinions—at least strong opinions. The question of eating animals hits chords that resonate deeply with our sense of self—our memories, desires, and values. Those resonances are potentially controversial, potentially threatening, potentially inspiring, but always filled with meaning. Food matters and animals matter and eating animals matters even more. The question of eating animals is ultimately driven by our intuitions about what it means to reach an ideal we have named, perhaps incorrectly, "being human."

THE FIRST THANKSGIVING OF MY CHILDHOOD

… However much we obfuscate or ignore it, we know that the factory farm is inhumane in the deepest sense of the word. And we know that there is something that matters in a deep way about the lives we create for the living beings most within our power. Our response to the factory farm is ultimately a test of how we respond to the powerless, to the most distant, to the voiceless—it is a test of how we act when no one is forcing us to act one way or another. Consistency is not required, but engagement with the problem is.

Historians tell a story about Abraham Lincoln, that while returning to Washington from Springfield, he forced his entire party to stop to help some small birds he saw in distress. When chided by the others, he responded, quite plainly, "I could not have slept tonight if I had left those poor creatures on the ground and not restored them to their mother." He did not make (though he might have) a case for the moral value of the birds, their worth to themselves or the ecosystem or God. Instead he observed, quite simply that once those suffering birds came into his view, a moral burden had been assumed. He could not be himself if he walked away. Lincoln was a hugely inconsistent personality, and of course he ate birds far more often than he aided them. But presented with the suffering of a fellow creature, he responded.

Whether I sit at the global table, with my family or with my conscience, the factory farm, for me, doesn't merely appear unreasonable. To accept the factory farm feels inhuman. To accept the factory farm—to feed the food it produces to my family, to support it with my money—would make me less myself, less my grandmother's grandson, less my son's father.

35 *This* is what my grandmother meant when she said, "If nothing matters, there's nothing to save."

(2009)

Questions

1. Foer wonders if "the imagined gaze of future generations" can "shame us" out of eating the Thanksgiving turkey (paragraph 12).
    a. Do you agree with Foer's implication that future generations will view factory farming as a shameful thing? Why or why not?
    b. Factory farming aside, what current practices do you think will be viewed by future generations as shameful?
2. As a guide to ethical behaviour, to what extent is it useful to imagine how our actions will be viewed from the future? Explain your view. Foer criticizes those who buy "ethical meat" when it is available but buy factory farmed meat at other times. What is his argument against this practice? Do you agree with it?
3. In your own eating, how do you reconcile ethical demands with other considerations, such as nutrition, flavour, and tradition?

JEANNETTE ARMSTRONG

EN'OWKIN: WHAT IT MEANS TO A SUSTAINABLE COMMUNITY

In this piece, Okanagan[1] *writer and activist Jeannette Armstrong addresses the meaning and importance of En'owkin, a multi-faceted concept traditional to the Okanagan people. "En'owkin: What It Means to a Sustainable Community" appeared in* Ecoliteracy: Mapping the Terrain *(2000), a sourcebook of readings published by the Center for Ecoliteracy in Berkeley, California.*

The word *En'owkin* comes from the high language of the Okanagan people and has its origin in a philosophy perfected to nurture voluntary cooperation, an essential foundation for everyday living.

The term is based on a metaphorical image created by the three syllables that make up the Okanagan word. The image is of liquid being absorbed drop by single drop through the head (mind). It refers to coming to understanding through a gentle integrative process.

En'owkin is also the name given our education centre by elders of the Okanagan; it is meant to assist and guide us in restoring to wholeness a community fragmented by colonization.

To the Okanagan People, as to all peoples practicing bio-regionally self-sufficient economies, the knowledge that the total community must be engaged in order to attain sustainability is the result of a natural process of survival. The practical aspects of willing teamwork within a whole-community system clearly emerged from experience delineated by necessity. However, the word cooperation is insufficient to describe the organic nature by which members continue to cultivate the principles basic to care-taking one another and other life forms, well beyond necessity.

Having been born into such a living community, albeit one becoming more 5
fragmented, I have come to the conclusion that its philosophy is supported by an infrastructure that governs the imperatives by which choices are made, and

1 *Okanagan* The Okanagan people are a First Nations people whose territory is the Okanagan region, which spans both sides of the Washington and British Columbia border.

that this structure solicits desired results. In this particular living community, the structure that implements the principles could be described as an organizational process, one profoundly deliberate in insuring an outcome that results in a community strengthened by the dynamics of deep collaboration—that is, collaboration at all levels over generations.

En'owkin, practised as a rules-to-order technique, solicits voluntary deep collaboration. As such, En'owkin is engaged in by the community as a customary procedure in order to ensure that the principles of sustainability will be incorporated in decision-making. The customs are cultural traditions arising as a worldview. In the En'owkin process, we do things in a way that enables us to experience collaboration as the most natural and right way to do things. To me the principles of the process seem simple: because they are so deeply imbedded, I cannot see how community could operate other than within these principles. Yet, through articulating them, I have come to discern the complexity and depth of their significance. The principles are most easily represented in a schematic, rather than in words, displaying the structurally integrative nature by which they intersect all levels of human experience.

INDIVIDUAL LAND FAMILY COMMUNITY

What can we come to expect from practising these life principles? First, we can expect each individual to fully appreciate that, while each person is singularly gifted, each actualizes full human potential only as a result of physical, emotional, intellectual, and spiritual well being, and that those four aspects of existence are always contingent on external things.

Second, as an individual, each person is a single facet of a transgenerational organism known as a family. Through this organism flows the powerful lifeblood of cultural transference designed to secure the best probability of well being for each generation.

Third, the family system is the foundation of a long-term living network called community. In its various configurations this network spreads its life force over centuries and across physical space; using its collective knowledge to secure the well being of all by the short- and long-term choices made via its collective process. Finally, a community is the living process that interacts with the vast and ancient body of intricately connected patterns operating in perfect unison called the land. The land sustains all life and must be protected from depletion in order to ensure its health and ability to provide sustenance across generations.

10 It is imperative that community—through the family and the individual—be seen as a whole system engaged in maintaining the principles that ensure its well-being. En'owkin is, to me, a philosophy expressed in the process

of being part of a community. The idea of community, as understood by my ancestors, encompassed a complex holistic view of interconnectedness. Within a contemporary Okanagan context, En'owkin achieves a process of inquiry and decision-making intended to continuously challenge complacency and rigidity.

I have found that it solicits a non-adversarial approach to collaborative decision-making culminating in true consensus making, which in turn encourages both harmony and empowerment.

The holistic parameters of En'owkin demand our responsibility to everything we are connected to—the heart of sustainability. I have most often observed its workings as a governing process, because En'owkin was most visibly engaged during decision-making in my community.

The word En'owkin in the Okanagan language elicits the metaphorical image of liquid being absorbed drop by single drop through the head (mind). It refers to coming to understanding through a gentle process of integration.

The Okanagan people used this word when there was a choice confronting the community. An elder would ask the people to engage in En'owkin, which requested each person contribute information about the subject at hand. What took place was not so much a debate as a process of clarification, incorporating bits of information from as many people as possible, no matter how irrelevant, trivial, or controversial these bits might seem, for in En'owkin, nothing is discarded or prejudged.

The process deliberately seeks no resolution in the first stage. Instead, it 15
seeks concrete information; then inquires how people are affected and how other things might be affected, both in the long and the short term. It seeks out diversity of opinion. Persons with good analytical skills or special knowledge are usually given opportunity to speak, as are spokespersons for individuals or families. Anyone may speak, but only to add new information or insight.

The next stage "challenges" the group to suggest directions mindful of each area of concern put forward. The challenge usually takes the form of questions put to the "elders," the "mothers," the "fathers," and the "youth." Here, the term *elders* refers to those who are like-minded in protecting traditions. The group seeks their spiritual insight as a guiding force of connection to the land. The term *mothers* refers to those who are like-minded in their concern about the daily well-being of the family. The group seeks from the mothers sound advice on policy and on workable systems based on human relations. The term *fathers* refers to those who are like-minded in their concern about the things necessary for security, sustenance, and shelter. Usually the group seeks from the fathers practical strategy, logistics, and action. The term *youth* refers to those who are like-minded in their tremendous creative energy as they yearn for change that will bring a better future. Usually the group seeks from the youths their creative and artistic prowess in theorizing the innovative possibilities and their engagement in carrying it out.

Using this process does not require a rigid meeting format in which information is solicited. Rather, it is imperative that each person play his or her strongest natural role, because that is how each person can best contribute to the community. Persons speaking usually identify the role they've assumed by saying, for example, "I speak as a mother," and proceed to outline what is understood that mothers are being challenged to contribute. Each role is then valued as indispensable to the unit.

YOUTH—innovative possibilities
FATHERS—security, sustenance, shelter
MOTHERS—policy, workable systems
ELDERS—connected to the land

Stated and unstated ground rules of the process "challenge" each member of the group to be considerate and compassionate to all others in the solution building. The process asks that each person be committed to creatively include in his or her own thinking the concerns of all others. It requires each person's understanding to expand to accommodate the whole of the community. The point of the process is not to persuade the community that you are right, as in a debate; rather, the point is to bring you, as an individual, to understand as much as possible the reasons for opposite opinions. Your responsibility is to see the views of others, their concerns and their reasons, which will help you to choose willingly and intelligently the steps that will create a solution—because it is in your own best interest that all needs are addressed in the community. While the process does not mean that everyone agrees—for that is never possible—it does result in everyone being fully informed and agreeing fully on what must take place and what each will concede or contribute.

The action finally taken will be the best possible action, taking into consideration all the short-term, concrete social needs of the community as well as long-term psychological and spiritual needs, because all are essential to a healthy community and to sustainability. This is where diversity of thought and ingenuity resides. The elders describe it as a decision-making process of the group mind at its best. The word they use means something like "our completeness." It creates complete solidarity in a group moving in the direction suggested, at the same time opening the door to a collaborative imagination and innovation much more likely to produce the best answer.

20 It seems to me that in diverse groups the En'owkin process is even more useful because there is a greater possibility of differing opinions. In modern

decision-making, the "Roberts rules of democratic process,"[2] in carrying out the will of the majority, creates great disparity and injustice to the minority, which in turn leads to division, polarity, and ongoing dissension. This type of process is in fact a way to guarantee the continuous hostility and division that give rise to aggressive actions that can destabilize the whole community, creating uncertainty, distrust, and prejudice. Different religions and ethnic origins, inequality of income levels, and inaccessible governing are the best reasons to invoke the En'owkin process.

Real democracy is not about power in numbers; it is about collaboration as an organizational system. Real democracy includes the right of the minority to a remedy, one that is unhampered by the tyranny of a complacent or aggressive majority. The En'owkin process is a mediation process especially designed for community. It is a process that seeks to build solidarity and develop remediated outcomes that will be acceptable, by informed choice, to all who will be affected. Its collaborative decision-making engages everyone in the process; decisions are not handed down by leaders "empowered" to decide for everyone. It is a negotiated process that creates trust and consensus because the solution belongs to everyone for all their own reasons. The process empowers the community, creating unity and strength for the long term. Because land is seen as a fundamental part of the self, along with family and community, it requires and ensures sustainable practice in its practice.

En'owkin as a community-building process makes even more sense as communities grow ever more diverse. While the human mind is naturally focused on survival; community-mind can be developed as a way to magnify the creativity of an individual mind and thus increase an individual's overall potential. A critical component of leadership today is the profit motive that affects us all at every level.

Our original communities have disintegrated; the long-term condition of the human species, and other life forms, has become secondary to short-term profit for the few, allowing for poor choices that have altered the health and lives of millions. I have come to understand that unless change occurs in the ways in which communities use the land, the well-being and survival of us all is at risk. We can change this. For these reasons, I choose to assist in changing the paradigm by joining in a collaborative process to devise a better future.

My contribution in the En'owkin process undertaken by the Center for Ecoliteracy is to share my insight and to assist with my view of an ages-old

---

2 *"Roberts rules of democratic process"* Reference to a book by General Henry M. Robert called *Robert's Rules of Order* (1876). Currently in its eleventh edition, the book outlines democratic parliamentary procedure, according to which decisions are made by vote; it is the most widely used manual of its kind in the United States.

technique perfected by my ancestors for building sustainability principles into community process. Today we human beings face the biggest of obstacles, and so the greatest challenges, to our creativity and responsibility.

Let us begin with courage and without limitations, and we will come up with surprising solutions.

(2000)

Questions

1. How does the En'owkin process differ from the parliamentary process?
2. In your opinion, would Canadians in general benefit from the En'owkin process being part of our governance system? What changes could it effect?
3. Armstrong differentiates between "democracy" as it is practised today and "real" democracy. What does she mean by "real" democracy and how is it different from our current practice?
4. Armstrong describes En'owkin as a decision-making practice ideally suited to communities. In your opinion, could it work for a large-scale community, like a country? Why or why not?

NEAL MCLEOD

CREE* POETIC DISCOURSE

Neal McLeod is a Cree poet, painter, and scholar. The following essay appeared in Across Cultures/Across Borders: Canadian Aboriginal and Native American Literatures, *a collection of creative and academic writing on Aboriginal culture in North America.*

INTRODUCTION

In many Indigenous Studies departments throughout Canada, the discipline has been put into the category of social science. Such an approach, while effective on some levels, does narrative violence to the integrity of Indigenous narrative knowing. By narrative violence, I mean that Indigenous narratives are sanitized and there is a conceptual shift that often takes the vitality away from Indigenous life-worlds. Within the United States, writers such as Robert Warrior, Paula Allen Gunn, and many others have encouraged the use of literary paradigms to examine Indigenous knowledge; they have also, in large part, resisted the narrative violence inflicted upon Indigenous knowing in the academic institutions within Canada.

Thinking poetically involves the movement away from the epistemological straitjacket* and the colonial box* that the social sciences have often placed on Indigenous narratives. Thinking poetically gives us a space to recreate, although imperfectly, the narrative thinking of the greatest of our kêhtê-ayak, Old Ones, and our storytellers. This metaphorical discourse, composed of symbolic and poetic descriptions of the world and our experiences, saturates and permeates Cree narrative memory. I call this way of understanding the world through sound Cree poetics: Cree poetics link human beings to the rest of the world through the process of mamâhtâwisiwin, the process of tapping into the Great Mystery, which, in turn, is mediated by historicity and wâhkôhtowin (kinship). Louise Halfe's poetic interpretation of the classical Cree story Cihcîpiscikwân (Rolling Head) exemplifies the idea of Cree poetics. Halfe's poetic discourse embodies and is part of what I call a "body poetic," which connects our living bodies to the living earth around us.

NARRATIVE VIOLENCE OF CONVENTIONAL ACADEMIC DISCOURSE

Academia has also, in many ways, become an extension of the process of the colonialism of Indigenous people and the subordination of Indigenous narrative knowing. This colonialism is done in a tacit manner, and many people who critique it are dismissed as "radicals." Consequently, these individuals are excluded from the old boys' academic clubs,* which are often exceptionally incestuous. Many of the adherents to the conventional academic disciplines pretend to be leading experts on Indigenous cultural and knowledge ways, which has been a particular problem in fields such as history and anthropology.

Vine Deloria, Jr.,[1] perhaps more than anyone, radically questioned the epistemological and narrative violence inflicted upon Indigenous people. He radically critiques the racism and colonialism that exist in the academy, as well as the culture of tokenism. What made Vine Deloria, Jr.'s critique of Western representations of Indigenous knowing so radical and effective was the fact that he did not care about the manufacturing of Indigenous knowledge within the academy. Ironically, he was hired because he radically attacked the status quo and grounded his position as a lawyer and social activist. While Vine Deloria, Jr. broke a great deal of ground conceptually, his position was like all positions, fundamentally limited because he did not make many culturally specific references within his work. In many ways, his work was a "negative sculpting"* of what Indigenous knowledge was not in relationship to Christianity, modernity, and colonialism. By negative sculpting, I mean the way in which Deloria defines what Indigenous knowledge is not, as opposed to what it is.

5 Our narratives have been guided and dissected by academia; what is needed now is a new wave of writing and a new wave of Indigenous scholarship. As contemporary Indigenous scholars, we need to ground our discourses in culturally specific metaphors and ground ourselves in the languages of the ancient pathways of Indigenous thinking. In essence, we need to build the "positive space"* of Indigenous knowledge. Writers such as Vine Deloria, Jr. were and are important because they were grounded in their communities and cultures; however, contemporary Indigenous scholarship must be one of cultural specificity. Nimosôm[2] (my grandfather), John R. McLeod, a pioneer in the development of Indian control of Indian education, once said that he wished for the "creation of an Indian-controlled institution where the finest

---

1 *Vine Deloria, Jr.* Influential Sioux intellectual and activist (1933–2005) whose work played a significant role in the development of Indigenous studies as a discipline.

2 [McLeod's note] Generally Cree does not use capitals, but the author chooses to use capitals when nouns are embedded in English text so as not to privilege the English language. Also, the author chooses not to use the convention of italicizing Cree so as to avoid the status of Cree as a "foreign language."

Indian thinking could occur." He thought poetically about our traditions by immersing himself in the stories, languages, and ceremonies of the kêhtê-ayak [Old Ones]. Part of this attempt to think poetically involved radically rethinking Christianity—just as Deloria did before him.

Ê-ânisko-âcimocik: Connecting through Storytelling

Ê-ânisko-âcimocik, literally translated, means "they connect through telling stories." The central strand in which Cree poetic discourse flourishes and continues is through the connection of contemporary storytellers and poets to the ancient poetic pathways of our ancestors. By drawing upon the epic and traditional narratives of our people, we can ground ourselves in culturally specific references and linguistic anchors, allowing us, in turn, to resist the onslaught of modernity and colonialism, which while related, are not the same.

One of the key components of Indigenous Studies involves the use of names. Names define and articulate a place within society and the world. Indigenous names are absolutely essential for the description of Indigenous realities. In order to describe this reality, we need words to shape and interpret it. For instance, we need to be able to name the process of poetry. In Cree, I would say that this process could be described as mamâhtâwisiwin [the process of tapping into the Great Mystery], which is mediated by our historicity and wâhkôhtowin (kinship). Because of this connection to other generations, there emerges an ethical dimension to Cree poetic discourse, namely, the moral responsibility to remember.

One of the challenges of linking to the old narrative memory is to keep the language and understandings inherent therein. My great-grandfather, Kôkôcîs, Peter Vandall, noted the importance of language and the need to preserve it in order to maintain ties between generations:

> êwako aya, tâpiskôc ôki anohc, namôya tâpsikoc kiskinahamâtowin ôki nêhiyâsisak, mitoni nitawêyihtamwak nêhiyawak kahkiyaw, tâpiskôt otawâsimisiwâwa môniyaw-kiskêyihtamowin kit-âyayit.
>
> It is that, for instance, the young Crees of today do not seem to want education, all of the Crees really want their children to have White-Man's knowledge. (Vandall 36)

Nicâpan (my great-grandfather) contrasts the western and Cree modes of education, and laments the way in which many Crees have seemingly turned their back on our narrative traditions. He describes how many have absorbed the epistemological and narrative violence inflicted upon our rich traditions. The consequence of this absorption is that we often do not value our traditions, turning, instead, to Western models and frameworks. It is precisely this internalization of colonization that Vine Deloria, Jr. radically attacked as well.

In contrast, Nicâpan notes the importance of having dignity and pride in our narrative traditions:

> êkwa namôya êkosi ta-kî-itôtahkik osk-âyak. ka-kî-kiskêyihtahkik ôma ê-nêhiyâwicik, êkwa onêhiyâwiwiniwâw anima namôya kakêtihk ê-itêyihtâkwaniyik.
>
> Now, the young people should not do that. They should know that they are Cree, and that their Creeness means a great deal. (Vandall 36)

It should be noted that Nicâpan uses terms such as "seems like" and "it appears" to describe the way in which many people, especially young people, have turned their backs on ancient Cree poetic pathways: the way in which kêhtê-ayak transmit culture through stories and narratives. Such a narrative strategy allows people to change their behaviour yet still save their honour in the process. It also invokes the power of ancient Cree poetic pathways as a way of restoring the dignity of his people, especially the younger ones. Within this process, there is a struggle to preserve a narrative genealogy, which differs from the trajectories of English-speaking scholarship and mainstream literatures. Our ancient poetic pathways are not a mimicry of colonial narrative structures,* but are rather grounded in our own traditions and worldviews.

MAMÂHTÂWISIWIN: CREE POETIC PROCESS

Poetic thinking involves dreaming, relying on the visceral, like a painter or jazz musician. A poetic way of thinking urges us to radically rethink the surface of things, like a dreamer. Such thinking allows us to bring back the words and the depth of the Great Mystery that the kêhtê-ayak have already charted out (Ermine). In a way, thinking poetically is radically historical and does not mean the "narrative space" is ordered chronologically. Poetic thinking involves the bending of time to a single point of consciousness. That is why Vine Deloria, Jr. in *God Is Red* so aptly noted that much Indigenous thinking is in terms of space instead of time. Mamâhtâwisiwin, the Cree poetic process, is mediated by not only historicity but also wâhkôhtowin, including our kinship to the land. The process of mamâhtâwisiwin involves spirituality and the belief that reality is more than what we understand on the surface.

10 The term ê-mamâhtâwisit, the verb form of mamâhtâwisiwin, means he or she is "spiritually gifted." It could also be translated perhaps as "they know something that you will never know." Once I asked my friend Edward Caisse from Green Lake, Saskatchewan, about a line from *Pulp Fiction*: "she is a funky dancer." He said, "ê-mamâhtâwisimot" or "she or he knows something that you will never know by the way she dances." Sometimes old Cree words become toys for anthropologists and other cultural tourists, but it should be noted that these terms and ideas have great relevance today. For instance, one Cree term

for computer is "mamâhtâwisi-âpacihcikan," which could be rendered as "the powerful machine."

"Ê-mamâhtâwisit Wisâhkêcâhk" is a common expression within Cree stories. It means that Kistêsinâw, our elder brother, "has the ability to tap into the Great Mystery." Because of this ability, Kistêsinâw was the first ceremonialist, trying to link living beings in this dimension to the force of life beyond our conscious reality. In the process, Wîsahkêcâhk transformed the world, made it safe for humans, and gave names and shapes to creation.

In Louise Halfe's powerful book *The Crooked Good*, the narrator Ê-kwêskît ("Turn around woman") talks about the origin of stories and the source of poetic insight as "[t]he gifted people of long ago, *kayâs kîmamâhtâwisiwak iyiniwak*" (Halfe 3). She adds:

> They never died. They are scattered here, there, everywhere, somewhere. They know the language, the sleep, the dream, the laws, these singers, these healers, *âtayôhkanak*, these ancient story keepers. (Halfe 3)

Just like Nôhtokwêw Âtayôhkan (the Old Grandmother Spirit) keeps the stories, the mamâhtâwisiwak, the poetic dreamers, keep ancient poetic pathways.

In *The Crooked Good*, Halfe discusses the classic Cree narrative Rolling Head and reframes it by retrieving the feminine voice through the sound of colonial imagination. In this work, Cree poetic memory is essential to the process of retrieving the hidden and submerged female perspective.

Ê-kwêskît: she notes that she is a "dreamer" (Halfe 4). She adds, "I dream awake. Asleep ... the day was the story" (Halfe 4). Part of the process is tapping into the Great Mystery, creating pathways for other dreamers. "The story" is always open and always open to re-examination: "So, every day, I am born" (Halfe 4). What Halfe means by this statement is that she can always add more to her journey through life and to her poetic pathway.

EMBODIED UNDERSTANDING

All poetic pathways are "embodied understandings" and are the poet- 15
dreamer's location in understanding the world and reality. In many ways, this idea is similar to Gadamer's notion of *Urteil* ("the original place"). Through an embodied sense of awareness, one is about to link one's own experiences with a larger narrative structure. Through this embodied understanding, one is able to expand one's own understanding and also, in a small way, the larger collective memory.

Often times, this embodied memory involves everyday experience and everyday events. Stories are not abstract and cut off from the living world around but rather are completely enmeshed in the concrete world of sensations and physical connections. Embodied memory is the connection to sensations of the body and also the connection to the sensations of the land.

Marilyn Dumont's poem "âcimowina" in *A Really Good Brown Girl* is an interesting example of this living memory. She does not describe the stories of her grandmother directly but rather the sensations that emerge from the concrete world around. She opens her poem by making the stories (âcimowina) of her grandmother embodied:

> my grandmother stories follow me,
> spill out of their bulging suitcases
> get left under beds
> hung on doorknobs (Dumont 70)

The stories exist within her living place, her house, and are around her in all of the daily sensations: "their stories smell of Noxzema,* mothballs and dried meat" (Dumont 70). The sensation of smell is indeed one of the strongest forms of awareness that we have. She also describes the stories in terms of medicines that are found around her house:

> their Polident dentures in old cottage cheese containers,
> Absorbine Junior, Buckley's and "rat root" take over my bathroom counters (Dumont 70)

By drawing upon Dumont's description and words, we can immerse ourselves in the embodied elements of her grandmother's stories. This poetics of embodiment, of wâhkôhtowin, is also found in various Treaty narratives wherein concepts such as forever (in terms of how long the Treaties would last), which sound very distant and abstract within the English narrative, are rendered poetically embodied through the discourse of traditional knowledge keepers. The well-respected Jim Kâ-Nîpitêhtêw recited the classical Cree phrasing of this:

> hâw, êkos êkwa, êkw ôma k-ês-âsotamâtakok, kâkikê, iskoyikohk pîsim ka-pimohtêt, iskoyikohk sîpiy ka-pimiciwahk, iskoyikohk maskosiya kê-sâkikihiki, êkospî isko ka-pimotêmakan ôma k-ês-âsotamâtân.
>
> Indeed, thus now the promises which I have made for you, forever, so long as the sun shall cross [walk - N.M.] the sky, so long as the rivers shall run, so long as the grass shall grow, that is how long these promises I have made to you will last. (Kâ-Nîpitêhtêw 113)

Forever, then, is understood in relation to the concrete, living earth, and we come to understand its meaning through our connection to these elements.

Central to an embodied, poetic understanding of the world is what I would call the "poetics of empathy," which could be translated into Cree by the term "wâhkôhtowin" (kinship/relationships). Through relations, we are able to create the web of understanding of our embodied locations and stretch it outwards to a wider context of collective historicity and through a poetics grounded in dialogue and an open-ended flow of narrative understanding. A poetics of wâhkôhtowin and empathy are key to a thorough engaging with history. These concepts are at the heart of Louise Halfe's *The Crooked Good*. In her book of poetry, Halfe radically questions the way in which Cihcîpiscikwân (Rolling Head) has been told and urges us to recover the hidden female voice that has been shattered and altered by colonialism and Christianity. Describing this re-imagining of the narrative mapping, she states, "The story gnawed, teased our infinite heavens" (Halfe 22).

In the disseminated versions, the Rolling Head is portrayed as a disembodied woman who has been unfaithful to her husband and who, in turn, has been beheaded. She is also portrayed as a mother who pursues her children and who scares them in her pursuit. What is missing in these accounts is the empathy that we could feel for the mother as well as the embodied understanding of her voice and position within the narrative.

Empathy to Cihcîpiscikwân dramatically enlarges our understanding of the narrative and also moves to correct some of the extreme distortions caused by Christianity, such as the limiting of the role of women, which has often accompanied the colonization of Indigenous women and peoples. Halfe's radical reinterpretation brings back lost elements through narrative imagination, while recreating and redrawing ancient themes and ancient poetic pathways. Cihcîpiscikwân, following and attempting to recover our sons, marks the land and sky in the same way that Wîsâhkêcâhk did. Thus, Cihcîpiscikwân is a dreamer and ancient Cree poet.

Halfe describes the loss of Cihcîpiscikwân and, in particular, the destruction of the home: "Their home eaten by fire" (Halfe 26). The home has been altered and destroyed by a series of factors, not simply because of Rolling Head's infidelity. Another key factor intimated by Halfe is the fact that the husband has been away a great deal because of hunting trips. Rolling Head, through the named narrator of Ê-kwêskît and Rib Woman, regains her character and her point of view. The reshaped narrative gives her position form and embodiment. Halfe notes that Cihcîpiscikwân "dig[s] through *okiskêyihtamawin*—her knowledge/sad and lonely/more than her bitter medicine" (Halfe 16). Cihcîpiscikwân is portrayed as having lost a great deal—the father has pushed things beyond livable limits. By presenting the narrative in this manner, the storyteller gives birth to understanding, and we are empathetic to Cihcîpiscikwân. We feel her pain, and we feel her sorrow.

CIHCÎPISCIKWÂN: THE ROLLING HEAD NARRATIVE

Central to understanding the innovative way in which Louise Halfe has opened the interpretation of the Rolling Head narrative, it would be helpful to examine the narrative in some detail through an intra-textual dialogue. Cree poetic consciousness rests on the notion that a narrative can never exhaust its possibilities, as there are always new embodiments and new interpretative locations. The conversation and dialogue between these interpretative locations and interpretative embodiments also enriches the conversation.

Each telling of a story is an embodiment—by telling I mean in both oral and written forms. Each understanding is, in turn, embodied. Thus, our understanding of poetic narrative pathways is an occasion of speaking and, in turn, an occasion of understanding. Each occasion of speaking/telling accounts for variations within the narratives and helps to explain differences between different accounts. The versions of narratives that have been committed to writing in various forms do not represent the totality of the speaker/teller, nor do they represent the totality of the possibilities of any narrative within a larger context. The occasion of speaking/telling, the demands of the audience, and the time in which the story is communicated alter the way in which the story is presented and, indeed, understood.

An interesting element in the occasion of the speaking/telling of the various versions of the Cihcîpiscikwân âtayôhkêwin (sacred story) is that one can analyze the narratives in the light of Christian influence. By examining the most "complete" version of the narrative, namely that of Edward Ahenakew, we see that the existence of the snake as a lover of Wîsakêcâhk's mother is most striking. A superficial reading would make it appear that the snake is perhaps a Christian influence, especially because Edward Ahenakew was an Anglican priest. What makes this hypothesis more plausible is that the Alanson Skinner text, recorded earlier, does not have the Trickster's mother's lover as a snake. Instead, the lover is simply in human form. It should be noted that there is a profound measure of overlap between the Plains Cree and the Plains Ojibway.

25 Skinner's representation of the lover in human form is also questionable because the Rolling Head and the Flood narrative cycle is scattered throughout Skinner's collection in fragments. From this, we can presume, apart from many of the narratives being summaries, that the stories would have also been told during shorter sessions. Thus, one of the ways in which we can account for the differences between these two representations is related to issues of transcription and also to the fact that Edward Ahenakew was a cultural insider, a Cree from the Sandy Lake reserve. He represented the narratives himself and not through the distorting lens of an outsider anthropologist.

Another argument that the snake is a pre-Christian element is that the Leonard Bloomfield version, which was recorded in the 1930s (a few years after the Ahenakew version), also has the lover as a snake. The decisive counter-evidence that the lover of Cihcîpiscikwân was not a human, but a snake, is in the Bloomfield version: the storyteller consciously juxtaposes his version of creation with the Christian creation story. This juxtaposition would seemingly imply that he was extremely conscious of any Christian influence that may have been operative in the Cree world at the time.

The motif of the snake figures strongly within Cree narrative traditions. Louise Halfe's interpretation of the narrative opens us to non-Christian interpretations of understanding this central figure within the narrative of Cihcîpiscikwân and of a return to older ways of understanding snakes. For instance, there is a story told to me by Charlie Burns of Kâ-Monakos, which is also the origin story for the place name of Maskihkiy Âstôtin (Medicine Hat). Within the narrative, the Crees are surrounded by the Blackfoot, and Kâ-Monakos calls upon his helper the snake to create a tunnel through which the Crees can escape. Thus, in this story, the snake is a helper and not an evil entity as in the Christian framework. Opening this understanding allows us to be more empathetic to Rolling Head's lover and also, in turn, to Rolling Head.

Towards a Critical Cree Poetic Consciousness

Cree narrative memory is essentially open-ended, and different elements of a story can be emphasized during a single performance, which can be characterized as the "occasion of speaking/telling." In other words, there can never be a "complete" authoritative performance of a narrative because the audience and the demands of the occasion will always vary. Furthermore, a narrative can never be fully exhausted because the dynamics between the teller and the listener will also vary: the story will always be understood in slightly different ways depending on the experiences of people in the group listening. Such open-endedness within Cree poetic consciousness is the foundation of critical thinking. I would argue that Cree poetics is a first order act of theory and critical thinking. The storytellers, kâ-mamâhtâwisiwak, engaged in this process open up new possibilities of narratives in a variety of ways: finding new ways of interpreting old narratives in light of new experiences, recovering old voice echoes lost due to colonialism, and discovering new understandings of narratives due to intra-narrative dialogue (âniskwâpitamâcimowin: "the act of inter-textual connecting"). This model of critical consciousness reframes the notion of theory. Instead of theory being abstract and detached from concrete experience, theory (critical poetic consciousness) emerges out of concrete situations and through conversation and storyteller. In this way, then, our Elders and storytellers could be thought of as theorists and critical thinkers.

It is important to remember that Indigenous poetic consciousness does not simply involve a glorification of tradition but rather a radical questioning of tradition, albeit one that is grounded in it. This is perhaps one of the most important contributions of Louise Halfe's book *The Crooked Good*. The title itself reminds me of another of the core elements of Cree poetic thinking. Good and evil are not binary opposites but exist in all possibilities, all moments, and all beings. As Derrida has pointed out, the West has done epistemological violence* to itself by thinking in terms of binaries, which distort a more holistic understanding of reality. This epistemological and narrative violence has by extension through colonialism been inflicted upon Indigenous people and their narratives and texts. Interestingly, the old narrative of Cihcîpiscikwân is described as a "nightmare" (Halfe 20) or an embodiment of trauma, which has occurred collectively through colonization but also existentially through the choices that we make in our daily lives.

In *The Crooked Good*, Louise Halfe helps us move beyond an essentialized understanding of the narrative of Cihcîpiscikwân. She moves towards an organic understanding of the story, and links a contemporary understanding to a past understanding, as evidenced in the last page of the book where the narrator Ê-kwêskît's words exist side by side with those of Rolling Head (Halfe 124). Through this intra-narrative dialogue, the ancient story becomes saturated with new layers and organically grows through the activity of narrative imagination. Narrative imaginations expand the interpretative possibilities of the sacred story and, in turn, the interpretative possibilities of the present moment and present reality. The narrative layering of the story engages our state of being embodied in a collective poetic pathway, allowing us to think critically of this positioning and, finally, to think of possibilities to reshape this embodied present. The central character, Cihcîpiscikwân, embodies this state of critical poetic consciousness: "*cihcipistikwân* stretches through her watery sleep/Phantom arms. Feels ... where does the gathering of the self begin?" (Halfe 19).

Mistasiniy: Linking to Ancient Poetic Pathways in My Own Work

In my own writing as poet, I have drawn heavily upon older Cree narratives. In particular, I have learned a great deal from Charlie Burns, storyteller from Nîhtâikihcikanisihk ("where there is good growing"—my reserve, the James Smith Cree reserve in north-eastern Saskatchewan). In particular, I remember one story, the story of Mistasiniy, which I included in my book *Cree Narrative Memory*. In my upcoming book of poetry, I rendered the narrative in the following way in excerpted form:

MISTASINIY

a boy was in a travois
wood cut earth
makes marks
tâpiskoc nêhiyawâsinahikan
like Cree writing, syllabics
pulled from sun
paths opened up
no light, and lets sun fall
through new cracks
napêsis with kôhkom
passing through prairie
travois holding baby body
loses in the pathway
paths of heard voices

boy was found
by a mosâpêw
buffalo bull
old, body cut
paths across prairie
his old body
memories of clustered
sun's passing
he sheltered the boy
from the wind
sâpowâstan, blowing through
another bull
younger challenged him
did not want
the orphan boy in the camp
he came from those
killed the buffalo, he said
they fought, raced
and the old buffalo won
keep the boy, and sheltered him
like trees hiding the earth
from open suspicious sky

as time gathered
created words and lost others

the boy was told
that he had to go home
mosôm buffalo gave stories
like body held memory
his body moving
ê-waskâwît

people in the boys camp
knew he was coming back
awa ê-kî-kôsapahtat
performed the ceremony
opened ground and sang songs
he came back, came home
but as he left
grandfather turned into stone (McLeod 2008)

Mistasiniy (the Grandfather stone) was destroyed in 1966 because two major waterways were to be joined in Saskatchewan. There was, indeed, a great campaign by many to try to save the stone or move it, but regrettably these efforts did not reach fruition. The narrative embodies the notion of wâhkôhtowin, as the stone embodies the relationship that people have to the buffalo. In addition, the narrative also marks the importance of adoption and the way in which we can raise children, who may not be ours biologically.

I adopted my son, Cody McLeod, and made sense of my adoption through thinking about the Mistasiniy. I wrote a poem about my understanding of the older narrative and I linked the older story organically to my life:

MEDITATIONS ON PASKWA-MOSTOS AWÂSIS

Buffalo Child
I remember
when you came to me vulnerable, shy
unprotected from prairie wind
sickly, dry pasty skin
tired of open spaces
valley loses shelter
trees wind
through the end

Buffalo Child, paskwa-mostos awâsis
wakes the prairie grass
promises of his grandfather

you give your hide
your house of being
sit on open prairie
heavy and old standing earth
broken by dynamite
tears the line of old relationship
but the ancient stone
becomes my body

Buffalo Child
paskwa-mostos awâsis
rock has fallen
clipped from valley's embrace
but the story lives through
this boy
his body becomes
this ancient stone
I took a boy in
like Old Buffalo Grandfather
as I tried my best to guide him
I thought of this story often

our bodies tattooed
with land's memories
with land speak, askiwêwin
even though the stone is gone
the story lives on
old stories give our bodies shape
and guide the path of sound
like trees guiding the wind (McLeod 2008)

I understood that my son Cody was a living embodiment of that story and that the kinship tie to him had been marked in the land by Mistasiniy. These old stories mark our bodies with meaning and live on within us, despite colonial encroachments such as the destruction of the stone. This poem is also an example of the organic nature in which old narratives become alive through our lives and experiences. Cree poetic consciousness radically questions the way in which the West has framed "history" in progressive and teleological terms. Rather, narratives are alive and are embodied in the moment and historicity of our understanding, never fixed and always changing organically, like the colours and shapes in the sky, like the folds and contours of water on lakes.

CONCLUSION

Cree poetic discourse is an old, ancient activity, stretching back to the beginning of Cree consciousness and ceremonies. Mamâhtâwisiwin, "tapping into the Great Mystery," describes this process within the Cree language. If we are to move towards Indigenous Studies as a unique discipline, with its own intellectual and narrative trajectories, we must draw upon conceptual frameworks within Indigenous languages and cultures. Cree poetic discourse connects to old voice echoes—to the stories and embodied experience of the ancestors. Through our dialogue with these older stories (âniskwâpitamâcimowin), pathways of understanding are retravelled and indeed expanded. These poetic pathways are embodied and emerge from a concrete, tactile engagement with the world.

Not only do the ancient, poetic pathways become embodied, they also, through the process of âniskwâpitamâcimowin, of inter-textual narrative interchange, allow us to see beyond the contingencies of the present. In turn, this critical Cree consciousness allows us to re-imagine narratives and to envision and imagine new possibilities for the future. Cree poetic discourse is profoundly grounded in land and territory and ancestral knowledge. At the same time, contemporary poets, writers, and contemporary storytellers extend Cree poetic discourse into the present.

(2010)

WORKS CITED

Ahenakew, Edward. "Cree Trickster Tales." *The Journal of American Folklore*, 42.166 (1929): 309-53.

Bloomfield, Leonard. *Plains Cree Texts*. New York: G.E. Stechert, 1934.

Burns, Charlie. "*kâ-monakos*" told orally to author many times since 2000.

Deloria, Vine, Jr. *God Is Red: A Native View of Religion*. 1972. Golden, CO: Fulcrum, 1994.

Dumont, Marilyn. *A Really Good Brown Girl*. London: Brick Books, 1996.

Ermine, Willie. "Aboriginal Epistemology." *First Nations Education in Canada: The Circle Unfolds*. Ed. Marie Battiste and Jean Barman. Vancouver: U British Columbia P, 1995. 101-12.

Gadamer, Hans-Georg. *Truth and Method*. 1960. New York: Seabury Press, 1975.

Halfe, Louise. *The Crooked Good*. Regina: Couteau Press, 2007.

Kâ-Nîpitêhtêw, Jim (*pimwêwêhahk*). "The Pipestem and the Making of Treaty Six." *ana kâ-pimwêwêhahk okakêskihkêmowina*. Ed. and trans. Freda Ahenakew and H.C. Wolfart. Winnipeg: U of Manitoba P, 1998. 106-19.

McLeod, Neal. *Gabriel's Beach*. Regina: Hagios Press, 2008.

Skinner, Alanson. "Plains Ojibway Tales." *The Journal of American Folklore* 32.124 (1919): 280-305.

Vandall, Peter (*kôkôcîs*). "Being Cree." *wâskahikaniwiyiniw-âcimowina: Stories of the House People*. Ed. and trans. Fred Ahenakew. Winnipeg: U of Manitoba P, 1987. 36-37.

Questions

1. McLeod uses Cree language in his essay, and many of his key concepts are expressed as Cree words.
   a) Explain the following in terms of their importance in the article: kêhtê-ayak, ê-ânisko-âcimocik, mamâhtâwisiwin, and wâhkôhtowin.
   b) Why does McLeod use the Cree words instead of English translations?
2. According to McLeod, why are "all poetic pathways ... 'embodied understandings'"?
3. In what way can Cree "Elders and storytellers ... be thought of as theorists and critical thinkers"?
4. In his poem "meditations on paskwa-mostos awâsis," how does McLeod see the relationship between the ancient story of Mistasiniy and his own life?
5. McLeod argues against the colonialism associated with conventional academic discourse. In terms of writing style and intellectual approach, how does this article compare with other academic essays you have read?
6. The approach to capitalization by McLeod and by a number of other Indigenous writers is to some degree unconventional. Identify some words capitalized in this selection that most writing guides would advise against capitalizing. What ethical or political point do you think the author may be making through his approach to capitalization? More generally, discuss his approach in the context of the tendency of many contemporary writers to employ capital letters much more frequently than writers of previous generations have done.
7. What do you take McLeod to mean when he says that "there can never be a 'complete' authoritative performance of a [Cree] narrative"? What are the advantages of this approach to narrative?
8. McLeod writes that there is "an ethical dimension to Cree poetic discourse, namely, the moral responsibility to remember." What does he mean by this? To what extent do poets and thinkers from other cultures have a similar moral responsibility to their own heritage, and to what extent is this ethical dimension unique to Indigenous discourses?

KRISTEN GILCHRIST

from "NEWSWORTHY" VICTIMS?

In December 2015, the federal government of Canada launched a National Inquiry into Missing and Murdered Indigenous Women. Aboriginal activists had for years been pressuring the government to respond to the disproportionate frequency of violent crime experienced by Aboriginal women: Aboriginal women constitute 2% of Canada's female population but 10% of the country's female homicide victims. Activists have questioned the roles of the government, police, and media in creating a situation in which the murders and disappearances of Aboriginal women have long gone underreported, and in which there has been a lack of public outcry outside Aboriginal communities. In the following article, Kristen Gilchrist analyzes trends in media coverage of the murders of white women and Aboriginal women. The article was first published in the journal Feminist Media Studies *in 2010.*

ABSTRACT

More than 500 Aboriginal women have gone missing or been murdered in Canada since the 1980s yet press attention to this violence is relatively minimal. This paper compares local press coverage of matched cases: three missing/murdered Aboriginal women from Saskatchewan and three missing/murdered White women from Ontario. Quantitative and qualitative content analyses indicate stark disparities in the amount and content of coverage between groups. The Aboriginal women received three and a half times less coverage; their articles were shorter and less likely to appear on the front page. Depictions of the Aboriginal women were also more detached in tone and scant in detail in contrast to the more intimate portraits of the White women. Drawing on feminist media studies and theories of intersectionality, this paper argues that the simultaneous devaluation of Aboriginal womanhood and idealization of middle-class White womanhood contributes to broader systemic inequalities which re/produce racism, sexism, classism, and colonialism. This paper raises concerns about the broader implications of the relative invisibility of missing/

murdered Aboriginal women in the press, and their symbolic annihilation from the Canadian social landscape.

INTRODUCTION

Accounting for 2 percent of Canada's population, Aboriginal women are over-represented as victims of sexual and physical violence and homicide.[1] Aboriginal women aged 25–44 are five times more likely to experience a violent death than any other Canadian woman (Department Of Indian & Northern Affairs 1996). Emerging research has shown that more than five hundred Aboriginal women from all walks of life have gone missing and/or been murdered in Canada since the 1980s—and this number continues to grow (Jacobs & Williams 2008; Native Women's Association of Canada [NWAC] 2008).[2] In the majority of cases the missing women were later found murdered, many in sexual homicides. Nearly half of murder cases remain unsolved (NWAC 2009).

This paper adopts a feminist intersectional approach emphasizing the multiple and connecting dimensions of inequality (Collins [1990] 2000). The intersectional/interlocking nature of racism, sexism, classism, and colonialism compound the vulnerabilities faced by Aboriginal women in Canada (Gilchrist 2008; Larocque 2007; McIvor 2007; Smith 2005). The racialization of Aboriginal women—the process by which they are racially marked and subjected to institutional and everyday racism (Jiwani & Young 2006)—is inextricably linked with and mutually constituted by these other oppressions (Monture-Angus 1995). The material effects of these interconnected disadvantages have led an advocacy group to proclaim Aboriginal women "the most victimized group in Canadian society" (The Elizabeth Fry Society of Saskatchewan, cited in Henry & Tator [2000] 2006, p. 121).

First, I draw on literature outlining the features of a newsworthy crime and victim, with particular emphasis on studies highlighting racial biases in news reporting of violent crimes against women. Next, I present research findings revealing significant disparities in press coverage of Aboriginal and White missing/murdered women. While the press demonstrated a continued, committed, and compassionate response to the White women, depicting them as "the girl next door," the Aboriginal women were largely ignored and thus relegated to the status of invisible "Others" (Jiwani & Young 2006). Links are made

1 [Gilchrist's note] The terms Aboriginal, Native, First Nations, and Indigenous are used interchangeably. These are umbrella terms used to describe various First Nations, Inuit, and Métis communities and Nations in Canada.

2 [Gilchrist's note] Missing refers to cases where women have disappeared under suspicious circumstances, with a strong likelihood that they may have been killed. Murdered refers to cases where missing women are found to be/identified as victims of homicide.

between the intersecting disadvantages experienced by Aboriginal women and the value judgments made by news organizations about what constitutes a crime or victim worthy of attention, or, who and what is *newsworthy*. Lastly, I explore how press disparities promote the symbolic annihilation, or systematic exclusion, trivialization, and marginalization of Aboriginal women's experiences (Sonwalkar 2005; Tuchman 1978).

NEWSMAKING AND NEWSWORTHINESS

5 Tuchman (1976, p. 97) referred to the news as "a constructed reality," while Cohen and Young (1973, p. 97) suggested that the news is "manufactured by journalists," and Schudson (1989, p. 265) pointed out that "news items are not simply selected but constructed." Rather than objectively reporting events and facts, newsmakers engage in a highly subjective and selective process of news production based on socially and culturally constructed criteria (Fowler 1991; Jewkes 2004; Zelizer 2005). Notably, decisions about who/what is newsworthy are filtered through a predominantly Western, White, heteronormative, middle-class, male lens (Henry & Tator [2000] 2006)....

GENDER, RACE, AND VIOLENCE IN THE NEWS

Hall (1973) argued that, of the millions of events that occur daily across the world, only a very tiny fraction will actually become part of the daily news landscape. Along the same lines, Meyers (1997) identified a hierarchy of crime operating in the news media, meaning that not all crimes are seen as equally newsworthy (see also Jewkes 2004). Severe violence, especially murder, is seen as most newsworthy, and young and elderly White females in particular receive considerable attention (Dowler 2004a, pp. 575–576). Sexually motivated homicides perpetrated by someone unknown to the victim will "invariably receive substantial, often sensational attention" (Jewkes 2004, p. 48). Previous literature has indicated that news stories exaggerate the risks of violent crimes faced by high-status White women (Reiner [1995] 2003, p. 386).

Carter (1998) and Jewkes (2004) have drawn attention to how particular forms of violence against women are deemed too routine or ordinary by newsmakers to be considered newsworthy. For instance, physical and sexual violence committed in the home, by acquaintances, and/or that is non-fatal, tends to fall at the bottom of the hierarchy of crime and is left off the news agenda. It is also useful to consider that the news media perpetuate a hierarchy of female victims, meaning that not all women who have experienced violence are treated equally. Media representations of violence against women often emphasize binary categories which differentiate "good" from "bad" women. "Good" women are seen as innocent and worth saving or avenging, whereas "bad" women are positioned as unworthy victims and beyond redemption

(Jiwani 2008). Like social relations in general, this binary is deeply tied to race and class. Traditionally, it has been middle-class White women who have been constructed as "innocent" and "good" (Collins [1990] 2000). The idealization, or placing of certain bodies in higher regard, subordinates and relegates bodies—in particular "raced" or racialized female bodies—to the status of "Others" (Crenshaw 1991; Mclaughlin 1991).

What must be underscored is that binaries of good/bad, worthy/unworthy, pure/impure, and the like, are relational and mutually dependent on one another. In other words, these binaries develop in the context of each other and each is inextricably bound to the other (Collins 1998). In order for there to be a "bad," "unworthy," "impure," "disreputable" woman/victim there must simultaneously be a "good," "worthy," "pure," and "respectable" woman/victim against whom she is judged. Simplistic binaries produce/reproduce hegemonic assumptions about acceptable and deviant expressions of femininity (Madriz 1997). Idealized depictions of heterosexual, able-bodied, middle-class, attractive White women have become the metaphor for "innocence" both in news discourse and in society more generally (Jewkes 2004; Wilcox 2005). The ideologies of human superiority and inferiority underlying these binaries encourage the valuing of some lives over others and act as powerful justifications for continued racial, gender, and class-based oppression (Collins [1990] 2000)....

Meyers (1997) argued that compared with high-status White women, poor and/or racialized crime victims are often depicted in the news as more blameworthy for their victimization. To illustrate, in sexual assault and sexual homicide cases, if a victim is judged to have deviated from patriarchal notions of appropriate feminine behaviour by drinking/using drugs, dressing provocatively (or not conservatively), and especially if she engages in sex for money, she is likely to be constructed as, at least partially, responsible for violence against her (Ardovi-Brooker & Caringella-Macdonald 2002; Jiwani & Young 2006; Madriz 1997). Likewise, Mclaughlin (1991) found that television representations of prostitution tended to align the dangers of sex work with the sex worker herself, and accordingly assigned victims rather than offenders blame for violence. As pointed out by Wilcox (2005, p. 529), the presumption in the news media is that male offenders are guilty only to the extent that their female victims are innocent.

In her analysis of Canadian news discourses of the more than sixty 10
missing/murdered women from a poverty-stricken area in Vancouver's Downtown Eastside, Jiwani (2008) argued that because many of the victims were poor sex workers and/or Aboriginal, the women were labelled as "high-risk," implying that violence occurred because women put themselves at risk because of their bad choices. This discourse blames women and obscures the unequal social conditions which governed and shaped "choices" made

under these circumstances. Aboriginal scholar Martin-Hill (2003) maintained that the disappearances/murders of the Downtown Eastside women and the high number of missing/murdered Aboriginal women in Canada, signals that Aboriginal women are viewed as disposable and so brutal victimization against them is justified because victims are stigmatized as prostitutes, street people, and addicts—even if they are not. The invocation of such stereotypes mitigates the seriousness of their victimization; signalling to the public that crimes against them do not matter. Degrading stereotypes also render racialized women's experiences of violence invisible, especially in relation to high-status White victims (Ardovi-Brooker & Caringella-Macdonald 2002)….

The racial and social status of female victims also influences whether crimes against them are reported at all (Chermak 1995; Dowler, Fleming & Muzzatti 2006). In a study of local crime newscasts in Canada and the United States, Dowler (2004b) established that minority crime victims received not just a less sympathetic tone of news reporting but also less media attention than White victims (cited in Dowler, Fleming & Muzzatti 2006; see also Meyers 1997). In the United States, Black and Hispanic male and female crime victims face a higher likelihood than Whites of receiving no coverage at all (Buckler & Travis 2005). Likewise, in his study of press coverage of crime in Toronto, Ontario, Canada, Wortley (2002) found that Black female crime victims rarely made it on the front page of the newspaper, were relegated to the back pages, or not mentioned at all. Entman and Rojecki's (2001) study of broadcast news in Chicago ascertained that the ratio of time spent on White (male and female) victims compared to Black victims exceeded three to one. Blacks while under-represented as victims were overrepresented as perpetrators….

Much of the Canadian literature about missing/murdered women focuses on the Downtown Eastside women and how their criminalized statuses as poor, drug-using, sex workers falling outside of societal expectations of the "good"/"worthy" victims influenced news reaction to the cases (Gilchrist 2008; Jiwani 2008; Jiwani & Young 2006; Martin-Hill 2003). My research diverges considerably from previous analyses in that it contrasts press coverage of Aboriginal and White missing/murdered women who are matched in other ways. The Aboriginal women in the study have been selected because they are those who by all accounts "fit in." Such a research design allowed me to build on the previous studies above by determining what difference it made to media coverage simply that women were Aboriginal or White, when they were very similar in other respects.

CASES

The focus of my analyses was on six cases. The disappearances/murders of three Aboriginal women from Saskatchewan: Daleen Bosse (age 26) who disappeared in Saskatoon, and Melanie Geddes (age 24) and Amber Redman (age 19) who disappeared in the Regina area. The coverage of these cases was contrasted with that of three White women from Ontario: Ardeth Wood (age 27) who went missing in Ottawa, Alicia Ross (age 25) who vanished in the Toronto area, and Jennifer Teague (age 18) who disappeared in the Ottawa area. All six women disappeared during the spring and summer months between 2003 and 2005. Four of the women, Amber Redman, Melanie Geddes, Alicia Ross, and Jennifer Teague disappeared within a seven week period in the summer of 2005. All six young women attended school or were working and maintained close connections with friends and family. None had known connections with the sex industry nor were they believed by their families to be runaways.[3]

METHODS AND FINDINGS

My objective was to explore whether there were identifiable differences in local press reporting of missing/murdered Aboriginal and White women. To gather data for comparison I utilized the *Canadian Newsstand* online newspaper database and searched for articles printed about each woman from the first day of coverage about her disappearance through November 30, 2006. Local newspapers were selected given Greer's (2003) emphasis on the importance of spatial and cultural proximity in determining the newsworthiness of an event. The most widely read local newspapers corresponding with the city where each woman disappeared/was murdered, were selected for quantitative and qualitative content analyses.[4] Quantitative content analysis is a methodological approach which codes print and visual text(s) into categories and then counts the frequencies and occurrences of each (Ahuvia 2001; Reason & Garcia 2007). The quantitative component of this research consisted of counting and comparing the number of times victims were mentioned in any capacity in their respective local newspapers, the number of articles addressing the victims and their cases specifically, the number of words printed about the victims in these articles, and the placement of articles within the newspaper.

---

3 [Gilchrist's note] During the time period explored for this research, all of the White women were found to be victims of homicide and White male perpetrators were criminally charged. By contrast, only Melanie Geddes was identified as murdered during this time. At the time of this article's publication, her perpetrator(s) remain at large. It was not until 2008 that evidence led police to the discovery of both Amber Redman and Daleen Bosse's remains. In early 2009, an Aboriginal man pled guilty to the second-degree murder of Amber Redman. A White man awaits trial in the murder of Daleen Bosse.

4 [Gilchrist's note] The *Saskatoon Star-Phoenix* was selected for Daleen Bosse and the *Regina Leader-Post* was selected for Amber Redman and Melanie Geddes. The *Toronto Star* was selected for Alicia Ross's case while the *Ottawa Citizen* was selected for its local coverage of Ardeth Wood and Jennifer Teague.

15 Interpretive content analysis goes beyond simply quantifying explicit elements of the text and thus was used to supplement my quantitative findings. A qualitative or interpretive analysis seeks to understand the subtle meanings and implications of the text(s) and is considered a more holistic approach to understanding context as well as content (Ahuvia 2001; Reason & Garcia 2007). Headlines, articles, and accompanying photographs were analyzed and specific attention was paid to the language used to describe and memorialize the victims, the general tone and themes in the coverage, information that was present in some articles but missing in others, and the types of photographs presented. Sixty articles—ten for each woman—were selected for in-depth analysis. Articles longer than three hundred words which discussed the cases at several integral points were selected, including the initial disappearance, subsequent searches, police investigations, memorials, community rallies, and vigils.

AMOUNT OF COVERAGE

When the number of articles mentioning the White and Aboriginal women in any capacity were counted, it was found that the White women were mentioned in the local press a total of 511 times compared with only eighty-two times for the Aboriginal women; more than six times as often (see Table 1).

When this analysis was broken down to include only articles discussing the missing/murdered women's cases specifically, disparities remained. The Aboriginal women garnered just fifty-three articles compared with 187 articles for the White women; representing three and a half times less coverage overall for the Aboriginal women (see Table 2).

There were 135,249 words published in articles related to the White women's disappearances/murders and 28,493 words about the Aboriginal women; representing a word count of more than four to one for the White women (see Table 3).

Further, articles about the White women averaged 713 words whereas Aboriginal women's articles averaged 518 words; 1.4 times fewer words (see Table 4).

PLACEMENT

20 Thirty-seven percent of articles about the White women appeared on the front page versus 25 percent of articles about Aboriginal women. It was not uncommon in the White women's cases—especially in the *Ottawa Citizen*'s coverage—for text and photographs to take up several pages of news or city sections. On the day that police/coroners identified the murdered body of Ardeth Wood there were nine articles printed about the case; two on the front page and seven in the "A"/news section.

TABLE 1

Comparison of Number of Articles That Mention Victims in Any Capacity

White victims	*Number of times mentioned in local press*	*Aboriginal victims*	*Number of times mentioned in local press*
Ardeth Wood	253	Daleen Bosse	16
Alicia Ross	61	Amber Redman	37
Jennifer Teague	197	Melanie Geddes	29
Total	511	Total	82
Average	170	Average	27

TABLE 2

Comparison of Number of Articles Discussing Victims/Case

White victims	*Number of articles written about case*	*Aboriginal victims*	*Number of articles written about case*
Ardeth Wood	82	Daleen Bosse	14
Alicia Ross	33	Amber Redman	26
Jennifer Teague	72	Melanie Geddes	13
Total	187	Total	53
Average	62	Average	18

TABLE 3

Comparison of Number of Words Printed about Victims (using Table 2 data)

White victims	*Number of words printed in articles*	*Aboriginal victims*	*Number of words printed in articles*
Ardeth Wood	61,809	Daleen Bosse	6,559
Alicia Ross	22,616	Amber Redman	15,638
Jennifer Teague	50,824	Melanie Geddes	6,296
Total	135,249	Total	28,493
Average	45,083	Average	9,498

TABLE 4

Comparison of Average Number of Words Printed about Victims (using Table 2 data)

White victims	*Average number of words per article*	*Aboriginal victims*	*Average number of words per article*
Ardeth Wood	747	Daleen Bosse	469
Alicia Ross	685	Amber Redman	601
Jennifer Teague	706	Melanie Geddes	484
Total	2,138	Total	1,554
Average	713	Average	518

Additional analysis of newspapers on microfiche obtained from the *National Archives of Canada* demonstrated that Aboriginal women's articles tended to be hidden amongst advertisements and soft news.[5]* In the majority of instances greater space and prominence was given to events of much lesser significance, for example, an article about an October snowfall entitled "Snowfalls in the southeast" (*Regina Leader-Post* 2005d, p. A1), a picture of two geese in the street with a caption that reads "A LITTLE OFF COURSE" (*Saskatoon Star-Phoenix* 2005a, p. A3), a photograph of classic cars accompanied by the headline, "CLASSICS: Summer is a great time for car lovers" (*Regina Leader-Post* 2005c, p. B1), and a photograph depicting flowers from "The Lily Society" (*Regina Leader-Post* 2005a, p. A12).

Articles discussing memorials to remember missing/murdered Aboriginal women were smaller in size than an advertisement offering a department store credit card (*Regina Leader-Post* 2005b, p. A12), and an ad for an automobile dealership offering customers an "Employee Discount" (*Saskatoon Star-Phoenix* 2005b, p. A5). Entman and Rojecki cautioned that poorly placed articles convey to readers that "events lack urgency and social importance," a condition which may "reduce the salience and emotional potency of stories whose content might otherwise be alarming or provoke hostility" (2001, p. 90). Articles about the (as yet) unsolved disappearances/murders of Aboriginal women were relegated to the periphery of the page and, by extension, of reader's consciousness.

HEADLINES

Having laid out the quantitative findings, I now move to outlining the qualitative dimensions of coverage, beginning with the headlines.[6] Headlines are a crucial element of press reporting given the limited space journalists have

5 [Gilchrist's note] This analysis draws on the sixty articles selected for qualitative/interpretive analysis.

6 [Gilchrist's note] Critics might argue that these findings are problematic given that the White women were from Ontario while the Aboriginal women were from Saskatchewan. Granted, Ontario is the most populous Canadian province and closer to the major national media markets influencing the amount of national media coverage for the White women. However, in selecting the most widely read local newspaper corresponding with the cities where the women disappeared/were murdered this largely resolves the problems of potential geographic and market differences between the provinces. Even though both Saskatchewan newspapers are smaller than the Ontario newspapers, they also have correspondingly less local news to cover, and one could reasonably expect that such a case would receive at least as much coverage in a Saskatchewan newspaper as an Ontario newspaper. In addition, the qualitative component of this research provides strong support that geographical differences do not account for/explain the stark disparities found along several other dimensions of coverage.

to communicate to readers the relevance of what has taken place (Teo 2000). Headlines printed about the Aboriginal women, often referred to them impersonally and rarely by name. For example, "RCMP identifies *woman's* remains" (Pruden 2006, p. A3; emphasis mine), "*Teen's* family keeping vigil" (Pruden 2005a, p. B1; emphasis mine), "Fear growing for family of missing *mom*" (Pruden 2005b, p. A1; emphasis mine), and "Trek raises awareness for missing *aboriginal* women" (Haight 2005, p. A3; emphasis mine). Detached descriptions of the Aboriginal women were in opposition to headlines about the White women referring to them by first and last names, and nicknames. Headlines were often also written as heartfelt personal messages from the victims' friends and family to the women, as with "*Ardeth Wood* 'lives in the light of God'" (Harvey 2003, p. B1; emphasis mine), "*Jenny* we love you, we miss you" (Mick 2005b, p. A1; emphasis mine), and "'Waiting for *Alicia*'" (Diebel 2005, p. A6; emphasis mine).

ARTICLES

As noted by Wortley (2002), how the news media depict a crime victim is almost as important as whether the crime is reported at all. Representations of both groups routinely invoked purported "good victim" characteristics. However, this tendency was amplified in the White women's coverage. The White women were discussed in glowing ways, using potent adjectives and imagery. For instance, Ardeth was described as "devout," "so beautiful," "imaginative," "promising," and possessing an "indomitable spirit," while Alicia was referred to as "cherished," "a lily among the thorns," "blossoming," "vibrant," "strong," and as having a "luminous smile." Similarly, Jennifer was said to be "gifted," "optimistic," and "a miniature dynamo" that "lit the room in life." Such complimentary adjectives were commonplace and often a single article would include multiple adjectives of this nature. There was also considerable overlap in the words used to describe the White women, especially adjectives describing their beauty and/or blondness.

Although adjectives like "shy," "nice," "caring," "a good mom," "pretty," 25
"educated," and "positive" were used to represent the three Aboriginal women, the impact of these words was in some ways neutralized because of their superficial and fleeting use. For instance, Melanie Geddes was described as a mother to three beautiful daughters and as the common-law wife of a very caring man, but this information was not bolstered with stories and memories as was the case for the White women. The amount of personal information included in accounts of the White women far outweighed the amount and depth of information presented about the Aboriginal women. Articles about the White women included what amounted to full biographies of their lives, offering thoroughly detailed accounts of their hobbies, idiosyncrasies, personalities,

families, goals, and other intimate personal information. For instance, listing Alicia Ross's music preferences as Led Zeppelin, Pink Floyd, and The Beatles is not particularly newsworthy nor does it assist police in generating leads about her disappearance/murder. However, it paints her as relatable to readers. Representations of Jennifer Teague and Alicia Ross portrayed them as the "girl next door" who shared the values, dreams, and experiences of an imagined [White] Canadian public. Ardeth Wood was typically represented as an angel whose chastity, grace, and godliness rendered her innocent but also vulnerable and fragile to her attacker (see Madriz 1997; Meyers 1997). Below is a passage taken from the *Ottawa Citizen*'s coverage of Jennifer Teague's murder:

> She shared her grandmother's stubborn spirit, her mother's gutsy determination, and according to those who loved her, a feisty spirit all her own. After 10 days of sleepless anxiety and hope, Jennifer Teague's family now knows the worst: that the teen who would sometimes make her brothers dinner before heading to work or soccer practice, is never coming home ... And that they have been robbed of their baby sister, only daughter, and bubbly friend—by a killer who walks free. (Hayley Mick 2005a, p. A1)

Given that articles about the Aboriginal women were considerably shorter, details of an intimate or personal nature were sporadic. Beyond superficial details, readers did not get the same sense of who the Aboriginal women were or what they meant to their loved ones or communities.

TONE AND THEMES

The tone of coverage for both groups was comparable, conveying a sense of desperation to locate the missing women and reunite them with their anguished loved ones. Faith and prayer were highlighted as ways for the families to cope with their tragic losses, and outpourings of compassion, grief, and support from their respective communities were displayed in coverage of both groups. Coverage of the White women, however, placed a heightened emphasis on the police and community doing "whatever it takes" to find the women and bring their killers to "justice" (Duffy & Mccooey 2005). Following the discovery of Ardeth Wood's remains, the *Ottawa Citizen* published some articles under the byline: "THE HUNT FOR ARDETH'S KILLER." Articles also communicated both a fear and outrage that violent predators are stalking our streets, fracturing our communities, and harming our daughters (Mick 2005a). Although articles about the Aboriginal women emphasized Native spirituality and communities as a place of solace for victims' families, this was depicted more as something *they* (Aboriginals) do to get through *their* grief over *their* missing daughters (Cowan 2005b; Polischuk 2005; see also Jiwani & Young 2006).

PHOTOGRAPHS

Visual images presented alongside text make the information presented more memorable, gives readers the feeling that they are experiencing or witnessing the events on a more personal level, and encourages them to identify with and become emotionally invested in the events (Graber 1996). Upon examination of the number and types of photographs found in the coverage of both groups, obvious qualitative differences were identified. Press coverage of the White women included photographs that were large, centrally placed, continued on in series for several pages, and often depicted the women as young children or alongside family members. Photographs also depicted police officers investigating the crimes alongside detailed maps and grids of search areas, images of community searchers, families in mourning, and sketches of suspects. By contrast, photographs of the Aboriginal women were considerably smaller, normally passport sized. If photographs were shown at all, they were less visible, not often centrally placed, and less intimate, as they rarely included images of victims' families and never included childhood photographs. The lack of visual imagery in these cases denied readers the same opportunity to identify with or become emotionally invested in the Aboriginal women's cases as they unfolded.

Overall, findings indicated identifiable quantitative and qualitative differences in local press coverage of the missing/murdered Aboriginal and White women. Disparities were found in the amount of coverage as well as in the wording, themes, tone, presentation, and placement of articles, headlines, and photographs. The Aboriginal women received three and a half times less coverage; their articles and photographs were smaller, less empathetic and provided minimal details. While violence against the White women was constructed as victimization done to or felt by all of us this was not replicated in the Aboriginal women's coverage….

CONCLUSION: CONSTITUTING AN INVISIBLE "OTHER"

Intersecting legacies of oppression have situated Aboriginal women on the margins of Canadian press and society (Gilchrist 2007; Jiwani & Young 2006). Jiwani and Young (2006, p. 912) argued bluntly that Aboriginal women are positioned "in the lowest rungs of the social order, thereby making them expendable and invisible, if not disposable." Jiwani (2008, p. 137) added that missing/murdered Aboriginal women are seen by the media "less as victims deserving rescue than as bodies that simply do not matter."

In stark contrast to the compassionate and in-depth coverage of the White women, the Aboriginal women were not seen to be "eminently newsworthy" (Jewkes 2004, p. 51) and were mostly "filtered out" of the press (Chermak

1995, p. 73); reinforcing the belief that White lives are more valuable (Entman & Rojecki 2001). Carter (1998, p. 230) cautioned that when newsmakers cease to report certain types of crime it creates the impression that they are no longer a cause for concern. The lack of coverage to missing/murdered Aboriginal women appears to suggest that their stories are not dramatic or worthy enough to tell, that Aboriginal women's victimization is too routine or ordinary, and/or irrelevant to (White) readers. The common news adage "if it bleeds it leads"* is not an accurate one as "it really depends on who is bleeding" (Dowler, Fleming & Muzzatti 2006, p. 841).

(2010)

REFERENCES[7]

AHUVIA, AARON (2001) 'Traditional, interpretive, and reception based content analyses: improving the ability to address issues of pragmatic and theoretical concern', *Social Indicators Research*, vol. 54, pp. 139–172.

ARDOVI-BROOKER, JOANNE & CARINGELLA-MACDONALD, SUSAN (2002) 'Media attributions of blame and sympathy in ten rape cases', *The Justice Professional*, vol. 15, pp. 3–18.

BUCKLER, KEVIN & TRAVIS, LAWRENCE (2005) 'Assessing the newsworthiness of homicide events: an analysis of coverage in the *Houston Chronicle*', *Journal of Criminal Justice and Popular Culture*, vol. 12, no. 1, pp. 1–25.

CARTER, CYNTHIA (1998) 'When the "extraordinary" becomes the "ordinary": everyday news of sexual violence', in *News, Gender and Power*, eds Cynthia Carter, Gill Branston & Stuart Allan, Routledge, London, pp. 219–232.

CHERMAK, STEVEN M. (1995) *Victims and the News: Crime and the American News Media*, Westview Press, Boulder.

COHEN, STANLEY & YOUNG, JOCK (eds) (1973) *The Manufacture Of News: A Reader*, Sage, Beverley Hills.

COLLINS, PATRICIA HILL [1990] (2000) *Black Feminist Thought: Knowledge, Consciousness, and the Politics of Empowerment*, 2nd edn, Routledge, New York.

COWAN, PAMELA (2005b) 'Family still clings to hope', *Regina Leader-Post*, 8 Oct., p. A6.

CRENSHAW, KIMBERLE (1991) 'Mapping the margins: intersectionality, identity politics, and violence against women of colour', *Stanford Law Review*, vol. 43, no. 6, pp. 1241–1299.

DEPARTMENT OF INDIAN AND NORTHERN AFFAIRS. (1996) *Aboriginal Women: A Demographic, Social, and Economic Profile*, Information Quality and Research Directorate, Information Management Branch, Corporate Services, Ottawa.

DIEBEL, LINDA (2005) 'Waiting for Alicia', *Toronto Star*, 28 Aug., p. A6.

DOWLER, KENNETH (2004a) 'Comparing American and Canadian local television crime stories: a content analysis', *Canadian Journal of Criminology and Criminal Justice*, vol. 46, no. 5, pp. 573–597.

DOWLER, KENNETH (2004b) 'Dual realities? Criminality, victimization, and the

7 *References* References have been excerpted to show only those cited in the excerpts reprinted here.

presentation of race on local television news', *Journal of Crime and Justice*, vol. 27, pp. 79–99.

DOWLER, KENNETH, FLEMING, THOMAS & MUZZATTI, STEPHEN L. (2006) 'Constructing crime: media, crime, and popular culture', *Canadian Journal of Criminology and Criminal Justice*, vol. 48, no. 6, pp. 837–866.

DUFFY, ANDREW & MCCOOEY, PAULA (2005) 'Why this two-year-old act of evil is still unsolved', *Ottawa Citizen*, 6 Aug., p. A1.

ENTMAN, ROBERT M. & ROJECKI, ANDREW (2001) *The Black Image in the White Mind: Media and Race in America*, The University of Chicago Press, Chicago.

FOWLER, ROGER (1991) *Language in the News: Discourse and Ideology in the Press*, London, Routledge.

GILCHRIST, KRISTEN (2007) *Invisible Victims: Disparity in Print-Media Coverage of Missing and Murdered Aboriginal and White Women*, MA Thesis, The University of Ottawa.

GILCHRIST, KRISTEN (2008) 'Multiple disadvantages: the missing and murdered women of Vancouver', in *Gender Relations in Canada: Intersectionality and Beyond*, eds Andrea Doucet & Janet Siltanen, Oxford University Press, New York, pp. 174–175.

GRABER, DORIS A. (1996) 'Say it with pictures', *Annals of the American Academy of Political and Social Science*, vol. 546, no. 1, pp. 85–96.

GREER, CHRIS (2003) *Sex Crime and the Media: Sex Offending and the Press in a Divided Society*, Willan, Cullompton.

HAIGHT, LANA (2005) 'Trek raises awareness for missing Aboriginal women', *Regina Leader-Post*, 23 July, p. A3.

HALL, STUART (1973) 'The determination of news photographs', in *The Manufacture of News:A Reader*, eds Stanley Cohen & Jock Young, Sage, Beverly Hills, pp. 176–190.

HARVEY, BOB (2003) 'Ardeth Wood "lives in the light of God"', *Ottawa Citizen*, 19 Aug., p. B1.

HENRY, FRANCES & TATOR, CAROL [2000] (2006) *The Colour of Democracy: Racism in Canadian Society*, 3rd edn, Nelson, Toronto.

JACOBS, BEVERLY & WILLIAMS, ANDREA (2008) 'Legacy of residential schools: missing and murdered Aboriginal women', in *From Truth to Reconciliation: Transforming the Legacy of Residential Schools*, eds Marlene Brant Castellano, Linda Archibald & Mike DeGagne, Aboriginal Healing Foundation, Ottawa, pp. 119–142.

JEWKES, YVONNE (2004) *Media & Crime*, Sage, London.

JIWANI, YASMIN (2008) 'Mediations of domination: gendered violence within and across borders', in *Feminist Intervention in International Communication: Minding the Gap*, eds Katherine Sarikakis & Leslie Regan Shade, Rowman & Littlefield, Plymouth, pp. 129–145.

JIWANI, YASMIN & YOUNG, MARYLYNN (2006) 'Missing and murdered women: reproducing marginality in news discourse', *Canadian Journal of Communication*, vol. 31, pp. 895–917.

LAROCQUE, EMMA (2007) 'Metis and feminist: ethical reflections on feminism, human rights and decolonization', in *Making Space for Indigenous Feminism*, ed. Joyce Green, Fernwood, Halifax, pp. 53–70.

MADRIZ, ESTHER (1997) *Nothing Bad Happens to Good Girls: Fear of Crime in Women's Lives*, The University of California Press, Berkeley.

MARTIN-HILL, DAWN (2003) 'She no speaks and other colonial constructs of "the traditional woman"', in *Strong Women Stories: Native Vision and Community Survival*, eds Bonita Lawrence & Kim Anderson, Sumach Press, Toronto, pp. 106–120.

MCIVOR, SHARON WITH KUOKKANEN, RAUNA (2007) 'Sharon McIvor: woman of action', in *Making Space for Indigenous Feminism*, ed. Joyce Green, Fernwood, Halifax, pp. 241–254.

MCLAUGHLIN, LISA (1991) 'Discourses of prostitution/discourses of sexuality', *Critical Studies in Mass Communication*, vol. 8, pp. 249–272.

MEYERS, MARIAN (1997) *News Coverage of Violence Against Women: Engendering Blame*, Sage, Newbury Park.

MICK, HAYLEY (2005a) 'Feisty, gutsy, vibrant', *Ottawa Citizen*, 20 Sept., p. A1.

MICK, HAYLEY (2005b) 'Jenny we love you, we miss you', *Ottawa Citizen*, 2 Oct., p. A1.

MONTURE-ANGUS, PATRICIA (1995) *Thunder in My Soul: A Mohawk Woman Speaks*, Fernwood, Halifax.

NATIVE WOMEN'S ASSOCIATION OF CANADA (2008) *Voices of our Sisters in Spirit: A Research and Policy Report to Families and Communities*, Native Women's Association of Canada, Ottawa.

NATIVE WOMEN'S ASSOCIATION OF CANADA (2009) *Voices of our Sisters in Spirit: A Research and Policy Report to Families and Communities*, 2nd edn, Native Women's Association of Canada, Ottawa.

POLISCHUK, HEATHER (2005) 'Mother still searching', *Regina Leader-Post*, 15 April, p. A1.

PRUDEN, JANA (2005a) 'Teen's family keeping vigil', *Regina Leader-Post*, 9 Aug., p. B1.

PRUDEN, JANA (2005b) 'Fear growing for family of missing mom', *Regina Leader-Post*, 18 Aug., p. A1.

PRUDEN, JANA (2006) 'RCMP identifies woman's remains', *Saskatoon Star-Phoenix*, 2 Feb., p. A3.

REASON, MATTHEW & GARCIA, BEATRIZ (2007) 'Approaches to the newspaper archive: content analysis and press coverage of Glasgow's year of culture', Media, Culture & Society, vol. 29, no. 2, pp. 304–331.

REGINA LEADER-POST (2005a) 'The Lily society', 23 July, p. A12.

REGINA LEADER-POST (2005b) Advertisement offering a department store credit card, 23 July, p. A12.

REGINA LEADER-POST (2005c) 'Classics: summer is a great time for car lovers', 22 Aug, p. B1.

REGINA LEADER-POST (2005d) 'Snowfalls in the southeast', 6 Oct., p. A1.

REINER, ROBERT (2003) 'Media made criminality: the representation of crime in the mass media', in *Oxford Handbook of Criminology*, 8th edn, eds Mike Maguire, Rod Morgan & Robert Reiner, Oxford University Press, Oxford, pp. 376–417.

SASKATOON STAR-PHOENIX (2005a) 'A little off course', 12 May, p. A3.

SASKATOON STAR-PHOENIX (2005b) 'Employee discount', 22 Aug., p. A5.

SCHUDSON, MICHAEL (1989) 'The sociology of news production', Media, Culture & Society, vol. 11, no. 3, pp. 263–282.

SMITH, ANDREA (2005) *Conquest: Sexual Violence and American Indian Genocide*, South End Press, Boston.

SONWALKAR, PRASUN (2005) 'Banal journalism: the centrality of the "us-them" binary in news discourse', in *Journalism: Critical Issues*, ed. Stuart Allan, Open University Press, New York, pp. 261–273.

TEO, PETER (2000) 'Racism in the news: a critical discourse analysis of news reporting in two Australian newspapers', *Discourse & Society*, vol. 11, no. 1, pp. 7–49.

TUCHMAN, GAYE (1976) 'Telling stories', *Journal of Communication*, vol. 26, fall, pp. 93–97.

TUCHMAN, GAYE (1978) 'Introduction: the symbolic annihilation of women by the mass media', in *Hearth and Home: Images of Women in the Mass Media*, eds Gaye Tuchman, Arlene Kaplan Daniels & James Benet, Oxford University Press, New York, pp. 3–38.

WILCOX, PAULA (2005) 'Beauty and the beast: gendered and raced discourse in news', *Social & Legal Studies*, vol. 14, no. 4, pp. 515–532.

WORTLEY, SCOT (2002) 'Misrepresentation or reality? The depiction of race and crime in the Toronto print media', in *Marginality & Condemnation: An Introduction to Critical Criminology*, eds Bernard Schissel & Carolyn Brooks, Fernwood, Halifax, pp. 55–82.

ZELIZER, BARBIE (2005) 'Journalism through the camera's eye', in *Journalism: Critical Issues*, ed. Stuart Allan, Open University Press, New York, pp. 167–176.

Questions

1. What does Gilchrist find through her qualitative analysis of the news coverage of these murders? In your opinion, is this kind of analysis as important, less important, or more important than the quantitative analyses?
2. What "broader systemic inequalities" does Gilchrist's study reveal?
3. According to Gilchrist's research, what informs mainstream ideas about what is "newsworthy"? What crimes are usually deemed newsworthy?
4. How do the presence and/or absence of victim photographs affect the rhetorical power of a newspaper or magazine article?
5. Compare Gilchrist's article with Sarah de Leeuw's creative non-fiction piece, "Soft Shouldered," which is also about missing and murdered Aboriginal women. In your opinion, which rhetorical approach to this topic is more effective? Why?
6. Find a news article, in a print or online newspaper, that reports a murder. Following Gilchrist's example, make a qualitative analysis determining the extent to which the murder is presented as important and emotionally impactful.

Michael Harris

The Unrepentant Whore

Many people in Vancouver's Downtown Eastside live in poverty, and the area is known for its drug and sex trades. In the 1990s, women from the community went missing (probably murdered) at the alarming rate of one every six weeks; most of the victims were sex workers, Aboriginal, and/or members of other groups that are disproportionately likely to experience violence. A full-scale investigation was not undertaken until 2001, and in 2002 police caught Robert Pickton, the serial killer responsible for about half the deaths (the exact number of women he killed remains unknown). A commission of inquiry would later find that the murder investigations had been hindered by "critical police failures" and that the Vancouver Police Department's "prostitution law enforcement strategies put women engaged in the survival sex trade at increased risk of violence, including serial predation."[1]

In 2013, three years after the following article was published, sex-work activists achieved a victory when Canada's supreme court unanimously found that several of the country's laws regarding prostitution were unconstitutional because they prevented sex workers from protecting their own safety. The outlawed activities included operating "common bawdy-houses" (brothels or other indoor places regularly used for sex work), making money from another person's sex work, and "communicating for the purposes of prostitution in public." Under the new laws implemented in 2014, it is still illegal to profit from another person's sex work, and it is now also illegal to pay for sexual services. Though the new laws are framed as targeting clients rather than sex workers, many of the activists who fought against the old laws argue that the new criminalization of the exchange is at least as harmful: both past and present laws prevent sex workers from hiring bodyguards or setting up brothels in which they can police each other's safety, and

1 See Wally T. Oppal, *Forsaken: The Report of the Missing Women Commission of Inquiry*, 19 November 2012.

both effectively force workers to meet clients in areas of town where nobody is likely to witness potential violence. (For a defense of the criminalization model, see "Buying Sex Should Not Be Legal," also included in this anthology.)

The following article, published in 2010, offers a portrait of Jamie Lee Hamilton, a Vancouver activist and politician known for her advocacy on behalf of sex workers.

One day in the deep end of winter, 1998, it rained on Vancouver's City Hall. It rained on the 6.9 Mercedes that pulled up to the entrance a little before noon. It rained on Jamie Lee Hamilton's good swing coat as she emerged from the car and lugged out four bulging garbage bags. It rained on the fourteen media crews that watched her carry the bags up the steps, hair plastered to her face. It rained on all of them as she dumped sixty-seven pairs of stilettos at the city's feet—one for every woman who she believed had gone missing from the Downtown Eastside.

Nobody knew that this was the start of the largest serial killer case in Canada's history; nor that Robert Pickton was still, then, taking women back to his pig farm on the outskirts of the city to mutilate and murder them; nor that, more than a decade later, in 2009, a constitutional appeal would argue that our country had systematically imperiled the lives of these women with brutal laws that forced them to work in untenable conditions. All Hamilton knew was that women—sex workers—were disappearing and nothing was being done.

If missing women are silenced women, Hamilton has made it her mission to be fully present and accounted for. An aboriginal, transsexual sex worker from one of the country's poorest neighbourhoods, she's a kind of activist polyglot,* able to speak with whatever voice best suits the situation. She presents as insistently at ease, adding "dear" and "honey" to her sentences like dollops of crème fraîche.* Still, mention her name, and journalists, politicos, and armchair commentators turtle in their heads with alternating fear and exasperation: she's infamous for her public and embarrassing arguments with anyone who crosses her. (Even one of her fiercest supporters told me, "You'd be safer writing a profile of a Mafia don.")

Perhaps that's why her letters requesting a meeting with the mayor had been ignored, leaving her no choice but to show up at City Hall in person—and her person can be as intimidating as her reputation. Her face is hearty and galvanized with energy, the strength of her shoulders set off against plunging necklines. When Mayor Philip Owen emerged, she picked up a red sequined stiletto to present to him, thinking she could ask for a meeting in front of rolling cameras. Owen bolted.

5 Following this initial embarrassment, she pitched a tent on the lawn of City Hall and slept there until, a few days later, it went missing. When she reported the theft from a phone inside the building, the police asked, "Do you have any suspects?" Yes, she said in her gravelly voice: Mayor Philip Owen. City Hall gave her back the tent. But still no meeting.

Her final stand was soon afterward, on February 3, when she walked into a council meeting (having neglected to proceed through the required channels) and demanded an audience. The room emptied. But she stood at the mike* for hours, anyway, waiting for a response. Once the media caught a whiff of "Crazy Shoe Lady, Part Three," city manager Ken Dobell delivered the news: "Okay, you've got your meeting."

"You're just the top city bureaucrat," returned Hamilton. "You get the mayor in his seat, on-camera, telling me I've got a meeting." So Owen did, and the struggle of sexual outliers had a new poster child.

In 1969, while a team of drag queens and friends rioted against police at New York's Stonewall Inn, sparking the North American gay rights movement, Jimmy Hamilton was a confused thirteen-year-old living in a Downtown Eastside housing project. His father—a union man who had worked at a foundry until silicosis of the lungs forced him into part-time work as a janitor at a burger joint—was furious that his son had turned out to be a "sissy." His mother, the revered aboriginal rights activist Alice Hamilton, took him to the REACH Community Health Centre, where a doctor asked Jimmy, "Do you think you're homosexual?"

Blink. "What do you mean?"

10 "Well," he said, searching for some delicate definition, "do you feel like a girl?"

"Oh, yes," Jimmy said, and was sent out. His mother was called in. Fifteen minutes later, when the boy poked his head around the door again, he found her in tears.

It could have been worse. Homosexuality was legalized in Canada that year, so instead of undergoing therapeutic "cures" (the sexual equivalent of an exorcism, and about as useful) Jimmy rode the bus from his housing project out to the University of British Columbia, where his counselling sessions were videotaped for research purposes by Dr. William Maurice in a room next to a daycare for psychiatric patients. Looking around, Jimmy asked his doctor, "Am I crazy?"

"No," said Maurice, "and don't let anyone tell you it's wrong."

Jimmy became the first boy in Canada to be medically sanctioned with a female identity—not that it made any difference at school. He was called "fag," "fairy," and "freak" by his schoolmates; phys ed classes, where he was forced to shower with boys, were particularly painful and alien. Jimmy's solution was simply to stop going. He had heard there was a burgeoning gay scene on the Granville strip, in particular at the White Lunch cafeteria (supposedly thus named to assure customers they didn't use Chinese cooks). There, he met five co-conspirators, all about fifteen years old.

One of his new friends told him about turning tricks beneath the stately Birks clock at Granville and Georgia. When Jimmy hit the hot spot, a pleasant man in his fifties rolled up and offered to pay for a blow job. They did the deed in the nearby Drake Steam Baths. "Easiest money I had ever made," Hamilton says, and growing up in the projects, easy was something money had never been before. He started hustling regularly: he could score forty bucks for oral or a hand job dressed as a boy, and double that if he was dressed as a girl.

The six friends would pool their resources and rent a room at the Palms Hotel, where they could practise applying makeup and walking in high heels; then they'd head over to the White Lunch to flirt and pick up men. Because transsexual sex workers are rare, they become a coveted, precious commodity. They become, often for the first time in their lives, beloved for who they are. The manager of the White Lunch, Molly, was not such an admirer. "You girls are dressing far too slutty," she finally spat. "You can't come in here till you learn how to dress like proper ladies."

The kids bridled at being ousted from the tiny space they'd carved out for themselves. They retreated to the Palms to plot their revenge. Ambushing the White Lunch dressed in even sluttier clothes—fishnet stockings, micro-miniskirts, loudest possible makeup—they lined up at the counter, reached their hands past the sneeze guard like a team of ballerinas at rehearsal, and stuck their fingers into a corresponding line of pies.

Behind any individual life looms a whorl of politics. In 1972, the vagrancy law,* outlawing pretty much all street life, was deemed a relic of ancient morality and replaced with what's called the soliciting law,* which meant sex-oriented vagrants could still be shuffled along. Hunky-dory, said the police. Fine, said the residents of aspirational neighbourhoods. Then, in 1978, the Supreme Court redefined soliciting as pressing or persistent behaviour; simply saying, "Want a date?" didn't qualify.

This proved problematic, since the murder of a twelve-year-old shoeshine boy in an apartment above a Yonge Street body rub parlour the year before had prompted raids of massage parlours in Toronto. (There had been similar campaigns in Vancouver even earlier.) Masses of sex workers were pushed onto the street. Needing a legal mechanism to shoo them, the government passed the communication law in 1985, which criminalized any communication for the purposes of prostitution in a public place (including cars).

20 It was the end of what Hamilton calls "the golden age of prostitution." By night, she would dress up as Cher and perform "Gypsies, Tramps, and Thieves" for audiences at a downtown Vancouver gay bar called BJs. By late night, she would join hundreds of other sex workers strolling the West End, a pimp-free "drive-in brothel"* where transsexuals, boys, and "fish" (biological women) could look out for one another and openly ply their trade.

Gordon Price, the director of the City Program at Simon Fraser University, was then leading CROWE (Concerned Residents of the West End) in the push to remove sex workers, and he remembers things differently. There were pimps, he says, dangerous ones, and everyone from schoolchildren to grandmothers was being solicited. Price becomes highly excitable when he discusses the past. "A new status quo, with sex workers working happily among residents, simply was not an option," he says. "It was us or them."

On the right side of Price's line in the sand: the West End's thriving gay community, which had moved with breathtaking speed toward empowerment since 1969. Fourteen years later, the gay bookstore Little Sister's and AIDS Vancouver, two totems of political will, came to life; by 1985, the city even had a gay newspaper. Homosexuals were real citizens, and capable of pushing other minorities around. Hamilton, who'd started on hormone therapy in 1977, thereby slowly and permanently distinguishing herself from the drag queens, remembers being barred from performing at one gay bar. Sex workers, meanwhile, were seen as "vermin that had to be exterminated," says Becki Ross, chair of the Women's and Gender Studies Department at UBC. "They had to be removed to give people a sense they were living in a 'contamination-free zone.'"

The pressure from residents grew to such a fever pitch that it finally resulted in a 1984 injunction by BC Supreme Court chief justice Allan McEachern; hundreds of sex workers were pushed out of the West End and, pursued by the communication law, into increasingly desolate spaces, until they were finally allowed to rest in the industrial no man's land of the Downtown Eastside. Since it had last been Hamilton's regular haunt, the city's central library, an Eaton's, and several offices had closed up shop, leaving a hole filled by deinstitutionalized psychiatric patients, whose presence encouraged a street-based drug trade, which in turn promoted theft and violent crime.

Pushing prostitutes there consolidated the city's undesirables into one messy (yet handily avoidable) package. "There was no precedent for this in Western jurisprudence," says Ross. And yet she points out that no one notable in the labour movement, the feminist movement, or the gay rights movement stepped forward to protect sex workers. Ross's research has led her to believe that their unchallenged relocation was the seedbed of the scores of Pickton murders that followed.

25 "I say the state created the killing fields of the Downtown Eastside," declares Hamilton, upping the ante, as ever. People tend to roll their eyes when she

makes such accusations. But she never had the luxury of being politically neutral. When Expo came in 1986, she organized protests against the displacement of those in low-income housing; she founded a sub-local of the Canadian Union of Public Employees, as well as a hot meal program and food bank for transsexuals. She became a Native Princess, a Ms. Gay Vancouver, and, inevitably, an honorary member of the travelling cast of *A Chorus Line*.

In the fall of 1996, Hamilton entered the municipal election race, winning herself pride of place as the first transsexual person in Canada to run for public office. When she didn't win the seat, she used her connections to open a now-infamous safe space on Hastings Street called Grandma's House, where sex workers could stop in to warm up, grab a coffee and spare clothing, and use the Internet. Angel funding came from two society women, Jacqui Cohen (heiress of the Army & Navy discount chain) and Cynnie Woodward (of the department store family). Provincial and city governments backed her with "about $27,000" each year.

But not even the beleaguered DTES community would put up with what it perceived as sanctioned sex work in its front yard. The local business association drove the outfit to a nearby residential street, where it again incurred the wrath of locals. Someone started making anonymous death threats on the phone. (When Hamilton alerted the police, the officer who came by said, "If I had a place like this in my neighbourhood, I don't think I'd be happy about it either.")

She was staffing Grandma's House one night when, at four in the morning, a slight aboriginal woman arrived with a pair of guys, drunk off their asses. A third was waiting in the car outside. "I've got nowhere to go," she said, eyes saucer wide. "Can I do this in one of the rooms here?" Hamilton was perfectly aware of the bawdy house law that made that an illegal option (it was introduced with the vagrancy law in the late nineteenth century). But she decided that sending this woman into a car with three overheated men wasn't an ethical option: "She'd have been violated. We knew by then there was a serial killer on the prowl, and I just couldn't send her away."

Over the next few months, at the height of Hamilton's celebrity (thanks to her antics at City Hall), rumours surfaced that other working girls were servicing johns at Grandma's House, and government funding was pulled in January of 2000. One day that August, Hamilton was stepping into a cab, en route to a radio interview with CKNW, when she was arrested on the sidewalk, charged with running a bawdy house. After eight hours, she was released on the condition that she shutter Grandma's House.

Hamilton is, famously, "an unrepentant whore." Is she also an unrepen- 30
tant madam? Sitting with her recently, I ask point-blank, "So, were you running a bawdy house?" She looks nonplussed: "Well, *yeah*." A hand flicks at some imaginary dirt on a cushion. "But so is every five-star hotel in this country.

"And you know what I really resented? They called it a *common* bawdy house. Listen, there was nothing common about it."

If Hamilton gets her way, of course, bawdy houses *will* become common, and some wonder whether the sex trade will be hurt by the trappings of legitimacy, such as income tax and EI* premiums. To some extent, minorities are ruined by their success; civil liberties denude civil righteousness. For better or worse, though, the long-distance destination for sex workers appears to be homogenization. The police, at least, are less interested in persecuting them. Between 1998 and 2008, total prostitution charges in Canada plummeted from 5,950 down to 2,535.

And Libby Davies, MP for Vancouver East, is among a small group of politicians who are starting to recognize this essentially useless voting demographic. "The laws we have are not protecting sex workers," she says. (Indeed, Hamilton has a list of twenty-five women she claims have gone missing since Pickton was arrested; it's increasingly likely there are more killers like him.) "The key point is this: I don't believe the state should be involved in shutting down consensual sexual activities between adults, whether money is involved or not. The state should only be involved where there's violence or exploitation."

Leading the charge to keep the state out of prostitutes' bedrooms is Alan Young, the gregarious, mustachioed Toronto lawyer who argued before the Superior Court of Ontario last year that Canada's laws deny sex workers the safety they are entitled to under the Constitution. Grandma's House was front and centre in his case. "Jamie created a safe house among the lowest of the low, and they shut 'em down," he says. "I needed to show the judge that even when you took measures to protect yourself, the law will sanction you. If the law prevents people from protecting themselves, that's not the law."

Whatever the outcome of Young's case, it will be appealed and appealed again. But it's the start of a multi-tiered approach, and after the preliminary fury of grassroots activism like Hamilton's it's only with the collaboration of suits like Young and Davies that real change can occur. Davies points to Vancouver's drug policy (which has pioneered safe injection sites) as a model for future work with the sex industry: "You've got academics, bureaucrats, elected people, drug users, West Side parents, and people in the media all in on the conversation. When they all converged on drug issues, it became something very powerful. The problem is that it's a much more fractious proposition once you start talking about sex."

You only have to look at the politically correct (and horribly cumbersome) string of letters that labels the LGBTTIQQ2S* community to know she's right. And it's almost taken for granted that gay men would break away from so much baggage. Why would they be concerned that sex workers are being murdered, or that transsexuals are still not explicitly protected from discrimination anywhere in Canada except the Northwest Territories? Well, maybe because it's not just hypocritical to desert another minority after you've gained your own civil rights; it's impolitic, too.

We gay folk may consider ourselves beyond the struggles of a person like Jamie Lee Hamilton (happily consuming our *Will & Grace** and purchasing our same-sex wedding cards with pride). But consider that while we report feelings of safety to our friends at Statistics Canada, the numbers tell us homosexuals are still two to four times more likely to be victims of violent crime. Nor has the wholesale absorption of hetero-normative marriage rights taken place: in the last census, only 7,460 people nationwide identified themselves as being part of a same-sex marriage. In the US, Maine's population recently approved a referendum overturning a same-sex marriage law; around the same time, New York and New Jersey both opted to disallow gay marriage. People change quickly (their minds, their genitals, whatever), but public opinion turns like a freighter.

When the New York State senate was preparing to vote on the rights of its gay constituents, straight senator Diane Savino—a supporter of same-sex marriage—said to her gay colleague, Senator Tom Dwayne, "My only hope, Tom, is that ... we can learn from you, and that you don't learn from us." What she may have been getting at is that there's value, irreplaceable value, in the minority experience. That the section of society that most discomfits the masses is precisely the one that can teach us something about the social hierarchy by which we all benefit and suffer to varying degrees.

The more time I spend with Hamilton, the more her multiple statuses (transsexual, sex worker, aboriginal, working class) appear to slip over my vision, like those successive lenses at the eye doctor's that finally bring the lowest letters into focus.

On Kingsway, the street that defies Vancouver's grid system and runs at a 40
disruptive angle across town, Hamilton has furnished a second-floor space with all the accoutrement necessary to create her idea of a community centre for trans women and their admirers. The door to Queens Cross is marked with the street address 1874½—a *Harry Potter*-esque* nod to the unregulated spaces in between.

My eyes have to adjust to the dim lighting. Hamilton—a proud shopkeep—sits behind a cash register in a vestibule. Normally, men pay a $20 entrance fee to socialize here. She gives me a free pass (it's a weekday, and early in the evening, so we're alone anyway). We lounge by candlelight on overstuffed white leather sofas. Around us, there are numerous mannequin heads sporting wigs. At the rear, I see a room with a massage table, and there's a video room to the left. The space drips with makeshift sensuality, but "it operates within city guidelines," she assures me.

Hamilton is at ease in her boudoir, her legs curled beneath her. She's finally given up on a career in politics, after three further failed attempts at public office in 1999, 2000, and 2008. She tells me she won't run again, because her sex work will always be used against her. "They'd only want me if I said I was *reformed.* But I'm not reformed. Listen, I'm fifty-four and can still work in the sex industry. I'm *glad.*" Her political will is too brazen, too tart, in any case, for her to serve in milquetoast council chambers. When a certain feminist group recently decided to inform Hamilton of her own safety interests, she told them the same thing she used to tell pimps who tried to work their way into the West End strolls: "If you really want to be an expert, you need to go home, put on a dress, and come suck some cock."

I ask her whether she considers herself lonely in her identity. Is she, hovering there at the multi-hued hub of her own Venn diagram,* a minority among minorities? She studies the flame from a red candle, then starts to answer: "You know, I just live my life ..." It's no more complicated than that.

"Be a gentleman," she urges, "and walk me to my bus stop."

(2010)

Questions

1. Hamilton's activist career is marked by her uncompromising expression of her personality and political opinions; Harris writes that "[h]er political will is too brazen, too tart, in any case, for her to serve in milquetoast council chambers." In terms of her activism, what are the advantages of this "brazen" public image? What are the disadvantages?
2. Comment on the balance between formal and colloquial language in this piece. Is this balance successful?
3. Who is this article likely to appeal to? Who is less likely to find it appealing? Consider the tone of the writing as well as the underlying political assumptions.
4. What relationship does Harris see between gay rights and the rights of "sexual outliers" such as transsexuals and sex workers?
5. What laws, if any, do you think there should be regarding prostitution? Why?
6. Since the publication of this article, there have been changes in Canadian law regarding prostitution, and the laws in the US differ significantly from those in Canada. Research the current laws in your area. Are these laws just? Why or why not?

J WALLACE

THE MANLY ART OF PREGNANCY

"The Manly Art of Pregnancy," educational consultant and activist j wallace's account of his pregnancy as a transgender man, first appeared in the essay collection Gender Outlaws: The Next Generation *in 2010.*

There are many ways to go about acquiring what they call "a beer belly."* I chose pregnancy. Beer and wings probably would have been an easier route, but I've never been one for the easy route, and I embraced the manly art of pregnancy. I'm a short, stocky guy who over the last year has gone from chunky, to having a great big gut, and back to chunky again. Along the way, I've also made a baby.

Judging by the resources available, one might assume that pregnancy is distinctly a woman's affair. Books have titles like *The Pregnant Mom's Guide, The Working Women's Guide, The Prospective Mother,* and *The Hip Mama's Survival Guide.* Most of the books for men make it clear that not only is pregnancy for women, but the only men interested in pregnancy are heterosexual males: *What to Expect When Your Wife Is Expecting* is typical. Even books which say *Dad's Pregnant* in large friendly letters on the cover turn out to be written for cisgender[1] men in heterosexual relationships, and about how to deal with your partner's pregnancy in your relationship. Books for pregnant men are hard to find indeed.

If the La Leche League[2] can encourage women everywhere to embrace *The Womanly Art of Breast Feeding,* I'm going to put in a plug for the Manly Art of Pregnancy. For those of you not yet familiar with pregnancy as a manly art, let me introduce it. The pregnant person is at once a biologist, a mechanic, a weight lifter, and someone providing for hir[3] family. Women can do those things, of course, but our culture still views them as masculine things, and

1 *cisgender* Identifying as the gender that matches the sex one was assigned at birth.

2 *La Leche League* International organization devoted to promoting breastfeeding through advocacy and educational support. *The Womanly Art of Breastfeeding*, a book first published by the league in 1958, has been updated and reissued numerous times.

3 *hir* Gender neutral pronoun used as an alternative to "him" or "her."

in this way pregnancy made me more of a man, not less of one. Before I was pregnant, I feared that pregnancy would make me into a woman or a lady. But it didn't; it made me more of a dude. I discovered that pregnancy is rife with things to worry about, and that after a while, gender stopped being one. Pregnancy became a manly act. Pregnancy helped me look, feel, and act more like an archetype of Man, and eventually lifted me to its pinnacle by making me a dad.

Let us begin with the aesthetics: Pregnancy is good for hair growth. Existing hair looks longer, darker, and thicker and new crops sprout up. I have new darker hairs on my chest, my leg hair is more visible, and even my beard is thicker. It's like taking testosterone all over again. Pregnant women often lament this, particularly when they are too pregnant to shave their own legs, but I loved it. The hair growth was so dramatic that I imagined pregnancy hormones being sold to people experiencing hair loss (because G-d knows they try to sell every other thing to people with hair loss). I imagined bald men rubbing Premarin[4] on the tops of their heads, with bald Before, and hirsute After photographs.

5 When I took testosterone, not having a period was my favourite physical change. I loved the freedom it gave, the extra energy, not having to pay an extra tax for the femaleness I found miserable anyway. Pregnancy is the same. There is no bleeding, I can go about the world, safe in the knowledge that I will not have to beg a tampon from a co-worker. I no longer worry that a spare tampon will leap out of my bag at an inopportune moment. I don't worry that my period will stain my favourite date underpants. I skip the feminine hygiene aisle at the drug store entirely, and I am happier for it.

I recognize that these changes can be part of anyone's pregnancy, regardless of gender. The people that make maternity clothes clearly have thought about how masculinizing the physical changes of pregnancy can be and have therefore designed maternity clothes to re-assert femininity. Why else would they invest so much time and attention in making maternity clothes so very feminine? Seriously. Maternity clothes are pink, pastel, or floral, or all of the above, with liberal use of lace, bows, and ribbon. Maternity clothes flaunt curves, and they *flow.* It's very hard to look serious in most maternity clothes. In addition to all that, many of them make you look like you are four. When I first told my boss that I was pregnant she was very clear with me that if I showed up to work in maternity clothes, she would send me home to change. I can assure you that she meant it in good humour, but her point was well taken. So, I figured out what paternity clothes look like. As it happens, you can get through much of a pregnancy in larger shirts, larger jeans with suspenders, chef

---

4 *Premarin* Estrogen hormone medication used in a variety of treatments.

pants, and overalls. If the clothes make the man, the masculine art of pregnancy ignores the rack of maternity clothes. The secret advantage to this is that without the maternity clothes, no-one knows you are pregnant. You can walk around hiding a whole tiny person in your abdomen. Never once did a stranger put hir hand on my belly, gush about how I was glowing and ask how far along I was. The masculine art of pregnancy retains at least a little privacy.

Of course the challenge to this was changes in my chest. Pregnancy makes your chest grow. Before being pregnant I was a happy binderwearing[5] guy, smoothing my lycra undershirt down over my boxer briefs, but rapid growth in the chest department necessitated the first-trimester purchase of chest restraining devices. I put it off as long as I could. I tried shopping for things on my own, discreetly, like a shy straight guy shopping for a new girlfriend—but apparently these things are sized, and it's not like they encourage the "shy straight guy" to go into the change room and try things on. It became clear that I would need to be fitted, and I eventually resigned myself to this. I chose a local shop where I heard they had good fitters, walked up to the counter and asked in a manly, clear voice for assistance fitting me with maternity/nursing bras. Manly pregnant people ask for help with perfect confidence that they are entitled to good assistance, and I found I got good assistance in return.

And then there's this—I grew a penis. Transition-wise I've never really wanted to have genital surgery. Sure, there have been times, in beds and in kayaks, when a penis would have been handy, but for me it's not worth actually having one surgically attached. That said, at our twenty-week ultrasound they showed me grainy black and white pictures of a tiny penis I'm growing. I know not all pregnancies go this way, and it's not as if I decided to grow a penis rather than a vagina, but here I am, growing a penis. Had I known that exposure to sperm would awaken this ability in my body I might have spent more time in bathhouses[6] and other seedy locations, but never mind, I can now add it to the list of things my body can do.

Pregnancy does mean making some life changes. I developed the art of seeming chivalrous while not lifting over forty pounds. I came to understand that sometimes, being manly is about knowing what tool to use. At seven months pregnant, the right tools to use to get a seized tire off one's car are a cell phone and roadside assistance. Crawling under one's car to strike at the tire with a hammer is not manly; protecting one's family and using a cell phone is. "Protecting one's family" is a manly pregnancy mantra. When the signs on

5 *binder* Article of clothing used to compress the chest, often worn by trans men in order to minimize the appearance of breasts.

6 *bathhouses* Establishments where people, usually gay men, can meet for casual sexual encounters.

the outside of a building warn that there has been an outbreak of fifth disease[7] and pregnant people should not enter the building—you obey them, you do not enter, even when it means recruiting a nice lady to go inside and explain that you are not coming. Even when she goes inside and says "There is some guy, outside, who says he cannot come in because he is pregnant...."

Pregnancy does not mean you lose access to your usual manly haunts, like the barber shop, and your local auto mechanic's. Even with the kid's kicks visible under the barber's towel, my barber did not notice my manly pregnant condition. We had the same conversation, and he gave me the same haircut and straight razor shave that he always does—and I gave him the same tip. The auto mechanics still called me sir and talked to me as if I know what the various engine parts are all supposed to do. It appears that if you're a guy, pregnancy does not make you a woman: it just makes you fat.

It's also easier to think about pregnancy as a manly activity if we butch up the language we use. I trained midwives, a doula,[8] Ob/Gyns, and even a lactation consultant to talk about "pregnant people" not "pregnant women," or "pregnant ladies." A number of ciswomen friends had also complained that when they became pregnant they went from being "women" to "ladies" and they found the prissiness of the word uncomfortable. They too found "pregnant person" a better fit, especially if it meant not being referred to as a "lady" all the time. If we talk about "nursing," focusing on the action of providing for one's child rather than "breastfeeding," focusing on a body part assumed to be feminine, even this activity can sound more manly.

Pregnancy made me a dad. Pregnancy has been making dads out of men since about nine months after sex was discovered. I know fine men who have become dads in a variety of ways, some by love, some by adoption and fostering, some by other means, and I do not believe that there is any one traditional way of going about it. There are more common and less common ways, but all of them have a history and tradition. I became a dad through pregnancy and birth. Along the way, people who love me created the language of "bearing father" and "seahorse papa."[9] We're queers, and we are well versed in creating the language we need to describe our realities. We will bring our world into being through words, as we bring babies into being through our bodies.

In the end, I gave birth to my son via a caesarean section. I have a small neat scar on my abdomen that I think of as "the baby escape hatch." Scars are

---

7 *fifth disease* Viral illness caused by parvovirus B19; while it is usually not serious, it carries some risk of miscarriage, so pregnant women are warned to avoid exposure.

8 *doula* Support person who aids new parents before, during, and/or after the birth of their baby.

9 *seahorse papa* Seahorse embryos grow in pouches in their fathers' abdomens.

manly. As I was recovering, I realized that the next time some intrusive person discovers I am trans and asks me if I have "had the surgery," I can say "yes" and go on to describe my c-section. They never say what surgery they mean, and a c-section is generally recognized as a gendered surgery.

In the hospital, after the birth, I was snuggled up in bed in my pajamas, holding my small son, when the public health nurse strolled in. She looked at me in the hospital bed, at the baby in my arms, and around the room. Then she looked again, and clearly did not find what she was looking for. "Where's the mom?" she asked. The simple answer is that there is no mom. Children need love and support from a parent, not a gender. Parents, not necessarily moms and dads, raise children, whether they are boys or girls. The public health nurse stammered an apology, and fled. I've been rehearsing better answers to that question since—better answers that say his family is not your business, keep your assumptions to yourself.

I've become a dad changing diapers, holding a baby, reading books to someone who can't really focus his eyes yet, a dad who was up many times last night with the baby and who is now blurry-eyed from lack of sleep. I do dadly things, including many things other dads do, and things I remember my dad doing. I'm also a dad who nurses, who gets up in the night to feed the baby without having to heat bottles, which I understand is an uncommon dad kind of thing to do. But I do it for my small person. I want the best for my child, which I understand is a common desire of good dads.

I'm a dad you might run into in the library reading to my small child, a dad in the park carrying my baby on my front, explaining the world to him, a dad who plans to teach my child to love insects and look at ants and caterpillars, a dad who'll head off in a canoe with his small person. I look forward to being the dad helping my child bake cupcakes and discover the joy of gardening, and celebrating his artwork. When you see me, what you see, and who or what you think I am has been totally eclipsed by the dad my small person sees, knows, and loves. I'm his dad, and in the tiny world of our family, that is what really matters.

(2010)

Questions

1. As a trans man, what particular challenges did wallace face during his pregnancy?
2. How does wallace use language to change the conventional narrative of pregnancy and child-bearing?
3. To what effect does wallace use humour in this essay? What other devices does he use to develop the essay's themes?

ZADIE SMITH

GENERATION WHY?

Best known as a novelist, Zadie Smith is also an acclaimed essayist. This review article (first published in the 25 November 2010 issue of The New York Review of Books*) discusses both David Fincher's then-newly released film* The Social Network *(with screenplay by Aaron Sorkin) and Jaron Lanier's then-bestselling book* You Are Not a Gadget: A Manifesto.

How long is a generation these days? I must be in Mark Zuckerberg's generation—there are only nine years between us—but somehow it doesn't feel that way. This despite the fact that I can say (like everyone else on Harvard's campus in the fall of 2003) that "I was there" at Facebook's inception, and remember Facemash[1] and the fuss it caused; also that tiny, exquisite movie star trailed by fan-boys through the snow wherever she went, and the awful snow itself, turning your toes grey, destroying your spirit, bringing a bloodless end to a squirrel on my block: frozen, inanimate, perfect—like the Blaschka glass flowers.[2] Doubtless years from now I will misremember my closeness to Zuckerberg, in the same spirit that everyone in '60s Liverpool met John Lennon.

At the time, though, I felt distant from Zuckerberg and all the kids at Harvard. I still feel distant from them now, ever more so, as I increasingly opt out (by choice, by default) of the things they have embraced. We have different ideas about things. Specifically we have different ideas about what a person is, or should be. I often worry that my idea of personhood is nostalgic, irrational, inaccurate. Perhaps Generation Facebook have built their virtual mansions in good faith, in order to house the People 2.0 they genuinely are, and if I feel uncomfortable within them it is because I am stuck at Person 1.0. Then again, the more time I spend with the tail end of Generation Facebook (in the shape of my students) the more convinced I become that some of the software currently

1 *Facemash* Precursor to Facebook created by Zuckerberg. The site displayed pictures of Harvard students two at a time and invited users to choose who was "hotter."

2 *Blaschka ... flowers* Botanically realistic glass models, crafted by Leopold Blaschka, on display at the Harvard Museum of Natural History.

shaping their generation is unworthy of them. They are more interesting than it is. They deserve better.

In *The Social Network* Generation Facebook gets a movie almost worthy of them, and this fact, being so unexpected, makes the film feel more delightful than it probably, objectively, is. From the opening scene it's clear that this is a movie about 2.0 people made by 1.0 people (Aaron Sorkin and David Fincher, forty-nine and forty-eight respectively). It's a *talkie,*[3] for goodness' sake, with as many words per minute as *His Girl Friday*.[4] A boy, Mark, and his girl, Erica, sit at a little table in a Harvard bar, zinging each other, in that relentless Sorkin style made famous by *The West Wing* (though at no point does either party say "Walk with me"—for this we should be grateful).[5]

But something is not right with this young man: his eye contact is patchy; he doesn't seem to understand common turns of phrase or ambiguities of language; he is literal to the point of offense, pedantic to the point of aggression. ("Final clubs,"[6] says Mark, correcting Erica, as they discuss those exclusive Harvard entities, "*Not* Finals clubs.") He doesn't understand what's happening as she tries to break up with him. ("Wait, wait, this is real?") Nor does he understand *why*. He doesn't get that what he may consider a statement of fact might yet have, for this other person, some personal, painful import:

ERICA: I have to go study.
MARK: You don't have to study.
ERICA: *How do you know I don't have to study?!*
MARK: *Because you go to B.U.!* [7]

Simply put, he is a computer nerd, a social "autistic": a type as recognizable 5
to Fincher's audience as the cynical newshound was to Howard Hawks's. To create this Zuckerberg, Sorkin barely need brush his pen against the page. We

---

3 *talkie* Film with spoken dialogue. (The term came into use in the late 1920s, as the silent film era was drawing to a close.)

4 *His Girl Friday* 1940 comedy film directed by Howard Hawks—an example of the 1930s and early 40s film genre known as "screwball comedy," in which everyone talks quickly and surprising things happen fast.

5 *Sorkin style ... be grateful* The television show *The West Wing*, which was created by Aaron Sorkin and ran from 1999 to 2006, was known for its rapid-fire dialogue, often spoken as characters were walking together through the west wing offices at the White House.

6 *Final clubs* Exclusive, male-only social clubs created and maintained by Harvard students.

7 *Because you go to B.U.!* Boston University (B.U.) is a less prestigious institution than Harvard.

came to the cinema expecting to meet this guy and it's a pleasure to watch Sorkin colour in what we had already confidently sketched in our minds. For sometimes the culture surmises an individual personality, collectively. Or thinks it does. Don't we all know why nerds do what they do? To get money, which leads to popularity, which leads to girls. Sorkin, confident of his foundation myth, spins an exhilarating tale of double rejection—spurned by Erica and the Porcellian, the Finaliest of the Final Clubs, Zuckerberg begins his spite-fuelled rise to the top. Cue a lot of betrayal. A lot of scenes of lawyers' offices and miserable, character-damning depositions. ("Your best friend is suing you!") Sorkin has swapped the military types of *A Few Good Men** for a different kind of all-male community in a different uniform: GAP hoodies, North Face sweats.

At my screening, blocks from NYU,* the audience thrilled with intimate identification. But if the hipsters and nerds are hoping for Fincher's usual pyrotechnics they will be disappointed: in a lawyer's office there's not a lot for Fincher to *do*. He has to content himself with excellent and rapid cutting between Harvard and the later court cases, and after that, the discreet pleasures of another, less-remarked-upon Fincher skill: great casting. It'll be a long time before a cinema geek comes along to push Jesse Eisenberg, the actor who plays Zuckerberg, off the top of our nerd typologies. The passive-aggressive, flat-line voice. The shifty boredom when anyone, other than himself, is speaking. The barely suppressed smirk. Eisenberg even chooses the correct nerd walk: not the sideways corridor shuffle (the *Don't Hit Me!*), but the puffed chest vertical march (the *I'm not 5'8", I'm 5'9"!*).

With rucksack, naturally. An extended four-minute shot has him doing exactly this all the way through the Harvard campus, before he lands finally where he belongs, the only place he's truly comfortable, in front of his laptop, with his blog:

> Erica Albright's a bitch. You think that's because her family changed their name from Albrecht or do you think it's because all B.U. girls are bitches?

Oh, yeah. We know this guy. Overprogrammed, furious, lonely. Around him Fincher arranges a convincing bunch of 1.0 humans, by turns betrayed and humiliated by him, and as the movie progresses they line up to sue him. If it's a three-act movie it's because Zuckerberg screws over more people than a two-act movie can comfortably hold: the Winklevoss twins and Divya Navendra (from whom Zuckerberg allegedly stole the Facebook concept), and then his best friend, Eduardo Saverin (the CFO* he edged out of the company), and finally Sean Parker, the boy king of Napster, the music-sharing program, although he, to be fair, pretty much screws himself. It's in Eduardo—in the actor Andrew Garfield's animate, beautiful face—that all these betrayals seem to converge, and become personal, painful. The arbitration scenes—that should be dull, being so terribly static—get their power from the eerie opposition between Eisenberg's unmoving countenance (his eyebrows hardly ever move; the real Zuckerberg's eyebrows never move) and Garfield's imploring disbelief, almost the way Spencer Tracy got all worked up opposite Frederic March's rigidity in another courtroom epic, *Inherit the Wind.*

Still, Fincher allows himself one sequence of (literal) showboating.* Halfway through the film, he inserts a ravishing but quite unnecessary scene of the pretty Winklevoss twins (for a story of nerds, all the men are surprisingly comely) at the Henley Regatta.[8] These two blond titans row like champs. (One actor, Armie Hammer, has been digitally doubled. I'm so utterly 1.0 that I spent an hour of the movie trying to detect any difference between the twins.) Their arms move suspiciously fast, faster than real human arms, their muscles seem outlined by a fine pen, the water splashes up in individual droplets as if painted by Caravaggio, and the music! Trent Reznor, of Nine Inch Nails, commits exquisite brutality upon Edward Grieg's already pretty brutal "In the Hall of the Mountain King." All synths and white noise. It's music video stuff—the art form in which my not-quite generation truly excels—and it demonstrates the knack for hyperreality that made Fincher's *Fight Club* so compelling while rendering the real world, for so many of his fans, always something of a disappointment. Anyway, the twins lose the regatta, too, by a nose, which allows Fincher to justify the scene by thematic reiteration: sometimes very close is simply not close enough. Or as Mark pleasantly puts it across a conference table: "If you guys were the inventors of Facebook you'd have invented Facebook."

10 All that's left for Zuckerberg is to meet the devil at the crossroads: naturally he's an Internet music entrepreneur. It's a Generation Facebook instinct to expect (hope?) that a pop star will fall on his face in the cinema, but Justin Timberlake, as Sean Parker, neatly steps over that expectation: whether or not you think he's a shmuck,* he sure plays a great shmuck. Manicured eyebrows, sweaty forehead, and that coked-up, wafer-thin self-confidence, always threatening to collapse into paranoia. Timberlake shimmies into view in the third act to offer the audience, and Zuckerberg, the very same thing, essentially, that he's been offering us for the past decade in his videos: a vision of the good life.

This vision is also wafer-thin, and Fincher satirizes it mercilessly. Again, we know its basic outline: a velvet rope, a cocktail waitress who treats you like a king, the best of everything on tap, a special booth of your own, fussy tiny expensive food ("Could you bring out some things? The lacquered pork with that ginger confit? I don't know, tuna tartar, some lobster claws, the foie gras and the shrimp dumplings, that'll get us started"), appletinis, a Victoria's Secret* model date, wild house parties, fancy cars, slick suits, cocaine, and

8 *Henley Regatta* Premier rowing competition.

a "sky's the limit" objective: "A million dollars isn't cool. You know what's cool?… A *billion* dollars." Over cocktails in a glamorous nightclub, Parker dazzles Zuckerberg with tales of the life that awaits him on the other side of a billion. Fincher keeps the thumping Euro house music turned up to exactly the level it would be in real life: the actors have to practically scream to be heard above it. Like many a nerd before him, Zuckerberg is too hyped on the idea that he's in heaven to notice he's in hell.

Generation Facebook's obsession with this type of "celebrity lifestyle" is more than familiar. It's pitiful, it pains us, and we recognize it. But would Zuckerberg recognize it, the real Zuckerberg? Are these really *his* motivations, *his* obsessions? No—and the movie knows it. Several times the script tries to square the real Zuckerberg's apparent indifference to money with the plot arc of *The Social Network*—and never quite succeeds. In a scene in which Mark argues with a lawyer, Sorkin attempts a sleight of hand, swapping an interest in money for an interest in power:

> Ma'am, I know you've done your homework and so you know that money isn't a big part of my life, but at the moment I could buy Harvard University, take the Phoenix Club and turn it into my ping pong room.

But that doesn't explain why the teenage Zuckerberg gave away his free app for an MP3 player (similar to the very popular Pandora, as it recognized your taste in music), rather than selling it to Microsoft. What power was he hoping to accrue to himself in high school, at seventeen? Girls, was it? Except the girl motivation is patently phony—with a brief interruption Zuckerberg has been dating the same Chinese-American, now a medical student, since 2003, a fact the movie omits entirely. At the end of the film, when all the suing has come to an end ("Pay them. In the scheme of things it's a parking ticket"), we're offered a Zuckerberg slumped before his laptop, still obsessed with the long-lost Erica, sending a "Friend request" to her on Facebook, and then refreshing the page, over and over, in expectation of her reply…. Fincher's contemporary window-dressing is so convincing that it wasn't until this very last scene that I realized the obvious progenitor of this wildly enjoyable, wildly inaccurate biopic. Hollywood still believes that behind every mogul there's an idée fixe.[9] Rosebud—meet Erica.[10]

---

9 *idée fixe* Idea fixed in the mind; obsession.

10 *Rosebud—meet Erica* Reference to Orson Welles's film *Citizen Kane* (1941), in which Welles stars as media mogul Charles Foster Kane. Kane dies with the name "Rosebud" on his lips.

If it's not for money and it's not for girls—what is it for? With Zuckerberg we have a real American mystery. Maybe it's not mysterious and he's just playing the long game, holding out: not a billion dollars but a hundred billion dollars. Or is it possible *he just loves programming*? No doubt the filmmakers considered this option, but you can see their dilemma: how to convey the pleasure of programming—if such a pleasure exists—in a way that is both cinematic and comprehensible? Movies are notoriously bad at showing the pleasures and rigours of art-making, even when the medium is familiar.

Programming is a whole new kind of problem. Fincher makes a brave stab at showing the intensity of programming in action ("He's wired in," people say to other people to stop them disturbing a third person who sits before a laptop wearing noise-reducing earphones) and there's a "vodka-shots-and-programming" party in Zuckerberg's dorm room that gives us some clue of the pleasures. But even if we spent half the film looking at those busy screens (and we do get glimpses), most of us would be none the wiser. Watching this movie, even though you know Sorkin wants your disapproval, you can't help feel a little swell of pride in this 2.0 generation. They've spent a decade being berated for not making the right sorts of paintings or novels or music or politics. Turns out the brightest 2.0 kids have been doing something else extraordinary. They've been making a world.

World makers, social network makers, ask one question first: How can I do it? Zuckerberg solved that one in about three weeks. The other question, the ethical question, he came to later: Why? Why Facebook? Why this format? Why do it like that? Why not do it another way? The striking thing about the real Zuckerberg, in video and in print, is the relative banality of his ideas concerning the "Why" of Facebook. He uses the word "connect" as believers use the word "Jesus," as if it were sacred in and of itself: "So the idea is really that, um, the site helps everyone connect with people and share information with the people they want to stay connected with…." Connection is the goal. The quality of that connection, the quality of the information that passes through it, the quality of the relationship that connection permits—none of this is important. That a lot of social networking software explicitly encourages people to make weak, superficial connections with each other (as Malcolm Gladwell has recently argued),[11] and that this might not be an entirely positive thing, seem to never have occurred to him.

He is, to say the least, dispassionate about the philosophical questions concerning privacy—and sociality itself—raised by his ingenious program. Watching him interviewed I found myself waiting for the verbal wit, the controlled

11 [Smith's note] See "Small Change: Why the Revolution Will Not Be Tweeted," *The New Yorker*, October 4, 2010.

and articulate sarcasm of that famous Zuckerberg kid—then remembered that was only Sorkin. The real Zuckerberg is much more like his website, on each page of which, once upon a time (2004), he emblazoned the legend: *A Mark Zuckerberg Production*. Controlled but dull, bright and clean but uniformly plain, non-ideological, affectless.[12]

In Zuckerberg's *New Yorker* profile it is revealed that his own Facebook page lists, among his interests, Minimalism, revolutions, and "eliminating desire."[13] We also learn of his affection for the culture and writings of ancient Greece. Perhaps this is the disjunct between real Zuckerberg and fake Zuckerberg: the movie places him in the Roman world of betrayal and excess, but the real Zuckerberg may belong in the Greek, perhaps with the Stoics* ("eliminating desire"?). There's a clue in the two Zuckerbergs' relative physiognomies: real Zuckerberg (especially in profile) is Greek sculpture, noble, featureless, a little like the Doryphorus[14] (only facially, mind—his torso is definitely not seven times his head). Fake Mark looks Roman, with all the precise facial detail filled in. Zuckerberg, with his steady relationship and his rented house and his refusal to get angry on television even when people are being very rude to him (he sweats instead), has something of the teenage Stoic about him. And of course if you've eliminated desire you've got nothing to hide, right?

It's that kind of kid we're dealing with, the kind who would never screw a groupie in a bar toilet—as happens in the movie—or leave his doctor girlfriend for a Victoria's Secret model. It's this type of kid who would think that giving people less privacy was a good idea. What's striking about Zuckerberg's vision of an open Internet is the very blandness it requires to function, as Facebook members discovered when the site changed their privacy settings, allowing more things to become more public, with the (unintended?) consequence that your Aunt Dora could suddenly find out you joined the group Queer Nation last Tuesday. Gay kids became un-gay, partiers took down their party photos, political firebrands put out their fires. In real life we can be all these people on our own terms, in our own way, with whom we choose. For a revealing moment Facebook forgot that. Or else got bored of waiting for us to change in the ways it's betting we will. On the question of privacy, Zuckerberg informed the world: "That social norm is just something that has evolved over time." On this occasion, the world protested, loudly, and so Facebook has responded with "Groups," a site revamp that will allow people to divide their friends into "cliques," some who see more of our profile and some who see less.

12 *affectless* Without displaying any sign of emotions or other feelings.

13 [Smith's note] See Jose Antonio Vargas, "The Face of Facebook: Mark Zuckerberg Opens Up," *The New Yorker*, September 20, 2010.

14 *Doryphorus* Ancient Greek sculpture of a muscular man.

How "Groups" will work alongside "Facebook Connect" remains to be 20
seen. Facebook Connect is the "next iteration of Facebook Platform," in which users are "allowed" to "'connect' their Facebook identity, friends and privacy to any site." In this new, open Internet, we will take our real identities with us as we travel through the Internet. This concept seems to have some immediate Stoical advantages: no more faceless bile, no more inflammatory trolling: if your name and social network track you around the virtual world beyond Facebook, you'll have to restrain yourself and so will everyone else. On the other hand, you'll also take your likes and dislikes with you, your tastes, your preferences, all connected to your name, through which people will try to sell you things.

Maybe it will be like an intensified version of the Internet I already live in, where ads for dental services stalk me from pillar to post* and I am continually urged to buy my own books. Or maybe the whole Internet will simply become like Facebook: falsely jolly, fake-friendly, self-promoting, slickly disingenuous. For all these reasons I quit Facebook about two months after I'd joined it. As with all seriously addictive things, giving up proved to be immeasurably harder than starting. I kept changing my mind: Facebook remains the greatest distraction from work I've ever had, and I loved it for that. I think a lot of people love it for that. Some work-avoidance techniques are onerous in themselves and don't make time move especially quickly: smoking, eating, calling people up on the phone. With Facebook hours, afternoons, entire days went by without my noticing.

When I finally decided to put a stop to it, once and for all, I was left with the question bothering everybody: Are you ever truly removed, once and for all? In an interview on *The Today Show*, Matt Lauer asked Zuckerberg the same question, but because Matt Lauer doesn't listen to people when they talk, he accepted the following answer and moved on to the next question: "Yeah, so what'll happen is that none of that information will be shared with anyone going forward."

You want to be optimistic about your own generation. You want to keep pace with them and not to fear what you don't understand. To put it another way, if you feel discomfort at the world they're making, you want to have a good reason for it. Master programmer and virtual reality pioneer Jaron Lanier (b. 1960) is not of my generation, but he knows and understands us well, and has written a short and frightening book, *You Are Not a Gadget*, which chimes with my own discomfort, while coming from a position of real knowledge and insight, both practical and philosophical. Lanier is interested in the ways in which people "reduce themselves" in order to make a computer's description of them appear more accurate. "Information systems," he writes, "need to have information in order to run, but information *underrepresents reality*" (my italics). In Lanier's view, there is no perfect computer analogue for what we call a "person." In life, we all profess to know this, but when we get online it becomes easy to forget. In Facebook, as it is with other online social networks, life is turned into a database, and this is a degradation, Lanier argues, which is

> based on [a] philosophical mistake … the belief that computers can presently represent human thought or human relationships. These are things computers cannot currently do.

We know the consequences of this instinctively; we feel them. We know that having two thousand Facebook friends is not what it looks like. We know that we are using the software to behave in a certain, superficial way toward others. We know what we are doing "in" the software. But do we know, are we alert to, what the software is doing to us? Is it possible that what is communicated between people online "eventually becomes their truth"? What Lanier, a software expert, reveals to me, a software idiot, is what must be obvious (to software experts): software is not neutral. Different software embeds different philosophies, and these philosophies, as they become ubiquitous, become invisible.

Lanier asks us to consider, for example, the humble file, or rather, to consider a world without "files." (The first iteration of the Macintosh, which never shipped, didn't have files.) I confess this thought experiment stumped me about as much as if I'd been asked to consider persisting in a world without "time." And then consider further that these designs, so often taken up in a slap-dash, last-minute fashion, become "locked in," and, because they are software, used by millions, too often become impossible to adapt, or change. MIDI, an inflexible, early-1980s digital music protocol for connecting different musical components, such as a keyboard and a computer, takes no account of, say, the fluid line of a soprano's coloratura;[15] it is still the basis of most of the tinny music we hear every day—in our phones, in the charts, in elevators—simply because it became, in software terms, too big to fail, too big to change.

Lanier wants us to be attentive to the software into which we are "locked in." Is it really fulfilling our needs? Or are we reducing the needs we feel in order to convince ourselves that the software isn't limited? As Lanier argues:

> Different media designs stimulate different potentials in human nature. We shouldn't seek to make the pack mentality as efficient as possible. We should instead seek to inspire the phenomenon of individual intelligence.

---

15 *coloratura* Elaborate vocal harmonics.

But the pack mentality* is precisely what Open Graph, a Facebook innovation of 2008, is designed to encourage. Open Graph allows you to see everything your friends are reading, watching, eating, so that you might read and watch and eat as they do. In his *New Yorker* profile, Zuckerberg made his personal "philosophy" clear:

> Most of the information that we care about is things that are in our heads, right? And that's not out there to be indexed, right?… It's like hardwired into us in a deeper way: you really want to know what's going on with the people around you.

Is that really the best we can do online? In the film, Sean Parker, during one of his coke-fuelled "Sean-athon monologues," delivers what is intended as a generation-defining line: "We lived on farms, then we lived in cities and now we're gonna live on the internet." To this idea Lanier, one of the Internet's original visionaries, can have no profound objection. But his sceptical interrogation of the "Nerd reductionism" of Web 2.0 prompts us to ask a question: What kind of life?[16] Surely not this one, where 500 million connected people all decide to watch the reality-TV show *Bride Wars* because their friends are? "You have to be somebody," Lanier writes, "before you can share yourself." But to Zuckerberg sharing your choices with everybody (and doing what they do) is being somebody.

Personally I don't think Final Clubs were ever the point; I don't think exclusivity was ever the point; nor even money. E Pluribus Unum[17]—that's the point. Here's my guess: he wants to be like everybody else. He wants to be liked. Those 1.0 people who couldn't understand Zuckerberg's apparently ham-fisted PR move of giving the school system of Newark $100 million on the very day the movie came out—they just don't get it. For our self-conscious generation (and in this, I and Zuckerberg, and everyone raised on TV in the Eighties and Nineties, share a single soul), *not being liked* is as bad as it gets. Intolerable to be thought of badly for a minute, even for a moment. He didn't need to just get out "in front" of the story. He had to get right on top of it and try to stop it breathing. Two weeks later, he went to a screening. Why? Because everybody liked the movie.

When a human being becomes a set of data on a website like Facebook, he or she is reduced. Everything shrinks. Individual character. Friendships.

---

16 [Smith's note] Lanier: "Individual web pages as they first appeared in the early 1990s had the flavour of personhood. MySpace preserved some of that flavour, though a process of regularized formatting had begun. Facebook went further, organizing people into multiple-choice identities, while Wikipedia seeks to erase point of view entirely."

17 *E Pluribus Unum* Out of many, one.

Language. Sensibility. In a way it's a transcendent experience: we lose our bodies, our messy feelings, our desires, our fears. It reminds me that those of us who turn in disgust from what we consider an overinflated liberal-bourgeois* sense of self should be careful what we wish for: our denuded networked selves don't look more free, they just look more owned.

With Facebook, Zuckerberg seems to be trying to create something like a Noosphere,[18] an Internet with one mind, a uniform environment in which it genuinely doesn't matter who you are, as long as you make "choices" (which means, finally, purchases). If the aim is to be liked by more and more people, whatever is unusual about a person gets flattened out. One nation under a format. To ourselves, we are special people, documented in wonderful photos, and it also happens that we sometimes buy things. This latter fact is an incidental matter, to us. However, the advertising money that will rain down on Facebook—if and when Zuckerberg succeeds in encouraging 500 million people to take their Facebook identities onto the Internet at large—this money thinks of us the other way around. To the advertisers, we are our capacity to buy, attached to a few personal, irrelevant photos.

Is it possible that we have begun to think of ourselves that way? It seemed significant to me that on the way to the movie theatre, while doing a small mental calculation (how old I was when at Harvard; how old I am now), I had a Person 1.0 panic attack. Soon I will be forty, then fifty, then soon after dead; I broke out in a Zuckerberg sweat, my heart went crazy, I had to stop and lean against a trashcan. Can you have that feeling, on Facebook? I've noticed—and been ashamed of noticing—that when a teenager is murdered, at least in Britain, her Facebook wall will often fill with messages that seem to not quite comprehend the gravity of what has occurred. You know the type of thing: *Sorry babes! Missin' you!!! Hopin' u iz with the Angles. I remember the jokes we used to have LOL! PEACE XXXXX*

When I read something like that, I have a little argument with myself: "It's only poor education. They feel the same way as anyone would, they just don't have the language to express it." But another part of me has a darker, more frightening thought. Do they genuinely believe, because the girl's wall is still up, that she is still, in some sense, alive? What's the difference, after all, if all your contact was virtual?[19]

---

18 *Noosphere* Sphere of human consciousness. Pierre Teilhard de Chardin postulated the Noosphere as an evolutionary stage to which humanity would ascend.

19 [Smith's note] Perhaps the reason why there has not been more resistance to social networking among older people is because 1.0 people do not use Web 2.0 software in the way 2.0 people do. An analogous situation can be found in the way the two generations use cell phones. For me, text messaging is simply a new medium for an old form of communication: I write to my friends in heavily punctuated, fully expressive, standard English sentences—

Software may reduce humans, but there are degrees. Fiction reduces humans, too, but bad fiction does it more than good fiction, and we have the option to read good fiction. Jaron Lanier's point is that Web 2.0 "lock-in" happens soon; is happening; has to some degree already happened. And what has been "locked in"? It feels important to remind ourselves, at this point, that Facebook, our new beloved interface with reality, was designed by a Harvard sophomore with a Harvard sophomore's preoccupations. What is your relationship status? (Choose one. There can be only one answer. People need to know.) Do you have a "life"? (Prove it. Post pictures.) Do you like the right sort of things? (Make a list. Things to like will include: movies, music, books and television, but not architecture, ideas, or plants.)

But here I fear I am becoming nostalgic. I am dreaming of a Web that 35
caters to a kind of person who no longer exists. A private person, a person who is a mystery, to the world and—which is more important—to herself. Person as mystery: this idea of personhood is certainly changing, perhaps has already changed. Because I find I agree with Zuckerberg: selves evolve.

Of course, Zuckerberg insists selves simply do this by themselves and the technology he and others have created has no influence upon the process. That is for techies and philosophers to debate (ideally techie-philosophers, like Jaron Lanier). Whichever direction the change is coming from, though, it's absolutely clear to me that the students I teach now are not like the student I once was or even the students I taught seven short years ago at Harvard. Right now I am teaching my students a book called *The Bathroom* by the Belgian experimentalist Jean-Philippe Toussaint—at least I used to *think* he was an experimentalist. It's a book about a man who decides to pass most of his time in his bathroom, yet to my students this novel feels perfectly realistic; an accurate portrait of their own denuded selfhood, or, to put it neutrally, a close analogue of the undeniable boredom of urban twenty-first-century existence.

In the most famous scene, the unnamed protagonist, in one of the few moments of "action," throws a dart into his girlfriend's forehead. Later, in the hospital they reunite with a kiss and no explanation. "It's just between them," said one student, and looked happy. To a reader of my generation, Toussaint's characters seemed, at first glance, to have no interiority—in fact theirs is not an absence but a refusal, and an ethical one. *What's inside of me is none of your business*. To my students, *The Bathroom* is a true romance.

Toussaint was writing in 1985, in France. In France philosophy seems to come before technology; here in the Anglo-American world we race ahead with technology and hope the ideas will look after themselves. Finally, it's the *idea*

---

and they write back to me in the same way. Text-speak is unknown between us. Our relationship with the English language predates our relationships with our phones.

of Facebook that disappoints. If it were a genuinely interesting interface, built for these genuinely different 2.0 kids to live in, well, that would be something. It's not that. It's the wild west of the Internet tamed to fit the suburban fantasies of a suburban soul. Lanier:

> These designs came together very recently, and there's a haphazard, accidental quality to them. Resist the easy grooves they guide you into. If you love a medium made of software, there's a danger that you will become entrapped in someone else's recent careless thoughts. Struggle against that!

Shouldn't we struggle against Facebook? Everything in it is reduced to the size of its founder. Blue, because it turns out Zuckerberg is red-green colour-blind. "Blue is the richest colour for me—I can see all of blue." Poking, because that's what shy boys do to girls they are scared to talk to. Preoccupied with personal trivia, because Mark Zuckerberg thinks the exchange of personal trivia is what "friendship" is. A Mark Zuckerberg Production indeed! We were going to live online. It was going to be extraordinary. Yet what kind of living is this? Step back from your Facebook Wall for a moment: Doesn't it, suddenly, look a little ridiculous? *Your* life in *this* format?

The last defense of every Facebook addict is: *but it helps me keep in contact with people who are far away!* Well, e-mail and Skype do that, too, and they have the added advantage of not forcing you to interface with the mind of Mark Zuckerberg—but, well, you know. We all know. If we *really* wanted to write to these faraway people, or see them, we would. What we actually want to do is the bare minimum, just like any nineteen-year-old college boy who'd rather be doing something else, or nothing.

At my screening, when a character in the film mentioned the early blog platform LiveJournal (still popular in Russia), the audience laughed. I can't imagine life without files but I can just about imagine a time when Facebook will seem as comically obsolete as LiveJournal. In this sense, *The Social Network* is not a cruel portrait of any particular real-world person called "Mark Zuckerberg." It's a cruel portrait of us: 500 million sentient people entrapped in the recent careless thoughts of a Harvard sophomore.

(2010)

Questions

1. What does Smith mean by "1.0 people" and "2.0 people"?
2. How does Zuckerberg view privacy? What does that mean for Facebook users?
3. What do Smith and Lanier mean when they say that software is not "neutral"? Do you agree with Smith's assessment that Facebook is not "neutral"? Why or why not?
4. How does Smith see the idea of personhood changing in the "2.0" world? Do you agree that personhood is changing in this way? If you disagree, explain why. If you agree, explain whether you see this change as a good, bad, or neutral development.
5. Consider a social media site other than Facebook (e.g., Twitter, Instagram, Tinder). How does the site you chose encourage particular ways of thinking or acting?

EDEN ROBINSON

from THE SASQUATCH AT HOME: TRADITIONAL PROTOCOLS AND STORYTELLING

This piece is an excerpt from the 2010 Canadian Literature Centre Kreisel Lecture, an annual lecture delivered at the University of Alberta by an important Canadian writer. The presentation excerpted here, by fiction writer Eden Robinson, was published in print form in 2011. Her lecture was divided into three parts; the following is the first of the three.

My name is Eden Robinson. My mother is Heiltsuk[1] from Bella Bella and my father is Haisla from Kitimaat village, both small reserves* on the northwest coast of British Columbia. My maternal grandmother's family was originally from Rivers Inlet. Since both sides of my family are matrilineal, technically, my clan name should have come from my mother's side and I should belong to the Eagle Clan. When I was ten years old, my father's family decided to give me and my sister Beaver Clan names at a Settlement Feast for a chief of the Beaver Clan who had died a year earlier.

When a chief died, his body was embalmed in a Terrace funeral home and then he was brought back to his house where he lay for at least three days, attended around the clock by family members or people hired by his family to keep him safe from harm as he rested in the living room. Community members paid respects by visiting him in his home and at his memorial. After the funeral itself, the Thank You Supper was held for people who had helped out emotionally, financially and organizationally. After a year of planning and

1 [Robinson's note] The Heiltsuk Nation's main reserve is Waglisla, BC, which is more commonly referred to as Bella Bella, the name given it by Spanish explorers. Kitamaat Village is known by its residents simply as the Village and was at first a winter camp and, later, a Methodist mission. It is currently the main reserve for the Haisla Nation. The reserve is also referred to as C'imotsa, "snag beach," because of all the stumps and logs that decorate the waterfront.

preparation, the family announced the date of the Settlement Feast and finally, of the headstone moving. Modern feasts are truncated affairs lasting six hours at the most. Much of the dancing has gone but the important dirges are sung, names are distributed and re-distributed to clan members, and people from the community are gifted according to status and involvement with the family. In general, headstone moving is considered an affair of the immediate family and close friends. Space in the graveyard is tight and imposing yourself on the family's grief is considered the height of rudeness.

You aren't supposed to attend a feast or a potlatch without an Indian[2] name and since we were living in Kitimaat Village, my mother, although annoyed, for the sake of convenience agreed to let us become Beaver Clan. My younger sister and I received our names at the Settlement Feast. Towards the end of the evening, we were told to go and line up with other children receiving names. I mostly remember being embarrassed to be standing in front of everyone and having no idea what I was supposed to do. One of my aunts told me if I wanted to learn more about my name, I should go visit my grandmother, my ma-ma-oo.[3]

The next day, we went to ma-ma-oo's house. She told my sister that her name was Sigadum'na'x, which meant Sent Back Chief Lady. A long time ago, a marriage was arranged between a high-ranking lady from up the line[4] and a Haisla chief. They fell deeply in love. Unfortunately, his other four wives became extremely jealous and kept trying to poison her. He couldn't divorce them because they came from powerful families and insulting them in this way would mean, at the very least, nasty feuds. So despite his feelings, he decided to send his love back to her home to save her life. He couldn't divorce her without causing her shame, so he made her a chief. I've since learned two other versions of the story behind my sister's name, but I like this one the best.

"Wow," I said when I heard the story. "What does my name mean?"

"Big lady."

"Um, what else does it mean?"

Ma-ma-oo paused. "Biiiiiig lady."

---

2 [Robinson's note] Indian, aboriginal, First Nations, native Canadian are used interchangeably in the context of this essay and most of my work. [In Canada the use of the words "Indian" and "Native" to describe First Nations people is controversial; some consider these words to be tainted by association with racist stereotypes, while some First Nations people continue to identify with both or either of the terms—and with Indian in particular, as it is used by the Canadian government for the designation of "Indian Status."]

3 [Robinson's note] Pronounced *ma*-MAH-*ew*.

4 *up the line* North.

I paused. Names come loaded with rights and histories. Within the Beaver Clan, the name of the Chief of All Haislas (Jasee) is hotly contested and has started many family quarrels. My father is one of the younger sons of a high-ranking family, so my siblings and I receive noble names, but nothing that garners too much prestige and thus requires extensive feasting or that can get me into too much trouble. Implied in my name, Wiwltxº, therefore, is a high rank as it was obtained through marriage and only given to women of noble birth. I was disappointed in my name, and it has nothing to do with rank: I had story envy. No heartbroken women were standing beside rivers with their long hair unbound as they sang their sadness to the world. Unfortunately, to change my name I'd have to throw a feast. Putting up a feast is like a cross between organizing a large wedding and a small conference. Family politics aside, the sheer cost will run you $5000 if you cheap out and just invite the chiefs and gift them to witness your event. But then your name would be marred by your miserliness and people would remember how poorly you'd done things long after you'd died. A real feast starts at $10,000 and goes up very, very quickly.

10 My aunts also gave my mother a name not long after she'd married my father. My mother had just returned to Bella Bella from residential school[5] in Port Alberni. Meanwhile, in the Village, my father was under pressure from his family to get married. At thirty-three years old, they were worried he was going to be an embarrassing bachelor forever. Ma-ma-oo was trying to arrange a marriage with someone suitable. My father decided to go fishing instead.

My maternal grandmother lived in a house near the docks in Bella Bella. One day my mother was looking out the front picture window when she saw my father coming up the gangplank. According to Gran, Mom said, "That's the man I'm going to marry." Mom's version is that she simply asked if she knew who he was.

They met later that night at a jukebox joint[6] held in a house. My father was a hottie and all the girls wanted to dance with him, but he only wanted to dance with my mother. They were getting along so well, they lost track of time. Back then, the air raid siren left over from a World War II naval base would sound and mark the time when the generator was shut off. The streets went dark. Mom's house was on the other side of the reserve. Dad offered to walk her home.

---

5 *residential school* Boarding school which many Aboriginal Canadian children were required to attend regardless of their parents' wishes. The purpose of the schools was to sever children's ties to their own communities and cultures and force them to adopt Euro-Canadian culture and language. Students were given a substandard education, poorly cared for, and often abused. The system was at its largest during the first half of the twentieth century, but the last residential school did not close until 1996.

6 *jukebox joint* Informal gathering often featuring food, drink, dancing, and gambling.

My father took my mother back to the Village after they were married. Dad's family was upset because mom was twelve years younger than Dad. She was annoyed that they thought she was too young for Dad and expressed her opinion forcefully. My aunts gifted her with an Indian name so she could attend the feasts in the Village. Mom's new name Halh.qala.ghum.ne'x, meant Sea Monster Turning the Other Way. Although it lacks the romance of my sister's name, I like the attitude it suggests and hope to inherit it.

I had been introduced to the concept of nusa[7] as a child, but had never really understood it until my trip to Graceland[8] with my mother. In 1997, I received £800 for winning the Royal Society of Literature's Winifred Holtby Memorial Prize.[9] After taxes and currency exchange, it worked out to $2000 CAD. One of my coworkers at the time suggested I put it into our RRSPs or at the very least a GIC,[10] but I had always wanted a black leather couch.[11] I spent a few weeks searching for just the right couch and anxiously awaited its delivery. Once it was in my apartment, it seemed monolithic. And it squeaked. And it felt sticky when it was hot. I returned it the next day, deciding what I really wanted was a tropical vacation.

I flipped through travel magazines, trying to insert myself into the happy, sunny pictures. Overwhelmed by the choices, I phoned my mother. I asked her if she could go anywhere in the world, where would she go?

"Graceland," Mom said.

"Really?"

"I would go in a heartbeat."

I was impressed by her certainty. "Okay."

She laughed and we chatted a bit longer. I spent the rest of the evening surfing the Internet for cheap flights and a passable hotel. There were some incredible deals on flights, but the cheapest ones had multiple connections. Mom hated flying, especially takeoffs and landings, so the fewer of those we could get away with the better. The Days Inn at Graceland promised Presley-inspired

---

7 [Robinson's note] *Nusa*: the traditional way of teaching children Haisla *nuyem*, or protocols.

8 *Graceland* Site of the home of musician Elvis Presley (1935–77) in Memphis, Tennessee.

9 *Royal ... Prize* Annual award for a distinguished work of fiction, non-fiction, or poetry. Robinson won for her short story collection *Traplines* (1996).

10 *RRSPs* Registered Retirement Savings Plans; *GIC* Guaranteed Investment Certificate, a form of low-risk investment.

11 [Robinson's note] I don't know why. I think it's because when I was a child, having a black leather couch was like wearing red lipstick or smoking skinny cigarettes—somehow it transformed you into a sophisticated grown-up.

décor, a guitar-shaped pool and a twenty-four-hour Elvis movie channel. The shoulder season rates were great and it was right beside Graceland, so we wouldn't have to rent a car or grab a cab to get there.

"Hey, how'd you like to spend your birthday in Graceland?" I said.

There was a prolonged silence over the phone. "Are you kidding?"

"I just wanted to make sure you really wanted to go because everything's non-refundable."

Another silence. "You're serious."

"Yeah, we've got a couple of options for flights, but I think our best bet is a connection out of Seattle."

"I don't think I can afford that."

I explained about the Royal Society prize money and the black leather couch and the desire to go somewhere I've never been before.

"That seems like a lot of money," she said.

"Do you want to go to Graceland?"

"Well, yes."

"Then let's go."

Dad wasn't interested in going to Graceland with us, so it was just Mom and me. Dad had his heart set on driving from Kitimaat to the 100th Anniversary of the Klondike Gold Rush* in Dawson City. Mom hates driving vacations, so she said she'd save her money for Graceland, which Dad said sounded like a glorified shopping trip. We drove up to Dawson that July in his denim-blue standard Ford F-150, but that is a story for another time.

Mom hadn't travelled much, except to visit her grandchildren in Ontario and her mother in Vancouver. Three weeks before we were scheduled to leave, her fears about flying were not soothed by the infamous crash of Swiss Air 111[12] near Peggy's Cove in Nova Scotia and the near constant media coverage of the wreckage and grieving relatives.

At that point, a series of hurricanes marched across the Gulf States, causing widespread damage and flooding. I had a shaky grasp of American geography, so trying to convince Mom that our plane would not be blown out of the sky was difficult.

"It's a sign," Mom said.

"It's not a sign."

"We aren't meant to go."

"The tickets are non-refundable."

And then our airline pilots went on strike. Which was probably why the tickets had been dirt cheap. Another airline offered to carry their rival's

---

12 *Swiss Air 111* In 1998 all 229 people aboard this flight from New York to Geneva, Switzerland, were killed when it crashed into the Atlantic Ocean.

passengers, but things were still iffy when mom flew into the Vancouver airport to meet up with me. From her pale complexion and bug-eyed expression, I knew the only things that could have got her on that plane were a) her grandchildren or b) Graceland.

We landed in Memphis at night. The cab ride to the hotel was quiet. We 40
were both exhausted. I think I was expecting a longer ride because the blue billboard announcing our arrival at Graceland seemed abrupt. After dragging our luggage to our room, I asked if she wanted to look around or just pass out.

"I'm going to the gates," Mom said.

We passed an Elvis-themed strip mall called Graceland Plaza. We peered in at the closed stores and then crossed the street. The Manor[13] was lit by floodlights. It seemed smaller than I'd been expecting. A stone wall surrounding it was covered in graffiti left there by fans, who were invited by a sign to use the black Sharpies provided to leave a note or signature. We took pictures of each other, and then other tourists took pictures of us together, looking shell-shocked.*

In the morning, we went straight to the ticket counter and bought the Platinum Tour, which included all four Elvis museums and the Manor. Mom wanted to go straight to the Manor. We were given audio headsets, which would guide us through the rooms. I put my headphones on. Mom left hers hanging around her neck, ignoring the flow of traffic and irritated glances as she slowly made her way through the entrance.

I turned my Walkman[14] on and began the tour. Halfway through the first room, I realized Mom wasn't with me. I found her staring at a white bedroom with purple furniture. I was about to explain the headphones to her when I realized she was trembling.

"This is his mother's room," she said. 45

We spent a week in Memphis, and I got the immersion course in Elvis. But there, at that moment, while Mom was telling me stories about Elvis and his mother, I was glad we'd come here together. You should not go to Graceland without an Elvis fan. It's like Christmas without kids—you lose that sense of wonder. The Manor wasn't that impressive if you just looked at it as a house. More importantly, as we walked slowly through the house and she touched the walls, everything had a story, and history. In each story was everything she valued and loved and wanted me to remember and carry with me.[15]

This is nusa.

(2010)

---

13 *The Manor* Mansion at Graceland.

14 *Walkman* Portable cassette or CD player.

15 [Robinson's note] To commemorate our trip, I wrote in a scene in *Monkey Beach* where my character took off for Graceland when he found out Elvis died.

Questions

1. What is nusa? What does Robinson's description of her visit to Graceland show us about nusa?
2. In this lecture, how does Robinson represent the relationship between tradition and contemporary life?
3. The Pueblo writer Leslie Marmon Silko says the following in the introduction to her essay "Language and Literature from a Pueblo Indian Perspective":

    > For those of you accustomed to being taken from point A to point B to point C, this presentation may be somewhat difficult to follow. Pueblo expression resembles something like a spider's web with many little threads radiating from the centre, crisscrossing each other. As with the web, the structure emerges as it is made and you must simply listen and trust, as the Pueblo people do, that meaning will be made.

    Though Silko is of course speaking of her own tradition, aspects of this approach to communication are common to some other Aboriginal North American cultures. To what extent does Silko's introduction describe the approach taken in Robinson's lecture?
4. Why is Robinson disappointed by her Indian name? What is the significance of this disappointment in the context of her lecture?

AMY SCHALET

from NOT UNDER MY ROOF: PARENTS, TEENS, AND THE CULTURE OF SEX

Sociologist Amy Schalet began in the mid 1990s to conduct comparative research into American and Dutch attitudes towards teenage sexuality. In 2000 she published a long article on the topic in the scholarly journal Body and Society *(under the title "Raging Hormones, Regulated Love"). She continued to publish scholarly articles on the subject through the first decade of this century.*

The excerpt included below from her book-length study Not Under My Roof *is from the book's first chapter (for which Schalet uses the same title she had used for her earlier article). Though* Not Under My Roof *is a scholarly monograph, it is written in a style accessible to non-specialists; the book has been both widely read and influential.*

Karel Doorman, a soft-spoken civil servant in the Netherlands, keeps tabs on his teenage children's computer use and their jobs to make sure neither are interfering with school performance or family time.[1] But Karel would not object if his daughter Heidi were to have a sexual relationship: "No," he explains. "She is sixteen, almost seventeen. I think she knows very well what matters, what can happen. If she is ready, I would let her be ready." If Heidi were to come home and say, "Dad, this is him," he says, "well, I hope I like him." Karel would also let Heidi spend the night with a steady boyfriend in her room, provided he did not show up "out of the blue." But Karel thinks that he would first "come by the house and that I will hear about him and that she'll talk about him and … that it really is a gradual thing." That said, Karel suspects his daughter might prefer a partner of her own sex. Karel would accept her orientation he says, though he grants, "the period of adjustment might take a little longer."

1 All names of people and places, and some occupations have been changed to preserve anonymity. All translations from Dutch are mine. [All notes to this essay are the author's original notes unless otherwise stated.]

Karel's approach stands in sharp contrast to that of his fellow parent, Rhonda Fursman, a northern California homemaker and former social worker. Rhonda tells her teenage son and daughter that premarital sex "at this point is really dumb." It is on the list with shoplifting, she explains, "sort of like the Ten Commandments: don't do any of those because if you do, you know, you're going to be in a world of hurt." It comes as no surprise therefore that Rhonda responds viscerally when asked whether she would let her fifteen-year-old son spend the night with a girlfriend. "No way, José!" She elaborates: "That kind of recreation … is just not something I would feel comfortable with him doing here." She ponders her reaction: "I tried to be very open and modern … but I am like, no, I'm not comfortable. I don't think I want to encourage that." She has a hard time imagining changing her position on permitting the sleepover, although maybe "if they are engaged or about to be married …"

Karel and Rhonda illustrate a puzzle: both white, middle class, and secular or moderately Christian, they belong to the one hundred and thirty Dutch and American parents and teenagers, mostly tenth-graders, whom I interviewed between the early 1990s and 2000. Despite the fact that both groups of parents are similar in education, religion, class, and race—features that often influence attitudes toward sexuality and childrearing—the vast majority of American parents oppose a sleepover for high-school-aged teenagers, while most Dutch parents permit it or consider doing so under the right circumstances. This book seeks to solve the puzzle of this striking difference, which is all the more surprising given the liberalization in sexual attitude and practices that took place throughout Europe and the United States since the 1960s. Given similar trends, why do the Dutch and American parents respond so differently? How do the parental approaches affect teenagers' experiences of sexuality and self? To answer these questions, we must look beyond sexuality at the different cultures of individualism that emerged in American and Dutch societies after the sexual revolution.

… Medical and public health literatures conceptualize adolescent sexuality primarily in terms of individual risk-taking and the factors that augment or lessen such risks.[2] American developmental psychologists tend to view adolescent sexuality as part of adolescents' separation from their parents and as an aspect of development that is especially perilous because of the disjuncture between teenagers' physical and cognitive development.[3] American sociologists have generally bypassed the parent-teenager nexus to focus on relationships

2 Michaud 2006.

3 This is especially true for classical (psychoanalytically informed) developmental psychology and evolutionary developmental psychology, in which separation from parents is a critical element of the individuation process. See also notes [54 and 55].

and networks *among* teenagers—in romance and in peer groups.* They have examined how peer cultures and networks and the status hierarchies within them impact adolescent sexuality.[4] Finally, gender scholars have examined how teenage girls' and teenage boys' experiences of sexuality are profoundly shaped by gender inequalities—including the sexual double standard.[5]

5 This book takes a different approach. It focuses on the negotiation of adolescent rights and responsibilities within the parent-teenager relationship as a particularly fruitful, and often overlooked, site for illuminating how youth come to relate to sexuality, themselves, and others. This cross-national comparison shows how much of what we take for granted about teenage sexuality—American folk,* professional, and academic wisdom—is the product of our cultural constructs and institutions. Indeed, the apparently trivial puzzle Karel Doorman and Rhonda Fursman introduce is not just a puzzle but a window onto two different ways of understanding and shaping individuals and social relationships in middle-class families and in the societies at large, which constitutes nothing less than two distinct cultures of individualism. Each culture of individualism comes with freedoms and sacrifices: the Dutch cultural templates provide teenagers with more support *and* subject them to deeper control, while American cultural templates make the experience of adolescent sexuality particularly conflict-ridden.

Adolescent Sexuality in America After the Sexual Revolution

Today most adolescents in the United States, like their peers across the industrial world, engage in sexual contact—broadly defined—before leaving their teens, typically starting around age seventeen.[6] Initiating sex and exploring romantic relationships, often with several successive partners before settling into long-term cohabitation or marriage, are normative parts of adolescence and young

---

4 Sociological classics on adolescent peer groups and status hierarchies include Waller 1937 and Coleman 1961. Contemporary sociological studies of adolescent networks and peer groups include Bearman and Brückner 2001; Bearman 2004; Anderson 1999; Eder, Evans, and Parker 1995; Bettie 2000; and Pascoe 2007.

5 See for instance Bettie 2000; Fine 1988; Nathanson 1991; Tolman 2002; Tolman, Striepe, and Harmon 2003; Vanwesenbeeck, Bekker, and van Lenning 1998; and Armstrong, Hamilton, and Sweeney 2006.

6 Abma et al. 2004; de Graaf et al. 2005; Darroch, Singh, and Frost 2001; and Mosher, Chandra, and Jones 2005. More than half of American and Dutch seventeen-year-olds (both girls and boys) have had oral sex with a same-sex and/or opposite-sex partner. Among seventeen-year-olds, a little under half of American girls and boys, 45 percent of Dutch boys, and six out ten Dutch girls have had vaginal intercourse (Mosher, Chandra, and Jones 2005; de Graaf et al. 2005).

adulthood across the developed world.[7] In the Netherlands, as in many countries of northwestern Continental Europe, adolescent sexuality has been what one might call *normalized*—treated as a normal part of individual and relational development, and discussible with adults in families, schools, and health care clinics.[8] But in the United States, teenage sex has been *dramatized*—fraught with cultural ambivalences, heated political struggles, and poor health outcomes, generating concern among the public, policymakers, and scholars.

In some respects, it is surprising to find adolescent sexuality treated as such a deep problem for the United States. Certainly, age at first intercourse has dropped since the sexual revolution, but not as steeply as often assumed. In their survey of the adult American population, *The Social Organization of Sexuality: Sexual Practices in the United States,* Edward Laumann and colleagues found that even in the 1950s and 1960s, only a quarter of men and less than half of women were virgins at age nineteen. The majority of young men had multiple sexual partners by age twenty.[9] And while women especially were supposed to enter marriage as virgins, the majority of those who came of age in the late 1950s and early 1960s had sexual intercourse before they married.[10] Still, a 1969 Gallup poll found that two-thirds of Americans said it was wrong for "a man and a woman to have sexual relations before marriage."

But by 1985, Gallup found that a slim majority of Americans no longer believed such relations were wrong.[11] Analyzing shifts in public opinion following the sexual revolution, sociologists Larry Petersen and Gregory Donnenwerth have shown that among Americans with a religious affiliation, only fundamentalist Protestants who attended church frequently remained unchanged. Among all other religious groups acceptance of premarital sex grew.[12] This growing acceptance of premarital sex did not, however, extend to teenagers: in their 1990s survey, Laumann and colleagues found that almost 80 percent of the American population continued to believe sex among teenagers was *always* or *almost always* wrong. Since then, two-thirds of Americans have consistently told interviewers of the General Social Survey that sex between fourteen and sixteen was always wrong. Interestingly, disapproval has remained widespread even among themselves: six in ten fifteen to nineteen-year-olds, surveyed in the National

7 Bozon and Kontula 1998.

8 Jones et al. 1986; Berne and Huberman 1999; and Rose 2005.

9 Laumann et al. 1994, 198 and 326.

10 Finer 2007.

11 The Gallup poll statistics come from Smith 1994.

12 Petersen and Donnenwerth 1997.

Survey of Family Growth, said it was not right for unmarried sixteen-year-olds who have "strong affection for each another" to have sexual intercourse.[13]

Part of the opposition to, and discomfort with, adolescent sexuality is its association with the high prevalence of unintended consequences, such as pregnancy and sexually transmitted diseases. In the United States, the rate of unintended pregnancies among teenagers rose during the 1970s and 80s and started dropping only in the 1990s.[14] However, despite almost a decade and a half of impressive decreases in pregnancy and birth rates, the teen birth rate remains many times higher in the United States than it is in most European countries. In 2007, births to fifteen to nineteen-year-old girls were eight times as high in the United States as they were in the Netherlands.[15] One reason for the different birth rates is that while condom use has improved among American teenagers, they remain far less likely to use the most effective methods of birth control, such as the pill.[16] Another reason is that, once pregnant, American girls are far more likely than their Dutch peers to carry their pregnancies to term.[17]

Nor are high rates of unintended pregnancies the only problems. Many 10
American teenagers have positive and enriching sexual experiences, yet researchers have also documented intense struggles. Sharon Thompson found that

---

13 Abma, Martinez, and Copen 2010; Abma et al. 2004; 2010.

14 Kost, Henshaw, and Carlin 2010.

15 In 2007, the birth rate was 5.2 [per thousand] for Dutch teenage girls and 42.5 for American girls (Garssen 2008; Hamilton, Martin, and Ventura 2009). During the early 1990s, Dutch teenage pregnancy rates were comparable to those in recent years (van Lee and Wijsen 2008). But early 1990s American rates were significantly higher than those in recent years, and the contrast between the two countries in teenage pregnancy rates was even starker.... During the second half of the 1990s, the Dutch teenage pregnancy rate increased, before steadily decreasing again in 2002. But in 2000, the Dutch teenage pregnancy rate was still approximately four times lower than the American rate....

16 Evert Ketting (1983; 1994) has attributed the low Dutch teenage pregnancy rate to the use of the pill primarily and to emergency contraception secondarily. In 1995, 63 percent of Dutch secondary school students always used the pill with their last sexual partner, and 42 percent always used condoms (another 31 percent sometimes used condoms) (Brugman et al. 1995). That same year, a quarter of American females and a third of American males, ages fifteen to nineteen, who had sex three months prior to being interviewed by the National Survey of Family Growth, used the pill at last intercourse. Thirty-eight percent of American females and 64 percent of American males used a condom. Since then, condom use among sexually active youth has increased in both countries. Indeed, ... condom use at first vaginal intercourse is relatively high in both countries. However, pill use and dual protection (condoms and hormonal methods combined) are much higher among Dutch teens than they are among American teens. International comparisons of contraceptive behaviour at last vaginal intercourse among sexually active fifteen-year-olds have found a similar pattern (Currie et al. 2008; Santelli, Sandfort, and Orr 2008; Godeau et al. 2008)....

17 See ... note [15].

only a quarter of the four hundred girls she interviewed about sexuality talked about their first sexual experiences as pleasurable. Among the girls Karin Martin interviewed, puberty and first intercourse decreased self-esteem. Psychologist Deborah Tolman found that most of the girls she interviewed struggled to fully own their sexual desires and experiences in the face of cultural constructs such as the double standard and the "slut" label* that stigmatize and deny girls' desires. Laura Carpenter illuminated another side of the double standard, finding that many of the young men she interviewed experienced their virginity as a stigma which they often sought to cast off as rapidly as possible. And in her ethnographic study *Dude, You're a Fag*,* C.J. Pascoe found that teenage boys were encouraged to treat girls as sex objects and risked social derogation if they openly expressed affection for their girlfriends.[18]

These qualitative studies are corroborated by national surveys that show that American teenagers feel widespread ambivalence and misgivings about their first sexual experiences, which suggests that they do not feel control over, or entitled to, their sexual exploration. In a national survey, a minority of young women and a small majority of young men in their early twenties reported that their first heterosexual intercourse was "really wanted." Almost half of the women and a sizable minority of men surveyed said they had mixed feelings.[19] In another poll, a majority of American girls and boys said they wished they had waited longer to have sex.[20] Research has also found that if girls are young relative to their peers when they first have sex, they are more likely to experience negative emotions afterward, especially if their relationship breaks up shortly thereafter. But even without intercourse, first romance can bring girls "down" because their relationship with their parents deteriorates.[21]

American teenagers have received uneven, and often very limited, support in navigating the challenges of sexuality and first relationships from adult institutions outside the family. Despite rising pregnancy rates, in the early 1970s American policymakers and physician organizations lagged in making contraception easily available to teenagers, and even today American youth face multiple barriers in accessing contraception, including confidentiality

---

18 See Thompson 1990; Thompson 1995; Martin 1996; Tolman 2002; Carpenter 2005; and Pascoe 2007.

19 Abma et al. 2004.

20 Albert 2004.

21 Meier found that the majority of teenagers do not experience negative mental health effects after first sex. However, some groups of girls do experience such effects, which depend on their age and relationship status during and after their first intercourse (Meier 2007). On the relationship between first romance and conflict with parents, see Joyner and Udry 2000.

concerns.[22] With few other venues for discussing sexuality, the media has been an important, although often unrealistic, source of sex education for many American teenagers. Describing the 1960s and 1970s when sex permeated the media, historians D'Emilio and Freedman write, "From everywhere sex beckoned, inciting desire, yet rarely did one find reasoned presentations of the most elementary consequences and responsibilities that sexual activity entailed."[23] Since then, researchers have noted that some media including magazines and Internet sites provide good sexual health information but not the interactive dialogue with adults that teenagers seek.[24]

Teenagers have been unlikely to find such dialogue in the classroom. Along with fights over the legal age of consent to contraceptive and abortion services, battles over sex education have been among the most heated sexuality-related political struggles in America.[25] Politically organized religious conservatives succeeded in institutionalizing a federal sex education policy that has required the schools it funded to teach "abstinence only until marriage." Initiated in the early 1980s, federal support for abstinence-only policy was institutionalized in the 1996 welfare reform bill. Generously funded for many years, this policy dictated that schools teach that sex outside heterosexual marriage is likely to be damaging, and it prohibited them from teaching about the health benefits of condoms and contraception.[26] Even in school districts not funded by this

22 In the late 1960s and early 1970s, Dutch policymakers and the organization of family physicians, who provide the bulk of primary care in the Netherlands, made a concerted effort to make contraception easily accessible to unmarried women, including teenage women (Ketting 1990). During the same period, Constance Nathanson argues, the majority of American physicians shied away from the issue of teenage sexuality and pregnancy prevention. Indeed in the 1970s, Nathanson reports the American Medical Association's House of Delegates, the organization's principal policymaking body, rejected the recommendation by its Committee on Maternal and Child Health to adopt a policy of "permitting physicians to offer contraceptive advice and methods to teenage girls whose sexual behaviour exposes them to possible pregnancy" (1991, 39). Policymakers also struggled with the issue: Nathanson argues that "neither Nixon in 1972 nor Carter in 1978 was prepared publicly to endorse birth control for unmarried adolescent women" (57).... Today, many states permit minors twelve and up to consent to contraceptive services. However, concerns about confidentiality and costs still constitute barriers to adolescents' obtaining reproductive health care (Lehrer et al. 2007; Ralph and Brindis 2010; Guttmacher Institute 2010).

23 D'Emilio and Freedman 1988, 342.

24 See Ward et al. 2006 and Steele 2002.

25 See Irvine 2002 and di Mauro and Joffe 2007.

26 Kantor et al. 2008. While the recent health-care reform act has included federal funding for schools that teach about condoms and contraception, it also allocated funds to support abstinence-only programs.

federal policy, sex education about contraception, pleasure, sexual diversity, and relationships has often been greatly constrained.[27]

Few survey findings have been as consistent as the finding that the general public supports sex education in schools.[28] In keeping with the surveys of the past decades, a 2004 national survey by NPR, the Kaiser Family Foundation, and Harvard University found that most parents wanted their children to learn about contraception and condoms. Yet, the same survey also gives some insight into why the abstinence-only policy nevertheless prevailed: while most parents did want their children to learn the information they needed to protect themselves, most respondents also wanted students to be taught that they should not engage in intercourse or other intimate sexual activities. And they accepted the "marriage only" framework: two-thirds of parents of middle and high-school students agreed that teenagers should be taught that abstaining from sexual activity outside of marriage is "the accepted standard for school-aged children."[29] Abstinence, most agreed, includes refraining from oral sex and intimate touching—sexual activities that most American youth, in actuality, start experimenting with in their mid-teens.[30]

Adolescent Sexuality in Dutch Society after the Sexual Revolution

15 In a late 1980s qualitative study with one hundred and twenty parents and older teenagers, Dutch sociologist Janita Ravesloot found that in most families the parents accepted that sexuality "from the first kiss to the first coitus" was part of the youth phase. In middle-class families, parents accepted their children's sexual autonomy, though lingering embarrassment kept them from engaging in elaborate conversations. Working-class parents were more likely to use authority to impose their norms, including that sex belonged only in steady relationships. In a few strongly religious families—Christian or Muslim—parents categorically opposed sex before marriage, which meant: "no overnights with steady boy or girlfriends at home."[31] But such families remain a minority: a 2003 national survey by *Statistics Netherlands* found that two-thirds of

27 See Lindberg, Santelli, and Singh 2006; Darroch, Landry, and Singh 2000; and Fields 2008.

28 Since the mid-1970s, the General Social Survey has found that at least four out of five Americans support sex education in schools.

29 *Sex Education in America* 2004.

30 See *Sex Education in America* 2004. Using 2002 NSFG data, Mosher and colleagues (2005) report that by age sixteen, the majority of American teenagers have engaged in some sexual contact—which could include oral sex or intimate touching—with another person (either the same or opposite sex).

31 See Ravesloot 1997.

Dutch teenagers, aged fifteen to seventeen, who had steady boy or girlfriends, said that their parents would allow their boy or girlfriend to spend the night in their bedrooms; girls and boys were just as likely to say they would be granted permission for a sleepover.[32]

The situation could hardly have been predicted in the 1950s. Then, women *and* men typically initiated intercourse in their early twenties, usually in a serious relationship if not engagement or marriage.[33] In a national survey in the late 1960s, the Dutch sociologist G.A. Kooij found that the majority of the Dutch population still rejected premarital sex if a couple was not married or was not planning to be married very shortly. After repeating the survey in the early 1980s, he noted a "moral landslide" had taken place in the interim, as evidenced by the fact that six out of ten of those surveyed no longer objected to a girl having sexual intercourse with a boy as long as she was in love with him.[34] Dutch sociologist Evert Ketting spoke of a "moral revolution": Not just a reluctant acceptance of sex outside of the context of heterosexual marriage, this revolution involved serious deliberation among medical professionals, the media, and the public at large—the result of a widely felt need to adjust the moral rules governing sexual life to real behaviour.[35]

Many groups in Dutch society played a role in this transition. In the 1950s and '60s, Dutch religious leaders had begun questioning traditional definitions of morality. The Dutch Catholic Church—which represented the nation's largest religious group—was early to embrace the use of oral contraception as a method of birth control.[36] The Dutch media played a key educational role.[37]

32 Centraal Bureau voor de Statistiek 2003.

33 Bozon and Kontula 1998; Ravesloot 1997; and Wouters 2004.

34 Kooij 1983.

35 Ketting 1990; Ketting and Visser 1994. See also note [22]. Schnabel (1990) has argued that there was wide support among the Dutch population for the changes of the sexual revolution, and that change was certainly not confined to a small group of students.

36 Jones et al. 1986, 178. Historian James C. Kennedy has also argued that during the 1950s and 1960s, Dutch religious leaders, especially within the Catholic Church, went much further than bishops in other countries in fundamentally changing doctrine and practice, replacing a morality based on individual compliance with an ethics based on universal human compassion and service to others (Kennedy 1995). The Dutch sociologist Kooij (1983) has also pointed toward the role of religious leaders in opening up discussions around sexuality in Dutch society of the 1960s and 1970s. It is notable that the new moral discourse did not only pertain to heterosexual couples....

37 One group that played an important role was the Dutch Association for Sexual Reform (NVSH), which in the mid-1960s had more than 200,000 members. The NVSH was a strong advocate for family planning and sex education—including through media—and it helped shape government policy as well as public opinion (Ketting and Visser 1994; Hekma 2004a)....

With television and radio time partially funded by, and divided among, groups with different religious and political perspectives, discussions about sexuality were widespread.[38] Remarking on such discussions throughout the 1970s, researchers for the Guttmacher Institute noted in 1986, "One might say the entire society had concurrently experienced a course in sex education."[39] From these public deliberations resulted, Evert Ketting has argued, new moral rules that cast sexuality as part of life to be governed by self-determination, mutual respect between sexual partners, frank conversations, and the prevention of unintended consequences.[40]

Notably, these new moral rules were applied to minors and institutionalized in Dutch health-care policies of the 1970s, which removed financial and emotional barriers to accessing contraceptives—including the requirement for parental consent and a pelvic examination.[41] Indeed, even as the age of first sexual intercourse was decreasing, the rate of births among Dutch teenagers dropped steeply between 1970 and 1996 to one of the lowest in the world. With their effective use of oral contraception, what distinguished Dutch teens from their Swedish counterparts, for instance, was that in addition to a very low fertility rate they also had a low abortion rate. Despite the AIDS crisis,* by the mid-1990s—just when American policymakers institutionalized "abstinence only until marriage"—Dutch funding agencies were so confident that, in the words of demographer Joop Garsen, youth were doing "wonderfully well," they decided that further study of adolescent sexual attitudes and behaviour was not warranted.[42]

---

38 ... Kees van der Haak and Leo van Snippenburg ... note ... that even after the legalization and expansion of commercial broadcasting in the 1980s and 1990s, the government was "intent on keeping the public part of the whole broadcasting system as strong as possible in a context of national and international competition in commercial broadcasting" (2001, 210).

39 Jones et al. 1986, 154. Survey research in the 1980s did not find strong effects of factors such as gender, class, religion, or urbanization on attitudes toward sexuality among the Dutch population (Van Zessen and Sandfort 1991).

40 Ketting 1994.

41 Ketting and Visser 1994 and Hardon 2003. Hardon describes the legal parameters and public sentiment: "Over age 16, patients are considered autonomous in decisions on health care, including contraception. Between ages 12 and 16 parental consent is needed, but if patients do not give consent and the minor wants treatment (e.g. contraception), a doctor can provide it if not doing so would have serious, negative consequences for the minor. The extent to which the Dutch respect the autonomy of minors is reflected in a recent survey in which 75 percent of respondents thought doctors should prescribe contraception without parental consent if that is what the minor needed and wanted" (61).

42 The confidence was challenged when Dutch teen pregnancies and abortions rose notably between 1996 and 2002. But the Netherlands' role as "guide country" with regard

Dutch researchers at that time noted similarities in boys' and girls' experiences of sexuality. Ravesloot found that the boys and girls she interviewed were equally as likely to feel controlled by their parents. Large-scale surveys from the early and mid-1990s found that boys and girls were approximating one another in combining feelings of being in love and lust as they pursued romantic relationships and initiated sexual experimentation.[43] At the same time, researchers found evidence of the double standard and sex-stereotyping—including the notion that boys were supposed to be more active and girls more passive in sexual interactions.[44] To counteract these "traditional" gender beliefs and roles, researchers recommended teaching negotiation or "interaction" skills, including the expression of sexual wishes and boundaries.[45] A 2005 national survey found high levels of such skills among both girls and boys, which include "letting the other person know exactly what feels good" and not doing things that one does not want.[46]

Indeed, the same study, which surveyed youth aged twelve through twenty-four, suggests Dutch adolescents feel more in control of their first sexual experiences and decision-making than their American peers, or alternatively, that the former feel more entitled or obliged than the latter to describe themselves as empowered sexual actors: four out of five Dutch youth describe their first sexual experiences—broadly defined to include different activities—as well timed, within their control, and fun. About their first intercourse, 86 percent of girls and young women and 93 percent of boys and young men said, "We both were equally eager to have it." At the same time, there were some notable gender differences. For instance, girls were much more likely to report having ever been forced to do something sexually. They were also more likely to regularly or always experience pain (11 percent) or have trouble reaching orgasm (27 percent) during sex than were boys. Nevertheless, the vast majority of both Dutch females and males were (very) satisfied with the pleasure and contact they felt with their partner during sex.

Emphasis on the positive aspects of sex and relationships—within the context of respect for self and others—is a key feature of Dutch sex education.

---

to teenage births and abortions remained intact and was strengthened by a sustained decrease in those rates between 2002 and 2007....

43 Brugman et al. 1995 and Vogels and van der Vliet 1990.

44 Cremer 1997 and Ravesloot 1997. Vanwesenbeeck and colleagues (1998) found that gendered patterns had persisted among Dutch college students of the 1990s; girls were likely to take a defensive approach to sexual interactions, while males were more likely to take an active,"go-get-it" approach.

45 Rademakers and Ravesloot (1993), for instance, state: "Sexual contact is a situation of negotiation in which both partners have an equal position.... Learning to talk about sex and contraception is particularly important, but also learning to negotiate in general" (277).

46 De Graaf et al. 2005.

Although they set national "attainment targets," Dutch policymakers avoided political controversy over sex education by delegating the task of reaching agreements on the content and delivery of sex education to professionals.[47] Sociologists Jane Lewis and Trudie Knijn have argued that like Dutch policymakers, Dutch sex educators have accepted teenage sexual exploration, viewing it as the result of societal changes. They teach students to view such issues as sexual diversity and diverse family formations in broader societal contexts as well. Sex education typically covers anatomy, reproduction, STDs,* contraception, and abortion. But in addition, sex education curricula often interweave the emotional and physical aspects of sex, emphasize relationships and developing mutual understanding, and openly discuss masturbation, homosexuality, and sexual pleasure.[48]

INVESTIGATING THE PUZZLE

The previous sections show how across an array of social institutions, adolescent sexuality has been viewed as a problem to be prevented in the United States, while in the Netherlands it has been accepted as part of teenage maturation to be guided by new moral rules. Why do adults in the two countries have such different approaches? This question is especially puzzling given that, in both countries, the generation in question lived through an era when attitudes toward sexuality outside the confines of heterosexual marriage changed rather dramatically. Indeed, of the two, the country in which it had been more common for teenagers to engage in sexual intercourse during the 1950s became, several decades later, the country in which teenage sexuality remained controversial.

Two factors immediately spring to mind when considering why adults in these two countries who lived through the sexual revolution—in which many themselves participated—would embrace such different approaches to the sexual socialization of the next generation. The first is religion. Americans are far more likely to be religiously devout than their Dutch counterparts, many of whom left their houses of worship in the 1960s and 1970s. As Laumann and colleagues found, Americans who do not view religion as a central force in their decision-making are much less likely to categorically condemn sex among teenagers. By the same token, devout Christians and Muslims in the Netherlands are more likely to hold attitudes towards sexuality and marriage that are similar to those of their American counterparts. That a larger proportion

47 Lewis and Knijn 2002; 2003.

48 Lewis and Knijn 2002, 687. But curricula are also adapted for religious audiences. An example of such adjustments included the emphasis on faithfulness over condoms and the exclusion of passages on masturbation and orgasm for a textbook used in schools of the Dutch Reformed Church (SOAIDS 2004).

of the American population than the Dutch population can be categorized as religiously conservative explains some of the difference between the countries.[49]

A second factor is economic security: as in most European countries, the Dutch government provides a range of what sociologists call "social rights" and what reproductive health advocates call "human rights."[50] These include the rights to housing, education, health care, and a minimum income. These rights ensure youth access to quality health care, including, if need be, free contraceptive and abortion services. Such supports—from universal children's allowances to college stipends—also make coming of age less perilous for both teenagers and parents, and they might make the prospect of sex derailing a child's life less haunting. Ironically, it is the lack of such rights in the United States, along with rates of childhood poverty that exceed those of most of Europe, that contributes to high rates of births among teenagers. Without adequate support systems or educational and job opportunities, young people everywhere, not just in the United Sates, are much more likely to start parenthood early in life.[51]

And yet, as Karel Doorman and Rhonda Fursman illustrated at the start of this chapter, there is more to the story: both parents are economically comfortable and neither attends church regularly, yet their answers to the question of the sleepover could not be more different. To understand why parents such as Rhonda and Karel reached such opposing conclusions about the sleepover, and how their different household practices affected teenagers, I interviewed one hundred and thirty members of the American and Dutch white, secular or moderately Christian and middle classes—fifty-eight individual parents or couples, thirty-two boys, and forty girls, with most of the teens in the tenth grade. To avoid only studying professionals, I included a spectrum of lower and upper-middle-class families, and interviewed parents of teenagers living in households where the breadwinners ranged from salespeople and bank clerks with little or no postsecondary education, to nurses and managers with four-year degrees, to psychotherapists and doctors with advanced degrees.

In both countries, most interviewees came from one of two locations: In the Netherlands, they lived in or around the medium-sized cities of Western and Eastern City, which are located in the more cosmopolitan, densely populated Western region and in the less cosmopolitan, less densely populated Eastern region respectively. In the United States, most interviewees lived in or around

---

49 In their analysis of fifteen nations, Kelley and de Graaf (1997) use a variety of measures for religiosity. They characterize the United States as an extraordinarily devout modern society and the Netherlands as a relatively secular one.

50 Goodin et al. 2000.

51 Singh, Darroch, and Frost 2001.

Corona, a medium-sized city in northern California, and Tremont, a small town in the Pacific Northwest. An additional group of American interviewees resided in Norwood, a New England suburb.[52] Avoiding the most cosmopolitan urban centres and liberal hotspots,* as well as the most conservative regions and remote rural areas, the two samples represent what I would call the "moderate middle" among the white middle class in the two countries. Comparing these population segments cannot illuminate important cultural differences *within* either nation—between classes, races, regions, ethnicities, and religions. But the comparison does illuminate differences between the two countries in the family cultures of two particularly influential groups—differences that are not accounted for by our prevailing theoretical perspectives on adolescent sexuality.

MEDICAL, SOCIAL SCIENCE, AND HISTORICAL PERSPECTIVES

In the United States, the prevailing perspective in the field of public policy and health has been that teenage sexual intercourse is a health risk—a potential sickness, which is to be ideally prevented altogether.[53] The primary focus of research in this field is on the various factors that increase and decrease the risks of adolescent sexuality—defined narrowly as acts of intercourse. The risk perspective is corroborated by one view from developmental psychology* which sees adolescents as inherently risk-prone and subject to impulses that they are not yet able to handle, given their stage of cognitive development.[54] Classical developmental psychology also conceptualizes sexuality as part of young people's separation process from parents.[55] This process, however, produces discord—between teenagers' impulses and their brains' capacities, between early onset of sexual feelings and their later proclivity for emotional intimacy, and between teenagers and parents whose job it is to communicate their values and to monitor and limit their children's opportunities for sex.

---

52 All of the American parent interviews informed the analyses and calculation of parents' answers to the questions of the sleepover. However, only Corona and Tremont parents are quoted in this book. For quotes from the interviews with Norwood parents, see Schalet 2000.

53 Michaud 2006 and Nathanson 1991.

54 Steinberg 2004.

55 American psychoanalytic developmental theory places a great emphasis on separation and on sexual development as one of the motors of separation (Erikson 1950; Freud 1958). For a fascinating analysis of how American psychoanalytic developmental psychology has been shaped by Anglo-American cultural traditions that emphasize among other things, self-reliance, resulting in an emphasis on separation as the marker of psychological health, see Kirschner 1990. Socio-biological evolutionary perspectives also place an emphasis on the necessity for separation between parents and adolescents (Collins, Welsh, and Furman 2009, 634)....

These perspectives from medicine and psychology do not explain the puzzle posed by the differences in approach to and experience of adolescent sexuality in two developed nations. If anything, the puzzle challenges their assumptions. While Dutch teenagers, like their American counterparts, must certainly navigate the potential health risks of sex, the variation between the two nations in negative outcomes of sexual activity shows that neither the level of sexual activity itself nor adolescents' inherent biological or psychological capacities are responsible for such outcomes. The normalization of adolescent sexuality in Dutch middle-class families challenges, moreover, the notion that teenage sexuality—and adolescence as a phase of life—causes a schism* between parents and teenagers that is often assumed in the United States to be an inevitable part of development, one in which parents and teenagers remain more closely connected and able to negotiate the potential disruptive elements of adolescent maturation....

A final perspective on adolescent sexuality places it in the context of historical change. French philosopher Michel Foucault has argued that in the modern era, governments are no longer able to rule large populations through repression and punishment alone. However, they have found in official discourses about "normal" heterosexual identities and reproductive behaviour effective methods for social control. Originating in religious, medical, scientific and penal institutions, disciplinary practices and discourses encourage self-disclosure, differentiate people into categories, and goad them into new self-conceptions. Unlike the "sovereign" power of authorities who impose harsh punishments, the power of discipline and discourse is harder to detect, which makes it effective. Modern power is "productive" rather than repressive, Foucault argues, because rather than forbid, it exhorts individuals to voluntarily shape their subjective sense of themselves according to confining understandings of what is normal, healthy, and desirable.[56]

Foucault's argument that, in the modern era, conceptions and practices around sexuality have been power-ridden and often serve the interests of authorities is useful but incomplete. Indeed, as we will see, the dramatization and normalization of adolescent sexuality are imbued with forms of social control. But Foucault's account does not help us understand why different discourses of adolescent sexuality have come to prevail in the institutions of two equally modern, post-sexual-revolution societies. Nor does it provide an explanation for why these different discourses—of adolescent-sexuality-as-risk in the United States, and of adolescent sexual self-determination in the Netherlands—resonate as they do among lay people. Finally, Foucault's argument about the effectiveness of modern power misses key ingredients.

56 Foucault 1977; 1978.

The successful use of contraception among Dutch girls appears a prime example of disciplinary power. But, I argue, this power "works" because girls remain connected to and supported by adult institutions and are able to develop self-mastery—parts of the puzzle Foucault bypasses....[57]

DRAMATIZATION AND NORMALIZATION

The first step to solve the puzzle of the sleepover is to see that Dutch and American parents engage in different cultural processes as they interpret and manage teenage sexuality. Culling words, expressions and modes of reasoning from interviews shows how the American parents engage in *dramatization*: highlighting difficulties and conflicts, they describe adolescent sexuality, first, as "raging hormones," individual, potentially overpowering forces that are difficult for teenagers to control and, second, as antagonistic heterosexual relationships in which girls and boys pursue love and sex respectively. Finally, parents see it as their obligation to encourage adolescents to establish autonomy—and gain the potential for financial self-sufficiency or marriage—before accepting their sexual activity as legitimate. And viewing sex as part of a process of separation in which parents must stand firm ground around certain key issues, the response to the question of a sleepover, even among many otherwise liberal parents is, "Not under my roof!"

The Dutch parents, by contrast, engage in a cultural process of normalization. Theirs is a conception of "regulated love": that is, the Dutch parents speak of sexual readiness (*era an toe zijn*), a process of becoming physically and emotionally ready that they believe young people can self-regulate, provided that they have been encouraged to pace themselves and prepare adequately by using the available means of contraception. But readiness does not happen in isolation. The Dutch parents talk about sexuality emerging from relationships, and they are strikingly silent about gender conflicts. And unlike their American counterparts, who are often sceptical about teenagers' capacities to fall in love, they assume that even those in their early teens do so. They also permit the sleepover for those in their mid and late teens, even if it requires an "adjustment" period to overcome their feelings of discomfort, because they feel obliged to accept the changes and to stay connected as relationships and sex become part of their children's lives.

The interplay of cultural frames that parents use to interpret adolescent sexuality, the capacities of young people, and the responsibilities of adults

57 This critique of Foucault has been partly inspired by the work of Norbert Elias, who offers an alternative and more optimistic view of the relationship between sexuality and control in the modern world (Elias 1994, 177; Smith 1999).

gives parents' responses to the question of the sleepover their cognitive, emotional, and moral common sense. These "webs of significance" thus create a more or less coherent cultural universe of meanings in which certain decisions and practices make intuitive sense while others do not. At the same time, there are holes in the webs: as significant as the cultural languages that parents have readily available are the silences, lacunae, and the ways in which dramatization and normalization do not adequately address aspects of parents' and teenagers' experiences. And although there are dominant tendencies in each middle-class culture, not everyone is on the same page. Indeed, as we will see, rather than constitute seamless wholes, dramatization and normalization often involve negotiations—between different people and between expectations and realities.

ADVERSARIAL AND INTERDEPENDENT INDIVIDUALISM

The second step in solving the puzzle is to see that the normalization and 35
dramatization of adolescent sexuality are embedded within different cultures of individualism and control that have come to prevail in Dutch and American societies. These different cultures of individualism and control build on longstanding traditions within each country. At the same time, they are also nation-specific responses to the changes in sexual, gender, and authority relations of the 1960s and 1970s: In the United States an "adversarial individualism" has prevailed, according to which individual and society stand opposed to each other, which leaves uncertainty about the basis for social bonds between people and for self-restraint within them. In the Netherlands an "interdependent individualism" has prevailed in which individual and society are conceptualized as mutually constitutive....

Each version of individualism has been accompanied by a distinct form of social control: Adversarial individualism permits, encourages even, individuals to attain autonomy by breaking away from social ties and dependencies, and only after that break form intimate relationships. However, because this definition of autonomy necessitates a disruption of social connectedness, it makes it difficult to envision social cohesion and self-restraint without some higher authority. Thus ironically, adversarial individualism calls for the use of overt external control, especially against those who have not (yet) attained full autonomy. Interdependent individualism, by contrast, encourages individuals to develop their autonomy in concert with ongoing relationships of interdependence. Because such relationships require, by their nature, a certain amount of mutual accommodation and self-restraint, the use of external controls appears less necessary. But while overtly egalitarian, interdependent individualism can obscure inequality and the fact that the less powerful parties in the relationships are expected to make the greater accommodations.*

The premises of adversarial and interdependent individualism—their assumptions about the relationship between self and other, and the relationship between different parts of the self—create cultural logics that undergird the dramatization and normalization of adolescent sexuality. Hence, American middle-class parents encourage adolescents to pursue individual interests and passions, break away from home, and establish themselves as emotionally and financially self-sufficient beings. At the same time, during the teenage years, American parents also view it as their responsibility to fight back, sometimes forcefully, against the passions that they at the same time encourage as signs of individuation but doubt that their teenage children are able to control. This template for adversarial individualism makes parents wary of adolescents' establishing intimate bonds. It also makes domesticating such bonds by permitting a sleepover out of the question.

The Dutch template of interdependent individualism provides a way for adolescents to develop their autonomy within relationships of interdependence. Such ongoing interrelatedness is not viewed as a matter of choice as much as an inherent human need and proclivity. Thus, adolescence does not bring the same rupture in the relationships with parents or in the self. An assumption of interdependent individualism is that even as they develop autonomy, individuals—parents and children alike—must demonstrate interpersonal attunement, which requires from adolescents the development of self-regulation. Within this framework of interdependent individualism, teenagers' intimate relationships do not pose a threat to the acquisition of autonomy, nor does their sexual component threaten parental authority within the home. By negotiating the sleepover, parents model the very interdependent individualism—integrating the needs of the self and the social—they encourage in their children.

Connection Through Control and Control Through Connection

Intergenerational cultural transmission takes place not just through cultural narratives but also through methods for maintaining control and connection that psychologically encode them.* As part of a new generation, young people's cultural universe only partially overlaps with that of their parents: they consume different media, are subject to different technological fluencies, participate in different institutions—school and peer culture—and are recipients of different formative "zeitgeists."* Having not been fully socialized and yet subject to multiple sources of socialization, young people are often "rawer" in their desires and tendencies than their parents. For all these reasons, one cannot assume that just because a cultural logic makes sense to parents, it will make sense to their children as well. Yet, as we will see, even as they are in process of forging their independent selves, young people do, in fact, reproduce through the interpretation and construction of their own experiences many of the same cultural categories their parents use.

Such cultural reproduction between the generations is not a matter of 40
course. In both countries, adolescent experimentation with sexuality and alcohol are sources of potential parent-adolescent conflict. However, the methods by which parents establish control and connection shape how those conflicts are experienced. Most American teenagers describe a parental strategy of *re-establishing connection through control*. Many American teenagers encounter parental policies much like those in the Fursman household—no sex or alcohol. And while most young people start their teenage "careers" as rule followers, sooner or later they start "sneaking around" to engage in forbidden activities, which in turn become vehicles through which they engage in a *psychology of separation*. But this secrecy also creates a disjuncture in the connection between parents and children. To re-establish that connection, parents must exert overt control and young people must "get caught."

In most Dutch families, by contrast, teenagers are subject to parental strategy of *maintaining control through connection*. With the belief widespread that it is not possible to keep young people from engaging in sex and drinking if they decide they want to, few teenagers find such exploratory activities outright forbidden. At the same time, they are expected to continue participation in family rituals that keep them connected to their parents even as they begin to experiment with sex, alcohol, and venturing into the world of nightlife. The "domestication" of their experimentations create bridges between the world of adults and the world of peers that their American counterparts lack, and it encourages in Dutch teenagers a *psychology of incorporation*. Those bridges are two-way streets: young people are able to integrate their experiences outside the home more easily with their roles as family members, but they are also subject to a deeper form of social control. This "soft" power is particularly effective when young people stay genuinely connected to their families not just out of duty but out of desire.[58]

Individualism and Gender

The different cultural templates for individualism and control also shape interpretations and experiences of gender. The American parents often mention differences and conflicts of interest between girls and boys. In fact, in some, though certainly not most families, the American boys report receiving implicit or explicit encouragement from fathers to pursue sexual interests. And while the interpretation and management of sexuality in American middle-class families led both girls and boys to use sex as a vehicle to engage in a psychology of separation, bifurcating sexuality and family life, this process tends to take a greater psychological toll on girls. While boys are expected to be "bad," girls

58 This plays on the title of Jane Collier's *From Duty to Desire: Remaking Families in a Spanish Village* (1997).

are encouraged to be "good." But with "good girl" status and sex viewed as incompatible, American girls often experience, or anticipate experiencing, difficulty reconciling their sexual maturation with good daughterhood.

Interdependent individualism shapes the language and experience of gender in Dutch middle-class families. As noted, the Dutch parents do not speak about adolescent sexuality in terms of girls' and boys' different positions of power or their "antagonistic gender strategies." Nor do they give evidence of treating sons and daughters differently with regard to sexuality and relationships. In keeping with national statistics and qualitative research, they suggest that daughters and sons are equally likely to receive permission for sleepovers. Like their female counterparts, most Dutch boys are subject to "soft control" that socializes them into a relationship-based experience of sexuality and self and that encourages negotiations within, rather than separation from, the household. But there are subtle gender differences: such negotiation tends to be more fraught for girls, and while few Dutch boys express reservations about actually bringing their girlfriends home for the night, a number of Dutch girls say that they would rather spend the night elsewhere, suggesting that they do feel more closely supervised by their parents.

Adversarial individualism and interdependent individualism also provide cultural templates with which the American and Dutch girls and boys navigate sex and sense of self within peer cultures. The different assumptions about people's inherent relational needs and proclivities—at the root of the two versions of individualism—shape teenage girls' and boys' dilemmas of gender. In both countries girls are confined by the potential slander of being called a slut, but that label is much more prominent in the interviews with American girls. One reason is that American girls encounter adult and peer cultures sceptical about teenagers' ability to sustain meaningful sexual relationships. This scepticism means that American girls lack the indisputable certainty that the Dutch girls possess about whether and when sex is culturally legitimate. But while Dutch adult and peer cultures validate sexual experience in relationships, uncritical validation of relationship-based sexuality can obscure conflicts of interest and power differences in heterosexual relationships.

45 To different degrees, the notion that boys want sex but not relationships has some currency in both American and Dutch peer and popular culture. But in both countries, the vast majority of boys describe themselves as quite romantic in their orientation, wanting to experience sex with someone with whom they are in love. The American boys tend to see themselves as unique for their romantic aspirations, calling to mind the icon of the lone cowboy opposing the crowd of hormone-driven boys and a peer and popular culture of soulless sex. Indeed, some American boys set the bar for love very high—defining it as a heroic relinquishing of self—thus distancing themselves not only from

other boys but from sexual pleasure itself. The Dutch boys describe themselves as normal in their pursuit of a combination of sex and relationships. Without the stark oppositions—between male and female, love and lust, and pleasure and responsibility—they evidence a more integrated experience of ideals and realities....

CULTURE'S COSTS

... Teenagers do better emotionally when they can remain connected to their parents during adolescence. But with sexuality culturally coded as a symbol of, and a means to attaining, separation between parents and children, an important developmental experience becomes a cause for disconnection in the parent-teenager relationship. This disconnect makes it more difficult for parents to serve as support when adolescents start their first sexual experiences during their mid-teens. And when teenagers must keep their sexual behaviour a secret or know it is a disappointment to their parents, it becomes more difficult to seek assistance from adults—to obtain contraception, assess their readiness, or discuss the qualities of a romantic relationship.

The ways in which the American culture of individualism conceptualizes autonomy and intimacy also do not serve adolescents well. The cultural narrative which dictates that one must attain financial and emotional autonomy before being ready for sex and emotional commitment leaves youth with a conception of autonomy they cannot attain until their mid-twenties, if ever. Such a conception does not provide the cultural tools to develop *internal* discernment and regulation necessary to exercise psychological autonomy within teenage sexual and romantic relationships.

As important, this narrative leaves young people and their parents without cultural templates for validating and assessing adolescent intimate relationships on their own terms. Strikingly, many American parents as well many American teenagers—girls and boys—use marriage as the ultimate intimacy that they are capable of and to strive for commitments they are not yet able to make.

The Dutch culture of interdependent individualism does not lead to the same psychological disconnect between parents and teenagers. Though the negotiation of adolescent sexuality is not tension-free, especially when it concerns the sexuality of girls, ultimately most of the Dutch girls and boys can integrate their sexual development with their relationship with their parents. This continued connectedness makes it easier for Dutch teenagers to draw on the support of parents and other adults as they move through their adolescent sexual and emotional explorations. With autonomy conceptualized as a matter of exercising self-direction within relationships, and with interdependence viewed as a matter of necessity rather than choice, Dutch teenagers also receive more cultural validation for their intimate relationships. At the same time, the cultural template of interdependent individualism makes it more difficult for Dutch teenagers and their parents to recognize and address conflicts of interest within relationships than it is for their American counterparts, who speak readily of conflicts and battles....

(2011)

References[59]

Abma, Joyce C., Gladys M. Martinez, and Casey E. Copen. 2010. Teenagers in the United States: Sexual Activity, Contraceptive Use, and Childbearing, National Survey of Family Growth 2006–2008. *Vital and Health Statistics,* ser. 23, no. 30. National Center for Health Statistics.

Abma, Joyce C., Gladys M. Martinez, William D. Mosher, and Brittany S. Dawson. 2004. Teenagers in the United States: Sexual Activity, Contraceptive Use, and Childbearing, 2002. *Vital and Health Statistics,* ser. 23, no. 24. National Center for Health Statistics.

Albert, Bill. 2004. *With One Voice 2004: America's Adults and Teens Sound Off About Teen Pregnancy*. Washington, DC: National Campaign to Prevent Teen Pregnancy.

Anderson, Elijah. 1999. *Code of the Street: Decency, Violence, and the Moral Life of the Inner City*. New York: W.W. Norton & Company.

Armstrong, Elizabeth A., Laura Hamilton, and Brian Sweeney. 2006. Sexual Assault on Campus: A Multilevel, Integrative Approach to Party Rape. *Social Problems* 53 (4): 483–99.

Bearman, Peter S., James Moody, and Katherine Stovel. 2004. Chains of Affection: The Structure of Adolescent Romantic and Sexual Networks. *American Journal of Sociology* 110 (1): 44–91.

Bearman, Peter S., and Hannah Brückner. 2001. Promising the Future: Virginity Pledges and First Intercourse. *American Journal of Sociology* 106 (4): 859–912.

Berne, Linda, and Barbara Huberman. 1999. *European Approaches to Adolescent Sexual Behavior and Responsibility*. Washington, DC: Advocates for Youth.

Bettie, Julie. 2000. Women Without Class: *Chicas, Cholas*, Trash, and the Presence/Absence of Class Identity. *Signs: Journal of Women in Culture and Society* 26 (1): 1–35.

Bozon, Michel, and Osmo Kontula. 1998. Sexual Initiation and Gender in Europe: A Cross-Cultural Analysis of Trends in the Twentieth Century. In *Sexual Behaviour and HIV/AIDS in Europe: Comparisons of National Surveys,* edited by M. Hubert, N. Bajos, and T. Sandfort. London: UCL Press.

Brugman, Emily, Hans Goedhart, Ton Vogels, and Gertjan van Zessen. 1995. *Jeugd en Seks 95: Resultaten van het Nationale Scholierenonderzoek*. Utrecht: SWP.

Carpenter, Laura M. 2005. *Virginity Lost: An Intimate Portrait of First Sexual Experiences*. New York: New York University Press.

Centraal Bureau voor de Statistiek. 2003. *Jeugd 2003: Cijfers en Feiten.* Voorburg/Heerlen: Centraal Bureau voor de Statistiek.

Coleman, James S. 1961. *The Adolescent Society: The Social Life of the Teenager and Its Impact on Education.* New York: The Free Press of Glencoe.

---

59 [Editors' note] References have been excerpted to show only those cited in the material included here.

Collins, W. Andrew, Deborah P. Welsh, and Wyndol Furman. 2009. Adolescent Romantic Relationships. *Annual Review of Psychology* 60: 631–52.

Cremer, Stephan W. 1997. Kwetsbaar en Grenzeloos: Experimenteren in Seks en Omgaan met Grenzen vanuit het Perspectief van Jongens. *Comenius* 17: 325–37.

Currie, Candace, Saoirse Nic Gabhainn, Emmanuelle Godeau, Chris Roberts, Rebecca Smith, Dorothy Currie, Will Picket, Matthias Richter, Antony Morgan, and Vivian Barnekow Rasmussen, eds. 2008. Inequalities in Young People's Health: International Report from 2005/2006 Survey. In *Health Policy for Children and Adolescents*, no. 5. Copenhagen: World Health Organization.

D'Emilio, John, and Estelle B. Freedman. 1988. *Intimate Matters: A History of Sexuality in America*. New York: Harper and Row.

Darroch, Jacqueline E., David J. Landry, and Susheela Singh. 2000. Changing Emphases in Sexuality Education in U.S. Public Secondary Schools, 1988–1999. *Family Planning Perspectives* 32 (5): 211–65.

Darroch, Jacqueline E., Susheela Singh, and Jennifer J. Frost. 2001. Differences in Teenage Pregnancy Rates among Five Developed Countries: The Roles of Sexual Activity and Contraceptive Use. *Family Planning Perspectives* 33 (60): 244–50 and 281.

De Graaf, Paul M., and Harry B.G. Ganzenboom. 1993. Family Background and Educational Attainment in the Netherlands for the 1891–1960 Birth Cohorts. In *Persistent Inequalities: A Comparative Study of Educational Attainment in Thirteen Countries*, edited by Y. Shavit and H.-P. Blossfeld, CO: Westview Press.

di Mauro, Diane and Carole Joffe. 2007. The Religious Right and the Reshaping of Sexual Policy: An Examination of Reproductive Rights and Sexuality Education. *Sexuality Research and Social Policy: A Journal of NSRC* 4 (1): 67–92.

Eder, Donna, Catherine Colleen Evans, and Stephen Parker. 1995. *School Talk: Gender and Adolescent Culture*. New Brunswick, NJ: Rutgers University Press.

Elias, Norbert. 1994. *The Civilizing Process*. Translated by E. Jephcott. Oxford: Blackwell.

Erikson, Erik H. 1950. *Childhood and Society*. New York: W.W. Norton & Co.

Fields, Jessica. 2008. *Risky Lessons: Sex Education and Social Inequality*. New Brunswick, NJ: Rutgers University Press.

Fine, Michelle. 1998. Sexuality, Schooling, and Adolescent Females: The Missing Discourse of Desire. *Harvard Educational Review* 58 (1): 29–53.

Finer, Lawrence B. 2007. Trends in Premarital Sex in the United States, 1954–2003. *Public Health Reports* 122 (January–February): 73–78.

Foucault, Michel. 1977. *Discipline and Punish: The Birth of the Prison*. Translated by A. Sheridan. New York: Vintage.

Freud, Anna. 1958. Adolescence. *Psychoanalytic Study of the Child* 15: 255–78.

Garssen, Joop. 2008. Sterke Daling Geboortecijfer Niet-westers Allochtone Tieners. *Bevolkings-trends* 56 (4): 14–21.

Godeau, Emmanuelle, Saoirse Nic Gabhainn, Celine Vignes, Jim Ross, Will Boyce, and Joanna Todd. 2008. Contraceptive Use by 15-year-old Students at Their Last Sexual Intercourse. *Archives of Pediatrics and Adolescent Medicine* 162 (1): 66–73.

Goodin, Robert E., Bruce Headey, Ruud Muffels, and Henk-Jan Dirven. 2000. The Real Worlds of Welfare Capitalism. In *The Welfare State: A Reader*, edited by C. Pierson and F.G. Castles, Cambridge, MA: Polity Press.

Graaf, Hanneke de, Suzanne Meijer, Jos Poelman, and Ine Vanwesenbeeck. 2005. *Seks onder je 25ste: Seksuele Gezondheid van Jongeren in Nederland Anno 2005*. Utrecht and Amsterdam: Rutgers Nisso Groep/Soa Aids Nederland.

Guttmacher Institute. 2010. *State Policies in Brief: An Overview of Minors' Consent Law*. New York: Guttmacher Institute.

Haak, Kees van der, and Leo van Snippenburg. 2001. Broadcasting in the Netherlands: The Rise and Decline of Segmentation. In *Western Broadcasting at the Dawn of the 21st Century*, edited by L. D'Haenens and F. Saeys. Berlin and New York: Mouton de Gruyter.

Hamilton, Brady E., Joyce A. Martin, and Stephanie J. Ventura. 2009. Births: Preliminary Data for 2007. *National Vital Statistics* 57 (12). National Center for Health Statistics.

Hardon, Anita. 2003. Reproductive Health Care in the Netherlands: Would Integration Improve It? *Reproductive Health Matters* 11 (21): 59–73.

Hekma, Gert. 2004a. The Decline of Sexual Radicalism in the Netherlands. In *Past and Present of Radical Sexual Politics,* edited by G. Hekma. Amsterdam: Mosse Foundation.

Irvine, Janice M. 2002. *Talk About Sex: The Battles over Sex Education in the United States*. Berkeley and Los Angeles: University of California Press.

Jones, Elise F., Jacqueline Darroch Forest, Noreen Goldman, Stanley Henshaw, Richard Lincoln, Jeannie I. Rosoff, Charles F. Westhoff, and Deidre Wulf. 1986. *Teenage Pregnancy in Industrialized Countries. A Study Sponsored by the Alan Guttmacher Institute*. New Haven: Yale University Press.

Joyner, Kara, and J. Richard Udry. 2000. You Don't Bring Me Anything but Down: Adolescent Romance and Depression. *Journal of Health and Social Behavior* 41 (4): 369–91.

Kantor, Leslie M., John S. Santelli, Julien Teitler, and Randall Balmer. 2008. Abstinence-Only Policies and Programs: An Overview. *Sexuality Research and Social Policy: A Journal of NSRC* 5 (3): 6–17.

Kelley, Jonathan, and Nan Dirk de Graaf. 1997. National Context, Parental Socialization, and Religious Belief: Results from 15 Nations. *American Sociological Review* 62 (4): 639–59.

Kennedy, James C. 1995. *Nieuw Babylon in Aanbouw: Nederland in de Jaren Zestig*. Amsterdam: Boom.

Ketting, Evert. 1983. Contraception and Fertility in the Netherlands. *Family Planning Perspectives* 15 (1): 19–25.

Ketting, Evert. 1990. De Seksuele Revolutie van Jongeren. In *Het Verlies van Onschuld: Seksualiteit in Nederland,* edited by G. Hekma, B. v. Stolk, B. v. Heerikhuizen, and B. Kruithof. Groningen: Wolters-Noordhoff.

Ketting, Evert. 1994. Is the Dutch Abortion Rate Really that Low? *Planned Parenthood in Europe* 23 (3): 29–32.

Ketting, Evert, and Adriaan P. Visser. 1994. Contraception in the Netherlands: The Low Abortion Rate Explained. *Patient Education and Counselling* 23 (3): 161–71.

Kirschner, Suzanne R. 1990. The Assenting Echo: Anglo-American Values in Contemporary Psychoanalytic Developmental Psychology. *Social Research* 57 (4): 821–57.

Kooij, G.A. 1983. *Sex in Nederland: Het Meest Recente Onderzoek naar Houding en Gedrag van de Nederlandse Bevolking*. Utrecht/Antwerp: Het Spectrum.

Kost, Kathryn, Stanley Henshaw, and Liz Carlin. 2010. *U.S. Teenage Pregnancies, Births and Abortions: National and State Trends and Trends by Race and Ethnicity*. Washington, DC: Guttmacher Institute.

Laumann, Edward O., John H. Gagnon, Robert T. Michael, and Stuart Michaels. 1994. *The Social Organization of Sexuality: Sexual Practices in the United States*. Chicago: University of Chicago Press.

Lee, Laura van, and Cecile Wijsen. 2008. *Landelijke Abortus Registratie 2007*. Utrecht, Netherlands: Rutgers Nisso Groep.

Lehrer, Jocelyn A., Robert Pantell, Kathleen Tebb, and Mary-Anne Shafer. 2007. Forgone Health Care among US Adolescents: Associations between Risk Characteristics and Confidentiality Concern. *Journal of Adolescent Health* 40 (3): 213–26.

Lewis, Jane, and Trudie Knijn. 2002. The Politics of Sex Education in England and Wales and the Netherlands since the 1980s. *Journal of Social Policy* 31(4): 669–94.

Lewis, Jane, and Trudie Knijn. 2003. Sex Education Materials in the Netherlands and in England and Wales: A Comparison of Content, Use and Teaching Practice. *Oxford Review of Education* 29 (1): 113–50.

Lindberg, Laura D., John S. Santelli, and Susheela Singh. 2006. Changes in Formal Sex Education: 1995–2002. *Perspectives on Sexual and Reproductive Health* 38 (4): 182–89.

Martin, Karin A. 1996. *Puberty, Sexuality, and the Self: Girls and Boys at Adolescence*. New York: Routledge.

Meier, Ann M. 2007. Adolescent First Sex and Subsequent Mental Health. *American Journal of Sociology* 112 (6): 1811–47.

Michaud, Pierre-Andre. 2006. Adolescents and Risks: Why Not Change Our Paradigm? *Journal of Adolescent Health* 38 (5): 481–83.

Mosher, William D., Anjani Chandra, and Jo Jones. 2005. Sexual Behavior and Selected Health Measures: Men and Women 15–44 Years of Age, United States, 2002. *Advance Data from Vital and Health Statistics,* n. 362. National Center for Health Statistics.

Nathanson, Constance. 1991. *Dangerous Passage: The Social Control of Sexuality in Women's Adolescence*. Philadelphia: Temple University Press.

Pascoe, C.J. 2007. *Dude, You're a Fag: Masculinity and Sexuality in High School*. Berkeley and Los Angeles: University of California Press.

Petersen, Larry R., and Gregory Donnenwerth. 1997. Secularization and the Influence of Religion on Beliefs about Premarital Sex. *Social Forces* 75 (93): 1071–88.

Rademakers, Jany, and Janita Ravesloot. 1993. Jongeren en Seksualiteit. In *Jeugd in Meervoud: Theorieën Modellen en Onderzoek van Leefwerelden van Jongeren*, edited by A.J. Dieleman, f.j.v.d. Linden and A.C. Perreijn. Utrecht: De Tijdstroom.

Ralph, Lauren J., and Claire D. Brindis. 2010. Access to Reproductive Healthcare for Adolescents: Establishing Healthy Behaviors at a Critical Juncture in the Lifecourse. *Current Opinion in Obstetrics and Gynecology* 22 (5): 369–74.

Ravesloot, Janita. 1997. *Seksualiteit in de Jeugdfase Vroeger en Nu: Ouders en Jongeren aan het Woord*. Amsterdam: Het Spinhuis.

Rose, Susan. 2005. Going Too Far? Sex, Sin and Social Policy. *Social Forces* 84 (2): 1207–32.

Santelli, John S., Theo G. Sandfort, and Mark Orr. 2008. Transnational Comparisons of Adolescent Contraceptive Use: What Can We Learn from These Comparisons? *Archives of Pediatrics and Adolescent Medicine* 162 (1): 92–94.

Schalet, Amy T. 2000. Raging Hormones, Regulated Love: Adolescent Sexuality and the Constitution of the Modern Individual in the United States and the Netherlands. *Body and Society* 6 (91): 75–105.

Schnabel, Paul. 1990. Het Verlies van de Seksuele Onschuld. In *Het Verlies van de Onschuld: Seksualiteit in Nederland*, edited by G. Hekma, B. v. Stolk, B. v. Heerikhuizen, and B. Kruithof. Gronigen: Wolters-Noordhoff.

Sex Education in America. An NPR/Kaiser/Kennedy School Poll. 2004. Washington, DC: National Public Radio, Kaiser Family Foundation, Harvard University Kennedy School of Government.

Singh, Susheela, Jacquelin E. Darroch, and Jennifer J. Frost. 2001. Socioeconomic Disadvantage and Adolescent Women's Sexual and Reproductive Behavior: The Case of Five Developed Countries. *Family Planning Perspectives* 33 (6): 251–58 and 289.

Smith, Dennis. 1999. *The Civilizing Process and the History of Sexuality:* Comparing Norbert Elias and Michel Foucault. *Theory and Society* 28 (1): 79–100.

Smith, Tom W. 1994. Attitudes toward Sexual Permissiveness: Trends, Correlates and Behavioral Connections. In *Sexuality Across the Life Course*, edited by A.S. Rossi. Chicago: University of Chicago Press.

Steele, Jeanne R. 2002. Teens and Movies: Something to Do, Plenty to Learn. In *Sexual Teens, Sexual Media: Investigating Media's Influence on Adolescent Sexuality,* edited by J. Brown, Jeanne Steele, and Kim Walsh-Childers. Mahwah, NJ: Lawrence Erlbaum Associates.

Steinberg, Laurence. 2004. Risk Taking Adolescence. What Changes and Why? *Annals of the New York Academy of Sciences* 1021: 51–58.

Thompson, Sharon. 1990. Putting a Big Thing into a Little Hole: Teenage Girls' Accounts of Sexual Initiation. *The Journal of Sex Research* 27 (3): 341–61.

Thompson, Sharon. 1995. *Going All the Way: Teenage Girls' Tales of Sex, Romance, and Pregnancy*. New York: Hill and Wang.

Tolman, Deborah L. 2002. *Dilemmas of Desire: Teenage Girls Talk about Sexuality.* Cambridge, MA: Harvard University Press.

Tolman, Deborah L., Meg L. Striepe, and Tricia Harmon. 2003. Gender Matters: Constructing a Model of Adolescent Sexual Health. *The Journal of Sex Research* 40: 4–12.

Vanwesenbeeck, Ine, Marrie Bekker, and Akeline van Lenning. 1998. Gender Attitudes, Sexual Meanings, and Interactional Patterns in Heterosexual Encounters among College Students in the Netherlands. *Journal of Sex Research* 35 (4): 317–27.

Waller, Willard. 1937. The Rating and Dating Complex. *American Sociological Review* 2 (5): 727–34.

Ward, L. Monique, Kyla M. Day, and Marina Epstein. 2006. Uncommonly Good: Exploring How Mass Media May Be a Positive Influence on Young Women's Sexual Health and Development. *New Directions for Child and Adolescent Development* 112: 57–70.

Wouters, Cas. 2004. *Sex and Manners: Female Emancipation in the West.* 1890–2000. Edited by M. Featherstone. Thousand Oaks, CA and London: Sage Publications.

Zessen, Gertjan van, and Theo Sandfort, eds. 1991. *Seksualiteit in Nederland: Seksueel Gerdrag, Risico en Preventie van AIDS*. Amsterdam: Swets & Zeitlinger.

Questions

1. Schalet contrasts Dutch and American parents' attitudes toward teenage sex.
   a. How does she characterize the prevailing attitudes in each country? What reasons does she give for the differences in attitude?
   b. Does Schalet present one of these prevailing attitudes as better than the other? In your view, *is* one better than the other?
   c. Which of the attitudes Schalet describes seems to you to be closer to the prevailing approach Canadian parents take toward teenage sex—the approach dominant in America, or the approach dominant in the Netherlands?
2. This article makes substantial use of footnotes. As a reader, do you find such extensive use of footnotes helpful or distracting? Explain your reasoning.
3. Research government policy on reproductive health education where you live. Considering the information offered by Schalet, evaluate the policy you find. Does it adequately meet the needs of teenagers? How, if at all, should it be changed?
4. How, according to Schalet, do American attitudes toward adolescent sex affect boys and girls differently?
5. Schalet gives examples of "dramatizing" and "normalizing" language that parents use regarding teen sex. Consider the language used regarding teen sex by parents you know. To what extent would you describe this language as "dramatizing"—or as "normalizing"?
6. What are "adversarial individualism" and "interdependent individualism"? How do these different cultures of individualism shape approaches to teen sex in the United States and the Netherlands, respectively?

IAN NICHOLSON

from "TORTURE AT YALE": EXPERIMENTAL SUBJECTS, LABORATORY TORMENT AND THE "REHABILITATION" OF MILGRAM'S "OBEDIENCE TO AUTHORITY"

Beginning in 1961, Stanley Milgram conducted a series of experiments in which participants were directed by an authority figure to administer what appeared to be more and more dangerous and painful electric shocks to another person (an actor who was also in on the experiment). As Milgram reported in his "Behavioural Study of Obedience" (also included in this anthology), more than half of the participants continued to obey until they had administered the highest available artificial shock, labelled 450 volts. According to Milgram's numerous supporters, the experiments should be celebrated for their astonishing insight into the readiness with which individuals will violate their own ethical boundaries if an authority figure tells them to. According to his detractors, however, the study was unethical and intellectually flawed. In this article from the journal Theory & Psychology, *psychologist Ian Nicholson delves into the historical archive surrounding the experiments and weighs in on the controversy surrounding Milgram's work.*

ABSTRACT

Stanley Milgram's experiments on "Obedience to Authority" are among the most criticized in all of psychology. However, over the past 20 years, there has been a gradual rehabilitation of Milgram's work and reputation, a reconsideration that is in turn closely linked to a contemporary "revival" of his Obedience experiments. This paper provides a critical counterpoint to this "Milgram revival" by drawing on archival material from participants in the

Obedience study and Milgram himself. This material indicates that Milgram misrepresented (a) the extent of his debriefing procedures, (b) the risk posed by the experiment, and (c) the harm done to his participants. The archival record also indicates that Milgram had doubts about the scientific value of the experiment, thereby compromising his principal ethical justification for employing such extreme methods. The article ends with a consideration of the implications of these historical revelations for contemporary efforts to revive the Milgram paradigm.

> "We couldn't possibly conceive that anybody would allow any torture to go through Yale University."
> Unnamed participant in the Obedience to Authority Experiment (Errera, 1963c, p. 10)

... Although much valuable work on the history of the Obedience experiments has been undertaken in recent years, several important elements of the Obedience experiments have been omitted or minimized, most crucially the experience of the participants themselves. This paper aims to bring the experiences of the participants back into play and in so doing provide a critical reexamination of both the ethics and meaning of the Obedience to Authority experiments.

Most scholarly discussions of the Obedience research take Milgram at his word on these matters, essentially paraphrasing what he said in his own defence when called to task for mistreating his participants. In his 1964 reply to Baumrind and again in his 1974 book, Milgram highlighted his extensive debriefing or "dehoaxing" procedures—unusual for the time—while citing the results of a quantitative follow-up study he undertook which indicated that 84% of participants were glad that they participated and that 4 out of 5 participants felt that more experiments of this sort should be carried out (Milgram, 1964). These are compelling numbers although as Benjamin & Simpson (2009) have noted, the numbers could well reflect a degree of cognitive dissonance on the part of the participants. Milgram did not consider this possibility and he maintained that the retrospective consent of participants justified the Obedience procedure. "The participant" Milgram insisted, "rather than the critic must be the ultimate source of judgment" (1974, p. 199), a verdict that contemporary Milgram enthusiasts seem happy to accept.

Milgram's apparent devotion to the importance of his participants' views is commendable, but scholarly consideration of the Obedience participants should not be restricted to a small number of quantitative survey items. What is largely absent from Milgram's own work and from the secondary literature is a consideration of the extensive participant feedback that Milgram gathered but chose to omit from his publications for reasons which in hindsight are clear: they cast doubt on the ethics of the study and the validity of its results. Milgram always publicly insisted that his research was ethical insofar as it involved a relatively minimal impact on his participants. Participants were stressed, yes, but it wasn't a matter of any consequence. Milgram also insisted that he took steps to minimize the physical and psychological impact of the extreme stress his experiment engendered. He repeatedly insisted in his published work that all participants were given a thorough and effective debriefing, or to use his term, "dehoaxing" immediately after the experiment (Milgram, 1964, p. 849). Despite this forceful and often-repeated insistence on the innocuous nature of the Obedience experiments, the qualitative records indicate that the debriefing procedures were nowhere near as thorough and effective as Milgram claimed.

5 The second insight to be gleaned from a consideration of participant narratives involves the very meaning of the study itself. Milgram did concede that his study was right on the line of what was ethically permissible, but he always insisted that the ethical riskiness of his work was more than offset by the extraordinary gains that were accrued, namely the revelation of something "dangerous": the tendency for people to harm others when ordered by an authority figure (Milgram, 1974, p. 188). The important question that arises is one that has, rather curiously, almost completely vanished from contemporary discussion: does the experiment actually reveal a "dangerous" propensity to obey destructive authority?

Milgram obscured this question by blending two definitions of obedience together. He defined "obedience" in operational terms as the "subject who complies with the entire series of experimental commands" (1965, p. 59). However, as Patten (1977a, 1977b) has noted, the cultural power of Milgram's experiment depended heavily on his extensive and largely unacknowledged use of a more comprehensive meaning of "obedience," one that relied on the participant's understanding of the situation. In this second definition of obedience, "one is obedient when one consistently responds to commands by performing acts which one has every reason to believe are immoral, merely because one is ordered to do so" (Patten, 1977b, p. 427). Milgram (1974) did not make a distinction between these two senses of "obedience," assuming that the act of going to the end of the board was something "obviously" and intrinsically unreasonable and "shockingly immoral" (p. 194). Feedback from participants raises doubts about Milgram's claim that it was "shockingly immoral" for his participants to have carried out the instructions of the experimenter.

Before discussing the participant feedback in detail, a note on sources. All of the participant feedback presented in this paper comes from Milgram's own papers at the Yale University Archives. There are two places within the Milgram papers that are relevant. The first series of documents contains brief written comments from participants that were obtained as part of a questionnaire that was sent out to all participants and that a remarkable 95% of participants returned

(Reaction of subjects, 1962). The second source of information comes from transcripts of 40 lengthy one-on-one and small-group interviews conducted by Paul Errera, an assistant professor of psychiatry at Yale. Unfortunately, most of these interviews are not yet available to researchers. The Yale Archives is in the process of "sanitizing" these documents—removing names and personal information. I have analyzed four of the interviews that have been sanitized (Errera, 1963a; 1963b; 1963c; 1963d). It is important to note therefore that the participant feedback that I am presenting is limited; however even this partial sample gives plenty of ways and reasons to rethink the ethics and meaning of the Obedience research.[1]

ETHICAL TREATMENT OF PARTICIPANTS

... The remarks of several participants make it clear that many were not debriefed after [the experiment] and that some were simply sent home to contemplate what had transpired. "I became somewhat irked when I received your first copy of the results, for after reading it, I felt that I was made a fool of, for I had no idea that this was preplanned." Another participant remarked that "I was pretty well shook up for a few days after the experiment. It would have helped if I had been told the facts shortly after." The psychological impact of being kept in the dark about the experiment is apparent in the remarks of other participants who were not debriefed: "I felt so bad afterward" one of these participants remarked. "I wanted to call and actually apologize ... and I went to the telephone book and looked up the name—he used the name Richardson or something and unfortunately there were three of them with exactly the same first and last name [so] I didn't make the call" (Subjects' conversation, 1963). It was not until weeks later when the participant received his participant report from Milgram that he learned that he had not physically harmed anyone. "I felt wonderful when I received that letter and know—realize that this fellow hadn't received any jolts." A similar combination of extreme discomfort and relief is evident in the remarks of another participant who stated that "I actually checked the death notices in the *New Haven Register* for at least two weeks after the experiment to see if I had been involved and a contributing factor in the death of the so called 'learner'—I was very relieved that his name did not appear in such a column" (Reaction of subjects, 1962).

In a relatively small city like New Haven, CT, word of the experiment soon spread and many participants criticized Milgram for not informing people

1 [Nicholson's Note] Australian psychologist and journalist Gina Perry (2008) interviewed some of the participants of the obedience experiment for a radio program "Beyond the Shock Machine" that was broadcast by the Australian Broadcasting Corporation.

about the "true" nature of the study immediately afterward: "From what I've learned from others who've taken part, it would seem you have been somewhat irresponsible in permitting disturbed subjects to leave without informing them that they didn't half kill the shockee" (Reaction of subjects, 1962). Milgram's ethical shortcomings in this matter were ably summarized by another participant:

> Upon reflection I seriously question the wisdom and ethics of not completely dehoaxing each subject immediately after the session. The standard decompression treatment I received was not successful in reducing my anger and concern below the boiling point. Probably not many subjects were in a position to take the matter directly to the principal investigator as I did so the question arises as to how many other subjects were more or less seriously disturbed by tensions that could have been resolved by full disclosure at the earliest possible time. Allowing subjects to remain deceived is not justified in my opinion even if such continued deception was thought necessary to avoid contamination. (Reaction of subjects, 1962)

It is clear from this feedback that Milgram deliberately misrepresented his post-experimental procedures in his published work. The reason for this "unsanctioned" deception may be found in the early scholarly reaction to the Obedience experiments. Professional criticism began to mount even before the first publication of his results in October, 1963. In 1962 a member of the Yale Psychology Department filed a complaint about Milgram's Obedience research with the American Psychological Association. Milgram was subsequently informed that his application for APA membership would be delayed pending an "informal" review by the Secretary of the Committee on Scientific and Professional Ethics and Conduct (Blass, 2004). The following year, Milgram (1963b) informed psychologist Dorwin Cartwright that he had been "clobbered" by professional criticism. If it emerged, in this context, that even a handful of participants had been sent home after so traumatic an experience without any debriefing Milgram's credibility as a responsible researcher would have been undermined. With the ethical integrity and possible future of the Obedience study on the line, Milgram evidently decided to lie his way through the criticism. When later pressed by Baumrind (1964) on the extent and efficacy of his dehoaxing procedure, he admitted that the debriefing changed over time and that the "exact content of the dehoax varied from condition to condition and with increasing experience on our part" (Milgram, 1964, p. 849). However, Milgram always insisted—dishonestly—that "all subjects" were told that the shocks were not real and that "procedures were undertaken to assure that the subject would leave the laboratory in a state of well being" (Milgram, 1963a, p. 374).

Serious though this misrepresentation of the extent and efficacy of the debriefing may be, it takes on an added significance in the context of the most serious ethical charge, namely that the Obedience research harmed participants. Milgram (1964) was again quite adamant about this, insisting that "at no point did they run the *risk* [emphasis added] of injurious effects" and that critics ought not to confuse "momentary excitement" with "harm" (p. 849). In the context of quantitative survey data, the characterization of participants' experiences as "momentary excitement" seems plausible enough, but a consideration of participant narratives puts a different complexion on the matter. Several participants commented on the toxicity of the experience. "My comment to my wife on arriving home was that this had been the most unpleasant night of my life" one participant remarked, a view echoed by several other participants. "I couldn't remember ever being quite as upset as I was during the experiment" (Reaction of subjects, 1962) one subject remarked while another stated that "I felt real remorse and when I came out—when the experiment was all over, I got home and told my family I had just gone through the most trying thing that I had ever subjected myself to" (Subjects' conversation, 1963). Others indicated that their experience was a matter of some consequence and had effects that extended well beyond the immediate laboratory moment. Some participants were full of strong feelings of self-recrimination after the study was over. "After completing the experiment I really was ashamed of myself. I kept thinking why didn't I refuse to give pain to my fellow man instead of going through as directed to the end [discussed with a friend who also participated and stopped exp.]. Thus I hated myself all the more for not doing the same." Another participant commented on his feelings of shame and how difficult it was to shake off a sense of personal diminishment: "Even now I'm ashamed of telling my friends that I took part in this experiment. I just want to forget it" (Reaction of subjects, 1962).

It is important to emphasize that most of Milgram's participants did not appear to take the experience to heart, and a majority indicated that they actually learned something about themselves in the experience. That said, several emotionally sensitive participants took the experience very hard indeed. For example, one participant remarked that his experience had badly jolted his self-image of being a caring, thoughtful, and morally superior person:

> It has bothered me that I went all the way ... I am a person who has had the opportunity to do a great deal of reading and reflecting ... I form my own opinions from the newspapers and mass periodicals ... I also read the smaller circulation publications such as *The Reporter*, *The Nation*, *The New Republic*, and similar publications. I consider

> myself better informed and I hope more cultured than the average non-college student. In spite of all this I gave the same performance that the average slob, taken off the street, would probably have done. This I consider frightening. (Reaction of subjects, 1962)

In addition to issues of self-image, some participants reported disturbed sleep and being upset for an extended period of time. "That night I couldn't sleep the test bothered me—even the next day I was upset" (Reaction of subjects, 1962). This view was echoed by another participant who commented on how difficult it was to shake off the traumatic impact of the experience: "I wouldn't want to do another experiment like that again for any amount of money. I'm still sorry I went to do it. It took me a couple of weeks before I was able to forget about it. I don't think it's right to put someone through such a nervous tension" (Reaction of subjects, 1962). The traumatic character of the experience was remarked upon by another participant who said that "the experiment left such an effect on me that I spent the night in a cold sweat and nightmares because of the fear that I might have killed the man in the chair" (Reaction of subjects, 1962). Another participant who identified himself as an alderman in the city of New Haven spoke of an intense but delayed reaction to his participation: "I sort of had a delayed reaction on this because I more or less forgot about it, but after speaking with Dr. Milgram ... I think I was really—I don't know how to describe it—just completely depressed for a while" (Errera, 1963b). For some participants, the intensity of the experiment carried over into the workplace and one participant reported that it led indirectly to him losing his job:

> By coincidence a fellow employee had taken part in the same experiment before me ... Later we compared notes and during one of our discussions, I got hot under the collar and said things I normally never would say, especially during working hours. Directly, I made a very bad impression on some people within hearing distance because I used some vulgar words and shortly thereafter because of other conditions I lost my job. (Reaction of subjects, 1962)

It would of course be unfair to lay all of the blame for this man's loss of employment at the feet of Milgram. However, it is clear from the archival record that Milgram did traumatize many of his participants and there is evidence that in several cases he did not help his participants adequately deal with what they had experienced. Indeed in several cases, Milgram does not appear to have debriefed his participants at all; he simply sent them home. It is clear in hindsight, that Baumrind (1964) was entirely justified in calling Milgram to task for brutalizing his participants while failing, at least in some instances, to deal with the consequences in even the most minimal of ways....

ETHICAL RISKS AND INTELLECTUAL REWARDS

Although Milgram never publicly disclosed the full extent of the harm he had inflicted, he did take on the ethical challenge of justifying the extreme nature of the experiment in relation to the intellectual benefits that accrued. Milgram claimed that the deception of participants and the "temporary" discomfort that many experienced was offset by the "revelation of certain difficult to get at truths" (1974, p. 198), namely that people have a tendency to obey any command that comes from a legitimate authority. While marshalling this argument, Milgram mobilized the ideal of the autonomous individual, while ignoring the powerful effect that context has on determining the meaning of any action. He insisted that his research was informed by the idea of the laboratory as a socially "neutral" space where each individual is free to act according to his or her conscience: "a person who comes to the laboratory is an active choosing adult capable of accepting or rejecting the prescriptions for action addressed to him" (Milgram, 1964, p. 852).

Here again, Milgram's vision of the experiment as a socially "neutral" test of autonomous individuals is undermined by the testimony of his participants. Many of his participants indicated that the context of the psychological experiment had a very significant impact on their actions. They saw the experiment as a social contract—a "bargain"—in which they had an obligation as participants to follow instructions as best they could (Errera, 1963c, p. 21). In return, they expected to be treated in a manner that would respect their dignity and physical and psychological well-being. Milgram breached this contract in a highly dramatic and stressful fashion and then in effect stood back and denied that any such contract existed. He manipulated his trusting participants into doing something that they would never ordinarily do and then once the experiment was over he shifted all the responsibility from himself onto the participants insisting that they were "free moral agents" (as cited in Abse, 1973, p. 126) and that a majority of them had behaved in a "shockingly immoral way" (Milgram, 1964, p. 849)....

A key element in the social contract of a psychological experiment is trust in the responsibility and competence of the scientific authority. Participants assume that the expert knows what he or she is doing and even if they have doubts, their lack of knowledge about the experimental situation combined with the repeated assurances of the expert is often enough to sustain compliance. As one obedient participant noted, "my main reason for not breaking off was the confidence I had in the experimenter knowing what he was doing" (Reaction of subjects, 1962). The participants had no reason not to trust the experimenter, a fact that Milgram was careful to exploit. When participants expressed concern for the "learner" and doubt as to whether they should proceed they were reassured in no uncertain terms: "although the shocks may seem painful, there is no permanent tissue damage, so please go on" (Milgram, 1963a, p. 374). It is impossible to know how many participants would have broken off the experiment without this reassurance, but it is likely that many took the experimenter at his word and continued on the basis of a declared commitment as to the safety of the procedure. "Giving the shocks did not upset me until the learner mentioned his heart, but I had faith in Yale that the doctor would stop the experiment if he thought it best" (Reaction of subjects, 1962).

In his analysis of the experiment, Milgram acknowledged that participants trust the experimenter and consequently transfer the responsibility for their behaviour from themselves to the scientific authority. "In the laboratory, through a set of simple manipulations, ordinary people no longer perceived themselves as a responsible part of the causal chain leading to action against a person" (Milgram, 1974, p. 175). However, as we have seen, there was nothing "simple" about Milgram's manipulations. Participants were placed in an unfamiliar and disorienting environment with little to rely on apart from their own senses and the expertise of the authority figure. Their doubts and concerns were ignored and they were expressly told that all was well and that they must continue. In his published work, Milgram never conceded the unfairness of the scenario he had constructed. A psychological test licenses unusual or unexpected challenges for participants but it brings with it extraordinarily strong expectations of ethical conduct on the part of the experimenter. Participants in an experiment know that all may not be what it seems but at a minimum they assume—correctly as it turned out—that however strange, however seemingly inexplicable an experimental situation may appear, no one is going to be physically harmed, much less killed. As noted earlier, Milgram explicitly reaffirmed this common-sense understanding of the benign character of psychological experimentation and turned it to his advantage by instructing participants reluctant to continue with the shocks that there was "no permanent tissue damage" (Milgram, 1963a, p. 374). Some participants explicitly stated that their awareness of being in a "psychological experiment" influenced their actions. Explaining why he continued, one participant remarked that "I have faith in psychological experiments and suspected that the learner was not being hurt as badly as he pretended to be" (Errera, 1963c, p. 10). Even those participants who thought that the shocks were real were reassured by the professional context of the experiment: "We couldn't possibly conceive that anybody would allow any torture to go through Yale University" (Errera, 1963c, p. 10)....

Milgram's experiment demonstrated little beyond the commonplace observation that people in unfamiliar environments will trust authority figures and as a consequence can be deceived, manipulated, and taken advantage of. Milgram claimed to be divining dark and hitherto unexamined reaches of human nature when what he was really doing was toying with his participants' self-worth and physical well-being for the sake of a psychological study and his own professional advantage. Many participants spoke of their feelings of anger at having their trust betrayed in such a manipulative and potentially dangerous manner. "I never expected to be hoodwinked at an outstanding university such as Yale. It tends to make one cynical." One participant felt so mistreated that he considered legal action. "After the experiment was completed and I had left the laboratory, I felt that I should report your actions to the police" (Reaction of subjects, 1962).

Milgram kept such concerns to himself and he publicly framed the experiment as something that actually benefitted his participants. The extreme circumstances of the experiment "provided people with an opportunity to learn something of importance about themselves" (Milgram, 1964, p. 850). To corroborate this claim, Milgram quoted several participants who framed their experience in a manner that reflected his own interpretation of the study as a moral test of character: Will the individual harm another? For these participants, the study helped "jar people out of complacency" by revealing obedient tendencies in themselves: "I think people should think more deeply about themselves and their relation to their world and to other people" (cited in Milgram, 1964, p. 850).

These were compelling testimonials and the majority of participants did indeed indicate that they had learned something through their participation. However, the self-knowledge was not always of the uplifting sort that Milgram reported. For many of Milgram's participants, the central test of the experiment was not "obedience to authority," but their own credulity. The experiment tested whether they were street-smart and savvy or easy "marks" who took too much on faith. Several participants indicated that the experiment taught them that they needed to be much more cynical in dealing with the world. "I've learned I am not as world-wise and sophisticated as I would like to believe. Your actors proved to me that I am a sucker for any two good con men. I now carry my wallet pinned in an inside pocket." Others commented on how instructive the study was for deepening their cynicism toward psychology. "Stay away from little men who try psychology without logic" one participant remarked (Reaction of subjects, 1962). For these participants, there was nothing especially edifying about being traumatized and manipulated and the study served only to underscore the importance of being mistrustful of everything—even something as seemingly benign as a study of "learning."

TORMENT IN THE LABORATORY: THE SEDUCTIVE APPEAL OF PSI-POWER

Milgram misrepresented three important components of the Obedience research: (a) the extent of his debriefing procedures, (b) the risk posed by the experiment, and (c) the harm done to some of his participants. In his defence, proponents of the Obedience research have argued that any alleged ethical lapses are still offset by the enormous intellectual gains that have come as a consequence of these studies. Milgram famously framed the study in terms of the Holocaust, and while he later conceded that there were a number of important differences between his American laboratory participants and German SS[2] guards (Milgram, 1964), he insisted throughout his career that his work contained vital insights into Nazi crimes. Indeed, for Milgram (1974), explaining the Holocaust was a relatively modest undertaking that sold the experiment short: "To focus only on the Nazis, however despicable their deeds ... is to miss the point entirely" he insisted. "For the studies are principally concerned with the ordinary and routine destruction carried out by everyday people following orders" (p. 178). Thus, publicly, the Obedience research had a clear meaning and ethical justification for Milgram. It was a dramatization of the weakness of our "unique personalities" in relation to "larger institutional structures" (p. 188). For Milgram and his contemporary enthusiasts, the price of such knowledge was high, but it was and is a price worth paying (see Elms, 1982; Miller, 2009).

This is an appealing and well-rehearsed defence, however it is undermined by other records from Milgram's papers. While Milgram (1963a) was running the study and routinely and knowingly subjecting people to "uncontrollable seizures" and "violent convulsions," he admitted in his notebook that he had strong reservations about the ethical status and meaning of his work (p. 375). As a graduate student, he spoke emphatically against the use of deception in psychological research: "My own view is that deception for any purposes [in psychology] is unethical and tends to weaken the fabric of confidence so desirable in human relations" (Milgram, 1959). Insisting as a graduate student that "truth is never to be pursued irresponsibly" (as cited in Evans, 1980, p. 193), Milgram soon reconciled himself to the use of deception in his research, although the matter evidently tugged at his conscience, for in a manner similar to contemporary verbal contortions over the word "torture," he carefully avoided the use of the term "deception" in favour of the euphemism "technical illusions." ...

... In a moment of extraordinary candour, Milgram admitted that the principal motivation for all this torment had little to do with high-minded sentiment. It was driven by curiosity and something darker:

> Considered as a personal motive of the author—the possible benefits that might rebound to humanity—withered to insignificance alongside

2 *SS* Abbreviation for *Shutzstaffel*, a Nazi organization. During the Holocaust, concentration camps and death camps were managed by a branch of the SS.

> the strident demands of intellectual curiosity. When an investigator keeps his eyes open throughout a scientific study he learns things about himself as well as his subjects and the conclusions do not always flatter. (Milgram, 1962b)

Milgram never specified what "unflattering" conclusions were to be drawn about himself concerning his role in these experiments, but it is not difficult to imagine the appeal of his experimental design to a young and physically small man. Most social psychological experiments place the experimenter in a position of power, but few confer upon the investigator the almost super-human capacity to psychologically crush other men, often individuals physically larger and older than oneself.[3] This fact was partly concealed by Milgram's emphasis on the "shockingly immoral" behaviour of his participants, however a close reading of the initial published report clearly reveals the immense power that the experimental design conferred upon the young assistant professor. The design did not simply "stress" participants; it temporarily obliterated their agency[4] and self-possession leaving them utterly at the mercy of experimenter. In his report, Milgram noted that on one occasion "we observed a seizure so violently convulsive that it was necessary to call a halt to the experiment" (Milgram, 1963a, p. 371). Such extraordinary manifestations of the experimenter's power were not rare, isolated occurrences. Milgram noted, in a matter-of-fact style, that extreme physiological stress reactions were "characteristic rather than exceptional responses to the experiment" (p. 375). And if that wasn't impressive enough, Milgram included a statement by an observer which summarized the experiment's psychologically destructive power:

> I observed a mature and initially poised businessman enter the laboratory smiling and confident. Within 20 minutes he was reduced to a twitching, stuttering wreck, who was rapidly approaching a point of nervous collapse. He constantly pulled an earlobe, and twisted his hands. At one point he pushed his fist into his forehead and muttered "Oh God, let's stop it." And yet he continued to respond to every word of the experimenter, and obeyed to the end. (cited in Milgram, 1963a, p. 377)

It is difficult to imagine how one could knowingly and regularly visit such anguish on so many innocent, unsuspecting people under any circumstances, let alone in the absence of a clear ethical goal. Milgram claimed that the torment was sustained by his "intellectual curiosity," but that just doesn't suffice

3 [Nicholson's Note] For a detailed analysis of the role of masculinity in the Obedience experiments, see Nicholson (2011).

4 *agency* Ability to make choices and act freely.

as an explanation in the face of such unrelenting brutality. What seems more likely, although it must remain at the level of speculation, are the all too common feelings of power and self-importance that often come to individuals put in a position (however briefly) of total control.

The extraordinary power and feelings of self-aggrandizement provided by the social psychology laboratory were very much in evidence in a letter that Milgram sent to his research assistant Alan Elms in 1961. Milgram outlined some of the logistical considerations for the obedience experiments and he explained that one of Elms' jobs would be to "think of ways to deliver more people to the laboratory":

> This is a very important practical aspect of the research. I will admit it bears some resemblance to Mr. Eichmann's position, but you at least should have no misconceptions of what we do with our daily quota. We give them a chance to resist the commands of a malevolent authority and assert their alliance with morality. (cited in Elms, 1995, p. 24)

The reference to Adolph Eichmann, senior SS officer and one of the architects of the Holocaust, was undoubtedly meant in jest, but it does suggest a level of ethical discomfort with what was about to unfold. Like Eichmann, Elms was to deliver innocent, unsuspecting people into an environment where they would be tormented. As we shall see later, inflicting anguish on the innocent did trouble Milgram slightly, but as this passage makes clear his extraordinary sense of moral entitlement was enough to allay such concerns. As a social psychologist, he saw himself as having the means and the authority to determine the ethical integrity of others according to a "test" of his own devising.

Milgram had set out to make his mark on the world and to develop the "boldest and most significant experimental research" he could think of (as cited in Blass, 2009, p. 40). He quickly discovered that the sustained torment and the temporary obliteration of his participants as autonomous moral agents was a pathway to professional success. Professional ambitions notwithstanding, there is evidence to indicate that Milgram enjoyed the brutality of the experiment and the sufferings of the participants. He never made so damning an admission in print (apart from his cryptic reference to learning things about himself that "do not always flatter"), but as a person, Milgram was known, even among friends, for his "off-putting, domineering, and prima donna-ish ways" (Blass, 2004, p. 185). Ever conscious of authority, Milgram's colleagues and former students noted that he was "routinely cruel to graduate students" (Pettigrew, 2005, p. 1778)....

The Obedience experiments provided plenty of opportunities for taking pleasure in the debasement of others. The special charm of the laboratory context for all this gruesomeness was the way it rendered the thrill of torment invisible. By tricking people in a laboratory instead of a "real world" setting such as a bank or school, ethical attention was shifted onto the actions of those being deceived rather than the people doing the manipulating. The laboratory setting cloaked the behaviour of the experimenters themselves in the socially uplifting language of science while enabling them to strike a pose of self-sacrifice: the world weary scientist who torments others for their own good and that of humanity....

In his published work, Milgram hid issues of power, sadism, and self-aggrandizement behind the Holocaust and the pose of disinterested science. However, Milgram's unpublished doubts concerning the ethics and meaning of the research suggest that darker, personal motivations were an important factor in the study. Milgram wanted to get ahead in psychology and short of physically harming someone he was clearly prepared to adopt the most extreme measures in order to achieve that goal. In pursuit of his goal to undertake the "boldest and most significant experimental research" (as cited in Blass, 2009, p. 40), he inflicted countless hours of at times gruesome torment on hundreds of unsuspecting innocent people, a fact which did at times weigh on him. In an unpublished reflection he remarked that "at times I have concluded that, although the experiment can be justified, there are still elements in it that are ethically questionable, that it is not nice to lure people into the laboratory and ensnare them into a situation that is stressful and unpleasant to them" (Milgram, n.d.). Publicly however, Milgram does not appear to have been even mildly concerned about the ethics of his actions. Indeed, he later indicated that he was "totally astonished" by ethical criticisms of Baumrind and others (Milgram cited in Evans, 1980, p. 193), a comment which in the context of his participants' feedback only serves to underscore his insensitivity and hubris. Milgram clearly felt that as a scientist he had the right to indulge his own intellectual interests, with little regard for the feelings of others, least of all his innocent participants. Quick to label his manipulated, "obedient" participants as nascent Nazis, he bristled at criticisms that his own work was excessive and complained that there was an "absence of any assumption of good will and good faith" (as cited in Evans, 1980, p. 194). In hindsight and in view of the archival record, it is apparent that Milgram's many critics in the 1960s and 1970s were entirely right to assume the worst.

CONCLUSION

... The experiment's enduring appeal is based in part on its theatricality—a fact readily conceded by Milgram himself (Nicholson, 2011). However, theatricality by itself is of little consequence; the study's remarkable capacity to fascinate comes from its ability to represent itself as a "scientific window" into graphic events of great historical consequence. Milgram famously framed the experiment as a kind of "mini-Holocaust," and the possibility of having even a portion of the Holocaust "laid-bare" in the comfort and safety of an American psychological laboratory has proven irresistible to many and an enormous boon to the legitimacy of social psychology. As Miller (2004) has noted, there is an "undeniable degree of prestige or intellectual status inherent in contributing significantly to an understanding of the Holocaust" (p. 227). More recently, the field has derived a similar prestige by applying Milgram to issues associated with the "War on Terror," most notably the torture of prisoners at Abu Ghraib[5] by American military police. Burger (2009) put the matter succinctly when he noted that Milgram gives social psychology a place at the table in discussions of "atrocities, massacres, and genocide" (p. 10). With so much on the line, continued disciplinary interest in Milgram and a kind of "willed indifference" to its extensive ethical and intellectual shortcomings is hardly surprising....

What accounts for the wider public interest in the Obedience experiment? Beyond the obvious tabloid allure of people "killing" each other in the laboratory, the experiment references the human capacity for extreme violence and it holds an appealing moral: one should not always "obey" a directive just because it comes from a duly constituted authority. This is a message readily available from a variety of other sources, but Milgram renders the moral in a scientific idiom while fostering the comforting illusion that we are on the path to "knowing" what causes atrocities and thereby "preventing more Holocausts, Abu Ghraibs and other examples of wanton cruelty" (Cohen, 2008, 11th para.). The fact that neither Milgram nor any of his contemporary imitators are able to offer any plausible theoretical insights into these horrific events is beside the point. It is the moral message that matters along with the dream of a human nature brought under laboratory control (see Brannigan, 1997; Lemov, 2005).

Having devoted my time to criticizing Milgram's work, I would conclude with an ironic endorsement of its value in understanding how "domains of brutality" come to be established and sustained. Whatever "lasting value" the study has in this respect lies not with the behaviour of the experimental participants but with the conduct of Milgram himself and that of his research associates. By invoking the ideal of scientific progress, Milgram was able to get a small team of researchers to deceive and torment nearly 1000 people. By all accounts, his research team were only too happy to comply; the rate of obedience for Milgram's research assistants was not 66% but 100%. Herein lies both the shortcoming and the value of Milgram's work. Taken at face value, the Obedience experiments provide little insight into the Holocaust since

5 *Abu Ghraib* A scandal occurred in 2004 when graphic and disturbing photographs emerged of torture at the military prison in Abu Ghraib, Iraq. Inmates were sexually humiliated, raped, and subjected to extreme violence.

the experience of Milgram's participants was quite unlike that of Nazi killers. Participants in the Obedience study found themselves in an unfamiliar, ethically ambiguous context where they were manipulated into doing something that most did not wish to do, in the face of considerable pressure from a physically present authority figure and a promise that their actions were causing "no permanent tissue damage" (Milgram, 1963a, p. 374). In contrast, members of the Nazi killing machine were fully aware of the killing and destruction they were carrying out and most required no coercion or "encouragement" from an immediate superior. As Goldhagen (1996) has noted, German police battalions willingly rampaged across eastern Europe torturing and murdering thousands, often at their own discretion and with a viciousness and thoroughness that frequently exceeded what they had been ordered to do. Most gladly did so with a clear conscience, convinced of the ethical basis of their actions given the magnitude of the "Jewish threat." As one Nazi police official noted, members of the police battalions "were motivated by a great hatred against the Jews" and consequently "were, with few exceptions, quite happy to take part in shootings of Jews. They had a ball!" (cited in Goldhagen, 1996, p. 396).

While the conduct of the participants in the Obedience experiments does little to "explain" the murderous rage of German police battalions, the attitude and actions of Milgram and his research team are consistent with the forms of justification noted by Goldhagen (1996). Unlike the Obedience study's often bullied, misled, and reluctant experimental participants, Milgram and his team were, almost from the outset of the study, well aware of the torment that they were to inflict on others. Like members of the German police battalions, they believed in what they were doing and they invoked a "high" ideal to justify their actions (Mandel, 1998). What the Obedience research thus reveals is not a fanciful "abandonment of humanity" or an equally outlandish "merger" of each individual's "unique personality into larger institutional structures" (Milgram, 1974, p. 188). The research unwittingly highlights instead the way in which an ideal—in this case the value of human experimentation—can underwrite a ready compliance with gratuitous torment.

If the recent revival of Milgram and his Obedience work is any guide, some psychologists seem ready to reassert this "scientific" ideal and test its power anew. It is my hope that this foray into Milgram's archive demonstrates not only the folly of this undertaking but of the need to be much more self-critical when examining the ethical justifications of human experimentation in psychology.

(2011)

FUNDING

This research was supported by a grant from the Social Science and Research Council of Canada (grant no. 410-2002-1448).

REFERENCES[6]

Abse, D. (1973). *The dogs of Pavlov*. London, UK: Vallentine Mitchell.

Baumrind, D. (1964). Some thoughts on ethics of research: After reading Milgram's "behavioral study of obedience". *American Psychologist, 19*, 421–423.

Benjamin, L., & Simpson, J. (2009). The power of the situation: The impact of Milgram's obedience studies on personality and social psychology. *American Psychologist, 64*, 12–19.

Blass, T. (2004). *The man who shocked the world: The life and legacy of Stanley Milgram.* New York, NY: Basic Books.

Blass, T. (2009). From New Haven to Santa Clara: A historical perspective on the Milgram obedience experiments. *American Psychologist, 64*, 37–45.

Brannigan, A. (1997). The postmodern experiment: Science and ontology in experimental social psychology. *British Journal of Sociology, 48*, 594–610.

Burger, J. (2009). Replicating Milgram: Would people still obey today? *American Psychologist, 64*(1), 1–11.

Cohen, A. (2008, December 29). Four decades after Milgram, we're still willing to inflict pain. *New York Times*, A24. Retrieved from http://www.nytimes.com/2008/12/29/opinion/29mon3. html?scp=1&sq=&st=nyt

Elms, A. (1982). Keeping deception honest: Justifying conditions for social scientific research stratagems. In T. Beauchamp, R. Faden, R.J. Wallace, & L. Walters (Eds.), *Ethical issues in social science research* (pp. 232–245). Baltimore, MD: John Hopkins University Press.

Elms, A. (1995). Obedience in retrospect. *Journal of Social Issues, 51*, 21–31.

Errera, P. (1963a, March 14). Defiant subjects. [Meeting conducted by Dr. Paul Errera]. Stanley Milgram Papers (Sanitized Data, Box 155A). Yale University Archives, New Haven, CT.

Errera, P. (1963b, April 11). Defiant subjects. [Meeting conducted by Dr. Paul Errera]. Stanley Milgram Papers (Sanitized Data, Box 155A). Yale University Archives, New Haven, CT.

Errera, P. (1963c, March 21). Obedient subjects. [Meeting conducted by Dr. Paul Errera]. Stanley Milgram Papers (Sanitized Data, Box 155A). Yale University Archives, New Haven, CT.

Errera, P. (1963d, April 4). Obedient subjects. [Meeting conducted by Dr. Paul Errera]. Stanley Milgram Papers (Sanitized Data, Box 155A). Yale University Archives, New Haven, CT.

Evans, R. (1980). *The making of social psychology*. New York, NY: Gardner Press.

Fenigstein, A. (1998). Were obedience pressures a factor in the Holocaust? *Analyse & Kritik, 20*, 54–73.

6 References have been excerpted to show only those cited in the above selection.

French TV contestants made to inflict "torture". (2010, March 18). *BBC News*. Retrieved from: http://news.bbc.co.uk/1/hi/8571929.stm

Goldhagen, D. (1996). *Hitler's willing executioners*. New York, NY: Knopf.

Lemov, R.M. (2005). *World as laboratory: Experiments with mice, mazes, and men* (1st ed.). New York, NY: Hill and Wang.

Mandel, D. (1998). The obedience alibi: Milgram's account of the Holocaust reconsidered. *Analyse & Kritik, 20*, 74–94.

Milgram, S. (1959). Note to self. Stanley Milgram Papers (Series I, Box 23, Folder 383). Yale University Archives, New Haven, CT.

Milgram, S. (1962b, August). Note to self. Stanley Milgram Papers (Series II, Box 46, Folder 173). Yale University Archives, New Haven, CT.

Milgram, S. (1963a). Behavioral study of obedience. *Journal of Abnormal & Social Psychology, 67*, 371–378.

Milgram, S. (1963b, April 17). Letter to Dorwin Cartwright. Stanley Milgram Papers (Series I, Box 1a, Folder 7). Yale University Archives, New Haven, CT.

Milgram, S. (1964). Issues in the study of obedience: A reply to Baumrind. *American Psychologist, 19*, 848–852.

Milgram, S. (1965). Some conditions of obedience and disobedience to authority. *Human Relations, 18*, 57–76.

Milgram, S. (1974). *Obedience to authority: An experimental view*. London, UK: Tavistock.

Milgram, S. (n.d.). An experimenter's dilemma. Stanley Milgram Papers (Series II, Box 46 Folder 173). Yale University Archives, New Haven, CT.

Miller, A. (2004). What can the Milgram obedience experiments tell us about the Holocaust? In A. Miller (Ed.), *Social psychology of good and evil* (pp. 193–239). New York, NY: Guilford.

Miller, A. (2009). Reflections on "Replicating Milgram" (Burger, 2009) [Peer commentary on the paper "Replicating Milgram: Would people still obey today?" by J.M. Burger]. *American Psychologist, 64*, 20–27.

Nicholson, I. (2011). "Shocking" masculinity: Stanley Milgram, "Obedience to Authority," and the crisis of manhood in Cold War America. *ISIS, 102*, 238–268.

Patten, S. (1977a). The case that Milgram makes. *Philosophical Review, 86*, 350–364.

Patten, S. (1977b). Milgram's shocking experiments. *Philosophy, 52*, 425–440.

Perry, G. (2008, October 11). Beyond the shock machine [Radio broadcast]. Australian Broadcasting Corporation.

Pettigrew, T. (2005). [Review of the book *The Man Who Shocked the World*, by T. Blass]. *SocialForces, 83*, 1778–1779.

Reaction of subjects. (1962). Stanley Milgram Papers (Series II, Box 44). Yale University Archives, New Haven, CT.

Subjects' conversation. (1963, February 28). Stanley Milgram Papers (Series II, Box 44). Yale University Archives, New Haven, CT.

Questions

1. How (if at all) does the evidence Nicholson offers change your perception of Milgram's experiment? Discuss.
2. Discuss Milgram's assertion that the "participant ... must be the ultimate source of judgment" of the morality of an experiment. Do you think this claim adequately justifies his experimental process?
3. According to this article, what problems with the experiment did the participants identify? After reading the extensive quotations from the participants, do you feel sympathetic toward them? Why or why not? What do you think your experience would have been, had you been a participant in the experiment?
4. The article suggests that Milgram's work confused two types of obedience. What are the two types, and, according to Nicholson's article, where does the confusion occur? Is Nicholson right to suggest that Milgram's experiment shows only the first type of obedience?
5. This paper contains speculation about Milgram's motivation, which is unusual for this type of social scientific paper. Is its inclusion warranted here? Why or why not?
6. Argue for or against the article's assertion that "Milgram's experiment demonstrated little beyond the commonplace observation that people in unfamiliar environments will trust authority figures and as a consequence can be deceived, manipulated, and taken advantage of."
7. Nicholson concludes his article with an "ironic endorsement of its value in understanding how 'domains of brutality' come to be established and sustained." Explain what he means by this. Do you find this reinterpretation of the experiment convincing?

Pico Iyer

The Terminal Check

A British-born novelist and non-fiction author of Indian background who was partly raised in California and has made his home in Japan, Pico Iyer is best known for his travel writing. The following short piece appeared in a 2011 volume of the literary magazine Granta. *Titled* Ten Years Later, *the volume addresses "the complexity and sorrow of life since 11 September 2001."*

I'm sitting in the expansive spaces of Renzo Piano's four-storey airport outside Osaka, sipping an Awake tea from Starbucks and waiting for my bus home. I've chosen to live in Japan for the past twenty years, and I know its rites as I know the way I need tea when feeling displaced, or to head for a right-hand window seat as soon as I enter a bus. A small, round-faced Japanese man in his early thirties, accompanied by a tall and somewhat cadaverous man of the same age, approaches me.

"Excuse me," says the small, friendly-seeming one; they look like newborn salarymen in their not-quite-perfect suits. "May I see your passport?"

When I look up, surprised, he flashes me a badge showing that he's a plainclothes policeman. Dazed after crossing sixteen time zones (from California), I hand him my British passport.

"What are you doing in Japan?"

"I'm writing about it." I pull out my business card with the red embossed 5
logo of *Time* magazine.

"*Time* magazine?" says the smiling cop, strangely impressed. "He works for *Time* magazine," he explains to his lanky and impassive partner. "Very famous magazine," he assures me. "High prestige!"

Then he asks for my address and phone number and where I plan to be for the next eighty-nine days. "If there is some unfortunate incident," he explains, "some terrorist attack" (he's sotto voce now), "then we will know you did it."

Six months later, I fly back to the country I love once more. This time I need to withdraw some yen from an ATM as I stumble out of my trans-Pacific plane, in order to pay for my bus home.

"You're getting some money?" says an attractive young Japanese woman, suddenly appearing beside me with a smile.

"I am. To go back to my apartment."

"You live here?" Few Japanese women have ever come up to me in public, let alone without an introduction, and shown such interest.

"I do."

"May I see your passport?" she asks sweetly, flashing a badge at me, much as the pair of questioners had done two seasons before.

"Just security," she says, anxious not to put me out, as my Japanese neighbours stream, unconcerned, towards the Gakuenmae bus that's about to pull out of its bay.

I tell my friends back in California about these small disruptions and they look much too knowing. It's 9/11, they assure me. Over the past decade, security has tightened around the world, which means that insecurity has increased proportionally. Indeed, in recent years Japan has introduced fingerprinting for all foreign visitors arriving at its airports, and takes photographs of every outsider coming across its borders; a large banner on the wall behind the immigration officers in Osaka—as angry-looking with its red-and-black hand-lettering as a student banner—explains the need for heightened measures in the wake of threats to national order.

But the truth of the matter is that, for those of us with darker skins, and from nations not materially privileged, it was ever thus. When I was eighteen, I was held in custody in Panama's airport (because of the Indian passport I then carried) and denied formal entry to the nation, while the roguish English friend from high school with whom I was travelling was free to enter with impunity and savour all the dubious pleasures of the Canal Zone. On my way into Hong Kong—a transit lounge of a city if ever there was one, a duty-free zone whose only laws seem to be those of the marketplace—I was hauled into a special cabin for a lengthy interrogation because my face was deemed not to match my (by then British) passport. In Japan I was strip-searched every time I returned to the country, three or four times a year—my lifelong tan moving the authorities to assume that I must be either Saddam Hussein's[1] cousin or an illegal Iranian (or, worst of all, what I really am, a wandering soul with Indian forebears). Once I was sent to a small room in Tokyo reserved for anyone of South Asian ancestry (where bejewelled women in saris loudly complained in exaggerated Oxbridge accents* about being taken for common criminals).

---

1 *Saddam Hussein* President of Iraq (1937–2006). Before their invasion of Iraq in 2003, the American and British governments accused him of involvement in the 11 September 2001 terrorist attacks on the United States, and of possessing weapons of mass destruction.

Another time, long before my Japanese neighbours had heard of Osama bin Laden,[2] I was even detained on my way *out* of Osaka—and the British Embassy hastily faxed on a Sunday night—as if any male with brown skin, passable English and a look of shabby quasi-respectability must be doing something wrong if he's crossing a border.

But now, having learned over decades to accept such indignities or injustices, I walk into a chorus of complaints every time I return to California, from my pale-skinned, affluent neighbours. They're patting us down now, my friends object, and they're confiscating our contact-lens fluid. They're forcing us to travel with tiny tubes of toothpaste and moving us to wear loafers when usually we'd prefer lace-ups. They're taking away every bottle of water—but only after bottles of water have been shown to be weapons of mass destruction; they're feeling us up with blue gloves, even here in Santa Barbara,* now that they know that underwear can be a lethal weapon.

I listen to their grousing and think that the one thing the 9/11 attacks have achieved, for those of us who spend too much time in airports, is to make suspicion universal; fear and discomfort are equal-opportunity employers now. The world is flat in ways the high-flying global theoreticians don't always acknowledge; these days, even someone from the materially fortunate parts of the world—a man with a ruddy complexion, a woman in a Prada suit—is pulled aside for what is quixotically known as "random screening."

20 It used to be that the rich corners of the world seemed relatively safe, protected, and the poor ones too dangerous to enter. Now, the logic of the terrorist attacks on New York and Washington has reversed all that. If anything, it's the rich places that feel unsettled. It used to be that officials would alight on people who look like me—from nations of need, in worn jeans, bearing the passports of more prosperous countries—as likely troublemakers; now they realize that even the well born and well dressed may not always be well-intentioned.

I understand why my friends feel aggrieved to be treated as if they came from Nigeria or Mexico or India. But I can't really mourn too much that airports, since 9/11, have become places where everyone may be taken to be guilty until proven innocent. The world is all mixed up these days, and America can no longer claim immunity. On 12 September 2001, *Le Monde*[3] ran its now famous headline: WE ARE ALL AMERICANS. On 12 September 2011, it might more usefully announce: WE ARE ALL INDIANS.

(2011)

---

2 *Osama bin Laden* Leader (1957–2011) of al-Qaeda, an Islamic fundamentalist organization responsible for several major terrorist attacks, including the 11 September 2001 attacks on the World Trade Center and other American targets.

3 *Le Monde* Major French newspaper.

Questions

1. Consider Iyer's statement that "over the past decade, security has tightened around the world, which means that insecurity has increased proportionally." What does he mean by this? Do you think this is true? Why or why not?
2. Who is disproportionally affected by "increased security measures" at borders? Has the situation improved, worsened, or stayed the same since 2011 (when this article was written)?
3. What does Iyer mean when he says that the 9/11 attacks contributed to making the "world flat"? Do you agree with him? Why or why not?

ETHAN KROSS, PHILIPPE VERDUYN, EMRE DEMIRALP, JIYOUNG PARK, DAVID SEUNGJAE LEE, NATALIE LIN, HOLLY SHABLACK, JOHN JONIDES, OSCAR YBARRA

from FACEBOOK USE PREDICTS DECLINES IN SUBJECTIVE WELL-BEING[1] IN YOUNG ADULTS

Ethan Kross is a social psychologist at the University of Michigan. Together with Philippe Verduyn, a researcher at the University of Leuven, as well as other colleagues at the University of Michigan, Kross conducted the study printed below, which examines how Facebook use influences young adults' self-reported happiness over time. It was originally published in PLoS ONE, *an online science journal.*

ABSTRACT

Over 500 million people interact daily with Facebook. Yet, whether Facebook use influences subjective well-being over time is unknown. We addressed this issue using experience-sampling, the most reliable method for measuring in-vivo[2] behaviour and psychological experience. We text-messaged people five times per day for two-weeks to examine how Facebook use influences the two components of subjective well-being: how people feel moment-to-moment and how satisfied they are with their lives. Our results

---

1 *Subjective Well-Being* Refers to how people experience their quality of life and includes both emotional reactions (affective well-being) and cognitive judgments (cognitive well-being).

NB To distinguish notes added for this anthology from the authors' note numbers referring to their list of references at the end of the article, subscript numbers have been used here for the latter.

2 *experience-sampling* Method of gathering experimental data by requiring participants to provide regular updates about their behaviour and feelings; *in vivo* Occurring within a complete, live organism.

indicate that Facebook use predicts negative shifts on both of these variables over time. The more people used Facebook at one time point, the worse they felt the next time we text-messaged them; the more they used Facebook over two-weeks, the more their life satisfaction levels declined over time. Interacting with other people "directly" did not predict these negative outcomes. They were also not moderated by the size of people's Facebook networks, their perceived supportiveness, motivation for using Facebook, gender, loneliness, self-esteem, or depression. On the surface, Facebook provides an invaluable resource for fulfilling the basic human need for social connection. Rather than enhancing well-being, however, these findings suggest that Facebook may undermine it.

INTRODUCTION

Online social networks are rapidly changing the way human beings interact. Over a billion people belong to Facebook, the world's largest online social network, and over half of them log in daily.[1] Yet, no research has examined how interacting with Facebook influences subjective well-being over time. Indeed, a recent article that examined every peer-reviewed publication and conference proceeding on Facebook between 1/2005 and 1/2012 (412 in total) did not reveal a single study that examined how using this technology influences subjective well-being over time.[2, [See also Supporting Information 1 at the end of the article.]]

Subjective well-being is one of the most highly studied variables in the behavioural sciences. Although significant in its own right, it also predicts a range of consequential benefits including enhanced health and longevity.[3-5] Given the frequency of Facebook usage, identifying how interacting with this technology influences subjective well-being represents a basic research challenge that has important practical implications.

This issue is particularly vexing because prior research provides mixed clues about how Facebook use should influence subjective well-being. Whereas some cross-sectional research reveals positive associations between online social network use (in particular Facebook) and well-being,[6] other work reveals the opposite.[7,8] Still other work suggests that the relationship between Facebook use and well-being may be more nuanced and potentially influenced by multiple factors including number of Facebook friends, perceived supportiveness of one's online network, depressive symptomatology,* loneliness, and self-esteem.[9,10,11]

5 So, how does Facebook usage influence subjective well-being over time? The cross-sectional approach[3] used in previous studies makes it impossible

3 *cross-sectional approach* Approach to gathering experimental data by observing an entire group at a specific time.

to know. We addressed this issue by using experience-sampling, the most reliable method for measuring in-vivo behaviour and psychological experience over time.[12] We text-messaged participants five times per day for 14-days. Each text-message contained a link to an online survey, which participants completed using their smartphones. We performed lagged analyses[4] on participants' responses, as well as their answers to the Satisfaction With Life Questionnaire (SWLS),[13] which they completed before and immediately following the 14-day experience-sampling period, to examine how interacting with Facebook influences the two components of subjective well-being: how people feel ("affective" well-being) and how satisfied they are with their lives ("cognitive" well-being).[14,15] This approach allowed us to take advantage of the relative timing of participants' natural Facebook behaviour and psychological states to draw inferences about their likely causal sequence.[16-19]

Methods

Participants

Eighty-two people (M_{age} = 19.52, SD_{age} = 2.17; 53 females;[5] 60.5% European American, 28.4% Asian, 6.2% African American, and 4.9% other) were recruited for a study on Facebook through flyers posted around Ann Arbor, Michigan. Participants needed a Facebook account and a touch-screen smartphone to qualify for the study. They received $20 and were entered into a raffle to receive an iPad2 for participating.

Ethics Statement

The University of Michigan Institutional Review Board approved this study. Informed written consent was obtained from all participants prior to participation.

Materials and Procedure

PHASE 1

Participants completed a set of questionnaires, which included the SWLS (M = 4.96, SD = 1.17), Beck Depression Inventory[20] (M = 9.02, SD = 7.20), the Rosenberg Self-Esteem Scale[21] (M = 30.40, SD = 4.96), and the Social Provision Scale[22] (M = 3.55, SD = .34), which we modified to assess perceptions of Facebook support. We also assessed participants' motivation for using

---

4 *lagged analyses* Identification of patterns in data collected over time.

5 *M* Mean; *SD* Standard Deviation, a number indicating the extent of difference within a group.

Facebook by asking them to indicate whether they use Facebook "to keep in touch with friends (98% answered yes)," "to find new friends (23% answered yes)," "to share good things with friends (78% answered yes)," "to share bad things with friends (36% answered yes)," "to obtain new information (62% answered yes)," or "other: please explain (17% answered yes)." Examples of other reasons included chatting with others, keeping in touch with family, and facilitating schoolwork and business.

PHASE 2

Participants were text-messaged 5 times per day between 10am and midnight over 14-days. Text-messages occurred at random times within 168-minute windows per day. Each text-message contained a link to an online survey, which asked participants to answer five questions using a slider scale: (1) How do you feel right now? (*very positive* [0] to *very negative* [100]; $M = 37.47$, $SD = 25.88$); (2) How worried are you right now? (*not at all* [0] to *a lot* [100]; $M = 44.04$, $SD = 30.42$); (3) How lonely do you feel right now? (*not at all* [0] to *a lot* [100]; $M = 27.61$, $SD = 26.13$); (4) How much have you used Facebook since the last time we asked? (*not at all* [0] to *a lot* [100]; $M = 33.90$, $SD = 30.48$); (5) How much have you interacted with other people "directly" since the last time we asked? (*not at all* [0] to *a lot* [100]; $M = 64.26$, $SD = 31.11$). When the protocol for answering these questions was explained, interacting with other people "directly" was defined as face-to-face or phone interactions. An experimenter carefully walked participants through this protocol to ensure that they understood how to answer each question and fulfill the study requirements.

10 Participants always answered the affect question first. Next the worry and loneliness questions were presented in random order. The Facebook use and direct social interaction questions were always administered last, again in random order. Our analyses focused primarily on affect (rather than worry and loneliness) because this affect question is the way "affective well-being" is typically operationalized.

PHASE 3

Participants returned to the laboratory following Phase 2 to complete another set of questionnaires, which included the SWLS ($M = 5.13$, $SD = 1.26$) and the Revised UCLA Loneliness Scale[23] ($M = 1.69$, $SD = .46$). Participants' number of Facebook friends ($M = 664.25$, $SD = 383.64$) was also recorded during this session from participants' Facebook accounts. [See Supporting Information 2 at the end of the article.]

RESULTS

Attrition and compliance

Three participants did not complete the study. As the methods section notes, participants received a text message directing them to complete a block of five questions once every 168 minutes on average (the text message was delivered randomly within this 168-minute window). A response to any question within a block was considered "compliant" if it was answered *before* participants received a subsequent text-message directing them to complete the next block of questions. Participants responded to an average of 83.6% of text-messages (range: 18.6%–100%). Following prior research,$_{24}$ we pruned the data[6] by excluding all of the data from two participants who responded to <33% of the texts, resulting in 4,589 total observations. The results did not change substantively when additional cutoff rates were used.

Analyses overview

We examined the relationship between Facebook use and affect using multilevel analyses to account for the nested data structure.[7] Specifically, we examined whether T_2[8] affect (i.e., How do you feel *right now?*) was predicted by T_{1-2} Facebook use (i.e., How much have you used Facebook *since the last time we asked?*), controlling for T_1 affect at level-1 of the model (between-day lags were excluded). Note that although this analysis assesses Facebook use at T_2, the question refers to usage between T_1 and T_2 (hence the notationT_{1-2}). This analysis allowed us to explore whether Facebook use during the time period separating T_1 and T_2 predicted changes in affect over this time span....

The relationship between mean Facebook use and life satisfaction was assessed using OLS regressions[9] because these data were not nested. Both

6 *pruned the data* Removed unnecessary data.

7 *multilevel analyses* Methods of analyzing data which recognize that there are multiple sources which may explain variations in data. Multilevel analyses are used specifically in research where data may be classified and organized at several levels; *nested data structure* Describes data that is obtained from multiple observations of individuals in particular groups, e.g., students in a particular class, or data that is obtained through repeated observation of the same individual over time.

8 *T_2* Refers to "Time $_2$," the moment when the participant receives an online survey to assess "Time $_{1-2}$," the period of Facebook usage beginning from the completion of the previous survey. "Time $_1$" is thus the moment a survey is completed.

9 *OLS regressions* Ordinary Least Squares regressions, models that calculate the relationship between a dependent variable and an independent variable in order to estimate the boundaries of the variables.

unstandardized (*B*) and standardized (*β*) OLS regression coefficients[10] are reported. [Supporting Information 3]

Facebook use and well-being

AFFECTIVE WELL-BEING

We examined whether people's tendency to interact with Facebook during the time period separating two text messages influenced how they felt at T_2, controlling for how they felt at T_1. Nested time-lag analyses indicated that the more people used Facebook the worse they subsequently felt, $B = .08$, $\chi^2 = 28.90$, $p < .0001$.[11] … The reverse pathway (T_1 Affect predicting T_{1-2} Facebook use, controlling for T_{0-1} Facebook use) was not significant, $B = -.005$, $\chi^2 = .05$, $p = .82$, indicating that people do not use Facebook more or less depending on how they feel. [See Supporting Information 4 and 5 at the end of the article.][…]

COGNITIVE WELL-BEING

To examine how Facebook use influenced "cognitive well-being," we analyzed whether people's average Facebook use over the 14-day period predicted their life satisfaction at the end of the study, controlling for baseline life satisfaction and average emotion levels over the 14-day period. The more participants used Facebook, the more their life satisfaction levels declined over time, $B = -.012$, $\boldsymbol{\beta} = -.124$, $t(73) = -2.39$,[12] $p = .02$.…

ALTERNATIVE EXPLANATIONS

An alternative explanation for these results is that any form of social interaction undermines well-being. Because we also asked people to indicate how frequently they interacted with other people "directly" since the last time we text messaged them, we were able to test this idea. Specifically, we repeated each of the aforementioned analyses substituting "direct" social interaction for Facebook use. In contrast to Facebook use, "direct" social interaction did not predict changes in cognitive well-being, $B = -.006$, $\beta = -.059$, $t(73) = 1.04$, $p = .30$, and predicted *increases* (not decreases) in affective well-being, $B = -.15$, $\chi^2 = 65.30$, $p<.0001$. Controlling for direct social interaction did not

---

10 *OLS regression coefficients* Numerical indications of the relationship between two variables.

11 χ^2 Chi squared, used in statistical tests to determine the probability that a set of data reflects a significant relationship between variables; *p* Probability, here an indication of the likelihood of getting the same experimental results as the ones observed if there were no relationship between the variables being studied.

12 *t* Variable used in *t*-tests to calculate the significance of the differences between two sets of data.

substantively alter the significant relationship between Facebook use and affective well-being, $B = .05$, $\chi^2 = 10.78$, $p<.01$.

Another alternative explanation for these results is that people use Facebook when they feel bad (i.e., when they are bored, lonely, worried or otherwise distressed), and feeling bad leads to declines in well-being rather than Facebook use per se. The analyses we reported earlier partially address this issue by demonstrating that affect does not predict changes in Facebook use over time and Facebook use continues to significantly predict declines in life satisfaction over time when controlling for affect. However, because participants also rated how lonely and worried they felt each time we text messaged them, we were able to test this proposal further.

We first examined whether worry or loneliness predicted changes in Facebook use over time (i.e., T_1 worry [or T_1 loneliness] predicting T_{1-2} Facebook use, controlling for T_{0-1} Facebook use). Worry did not predict changes in Facebook use, $B = .04$, $\chi^2 = 2.37$, $p = .12$, but loneliness did, $B = .07$, $\chi^2 = 8.54$, $p<.01$. The more lonely people felt at one time point, the more people used Facebook over time. Given this significant relationship, we next examined whether controlling for loneliness renders the relationship between Facebook use and changes in affective and cognitive well-being non-significant—what one would predict if Facebook use is a proxy for loneliness. This was not the case. Facebook use continued to predict declines in affective well-being, $B = .08$, $\chi^2 = 27.87$, $p<.0001$, and cognitive well-being, $B = -.012$, $\beta = -.126$, $t(72) = 2.34$, $p = .02$, when loneliness was controlled for in each analysis. Neither worry nor loneliness interacted significantly with Facebook use to predict changes in affective or cognitive well-being ($ps>.44$).

MODERATION

Next, we examined whether a number of theoretically relevant individual- 20
difference variables[13] including participants' number of Facebook Friends, their perceptions of their Facebook network support, depressive symptoms, loneliness, gender, self-esteem, time of study participation, and motivation for using Facebook (e.g., to find new friends, to share good or bad things, to obtain new information) interacted with Facebook use to predict changes in affective or cognitive well-being. [See Supporting Information 6 at the end of the article.] In no case did we observe any significant interactions ($ps>.16$).

---

13 *individual-difference variables* Variables indicating characteristics that individual participants already possess, which may affect study results but are not controlled by the study.

EXPLORATORY ANALYSES

Although we did not have *a priori* predictions[14] about whether Facebook use and direct social contact would interact to predict changes in affective and cognitive well-being, we nevertheless explored this issue in our final set of analyses. The results of these analyses indicated that Facebook use and direct social contact interacted significantly to predict changes in affective well-being, $B = .002$, $\chi^2 = 19.55$, $p<.0001$, but not changes in cognitive well-being, $B = .000$, $\beta = .129$, $t(71)=.39$, $p = .70$. To understand the meaning of the former interaction, we performed simple slope analyses.[15] These analyses indicated that the relationship between Facebook use and declines in affective well-being increased linearly with direct social contact. Specifically, whereas Facebook use did not predict significant declines in affective well-being when participants experienced low levels of direct social contact (i.e., 1 standard deviation below the sample mean for direct social contact; $B = .00$, $\chi^2 = .04$, $p = .84$), it did predict significant declines in well-being when participants experienced moderate levels of direct social contact (i.e., at the sample mean for direct social contact; $B = .05$, $\chi^2 = 11.21$, $p<.001$) and high levels of direct social contact (i.e., 1 standard deviation above the sample mean for direct social contact; $B = .10$, $\chi^2 = 28.82$, $p<.0001$).

DISCUSSION

Within a relatively short timespan, Facebook has revolutionized the way people interact. Yet, whether using Facebook predicts changes in subjective well-being over time is unknown. We addressed this issue by performing lagged analyses on experience sampled data, an approach that allowed us to take advantage of the relative timing of participants' naturally occurring behaviours and psychological states to draw inferences about their likely causal sequence.[17,18] These analyses indicated that Facebook use predicts declines in the two components of subjective well-being: how people feel moment to moment and how satisfied they are with their lives.

Critically, we found no evidence to support two plausible alternative interpretations of these results. First, interacting with other people "directly" did not predict declines in well-being. In fact, direct social network interactions led people to feel *better* over time. This suggests that Facebook use may constitute a unique form of social network interaction that predicts impoverished well-being. Second, multiple types of evidence indicated that it was not the case that Facebook use led to declines in well-being because people are more likely to

---

14 *a priori predictions* Predictions made before research began.

15 *slope analyses* Analyses showing the incline of the line that would be formed if a set of data were depicted in a graph.

use Facebook when they feel bad—neither affect nor worry predicted Facebook use and Facebook use continued to predict significant declines in well-being when controlling for loneliness (which did predict increases in Facebook use and reductions in emotional well-being).

Would engaging in any solitary activity similarly predict declines in well-being? We suspect that they would not because people often derive pleasure from engaging in some solitary activities (e.g., exercising, reading). Supporting this view, a number of recent studies indicate that people's *perceptions* of social isolation (i.e., how lonely they feel)—a variable that we assessed in this study, which did not influence our results—are a more powerful determinant of well-being than *objective* social isolation.[25] A related question concerns whether engaging in any Internet activity (e.g., email, web surfing) would likewise predict well-being declines. Here too prior research suggests that it would not. A number of studies indicate that whether interacting with the Internet predicts changes in well-being depends on how you use it (i.e., what sites you visit) and who you interact with.[26]

Future research

Although these findings raise numerous future research questions, four stand 25
out as most pressing. First, do these findings generalize? We concentrated on young adults in this study because they represent a core Facebook user demographic. However, examining whether these findings generalize to additional age groups is important. Future research should also examine whether these findings generalize to other online social networks. As a recent review of the Facebook literature indicated[2] "[different online social networks] have varied histories and are associated with different patterns of use, user characteristics, and social functions" (p. 205). Therefore, it is possible that the current findings may not neatly generalize to other online social networks.

Second, what mechanisms underlie the deleterious effects of Facebook usage on well-being? Some researchers have speculated that online social networking may interfere with physical activity, which has cognitive and emotional replenishing effects[27] or trigger damaging social comparisons.[8,28] The latter idea is particularly interesting in light of the significant interaction we observed between direct social contact and Facebook use in this study—i.e., the more people interacted with other people directly, the more strongly Facebook use predicted declines in their affective well-being. If harmful social comparisons explain how Facebook use predicts declines in affective well-being, it is possible that interacting with other people directly either enhances the frequency of such comparisons or magnifies their emotional impact. Examining whether these or other mechanisms explain the relationship between

Facebook usage and well-being is important both from a basic science and practical perspective.

Finally, although the analytic approach we used in this study is useful for drawing inferences about the likely causal ordering of associations between naturally occurring variables, experiments that manipulate Facebook use in daily life are needed to corroborate these findings and establish definitive causal relations. Though potentially challenging to perform—Facebook use prevalence, its centrality to young adult daily social interactions, and addictive properties may make it a difficult intervention target—such studies are important for extending this work and informing future interventions.*

Caveats

Two caveats* are in order before concluding. First, although we observed statistically significant associations between Facebook usage and well-being, the sizes of these effects were relatively "small." This should not, however, undermine their practical significance.[29] Subjective well-being is a multiply determined outcome—it is unrealistic to expect any single factor to powerfully influence it. Moreover, in addition to being consequential in its own right, subjective well-being predicts an array of mental and physical health consequences. Therefore, identifying any factor that systematically influences it is important, especially when that factor is likely to accumulate over time among large numbers of people. Facebook usage would seem to fit both of these criteria.

Second, some research suggests that asking people to indicate how good or bad they feel using a single bipolar scale,* as we did in this study, can obscure interesting differences regarding whether a variable leads people to feel less positive, more negative or both less positive and more negative. Future research should administer two unipolar affect questions to assess positive and negative affect separately to address this issue.

CONCLUDING COMMENT

30 The human need for social connection is well established, as are the benefits that people derive from such connections.[30-34] On the surface, Facebook provides an invaluable resource for fulfilling such needs by allowing people to instantly connect. Rather than enhancing well-being, as frequent interactions with supportive "offline" social networks powerfully do, the current findings demonstrate that interacting with Facebook may predict the opposite result for young adults—it may undermine it.

(2013)

ACKNOWLEDGMENTS: We thank Emily Kean for her assistance running the study and Ozlem Ayduk and Phoebe Ellsworth for their feedback.

AUTHOR CONTRIBUTIONS: Conceived and designed the experiments: EK ED JP DSL NL JJ OY. Performed the experiments: HS NL. Analyzed the data: PV ED. Wrote the paper: EK ED PV JJ OY. Discussed the results and commented on the manuscript: EK PV ED JP DSL NL HS JJ OY.

SUPPORTING INFORMATION:

1: We do not imply that no longitudinal research on Facebook has been performed. Rather, no published work that we are aware of has examined how Facebook influences subjective well-being over time (i.e., how people feel and their life satisfaction).
2: Additional measures were administered during Phases 1 and 2 for other purposes. The measures reported in the MS are those that were theoretically motivated.
3: Raw data are available upon request for replication purposes.
4: We also examined whether T_{0-1} (rather than T_{1-2}) Facebook use influences T_2 affect, controlling for T_1 affect. Nested time-lagged analyses indicated that this was also true, $B = .03$, $\chi^2 = 4.67$, $p = .03$.
5: Some research suggests that affect fluctuates throughout the day. Replicating this work, time of day was related to affective well-being such that people reported feeling better as the day progressed ($B = -1.06$, $\chi^2 = 21.49$, $p < .0001$). Controlling for time of day did not, however, substantively influence any of the results.
6: 98% of participants reported using Facebook to "keep in touch with friends." Therefore, we did not test for moderation with this variable.

REFERENCES

1. FacebookInformation (2012) Facebook Newsroom Website. Available: http://newsroom.fb.com/content/default.aspx?NewsAreaId=22. Accessed 2012 April 23.
2. Wilson RE, Gosling SD, Graham LT (2012) A Review of Facebook Research in the Social Sciences. Perspect Psychol Sci 7: 203–220.
3. Steptoe A, Wardle J (2011) Positive affect measured using ecological momentary assessment and survival in older men and women. Proc Natl Acad Sci USA 108: 18244–18248. doi: 10.1073/pnas.1110892108.
4. Boehm JK, Peterson C, Kivimaki M, Kubzansky L (2011) A prospective study of positive psychological well-being and coronary heart disease. Health Psychol 30: 259–267. doi: 10.1037/a0023124.
5. Diener E (2011) Happy people live longer: Subjective well-being contributes to health and longevity. Appl Psychol Health Well Being 3: 1–43. doi: 10.1111/j.1758-0854.2010.01045.x.
6. Valenzuela S, Park N, Kee KF (2009) Is There Social Capital in a Social Network Site?: Facebook Use and College Students' Life Satisfaction, Trust, and Participation. J Comput Mediat Commun 14: 875–901. doi: 10.1111/j.1083-6101.2009.01474.x.
7. Huang C (2010) Internet use and psychological well-being: A meta-analysis. Cyberpsychol Behav Soc Netw 13: 241–248.
8. Chou H, Edge N (2012) 'They are happier and having better lives than I am': The impact of using Facebook on perceptions of others' lives. Cyberpsychol Behav Soc Netw 15: 117–120. doi: 10.1089/cyber.2011.0324.

9. Forest AL, Wood JV (2012) When Social Networking Is Not Working: Individuals With Low Self-Esteem Recognize but Do Not Reap the Benefits of Self-Disclosure on Facebook. Psychol Sci 23: 295–302. doi: 10.1177/0956797611429709.
10. Manago AM, Taylor T, Greenfield PM (2012) Me and my 400 friends: The anatomy of college students' Facebook networks, their communication patterns, and well-being. Dev Psychol 48: 369–380. doi: 10.1037/a0026338.
11. Kim J, LaRose R, Peng W (2009) Loneliness as the cause and the effect of problematic Internet use: The relationship between Internet use and psychological well-being. Cyberpsychology & behavior: The impact of the Internet, multimedia and virtual reality on behavior and society 12: 451–455. doi: 10.1089/cpb.2008.0327.
12. Kahneman D, Krueger AB, Schkade DA, Schwarz N, Stone AA (2004) A survey method for characterizing daily life experience: The day reconstruction method. Science 306: 1776–1780. doi: 10.1126/science.1103572.
13. Diener E, Emmons RA, Larsen RJ, Griffin S (1985) The Satisfaction with Life Scale. J Pers Assess 49: 71–74. doi: 10.1207/s15327752jpa4901_13.
14. Kahneman D, Deaton A (2010) High income improves evaluation of life but not emotional well-being. Proc Natl Acad Sci USA 107: 16489–16493. doi: 10.1073/pnas.1011492107.
15. Diener E (1984) Subjective Well-Being. Psychol Bull 95: 542–575. doi: 10.1037/0033-2909.95.3.542.
16. Hofmann W, Vohs KD, Baumeister RF (2012) What people desire, feel conflicted about, and try to resist in everyday life. Psychol Sci doi: 10.1177/0956797612437426.
17. Bolger N, Davis A, Rafaeli E (2003) Diary methods: Capturing life as it is lived. Annu Rev Psychol 54: 579–616. doi: 10.1146/annurev.psych.54.101601.145030.
18. Adam EK, Hawkley LC, Kudielka BM, Cacioppo JT (2006) Day-to-day dynamics of experience–cortisol associations in a population-based sample of older adults. Proc Natl Acad Sci USA 103: 17058–17063. doi: 10.1073/pnas.0605053103.
19. Killingsworth MA, Gilbert DT (2010) A Wandering Mind Is an Unhappy Mind. Science 330: 932–932. doi: 10.1126/science.1192439.
20. Beck AT, Steer RA, Brown GK (1996) BDI-II Manual. San Antonio: Harcourt Brace & Company.
21. Rosenberg M (1965) Society and the adolescent self-image. Princeton: Princeton University Press.
22. Cutrona CE (1989) Ratings of social support by adolescents and adult informants: Degree of correspondence and prediction of depressive symptoms. Journal of Personality and Social Psychology 57: 723–730. doi: 10.1037//0022-3514.57.4.723.
23. Russell D, Peplau LA, Cutrona CE (1980) The revised UCLA Loneliness Scale: Concurrent and discriminant validity evidence. J Pers Soc Psychol 39: 472–480. doi: 10.1037//0022-3514.39.3.472.
24. Moberly NJ, Watkins ER (2008) Ruminative self-focus, negative life events, and negative affect. Behav Res Ther 46: 1034–1039. doi: 10.1016/j.brat.2008.06.004.
25. Cacioppo JT, Hawkley LC, Norman GJ, Berntson GG (2011) Social isolation. Ann N Y Acad Sci 1231: 17–22. doi: 10.1111/j.1749-6632.2011.06028.x.
26. Bessiére K, Kiesler S, Kraut R, Boneva BS (2008) Effects of Internet use and social resources on changes in depression. Information, Communication, and Society 11: 47–70.

27. Kaplan S, Berman MG (2010) Directed Attention as a Common Resource for Executive Functioning and Self-Regulation. Perspect Psychol Sci 5: 43–57. doi: 10.1177/1745691609356784.
28. Haferkamp N, Kramer NC (2011) Social Comparison 2.0: Examining the Effects of Online Profiles on Social-Networking Sites. Cyberpsychol Behav Soc Netw 14: 309–314. doi: 10.1089/cyber.2010.0120.
29. Prentice DA, Miller DT (1992) When small effects are impressive. Psychological Bulletin 112: 160–164. doi: 10.1037/0033-2909.112.1.160.
30. Baumeister RF, Leary MR (1995) The need to belong: desire for interpersonal attachments as a fundamental human motivation. Psychol Bull 117: 497–529. doi: 10.1037/0033-2909.117.3.497.
31. Kross E, Berman MG, Mischel W, Smith EE, Wager TD (2011) Social rejection shares somatosensory representations with physical pain. Proc Natl Acad Sci USA 108: 6270–6275. doi: 10.1073/pnas.1102693108.
32. Eisenberger NI, Cole SW (2012) Social neuroscience and health: neurophysiological mechanisms linking social ties with physical health. Nat Neurosci 15: 669–674. doi: 10.1038/nn.3086.
33. House JS, Landis KR, Umberson D (1988) Social relationships and health. Science 241: 540–545. doi: 10.1126/science.3399889.
34. Ybarra O, Burnstein E, Winkielman P, Keller MC, Chan E, et al. (2008) Mental exercising through simple socializing: Social interaction promotes general cognitive functioning. Pers Soc Psychol Bull 34: 248–259. doi: 10.1177/0146167207310454.

Questions

1. The article states that "[s]ubjective well-being is one of the most highly studied variables in the behavioural sciences." What reasons did the authors give in the article for their choice to examine this variable? What (if any) potential drawbacks to this choice can you identify?
2. Why do you think the authors might have chosen to text-message study participants to gather data? What are the benefits and drawbacks of this choice? Name another way they could have gathered similar data, and explain why that would or would not have been a better choice.
3. What is the difference between "affective" and "cognitive" well-being, according to the article? Does this experiment adequately address both components of subjective well-being? Explain your answer.
4. The article considers and rejects alternative explanations of the study data. Are all of these alternative explanations adequately addressed? Explain.

NADINE BACHAN

OL' TALK

The following article by Trinidadian-Canadian essayist and editor Nadine Bachan first appeared in 2014 in Maisonneuve, *an arts, culture, and politics quarterly based in Montreal.*

"Dis boi will eat up he family in trut."

I read the line aloud with its Trinidadian inflections, in the way I believed the character would have actually spoken it. The words—uttered with unease by the protagonist's father in V.S. Naipaul's[1] novel *A House for Mr. Biswas*—flowed out of me, and it felt good. Better than good. It had been a very long time since I'd last sat alone and felt compelled to use dialect. Like a comforting scent, the lyrical highs and lows triggered familiar feelings both warm and conflicted, much more complicated than nostalgia.

In the novel, this line, along with all of the dialogue, is written in British English:

"This boy will eat up his family in truth."

5 I was a seen-and-not-heard child.* Raised to be polite and tight-lipped, my meekness allowed my presence among adults to go mostly unnoticed. Always within earshot of lively conversation—fast-talking, grin-inducing and punctuated with laughter—I took in all the unfiltered chatter.

When I was six years old, I was at one of the countless house parties my family was invited to in the early years of our new life in Canada. We revelled in our own little social village then, made up mostly of relatives and close friends who were also recent immigrants from Trinidad. There was always some birthday or milestone celebration, or holiday get-together, or just-because-we-deserve-a-bit-of-fun fête* to attend.

A man in the crowd began to look around the room, trying to locate his wife. He asked the people nearest to him if they had seen her. I could have asked, "Where is she?" but a choice phrase came to my mind, something I had

---

1 *V.S. Naipaul* Trinidadian-born British writer and recipient of the 2001 Nobel Prize for Literature. *A House for Mr. Biswas* (1961), one of several novels he set in Trinidad, is considered one of his most important works.

heard earlier and logged away as one of those fun little idioms. I yelled out: "Whey she dey dey?"

Several people around me laughed, loudly. I delighted in the attention until I saw my mother's face. Her smile was pursed and forced. Her eyes stared down at me in that tell-tale way. I'd done something wrong. She took me by the hand, led me aside and reprimanded me to tears.

In Trinidad, "Whey she dey dey?" scrapes the bottom of the inevitable hierarchy of speech that exists in any language. Saying the phrase at my tender age was akin to a toddler blurting out an expletive after stubbing a toe. I hadn't cussed, but my mother corrected me as if I had; what I had said was improper, coarse, foul—I was never to speak that way again.

From then on, I did as children do when they want to learn how to navigate 10
the world: I followed the cues of my parents. I listened with a turned ear whenever they spoke to Canadians. Although my parents' Trinidadian accents were never fully erased, their diction and tone would shift to something deliberate, with much of the colour wrung out.

I have always been conscious of the way I speak, hyper-aware of the sounds that fight to be the first out of my mouth. My group classroom portraits when I was young were quintessentially multicultural—rows upon rows of toothy, chubby-cheeked faces of nearly every ethnicity a person could imagine. However, most of my young schoolmates were born and raised in Canada and spoke with Canadian accents like all of my teachers. Before I understood what the word meant, assimilation was my goal.

While my accent is now dominantly Canadian, there are still occasions when I speak in slang, with a somewhat garbled and uneven Caribbean articulation. I'm prone to over-think and over-enunciate, worried that I'm saying things wrong. Whatever "wrong" is. Attempting to reconcile the polarity of being a Trinidadian-Canadian—and the tug-of-war of allegiances that goes with the attempt—is an exercise in self-discovery that has been both enriching and exhaustingly circular.

Nature drives us to adjust to our circumstances. The mimic octopus will twist and turn and fold its body to look like various kinds of fish, or snakes, or to simply disappear into the sea bed. The lyrebird will reproduce the sounds of its environment, including the mating call of other birds and animals. Assimilation may begin as a survival tactic of sorts, but it's also a matter of choice. And unlike my animal comrades, I get to be cognitively conflicted about what I do and why.

The intricacy of verbal indicators—language, word choice, even something as simple as an upward inflection—can speak volumes about a person. Hearing a familiar accent or a hometown turn-of-phrase in public is like detecting a homing beacon. Everything else fades into white noise. "Language is such an emotional issue for everyone," says Molly Babel, an aptly-named professor of linguistics at the University of British Columbia (UBC) who focuses on speech perception in societies with a range of dialects. "It is a huge part of our presentation of our identities and others use it—for better or worse—to label and categorize us."

The biggest misconception, Babel says, is probably "that some dialects or accents are better than others." She cites the North American perception that a British accent sounds intelligent and elegant, while an accent from the southern United States sounds unsophisticated. "In a nutshell, we are more likely to imitate the speech patterns of others when we have positive feelings towards that individual or what that individual's speech patterns represent." On the other hand, linguistic discrimination is the act of prejudice against a person because of the way they speak. It's wrapped up in the notion that speech indicates upbringing, education, economic status, prestige, sociocultural environment and a plethora of other factors that serve to maintain an audible pecking order. Dialect is interpreted as a barometer of strength and weakness. Of intelligence and stupidity. George Orwell called it being "branded on the tongue."

When I was still a child, one of my cousins was forced to enrol in speech therapy, the elementary school's attempt to fix how he spoke. While his mother was earning her master's degree in Guelph, Ontario, he lived with my family in the Etobicoke suburbs of Toronto and enrolled in school with me and my siblings. He was diagnosed with a long list of "problematic" speech patterns that were really nothing more than a Trinidadian accent. He didn't pronounce the th at the beginnings of words. Thing was ting. The was dee. Them was dem. He also didn't pronounce the er at the end of words. Water was wat-ah. Teacher was teach-ah.

He attended therapy diligently, but the vocal exercises didn't stick. He pronounced all of the words exactly as he was instructed, then walked out of the room and immediately fell back into his natural way of speaking. In the end, it didn't matter. Although it had been their initial plan to stay in Canada, my aunt and cousin decided they ought to return to Trinidad. From time to time, my cousin will talk about how much he disliked going to those sessions. To this day, whenever I speak to him, he affects an exaggerated Canadian accent to tease me: "How's the weather up there in Ca-na-der?" I suspect the voice he employs is that of his former speech therapist.

My cousin would be pleased to learn that in her forty-plus-year career, Barbara May Bernhardt—a clinical speech pathologist who teaches at UBC's School of Audiology and Speech Sciences—has seen a significant turnaround in how speech-language pathologists approach accent reduction. "Pronunciation-wise, there are often misconceptions when considering speech without dialect.

It can be sometimes misconstrued as 'development errors,' which would be an incorrect assessment when a person's cultural upbringing is not considered." Mis-diagnosing dialect as language difficulty or impairment can result in detrimental long-term effects, including feelings of low self-worth and negative attitudes towards education.

Unlike the lessons experienced by my cousin, the British Columbia school system's practices incorporate a "bidialectal" approach, which respects both the standard and the dialect. Standard English as a Second Language is a linguistic phenomenon that is now recognized in schools in indigenous communities in the province. One of the core beliefs of the American Speech-Language-Hearing Association is that no dialectal variety of American English is a disorder or a pathological form of speech or language. And, all across the globe, variants of World English (also known as International English, which includes dialects of all forms) are becoming more prevalent and accepted.

20 However, both Babel and Bernhardt acknowledge that discrimination based on voice still exists. The first impression when interviewing for a job or meeting new colleagues is so important to professional development and is influenced by several factors, including how we speak. Because of this, some adults opt for accent reduction therapy.

I used to describe the way my parents and most of my relatives spoke as broken English. I had heard more than a few people use the term during my childhood. For years, no one corrected me. I was eventually told by my sister, who was enthusiastically contemplating all manner of things in her undergraduate studies at the time, that the language Trinidadians speak is not broken English but, rather, a dialect.

Some would argue that there isn't much of a difference between language and dialect. Max Weinreich, a Yiddish* sociolinguist, popularized the saying, "A language is a dialect with an army and a navy." As the writer Lauren Webb asks, "Why is it that one language is classed as a language, and another is classed a dialect? Some dialects have hundreds of thousands of speakers, whereas some languages have less than one thousand." But my feeling that Trinidadian English was somehow lesser than the Queen's English* continued to plague me for many years.

My mother and father both speak in a dialect associated with the southern region of Trinidad, comprised mostly of small towns and farming communities. Their accent indicates a middle- or working-class background. The difference is subtle, but makes for an emphatic social marker that separates most of my family from those who live north, in and near the capital city Port of Spain, a region associated with upper-class sensibilities.

My aunt has lived in southern Trinidad her entire life. She and I share a quietness; we are listeners in a very vocal family. Her childhood stories are seldom told, which invests anything she tells me with added resonance.

As a scrappy ten-year-old, my aunt once ran through her father's garden in bare feet and stepped on a thorn. She hobbled inside, yelling:

"Someting jook my foot!"

At the time, one of her own aunts (my great-aunt or Tanty) had been entertaining a suitor. They were enjoying an afternoon tea on my grandmother's Royal Doulton, the china set she kept on the highest shelf in her living room display case. The suitor—a wealthy man from a gated community in the north—turned to my aunt and said, "Say that again."

She repeated herself. "Someting jook me."

He smirked at her. "Now, I don't think that's the right word. Do you?"

She was confused. She had no idea what he was talking about.

He continued, "Jook. Jook is not correct. What is the proper word?"

He spoke the word "jook" as though it was a bad taste in his mouth and made her stand in the middle of the room, waiting while she grew mortified and close to tears. After several minutes of silence, he finally let her off the hook.

"The correct word is jab. Or prick," he said before waving her away.

Prick, indeed.

By the time I was a teenager—engulfed by the turmoil of finding my footing in high school—my Canadian accent became my dominant voice, both in public and at home. However, I had the ability to "turn off" the Canadian and "turn on" the Trinidadian when the situation called for it. Sometimes, my classmates would ask me to "say something in Trini." I always shrank at the thought and they always urged me on. I would close my eyes and feel the stretch of my embarrassed grin, uncomfortable on the centre stage. They'd give me a sentence to convert and I'd do it for them like I was performing a party trick.

Eventually, I refused to flaunt my Trinidadian accent for kicks with friends. It felt degrading. I was tired of being pointed out for what made me different and politely denied the requests until I simply lost the ability to "turn it on." I couldn't switch to the Trinidadian dialect outside of my home anymore, and that was fine by me. By then, I had been living in Canada for fifteen years, and I was feeling all that much closer to being a true citizen of the Great White North.

My connection to dialect now exists predominantly in the speech of others, but I fall into that way of speaking whenever I'm in the presence of close company. A word here or there will flourish at the end when I chat with my mother and father, or I might use a certain expression to make a point when conversing with my brother and sister. Speaking to each other in this subtly fluctuating way is just one facet of our family's intimacy. Still, whatever the occasion may be, I would always become aware of the shift and it never sounded right. I had come to terms with the fact that I had lost the ability to enjoy speaking in my dialect until I began to read *A House for Mr. Biswas.*

The Trinidadian opinion of V.S. Naipaul is fascinating. Although he was born and raised in Trinidad, he moved to England at the age of eighteen. The novel has been perceived as a fictional re-telling of Naipaul's father's life, based on the writer's childhood memories. Mohun, the protagonist, steers away from expectations dictated by generations of deeply-rooted tradition; his is a lifelong struggle with "culture," trying to be his own man. The book earned Naipaul international acclaim and established him as one of the best writers of his time. Despite this success, there is a sizeable group of Trinidadians who call him a traitor, a man who left the country only to exploit it years later for literary fame. He has been judged for misrepresenting the land and its people. While there are many reasons for the contempt—Naipaul is notoriously thorny and unaccommodating—his careful Oxbridge accent* is one very noticeable indication of his distance from his birthplace.

An incident supposedly occurred several years ago during one of Naipaul's visits to Trinidad, not long after he received the Nobel Prize. It's a story that has made its rounds viva voce,[2] certainly shifting and evolving as it passes from mouth to mouth. A large crowd had gathered at an event to celebrate the author's literary work and achievements. Several people asked him questions about his writing, his inspiration and his life in England. One frowning man stood up and, in a very strong accent, said simply, "I knew your father." Four words meant to pull him down, to remind him that he had come from humble beginnings. Four words meant to jook what some have deemed an inflated ego.

Naipaul made his choice very firmly and relatively simply: he would become an English gentleman and leave Trinidad mostly behind. For many of us, it's not so easy. Jodi Picoult wrote it best in *Change of Heart*: "In the space between yes and no, there's a lifetime. It's the difference between the path you walk and the one you leave behind; it's the gap between who you thought you could be and who you really are."

During one of our cross-country video-chats, I tell my parents that I'm finally reading the Naipaul novel. We discuss the beauty of the book's narrative and language and my father's face lights up, as it always does when he tells me about his youth. His words are rich with cherished memory. He smiles inwardly at things I will never fully understand.

---

2 *viva voce* By word of mouth (rather than in writing).

For a long time, I was envious that I didn't have that same strong connection to the place where I was born. Yet, somehow, it feels much more precious, seeing those people and places entirely through his telling—through his voice.

(2014)

Questions

1. How do class dynamics affect Bachan's feelings about her accent?
2. In this piece, how are Bachan and her relatives pushed into certain ways of speaking by fellow Trinidadians? By fellow Canadians without Trinidadian roots?
3. Near the end of the article, Bachan quotes Jodi Picoult. What does that quotation mean in the context of this essay?
4. "Ol' Talk" is a personal essay. What does this genre allow Bachan to say about Canadian immigrant experience that could not be as easily said in an essay without a personal component? How much of what is said in this essay is applicable outside Bachan's own family?

CARL WILSON

I KNEW ABOUT JIAN GHOMESHI

In 2014, Canadian radio celebrity Jian Ghomeshi was fired from the CBC, as allegations began to surface that he had committed nonconsensual violent acts against women in sexual contexts. Late in the same year, Ghomeshi was arrested and charged with four counts of sexual assault and one count of overcoming resistance by choking. The trial began in February 2016, and Ghomeshi was cleared of all charges in March 2016, as the judge found the key testimonies to be internally inconsistent and therefore unreliable. (A portion of the court decision is also included in this anthology.) The arrest and trial of Ghomeshi led to an impassioned discourse in Canada about the culture of sexual assault (or "rape culture") and the way in which the criminal justice system deals with sexual assault. The following article appeared in* Slate Magazine *in November 2014, after the allegations surfaced but before the trial.*

You know Jian, of course. So does almost everyone else you know.

You are all part of the downtown-Toronto arts scene. Jian is the host of the popular public-radio culture show *Q*, heard across Canada every weekday morning and syndicated to 180 U.S. stations—a rare CBC success at reaching beyond retirees.

As a critic and author, you have been a guest on *Q* a half-dozen times, most recently in early summer, to discuss a *Slate* piece you'd written. You enjoy doing it, and you value it professionally: It is by far the highest-profile Canadian broadcast venue that consistently engages with the kind of work you do. You think you and Jian have a good on-air rapport.

Then again, you are a man. You are well-aware that to many of the women you know, Jian is a creep.

You run into him constantly around town. Awards ceremonies, panel 5
discussions, fashion events, charitable and cultural galas of all kinds—Jian is there, and he is subsequently pictured online and in the society pages, often with his arms around a couple of young women in cocktail dresses. He might

as well have been appointed Host Laureate[1] by the Canadian parliament. It is a function of Canada's small population, and its colonial propensity to stick with the familiar, that there is usually just one such inescapable person in this country. For the past five years, it has been Jian.

Because he is post-boomer and Iranian Canadian, he is embraced as the embodiment of the New Canada: multicultural, tuned-in,* no longer parochial. But as a well-read, affable, stylish liberal, he does not make the Old Canada too uncomfortable, either.

He does make some people uncomfortable. Female friends often remark that they would never date him, that they've "heard things." You've heard things too.

You and Jian are about the same age. You met him before his brief celebrity as the leader of a goofy college-circuit folk-rock band[2] in the mid-1990s. (The only sin you knew of there was against decent music.) Some of your friends had worked with him before *Q*, and when it was launched others got jobs there.

There was chatter at parties, stories of pushed boundaries, of Jian hitting on* woman after woman. You'd heard this kind of talk about journalists in town before, but usually about men of an older generation, not your own. The gossip was sometimes kind of funny, sometimes simply gross. On one or two occasions, a little darker, in ways you couldn't really parse.

10 Then, one weekend years later, Jian abruptly goes on leave from the CBC. At brunch the next morning, friends tell you it's because a freelance writer you know (he interviewed you for his podcast[3] just a few weeks ago) is about to publish an exposé of Jian's treatment of women, in the office and in his private life.

Your friends laugh at your startled expression—which is not because there are allegations (though you don't yet know their depth), but because someone is finally reporting them. As another journalist said, whenever there is a profile of Jian in a paper or a magazine, you wonder if it will confront the subject. It never does, not seriously. Until now. In the next couple of days it all begins to come out, and keeps coming.

There were the parts you'd anticipated: allegations of workplace harassment, aggression, inappropriate behaviour. But by the end of the week, eight women have accused him of assaulting them violently on dates, most

---

1 *Host Laureate* Wilson is playing on the government-conferred appointment of the "Poet Laureate," a poet who is commissioned to write pieces for state occasions. Wilson is suggesting that Ghomeshi, as a radio host, had a similar status in Canada's elite circles.

2 *folk-rock band* Ghomeshi played drums and sang for the band Moxy Früvous from 1989 to 2001.

3 *freelance writer* Jesse Brown, Canadian journalist; *podcast* Brown's podcast, *Canadaland*, focuses on media criticism.

anonymously, but two by name. The allegations include belts and bruises and concrete walls. Toronto police announce that they are investigating three complaints.

As you follow all of this, you remember reading the words of Pope Francis when he held a special Mass at the Vatican this summer for visiting survivors of clerical sexual abuse: He spoke of "despicable actions, camouflaged by a complicity that cannot be explained."

You were brought up in the Church, sort of. But as a nonbeliever, you bolted like a cat as early as you could. As the international scandal about priests and young boys unfolded over the ensuing decades, you were grateful you'd distanced yourself when you did. You watched mostly with an outsider's outraged disbelief: How could these parishes and hierarchies have tolerated and hushed up these patterns for so long? That question, and that quotation, return to haunt you now.

Despite what you knew, when you were invited on Jian's show, you went. And went again. Though you found his manner slick and off-putting, you were friendly with him. You played nice. You never saw each other socially, but you chatted. His interview style sometimes seemed patronizing, particularly with female guests; you were surprised so much of the audience found him charming, rather than smarmy. Then again, he was always well-prepared and well-scripted.

The banter about Jian's annoying pick-up-artist persona continued. One summer evening at a Toronto outdoor indie-rock festival, a friend was tipsy, talking about him a bit loudly, when you noticed Jian right behind you, holding a beer. You shushed her. You nodded hi and hoped he hadn't heard, because you wanted to continue being invited on the show. Which you were.

You're sceptical about calling every professional network a community. "I'm a member of the sports-equipment-public-relations community." Come off it. But when you discover that the gauche figure in your field whom you've all grumbled and laughed about is possibly something much worse, you realize it is a community. Because you feel associated. You feel responsible. You stood by. You grinned and took the man's hand.

It's as if no matter where you go, you are in the position so many Catholics have unwillingly found themselves in: You are always in some way part of a community that is studiously ignoring the wrong some man is doing. In this case it was the Canadian arts and media scene. But friends have told you these patterns occur among scientific researchers. In education. In medicine. In theatre. In an activist group, an ethnic community, a queer community, a kibbutz. Men at the top, abusing their influence. Objections murmured mostly behind their backs.

There was a round of similar allegations against men in the literary world just a few weeks ago. Some of your friends knew the accused parties. Some knew the aggrieved women. Not all of the stories were straightforward. Some friends felt torn about accounts being aired online, in public, destroying reputations—about whether to call certain incidents "rape." Others had no such hesitations. Tempers flared.

20 What do you do, you thought then, about actions that make women feel unsafe, violated, but do not cross the line of criminality? About grey zones?* About the creeps in your midst?

Now, you think: If something seems kind of wrong, it is all too possible that it is very wrong.

In Jian's case, you didn't know, of course. But you knew. There was doublethink,* a split consciousness. "Everybody" knew, so perhaps you had no special burden, not compared to his employers, for example. A former *Q* staffer says that after she complained, a CBC executive reminded her to be "malleable." There remain a lot of questions about what happened there.

But maybe you, too, downplayed the problem because facing it might mean making a sacrifice: You liked doing that show. Just as the CBC and the U.S. stations liked having that show. As his publisher liked selling his 1980s memoir. As organizations liked having Jian host. As websites and newspapers liked printing his handsome photos.

And so it went on. And more women ended up hurt. While he allegedly turned his teddy-bear face away.[4]

25 (You contacted Jian to tell him you were writing this piece and get his comment, but he did not respond.)

So what should you have done, back when there were only rumours and snaky vibes?* Refused to be a guest on *Q*? Scowled and been uncivil to Jian in public? Should you have tried to expose him? You didn't have much to go on, and you are not an investigative reporter. Then again, you used to work as an editor at a Toronto newspaper. You could have urged someone to look into it. It just didn't seem clear enough. So you took it too lightly.

If things are fuzzy, the human default is often to do nothing. It's genuinely difficult to conceive and accept that something extreme may be happening, unless you witness it firsthand. Unless it happens to you. And as some of the women's accounts make clear, it can be hard to absorb even then.

The worst thing, you realize, is that you tended to look down on Jian's conquests. As if anyone who fell for his come-ons was a fool, instead of merely lacking the advantage of inside knowledge.

No wonder the women didn't hope to be taken seriously. No wonder most filed no grievances, and none of them laid charges, nor spoke out in public, until they learned they were not alone. They expected not to be believed, and

---

4 *teddy-bear face away* Ghomeshi allegedly turned his teddy bear to face the wall during sexual encounters.

worse, that they would be hounded and humiliated—and the way many *Q* fans have treated them on social media proves them right. Neither did they trust the legal system, for good reason. A lot of your older male journalist friends don't get that: "Why not go to court?" they say on Twitter.

And then, some of the women say they feared that speaking out might 30
jeopardize their careers in Canadian media. "I felt like Jian was CBC god," as one of them puts it. And this is where you feel most implicated, along with your colleagues. In a small country, in an insular profession, the tightness of interconnection holds everything in place, maintains the status quo. Even in a field whose task is allegedly to question the status quo. Where, nonetheless, most of the bosses are still men.

"A complicity that cannot be explained," said the Catholic patriarch. That was bold, but too facile. This denial, the church's in a massive sexual-abuse cover-up, or yours in your cultural circles, was not a fog ordained by God to cloud the mortal mind. It served functions. It was not just something that was broken. It was something that was working all too well. Complicity can be explained. And it must be, because you need to figure out how to break it.

For days, a dynamic, tense discussion unfolds among everyone you know. Friends in the music community speak out. Petitions are started. You exchange links to essays about women's voices, being silenced. How sexual violence is treated unlike other crimes. You post on Facebook about your unsettled feelings about your role, about having played nice.

Your friend Becky, an improv comedian, remarks: "One always has a responsibility not to play nice when one knows one shouldn't. Unfortunately, having a responsibility does not make actions easier or more possible. It's just that we live in hell and awful people are in charge." That makes you laugh, which helps.

But it doesn't help enough. Already, amid the racket, you have heard new whispers, about other men. You don't want to believe them. But you do. So far, you have done nothing about it.

(2014)

Questions

1. Do you think that members in "cultural circles" such as Wilson's in Toronto (the downtown arts scene) were complicit in keeping Ghomeshi's "creepiness" under wraps? What responsibility do people have to respond to persistent rumours about someone in their community?
2. How did Ghomeshi's position in the arts and media community in Toronto affect the author's behaviour towards him? How do the dynamics of power affect the reporting of, and prosecution of, sexual assault?

Jessamyn Hope

The Reverse

This memoir essay was originally published in PRISM International, *a Vancouver-based literary magazine. It later appeared in* Best Canadian Essays 2015 *and received a Pushcart Prize honourable mention.*

3:30

"Today's the day," said Andrea, my diving coach, standing with her thick legs apart, back arched, meaty arms crossed over her large bosom. "Today's the goddamn day."

I nodded. My crotch tingled as if I needed to pee, but I knew that was impossible. Before leaving the locker room, I had balanced over the toilet three times, the last time unable to squeeze out a single drop of fear.

Andrea squinted at the bleachers on the other side of the indoor swimming pool, where my friend Theresa sat like a small sun, her light-blond bangs shooting ten centimetres into the air and fanning open. To achieve this gravity-defying look Theresa would soak her bangs in hairspray and then press them, panini-style, between two books. The rest of her hair fell softly to her shoulders, framing her small, vulpine face, which was twisting around a jawbreaker. Without the bangs, scrawny Theresa barely made five feet.

Andrea ran her hand through her short, russety hair and said, "What is that punk doing here again? Does she have a crush on you? Tell your lesbo friend to take off."

5 "She's not a lesbian," I said, having only a vague idea of what a lesbian was and no idea of what a lesbian did. Actually, my sole image of a lesbian was Andrea, because that's what one of the older divers had called her last week, the same boy who, to my utter bafflement, always called Greg Louganis "Greg Loose-Anus."

Andrea clapped her hands and pointed at me between the eyes. "Listen, my little Star of David,* if you don't do the reverse dive today, you're out. Off the team! You've been wriggling your way out of it for months. If you don't do the dive by"—Andrea looked toward the big round clock hanging high on the cement wall—"four o'clock, that's it. You can walk your coward's ass on out of here, clean out your locker, and never show your face at this pool again."

3:36

I took my time going through the warm-up exercises on the blue gym mats to the left of the boards. I grimaced through twenty lunges and fifteen push-ups.

While doing my sixty sit-ups, I pictured how nice it was going to be two hours from now—diving practice behind me, Theresa and I down at the shops, eating poutine out of Styrofoam containers, a full twenty-two hours to go before I had to be at the pool again.

The Pointe-Claire municipal pool had no windows, yet somehow a sense of the January outside—already dark at this early hour and twenty-five below—mingled with the smell of chlorine. Under a very steep, church-like roof, high enough to accommodate a ten-metre diving platform, lay Canada's first Olympic-sized swimming pool, built in 1967. Twenty-one years later, it was still the training ground for the country's best swimming and diving team, and a number of Olympic medalists and World Record holders were diving off its boards that very afternoon. All around me were strong, beautiful bodies: practicing handstands, somersaulting high above the trampoline, bounding off the springboards and soaring into the air as if they had a different relationship with gravity, seeming to suspend a moment, arms spread open, before falling toward the water straight as a spear. After emerging from the pool, wet and glistening, they would grab their pastel shammies* and whip each other's bums, joking and laughing as if we were doing something fun here.

I lay back on the blue mat and stared up at the roof's crisscrossing rafters. 10
That I would sooner or later have to do a reverse dive—where a diver jumps off the board facing forward, but then flips backward, toward the board—had been haunting me for over a year. When I set off for my first diving practice, my dad said he was allowing me to take up the sport on one condition: that I never, ever do a reverse dive, which in his South African English accent he called "a gainer." To make doubly sure I obeyed, he claimed that on any summer day, half the people in an emergency room were there thanks to gainers.

Why was Dad so alarmist about reverse dives? Probably because five years earlier in Edmonton, a diver from the Soviet Union named Sergei Chalibashvili smacked his head while doing a reverse dive and died. I was too young to remember the accident, but it must have been in all the Canadian papers because Chalibashvili, to this day, is the only diver to be killed during an international competition. What happened after the medics carried Chalibashvili away is diving lore: Greg Louganis, who'd been standing on the ten-metre platform when Chalibashvili's head hit it, after peeking over the edge and seeing the water filled with blood, had to go ahead and do the exact same dive—a reverse with three-and-a-half somersaults—a dive Louganis himself had hit his head doing a few years earlier in Tbilisi, USSR, which just so happened to be Chalibashvili's hometown.

I had recently seen the video of Louganis hitting his head back in 1979 in Tbilisi. They had replayed it on TV that past October after he once again hit his head doing a reverse at the Summer Games in Seoul. If I hadn't already been terrified of the dive, I would have been after seeing that old black-and-white footage. It came to me again as I lay on the blue mat, Louganis smashing his skull against the hard platform and then, head joggling as if he were a bobblehead doll, losing consciousness in midair and just falling, limply falling, until he met the water with a flat back.

"Hey there, Sleeping Beauty." Andrea's ruddy face stared down at me. She was bent over, hands on her knees, the roof sloping up behind her. "Would you like a pillow?"

3:41

My first warm-up dive—a simple front dive from the one-metre—did not go well.

"Like piss hitting a plate," Andrea said as I pushed out of the pool. She was leaning back in her steel fold-up chair, one ankle resting on her knee, her hands propped on her wide waist.

I grabbed my blue shammy off the bleacher and wiped down my arms and legs.

Eyeing my white thighs, Andrea said, "You're not the skinnymalink you were a few months ago. You're getting boobs and hips, eh? Too bad. Harder to slice the water like a knife when you've got bags of fat hanging off you. Not impossible, but harder."

I nodded as if I were to blame for the new breasts pushing against the plasticky white windmill on the front of my swimsuit. The team emblem was the Pointe-Claire Windmill, "the oldest windmill in Montreal," built by Sulpician priests[1] in 1709, when the only other people leaving snow prints on this part of the island were the Iroquois.* That was hundreds of years before the land became a suburb of the city, covered in track homes and strip malls, and more than 250 years before my parents would immigrate to Canada, but it never occurred to me that this windmill wasn't a part of my history. I was very proud of that team swimsuit. The first time I put it on, I stood in front of my bedroom mirror, hands down at my sides, chin raised like a soldier at attention, thinking, Look at that, you're an athlete now.

---

1 *Sulpician priests* Members of the Society of Saint-Sulpice, an organization of Catholic priests. Founded in Paris, the society played a substantial role in Montreal's early history.

Back in line for the board, I waited behind Jackie, a buck-toothed girl who was, it could not be denied, a truly good diver now. When the two of us first made the team, I bad been a far better diver. I had been the best of all the rookies. Until recently I had always been the best at whatever I did: the fastest runner on the street, the highest climber of trees, the top student in Greendale Elementary. I had played Snow White in a production downtown, singing and dancing for an audience of hundreds while an understudy almost twice my age waited in the wings. But lately, everything had become a lot harder. My last report card, hidden under my mattress since the summer, had been a column of Cs. My parents were too preoccupied, first fighting over Dad's friendship with his new secretary, then driving Mom back and forth to the Royal Vic for "treatments," to notice I never gave it to them. Six months later I was still debating whether I had the moral obligation to bring the shameful report card to their attention. The director of my drama school, after failing to give me a lead role in *West Side Story*,* asked, "Whatever happened, Jessamyn, to your beautiful voice?" And all the other new divers had gotten better, executing dives with higher and higher degrees of difficulty, while my dives stayed the same, leaving me the worst diver on the team.

I have to do this dive today, I thought. I have to do it. It would be proof 20
that I wasn't going to be a failure from here on out, that I wasn't going to be the remarkable little girl who grew up to be a big sad disappointment, that I was still on track to be a remarkable woman, the kind of woman who didn't let fear stand in her way. If I didn't do this dive, I would officially be a coward. Never to do anything great. Never to be admired. Or loved, not truly loved, the way Gilbert Blythe loved Anne Shirley. Gilbert never would've been so taken by Anne, yearning for her year after year, if she hadn't been the bravest and most talented girl he had ever met. This was my last chance to prove that I was an Anne of Green Gables, Jo March, Scarlett O'Hara.[2]

3:47

After messing up another front dive, I swam for the pool's edge without coming up for air. The world above was a muffled blur. As long as I was underwater, everything was on hold.

Andrea pretended I was invisible when I climbed out of the pool, looking all around except at me, as if my dive had been too terrible to be real.

I got back in line for the board, teeth chattering. Squeezing the water out of my black braid, I peeked up at the clock. Thirteen more minutes. Maybe I really did have to pee now?

---

2 *Anne of Green Gables* Protagonist of the classic 1908 novel of the same name, by Lucy Maud Montgomery; *Jo March* Protagonist of *Little Women* (1868–69), another classic novel; *Scarlett O'Hara* Protagonist of Margaret Mitchell's 1936 classic *Gone with the Wind*. All three of the characters mentioned here are young, dynamic women.

I looked over at Theresa, still sitting on the bleacher, chewing her jawbreaker. Catching my eyes on her, she lifted her small hand and turned up her small mouth. I smiled back, thinking, Why? Why did she come with me, every afternoon, across the slushy boulevard from our high school to the pool? I knew Theresa was needy, everybody knew it. There wasn't a girl in our grade Theresa hadn't dragged into a photobooth, as if she required evidence she had friends. Still, lonely or not, how could she stand it, sitting on that bleacher, day after day, watching other kids work hard to get good at something? Didn't it bother her that she wasn't good at anything?

When I first started spending my evenings with Theresa, hanging at the shops and staying late at her townhouse, often sleeping over since Theresa lived around the corner from our high school, my mom didn't like it. She said, "'Theresa's mom's never home. All you eat there are microwaved hotdogs"—a comment so out of character for my mother, a woman who made Toblerone* fondue for dinner, that it still niggles at me decades later. My mother was an Italian immigrant, a stay-at-home mom, but she never said conventional "mom" things, never scrunched her nose at other women and their homes, and there's just something about that microwaved-hotdog comment that I can't quite put my finger on.

Mom didn't press the point, though. How could she, when we weren't eating much better at home? Not since the breast cancer came back for the third time, and Mom and Dad finally told me about the other two times, because this time was guaranteed to be the last. If Mom wasn't at the hospital, she was either sitting in the family room on the puffy black recliner, wearing her oversized auburn wig, a neck brace, and a scowl, or she was locked in her bedroom with the silver vomit dish, mostly in silence, though once I heard her cry out: "Please, dear God, just kill me already!" As for Theresa's mom, I had no idea where she was. I never asked. I just made the most of her absence.

A full year of school nights at Theresa's townhouse, and all I'm left with now are a few flashes: my hands bringing a plate of frozen hotdogs up to the microwave; Theresa cackling as she pulled a strand of condoms out of her mother's half-packed suitcase; sitting cross-legged on the beige carpet, passing the telephone back and forth while we talked on the Party Line to "Nine-Inch Brian," whom Theresa told, unable to suppress her cackle, that we were Catholic schoolgirls.

Who would have thought that an adult man would desire a schoolgirl? But Theresa knew things at a time, in those last years before the internet, when it wasn't so easy to find things out. It wasn't a prudish era; sex was everywhere—Calvin Klein ads, slapstick comedies, music videos (George Michael wanted yours)—but exactly what everybody was talking about could remain, sometimes for years, unclear, a little fuzzy, like those scrambled soft-core movies that came on after midnight. Only Theresa, between "fuck this" and "fuck that," bandied about terms like *blowjob* and *rimmer* and *double-team* like she totally knew what they meant, always followed by her machine-gun HA HA HA HA HA!

That's why it was such a surprise when, earlier that year, in the middle of Sex Ed, while we were watching a close-up of a baby's hairy head pushing out of a stretched vagina, Theresa fainted. She timbered out of her chair—the shadow of her spiky bangs passing over the screen—and landed with a crash in front of the film projector.

3:50

"Show time!" Andrea said, when I popped my head out of the water after finally 30
doing a decent front dive. "Time to shine, Star of David."

I looked to the clock. "You said I had until four!"

"Jessamyn!"

"Please," I begged, clasping the side of the pool. "Can't I do a few more warm-up dives?"

"One more," Andrea said, holding a finger up in front of her face as if I didn't know what one meant.

I glanced back at Theresa who shook her head like "fuck that." Andrea 35
followed my eyes and ordered me to go tell my loser friend to get lost.

I said, "I won't look at her again, I promise."

"She's creepy. Tell her to go home."

I walked around the pool, hunched, arms twisted in front of my chest. Instead of walking around the boards, I took the long way, circumnavigating the swimming lanes with their furious back-and-forth of goggled swimmers. At the far end of the pool, I paused to watch Katherine, only one year older than me, all the way up on the ten-metre platform, standing still, mentally preparing for her dive. When she started to run, my chest rose and the breath caught in my throat. She leapt off the platform with her arms above her head, whipped them forward, and started falling while spinning, not in a ball, but bent in two at the waist, arms wrapped around her straight legs, going round and round, and opening up just in time to pierce the water. I exhaled, and thought about how good it must feel to be a work of art.

"Coach says you have to go."

Theresa's eyes were as blue and clear as the pool. Judging by her tongue 40
and lips, her jawbreaker had been blue too.

"Bitch," Theresa said. "I still don't get why she keeps calling you Star of David. Who the fuck is David?"

"Seriously, you have to leave right now."

"You don't have to do it, you know."

"Yeah, I do. You need a reverse to compete."

"Why do you have to compete?"

"Because that's what it means to do a sport, Theresa," I said, although I knew that I no longer had to do the reverse to compete. I had to do it to quit. Do this one last dive, and I could walk away with dignity. "I told you, I have to push myself."

"Why do you have to push yourself?"

I glanced back at Andrea who opened her hands in a "What's taking so long?" gesture.

Turning back to Theresa, I said, "Honestly, I don't know why I hang out with you."

"Fuck you!" Theresa said with a cackle-laugh and picked up her army backpack. "I'll wait for you in the foyer."

As I walked back around the pool, again the long way, again hunched with my arms folded in front of my chest, a doughnut popped into my head—a soft white yeasty doughnut topped with chocolate icing and pink and blue sprinkles. Without fail, this doughnut came to me every practice. I could see it, smell it, almost taste it. The vision of this doughnut, sitting on a piece of wax paper on a red counter in front of a giant mirror bordered by vanity lights, was at once ironclad and hazy, as first memories tend to be. When I was four years old and taking swimming lessons at the indoor pool closer to our house in Dollard-des-Ormeaux, my mom would buy me a doughnut to eat afterward, and this doughnut would be in the locker room waiting for me to finish changing into dry cloches. Cavernous indoor pool, fear of drowning, followed by a doughnut.

3:57

Upon my return, Andrea said, "That took too long. No more warm-up dives."

I looked to the clock. "You said I had until four!"

"Jesus Christ, Jessamyn! Have some mercy on me."

"You said I had until four."

"By the time you're on the board, it'll be four."

3:58

Jackie climbed onto the green springboard, and I moved to next in line. One year younger than me, Jackie still had her childhood body. She adjusted the fulcrum,[3] moving the knob back with her pale foot and spindly leg.

Crossing my legs against the pee feeling, I ran through the reverse in my head, because that was what all the great athletes said you should do. Never think while moving, they said. Imagine yourself doing the perfect dive (or

---

3 *fulcrum* Mechanism to set the amount of spring on a diving board.

dunk or catch or whatever) over and over again, so when the time comes, your body just does it, automatically, with grace.

I'm standing in the middle of the board, facing the pool. I take the first step of the three-step hurdle. The second step, the third. I jump onto both feet at the end of the board and, as it's bowing beneath me, I bend my knees and jump as it springs back, jump high, not out, and when I'm as high as I'll go, no sooner, I open my arms while looking back ...

But if I did as I was supposed to, and only thought about jumping high 60
off the board, not away from it, how was I supposed to make sure I didn't hit my head? And if those great athletes were right, that you'll naturally do what you've been imagining, then what was going to happen after I've been imagining smacking my head all day?

3:59

Jackie stood at the end of the board, her back to the pool as if she were going to do a back dive, but she was preparing to do an inward, where a diver jumps backward and then flips inward, toward the board. Her pale, freckled face was stern, her big blue eyes focussed. Her long black lashes were in wet, doll-like clumps. Jackie would have been one of the prettiest girls on the team if not for the gigantic buckteeth that prevented her from ever fully closing her mouth.

When she raised her hands above her head, I thought, oh god, here we go. In two seconds, she'll be done, and I'm up. Jackie jumped, whipped her hands forward, somersaulted in a fast tight tuck, and opened up—

I gasped. Andrea did too.

Jackie's face met the board. She didn't skim her forehead. Her entire face smashed into the board, flat down. The board bent under the pressure and lobbed Jackie off, in an arc, blood sputtering off her face like a summer sprinkler. She landed on her back, the water swallowing her and blooming red.

It felt as if I had wished this on her, as if my imaginings had been that 65
powerful. And yet, that wasn't why I felt so guilty. No, the guilt came with the sweet giddy relief, the weightless tingly sense of good fortune. Now I wouldn't have to do the reverse. Maybe tomorrow, but not today.

"Call 9-1-1!" Andrea shouted as she ran and dove into the water. She surfaced with Jackie and sidestroked back with her under her arm. Jackie fumbled for the steel ladder—at least she was conscious. After managing to climb a rung, Jackie stopped, opened her mouth, and the blood waterfalled out. All of her ugly teeth were gone.

A lifeguard pressed a towel against Jackie's mouth, while another lifeguard, wrapping a towel around her shoulders, said, "You're okay, you're okay, you're okay."

"An ambulance is on the way," came a cry from across the pool.

Everyone stood and watched from the deck, the one-metre boards, the threemetres, the seven, and the ten, as the lifeguards escorted Jackie out.

4:14

70 "Okay, your reverse," Andrea said, towelling off her hair.

I widened my eyes at her

The rest of the divers, after respectfully waiting for Jackie to disappear into the locker room, had gone back to work. The blood had dissipated into the giant pool, been disinfected by the chlorine. The place was loud again with the thud of boards and the swimming coaches' impatient whistles.

Andrea said, "If you don't do it now, you'll never do it. It's a falling off the horse sort of thing."

Louganis after Chalibashvili.

75 This had become an even bigger test of my heroism.

"Go on," Andrea said. "The longer you wait, the scarier it's going to be."

I turned from Andrea and walked toward the board. I climbed its ladder with my heart pounding hard and fast. No urge to pee. I hardly felt my body. Only the thudding heart. How was I going to control my body if I couldn't feel it?

"Hey!" Andrea said, approaching the side of the board with her hands held high, making a triangle with her thumbs and forefingers.

I made the same triangle but upside-down, and we brought our triangles together.

80 She said, "Star of David! Powers activate!"

Andrea forced me to do this ritual she had invented every time I was attempting a new or difficult dive. Was she laughing at my being a Jew? Maybe a little. But mostly, I think, she was trying to give me a laugh and wish me good luck. Whenever she said it, I thought of this gold pendant Dad used to wear, a rather large, slanted Star of David that nestled in his chest hair while we played in the swimming pools of Daytona. My favourite game was "The Rocket," where Dad would crouch underwater and I would climb onto his shoulders and he would spring up and I would go rocketing into the air. That was back when I wore a Wonder Woman swimsuit and Mom still had hair, dyed-red, carefully curled hair, which is why she would only wade around in the shallow end, careful to keep her head above the water and out of the way of The Rocket. But I always assumed she was watching me soar into the air, thinking, My daughter, such a daredevil!

Andrea stepped back. I took my position in the middle of the board. I brought my feet together, straightened my back, and lowered my hands by my sides.

4:16

"One!" shouted Andrea when minutes later I was still standing in place.

I didn't turn to look at her. I stayed in position, eyes forward, but she haunted my peripheral vision with her hands cupped around her mouth.

"Two! If I get to ten and you still haven't done it, that's it! You're done!"

What was she doing? How was I supposed to concentrate with her yelling like that?

"Three!"

Her voice boomed everything else into silence. The thud of the boards ceased again. I tried not to look, but my eyes leapt about against my will. Everyone, the Olympic hopefuls and medalists, the other coaches, the newbies who were far better than me now, had all stopped to watch. Even a few swimmers had gathered to the right of my board.

"Four!"

You have to do this, I thought. You have to do it. Do it.

"Five!"

The doughnut. What? Why the doughnut now!

"Six!"

I knew what those great athletes meant by not thinking, I really did. Once I had been able to do it, to simply be, simply move, trust, trust that things were going to be fine, better than fine, good, perfect, but now I couldn't get my mind to shut up to shut up to shut up just shut up and go go go

"Seven!"

Go go go go go go go

"Eight!"

Oh my god, oh my god, I'm going. I'm going! Look, my bare foot taking the first step.

"Nine!"

The second step, oh oh am I really doing this, the third step, I'm still not sure, I'm jumping onto both feet at the end of the board, bending my legs, and—

There I remained. Frozen. On bent knees. The very picture of a cower.

Andrea didn't bother with "Ten." Everyone watched as I straightened my legs, but not my shoulders, turned around, and made my way back down the board.

Andrea shook her head. "Go pack your stuff."

4:33

Alone in the communal showers, under a jet of hot water, I stood for a long time, half hoping Andrea would come and tell me that it was okay, she was just trying to play hard ball, I was still on the team, and half hoping I would never lay eyes on her again. It dawned on me that I was in the middle of a second test, that Andrea was out there right now, standing by the board, waiting to see if I would come back and beg for a second chance to prove myself.

5:00

105 Out in the foyer, Theresa looked up from her paperback copy of *Cujo*.[4]

She asked, "Did you do it?"

I shook my head. My backpack was filled with all the things I wouldn't be needing anymore: Ultraswim shampoo, the shammy, the swimsuit with the iron-on windmill.

"Good," Theresa said, slipping her arm through mine.

I shoved her arm away and pushed through the glass doors into the wintery night. Since it was considered nerdy to acknowledge the cold, neither one of us wore hats, mitts, or boots, just acid-wash jean jackets, Theresa's hanging off her shoulders, and Converse high-tops. In seconds my wet hair would harden into Medusa[5]-like icicles.

110 The sidewalk in front of the building was lined with cars, parents waiting in the drivers' seats, headlights on. My mom's face used to wait for me behind the windshield of an old boxy white Buick—her high, plump cheeks, thin lips, green angora beret over her red hair, black winged eyeliner magnifying her already big, black eyes. I could always tell when her eyes caught sight of me coming toward the car. She didn't smile or wave, but she just looked happier, reanimated, as she turned the key in the ignition. I would climb into the heated Buick and Billy Joel* would sing us down Saint John's Boulevard, past the big shopping centre and fast food huts. If we didn't pick up Harvey's* or McDonald's on the way home, she would make a huge bowl of her chunky french fries with the skins still on, which I would soak in salt and vinegar and eat sitting on the brown carpet behind the coffee table, watching *Today's Special*, followed by *The Cosby Show*, *Family Ties*, *Cheers*, *Night Court*.[6] There were no quotas on TV in our house.

And it hits me, not then, but today, thirty years later. Thirty years too late. I'm lying on my side in bed, my husband asleep behind me, and I'm nodding off after a day spent writing out this memory—the reverse, the reverse—when my eyes pop open. I clutch the comforter and stare into the darkness of the

---

4 *Cujo* Popular 1981 horror novel by Stephen King.

5 *Medusa* Monstrous woman of Greek mythology with snakes instead of hair.

6 *Today's Special* Canadian television show for children featuring a store mannequin who comes to life at night; *The Cosby ... Night Court* American television comedies popular during the 1980s.

bedroom, a dark bedroom in New York City, so far away from there, from then, from that autumn morning Mom stood in the sunlit foyer in her red velvet housecoat and, watching me put on my jean jacket, asked whether I was planning to go to Theresa's again after diving. Mom probably no longer filled out the red housecoat; it probably hung on hunched, bony shoulders. She probably no longer filled out her face, but I can't say for sure because I wouldn't look at her face, at those harrowed black eyes. She said, "I don't like it. All you eat there are microwaved hotdogs," as I walked out the door. No wonder those words wouldn't go away. How could I have been so slow? Knowing she had only a few months left with her daughter, Mom was saying, hey, instead of going to Theresa's every night, I would really like it if you came home. But she couldn't say that, knowing the whole reason I wasn't coming home was because she was there, dying.

Theresa said, "Hey, Jess. You have no reason to be mad at me. I didn't do anything. I didn't kick you off the team."

Theresa was right, so I nodded, but I still couldn't look at her. We crossed the snowy parking lot, its streetlamps throwing small circles of light on the compacted snow. Empty white spotlights. The grief was breathtaking. Not for Mom yet, but for me.

I was gone.

(2014)

Questions

1. How might the reverse dive be read as a symbol in this piece?
2. Consider the last line of this essay: "I was gone." What does it mean?
3. In this essay a few insensitive terms, such as "lesbo" and "Star of David," are used in reference to people. What functions do these play in the essay?
4. This essay incorporates three major elements: the author's experience on the diving team, her friendship with Theresa, and the terminal illness of the author's mother. How are these elements related?

IRA BOUDWAY

NBA REFS LEARNED THEY WERE RACIST, AND THAT MADE THEM LESS RACIST

The following article, reporting on the results of a study by Devin Pope, Joseph Price, and Justin Wolfers, was posted on the Bloomberg news website 7 February 2014. The 2013 study that the article describes was a follow-up to a 2007 study—Price and Wolfers' "Racial Discrimination among NBA Referees." Both the 2007 and the 2013 studies were widely reported in the media. (The 2013 study is also referenced in a Nicholas Kristof column that is included in these pages.)

In some scholarly disciplines there can be a long lag between initial publication of preliminary research results and final publication in a scholarly journal. In this case, both the 2007 study and the more recent one were initially published as working papers; the working paper presenting the research results discussed in Boudway's article appeared in December 2013 as "National Bureau of Economic Research Working Paper No. 19765," and also in February of 2014 in the Brookings Institution's Working Paper series. A revised version of the 2007 study was published in 2010 in The Quarterly Journal of Economics*; as of June 2017 a revised version of the 2013 study had yet to appear in a scholarly journal.*

Seven years ago, a pair of scholars released a study of NBA* referees that found white officiating crews more likely to call fouls against black players—and, to a lesser degree, black officiating crews more likely to call fouls against white players. The study drew broad media attention and caused a small stir in the league. Then-Commissioner David Stern, questioned its validity in the *New York Times*, and players weighed in on sports-talk radio and ESPN.*

The same scholars, Justin Wolfers of the University of Michigan and Joseph Price of Brigham Young University, returned to the subject of racially biased referees in a working paper released in December with an astounding result.

Once the results of the original study were widely known, the bias disappeared. "When we conduct the same tests for own-race bias in the period immediately following the media coverage," they wrote, "we find none exists."

The original data set came from the 1991–2002 NBA seasons. In the new study, in which the original scholars worked with Devin Pope of the Booth School of Business, the authors looked both at a sample from the 2003–2006 seasons—after the original data but before the public attention—and from 2007–2010. From 2003 to 2006, the bias persisted at the same level, roughly an extra fifth of a foul every 48 minutes. But from 2007 to 2010, they found no significant bias in either direction.

In explaining why this happened, the authors argue that public awareness itself shaped referee behaviour. The NBA, they wrote, did not increase the frequency of mixed-race officiating crews or otherwise take action after the release of the initial study:

> A phone conversation with NBA league administrators who oversee the NBA's officiating department suggests that the NBA did not take any specific action to eliminate referee discrimination. Specifically, the administrators to whom we spoke denied that the NBA spoke with the referees about the Price and Wolfers study. They also indicated that the study did not lead to a change in referee incentives or a change in the way they train their referees.

Simply knowing that bias was present and that other people knew, they wrote, made it go away:

> We argue that this dramatic decrease in bias is a causal result of the awareness associated with the treatment—the release and subsequent publicity surrounding the original academic study in 2007.

The study may hold implications for any organization looking to reduce group bias. In the realms of public policy and education, the focus is often on increased exposure and proximity to out groups. But bias, as the original referee study showed, can sometimes withstand proximity. The remedy might be to locate bigotry and bring it into the light. As Louis Brandeis famously wrote in 1913:[1] "Publicity is justly commended as a remedy for social and industrial diseases. Sunlight is said to be the best of disinfectants; electric light the most efficient policeman."

(2014)

---

1 *Louis Brandeis ... 1913* This well-known quotation from Brandeis (who later became a member of the Supreme Court), first appeared in *Harper's Weekly* magazine in an article entitled "What Publicity Can Do."

Questions

1. What are the findings of the study examining the 1991–2002 NBA seasons, and how do they compare to the same authors' findings regarding the 2003–2006 seasons? What about the 2007–2010 seasons? How do the authors account for the pattern of similarities and differences over time?
2. Do the reported findings adequately justify the title of this piece? What evidence does the article cite to prove the title's causal claim about learning and behaviour?
3. What strategy does Boudway suggest for eliminating racial bias beyond the NBA? Under what (if any) circumstances do you think this strategy would be effective? Under what (if any) circumstances do you think it would be ineffective?

Rebecca Solnit

Climate Change Is Violence

The first of the two selections reprinted here appeared in Solnit's 2014 book The Encyclopedia of Trouble and Spaciousness, *an alphabetically arranged collection of 29 essays on politics, history, geography, and culture; other entries under "C" include "Cults, Creeps, California in the 1970s," "Concrete in Paradise," and "The Colorado River and Hydrological Madness of the West."*

The second Solnit essay included here was first published in the October 2015 issue of Harper's *magazine.*

Climate change is global-scale violence against places and species, as well as against human beings. Once we call it by name, we can start having a real conversation about our priorities and values.

But if you're tremendously wealthy, you can practise industrial-scale violence without any manual labour on your own part. You can, say, build a sweatshop factory that will collapse in Bangladesh and kill more people than any hands-on mass murderer ever did,* or you can calculate risk and benefit about putting poisons or unsafe machines into the world, as manufacturers do every day. If you're the leader of a country, you can declare war and kill by the hundreds of thousands or millions. And the nuclear superpowers—the United States and Russia—still hold the option of destroying quite a lot of life on Earth.

So do the carbon barons. But when we talk about violence, we almost always talk about violence from below, not above.

Or so I thought when I received a press release from a climate group announcing that "scientists say there is a direct link between changing climate and an increase in violence." What the scientists actually said, in a not-so-newsworthy article in *Nature* a few years ago, is that there is higher conflict in the tropics in El Nino years and that perhaps this will scale up to make our age of climate change also an era of civil and international conflict.

The message is that ordinary people will behave badly in an era of intensi- 5
fied climate change. All this makes sense, unless you go back to the premise

and note that climate change is itself violence. Extreme, horrific, long-term, widespread violence.

Climate change is anthropogenic—caused by human beings, some much more than others. We know the consequences of that change: the acidification of oceans and decline of many species in them, the slow disappearance of island nations such as the Maldives, increased flooding, drought, crop failure leading to food-price increases and famine, increasingly turbulent weather. (Think Hurricane Sandy and the recent typhoon in the Philippines and heat waves that kill elderly people by the tens of thousands.)

Climate change is violence.

So if we want to talk about violence and climate change, then let's talk about climate change as violence. Rather than worrying about whether ordinary human beings will react turbulently to the destruction of the very means of their survival, let's worry about that destruction—and their survival.

Of course, water failure, crop failure, flooding, and more will lead to mass migration and climate refugees—they already have—and this will lead to conflict. Those conflicts are being set in motion now.

10 You can regard the Arab Spring,[1] in part, as a climate conflict: the increase in wheat prices was one of the triggers for that series of revolts that changed the face of northernmost Africa and the Middle East. On the one hand, you can say, how nice if those people had not been hungry in the first place. On the other, how can you not say, how great is it that those people stood up against being deprived of sustenance and hope? And then you have to look at the systems that created that hunger—the enormous economic inequalities in places such as Egypt and the brutality used to keep down the people at the lower levels of the social system, as well as the weather.

People revolt when their lives are unbearable. Sometimes material reality creates that unbearableness: droughts, plagues, storms, floods. But food and medical care, health and well-being, access to housing and education—these things are also governed by economic means and government policy. That's what the revolt called Occupy Wall Street* was against.

Climate change will increase hunger as food prices rise and food production falters, but we already have widespread hunger on Earth, and much of it is due not to the failures of nature and farmers, but to systems of distribution. Almost 16 million children in the United States now live with hunger, according to the U.S. Department of Agriculture, and that is not because the vast, agriculturally rich United States cannot produce enough to feed all of us. We are a country whose distribution system is itself a kind of violence.

---

1 *Arab Spring* Series of popular uprisings in Tunisia, Egypt, and other Middle Eastern countries in the spring of 2011. In several countries these uprisings led to an overthrow of the government.

Climate change is not suddenly bringing about an era of equitable distribution. I suspect people will be revolting in the coming future against what they revolted against in the past: the injustices of the system. They should revolt, and we should be glad they do, if not so glad that they need to. (Though one can hope they'll recognize that violence is not necessarily where their power lies.) One of the events prompting the French Revolution was the failure of the 1788 wheat crop, which made bread prices skyrocket and the poor go hungry. The insurance against such events is often thought to be more authoritarianism and more threats against the poor, but that's only an attempt to keep a lid on what's boiling over; the other way to go is to turn down the heat.

The same week during which I received that ill-thought-out press release about climate and violence, Exxon Mobil Corporation issued a policy report. It makes for boring reading, unless you can make the dry language of business into pictures of the consequences of those acts undertaken for profit. Exxon says, "We are confident that none of our hydrocarbon reserves are now or will become 'stranded.' We believe producing these assets is essential to meeting growing energy demand worldwide."

Stranded assets. That means carbon assets—coal, oil, gas still under- 15
ground—would become worthless if we decided they could not be extracted and burned in the near future. Because scientists say that we need to leave most of the world's known carbon reserves in the ground if we are to go for the milder rather than the more extreme versions of climate change. Under the milder version, countless more people, species, and places will survive. In the best-case scenario, we damage the Earth less. We are currently wrangling about how much to devastate the Earth.

In every arena, we need to look at industrial-scale and systemic violence, not just the hands-on violence of the less powerful. When it comes to climate change, this is particularly true. Exxon has decided to bet that we can't make the corporation keep its reserves in the ground, and the company is reassuring its investors that it will continue to profit off the rapid, violent, and intentional destruction of the Earth.

That's a tired phrase, the destruction of the Earth, but translate it into the face of a starving child and a barren field—and then multiply that a few million times. Or just picture the tiny bivalves: scallops, oysters, Arctic sea snails that can't form shells in acidifying oceans right now. Or another superstorm tearing apart another city. Climate change is global-scale violence against places and species, as well as against human beings. Once we call it by name, we can start having a real conversation about our priorities and values. Because the revolt against brutality begins with a revolt against the language that hides that brutality.

(2014)

Questions

1. Solnit claims that "the revolt against brutality begins with a revolt against the language that hides that brutality" (paragraph 17).
   a. Give an example of a place in this article where Solnit describes a political, economic, or environmental phenomenon in terms other than those normally used by those in power. What (if any) rhetorical impact does this have?
   b. Argue for or against Solnit's statement. Is a change in the language we use a necessary precursor to political change?
2. What, according to Solnit, is the relationship between global climate change and the world's socioeconomic system?
3. Read the article "Dr. Bjorn Lomborg Argues the Climate Change Fight Isn't Worth the Cost," also included in this anthology. How do you think Solnit might respond to Lomborg's argument?

THE MOTHER OF ALL QUESTIONS

I gave a talk on Virginia Woolf[2] a few years ago. During the question-and-answer period that followed it, the subject that seemed to most interest a number of people was whether Woolf should have had children. I answered the question dutifully, noting that Woolf apparently considered having children early in her marriage, after seeing the delight that her sister, Vanessa Bell, took in her own. But over time Woolf came to see reproduction as unwise, perhaps because of her own psychological instability. Or maybe, I suggested, she wanted to be a writer and to give her life over to her art, which she did with extraordinary success. In the talk I had quoted with approval her description of murdering "the angel of the house,"[3] the inner voice that tells many women to be self-sacrificing handmaidens to domesticity and male vanity. I was surprised that advocating for throttling the spirit of conventional femininity should lead to this conversation.

---

2 *Virginia Woolf* English novelist and essayist (1882–1941) who played a central role in the development of modernism.

3 *the angel of the house* "The Angel in the House" is an 1854 poem by Coventry Patmore depicting the Victorian ideal of the selfless, domestic wife and mother; the phrase "angel in the house" later became shorthand for this ideal. In her 1931 speech "Professions for Women," Woolf argues that one of the tasks of a woman writer is to kill "the angel in the house."

What I should have said to that crowd was that our interrogation of Woolf's reproductive status was a soporific and pointless detour from the magnificent questions her work poses. (I think at some point I said, "Fuck this shit," which carried the same general message and moved everyone on from the discussion.) After all, many people have children; only one made *To the Lighthouse* and *The Waves*,[4] and we were discussing Woolf because of the books, not the babies.

The line of questioning was familiar enough to me. A decade ago, during a conversation that was supposed to be about a book I had written on politics, the British man interviewing me insisted that instead of talking about the products of my mind, we should talk about the fruit of my loins,* or the lack thereof. Onstage, he hounded me about why I didn't have children. No answer I gave could satisfy him. His position seemed to be that I must have children, that it was incomprehensible that I did not, and so we had to talk about why I didn't, rather than about the books I did have.

As it happens, there are many reasons why I don't have children: I am very good at birth control; though I love children and adore aunthood, I also love solitude; I was raised by unhappy, unkind people, and I wanted neither to replicate their form of parenting nor to create human beings who might feel about me the way that I felt about my begetters; I really wanted to write books, which as I've done it is a fairly consuming vocation. I'm not dogmatic about not having kids. I might have had them under other circumstances and been fine—as I am now.

5 But just because the question can be answered doesn't mean that I ought to answer it, or that it ought to be asked. The interviewer's question was indecent, because it presumed that women should have children, and that a woman's reproductive activities were naturally public business. More fundamentally, the question assumed that there was only one proper way for a woman to live.

But even to say that there's one proper way may be putting the case too optimistically, given that mothers are consistently found wanting, too. A mother may be treated like a criminal for leaving her child alone for five minutes, even a child whose father has left it alone for several years. Some mothers have told me that having children caused them to be treated as bovine non-intellects who should be disregarded. Other women have been told that they cannot be taken seriously professionally because they will go off and reproduce at some point. And many mothers who do succeed professionally are presumed to be neglecting someone. There is no good answer to being a woman; the art may instead lie in how we refuse the question.

We talk about open questions, but there are closed questions, too, questions to which there is only one right answer, at least as far as the interrogator is concerned. These are questions that push you into the herd or nip at you for

4 *To the ... The Waves* Two of Woolf's most acclaimed novels.

diverging from it, questions that contain their own answers and whose aim is enforcement and punishment. One of my goals in life is to become truly rabbinical, to be able to answer closed questions with open questions, to have the internal authority to be a good gatekeeper when intruders approach, and to at least remember to ask, "Why are you asking that?" This, I've found, is always a good answer to an unfriendly question, and closed questions tend to be unfriendly. But on the day of my interrogation about having babies, I was taken by surprise (and severely jet-lagged), and so I was left to wonder—why do such bad questions so predictably get asked?

Maybe part of the problem is that we have learned to ask the wrong things of ourselves. Our culture is steeped in a kind of pop psychology* whose obsessive question is: Are you happy? We ask it so reflexively that it seems natural to wish that a pharmacist with a time machine could deliver a lifetime supply of tranquilizers and antipsychotics to Bloomsbury,[5] so that an incomparable feminist prose stylist could be reoriented to produce litters of Woolf babies.

Questions about happiness generally assume that we know what a happy life looks like. Happiness is understood to be a matter of having a great many ducks lined up in a row—spouse, offspring, private property, erotic experiences—even though a millisecond of reflection will bring to mind countless people who have all those things and are still miserable.

10 We are constantly given one-size-fits-all recipes, but those recipes fail, often and hard. Nevertheless, we are given them again. And again and again. They become prisons and punishments; the prison of the imagination traps many in the prison of a life that is correctly aligned with the recipes and yet is entirely miserable.

The problem may be a literary one: we are given a single story line about what makes a good life, even though not a few who follow that story line have bad lives. We speak as though there is one good plot with one happy outcome, while the myriad forms a life can take flower—and wither—all around us.

Even those who live out the best version of the familiar story line might not find happiness as their reward. This is not necessarily a bad thing. I know a woman who was lovingly married for seventy years. She has had a long, meaningful life that she has lived according to her principles. But I wouldn't call her happy; her compassion for the vulnerable and concern for the future have given her a despondent worldview. What she has had instead of happiness requires better language to describe. There are entirely different criteria for a good life that might matter more to a person—honour, meaning, depth, engagement, hope.

---

5 *Bloomsbury* Woolf was a member of the Bloomsbury Group, a circle of writers, artists, and other intellectuals centred in the Bloomsbury neighborhood of London.

Part of my own endeavour as a writer has been to find ways to value what is elusive and overlooked, to describe nuances and shades of meaning, to celebrate public life and solitary life, and—in John Berger's phrase—to find "another way of telling," which is part of why getting clobbered by the same old ways of telling is disheartening.

The conservative "defense of marriage,"* which is really nothing more than a defense of the old hierarchical arrangement that straight marriage* was before feminists began to reform it, has bled over into the general culture, entrenching the devout belief that there is something magically awesome for children about the heterosexual two-parent household, which leads many people to stay in miserable marriages. I know people who long hesitated to leave horrible marriages because the old recipe insists that somehow a situation that is terrible for one or both parents will be beneficent for the children. Even women with violently abusive spouses are often urged to stay in situations that are supposed to be so categorically wonderful that the details don't matter. Form wins out over content. And yet an amicably divorced woman recently explained to me how ideal it was to be a divorced parent: she and her former spouse both had plenty of time with and without their children.

After I wrote a book about me and my mother, who married a brutal profes- 15
sional man and had four children and often seethed with rage and misery, I was ambushed by an interviewer who asked whether my abusive father was the reason I had failed to find a life partner. Her question was freighted with astonishing assumptions about what I had intended to do with my life. The book, *The Faraway Nearby,* was, I thought, in a quiet, roundabout way about my long journey toward a really nice life, and an attempt to reckon with my mother's fury (including the origin of that fury in her entrapment in conventional feminine roles and expectations).

I have done what I set out to do in my life, and what I set out to do was not what the interviewer presumed. I set out to write books, to be surrounded by generous, brilliant people, and to have great adventures. Men—romances, flings, and long-term relationships—have been some of those adventures, and so have remote deserts, arctic seas, mountaintops, uprisings and disasters, and the exploration of ideas, archives, records, and lives.

Society's recipes for fulfillment cause a great deal of unhappiness, both in those who are stigmatized for being unable or unwilling to carry them out and in those who obey but don't find happiness. Of course there are people with very standard-issue lives who are very happy. I know some of them, just as I know very happy childless and celibate monks, priests, and abbesses, gay divorcees, and everything in between. Last summer my friend Emma was walked down the aisle by her father, with his husband following right behind on Emma's mother's arm; the four of them, plus Emma's new husband, are an exceptionally loving and close-knit family engaged in the pursuit of justice through politics. This summer, both of the weddings I went to had two grooms and no brides; at the first, one of the grooms wept because he had been excluded from the right to marry for most of his life, and he had never thought he would see his own wedding. I'm all for marriage and children, when it and they are truly what people want from their lives.

In the traditional worldview happiness is essentially private and selfish. Reasonable people pursue their self-interest, and when they do so successfully they are supposed to be happy. The very definition of what it means to be human is narrow, and altruism, idealism, and public life (except in the forms of fame, status, or material success) have little place on the shopping list. The idea that a life should seek meaning seldom emerges; not only are the standard activities assumed to be inherently meaningful, they are treated as the only meaningful options.

People lock onto motherhood as a key to feminine identity in part from the belief that children are the best way to fulfill your capacity to love, even though the list of monstrous, ice-hearted mothers is extensive. But there are so many things to love besides one's own offspring, so many things that need love, so much other work love has to do in the world.

20 While many people question the motives of the childless, who are taken to be selfish for refusing the sacrifices that come with parenthood, they often neglect to note that those who love their children intensely may have less love left for the rest of the world. Christina Lupton, a writer who is also a mother, recently described some of the things she relinquished when motherhood's consuming tasks had her in their grasp, including all the ways of tending to the world that are less easily validated than parenting, but which are just as fundamentally necessary for children to flourish. I mean here the writing and inventing and the politics and the activism; the reading and the public speaking and the protesting and the teaching and the filmmaking.... Most of the things I value most, and from which I trust any improvements in the human condition will come, are violently incompatible with the actual and imaginative work of childcare.

One of the fascinating things about Edward Snowden's[6] sudden appearance a little more than two years ago was the inability of many people to comprehend

6 *Edward Snowden* Controversial ex-CIA employee (b. 1983) who copied a large number of classified government documents and released them to journalists in order to expose secret mass surveillance being conducted by the National Security Agency.

why a young man might give up on the recipe for happiness—high wages, secure job, Hawaiian home—to become the world's most sought-after fugitive. Their premise seemed to be that since all people are selfish, Snowden's motive must be a self-serving pursuit of attention or money.

During the first rush of commentary, Jeffrey Toobin, *The New Yorker*'s legal expert, wrote that Snowden was "a grandiose narcissist who deserves to be in prison." Another pundit announced, "I think what we have in Edward Snowden is just a narcissistic young man who has decided he is smarter than the rest of us." Others assumed that he was revealing U.S. government secrets because he had been paid by an enemy country.

Snowden seemed like a man from another century. In his initial communications with journalist Glenn Greenwald he called himself Cincinnatus—after the Roman statesman who acted for the good of his society without seeking self-advancement. This was a clue that Snowden formed his ideals and models far away from the standard-issue formulas for happiness. Other eras and cultures often asked other questions than the ones we ask now: What is the most meaningful thing you can do with your life? What is your contribution to the world or your community? Do you live according to your principles? What will your legacy be? What does your life mean? Maybe our obsession with happiness is a way not to ask those other questions, a way to ignore how spacious our lives can be, how effective our work can be, and how far-reaching our love can be.

There is a paradox at the heart of the happiness question. Todd Kashdan, a psychology professor at George Mason University, reported a few years ago on studies that concluded that people who think being happy is important are more likely to become depressed: "Organizing your life around trying to become happier, making happiness the primary objective of life, gets in the way of actually becoming happy."

I did finally have my rabbinical moment* in Britain. After the jet lag was 25
over, I was interviewed onstage by a woman with a plummy, fluting accent. "So," she trilled, "you've been *wounded* by humanity and *fled* to the landscape for refuge." The implication was clear: I was an exceptionally sorry specimen on display, an outlier in the herd. I turned to the audience and asked, "Have any of you ever been wounded by humanity?" They laughed with me; in that moment, we knew that we were all weird, all in this together, and that addressing our own suffering, while learning not to inflict it on others, is part of the work we're all here to do. So is love, which comes in so many forms and can be directed at so many things. There are many questions in life worth asking, but perhaps if we're wise we can understand that not every question needs an answer.

(2015)

Questions

1. Consider how the last paragraph of this essay relates to the structure of the rest of the piece. How does this paragraph connect to earlier portions of the essay?
2. What alternative or alternatives to the pursuit of happiness does Solnit propose? To what extent does it (or do they) seem to you likely to lead to a good life?
3. Explain Solnit's statement "There is no good answer to being a woman; the art may instead lie in how we refuse the question" (paragraph 6). What are some ways of "refusing the question"?

Claudia Rankine

from Citizen: An American Lyric [On Serena Williams]

In 2014, for the first time in the history of the National Book Critics Circle Awards, the same book was nominated in two different categories: Claudia Rankine's Citizen, *a short, heavily illustrated book exploring various aspects of African American experience in unconventional ways, was a finalist in the Criticism category, and the winner in the Poetry category.*

The excerpt included here is the second of the book's seven, unnamed chapters.

Hennessy Youngman aka Jayson Musson, whose *Art Thoughtz* take the form of tutorials on YouTube, educates viewers on contemporary art issues. In one of his many videos, he addresses how to become a successful black artist, wryly suggesting black people's anger is marketable. He advises black artists to cultivate "an angry nigger exterior"* by watching, among other things, the Rodney King video[1] while working.

Youngman's suggestions are meant to expose expectations for blackness as well as to underscore the difficulty inherent in any attempt by black artists to metabolize real rage. The commodified anger his video advocates rests lightly on the surface for spectacle's sake. It can be engaged or played like the race card* and is tied solely to the performance of blackness and not to the emotional state of particular individuals in particular situations.

On the bridge between this sellable anger and "the artist" resides, at times, an actual anger. Youngman in his video doesn't address this type of anger: the anger built up through experience and the quotidian struggles against dehumanization every brown or black person lives simply because of skin colour. This

1 *the Rodney King video* Video footage from 3 March 1991 showed the violent beating of African American taxi driver Rodney King (1965–2012) by four white Los Angeles police officers. The event heightened awareness of racism in law enforcement, and the subsequent acquittal of the police officers prompted the 1992 Los Angeles Riots.

other kind of anger in time can prevent, rather than sponsor, the production of anything except loneliness.

You begin to think, maybe erroneously, that this other kind of anger is really a type of knowledge: the type that both clarifies and disappoints. It responds to insult and attempted erasure simply by asserting presence, and the energy required to present, to react, to assert is accompanied by visceral disappointment: a disappointment in the sense that no amount of visibility will alter the ways in which one is perceived.

5 Recognition of this lack might break you apart. Or recognition might illuminate the erasure the attempted erasure triggers. Whether such discerning creates a healthier, if more isolated self, you can't know. In any case, Youngman doesn't speak to this kind of anger. He doesn't say that witnessing the expression of this more ordinary and daily anger might make the witness believe that a person is "insane."

And insane is what you think, one Sunday afternoon, drinking an Arnold Palmer,* watching the 2009 Women's US Open semifinal, when brought to full attention by the suddenly explosive behaviour of Serena Williams.[2] Serena in HD before your eyes becomes overcome by a rage you recognize and have been taught to hold at a distance for your own good. Serena's behaviour, on this particular Sunday afternoon, suggests that all the injustice she has played through all the years of her illustrious career flashes before her and she decides finally to respond to all of it with a string of invectives. Nothing, not even the repetition of negations ("no, no, no") she employed in a similar situation years before as a younger player at the 2004 US Open, prepares you for this. Oh my God, she's gone crazy, you say to no one.

What does a victorious or defeated black woman's body in a historically white space look like? Serena and her big sister Venus Williams brought to mind Zora Neale Hurston's[3] "I feel most coloured when I am thrown against a sharp white background." This appropriated line, stenciled on canvas by Glenn Ligon, who used plastic letter stencils, smudging oil sticks, and graphite to transform the words into abstractions, seemed to be ad copy[4] for some aspect of life for all black bodies.

---

2 *US Open* One of the four most important annual tennis tournaments, which together comprise the Grand Slam; *Serena Williams* African American tennis player (b. 1981), often considered the best female tennis player of all time.

3 *Zora Neale Hurston* African American writer (1891–1960), best known for her novel *Their Eyes Were Watching God* (1937). The quotation here appears in her essay "How It Feels to Be Coloured Me," also included in this anthology.

4 *Glenn Ligon* African American artist (b. 1960); *ad copy* Text of an advertisement.

Hurston's statement has been played out on the big screen by Serena and Venus: they win sometimes, they lose sometimes, they've been injured, they've been happy, they've been sad, ignored, booed mightily (see Indian Wells,[5] which both sisters have boycotted for more than a decade), they've been cheered, and through it all and evident to all were those people who are enraged they are there at all—graphite against a sharp white background.

For years you attribute to Serena Williams a kind of resilience appropriate only for those who exist in celluloid. Neither her father nor her mother nor her sister nor Jehovah her God nor NIKE camp could shield her ultimately from people who felt her black body didn't belong on their court, in their world. From the start many made it clear Serena would have done better struggling to survive in the two-dimensionality of a Millet painting, rather than on their tennis court—better to put all that strength to work in their fantasy of her working the land, rather than be caught up in the turbulence of our ancient dramas, like a ship fighting a storm in a Turner[6] seascape.

The most notorious of Serena's detractors takes the form of Mariana Alves, 10
the distinguished tennis chair umpire.[7] In 2004 Alves was excused from officiating any more matches on the final day of the US Open after she made five bad calls against Serena in her quarterfinal matchup against fellow American Jennifer Capriati. The serves and returns Alves called out were landing, stunningly unreturned by Capriati, inside the lines, no discerning eyesight needed. Commentators, spectators, television viewers, line judges, everyone could see the balls were good, everyone, apparently, except Alves. No one could understand what was happening. Serena, in her denim skirt, black sneaker boots, and dark mascara, began wagging her finger and saying "no, no, no," as if by negating the moment she could propel us back into a legible world. Tennis superstar John McEnroe,[8] given his own keen eye for injustice during his professional career, was shocked that Serena was able to hold it together after losing the match.

---

5 *Indian Wells* Tennis tournament held annually in Indian Wells, California. In 2001, the Williams sisters and their father Richard Williams were booed, and some in the crowd shouted racial slurs.

6 *Millet* Jean-François Millet (1815–75), French painter best known for paintings depicting peasant farmers; *Turner* J.M.W. Turner (1775–1851), English painter whose works often depicted scenes of ships in stormy seas. (Rankine includes reproductions of his painting *Slave Ship* and of a detail from the painting as the final images in *Citizen*.)

7 *chair umpire* In tennis, person who holds final authority to decide questions, doubts, and disputes during a match.

8 *John McEnroe* American tennis player (b. 1959), often considered one of the all-time best players.

Though no one was saying anything explicitly about Serena's black body, you are not the only viewer who thought it was getting in the way of Alves's sight line. One commentator said he hoped he wasn't being unkind when he stated, "Capriati wins it with the help of the umpires and the line judges." A year later that match would be credited for demonstrating the need for the speedy installation of Hawk-Eye, the line-calling technology that took the seeing away from the beholder. Now the umpire's call can be challenged by a replay; however, back then after the match Serena said, "I'm very angry and bitter right now. I felt cheated. Shall I go on? I just feel robbed." And though you felt outrage for Serena after that 2004 US Open, as the years go by, she seems to put Alves, and a lengthening list of other curious calls and oversights, against both her and her sister, behind her as they happen.

Yes, and the body has memory. The physical carriage hauls more than its weight. The body is the threshold across which each objectionable call passes into consciousness—all the unintimidated, unblinking, and unflappable resilience does not erase the moments lived through, even as we are eternally stupid or everlastingly optimistic, so ready to be inside, among, a part of the games.

And here Serena is, five years after Alves, back at the US Open, again in a semifinal match, this time against Belgium's Kim Clijsters. Serena is not playing well and loses the first set. In response she smashes her racket on the court. Now McEnroe isn't stunned by her ability to hold herself together and is moved to say, "That's as angry as I've ever seen her." The umpire gives her a warning; another violation will mean a point penalty.

She is in the second set at the critical moment of 5–6 in Clijsters's favour, serving to stay in the match, at match point. The line judge employed by the US Open to watch Serena's body, its every move, says Serena stepped on the line while serving. What? (The Hawk-Eye cameras don't cover the feet, only the ball, apparently.) What! Are you serious? She is serious; she has seen a foot fault, one no one else is able to locate despite the numerous replays. "No foot fault, you definitely do not see a foot fault there," says McEnroe. "That's overofficiating for certain," says another commentator. Even the ESPN tennis commentator, who seems predictable in her readiness to find fault with the Williams sisters, says, "Her foot fault call was way off." Yes, and even if there had been a foot fault, despite the rule, they are rarely ever called at critical moments in a Grand Slam match because "You don't make a call," tennis official Carol Cox says, "that can decide a match unless it's flagrant."

15 As you look at the affable Kim Clijsters, you try to entertain the thought that this scenario could have played itself out the other way. And as Serena turns to the lineswoman and says, "I swear to God I'm fucking going to take this fucking ball and shove it down your fucking throat, you hear that? I swear to God!" As offensive as her outburst is, it is difficult not to

applaud her for reacting immediately to being thrown against a sharp white background. It is difficult not to applaud her for existing in the moment, for fighting crazily against the so-called wrongness of her body's positioning at the service line.

She says in 2009, belatedly, the words that should have been said to the umpire in 2004, the words that might have snapped Alves back into focus, a focus that would have acknowledged what actually was happening on the court. Now Serena's reaction is read as insane. And her punishment for this moment of manumission[9] is the threatened point penalty resulting in the loss of the match, an $82,500 fine, plus a two-year probationary period by the Grand Slam Committee.

Perhaps the committee's decision is only about context, though context is not meaning. It is a public event being watched in homes across the world. In any case, it is difficult not to think that if Serena lost context by abandoning all rules of civility, it could be because her body, trapped in a racial imaginary, trapped in disbelief—code for being black in America—is being governed not by the tennis match she is participating in but by a collapsed relationship that had promised to play by the rules. Perhaps this is how racism feels no matter the context—randomly the rules everyone else gets to play by no longer apply to you, and to call this out by calling out "I swear to God!" is to be called insane, crass, crazy. Bad sportsmanship.

Two years later, September 11, 2011, Serena is playing the Australian Sam Stosur in the US Open final. She is expected to win, having just beaten the number-one player, the Dane Caroline Wozniacki, in the semifinal the night before. Some speculate Serena especially wants to win this Grand Slam because it is the tenth anniversary of the attack on the Twin Towers.[10] It's believed that by winning she will prove her red-blooded American patriotism and will once and for all become beloved by the tennis world (think Arthur Ashe[11] after his death). All the bad calls, the boos, the criticisms that she has made ugly the game of tennis—through her looks as well as her behaviour—that entire cluster of betrayals will be wiped clean with this win.

One imagines her wanting to say what her sister would say a year later after being diagnosed with Sjögren's syndrome[12] and losing her match to shouts

---

9 *manumission* Release from slavery.

10 *tenth anniversary ... Twin Towers* In the terrorist attacks by al-Qaeda on September 11, 2001, the Twin Towers of the World Trade Center in New York were destroyed; almost 3000 people died.

11 *Arthur Ashe* American tennis player (1943–93), winner of three Grand Slam tournaments. An African American, Ashe was often the target of racism during his lifetime, but he became almost universally revered after his death.

12 *Sjögren's syndrome* Autoimmune disorder which typically causes dry mouth, dry eyes, joint pain, and fatigue, as well as often being the cause of other complications.

of "Let's go, Venus!" in Arthur Ashe Stadium: "I know this is not proper tennis etiquette, but this is the first time I've ever played here that the crowd has been behind me like that. Today I felt American, you know, for the first time at the US Open. So I've waited my whole career to have this moment and here it is."

20 It is all too exhausting and Serena's exhaustion shows in her playing; she is losing, a set and a game down. Yes, and finally she hits a great shot, a big forehand, and before the ball is safely past Sam Stosur's hitting zone, Serena yells, "Come on!" thinking she has hit an irretrievable winner. The umpire, Eva Asderaki, rules correctly that Serena, by shouting, interfered with Stosur's concentration. Subsequently, a ball that Stosur seemingly would not have been able to return becomes Stosur's point. Serena's reply is to ask the umpire if she is trying to screw her again. She remembers the umpire doing this to her before. As a viewer, you too, along with John McEnroe, begin to wonder if this is the same umpire from 2004 or 2009. It isn't—in 2004 it was Mariana Alves and in 2009 it was Sharon Wright; however, the use of the word "again" by Serena returns her viewers to other times calling her body out.

Again Serena's frustrations, her disappointments, exist within a system you understand not to try to understand in any fair-minded way because to do so is to understand the erasure of the self as systemic, as ordinary. For Serena, the daily diminishment is a low flame, a constant drip. Every look, every comment, every bad call blossoms out of history, through her, onto you. To understand is to see Serena as hemmed in as any other black body thrown against our American background. "Aren't you the one that screwed me over last time here?" she asks umpire Asderaki. "Yeah, you are. Don't look at me. Really, don't even look at me. Don't look my way. Don't look my way," she repeats, because it is that simple.

Yes, and who can turn away? Serena is not running out of breath. Despite all her understanding, she continues to serve up aces while smashing rackets and fraying hems. In the 2012 Olympics she brought home two of the three gold medals the Americans would win in tennis. After her three-second celebratory dance on centre court at the All England Club, the American media reported, "And there was Serena … Crip-Walking[13] all over the most lily-white place in the world.… You couldn't help but shake your head.… What Serena did was akin to cracking a tasteless, X-rated* joke inside a church.… What she did was immature and classless."

Before making the video *How to Be a Successful Black Artist*, Hennessy Youngman uploaded to YouTube *How to Be a Successful Artist*. While putting forward the argument that one needs to be white to be truly successful, he adds, in an aside, that this might not work for blacks because if "a nigger paints a

---

13 *Crip-Walking* Dance move originated by the Los Angeles Crip gang in the 1970s.

flower it becomes a slavery flower, flower de *Amistad*,"[14] thereby intimating that any relationship between the white viewer and the black artist immediately becomes one between white persons and black property, which was the legal state of things once upon a time,* as Patricia Williams has pointed out in *The Alchemy of Race and Rights*: "The cold game of equality staring makes me feel like a thin sheet of glass.… I could force my presence, the real me contained in those eyes, upon them, but I would be smashed in the process."

Interviewed by the Brit Piers Morgan after her 2012 Olympic victory, Serena is informed by Morgan that he was planning on calling her victory dance "the Serena Shuffle"; however, he has learned from the American press that it is a Crip Walk, a gangster dance. Serena responds incredulously by asking if she looks like a gangster to him. Yes, he answers. All in a day's fun, perhaps, and in spite and despite it all, Serena Williams blossoms again into Serena Williams. When asked if she is confident she can win her upcoming matches, her answer remains, "At the end of the day, I am very happy with me and I'm very happy with my results."

25 Serena would go on to win every match she played between the US Open and the year-end 2012 championship tournament, and because tennis is a game of adjustments, she would do this without any reaction to a number of questionable calls. More than one commentator would remark on her ability to hold it together during these matches. She is a woman in love, one suggests. She has grown up, another decides, as if responding to the injustice of racism is childish and her previous demonstration of emotion was free-floating and detached from any external actions by others. Some others theorize she is developing the admirable "calm and measured logic" of an Arthur Ashe, who the sportswriter Bruce Jenkins felt was "dignified" and "courageous" in his ability to confront injustice without making a scene. Jenkins, perhaps inspired by Serena's new comportment, felt moved to argue that her continued boycott of Indian Wells in 2013, where she felt traumatized by the aggression of racist slurs hurled at her in 2001, was lacking in "dignity" and "integrity" and demonstrated "only stubbornness and a grudge." (Serena lifted her boycott in 2015, though Venus continues to boycott Indian Wells.)

Watching this newly contained Serena, you begin to wonder if she finally has given up wanting better from her peers or if she too has come across Hennessy's *Art Thoughtz* and is channelling his assertion that the less that is communicated the better. Be ambiguous. This type of ambiguity could also be diagnosed as dissociation and would support Serena's claim that she has had to split herself off from herself and create different personae.

---

14 *Amistad* The reference is to *La Amistad*, a nineteenth-century schooner on which a slave revolt occurred in 1839.

Now that there is no calling out of injustice, no yelling, no cursing, no finger wagging or head shaking, the media decides to take up the mantle when on December 12, 2012, two weeks after Serena is named WTA[15] Player of the Year, the Dane Caroline Wozniacki, a former number-one player, imitates Serena by stuffing towels in her top and shorts, all in good fun, at an exhibition match. Racist? CNN* wants to know if outrage is the proper response.

It's then that Hennessy's suggestions about "how to be a successful artist" return to you: be ambiguous, be white. Wozniacki, it becomes clear, has finally enacted what was desired by many of Serena's detractors, consciously or unconsciously, the moment the Compton[16] girl first stepped on court. Wozniacki (though there are a number of ways to interpret her actions—playful mocking of a peer, imitation of the mimicking antics of the tennis player known as the joker, Novak Djokovic) finally gives the people what they have wanted all along by embodying Serena's attributes while leaving Serena's "angry nigger exterior" behind. At last, in this real, and unreal, moment, we have Wozniacki's image of smiling blond goodness posing as the best female tennis player of all time.

(2014)

Questions

1. Rankine discusses two types of anger at the beginning of the essay. How would you characterize them, and how are they different? What does Rankine say about anger and the body?
2. How does Rankine interpret Serena Williams's outburst during the 2009 US Open? How does she use the tennis match as a metaphor to make a larger argument?
3. The book from which this essay was drawn was a finalist for the National Book Award in two categories, Poetry and Criticism. To what extent do you think it appropriate to place her writing in both these categories?

---

15 *WTA* Women's Tennis Association.

16 *Compton* City in California, south of Los Angeles.

NIKOLE HANNAH-JONES

HOW SCHOOL SEGREGATION DIVIDES FERGUSON—AND THE UNITED STATES

On 9 August 2014, police officer Darren Wilson shot and killed unarmed teenager Michael Brown in Ferguson, Missouri (a suburb of St. Louis); when no charges were filed against Wilson, the incident became a focus of widespread anger. Protests carried on for many weeks, bringing race relations in America to the forefront of public discussion. The full version of the following article was originally published on 19 December 2014 in the online magazine ProPublica *under the title "School Segregation: The Continuing Tragedy of Ferguson." The abridged version reprinted here appeared in* The New York Times.

On Aug. 1, five students in satiny green-and-red robes and mortarboards* waited in an elementary school classroom to hear their names called as graduates of Normandy High School. This ceremony, held months after the official graduation, was mostly for students who had been short of credits in May.

One of those new graduates was Michael Brown. He was 18, his mother's oldest son. He had been planning to start college in September.

Eight days later, he was dead, killed in the streets of nearby Ferguson, Mo., by a white police officer in a shooting that ignited angry protests and a painful national debate about race, policing and often elusive justice. Many news reports after Mr. Brown's death noted his graduation and his college plans. The implication was that these scholarly achievements magnified the sorrow.

But if Michael Brown's educational experience was a success story, it was a damning one.

The Normandy school district is among the poorest and most segregated 5
in Missouri. It ranks last in overall academic performance. Its rating on an annual state assessment was so dismal that by the time Mr. Brown graduated the district had lost its state accreditation.

About half of black male students at Normandy High never graduate. Just one in four graduates makes it to a four-year college. The college where

Mr. Brown was headed is a for-profit trade school that recruits those it once described in internal documents as "Unemployed, Underpaid, Unsatisfied, Unskilled, Unprepared, Unsupported, Unmotivated, Unhappy, Underserved!"

Just five miles down the road from Normandy lies Clayton, the wealthy county seat where a grand jury recently deliberated the fate of Darren Wilson, the officer who killed Mr. Brown. Success there looks very different. The Clayton public schools are predominantly white, with almost no poverty to speak of. The district is regularly ranked in the top 10 percent in the state. More than 96 percent of its students graduate. Eighty-four percent head to four-year universities.

Decades of public and private housing discrimination made St. Louis one of the most racially segregated metropolitan areas in the country. A network of school district boundaries has, to this day, divided students in racially separate schools as effectively as any Jim Crow law.*

Michael Brown's education was not exceptional, then, but all too typical, and it illustrates the vast disparity in resources and expectations for black children in America's segregated school systems.

10 As hundreds of school districts across the nation have been released from court-enforced integration* over the past 15 years, the number of what researchers call "apartheid schools"—in which the white population is 1 percent or less—has shot up. The achievement gap, narrowed during the height of school integration, has widened.

According to data compiled by the Department of Education, black and Latino children nationwide are the least likely to be taught by a qualified, experienced teacher; to be offered courses such as chemistry and calculus; or to have access to technology.

"American schools are disturbingly racially segregated—period," Catherine Lhamon, head of the Education Department's civil rights office, said in a speech in October.

Since Aug. 9, the day Mr. Brown's lifeless body lay for hours under a hot summer sun, St. Louis County has come to illustrate the country's racial fault lines in police conduct and the criminalization of black youth. But most black youth will not die at the hands of the police.

They share the fate that was already Michael Brown's.

15 In 1954, when the United States Supreme Court rejected the notion of separate but equal schools in its Brown v. Board of Education[1] decision, St. Louis ran the second-largest segregated school district in the country.

---

1 *Brown v. Board of Education* This ruling established that state laws allowing separate public schools for black and white students was unconstitutional.

After the ruling, school officials promised to integrate voluntarily. But the acceleration of white flight and the redrawing of school district lines around black and white neighbourhoods allowed metropolitan St. Louis to preserve its racial divide. Nearly 30 years later, 90 percent of black children in St. Louis still attended predominantly black schools.

In 1983, a federal judge ordered a desegregation plan for the entire metropolitan area. At its peak, some 15,000 St. Louis public school students a year attended 16 heavily white suburban districts. Another 1,300 white students headed in the opposite direction to 27 new magnet schools in St. Louis.

The program left another 15,000 of St. Louis's black students in segregated, inferior schools. But for the transfer students who rode buses out of the city, the plan successfully broke the deeply entrenched connection between race, ZIP code and opportunity. Test scores for eighth- and 10th-grade transfer students rose. The transfer students were more likely to graduate and go on to college. In surveys, white students overwhelmingly said they had benefitted from the opportunity to be educated alongside black students. The St. Louis model was heralded as the nation's most successful metropolitan desegregation program.

But from the moment it started, the St. Louis desegregation plan was under assault. The cost would eventually reach $1.7 billion. In 1999 the program was made entirely voluntary. Today, about 5,000 students get to escape the troubles of the St. Louis public schools—a small fraction of the number who apply for the privilege of doing so.

Incorporated in 1945, Normandy became a destination for St. Louis's fleeing white working class.

Nedra Martin's family was among the black strivers who began to make their way to Normandy in the 1970s. Ms. Martin, who still lives in Normandy and works in human resources at Walmart, said her parents settled in the town in 1975. They both worked in government jobs—her dad was a welder for the city, her mom an aide in a state group home. But as black families like the Martins moved in, "For Sale" signs went up and whites fled to new exurbs.

After 1970, black enrollment in the Normandy schools exploded, more than doubling within eight years to 6,200. By 1978, only St. Louis itself enrolled more black students than Normandy.

For years, Normandy's schools struggled to meet minimum state requirements for student achievement. Then, in 2009, the state decided that the Normandy school district would absorb the ailing Wellston school district.

Wellston was also high-poverty, and Missouri's only 100 percent black school system. State officials had called conditions in Wellston's schools "deplorable" and "academically abusive."

But its students were not sent to the high-performing, mostly white districts nearby. Michael Jones, a state board of education official, was blunt about the reason: "You'd have had a civil war."

By the time Michael Brown was a high school junior, he had spent most of his educational career in racially segregated and financially disadvantaged schools. Behind in credits, he entered Normandy High in the spring of 2013.

The state's most recent assessment of Normandy's schools was spectacularly bleak: Out of Missouri's 520 school districts, Normandy, among the state's poorest and 98 percent black, was marooned at the very bottom.

But last year, the Normandy district was thrown an unlikely lifeline. Its schools had failed so badly that the state had formally stripped it of its accreditation. And the Missouri State Supreme Court had just upheld a state law allowing students in unaccredited districts to transfer to accredited ones.

Nedra Martin, had a daughter stuck in Normandy's failing schools. Just like that, the state's decision erased the invisible, impenetrable lines of segregation that had trapped her child. "I was elated," Ms. Martin said. "Just elated."

30 Parents in the school district that had to take Normandy's students—Francis Howell, an 85 percent white district 26 miles away—were not. Officials there held a public forum to address community concerns. More than 2,500 parents packed into the high school gym.

Would the district install metal detectors? What about the violence their children would be subjected to, an elementary school parent asked. Wouldn't test scores plummet? The issue wasn't about race, one parent said, "but trash."

Mah'Ria Pruitt-Martin, a rising eighth grader, was sitting in the audience that night with her mother. Hers was one of the few brown faces there, and the girl said she wiped away tears.

"It made me heartbroken because they were putting us in a box," Mah'Ria said. "I was sitting there thinking, 'Would you want some other parents talking about your kid that way?'"

In the fall of 2013, nearly 1,000 Normandy students—about a quarter of the district's enrollment—switched to schools in accredited districts. More than 400 headed to Francis Howell.

35 Mah'Ria said that she was, in fact, welcomed into her new middle school by students and teachers. Despite the fears, recently released state data show that with the exception of one district, test scores in the transfer schools did not drop.

But there was a cruel twist. The state required any failing district whose students were allowed to transfer to pay the costs of their education in the adjoining districts. The payments drained Normandy's finances. Normandy closed a school and laid off 40 percent of its staff.

"In order to save the district, they killed the district," said John Wright, who spent stints as superintendent in both St. Louis and Normandy.

The state then announced that it was taking over the Normandy Public Schools district and reconstituting it as the Normandy Schools Collaborative. As a new educational entity, the district got a clean slate. It no longer was unaccredited, but operated as a "state oversight district." The transfer law, the state claimed, no longer applied. One by one, transfer districts announced that Normandy children were no longer welcome.

Ms. Martin and other parents sued, asserting that the state had no legal authority to reconstitute the district to change its accreditation status. On Aug. 15, after the school year had begun in some districts, a state judge granted a temporary injunction allowing the plaintiffs to enroll their children in the transfer districts.

"Every day a student attends an unaccredited school," the judge wrote, the child "could suffer harm that cannot be repaired." The state is fighting the ruling, but most school districts have reopened their doors to the transfer students.

When asked whether black children in Missouri were receiving an equal education, Commissioner Chris Nicastro, the state's top education official, paused, then inhaled deeply. "Do I think black children in Missouri are getting in all cases the same education as their white counterparts?" Ms. Nicastro said. "I'd have to say no."

Students who spend their careers in segregated schools can look forward to a life on the margins, according to a 2014 study on the long-term impacts of school desegregation by Rucker C. Johnson, an economist at the University of California, Berkeley. They are more likely to be poor. They are more likely to go to jail. They are less likely to graduate from high school, to go to college, or to finish if they go. They are more likely to live in segregated neighbourhoods as adults. Their children are more likely to attend segregated schools, repeating the cycle.

"You know how hard it was for me to get him to stay in school and graduate?" Michael Brown's mother, Lesley McSpadden, cried on the August day he died. "You know how many black men graduate? Not many."

Michael Brown was buried in the old St. Peter's Cemetery.

It lies next to Normandy High School.

(2014)

Questions

1. How does Hannah-Jones's analysis of Michael Brown's education deepen and complicate the tragedy of his death?
2. What is an "apartheid school"? Why are there more now than in the recent past?
3. In the final paragraph of this article, Hannah-Jones mentions the proximity of St. Peter's Cemetery to Normandy High School. What is she suggesting here about the fate of black students in Normandy? Is this true in other parts of America?

Ta-Nehisi Coates

The Case for Reparations

Ta-Nehisi Coates, whose bestselling Between the World and Me *won the National Book Award for Non-fiction in 2015, came into prominence the previous year with this long essay, published in the June 2014 issue of* The Atlantic. *The essay helped to inspire the Black Lives Matter movement—and helped as well to change many minds on the issue of whether or not reparations for slavery would be appropriate. (Coates had himself changed his mind on the issue—as he recounted in a May 22 online background piece for* The Atlantic, *"The Case for Reparations: An Intellectual Autopsy.")*

And if thy brother, a Hebrew man, or a Hebrew woman, be sold unto thee, and serve thee six years; then in the seventh year thou shalt let him go free from thee. And when thou sendest him out free from thee, thou shalt not let him go away empty: thou shalt furnish him liberally out of thy flock, and out of thy floor, and out of thy winepress: of that wherewith the LORD thy God hath blessed thee thou shalt give unto him. And thou shalt remember that thou wast a bondman in the land of Egypt, and the LORD thy God redeemed thee: therefore I command thee this thing today.—Deuteronomy 15: 12–15

Besides the crime which consists in violating the law, and varying from the right rule of reason, whereby a man so far becomes degenerate, and declares himself to quit the principles of human nature, and to be a noxious creature, there is commonly injury done to some person or other, and some other man receives damage by his transgression: in which case he who hath received any damage, has, besides the right of punishment common to him with other men, a particular right to seek reparation.—John Locke, "Second Treatise"

By our unpaid labour and suffering, we have earned the right to the soil, many times over and over, and now we are determined to have it.—Anonymous, 1861

Clyde Ross was born in 1923, the seventh of 13 children, near Clarksdale, Mississippi, the home of the blues.* Ross's parents owned and farmed a 40-acre tract of land, flush with cows, hogs, and mules. Ross's mother would drive to Clarksdale to do her shopping in a horse and buggy, in which she invested all the pride one might place in a Cadillac. The family owned another horse, with a red coat, which they gave to Clyde. The Ross family wanted for little, save that which all black families in the Deep South then desperately desired—the protection of the law.

In the 1920s, Jim Crow Mississippi[1] was, in all facets of society, a kleptocracy.[2] The majority of the people in the state were perpetually robbed of the vote—a hijacking engineered through the trickery of the poll tax and the muscle of the lynch mob.* Between 1882 and 1968, more black people were lynched in Mississippi than in any other state. "You and I know what's the best way to keep the nigger from voting," blustered Theodore Bilbo, a Mississippi senator and a proud Klansman.* "You do it the night before the election."

The state's regime partnered robbery of the franchise with robbery of the purse. Many of Mississippi's black farmers lived in debt peonage,[3] under the sway of cotton kings who were at once their landlords, their employers, and their primary merchants. Tools and necessities were advanced against the return on the crop, which was determined by the employer. When farmers were deemed to be in debt—and they often were—the negative balance was then carried over to the next season. A man or woman who protested this arrangement did so at the risk of grave injury or death. Refusing to work meant arrest under vagrancy laws and forced labour under the state's penal system.

Well into the 20th century, black people spoke of their flight from Mississippi in much the same manner as their runagate[4] ancestors had. In her 2010 book, *The Warmth of Other Suns*, Isabel Wilkerson tells the story of Eddie Earvin, a spinach picker who fled Mississippi in 1963, after being made to work at gunpoint. "You didn't talk about it or tell nobody," Earvin said. "You had to sneak away."

When Clyde Ross was still a child, Mississippi authorities claimed his fa- 5
ther owed $3,000 in back taxes. The elder Ross could not read. He did not have a lawyer. He did not know anyone at the local courthouse. He could not expect the police to be impartial. Effectively, the Ross family had no way to contest the claim and no protection under the law. The authorities seized the land. They

---

1 *Jim Crow Mississippi* Mississippi under the Jim Crow laws, which enforced segregation.

2 *kleptocracy* Jurisdiction in which theft is central to the operation of society.

3 *debt peonage* Forced servitude to one's creditors.

4 *runagate* Runaway, especially one who has broken the law.

seized the buggy. They took the cows, hogs, and mules. And so for the upkeep of separate but equal, the entire Ross family was reduced to sharecropping.*

This was hardly unusual. In 2001, the Associated Press published a three-part investigation into the theft of black-owned land stretching back to the antebellum period.* The series documented some 406 victims and 24,000 acres of land valued at tens of millions of dollars. The land was taken through means ranging from legal chicanery to terrorism. "Some of the land taken from black families has become a country club in Virginia," the AP reported, as well as "oil fields in Mississippi" and "a baseball spring training facility in Florida."

Clyde Ross was a smart child. His teacher thought he should attend a more challenging school. There was very little support for educating black people in Mississippi. But Julius Rosenwald, a part owner of Sears, Roebuck, had begun an ambitious effort to build schools for black children throughout the South. Ross's teacher believed he should attend the local Rosenwald school. It was too far for Ross to walk and get back in time to work in the fields. Local white children had a school bus. Clyde Ross did not, and thus lost the chance to better his education.

Then, when Ross was 10 years old, a group of white men demanded his only childhood possession—the horse with the red coat. "You can't have this horse. We want it," one of the white men said. They gave Ross's father $17.

"I did everything for that horse," Ross told me. "Everything. And they took him. Put him on the racetrack. I never did know what happened to him after that, but I know they didn't bring him back. So that's just one of my losses."

10 The losses mounted. As sharecroppers, the Ross family saw their wages treated as the landlord's slush fund. Landowners were supposed to split the profits from the cotton fields with sharecroppers. But bales would often disappear during the count, or the split might be altered on a whim. If cotton was selling for 50 cents a pound, the Ross family might get 15 cents, or only five. One year Ross's mother promised to buy him a $7 suit for a summer program at their church. She ordered the suit by mail. But that year Ross's family was paid only five cents a pound for cotton. The mailman arrived with the suit. The Rosses could not pay. The suit was sent back. Clyde Ross did not go to the church program.

It was in these early years that Ross began to understand himself as an American—he did not live under the blind decree of justice, but under the heel of a regime that elevated armed robbery to a governing principle. He thought about fighting. "Just be quiet," his father told him. "Because they'll come and kill us all."

Clyde Ross grew. He was drafted into the Army. The draft officials offered him an exemption if he stayed home and worked. He preferred to take his chances with war. He was stationed in California. He found that he could go into stores without being bothered. He could walk the streets without being harassed. He could go into a restaurant and receive service.

Ross was shipped off to Guam. He fought in World War II to save the world from tyranny. But when he returned to Clarksdale, he found that tyranny had followed him home. This was 1947, eight years before Mississippi lynched Emmett Till[5] and tossed his broken body into the Tallahatchie River. The Great Migration,* a mass exodus of 6 million African Americans that spanned most of the 20th century, was now in its second wave. The black pilgrims did not journey north simply seeking better wages and work, or bright lights and big adventures. They were fleeing the acquisitive warlords of the South. They were seeking the protection of the law.

Clyde Ross was among them. He came to Chicago in 1947 and took a job as a taster at Campbell's Soup. He made a stable wage. He married. He had children. His paycheck was his own. No Klansmen stripped him of the vote. When he walked down the street, he did not have to move because a white man was walking past. He did not have to take off his hat or avert his gaze. His journey from peonage to full citizenship seemed near-complete. Only one item was missing—a home, that final badge of entry into the sacred order of the American middle class of the Eisenhower years.*

In 1961, Ross and his wife bought a house in North Lawndale, a bustling community on Chicago's West Side. North Lawndale had long been a predominantly Jewish neighbourhood, but a handful of middle-class African Americans had lived there starting in the '40s. The community was anchored by the sprawling Sears, Roebuck headquarters. North Lawndale's Jewish People's Institute actively encouraged blacks to move into the neighbourhood, seeking to make it a "pilot community for interracial living." In the battle for integration then being fought around the country, North Lawndale seemed to offer promising terrain. But out in the tall grass, highwaymen,* nefarious as any Clarksdale kleptocrat, were lying in wait.

Three months after Clyde Ross moved into his house, the boiler blew out. This would normally be a homeowner's responsibility, but in fact, Ross was not really a homeowner. His payments were made to the seller, not the bank. And Ross had not signed a normal mortgage. He'd bought "on contract": a predatory agreement that combined all the responsibilities of homeownership with all the disadvantages of renting—while offering the benefits of neither. Ross had bought his house for $27,500. The seller, not the previous homeowner but a new kind of middleman, had bought it for only $12,000 six months before selling it to Ross. In a contract sale, the seller kept the deed until the contract was paid in full—and, unlike with a normal mortgage, Ross would acquire no equity in

5 *Emmett Till* 14-year-old boy whose murder became emblematic of racial injustice.

the meantime. If he missed a single payment, he would immediately forfeit his $1,000 down payment, all his monthly payments, and the property itself.

The men who peddled contracts in North Lawndale would sell homes at inflated prices and then evict families who could not pay—taking their down payment and their monthly installments as profit. Then they'd bring in another black family, rinse, and repeat. "He loads them up with payments they can't meet," an office secretary told *The Chicago Daily News* of her boss, the speculator Lou Fushanis, in 1963. "Then he takes the property away from them. He's sold some of the buildings three or four times."

Ross had tried to get a legitimate mortgage in another neighbourhood, but was told by a loan officer that there was no financing available. The truth was that there was no financing for people like Clyde Ross. From the 1930s through the 1960s, black people across the country were largely cut out of the legitimate home-mortgage market through means both legal and extralegal. Chicago whites employed every measure, from "restrictive covenants"[6] to bombings, to keep their neighbourhoods segregated.

Their efforts were buttressed by the federal government. In 1934, Congress created the Federal Housing Administration. The FHA insured private mortgages, causing a drop in interest rates and a decline in the size of the down payment required to buy a house. But an insured mortgage was not a possibility for Clyde Ross. The FHA had adopted a system of maps that rated neighbourhoods according to their perceived stability. On the maps, green areas, rated "A," indicated "in demand" neighbourhoods that, as one appraiser put it, lacked "a single foreigner or Negro." These neighbourhoods were considered excellent prospects for insurance. Neighbourhoods where black people lived were rated "D" and were usually considered ineligible for FHA backing. They were coloured in red. Neither the percentage of black people living there nor their social class mattered. Black people were viewed as a contagion. Redlining[7] went beyond FHA-backed loans and spread to the entire mortgage industry, which was already rife with racism, excluding black people from most legitimate means of obtaining a mortgage.

20 "A government offering such bounty to builders and lenders could have required compliance with a nondiscrimination policy," Charles Abrams, the urban-studies expert who helped create the New York City Housing Authority, wrote in 1955. "Instead, the FHA adopted a racial policy that could well have been culled from the Nuremberg laws."[8]

---

6 *restrictive covenants* Clauses in property owners' deeds or leases that limit how a given property can be used. In the cases mentioned here, covenants often permitted the sale of homes only to white buyers.

7 *Redlining* Withholding services to people because of the racial or ethnic makeup of the neighbourhoods they live in.

8 *Nuremberg laws* Laws that governed policies regarding "racial purity" in Nazi Germany.

The devastating effects are cogently outlined by Melvin L. Oliver and Thomas M. Shapiro in their 1995 book, *Black Wealth/White Wealth*:

> Locked out of the greatest mass-based opportunity for wealth accumulation in American history, African Americans who desired and were able to afford home ownership found themselves consigned to central-city communities where their investments were affected by the "self-fulfilling prophecies" of the FHA appraisers: cut off from sources of new investment[,] their homes and communities deteriorated and lost value in comparison to those homes and communities that FHA appraisers deemed desirable.

In Chicago and across the country, whites looking to achieve the American dream could rely on a legitimate credit system backed by the government. Blacks were herded into the sights of unscrupulous lenders who took them for money and for sport. "It was like people who like to go out and shoot lions in Africa. It was the same thrill," a housing attorney told the historian Beryl Satter in her 2009 book, *Family Properties*. "The thrill of the chase and the kill."

The kill was profitable. At the time of his death, Lou Fushanis owned more than 600 properties, many of them in North Lawndale, and his estate was estimated to be worth $3 million. He'd made much of this money by exploiting the frustrated hopes of black migrants like Clyde Ross. During this period, according to one estimate, 85 percent of all black home buyers who bought in Chicago bought on contract. "If anybody who is well established in this business in Chicago doesn't earn $100,000 a year," a contract seller told *The Saturday Evening Post* in 1962, "he is loafing."

Contract sellers became rich. North Lawndale became a ghetto.

Clyde Ross still lives there. He still owns his home. He is 91, and the 25
emblems of survival are all around him—awards for service in his community, pictures of his children in cap and gown. But when I asked him about his home in North Lawndale, I heard only anarchy.

"We were ashamed. We did not want anyone to know that we were that ignorant," Ross told me. He was sitting at his dining-room table. His glasses were as thick as his Clarksdale drawl. "I'd come out of Mississippi where there was one mess, and come up here and got in another mess. So how dumb am I? I didn't want anyone to know how dumb I was.

"When I found myself caught up in it, I said, 'How? I just left this mess. I just left no laws. And no regard. And then I come here and get cheated wide open.' I would probably want to do some harm to some people, you know, if I had been violent like some of us. I thought, 'Man, I got caught up in this stuff. I can't even take care of my kids.' I didn't have enough for my kids. You could fall through the cracks easy fighting these white people. And no law."

But fight Clyde Ross did. In 1968 he joined the newly formed Contract Buyers League—a collection of black homeowners on Chicago's South and West Sides, all of whom had been locked into the same system of predation. There was Howell Collins, whose contract called for him to pay $25,500 for a house that a speculator had bought for $14,500. There was Ruth Wells, who'd managed to pay out half her contract, expecting a mortgage, only to suddenly see an insurance bill materialize out of thin air—a requirement the seller had added without Wells's knowledge. Contract sellers used every tool at their disposal to pilfer from their clients. They scared white residents into selling low. They lied about properties' compliance with building codes, then left the buyer responsible when city inspectors arrived. They presented themselves as real-estate brokers, when in fact they were the owners. They guided their clients to lawyers who were in on the scheme.

The Contract Buyers League fought back. Members—who would eventually number more than 500—went out to the posh suburbs where the speculators lived and embarrassed them by knocking on their neighbours' doors and informing them of the details of the contract-lending trade. They refused to pay their installments, instead holding monthly payments in an escrow account. Then they brought a suit against the contract sellers, accusing them of buying properties and reselling in such a manner "to reap from members of the Negro race large and unjust profits."

THE STORY OF CLYDE ROSS AND THE CONTRACT BUYERS LEAGUE

30 In return for the "deprivations of their rights and privileges under the Thirteenth and Fourteenth Amendments,"* the league demanded "prayers for relief"—payback of all moneys paid on contracts and all moneys paid for structural improvement of properties, at 6 percent interest minus a "fair, nondiscriminatory" rental price for time of occupation. Moreover, the league asked the court to adjudge that the defendants had "acted willfully and maliciously and that malice is the gist of this action."

Ross and the Contract Buyers League were no longer appealing to the government simply for equality. They were no longer fleeing in hopes of a better deal elsewhere. They were charging society with a crime against their community. They wanted the crime publicly ruled as such. They wanted the crime's executors declared to be offensive to society. And they wanted restitution for the great injury brought upon them by said offenders. In 1968, Clyde Ross and the Contract Buyers League were no longer simply seeking the protection of the law. They were seeking reparations.

According to the most-recent statistics, North Lawndale is now on the wrong end of virtually every socioeconomic indicator. In 1930 its population was

112,000. Today it is 36,000. The halcyon talk of "interracial living" is dead. The neighbourhood is 92 percent black. Its homicide rate is 45 per 100,000—triple the rate of the city as a whole. The infant-mortality rate is 14 per 1,000—more than twice the national average. Forty-three percent of the people in North Lawndale live below the poverty line—double Chicago's overall rate. Forty-five percent of all households are on food stamps—nearly three times the rate of the city at large. Sears, Roebuck left the neighbourhood in 1987, taking 1,800 jobs with it. Kids in North Lawndale need not be confused about their prospects: Cook County's Juvenile Temporary Detention Center sits directly adjacent to the neighbourhood.

North Lawndale is an extreme portrait of the trends that ail black Chicago. Such is the magnitude of these ailments that it can be said that blacks and whites do not inhabit the same city. The average per capita income of Chicago's white neighbourhoods is almost three times that of its black neighbourhoods. When the Harvard sociologist Robert J. Sampson examined incarceration rates in Chicago in his 2012 book, *Great American City*, he found that a black neighbourhood with one of the highest incarceration rates (West Garfield Park) had a rate more than 40 times as high as the white neighbourhood with the highest rate (Clearing). "This is a staggering differential, even for community-level comparisons," Sampson writes. "A difference of kind, not degree."

In other words, Chicago's impoverished black neighbourhoods—characterized by high unemployment and households headed by single parents—are not simply poor; they are "ecologically distinct." This "is not simply the same thing as low economic status," writes Sampson. "In this pattern Chicago is not alone."

The lives of black Americans are better than they were half a century 35
ago. The humiliation of Whites Only signs are gone. Rates of black poverty have decreased. Black teen-pregnancy rates are at record lows—and the gap between black and white teen-pregnancy rates has shrunk significantly. But such progress rests on a shaky foundation, and fault lines are everywhere. The income gap between black and white households is roughly the same today as it was in 1970. Patrick Sharkey, a sociologist at New York University, studied children born from 1955 through 1970 and found that 4 percent of whites and 62 percent of blacks across America had been raised in poor neighbourhoods. A generation later, the same study showed, virtually nothing had changed. And whereas whites born into affluent neighbourhoods tended to remain in affluent neighbourhoods, blacks tended to fall out of them.

This is not surprising. Black families, regardless of income, are significantly less wealthy than white families. The Pew Research Center estimates that white households are worth roughly 20 times as much as black households, and that whereas only 15 percent of whites have zero or negative wealth, more than a third of blacks do. Effectively, the black family in America is working without a safety net. When financial calamity strikes—a medical emergency, divorce, job loss—the fall is precipitous.

And just as black families of all incomes remain handicapped by a lack of wealth, so too do they remain handicapped by their restricted choice of neighbourhood. Black people with upper-middle-class incomes do not generally live in upper-middle-class neighbourhoods. Sharkey's research shows that black families making $100,000 typically live in the kinds of neighbourhoods inhabited by white families making $30,000. "Blacks and whites inhabit such different neighbourhoods," Sharkey writes, "that it is not possible to compare the economic outcomes of black and white children."

The implications are chilling. As a rule, poor black people do not work their way out of the ghetto—and those who do often face the horror of watching their children and grandchildren tumble back.

Even seeming evidence of progress withers under harsh light. In 2012, the Manhattan Institute cheerily noted that segregation had declined since the 1960s. And yet African Americans still remained—by far—the most segregated ethnic group in the country.

40 With segregation, with the isolation of the injured and the robbed, comes the concentration of disadvantage. An unsegregated America might see poverty, and all its effects, spread across the country with no particular bias toward skin colour. Instead, the concentration of poverty has been paired with a concentration of melanin.[9] The resulting conflagration has been devastating.

One thread of thinking in the African American community holds that these depressing numbers partially stem from cultural pathologies that can be altered through individual grit and exceptionally good behaviour. (In 2011, Philadelphia Mayor Michael Nutter, responding to violence among young black males, put the blame on the family: "Too many men making too many babies they don't want to take care of, and then we end up dealing with your children." Nutter turned to those presumably fatherless babies: "Pull your pants up and buy a belt, because no one wants to see your underwear or the crack of your butt.") The thread is as old as black politics itself. It is also wrong. The kind of trenchant racism to which black people have persistently been subjected can never be defeated by making its victims more respectable. The essence of American racism is disrespect. And in the wake of the grim numbers, we see the grim inheritance.

The Contract Buyers League's suit brought by Clyde Ross and his allies took direct aim at this inheritance. The suit was rooted in Chicago's long history of segregation, which had created two housing markets—one legitimate and backed by the government, the other lawless and patrolled by predators.

---

9 *melanin* Pigment in skin (darker shades are produced by more melanin).

The suit dragged on until 1976, when the league lost a jury trial. Securing the equal protection of the law proved hard; securing reparations proved impossible. If there were any doubts about the mood of the jury, the foreman removed them by saying, when asked about the verdict, that he hoped it would help end "the mess Earl Warren made with *Brown v. Board of Education*[10] and all that nonsense."

The Supreme Court seems to share that sentiment. The past two decades have witnessed a rollback of the progressive legislation of the 1960s. Liberals have found themselves on the defensive. In 2008, when Barack Obama was a candidate for president, he was asked whether his daughters—Malia and Sasha—should benefit from affirmative action.* He answered in the negative.

The exchange rested upon an erroneous comparison of the average American white family and the exceptional first family. In the contest of upward mobility, Barack and Michelle Obama have won. But they've won by being twice as good—and enduring twice as much. Malia and Sasha Obama enjoy privileges beyond the average white child's dreams. But that comparison is incomplete. The more telling question is how they compare with Jenna and Barbara Bush—the products of many generations of privilege, not just one. Whatever the Obama children achieve, it will be evidence of their family's singular perseverance, not of broad equality.

In 1783, the freedwoman* Belinda Royall petitioned the commonwealth of 45
Massachusetts for reparations. Belinda had been born in modern-day Ghana. She was kidnapped as a child and sold into slavery. She endured the Middle Passage and 50 years of enslavement at the hands of Isaac Royall and his son. But the junior Royall, a British loyalist, fled the country during the Revolution.* Belinda, now free after half a century of labour, beseeched the nascent Massachusetts legislature:

> The face of your Petitioner, is now marked with the furrows of time, and her frame bending under the oppression of years, while she, by the Laws of the Land, is denied the employment of one morsel of that immense wealth, apart whereof hath been accumilated by her own industry, and the whole augmented by her servitude.
>
> WHEREFORE, casting herself at your feet if your honours, as to a body of men, formed for the extirpation of vassalage, for the reward of Virtue, and the just return of honest industry—she prays, that such allowance may be made her out of the Estate of Colonel Royall, as

10 *Brown v. Board of Education* Landmark 1954 decision in which the Supreme Court decreed segregation in schools to be unconstitutional.

> will prevent her, and her more infirm daughter, from misery in the greatest extreme, and scatter comfort over the short and downward path of their lives.

Belinda Royall was granted a pension of 15 pounds and 12 shillings, to be paid out of the estate of Isaac Royall—one of the earliest successful attempts to petition for reparations. At the time, black people in America had endured more than 150 years of enslavement, and the idea that they might be owed something in return was, if not the national consensus, at least not outrageous.

"A heavy account lies against us as a civil society for oppressions committed against people who did not injure us," wrote the Quaker* John Woolman in 1769, "and that if the particular case of many individuals were fairly stated, it would appear that there was considerable due to them."

As the historian Roy E. Finkenbine has documented, at the dawn of this country, black reparations were actively considered and often effected. Quakers in New York, New England, and Baltimore went so far as to make "membership contingent upon compensating one's former slaves." In 1782, the Quaker Robert Pleasants emancipated his 78 slaves, granted them 350 acres, and later built a school on their property and provided for their education. "The doing of this justice to the injured Africans," wrote Pleasants, "would be an acceptable offering to him who 'Rules in the kingdom of men.'"

Edward Coles, a protégé of Thomas Jefferson* who became a slaveholder through inheritance, took many of his slaves north and granted them a plot of land in Illinois. John Randolph, a cousin of Jefferson's, willed that all his slaves be emancipated upon his death, and that all those older than 40 be given 10 acres of land. "I give and bequeath to all my slaves their freedom," Randolph wrote, "heartily regretting that I have been the owner of one."

In his book *Forever Free*, Eric Foner recounts the story of a disgruntled planter reprimanding a freedman loafing on the job:

> Planter: "You lazy nigger, I am losing a whole day's labour by you."
>
> Freedman: "Massa, how many days' labour have I lost by you?"

In the 20th century, the cause of reparations was taken up by a diverse cast that included the Confederate veteran Walter R. Vaughan, who believed that reparations would be a stimulus for the South; the black activist Callie House; black-nationalist* leaders like "Queen Mother" Audley Moore; and the civil-rights activist James Forman. The movement coalesced in 1987 under an umbrella organization called the National Coalition of Blacks for Reparations in America (N'COBRA). The NAACP* endorsed reparations in 1993. Charles J. Ogletree Jr., a professor at Harvard Law School, has pursued reparations claims in court.

But while the people advocating reparations have changed over time, the response from the country has remained virtually the same. "They have been taught to labour," the *Chicago Tribune* editorialized in 1891. "They have been taught Christian civilization, and to speak the noble English language instead of some African gibberish. The account is square with the ex-slaves."

Not exactly. Having been enslaved for 250 years, black people were not left to their own devices. They were terrorized. In the Deep South, a second slavery ruled.* In the North, legislatures, mayors, civic associations, banks, and citizens all colluded to pin black people into ghettos, where they were overcrowded, overcharged, and undereducated. Businesses discriminated against them, awarding them the worst jobs and the worst wages. Police brutalized them in the streets. And the notion that black lives, black bodies, and black wealth were rightful targets remained deeply rooted in the broader society. Now we have half-stepped away from our long centuries of despoilment, promising, "Never again." But still we are haunted. It is as though we have run up a credit-card bill and, having pledged to charge no more, remain befuddled that the balance does not disappear. The effects of that balance, interest accruing daily, are all around us.

Broach the topic of reparations today and a barrage of questions inevitably follows: Who will be paid? How much will they be paid? Who will pay? But if the practicalities, not the justice, of reparations are the true sticking point, there has for some time been the beginnings of a solution. For the past 25 years, Congressman John Conyers Jr., who represents the Detroit area, has marked every session of Congress by introducing a bill calling for a congressional study of slavery and its lingering effects as well as recommendations for "appropriate remedies."

A country curious about how reparations might actually work has an easy 55
solution in Conyers's bill, now called HR 40, the Commission to Study Reparation Proposals for African Americans Act. We would support this bill, submit the question to study, and then assess the possible solutions. But we are not interested.

"It's because it's black folks making the claim," Nkechi Taifa, who helped found N'COBRA, says. "People who talk about reparations are considered left lunatics. But all we are talking about is studying [reparations]. As John Conyers has said, we study everything. We study the water, the air. We can't even study the issue? This bill does not authorize one red cent to anyone."

That HR 40 has never—under either Democrats or Republicans—made it to the House floor suggests our concerns are rooted not in the impracticality of reparations but in something more existential. If we conclude that the conditions in North Lawndale and black America are not inexplicable but are instead precisely what you'd expect of a community that for centuries has lived in America's crosshairs, then what are we to make of the world's oldest democracy?

One cannot escape the question by hand-waving at the past, disavowing the acts of one's ancestors, nor by citing a recent date of ancestral immigration. The last slaveholder has been dead for a very long time. The last soldier to endure Valley Forge[11] has been dead much longer. To proudly claim the veteran and disown the slaveholder is patriotism à la carte.* A nation outlives its generations. We were not there when Washington crossed the Delaware,* but Emanuel Gottlieb Leutze's rendering[12] has meaning to us. We were not there when Woodrow Wilson took us into World War I, but we are still paying out the pensions. If Thomas Jefferson's genius matters, then so does his taking of Sally Hemings's[13] body. If George Washington crossing the Delaware matters, so must his ruthless pursuit of the runagate Oney Judge.[14]

In 1909, President William Howard Taft told the country that "intelligent" white southerners were ready to see blacks as "useful members of the community." A week later Joseph Gordon, a black man, was lynched outside Greenwood, Mississippi. The high point of the lynching era has passed. But the memories of those robbed of their lives still live on in the lingering effects. Indeed, in America there is a strange and powerful belief that if you stab a black person 10 times, the bleeding stops and the healing begins the moment the assailant drops the knife. We believe white dominance to be a fact of the inert past, a delinquent debt that can be made to disappear if only we don't look.

There has always been another way. "It is in vain to allege, that *our ancestors* brought them hither, and not we," Yale President Timothy Dwight said in 1810.

> We inherit our ample patrimony with all its incumbrances; and are bound to pay the debts of our ancestors. *This* debt, particularly, we are bound to discharge: and, when the righteous Judge of the Universe comes to reckon with his servants, he will rigidly exact the payment at our hands. To give them liberty, and stop here, is to entail upon them a curse.

America begins in black plunder and white democracy, two features that are not contradictory but complementary. "The men who came together to found the independent United States, dedicated to freedom and equality, either held

---

11 *Valley Forge* Site of a Revolutionary War-era military camp where American forces spent the winter of 1777 with inadequate provisions; thousands died.

12 *Emanuel ... rendering* Emanuel Gottlieb Leutze's 1857 painting *Washington Crossing the Delaware* is an iconic image of the event.

13 *Sally Hemings* Hemings (1773–1835) was a slave of Thomas Jefferson with whom he had a long-term sexual relationship.

14 *Oney Judge* Judge (c. 1773–1848) was a slave of George Washington who escaped; Washington tried repeatedly to secure her return.

slaves or were willing to join hands with those who did," the historian Edmund S. Morgan wrote. "None of them felt entirely comfortable about the fact, but neither did they feel responsible for it. Most of them had inherited both their slaves and their attachment to freedom from an earlier generation, and they knew the two were not unconnected."

When enslaved Africans, plundered of their bodies, plundered of their families, and plundered of their labour, were brought to the colony of Virginia* in 1619, they did not initially endure the naked racism that would engulf their progeny. Some of them were freed. Some of them intermarried. Still others escaped with the white indentured servants who had suffered as they had. Some even rebelled together, allying under Nathaniel Bacon to torch Jamestown in 1676.

One hundred years later, the idea of slaves and poor whites joining forces would shock the senses, but in the early days of the English colonies, the two groups had much in common. English visitors to Virginia found that its masters "abuse their servantes with intollerable oppression and hard usage." White servants were flogged, tricked into serving beyond their contracts, and traded in much the same manner as slaves.

This "hard usage" originated in a simple fact of the New World—land was boundless but cheap labour was limited. As life spans increased in the colony, the Virginia planters found in the enslaved Africans an even more efficient source of cheap labour. Whereas indentured servants were still legal subjects of the English crown and thus entitled to certain protections, African slaves entered the colonies as aliens. Exempted from the protections of the crown, they became early America's indispensable working class—fit for maximum exploitation, capable of only minimal resistance.

For the next 250 years, American law worked to reduce black people to a class of untouchables[15] and raise all white men to the level of citizens. In 1650, Virginia mandated that "all persons except Negroes" were to carry arms. In 1664, Maryland mandated that any Englishwoman who married a slave must live as a slave of her husband's master. In 1705, the Virginia assembly passed a law allowing for the dismemberment of unruly slaves—but forbidding masters from whipping "a Christian white servant naked, without an order from a justice of the peace." In that same law, the colony mandated that "all horses, cattle, and hogs, now belonging, or that hereafter shall belong to any slave" be seized and sold off by the local church, the profits used to support "the poor of the said parish." At that time, there would have still been people alive who could remember blacks and whites joining to burn down Jamestown only 29 years before. But at the beginning of the 18th century, two primary classes were enshrined in America.

---

15 *untouchables* Lowest members in India's elaborate class hierarchy.

65 "The two great divisions of society are not the rich and poor, but white and black," John C. Calhoun, South Carolina's senior senator, declared on the Senate floor in 1848. "And all the former, the poor as well as the rich, belong to the upper class, and are respected and treated as equals."

In 1860, the majority of people living in South Carolina and Mississippi, almost half of those living in Georgia, and about one-third of all Southerners were on the wrong side of Calhoun's line. The state with the largest number of enslaved Americans was Virginia, where in certain counties some 70 percent of all people laboured in chains. Nearly one-fourth of all white Southerners owned slaves, and upon their backs the economic basis of America—and much of the Atlantic world—was erected. In the seven cotton states, one-third of all white income was derived from slavery. By 1840, cotton produced by slave labour constituted 59 percent of the country's exports. The web of this slave society extended north to the looms of New England,* and across the Atlantic to Great Britain, where it powered a great economic transformation and altered the trajectory of world history. "Whoever says Industrial Revolution," wrote the historian Eric J. Hobsbawm, "says cotton."

The wealth accorded America by slavery was not just in what the slaves pulled from the land but in the slaves themselves. "In 1860, slaves as an asset were worth more than all of America's manufacturing, all of the railroads, all of the productive capacity of the United States put together," the Yale historian David W. Blight has noted. "Slaves were the single largest, by far, financial asset of property in the entire American economy." The sale of these slaves—"in whose bodies that money congealed," writes Walter Johnson, a Harvard historian—generated even more ancillary wealth. Loans were taken out for purchase, to be repaid with interest. Insurance policies were drafted against the untimely death of a slave and the loss of potential profits. Slave sales were taxed and notarized. The vending of the black body and the sundering of the black family became an economy unto themselves, estimated to have brought in tens of millions of dollars to antebellum America. In 1860 there were more millionaires per capita in the Mississippi Valley than anywhere else in the country.

Beneath the cold numbers lay lives divided. "I had a constant dread that Mrs. Moore, her mistress, would be in want of money and sell my dear wife," a freedman wrote, reflecting on his time in slavery. "We constantly dreaded a final separation. Our affection for each was very strong, and this made us always apprehensive of a cruel parting."

Forced partings were common in the antebellum South. A slave in some parts of the region stood a 30 percent chance of being sold in his or her lifetime. Twenty-five percent of interstate trades destroyed a first marriage and half of them destroyed a nuclear family.

When the wife and children of Henry Brown, a slave in Richmond, Vir- 70
ginia, were to be sold away, Brown searched for a white master who might buy his wife and children to keep the family together. He failed:

> The next day, I stationed myself by the side of the road, along which the slaves, amounting to three hundred and fifty, were to pass. The purchaser of my wife was a Methodist minister, who was about starting for North Carolina. Pretty soon five waggon-loads of little children passed, and looking at the foremost one, what should I see but a little child, pointing its tiny hand towards me, exclaiming, "There's my father; I knew he would come and bid me good-bye." It was my eldest child! Soon the gang approached in which my wife was chained. I looked, and beheld her familiar face; but O, reader, that glance of agony! may God spare me ever again enduring the excruciating horror of that moment! She passed, and came near to where I stood. I seized hold of her hand, intending to bid her farewell; but words failed me; the gift of utterance had fled, and I remained speechless. I followed her for some distance, with her hand grasped in mine, as if to save her from her fate, but I could not speak, and I was obliged to turn away in silence.

In a time when telecommunications were primitive and blacks lacked freedom of movement, the parting of black families was a kind of murder. Here we find the roots of American wealth and democracy—in the for-profit destruction of the most important asset available to any people, the family. The destruction was not incidental to America's rise; it facilitated that rise. By erecting a slave society, America created the economic foundation for its great experiment in democracy. The labour strife that seeded Bacon's rebellion was suppressed. America's indispensable working class existed as property beyond the realm of politics, leaving white Americans free to trumpet their love of freedom and democratic values. Assessing antebellum democracy in Virginia, a visitor from England observed that the state's natives "can profess an unbounded love of liberty and of democracy in consequence of the mass of the people, who in other countries might become mobs, being there nearly altogether composed of their own Negro slaves."

The consequences of 250 years of enslavement, of war upon black families and black people, were profound. Like homeownership today, slave ownership was aspirational, attracting not just those who owned slaves but those who wished to. Much as homeowners today might discuss the addition of a patio or the painting of a living room, slaveholders traded tips on the best methods for breeding workers, exacting labour, and doling out punishment. Just as a homeowner today might subscribe to a magazine like *This Old House*, slaveholders had journals such as *De Bow's Review*, which recommended the best practices for wringing profits from slaves. By the dawn of the Civil War, the enslavement of black America was thought to be so foundational to the country that those who sought to end it were branded heretics worthy of death. Imagine what would happen if a president today came out in favour of taking all American homes from their owners: the reaction might well be violent.

"This country was formed for the *white*, not for the black man," John Wilkes Booth wrote, before killing Abraham Lincoln. "And looking upon *African slavery* from the same standpoint held by those noble framers of our Constitution, I for one have ever considered it one of the greatest blessings (both for themselves and us) that God ever bestowed upon a favoured nation."

In the aftermath of the Civil War, Radical Republicans attempted to reconstruct the country upon something resembling universal equality—but they were beaten back by a campaign of "Redemption," led by White Liners, Red Shirts,[16] and Klansmen bent on upholding a society "formed for the *white*, not for the black man." A wave of terrorism roiled the South. In his massive history *Reconstruction*, Eric Foner recounts incidents of black people being attacked for not removing their hats; for refusing to hand over a whiskey flask; for disobeying church procedures; for "using insolent language"; for disputing labour contracts; for refusing to be "tied like a slave." Sometimes the attacks were intended simply to "thin out the niggers a little."

75 Terrorism carried the day. Federal troops withdrew from the South in 1877. The dream of Reconstruction* died. For the next century, political violence was visited upon blacks wantonly, with special treatment meted out toward black people of ambition. Black schools and churches were burned to the ground. Black voters and the political candidates who attempted to rally them were intimidated, and some were murdered. At the end of World War I, black veterans returning to their homes were assaulted for daring to wear the American uniform. The demobilization of soldiers after the war, which put white and black veterans into competition for scarce jobs, produced the Red Summer of 1919: a succession of racist pogroms against dozens of cities ranging from Longview, Texas, to Chicago to Washington, D.C. Organized white violence against blacks continued into the 1920s—in 1921 a white mob levelled Tulsa's "Black Wall Street,"* and in 1923 another one razed the black town of Rosewood, Florida—and virtually no one was punished.

The work of mobs was a rabid and violent rendition of prejudices that extended even into the upper reaches of American government. The New Deal* is today remembered as a model for what progressive government should do—cast a broad social safety net that protects the poor and the afflicted

---

16 *White Liners, Red Shirts* Groups of white supremacists.

while building the middle class. When progressives wish to express their disappointment with Barack Obama, they point to the accomplishments of Franklin Roosevelt. But these progressives rarely note that Roosevelt's New Deal, much like the democracy that produced it, rested on the foundation of Jim Crow.

"The Jim Crow South," writes Ira Katznelson, a history and political-science professor at Columbia, "was the one collaborator America's democracy could not do without." The marks of that collaboration are all over the New Deal. The omnibus programs passed under the Social Security Act in 1935 were crafted in such a way as to protect the southern way of life. Old-age insurance (Social Security proper) and unemployment insurance excluded farmworkers and domestics—jobs heavily occupied by blacks. When President Roosevelt signed Social Security into law in 1935, 65 percent of African Americans nationally and between 70 and 80 percent in the South were ineligible. The NAACP protested, calling the new American safety net "a sieve with holes just big enough for the majority of Negroes to fall through."

The oft-celebrated G.I. Bill* similarly failed black Americans, by mirroring the broader country's insistence on a racist housing policy. Though ostensibly colour-blind, Title III of the bill, which aimed to give veterans access to low-interest home loans, left black veterans to tangle with white officials at their local Veterans Administration as well as with the same banks that had, for years, refused to grant mortgages to blacks. The historian Kathleen J. Frydl observes in her 2009 book, *The GI Bill*, that so many blacks were disqualified from receiving Title III benefits "that it is more accurate simply to say that blacks could not use this particular title."

In Cold War America,* homeownership was seen as a means of instilling patriotism, and as a civilizing and anti-radical force. "No man who owns his own house and lot can be a Communist," claimed William Levitt, who pioneered the modern suburb with the development of the various Levittowns, his famous planned communities. "He has too much to do."

But the Levittowns were, with Levitt's willing acquiescence, segregated 80
throughout their early years. Daisy and Bill Myers, the first black family to move into Levittown, Pennsylvania, were greeted with protests and a burning cross.* A neighbour who opposed the family said that Bill Myers was "probably a nice guy, but every time I look at him I see $2,000 drop off the value of my house."

The neighbour had good reason to be afraid. Bill and Daisy Myers were from the other side of John C. Calhoun's dual society. If they moved next door, housing policy almost guaranteed that their neighbours' property values would decline.

Whereas shortly before the New Deal, a typical mortgage required a large down payment and full repayment within about 10 years, the creation of the Home Owners' Loan Corporation in 1933 and then the Federal Housing Administration the following year allowed banks to offer loans requiring no more than 10 percent down, amortized over 20 to 30 years. "Without federal intervention in the housing market, massive suburbanization would have been impossible," writes Thomas J. Sugrue, a historian at the University of Pennsylvania. "In 1930, only 30 percent of Americans owned their own homes; by 1960, more than 60 percent were home owners. Home ownership became an emblem of American citizenship."

That emblem was not to be awarded to blacks. The American real-estate industry believed segregation to be a moral principle. As late as 1950, the National Association of Real Estate Boards' code of ethics warned that "a Realtor should never be instrumental in introducing into a neighbourhood ... any race or nationality, or any individuals whose presence will clearly be detrimental to property values." A 1943 brochure specified that such potential undesirables might include madams, bootleggers, gangsters—and "a coloured man of means who was giving his children a college education and thought they were entitled to live among whites."

The federal government concurred. It was the Home Owners' Loan Corporation, not a private trade association, that pioneered the practice of redlining, selectively granting loans and insisting that any property it insured be covered by a restrictive covenant—a clause in the deed forbidding the sale of the property to anyone other than whites. Millions of dollars flowed from tax coffers into segregated white neighbourhoods.

85 "For perhaps the first time, the federal government embraced the discriminatory attitudes of the marketplace," the historian Kenneth T. Jackson wrote in his 1985 book, *Crabgrass Frontier*, a history of suburbanization. "Previously, prejudices were personalized and individualized; FHA exhorted segregation and enshrined it as public policy. Whole areas of cities were declared ineligible for loan guarantees." Redlining was not officially outlawed until 1968, by the Fair Housing Act. By then the damage was done—and reports of redlining by banks have continued.

The federal government is premised on equal fealty from all its citizens, who in return are to receive equal treatment. But as late as the mid-20th century, this bargain was not granted to black people, who repeatedly paid a higher price for citizenship and received less in return. Plunder had been the essential feature of slavery, of the society described by Calhoun. But practically a full century after the end of the Civil War and the abolition of slavery, the plunder—quiet, systemic, submerged—continued even amidst the aims and achievements of New Deal liberals.

Today Chicago is one of the most segregated cities in the country, a fact that reflects assiduous planning. In the effort to uphold white supremacy at every level down to the neighbourhood, Chicago—a city founded by the black fur trader Jean Baptiste Point du Sable—has long been a pioneer. The efforts began in earnest in 1917, when the Chicago Real Estate Board, horrified by the influx of southern blacks, lobbied to zone the entire city by race. But after the Supreme Court ruled against explicit racial zoning that year, the city was forced to pursue its agenda by more-discreet means.

Like the Home Owners' Loan Corporation, the Federal Housing Administration initially insisted on restrictive covenants, which helped bar blacks and other ethnic undesirables from receiving federally backed home loans. By the 1940s, Chicago led the nation in the use of these restrictive covenants, and about half of all residential neighbourhoods in the city were effectively off-limits to blacks.

It is common today to become misty-eyed about the old black ghetto, where doctors and lawyers lived next door to meatpackers and steelworkers, who themselves lived next door to prostitutes and the unemployed. This segregationist nostalgia ignores the actual conditions endured by the people living there—vermin and arson, for instance—and ignores the fact that the old ghetto was premised on denying black people privileges enjoyed by white Americans.

90 In 1948, when the Supreme Court ruled that restrictive covenants, while permissible, were not enforceable by judicial action, Chicago had other weapons at the ready. The Illinois state legislature had already given Chicago's city council the right to approve—and thus to veto—any public housing in the city's wards. This came in handy in 1949, when a new federal housing act sent millions of tax dollars into Chicago and other cities around the country. Beginning in 1950, site selection for public housing proceeded entirely on the grounds of segregation. By the 1960s, the city had created with its vast housing projects what the historian Arnold R. Hirsch calls a "second ghetto," one larger than the old Black Belt but just as impermeable. More than 98 percent of all the family public-housing units built in Chicago between 1950 and the mid-1960s were built in all-black neighbourhoods.

Governmental embrace of segregation was driven by the virulent racism of Chicago's white citizens. White neighbourhoods vulnerable to black encroachment formed block associations for the sole purpose of enforcing segregation. They lobbied fellow whites not to sell. They lobbied those blacks who did manage to buy to sell back. In 1949, a group of Englewood Catholics formed block associations intended to "keep up the neighbourhood." Translation: keep black people out. And when civic engagement was not enough, when government failed, when private banks could no longer hold the line, Chicago turned to an old tool in the American repertoire—racial violence. "The pattern of terrorism is easily discernible," concluded a Chicago civic group in the 1940s. "It is at the seams of the black ghetto in all directions." On July 1 and 2 of 1946, a mob of thousands assembled in Chicago's Park Manor neighbourhood, hoping to eject a black doctor who'd recently moved in. The mob pelted the house with rocks and set the garage on fire. The doctor moved away.

In 1947, after a few black veterans moved into the Fernwood section of Chicago, three nights of rioting broke out; gangs of whites yanked blacks off streetcars and beat them. Two years later, when a union meeting attended by blacks in Englewood triggered rumours that a home was being "sold to niggers," blacks (and whites thought to be sympathetic to them) were beaten in the streets. In 1951, thousands of whites in Cicero, 20 minutes or so west of downtown Chicago, attacked an apartment building that housed a single black family, throwing bricks and firebombs through the windows and setting the apartment on fire. A Cook County grand jury declined to charge the rioters—and instead indicted the family's NAACP attorney, the apartment's white owner, and the owner's attorney and rental agent, charging them with conspiring to lower property values. Two years after that, whites picketed and planted explosives in South Deering, about 30 minutes from downtown Chicago, to force blacks out.

When terrorism ultimately failed, white homeowners simply fled the neighbourhood. The traditional terminology, white flight, implies a kind of natural expression of preference. In fact, *white flight* was a triumph of social engineering, orchestrated by the shared racist presumptions of America's public and private sectors. For should any nonracist white families decide that integration might not be so bad as a matter of principle or practicality, they still had to contend with the hard facts of American housing policy: When the mid-20th-century white homeowner claimed that the presence of a Bill and Daisy Myers decreased his property value, he was not merely engaging in racist dogma—he was accurately observing the impact of federal policy on market prices. Redlining destroyed the possibility of investment wherever black people lived.

Speculators in North Lawndale, and at the edge of the black ghettos, knew there was money to be made off white panic. They resorted to "block-busting"—spooking whites into selling cheap before the neighbourhood became black. They would hire a black woman to walk up and down the street with a stroller. Or they'd hire someone to call a number in the neighbourhood looking for "Johnny Mae."* Then they'd cajole whites into selling at low prices, informing them that the more blacks who moved in, the more the value of their homes would decline, so better to sell now. With these white-fled homes in hand, speculators then turned to the masses of black people who had streamed northward as part of the Great Migration, or who were desperate to escape the ghettos: the speculators would take the houses they'd just bought cheap through block-busting and sell them to blacks on contract.

95 To keep up with his payments and keep his heat on, Clyde Ross took a second job at the post office and then a third job delivering pizza. His wife took a job working at Marshall Field.* He had to take some of his children out of private school. He was not able to be at home to supervise his children or help them with their homework. Money and time that Ross wanted to give his children went instead to enrich white speculators.

"The problem was the money," Ross told me. "Without the money, you can't move. You can't educate your kids. You can't give them the right kind of food. Can't make the house look good. They think this neighbourhood is where they supposed to be. It changes their outlook. My kids were going to the best schools in this neighbourhood, and I couldn't keep them in there."

Mattie Lewis came to Chicago from her native Alabama in the mid-'40s, when she was 21, persuaded by a friend who told her she could get a job as a hairdresser. Instead she was hired by Western Electric, where she worked for 41 years. I met Lewis in the home of her neighbour Ethel Weatherspoon. Both had owned homes in North Lawndale for more than 50 years. Both had bought their houses on contract. Both had been active with Clyde Ross in the Contract Buyers League's effort to garner restitution from contract sellers who'd operated in North Lawndale, banks who'd backed the scheme, and even the Federal Housing Administration. We were joined by Jack Macnamara, who'd been an organizing force in the Contract Buyers League when it was founded, in 1968. Our gathering had the feel of a reunion, because the writer James Alan McPherson had profiled the Contract Buyers League for *The Atlantic* back in 1972.

Weatherspoon bought her home in 1957. "Most of the whites started moving out," she told me. "'The blacks are coming. The blacks are coming.' They actually said that. They had signs up: Don't sell to blacks."

Before moving to North Lawndale, Lewis and her husband tried moving to Cicero after seeing a house advertised for sale there. "Sorry, I just sold it today," the Realtor told Lewis's husband. "I told him, 'You know they don't want you in Cicero,'" Lewis recalls. "'They ain't going to let nobody black in Cicero.'"

100 In 1958, the couple bought a home in North Lawndale on contract. They were not blind to the unfairness. But Lewis, born in the teeth of Jim Crow, considered American piracy—black people keep on making it, white people keep on taking it—a fact of nature. "All I wanted was a house. And that was the only way I could get it. They weren't giving black people loans at that time," she said. "We thought, 'This is the way it is. We going to do it till we die, and they ain't never going to accept us. That's just the way it is.'

"The only way you were going to buy a home was to do it the way they wanted," she continued. "And I was determined to get me a house. If everybody else can have one, I want one too. I had worked for white people in the South. And I saw how these white people were living in the North and I thought, 'One day I'm going to live just like them.' I wanted cabinets and all these things these other people have."

Whenever she visited white co-workers at their homes, she saw the difference. "I could see we were just getting ripped off," she said. "I would see things and I would say, 'I'd like to do this at my house.' And they would say, 'Do it,' but I would think, 'I can't, because it costs us so much more.'"

I asked Lewis and Weatherspoon how they kept up on payments.

"You paid it and kept working," Lewis said of the contract. "When that payment came up, you knew you had to pay it."

105 "You cut down on the light bill. Cut down on your food bill," Weatherspoon interjected.

"You cut down on things for your child, that was the main thing," said Lewis. "My oldest wanted to be an artist and my other wanted to be a dancer and my other wanted to take music."

Lewis and Weatherspoon, like Ross, were able to keep their homes. The suit did not win them any remuneration. But it forced contract sellers to the table, where they allowed some members of the Contract Buyers League to move into regular mortgages or simply take over their houses outright. By then they'd been bilked for thousands. In talking with Lewis and Weatherspoon, I was seeing only part of the picture—the tiny minority who'd managed to hold on to their homes. But for all our exceptional ones, for every Barack and Michelle Obama, for every Ethel Weatherspoon or Clyde Ross, for every black survivor, there are so many thousands gone.

"A lot of people fell by the way," Lewis told me. "One woman asked me if I would keep all her china. She said, 'They ain't going to set you out.'"

On a recent spring afternoon in North Lawndale, I visited Billy Lamar Brooks Sr. Brooks has been an activist since his youth in the Black Panther Party,* when he aided the Contract Buyers League. I met him in his office at the Better Boys Foundation, a staple of North Lawndale whose mission is to direct local kids off the streets and into jobs and college. Brooks's work is personal. On June 14, 1991, his 19-year-old son, Billy Jr., was shot and killed. "These guys tried to stick him up," Brooks told me. "I suspect he could have been involved in some things … He's always on my mind. Every day."

110 Brooks was not raised in the streets, though in such a neighbourhood it is impossible to avoid the influence. "I was in church three or four times a week. That's where the girls were," he said, laughing. "The stark reality is still there. There's no shield from life. You got to go to school. I lived here. I went to Marshall High School. Over here were the Egyptian Cobras. Over there were the Vice Lords."[17]

17 *Egyptian Cobras ... Vice Lords* Gang names.

Brooks has since moved away from Chicago's West Side. But he is still working in North Lawndale. If "you got a nice house, you live in a nice neighbourhood, then you are less prone to violence, because your space is not deprived," Brooks said. "You got a security point. You don't need no protection." But if "you grow up in a place like this, housing sucks. When they tore down the projects here, they left the high-rises and came to the neighbourhood with that gang mentality. You don't have nothing, so you going to take something, even if it's not real. You don't have no street, but in your mind it's yours."

We walked over to a window behind his desk. A group of young black men were hanging out in front of a giant mural memorializing two black men: In Lovin Memory Quentin aka "Q," July 18, 1974 ❤ March 2, 2012. The name and face of the other man had been spray-painted over by a rival group. The men drank beer. Occasionally a car would cruise past, slow to a crawl, then stop. One of the men would approach the car and make an exchange, then the car would drive off. Brooks had known all of these young men as boys.

"That's their corner," he said.

We watched another car roll through, pause briefly, then drive off. "No respect, no shame," Brooks said. "That's what they do. From that alley to that corner. They don't go no farther than that. See the big brother there? He almost died a couple of years ago. The one drinking the beer back there … I know all of them. And the reason they feel safe here is cause of this building, and because they too chickenshit to go anywhere. But that's their mentality. That's their block."

Brooks showed me a picture of a Little League team he had coached. He 115
went down the row of kids, pointing out which ones were in jail, which ones were dead, and which ones were doing all right. And then he pointed out his son—"That's my boy, Billy," Brooks said. Then he wondered aloud if keeping his son with him while working in North Lawndale had hastened his death. "It's a definite connection, because he was part of what I did here. And I think maybe I shouldn't have exposed him. But then, I had to," he said, "because I wanted him with me."

From the White House on down, the myth holds that fatherhood is the great antidote to all that ails black people. But Billy Brooks Jr. had a father. Trayvon Martin had a father. Jordan Davis[18] had a father. Adhering to middle-class norms has never shielded black people from plunder. Adhering to middle-class norms is what made Ethel Weatherspoon a lucrative target for rapacious speculators. Contract sellers did not target the very poor. They targeted black

---

18 *Trayvon Martin ... Jordan Davis* Martin and Davis were both African American teens who were shot and killed in 2012 by civilians while breaking no law.

people who had worked hard enough to save a down payment and dreamed of the emblem of American citizenship—homeownership. It was not a tangle of pathology that put a target on Clyde Ross's back. It was not a culture of poverty that singled out Mattie Lewis for "the thrill of the chase and the kill." Some black people always will be twice as good. But they generally find white predation to be thrice as fast.

Liberals today mostly view racism not as an active, distinct evil but as a relative of white poverty and inequality. They ignore the long tradition of this country actively punishing black success—and the elevation of that punishment, in the mid-20th century, to federal policy. President Lyndon Johnson may have noted in his historic civil-rights speech at Howard University in 1965 that "Negro poverty is not white poverty." But his advisers and their successors were, and still are, loath to craft any policy that recognizes the difference.

After his speech, Johnson convened a group of civil-rights leaders, including the esteemed A. Philip Randolph and Bayard Rustin, to address the "ancient brutality." In a strategy paper, they agreed with the president that "Negro poverty is a special, and particularly destructive, form of American poverty." But when it came to specifically addressing the "particularly destructive," Rustin's group demurred, preferring to advance programs that addressed "all the poor, black and white."

The urge to use the moral force of the black struggle to address broader inequalities originates in both compassion and pragmatism. But it makes for ambiguous policy. Affirmative action's precise aims, for instance, have always proved elusive. Is it meant to make amends for the crimes heaped upon black people? Not according to the Supreme Court. In its 1978 ruling in *Regents of the University of California v. Bakke*, the Court rejected "societal discrimination" as "an amorphous concept of injury that may be ageless in its reach into the past." Is affirmative action meant to increase "diversity"? If so, it only tangentially relates to the specific problems of black people—the problem of what America has taken from them over several centuries.

120 This confusion about affirmative action's aims, along with our inability to face up to the particular history of white-imposed black disadvantage, dates back to the policy's origins. "There is no fixed and firm definition of affirmative action," an appointee in Johnson's Department of Labor declared. "Affirmative action is anything that you have to do to get results. But this does not necessarily include preferential treatment."

Yet America was built on the preferential treatment of white people—395 years of it. Vaguely endorsing a cuddly, feel-good diversity does very little to redress this.

Today, progressives are loath to invoke white supremacy as an explanation for anything. On a practical level, the hesitation comes from the dim view the Supreme Court has taken of the reforms of the 1960s. The Voting Rights Act has been gutted. The Fair Housing Act might well be next. Affirmative action is on its last legs. In substituting a broad class struggle for an anti-racist struggle, progressives hope to assemble a coalition by changing the subject.

The politics of racial evasion are seductive. But the record is mixed. Aid to Families With Dependent Children was originally written largely to exclude blacks—yet by the 1990s it was perceived as a giveaway to blacks. The Affordable Care Act* makes no mention of race, but this did not keep Rush Limbaugh* from denouncing it as reparations. Moreover, the act's expansion of Medicaid was effectively made optional, meaning that many poor blacks in the former Confederate states do not benefit from it. The Affordable Care Act, like Social Security, will eventually expand its reach to those left out; in the meantime, black people will be injured.

"All that it would take to sink a new WPA program[19] would be some skillfully packaged footage of black men leaning on shovels smoking cigarettes," the sociologist Douglas S. Massey writes. "Papering over the issue of race makes for bad social theory, bad research, and bad public policy." To ignore the fact that one of the oldest republics in the world was erected on a foundation of white supremacy, to pretend that the problems of a dual society are the same as the problems of unregulated capitalism, is to cover the sin of national plunder with the sin of national lying. The lie ignores the fact that reducing American poverty and ending white supremacy are not the same. The lie ignores the fact that closing the "achievement gap" will do nothing to close the "injury gap," in which black college graduates still suffer higher unemployment rates than white college graduates, and black job applicants without criminal records enjoy roughly the same chance of getting hired as white applicants *with* criminal records.

Chicago, like the country at large, embraced policies that placed black 125
America's most energetic, ambitious, and thrifty countrymen beyond the pale of society and marked them as rightful targets for legal theft. The effects reverberate beyond the families who were robbed to the community that beholds the spectacle. Don't just picture Clyde Ross working three jobs so he could hold on to his home. Think of his North Lawndale neighbours—their children, their nephews and nieces—and consider how watching this affects them. Imagine yourself as a young black child watching your elders play by all the rules only

19 *WPA program* Works Progress Administration program, a part of the New Deal in which unemployed workers were given employment building schools, roads, and other public works.

to have their possessions tossed out in the street and to have their most sacred possession—their home—taken from them.

The message the young black boy receives from his country, Billy Brooks says, is "'You ain't shit. You not no good. The only thing you are worth is working for us. You will never own anything. You not going to get an education. We are sending your ass to the penitentiary.' They're telling you no matter how hard you struggle, no matter what you put down, you ain't shit. 'We're going to take what you got. You will never own anything, nigger.'"

When Clyde Ross was a child, his older brother Winter had a seizure. He was picked up by the authorities and delivered to Parchman Farm, a 20,000-acre state prison in the Mississippi Delta region.*

"He was a gentle person," Clyde Ross says of his brother. "You know, he was good to everybody. And he started having spells, and he couldn't control himself. And they had him picked up, because they thought he was dangerous."

Built at the turn of the century, Parchman was supposed to be a progressive and reformist response to the problem of "Negro crime." In fact it was the gulag[20] of Mississippi, an object of terror to African Americans in the Delta. In the early years of the 20th century, Mississippi Governor James K. Vardaman used to amuse himself by releasing black convicts into the surrounding wilderness and hunting them down with bloodhounds. "Throughout the American South," writes David M. Oshinsky in his book *Worse Than Slavery*, "Parchman Farm is synonymous with punishment and brutality, as well it should be … Parchman is the quintessential penal farm, the closest thing to slavery that survived the Civil War."

130 When the Ross family went to retrieve Winter, the authorities told them that Winter had died. When the Ross family asked for his body, the authorities at Parchman said they had buried him. The family never saw Winter's body.

And this was just one of their losses.

Scholars have long discussed methods by which America might make reparations to those on whose labour and exclusion the country was built. In the 1970s, the Yale Law professor Boris Bittker argued in *The Case for Black Reparations* that a rough price tag for reparations could be determined by multiplying the number of African Americans in the population by the difference in white and black per capita income. That number—$34 billion in 1973, when Bittker wrote his book—could be added to a reparations program each year for a decade or two. Today Charles Ogletree, the Harvard Law School professor,

---

20 *gulag* In the former Soviet Union, gulags were prisons to which political dissidents were sent. Such prisons were known for brutally harsh conditions; many prisoners died before the end of their sentence.

argues for something broader: a program of job training and public works that takes racial justice as its mission but includes the poor of all races.

Perhaps no statistic better illustrates the enduring legacy of our country's shameful history of treating black people as sub-citizens, sub-Americans, and sub-humans than the wealth gap. Reparations would seek to close this chasm. But as surely as the creation of the wealth gap required the cooperation of every aspect of the society, bridging it will require the same.

Perhaps after a serious discussion and debate—the kind that HR 40 proposes—we may find that the country can never fully repay African Americans. But we stand to discover much about ourselves in such a discussion—and that is perhaps what scares us. The idea of reparations is frightening not simply because we might lack the ability to pay. The idea of reparations threatens something much deeper—America's heritage, history, and standing in the world.

The early American economy was built on slave labour. The Capitol and the 135
White House were built by slaves. President James K. Polk traded slaves from the Oval Office. The laments about "black pathology,"[21] the criticism of black family structures by pundits and intellectuals, ring hollow in a country whose existence was predicated on the torture of black fathers, on the rape of black mothers, on the sale of black children. An honest assessment of America's relationship to the black family reveals the country to be not its nurturer but its destroyer.

And this destruction did not end with slavery. Discriminatory laws joined the equal burden of citizenship to unequal distribution of its bounty. These laws reached their apex in the mid-20th century, when the federal government—through housing policies—engineered the wealth gap, which remains with us to this day. When we think of white supremacy, we picture COLOURED ONLY signs,* but we should picture pirate flags.

On some level, we have always grasped this.

"Negro poverty is not white poverty," President Johnson said in his historic civil-rights speech.

> Many of its causes and many of its cures are the same. But there are differences—deep, corrosive, obstinate differences—radiating painful roots into the community and into the family, and the nature of the individual. These differences are not racial differences. They are solely and simply the consequence of ancient brutality, past injustice, and present prejudice.

---

21 *black pathology* Allegedly diseased nature of African American culture.

We invoke the words of Jefferson and Lincoln because they say something about our legacy and our traditions. We do this because we recognize our links to the past—at least when they flatter us. But black history does not flatter American democracy; it chastens it. The popular mocking of reparations as a harebrained scheme authored by wild-eyed lefties and intellectually unserious black nationalists is fear masquerading as laughter. Black nationalists have always perceived something unmentionable about America that integrationists dare not acknowledge—that white supremacy is not merely the work of hotheaded demagogues, or a matter of false consciousness, but a force so fundamental to America that it is difficult to imagine the country without it.

140 And so we must imagine a new country. Reparations—by which I mean the full acceptance of our collective biography and its consequences—is the price we must pay to see ourselves squarely. The recovering alcoholic may well have to live with his illness for the rest of his life. But at least he is not living a drunken lie. Reparations beckons us to reject the intoxication of hubris and see America as it is—the work of fallible humans.

Won't reparations divide us? Not any more than we are already divided. The wealth gap merely puts a number on something we feel but cannot say—that American prosperity was ill-gotten and selective in its distribution. What is needed is an airing of family secrets, a settling with old ghosts. What is needed is a healing of the American psyche and the banishment of white guilt.

What I'm talking about is more than recompense for past injustices—more than a handout, a payoff, hush money, or a reluctant bribe. What I'm talking about is a national reckoning that would lead to spiritual renewal. Reparations would mean the end of scarfing hot dogs on the Fourth of July while denying the facts of our heritage. Reparations would mean the end of yelling "patriotism" while waving a Confederate flag. Reparations would mean a revolution of the American consciousness, a reconciling of our self-image as the great democratizer with the facts of our history.

We are not the first to be summoned to such a challenge.

In 1952, when West Germany began the process of making amends for the Holocaust, it did so under conditions that should be instructive to us. Resistance was violent. Very few Germans believed that Jews were entitled to anything. Only 5 percent of West Germans surveyed reported feeling guilty about the Holocaust, and only 29 percent believed that Jews were owed restitution from the German people.

145 "The rest," the historian Tony Judt wrote in his 2005 book, *Postwar*, "were divided between those (some two-fifths of respondents) who thought that only people 'who really committed something' were responsible and should pay,

and those (21 percent) who thought 'that the Jews themselves were partly responsible for what happened to them during the Third Reich.'"

Germany's unwillingness to squarely face its history went beyond polls. Movies that suggested a societal responsibility for the Holocaust beyond Hitler were banned. "The German soldier fought bravely and honourably for his homeland," claimed President Eisenhower, endorsing the Teutonic national myth. Judt wrote, "Throughout the fifties West German officialdom encouraged a comfortable view of the German past in which the Wehrmacht[22] was heroic, while Nazis were in a minority and properly punished."

Konrad Adenauer, the postwar German chancellor, was in favour of reparations, but his own party was divided, and he was able to get an agreement passed only with the votes of the Social Democratic opposition.

Among the Jews of Israel, reparations provoked violent and venomous reactions ranging from denunciation to assassination plots. On January 7, 1952, as the Knesset—the Israeli parliament—convened to discuss the prospect of a reparations agreement with West Germany, Menachem Begin, the future prime minister of Israel, stood in front of a large crowd, inveighing against the country that had plundered the lives, labour, and property of his people. Begin claimed that all Germans were Nazis and guilty of murder. His condemnations then spread to his own young state. He urged the crowd to stop paying taxes and claimed that the nascent Israeli nation characterized the fight over whether or not to accept reparations as a "war to the death." When alerted that the police watching the gathering were carrying tear gas, allegedly of German manufacture, Begin yelled, "The same gases that asphyxiated our parents!"

Begin then led the crowd in an oath to never forget the victims of the Shoah,[23] lest "my right hand lose its cunning" and "my tongue cleave to the roof of my mouth." He took the crowd through the streets toward the Knesset. From the rooftops, police repelled the crowd with tear gas and smoke bombs. But the wind shifted, and the gas blew back toward the Knesset, billowing through windows shattered by rocks. In the chaos, Begin and Prime Minister David Ben-Gurion exchanged insults. Two hundred civilians and 140 police officers were wounded. Nearly 400 people were arrested. Knesset business was halted.

Begin then addressed the chamber with a fiery speech condemning the actions the legislature was about to take. "Today you arrested hundreds," he said. "Tomorrow you may arrest thousands. No matter, they will go, they will sit in prison. We will sit there with them. If necessary, we will be killed with them. But there will be no 'reparations' from Germany."

---

22 *Wehrmacht* Term for the armed forces in Nazi Germany.

23 *Shoah* Hebrew term for the Holocaust.

Survivors of the Holocaust feared laundering the reputation of Germany with money, and mortgaging the memory of their dead. Beyond that, there was a taste for revenge. “My soul would be at rest if I knew there would be 6 million German dead to match the 6 million Jews,” said Meir Dworzecki, who’d survived the concentration camps of Estonia.

Ben-Gurion countered this sentiment, not by repudiating vengeance but with cold calculation: “If I could take German property without sitting down with them for even a minute but go in with jeeps and machine guns to the warehouses and take it, I would do that—if, for instance, we had the ability to send a hundred divisions and tell them, ‘Take it.’ But we can’t do that.”

The reparations conversation set off a wave of bomb attempts by Israeli militants. One was aimed at the foreign ministry in Tel Aviv. Another was aimed at Chancellor Adenauer himself. And one was aimed at the port of Haifa, where the goods bought with reparations money were arriving. West Germany ultimately agreed to pay Israel 3.45 billion deutsche marks, or more than $7 billion in today’s dollars. Individual reparations claims followed—for psychological trauma, for offense to Jewish honour, for halting law careers, for life insurance, for time spent in concentration camps. Seventeen percent of funds went toward purchasing ships. “By the end of 1961, these reparations vessels constituted two-thirds of the Israeli merchant fleet,” writes the Israeli historian Tom Segev in his book *The Seventh Million*. “From 1953 to 1963, the reparations money funded about a third of the total investment in Israel’s electrical system, which tripled its capacity, and nearly half the total investment in the railways.”

Israel’s GNP tripled during the 12 years of the agreement. The Bank of Israel attributed 15 percent of this growth, along with 45,000 jobs, to investments made with reparations money. But Segev argues that the impact went far beyond that. Reparations “had indisputable psychological and political importance,” he writes.

155 Reparations could not make up for the murder perpetrated by the Nazis. But they did launch Germany’s reckoning with itself, and perhaps provided a road map for how a great civilization might make itself worthy of the name.

Assessing the reparations agreement, David Ben-Gurion said:

> For the first time in the history of relations between people, a precedent has been created by which a great State, as a result of moral pressure alone, takes it upon itself to pay compensation to the victims of the government that preceded it. For the first time in the history of a people that has been persecuted, oppressed, plundered and despoiled for hundreds of years in the countries of Europe, a persecutor and despoiler has been obliged to return part of his spoils and has even undertaken to make collective reparation as partial compensation for material losses.

Something more than moral pressure calls America to reparations. We cannot escape our history. All of our solutions to the great problems of health care, education, housing, and economic inequality are troubled by what must go unspoken. "The reason black people are so far behind now is not because of now," Clyde Ross told me. "It's because of then." In the early 2000s, Charles Ogletree went to Tulsa, Oklahoma, to meet with the survivors of the 1921 race riot that had devastated "Black Wall Street." The past was not the past to them. "It was amazing seeing these black women and men who were crippled, blind, in wheelchairs," Ogletree told me. "I had no idea who they were and why they wanted to see me. They said, 'We want you to represent us in this lawsuit.'"

A commission authorized by the Oklahoma legislature produced a report affirming that the riot, the knowledge of which had been suppressed for years, had happened. But the lawsuit ultimately failed, in 2004. Similar suits pushed against corporations such as Aetna (which insured slaves) and Lehman Brothers (whose co-founding partner owned them) also have thus far failed. These results are dispiriting, but the crime with which reparations activists charge the country implicates more than just a few towns or corporations. The crime indicts the American people themselves, at every level, and in nearly every configuration. A crime that implicates the entire American people deserves its hearing in the legislative body that represents them.

John Conyers's HR 40 is the vehicle for that hearing. No one can know what would come out of such a debate. Perhaps no number can fully capture the multi-century plunder of black people in America. Perhaps the number is so large that it can't be imagined, let alone calculated and dispensed. But I believe that wrestling publicly with these questions matters as much as—if not more than—the specific answers that might be produced. An America that asks what it owes its most vulnerable citizens is improved and humane. An America that looks away is ignoring not just the sins of the past but the sins of the present and the certain sins of the future. More important than any single cheque cut to any African American, the payment of reparations would represent America's maturation out of the childhood myth of its innocence into a wisdom worthy of its founders.

In 2010, Jacob S. Rugh, then a doctoral candidate at Princeton, and the soci- 160
ologist Douglas S. Massey published a study of the recent foreclosure crisis.* Among its drivers, they found an old foe: segregation. Black home buyers—even after controlling for factors like creditworthiness—were still more likely than white home buyers to be steered toward subprime loans.* Decades of racist housing policies by the American government, along with decades of racist housing practices by American businesses, had conspired to concentrate African Americans in the same neighbourhoods. As in North Lawndale half a

century earlier, these neighbourhoods were filled with people who had been cut off from mainstream financial institutions. When subprime lenders went looking for prey, they found black people waiting like ducks in a pen.

"High levels of segregation create a natural market for subprime lending," Rugh and Massey write, "and cause riskier mortgages, and thus foreclosures, to accumulate disproportionately in racially segregated cities' minority neighbourhoods."

Plunder in the past made plunder in the present efficient. The banks of America understood this. In 2005, Wells Fargo promoted a series of Wealth Building Strategies seminars. Dubbing itself "the nation's leading originator of home loans to ethnic minority customers," the bank enrolled black public figures in an ostensible effort to educate blacks on building "generational wealth." But the "wealth building" seminars were a front for wealth theft. In 2010, the Justice Department filed a discrimination suit against Wells Fargo alleging that the bank had shunted blacks into predatory loans regardless of their creditworthiness. This was not magic or coincidence or misfortune. It was racism reifying itself. According to *The New York Times*, affidavits found loan officers referring to their black customers as "mud people" and to their subprime products as "ghetto loans."

"We just went right after them," Beth Jacobson, a former Wells Fargo loan officer, told *The Times*. "Wells Fargo mortgage had an emerging-markets unit that specifically targeted black churches because it figured church leaders had a lot of influence and could convince congregants to take out subprime loans."

In 2011, Bank of America agreed to pay $355 million to settle charges of discrimination against its Countrywide unit. The following year, Wells Fargo settled its discrimination suit for more than $175 million. But the damage had been done. In 2009, half the properties in Baltimore whose owners had been granted loans by Wells Fargo between 2005 and 2008 were vacant; 71 percent of these properties were in predominantly black neighbourhoods.

(2014)

Questions

1. How do the three epigraphs for this essay begin the argument for reparations? Who wrote them? Why is their authorship significant?
2. What means did white people use to steal land from African Americans?
3. What did Clyde Ross find when he was stationed in California? What did he find in Mississippi when he returned after World War II?

4. What is redlining?
5. What was the Contract Buyers League? How did they seek justice? Were they successful?
6. How is slavery the basis of American democracy and wealth?
7. Anne-Marie Slaughter wrote a response to this essay in a Facebook post on 22 November 2015. She said: "I started reading Ta-Nehisi Coates' article … firmly convinced that I was opposed to reparations…. I finished it convinced that he was right." What was your experience reading this essay? Were you convinced by the arguments?
8. What are some of the reasons for resistance to reparations? What impact—positive and/or negative—would reparations have on American society?
9. Consider what you know of Canadian history. Are there any Canadian groups about which one could make arguments parallel to Coates's?

Nicholas Kristof

When Whites Just Don't Get It

The 9 August 2014 shooting by police officer Darren Wilson of unarmed teenager Michael Brown in Ferguson, Missouri (a suburb of St. Louis) became a cause célèbre when no charges were filed against the officer responsible. Protests carried on for many weeks, and the incident prompted many to ask fresh questions about race relations in America. New York Times *columnist Nicholas Kristof's piece on the topic generated a variety of passionate responses, and he followed up with several more columns under the same heading. Included here are the first and the sixth in the series (30 August 2014 and 6 April 2016, respectively).*

Many white Americans say they are fed up with the coverage of the shooting of Michael Brown in Ferguson, Mo. A plurality of whites in a recent Pew survey said that the issue of race is getting more attention than it deserves.

Bill O'Reilly of Fox News reflected that weariness, saying: "All you hear is grievance, grievance, grievance, money, money, money."

Indeed, a 2011 study by scholars at Harvard and Tufts found that whites, on average, believed that anti-white racism was a bigger problem than anti-black racism.

Yes, you read that right!

5 So let me push back at what I see as smug white delusion. Here are a few reasons race relations deserve more attention, not less:

- The net worth of the average black household in the United States is $6,314, compared with $110,500 for the average white household, according to 2011 census data. The gap has worsened in the last decade, and the United States now has a greater wealth gap by race than South Africa did during apartheid. (Whites in America on average own almost 18 times as much as blacks; in South Africa in 1970, the ratio was about 15 times.)
- The black-white income gap is roughly 40 percent greater today than it was in 1967.
- A black boy born today in the United States has a life expectancy five years shorter than that of a white boy.

- Black students are significantly less likely to attend schools offering advanced math and science courses than white students. They are three times as likely to be suspended and expelled, setting them up for educational failure.
- Because of the catastrophic experiment in mass incarceration, black men in their 20s without a high school diploma are more likely to be incarcerated today than employed, according to a study from the National Bureau of Economic Research. Nearly 70 percent of middle-aged black men who never graduated from high school have been imprisoned.

All these constitute not a black problem or a white problem, but an American problem. When so much talent is underemployed and over-incarcerated, the entire country suffers.

Some straight people have gradually changed their attitudes toward gays after realizing that their friends—or children—were gay. Researchers have found that male judges are more sympathetic to women's rights when they have daughters. Yet because of the de facto* segregation of America, whites are unlikely to have many black friends: A study from the Public Religion Research Institute suggests that in a network of 100 friends, a white person, on average, has one black friend.

That's unfortunate, because friends open our eyes. I was shaken after a well-known black woman told me about looking out her front window and seeing that police officers had her teenage son down on the ground after he had stepped out of their upscale house because they thought he was a prowler. "Thank God he didn't run," she said.

One black friend tells me that he freaked out when his white fiancée purchased an item in a store and promptly threw the receipt away. "What are you doing?" he protested to her. He is a highly successful and well-educated professional but would never dream of tossing a receipt for fear of being accused of shoplifting.

Some readers will protest that the stereotype is rooted in reality: Young 10
black men are disproportionately likely to be criminals.

That's true—and complicated. "There's nothing more painful to me," the Rev. Jesse Jackson once said, "than to walk down the street and hear footsteps and start thinking about robbery—and then look around and see somebody white and feel relieved."

All this should be part of the national conversation on race, as well, and prompt a drive to help young black men end up in jobs and stable families rather than in crime or jail. We have policies with a robust record of creating opportunity: home visitation programs like Nurse-Family Partnership; early education initiatives like Educare and Head Start; programs for troubled adolescents like

Youth Villages; anti-gang and anti-crime initiatives like Becoming a Man; efforts to prevent teen pregnancies like the Carrera curriculum; job training like Career Academies; and job incentives like the earned-income tax credit.

The best escalator to opportunity may be education, but that escalator is broken for black boys growing up in neighbourhoods with broken schools. We fail those boys before they fail us.

So a starting point is for those of us in white America to wipe away any self-satisfaction about racial progress. Yes, the progress is real, but so are the challenges. The gaps demand a wrenching, soul-searching excavation of our national soul, and the first step is to acknowledge that the central race challenge in America today is not the suffering of whites.

(2014)

WHEN WHITES JUST DON'T GET IT, PART 6

Let's start with a quiz. When researchers sent young whites and blacks out to interview for low-wage jobs in New York City armed with equivalent résumés, the result was:

a) Whites and blacks were hired at similar rates.
b) Blacks had a modest edge because of affirmative action.
c) Whites were twice as likely to get callbacks.

The answer is C, and a black applicant with a clean criminal record did no better than a white applicant who was said to have just been released from 18 months in prison.

A majority of whites believe that job opportunities are equal for whites and blacks, according to a PBS poll, but rigorous studies show that just isn't so.

Back in 2014, I did a series of columns called "When Whites Just Don't Get It" to draw attention to inequities, and I'm revisiting it because public attention to racial disparities seems to be flagging even as the issues are as grave as ever.

5 But let me first address some reproaches I've received from indignant whites, including the very common: You would never write a column about blacks not getting it, and it's racist to pick on whites. It's true that I would be wary as a white person of lecturing to blacks about race, but plenty of black leaders (including President Obama) have bluntly spoken about shortcomings in the black community.

Toni Morrison in her novels writes searingly about a black world pummelled by discrimination but also by violence, drunkenness and broken families. In a CNN poll, 86 percent of blacks said family breakdown was a reason for difficulties of African-Americans today, and 77 percent cited "lack of motivation and unwillingness to work hard."

Frankly, the conversation within the black community seems to me to be more mature and honest than the one among whites, and considering how much of the white conversation about race invokes "personal responsibility," maybe it's time for whites to show more.

Obama's election reinforced a narrative that we're making progress. We are in some ways, but the median black household in America still has only 8 percent of the wealth of the median white household. And even for blacks who have "made it"—whose incomes are in the upper half of American incomes—60 percent of their children tumble back into the lower half in the next generation, according to a Federal Reserve study. If these trends continue, the Fed study noted, "black Americans would make no further relative progress."

Most of the public debate about race focuses on law enforcement. That's understandable after the shootings of unarmed blacks and after the U.S. Sentencing Commission found that black men received sentences about 20 percent longer than white men for similar crimes. But that's just the tip of the iceberg. Lead poisoning, for example, is more than twice as common among black children as among white children, and in much of the country, it's even worse than in Flint, Mich.[1]

Three generations after *Brown v. Board of Education*,[2] American schools 10
are still often separate and unequal. The average white or Asian-American student attends a school in at least the 60th percentile in test performance; the average black student is at a school at the 37th percentile. One reason is an unjust school funding system that often directs the most resources to privileged students.

So if we're going to address systemic disadvantage of black children, we have to broaden the conversation to unequal education. There's a lot of loose talk among whites about black boys making bad decisions, but we fail these kids before they fail us. That's unconscionable when increasingly we have robust evidence about the kinds of initiatives (like home visitation, prekindergarten and "career academies") that reduce disparities.

---

1 *Flint, Mich.* The revelation in 2014 of dangerous levels of lead contamination in the drinking water of Flint caused a considerable scandal.

2 *Brown v. Board of Education* Landmark 1954 Supreme Court case, which declared enforced segregation of schoolchildren on the basis of race to be unconstitutional.

Reasons for inequality involve not just institutions but also personal behaviours. These don't all directly involve discrimination. For instance, black babies are less likely to be breast-fed than white babies, are more likely to grow up with a single parent and may be spoken to or read to less by their parents. But racial discrimination remains ubiquitous even in crucial spheres like jobs and housing.

In one study, researchers sent thousands of résumés to employers with openings, randomly using some stereotypically black names (like Jamal) and others that were more likely to belong to whites (like Brendan). A white name increased the likelihood of a callback by 50 percent.

Likewise, in Canada researchers found that emails from stereotypically black names seeking apartments are less likely to get responses from landlords. And in U.S. experiments, when blacks and whites go in person to rent or buy properties, blacks are shown fewer options.

Something similar happens even with sales. Researchers offered iPods for sale online and found that when the photo showed the iPod held by a white hand, it received 21 percent more offers than when held by a black hand.

Discrimination is also pervasive in the white-collar world.* Researchers found that white state legislators, Democrats and Republicans alike, were less likely to respond to a constituent letter signed with a stereotypically black name. Even at universities, emails sent to professors from stereotypically black names asking for a chance to discuss research possibilities received fewer responses.

Why do we discriminate? The big factor isn't overt racism. Rather, it seems to be unconscious bias among whites who believe in equality but act in ways that perpetuate inequality.

Eduardo Bonilla-Silva, an eminent sociologist, calls this unconscious bias "racism without racists," and we whites should be less defensive about it. This bias affects blacks as well as whites, and we also have unconscious biases about gender, disability, body size and age. You can explore your own unconscious biases in a free online test, called the implicit association test.

One indication of how deeply rooted biases are: A rigorous study by economists found that even N.B.A. referees were more likely to call fouls on players of another race. Something similar happens in baseball, with researchers finding that umpires calling strikes are biased against black pitchers.

If even professional referees and umpires are biased, can there be any hope for you and me as we navigate our daily lives? Actually, there is.

The N.B.A. study caused a furor (the league denied the bias), and a few years later there was a follow-up by the same economists, and the bias had disappeared. It seems that when we humans realize our biases, we can adjust and act in ways that are more fair. As the study's authors put it, "Awareness reduces racial bias."

That's why it's so important for whites to engage in these uncomfortable discussions of race—because we are (unintentionally) so much a part of the problem. It's not that we're evil, but that we're human. The challenge is to recognize that unconscious bias afflicts us all—but that we just may be able to overcome it if we face it.

(2016)

Questions

1. Discuss Kristof's argument about the way friends and relatives can help one overcome one's prejudices. Do you agree? Why or why not?
2. What was the predominant white reaction to the media attention following the shooting of Michael Brown? How does Kristof challenge the validity of that reaction?
3. List five of the statistics that Kristof uses to reinforce his message that "Whites Just Don't Get It." Do these numbers change your point of view on the narrative of progress in America?
4. What kinds of reactions does Kristof report that he received from whites in response to this series of articles? How does he refute them? Evaluate his refutation.

LAWRENCE G. PROULX

A GROUP YOU CAN SAFELY ATTACK

Nicholas Kristof's series of columns entitled "When Whites Just Don't Get It" (see above) sparked a wide range of reactions. Some suggested that he was not going far enough in his criticisms; in the online Observer, *for example, Lincoln Mitchell opined that "calling for another conversation about race is a serious sounding way of doing nothing." A more frequently heard criticism of Kristof, however, went along the lines suggested by Norman Leahy and Paul Goldman in their* Washington Post *blog: "staining a whole group with such a broad journalistic brush [as Kristof uses] would be considered ignorant if not racist had it been written about anyone but white people."*[1] *That argument is made at greater length by Lawrence Proulx in the 2 September 2015* Providence Journal *column reprinted here.*

Every age has propositions that it is happy to hear and repeat and others that it is loath to. In times of war, people want to hear praise of their side, not of the enemy. In times of tragedy, criticism of the victims is intolerable. Honesty is no excuse.

Our age is no different.

In America today, people generally find it distasteful to hear general categories of human beings discussed in a negative way. But there are two prominent exceptions: white people and men. I belong to both categories.

In my work, I read one of the world's great newspapers;[2] in my leisure time I read other general-interest papers and magazines. And I have slowly gotten the impression that white people and men are treated in a particular, unenviable, way. They are, in reporting and commentary, what you might call fair game. Where writers are generally reluctant to call attention to the sex,

---

1 *online ... white people* See Lincoln Mitchell, "Honestly, Talking about Race Changes Nothing in America," *Observer*, 4 December 2014; and Norman Leahy and Paul Goldman, "When 'Whites' Don't Get It—a Rebuttal," *Washington Post*, 23 October 2014.

2 *In my work ... newspapers* The author works as a copyeditor for the *International New York Times* in France.

ethnicity, religion or race of people when the result would be unflattering, they make an exception for whites and for men. There is something in the air that implicitly imparts the message that white people and men have it coming.

5 In news articles it is common to have it pointed out to us when men or white people predominate in a criticizable practice. If they enjoy an advantage or apparent advantage, the mere fact is offered as an obvious case of injustice.

An example. Starting on Aug. 30 of last year, *The New York Times* published five columns by Nicholas Kristof on "When Whites Just Don't Get It," the thrust of which was that white people just don't realize how badly they behave toward black people.

Kristof has every right to express his opinions. But I have the uncomfortable feeling that his criticisms of white people were welcomed by the *Times* in a way that criticisms of other categories of people would not have been.

Tell me if I'm wrong. Can you recall the *Times* or *The Wall Street Journal* or any other newspaper running articles about "When Blacks Just Don't Get It" or "When Homosexuals Just Don't Get It" or "When Jews Just Don't Get It"? Am I just paranoid? Was I napping when they ran?

Another example: In November, in a *Washington Post* interview, Meghan McCain, co-host of a show on the Pivot network, was asked what she would do if she were ruler of the universe. She said, "I would just like to have less old white men ruling everything in the media."

10 She, too, has the right to her opinions. But imagine that instead of "old white men" she had talked of "old Jews" and had opined that she would "just like to have less old Jews ruling everything at the Federal Reserve." Or that she wished there weren't so many "young black men" on television. Would the *Post* still have treated her remark as a cute part of her "dishing" with its gossip columnist? Again, I suspect the answer is no. What is considered indecent in relation to some groups is perfectly fine for others.

Generalizations, whether positive or negative, can be valid or invalid. It depends on the facts, and people must be free to propose and debate them. But a situation where some groups are off-limits and others are ganged up on is hard to defend on any principle of logic or fairness.

Is what would be considered rude and unacceptable in relation to Jews or women or black people not also rude and unacceptable in relation to white people and men? If not, why not?

Surely writers and editors give consideration to some people's sensibilities not because these people have special rights but because they fully possess rights that are universal.

So, I submit, do white people and men.

(2015)

Questions

1. Do you agree with Proulx that white men are "fair game" in Western society?
2. What might be some of the reasons why it is important for white people, and for white men in particular, to think critically about themselves, and for others to think critically about them?
3. Does criticism of white men infringe on their universal rights? Why or why not?
4. Two of Kristof's "When Whites Just Don't Get It" columns are published in this anthology. In your opinion, does Kristof "beat up" on whites in these articles? Why or why not? Offer a few quotations from the Kristof articles to back up your opinion.

Roxane Gay

Bad Feminist: Take One

Gay's 2014 collection Bad Feminist: Essays *draws on feminist theory and personal experience to address political issues such as abortion rights and racism, together with elements of popular culture—from the films of Quentin Tarantino to the hit song "Blurred Lines" to the world of competitive Scrabble. The following essay offers a case study of Sheryl Sandberg's bestseller* Lean In: Women, Work, and the Will to Lead *(2013), a book that considers gender in the workplace and offers advice to ambitious women. Upon its release* Lean In *was both praised as an exemplary text and slammed by numerous feminist critics as a work of "faux feminism" useful only to a white upper-class audience.*

My favourite definition of a "feminist" is one offered by Su, an Australian woman who, when interviewed for Kathy Bail's 1996 anthology *DIY Feminism*, said feminists are "just women who don't want to be treated like shit." This definition is pointed and succinct, but I run into trouble when I try to expand that definition. I fall short as a feminist. I feel like I am not as committed as I need to be, that I am not living up to feminist ideals because of who and how I choose to be.

I feel this tension constantly. As Judith Butler[1] writes in her 1988 essay "Performative Acts and Gender Constitution," "Performing one's gender wrong initiates a set of punishments both obvious and indirect, and performing it well provides the reassurance that there is an essentialism of gender identity after all." This tension—the idea that there is a right way to be a woman, a right way to be the most essential woman—is ongoing and pervasive.

We see this tension in socially dictated beauty standards—the right way to be a woman is to be thin, to wear makeup, to wear the right kind of clothes (not

1 *Judith Butler* Feminist theorist (b. 1956) whose works such as *Gender Trouble* and *Bodies that Matter* have outlined her influential theory of gender performativity, according to which gender is not biologically innate but is constructed through behaviour.

too slutty, not too prudish—show a little leg, ladies), and so on. Good women are charming, polite, and unobtrusive. Good women work but are content to earn 77 percent of what men earn or, depending on whom you ask, good women bear children and stay home to raise those children without complaint. Good women are modest, chaste, pious, submissive. Women who don't adhere to these standards are the fallen, the undesirable; they are bad women.

Butler's thesis could also apply to feminism. There is an essential feminism or, as I perceive this essentialism, the notion that there are right and wrong ways to be a feminist and there are consequences for doing feminism wrong.

5 Essential feminism suggests anger, humourlessness, militancy, unwavering principles, and a prescribed set of rules for how to be a proper feminist woman, or at least a proper white, heterosexual feminist woman—hate pornography, unilaterally decry the objectification of women, don't cater to the male gaze,[2] hate men, hate sex, focus on career, don't shave. I kid, mostly, with that last one. This is nowhere near an accurate description of feminism, but the movement has been warped by misperception for so long that even people who should know better have bought into this essential image of feminism.

Consider Elizabeth Wurtzel, who, in a June 2012 *Atlantic* article, says, "Real feminists earn a living, have money and means of their own." By Wurtzel's thinking, women who don't "earn a living, have money and means of their own," are fake feminists, undeserving of the label, disappointments to the sisterhood. She takes the idea of essential feminism even further in a September 2012 *Harper's Bazaar* article where she suggests that a good feminist works hard to be beautiful. She says, "Looking great is a matter of feminism. No liberated woman would misrepresent the cause by appearing less than hale and happy." It's too easy to dissect the error of such thinking. She is suggesting that a woman's worth is, in part, determined by her beauty, which is one of the very things feminism works against.

The most significant problem with essential feminism is how it doesn't allow for the complexities of human experience or individuality. There seems to be little room for multiple or discordant points of view. Essential feminism has, for example, led to the rise of the phrase "sex-positive feminism," which creates a clear distinction between feminists who are positive about sex and feminists who aren't—which, in turn, creates a self-fulfilling essentialist prophecy.

---

2 *male gaze* Term coined by film theorist Laura Mulvey, who argued that Hollywood films of the 1950s and 60s tended to be made with a male audience in mind, such that the viewer is encouraged to identify with male characters and objectify female ones. The term has since been adapted to other contexts.

I sometimes cringe when I am referred to as a feminist, as if I should be ashamed of my feminism or as if the word "feminist" is an insult. The label is rarely offered in kindness. I am generally called a feminist when I have the nerve to suggest that the misogyny deeply embedded in our culture is a real problem requiring relentless vigilance. The essay in this collection about Daniel Tosh and rape jokes originally appeared in *Salon*.[3] I tried not to read the comments because they get vicious, but I couldn't help but note one commenter who told me I was an "angry blogger woman," which is simply another way of saying "angry feminist." All feminists are angry instead of, say, passionate.

A more direct reprimand came from a man I was dating during a heated discussion that wasn't quite an argument. He said, "Don't you raise your voice to me," which was strange because I had not raised my voice. I was stunned because no one had ever said such a thing to me. He expounded, at length, about how women should talk to men. When I dismantled his pseudo-theories, he said, "You're some kind of feminist, aren't you?" There was a tone to his accusation, making it clear that to be a feminist was undesirable. I was not being a good woman. I remained silent, stewing. I thought, *Isn't it obvious I am a feminist, albeit not a very good one?* I also realized I was being chastised for having a certain set of beliefs. The experience was disconcerting, at best.

I'm not the only outspoken woman who shies away from the feminist 10
label, who fears the consequences of accepting the label.

In an August 2012 interview with *Salon*'s Andrew O'Hehir, actress Melissa Leo,[4] known for playing groundbreaking female roles, said, "Well, I don't think of myself as a feminist at all. As soon as we start labelling and categorizing ourselves and others, that's going to shut down the world. I would never say that. Like, I just did that episode with Louis C.K."[5] Leo is buying into a great many essential feminist myths with her comment. We are categorized and labelled from the moment we come into this world by gender, race, size, hair colour, eye colour, and so forth. The older we get, the more labels and categories we collect. If labelling and categorizing ourselves is going to shut the world down, it has been a long time coming. More disconcerting, though, is the assertion that a feminist wouldn't take a role on Louis C.K.'s sitcom, *Louie*, or that a feminist would be unable to find C.K.'s brand of humour amusing. For

---

3 *essay ... Salon* "Daniel Tosh and Rape Jokes: Still Not Funny" (2012), Gay's essay addressing the controversy over stand-up comedian Daniel Tosh telling a rape joke in response to criticism from a female audience member.

4 *Melissa Leo* American actor (b. 1960).

5 *Louis C.K.* Stand-up comedian (b. 1967); since 2010, he has written, directed, and starred in the comedy-drama *Louie*, known for its brash, satirical tone.

Leo, there are feminists and then there are women who defy categorization and are willing to embrace career opportunities.

Trailblazing female leaders in the corporate world tend to reject the feminist label too. Marissa Mayer, who was appointed president and CEO of Yahoo! in July 2012, said in an interview,

> I don't think that I would consider myself a feminist. I think that I certainly believe in equal rights, I believe that women are just as capable, if not more so in a lot of different dimensions, but I don't, I think, have, sort of the militant drive and the sort of, the chip on the shoulder that sometimes comes with that. And I think it's too bad, but I do think that "feminism" has become in many ways a more negative word. You know, there are amazing opportunities all over the world for women, and I think that there is more good that comes out of positive energy around that than comes out of negative energy.

For Mayer, even though she is a pioneering woman, feminism is associated with militancy and preconceived notions. Feminism is negative, and despite the feminist strides she has made through her career at Google and now Yahoo!, she'd prefer to eschew the label for the sake of so-called positive energy.

Audre Lorde[6] once stated, "I am a Black Feminist. I mean I recognize that my power as well as my *primary* oppressions come as a result of my blackness as well as my womanness, and therefore my struggles on both of these fronts are inseparable." As a woman of colour, I find that some feminists don't seem terribly concerned with the issues unique to women of colour—the ongoing effects of racism and postcolonialism, the status of women in the Third World, the fight against the trenchant archetypes black women are forced into (angry black woman, mammy, Hottentot,[7] and the like).

White feminists often suggest that by believing there are issues unique to women of colour, an unnatural division occurs, impeding solidarity, sisterhood. Other times, white feminists are simply dismissive of these issues. In 2008, prominent blogger Amanda Marcotte was accused of appropriating ideas for her article "Can a Person Be Illegal?" from the blogger "brownfemipower," who

---

6 *Audre Lorde* African American poet and theorist (1924–92) whose celebrated works address racism, feminism, and heterosexism.

7 *mammy* Racist stock figure of a jolly maternal domestic slave or paid worker; *Hottentot* Offensive term for the Khoekhoe peoples of Southern Africa. The term conjures the image of Sara Baartman, a South African woman brought to London in 1810 and displayed to white spectators under the title "Hottentot Venus." The Hottentot stereotype that endured concerns an exoticized, sexualized figure with exaggerated buttocks.

posted a speech she gave on the same subject a few days prior to the publication of Marcotte's article. The question of where original thought ends and borrowed concepts begin was complicated significantly in this case by the sense that a white person had yet again taken the creative work of a person of colour.

The feminist blogosphere engaged in an intense debate over these issues, at times so acrimonious that black feminists were labelled "radical black feminists," were accused of overreacting and, of course, "playing the race card."*

Such willful ignorance, such willful disinterest in incorporating the issues and concerns of black women into the mainstream feminist project, makes me disinclined to own the feminist label until it embraces people like me. Is that my way of essentializing feminism, of suggesting there's a right kind of feminism or a more inclusive feminism? Perhaps. This is all murky for me, but a continued insensitivity, within feminist circles, on the matter of race is a serious problem.

There's also this. Lately, magazines have been telling me there's something wrong with feminism or women trying to achieve a work-life balance or just women in general. *The Atlantic* has led the way in these lamentations. In the aforementioned June 2012 article, Wurtzel, author of *Prozac Nation*,[8] wrote a searing polemic about "1% wives"* who are hurting feminism and the progress of women by choosing to stay at home rather than enter the workplace. Wurtzel begins the essay provocatively, stating,

> When my mind gets stuck on everything that is wrong with feminism, it brings out the 19th century poet in me: *Let me count the ways*.[9] Most of all, feminism is pretty much a nice girl who really, really wants so badly to be liked by everybody—ladies who lunch,* men who hate women, all the morons who demand choice and don't understand responsibility—that it has become the easy lay* of social movements.

There are problems with feminism. Wurtzel says so, and she is vigorous in defending her position. Wurtzel knows the right way for feminism. In that article, Wurtzel goes on to state there is only one kind of equality, economic equality, and until women recognize that and enter the workforce en masse, feminists, and wealthy feminists in particular, will continue to fail. They will continue to be bad feminists, falling short of essential ideals of feminism.

---

8 *Prozac Nation* Wurtzel's 1994 memoir about her experiences with mental illness during her formative years. The book, which garnered both praise and derision from critics, was made into a film in 2001.

9 *Let me count the ways* Reference to Elizabeth Barrett Browning's Sonnet 43 ("How do I love thee? Let me count the ways").

Wurtzel isn't wrong about the importance of economic equality, but she is wrong in assuming that with economic equality, the rest of feminism's concerns will somehow disappear.

In the July/August 2012 *Atlantic*, Anne-Marie Slaughter wrote more than twelve thousand words about the struggles of powerful, successful women to "have it all." Her article was interesting and thoughtful, for a certain kind of woman—a wealthy woman with a very successful career. She even parlayed the piece into a book deal. Slaughter was speaking to a small, elite group of women while ignoring the millions of women who don't have the privilege of, as Slaughter did, leaving high-powered positions at the State Department to spend more time with their sons. Many women who work do so because they have to. Working has little to do with having it all and much more to do with having food on the table.

Slaughter wrote,

> I'd been the woman congratulating herself on her unswerving commitment to the feminist cause, chatting smugly with her dwindling number of college or law-school friends who had reached and maintained their place on the highest rungs of their profession. I'd been the one telling young women at my lectures that you can have it all and do it all, regardless of what field you are in.

The thing is, I am not at all sure that feminism has ever suggested women can have it all. This notion of being able to have it all is always misattributed to feminism when really, it's human nature to want it all—to have cake and eat it too* without necessarily focusing on how we can get there and how we can make "having it all" possible for a wider range of people and not just the lucky ones.

Alas, poor feminism. So much responsibility keeps getting piled on the shoulders of a movement whose primary purpose is to achieve equality, in all realms, between men and women. I keep reading these articles and getting angry and tired because they suggest there's no way for women to ever *get it right*. These articles make it seem like, as Butler suggests, there is, in fact, a right way to be a woman and a wrong way to be a woman. The standard for the right way to be a woman and/or a feminist appears to be ever changing and unachievable.

In the weeks leading up to the publication of Sheryl Sandberg's *Lean In*, critics had plenty to say about the Facebook chief operating officer's ideas about being a woman in the workplace—even though few had actually read the tome. Many of the resulting discussions bizarrely mischaracterized *Lean In*, tossing around misleading headlines, inaccurate facts, and unfair assumptions.

As it turns out, not even a fairly average entry into the world of corporate advice books is immune from double standards.

Sandberg intersperses personal anecdotes from her remarkable career (a 25
vice presidency at Google, serving as the US Treasury's chief of staff during the Clinton administration)* with observations, research, and pragmatic advice for how women can better achieve professional and personal success. She urges women to "lean in" to their careers and to be "ambitious in any pursuit." *Lean In* is competently written, blandly interesting, and it does repeat a great deal of familiar research—although it isn't particularly harmful to be reminded of the challenges women face as they try to get ahead.

Intentionally or not, much of the book is a stark reminder of the many obstacles women face in the workplace. I cannot deny that parts resonated, particularly in Sandberg's discussion about "impostor syndrome"[10] and how women are less willing to take advantage of potential career opportunities unless they feel qualified.

But Sandberg is rigidly committed to the gender binary, and *Lean In* is exceedingly heteronormative. Professional women are largely defined in relation to professional men; *Lean In*'s loudest unspoken advice seems to dictate that women should embrace traditionally masculine qualities (self-confidence, risk taking, aggression, etc.). Occasionally, this advice backfires because it seems as if Sandberg is advocating, *If you want to succeed, be an asshole*. In addition, Sandberg generally assumes a woman will want to fulfill professional ambitions while also marrying a man and having children. Yes, she says, "Not all women want careers. Not all women want children. Not all women want both. I would never advocate that we should all have the same objectives." But she contradicts herself by placing every single parable within the context of heterosexual women who want a wildly successful career and a rounded-out nuclear family. Accepting that Sandberg is writing to a very specific audience, and has little to offer those who don't fall within that target demographic, makes enjoying the book a lot easier.

One of the main questions that has arisen in the wake of *Lean In*'s publication is whether Sandberg has a responsibility to women who don't fall within her target demographic. Like Slaughter, Sandberg is speaking to a rather narrow group of women. In the *New York Times*, Jodi Kantor writes, "Even [Sandberg's] advisers acknowledge the awkwardness of a woman with double Harvard degrees, dual stock riches (from Facebook and Google, where she also worked), a 9,000-square-foot house and a small army of household help urging less fortunate women to look inward and work harder."

---

10 *impostor syndrome* Term coined by psychologists Pauline Rose Clance and Suzanne Imes to describe the feeling of self-doubt and inadequacy some people experience despite achieving success.

At times the inescapable evidence of Sandberg's fortune is grating. She casually discusses her mentor Larry Summers,[11] working for the Treasury department, her doctor siblings, and her equally successful husband, David Goldberg. (As CEO of SurveyMonkey, Goldberg moved the company headquarters from Portland to the Bay Area so he could more fully commit to his family.) She gives the impression that her movement from one ideal situation to the next is easily replicable.

30 Sandberg's life is so absurd a fairy tale, I began to think of *Lean In* as a snow globe, where a lovely little tableau was being nicely preserved for my delectation and irritation. I would not be so bold as to suggest Sandberg has it all, but I need to believe she is pretty damn close to whatever "having it all" might look like. Common sense dictates that it is not realistic to assume anyone could achieve Sandberg's successes simply by "leaning in" and working harder—but that doesn't mean Sandberg has nothing to offer, or that *Lean In* should be summarily dismissed.

Cultural critics can get a bit precious and condescending about marginalized groups, and in the debate over *Lean In*, "working-class women" have been lumped into a vaguely defined group of women who work too hard for too little money. But very little consideration has been given to these women as actual people who live in the world, and who maybe, just maybe, have ambitions too.

There has been, unsurprisingly, significant pushback against the notion that leaning in is a reasonable option for working-class women, who are already stretched woefully thin. Sandberg is not oblivious to her privilege, noting:

> I am fully aware that most women are not focused on changing social norms for the next generation but simply trying to get through each day. Forty percent of employed mothers lack sick days and vacation leave, and about 50 percent of employed mothers are unable to take time off to care for a sick child. Only about half of women receive any pay during maternity leave. These policies can have severe consequences; families with no access to paid family leave often go into debt and can fall into poverty. Part-time jobs with fluctuating schedules offer little chance to plan and often stop short of the forty-hour week that provides basic benefits.

It would have been useful if Sandberg offered realistic advice about career management for women who are dealing with such circumstances. It would also be useful if we had flying cars. Assuming Sandberg's advice is completely useless for working-class women is just as shortsighted as claiming her advice

---

11 *Larry Summers* Economist who served as Secretary of the Treasury from 1999 to 2001 and president of Harvard University from 2001 to 2006.

needs to be completely applicable to all women. And let's be frank: if Sandberg chose to offer career advice for working-class women, a group she clearly knows little about, she would have been just as harshly criticized for overstepping her bounds.

The critical response to *Lean In* is not entirely misplaced, but it is emblematic of the dangers of public womanhood. Public women, and feminists in particular, have to be everything to everyone; when they aren't, they are excoriated for their failure. In some ways, this is understandable. We have come far, but we have so much further to go. We need so very much, and we hope women with a significant platform might be everything we need—a desperately untenable position. As Elizabeth Spiers notes in *The Verge*,

> When's the last time someone picked up a Jack Welch (or Warren Buffett,[12] or even Donald Trump) bestseller and complained that it was unsympathetic to working class men who had to work multiple jobs to support their families? … And who reads a book by Jack Welch and defensively feels that they're being told that they have to adopt Jack Welch's lifestyle and professional choices or they are lesser human beings?

Lean In cannot and should not be read as a definitive text, or a book offering universally applicable advice to all women, everywhere. Sandberg is confident and aggressive in her advice, but the reader is under no obligation to do everything she says. Perhaps we can consider *Lean In* for what it is—just one more reminder that the rules are always different for girls, no matter who they are and no matter what they do.

(2014)

Questions

1. Why is Gay particularly reluctant to "own" the feminist label for herself?
2. What challenges do public women face that their male counterparts do not?
3. Do you agree that "feminism" has become "a more negative word"?
4. What is the tone of this essay? What does this tone suggest about Gay's approach to feminism?

---

12 *Jack Welch* American businessperson (b. 1935) and one-time CEO of General Electric, known for his domineering corporate leadership; *Warren Buffett* American businessperson (b. 1930) whose investing prowess has made him one of the wealthiest people in the world.

NOURIEL ROUBINI

ECONOMIC INSECURITY AND THE RISE OF NATIONALISM[1]

In 2016, as the United States elected Donald Trump as president and as the United Kingdom voted to leave the European Union, many political commentators interpreted these events as part of a larger, global pattern of growth in right-wing nationalist movements. In the following article—published in The Guardian *in June 2014, two years before either Trump's election or the Brexit vote—economist Nouriel Roubini discusses the causes of this pattern and speculates as to what might happen next.*

In the immediate aftermath of the 2008 global financial crisis, policymakers' success in preventing the Great Recession from turning into Great Depression II[2] held in check demands for protectionist and inward-looking measures.[3] But now the backlash against globalization[4]—and the freer movement of goods, services, capital, labour, and technology that came with it—has arrived.

1 *Nationalism* In this context, prioritization of the needs of one's own nation without regard for the needs of other nations; or, the belief that one's own nation is more important or better than other nations.

2 *2008 global financial crisis* International banking crisis during which governments across the world bailed out banks to avoid a collapse of the international financial system; *Great Recession* The 2008 financial crisis resulted in a worldwide recession during the late 2000s and early 2010s, now known as the Great Recession; *Great Depression II* Term for what could have happened if the global system had collapsed after the 2008 crisis. The Great Depression of the 1930s was the worst global economic depression of the twentieth century; this term implies that without the government bailouts to the financial sector, the Great Recession could have been on a similar scale.

3 *protectionist ... measures* Economic policies that seek to safeguard domestic industries from foreign competition, usually by means of tariffs or duties on foreign goods.

4 *globalization* Economic, political, and cultural integration of the world's countries. Though historians disagree as to when globalization began, it is generally agreed that it sped up in the twentieth and twenty-first centuries because of technological advances

This new nationalism takes different economic forms: trade barriers, asset protection, reaction against foreign direct investment, policies favouring domestic workers and firms, anti-immigration measures, state capitalism, and resource nationalism. In the political realm, populist,[5] anti-globalization, anti-immigration, and in some cases outright racist and antisemitic parties are on the rise.

These forces loathe the alphabet soup* of supranational governance institutions—the EU, the UN, the WTO, and the IMF,[6] among others—that globalization requires. Even the internet, the epitome of globalization for the past two decades, is at risk of being balkanized[7] as more authoritarian countries—including China, Iran, Turkey, and Russia—seek to restrict access to social media and crack down on free expression.

The main causes of these trends are clear. Anemic economic recovery has provided an opening for populist parties, promoting protectionist policies, to blame foreign trade and foreign workers for the prolonged malaise. Add to this the rise in income and wealth inequality in most countries, and it is no wonder that the perception of a winner-take-all economy that benefits only elites and distorts the political system has become widespread. Nowadays, both advanced economies (like the United States, where unlimited financing of elected officials by financially powerful business interests is simply legalized corruption) and emerging markets (where oligarchs often dominate the economy and the political system) seem to be run for the few.

5 For the many, by contrast, there has been only secular stagnation, with depressed employment and stagnating wages. The resulting economic insecurity for the working and middle classes is most acute in Europe and the eurozone,[8] where in many countries populist parties—mainly on the far-right—outperformed mainstream forces in last weekend's [May 2014] European parliament election. As in the 1930s, when the Great Depression gave rise to authoritarian governments in Italy, Germany and Spain—and a similar trend now may be underway.

---

in transportation and communication. Some critics of globalization are concerned that it threatens local culture and helps wealthy countries to exploit less wealthy ones.

5 *populist* Populist political movements claim to represent the interests of the common people (as opposed to elite interests). While it is a familiar feature of democratic policies on both the left and the right, mass populism has also played a role in the emergence of fascist regimes.

6 *EU* European Union; *UN* United Nations; *WTO* World Trade Organization; *IMF* International Monetary Fund.

7 *balkanized* Fragmented into small, mutually hostile parts.

8 *eurozone* Union of 19 of the 28 countries in the EU that adopted the monetary unit of the Euro.

If income and job growth do not pick up soon, populist parties may come closer to power at the national level in Europe, with anti-EU sentiments stalling the process of European economic and political integration. Worse, the eurozone may again be at risk: some countries (the UK) may exit the EU; others (the UK, Spain, and Belgium) eventually may break up.

Even in the US, the economic insecurity of a vast white underclass that feels threatened by immigration and global trade can be seen in the rising influence of the extreme right and Tea Party[9] factions of the Republican party. These groups are characterized by economic nativism,[10] anti-immigration and protectionist leanings, religious fanaticism, and geopolitical isolationism.

A variant of this dynamic can be seen in Russia and many parts of eastern Europe and central Asia, where the fall of the Berlin Wall[11] did not usher in democracy, economic liberalization, and rapid output growth. Instead, nationalist and authoritarian regimes have been in power for most of the past quarter-century, pursuing state-capitalist growth models that ensure only mediocre economic performance. In this context, President Vladimir Putin's[12] destabilization of Ukraine cannot be separated from his dream of leading a "Eurasian Union"—a thinly disguised effort to recreate the former Soviet Union.*

In Asia, too, nationalism is resurgent. New leaders in China, Japan, South Korea, and now India are political nationalists in regions where

---

9 *Tea Party* Movement within the US Republican party that advocates for limited government and reduced government spending (particularly in reaction to the government bailouts after the Great Recession of 2008). During the Obama administration, The Tea Party viewed the White House, Congress, and the media with distrust and scepticism.

10 *nativism* Attitude that places the needs of native-born inhabitants above the needs of immigrants.

11 *fall ... Berlin Wall* After the end of World War II, Germany was occupied by the Allied Nations it had fought against. In 1961, Soviet Russia constructed a wall that encircled West Berlin (occupied by France, Britain, and the US) to prevent the inhabitants of Soviet-occupied East Berlin and East Germany from migrating across the border. The wall came to represent the "Iron Curtain," the closing off of the Soviet Union and its allies from Western Europe during the Cold War. Political unrest and the weakening of Soviet Russia led to the fall of the Berlin Wall in November 1989.

12 *Vladimir Putin* President of the Russian Federation (entering office in 2012). He was Prime Minister from 1999 to 2000, President from 2000 to 2008, and Prime Minister from 2008 to 2012. Putin wields unconstrained power over the Russian Federation. In Ukraine, Putin has supported the efforts of pro-Russian factions to oppose association with the EU. After Ukraine's pro-Russian President Yanukovych was unseated by protesters in 2014, Putin seized the region of Crimea, an area dominated by Russian speakers. Conflict between the post-revolutionary government and pro-Russian factions has since continued to escalate in Ukraine.

territorial disputes remain serious and long-held historical grievances fester. These leaders—as well as those in Thailand, Malaysia, and Indonesia, who are moving in a similar nationalist direction—must address major structural-reform challenges if they are to revive falling economic growth and, in the case of emerging markets, avoid a middle-income trap. Economic failure could fuel further nationalist, xenophobic tendencies—and even trigger military conflict.

The Middle East remains a region mired in backwardness. The Arab spring[13]—triggered by slow growth, high youth unemployment, and widespread economic desperation—has given way to a long winter in Egypt and Libya, where the alternatives are a return to authoritarian strongmen and political chaos. In Syria and Yemen, there is civil war; Lebanon and Iraq could face a similar fate; Iran is both unstable and dangerous to others; and Afghanistan and Pakistan look increasingly like failed states.

In all of these cases, economic failure and a lack of opportunities and hope for the poor and young are fuelling political and religious extremism, resentment of the West and, in some cases, outright terrorism.

In the 1930s, the failure to prevent the Great Depression empowered authoritarian regimes in Europe and Asia, eventually leading to the Second World War. This time, the damage caused by the Great Recession is subjecting most advanced economies to secular stagnation and creating major structural growth challenges for emerging markets.

This is ideal terrain for economic and political nationalism to take root and flourish. Today's backlash against trade and globalization should be viewed in the context of what, as we know from experience, could come next.

(2014)

Questions

1. Roubini is rather famous for the accuracy of his economic predictions; he has been given the nicknames "Cassandra" (a famous Classical seer) and "Dr. Doom." He was one of few economists to foresee the global economic crisis of 2008, for example. To what extent were Roubini's concerns in this 2014 article borne out by events in the years that followed?

13 *Arab spring* Term used to refer to a series of democratic uprisings that occurred in several Arab countries in 2011.

2. Why is there a "backlash" against globalization? To what extent (if at all) do you think this backlash is warranted?
3. Roubini sees the political backlash primarily as being against "trade and globalization." Are populist arguments against international trade agreements and globalization only coming from the right? How do left-wing parties view these issues?

Sarah de Leeuw

Soft Shouldered

Between 1969 and 2011, at least 19 girls and women disappeared or were murdered along BC's Highway 16, known as the "Highway of Tears." Aboriginal organizations place the number at over 40 victims, including women who have disappeared farther away from the road. The 720-kilometre stretch of highway between Prince George and Prince Rupert borders 23 Aboriginal communities, and more than half of the 19 "official" victims have been of Aboriginal descent. The resolution rate of the crimes—only one of the murders has been solved—and the lack of resources dedicated to the cases led many to suspect racism in the police and media response. The disappearance of a white woman, Nicole Hoar, in 2002 was the first incident to spark media attention in major newspapers. In 2005 the RCMP finally launched E-PANA, a large-scale investigation into all the cases of missing and murdered women from Highway 16.

The Highway of Tears victims are part of a larger trend of violence against Aboriginal women in Canada; between 1980 and 2012, there have been 1,181 missing and murdered Aboriginal women across the country. On 8 December 2015, in response to a decade-long protest campaign organized by Aboriginal activists, the Government of Canada launched an independent national inquiry to address the disproportionate number of murdered and missing Aboriginal girls and women. "Soft Shouldered" appeared in Prism *magazine in the fall of 2013; it was subsequently nominated for a National Magazine Award and printed in the 2014 edition of* Best Canadian Essays.

This part is true.

It is true because it is named and found. People have investigated and made inquiries. And inquires result in findings and findings can be documented and published and circulated and so people pay attention and they search for solutions.

Dystocia is the name given to any difficult childbirth or abnormal labour. During childbirth, when the anterior shoulders of the infant cannot pass below the mother's pubic symphysis,[1] when a baby's shoulders are wider than the opening in a mother's pelvic bone, it is called Shoulder Dystocia. Imagine an infant gasping for breath, trying to emerge into the world. Imagine watery panic. Contractions. Bone against bone, unyielding.

The quickest solution is to break the baby's clavicle bones.[2] Reach inside, first one side and then the other, thumb on tiny collarbone, hand grasping around the curve of shoulders, fingers on shoulder blades. And snap. Yes. Snap. This must be done with force and conviction. A clear fracture heals with fewer complications. We tell mothers that their babies will not remember that excruciating pain. We tell mothers that their children, their daughters, will cross a threshold into life with limp and broken shoulders. But the bones will bind themselves back together again and the breaks will set and arms will again stretch out strong, poised for running, running, and being alive with breath pulled deep into lungs. It's enough to make a person cry. With relief.

5 This next part is no less true.

And it hurts no less.

But there is nothing named or found and so nothing is documented or published. The sparseness of findings and inquiries has resulted in almost nothing and so nothing has been circulated and solutions are slippery and invisible.

No name is given to a child born to vanish. There is no diagnostic term for those who slip into this world born to disappear.

There are no solutions or diagrams or carefully recorded scientific data about the daughters who effortlessly take their first breath, who pull air into their lungs for years and years but for whom each breath is a breath closer to the moment when, on the shoulder of a highway, they will go missing.

10 This too is enough to make a person cry. With anticipation of what is coming.

And it too begins at birth, the edge of life, a life running and rushing, arms outstretched, towards a vanishing.

So begin with me at the edge. That borderland where pavement ends and soft shoulder begins. This is a land bordered by a wall of green so dark it might be black. At highway speeds, this is how Engelmann spruce trees[3] appear. Through a car's passenger window, branches blur and trunks transform. Things get hazy and things get lost. The details disappear.

Asphalt dissipates into gravel, gravel touches mud that curves into ditches scarred and slashed by the bulldozers and the D-9 Cats[4] sent to scrape the

---

1 *anterior shoulders* Front of the shoulders; *pubic symphysis* Joint connecting the two halves of the pelvis bone.

2 *clavicle bones* Collar bones.

3 *Engelmann spruce trees* Species of evergreen tree native to the alpine areas on the west coast of North America.

4 *D-9 Cats* Large track-type tractors made by Caterpillar.

foliage, the never-ending efforts of devil's club, slide alder, Indian paintbrush, and salmonberry bushes.[5] This is a space where everything is feral and weedy, growing and growing, creeping up past the boundaries that separate the regulated and patrolled highway and the wild, wild, western wilderness. Soft shoulder of road, slip of pavement, downward slope from the centre line, a space of refuse and discard.

You are in northern British Columbia. Nowhere most of the world will ever go. A land bordering on the lost. An unseen. A beyond cities, a far outside the imaginings of most.

Still, it is worth looking at. It is worth looking closely at, if only to see what has disappeared, what is missing. Look into the thin shoulder space that borders this highway. Here is what you might find.

Broken beer bottles tossed from cars. Can you hear the hilarity, teenagers partying, driving drunk on unpatrolled roads, sweaty and in love during the few days of heat that summer offers up? Ice-cold beer and the freedom speed of a car, a carborator-smoking-nearly-used-up-bought-off-a-neighbour-car with the windows rolled down and the wind rolling in. Yes, oh yes, toss those beer bottles, watch them shatter, just because you can. Nobody is patrolling you.

Plastic bags, snagged on brambles and translucent as lungs, filled with wind and the rushing exhaust of cars.

Mufflers rotting into metal rust, patterns like muscled lace in thin seepages of water.

Thick black curls of rubber, the ruins of wheels from transport trucks, skid marks like scabs.

Carcasses of broken deer, necks snapped and smears of blood, legs always, always, bent in that running position, some frozen reminder of a futile attempt at escape.

Fallen rocks and the remnants of blasting caps. What is left after dynamite has done its job and the fireweed has come back to ignite the dips and drops; first there are the bright purple flowers, then during pollination the fluffy cotton white. And as it dies, the fireweed gasps into red, a red so red it looks like fresh meat, road kill.

Things decay and things are consumed in the ditches and crevices on the edge of Highway 16. There is meat and metal and flowers and there is rot and there is rejuvenation. These shoulders are thin and strong, exposed and jutting. Imagine the shoulders of a very young dancer, clavicle bones jutting through flesh. The ever-present risk of breaking.

Broken shoulders.

---

5 *devil's club ... salmonberry bushes* Brambles, shrubs, and weeds native to the northern west coast of North America.

Soft shoulders and sharp shoulders and oh, oh, such are the shoulders of a sinewy highway, Highway 16.

Things go missing at 120 km per hour on long desolate stretches of road, straight shots between one place that almost no one has heard of and another place even fewer know about. Truck stops and Indian reserves, logging camps and precarious towns clinging to the edges of giant gouges, open pit mines exhaling molybdenum. Endako and Gitsegukla. Kitwanga, Kispiox, and New Hazelton. Usk and Rosswood. Smithers and Moricetown.

We have stopped many times on the shoulders of that highway and the time we stopped years ago was not so much different, a detour to the edge.

Pulling off onto the highway's soft shoulder for a soft-shouldered young woman, standing there on the edge of the road on the edge of a town that seems to have no hard and fast boundaries. Smithers simply evaporates. Slowly. From downtown core to mountains, from Main Street to railway track to cabins on lakes to glaciers that trail like tongues up the valleys and into sky.

And the sky is blue the day we stop for her, her in a tight black tank-top and tight jeans and jaunt and confidence on the side of Highway 16, walking backwards on the right shoulder of the road, right hand out, thumb spiked skyward.

By the time we reach Smithers we have already been driving for five hours. We left late but the long summer days make driving all night seem possible. The air is warm. Our car windows are unrolled, our dog is riding in the back seat, head hanging out the window, face streamlined in glee and we have passed rigs* and beehive burners[6] with sparks like fireflies in the long light of late August. We have counted seven black bears, fish-fat fed and glossy handsome, lumbering along the highway's edge. Our dog has barked. The evening has remained warm but we know it will grow cool before the girl will make it to where she surely must be going. And that is part of the reason we stop.

We do not want her to get cold on the edge of the highway.

And of course there is something else.

Moricetown, she says, slipping into the front seat beside me. I'm going to Moricetown.

We have decided I will drive, you will sit in the back seat with our dog, and the girl from the edge of the highway will sit in the front seat beside me. We do not want our dog to make her uncomfortable. So soon she is settled in, all smiles and teeth and chitter-chatter and stories of summer basketball games in Smithers. Stories about kids from the reserves hitching "into town."

---

6 *beehive burners* Wood waste burners used at sawmills and logging yards; the steel structures are shaped like beehives and are at least 30 feet tall.

Into town, that descriptor that covers every place that is not the reserve, not her reserve with the Moricetown Canyon at its heart, a canyon through which waters boil, waters that men tether themselves over, strapped onto rock faces, spears in hand, the gut-blood of speared salmon spewing into the fine mist that sprays up from the Bulkley River, narrowed for such a breathtakingly short span, dizzying, fish leaping. Salmon by the hundreds for canning and smoking, fillets of red meat crisscrossed and hatched and slung over ladders made of green sapling alder bound with cord and bendable enough to withstand the winds that careen in. The wind smells of all of this and more.

And it is precisely this, this smoky-sugared scent of drying fish and the 35
slippery sweat of men tethered to canyon walls, which is everything she wants to escape.

Hitchhiking into town. Because in Smithers the smell of reserve smoke disappears.

How old is she? Fourteen. Going into Grade 9 in the fall. The call of new jeans, runners white and unscuffed, crisp pages of notebooks, and moist bright highlighter pens. Geometry sets with not a single missing piece, the protractor's needle perfectly sharp. These are the things she is looking forward to, things she dreams will unfold come the early days of September, come the first whispers of frost.

We curve into Moricetown. Past the roadside hut selling smoked salmon, past the bridge over the canyon, past the Band Office and the community hall and up the hill on the other side of the reserve and onto the shoulder once again. She points out a trail. An almost invisible cleft in the ditch's vegetation, a path through bush and bramble that we would never have seen had she not known just where to look. We let her out, sun-setting light on her swinging arms as she crosses the highway's shoulder, descends the cupped lip of the ditch and then up the other side and back to her home hidden beyond the tree line.

Our hitchhiker crosses a borderland, walks over the highway's soft shoulder and is lost from our sight. Enveloped by all that grows on the sides of roads.

I have picked up other women hitching their way home. Once there was a 40
woman in Gitsegukla, perched on a stack of Coors Light cases, teetering in the dark, hitching back to Kitwanga. I round the curve and my headlights catch her eyes no differently than headlights would catch the eyes of a highway coyote, trotting along the side of the road. Glowing illuminated metallic yellow like asteroids. She is so drunk I take her in my arms and fold her into the seat beside me. I pack all the cases of beer into the trunk of my car and I do not argue about the can she keeps in her hand.

She tells me stories as we drive, warm boozy breath wrapping around descriptions of her daughter, her cousins, tales of picking berries or heading down to Vancouver. She is heading home to her auntie's house and in the morning there will be tea. She calls it angel's tea, tea so milky white, warm and sweet, it is like the clouds we see in pictures of heaven. She is certain of this tea, this tea that awaits her. It will mark her return home. And my headlights shine and the ditches on the edge of the highway fade into blackness beyond the light of high beams and her voice hits the pitch of tires on asphalt and we are hurtling together down a mean, mean, road.

Think of this highway as a cut. A slice through darkness or wilderness or vegetation or the towns from which we all run.

And now think of this.

A slash right down to the bone can be done in less than three seconds. A slice so deep the skin may never bind, the scar will most assuredly never fade.

Now think of that highway once again and hold your breath and contemplate all the soft shoulders you have touched. Close your eyes and feel the softest slope in the world, the slope at the top of a baby's arm, curve up to neck. The landscape of your lover's clavicle bone, rising and falling with the deep breathing of calm sleep, facing you and the early morning sunlight with a familiarity that knots your stomach and makes you reach out, again and again, just to touch that beautiful skin. Think about every shoulder you have ever touched, ever loved. Think about every person you hold dear.

May you never know what it is to lose your daughter. May you never know a disappearance never explained. A missing without reason or answer or end. May you never dream of your daughter's shoulders buckled and torn in the mud and silt of a ditch. May you never know what mothers know in Moricetown, in Kitwanga, in Burns Lake, Kitwankool, Terrace, Hazelton Kitimat Prince Rupert or in Kispiox. May you never think of your daughter as roadside prey.

May you never be the mother of the daughter gone missing from the shoulder of Highway 16 in July, in July when the days can be so cruel. A month of forest fires, a month thick with mosquitoes and decomposition. Fish rot. Of course there are daughters for almost every month of the year because slaughter has no timeline. Thirty-three murdered and missing daughters, sometimes at a rate of more than one per year.

The missing daughter of July was a treeplanter. Hitchhiking between Smithers and Prince George, backpack and hemp necklace and a shadow cast on the shoulder of Highway 16. When I think of her I think of long moments when nothing is audible but the sound of wind on the leaves of aspen trees. I think of sun on pavement and the rustle of shrubs and blood red fists of elderberry thick with juices that birds will drink come fall. I think of the safe stretch of time that existed for her between cars passing. Yes, there would have been that flicker of disappointment when the minivan with a mother and two children did not stop or when that fully loaded logging truck barrelled on past. But as long as she was walking, as long as a killer did not stop, that July daughter was safe.

In Moricetown there is a billboard on the side of the highway. "Girls, don't go hitchhiking. Killer on the loose."

They search for her in waves, ripples of people winding through the ditches. They sift through the foliage and the growth and the rot. Where the roadside slips into fields, they use long sticks and methodically beat back the wheat and alfalfa swaying in the wind. In those roadside tides of green, search crews hope one of them will stumble upon her body. Even a piece of her would be a clue. Please, they think, please let this stick connect with a portion, any broken portion, of the family's daughter.

Let her not have gone missing without a trace, let the soft shoulders of this highway reveal something.

These daughters go missing in the spring and in the winter. They are only occasionally found, frozen and crumpled amongst the roots of alder trees, left torn with pine needles resting on their eyelids, tossed without concern and scratched at by eagles and ravens that draw no distinction between someone's child and the body of a porcupine clipped by a careless driver. Blood on the shoulder of a highway is blood on the shoulder of a highway. So may you never think of your daughter as roadside prey, shoulders soft as dawn, shattered in a ditch overlooked when we travel at highway speeds.

May you never know this truth.

(2013)

Questions

1. Why does de Leeuw open her piece with a description of Shoulder Dystocia? How does she connect this procedure with the murders along the Highway of Tears? What are the similiarities, and what are the differences, between these two traumatic events?
2. Consider de Leeuw's description of Highway 16. What words does she repeat in her description? What verbs does she use? What similes? How does this language contribute to your imagining of the highway?
3. How does the narrator's personal story of picking up hitchhikers on the highway contribute to your understanding of the highway's tragic history?
4. De Leeuw draws a distinction between traumas that are recorded and documented and those that aren't. Why does documentation of a trauma matter?

Margo Pfeiff

When the Vikings Were in Nunavut

This piece appeared in the July/August 2013 issue of Up Here, *a magazine about Canada's North, and was later reprinted in* Best Canadian Essays 2014. *The subject of the story, the work of Canadian Arctic archeologist Patricia Sutherland, has received a great deal of media attention within Canada and beyond.*

Look at this!" says Patricia Sutherland. It's 2002 and she's kneeling on the tundra, pointing her trowel at a whale bone at the bottom of the muddy trench she's been excavating. The bone has been fashioned into a spade to cut sod into building blocks, the kind of artifact she would expect to find in old Norse[1] sites in Greenland. To Sutherland, one of Canada's top Arctic archeologists, the sod-chopper isn't the only thing that seems out of place at the Nanook archeological dig. Here on the treeless barrens just outside Kimmirut, Nunavut, the structure that she's unearthing—a large, rectangular foundation of rock and sod—just doesn't fit with the landscape.

That's exactly what American archeologist Moreau Maxwell thought when he first began digging here in the 1960s. "He couldn't explain the structures he was finding," says Sutherland. "He said it was complicated."

Complicated—that's exactly what Nanook has proven to be for Sutherland, a former curator of archeology for Ottawa's Museum of Civilization. But now, after seven summers of excavation here, and 12 years of meticulously poring over artifacts and piecing together clues, she thinks she's got the site figured out.

She says that here, on southern Baffin Island, was a trading post occupied by the ancient Norse. Her theory is controversial. But if it's correct, it could rewrite the history books.

5 It's long been known that the Norse were active in the far reaches of the North Atlantic. About a millennium ago, seafaring Norwegian traders, some

1 *Norse* Medieval Scandinavian. Norse are sometimes referred to as "Vikings."

worshipping Odin[2] and others having converted to Christianity, island-hopped in search of resources. They sailed from Scandinavia to the Shetlands, Orkney Islands, Ireland, the Faroes, Iceland, and finally to the western shore of Davis Strait, where colonies were established by Erik the Red, a convicted murderer and charismatic marketer. He named this new place "Greenland," convincing settlers to join him in the protected fjords of the island's southwest. For centuries, the Norse thrived there, supporting themselves by farming and sending trade goods to Europe—everything from walrus ivory to live polar bears for Old World royal courts.

It was during the colonization of Greenland that the snow-capped mountains of Baffin Island were most likely sighted far to the west. A cryptic reference to Baffin was first penned by a 14th-century Icelandic scribe who recorded events that had taken place more than two centuries earlier. In the Saga of Erik the Red, Erik's adventurous son, Leif Erikson, sailed westward from Greenland around 1000 AD, soon encountering a desolate stretch of land. Rowing ashore, he was unimpressed: "[T]he land was like a single flat slab of rock to the sea. This land seemed of little use." Erikson dubbed it Helluland—"land of stone slabs"—and turned his back on it, heading southwards. Soon he found Markland ("land of forests," possibly Labrador) and then Vinland ("land of wine" or "of pasture"—Newfoundland). At a site now called L'Anse aux Meadows, he built a small station for repairing ships and gathering cargo before returning to Greenland the following spring. Helluland barely received another mention, and by the mid-1400s, the Norse had vanished even from Greenland.

Despite this, or perhaps because of it, whispers of Norse in Canada's Northland have lingered for centuries. Mentions of "blonde Eskimos" appeared from 1821 onwards in the journals of explorers William Parry, John Ross, John Rae and John Franklin. In 1910, Arctic ethnologist Vilhjalmur Stefansson, an Icelandic-Canadian, wrote in his diary about an isolated group of tall Inuit on southwest Victoria Island: "There are three men here whose beards are almost the colour of mine, and who look like typical Scandinavians." But DNA testing on the Victoria Islanders revealed no Nordic genes.

In the 1970s, archeologist Peter Schledermann of the Arctic Institute of North America found Norse artifacts at several sites on Ellesmere's east coast. There were knife blades, pieces of oak with inset wooden dowels, copper, medieval chainmail, ship rivets and woven woollen cloth. These relics dated from between the 13th and 15th centuries, many proven to have originated in Norse settlements in southern Greenland. Fragments of objects made of smelted metal have also turned up on Bathurst and Devon Islands. Had Inuit or their

---

2 *Odin* One of the gods worshipped in Norse mythology.

predecessors, the Dorset,[3] scavenged them from Norse shipwrecks? Had they journeyed to Greenland and brought them back? Or had the Norse themselves come here, seeking to trade?

Not long ago, this last theory was commonly accepted: The Norse had ventured west, possibly well into Nunavut, Nunavik and the gulf of St. Lawrence, to exchange goods with the aboriginals of North America. "But that idea fell out of favour," says Sutherland. So it was controversial when Newfoundland's L'Anse aux Meadows was declared to be a Norse outpost. And when National Museum of Canada archeologist Tom Lee announced in the 1960s that he'd uncovered Norse camps on Quebec's Ungava Bay, "he brought the wrath of the entire archeological community on his head," says Sutherland. After that, most scholars shied away.

10 Then Pat Sutherland came along. In 1977, as an expert in indigenous archeology, she was hired by Parks Canada to do a survey of potential archeological sites in what would become Quttinirpaaq National Park on Ellesmere Island. She'd just arrived when, amidst the lingering June snow, she spotted something lying on a bald patch of tundra.* It was a long, thin piece of metal. Not being familiar with Norse artifacts, she had no idea what it was. But the Parks expert to whom she showed it was shocked. "It was one arm of a bronze balance used by professional Norse traders in the Old world for weighing silver," says Sutherland.

Six years later, on Axel Heiberg Island, Sutherland again stumbled across a strange artifact. Carved on a single piece of antler were two radically dissimilar faces—one with typical round Dorset features, and another, long and thin, with what appeared to be a beard and heavy eyebrows. To her it was an iconic portrayal of two very different cultures. She puzzled over it for a long time, and began to rethink the long-held belief that Norse had not crossed paths with the Dorset.

In 1993 Sutherland was invited to join a dig at a medieval Greenlandic farm called Garden Under Sandet in Greenland. Here, she quickly learned about all things Norse. One of the finds made there was part of a loom with threads of yarn still attached. Six years later, while studying artifacts at the Museum of Civilization,[4] she sifted through a collection excavated in the 1970s and 80s by Father Guy Mary-Rousselière, a French-Canadian anthropologist and missionary based in Pond Inlet.[5] She stopped dead at the sight of two soft pieces of yarn, three metres long, that looked exactly like the wool she'd seen in

3 *Dorset* Dorset people lived in the central and eastern Canadian Arctic until about 500 years ago.

4 *Museum of Civilization* Canada's national museum.

5 *Pond Inlet* Northern Baffin Island.

Greenland. Sure enough, when she took them to a textiles expert, they matched precisely with wool woven at Garden Under Sandet in the late 13th century.

Sutherland knew she was on to something. She hunkered down in the museum's collection, searching through more than 15,000 Arctic objects and comparing them to confirmed Norse artifacts from Greenland, Russia and Europe. Over 100 strands of yarn came to light, hailing from previously excavated sites ranging from northern Baffin Island to northern Labrador. The Inuit and their predecessors, Sutherland knew, didn't use wool—but the Norse did, making garments and even sails from it. The yarn was identified as having been spun with a spindle,[6] requiring great skill to bind the short, smooth fibres of wild animals like Arctic hare. It would have been a laborious task, but the result was yarn that was very soft—and very European. Armed with this knowledge, Sutherland set off in the year 2000 to re-open the most tantalizing site on Baffin Island: Maxwell Moreau's puzzling Nanook dig in Tanfield Valley, about 20 kilometres from Kimmirut. In Sutherland's eyes, Nanook would have been a perfect spot for the Norse: It had ample sod, a sheltered harbour large enough for wooden ocean-going ships, and plentiful wildlife—especially Arctic fox, the same creatures that prompted the Hudson's Bay Company* to choose Kimmirut as their first Baffin post. It was barely 300 kilometres from Greenland—two or three days' sailing. "Why people have trouble accepting that Norse would have been here is crazy," Sutherland says.

After six centuries, Helluland was back in the press and Sutherland's fellow archeologists closely followed her progress. "I knew the project was controversial because everything to do with Norse is controversial," she says. "It had the potential to shift the paradigm about what was happening in the Arctic 1,000 years ago."

Known to be single-minded and unflinchingly committed, Sutherland was 15
prepared for the uphill battle. She had received her share of criticism over the years, as is the norm in a field where radical new concepts are fiercely scrutinized. So to test the strength of her own thesis, she analyzed multiple lines of evidence simultaneously. She excavated new artifacts while at the same time working with experts in fields as diverse as Norse architecture, ancient textiles, insect remains and DNA. Her challenge was to build a multi-pronged case that the ancient Norse had lived in Nunavut.

It wasn't easy. During long days of fieldwork at Nanook, the site became increasingly complex. Moreau Maxwell's excavations had damaged the walls of the mysterious stone dwelling, but she soon discovered a new wall: layers of sod chunks alternating with large stones, some cut and shaped in a style reminiscent of European stone-masonry. Nanook also yielded a trove of artifacts not

6 *spindle* Straight shaft used to spin fibre into yarn.

usually associated with the Inuit or Dorset, including the whalebone spade, and notched wooden "tally sticks" to record trade transactions. There were remains of European rats that couldn't have survived long in the Canadian Arctic, more strands of Scandinavian-style spun yarn, and European whetstones designed for sharpening metal knives that didn't exist in indigenous Northerners' toolboxes. One particularly intriguing item was a carved wooden figure with a beard and heavy ridge over his eyes: either eyebrows or the edge of a cap common among medieval European merchants.

It wasn't a straightforward dig. Among this jumble were classic hunter-gatherer artifacts like fur-cleaning tools and needles—things Inuit or Dorset might use. And there were issues with the radio-carbon dating: results pointing to the 8th century, hundreds of years before the Norse arrived even in Greenland. Part of the problem, says Sutherland, is that "everything on the site was saturated with seal, walrus and whale oil." Marine-mammal materials are known to skew radio-carbon results, dating them too old. The site seems to point at having been occupied several times, and one radio-carbon date confirms Tanfield Valley was occupied in the 14th century, at the very time Norse settlers lived along nearby Greenland.

Sutherland approached the Geological Survey of Canada to unearth more clues. Using a process not commonly employed in archeology, a technique called energy-dispersive spectroscopy, they painstakingly scanned wear-grooves on more than 20 whetstones from Nanook and similar sites, looking for smelted metal. The results were spectacular: microscopic streaks of bronze, brass and smelted iron, forming positive evidence of European metallurgy. To some scholars—even Sutherland's sceptics—this was the smoking gun. She presented her preliminary results at a meeting of the Council for Northeast Historical Archaeology in St. John's in October of last year. Afterwards, James Tuck, professor emeritus of archeology at Memorial University, declared, "While her evidence was compelling before, I find it convincing now."

Sutherland, with more than three decades of Arctic archeology under her trowel and by now also a research fellow at the University of Aberdeen and an adjunct professor of archeology at Newfoundland's Memorial University, is convinced Nanook was the site of a Norse outpost dating from the 13th century or so. The structures there strongly resemble confirmed Greenlandic Norse sites, right down to the shallow, stone-lined drainage system to funnel water from the site. Sutherland says the stone-and-sod walls seem to have been hastily constructed in comparison to similar buildings in Greenland, perhaps in a race against a rapidly approaching winter. The close proximity of Dorset artifacts and other remains suggests small bands of hunters likely camped nearby.

Sutherland believes the Norse travelled the Baffin and Labrador coasts for 20
roughly 400 years, from AD 1000 to AD 1400, to ply trade. While it's not clear how many Europeans were at Nanook, nor whether they overwintered or just visited during the warm summers, she speculates that it was just one of many sites throughout the region where Norse traded iron and wood for furs and ivory, luxury items coveted in Europe.

If she's right, Nanook would become only the second confirmed Norse site in North America, after Leif Erikson's L'Anse aux Meadows. But while Erikson only stayed for a winter, and had no apparent dealings with the local aboriginals, Nanook is very different.

"The Northern world," says Sutherland, "was not a remote, marginal place 1,000 years ago, where nothing ever happened. The Norse push west from Norway was a commercial enterprise, for resource exploitation and trade. It was the start of early globalization."

For the 63-year-old Sutherland, 2012 looked to be her bonanza year: She presented her metallurgy findings and in November was featured in a major *National Geographic** article. That same month, she was in a documentary broadcast on the popular CBC show *The Nature of Things*.

But in April of that year, she'd been abruptly dismissed from her 28-year-long tenure at the Museum of Civilization, and her Nanook Project had been put on ice. Her husband, legendary Arctic archeologist Robert McGhee, was stripped of the emeritus status the museum bestowed on him in 2008. Neither Sutherland nor the museum will comment on the dismissals at the present time.[7]

Sutherland's firing, coming on the heels of the federal government's 25
roll call of shutdowns, funding cuts, media-muzzlings and layoffs in the science community,[8] created a furor. One of her many supporters, Memorial

---

7 *Neither ... time* In an interview conducted by the CBC and broadcast on the radio program *As It Happens*, Sutherland claimed that she had been targeted by the federal government because the content of her research did not fit a historical narrative that legitimized Canadian claims to sovereignty in the Arctic (and therefore a right to exploit its natural resources). In response, the Canadian Museum of History released a statement claiming that "Dr. Sutherland was terminated for harassment following an 18-month investigation done by an independent third party." A January 2014 investigation of these allegations by the CBC program *The Fifth Estate* characterized the investigation's findings as a portrait of "a perfectionist who sometimes spoke too bluntly" and implied that the findings were politically motivated.

8 *federal government's ... community* The Federal Government of Canada, under the leadership of Prime Minister Stephen Harper, implemented drastic cuts to funding for scientific research between 2009 and 2014, and beginning in 2008 severely curtailed

University's Tuck, speculated to *Maclean's* that Sutherland's reinterpretation of Canadian history might not be in tune with the new mandate of her old institution, which is changing its name to the Canadian Museum of History and focusing narrowly on the country's past 150 years. Other rumours are swirling that with the Harper government's ardent focus on Arctic sovereignty, evidence of Norwegians having set up shop in the Arctic a millennium ago might be too inconvenient to tolerate.

For Sutherland, the hardest blow is having been cut off from her 12 years' worth of research material.[9] For now the remarkable Nanook site lies fallow. "More than anything, I want to finish this project," she says. "At this point in my life I feel it's my legacy." The full saga of the Norse on Baffin has waited 1,000 years to be told, but even now, the ending of the story remains a mystery.

(2013)

Questions

1. At the time this article was written, a great deal of controversy surrounded Patricia Sutherland's firing, but the article does not mention the firing until the final few paragraphs. What effect does this have?
2. The article suggests that the Harper government was not supportive of Sutherland's research. Why was this the case?
3. Pfeiff puts forward the evidence for Norse habitation on Baffin Island in the order in which Sutherland discovered it. What are some alternative ways this information could have been organized? What are the advantages and disadvantages of presenting it as Pfeiff has?
4. Assuming Sutherland is correct in her belief that Norse traded in Canada's Arctic for hundreds of years, what (if any) impact does this have on Canadian national identity?

---

government scientists' freedom to share the results of their research with the public. Canada's scientific community responded with outrage.

9 *For Sutherland ... research material* In 2015, Sutherland was offered a research budget and access to her materials, but only outside "regular working hours"—an impediment she has claimed unreasonably limits her ability to complete her work.

JAMES SUROWIECKI

A FAIR DAY'S WAGE

The New Yorker *magazine often features a "Financial Page," a brief article by business writer James Surowiecki addressing a matter of economic importance. The following Surowiecki column discusses a decision made by the C.E.O. of Aetna, an American health insurance company, to pay its lowest-earning workers more.*

It's no secret that the years since the Great Recession[1] have been hard on American workers. Though unemployment has finally dipped below six per cent, real wages for most have barely budged since 2007. Indeed, the whole century so far has been tough: wages haven't grown much since 2000. So it was big news when, last month, Aetna's C.E.O., Mark Bertolini, announced that the company's lowest-paid workers would get a substantial raise—from twelve to sixteen dollars an hour, in some cases—as well as improved medical coverage. Bertolini didn't stop there. He said that it was not "fair" for employees of a Fortune 50 company[2] to be struggling to make ends meet. He explicitly linked the decision to the broader debate about inequality, mentioning that he had given copies of Thomas Piketty's *Capital in the Twenty-first Century*[3] to all his top executives. "Companies are not just money-making machines," he told me last week. "For the good of the social order, these are the kinds of investments we should be willing to make."

Such rhetoric harks back to an earlier era in U.S. labour relations. These days, most of the benefits of economic growth go to people at the top of the income ladder. But in the postwar era,* in particular, the wage-setting process was shaped by norms of fairness and internal equity. These norms were bolstered by the strength of the U.S. labour movement, which emphasized the idea

1 *the Great Recession* Worldwide economic decline that occurred towards the end of the first decade of the twenty-first century; in the United States, it is generally considered to have lasted from 2007 to 2009.

2 *Fortune 50 company* One of the fifty largest companies in the United States, according to annual rankings published by *Fortune* magazine.

3 *Thomas ... Century* Influential 2013 book on economic inequality; in it, Piketty proposes redistributing world wealth by means of taxation.

of the "living" or "family" wage—that someone doing a full day's work should be paid enough to live on. But they were embraced by many in the business class, too. Economists are typically sceptical that these kinds of norms play any rôle in setting wages. If you want to know why wages grew fast in the nineteen-fifties, they would say, look to the economic boom and an American workforce that didn't have to compete with foreign workers. But this is too narrow a view: the fact that the benefits of economic growth in the postwar era were widely shared had a lot to do with the assumption that companies were responsible not only to their shareholders but also to their workers. That's why someone like Peter Drucker, the dean of management theorists, could argue that no company's C.E.O. should be paid more than twenty times what its average employee earned.

That's not to imply that there aren't solid business reasons for paying workers more. A substantial body of research suggests that it can make sense to pay above-market wages—economists call them "efficiency wages." If you pay people better, they are more likely to stay, which saves money; job turnover was costing Aetna a hundred and twenty million dollars a year. Better-paid employees tend to work harder, too. The most famous example in business history is Henry Ford's decision, in 1914, to start paying his workers the then handsome sum of five dollars a day. Working on the Model T assembly line was an unpleasant job. Workers had been quitting in huge numbers or simply not showing up for work. Once Ford started paying better, job turnover and absenteeism plummeted, and productivity and profits rose.

Subsequent research has borne out the wisdom of Ford's approach. As the authors of a just published study of pay and performance in a hotel chain wrote, "Increases in wages do, in fact, pay for themselves." Zeynep Ton, a business-school professor at M.I.T., shows in her recent book, "The Good Jobs Strategy," that one of the reasons retailers like Trader Joe's and Costco have flourished is that, instead of relentlessly cost-cutting, they pay their employees relatively well, invest heavily in training them, and design their operations to encourage employee initiative. Their upfront labour costs may be higher, but, as Ton told me, "these companies end up with motivated, capable workers, better service, and increased sales." Bertolini—who, as it happens, once worked on a Ford rear-axle assembly line—makes a similar argument. "It's hard for people to be fully engaged with customers when they're worrying about how to put food on the table," he told me. "So I don't buy the idea that paying people well means sacrificing short-term earnings."

5 That hardly seems like a radical position. But it certainly makes Bertolini an outlier in today's corporate America. Since the nineteen-seventies, a combination of market forces, declining union strength, and ideological changes has led to what the economist Alan Krueger has described as a steady "erosion

of the norms, institutions and practices that maintain fairness in the U.S. job market." As a result, while companies these days tend to pay lavishly for talent on the high end—Bertolini made eight million dollars in 2013—they tend to treat frontline workers as disposable commodities.

This isn't because companies are having trouble making money: corporate America, if not the rest of the economy, has done just fine over the past five years. It's that all the rewards went into profits and executive salaries, rather than wages. That arrangement is the result not of some inevitable market logic but of a corporate ethos that says companies should pay workers as little as they can, and no more. This is what Bertolini seems to be challenging. His move may well turn out to be merely a one-off, rather than a harbinger of bigger change. But inequality and the shrinking middle class have become abiding preoccupations on Main Street and in Washington. It's only fair that these concerns have finally reached the executive suite.

(2015)

Questions

1. This article describes American employers' current attitudes toward wages. In your experience, to what extent do Canadian employers share these attitudes?
2. Why, according to Surowiecki, are wage increases good for businesses? Name a few other effects—positive or negative—wage increases might have on businesses.
3. Surowiecki quotes Bertolini's assertion that "'Corporations are not just money-making machines.'" What, if anything, other than making money should be the goals of corporations?

Jonathan M. Metzl and Kenneth T. MacLeish

from Mental Illness, Mass Shootings, and the Politics of American Firearms

This academic article from the American Journal of Public Health *questions several assumptions often made about gun violence. The article focuses in particular on the links that are often presumed to exist between such violence and mental illness. The researchers conclude that "notions of mental illness that emerge in relation to mass shootings frequently reflect larger cultural stereotypes and anxieties about matters such as race/ethnicity, social class, and politics; these issues become obscured when mass shootings come to stand in for all gun crime, and when 'mentally ill' ceases to be a medical designation and becomes a sign of violent threat." Excerpted here is the first of four sections on particular assumptions discussed in the article.*

The Assumption That Mental Illness Causes Gun Violence

The focus on mental illness in the wake of recent mass shootings[1] reflects a decades-long history of more general debates in psychiatry and law about guns, gun violence, and "mental competence." Psychiatric articles in the 1960s deliberated ways to assess whether mental patients were "of sound mind enough" to possess firearms.$_{21}$ Following the 1999 mass shooting at Columbine High School,* Breggin decried the toxic combination of mental illness, guns,

1 *recent mass shootings* This article was published online in February 2015. High-profile mass shootings in the United States in the immediately preceding years included incidents in Newtown, CT (2012, 27 dead); Washington, DC (2013, 12 dead); and Isla Vista, CA (2014, 6 dead).

NB To distinguish notes added for this anthology from the authors' note numbers referring to their list of references at the end of the article, subscript numbers have been used here for the latter.

and psychotropic medications that contributed to the actions of shooter Eric Harris.[22] After the 2012 shooting at Newtown,* Torrey amplified his earlier warnings about dangerous "subgroups" of persons with mental illness who, he contended, were perpetrators of gun crimes. Speaking to a national television audience, Torrey, a psychiatrist, claimed that "about half of … mass killings are being done by people with severe mental illness, mostly schizophrenia, and if they were being treated they would have been preventable."[23] Similar themes appear in legal dialogues as well. Even the US Supreme Court, which in 2008 strongly affirmed a broad right to bear arms,* endorsed prohibitions on gun ownership "by felons and the mentally ill" because of their special potential for violence.[24]

Yet surprisingly little population-level evidence supports the notion that individuals diagnosed with mental illness are more likely than anyone else to commit gun crimes. According to Appelbaum,[25] less than 3% to 5% of US crimes involve people with mental illness, and the percentages of crimes that involve guns are lower than the national average for persons not diagnosed with mental illness. Databases that track gun homicides, such as the National Center for Health Statistics, similarly show that fewer than 5% of the 120,000 gun-related killings in the United States between 2001 and 2010 were perpetrated by people diagnosed with mental illness.[26]

Meanwhile, a growing body of research suggests that mass shootings represent anecdotal distortions of, rather than representations of, the actions of "mentally ill" people as an aggregate group. By most estimates, there were fewer than 200 mass shootings reported in the United States—often defined as crimes in which four or more people are shot in an event, or related series of events—between 1982 and 2012.[27,28] Recent reports suggest that 160 of these events occurred after the year 2000[29] and that mass shootings rose particularly in 2013 and 2014.[28] As anthropologists and sociologists of medicine have noted, the time since the early 1980s also marked a consistent broadening of diagnostic categories and an expanding number of persons classifiable as "mentally ill."[30] Scholars who study violence prevention thus contend that mass shootings occur far too infrequently to allow for the statistical modelling and predictability—factors that lie at the heart of effective public health interventions. Swanson argues that mass shootings denote "rare acts of violence"[31] that have little predictive or preventive validity in relation to the bigger picture of the 32,000 fatalities and 74,000 injuries caused on average by gun violence and gun suicide each year in the United States.[32]

Links between mental illness and other types of violence are similarly contentious among researchers who study such trends. Several studies[33–35] suggest that subgroups of persons with severe or untreated mental illness might be at increased risk for violence in periods surrounding psychotic episodes or psychiatric hospitalizations. Writing in the *American Journal of Psychiatry*, Keers et al. found that the emergence of "persecutory delusions" partially explained associations between untreated schizophrenia and violence.[36] At the same time, a number of seminal studies asserting links between violence and mental illness—including a 1990 study by Swanson et al.[37] cited as fact by the *New York Times* in 2013[38]—have been critiqued for overstating connections between serious mental illness and violent acts.[39]

5 Media reports often assume a binary distinction between mild and severe mental illness, and connect the latter form to unpredictability and lack of self-control. However, this distinction, too, is called into question by mental health research. To be sure, a number of the most common psychiatric diagnoses, including depressive, anxiety, and attention-deficit disorders, have no correlation with violence whatsoever.[18] Community studies find that serious mental illness without substance abuse is also "statistically unrelated" to community violence.[40] At the aggregate level, the vast majority of people diagnosed with psychiatric disorders do not commit violent acts—only about 4% of violence in the United States can be attributed to people diagnosed with mental illness.[41,42]

A number of studies also suggest that stereotypes of "violent madmen" invert on-the-ground realities. Nestor theorizes that serious mental illnesses such as schizophrenia actually reduce the risk of violence over time, as the illnesses are in many cases marked by social isolation and withdrawal.[43] Brekke et al. illustrate that the risk is exponentially greater that individuals diagnosed with serious mental illness will be assaulted by others, rather than the other way around. Their extensive surveys of police incident reports demonstrate that, far from posing threats to others, people diagnosed with schizophrenia have victimization rates 65% to 130% higher than those of the general public.[44] Similarly, a meta-analysis by Choe et al. of published studies comparing perpetuation of violence with violent victimization by and against persons with mental illness concludes that "victimization is a greater public health concern than perpetration."[33(p153)] Media reports sound similar themes: a 2013 investigation by the *Portland Press Herald* found that "at least half" of persons shot and killed by police in Maine suffered from diagnosable mental illness.[45–48]

This is not to suggest that researchers know nothing about predictive factors for gun violence. However, credible studies suggest that a number of risk factors more strongly correlate with gun violence than mental illness alone. For instance, alcohol and drug use increase the risk of violent crime by as much as 7-fold, even among persons with no history of mental illness—a concerning statistic in the face of recent legislation that allows persons in certain US states to bring loaded handguns into bars and nightclubs.[49,50] According to Van Dorn et al., a history of childhood abuse, binge drinking, and male gender are all predictive risk factors for serious violence.[51]

A number of studies suggest that laws and policies that enable firearm access during emotionally charged moments also seem to correlate with gun violence more strongly than does mental illness alone. Belying Lott's argument that "more guns" lead to "less crime,"[52] Miller et al. found that homicide was more common in areas where household firearms ownership was higher.[53] Siegel et al. found that states with high rates of gun ownership had disproportionately high numbers of deaths from firearm-related homicides.[54] Webster's analysis uncovered that the repeal of Missouri's background check law led to an additional 49 to 68 murders per year,[55] and the rate of interpersonal conflicts resolved by fatal shootings jumped by 200% after Florida passed "stand your ground"[2] in 2005.[56] Availability of guns is also considered a more predictive factor than is psychiatric diagnosis in many of the 19,000 US completed gun suicides each year.[11,57,58] (By comparison, gun-related homicides and suicides fell precipitously, and mass-shootings dropped to zero, when the Australian government passed a series of gun-access restrictions in 1996.[59])

Contrary to the image of the marauding lone gunman, social relationships also predict gun violence. Regression analyses by Papachristos et al. demonstrate that up to 85% of shootings occur within social networks.[60] In other words, people are far more likely to be shot by relatives, friends, enemies, or acquaintances than they are by lone violent psychopaths. Meanwhile, a report by the police department of New York City found that, in 2013, a person was "more likely to die in a plane crash, drown in a bathtub or perish in an earthquake" than be murdered by a crazed stranger in that city.[61]

Again, certain persons with mental illness undoubtedly commit violent 10
acts. Reports argue that mental illness might even be underdiagnosed in people who commit random school shootings.[62] Yet growing evidence suggests that mass shootings represent statistical aberrations that reveal more about particularly horrible instances than they do about population-level events. To use Swanson's phrasing, basing gun crime–prevention efforts on the mental health histories of mass shooters risks building "common evidence" from "uncommon things."[31] Such an approach thereby loses the opportunity to build common evidence from common things—such as the types of evidence that clinicians of many medical specialties might catalogue, in alliance with communities, about substance abuse, domestic violence, availability of firearms, suicidality, social networks, economic stress, and other factors.

Gun crime narratives that attribute causality to mental illness also invert the material realities of serious mental illness in the United States. Commentators

2 *stand your ground* Colloquial way of referring to a law authorizing people to use deadly force if they believe it necessary for self-defence, with no duty to attempt to escape from rather than killing a potential attacker.

such as Coulter[3] blame "the mentally ill" for violence, and even psychiatric journals are more likely to publish articles about mentally ill aggression than about victimhood.[5] But, in the real world, these persons are far more likely to be assaulted by others or shot by the police than to commit violent crime themselves. In this sense, persons with mental illness might well have more to fear from "us" than we do from "them." And blaming persons with mental disorders for gun crime overlooks the threats posed to society by a much larger population—the sane....

(2015)

REFERENCES

5. Kaplan T, Hakim D. New York lawmakers reach deal on new gun curbs. New York Times. January 14, 2013: NY/Region. Available at: http://www.nytimes.com/2013/01/15/nyregion/new-york-legislators-hope-for-speedy-vote-on-gun-laws.html. Accessed July 23, 2014....

11. Martin A. Asperger's is accused but still not guilty. Huffington Post. June 6, 2014. Available at: http://www.huffingtonpost.com/areva-martin/aspergers-is-accused-but-_b_5434413.html. Accessed July 20, 2014....

18. Johns Hopkins Center for Gun Policy and Research. Guns, public health and mental illness: an evidence-based approach for state policy. Consortium for Risk-Based Firearm Policy. 2013. Available at: http://www.jhsph.edu/research/centers-and-institutes/johns-hopkins-center-for-gun-policy-and-research/publications/GPHMI-State.pdf. Accessed October 1, 2014....

21. Rotenberg LA, Sadoff RL. Who should have a gun? Some preliminary psychiatric thoughts. Am J Psychiatry. 1968;125(6):841–843.

22. Breggin P. Reclaiming Our Children: A Healing Plan for a Nation in Crisis. New York, NY: Basic Books; 2000.

23. Preview: imminent danger. *60 Minutes*. CBS. 2013. Available at: http://www.cbsnews.com/videos/preview-imminent-danger. Accessed July 23, 2014.

24. *District of Columbia v Heller*, 07–290 (DC Cir 2008).

25. Appelbaum PS. Violence and mental disorders: data and public policy. Am J Psychiatry. 2006;163(8):1319–1321.

26. Centers for Disease Control and Prevention. Leading causes of death reports, National and regional, 1999–2010. February 19, 2013. Available at: http://webappa.cdc.gov/sasweb/ncipc/leadcaus10_us.html. Accessed July 23, 2014.

27. Follman M, Aronsen G, Pan D. A guide to mass shootings in America. Mother Jones. May 24, 2014. Available at: http://www.motherjones.com/politics/2012/07/mass-shootings-map?page=2. Accessed July 20, 2014.

28. Mass shooting tracker. Available at: http://shootingtracker.com/wiki/Main_Page. Accessed July 20, 2014.

29. US Department of Justice. A study of active shooter incidents in the United States between 2000 and 2013. Available at: http://www.fbi.gov/news/stories/2014/september/

---

3 *Coulter* Ann Coulter (b. 1961), controversial conservative commentator.

fbi-releases-study-on-active-shooter-incidents/pdfs/a-study-of-active-shooter-incidents-in-the-u.s.-between-2000-and-2013. Accessed October 1, 2014.
30. Horwitz AV. Creating Mental Illness. Chicago, IL: University of Chicago Press; 2003.
31. Swanson JW. Explaining rare acts of violence: the limits of evidence from population research. Psychiatr Serv. 2011;62(11):1369–1371.
32. Firearm and Injury Center at Penn. Firearm injury in the U.S. 2009. Available at: http://www.uphs.upenn.edu/ficap/resourcebook/Final%20Resource%20Book%20Updated%202009%20Section%201.pdf. Accessed July 23, 2014.
33. Choe JY, Teplin LA, Abram KM. Perpetration of violence, violent victimization, and severe mental illness: balancing public health concerns. Psychiatr Serv. 2008;59(2):153–164.
34. McNiel DE, Weaver CM, Hall SE. Base rates of firearm possession by hospitalized psychiatric patients. Psychiatr Serv. 2007;58(4):551–553.
35. Large MM. Treatment of psychosis and risk assessment for violence. Am J Psychiatry. 2014;171(3):256–258.
36. Keers R, Ullrich S, DeStavola BL, Coid JW. Association of violence with emergence of persecutory delusions in untreated schizophrenia. Am J Psychiatry. 2014;171(3):332–339.
37. Swanson JW, Holzer CE, Ganju VK, Jono RT. Violence and psychiatric disorder in the community: evidence from the epidemiologic catchment area surveys. Psychiatr Serv. 1990;41(7):761–770.
38. Luo M, Mcintire M. When the right to bear arms includes the mentally ill. New York Times. December 21, 2013: US. Available at: http://www.nytimes.com/2013/12/22/us/when-the-right-to-bear-arms-includes-the-mentally-ill.html. Accessed July 23, 2014.
39. Grohol J. Violence and mental illness: simplifying complex data relationships. Psych Central. Available at: http://psychcentral.com/blog/archives/2007/05/02/violence-and-mental-illness-simplifying-complex-data-relationships. Accessed July 1, 2014.
40. Elbogen EB, Johnson SC. The intricate link between violence and mental disorder: results from the National Epidemiologic Survey on Alcohol and Related Conditions. Arch Gen Psychiatry. 2009;66(2):152–161.
41. Fazel S, Grann M. The population impact of severe mental illness on violent crime. Am J Psychiatry. 2006;163(8):1397–1403.
42. Friedman R. A misguided focus on mental illness in gun control debate. New York Times. December 17, 2012: Health. Available at: http://www.nytimes.com/2012/12/18/health/a-misguided-focus-on-mental-illness-in-gun-control-debate.html. Accessed July 23, 2014.
43. Nestor PG. Mental disorder and violence: personality dimensions and clinical features. Am J Psychiatry. 2002;159(12):1973–1978.
44. Brekke JS, Prindle C, Bae SW, Long JD. Risks for individuals with schizophrenia who are living in the community. Psychiatr Serv. 2001;52(10):1358–1366.
45. Deadly force. Police and the mentally ill. Portland Press Herald. Available at: http://www.pressherald.com/special/Maine_police_deadly_force_series_Day_1.html. Accessed March 23, 2014.
46. Steadman HJ, Mulvey EP, Monahan J. et al. Violence by people discharged from acute psychiatric inpatient facilities and by others in the same neighborhoods. Arch Gen Psychiatry. 1998;55(5):393–401.

47. Soliman AE, Reza H. Risk factors and correlates of violence among acutely ill adult psychiatric inpatients. Psychiatr Serv. 2001;52(1):75–80.
48. Rapoport A. Guns—not the mentally ill—kill people. Am Prospect. February 7, 2013. Available at: http://prospect.org/article/guns%E2%80%94not-mentally-ill%E2%80%94kill-people. Accessed July 23, 2014.
49. Brammer J. Kentucky Senate approves bill allowing concealed guns in bars if owner doesn't drink. February 20, 2014. Available at: http://www.kentucky.com/2014/02/20/3100119/kentucky-senate-approves-bill.html. Accessed July 23, 2014.
50. Monahan J, Steadman H, Silver E. Rethinking Risk Assessment: The MacArthur Study of Mental Disorder and Violence. New York, NY: Oxford University Press; 2001.
51. Van Dorn R, Volavka J, Johnson N. Mental disorder and violence: is there a relationship beyond substance use? Soc Psychiatry Psychiatr Epidemiol. 2012;47(3):487–503.
52. Lott JR. More Guns, Less Crime: Understanding Crime and Gun-Control Laws. Chicago, IL: The University of Chicago Press; 2010.
53. Miller M, Azrael D, Hemenway D. Rates of household firearm ownership and homicide across US regions and states, 1988–1997. Am J Public Health. 2002;92(12):1988–1993.
54. Siegel M, Ross CD, King C. The relationship between gun ownership and firearm homicide rates in the United States, 1981–2010. Am J Public Health. 2013;103(11):2098–2105.
55. Webster D, Crifasi CK, Vernick JS. Effects of the repeal of Missouri's handgun purchaser licensing law on homicides. J Urban Health. 2014;9(2):293–302.
56. The Editorial Board. Craven statehouse behavior. New York Times. March 14, 2014. Available at: http://www.nytimes.com/2014/03/15/opinion/craven-statehouse-behavior.html. Accessed July 23, 2014.
57. Lewiecki EM, Miller SA. Suicide, guns, and public policy. Am J Public Health. 2013;103(1):27–31.
58. Centers for Disease Control and Prevention. FASTSTATS - Suicide and self-inflicted injury. December 30, 2013. Available at: http://www.cdc.gov/nchs/fastats/suicide.htm. Accessed July 23, 2014.
59. Chapman S, Alpers P, Agho K, Jones M. Australia's 1996 gun law reforms: faster falls in firearm deaths, firearm suicides, and a decade without mass shootings. Inj Prev. 2006;12(6):365–372.
60. Papachristos AV, Braga AA, Hureau DM. Social networks and the risk of gunshot injury. J Urban Health. 2012;89(6):992–1003.
61. Hamilton B. Odds that you'll be killed by a stranger in NYC on the decline. New York Post. January 5, 2014. Available at: http://nypost.com/2014/01/05/odds-that-youll-be-killed-by-a-stranger-in-nyc-on-the-decline. Accessed July 23, 2014.
62. US Secret Service and US Department of Education. Final report and findings of the safe school initiative: implications for the prevention of school attacks in the United States. Available at: http://www2.ed.gov/admins/lead/safety/preventingattacksreport.pdf. Accessed July 20, 2014.

Questions

1. Did anything in this article surprise you? Why or why not?
2. Metzl and MacLeish claim that mass shootings "represent statistical aberrations that reveal more about particularly horrible instances than they do about population-level events." What do they mean by this? Why do you think there is so much more attention paid to mass shootings than to more common types of gun crime? Is this degree of attention justified?
3. Evaluate the persuasiveness of the statistics used in this article.
4. According to the studies cited by Metzl and MacLeish, what factors increase the likelihood of gun violence? Based on these studies, what public policy regarding guns do you think would be more effective than limiting purchases by those diagnosed with mental illness?

NATHANAEL JOHNSON

IS THERE A MORAL CASE FOR MEAT?

This essay is by the food editor for Grist, *an online source of news and commentary, primarily on matters relating to the environment; Johnston is also the author of the 2013 book* All Natural: A Skeptic's Quest to Discover If the Natural Approach to Diet, Childbirth, Healing, and the Environment Really Keeps Us Healthier and Happier. *"Is There a Moral Case for Meat?" was published on the* Grist *site on 20 July 2015.*

Where are the philosophers arguing that eating meat is moral?

When I started researching this piece, I'd already read a lot of arguments against meat, but I hadn't seen a serious philosophical defense of carnivores. So I started asking around. I asked academics, meat industry representatives, and farmers: Who was the philosophical counterweight to Peter Singer?

In 1975, Singer wrote *Animal Liberation*, which launched the modern animal rights movement with its argument that causing animal suffering is immoral. There are plenty of other arguments against eating animals besides Singer's, going back to the ancient Greeks and Hindus. There are even arguments that Christianity contains a mandate for vegetarianism. Matthew Scully's *Dominion* argues against animal suffering; Scully rejects Singer's utilitarian assertion that humans and animals are equal but says that, since God gave people "dominion over the fish of the sea and the fowl of the air, and over the cattle, and over all the earth," so we have a responsibility to care for them and show them mercy.

The arguments against eating animals are pretty convincing. But surely, I thought, there were also intellectuals making convincing counterarguments. Right? Nope. Not really.

5 There is the Cartesian[1] idea that animals are unfeeling machines, incapable of suffering—but I just wasn't buying that. It's clear that animals have an aversive response to pain, and careful, well-respected scientists are saying that animals are probably capable of feeling and consciousness. Once we admit even the possibility that animals are sentient, the ethical game is on: It doesn't

1 *Cartesian* Associated with the work of René Descartes (1596–1650), an influential French philosopher.

matter that an animal is *just an animal*; if you're against suffering and you agree animals can feel pain, it's pretty hard to justify eating them. (Of course, the further you get from humans the harder it is to judge—plants may be sentient in a totally alien way! Singer says we can stop caring somewhere between a shrimp and oyster.)

My enquiries didn't turn up any sophisticated defense of meat. Certainly there are a few people here and there making arguments around the edges, but nothing that looked to me like a serious challenge to Singer. In fact, the lack of philosophical work to justify meat eating is so extreme that people kept referring me not to scholarly publications, but to an essay contest that the *New York Times* held back in 2012. Ariel Kaminer organized that contest after noticing the same gaping hole in the philosophical literature that I'd stumbled upon. Vegetarians have claimed the ethical high ground with book after book and, Kaminer wrote:

> In response, those who love meat have had surprisingly little to say. They say, of course, that, well, they love meat or that meat is deeply ingrained in our habit or culture or cuisine or that it's nutritious or that it's just part of the natural order.... But few have tried to answer the fundamental ethical issue: Whether it is right to eat animals in the first place, at least when human survival is not at stake.

The winner of that contest, Jay Bost, didn't take it much farther than that, basically arguing that "meat is just part of the natural order," because animals are an integral part of the food web. That's a start, but I'd want a lot more than a 600-word essay to flesh out the idea and respond to the obvious criticisms—since almost all the animals we eat are far removed from natural food webs, it's still basically a prescription for veganism. Plus, where do you draw the line on what's natural?

I found several beginnings of arguments like this—no real philosophical shelter for a meat eater, but a few foundational observations that you might build something upon if you carefully thought through all the implications.

Animal welfare expert Temple Grandin offered one potential plank for building a defense of meat eating. "We've gotta give animals a life worth living," she told me. Later in the interview, she reminded me that most farm animals wouldn't have a life at all if no one ate meat. Combine these points and you could argue that it's better to have a life worth living than no life at all—even if it ends with slaughter and consumption.

When I bounced this argument off the ethicist Paul Thompson, he said, "That may be a defensible position, but a philosopher should also be prepared to apply it to humans."

Right. It's hard to limit the "a life worth living is better than no life at all" 10
argument to farm animals. Using the same argument we might raise children

for the purpose of producing organs: As long as they were well cared for, ignorant of their fate, and painlessly slaughtered, you could say they had a life worth living. The clone gets a (short) life, a dying girl gets a new heart, everyone wins! It's rationally consistent, but certainly doesn't feel right to me.

Perhaps some brilliant philosopher will develop these points, but, since I am not one of those, I was left with the conclusion that the vegans were right. Oddly, however, that didn't make me think twice about laying sliced turkey on my sandwich the next day. I was convinced on a rational level, but not in an embodied, visceral way.

"*Animal Liberation* is one of those rare books that demand that you either defend the way you live or change it," Michael Pollan once wrote. I know what he means—when I first read it, I felt battered and stupefied by the horrors of animal suffering that Singer paraded before me. Nevertheless, despite my inability to muster a defense for my meat eating, I didn't change my way of life. Pollan didn't, either: His piece is set up as a stunt—he's reading *Animal Liberation* while eating rib-eye in a steakhouse. And, though Pollan finds himself agreeing with Singer, he has no problem finishing his steak.

I tend to think of rational argument as a powerful force, certainly more powerful than the trivial pleasure of eating meat. But it turns out that's backwards: Rational morality tugs at us with the slenderest of threads, while meat pulls with the thick-twined cords of culture, tradition, pleasure, the flow of the crowd, and physical yearning—and it pulls at us three times a day. Thousands, convinced by Singer and the like, become vegetarians for moral reasons. And then most of those thousands start eating meat again. Vaclav Smil notes: "Prevalence of all forms of 'vegetarianism' is no higher than 2–4 percent in any Western society and that long-term (at least a decade) or life-long adherence to solely plant-based diets is less than 1 percent." As the psychologist Hal Herzog told *Grist*'s Katie Herzog in this podcast, "It's the single biggest failure of the animal rights movement."

How do we deal with this? Some people just shrug and say, "Whatever, animals are different, it's OK to kill them." I can't quite bring myself to do that, because I value rational consistency. And yet, I don't feel immoral when I eat meat—I actually feel pretty good.

15 Whenever you have lots of people agreeing in principle to a goal that is impossible for most to achieve in practice, you have something resembling religion. Religions are all about setting standards that most people will never live up to. And Thompson thinks they have something to teach us on this issue.

Thompson's solution is to treat vegetarianism the way religious traditions treat virtues. Christians strive to love their neighbours, but they don't say that people who fail to reach Jesus-level self-sacrifice are immoral. Buddhists strive for detachment, but they don't flagellate themselves when they fail to achieve it.

Thompson suggests that we should strive to do better by animals, but that doesn't mean we should condemn ourselves for eating meat. There are lots of cases like this, he told me. "Some people are going to take these issues up in a way that other people would find really difficult," Thompson said. "For instance, we all respect Mother Theresa for taking on amazing burdens, but we don't say that you are evil for not doing it."

This makes sense to me. Louis CK* can make a pretty solid argument that people who have enough money to buy a nice car (or to spend time reading long essays about meat philosophy) should be donating 90 percent of their income to the poor.

And yet most of us don't give up our luxuries. By Thompson's reasoning, that doesn't make us immoral. In fact, he says, it's just wrong to condemn people who eat meat. When people rise out of extreme poverty, that is, when they start earning $2.60 a day, they almost invariably spend that newfound money on animal protein: milk, meat, or eggs. Now, you might roll your eyes and say that *of course* the desperate should be excused from the moral obligation—but wait. As Thompson writes in his book, *From Field to Fork: Food Ethics for Everyone*:

> [T]his response misses my point. Excuses apply in extenuating circumstances, but the logic of excuses implies that the action itself is still morally wrong. A poor person might be excused for stealing a loaf of bread. Theft might be excused when a poor person's situation takes a turn for the worse, but in the case at hand, their situation has taken a turn toward the better. Under modestly improved circumstances, the extremely poor add a little meat, milk, or eggs into their diet. My claim is that there is something curious with a moral system that reclassifies legally and traditionally sanctioned conduct of people at the utter margins of society as something that needs to be excused.

Is it morally wrong for a hungry child in India to eat an egg? This isn't just a thought experiment—it's a real controversy. It's not enough to wave it off by saying it's easy to provide vegan alternatives, because those alternatives just don't exist for many people. Often, the cheapest high-quality protein available to the poor comes from animals. Thompson's point is that allowing people to access that protein should be *moral*, not just an excusable lapse.

If we accept Thompson's formulation (and I'm inclined to), it lets us stop 20
wringing our hands over our hypocrisy and strive to improve conditions for animals. That's what Temple Grandin does. She didn't have much patience for my philosophical questions. Instead, she is focused on the realistic changes that will give animals better lives. And as I talked to her, she served up surprise after surprise. Many of the elements in confined animal feeding operations

(CAFOs) that people find most abhorrent, she said, may be fine from the animal's perspective. For instance, consider egg-laying hens: What's better for them—an open barn or stacked cages? Small battery cages, with several hens packed inside each, are bad news, according to Grandin, but enriched cages are a really good alternative.

"There are objective ways to measure a hen's motivation to get something she wants—like a private nest box," Grandin told me. "How long is she willing to not eat to get it, or how heavy a door will she push to get it? How many times will she push a switch to get it? A private nest box is something she wants, because in the wild she has an instinct to hide in the bushes so that a fox doesn't get [her eggs]. Give her some pieces of plastic to hang down that she can hide behind. Give her a little piece of astroturf to lay [her eggs] on. Give her a perch, and a piece of plastic to scratch on, and at least enough cage height so she can walk normally. I'm gonna call that apartment living for chickens. Do they need natural elements? Being outside? Science can't answer that. I mean, there are people in New York that hardly go outside."

I pressed her: Can't you use those same objective measurement techniques to see how badly the hens want to go outside and scratch for bugs?

"Well you can," Grandin said, "and the motivation is pretty weak compared to something like the nest box, which is hardwired. Take dust bathing. For a hen dust bathing is nice to do, but it's kind of like, yes, it's nice to have a fancy hotel room, but the EconoLodge* will do too."

And in fact, the free-range system that I would instinctively choose for chickens may be worse than an enriched cage—because the birds get sick and injured a lot more. And laying hens, unlike meat chickens, are pretty nasty about setting up pecking orders. As Thompson observes in his book, "This is well and good in the flocks of 10 to 20 birds, as might be observed among wild jungle fowl, and it is probably tolerable in a flock of 40 to 60 birds that might have been seen on a typical farmstead in 1900.... But a cage-free/free-range commercial egg barn will have between 150,000 to 500,000 hens occupying the same space. If you are a hen at the bottom end of the pecking order in an environment like that, you are going to get pecked. A lot."

25 Even small farms with pastured hens that produce $9-a-dozen eggs often have hundreds of birds, which means the most submissive hens are going to get beat up. I certainly prefer Joel Salatin's 400-bird Eggmobile[2] on lush grass, because to my human eyes it's beautiful—and chicken cages look horrible. But I have real doubt as to what's better from the chicken's perspective.

There are a lot of counterintuitive things like this when it comes to animal farming.... So I asked Grandin how we should feel about animal agriculture in the United States as it's currently practised: Do these animals really have a life worth living?

---

2 *Eggmobile* Portable henhouse.

It varies greatly, she said, but some CAFOs really are good. "I think cattle done right have a decent life," she said. I couldn't get her to give a simple thumbs up or down to chicken or pork CAFOs.

Talking to Grandin didn't make me want to go stock up on corn-fed beef, but it did significantly soften my (negative) feelings about industrial animal production. And talking to Thompson made me realize that I was willing to compromise the needs of animals for the needs of humans if they come into direct conflict. In that way I'm a speciesist—I have an unshakeable favouritism for humans. Perhaps it's irrational, but I really want that little girl in India to get her egg, even if it means hens suffer, even if there's a good vegan alternative for a slightly higher cost.

Perhaps there's a philosophical argument to be made in defense of killing animals, but no one has spelled that out in a way that I found convincing. Does this mean that we should join the vegans?

I think the answer is yes, but in a very limited way—in the same way that 30
we all *should* take vows of poverty and stop thinking impure thoughts. Ending deaths and suffering is a worthy moral goal for those of us who have the wealth to make choices. But saying that it's wrong and immoral to eat meat is just too absolutist. I mean, even the Dalai Lama, who says vegetarianism is preferable, eats meat twice a week.

The binary, good-or-evil view of meat is pragmatically counterproductive—the black and white strategy hasn't gotten many people to become vegan. Instead, let's focus on giving farm animals a life worth living.

(2015)

Questions

1. What arguments in favour of meat eating does Johnson advance? Of these, which do you find the most persuasive? What about it do you find persuasive? Are there any compelling counterarguments to the argument you chose?
2. Compare this essay with the excerpt from Jonathan Safran Foer's *Eating Animals* included in this anthology. What similarities can you find in Foer's and Johnson's arguments? What differences can you find? Which piece do you find most persuasive?
3. If you eat meat, does this article make you feel better about this choice? If you don't eat meat, does this article influence the way you feel about the morality of meat eating? Why or why not?
4. In the first pages of "Is There a Moral Case for Meat," Johnson refers to Peter Singer's *Animal Liberation* several times. Read the excerpt from *Animal Liberation* included in this volume. How accurately does Johnson represent Singer's work?

MICHAEL POLLAN

WHY "NATURAL" DOESN'T MEAN ANYTHING ANYMORE

Pollan became famous with two bestselling books on food and the environment, The Omnivore's Dilemma *(2006) and* In Defense of Food *(2008). He has continued since then to publish both on those topics and on related issues—as in the essay included here, in which he explores belief systems around the nature, and assumed superiority, of "natural" states. The piece first appeared in the 28 April 2015 issue of* The New York Times Magazine. *The above title was assigned to the piece online; in print, it was entitled "Altered State."*

It isn't every day that the definition of a common English word that is ubiquitous in common parlance* is challenged in federal court, but that is precisely what has happened with the word "natural." During the past few years, some 200 class-action suits have been filed against food manufacturers, charging them with misuse of the adjective in marketing such edible oxymorons as "natural" Cheetos Puffs, "all-natural" Sun Chips, "all-natural" Naked Juice, "100 percent all-natural" Tyson chicken nuggets and so forth. The plaintiffs argue that many of these products contain ingredients—high-fructose corn syrup, artificial flavours and colourings, chemical preservatives and genetically modified organisms—that the typical consumer wouldn't think of as "natural."

Judges hearing these cases—many of them in the Northern District of California—have sought a standard definition of the adjective that they could cite to adjudicate these claims, only to discover that no such thing exists.

Something in the human mind, or heart, seems to need a word of praise for all that humanity hasn't contaminated, and for us that word now is "natural." Such an ideal can be put to all sorts of rhetorical uses. Among the antivaccination crowd,* for example, it's not uncommon to read about the superiority of something called "natural immunity," brought about by exposure to the pathogen in question rather than to the deactivated (and therefore harmless) version of it made by humans in laboratories. "When you inject a vaccine into the body," reads a post on an antivaxxer website, Campaign for Truth in Medicine, "you're actually performing an unnatural act." This, of course, is the very same term once used to decry homosexuality and, more recently, same-sex marriage, which the Family Research Council[1] has taken to comparing unfavourably to what it calls "natural marriage."

If nature offers a moral standard by which we measure ourselves, and a set of values to which we should aspire, exactly what sort of values are they?

So what are we really talking about when we talk about natural? It depends; 5
the adjective is impressively slippery, its use steeped in dubious assumptions that are easy to overlook. Perhaps the most incoherent of these is the notion that nature consists of everything in the world except us and all that we have done or made. In our heart of hearts, it seems, we are all creationists.*

In the case of "natural immunity," the modifier implies the absence of human intervention, allowing for a process to unfold as it would if we did nothing, as in "letting nature take its course." In fact, most of medicine sets itself against nature's course, which is precisely what we like about it—at least when it's saving us from dying, an eventuality that is perhaps more natural than it is desirable.

Yet sometimes medicine's interventions are unwelcome or go overboard, and nature's way of doing things can serve as a useful corrective. This seems to be especially true at the beginning and end of life, where we've seen a backlash against humanity's technological ingenuity that has given us both "natural childbirth" and, more recently, "natural death."*

This last phrase, which I expect will soon be on many doctors' lips, indicates the enduring power of the adjective to improve just about anything you attach it to, from cereal bars all the way on up to dying. It seems that getting end-of-life patients and their families to endorse "do not resuscitate" orders has been challenging. To many ears, "D.N.R."[2] sounds a little too much like throwing Grandpa under the bus. But according to a paper in *The Journal of Medical Ethics*, when the orders are reworded to say "allow natural death," patients and family members and even medical professionals are much more likely to give their consent to what amounts to exactly the same protocols.

The word means something a little different when applied to human behaviour rather than biology (let alone snack foods). When marriage or certain sexual practices are described as "natural," the word is being strategically deployed as a synonym for "normal" or "traditional," neither of which carries nearly as much rhetorical weight. "Normal" is by now too obviously soaked in moral bigotry; by comparison, "natural" seems to float high above human squabbling, offering a kind of secular version of what used to be called divine law.* Of course, that's exactly the role that "natural law" played for America's

1 *Family Research Council* Christian public policy ministry in Washington, D.C.

2 *D.N.R.* Do Not Resuscitate.

founding fathers, who invoked nature rather than God as the granter of rights and the arbiter of right and wrong.

10 "Traditional" marriage might be a more defensible term, but traditional is a much weaker modifier than natural. Tradition changes over time and from culture to culture, and so commands a fraction of the authority of nature, which we think of as timeless and universal, beyond the reach of messy, contested history.

Implicit here is the idea that nature is a repository of abiding moral and ethical values—and that we can say with confidence exactly what those values are. Philosophers often call this the "naturalistic fallacy": the idea that whatever is (in nature) is what ought to be (in human behaviour). But if nature offers a moral standard by which we can measure ourselves, and a set of values to which we should aspire, exactly what sort of values are they? Are they the brutally competitive values of "nature, red in tooth and claw," in which every individual is out for him- or herself? Or are they the values of cooperation on display in a beehive or ant colony, where the interests of the community trump* those of the individual? Opponents of same-sex marriage can find examples of monogamy in the animal kingdom, and yet to do so they need to look past equally compelling examples of animal polygamy as well as increasing evidence of apparent animal homosexuality. And let's not overlook the dismaying rates of what looks very much like rape in the animal kingdom, or infanticide, or the apparent sadism of your average house cat.

The American Puritans* called nature "God's Second Book," and they read it for moral guidance, just as we do today. Yet in the same way we can rummage around in the Bible and find textual support for pretty much whatever we want to do or argue, we can ransack nature to justify just about anything. Like the maddening whiteness of Ahab's whale,[3] nature is an obligingly blank screen on which we can project what we want to see.

So does this mean that, when it comes to saying what's natural, anything goes? I don't think so. In fact, I think there's some philosophical wisdom we can harvest from, of all places, the Food and Drug Administration.* When the federal judges couldn't find a definition of "natural" to apply to the class-action suits before them, three of them wrote to the F.D.A., ordering the agency to define the word. But the F.D.A. had considered the question several times before, and refused to attempt a definition. The only advice the F.D.A. was willing to offer the jurists was that a food labelled "natural" should have "nothing artificial or synthetic" in it "that would not normally be expected in the food." The F.D.A. states on its website that "it is difficult to define a food product as

---

3 *Ahab's whale* Reference to Herman Melville's classic novel *Moby-Dick* (1851), in which Captain Ahab is obsessed with seeking revenge on the whale who destroyed his previous ship.

'natural' because the food has probably been processed and is no longer the product of the earth," suggesting that the industry might not want to press the point too hard, lest it discover that nothing it sells is natural.

The F.D.A.'s philosopher-bureaucrats are probably right: At least at the margins, it's impossible to fix a definition of "natural." Yet somewhere between those margins there lies a broad expanse of common sense. "Natural" has a fairly sturdy antonym—artificial, or synthetic—and, at least on a scale of relative values, it's not hard to say which of two things is "more natural" than the other: cane sugar or high-fructose corn syrup? Chicken or chicken nuggets? G.M.O.s or heirloom seeds?* The most natural foods in the supermarket seldom bother with the word; any food product that feels compelled to tell you it's natural in all likelihood is not.

But it is probably unwise to venture beyond the shores of common sense, 15
for it isn't long before you encounter either Scylla or Charybdis.[4] At one extreme end of the spectrum of possible meanings, there's nothing but nature. Our species is a result of the same process—natural selection—that created every other species, meaning that we and whatever we do are natural, too. So go ahead and call your nuggets natural: It's like saying they're made with matter, or molecules, which is to say, it's like saying nothing at all.

And yet at the opposite end of the spectrum of meaning, where humanity in some sense stands outside nature—as most of us still unthinkingly believe—what is left of the natural that we haven't altered in some way? We're mixed up with all of it now, from the chemical composition of the atmosphere to the genome of every plant or animal in the supermarket to the human body itself, which has long since evolved in response to cultural practices we invented, like agriculture and cooking. Nature, if you believe in human exceptionalism,[5] is over. We probably ought to search elsewhere for our values.

(2015)

Questions

1. Is naturalness inherently good? Why or why not?
2. Why is it so difficult to reach a consensus about the meaning of the word "natural"?
3. Discuss an instance where an "unnatural" state may be preferable to a "natural" one.

---

4 *before you ... Charybdis* I.e., before you have to choose between two evils. (The reference is to a story in Greek mythology.)

5 *human exceptionalism* The belief that humans are different from (and superior to) all other animals.

LAILA LALAMI

MY LIFE AS A MUSLIM IN THE WEST'S "GREY ZONE"

This essay discussing the position of Muslims in Western societies since 2001 was first published in the 20 November 2015 issue of The New York Times Magazine.

Some months ago, I gave a reading from my most recent novel in Scottsdale, Ariz. During the discussion that followed, a woman asked me to talk about my upbringing in Morocco. It's natural for readers to be curious about a writer they've come to hear, I told myself. I continued to tell myself this even after the conversation drifted to Islam, and then to ISIS. Eventually, another woman raised her hand and said that the only Muslims she saw when she turned on the television were extremists. "Why aren't we hearing more from people like you?" she asked me.

"You are," I said with a nervous laugh. "Right now." I wanted to tell her that there were plenty of ordinary Muslims in this country. We come in all races and ethnicities. Some of us are more visible by virtue of beards or head scarves. Others are less conspicuous, unless they give book talks and it becomes clear that they, too, identify as Muslims.

To be fair, I'm not a very good Muslim. I don't perform daily prayers anymore. I have never been on a pilgrimage to Mecca.[1] I partake of the forbidden drink.[2] I do give to charity whenever I can, but I imagine that this would not be enough to save me were I to have the misfortune, through an accident of birth or migration, to live in a place like Raqqa, Syria, where in the last two years, the group variously known as Daesh, ISIL or ISIS has established a caliphate: a successor to past Islamic empires. Life in Raqqa reportedly follows rules that range from the horrifying to the absurd: The heads of people who have been executed are posted on spikes in the town's main square; women must wear a

1 *pilgrimage to Mecca* The Hajj is an annual journey to Saudi Arabia to visit the most holy city in Islam; making this pilgrimage at least once in an adult's lifetime is a religious requirement within most branches of Islam.

2 *forbidden drink* Alcohol, which is forbidden in the Qur'an.

niqab[3] and be accompanied by a male companion when they go out; smoking and swearing are not allowed; chemistry is no longer taught in schools and traffic police are not permitted to have whistles because ISIS considers them un-Islamic.

As part of its efforts to spread its message outside the territory it controls, ISIS puts out an English-language magazine, *Dabiq*, which can be found online. In February, *Dabiq* featured a 12-page article, complete with high-resolution photos and multiple footnotes, cheering the terrorist attacks of Sept. 11 and claiming that they made manifest for the world two camps: the camp of Islam under the caliphate and the camp of the West under the crusaders. The article ran under the title "The Extinction of the Greyzone." The grey zone is the space inhabited by any Muslim who has not joined the ranks of either ISIS or the crusaders. Throughout the article, these Muslims are called "the greyish," "the hypocrites" and, for variety, "the greyish hypocrites."

On Nov. 13, men who had sworn allegiance to ISIS struck the city of Paris, 5
killing 130 people at different locations mostly in the 10th and 11th arrondissements, neighbourhoods that are known for their multiculturalism. As soon as I heard about the attacks, I tried to reach a cousin of mine, who is studying in Paris. I couldn't. I spent the next two hours in a state of crushing fear until he posted on Facebook that he was safe. Relieved, I went back to scrolling through my feed, which is how I found out that my friend Najlae Benmbarek, a Moroccan journalist, lost her cousin. A recently married architect, Mohamed Amine Ibnolmobarak was eating dinner with his wife at the Carillon restaurant when an ISIS terrorist killed him.

It was probably not a coincidence that the Paris attacks were aimed at restaurants, a concert hall and a sports stadium, places of leisure and community, nor that the victims included Muslims. As *Dabiq* makes clear, ISIS wants to eliminate coexistence between religions and to create a response from the West that will force Muslims to choose sides: either they "apostatize and adopt" the infidel religion of the crusaders[4] or "they perform *hijrah*[5] to the Islamic State and thereby escape persecution from the crusader governments and citizens." For ISIS to win, the grey zone must be eliminated.

Whose lives are grey? Mine, certainly. I was born in one nation (Morocco) speaking Arabic, came to my love of literature through a second language (French) and now live in a third country (America), where I write books and teach classes in yet another language (English). I have made my home in

---

3 *niqab* Cloth to cover the face.

4 *apostatize and ... crusaders* I.e., relinquish Islam and adopt Christianity.

5 *hijrah* Migration for religious purposes; "the Hijrah" typically refers to Muhammad's migration from Mecca to Medina to escape assassination.

between all these cultures, all these languages, all these countries. And I have found it a glorious place to be. My friends are atheists and Muslims, Jews and Christians, believers and doubters. Each one makes my life richer.

This grey life of mine is not unique. I share it with millions of people around the world. My brother in Dallas is a practising Muslim—he prays, he fasts, he attends mosque—but he, too, would be considered to be in the grey zone, because he despises ISIS and everything it stands for.

Most of the time, grey lives go unnoticed in America. Other times, especially when people are scared, grey lives become targets. Hate crimes against Muslims spike after every major terrorist attack. But rather than stigmatize this hate, politicians and pundits often stoke it with fiery rhetoric, further diminishing the grey zone. Every time the grey zone recedes, ISIS gains ground.

10 The language that ISIS uses may be new, but the message is not. When President George W. Bush spoke to a joint session of Congress after the terrorist attacks of Sept. 11, he declared, "Either you are with us or you are with the terrorists." It was a decisive threat, and it worked well for him in those early, confusing days, so he returned to it. "Either you are with us," he said in 2002, "or you are with the enemy. There's no in between." This polarized thinking led to the United States invasion of Iraq, which led to the destabilization of the Middle East, which in turn led to the creation of ISIS.

Terrorist attacks affect all of us in the same way: We experience sorrow and anger at the loss of life. For Muslims, however, there is an additional layer of grief as we become subjects of suspicion. Muslims are called upon to condemn terrorism, but no matter how often or how loud or how clear the condemnations, the calls remain. Imagine if, after every mass shooting in a school or a movie theatre in the United States, young white men in this country were told that they must publicly denounce gun violence. The reason this is not the case is that we presume each young white man to be solely responsible for his actions, whereas Muslims are held collectively responsible. To be a Muslim in the West is to be constantly on trial.

The attacks in Paris have generated the same polarization as all previous attacks have. Even though most of the suspects were French and Belgian nationals who could have gained entry to the United States on their passports, Republican governors in 30 states say that they will refuse to take in any refugees from Syria without even more stringent screening. Barely two days after the attacks, Jeb Bush* told CNN's Jake Tapper that the United States should focus its efforts only on helping Syrian refugees who are Christian.

Ted Cruz* went a step further, offering to draft legislation that would ban Muslim Syrian refugees from the United States. When he was asked by Dana Bash of CNN what would have happened to him if his father, a Cuban refugee who was fleeing communism, had been refused entry, he implied that it was a different situation because of the special risks associated with ISIS.

As it happens, I am married to a son of Cuban refugees. Like Cruz's father, they came to this country because America was a safe haven. What would have been their fate if an American legislator said that they could not be allowed in because the Soviet Union was trying to infiltrate the United States?

The other day, my daughter said to me, "I want to be president." She has been saying this a lot lately, usually the morning after a presidential debate, when our breakfast-table conversation veers toward the elections. My daughter is 12. She plays the violin and the guitar; she loves math and history; she's quick-witted and sharp-tongued and above all she's very kind to others. "I'd vote for you," I told her. And then I looked away, because I didn't have the heart to tell her that half the people in this country—in her country—say they would not vote for a Muslim presidential candidate.

I worry about her growing up in a place where some of the people who are seeking the highest office in the land cannot make a simple distinction between Islam and ISIS, between Muslim and terrorist. Ben Carson* has said he "would not advocate that we put a Muslim in charge of this nation."

Right now, my daughter still has the innocence and ambition that are the natural attributes of the young. But what will happen when she comes of age and starts to realize that her life, like mine, is constantly under question? How do you explain to a child that she is not wanted in her own country? I have not yet had the courage to do that. My daughter has never heard of the grey zone, though she has lived in it her entire life. Perhaps this is my attempt at keeping the world around all of us as grey as possible. It is a form of resistance, the only form of resistance I know.

(2015)

Questions

1. According to Lalami, what is the grey zone, and who occupies it?
2. Lalami writes that whenever "the grey zone recedes, ISIS gains ground." What causes the grey zone to recede? Why is this good for ISIS and bad for the West?
3. Lalami contrasts the public response to mass killings conducted by Muslims with the public response to mass killings conducted by young white men. How and why, according to Lalami, do these events tend to be treated differently? To what extent (if at all) is this difference justified?

4. What prejudices are revealed by the questions asked at the book signing described in the opening paragraph?
5. Lalami lives in the United States. How similar is the majority attitude toward Muslims in Canada to the attitude Lalami describes as dominant in America?
6. Lalami writes that "rather than stigmatize [hatred of Muslims], politicians and pundits often stoke it with fiery rhetoric." Look online and find an example of such rhetoric quoted in a news article from this week.
7. Who is the intended audience for this piece? How is the piece crafted to be persuasive to this particular audience?

SARAH KURCHAK

AUTISTIC PEOPLE ARE NOT TRAGEDIES

This opinion piece was published online at the end of April 2015 on the website of The Guardian, *a British newspaper with a worldwide audience.*

The existence of autistic people like me is not a "tragedy." Yet many autism awareness narratives[1] insist it is because they prioritize the feelings of neurotypicals (non-autistic people) and dismiss the rest of us as little more than zombies. And when people buy into this idea, it actively hurts autistic people.

When I was finally diagnosed with autism spectrum disorder six years ago, I wouldn't shut up about it. In part, this was because I, like many autistics, tend to perseverate[2] about the things that intensely fascinate me and, at that moment, there was nothing more fascinating to me than discovering that there was an explanation for all of my sensory sensitivities, social issues, repetitive behaviours and obsessive interests. I also believed in the importance of autism awareness.

But once I started participating in awareness campaigns I found the same overly simplistic and fear-mongering message over and over again: autism is a "crisis." According to the highly influential charity Autism Speaks (which doesn't have a single autistic person on its board), autistic people are "missing"—we leave our family members "depleted. Mentally. Physically. And especially emotionally." Defining our existences solely as a tragedy for non-autistic people is hurtful on a personal level. No one deserves to be told that they are nothing but a burden to the people who love them and everyone has the right to feel like their lives have value.

But it also has troubling implications for public policy.

If autism is only presented as an unequivocally terrible curse that must be 5
"cured" and eliminated, then charities that are primarily focused on finding a

---

1 *autism awareness narratives* The piece appeared at the end of April, the month that has been put forward by Autism Speaks and many other autism organizations as World Autism Awareness Month.

2 *perseverate* Continue to do or think about something after the reason for the original thought or action has passed.

cure—like Autism Speaks—will continue to receive the bulk of ASD[3]-related funding and volunteer hours. Even if a cure is possible or preferable (both of which are arguable) these wild stabs at hunting down genetic bogeymen in the hopes of eliminating them in the future do nothing to improve the lives of the autistic people and their caregivers who are struggling with a scarcity of both resources and understanding right now.

This line of thought also eclipses more nuanced discussions that might help to make life more manageable for the people who make up this so-called autism epidemic. If you spend time following hashtags like #ActuallyAutistic and the work of organizations like the Autistic Self Advocacy Network and the Autism Women's Network, a cure is the last thing on any of our minds.

We want to talk about autism acceptance. We want people to understand that everyone on the spectrum, verbal or otherwise,[4] has value and we want to work so that everyone has a voice, be it verbal, written, assisted or otherwise. We want to talk about which therapies and treatments are actually effective for us and which ones are detrimental to our well-being. And we want to know how we can create an environment in which autistic children are not at constant risk of wildly disproportionate punishment due to misunderstanding and fear. This is a particular concern with autistic children of colour who face both ableism[5] and racism, like 12-year-old Kayleb Moon-Robinson, who was charged with a felony after kicking a garbage can.

Genuine awareness of autistic people, of our lives, our needs and our value, could greatly improve the lives of people both on and off the spectrum. Autistic people and our allies just need the rest of the world to stop spreading "autism awareness" long enough to actually listen and gain some.

(2015)

Questions

1. As autistic children mature into autistic adults, they are more able to share their experiences in the media. Why is it useful to hear from autistic people themselves?

---

3 *ASD* Autism spectrum disorder.

4 *verbal or otherwise* Communication skills and styles in autistic people range from excellent to extremely impaired. Augmentative communication devices, specialized apps, and other strategies facilitate communication for many who would otherwise be perceived as cognitively disabled.

5 *ableism* Discrimination against people with disabilities.

2. In autism awareness campaigns and narratives, how is autism portrayed? How does this portrayal affect how autistic people perceive themselves?
3. There are different forms of ableism. Is searching for a cure for autism ableist? Why or why not?
4. What might it look like to be an "autism ally"?

EMILY NUSSBAUM

THE PRICE IS RIGHT: WHAT ADVERTISING DOES TO TV

Mad Men, *a highly popular television show about the world of New York advertising firms in the 1960s, ran from 2007 to 2015 on the American basic cable network AMC. In this essay, a television critic for* The New Yorker *magazine is prompted by the conclusion of that program to consider the role advertising itself plays in shaping television and popular culture. The article was published in the 12 October 2015 issue of* The New Yorker.

Ever since the finale of "Mad Men," I've been meditating on its audacious last image. Don Draper,* sitting cross-legged and purring "Ommmm," is achieving inner peace at an Esalen[1]-like retreat. He's as handsome as ever, in khakis and a crisp white shirt. A bell rings, and a grin widens across his face. Then, as if cutting to a sponsor, we move to the iconic Coke ad from 1971—a green hillside covered with a racially diverse chorus of young people, trilling, in harmony, "I'd like to teach the world to sing." Don Draper, recently suicidal, has invented the world's greatest ad. He's back, baby.

The scene triggered a debate online. From one perspective, the image looked cynical: the viewer is tricked into thinking that Draper has achieved Nirvana,* only to be slapped with the source of his smile. It's the grin of an ad-man who has figured out how to use enlightenment to peddle sugar water, co-opting the counterculture as a brand. Yet, from another angle, the scene looked idealistic. Draper has indeed had a spiritual revelation, one that he's expressing in a beautiful way—through advertising, his great gift. The night the episode aired, it struck me as a dark joke. But, at a discussion a couple of days later, at the New York Public Library, Matthew Weiner, the show's creator, told the novelist A.M. Homes that viewers should see the hilltop ad as "very pure," the product of "an enlightened state." To regard it otherwise, he warned, was itself the symptom of a poisonous mind-set.

---

1 *Esalen* New Age educational facility.

The question of how television fits together with advertising—and whether we should resist that relationship or embrace it—has haunted the medium since its origins. Advertising is TV's original sin. When people called TV shows garbage, which they did all the time, until recently, commercialism was at the heart of the complaint. Even great TV could never be good art, because it was tainted by definition. It was there to sell.

That was the argument made by George W.S. Trow in this magazine, in a feverish manifesto called "Within the Context of No Context." That essay, which ran in 1980, became a sensation, as coruscating denunciations of modernity so often do. In television, "the trivial is raised up to power," Trow wrote. "The powerful is lowered toward the trivial." Driven by "demography"—that is, by the corrupting force of money and ratings—television treats those who consume it like sales targets, encouraging them to view themselves that way. In one of several sections titled "Celebrities," he writes, "The most successful celebrities are products. Consider the real role in American life of Coca-Cola. Is any man as well-loved as this soft drink is?"

5 Much of Trow's essay, which runs to more than a hundred pages, makes little sense. It is written in the style of oracular[2] poetry, full of elegant repetitions, elegant repetitions that induce a hypnotic effect, elegant repetitions that suggest authority through their wonderful numbing rhythms, but which contain few facts. It's élitism in the guise of hipness. It is more nostalgic than *Mad Men* ever was for the era when Wasp* men in hats ran New York. It's a screed against TV written at the medium's low point—after the energy of the sitcoms of the seventies had faded but before the innovations of the nineties—and it paints TV fans as brainwashed dummies.

And yet there's something in Trow's manifesto that I find myself craving these days: that rude resistance to being sold to, the insistence that there is, after all, such a thing as selling out. Those of us who love TV have won the war. The best scripted shows are regarded as significant art—debated, revered, denounced. TV showrunners are embraced as heroes and role models, even philosophers. At the same time, television's business model is in chaos, splintered and re-forming itself, struggling with its own history. Making television has always meant bending to the money—and TV history has taught us to be cool with any compromise. But sometimes we're knowing about things that we don't know much about at all.

Once upon a time, TV made sense, economically and structurally: a few dominant network shows ran weekly, with ads breaking them up, like choruses between verses. Then came pay cable, the VCR, the DVD, the DVR, and the

---

2 *oracular* Prophetic.

Internet. At this point, the model seems to morph every six months. Oceanic flat screens give way to palm-size iPhones. A cheap writer-dominated medium absorbs pricey Hollywood directors. You can steal TV; you can buy TV; you can get it free. Netflix, a distributor, becomes a producer. On Amazon, customers vote for which pilots will survive. Shows cancelled by NBC jump to Yahoo, which used to be a failing search engine. The two most ambitious and original début series this summer came not from HBO or AMC but from a pair of lightweight cable networks whose slogans might as well be "Please underestimate us": Lifetime, with *UnREAL*, and USA Network, with *Mr. Robot*. That there is a summer season at all is a new phenomenon. This fall, as the networks launch a bland slate of pilots, we know there are better options.

A couple of months ago, at a meeting of the Television Critics Association, the C.E.O. of FX,[3] John Landgraf, delivered a speech about "peak TV," in which he lamented the exponential rise in production: three hundred and seventy-one scripted shows last year, more than four hundred expected this year—a bubble, Landgraf said, that would surely deflate. He got some pushback: Why now, when the door had cracked open to more than white-guy antiheroes, was it "too much" for viewers? But just as worrisome was the second part of Landgraf's speech, in which he wondered how the industry could fund so much TV. What was the model, now that the pie had been sliced into slivers? When Landgraf took his job, in 2005, ad buys made up more than fifty per cent of FX's revenue, he said. Now that figure was thirty-two per cent. When ratings drop, ad rates drop, too, and when people fast-forward producers look for new forms of access: through apps, through data mining, through deals that shape the shows we see, both visibly and invisibly. Some of this involves the ancient art of product integration, by which sponsors buy the right to be part of the story: these are the ads that can't be fast-forwarded.

This is both a new crisis and an old one. When television began, it was a live medium. Replicating radio, it was not merely supported by admen; it was run by them. In TV's early years, there were no showrunners: the person with ultimate authority was the product representative, the guy from Lysol or Lucky Strike.[4] Beneath that man (always a man) was a network exec. A layer down were writers, who were fungible, nameless figures, with the exception of people like Paddy Chayefsky, machers[5] who often retreated when they grew frustrated by the industry's censorious limits. The result was that TV writers developed a complex mix of pride and shame, a sense that they were hired

3 *FX* Basic cable network known for the quality of its original programming.

4 *Lucky Strike* Cigarette brand. Though Lucky Strike is a real company, Draper's firm advertises for it in *Mad Men*.

5 *machers* People with influence, but lacking substance.

hands, not artists. It was a working-class model of creativity. The shows might be funny or beautiful, but their creators would never own them.

Advertisements shaped everything about early television programs, in- 10
cluding their length and structure, with clear acts to provide logical inlets for ads to appear. Initially, there were rules governing how many ads could run: the industry standard was six minutes per hour. (Today, on network, it's about fourteen minutes.) But this didn't include the vast amounts of product integration that were folded into the scripts. (Product placement,* which involves props, was a given.) Viewers take for granted that this is native to the medium, but it's unique to the U.S.; in the United Kingdom, such deals were prohibited until 2011. Even then, they were barred from the BBC, banned for alcohol and junk food, and required to be visibly declared—a "P" must appear onscreen.

In *Brought to You By: Postwar Television Advertising and the American Dream*, Lawrence R. Samuel describes early shows like NBC's *Coke Time*, in which Eddie Fisher sipped the soda. On an episode of *I Love Lucy* called "The Diet," Lucy and Desi smoked Philip Morris cigarettes. On *The Flintstones*, the sponsor Alka-Seltzer ruled that no character get a stomach ache, and that there be no derogatory presentations of doctors, dentists, or druggists. On *My Little Margie*, Philip Morris reps struck the phrase "I'm real cool!," lest it be associated with their competitors Kool cigarettes. If you were a big name—like Jack Benny, whom Samuel calls "the king of integrated advertising"—"plugola"* was par for the course. (Benny once mentioned Schwinn bikes, then looked directly into the camera and deadpanned, "Send three.") There were only a few exceptions, including Sid Caesar, who refused to tout brands on *Your Show of Shows*.

Sponsors were a conservative force. They helped blacklist* writers suspected of being Communists, and, for decades, banned plots about homosexuality and "miscegenation."[6] In Jeff Kisseloff's oral history *The Box*, from 1995, Bob Lewine, of ABC, describes pitching Sammy Davis, Jr.,[7] in an all-black variety show: Young & Rubicam execs walked out, so the idea was dropped. This tight leash affected even that era's version of prestige TV. In *Brought to You By*, Samuel lists topics deemed off limits as "politics, sex, adultery, unemployment, poverty, successful criminality and alcohol"—now the basic food groups of cable. In one notorious incident, the American Gas Association sponsored CBS's anthology series *Playhouse 90*. When an episode called "Portrait of a Murderer" ended, it created an unfortunate juxtaposition: after the killer was executed, the show cut to an ad with the slogan "Nothing but gas does so many jobs so well." Spooked, American Gas took a closer

---

6 *miscegenation* Conception of children by or marriage between people of different races.

7 *Sammy Davis, Jr.* African American actor, dancer, and musician (1925–90).

look at an upcoming project, George Roy Hill's *Judgment at Nuremberg*. The company objected to any mention of the gas chambers—and though the writers resisted, the admen won.

This sponsor-down model held until the late fifties, around the time that the quiz-show scandals[8] traumatized viewers: producers, in their quest to please ad reps, had cheated. Both economic pressures and the public mood contributed to increased creative control by networks, as the old one-sponsor model dissolved. But the precedent had been established: when people talked about TV, ratings and quality were existentially linked, the business and the art covered by critics as one thing. Or, as Trow put it, "What is loved is a hit. What is a hit is loved."

Kenya Barris's original concept for the ABC series *Black-ish*, last year's smartest network-sitcom début, was about a black writer in a TV writers' room. But then he made the lead role a copywriter at an ad agency, which allowed the network to cut a deal with Buick, so that the show's hero, Dre, is seen brainstorming ads for its car. In *Automotive News*, Buick's marketing manager, Molly Peck, said that the company worked closely with Barris. "We get the benefit of being part of the program, so people are actually watching it as opposed to advertising where viewers often don't watch it."

15 Product integration is a small slice of the advertising budget, but it can take on outsized symbolic importance, as the watermark of a sponsor's power to alter the story—and it is often impossible to tell whether the mention is paid or not. *The Mindy Project* celebrates Tinder. An episode of *Modern Family* takes place on iPods and iPhones. On the ABC Family drama *The Fosters*, one of the main characters, a vice-principal, talks eagerly about the tablets her school is buying. "Wow, it's so light!" she says, calling the product by its full name, the "Kindle Paperwhite e-reader," and listing its useful features. On last year's most charming début drama, the CW's *Jane the Virgin*, characters make trips to Target, carry Target bags, and prominently display the logo.

Those are shows on channels that are explicitly commercialized. But similar deals ripple through cable television and the new streaming producers. FX cut a deal with MillerCoors, so that every character who drinks or discusses a beer is drinking its brands. (MillerCoors designs retro bottles for *The Americans*.) According to *Ad Age*, Anheuser-Busch struck a deal with *House of Cards*, trading supplies of booze for onscreen appearances; purportedly, Samsung struck another, to be the show's "tech of choice." Unilever's Choco Taco paid for integration on Comedy Central's *Workaholics*, aiming to

---

8 *quiz-show scandals* In the 1950s, the public discovered that several popular game shows were rigged.

be "the dessert for millennials." On NBC, Dan Harmon's avant-garde comedy, *Community*, featured an anti-corporate plot about Subway paid for by Subway. When the show jumped to Yahoo, the episode "Advanced Safety Features" was about Honda. "It's not there were just a couple of guys driving the car; it was the whole episode about Honda," Tom Peyton, an assistant V.P. of marketing at Honda, told *Ad Week*. "You hold your breath as an advertiser, and I'm sure they did too—did you go too far and commercialize the whole thing and take it away from it?—but I think the opposite happened.... Huge positives."

Whether that bothers you or impresses you may depend on whether you laughed and whether you noticed. There's a common notion that there's good and bad integration. The "bad" stuff is bumptious—unfunny and in your face. "Good" integration is either invisible or ironic, and it's done by people we trust, like Stephen Colbert or Tina Fey. But it brings out my inner George Trow. To my mind, the cleverer the integration, the more harmful it is. It's a sedative designed to make viewers feel that there's nothing to be angry about, to admire the ad inside the story, to train us to shrug off every compromise as necessary and normal.

Self-mocking integration used to seem modern to me—the irony of a post-*Simpsons* generation—until I realized that it was actually nostalgic: Jack Benny did sketches in which he playfully "resisted" sponsors like Lucky Strike and Lipton tea. Alfred Hitchcock, on *Alfred Hitchcock Presents*, made snide remarks about Bristol-Myers. The audience had no idea that those wisecracks were scripted by a copywriter who had submitted them to Bristol-Myers for approval.

A few weeks ago, Stephen Colbert began hosting CBS's *Late Show*. In his first show, he pointed to a "cursed" amulet. He was under the amulet's control, Colbert moaned, and thus had been forced to "make certain"—he paused—"regrettable compromises." Then he did a bit in which he slavered over Sabra hummus and Rold Gold pretzels. Some critics described the act as satire, but that's a distinction without a difference. Colbert embraced "sponsortunities" when he was on Comedy Central, too, behind the mask of an ironic persona; it's likely one factor that made him a desirable replacement for Letterman, the worst salesman on late-night TV.

During this summer of industry chaos, one TV show did make a pungent 20
case against consumerism: *Mr. Robot*, on USA Network. A dystopian thriller with Occupy-inflected politics,[9] the series was refreshing, both for its melancholy beauty and for its unusually direct attack on corporate manipulation. *Mr. Robot* was the creation of a TV newcomer, Sam Esmail, who found himself

9 *Occupy-inflected politics* Reference to the Occupy Wall Street movement against economic inequality.

in an odd position: his anti-branding show was itself rebranding an aggressively corporate network, known for its "blue sky"[10] procedurals—a division of NBCUniversal, a subsidiary of Comcast.

Mr. Robot tells the story of Elliott Alderson, corporate cog by day, hacker by night, a mentally unstable junkie who is part of an Anonymous-like[11] collective that conspires to delete global debt. In one scene, Elliott fantasizes about being conventional enough for a girlfriend: "I'll go see those stupid Marvel movies with her. I'll join a gym. I'll heart things on Instagram." He walks into his boss's office with a Starbucks vanilla latte, the most basic of beverages. This sort of straightforwardly hostile namecheck is generally taboo, both to avoid offending potential sponsors and to leave doors open for their competitors. Esmail says he fought to get real brands in the story, citing *Mad Men* as precedent, as his phone calls with the network's lawyers went from "weekly to daily."

Were any of these mentions paid for? Not in the first season—although Esmail says that he did pursue integrations with brands, some of which turned him down and some of which he turned down (including tech companies that demanded "awkward language" about their features). He's open to these deals in Season 2. "If the idea is to inspire an interesting debate over capitalism, I actually think (depending on how we use it) it can help provoke that conversation even more," he said. As long as such arrangements are "organic and not forced," they're fine with him—what's crucial is not the money but the verisimilitude that brands provide. Only one major conflict came up, Esmail said, in the finale, when Elliott's mysterious alter ego screams in the middle of Times Square, "I'm no less real than the fucking meat patty in your Big Mac." Esmail and USA agreed to bleep "Big Mac"—"to be sensitive to ad sales," Esmail told me—but they left it in for online airings. Esmail said he's confident that the network fought for him. "Maybe Comcast has a relationship with McDonald's?" he mused. (USA told me that the reason was "standards and practices.")

"Are you asking me how I feel about product integration?" Matt Weiner said. "I'm for it." Everything on TV is an ad for something, he pointed out, down to Jon Hamm's beautifully pomaded hair—and he argued that a paid integration is far less harmful than other propaganda embedded in television, such as how cop shows celebrate the virtues of the state. We all have our sponsors. Michelangelo painted for the Pope! What's dangerous about modern TV isn't advertisers, Weiner told me; it's creatives not getting enough of a cut of the proceeds.

Weiner used to work in network television, in a more restrictive creative environment, until he got his break, on *The Sopranos*. Stepping into HBO's

10 *blue sky* Optimistic and pleasantly escapist.

11 *Anonymous-like* Anonymous is an Internet-based anarchic collective of activists.

subscription-only chamber meant being part of a prestige brand: no ads, that gorgeous hissing logo, critical bennies.[12] The move to AMC, then a minor cable station, was a challenge. Weiner longed for the most elegant model, with one sponsor—the approach of *Playhouse 90*. But getting ads took hustle, even in a show about them. Weiner's description of the experience of writing integrations is full of cognitive dissonance. On the one hand, he said, wistfully, he didn't realize at first that he could say no to integrations. Yet he was frustrated by the ones he couldn't get, like attaching Revlon to Peggy's "Basket of Kisses" plot about lipstick. Such deals were valuable—"money you don't leave on the floor"—but it was crucial that the audience not know about them, and that there be few.

The first integration on *Mad Men*, for Jack Daniel's,* was procured before Weiner got involved; writing it into the script made him feel "icky." (Draper wouldn't drink Jack Daniel's, Weiner told me.) Pond's cold cream was a more successful fit. But he tried to impose rules: the sponsor could see only the pages its brand was on; dialogue would mention competitors; and, most important, the company couldn't run ads the night its episode was on the air. Unilever cheated, Weiner claimed—and AMC allowed it. The company filmed ads mimicking the *Mad Men* aesthetic, making the tie with the show visible. If viewers knew that Pond's was integrated, they wouldn't lose themselves in the story, Weiner worried.

In the end, he says, he did only three—Heineken was the third (an integration procured after Michelob backed out). I naïvely remarked that Jaguar couldn't have paid: who would want to be the brand of sexual coercion? "You'd be surprised," he said. Jaguar didn't buy a plug, but the company loved the plot—and hired Christina Hendricks to flack the car,* wearing a bright-red pantsuit.

Weiner had spent the Television Critics Association convention talking up *Mr. Robot* and he told me that he was "stunned" by Esmail's show, which he called American TV's "first truly contemporary anti-corporate message." Then again, he said, "show business in general has been very good at co-opting the people that bite the hands that feed them." NBCUniversal was wise to buy into Esmail's radical themes, he said, because these are ideas that the audience is ready for—"even the Tea Party* knows we don't want to give the country over to corporations."

Weiner made clear that Coke hadn't paid for any integration; he mentioned it a few times. Finally, I asked, Why not? *Mad Men* ended in a way that both Coke and viewers could admire. Why not take the money? Two reasons, he

---

12 *critical bennies* Critical "buzz." ("Bennies" is a slang term for benzedrine, an amphetamine.)

said. First, Coca-Cola could "get excited and start making demands." But, really, he didn't want to "disturb the purity of treating that ad as what it was." Weiner is proud that *Mad Men* had a lasting legacy, influencing how viewers saw television's potential, how they thought about money and power, creativity and the nature of work. He didn't want them to think that Coke had bought his finale.

There is no art form that doesn't run a three-legged race with the sponsors that support its production, and the weaker an industry gets (journalism, this means you; music, too) the more ethical resistance flags. But readers would be grossed out to hear that Karl Ove Knausgaard[13] had accepted a bribe to put the Talking Heads into his childhood memories. They'd be angry if Stephen Sondheim[14] slipped a Dewar's jingle into *Company*. That's not priggishness or élitism. It's a belief that art is powerful, that storytelling is real, that when we immerse ourselves in that way it's a vulnerable act of trust. Why wouldn't this be true for television, too?

30 Viewers have little control over how any show gets made; TV writers and directors have only a bit more—their roles mingle creativity and management in a way that's designed to create confusion. Even the experts lack expertise, these days. But I wonder if there's a way for us to be less comfortable as consumers, to imagine ourselves as the partners not of the advertisers but of the artists—to crave purity, naïve as that may sound. I miss *Mad Men*, that nostalgic meditation on nostalgia. But embedded in its vision was the notion that television writing and copywriting are and should be mirrors, twins. Our comfort with being sold to may look like savvy, but it feels like innocence. There's something to be said for the emotions that Trow tapped into, disgust and outrage and betrayal—emotions that can be embarrassing but are useful when we're faced with something ugly.

Perhaps this makes me sound like a drunken twenty-two-year-old waving a battered copy of Naomi Klein's *No Logo*.[15] But that's what happens when you love an art form. In my imagination, television would be capable of anything. It could offend anyone; it could violate any rule. For it to get there, we might have to expect of it what we expect of any art.

(2015)

---

13 *Karl Ove Knausgaard* Author of *My Struggle*, a six-volume autobiography that has been much discussed in the literary world.

14 *Stephen Sondheim* Songwriter known for acclaimed musicals such as *Company* and *West Side Story*.

15 *No Logo* Influential 1999 book critiquing corporate branding.

Questions

1. To what extent do you value TV shows as "significant art"? Explain.
2. In this article, Nussbaum condemns the use of product integration as a means of financing TV shows. List all the arguments you can think of for and against the use of product integration—both those given in the article and any others you can think of. After considering these arguments, do you agree or disagree with Nussbaum?
3. Nussbaum describes "Weiner's description of experience of writing integrations" as being "full of cognitive dissonance" (paragraph 24). Where is this cognitive dissonance displayed? What is its cause?
4. Nussbaum writes that "[m]aking television has always meant bending to the money—and TV history has taught us to be cool with any compromise" (paragraph 6). Consider the short history of TV production that Nussbaum offers. How have history and economics come together to shape the current role advertising plays in TV production?

RACHEL MORAN

BUYING SEX SHOULD NOT BE LEGAL

In recent years many governments and organizations have called for changes to laws governing the sale of sex, in the hopes of protecting the human rights of those involved in the sex trade. The complete decriminalization of commercial sex and of associated activities such as buying, soliciting, and organizing sex work has been suggested as one solution; many have argued that decriminalization allows for a better-regulated industry in which sex workers are less likely to be subjected to police harassment and better able to protect their own safety. (See "The Unrepentant Whore," elsewhere in this anthology, for an articulation of this view.) Written for The New York Times *in August 2015, the following piece by activist Rachel Moran criticizes the decriminalization approach.*

Dublin—Here in my city, earlier this month, Amnesty International's[1] international council endorsed a new policy calling for the decriminalization of the global sex trade. Its proponents argue that decriminalizing prostitution is the best way of protecting "the human rights of sex workers," though the policy would apply equally to pimps, brothel-keepers and johns.*

Amnesty's stated aim is to remove the stigma from prostituted women, so that they will be less vulnerable to abuse by criminals operating in the shadows. The group is also calling on governments "to ensure that sex workers enjoy full and equal legal protection from exploitation, trafficking and violence."

The Amnesty vote comes in the context of a prolonged international debate about how to deal with prostitution and protect the interests of so-called sex workers. It is a debate in which I have a personal stake—and I believe Amnesty is making a historic mistake.

I entered the sex trade—as most do—before I was even a woman. At age 14, I was placed in the care of the state after my father committed suicide and because my mother suffered from mental illness.

---

1 *Amnesty International* Respected international non-governmental organization which advocates for the prevention of human rights violations across the globe.

Within a year, I was on the streets with no home, education or job skills. 5
All I had was my body. At 15, I met a young man who thought it would be a good idea for me to prostitute myself. As "fresh meat,"* I was a commodity in high demand.

For seven years, I was bought and sold. On the streets, that could be 10 times in a night. It's hard to describe the full effect of the psychological coercion, and how deeply it eroded my confidence. By my late teens, I was using cocaine to dull the pain.

I cringe when I hear the words "sex work." Selling my body wasn't a livelihood. There was no resemblance to ordinary employment in the ritual degradation of strangers' using my body to satiate their urges. I was doubly exploited—by those who pimped me and those who bought me.

I know there are some advocates who argue that women in prostitution sell sex as consenting adults. But those who do are a relatively privileged minority—primarily white, middle-class, Western women in escort agencies*—not remotely representative of the global majority. Their right to sell doesn't trump my right and others' *not* to be sold in a trade that preys on women already marginalized by class and race.

The effort to decriminalize the sex trade worldwide is not a progressive movement. Implementing this policy will simply calcify into law men's entitlement to buy sex, while decriminalizing pimping will protect no one but the pimps.

In the United States, prostitution is thought to be worth at least $14 billion 10
a year. Most of that money doesn't go to girls like my teenage self. Worldwide, human trafficking is the second largest enterprise of organized crime, behind drug cartels but on a par with gunrunning.*

In countries that have decriminalized the sex trade, legal has attracted illegal. With popular support, the authorities in Amsterdam have closed down much of the city's famous red light district[2]—because it had become a magnet for criminal activity.

In Germany, where prostitution was legalized in 2002, the industry has exploded. It is estimated that one million men pay to use 450,000 girls and women every day. Sex tourists are pouring in, supporting "mega-brothels" up to 12 stories high.

In New Zealand, where prostitution was decriminalized in 2003, young women in brothels have told me that men now demand more than ever for less

---

2 *red light district* Section of an urban area which houses a high concentration of brothels and other sex-centred businesses. The city of Amsterdam in the Netherlands, where prostitution has been fully legal since 2000, has been well-known internationally for its several red lights districts, which were significant tourist attractions.

than ever. And because the trade is socially sanctioned, there is no incentive for the government to provide exit strategies for those who want to get out of it. These women are trapped.

There is an alternative: an approach, which originated in Sweden, that has now been adopted by other countries such as Norway, Iceland and Canada and is sometimes called the "Nordic model."

The concept is simple: Make selling sex legal but buying it illegal—so that women can get help without being arrested, harassed or worse, and the criminal law is used to deter the buyers, because they fuel the market. There are numerous techniques, including hotel sting operations,* placing fake ads to inhibit johns, and mailing court summonses to home addresses, where accused men's spouses can see them.

Since Sweden passed its law, the number of men who say they have bought sex has plummeted. (At 7.5 percent, it's roughly half the rate reported by American men.) In contrast, after neighbouring Denmark decriminalized prostitution outright, the trade increased by 40 percent within a seven-year period.

Contrary to stereotype, the average john is not a loner or a loser. In America, a significant proportion of buyers who purchase sex frequently have an annual income above $120,000 and are married. Most have college degrees, and many have children. Why not let fines from these privileged men pay for young women's counselling, education and housing? It is they who have credit cards and choices, not the prostituted women and girls.

Amnesty International proposes a sex trade free from "force, fraud or coercion," but I know from what I've lived and witnessed that prostitution cannot be disentangled from coercion. I believe that the majority of Amnesty delegates who voted in Dublin wished to help women and girls in prostitution and mistakenly allowed themselves to be sold the notion that decriminalizing pimps and johns would somehow achieve that aim. But in the name of human rights, what they voted for was to decriminalize *violations* of those rights, on a global scale.

The recommendation goes before the board for a final decision this autumn. Many of Amnesty's leaders and members realize that their organization's credibility and integrity are on the line. It's not too late to stop this disastrous policy before it harms women and children worldwide.

(2015)

Questions

1. How (if at all) does Moran's personal experience of prostitution affect how you perceive her argument? Does her experience give her argument added weight? Does it make her biased?
2. Apart from the Nordic model, what ways might governments, organizations, and societies attempt to reduce prostitution and the human rights violations associated with it? Do any of these other approaches strike you as better than the Nordic model? Why or why not?
3. Does the continued criminalization of the sex trade impinge upon the freedom of those who voluntarily choose prostitution to do what they want with their own bodies? Is it possible to reconcile some people's "right to sell" with the right of others *not* to sell sex?
4. Were you surprised by any of the statistics Moran cites? Why or why not?
5. Read "The Unrepentant Whore," also included in this anthology, and consider the argument that article advances in favour of decriminalization. Which argument do you find more persuasive, and why?

Desmond Cole

The Skin I'm In

In this 2015 piece for Toronto Life *magazine, Desmond Cole chronicles his experiences with police as a black Canadian. Raised in Ontario, this high-profile columnist and activist continues to advocate against what he sees as institutionalized policies supporting racial profiling in the province. Among these policies is the controversial police practice of "carding": stopping people who are not suspected of a specific crime, requesting identification, questioning them, and documenting the interactions. Since "The Skin I'm In" was published, new provincial regulations have instituted a requirement that, when carding, officers inform individuals that they are not required to give personal information. The regulations, which went into effect at the beginning of 2017, also limit access to the records collected through carding. Cole has dismissed these regulations as a "reaffirmation of police carding" that allows police to preserve the practice with little more than an unenforced "promise not to target people based on the colour of their skin."*

The summer I was nine, my teenage cousin Sana came from England to visit my family in Oshawa. He was tall, handsome and obnoxious, the kind of guy who could palm a basketball like Michael Jordan. I was his shadow during his visit, totally in awe of his confidence—he was always saying something clever to knock me off balance.

One day, we took Sana and his parents on a road trip to Niagara Falls. Just past St. Catharines, Sana tossed a dirty tissue out the window. Within seconds, we heard a siren: a cop had been driving behind us, and he immediately pulled us onto the shoulder. A hush came over the car as the stocky officer strode up to the window and asked my dad if he knew why we'd been stopped. "Yes," my father answered, his voice shaky, like a child in the principal's office. My dad isn't a big man, but he always cut an imposing figure in our household. This was the first time I realized he could be afraid of something. "He's going to pick it up right now," he assured the officer nervously, as Sana exited the car to retrieve the garbage. The cop seemed casually uninterested, but everyone in the car thrummed with tension, as if they were bracing for something catastrophic. After Sana returned, the officer let us go. We drove off, overcome with silence until my father finally exploded. "You realize everyone in this car is black, right?" he thundered at Sana. "Yes, Uncle," Sana whispered, his head down and shoulders slumped. That afternoon, my imposing father and cocky cousin had trembled in fear over a discarded Kleenex.

My parents immigrated to Canada from Freetown, Sierra Leone, in the mid-1970s. I was born in Red Deer, Alberta, and soon after, we moved to Oshawa, where my father was a mental health nurse and my mother a registered nurse who worked with the elderly. Throughout my childhood, my parents were constantly lecturing me about respecting authority, working hard and preserving our family's good name. They made it clear that although I was the same as my white peers, I would have to try harder and achieve more just to keep up. I tried to ignore what they said about my race, mostly because it seemed too cruel to be true.

In high school, I threw myself into extra-curricular activities—student council, choir, tennis, soccer, fundraising drives for local charities—and I graduated valedictorian of my class. Despite my misgivings about my parents' advice, I was proud to be living up to their expectations. In 2001, I earned admission to Queen's University. I was enticed by the isolated, scenic campus—it looked exactly like the universities I'd seen in movies, with stately buildings and waterfront views straight out of *Dead Poets Society*.[1] When I told my older sister, who was studying sociology at Western, she furrowed her brow. "It's so *white,*" she bristled. That didn't matter much to me: Oshawa was just as white as Kingston, and I was used to being the only black kid in the room. I wasn't going to let my race dictate my future.

At Queen's, I was one of about 80 black undergrads out of 16,000. In 5
second year, when I moved into the student village, I started noticing cops following me in my car. At first, I thought I was being paranoid—I began taking different roads to confirm my suspicions. No matter which route I took, there was usually a police cruiser in my rear-view mirror. Once I felt confident I was being followed, I became convinced that if I went home, the police would know where I lived and begin following me there too. I'd drive around aimlessly, taking streets I didn't know.

I had my first face-to-face interaction with the Kingston police a few months into second year, when I was walking my friend Sara, a white woman, back to her house after a party. An officer stopped us, then turned his back to me and addressed Sara directly. "Miss, do you need assistance?" he asked her. Sara was stunned into silence. "No," she said twice—once to the officer, and

---

1 *Dead Poets Society* 1989 film set at an expensive New England private school.

once to reassure herself that everything was all right. As he walked away, we were both too shaken to discuss what had happened, but in the following days we recounted the incident many times over, as if grasping to remember if it had really occurred. The fact that my mere presence could cause an armed stranger to feel threatened on Sara's behalf shocked me at first, but shock quickly gave way to bitterness and anger.

As my encounters with police became more frequent, I began to see every uniformed officer as a threat. The cops stopped me anywhere they saw me, particularly at night. Once, as I was walking through the laneway behind my neighbourhood pizza parlour, two officers crept up on me in their cruiser. "Don't move," I whispered to myself, struggling to stay calm as they got out of their vehicle. When they asked me for identification, I told them it was in my pocket before daring to reach for my wallet. If they thought I had a weapon, I was convinced that I'd end up being beaten, or worse. I stood in the glare of the headlights, trying to imagine how I might call out for help if they attacked me. They left me standing for about 10 minutes before one of them—a white man who didn't look much older than me—approached to return my identification. I summoned the courage to ask why he was doing this. "There's been some suspicious activity in the area," he said, shrugging his shoulders. Then he said I could go. Another time, an officer stopped me as I was walking home from a movie. When I told him I wasn't carrying ID, he twisted his face in disbelief. "What do you mean?" he asked. "Sir, it's important that you always carry identification," he said, as if he was imparting friendly advice. Everywhere I went, he was saying, I should be prepared to prove I wasn't a criminal, even though I later learned I was under no legal obligation to carry ID. When I told my white friends about these encounters with police, they'd often respond with scepticism and dismissal, or with a barrage of questions that made me doubt my own sanity. "But what were you doing?" they'd badger, as if I'd withheld some key part of the story that would justify the cops' behaviour.

When I was 22, I decided to move to Toronto. We'd visited often when I was a kid, driving into the city for festivals and fish markets and dinners with other families from Sierra Leone. In Toronto, I thought I could escape bigotry and profiling, and just blend into the crowd. By then, I had been stopped, questioned and followed by the police so many times I began to expect it. In Toronto, I saw diversity in the streets, in shops, on public transit. The idea that I might be singled out because of my race seemed ludicrous. My illusions were shattered immediately.

My skin is the deep brown of a well-worn penny. My eyes are the same shade as my complexion, but they light up amber in the sun, like a glass of whiskey. On a good day, I like the way I look. At other times, particularly when people point out how dark I am, I want to slip through a crack in the ground and disappear. White people often go out of their way to say they don't see colour when they look at me—in those moments, I'm tempted to recommend an optometrist. I know they're just expressing a desire for equality, but I don't want to be erased in the process. When I walk down the street, I find myself imagining that strangers view me with suspicion and fear. This phenomenon is what the African-American writer and activist W.E.B. Du Bois described as "double-consciousness": how blacks experience reality through their own eyes and through the eyes of a society that prejudges them.

I hate it when people ask me where I'm from, because my answer is often 10
followed by, "But where are you *really* from?" When they ask that question, it's as though they're implying I don't belong here. The black diaspora[2] has rippled across Toronto: Somalis congregate in Rexdale, Jamaicans in Keelesdale, North Africans in Parkdale. We make up 8.5 per cent of the city's population, but the very notion of a black Torontonian conflates hundreds of different languages, histories, traditions and stories. It could mean dark-skinned people who were born here or elsewhere, who might speak Arabic or Patois or Portuguese, whose ancestors may have come from anywhere in the world. In the National Household Survey,[3] the term "black" is the only classification that identifies a skin colour rather than a nation or region.

There's this idea that Toronto is becoming a post-racial city, a multicultural utopia where the colour of your skin has no bearing on your prospects. That kind of thinking is ridiculously naïve in a city and country where racism contributes to a self-perpetuating cycle of criminalization and imprisonment. Areas where black people live are heavily policed in the name of crime prevention, which opens up everyone in that neighbourhood to disproportionate scrutiny. We account for 9.3 per cent of Canadian prisoners, even though we only make up 2.9 per cent of the populace at large. And anecdotal evidence suggests that more and more people under arrest are pleading guilty to avoid pretrial detention—which means they're more likely to end up with a criminal record. Black people are also more frequently placed in maximum-security institutions, even if the justice system rates us as unlikely to be violent or to reoffend: between 2009 and 2013, 15 per cent of black male inmates were assigned to maximum-security, compared to 10 per cent overall. If we're always presumed guilty, and

---

2 *diaspora* Group of people who have dispersed from their original or traditional homeland. The term "African diaspora" or "black diaspora" refers to the movement of African people out of Africa over the past centuries—with a particular emphasis on enforced movement via the slave trade.

3 *National Household Survey* Voluntary long-form survey component of the Canada 2011 Census. In 2016 Statistics Canada withdrew the NHS and reinstated the mandatory long-form census for some households.

if we receive harsher punishments for the same crimes, then it's no surprise that many of us end up in poverty, dropping out of school and reoffending.

About a decade ago, the Toronto Police Service established carding, a controversial practice that disproportionately targets young black men and documents our activities across the city. According to police parlance, it's a voluntary interaction with people who are not suspected of a crime. Cops stop us on the street, demand identification, and catalogue our race, height, weight and eye colour. Until early this year, these fill-in-the-blanks forms—known as Field Information Reports—also had slots to identify a civilian as a "gang member" or "associate"; to record a person's body markings, facial hair and cellphone number; and, for minors, to indicate whether their parents were divorced or separated. All that information lives in a top-secret database, ostensibly in the interest of public safety, but the police have never provided any evidence to show how carding reduces or solves crime. They've also failed to justify carding's excessive focus on black men. The *Toronto Star* crunched the numbers and found that in 2013, 25 per cent of people carded were black. At that time, I was 17 times more likely than a white person to be carded in Toronto's downtown core.

In late March, the TPS revamped their carding policy, announcing with much self-congratulatory back-slapping that they'd rebranded the FIR cards as "community engagement reports," implemented a plan for racial sensitivity training and eliminated carding quotas for officers. But when you look at the fine print, it's clear that little has changed. Under their new procedures, police do not have to inform civilians that a carding interaction is voluntary, that they can walk away at any time. Cops won't be required to tell civilians why they are being stopped, and their internal justifications for a stop are so broad they might as well not exist. Worst of all, the database where police have been storing this information will still be used.

In a recent report to the Toronto Police Services Board, residents in 31 Division, which includes several low-income and racialized neighbourhoods in northwest Toronto, were candid about their views of police. Many said our cops disrespect them, stop them without cause and promote a climate of constant surveillance in their neighbourhoods. Some respondents to the TPSB survey said they now avoid certain areas within their own neighbourhoods for fear of encountering police. Black respondents were most likely to report that police treated them disrespectfully, intimidated them or said they fit the description of a criminal suspect. "Police are supposed to serve and protect, but it always feels like a battle between us and them," one survey participant said.

15 I have been stopped, if not always carded, at least 50 times by the police in Toronto, Kingston and across southern Ontario. By now, I expect it could happen in any neighbourhood, day or night, whether I am alone or with friends.

These interactions don't scare me anymore. They make me angry. Because of that unwanted scrutiny, that discriminatory surveillance, I'm a prisoner in my own city.

When I arrived in Toronto in 2004, I had no idea what I wanted to do other than escape my suburban hometown and the bigotry I'd faced in Kingston. For the first few months, I crashed with my childhood friend Matthew at his grandfather's East York home. I didn't have much money, so I spent a lot of time wandering downtown, sitting in parks or coffee shops, marvelling at the diversity I saw on the streets. I was enjoying an anonymity I had never experienced before. One night I set out, journal in hand, to find somewhere to write. Less than a minute into my stroll, a police cruiser stopped me on Holborne Avenue, near Woodbine and Cosburn.

"How are you doing this evening?" one of the two officers asked from the car. By now I was familiar with this routine. I'd been stopped a dozen times in Kingston and followed so frequently I'd lost count. "I'm okay," I replied, trying to stay calm. "What are you doing?" the officer continued. "Walking," I said with a glare. When he asked me if I lived around there, I replied that I didn't have to disclose that information. My mouth was dry and my heart was racing—I didn't usually refuse police requests during confrontations, but my frustration had got the better of me. "Could you tell me what street we're on right now?" the cop asked. I was quaking with rage at this unsolicited game of 20 questions. "Anyone can tell you that," I shot back, trying not to raise my voice. "There's a street sign right in front of you."

My parents would have been furious—they'd always taught me to politely answer any questions I was asked. The police had the upper hand. But I'd lost patience. I demanded to know why I was being stopped. "We've had some break-and-enters in this area recently," the officer replied, as if that explained everything. "Well, unless you think I'm the culprit, I have the right to walk in peace." The officer seemed taken aback. He quickly wished me good night, and they drove off. I was so shaken I could have sat down and cried, but I realized the street I was living on was no longer a safe place to stand at night. I walked briskly to the Danforth, where I escaped into a bar.

After bouncing all over the city trying to find work, I eventually got a job at a drop-in centre for homeless youth at Queen and Spadina. As I settled into my life in Toronto, unwanted attention followed me everywhere I went. That year was 2005, the Summer of the Gun, when a streak of Toronto murders made headlines around the country. Most of the shooting victims and suspects were young black men, many of them alleged gang members, and the surge of violence stoked a culture of racial anxiety. I read about these shootings with sadness, but also with fear that people were reflexively associating me with gun crimes. If someone ignored me when I asked for directions on the street, or left the seat next to me vacant on the streetcar, I wondered if they were afraid of me.

In Kingston, I was used to women crossing the street when they saw me approaching, but until I moved to Toronto, I'd never seen them run. One night, I stepped off a bus on Dufferin Street at the same time as a young woman in her 20s. She took a couple of steps, looked over her shoulder at me, and tore into a full sprint. I resisted the urge to call out in my own defence. In 2006, I ran for Toronto city council in Trinity-Spadina. As I canvassed houses along Bathurst Street, a teenage girl opened the door, took one look at me, and bolted down the hallway. She didn't even close the door. When her mother appeared a moment later and apologized, I couldn't tell which of us was more embarrassed.

That same year, I was denied entry to a popular bar on College Street. The bouncer told me I couldn't come in with the shoes I had on, a pair of sneakers that resembled those of countless other guys in the queue. Fuming, I began to object, but I quickly realized that a black guy causing a scene at a nightclub was unlikely to attract much sympathy. I didn't want to embarrass the half-dozen friends I'd come with. We left quietly, and I've never gone back.

Shortly after my (unsuccessful) election campaign, I went to a downtown pub to watch hockey with some friends and my girlfriend at the time, a white child-care worker named Heather. The Leafs won, and the place turned into a party. Heather and I were dancing, drinking and having a great time. On my way back from the washroom, two bouncers stopped me and said I had to leave. "We just can't have that kind of stuff around here," one of them informed me. I asked what "stuff" he meant, but he and his partner insisted I had to go. They followed closely behind me as I went back upstairs to inform Heather and my friends that I was being kicked out. My friends seemed confused and surprised, but none made a fuss or questioned the bouncers who stood behind me. People stopped dancing to see what was going on and, recognizing that security was involved, kept their distance. I tried not to make eye contact with anyone as the guards escorted me out of the bar.

I have come to accept that some people will respond to me with fear or suspicion—no matter how irrational it may seem. After years of needless police scrutiny, I've developed habits to check my own behaviour. I no longer walk through upscale clothing stores like Holt Renfrew or Harry Rosen, because I'm usually tailed by over-attentive employees. If I'm paying cash at a restaurant, I will hand it to the server instead of leaving it on the table, to make sure no one accuses me of skipping out on the bill. If the cops approach, I immediately ask if I am being detained. Anyone who has ever travelled with me knows I experience serious anxiety when dealing with border officials—I'm terrified of anyone with a badge and a gun, since they always seem excessively interested in who I am and what I'm doing. My eyes follow every police car that passes me. It has become a matter of survival in a city where, despite all the talk of harmonious multi-culturalism, I continue to stand out.

I was carded for the first time in 2007. I was walking my bike on the sidewalk on Bathurst Street just south of Queen. I was only steps from my apartment when a police officer exited his car and approached me. "It's illegal to ride your bike on the sidewalk," he informed me. "I know, officer, that's why I'm walking it," I replied edgily. Then the cop asked me for ID. After sitting in front of the computer inside his car for a few minutes, the officer returned nonchalantly and said, "Okay, you're all set." I wanted to tell him off, but thought better of it and went home. I still don't know what he saw when he ran my name.

Over the next seven years, I was carded at least a dozen times. One summer evening in 2008, two friends and I were stopped while walking at night in a laneway just north of my apartment, only a few hundred metres from where I was carded the first time. Two officers approached in their cruiser, briefly turning on their siren to get our attention. Once they got out of the car, they asked us what we were doing. "We're just walking, bro," I said. The cops immediately asked all of us to produce identification. While one officer took our drivers' licences back to his car, the other got on his radio. I heard him say the word "supervisor," and my stomach turned. Within 60 seconds, a second cruiser, marked S2, arrived in the laneway, and the senior officer at the wheel got out to join his colleagues.

The officer who had radioed for backup returned and asked us to empty our pockets. As the supervisor watched, the radio officer approached us one at a time, took our change and wallets and inspected them. He was extremely calm, as if he was thoroughly accustomed to this routine. "I'm going to search each of you now to make sure you didn't miss anything," he explained. I knew it was my legal right to refuse, but I couldn't muster the courage to object. The search officer approached me first. "Before I search you, I want you to tell me if I'm going to find anything you shouldn't have," he said gravely. "I don't have anything," I replied, my legs trembling so violently I thought they'd give out from under me. The officer patted down my pockets, my pant legs, my jacket, my underarms. He then repeated the search with my two friends, asking each of them before touching them if he would find anything. One of my friends spoke up: "I have a weed pipe in my back pocket, but there's nothing in it." The officer took the pipe and walked with the supervisor to the car with the officer who had taken our ID. As the policemen huddled for what felt like an hour, my friend apologized. "It's not your fault," I replied. I cursed myself for choosing that route rather than staying on Queen Street, where hundreds of people would have been walking. Here, we had no witnesses.

When the officers finally came back, they returned the pipe to my friend. "Are any of you currently wanted on an out-standing warrant?" asked the search officer. We all said no. "Okay, guys, have a good night," he said. I was still too scared to move, and apparently my friends were too; we just stood there and looked at the cops for a second. "You can go," the officer assured us. I made sure not to look back for fear they'd interpret some outstanding guilt on my part. I was certain that the police had just documented my name along with the names of my friends, one of whom was carrying a pipe for smoking an illegal substance. This information would be permanently on my record.

Another time, as I smoked a cigarette outside a local community centre on Bloor West near Dufferin, a police officer sat parked in his car, glaring at me and scribbling notes. After five minutes of this, I walked over to his cruiser. "Is there a problem, officer?" I asked. The cop, a 30-something white guy, asked, "Oh, are you lost? You look like you're lost." His response was so ridiculous I almost laughed in exasperation, but instead I just repeated that I was fine. After a brief pause the officer rejoined, "Really? 'Cause you seemed lost." I had to remind myself that I wasn't going crazy. "I know why you're doing this," I told him before dashing my cigarette and going back inside. Whether it was motivated by ignorance, training, police culture or something else, the officer's behaviour sent a clear message: I didn't belong.

When I was a boy in Oshawa, my parents always greeted black strangers we passed on the street. As an adult, I have taken up this ritual in Toronto—it's an acknowledgment of a shared (if unwanted) experience. These days, when I meet other black people who want to talk about race, I feel comfort and reassurance. I was shopping at my local grocery store recently when an elderly white fellow tapped me on the arm and pointed to a black clerk shelving goods down the aisle. "You guys, you brothers," he said in broken English. It was one of those moments I was grateful for dark skin, to hide my embarrassment. "What do you mean?" I asked him. "You know, you and him, you guys brothers," the man repeated. "But aren't we brothers too, you and I?" I asked. He paused and smiled. "Oh, yes, yes!" As he left, the clerk and I exchanged a smile. It's nice to be around other people who know what you're going through.

After years of being stopped by police, I've started to internalize their scrutiny. I've doubted myself, wondered if I've actually done something to provoke them. Once you're accused enough times, you begin to assume your own guilt, to stand in for your oppressor. It's exhausting to have to justify your freedoms in a supposedly free society. I don't talk about race for attention or personal gain. I would much rather write about sports or theatre or music than carding and incarceration. But I talk about race to survive. If I diminish the role my skin colour plays in my life, and in the lives of all racialized people, I can't change anything.

Last winter, I asked the cops if I could look at my file. I was furious when they told me no: that the only way I could see that information was to file a Freedom of Information request. Each one can take months to process. One of my friends, a law student at Osgoode Hall, recently had his FOI request approved. When he finally saw his file, he learned that over the years cops had labelled him as "Jamaican," "Brown East African" and "Black North African." They said he was "unfriendly" with them, and that he believed he was being racially profiled.

I have no idea what I'll find in my file. Does it classify me as Black West African or Brown Caribbean? Are there notes about my attitude? Do any of the cops give a reason as to why they stopped me? All I can say for certain is that over the years, I've become known to police. That shorthand has always troubled me—too many black men are "known" through a foggy lens of suspicion we've done nothing to earn. Maybe if they really got to know us, they'd treat us differently.

(2015)

Questions

1. Consider your own identity—your race, class, gender, age, and so on. How does your identity affect the nature and frequency of your interactions with police?
2. In this article, Cole makes use of personal anecdotes and of statistics. Which do you find more persuasive? Why?
3. Does anything about Cole's portrayal of police interactions with black Canadians surprise you? Why or why not?
4. In rhetorical theory, a writer's *ethos*, the impression given of the writer's character, is an important part of creating a forceful argument. How would you describe Cole's *ethos*? How does it affect your assessment of his argument?
5. Consider the police interactions with Aboriginal Canadians described in "A Different Kind of Simakanis," excerpted elsewhere in this anthology. How is Cole's relationship to police similar to Aboriginal Canadians' relationships to police as portrayed in that article? How is it different?

CARISSA HALTON

from A DIFFERENT KIND OF SIMAKANIS

The following article, written for the Edmonton-based magazine Eighteen Bridges, *received a National Magazine Award in 2016. Its focus is the relationship between police officers and Aboriginal civilians in Edmonton, which has one of the largest Aboriginal populations of any Canadian city. Interactions between Aboriginal people and police have long been characterized by animosity and discrimination; now, Halton asks, "what happens when police forces start to listen" to the communities they are meant to serve?*

It was not quite midnight as I drove home north on 95th Street from downtown Edmonton, past the glowing Burger Baron sign, the dark pawnshops, the queasy light from various convenience store windows and the ever-present drug trade hopping off and on bikes, out of backpacks, through car windows, into cupped hands. I craned to watch the action, but when I looked forward again I had to quickly stomp on the brake pedal. Just ahead of me on the road was a woman walking with a slight sidestep, as if she'd been riding a horse too long or had wet her pants. Her acid-wash skinny jeans glowed like moonbeams under the car headlights.

I'd come across walkers in the middle of the road here before. They often staggered or shouted, or weaved in the disoriented way of frat boys after midnight. This woman in platform shoes, however, walked straight on the centre line.

I rolled down my window. "Can I help?"

The salt tracks on her brown cheeks shone in the light of a truck behind us that would not pass. She glanced back, and when she met my gaze there was no fear, no relief—just something closer to confusion. A scar followed the curve of her eye until it disappeared into her shoulder-length black hair.

5 "I need to get away from those guys," she said, gesturing back towards the truck. Before I could respond, she walked around the front of my vehicle to the passenger door.

This woman—possibly in danger, possibly high, and possibly about to rob me—was about to get into my car. Too many things were unfolding to process fully: the men behind, the woman in front, the ghosts of so many missing and murdered women all around.[1] And inside my head was the voice of a former gang member I'd met. "I have a place," she'd tell johns,* directing them to a trap. Her words skipped like a record in my head. "I robbed people alone, too. I'd just pull a shank."*

When the woman in the acid-wash jeans reached out, I instinctively locked the door but rolled down the window. "I'm sorry, I don't feel comfortable letting you in my car."

Of course. Her face fell into resignation. *Of course*.

"Can I call someone?"

I turned on my hazard lights, which blinked far slower than my pulse. Her hand dropped to her side and she moved to the dark sidewalk. I followed her, slowly, while my mind raced. *Why is that truck still behind me? How could I have left her out there?*

The truck passed. I pulled up beside her again and asked if she wanted me to call the Crossroads outreach[2] line.

She was slight and small, and her resolve had blocked her tears. "Just forget it."

"Please, can I call anyone?"

"No one cares a fuck about me," she said. Her voice was flat. She waved a limp arm at me. "Forget it." She stopped and said more urgently: "Don't call the cops."

I had to pull out and ease around a couple of parked cars. I stopped further down the road and looked in my rear-view mirror. Her moonbeam legs raced on to the road towards a stopped truck. Boxy front grill and lights. They'd just gone around the block. The door opened and the truck's cab swallowed her up. *No one cares a fuck.* The flatness of those words struck me only slightly harder than the insistence of the last thing she said to me: *Don't call the cops.*

Lynn Jackson, Rachel Quinney and Bonnie Jack all disappeared from the streets of Edmonton and their bodies were eventually found dumped along nearby rural roads. Twenty-six sex-trade workers, many of them aboriginal, went missing or were murdered in Edmonton between 1988 and 2014. Inspector Dan Jones with the Edmonton Police Service (EPS) knew many of them.

---

1 *the ghosts ... all around* Allusion to the high proportion of Aboriginal women in Canada who are known to have gone missing in recent decades, many of whom were murdered or are presumed to have been. The RCMP reports that almost 1,200 women went missing or were murdered between 1980 and 2012—though many more cases may be undocumented—and many cases remain unresolved.

2 *Crossroads outreach* Edmonton non-profit service providing support for "folks involved in street-based sex work and for those who are engaging in survival sex."

He worked the 95th Street and 118th Avenue beat between 2000 and 2004, early in his career. Not only did he recognize every unflattering mugshot, he often knew the women's partners, kids and parents, too.

This was the same beat Jones's father had walked. He has photos of his dad lighting cigarettes for homeless people at a time when new community law-enforcement models transformed many police "forces" into police "services." Becoming part of the streetscape—walking, biking, drinking coffee—was one element in a broader strategy. For officers, crisis response was secondary to building relationships.

But when it came to race issues, there were limits to what progressive community policing could do. Jones's dad had told him about the "Indian List." It was the early 1970s, and aboriginal people weren't allowed to buy alcohol or go into bars. If someone somewhere worried an individual would break the law, their name was added to the list, and they could be arrested at any time, without cause.

There was no Indian List when Dan Jones walked the beat in the early aughts,* but there were proportionally more aboriginal people—Cree and Inuit, Ojibwa and Blackfoot, who made their home in the inner city.

20 In 2013, Jones was assigned a lead role in the police department's newly formed aboriginal relations unit. An aboriginal strategy was released in 2014, and that same year Edmonton hosted the final event in the Truth and Reconciliation Commission of Canada, which had been created in 2008 to document experiences of those affected by Indian residential schools. Edmonton's mayor proclaimed 2014 to be the "Year of Reconciliation." It was also a year in which the EPS faced backlash for promoting officer Mike Wasylyshen, the son of a former police chief, to sergeant. In 2002, Wasylyshen found 16-year-old Randy Fryingpan passed out in the back seat of a truck. He tasered* Fryingpan six times in just over a minute. Fryingpan survived. The judge called it "cruel and unusual treatment." Wasylyshen's sentence was a 120-hour suspension and a decade of delayed promotion.

Many in the aboriginal community challenged the spirit of the promotion. Taz Bouchier, an aboriginal elder who worked at the Edmonton Remand Centre, protested at a police commission meeting. "For many people, a police uniform is a trigger* and promoting Wasylyshen promotes mistrust," she told reporters at the time. "He has a criminal history that is violent," Bouchier said. "It makes it difficult for the aboriginal community to access services when they cannot have trust and a relationship."

The goal of the EPS's aboriginal strategy was to build the kind of trust Bouchier was talking about. In 2017, Edmonton will have the largest population of urban aboriginals in Canada. Two out of five already live below the poverty line. While aboriginal people represent almost a quarter of the national incarceration rate (this proportion only continues to grow), half of the inmates housed in Edmonton's national maximum security facilities are aboriginal. In the city's women's institution, that number is closing in on two-thirds. Aboriginal people are twice as likely as non-aboriginals to be a victim of a violent assault, and they are seven times more likely to be murdered.

"Collaboration is key to success," reads the strategy. "Crime prevention and public safety are most effective at the grassroots* level, working side-by-side with the community." But according to Jones, history and habit can stand in the way. It was often the role of the local RCMP officers to collect the children for residential schools.[3] Authority figures such as Indian agents,[4] social workers, police officers and parole officers, not to mention prison guards and security personnel, have not always helped the community. "For many aboriginals, simakanis are simakanis are simakanis," Jones said to me, using the Cree word for law officer. (Simakanis or simakanisak traditionally translates more broadly to "protectors that surround the living area.") "It's our job," he added, "to help people understand that we're not all the same." ...

... If you are born with the name Moostoos—or Cardinal or Whiskeyjack or Callihoo—no matter your education or career, your chances of meeting a simakanis are exponentially greater, for exponentially more serious things.

In Alberta, a kid with the name Moostoos is nine times more likely to go to jail than the same kid named Jones who claims no indigenous ancestry. If Moostoos moved to Saskatchewan, he would be 30 times more likely to go to jail.

While youthful demographics, lower employment and education rates all impact the higher proportion of aboriginal people in jail, they aren't the only reasons for the inequality. Take an Albertan child named Moostoos and raise him alongside his adopted, non-aboriginal brother named Jones. Give both the same education and the same jobs. Then watch. Moostoos would still be five times more likely than his brother to spend time in jail. The Moostoos boy

---

3 *residential schools* Boarding schools which many Aboriginal Canadian children were required to attend regardless of their parents' wishes. The purpose of the schools was to sever children's ties to their own communities and cultures and force them to adopt Euro-Canadian culture and language. Students were given a substandard education, poorly cared for, and often abused. The system was at its largest during the first half of the twentieth century, but the last residential school did not close until 1996.

4 *Indian agents* Officials responsible for the implementation of government policy on reserves. The primary goal of these policies was to extinguish First Nations cultures and force First Nations people to adopt Euro-Canadian ways of living, and Indian agents exercised a great deal of power over nearly every aspect of the lives of the people on the reserves they managed. The position was phased out in the 1960s.

would be more likely to get a traffic ticket. He would be more likely to get arrested. When arrested, he would be more likely to get convicted, and when convicted, he would receive a longer sentence than his adopted brother Jones would for the same crime. Moostoos would be less likely to get parole. When he finally got parole, he would face harsher probation terms than his brother. On finally gaining his freedom, Moostoos would be less likely to be offered a job and more likely to again see the inside of a police car, courtroom and jail cell. As victims, aboriginal Canadians are more likely to be sexually assaulted, murdered or robbed.

In the face of all this, the real Jones, Dan Jones, forges on....

... "Officers all start the job wanting to help," Jones said to me.... "They believe everyone is good." He wrote this at the top of an inverted pyramid he drew for me to illustrate the challenge police officers face in responding with compassion. "The Reverse Asshole Theory of Policing" is from Kevin Gilmartin's book *Emotional Survival for Law Enforcement*. As officers meet people—both victims and perpetrators—over and over and over in their absolute worst moments, their hope in people falters.

Jones's finger continued down the funnel, following a tragic, emotional trajectory. At some point, many cops begin to feel that only cops are good. Then they believe only their division is good. Then only their squad. Then just their partners. His finger came to rest at the bottom of the funnel: *Me*. An officer, utterly isolated.

30 "Just look at the number of suicides by first responders," Jones said, referring to the impact of protective isolation. In January of 2015, five first responders killed themselves in Canada. On average, for every one cop that dies on the job, three kill themselves—a gap that Jones believes is widening. "We can have a lack of empathy that comes across, to protect us," he said, "but that same lack of empathy takes away who we are. In the end, it kills us."

... Maskwacis, the town formerly known as Hobbema[, is] shared by four Plains Cree nations: Samson, Ermineskin, Louis Bull and Montana.... When the gang wars terrorized these communities, shots were exchanged by rival gangs across [Highway 611]. It happens less often now that the number of gangs has dropped from a high of 13 in 2008 to three in 2015.

Roy and Judy Louis remembered those days as a time of fear. In 2008, there were 365 shootings in six months. The community's 16,000 people were terrified, and most had nothing to do with the violence. Like five-year-old Ethan Yellowbird, who was hit by a stray bullet as he slept in his bed. Or an 18-month girl who was shot while eating lunch at her grandfather's table. She survived. Ethan Yellowbird did not....

"It developed into a full-blown war, basically," [Roy] said. "Kids weren't playing outside because they were afraid of gunshots."

"People weren't smoking on their deck because they were afraid of gun fire," Judy added.

"There were three hundred gang members in the four nations," Roy said.

"But there was another incident, almost as significant as gang members," Judy completed his thought. "During a sundance[5] ceremony one of the RCMP drove right through the sacred grounds. The community chastised the RCMP and, I can tell you, we didn't need any more animosity towards the police."

The RCMP asked the Louises if they'd facilitate a two-hour cultural awareness training for officers at the Maskwacis detachment. The two hours grew to become a two-day workshop, the first held in a classroom and the second day in a more traditional manner, starting with a pipe ceremony, then a sweat,[6] and finishing with a feast.

The impact of the training showed in many ways, one of them being the very nature of calls the detachment received. Slowly, the RCMP saw a change from always being asked the question *What are you doing?* to asking themselves the question *What can we do?*

Roy looked out the dining room window at ground covered with medicines and low brush, noting for me that this land has hosted many sweats specifically for simakanisak. Top-ranking provincial RCMP officers have sat with the Louises under the willow branches and canvas of a sweat lodge. "The warm water and the heat allows the officers to dump everything, to get rid of some of that stuff they're carrying around," said Judy Louis. "And sometimes even to talk about it."

In 2012, senior EPS officers came to the rather belated realization that they had no aboriginal strategy or aboriginal relations unit. The EPS hierarchy, many with former RCMP ties to the Maskwacis area, connected Dan Jones with Roy and Judy Louis. Later that year, various EPS members shared bannock* at the Louis's dining table and developed a day-long curriculum based on much of what the Louises had done for the RCMP.

---

5 *sundance* Ceremony important to many indigenous nations, especially in North America's Plains region. The features of a sun dance vary greatly across cultures and communities, but among Cree people of Alberta the ceremony usually involves a large community gathering, fasting, prayer, and the performance of a sacred dance.

6 *pipe ceremony* Ceremonial pipes are used for prayer and other solemn purposes in many North American Aboriginal cultures; *sweat* Ceremony held in a sweat lodge, a small structure whose interior is heated to a very high temperature in order to induce sweating in participants. The ceremony is one of spiritual healing and cleansing.

"We hit on four themes: colonization, residential schools, treaties and the Indian Act[7] because they all impact First Nations people across the country," said Roy.

"And the most important thing we identified," said Judy, "was that we need to help officers identify and understand how stereotypes and biases impact aboriginal communities and their relationships with the police."

The training was called "Learning Together: Wahkotowin." Each of the training days, held at Bent Arrow Traditional Healing Centre, was opened by one of the three most senior EPS members. The chief and his deputies created the tone for the sharing circle that followed. "Then, we'd start every day with a talking circle and a smudge," said Roy. Holding the eagle feather, each member shared his or her hope for the day. Then, Louis released the officers to view pictures posted on the wall. "Write the first thing that comes to your brain when you look at the pictures," he instructed. "No political correctness allowed."

"I tell you, it could be brutal," Judy said.

"The different myths and misconceptions came up," said Roy, "Like: *You're a drain on society. You're a menace because you are filling the jails and overcrowding the child welfare system.* They were expressing their beliefs and that was OK. We needed to deal with that right off the bat."

In one photo, a dark haired man with a sparse moustache hugged his four smiling kids. The officers wrote: *A man on a supervised visit with his kids.*

"Who's taking the picture?" Louis asked. *His case officer.*

In fact, this was a prominent aboriginal activist out with his family. His wife had taken the picture.

In another, a light-skinned family of four knelt in traditional aboriginal dress. The father wore a knee-length headdress, while the mother and kids smiled in elaborately beaded shawls. *People dressing up for Halloween.* It was in reality a Mi'kmaq family preparing for ceremony.

A third picture showed a set of handcuffs. *Justice*, wrote the officers. These were, in fact, the tiny handcuffs used to punish kids in residential schools.

What followed was a frenzied march through an often wretched history, from pre- and post-contact, to the impact of colonialism and residential schools. Louis presented dizzying facts that were new to most of the participants. The last residential school in Canada closed in 1996. South Africa's

---

7 *Indian Act* Federal law in Canada, first passed in 1876, presiding over the relationship between First Nations people and the federal government. The Act defines "Indian status" and delineates the government's obligations to people with status. It also has a long history of including damaging and severely discriminatory policies, such as those regarding residential schools and the powers of the Indian agent; despite many reforms, aspects of the Act are still widely criticized.

apartheid[8] system was heavily influenced by Canada's Indian policies. The workshop participants were reminded that Duncan Campbell Scott, who held the fate of many aboriginal communities in his hands as federal deputy minister of Indian Affairs from 1913 until 1932, had said: "I want to get rid of the Indian problem. Our objective is to continue until there is not a single Indian in Canada that has not been absorbed into the body politic and there is no Indian question, and no Indian Department."

Jones jumped in every time he thought the officers at the training sessions were becoming defensive. Louis covered the facts and Jones, as a high-ranking officer, offered the commentary.

After lunch, Teresa Strong shared her experiences from the inside of an aboriginal-based street gang, and talked about how her life changed since then. In one session, as Strong described the robbery that would lead to her final sentence, an officer audibly gasped. She remembered the crime scene, because she had been a first responder—one of the first to see Strong's victim beaten, bloodied and terrified.

"It's just hard to believe," the officer said. Her response was visceral and raw. "It's hard to believe that you've changed."

Strong shrugged. "I don't have to prove it to you." 55

Jones interjected. "We are not here to judge."

The officers, inspired by Strong's story, then gave some reflections of their own. On every call, they do their job and leave. They rarely discovered what happened to the people involved in offences, or gained insight about them. Now they had heard a survival story. The officers gave Strong her first standing ovation.

Because they started with a circle, the training closed with a sharing circle. In almost every session, as the eagle feather travelled clockwise, a police officer disclosed aboriginal heritage that he or she hadn't mentioned when the day began. Close to five percent of EPS officers have aboriginal heritage. "It's probably significantly higher because there are many on this job who have never disclosed that they are aboriginal on their file," said Jones. "As a nation, we have really marginalized a group of people and made it not OK for them to be proud to be who they are."

As the simakanisak rolled out from Bent Arrow on to the streets in their patrol cars and bikes, they began to use the Louis's advice on building rapport with aboriginal people. One officer started showing up at Bent Arrow on his days off to play floor hockey with kids. Another listened to a Cree language app. He learned enough of the language that when he was called to a violent domestic dispute, he de-escalated the situation almost entirely in Cree. Not long ago,

---

8 *apartheid* From 1948 to 1991, a system of enforced racial segregation of white and black South Africans.

another simakanis responded to a call at a Light Rail Transit station. A heavily intoxicated and belligerent man was threatening riders while slumped against a brick wall near the tracks. The officer approached and removed her black leather glove. She offered him her hand. "Tanisi," she said. It is a simple greeting.

"I think I need to sober up so I can teach you more Cree," the man said.

"I'd like that," said the officer. "But how about you sober up outside the station." The man complied.

After almost every session, Roy and Judy Louis received emails from officers seeking resources and advice. Many officers now carry a small supply of cigarettes in their ticket boxes (though not all Nations use tobacco as protocol).

In 2015, Learning Together: Wahkotowin will be repeated for all new recruits and the remainder of the EPS officers who haven't yet participated (high-ranking members and specialized units). A more in-depth optional four-day training program is being developed. "It's a small drop in the bucket," said Jones. "But we have a lot of great cops who are very relationship-oriented. Those are the ones we need to champion change for." …

(2015)

Questions

1. Does this article have a central argument or thesis? If so, what is it?
2. Halton raises the example of a hypothetical Aboriginal child named Moostoos, whose life is compared to that of a hypothetical white child named Jones. What disparities does this comparison identify? What causes these disparities? What can be done to reduce them?
3. Discuss the value of empathy in policing, especially in relation to the "Reverse Asshole Theory of Policing" that Halton cites. How realistic do you think it is to expect that police officers retain their sense of compassion for the duration of their careers? What (if anything) can help them to do this?
4. At the beginning of this article, Halton describes a personal encounter with a stranger. How does this passage relate to the remainder of the article? What impact did it have on the way you approached the rest of the piece?
5. Halton uses the Cree word "simakanis" throughout her article and in the title. What effect does the repeated use of this word have?
6. This article incorporates statistics alongside anecdotal stories as evidence that the relationship between Aboriginal Canadians and law enforcement is seriously damaged. As a reader, which do you find more impactful: the statistics or the anecdotes? Why?

MARGARET MACMILLAN

from HISTORY'S PEOPLE: PERSONALITIES AND THE PAST [VICTOR KLEMPERER]

The CBC Massey Lectures are an annual lecture series delivered by a prominent intellectual—usually a Canadian—who offers original scholarship on a topic in the humanities. The lectures are customarily delivered at various Canadian universities, broadcast nationally on CBC radio, and later published in book form. History's People*, the Massey Lecture series given in 2015 by historian Margaret MacMillan, examines the relationship of the individual to history. In the five-part series, the first four lectures each focus on a specific quality found in those individuals who have shaped history: persuasion, hubris, daring, and curiosity. The following excerpt is from the final lecture, titled "Observers," which focuses on lesser-known historical figures who reflected intelligently on the times in which they lived.*

Victor Klemperer, from an assimilated, cultivated German Jewish family (the conductor Otto Klemperer was a cousin), had tried a career in journalism but eventually became a professor of Roman languages in Dresden. Although he took his academic writing very seriously, we remember him now for his diary, which provides a detailed account of what it was like to live in the Germany of the 1930s, as the Nazi hold on power tightened, and then in the 1940s during Hitler's war. Because he was married to an Aryan,[1] under the deranged Nazi bureaucratic rules he was not sent to the camps. Rather he and his wife were obliged to move into a special Jews' House for mixed couples.

---

1 *Aryan* Term used since the mid-nineteenth century to refer to blonde-haired people of Northern European descent. The term is associated with racist ideologies such as that of Arthur de Gobineau (1816–82), who claimed that Aryans had developed all the world's major civilizations. The supposed racial purity of Aryans was an important part of the Nazi Party's platform.

The English translations of the diaries start in 1933 with the Nazis assuming power. Klemperer complains, as he is going to do throughout, about his health. He is, he notes, exhausted, lethargic, and depressed. He suffers from one ailment after another and constantly lives with the fear that his heart or eyes or kidneys are about to give out. He is sure, and says so repeatedly, that he will not live to see the end of the Third Reich.[2] Yet he keeps researching and writing. He works on his biography and on studies of French writers. He also starts a project on Nazi language, noting the hyperbole, the frequent references to heroism or bravery, the many superlatives—the biggest victory, the greatest success—and the repeated use of military terms. He also notes how the Nazis dehumanize the objects of their hatred by referring to "the Jew" or "the Communist" or how they vaunt irrationality so that it now becomes praise to describe someone as a fanatic or possessed by blind rage. And Klemperer doggedly keeps his diary, noting down the daily details of his life: the growing restrictions that surround him; the petty humiliations; the happy moments that, in spite of all, he and his beloved wife enjoy; and his own thoughts and reactions as he sees Germany changing. He comments on politics and the war, but his purpose, as he says, is not to provide a history of his times but of himself and his own small world, of the view from below.

As the Nazis stamped out all opposition, it became increasingly dangerous to keep anything from a book to a drawing that could be interpreted as subversive or critical of the regime. The German secret police, the Gestapo, made unscheduled searches, and suspicious material or forbidden objects frequently meant death. "I shall go on writing," Klemperer wrote in 1942. "That is *my* heroism. I will bear witness, precise witness!" His wife, who as an Aryan was still allowed to travel freely, smuggled the pages out of the house and took them to a woman doctor friend, who risked her own life to keep them safe.

Klemperer, against all odds, did survive the Nazis and the war, and so did his diary. He was determined to keep going, partly by his deep love for his wife and the hope that one day he would see the end of the Nazi criminals. With many complaints, fears, and worries, he did indeed bear witness, week after week, month after month, and year after year. There is no account of life in Nazi Germany quite like it. What makes the diaries such a powerful and compelling record is that we go along with him step by step: from the first time when as a Jew he is singled out for persecution; through the grinding, unending series of privations, meannesses, and prohibitions; to the ever-growing fear of death, either at the hands of the Nazis or by Allied[3] bombing. Like Klemperer

---

2 *Third Reich* Term referring to Germany from 1933 to 1945 under the rule of Adolf Hitler.

3 *Allied* The countries that combined forces against Germany during World War II were known as the "Allies."

himself, we move from being shocked at the first revelation of what is happening to Germany under the Third Reich to absorbing greater and greater horrors. Unlike him, however, we always know how much worse it is going to get.

The first signs of what was to come appeared early in 1933. Klemperer notes that more and more people were using the greeting "Heil Hitler,"[4] and then that it had become compulsory. The Klemperers' social circle started to narrow as some they knew joined the Nazi Party while others decided to leave Germany. Conversations became increasingly circumspect as people grew wary of uttering any criticism of the regime, and dissidents started to disappear into the first concentration camps. It was increasingly clear that the state itself was waging war on many of its own citizens. Jew-baiting[5] had now become acceptable and open as the Nazi-controlled press filled with wild stories and accusations about Jews; signs started to appear throughout Dresden saying, "Who buys from a Jew is a traitor to the nation" or "No Jews wanted here." Klemperer resisted pressure to join the body known as the Jewish Community; he kept insisting that he was a Protestant* by religion and a German by nationality. He gradually gave up hope that the German people would tire and overthrow the regime. As he noted in his diary, ordinary Germans might grumble about the Nazis, but many felt they were preferable to the Communists.

For a time his life went on relatively normally. He and his wife Eva continued to see the films they enjoyed so much. In evenings at home, as he had always done, he read out loud to her. Although he worried constantly about his finances, he also bowed to pressure from Eva and agreed to build a small house in the village of Dölzschen. He was touched and delighted by the pleasure she took in the house and its garden and pleasantly surprised that they were able to manage it at such a time. "Why," he asks in a moment of optimism, "should there not be further miracles?" He also decided to learn to drive and bought a small car in which he and Eva made a series of excursions around Germany.

In 1934 the first of what was to be a lengthening and increasingly punitive series of exclusions for Jews started as he learned that German clubs for owners of cats were now only for Aryans. At the university, his students dwindled and he was squeezed out of responsibilities. The following year, he was made redundant, but he was luckier than some of his colleagues because he still kept part of his pension. His money started to run short, however, and he started pawning his possessions. In Dölzschen the local police came to the house to carry out searches for radios or weapons to confiscate or cultural treasures of the German people which had to be removed to be "safeguarded." When they found the rusty sabre he had kept from his military service in the First

---

4 *Heil Hitler* Greeting coupled with the right arm raised straight and upward in salute.

5 *Jew-baiting* Persecution of Jews.

World War, he was obliged to report to the police station, but at this stage he was still treated with courtesy. In September 1935 the government passed the Nuremberg Laws,[6] for the "protection of German blood and German honour," which served further to isolate and exclude Jews from German society. In 1936 Klemperer celebrated what he described as "the worst birthday of my life." He was first banned from the reading room at the library and then told by a weeping librarian that he was no longer allowed to borrow books.

The petty humiliations and the more serious exclusions intensified. In 1938 the Klemperers' cleaning lady was summoned by an official and told it would harm her son's and daughter's prospects if she continued to work for a Jew. The couple unhappily took up housework; at first it took them three hours to wash the dishes. By this time Jews could not go to film theatres, nor were they allowed to have driving licences, so Klemperer was obliged to give up the car which had given them so much enjoyment. The first prohibitions on Jews practising certain professions were enacted: all Jewish doctors were struck from the medical register. Jews now had to carry special yellow cards if they wanted to visit the public baths, and all Jews had to have an identity card with a Jewish forename. Klemperer became Victor-Israel. He was disappointed in his fellow Germans for going along with the Nazis, but especially in the intellectuals—his colleagues who did not lift a finger to support him, or the professors who joined the Academic Society for Research into Jewry and wrote papers about the eternal engrained characteristics of the Jews, such as cruelty, violent emotion, adaptability, or ancient Asiatic hate. In his diary he wrote that he felt that he and his wife were being buried alive and that they were just waiting for the last shovelsful.

The Anschluss of March 1938, when Germany easily took over Austria, increased Nazi self-confidence and brutality—and anti-Semitism. Hitler repeatedly attacked what he called the Jewish-Bolshevist[7] world enemy, and the Nazi press was filled with stories of Jewish wickedness. That November the Nazis attacked Jews and synagogues and Jewish businesses across Germany in what came to be called Kristallnacht, the night of broken glass. A friend of the Klemperers described what she saw in Leipzig, where storm troopers[8] poured gasoline into a synagogue and a Jewish department store and then prevented

---

6 *Nuremberg Laws* Laws that governed policies regarding "racial purity" in Nazi Germany.

7 *Jewish-Bolshevist* An unfounded anti-Semitic belief was that Jews were the founders and orchestrators of the world's communist movements. Though the Bolsheviks were a specific Russian political faction, Nazis used "Bolshevist" as a blanket derogatory term for a communist.

8 *storm troopers* Specialized German Army soldiers who acted as a paramilitary force for the Nazi party.

the fire department from putting out the blaze. Klemperer was in despair over the supine reaction of the democracies. In Dölzschen someone stuck handbills with the Yellow Star of David[9] on their fence.

More and more people were disappearing into the concentration camps. Klemperer picked up scraps of information coming out of Buchenwald, where, it was said, twenty to thirty people a day were dying. Increasingly he was hearing of others who were committing suicide. He and his wife talked of leaving—and they now knew many who had—but something always held them back. Eva did not think she could start another life in a strange land. She did not want to leave Germany or her house and garden, and Victor did not want to make her unhappy. "We are digging ourselves in," Klemperer wrote shortly before the war, "and shall perish here." And his pride was a factor as well. He did not want to be dependent on his relatives who had already left Germany, in particular his older, more successful brother Georg, who was established in the United States. Victor was obliged again and again to accept the money which Georg so freely offered, but resented being patronized,* as he saw it. Nevertheless Klemperer made stabs at leaving, even if his heart was never really in it: he got the addresses of people abroad who might help him; he sent offers to come and teach or give lectures; he even tried, in a desultory fashion, to learn English. He and Eva discussed booking passage for Australia or Cuba, where it was still easy for Jews to be admitted. At one point they contemplated moving to Rhodesia (now Zimbabwe) and starting a mineral water factory. (He completely ruled out emigrating to Palestine: he was firmly anti-Zionist.[10]) In a way he was relieved when it became clear by the summer of 1941 that there was no longer any chance of leaving. "That suits us entirely. All vacillation is now at an end." Either he and Eva would die or they would survive.

What also held him in Germany was that, as far as he was concerned, he remained German. As he wrote in April 1942, "I *think* German, I *am* German—I did not give it to myself, I cannot tear it out of *myself*." Although at times he felt that he would never belong in Germany or trust his fellow Germans again, at others he felt that it was all a bad dream. "I am German," he wrote, also in 1942, "and waiting for the Germans to return.... They have gone into hiding somewhere."

On New Year's Day 1939, while the world was still at peace, Klemperer looked back at the dismal events of the previous year. Perhaps, he wondered, the lowest circle of hell had been reached. We the readers know of course that

---

9 *Yellow Star of David* Symbol used to mark Jewish shops—and later worn as a mandatory badge by Jewish people—during Nazi rule.

10 *anti-Zionist* Opposed to the establishment of a Jewish state in what was then officially called Mandatory Palestine (Israel was established there in 1947).

he was wrong. With the outbreak of war in the autumn, conditions became much worse for the Jews. In 1940 Klemperer received an order to leave his house, even though he was still obliged to pay the taxes and upkeep. Because his wife was Aryan, he was assigned two rooms, where most Jews would have had only one. The couple moved into their first Jews' House, a "superior concentration camp," as Klemperer described it, where they endured the pinpricks and frustrations of being forced to live at close quarters with others. Klemperer got tired of the quarrels over who was using too much hot water or who had taken someone's sugar ration. He was irritated by some of his fellow Jews who remained intensely patriotic, still hoping for a German victory. He himself believed that only defeat would end the Nazi regime. Klemperer was also snobbish about the lack of education of several of his fellow inmates and was driven to distraction by the goodhearted Frau Voss, the Jewish widow of an Aryan, whose house they now found themselves living in. She was endlessly talkative and given to popping in without being invited.

The inmates of the house also had to endure the mindless bullying and brutality of the Gestapo officers, such as those they nicknamed the Spitter and the Boxer. The secret police made repeated house searches, emptying cupboards and drawers, throwing powder and sugar about, and smashing everything from pills to Christmas decorations. After one search, the Klemperers found a head of garlic cut to pieces and hidden around their rooms. The Gestapo stole valuables, from bottles of wine to Klemperer's Service Cross from the First World War. (Klemperer notices that they did not usually take books.) They asked the Jews why they didn't hang themselves and slapped Aryan women such as Eva, calling them whores and pigs for marrying Jews. Often Jews were taken off to Gestapo headquarters to endure even more abuse; sometimes they never returned, and their families were told that they had died of a "heart attack."

The list of prohibitions and restrictions lengthens. Jews can no longer buy foods such as chocolate, gingerbread, coffee, certain fresh vegetables, oranges, eggs, or ice cream. They cannot buy flowers, tobacco, or newspapers. If they own furs, opera glasses, or typewriters they must surrender them to the authorities. They cannot have telephones or pets (the Klemperers have to put down their beloved cat). If they had military medals, as Klemperer does, they could no longer wear them. As the months and years went by Jews were also forbidden to eat in restaurants, go to concerts, ride on trams, or walk in Dresden's main parks or along certain streets. They also had to observe a curfew. Shops were forbidden to deliver to Jews, so Klemperer now had to spend much of the day queuing for food or coal and dragging what he could find home in a knapsack or on a borrowed handcart. Jews were no longer eligible for clothing coupons but had to apply to the Jewish Community for clothes. At first Klemperer was appalled to receive second-hand clothes from dead men; later he was glad to get anything he could. Although he felt increasingly shabby, he never forgot he was a professor. When his shirts wore out, he continued to wear a detachable collar and a tie.

15 The diaries catalogue the dreary daily struggle to keep going, the disappointments when there is no food to be had, or the small triumphs—when, for example, he gets an extra piece of meat or sack of potatoes. Where once he felt shame borrowing money, his main feeling now was relief that they could survive for a bit longer. And fear was always very close to the surface. He and his wife never knew, when either went out, if they would see each other again. In March 1941 he had a close call when he was sentenced to a week in prison because there was a chink in their blackout.[11] There he endured fresh degradation, having to hold up his trousers because his belt had been taken away and not being allowed his glasses or anything to read. He passed the time thinking about his work and wondering whether he had been a good husband to Eva. He was fortunate in that, unlike so many others, he did not die mysteriously in custody.

In September 1941 there came a fresh humiliation. All Jews now had to wear the Yellow Star when they went out in public. At first Klemperer could not bring himself to venture forth, but in time he got used to this, as he had to the other, earlier humiliations, even when members of the Hitler Youth shouted "Yid"[12] at him on the street. On the other hand he notes down the acts of sympathy: the butcher who slipped him extra meat, the grocer who gave him chocolate, or the housewife who bought him vegetables, which as a Jew he could not purchase. Complete strangers greeted him courteously on the streets and said quietly that what was happening to the Jews was all wrong. In Dölzschen the trustee appointed by the authorities to look after his house did his best to keep it safe for him and talked frankly about how much he disliked the Nazis. Aryan friends brought the Klemperers food and passed on news from the broadcasts that Germans were forbidden to listen to.

As the war went on, Klemperer, like other Germans, listened avidly to rumours and tried to read between the lines of the official Nazi bulletins. Soldiers back from the front, he reports, were talking of fierce fighting in the east and heavy German losses. By 1943 he started to hope that the end might be approaching. The Allied victories in North Africa, their landings in Italy and then the armistice with a new Italian government, and finally the Soviet

---

11 *chink in their blackout* Crack in their window covering. Blackout regulations required that no light escape from houses, so as to make it more difficult for Allied planes to target populated areas during night raids.

12 *Yid* Derogatory term for a Jewish person.

victory at Stalingrad, all gave him hope. The question in his mind, however, was whether he and Eva would survive to see the end of the war.

By this point they had been moved into a smaller, more crowded Jews' House, where they had to share a kitchen and lavatory with several other families. Food was now much scarcer, and German cities, although not yet Dresden, were being destroyed by Allied bombing. Ominously more and more Jews were being taken away from Germany; to what fate was not yet clear.

The diaries show that the full realization of the full meaning of the Final Solution[13] dawned slowly on Klemperer. As early as 1941 he knew that Jews were being deported eastwards into Nazi-occupied Poland, but he still was inclined to believe that they were being used for labour, perhaps even getting good rations and decent treatment in the factories where they were forced to work. By 1942, however, he was hearing reports of Jews being shot on the way east. A nurse told him of the brutality of the evacuation, how the elderly, many of them sick, were crowded into trucks without any provision for their care. Klemperer started to suspect that those who could not work would secretly be disposed of in isolated camps such as Theresienstadt. He was relieved that his oldest sister, who was designated to be sent east, died before she could go. He heard too that Auschwitz was a particularly dreadful concentration camp where people were dying of overwork. He described it as "a swift-working slaughter-house" and no longer expected that anyone sent east would return, but he did not yet get the full horror of what the Nazis were doing. When he learned in 1944 that the BBC was reporting that Jews were being gassed, he still wondered if the report was wrong but gradually he became convinced that it was correct. A soldier back in Dresden from Poland spotted the Yellow Star on an acquaintance of Klemperer's and said to its wearer: "I've seen such awful things in Poland, such awful things! It will have to be paid for." Klemperer heard stories of German soldiers having to be given schnapps before they would carry out their orders, or committing suicide rather than obey.

20 In 1933 there had been 4,600 Jews, defined by religion, in Dresden; by 1945 198 were left. Klemperer had been spared to this point because of his marriage, but it now appeared that his end had come. On Tuesday, February 13, all remaining Jews in Dresden who were capable of working were told to report for deportation. That night the British bombed Dresden, and in the chaos of the ruined and burning city, the Klemperers left the Jews' House. He pulled off his Yellow Star and managed to obtain a ration card as an Aryan. Walking and occasionally finding rides on trams or carts, the couple wandered through the countryside, finding food and lodging as they could. On May 7 Germany

13 *the Final Solution* Nazi Party euphemism for the plan to eliminate the Jewish people. Mass killing at concentration camps was a major component of the plan.

surrendered and the Klemperers headed to Dölzschen by a roundabout route. On June 10 they walked up a hill into the town. Their house was waiting for them.

When the Cold War divided Germany,[14] Klemperer chose to stay on in the East. He resumed teaching and published books on Voltaire and Rousseau[15] as well as his work on Nazi language. He died in 1960 at the age of seventy-eight. His diaries survived the Communists just as they had the Nazis.

(2015)

Questions

1. In what ways was Klemperer more privileged than many other German Jews? How much of an impact did this privilege have on his experience of the Nazi regime?
2. Based on MacMillan's synopsis of Klemperer's diaries, to what extent (if at all) should ordinary Germans of the period be held responsible for the persecution Klemperer experienced?
3. Paragraph 14 (beginning "The list of prohibitions ...") employs the historical present tense. What effect does this have?
4. To what extent (if at all) could the Klemperers be described as resisting the Nazi regime?
5. *History's People* is described in its publication material as an examination of the "complex relationship between ... individuals and their times." What does the portion of the book excerpted here suggest about the relationship between individuals and their historical context?

---

14 *Cold War* Name given to a long period of political unrest in the mid- to late-twentieth century, during which the United States, much of the western part of Europe, and their allies conflicted with the Soviet Union and its allies; *divided Germany* In the years following the war, Germany was split into two countries: West Germany, a democracy allied with the United States; and East Germany, under the control of the Soviet Union. Germany became a single nation again in 1990.

15 *Voltaire* Pen name of French historian and writer François-Marie Arouet (1694–1778); *Rousseau* French writer, historian, and political philosopher Jean-Jacques Rousseau (1712–78).

from HONOURING THE TRUTH, RECONCILING FOR THE FUTURE: SUMMARY OF THE FINAL REPORT OF THE TRUTH AND RECONCILIATION COMMISSION OF CANADA[1]

In 1992, the Canadian government established a Royal Commission to investigate issues affecting Aboriginal communities. The Commission published its report in 1996 and made important recommendations for furthering Aboriginal self-government and preserving Aboriginal languages and culture. In response to the Commission, the government also began a process of acknowledging and, in so far as it is possible, redressing the infliction of cultural genocide on Aboriginal peoples. The Residential School system, in which Aboriginal children were separated from their families and relocated to church-run schools, was one of the means by which this genocide was perpetrated. In November 2005, the government announced a compensation package for former students of the Residential Schools, the Indian Residential Schools Settlement Agreement (IRSSA). The agreement entailed financial compensation to all the survivors, as well as additional compensation to the many students who had suffered physical and/or sexual abuse at the schools. In addition to this financial reparation, the IRSSA included funds to create the Truth and Reconciliation Commission (TRC). The Commission's mandate was to listen to, and to document, the experiences of the survivors of the Residential School system. The TRC was launched in 2008 and was completed in December 2015. The archive gathered through this process is now located at the National Centre for Truth and Reconciliation at the University of Manitoba. Below is an excerpt from the Commission's Final Report.

---

1 *Honouring ... Canada* Bibliographical notes from the original report have been removed from this excerpt. For the full summary report, see www.nctr.ca/assets/reports/Final%20Reports/Executive_Summary_ English_Web.pdf.

FROM INTRODUCTION

For over a century, the central goals of Canada's Aboriginal policy were to eliminate Aboriginal governments; ignore Aboriginal rights; terminate the Treaties;[2] and, through a process of assimilation, cause Aboriginal peoples to cease to exist as distinct legal, social, cultural, religious, and racial entities in Canada. The establishment and operation of residential schools were a central element of this policy, which can best be described as "cultural genocide."

Physical genocide is the mass killing of the members of a targeted group, and biological genocide is the destruction of the group's reproductive capacity. Cultural genocide is the destruction of those structures and practices that allow the group to continue as a group. States that engage in cultural genocide set out to destroy the political and social institutions of the targeted group. Land is seized, and populations are forcibly transferred and their movement is restricted. Languages are banned. Spiritual leaders are persecuted, spiritual practices are forbidden, and objects of spiritual value are confiscated and destroyed. And, most significantly to the issue at hand, families are disrupted to prevent the transmission of cultural values and identity from one generation to the next.

In its dealing with Aboriginal people, Canada did all these things.

Canada asserted control over Aboriginal land. In some locations, Canada negotiated Treaties with First Nations;* in others, the land was simply occupied or seized. The negotiation of Treaties, while seemingly honourable and legal, was often marked by fraud and coercion, and Canada was, and remains, slow to implement their provisions and intent.

On occasion, Canada forced First Nations to relocate their reserves from agriculturally valuable or resource-rich land onto remote and economically marginal reserves.

Without legal authority or foundation, in the 1880s Canada instituted a "pass system"[3] that was intended to confine First Nations people to their reserves.

---

2 *the Treaties* Treaties are constitutionally recognized agreements between Aboriginal peoples and the Crown. They are usually agreements whereby Aboriginal peoples agree to share their ancestral lands in return for payments or promises.

3 *"pass system"* The pass system was a means of keeping Aboriginal people segregated on reservations. To leave the reservation, any person had to describe the purpose and duration of the trip and get a pass approved by the Indian agent (the government official in charge of the reservation). The pass system ended in 1941, and its existence was subsequently covered up; few passes remain as documentary evidence.

Canada replaced existing forms of Aboriginal government with relatively powerless band councils whose decisions it could override and whose leaders it could depose. In the process, it disempowered Aboriginal women, who had held significant influence and powerful roles in many First Nations, including the Mohawks, the Carrier, and Tlingit.

Canada denied the right to participate fully in Canadian political, economic, and social life to those Aboriginal people who refused to abandon their Aboriginal identity.

Canada outlawed Aboriginal spiritual practices, jailed Aboriginal spiritual leaders, and confiscated sacred objects.

10 And, Canada separated children from their parents, sending them to residential schools. This was done not to educate them, but primarily to break their link to their culture and identity. In justifying the government's residential school policy, Canada's first prime minister, Sir John A. Macdonald, told the House of Commons in 1883:

> When the school is on the reserve the child lives with its parents, who are savages; he is surrounded by savages, and though he may learn to read and write his habits, and training and mode of thought are Indian. He is simply a savage who can read and write. It has been strongly pressed on myself, as the head of the Department, that Indian children should be withdrawn as much as possible from the parental influence, and the only way to do that would be to put them in central training industrial schools where they will acquire the habits and modes of thought of white men.

These measures were part of a coherent policy to eliminate Aboriginal people as distinct peoples and to assimilate them into the Canadian mainstream against their will. Deputy Minister of Indian Affairs Duncan Campbell Scott outlined the goals of that policy in 1920, when he told a parliamentary committee that "our object is to continue until there is not a single Indian in Canada that has not been absorbed into the body politic." These goals were reiterated in 1969 in the federal government's Statement on Indian Policy (more often referred to as the "White Paper"), which sought to end Indian status and terminate the Treaties that the federal government had negotiated with First Nations.

The Canadian government pursued this policy of cultural genocide because it wished to divest itself of its legal and financial obligations to Aboriginal people and gain control over their land and resources. If every Aboriginal person had been "absorbed into the body politic," there would be no reserves, no Treaties, and no Aboriginal rights.

Residential schooling quickly became a central element in the federal government's Aboriginal policy. When Canada was created as a country in 1867,

Canadian churches were already operating a small number of boarding schools for Aboriginal people. As settlement moved westward in the 1870s, Roman Catholic and Protestant missionaries established missions and small boarding schools across the Prairies, in the North, and in British Columbia. Most of these schools received small, per-student grants from the federal government. In 1883, the federal government moved to establish three large residential schools for First Nation children in western Canada. In the following years, the system grew dramatically. According to the Indian Affairs annual report for 1930, there were eighty residential schools in operation across the country. The Indian Residential Schools Settlement Agreement provided compensation to students who attended 139 residential schools and residences. The federal government has estimated that at least 150,000 First Nation, Métis,* and Inuit* students passed through the system.

Roman Catholic, Anglican, United, Methodist, and Presbyterian churches were the major denominations involved in the administration of the residential school system. The government's partnership with the churches remained in place until 1969, and, although most of the schools had closed by the 1980s, the last federally supported residential schools remained in operation until the late 1990s. For children, life in these schools was lonely and alien. Buildings were poorly located, poorly built, and poorly maintained. The staff was limited in numbers, often poorly trained, and not adequately supervised. Many schools were poorly heated and poorly ventilated, and the diet was meagre and of poor quality. Discipline was harsh, and daily life was highly regimented. Aboriginal languages and cultures were denigrated and suppressed. The educational goals of the schools were limited and confused, and usually reflected a low regard for the intellectual capabilities of Aboriginal people. For the students, education and technical training too often gave way to the drudgery of doing the chores necessary to make the schools self-sustaining. Child neglect was institutionalized, and the lack of supervision created situations where students were prey to sexual and physical abusers.

In establishing residential schools, the Canadian government essentially declared Aboriginal people to be unfit parents. Aboriginal parents were labelled as being indifferent to the future of their children—a judgment contradicted by the fact that parents often kept their children out of schools because they saw those schools, quite accurately, as dangerous and harsh institutions that sought to raise their children in alien ways. Once in the schools, brothers and sisters were kept apart, and the government and churches even arranged marriages for students after they finished their education. The residential school system was based on an assumption that European civilization and Christian religions were superior to Aboriginal culture, which was seen as being savage and brutal. Government officials also were insistent that children be discouraged—and often prohibited—from speaking their own languages. The missionaries who ran the schools played prominent roles in the church-led campaigns to ban Aboriginal spiritual practices such as the Potlatch and the Sun Dance (more properly called the "Thirst Dance"), and to end traditional Aboriginal marriage practices. Although, in most of their official pronouncements, government and church officials took the position that Aboriginal people could be civilized, it is clear that many believed that Aboriginal culture was inherently inferior.

This hostility to Aboriginal cultural and spiritual practice continued well into the twentieth century. In 1942, John House, the principal of the Anglican school in Gleichen, Alberta, became involved in a campaign to have two Blackfoot chiefs deposed, in part because of their support for traditional dance ceremonies. In 1947, Roman Catholic official J.O. Plourde told a federal parliamentary committee that since Canada was a Christian nation that was committed to having "all its citizens belonging to one or other of the Christian churches," he could see no reason why the residential schools "should foster aboriginal beliefs." United Church official George Dorey told the same committee that he questioned whether there was such a thing as "native religion."

Into the 1950s and 1960s, the prime mission of residential schools was the cultural transformation of Aboriginal children. In 1953, J.E. Andrews, the principal of the Presbyterian school in Kenora, Ontario, wrote that "we must face realistically the fact that the only hope for the Canadian Indian is eventual assimilation into the white race." In 1957, the principal of the Gordon's Reserve school in Saskatchewan, Albert Southard, wrote that he believed that the goal of residential schooling was to "change the philosophy of the Indian child. In other words since they must work and live with 'whites' then they must begin to think as 'whites.'" Southard said that the Gordon's school could never have a student council, since "in so far as the Indian understands the department's policy, he is against it." In a 1958 article on residential schools, senior Oblate Andre Renaud echoed the words of John A. Macdonald, arguing that when students at day schools went back to their "homes at the end of the school day and for the weekend, the pupils are re-exposed to their native culture, however diluted, from which the school is trying to separate them." A residential school, on the other hand, could "surround its pupils almost twenty-four hours a day with non-Indian Canadian culture through radio, television, public address system, movies, books, newspapers, group activities, etc."

Despite the coercive measures that the government adopted, it failed to achieve its policy goals. Although Aboriginal peoples and cultures have been badly damaged, they continue to exist. Aboriginal people have refused to surrender their identity. It was the former students, the Survivors of Canada's residential schools, who placed the residential school issue on the public agenda. Their efforts led to the negotiation of the Indian Residential Schools Settlement Agreement that mandated the establishment of a residential school Truth and Reconciliation Commission of Canada (TRC). The Survivors acted with courage and determination. We should do no less. It is time to commit to a process of reconciliation. By establishing a new and respectful relationship, we restore what must be restored, repair what must be repaired, and return what must be returned.

RECONCILIATION AT THE CROSSROADS

To some people, reconciliation is the re-establishment of a conciliatory state. However, this is a state that many Aboriginal people assert never has existed between Aboriginal and non-Aboriginal people. To others, reconciliation, in the context of Indian residential schools, is similar to dealing with a situation of family violence. It's about coming to terms with events of the past in a manner that overcomes conflict and establishes a respectful and healthy relationship among people, going forward. It is in the latter context that the Truth and Reconciliation Commission of Canada has approached the question of reconciliation.

To the Commission, reconciliation is about establishing and maintaining a mutually respectful relationship between Aboriginal and non-Aboriginal peoples in this country. In order for that to happen, there has to be awareness of the past, acknowledgment of the harm that has been inflicted, atonement for the causes, and action to change behaviour.

We are not there yet. The relationship between Aboriginal and non- 20
Aboriginal peoples is not a mutually respectful one. But, we believe we can get there, and we believe we can maintain it. Our ambition is to show how we can do that....

The urgent need for reconciliation runs deep in Canada. Expanding public dialogue and action on reconciliation beyond residential schools will be critical in the coming years. Although some progress has been made, significant barriers to reconciliation remain. The relationship between the federal government and Aboriginal peoples is deteriorating. Instead of moving towards reconciliation, there have been divisive conflicts over Aboriginal education, child welfare, and justice. The daily news has been filled with reports of controversial issues ranging from the call for a national inquiry on violence towards Aboriginal women and girls to the impact of the economic development of lands and resources on Treaties and Aboriginal title and rights. The courts continue to hear Aboriginal rights cases, and new litigation has been filed by Survivors of day schools not covered under the Indian Residential Schools Settlement Agreement, as well as by victims of the "Sixties Scoop," which was a child-welfare policy that removed Aboriginal children from their homes and placed them with non-Aboriginal families. The promise of reconciliation, which seemed so imminent back in 2008 when the prime minister, on behalf of all Canadians, apologized[4] to Survivors, has faded.

Too many Canadians know little or nothing about the deep historical roots of these conflicts. This lack of historical knowledge has serious consequences for First Nations, Inuit, and Métis peoples, and for Canada as a whole. In government circles, it makes for poor public policy decisions. In the public realm, it reinforces racist attitudes and fuels civic distrust between Aboriginal peoples and other Canadians. Too many Canadians still do not know the history of Aboriginal peoples' contributions to Canada, or understand that by virtue of the historical and modern Treaties negotiated by our government, we are all Treaty people. History plays an important role in reconciliation; to build for the future, Canadians must look to, and learn from, the past.

As Commissioners, we understood from the start that although reconciliation could not be achieved during the TRC's lifetime, the country could and must take ongoing positive and concrete steps forward. While the Commission has been a catalyst for deepening our national awareness of the meaning and potential of reconciliation, it will take many heads, hands, and hearts, working together, at all levels of society to maintain momentum in the years ahead. It will also take sustained political will at all levels of government and concerted material resources.

The thousands of Survivors who publicly shared their residential school experiences at TRC events in every region of this country have launched a much-needed dialogue about what is necessary to heal themselves, their families, communities, and the nation. Canadians have much to benefit from listening to the voices, experiences, and wisdom of Survivors, Elders, and Traditional Knowledge Keepers—and much more to learn about reconciliation. Aboriginal peoples have an important contribution to make to reconciliation. Their knowledge systems, oral histories, laws, and connections to the land have vitally informed the reconciliation process to date, and are essential to its ongoing progress….

Over the past five years, the Truth and Reconciliation Commission of Canada urged Canadians not to wait until our final report was issued before contributing to the reconciliation process. We have been encouraged to see that across the country, many people have been answering that call....

4 *prime minister... apologized* On 11 June 2008, Prime Minister Stephen Harper apologized "on behalf of the Government of Canada, and all Canadians, for the forcible removal of Aboriginal children from their homes and communities to attend Indian residential schools."

Aboriginal and non-Aboriginal Canadians from all walks of life spoke to us about the importance of reaching out to one another in ways that create hope for a better future. Whether one is First Nations, Inuit, Métis, a descendant of European settlers, a member of a minority group that suffered historical discrimination in Canada, or a new Canadian, we all inherit both the benefits and obligations of Canada. We are all Treaty people who share responsibility for taking action on reconciliation.

Without truth, justice, and healing, there can be no genuine reconciliation. Reconciliation is not about "closing a sad chapter of Canada's past," but about opening new healing pathways of reconciliation that are forged in truth and justice. We are mindful that knowing the truth about what happened in residential schools in and of itself does not necessarily lead to reconciliation. Yet, the importance of truth telling in its own right should not be underestimated; it restores the human dignity of victims of violence and calls governments and citizens to account. Without truth, justice is not served, healing cannot happen, and there can be no genuine reconciliation between Aboriginal and non-Aboriginal peoples in Canada ….

At the TRC Victoria Regional Event, Brother Tom Cavanaugh, the district superior of the Oblates[5] of Mary Immaculate for British Columbia and the Yukon, spoke about his time as a supervisor at the Christie residential school.

> What I experienced over the six years I was at Christie residential school was a staff, Native and non-Native alike, working together to provide as much as possible, a safe loving environment for the children attending Christie school. Was it a perfect situation? No, it wasn't a perfect situation ... but again, there didn't seem to be, at that time, any other viable alternative in providing a good education for so many children who lived in relatively small and isolated communities.

Survivors and family members who were present in the audience spoke out, saying, "Truth, tell the truth." Brother Cavanaugh replied, "If you give me a chance, I will tell you the truth." When TRC Chair Justice Murray Sinclair intervened to ask the audience to allow Brother Cavanaugh to finish his statement, he was able to do so without further interruption. Visibly shaken, Cavanaugh then went on to acknowledge that children had also been abused in the schools, and he condemned such actions, expressing his sorrow and regret for this breach of trust.

> I can honestly say that our men are hurting too because of the abuse scandal and the rift that this has created between First Nations and church representatives. Many of our men who are still working with

5 *Oblates* In Christian monasteries, an oblate is a person dedicated to God.

> First Nations have attended various truth and reconciliation sessions as well as Returning to Spirit sessions, hoping to bring about healing for all concerned. The Oblates desire healing for the abused and for all touched by the past breach of trust. It is our hope that together we can continue to build a better society.

Later that same day, Ina Seitcher, who attended the Christie residential school, painted a very different picture of the school from what Brother Cavanaugh had described.

> I went to Christie residential school. This morning I heard a priest talking about his Christie residential school. I want to tell him [about] my Christie residential school. I went there for ten months. Ten months that impacted my life for fifty years. I am just now on my healing journey.... I need to do this, I need to speak out. I need to speak for my mom and dad who went to residential school, for my aunts, my uncles, all that are beyond now.... All the pain of our people, the hurt, the anger.... That priest that talked about how loving that Christie residential school was—it was not. That priest was most likely in his office not knowing what was going on down in the dorms or in the lunchroom.... There were things that happened at Christie residential school, and like I said, I'm just starting my healing journey. There are doors that I don't even want to open. I don't even want to open those doors because I don't know what it would do to me.

These two, seemingly irreconcilable, truths are a stark reminder that there are no easy shortcuts to reconciliation. The fact that there were few direct exchanges at TRC events between Survivors and former school staff indicates that for many, the time for reconciliation had not yet arrived. Indeed, for some, it may never arrive. At the Manitoba National Event in 2010, Survivor Evelyn Brockwood talked about why it is important to ensure that there is adequate time for healing to occur in the truth and reconciliation process. She said,

> When this came out at the beginning, I believe it was 1990, about residential schools, people coming out with their stories, and ... I thought the term, the words they were using, were truth, healing and reconciliation. But somehow it seems like we are going from truth telling to reconciliation, to reconcile with our white brothers and sisters. My brothers and sisters, we have a lot of work to do in the middle. We should really lift up the word healing.... Go slow, we are going too fast, too fast.... We have many tears to shed before we even get to the word reconciliation.

To determine the truth and to tell the full and complete story of residential schools in this country, the TRC needed to hear from Survivors and their families, former staff, government and church officials, and all those affected by residential schools.

Canada's national history in the future must be based on the truth about what happened in the residential schools. One hundred years from now, our children's children and their children must know and still remember this history, because they will inherit from us the responsibility of ensuring that it never happens again ….

(2015)

Questions

1. In your own education in Canadian history, what (if anything) did you learn about Residential Schools specifically, and more generally about the Canadian government's treatment of Aboriginal people? How (if at all) did reading this excerpt from the Truth and Reconciliation report change your understanding of Canada's past?
2. Some people have been critical of the use of the term "reconciliation" in the name of the Commission, as it suggests a return to a former harmonious state between Aboriginal communities and non-Aboriginal settlers—a harmonious state that never in fact existed. How does the Commission respond to these critics? Do you think it is a sufficient response? Why or why not?
3. Based on this report, what do you think the Canadian government should do now? What should Canadian citizens do?
4. Consider the quotations from Brother Tom Cavanaugh and Ina Seitcher. The Commission describes their words as "two irreconcilable truths." Do you agree with this description? Why or why not?
5. What does it mean to say that "we are all Treaty people"? How could this way of seeing things change the way we exercise citizenship in Canada today?

BARTON SWAIM

HOW DONALD TRUMP'S LANGUAGE WORKS FOR HIM

In November 2016, Donald Trump was elected the 45th President of the United States. His election came as a surprise to many, as the mainstream media and the majority of polls had predicted a win for the Democratic candidate Hillary Clinton. Trump's rise to power, and the source of his appeal to voters, have been widely discussed by the press and by political analysts. In the following piece, speechwriter Barton Swaim considers how Trump's use of language may have contributed to his success with voters.

Almost every political commentator in America has now written at least one piece attempting to explain the mystery of Donald Trump's appeal. Most have dealt with the man's demeanour, his talent for attracting media coverage and his disdain for party and intellectual elites. Some of these I find cogent.

The thing I find most distinctive about Trump, though—and perhaps it's at least a component of his success so far—is the structure of his language.

Everybody senses that Trump doesn't speak like other politicians. But how is his speech different, exactly? Is it just the swagger, the dismissive tone and clipped accent? Maybe in part. Trump does seem emotionally engaged in a way none of his competitors do; he is perpetually annoyed—exasperated that things aren't as they should be—but somehow also good-humoured about it. (Chris Christie and John Kasich[1] seem perpetually annoyed, too, but there is nothing funny or cheerful about their versions.)

To get at what makes Trump's language different, take a look at the shape of his sentences. They don't work the way modern political rhetoric does—they work the way punchlines work: short (sometimes very short) with the most important words at the end.

---

1 *Chris Christie* Christopher Christie (b. 1962) is a lawyer and Republican politician. He was re-elected Governor of New Jersey in 2014; *John Kasich* Republican politician and former television host, Kasich (b. 1952) was re-elected Governor of Ohio in 2014.

5 That's rare among modern politicians, and not simply because they lack Trump's showmanship or comedic gifts. It's rare because most successful modern politicians are habitually careful with their language. They are keenly aware of the ways in which any word they speak may be interpreted or misinterpreted by journalists and partisan groups and constituencies and demographic groups.

And so in important situations—situations in which they know a lot depends on what they say or don't say—their language takes on (at least) two peculiar characteristics. First, their syntax tends to abstraction. They speak less about particular things and people—bills, countries, identifiable officials—and more about "legislation" and "the international community" and "officials" and "industry" and "Washington" and "government."

Second, their sentences take on a higher number of subordinate clauses and qualifying phrases—"over the last several years," "in general," "in effect," "what people are telling me," and so on. This is the kind of language you use when you're aware that your words might be misinterpreted or used against you.

When used well, it conveys competence and assures listeners that the speaker thinks coherent thoughts and holds reasonable positions. It suggests that the speaker cares about the truth of his claims. But politicians are frequently too careful with their language, and this conscientiousness can begin to sound like deceit or cowardice. When they rely too heavily on abstractions, when they avoid concrete nouns, when all their statements seem always hedged by qualifying phrases, they sound like politicians, in the worst sense of the word. To my ear, anyway, Hillary Clinton sounds this way almost all the time.

Whether used well or poorly, however, the language of a typical modern politician has a distinctive sound to it. It sounds complex and careful—sometimes sophisticated, sometimes emotive, sometimes artificial or over-scripted, but always circumspect and inevitably disingenuous.

10 Trump's language is from another rhetorical tradition entirely. Consider his hour-long media availability on Sept. 3, just after he'd signed a "loyalty pledge" that he wouldn't run as a third-party candidate if he loses the GOP nomination. Some of his answers last only a few seconds, some are slightly longer, but almost all consist of simple sentences, grammatically and conceptually, and most of them withhold their most important word or phrase until the very end. Trump's sentences end with a pop, and he seems to know instinctively where to put the emphasis in each one.

Near the beginning of the news conference, he says: "I don't need money. I don't want money. And this is going to be a campaign, I think, like no other. I'm not controlled by lobbyists. I'm not controlled by anybody."

This is not the language of a typical politician.

Someone asks Trump about New Jersey Gov. Chris Christie's (R) remark that he, Christie, didn't need the chairman of the Republican National Committee to meet with him in order to beg him to sign a loyalty pledge. Another politician—a politician wanting to take a shot at Christie—might have answered, "Well I'm not sure why anybody would need Gov. Christie to sign a loyalty pledge, given his standing in the polls right now."

That would have gotten a chuckle. But Trump worded his answer far better: "Well, you don't have to be met when you're at 2 percent."

His comedic instinct, I think, told him it was worth some awkward wording at the beginning of the sentence ("you don't have to be met") in order to put the words "2 percent" at the very end. Pop. Hardy laughter.

Trump's lengthier answers, too, involve mostly short, grammatically uncomplicated sentences, with very few of the complicating phrases you hear from an ordinary politician who's trying hard not to say something obviously false or stupid. Oftentimes his answers, when transcribed one sentence per line, read like free verse poetry. Asked a question about Jeb Bush,[2] for instance, Trump replies:

> Jeb Bush is a very nice man.
>
> I'll be honest; I think he's a very nice person.
>
> I think he's a very low-energy person, and I don't think that's what the country needs.
>
> I hear that he's going to spend a lot of money on negative ads on me, and honestly—look, he's getting the money from special interests.
>
> He's getting the money from lobbyists and his donors.
>
> And they're making him do it because he's crashing in the polls.
>
> So I don't know what's gonna happen.
>
> If he spends $20 million or $25 million on negative ads, I don't know.
>
> I know that my life will continue.
>
> I just don't know.
>
> I mean, nobody's ever spent money on ads against me.
>
> But he probably has to do that, although it would not be the way I would do it.

---

2 *Jeb Bush* John Ellis Bush Sr. (b. 1953), an American politician; he is brother to former President George W. Bush and son to former President George H.W. Bush.

His sentences get even shorter when he lapses into his campaign boilerplate.* Politicians do this all the time. When the question is general enough, they move quickly from answering it to expatiating on general themes. But when Trump does it, his sentences contract to little more than a subject, a verb, and usually a direct object. Most range between five and fifteen syllables.

Our country could be doing much better.

We have deficits that are enormous.

We have all bad trade agreements.

We have an army that the head [Gen. Raymond Odierno] said is not prepared.

We have a military that needs help, and especially in these times.

We have nuclear weapons that—you look at *60 Minutes**—they don't even work.

The phones don't work.

They're 40 years old.

They have wires that are no good.

Nothing works.

Our country doesn't work.

Everybody wins except us.

We need victories in this country.

We don't have victories anymore.

Our country will be great again, but right now our country has major problems.

The words themselves are mostly preposterous. Other than "We have deficits that are enormous" and the one about Odierno, they range between laughable exaggeration and nonsense. What makes them effective in their way is that they don't sound like political speech. Politicians in modern democracies just don't talk this way.

Trump makes no effort—or seems to make no effort—to measure the effect of his propositions on different constituencies. He seems genuinely unaware that anybody might try to pick them apart. He makes no effort to hedge his statements or phrase them in such a way that they are at least defensible. Indeed, you don't feel you're listening to a politician at all. You feel you're listening to a man who has rejected the conventions of electoral politics altogether—someone who's opted out of the whole charade.

The result, for probably the great majority of people who follow politics, is alternately comical and horrifying. But for people who've grown weary of politicians using vague and convoluted language to lull or impress their listeners, to preserve their options and to avoid criticism, Trump sounds refreshingly clear and forthright. I don't share their view, but I find it hard to blame them.

(2015)

Questions

1. George Orwell, in "Politics and the English Language," writes that "the great enemy of clear language is insincerity. When there is a gap between one's real and one's declared aims, one turns as it were instinctively to long words and exhausted idioms, like a cuttlefish squirting out ink." According to Swaim, how has political language come to seem insincere? How does he argue Trump's language is different? Do you agree with this assessment?
2. What, according to Swaim, are the characteristics of the way politicians typically speak? Find a sample of language used by a Canadian politician (look up responses to a press conference, for example, or responses to an interview) and discuss whether it matches Swaim's description of typical political speech. How does the politician's way of speaking shape your belief in his or her sincerity and trustworthiness?
3. Trump is fond of Twitter as a platform for communicating his views. Considering Swaim's analysis of Trump's use of language, why might Twitter be an ideal vehicle for Trump's words and ideas? Compare Trump's Twitter account with Justin Trudeau's, or with that of another politician. What are the differences and similarities?
4. Barton Swaim self-identifies as a conservative. What—if any—political bias can you detect in this article?

Andrew Coyne

Guarantee a Minimum Income, Not a Minimum Wage

Alberta's May 2015 election ended 44 years of Progressive Conservative government in the province, as a majority of seats went to the Alberta New Democratic Party, led by Rachel Notley. This National Post *op-ed was first published shortly afterward; in it, Canadian columnist Andrew Coyne discusses the new government's promised endeavours to reduce poverty in the province. For an alternative view on guaranteed minimum income, one of the policies proposed, see "'Basic Income' Is Tempting—But It Could Backfire," also included in this anthology.*

With a new government—the first really new government in 44 years—Alberta politics is alive with possibilities for new directions and fresh approaches. Two ideas in particular have the province's political class abuzz.

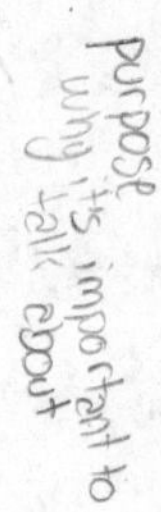

The first is the possible introduction of a guaranteed minimum income, known to be an area of interest to the province's new finance minister, the former city alderman and poverty activist Joseph Ceci. The second is an increase in the province's minimum wage to $15, as promised in the NDP's election manifesto.

The two might be thought to work in parallel, both with "minimum" in their name, both aiming—or professing to do so—to improve the lot of the worst off in society. In fact, they are opposites.

The guaranteed minimum income has been the desideratum[1] of generations of economists and welfare theorists, from the left and the right. The idea is to combine a number of existing income support and benefit programs into one, for which every citizen would qualify as of right: no forms to fill out, no eligibility criteria, just a basic entitlement.

The benefit would start at a relatively low level, for those with no income 5
at all, but would be withdrawn relatively gradually as earned income increased,

1 *desideratum* Thing that is desired.

thus ensuring recipients were not unduly penalized for taking a job and advancing themselves. The easiest objection to the guaranteed minimum income—that it would leave people with no incentive to work—is thus the most easily rebuffed. The real disincentive to work arises not from giving money to people who don't work, but taking it away from them when they do.

But notice how it works. The benefit is a social obligation; thus, it is socially financed, i.e., through the tax and transfer system. Everybody pays for it (though the more you make the more you pay) and everybody is eligible for it (though the more you make the less you receive). It is available whether you are in work or out, and has no impact either on the willingness of workers to supply their labour or the willingness of employers to demand it.

Now contrast all this to the minimum wage. This makes no pretence to be available to all. To benefit from it, you must have a job. Moreover, rather than being financed collectively, through a levy that all must pay, the cost is borne entirely by employers—at least in theory.

But of course, employers have a simple means of avoiding this obligation that the rest of us have seen fit to thrust upon them: by hiring fewer workers. And the higher the minimum wage, the greater an employer's incentive to take this exit. It need not mean actually laying people off; it may simply be that they take on fewer new hires than they otherwise would. But all the legislation in the world can't force a company to pay a worker who isn't in their employ.

Of course, the minimum wage benefits some workers: those who are employed make more than they otherwise would. Surprisingly few workers are actually at the minimum wage—just five per cent of the labour force—and few of these work full-time or serve as a family's principal source of income. But there's also some evidence that minimum wages tend to push up wages at higher levels, to the extent wage bargainers work off the difference between the two.

10 But this is hardly social justice. A just society concerns itself first with the lot of those worst off, and the very worst off are surely those, not on low income, but no income at all; not those in work, but those out of work, priced out of the market by the tariff the state has thoughtfully placed on their labour.

A government that wanted to help those whose lack of skills or experience left them unable to earn what the rest of us would regard as a decent level of income would therefore prefer the minimum income to the minimum wage—that is, a government that valued results, rather than just good intentions, would do so.

Indeed, it wouldn't bring in a minimum income in addition to the minimum wage, but as its replacement, acknowledging that, just as the estimation of what is the decent minimum anyone should be expected to live on is a collective judgment, so the fulfilment of that objective is a collective obligation.

It's simply not good enough just to fix wages, cross our fingers, and hope for the best.

Why, then, do we do that? I think it is out of a desire to pretend that we are not intervening in the economy when, in fact, we are. A guaranteed minimum income sounds like utopian socialism (it was first proposed by Milton Friedman,[2] who called it a "negative income tax"). Whereas a minimum wage, well that's just the market at work, isn't it—albeit with a little "help" from the state.

Well, no. The market can do many things, but one of the things it can't do is bring about a just distribution of income. Markets are about the fulfilment of individual wants, not collective judgments. That doesn't change because you start messing about with wages and prices. In fact, it makes things worse: so far as we are preventing wages from doing what they are supposed to do, which is to bring the supply and demand for labour into balance, the result will be surplus labour, or what is more usually called unemployment.

Distributional equity is the state's work. The tools for achieving it are taxes and transfers. Allocating resources efficiently is the market's job, the tools for which are prices. Wages are prices: let them do what they can do, and help the poorest through the state instead. It's a minimum income we should wish to guarantee, not a minimum wage.

(2015)

Questions

1. Coyne anticipates some objections to guaranteed minimum income. What are these objections, and how effectively does he refute them? What other objections might opponents raise, and how persuasive do you find them?
2. Coyne claims that "The real disincentive to work arises not from giving money to people who don't work, but taking it away from them when they do." What does he mean by this? Does this point indicate a problem with Canada's present social assistance programs?
3. Consider Coyne's statement that "A just society concerns itself first with the lot of those worst off." Do you agree with his conception of social justice? What else (if anything) should a just society prioritize?
4. Would there be any social benefit to simultaneously introducing a guaranteed minimum income *and* increasing the minimum wage? Any disadvantages?

---

2 *Milton Friedman* Nobel Prize-winning American economist (1912–2006) who favoured free-market capitalism with very little government intervention.

ANONYMOUS [THE TORONTO STAR]

"BASIC INCOME" IS TEMPTING—BUT IT COULD BACKFIRE

The possibility of offering every citizen a basic income (also called "guaranteed annual income" or "minimum income") has long been discussed in Canada, but the mid-2010s saw a resurgence of interest in the policy on both federal and provincial levels. This February 2016 editorial from the Toronto Star *enters this contemporary conversation. For an alternative view, see "Guarantee a Minimum Income, Not a Minimum Wage," elsewhere in this anthology.*

An old idea is having a new moment. The idea goes by various labels—guaranteed annual income, basic minimum income, negative income tax. But it comes down to much the same thing: give everybody a minimum yearly income, no strings attached.

It's been a favourite intellectual plaything of economists and social theorists for decades. But some new developments are bringing it back into the limelight.

Over in Europe, Finland has announced it plans to experiment with the concept by paying all its people 800 euros (about $1,250) a month. Closer to home, Justin Trudeau's* minister in charge of social programs, Jean-Yves Duclos, says he thinks it's worth a look. His counterpart in Quebec, François Blais, has also been asked to study the idea by Premier Philippe Couillard.

On the surface, a guaranteed annual income, or GAI, is indeed a seductive idea. It appeals to notions of economic justice: surely in a rich country like Canada we should make sure no one falls below a minimum standard of living—regardless of whether they work or not. Proponents say it would abolish poverty, reduce inequality, improve health and cut crime.

5 For others (those on the libertarian[1] right) it appeals to ideas of efficiency. Rather than employ a small army of welfare workers, snoops and bureaucrats

1 *libertarian* Libertarianism is a political ideology emphasizing individual liberty and autonomy; libertarians are generally sceptical towards social programs and other forms of government intervention.

to enforce the rules on a host of social programs, they ask, why not just give people a monthly cheque and let them use it as they wish?

Sounds great, especially in an era of precarious work when our social safety net seems increasingly inadequate. But before we go too far down this road it's worth considering some thorny issues that have always made GAI a tempting idea in theory—but a minefield in practice. Progressive-minded voters, in particular, need to keep in mind that depending on how it's designed, a GAI plan could turn out to be an alluring trap that actually undermines efforts to achieve more social justice:

Cost: The cost of a GAI obviously depends on where the basic income floor is set. But every available study suggests that to guarantee a decent minimum such a plan would cost an awful lot—estimates vary wildly from about $17 billion a year to as much as $400 billion.

Proponents argue the net costs would be manageable, since other forms of social assistance would be abolished. So take away the costs of welfare, disability payments, Employment Insurance, Old Age Security, workers' compensation, child benefit and so on. And subtract the cost of employing the many thousands of people who run those programs. Then further calculate savings that would be realized in health costs, prisons and mental health caused by poverty, they say.

Those savings, though, would depend on dismantling the social safety net constructed over past decades. How believable is it that that could be done without enormous resistance? Some poor people would be better off, but others would inevitably end up worse off. Are we prepared to accept that? And is it realistic to think the tens of thousands of people who are paid to oversee current social programs will just disappear from their jobs?

Fairness: Equal, unconditional payments for everyone might seem like the fair- 10
est possible system. But people aren't the same; their needs vary enormously. For example, would disabled people with life-long issues get the same benefit as able-bodied people facing short-term unemployment?

What about those with accumulated or inherited resources? A fairly modest annual payment might be fine for them, but for someone with no savings it would just guarantee perpetual poverty.

And what about housing? It's the biggest cost for most people, so those in areas with cheap housing (or those lucky enough to have no housing costs, such as young people living at home) would get a windfall.* Many poorer people can't just leave the big, expensive cities, so they would be left struggling with sky-high rents.

Of course, all that could be dealt with by assessing everyone's needs and costs, and adjusting payments accordingly. But that would just drive the system back to means-testing, and undo most of the advantages that proponents claim for GAI.

Social planning: There's a reason why some right-wing theorists love the idea of a basic minimum income—and it's not that they've suddenly fallen in love with social justice. It's no accident, either, that the Finnish experiment that has GAI proponents excited actually comes from a right-wing government pushing an austerity agenda.

For libertarian conservatives, a basic income would essentially be a way of junking the tangled web of social programs developed over the past 70 years or so. These programs may be inefficient or inadequate, but they are at least aimed at helping people with various needs—disability, mental illness, child care, unemployment and so on. A one-size-fits-all payment risks leaving many worse off.

That's why some progressive-minded theorists are very sceptical about GAI. In a 2009 study for the Canadian Centre for Policy Alternatives, for example, Margot Young and James Mulvale warned it could simply "reinforce the individualism and market focus of neo-liberalism" and lead to results that are "regressive and less just." Not a pretty picture—at least, not one that would make social justice advocates happy.

Of course, no one is proposing to enact such a program in Canada anytime soon. In many ways, it's less of a plan than a vision—of a country in which no one is left behind. Thought of like that, it may well be expressed in many ways in a federal country like ours, rather than as one uniform scheme. It may be wiser to boost and expand the existing patchwork of programs, rather than replace them entirely.

There's a pressing need for fresh thinking about the social safety net as the labour market becomes increasingly dominated by precarious employment, and benefits attached to stable, long-term jobs vanish. GAI—or some variation on that theme—could be an important part of the solution. But proponents have plenty of work to do to come up with a workable (and politically saleable) plan.

(2016)

Questions

1. Assuming that basic annual income might free up the potential for people to work fewer hours if they choose, can you think of any social, moral, and/or economic benefits that would come from giving people the option of working less? Any disadvantages?
2. Why does the author say that GAI is "less of a plan than a vision"? Do you agree with this assessment?
3. Read Andrew Coyne's article "Guarantee a Minimum Income, Not a Minimum Wage," also in this anthology, and consider the two articles together.
   a. Try to find some common ground between the opinions put forward in each article. Are there any ways in which the two seemingly opposed arguments are in fact alike?
   b. Now that you have read both articles on this topic, does basic minimum income ultimately seem like a more economically conservative or progressive program? Why?
   c. Considering the arguments made in each article, what approach do you think is best for Canada: a minimum income? a minimum wage? both? neither? something else?
   d. Which article do you think makes the best use of rhetorical strategies to convince readers?

ALEX BOZIKOVIC

CHICAGO ARCHITECT AIMS TO REPAIR RELATIONS BETWEEN POLICE AND RESIDENTS

Architect Jeanne Gang has received considerable attention worldwide for the striking appearance of many of the buildings she designs—and for her progressive ideas about architecture and society. The article included here, by the architecture critic for The Globe and Mail, *was first published on 3 April 2016. The above title is that given to the piece online; in the print newspaper it bore the following title and subtitle: "Remaking Space to Remake a Culture: Architect Espouses Rounded Vision of What Design Is About—Beauty, But Also Prosperity and Justice."*

Designing a building, or a block: This is an architect's job. But what about repairing the relationship between police departments and urban residents?

The Chicago architect Jeanne Gang is aiming for exactly that. By altering police stations from fortresses to community hubs, you can change the mindset of officers and of the community around them. "Spaces and environments are a huge influence on how we behave," Gang suggests. "It's a small example, but a police station could be welcoming. Why not make it a space where there's free WiFi and free computers? That way, it can serve a policing function and a community function at the same time.

"And if you can remake space, you can change a culture."

That sort of statement has been too rare; for a generation, architects have eschewed[1] such social ambition and the responsibility that comes with it. But Gang, an intellectual leader in the field, is trying to knit together the work of making beautiful buildings and the larger job of building a city that holds together. It's a rounded vision of what design is about: beauty, but also prosperity and justice.

1 *eschewed* Avoided using.

“It’s what I call actionable idealism,” says Gang, 52, who spoke earlier 5
this month at Carleton University. “We want to help our cities, and help in a physical sense.”

Out of that comes Polis Station, a proposal from her office Studio Gang that was a highlight at the Chicago Architecture Biennial[2] last fall. Working in their home city, Gang’s team of architects and urbanists looked at a typical [police] station on the troubled West Side. Their proposal reimagines the station house, placing the secure areas at the back and a variety of public services—a library, daycare, mental-health-care providers and a community room—all sharing a grand public entrance and adjacent to new park space.

“When you have a fire station in your neighbourhood, people feel comfortable going there for help,” Gang says. “People have a relationship with the workers. It’s nice, and friendly. I was struck thinking about the architecture of police stations: People are scared to go inside.”

Polis Station would change that. Although speculative, it is technically and economically feasible. It is also deeply relevant, a response to the Black Lives Matter movement,* the controversy in Chicago over the 2014 police shooting of Laquan McDonald, and to an increasing sense that urban police departments are detached, even after a long vogue for “community policing,” from many of the people they serve. (Canadians shouldn’t feel superior about any of this; urban police stations here are much the same. The best contemporary example I’ve seen, Toronto’s 14 Division by architects Stantec, is essentially a handsome fortress.)

But it’s a sign of the times that Studio Gang is even interested in such questions; Gang, who won a “genius grant” McArthur Fellowship in 2011, is a star in the field. She was recently named Architect of the Year in *Architectural Review*’s 2016 Women in Architecture Awards. She and her firm could focus on easier and far more profitable things. They recently won the plum job to expand the American Museum of Natural History in New York, and a new American embassy in Brasilia.

Gang founded her practice in 1997 after school in Switzerland and at Har- 10
vard; she spent several years at OMA, the Dutch office led by Rem Koolhaas that was, and remains, an intellectual hotbed.

She rose to prominence back in Chicago (she is from rural Illinois) with a mix of commercial and institutional projects. The former offered scale and revenue; the latter, creative freedom and the budgets to innovate. But her office has proved its ability to innovate on all types of projects.

With the 87-storey Aqua tower in Chicago, she found a way to turn the boxy residential tower into sculpture—by working with the balconies on its outside. Their curvy contours ripple down the surface of the high-rise. That

2 *Biennial* Exhibition.

move was brilliant and economical—just as beautiful in real life as in drawings—and it has been widely borrowed.

And yet, she argues, even that building is not merely an object. "It is closely connected to the city fabric," she argues. "There is a ripple in our work, that's getting bigger, from what was present there: a concern for cities in North America."

On a current project for a developer, the 500,000-square-foot City Hyde Park, Studio Gang designed a complex weave of balconies and sunshades that will allow residents to actually see and speak to their neighbours. "For us, residential buildings are about creating community," she says, "and that's true in a tower building as well. What does a balcony mean? What can it do in the city?"

Coming from Gang, that is not just lip service.* Buildings like that one share an ethic with the firm's civic work, such as the Polis Station proposal; planner Gia Biagi is the studio's senior director for urbanism and civic impact. Their work includes the master plan for the 91-acre Northerly Island Park in Chicago, now under construction.

The collective message of all this work, much of it now being realized, is a broader sense of architecture's role in society, one that captures the growing spirit of public service in the world of architecture. "It's an exciting time of engagement between the profession and the world," Gang says.

And yet, beauty matters, too. "Architecture doesn't work unless it gives you this element of wonder and joy," Gang adds, "and you want to be there and you want to go out of your way to see it. That's the thing that ties together the generation that created eye-popping structures with the one that is now looking more at cities.

"I think what's happening now is looking beyond the buildings themselves to make a city that's even stronger," Gang says. "A building can have a magnetic presence that changes the place it's in." Even a police station.

(2015)

Questions

1. Notice the buildings in your community. Are they compelling to look at? Why or why not?
2. Does your hometown have a "signature" building, perhaps built by a well-known architect, that residents and tourists go out of their way to see? If so, what role does this building play in your community?
3. If and when it is built in Chicago, how much impact do you think Polis Station will have on the city? Why?
4. If you were to design something like Polis Station for your hometown, what features would you want it to have? Why?

GLORIA GALLOWAY

DR. BJORN LOMBORG ARGUES THE CLIMATE CHANGE FIGHT ISN'T WORTH THE COST

The views of political scientist Bjorn Lomborg on climate change stand in marked contrast to those of Rebecca Solnit (see above). This article summarizing his approach for a general audience was published in the 12 June 2015 issue of The Globe and Mail. *(The online title is provided here; in the newspaper's print version the article was entitled, "Climate-change Emphasis Is Misguided, Professor Says.")*

Bjorn Lomborg says he is not a climate-change denier; he is a realist who knows better ways of improving the world than a head-on assault on global warming.

It's not easy to take a public stand against the internationally agreed upon goal of limiting the increase in average temperatures to 2 degrees Celsius above pre-industrial levels—a rise that some scientists describe as a tipping point that would be followed by the collapse of ice sheets, rising sea levels and an onslaught of dramatic weather events.

But Dr. Lomborg has, for years, been arguing that the target is simply too difficult and too expensive to achieve and the world's development dollars would be put to better use in reducing poverty, preventing disease, educating the illiterate and feeding the hungry. And, yes, he would also protect the environment, but in smaller, more achievable ways.

Dr. Lomborg, a Danish political scientist and a man who has been named by *Time* magazine as one of the most influential people in the world, is the director of the Copenhagen Consensus Centre. It is a think tank that engages top economists to apply a cost-benefit analysis to major problems so policy-makers will know where development money is best spent. And, he says, the 2-degree global warming target is a bad investment.

5 "We have problems that are huge and we don't know how to fix them," he said in an interview with *The Globe and Mail* on a recent visit to Ottawa. "So we say let's spend the money where we know how to fix them."

Dr. Lomborg's message comes as the members of the United Nations prepare to set global sustainable development goals that will influence how $2.5-trillion (U.S.) in aid is spent between 2015 to 2030. The list of goals is expected to be finalized at a summit in New York in September and follows on the eight Millennium Development Goals and 18 associated targets which end this year.

At the moment, there are 17 proposed new goals and 169 proposed new targets. They advocate ambitious actions as diverse as eradicating extreme poverty, ending epidemics of deadly diseases, putting a stop to violence against women, ensuring affordable access to energy and halting climate change.

"The thing that's wrong in this process is, basically, we are promising everything to everyone everywhere at all times," said Dr. Lomborg. "Which, of course, is really really nice but it's not going to do very much because we are just going to spend a tiny bit of money everywhere."

The analysis done by his institute says that, if the world's aid money is distributed evenly over all of the 169 targets, it would do about $7 worth of good for every dollar spent. But, if the number of targets were reduced to the most economically efficient 19, the money would do about $32 worth of good for every dollar spent.

10 The best thing the world could do, according to the economists enlisted by Dr. Lomborg, would be to reduce world trade restrictions by successfully completing the Doha round of World Trade Organization talks. That, they say, would make the world richer by $11-trillion by the year 2030 and lift 160 million people out of poverty.

Instead of going after headline-grabbing diseases like Ebola, which, in its worst year, killed 20,000 people, Dr. Lomborg says the economic analysis points to targeting malaria which kills 600,000 people annually and tuberculosis which kills 1.3 million.

And, instead of holding steadfast to the goal of keeping global temperatures within 2 degrees above pre-industrial levels, Dr. Lomborg advocates the elimination of subsidies on fossil fuels and the introduction of carbon taxes. Neither measure would be a solution, he said, but would at least "nibble away" at the problem.

Dr. Lomborg's ideas have made him unpopular with many environmentalists who argue that, unless tackling climate change is the world's top priority and the 2-degree goal is met, the ensuing devastation will make all other problems pale by comparison. They argue with his numbers and have created websites to list what they say are factual holes in his arguments.

He remains undaunted.

"The UN climate panel estimates that, by the mid-'70s, global warming 15
is going to cost somewhere between 0.2 per cent and 2 per cent of GDP every year," said Dr. Lomborg. "That's not a trivial cost. But of course it's also important to say it's not the end of the world."

World leaders have talked a lot about the importance of the possibly unachievable goal of the 2-degree limit but, in the end, none have taken the measures that are needed to achieve it, said Dr. Lomborg.

"By focusing on the things that will do the most good, we will do much more good but we will feel less virtuous," he said. "And that's the real challenge."

(2015)

Questions

1. Galloway quotes Lomborg's statement that "'The UN climate panel estimates that, by the mid-'70s, global warming is going to cost somewhere between 0.2 per cent and 2 per cent of GDP every year'" (paragraph 15). Besides this financial impact, what other "costs" can we expect global warming to have?
2. What is cost-benefit analysis? Is it, in your opinion, a useful tool for deciding international policy? What (if any) drawbacks are there to this approach?
3. When this article ran in *The Globe and Mail,* its title was "Climate Change Emphasis Is Misguided, Professor Says." On the *Globe and Mail* website, it appears under the title "Dr. Bjorn Lomborg Argues the Climate Change Fight Isn't Worth the Cost." What is the rhetorical effect of this change? Does one version seem more objective than the other?
4. Read the excerpt from Naomi Klein's article "Let Them Drown" that appears elsewhere in this anthology. Based on that article, how do you think Klein might counter Lomborg's argument?

Jonathan Kay

How Political Correctness Is Hurting the Poor

In April 2016, this piece by Jonathan Kay appeared on the website for The Walrus *magazine, of which Kay was then editor-in-chief. It was then published in the May 2016 print edition of the magazine under the title "Vancouver's Offshore Problem" as a companion piece to that issue's cover story, "The Highest Bidder: How Foreign Investors Are Squeezing Out Vancouver's Middle Class."*

The median sale price for a house in Vancouver is about $750,000—making the city Canada's most expensive real-estate market by far. How do middle-class firefighters, teachers, and business owners pay that sum off on an average individual income of $43,000?

The answer is, they don't. They rent. Or bunk up in someone's basement. Or move to a distant suburb.

If they do buy in, it's often with their parents' money. Which means the system shuts out extended families lacking accumulated wealth—thereby locking in the socio-economic status quo. This is not how a healthy real-estate market works. This is not how a healthy society works.

Why Vancouver? Why not Toronto, Montreal, Calgary, or Halifax? As Kerry Gold explains in our cover story, the answer isn't complicated: the city's real-estate market has become a speculative playground for wealthy Chinese immigrants looking for a safe place to park their capital while still living on the other side of the Pacific. As a result, some neighbourhoods have become ghost towns, largely stripped of street life. Again: not how a healthy society works.

5 "Global money is boosting Vancouver's prices, and local dollars can't compete," Gold writes. Much of the cash, she notes, appears connected to the movement of illegal currency. "Most troubling is that homeowners are now selling directly to buyers in China, listing their homes in real-estate exhibitions in Beijing and Shanghai.... Average-earning buyers are being entirely cut out of the purchasing loop."

Canada has a shameful legacy of anti-Asian racism. This helps explain why Andy Yan's groundbreaking 2015 report on foreign buyers in Vancouver—the statistical basis for Gold's analysis—was greeted with headlines such as "Foreign ownership research prompts cries of racism." Mayor Gregor Robertson suggested Yan was turning his findings into a "race issue." (The city, meanwhile, has done nothing to address the problem.)[1] An urban planner expressed worry that Yan's research would incite "racism" and "intolerance."

But Yan's research isn't racist. He focuses not on the colour of homebuyers' skin but on the massive economic distortion that results when billions of dollars get mainlined into a geographically concentrated real-estate market. The scope of distortion would be identical if these buyers hailed from Kuwait, Norway, or Seattle.

It's troubling that a prominent left-wing politician such as Robertson—a former NDP* member of the provincial legislature who has a strong social-justice resumé—would prefer to stare at his shoes and offer bromides about tolerance rather than meaningfully engage with a phenomenon that affects every one of the 2.1 million people living in the Greater Vancouver Area. His overriding concern, shared by the media, is to avoid any hint of political incorrectness.

In this way, Robertson exemplifies a larger trend: a narrow fixation on identity politics has compromised the left's traditional focus on wide-angle issues of socio-economic stratification, poverty, and income inequality.

This is a critical period in the history of the Canadian social contract. The labour movement continues to disintegrate. The sharing economy threatens the livelihoods of taxi drivers and hotel staffers. Driverless cars and other robotic technologies will soon extinguish whole fields of work. Full-time employment is being replaced by contract positions. Entry-level journalists laugh mirthlessly when I ask if they ever plan to buy a house. Most of them can't even afford to ante up for RRSPs.*

The left now has a golden opportunity to push for bold policies that would go to the heart of income inequality in our class-based society: guaranteed income, universal access to care for those suffering from mental illness, and, yes, tax and regulatory policies that discourage hot money from overinflating local real-estate markets. But from what I've read on social media and in *Walrus* editorial submissions, many activists and pundits seem far more comfortable striking positions on highly compartmentalized identity-politics issues that can

1 *The city ... problem* Some steps have been taken since the first publication of this article. For example, in August 2016 the province of British Columbia instituted a fifteen per cent tax on foreign real estate purchases, and in November 2016 the City of Vancouver approved a one per cent tax on empty homes to take effect in 2017.

be reduced to succinct, tweet-able messages. Accusations of racism, sexism, and homophobia, in particular, can encourage a pack mentality—and so politicians such as Robertson are (understandably) terrified of arousing accusations that they harbour impure thoughts.

Consider this longitudinal case study: a generation ago, opposition to the Canada–United States free-trade deal and NAFTA* were the dominant obsessions of the Canadian left. And rightly so. Globalization has revolutionized our economy, creating whole new classes of winners and losers. By contrast, news of last year's Trans-Pacific Partnership—the largest trade deal in history—was treated for the most part as an obscurity. Progressive media were far more interested in culture-war battles over the likes of #OscarsSoWhite, *niqabs*,[2] and Donald Trump. Important Canadian stories with enormous economic impact continue to get short shrift.

That includes the story of how a flood of overseas money has made Vancouver all but unlivable. And I hope Kerry Gold's reporting finally spurs policies that help poor and middle-class Vancouverites find a lasting place in their city.

(2016)

Questions

1. What does Kay mean when he says that "a narrow fixation on identity politics has compromised the left's traditional focus on wide-angle issues of socio-economic stratification, poverty, and income inequality"? To what extent is this true?
2. Apart from matters of political correctness, what else might have motivated politicians to avoid giving attention to foreign ownership in Vancouver's real estate market? Does political correctness strike you as the most likely primary motive?
3. Kay reports many politicians expressing concern that a focus on the impact of wealthy Chinese buyers is racist or could provoke a racist response. To what extent (if any) is this a legitimate concern?

---

2 *#OscarsSoWhite* Twitter hashtag associated with a boycott protesting the 2016 Academy Awards. All the nominees in the Best Actor, Best Actress, Best Supporting Actor, and Best Supporting Actress categories that year were white; *niqabs* Head coverings that conceal most of the face, worn for religious reasons by some Muslim women. The question of whether new citizens should be allowed to wear *niqabs* during their citizenship ceremonies was a major controversy during Canada's 2015 federal election.

Malik Jalal

I'm on the Kill List. This Is What It Feels Like to Be Hunted by Drones

In 2001 the CIA began using the remote-controlled Predator drone to carry out attacks on enemies in war zones and individuals suspected of terrorism. More than 400 drone strikes have been carried out in the tribal regions of Pakistan; though accurate records of the identities and numbers of the casualties of these attacks are not available, of the several thousand people killed, hundreds have been civilians rather than members of terrorist organizations. (The American government has not released an estimate. While the New America Foundation estimates 286 civilian deaths between 2004 and February 2016 and the Bureau of Investigative Journalism estimates between 423 and 965 for the same period, a review by the Columbia Law School Human Rights Clinic suggests that these estimates may be low.)

A tribal elder in Waziristan, a region in Pakistan near the border with Afghanistan, Malik Jalal claims to have narrowly avoided multiple drone strikes and believes that his name is on the US government's notoriously secret "kill list." (Jalal is a member of the North Waziristan Peace Committee, which he describes as an organization that negotiates with the Taliban to maintain peace; American and British intelligence view the organization as offering refuge to the Taliban.) In 2016 Jalal visited the United Kingdom to share his personal experience with a world audience. His essay "I'm on the Kill List" was published by the Independent, *a UK newspaper.*

I am in the strange position of knowing that I am on the "Kill List." I know this because I have been told, and I know because I have been targeted for death over and over again. Four times missiles have been fired at me. I am extraordinarily fortunate to be alive.

I don't want to end up a "Bugsplat"—the ugly word that is used for what remains of a human being after being blown up by a Hellfire missile[1] fired from a Predator drone. More importantly, I don't want my family to become victims, or even to live with the droning engines overhead, knowing that at any moment they could be vaporized.

I am in England this week because I decided that if Westerners wanted to kill me without bothering to come to speak with me first, perhaps I should come to speak to them instead. I'll tell my story so that you can judge for yourselves whether I am the kind of person you want to be murdered.

I am from Waziristan, the border area between Pakistan and Afghanistan. I am one of the leaders of the North Waziristan Peace Committee (NWPC), which is a body of local Maliks (or community leaders) that is devoted to trying to keep the peace in our region. We are sanctioned by the Pakistan government, and our main mission is to try to prevent violence between the local Taliban and the authorities.

5 In January 2010, I lent my vehicle to my nephew, Salimullah, to drive to Deegan for an oil change and to have one of the tires checked. Rumours had surfaced that drones were targeting particular vehicles, and tracking particular phone signals. The sky was clear and there were drones circling overhead.

As Salimullah conversed with the mechanic, a second vehicle pulled up next to mine. There were four men inside, just local chromite miners. A missile destroyed both vehicles, killed all four men, and seriously injured Salimullah, who spent the next 31 days in hospital.

Upon reflection, because the drones target the vehicles of people they want to kill in Waziristan, I was worried that they were aiming for me.

The next attack came on 3 September 2010. That day, I was driving a red Toyota Hilux Surf SUV to a "Jirga," a community meeting of elders. Another red vehicle, almost identical to mine, was some 40 metres behind. When we reached Khader Khel, a missile blew up the other vehicle, killing all four occupants. I sped away, with flames and debris in my rear view mirror.

Initially I thought the vehicle behind was perhaps being used by militants, and I just happened to be nearby. But I learned later the casualties were four local labourers from the Mada Khel tribe, none of whom had any ties to militant groups. Now it seemed more likely that I was the target.

10 The third drone strike came on 6 October 2010. My friend Salim Khan invited me to dinner. I used my phone to call Salim to announce my arrival, and

---

1 *Hellfire missile* American-created missile fired at tanks and other targets on the ground from the air.

just before I got there a missile struck, instantly killing three people, including my cousin, Kaleem Ullah, a married man with children, and a mentally handicapped man. Again, none of the casualties were involved in extremism.

Now I knew for certain it was me they were after.

Five months later, on 27 March 2011, an American missile targeted a Jirga, where local Maliks—all friends and associates of mine—were working to resolve a local dispute and bring peace. Some 40 civilians died that day, all innocent, and some of them fellow members of the NWPC. I was early to the scene of this horror.

Like others that day, I said some things I regret.[2] I was angry, and I said we would get our revenge. But, in truth, how would we ever do such a thing? Our true frustration was that we—the elders of our villages—are now powerless to protect our people.

I have been warned that Americans and their allies had me and others from the Peace Committee on their Kill List. I cannot name my sources, as they would find themselves targeted for trying to save my life. But it leaves me in no doubt that I am one of the hunted.

I soon began to park any vehicle far from my destination, to avoid making 15
it a target. My friends began to decline my invitations, afraid that dinner might be interrupted by a missile.

I took to the habit of sleeping under the trees, well above my home, to avoid acting as a magnet of death for my whole family. But one night my youngest son, Hilal (then aged six), followed me out to the mountainside. He said that he, too, feared the droning engines at night. I tried to comfort him. I said that drones wouldn't target children, but Hilal refused to believe me. He said that missiles had often killed children. It was then that I knew that I could not let them go on living like this.

I know the Americans think me an opponent of their drone wars. They are right; I am. Singling out people to assassinate, and killing nine of our innocent children for each person they target, is a crime of unspeakable proportions. Their policy is as foolish as it is criminal, as it radicalizes the very people we are trying to calm down.

I am aware that the Americans and their allies think the Peace Committee is a front, and that we are merely creating a safe space for the Pakistan Taliban. To this I say: you are wrong. You have never been to Waziristan, so how would you know?

The mantra that the West should not negotiate with "terrorists" is naive. There has hardly ever been a time when terrorists have been brought back into

2 *I said ... regret* Jalal made a statement in support of "blood revenge" against the United States.

the fold of society without negotiation. Remember the IRA;[3] once they tried to blow up your prime minister, and now they are in parliament. It is always better to talk than to kill.

I have travelled half way across the world because I want to resolve this dispute the way you teach: by using the law and the courts, not guns and explosives.

Ask me any question you wish, but judge me fairly—and please stop terrorizing my wife and children. And take me off that Kill List.

(2016)

Questions

1. In *Objective Troy*, a recent book about President Obama's use of drone warfare, Scott Shane writes that "by comparison with the two big ground wars Obama had inherited, the toll of non-combatants killed in drone strikes was very small—hundreds, versus hundreds of thousands." Does the "smaller" number of deaths involved justify the use of drone killings?
2. Jalal writes that the American mandate to "not negotiate with terrorists" is naïve and must be changed if progress toward peace is to be made. Do you agree?
3. Do you agree with Jalal that drone attacks lead to more radicalization? Why or why not?
4. According to the Director of National Intelligence (DNI), between 2,372 and 2,581 combatants, and between 64 and 116 non-combatants were killed in drone strikes between 2009 and 2015. Do these numbers accord with Jalal's claims? In this context, can we trust numbers made public by the government?

---

3 *IRA* Irish Republican Army, a paramilitary organization whose members sought to gain independence for Ireland through violent attacks on British targets. The conflict over Irish independence lasted for decades in the late twentieth century until negotiations involving the IRA resulted in the Good Friday Agreement (1998), which brought an almost complete end to the violence.

Ross Finnie, Kaveh Afshar, Eda Bozkurt,
Masashi Miyairi, and Dejan Pavlic

from Barista* or Better? New Evidence on the Earnings of Post-Secondary Education Graduates: A Tax Linkage Approach

The Education Policy Research Initiative (EPRI), at the University of Ottawa, researches matters related to "education, skills and the labour market." The following executive summary outlines the results of one such research project, which used information from the tax records of college and university graduates to examine the relationship between postsecondary education and income in Canada. Published in July 2016, the report was widely discussed in Canadian newspapers and news magazines; an article on the subject from The Globe and Mail *is also included in this anthology.*

Executive Summary

The skills that individuals develop play a pivotal role in determining their labour-market opportunities and life chances in general, and are of vital importance to a country's economic performance and many social outcomes. Post-secondary education (PSE) is a primary means by which Canadians obtain the skills that they need.

It is therefore essential to have accurate, up-to-date, and relevant learning and labour market information (LLMI) that is widely available so that all players in the PSE system—students making their PSE choices, PSE institutions deciding which programs to offer, policy makers, and the general public—can make informed decisions.

This is especially relevant at a time when we are often confronted with the now familiar barista trope—the suggestion (even assumption) that going to university, or college, particularly in a non-STEM (Science, Technology,

Engineering, Mathematics) field of study, is a waste of time and will leave graduates stuck in a job with low earnings and little opportunity for career advancement.

Empirical data on PSE graduates' earnings constitute a critical element of the information that is needed. Current data sources, however, have significant shortcomings, including their relatively short-term nature.

In this context, the Education Policy Research Initiative (EPRI), a national policy-focused research organization based at the University Ottawa, has undertaken an innovative research project that uses administrative data on students provided by 14 PSE institutions from four Canadian provinces linked to tax records held at Statistics Canada to track the labour market outcomes of Canadian college (diploma) and university (bachelor's) graduates from 2005 through 2013.

MAIN FINDINGS

Funded by Employment and Social Development Canada (ESDC) and undertaken in partnership with Statistics Canada, the study has produced a range of findings, which both support and, conversely, sometimes challenge popular preconceptions:

- Overall, 2005 bachelor's degree graduates had average annual earnings of $45,200 (in 2014 dollars) in the first year after graduation, growing by 66% to reach $74,900 eight years out.
- College diploma graduates who finished their studies in 2005 had mean[1] annual earnings of $33,900 (in 2014 dollars) in the first year following graduation, growing by 59% to $54,000 eight years after graduation.
- Engineering, Mathematics & Computer Science, and Business graduates generally had higher incomes and greater earnings growth than others, but graduates of almost all other fields of study, including the oft-maligned* Humanities and Social Sciences bachelor's graduates, also performed well. Fine Arts graduates had the lowest earnings levels. Very few graduates had truly barista-level earnings even to start, and they increasingly moved even further from that level as they gained labour market experience.
- Later cohorts[2] of graduates generally had similar earnings patterns and the ranking of fields of study remained consistent as well, although some

---

1 *mean* Average.

2 *cohorts* In statistics, groups of people with shared characteristics (here, the shared characteristic being that they graduated in the same year).

fields of study did have greater differences in earnings across cohorts than others.

- Immediately following the 2008 financial crisis,[3] first year earnings of all graduates taken together (i.e., across all fields of study) first dipped, after having risen the two preceding years, but stabilized in 2010. Across the entire 2005–2012 period, earnings rose for later cohorts of graduates of certain fields of study, were stable for others, and declined for another set, but those declines could be described as moderate to substantial (at worst), rather than calamitous....

THE BIGGER PICTURE

... A broader research agenda should, in particular, involve identifying the full range of skill sets that matter and determining the potential role of PSE in helping individuals develop these skills. These should include not only conventional discipline-specific skills, but also essential skills, higher order cognitive skills, and—in particular—"transferable" skills such as various communications skills, being able to work in a (multi-disciplinary) team environment, and to be continuously looking for opportunities to foster innovation that have been gaining so much interest in recent years. The research platform established in this study could play a key role in making progress on this new skills agenda....

(2016)

Questions

1. Does anything about Finnie et al.'s findings surprise you? Why or why not?
2. Compare the tone of this summary to that of Barrie McKenna's article "It's Time to Retire the Myth of the Educated Barista," also included in this anthology. How do differences in tone reflect differences in the intended audience of each piece?
3. Why do you think the humanities and social sciences are "oft-maligned"?
4. To what extent do financial prospects shape your choice of educational path? What other factors do you consider? Which are most important to you?

---

3 *2008 financial crisis* Economic crisis that resulted in a global recession, considered by many economists to have been the worst financial recession since the 1930s.

Barrie McKenna

It's Time to Retire the Myth of the Educated Barista*

In 2016, the Education Policy Research Initiative at the University of Ottawa published a study examining the earnings of Canadian college and university graduates. The following piece, written for The Globe and Mail *in July 2016, summarizes and comments on the results of that study. An excerpt from the executive summary of the study itself, "Barista or Better? New Evidence on the Earnings of Post-Secondary Education Graduates," is also included in this anthology.*

Perhaps you know her—the Starbucks barista with a masters in English literature.

No? It turns out she's more urban legend* than reality.

Worse, the cliché sends the distressing message to young people that education doesn't matter and that a degree in anything other than engineering or science is virtually worthless.

The perception is patently false. All of the available data overwhelmingly show that education and training matter a lot. People with postsecondary education make more money, they're less likely to be unemployed and they land better jobs. And if you have dreams of reaching the top 1 per cent of income earners, stay in school. Two-thirds of one-percenters* have at least one university degree, according to Statistics Canada. Of course, there are examples of overeducated graduates working in low-skilled jobs. But they arc the exception, not the rule. The key lesson here is that more education beats less education virtually every time.

5 Groundbreaking new research by a team headed by University of Ottawa labour economist Ross Finnie and funded by the federal government examined the earnings of university and college graduates in the years after they leave school. The study, titled *Barista or Better*, matched 340,000 graduates from 14 colleges and universities across four provinces with income tax data from 2005 to 2013 to create a refreshingly clear and dynamic portrait of outcomes.

And guess what? Average incomes rose rapidly in the years after graduation across all fields, including the "oft* maligned*" humanities and social sciences, according to the study, the first of its kind in Canada. Over all, the class of 2005 earned an average of $42,500 in the first year after graduation, growing 66 per cent to nearly $75,000 by year eight.

That's an annual growth rate of better than 8 per cent, even through the depths of the 2008–09 recession.[1] Not bad, all things considered.

"We've been torturing our children, inappropriately and wrongly, based on bad data," Mr. Finnie, director of the university's Education Policy Research Initiative, lamented in an interview. "The debunking [of the barista myth] is critical."

As it turned out, the study found that very few of the graduates had "truly barista-level earnings even to start, and they increasingly moved further from that level as they gained labour market experience."

University graduates generally did better than college graduates. And some graduates did much better than the average, notably those with engineering, mathematics, computer science and business degrees. Engineers, for example, topped $100,000 in annual earnings by year eight, according to the study, which excluded those who pursued degrees beyond college diplomas or bachelor's degrees.

That's understandable. These are more technical fields, where workers are in higher demand and graduates more scarce.

The most encouraging aspect of the research is that even English or history graduates are finding their degrees have substantial value in the Canadian workplace. Maybe these graduates don't know about fluid dynamics* and stress loads,* but chances are they're good communicators, team workers and problem solvers—skills that employers also value highly.

Indeed, a common complaint among technology companies is that too many recruits lack the softer skills* that are so essential in the business world. And these are talents that are often more developed among social science graduates.

"It is not because someone has read Plato or Aristotle* that they are being hired," Mr. Finnie explained to *The Globe and Mail*'s Rachelle Younglai. "They don't have training for what you see in job ads.... They have other skills, like critical thinking."

There is, of course, much we still don't know about factors that affect the incomes of recent graduates, including race, socioeconomic background and

---

1 *2008–09 recession* Global recession sometimes called the "Great Recession." It is widely considered the worst economic recession since the 1930s.

the specifics of their college or university program. Do co-op programs,[2] for example, lead to better wages after graduation, and how can schools tailor what they do to improve students' job prospects?

Obviously, there is a need in Canada to better match the education system to the evolving needs of employers. Colleges and universities can always do a better job of churning out workers the market needs. And companies need to invest more in training to turn new recruits into the employees they want.

What we do know is that a low level of education is a sentence to a life of low wages and bad jobs.

It's time to retire the barista myth.

(2016)

Questions

1. How often have you encountered the "educated barista" myth? Has it affected your approach to your own education, or your opinions of the educations of others?
2. McKenna suggests that postsecondary institutions "can always do a better job of churning out workers the market needs." Apart from producing employable workers, what other purposes might postsecondary education serve? How important are these in comparison to worker education?
3. Compare McKenna's article to the executive summary of the original research conducted by Ross Finnie et al., also included in this anthology. Does it seem to you that McKenna's is a relatively neutral presentation of the study's research and results, or does he put forward his own opinion in addition?
4. Do you ultimately find this essay to be a strong defense of the humanities and social sciences? Why or why not?

2 *co-op programs* Programs in which students gain academic credit for participating in relevant job experiences.

NATHAN HELLER

THE FAILURE OF FACEBOOK DEMOCRACY

As an increasing number of people access news online, particularly via social media sites such as Facebook, questions have arisen about the effects of the Internet on the types of news we encounter. Algorithms on sites such as Google and Facebook tailor the information we receive to match our interests. These so-called "filter bubbles" are particularly prevalent on social media sites, where, it is argued, communities of friends or followers tend to share similar views and filter out opposing ones. A related concern is that the news people access through Facebook is often not fact-checked, so that "fake news" has begun to exert a significant influence on public discourse. The following article discusses the effects of filter bubbles and fake news on the democratic process; it first appeared in The New Yorker *on 18 November 2016, shortly after Donald Trump was elected President of the United States.*

In December of 2007, the legal theorist Cass R. Sunstein wrote in *The Chronicle of Higher Education* about the filtering effects that frequently attend the spread of information on the Web. "As a result of the Internet, we live increasingly in an era of enclaves and niches—much of it voluntary, much of it produced by those who think they know, and often do know, what we're likely to like," Sunstein noted. In the piece, "The Polarization of Extremes," Sunstein argued that the trend promised ill effects for the direction—or, more precisely, the misdirection—of public opinion. "If people are sorted into enclaves and niches, what will happen to their views?" he wondered. "What are the eventual effects on democracy?"

This month has provided a jarring answer. The unexpected election of Donald Trump is said to owe debts to both niche extremism and rampant misinformation. Facebook, the most pervasive of the social networks, has received much scrutiny and blame. During the final weeks of the campaigns, it grew apparent that the site's "news" algorithm—a mechanism that trawls posts from one's online friends and rank-displays those deemed of interest—was not distinguishing between real news and false information: the sort of tall tales, groundless conspiracy theories, and oppositional propaganda that, in the Cenozoic era,[1] circulated mainly via forwarded e-mails. (In the run-up to the election, widely shared false stories included reports that Pope Francis has endorsed Donald Trump and that Hillary Clinton had commissioned murders.) On Thursday, the *Washington Post* published an interview with what it called an "impresario[2] of a Facebook fake-news empire." He took responsibility. "I think Trump is in the White House because of me," he said. "His followers don't fact-check anything—they'll post everything, believe anything."

Facebook is not the only network to have trafficked phony news, but its numbers have been striking. A much-cited Pew survey, released in May, suggested that forty-four per cent of the general population used Facebook as a news source, a figure unrivalled by other social networks. An analysis this week by Craig Silverman, of *BuzzFeed*, found that the twenty top-performing fake news stories on the network outperformed the twenty top real-news stories during the final three months before the election—and that seventeen of those fakes favoured the Trump campaign. Trump's exponents, including the candidate himself, routinely cited fake information on camera. In the eyes of critics, Facebook's news feed has become a distribution channel for propagandistic misinformation. "As long as it's on Facebook and people can see it ... people start believing it," President Obama said right before the election. "It creates this dust cloud of nonsense."

The criticism has been hard to shake. Mark Zuckerberg, Facebook's founder and C.E.O., dismissed complaints at a conference late last week and again in a lengthy post over the weekend. "The hoaxes that do exist are not limited to one partisan view, or even to politics. Over all, this makes it extremely unlikely hoaxes changed the outcome of this election in one direction or the other," he wrote. "I believe we must proceed very carefully though. Identifying the 'truth' is complicated." Few members of the public were appeased (not least because Facebook's advertising strategy is premised on the idea that it can move the needle of public opinion), and even some Facebook employees were uneasy. On Monday, *BuzzFeed*'s Sheera Frenkel reported on an anonymous cabal of "renegade Facebook employees" who found Zuckerberg's claims dishonest. They were working to develop formal recommendations for change.

---

1 *Cenozoic era* Current geologic era spanning the past 66 million years; it followed the Mesozoic era. Heller is using the term playfully to refer to a recent "era" of technology (when we received news from friends via forwarded emails).

2 *impresario* Italian: person who organizes a show or entertainment (concert, circus, opera).

"You don't have to believe Facebook got Trump elected to be a little chilled by its current estrangement from fact," Brian Phillips observed in a cutting piece on MTV.com. "One of the conditions of democratic resistance is having an accurate picture of what to resist."

The democratic effects of widespread misinformation were Sunstein's preoccupation when he wrote about "self-sorting" in 2007. He cited an experiment previously run in Colorado. The study used liberal subjects from Boulder and conservative subjects from Colorado Springs. Participants had been divided into groups and instructed to discuss controversial issues: same-sex unions, global warming, affirmative action.* Researchers recorded individual opinions before and after fifteen minutes of discussion. Trends emerged. When participants spoke with politically like-minded people, their opinions usually became more extreme. Liberals grew more liberal in their thinking on a given issue; conservatives, more conservative. The range of opinion narrowed, too. Like-minded participants drifted toward consensus.

Sunstein projected that a similar drift would occur online, where information in support of preëxisting views was readily available (and even hard to avoid, due to the way Internet browsing works). He called the polarization that it produced "enclave extremism." One contributing factor, he contended, was the social flow of information: people who hung out with people of a similar view were apt to encounter a disproportionate amount of information in support of that view, intensifying their support. He thought more purely social effects were involved, too: "People want to be perceived favourably by other group members." Most citizens, on most issues, don't know precisely what they think, and are susceptible to minor suasion.[3] Enclave opinion, which builds confidence in one's views, allows general thoughts to sharpen and intensify. The risk was that bad ideas could gain wide adherence if the self-sorting worked out right.

Sunstein did not account for Facebook algorithms or the spread of demonstrably false information. The first factor amplifies the enclave effect he described; the second nurtures confident extremism. Even when information is accurate, enclave extremism helps explain how those who trade in fact, such as journalists, could manage to get the big-picture stuff, such as the electoral mood of the country, completely wrong.[4] In the days after Trump's election, many bemused coastal pundits lamented what the writer Eli Pariser has called a "filter bubble": an echo chamber of information and opinion which, in this

---

3 *suasion* Influence; persuasion.

4 *fact ... wrong* In the weeks leading up to the November 2016 election, most mainstream media outlets in the US expressed confidence that Hillary Clinton was on track to win the presidency.

case, led those writing the news to be disproportionately exposed to information in line with their existing theories. The more we rely on the digital sphere as our window onto the world, the more vulnerable to its weaknesses we are.

A couple of years ago, reporting from San Francisco, I noted an erosion of public meaning which seemed to be getting in the way of civic progress. A key cause, I suggested at the time, was technology's filtering effects—the way that, as we lived more of our lives in a personal bespoke,[5] we lost touch with the common ground, and the common language, that made meaningful public work possible. Perhaps filtering effects are at play, but nothing I've seen since has changed my mind. The most dangerous intellectual spectre today seems not to be lack of information but the absence of a common information sphere in which to share it across boundaries of belief.

Pauline Kael, a *New Yorker* film critic for many years, once famously quipped, in a speech, "I live in a rather special world. I only know one person who voted for Nixon."* Enclave extremism isn't new, in other words. What may be fresher is our oblivion of the moments when we're living in its thrall. If a majority of Americans are getting their news from Facebook, then Facebook surely has a civic obligation to ensure the information it disseminates is sound. The long-term effects of enclave extremism, Sunstein observed, can be bad news for democracy: "Those who flock together, on the Internet or elsewhere, will end up both confident and wrong, simply because they have not been sufficiently exposed to counterarguments. They may even think of their fellow citizens as opponents or adversaries in some kind of 'war.'" A Presidential Administration with that outlook is dangerous. But a confident, misinformed public is much worse.

(2016)

Questions

1. If you are a member of any social networks (Facebook, Twitter, Instagram, Snapchat, etc.), do you think your membership in those networks has sorted you into a "niche" of friends with like-minded views? What effect (if any) does discourse with your social media friends have on your political and ethical opinions?
2. Do you think Facebook has a responsibility to fact check its newsfeed? Why or why not? What do you think of Zuckerberg's statement that "identifying the truth is complicated"?

---

5 *bespoke* Made to order, tailor-made.

3. Heller argues that the more we rely on the Internet as our sphere of public discourse, the more "vulnerable we are to its weaknesses." What are these weaknesses? Does the Internet have strengths as a sphere of public discourse that counteract these weaknesses?
4. Heller argues that "enclave extremism" leads people in different groups to be both "confident and wrong," increasing the intensity of animosity between people with different values. To what extent do you see this phenomenon reflected in Canada's present-day political landscape?
5. In what ways could politicians and corporations profit from a culture that is distancing itself from caring about fact and truth?

DOUG SAUNDERS

DON'T BLAME DARK VOTING TRENDS ON ONLINE THOUGHT BUBBLES

This opinion piece originally appeared as part of Doug Saunders's weekly column in The Globe and Mail*; in online publication it was assigned the title "Bursting the bubble of 'online filter bubbles.'" As Saunders's work often does, the following piece distills the results of academic research for a general audience. The studies he refers to are Andrew Guess, "Media Choice and Moderation: Evidence from Online Tracking Data"; Seth Flaxman, Sharad Goel, and Justin Rao, "Filter Bubbles, Echo Chambers, and Online News Consumption"; Matthew Gentzkow and Jesse M. Shapiro, "Ideological Segregation Online and Offline"; and Kartik Hosanagar, Daniel M. Fleder, Dokyun Lee, and Andreas Buja, "Will the Global Village Fracture into Tribes: Recommender Systems and Their Effects on Consumers."*

When I watch election polls rolling out of the United States and Europe, with big margins of voters willing to back the previously unthinkable, my mind keeps straying back to the story, reported this summer, of Timothy Trespas.

Mr. Trespas, an unemployed guy in his early 40s who lives in New York, began noticing a problem a few years ago: He is being stalked by strangers. Dozens of people are following him all the time, and they occasionally whisper mysterious things in his ear. He went online to see what was wrong. A search revealed tens of thousands of people plagued with similar "gang-stalking" problems. They call themselves "targeted individuals," or TIs, and they've created hundreds of YouTube videos and dozens of e-books on the phenomenon, explaining the government plots behind it. They've organized support groups (key advice: don't see a psychiatrist). Mr. Trespas, as he told Mike McPhate of *The New York Times*, lost his friends and became more fearful and withdrawn. He only believes news from TI sites.

Gang-stalking theories are well known to the psychiatric community: They are classic symptoms of schizophrenia and other delusion-based diseases. In recent years, professionals have reacted with alarm as people have stopped reaching out for help and instead reach for their browsers. There they find only confirmation of their delusions. If you come to suspect that vapour trails* are actually mind-control chemicals, or that the "spherical-Earth theory"* is a fraud, you will find limitless amounts of support, and a welcoming community that protects you from alternative views.

It is tempting to think of Mr. Trespas as the very model of the modern voter. Are many of our fellow citizens, like him, getting information only from sources that confirm their ideologies, preconceptions and pathologies?

It's not difficult to find people on Twitter or Facebook, or sometimes at 5
family gatherings, who seem to live in ideologically isolated, self-confirming worlds—or, in the phrase coined by Internet entrepreneur Eli Pariser, "filter bubbles." But, it turns out, such people are both very rare and also very atypical—perhaps increasingly so, studies keep showing.

The most recent research, by Andrew Guess of New York University, assembled a representative sample of 1,400 people across the United States, sorted them by self-declared ideology and monitored everything they viewed and shared for three weeks. It found that the online sources used by almost all Republicans were almost identical to those used by most Democrats, and those were mainly the less ideologically polarized, big-tent mass media everyone uses—except at rare, intense moments, when they would glance at Fox News or Breitbart[1] or some other partisan website, then return to the centre. But for the most part, everyone was hearing everyone else's voices.

Another study, completed in March by three researchers at Oxford, Stanford and Microsoft Research, looked at the activities of 50,000 Americans. It found that social media are indeed increasing "the ideological distance between individuals"—people are fighting from partisan positions—but that "these same channels also are associated with an increase in an individual's exposure to material from his or her less-preferred side of the political spectrum," and that mainstream news sources still account for the "vast majority" of what ideologically polarized people visit.

A large-scale study by Matthew Gentzkow and Jesse Shapiro of the University of Chicago similarly found "no evidence that the Internet is becoming more segregated over time." And a 2014 study by four scholars at the Wharton

1 *Fox News* American News network that has been widely condemned for pro-Republican bias; *Breitbart* American news and political commentary website associated with right-wing extremism.

School found that Internet filtering was causing not fragmentation but, in fact, an "increase in commonality with others."

It appears, from this work, that people are not being isolated into self-confirming thought ghettos; rather, they have more sources than ever before, and prefer the credible ones—but they're also members of communities of believers who influence them, sometimes darkly. It is community, not content, that causes extremism.

As those studies show, the Internet has compartments, but it also has a lot of cracks. They're how the light gets in.* A lot of people have been won over by bad ideas, but they're able and willing to listen—so it's worth the effort to try to persuade them otherwise.

(2016)

Questions

1. Explicate the analogy Saunders draws between Timothy Trespas's online community and "alt-right" voters in the US election. What conclusion does Saunders draw about this analogy? Do you agree with him? Why or why not?
2. Do you think "filter bubbles" (i.e., online communities that reinforce and support extreme views while filtering out opposing ones) are a significant problem? Explain your answer and provide some examples to support it.
3. This article was written before the 2016 US election and before the associated increase in concern about social media circulating "fake news"—stories that appear to be news but are not fact-checked and are often outrageously inaccurate. Does the rise of "fake news" affect the persuasiveness of Saunders's argument? Why or why not?
4. Saunders claims that it is "community" not "content" that causes extremism. What does this mean? Do you agree? Why or why not?

Ron Srigley

from Pass, Fail

Ron Srigley is a professor of religious studies at Prince Edward Island University. His research interests span classical philosophy, religion, and contemporary critiques of modernity; much of his work during the 2010s focuses on technology and the promises and dangers of globalization. "Pass, Fail" was first published in The Walrus, *a Canadian magazine that features independent journalism and short fiction.*

For the past seven years, I've polled my students at the University of Prince Edward Island on two questions. First: If you were told today that a university education was no longer a requirement for high-quality employment, would you quit? Second: If you decided to stay, would you then switch programs?

Positive responses to both questions run consistently in the 50 percent range. That means at least half of my humanities students—or about 750 since 2007—don't want to be there.

Why not? A university degree, after all, is a credential crucial for economic success. At least, that's what we're told. But as with all such credentials—those sought for the ends they promise rather than the knowledge they represent—the trick is to get them cheaply, quickly, and with as little effort as possible. My students' disaffection is the real face of this ambition.

I teach mostly bored youth who find themselves doing something they neither value nor desire—and, in some cases, are simply not equipped for—in order to achieve an outcome they are repeatedly warned is essential to their survival. What a dreadful trap. Rather than learning freely and excelling, they've become shrewd managers of their own careers and are forced to compromise what is best in themselves—their honesty or character—in order to "make it" in the world we've created for them.

The credentialing game can be played for only so long before the market 5
gets wise and values begin to decline. I have been an educator in Canadian universities for over fourteen years, having taught some eighty-five liberal arts courses. During that time, evidence has mounted showing that a bachelor's degree from a Canadian university brings with it less and less economic earning

power. Last year, the Council of Ontario Universities released the results of the Ontario Graduates' Survey for the class of 2012. It's one of the few documents in Canada that tracks the employment rates and earnings of university graduates. Six months after graduation, the class of 2012 had an average income 7 percent below that of the class of 2005. Two years after graduation, incomes dropped to 14 percent below those of the 2005 class.

Though there are likely several reasons for this decline (increases in the number of graduates, demographic shifts in markets, precarious labour), one in particular matches perfectly with the type of change I've observed on my watch: the eradication of content from the classroom.*

What kind of students are produced by such contentless environments? A couple of years ago, I dimmed the lights in order to show a clip of an interview. I was trying to make a point about the limits of human aspiration, a theme discussed in one of our readings, and I'd found an interview with Woody Allen in which he urged that we recognize the ultimate futility of all endeavours (a tough sell in today's happiness market). The moment the lights went down, dozens and dozens of bluish, iPhone-illumined faces emerged from the darkness. That's when I understood that there were several entertainment options available to students in the modern university classroom, and that lectures rank well below Twitter, Tumblr, or Snapchat.

Yet you can't get mad at students for being distracted and inattentive, not like in the old days. "Hey, you, pay attention! This is important." Say that today, and you won't be met with anger or shame. You'll hear something like "Oh, sorry sir. My bad. I didn't mean anything." And they don't. They don't mean anything. They are not dissing* you. They are not even thinking about you, so it's not rebellion. It's just that the ground has shifted and left the instructor hanging there in empty space, like Wile E. Coyote.[1] Just a few more moments (or years), and down we'll all fall. These people look like students. They have arms and legs and heads. They sit in a class like students; they have books and write papers and take exams. But they are not students, and you are not a professor. And there's the rub.[2] ...

... This is the classroom in which our sons or daughters (or you) very likely sit each day, so let's map the contours of its nihilism a little more systematically.

1 *Wile E. Coyote* Character from the cartoon series *Looney Tunes* (1930–69). Wile E. Coyote tries repeatedly, and unsuccessfully, to capture and eat the Road Runner; his foiled plots sometimes send him off a cliff, where he hangs suspended in the air before plummeting to the ground.

2 *there's the rub* Phrase from Shakespeare's *Hamlet* 3.1 meaning "this is the problem."

Students today read very little. In 2009, the Canadian Council on Learning reported that 20 percent of all university graduates in Canada fell below Level 3 (the minimum level of proficiency) on a prose literacy scale provided by the Programme for International Student Assessment. That proportion was expected to rise.

I see ample evidence of this at UPEI. In one course I co-taught with several other faculty members, the readings were posted online, which allowed us to map access patterns. In that course, readings were accessed—not necessarily read—by 5 to 15 percent of the enrolled students. The same pattern was confirmed by textbook sales in a course from the previous year. I was teaching George Orwell's *Nineteen Eighty-Four*, and I had ordered 230 copies based on enrolment numbers. At the end of term, the bookstore had sold only eighteen copies, a hit rate of about 8 percent.

It may be that some students already had the book or had purchased it from another source. But the quality of the essays and mid-term exams suggested a different story, as did students' own explanations of their actions. Remove your professor hat for a moment and students will speak frankly. They will tell you that they don't read because they don't have to. They can get an A without ever opening a book....

... Over the past fourteen years of teaching, my students' grade-point averages have steadily gone up while real student achievement has dropped. Papers I would have failed ten years ago on the grounds that they were unintelligible and failed to meet the standard of university-level work, I now routinely assign grades of C or higher. Each time I do so, I rub another little corner of my conscience off and cheat your son or daughter of an honest low grade or of a failure that might have given rise to a real success.

I am speaking, of course, of grade inflation. For faculty, the reasons for it vary. It can help them avoid time-consuming student appeals, create a level playing field for their own students in comparison to others, or boost subscription rates. Since most degrees involve no real content, it doesn't matter how the achievement is assessed. Beyond questions of mere style, there are no grounds for assigning one ostensibly well-considered paper an A and another a B when both marks are effectively illusory. Let the bottom rise to whatever height is necessary in your particular market, so long as there remains some type of performance arc that will maintain the appearance of merit.

But as practices change, so do habits of mind and expectations. If students are awarded ever-higher grades, they will eventually believe they deserve such grades. If this practice begins early enough, say in middle or secondary school, it will become so entrenched that, by the time they reach university, any violation of it will be taken as a grievous and unwarranted denigration of their abilities.

15 Perhaps somewhere deep down, they know their degrees are worthless. But anyone who challenges them will likely be hauled before an appeal board and asked to explain how she has the temerity to tell students their papers are hastily compiled and undigested piles of drivel unacceptable as university-level work. The customer is always right. One university vice-president I know promises on her website that she will provide "one-stop shops" and "exceptional customer service" to all. Do not let the stupidity of this statement fool you into believing it is in any way benign. We no longer have "students"—only "customers."

Online courses are perhaps one of the most complete expressions of the denigration of university education. At least half of all Canadian universities offer students some kind of online programming....

Increasingly, these courses are preferred even by students who attend the university full time and live on campus. Why go to class when you can watch a video online and then do a quiz? If your learning style is visual (i.e. you can't read) and your range of concentration is fifteen minutes (i.e. you have no attention span), then you can watch the video in fifteen-minute chunks. And if you don't like what you're hearing, you can just turn it off and ask your friend about it later. And if you don't understand what is being said, don't worry. Who will know?

No one will ever ask you a difficult question that makes it apparent you haven't done your readings; it is much easier to fudge online assignments or to plagiarize them outright; the assignments themselves will tend to be simplistic, multiple choice-style tests and quizzes that fit the technical structure of the medium much better than more complex forms of writing. All of this comes with the added perk for professors of not having to read long and often poorly written essays and reviews....

... If you are mocked and denigrated for years on end, whether passive-aggressively through the slow clawing back of your budgets or through the Disneyfication of your course offerings (Religious Studies 211—"The Whore of North Africa: Augustine Gone Wild in Carthage")[3] by more "progressive" colleagues, sooner or later your rational self might tell you that the game is up, and you might stop doing what it is you do (serious study of texts and historical events, honest lectures with real content) and start doing what you are expected

---

3 *Augustine* Augustine of Hippo (354–430), important early Christian philosopher whose *Confessions* recounts his morally dissolute youth and eventual conversion to Christianity; *Carthage* Ancient city in northern Africa.

to do (keep an increasingly disengaged and intellectually limited group of young people entertained or otherwise distracted for three hours a week).

Though entirely understandable, this is a self-defeating strategy. You dumb down your lectures to keep your subscriptions up and to justify your courses in the eyes of the administration. The dumber they become, the less justification there is for continuing them and the more the administration sneers when it hears your defence of the ennobling powers of the humanities and the arts. So why wouldn't you just go along? Why not inflate Susan's and Bill's grades to ensure that they have a nice experience and don't feel disrespected? Why not indeed, if doing so comes with the added perk of avoiding catching hell from students and administrators for refusing to say that two plus two equals five?

Because the worst fate for our children, yours and mine, is yet to come. Because when the easy pleasures of youth run out and self-affirmation is all students have left, what will remain? Not just bad work and the dreary distractions of the modern entertainment industry—all of which can be tolerated, as bad as they may be—but the absence of something to live for, the highest and most beautiful activity of their intelligence. To cheat them of that is the real crime, and the most profound way in which modern universities have betrayed the trust of an entire generation of young people.

(2016)

Questions

1. What are the practices of the modern university that Srigley argues "cheats" students of the opportunity to develop their intelligence? Do you agree? Why or why not?
2. Are students becoming "customers"? What does being a student imply, and what does being a customer imply? Which would you rather be, and why?
3. Find 5 choices of diction (word choice) in Srigley's article that reveal a value judgment by the author. How does the author's attitude toward his subject affect the impact of his article?
4. How does Srigley describe the motivations of his students? Does this description align with what motivates you in the pursuit of your own post-secondary education? Does it match how you perceive the motivations of your peers?

DARRYL WHETTER

THE KIDS ARE ALRIGHT

Darryl Whetter is a Canadian writer and professor of English at the Université Sainte-Anne in Pointe-de-l'Église, Nova Scotia. "The Kids Are Alright" was first published in The Walrus *in 2016 in response to another article that also appeared in the magazine. That article—"Pass, Fail," a condemnation of Canada's institutions of higher education by professor and writer Ron Srigley—is excerpted in this anthology.*

"Witness!" the shirtless War Boys yell to their comrades in *Mad Max: Fury Road*[1] when they risk their lives to serve their army. I play clips of that post-apocalyptic film when teaching Cormac McCarthy's post-apocalyptic novel *The Road*[2] to my first-year English undergrads, most of whom will not major in English at my tiny francophone university. They are, like many of the students profiled in Ron Srigley's recent article "Pass, Fail," intellectual tourists (or conscripts) passing through a Humanities course. Srigley would presumably find my madmaxing, with its "loud soundtrack," culpable in his lament of the "eradication of content from the classroom." *Au contraire*.[3] I follow this film clip by quoting a tenth-century section of the Eddic poem *Hávamál*,[4] and its similar insistence on earning a reputation for a noble death. Invoke a little contemporary ISIS and jihad,[5] circle back to McCarthy's *The Road* and its inculcation by oral legends in a post-print world—lesson made.

1 *Mad Max: Fury Road* Highly acclaimed 2015 action film involving a violent journey through a desert wasteland.

2 *The Road* Pulitzer Prize-winning 2006 novel in which the protagonist and his son travel through a damaged landscape.

3 *Au contraire* French: On the contrary.

4 *Eddic poem Hávamál* Old Norse poem offering proverbial advice. It is preserved in the thirteenth-century Codex Regius.

5 *ISIS* Acronym for the Islamic State of Iraq and Syria, a fundamentalist and militant group designated as a terrorist organization by the United Nations; *jihad* Arabic term referring to a complex concept in Islamic faith. The term, which refers to "struggle," is used by fundamentalist terrorists to justify violence in the name of Islam—but a majority

Like Srigley, I have to admit that for all my hope and planning, this lesson won't change the souls of some of my students. Unlike Srigley, I don't think that because they have smartphones and I use film clips that "they are not students, and [I am] not a professor." Distracted students have always been distracted and great students are still great students.

Yes, university education, now as always, has many flaws, but attacking students for being the net natives that they are isn't a fruitful lament. While Srigley's dissatisfaction with the ever-expanding and overpaid university administrative class is laudable, he forgets several fundamentals of teaching that are manifest in any learning environment, from grade five to the online courses he loathes: intelligence, and learning style, come in various forms. All education, he implies, should be the education that works for him as learner and teacher: verbal lectures with heavy reading. This constitutes the same narcissistic "mirroring" he bemoans in curricula designed to please. Forget that Richard Feynman[6] couldn't do his physics without sometimes setting aside the graph paper to reach for his bongos. If only we could have kept Einstein away from that pesky violin.

True, a proper university education does not exist without heavy reading. But edutainment* that sacrifices content to please crowds, and the administrative insistence on education as customer service, are not the new post-millennial threats Srigley suggests. Just one hundred years ago, studying literature in your native language—the same literature Srigley worries we don't read enough of now—was considered facile and popular-therefore-bad. For the majority of their history, Western universities reserved the study of literature to Greek and Roman literature, not anything so down-market as novels in your own language. As Terry Eagleton,[7] royal chronicler of anglo-literary study, describes, "In the early 1920s it was desperately unclear why English was worth studying at all; by the early 1930s it had become a question of why it was worth wasting your time on anything else." As soon as the once-revolutionary English gained centrality, it became (and largely remains) just as hostile towards the upstart creative writing as the Edwardian[8] philologists and classicists had been towards it. Genuine education of the kind, I hope, both Srigley and I seek (in our different ways), is always under threat, and there were never any good ol' days.* Try to find a soldier or doctor who doesn't think today's new recruits

---

of Muslims use the term in reference to personal spiritual striving, without violent associations.

6 *Richard Feynman* Nobel Prize-winning physicist (1918–88).

7 *Terry Eagleton* Influential literary theorist (b. 1943).

8 *Edwardian* The Edwardian era was the first decade of the twentieth century.

and med students have it too easy compared to their day. "Nostalgia," Douglas Coupland[9] warns, "is a weapon."

According to Horace,[10] good literature must both "delight and instruct." Why, if you want your lessons to be remembered, shouldn't your teaching strive for the same? Yes, simply offering student "customers" what they already want to buy is cowardly and ruinous. *Harry Potter* books and vampire television have already been consumed before university, and they should only ever be spices in it, never entrées. However, we always teach in a now, never a vacuum, and our now is wired, wired, wired. Smartphones and the online networks Srigley decries are the contemporary distractions for a humanity, not just a student body, that is always distracted. In the early 1700s, Cambridge professors lamented how much time students wasted in coffee houses. Student union buildings, my parents' generation tell me, were once giant games of bridge.* Srigley risks sounding like Saint Bernard of Clairvaux, the twelfth-century French abbot who wanted to shut down the new technology of flour mills. The mills were not only becoming popular with farmers, Clairvaux warned, but were attracting prostitutes. Curbing prostitution (or student e-distraction) won't happen by banning the mills (or digital networks) we can no longer live without.

The Pareto principle holds that 80 percent of effects usually come from 20 percent of causes (in everything from sales to sports teams to organizational productivity). Take any classroom of students anywhere in the privileged West, and, true, the majority of them may not be putting enough into their liberal arts educations to have their lives transformed. But no education, at any time, will transform everyone. Only a small fraction of students will be deepened and expanded by their studies. When briefly living by my pen outside academia, I supplemented my writing income as a supply teacher.* A gym class with grade-three students had me supervising a cooperative game involving a rubber chicken and several bean bags.* 20 percent of the students chased those bean bags like they were keys to save the planet. 80 percent wandered around. Same as it ever was.

(2016)

---

9 *Douglas Coupland* Canadian artist and novelist, perhaps best known for the bestseller *Generation X: Tales for an Accelerated Culture* (1991).

10 *Horace* Eminent Roman lyric poet (65–8 BCE).

Questions

1. To what extent—if at all—would your ideal post-secondary humanities classroom include technology? Why?
2. To what extent—if at all—would your ideal post-secondary humanities classroom address works of contemporary popular culture? Why?
3. Do you think students are less engaged with their educations today than they were before the existence of social media and other technologies? Why or why not?
4. Whetter argues against Srigley's assertion that there has been a great decline in post-secondary student attention. What points does Srigley make, and how does Whetter refute them? Whose argument do you think is stronger?

GEOFFREY YORK

COULD A LEGAL HORN "HARVEST" AND TRADE SAVE THE RHINO?

Four of the five species of rhinoceros are endangered; white rhinos, the only species not considered endangered, once faced extinction but have reached "near threatened" status only through extensive conservation efforts. Most of the world's rhino population lives in conservation areas, but habitat destruction is not the only threat to their survival. The illegal trade in rhinoceros horn, which is an extremely valuable commodity in China and Vietnam, resulted in the poaching of more than 1,300 rhinos in 2015 alone. How best to solve this problem is a subject of ongoing international controversy, and one proposed approach is to legalize and regulate the trade.

The following piece appeared in The Globe and Mail *online in September 2016 under the title "Can 'Harvesting' Its Horns Save the Rhino?" and later in the newspaper's print edition under the title that appears here. Its publication coincided with the fall 2016 conference of The Convention on International Trade in Endangered Species of Wild Fauna and Flora, where a proposal to legalize the trade of rhinoceros horn was being considered. The proposal was defeated shortly after this article was written.*

In the scrubby grasslands and thorn trees southwest of Johannesburg, the world's biggest rhino breeder is harvesting one of the planet's most lucrative products.

The stockpile of rhino horn on John Hume's ranch could be worth up to $300-million on the streets of Vietnam or China. With a retail value of up to $60,000 (U.S.) a kilogram, rhino horn has become more valuable than gold or cocaine.

Mr. Hume, a gruff, 74-year-old millionaire, owns a total of 1,410 rhinos—far more than most African countries these days. He has already harvested five tonnes of horn, which his workers cut off the animals with a hacksaw in a 20-minute operation that he compares to a trip to the dentist.

Animal-rights activists have denounced him as cruel and unethical, but Mr. Hume says he finds it unfair that he is portrayed as the "ogre" of the wildlife industry. He is convinced he is saving a magnificent species from extinction by pioneering a sustainable commercial use for its horns, while making the rhinos less of a lure for poachers.

His $300-million stockpile is just one of the prizes up for grabs in the 5
high-stakes negotiations that began this week at a global treaty convention in Johannesburg. The larger issue—and the crucial question for the fate of elephants, rhinos and other species—is whether to ban all trade in these animals and their products, or instead allow hunters and ranchers to find commercial value in them, a policy that could expand their habitat and population.

The global treaty, known as the Convention on International Trade in Endangered Species (CITES), sets the legally binding rules for the trade of animal and plant products for 183 nations. Its 12-day meeting, attended by about 3,500 delegates and observers, is the biggest-ever global wildlife conference, with a record number of nations and agenda items.

It's a crucial moment for Africa's wildlife. Rhinos and elephants have been decimated by illegal trafficking in recent years. A study released this week found a shocking loss of 111,000 elephants across Africa in the past decade, largely due to poaching for ivory.

Last week, just before visiting Canada, the Duke of Cambridge issued a passionate warning that elephants could become extinct within 25 years. At the same time, Africa lost a record total of 1,338 rhinos to poachers last year, leaving the future of that species hanging in the balance, too.

Now CITES must decide whether a limited commercial trade—the sale of existing stockpiles of ivory and rhino horn—could reduce poaching and generate revenue for conservation.

But behind this immediate challenge is a larger debate, involving many of 10
the same issues raised by the legalization of drugs or other products. Private rhino owners argue, for example, that prohibition has never succeeded against marijuana or alcohol. Legalization, they say, might even reduce the consumption of rhino horn, by forcing out the poachers and illegal traders and replacing them with a carefully regulated trade.

Their critics disagree. Even a small legal trade, they say, could open a Pandora's box* of unpredictable consequences. Instead of replacing the poached ivory and rhino horn with regulated products, a legal trade could stimulate new demand and make it easier for poachers to hide their illegal goods, they say.

Mr. Hume left his remote farm and drove into Johannesburg this week to watch the CITES debates. He was infuriated to see the animal-rights activists with the upper hand—which probably means a continued ban on the rhino trade.

"They are determined to keep the criminals earning all the money," he told *The Globe and Mail*. "It's incredibly frustrating how the world is determined to go on persecuting the rhino.

"What the world is making us do to the rhinos will make them go extinct—unless we change our policy and stop destroying the horns, which only raises the black-market price and makes it more profitable for the criminal."

15 This is the first time in nearly 20 years that the CITES conference has ventured into southern Africa, where the private hunting and ranching lobby is strongest. These are multimillion-dollar industries here, employing thousands of people and generating huge revenue for private companies and governments.

While the CITES delegates meet in a vast room of airport-hangar dimensions at the top of a convention centre in Johannesburg's affluent Sandton suburb, the real negotiations and strategy sessions are under way in the backrooms of the floors below.

In a lower-floor exhibition hall, the contrasts are extreme: pro-hunting and ranching groups sit uneasily in their booths, cheek-by-jowl* with the colourful stands of the animal-rights lobbyists. It's a political battleground, symbolized by the global furor over the Minnesota dentist who killed a Zimbabwean lion named Cecil last year. The private rhino owners, struggling to make their case, are launching a $70,000 campaign to get their message out on social media, where they are routinely beaten up by outraged animal-rights activists.

"I ALWAYS BACK THE UNDERDOG"

Mr. Hume made his fortune in business by developing South African holiday resorts. In 1992, he set up a game farm with antelope and buffalo. Then he decided that his life's work was to save the rhino from extinction. Today he owns more of the lumbering prehistoric-looking creatures than any other private farmer in the world—more, in fact, than any country except Namibia and South Africa.

"I have a fatal flaw in my personality—I always back the underdog, which invariably means that I back the loser," he says. "When I got to know rhinos, I found they had wonderful personalities, better than any other animal. You've got to get to know them. Even the black rhinos [considered more aggressive]—they're all bluster."

20 His ambition, he says, is to breed 200 rhinos every year. So far, since the 1990s, he has bred 960 in total, including white rhinos and the less common black rhinos.

But the cost of protecting his rhinos has soared exponentially as the poaching crisis grows worse. In 2007, barely a dozen rhinos were killed by poachers in South Africa. Since then, the illegal trade has swollen into a national disaster.

Poachers killed 1,175 rhinos here last year, fuelled by demand from newly affluent consumers in Vietnam and China, where rhino horn has become a status symbol and a trendy "cure" for hangovers and other ailments, ground up into a powder and consumed with water. (Rhino horn consists of keratin, which is similar to human hair and fingernails—and medically useless.)

Until five years ago, Mr. Hume didn't need to spend anything on security. Then he lost several rhinos to poachers, and today he is spending about $215,000 a month to guard his herd.

He says he just wants to recover these costs by selling rhino horn legally. But he can't sell the horn to Asian buyers because of the CITES rules, and he can't sell to domestic buyers because of a South African moratorium, imposed in 2009.

That could be about to change. This year, Mr. Hume and another rhino owner persuaded a South African court to quash the moratorium, on the grounds that the government had failed to consult owners before banning their products. The government has appealed to the highest court, the Constitutional Court, but is expected to lose—which would allow Mr. Hume to begin selling horns domestically.

"In South Africa, we have 400,000 ethnic Chinese," he says. "To me, the ethnic Chinese are a very good bet to target. It won't put jam on the bread, but it will certainly buy the bread—the cost of protecting my rhinos and letting them breed."

The domestic trade, he says, could become a "wedge" to force open the international trade, even if it leads to breaches of the legal ban on selling to Asia. "The animal-rights people say, 'Wouldn't it be terrible if someone smuggled one of my horns to Vietnam?' But if my horn gets to Vietnam, it might save an order that would otherwise go to the poachers. Why should I support laws that I believe are killing my rhinos?"

Mr. Hume is supported by activists such as Eugene Lapointe, a Canadian hunting enthusiast and former Ottawa bureaucrat who headed CITES from 1982 until he was forced out in 1990 by opponents who disliked his lobbying against the ivory-trade ban. Today, as head of a Swiss-based conservation trust, Mr. Lapointe remains an active lobbyist. Criticizing the "hysteria" over the ivory trade, he argues that the ban has failed to stop large-scale poaching. He describes the burning of ivory stockpiles, as Kenya has done, as a modern form of witch-burning—an irrational "inquisition."

At the age of 77, Mr. Lapointe still hunts moose and deer in the wilderness of Quebec, just as he did in his childhood. He calls for a balance between the competing uses of wildlife resources, including commercial uses. Ranchers such as Mr. Hume can play a major role in wildlife conservation, he says.

30 The South African government, swayed by the arguments of its hunting and ranching industries, came close to proposing a legalized rhino-horn trade at CITES this year. But at the last minute it backed away, and the legalization proposal is instead being made by tiny Swaziland, which has only 73 rhinos in its national parks and wildlife sanctuaries.

Ted Reilly is the legendary conservation guru who created Swaziland's national park system in the 1960s when much of its wildlife had vanished. He argues that the trade ban is failing. "The best way to emasculate criminals is to decriminalize their contraband," he says in the Swazi proposal to CITES.

A similar proposal is being made by Namibia and Zimbabwe to sell their ivory stockpiles. They have unofficial support from many other countries in southern Africa, where—unlike the rest of the continent—the elephant population has soared.

Some southern African governments even support the export of live elephants (China is the biggest buyer)—a practice that has become common in Zimbabwe. "Good conservation produces surpluses," Mr. Reilly told CITES this week.

In many of southern Africa's most famous game parks, the elephant population has grown too big, leading to massive damage to trees and bushes. Chobe National Park in Botswana, for example, is estimated to have as many as 120,000 elephants. As a result, its forests are so damaged that they "look like a war zone," according to Stan Burger, president of the Professional Hunters Association of South Africa. He argues that 3 to 5 per cent of southern Africa's elephants can be hunted without jeopardizing the population.

35 Professional hunters believe their revenue-generating activities have helped expand the wildlife habitat in southern Africa, by providing a financial incentive for protecting animals. Trophy hunting may have actually boosted the number of lions and other animals in southern Africa, encouraging farmers to turn their land into wildlife ranches.

CHARGES OF "ECO-COLONIALISM"

There is also a political dimension to the wildlife debates. Southern African governments, pushing for legalized trade, have complained that they are victims of "eco-colonialism" by wealthy developed countries that want to impose their restrictions on Africa. This argument is undermined, however, by the fact that 29 countries in the rest of Africa have banded together to seek a stronger ivory-trade ban.

The rhino and ivory legalization proposals are likely to be defeated when they reach a vote at CITES on Monday. But the battle is not over. In his speech to the conference, South African President Jacob Zuma spoke approvingly of the "sustainable use" of wildlife—one of the slogans of the hunting and ranching industry. His environment minister, Edna Molewa, told *The Globe* that her government could revive the rhino trade proposal in time for the next CITES conference in 2019.

Yet legalization would be a dangerous step into the unknown. When a South African government committee asked economists to study whether a legalized rhino-horn trade would stimulate new demand from Asian consumers, it couldn't get a clear answer. It admitted that legalization could lead to "increased uncertainty and risks."

A legalized ivory trade has the same risks. Its proponents tend to make unrealistic assumptions, according to Ross Harvey, a researcher at the South African Institute of International Affairs.

"Ivory tends to be treated as though it is perfectly renewable," he said in an academic analysis this year. "The major risk of this approach is that, if the sale of legally stockpiled ivory onto the market failed to reduce the price, and inadvertently expanded demand, species extinction could be quickened."

That may not be a risk the world is ready to take.

(2016)

Questions

1. What are the possible advantages to legalizing a trade in rhino horn? What are the possible disadvantages? What do you see as the best approach?
2. York compares the ban on rhino horn to drug and alcohol prohibition. How are these things similar? How are they different? How persuasive do you find the analogy?
3. York mentions several times that "animal-rights activists" oppose a legalized rhino horn trade, but does not explain this group's reasoning. Do some research of your own and find out why many activists oppose legalization. Evaluate the arguments you find.
4. How biased is this article? How can you tell?

NAOMI KLEIN

from LET THEM DROWN: THE VIOLENCE OF OTHERING[1] IN A WARMING WORLD

In May 2016, Naomi Klein delivered the Edward W. Said lecture in London. The lecture series, established in memory of the literary critic and activist Edward Said (1935–2003), aims to honour his work by examining the links between culture, politics, and ideology in the Middle East and across the world. Klein's lecture "Let Them Drown" is inspired by Said's incisive analysis of the intellectual underpinnings of colonialism. She takes a look at how the propensity for the powerful to exploit and disregard the less powerful is at the heart of many global crises today—including the crisis of climate change. The following excerpt is from the text of her lecture, which was printed in The London Review of Books *in June 2016.*

... Fossil fuels aren't the sole driver of climate change—there is industrial agriculture, and deforestation—but they are the biggest. And the thing about fossil fuels is that they are so inherently dirty and toxic that they require sacrificial people and places: people whose lungs and bodies can be sacrificed to work in the coal mines, people whose lands and water can be sacrificed to open-pit mining and oil spills. As recently as the 1970s, scientists advising the US government openly referred to certain parts of the country being designated "national sacrifice areas." Think of the mountains of Appalachia,[2] blasted off for coal mining—because so-called "mountain top removal" coal mining is cheaper than digging holes underground. There must be theories of othering to justify sacrificing an entire geography—theories about the people who lived there being so poor and backward that their lives and culture don't deserve

1 *Othering* Categorizing another person or group of people as alien from, and usually subordinate to, another more powerful group.

2 *Appalachia* Region in the Eastern United States comprising the central and southern range of the Appalachian mountains (from southern New York state to northern Alabama and Mississippi).

protection. After all, if you are a "hillbilly,"[3] who cares about your hills? Turning all that coal into electricity required another layer of othering too: this time for the urban neighbourhoods next door to the power plants and refineries. In North America, these are overwhelmingly communities of colour, black and Latino, forced to carry the toxic burden of our collective addiction to fossil fuels, with markedly higher rates of respiratory illnesses and cancers. It was in fights against this kind of "environmental racism" that the climate justice movement[4] was born.

Fossil fuel sacrifice zones dot the globe. Take the Niger Delta, poisoned with an Exxon Valdez-worth[5] of spilled oil every year, a process Ken Saro-Wiwa,[6] before he was murdered by his government, called "ecological genocide." The executions of community leaders, he said, were "all for Shell."[7] In my country, Canada, the decision to dig up the Alberta tar sands—a particularly heavy form of oil—has required the shredding of treaties with First Nations, treaties signed with the British Crown that guaranteed Indigenous peoples the right to continue to hunt, fish and live traditionally on their ancestral lands. It required it because these rights are meaningless when the land is desecrated, when the rivers are polluted and the moose and fish are riddled with tumours. And it gets worse: Fort McMurray—the town at the centre of the tar sands boom, where many of the workers live and where much of the money is spent—is currently

---

3 *hillbilly* Pejorative term for a person living in a remote, mountainous area (particularly for those living in Appalachia).

4 *climate justice movement* Movement that sees global warming as a political and ethical issue rather than simply as a physical one. The movement believes that those least responsible for climate change are the ones who will most quickly and severely suffer its consequences.

5 *Exxon Valdez-worth* The *Exxon Valdez* oil spill took place in Alaska in 1989, when the *Exxon Valdez* tanker struck a reef and spilled 11 to 38 million gallons of crude oil over the following days. It is considered one of the worst human-caused environmental disasters in history.

6 *Ken Saro-Wiwa* Nigerian writer and environmental activist. Saro-Wiwa (1941–95) was a member of the Ogoni people, whose homeland in the Niger Delta has been degraded and poisoned by oil dumping as a result of crude oil extraction. During his non-violent campaign against the environmental destruction of the Niger Delta, Saro-Wiwa was accused of masterminding the murder of Ogoni chiefs at a meeting with government officials, and hanged after an unjust trial.

7 *Shell* The Shell Oil Company is a subsidiary of Royal Dutch Shell, the multinational oil company responsible for oil extraction in the Niger Delta. Some of the witnesses who testified against Saro-Wiwa later admitted to having been bribed by Shell.

in an infernal blaze.[8] It's that hot and that dry. And this has something to do with what is being mined there.

Even without such dramatic events, this kind of resource extraction is a form of violence, because it does so much damage to the land and water that it brings about the end of a way of life, a death of cultures that are inseparable from the land. Severing Indigenous people's connection to their culture used to be state policy in Canada—imposed through the forcible removal of Indigenous children from their families to boarding schools where their language and cultural practices were banned, and where physical and sexual abuse were rampant. A recent truth and reconciliation report called it "cultural genocide." The trauma associated with these layers of forced separation—from land, from culture, from family—is directly linked to the epidemic of despair ravaging so many First Nations communities today. On a single Saturday night in April, in the community of Attawapiskat—population 2000—11 people tried to take their own lives. Meanwhile, DeBeers runs a diamond mine on the community's traditional territory; like all extractive projects, it had promised hope and opportunity. "Why don't the people just leave?," the politicians and pundits ask. But many do. And that departure is linked, in part, to the thousands of Indigenous women in Canada who have been murdered or gone missing, often in big cities. Press reports rarely make the connection between violence against women and violence against the land—often to extract fossil fuels—but it exists. Every new government comes to power promising a new era of respect for Indigenous rights. They don't deliver, because Indigenous rights, as defined by the United Nations Declaration on the Rights of Indigenous People, include the right to refuse extractive projects—even when those projects fuel national economic growth. And that's a problem because growth is our religion, our way of life. So even Canada's hunky and charming new prime minister[9] is bound and determined to build new tar sands pipelines, against the express wishes of Indigenous communities who don't want to risk their water, or participate in the further destabilizing of the climate.

Fossil fuels require sacrifice zones: they always have. And you can't have a system built on sacrificial places and sacrificial people unless intellectual theories that justify their sacrifice exist and persist: from Manifest Destiny to Terra Nullius to Orientalism, from backward hillbillies to backward Indians.[10]

---

8 *currently in an infernal blaze* In May 2016 the largest and costliest wildfire in Alberta history began just southwest of Fort McMurray and spread across northern Alberta into Saskatchewan. The fire was declared under control on 5 June 2016.

9 *new prime minister* Justin Trudeau assumed office as Prime Minister of Canada in November 2015.

10 *Manifest Destiny* Nineteenth-century belief that American expansion from coast to coast was not only possible but destined to happen. This attitude supported settlement in

We often hear climate change blamed on "human nature," on the inherent greed and short-sightedness of our species. Or we are told we have altered the earth so much and on such a planetary scale that we are now living in the Anthropocene[11]—the age of humans. These ways of explaining our current circumstances have a very specific, if unspoken meaning: that humans are a single type, that human nature can be essentialized to the traits that created this crisis. In this way, the systems that certain humans created, and other humans powerfully resisted, are completely let off the hook. Capitalism, colonialism, patriarchy—those sorts of systems. Diagnoses like this erase the very existence of human systems that organized life differently: systems that insist that humans must think seven generations in the future; must be not only good citizens but also good ancestors; must take no more than they need and give back to the land in order to protect and augment the cycles of regeneration. These systems existed and still exist, but they are erased every time we say that the climate crisis is a crisis of "human nature" and that we are living in the "age of man." And they come under very real attack when megaprojects are built, like the Gualcarque hydroelectric dams in Honduras, a project which, among other things, took the life of the land defender Berta Cáceres,[12] who was assassinated in March.

Some people insist that it doesn't have to be this bad. We can clean up resource 5
extraction, we don't need to do it the way it's been done in Honduras and the Niger Delta and the Alberta tar sands. Except that we are running out of cheap and easy ways to get at fossil fuels, which is why we have seen the rise of

---

the west, the removal of Aboriginal people, and war with Mexico; *Terra Nullius* Latin: no-one's land. The term in international law refers to territory that has never been subject to a state and can thus be acquired through occupation; *Orientalism* View that the cultures of Asia and the Middle East share a variety of characteristics, and that it is thus appropriate to class them together, usually in contrast to Western or "Occidental" societies, which are considered superior according to this ideology. Edward Said famously analyzed these thought patterns and their consequences in his influential book *Orientalism* (1978); *Indians* Term for Aboriginal peoples that is considered pejorative in Canada (though it is also used in Canadian government documents).

11 *Anthropocene* The boundaries of a geological epoch are determined by significant global changes in the rock layers associated with a given time period; an epoch is typically millions of years long. The term "anthropocene" is used by a growing number of scientists to suggest that the environmental impact of recent technologies is so great it will be evident in the geologic record.

12 *Berta Cáceres* Honduran environmental activist who received the Goldman Environmental Prize in 2015 for successfully pressuring the world's largest dam builder to pull out of the Agua Zarc Dam. She was assassinated in her home in 2016 after years of threats to her life.

fracking[13] and tar sands extraction in the first place. This, in turn, is starting to challenge the original Faustian pact[14] of the industrial age: that the heaviest risks would be outsourced, offloaded, onto the other—the periphery abroad and inside our own nations. It's something that is becoming less and less possible. Fracking is threatening some of the most picturesque parts of Britain as the sacrifice zone expands, swallowing up all kinds of places that imagined themselves safe. So this isn't just about gasping at how ugly the tar sands are. It's about acknowledging that there is no clean, safe, non-toxic way to run an economy powered by fossil fuels. There never was.

There is an avalanche of evidence that there is no peaceful way either. The trouble is structural. Fossil fuels, unlike renewable forms of energy such as wind and solar, are not widely distributed but highly concentrated in very specific locations, and those locations have a bad habit of being in other people's countries. Particularly that most potent and precious of fossil fuels: oil. This is why the project of Orientalism, of othering Arab and Muslim people, has been the silent partner of our oil dependence from the start—and inextricable, therefore, from the blowback that is climate change. If nations and peoples are regarded as other—exotic, primitive, bloodthirsty, as Said documented in the 1970s—it is far easier to wage wars and stage coups when they get the crazy idea that they should control their own oil in their own interests. In 1953 it was the British-US collaboration to overthrow the democratically elected government of Muhammad Mossadegh after he nationalised the Anglo-Iranian Oil Company (now BP). In 2003, exactly fifty years later, it was another UK-US co-production—the illegal invasion and occupation of Iraq. The reverberations from each intervention continue to jolt our world, as do the reverberations from the successful burning of all that oil. The Middle East is now squeezed in the pincer of violence caused by fossil fuels, on the one hand, and the impact of burning those fossil fuels on the other.

In his latest book, *The Conflict Shoreline*, the Israeli architect Eyal Weizman has a groundbreaking take on how these forces are intersecting. The main way we've understood the border of the desert in the Middle East and North Africa, he explains, is the so-called "aridity line," areas where there is on average 200 millimetres of rainfall a year, which has been considered the minimum for growing cereal crops on a large scale without irrigation. These meteorological boundaries aren't fixed: they have fluctuated for various

---

13 *fracking* Drilling down into the earth and then injecting high-pressure water, sand, and chemicals at the rock to release gas trapped inside. The process has disastrous effects on the environment, poisoning water and air, as well as triggering earthquakes.

14 *Faustian pact* In German legend, Faust makes a pact with the Devil, offering his soul in return for power, knowledge, and worldly pleasures.

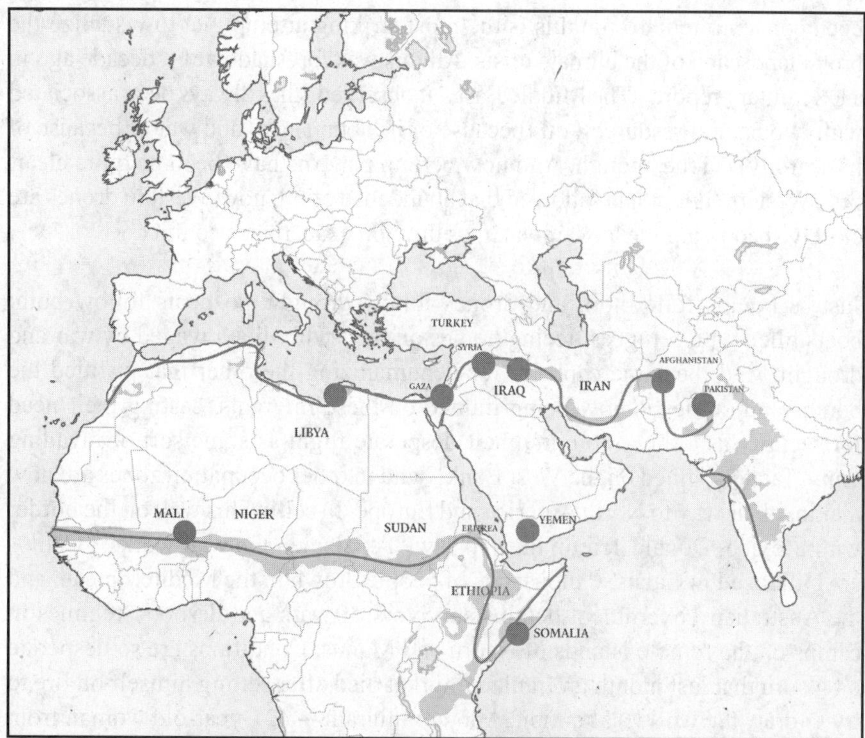

reasons, whether it was Israel's attempts to "green the desert" pushing them in one direction or cyclical drought expanding the desert in the other. And now, with climate change, intensifying drought can have all kinds of impacts along this line. Weizman points out that the Syrian border city of Daraa falls directly on the aridity line. Daraa is where Syria's deepest drought on record brought huge numbers of displaced farmers in the years leading up to the outbreak of Syria's civil war, and it's where the Syrian uprising broke out in 2011. Drought wasn't the only factor in bringing tensions to a head. But the fact that 1.5 million people were internally displaced in Syria as a result of the drought clearly played a role. The connection between water and heat stress and conflict is a recurring, intensifying pattern all along the aridity line: all along it you see places marked by drought, water scarcity, scorching temperatures and military conflict—from Libya to Palestine, to some of the bloodiest battlefields in Afghanistan and Pakistan.

But Weizman also discovered what he calls an "astounding coincidence." When you map the targets of Western drone strikes onto the region, you see that "many of these attacks—from South Waziristan through northern Yemen, Somalia, Mali, Iraq, Gaza and Libya—are directly on or close to the 200 mm aridity line." The … dots on the map above represent some of the areas where strikes have been concentrated. To me this is the most striking attempt yet to visualize the brutal landscape of the climate crisis. All this was foreshadowed a decade ago in a US military report. "The Middle East," it observed, "has always been associated with two natural resources, oil (because of its abundance) and water (because of its scarcity)." True enough. And now certain patterns have become quite clear: first, Western fighter jets followed that abundance of oil; now, Western drones are closely shadowing the lack of water, as drought exacerbates conflict.

Just as bombs follow oil, and drones follow drought, so boats follow both: boats filled with refugees fleeing homes on the aridity line ravaged by war and drought. And the same capacity for dehumanizing the other that justified the bombs and drones is now being trained on these migrants, casting their need for security as a threat to ours, their desperate flight as some sort of invading army. Tactics refined on the West Bank[15] and in other occupation zones are now making their way to North America and Europe. In selling his wall on the border with Mexico, Donald Trump likes to say: "Ask Israel, the wall works." Camps are bulldozed in Calais,[16] thousands of people drown in the Mediterranean, and the Australian government detains survivors of wars and despotic regimes in camps on the remote islands of Nauru and Manus. Conditions are so desperate on Nauru that last month an Iranian migrant died after setting himself on fire to try to draw the world's attention. Another migrant—a 21-year-old woman from Somalia—set herself on fire a few days later. Malcolm Turnbull, the prime minister, warns that Australians "cannot be misty-eyed about this" and "have to be very clear and determined in our national purpose." It's worth bearing Nauru in mind the next time a columnist in a Murdoch paper declares, as Katie Hopkins[17] did last year, that it's time for Britain "to get Australian. Bring on the gunships, force migrants back to their shores and burn the boats." In another bit of symbolism Nauru is one of the Pacific Islands very vulnerable to sea-level rise. Its residents, after seeing their homes turned into prisons for others, will very possibly have to migrate themselves. Tomorrow's climate refugees have been recruited into service as today's prison guards.

---

15 *West Bank* Territory west of the Jordan river, bordered by Israel and Jordan; the territory is disputed between Israel and Palestine and is currently under Israeli military occupation.

16 *Camps ... in Calais* The so-called "Calais Jungle" was a refugee camp in Calais, France. In February 2016 the French government began evicting refugees; by the end of October 2016 the camp was dismantled.

17 *Murdoch paper* Newspaper owned by Rupert Murdoch, media mogul in charge of the News Corporation conglomerate; *Katie Hopkins* Newspaper columnist for *The Sun* (a paper owned by Rupert Murdoch).

We need to understand that what is happening on Nauru, and what is 10
happening to it, are expressions of the same logic. A culture that places so little value on black and brown lives that it is willing to let human beings disappear beneath the waves, or set themselves on fire in detention centres, will also be willing to let the countries where black and brown people live disappear beneath the waves, or desiccate in the arid heat. When that happens, theories of human hierarchy—that we must take care of our own first—will be marshalled to rationalize these monstrous decisions. We are making this rationalization already, if only implicitly. Although climate change will ultimately be an existential threat to all of humanity, in the short term we know that it does discriminate, hitting the poor first and worst, whether they are abandoned on the rooftops of New Orleans during Hurricane Katrina[18] or whether they are among the 36 million who according to the UN are facing hunger due to drought in Southern and East Africa.

This is an emergency, a present emergency, not a future one, but we aren't acting like it. The Paris Agreement commits to keeping warming below 2°c. It's a target that is beyond reckless. When it was unveiled in Copenhagen in 2009, the African delegates called it "a death sentence." The slogan of several low-lying island nations is "1.5 to stay alive." At the last minute, a clause was added to the Paris Agreement that says countries will pursue "efforts to limit the temperature increase to 1.5°c." Not only is this non-binding but it is a lie: we are making no such efforts. The governments that made this promise are now pushing for more fracking and more tar sands development—which are utterly incompatible with 2°c, let alone 1.5°c. This is happening because the wealthiest people in the wealthiest countries in the world think they are going to be OK, that someone else is going to eat the biggest risks, that even when climate change turns up on their doorstep, they will be taken care of.

When they're wrong things get even uglier. We had a vivid glimpse into that future when the floodwaters rose in England last December and January, inundating 16,000 homes. These communities weren't only dealing with the wettest December on record. They were also coping with the fact that the government has waged a relentless attack on the public agencies, and the local councils, that are on the front lines of flood defence. So understandably, there were many who wanted to change the subject away from that failure. Why, they asked, is Britain spending so much money on refugees and foreign aid

18 *Hurricane Katrina* More than 1,200 people died in this 2005 hurricane, many of them as a result of flooding in New Orleans that occurred because the city's floodwalls had been cheaply constructed. Most of the people who died were poor and black, and the federal government was criticized for its slow response to the crisis.

when it should be taking care of its own? "Never mind foreign aid," we read in the *Daily Mail*. "What about national aid?" "Why," a *Telegraph* editorial demanded, "should British taxpayers continue to pay for flood defences abroad when the money is needed here?" I don't know—maybe because Britain invented the coal-burning steam engine and has been burning fossil fuels on an industrial scale longer than any nation on Earth? But I digress. The point is that this could have been a moment to understand that we are all affected by climate change, and must take action together and in solidarity with one another. It wasn't, because climate change isn't just about things getting hotter and wetter: under our current economic and political model, it's about things getting meaner and uglier.

The most important lesson to take from all this is that there is no way to confront the climate crisis as a technocratic problem, in isolation. It must be seen in the context of austerity[19] and privatization, of colonialism and militarism, and of the various systems of othering needed to sustain them all. The connections and intersections between them are glaring, and yet so often resistance to them is highly compartmentalized. The anti-austerity people rarely talk about climate change, the climate change people rarely talk about war or occupation. We rarely make the connection between the guns that take black lives on the streets of US cities and in police custody and the much larger forces that annihilate so many black lives on arid land and in precarious boats around the world.

Overcoming these disconnections—strengthening the threads tying together our various issues and movements—is, I would argue, the most pressing task of anyone concerned with social and economic justice. It is the only way to build a counterpower sufficiently robust to win against the forces protecting the highly profitable but increasingly untenable status quo. Climate change acts as an accelerant to many of our social ills—inequality, wars, racism—but it can also be an accelerant for the opposite, for the forces working for economic and social justice and against militarism. Indeed the climate crisis—by presenting our species with an existential threat and putting us on a firm and unyielding science-based deadline—might just be the catalyst we need to knit together a great many powerful movements, bound together by a belief in the inherent worth and value of all people and united by a rejection of the sacrifice zone mentality, whether it applies to peoples or places. We face so many overlapping and intersecting crises that we can't afford to fix them one at a time. We need integrated solutions, solutions that radically bring down emissions, while creating huge numbers of good, unionized jobs and delivering meaningful justice

19 *austerity* Economic policies that aim to reduce government deficits, for example by cutting spending and raising taxes.

to those who have been most abused and excluded under the current extractive economy.…

(2016)

Questions

1. What are sacrifice zones? Give an example of a sacrifice zone discussed by Klein. How do the corporations and governments involved justify its existence?
2. What is the "aridity line," and why is it significant?
3. What does Klein argue we should do to best address the problem of climate change?
4. What is "environmental racism"? What can be done in response to it?
5. How is our "religion" of growth preventing Canada from granting key rights to First Nations people?
6. Klein claims that we "face so many overlapping and intersecting crises that we can't afford to fix them one at a time." Is it in your view realistic to try to achieve this kind of sweeping change? Given the serious threat posed by climate change and the current world order, is it realistic to aim for anything else?

Charlotte McDonald-Gibson

The Human Face of the Refugee Crisis

The European refugee crisis is one of the defining issues of the 2010s. As war and oppressive regimes in the Middle East and North Africa make living conditions untenable for many citizens, the number of refugees fleeing by sea across the Mediterranean or by land over Southeastern Europe has increased dramatically. In 2015 alone, the EU member states received 1.2 million first-time asylum applications, more than twice the number of the previous year. The European Union has struggled to cope with the crisis, and right-wing reaction to increased immigration has had political ramifications across the world.

In the following extract from Charlotte McDonald-Gibson's Cast Away: Stories of Survival from Europe's Refugee Crisis *(2016), a woman referred to as Sina (not her real name) makes a perilous journey to Greece from her home country of Eritrea. Eritrea is a nation on the horn of Africa, bordering the Red Sea. According to Human Rights Watch, it has one of the worst human rights records in the world. Sina's story was first published in* The Guardian *in May 2016.*

2012

Dani was unlike anyone Sina had ever met in Eritrea. Here, people tended to keep their thoughts, feelings, talents and any dissenting opinions to themselves. Spies lurked in every classroom, every workplace, sometimes in your own home. People heard rumours that life was similar in North Korea,[1]

1 *North Korea* The Democratic People's Republic of Korea has a centralized one-party government that exercises a great deal of control over its people, including the media. The government controls where people live, if they travel, and what they wear and eat. Mass surveillance monitors all forms of communication, including text messages and cell phone calls.

but at least the rest of the world knew how awful that country was. In Eritrea you just tried to stay under the radar and out of prison.

But Dani was the kind of man who could not contain his intelligence, and Sina was smitten from the moment she joined his drawing class in her second year of a chemical engineering degree. Now he was asking Sina to spend the rest of her life with him, and suddenly everything made sense. Optimism seized the young woman. This marriage would be a genuine choice in a society where self-determination was rare. In Eritrea, no one got to make their own decisions about their life. You couldn't choose where you lived, where you worked, which God you worshipped, which political group you supported, what you owned, or where you travelled. It was all decided by a dictatorship still using two painful wars with neighbouring Ethiopia as an excuse to keep the entire population in perpetual servitude. But Sina could only see the good in the world as she imagined her and Dani's future together, despite the threat of indefinite military service hanging over the couple.

President Isaias Afewerki—a veteran of the independence struggle, who took power when Eritrea became a state in 1993 and never gave it up—introduced compulsory military service for all men and women in 1995, notionally to protect the young state from future threats and promote self-sufficiency. Everyone in the nation of 5 million people would be drafted, starting with gruelling boot camp in the last year of high school, then returning to the ranks upon graduation from school or university. Not completing your service or deserting was one of the many crimes that could get you locked up in the nation's jail network for an indefinite period of time, or even killed. Never mind that military service could amount to a life sentence of torture, abuse, arbitrary detention and forced labour.

Sina thrived at school, and had won a 21-inch flatscreen TV as a reward for coming top of her year in all subjects. That didn't exempt her from life as a soldier, however, and in her 12th-grade year—at the age of 16—she was torn away from her family and sent to Sawa. The short, melodic name of the military base belied the fear it inspired in Eritrea's youth.

Stripped of everything they knew, and abused—mentally, physically and, 5
for some female conscripts, sexually—they either broke down with psychological problems they would bear for years to come, or if they were strong enough they quickly adapted to survive. Sina turned out to be a strong one, and for the rest of the year of study and service, her mindset shifted. *I am not a student, I am a soldier.* In this way she got through it. And after the pain of Sawa, university was a relief.

Chemical engineering was fascinating, friends came easily, her teachers—including Dani—encouraged her, and she got a paid part-time job at a western pharmaceutical company—albeit in secret as she did not have government permission. Just like in high school, Sina shone at university, receiving her degree with a distinction. After graduation in 2009, the government decided she would be one of the rare few spared from active military duty, and allowed her to practise her profession.

For Sina, home would now be a dusty town in northern Eritrea, where she would work as a chemical engineer for a government firm. But she felt blessed: at least she could put her intellect to use working as a supervisor of a small team. Her job was still considered part of her national service, so for working 12-hour days with no breaks she got paid 450 nakfa ($30) a month. Her future husband had not been so fortunate in his career. He was a fully qualified civil engineer and a talented teacher, but had been pulled out of the university when Sina was in her third year and told to report to the barracks for his new life as a soldier.

As the year went on, his supervisor became a little more relaxed, and turned a blind eye when Dani started to work part time as a private teacher. The young couple still had to depend on their parents. But when Dani proposed, Sina could imagine a future. Leaving Eritrea never entered her mind.

2013

After months of excited planning, Sina and Dani's wedding day finally arrived. They had decided on a traditional Eritrean ceremony, and on 17 July 2013, more than 300 friends and family gathered to watch the young couple exchange their vows.

10 But when Sina glanced around the room, she couldn't help but notice the absences. Many friends had already fled Eritrea and were living in refugee camps in Sudan and Kenya. Some had travelled further afield to try to escape the long arm of the Eritrean security apparatus. No matter where you went in sub-Saharan Africa, if you had left Eritrea illegally the state could reach well outside national borders and drag you back for a cruel punishment. Security forces in at least four countries had colluded in the forced repatriation of Eritreans, so many people had decided to try and reach Europe, the only place where they would feel safe.

Not that Sina would ever discuss these disappearances. That alone could be enough to be thrown into a cell. The most brutal retribution was reserved for those the government deemed traitors. A simple slip-up like asking the wrong person about a missing friend or discussing general government policy could be enough to warrant the accusation of betraying your country. Other "crimes" included practising a banned religion, plotting to leave the country, wandering too close to an external border, working for a foreign company, or simply being related to someone suspected of deviant behaviour.

Given the number of people President Afewerki was locking away, there was a need for creativity when it came to the logistics of incarceration. The official prisons were supplemented with secret facilities that included caves, holes, open-air camps and converted old buildings. A particularly horrific innovation was the underground dungeon, a metal shipping container measuring 20ft by 8ft buried in the desert. No light could seep in, temperatures reached 44C, and screams would echo around the metal box, the sound unable to penetrate the soil above.

Conditions in all facilities were inhuman, with inmates crammed into small spaces with no toilets, forced to sleep in their own waste. Sickness was common, and many people died of illness. Others took their own lives.

Imprisonment was an everyday occurrence—everyone knew someone who had disappeared—and that was exactly how the regime wanted it. Fear was its most powerful weapon, and it sowed it with expertise.

So deserting was not an option for Dani. Instead, the couple decided to ask the military to transfer Dani to a post near Sina's office in the north of the country. The request was turned down. Dani's supervisor had another plan for him. He was to be sent 500km south of Asmara[2] to take up his new post as a guard on the border with the neighbouring nation of Djibouti.

Sina and Dani spent just two and a half precious months together as man and wife before Dani boarded a bus down to the southern city of Assab. There he would spend his days standing in the desert heat on the sun-baked southern plains of Eritrea, notionally keeping watch to prevent some of the tens of thousands of border jumpers escaping to Djibouti and other neighbouring countries.

2014

Sina and Dani tried so hard to play by Eritrea's arbitrary rules, but it wasn't enough. After a few months at the border, Dani disappeared. It was only when he contracted an intestinal disorder in the filth and misery of his jail cell and was transported to Asmara for medical treatment that Sina learned what had happened.

Although Dani was an Orthodox Christian, some of his friends were Pentecostal—a banned religion in Eritrea—and one evening they were holding a prayer meeting in a room in the building where Dani lived. Someone tipped off the military police, and every person living in the building was arrested and thrown in jail, no matter what religion they practised.

When Dani's treatment at the Asmara hospital ended in early summer 2014, he walked out the door and home to his wife. With limited resources and

2 *Asmara* Capital city of Eritrea.

plenty of deserters to worry about, it would take a few months for the authorities in the south to realize that Dani was missing. Sina was determined to enjoy that time together, and for a while they were able to live under the illusion that they were just like any other young couple in the world.

20 They could enjoy long walks together again, meals in Asmara's restaurants, time spent with their brothers, sisters, cousins and parents. One day in August, Dani and Sina went to the clinic together. The doctor smiled. They were expecting a baby. It was a bittersweet moment. Happiness at the growing life was tempered by all the problems they would have to overcome to be able to give their baby a safe and secure home.

It was the summer of 2014. Their baby was due on 15 April the following year. They had nine months to try to make a future worthy of the tiny life they had created. But every moment of joy was overshadowed by fear. The military police had finally started to look for Dani. If he returned to prison, he would never be released, and Sina would have to bring up their child alone. She too could be jailed for aiding a deserter. Going on the run was their only choice.

2015

Their smuggler had driven them with relative ease through the border to Sudan and on to South Sudan, but the only way across the border to Uganda was on foot. Sina didn't complain. All those marches during military service and the hardships of life in the field as a chemical engineer had prepared her well, and she followed Dani and the smuggler through thick forest tracts for two hours. When they reached Uganda, she gratefully sank into the car that would take them to the capital.

Sina and Dani contacted a smuggler called Kibrat. For $14,000, he would prepare everything for their passage to Turkey, but he warned it could take a while. The weeks passed, and Sina's belly grew. After two months, Kibrat called. Their fake passports were ready, and the couple could continue their journey and fly to Istanbul that coming Sunday—16 March. His call came just in time: Sina was eight months pregnant and starting to worry that she would never reach a safe place in time to give birth.

Then on Saturday, Kibrat called back. There had been a change of plan. Sina would have to fly alone and Dani would follow a few days later. "You have to go now," he said. "You are pregnant, and very pregnant people can't fly."

25 His advice seemed to make sense, so on Sunday morning Dani and Sina got into a car to go to the airport. Just before the passenger drop-off point, Kibrat pulled over—Sina had to enter the airport alone. The couple held each other by the roadside. "Take care of yourself," Dani said. Sina just smiled—she would see him again in a few days. Her car was waiting.

When she landed, an Eritrean smuggler called Mehari was waiting for her at the airport. For a week, Sina stayed in Mehari's filthy apartment waiting for Dani. But Dani never came.

Kibrat had stopped answering his phone. After a week, his number was disconnected. He had disappeared with the money, and Dani was left alone and penniless in Kampala, just a voice at the end of the phone promising Sina he was doing everything he could to get back to her. Within a week, the promise of their new life together which had begun with such hope on New Year's Day was beginning to collapse.

When Mehari arrived at the apartment in Istanbul on 19 April and told her to get ready to travel to Greece, Sina was terrified. She was past her due date and feared going into labour at sea, but Mehari was aggressive and left her with no choice.

When Sina looked out to sea [having arrived by bus at the Turkish port of Marmaris], she saw a wooden sailing boat about 30 metres long approach the beach. For a moment, she could not speak—it looked so old, its naked masts reaching into the darkness and rocking the boat back and forth in the low swell.

Mehari promised that a large ship with lifejackets was waiting just off-shore, so Sina stepped aboard. Perhaps in her heart Sina always knew there was not going to be another ship. She had to believe the lie to get on the boat, as there was no one to accompany her on a two-hour trek back over the hills to the nearest road, to drive her for 10 hours back to Istanbul, and to give her a place to stay and to look after her when the child arrived.

When they cast off, Sina looked around her: people were doubled over and vomiting in response to the violent rocking and the stink of rotten fish. As the boat tipped from side to side, the bodies crammed in the small space would skid in the stagnant water, and the sick and the stench was overwhelming. Sina put her hands over her face, blocking out the sight, the sounds, the smell. *If I start to vomit, I will deliver my baby here.* All she could do was focus on keeping her baby inside her for a few hours more.

Eventually, the flickering bulb that threw ghoulish shadows across the decaying wood went out. Darkness enveloped the hold just as people started to notice the seawater seeping through the planks. Sina put her hand to the floor. Cold water pooled around the tire where she sat. One after another the passengers realized that calamity was approaching, and cries of terror spread back and forth through the throng of people, an anguished call and response. *We are almost dead,* Sina thought.

The sailing boat was disintegrating beneath her feet: it had been ripped in two when it had attempted to turn at speed in the rough conditions. Huge waves tore parts of the boat away, and all Sina could hear was the sound of splintering wood—a racking, shuddering sound—and the cries of the people flinging themselves into the water. The coast was in sight, but it didn't matter now. Sina grabbed on to a rope dangling by her hand, and thought of Dani. Sina looked out to sea and felt the wood beneath her feet give way and slide into the water, taking her with it. First she went down, then up again, desperately trying to keep hold of the slippery rope. Then there was nothing to hold on to any more. She was in the water. Sina heard a voice. "Please help us, we have a nine-month-pregnant woman, help her, she is here." Then everything went black.

Antonis Deligiorgis, a sergeant in the Greek army, had just dropped his six-year-old son and 12-year-old daughter off at school and was having a coffee by Zefiros beach on the Greek island of Rhodes. His eyes lazily drifted over the brilliant blue of the Mediterranean, a little rough that day but still beautiful in the early spring sunshine. He had seen plenty of suffering that year: Antonis had worked night-time rescues, saving people from the fragile inflatable dinghies to which they had entrusted their lives. But on 20 April at 9.30 am, he was off duty, and enjoying spending time with his wife.

He didn't see the tall sailing ship that had swerved in a tight turn to avoid the rocks on approach to Zefiros, the force of the manoeuvre snapping the craft in the middle. But by the time the sirens grew louder and crowds had gathered on the port, he was up and ready to do what he could. "Whoever is a good swimmer can help," a passing police officer shouted.

When Antonis reached the wreck, the water was slick with oil and wood, and all around him screams battled to be heard over the roar of the waves. He saw wild eyes filled with terror; he saw panicked people vomiting into the water, their bodies trying to process the exhaustion, the mouthfuls of seawater, the fear of death. One by one, Antonis grabbed thrashing bodies and dragged them through the water to the shore: children, women, an old man missing a leg.

A heavily pregnant woman clung to a life jacket. She was close to the rocks, and her exhausted eyes darted with fear as she tried to battle the swell dragging her towards sharp crags. The waves had already churned up the wood and glass from the broken boat and ground them into her flesh. Antonis reached Sina just in time, pushing her into the arms of two men on the shore. "Thank you, thank you," Sina repeated over and over again, "you are saving my life."

Ninety-three Eritreans and Syrians were rescued that day, but Antonis remembered the ones who were lost. Most people had survived because the boat broke up in daylight within yards of the Greek coastline, but three people perished: a Syrian man who died of a heart attack, and an Eritrean woman and her six-year-old son.

Sina was taken to the hospital in Rhodes, where she was treated for cuts all over her body. Doctors kept her under observation for a couple of days while her body regained its strength, then took her to the operating theatre for a caesarean section. On 23 April, Sina gave birth to a healthy baby boy. Andonis Georgis—named after his saviour—was born at 9pm weighing 9.9lb, strong like his mother and destined to keep her going through the days ahead.

On 20 July, Dani finally left Kampala and went with a smuggler back through South Sudan and into Sudan, renting a hotel room in Khartoum. He called the next day from the Sudanese capital, and told Sina that he had an appointment with the Greek embassy there in a few days' time. Soon they would be together again, and he would be able to hold his son in his arms for the first time.

On the morning of Sunday 26 July, Sina got up [by now in Athens], fed Andonis and went for breakfast in the hotel restaurant. Just like they did every other morning, many of the regular guests asked after Dani. They were so used to seeing this cheerful young woman tending her baby with one hand and clutching her mobile phone in the other, chatting away to her husband as if he were right there beside her.

But that morning, Sina was not her usual sunny self. She had not spoken to Dani in five days. The last news she had had from him was on 21 July, when he had arrived in Khartoum and called to say he had an appointment at the Greek embassy. Then there was silence. His phone just rang and rang.

(2016)

Questions

1. How does Sina's story affect your understanding of the refugee crisis in Europe?
2. In your opinion, what responsibilities do wealthier, more stable countries have toward refugees from autocratic and war-torn countries?
3. What has been Canada's response to the refugee crisis? How do we compare with Germany, the United Kingdom, or Italy?
4. What techniques does the writer use to make Sina's story vivid and immediate?

Adam Gopnik

Does *Mein Kampf* Remain a Dangerous Book?

Adolf Hitler published Mein Kampf *in 1925, at which time he was the leader of the Nazi party but the Nazis had not yet taken control of the German government. Part memoir and part political treatise, the book articulates the abhorrent anti-Semitic ideology he would later use to justify the Holocaust. For 70 years after World War II, the Finance Ministry of the State of Bavaria managed Hitler's intellectual property rights, and chose to prevent the book's republication in Germany. In January 2016, the copyright for* Mein Kampf *expired, and Germany faced a difficult decision regarding whether to lift the ban on Hitler's text. In the end, the German government chose to publish the book, but only in a heavily annotated scholarly edition. Weighing 12 pounds and with 3,700 footnotes, the edition carefully exposes the ideology behind Hitler's words and the genocidal results of his "new world order." In the months following its publication, it became a bestseller in Germany. Adam Gopnik's "Does* Mein Kampf *Remain a Dangerous Book?" was originally published in* The New Yorker.

There was a lot said last week about the reemergence, in Germany, of Adolf Hitler's *Mein Kampf* (*My Struggle*)—which just became legal to publish and sell there, for the first time since the end of the Second World War, albeit in a heavily hedged "scholarly" edition.[1] Did providing a public place for the autobiographical testament of the Nazi dictator, written when he was briefly imprisoned in Bavaria, in the nineteen-twenties, in some way legitimize it, people asked, even if the text was surrounded by a trench work of scholarly addenda designed to italicize its lies and manias?

1 *hedged "scholarly" edition* Heavily annotated academic version that exposes the ideologies at work in the text.

I read *Mein Kampf* right through for the first time last year, while working on a piece about Timothy Snyder's history of the Holocaust as it happened in the Slavic and Baltic states during the Second World War. (Snyder reads Hitler in a somewhat original and provocative way, derived in part from his reading of *Mein Kampf*.) I read it in the first English translation, from 1933, with the German version alongside, online, and a crib of graduate-school German grammar nearby. (I've since reread sections, in Ralph Manheim's later translation.) The question of what to do with *Mein Kampf* is, in some sense, independent of the book's contents—buying it is a symbolic act before it's any kind of intellectual one, and you can argue that it's worth banning on those grounds alone. A good opposing case can be made on similarly symbolic grounds: that making it public in Germany is a way of robbing it of the glamour of the forbidden.

However that may be, the striking thing about the text as a text is that it is not so much diabolical or sinister as *creepy*.* It is the last book in the world that you would expect a nascent Fascist dictator to write. Most of us—and most politicians in particular, even those who belong to extremist movements—try to draw a reasonably charismatic picture of our histories and ourselves. We want to look appealing. An evil force may emerge and temporarily defeat the narrator, but that force is usually placed against a childhood of a purer folk existence, now defiled. That's the way most politicians' campaign memoirs still work, for instance.

Hitler, whom we suspect of being an embittered, envious, traumatized loser, presents himself as ... an embittered, envious, traumatized loser. The weirdness of this is especially evident in the earlier autobiographical chapters. His resentments are ever-present. His father was dense, mean, unforgiving, and opaque. ("My father forbade me to nourish the slightest hope of ever being allowed to study art. I went one step further and declared that if that was the case I would stop studying altogether. As a result of such 'pronouncements,' of course, I drew the short end; the old man began the relentless enforcement of his authority.") His schoolmates were combative, his schoolmasters unappreciative. The petty rancour and unassuaged disappointments of a resentment-filled life burn on every page, in ways one would think might be more demoralizing than inspiring to potential followers. His embittered account of his final rejection at Vienna's Academy of Fine Arts is typical:

> I had set out with a pile of drawings, convinced that it would be child's play to pass the examination. At the *Realschule*[2] I had been by far the best in my class at drawing, and since then my ability had developed amazingly; my own satisfaction caused me to take a joyful pride in

2 *Realschule* Secondary school in Germany. Students attend from the ages of 10 or 11 until 16 or 17.

> hoping for the best.... I was in the fair city for the second time, waiting with burning impatience, but also with confident self-assurance, for the result of my entrance examination. I was so convinced that I would be successful that when I received my rejection, it struck me as a bolt from the blue. Yet that is what happened. When I presented myself to the rector, requesting an explanation for my non-acceptance at the Academy's school of painting, that gentleman assured me that the drawings I had submitted incontrovertibly showed my unfitness for painting.

The triviality of the injury and the length and intensity with which it's recalled—in a book intended, after all, to attract fanatical followers to a fanatical cause—would seem to be more unsettling than seductive. And many similar passages of equally irrelevant self-pity follow. His description of his hunger while footloose* in Vienna is pointillist.[3]

Mussolini's[4] autobiography, to take the obvious comparison, though ghostwritten—by a former American Ambassador to Italy, apparently!—nonetheless reflects his sense of the best self to put forward; the youthful memories are more predictably of a concord between the young Italian and the national landscape he inhabits. (The Masons[5] play the same role for Mussolini that the Jews did for Hitler: the cosmopolitan force interrupting the natural harmony between the people and their home, the blood and the birthplace.) Mussolini's is a Fascist dictator's memoir written as you would expect a Fascist dictator to write it. To be sure, Hitler is writing at the bottom of the ascent and Mussolini at the top, but the temperamental difference is arresting nonetheless.

Indeed, strangely, the "lesser" Fascist and extreme right-wing European figures of the period are closer to the idealized image of a national saviour than Hitler even pretends to be. Corneliu Codreanu,[6] in Romania, for instance—who was, hard to believe, an even more violent anti-Semite than Hitler—was a model of the charismatic national leader, providing a mystical religious turn as well. Even Oswald Mosley,[7] in England—for all that P.G. Wodehouse nicely

---

3 *pointillist* Pointillism is a technique in painting in which small dots of colour are applied on a canvas in patterns to create images.

4 *Mussolini* Benito Mussolini (1883–1945) was an Italian dictator and leader of the National Fascist Party. He was Prime Minister of Italy from 1922 to 1943.

5 *Masons* Freemasons are members of fraternal organizations that follow a code of morality revealed in symbols. Mussolini viewed Masonry as incompatible with Fascism, and he banned the organizations in 1925.

6 *Corneliu Codreanu* Romanian politician (1899–1938) and the founding leader of the Iron Guard, an anti-Semitic and nationalistic organization.

7 *Oswald Mosley* British politician (1896–1980) and the founding leader of the British Union of Fascists (BUF).

mocked him in his figure of Roderick Spode[8]—had many of the traits of a genuinely popular, charismatic figure, worryingly so. Hitler's self-presentation has none of that polished charisma. He is a victim and a sufferer first and last—a poor soldier who is gassed, a failed artist who is desperately hungry and mocked by all. The creepiness extends toward his fanatical fear of impurity—his obsession with syphilis is itself pathological—and his cult of strong bodies. Pathos is the weirdly strong emotion, almost the strongest emotion, in the memoir.

Yet the other striking—and, in its way, perhaps explanatory—thing about the book is how petty-bourgeois[9] (in the neutral, descriptive sense that Marx, or, for that matter, Kierkegaard,[10] used the term) its world picture is, even including the petty-bourgeois bias toward self-contempt. The class nature of Hitler's experience is as clear to him as it is to the reader—he is, he knows, a child of the lower middle classes, and his view of the world is conditioned by that truth.

His pervasive sense of resentment must have vibrated among those who know resentment as a primary emotion. Creepy and miserable and uninspiring as the book seems to readers now, its theme of having been dissed* and disrespected by every authority figure and left to suffer every indignity must have resonated with a big chunk of an entire social class in Germany after war and inflation. Even his Jew-hating bears the traces of personal rancour as much as of "scientific" racial ideology. The poison of anti-Semitism comes in many flavours, after all, but the kind that, for instance, Drumont, in France, or Chesterton and Belloc,[11] in Britain, had until then favoured was aristocratic in pretension. It assumed that Jews have a secret, conspiratorial power. Admiration is

---

8 *P.G. Wodehouse ... Spode* English writer P.G. Wodehouse (1881–1975) is the author of the *Jeeves* series of stories and novels. They include a fictional character based on Mosley named Sir Roderick Spode, a Nazi sympathizer and "amateur dictator."

9 *petty-bourgeois* Karl Marx used the term "petite bourgeoisie" ("small bourgeoisie") to refer to a sub-stratum of the middle class that included shopkeepers and the workers who managed larger capitalist enterprises owned by the upper-middle classes. The petty-bourgeois belong to what we would think of today as the lower middle class.

10 *Kierkegaard* Søren Kirkegaard (1813–55) was a Danish philosopher and religious writer. In *The Sickness unto Death* (1849), he describes the petty bourgeois as "spiritless," "[d]evoid of imagination," and limited to "a certain orbit of trivial experiences."

11 *Drumont* Édouard Adolphe Drumont (1844–1917), a French writer who started the Antisemitic League of France in 1889; *Chesterton* G.K. Chesterton (1874–1936), an English writer who, though opposed to Nazism, nonetheless made anti-Semitic comments; *Belloc* Hilaire Belloc (1870–1953), an Anglo-French writer who collaborated with Chesterton. His anti-Semitism centred on the belief that Jews had inordinate control over the world of finance and over society in general.

mixed with disgust, as with the parallel "yellow peril"[12] of the Asians—they're so smart that they're sinister.

Hitler's anti-Semitism seems a purer case of petit-bourgeois paranoia. It resents not the newcomer who invades the sanctuary but the competitor in the shop down the street, who plays by unfair rules. ("I didn't know what to be more amazed at: the agility of their tongues or their virtuosity at lying.") It's telling that his anti-Semitism in *Mein Kampf* is, early on, entangled with his Francophobia.[13] The Jews are like the French: they are, in plain English, the people who get to go to art school. Both the Francophobia and the anti-Semitism are part of the same petty-bourgeois suspicion: They think they're superior to us! They think they're better than us because they're slicker than we are! They look down on us, and it is intolerable to have anyone look down on us! That fear of mockery and of being laughed at is so strong in Hitler that it filled his speeches as late as the onset of the war: the Jews and the English are laughing at me, and they won't be allowed to laugh for long! That someone would feel this sense of impending shame as a motive for violence is commonplace. But that someone would choose to make so overt that his love of violence arises from a fear of being mocked, and that he would use this as the source of his power seems weirdly naked and unprotected.

10 Here we touch on a potentially absurd but also possibly profound point. The resemblance of Charlie Chaplin to Hitler is one of the fearful symmetries[14] of twentieth-century life, one that could hardly have been imagined if it were not so—Chaplin even writes in his autobiography that, when he was shown postcards of Hitler giving a speech, he thought that the German leader was doing "a bad imitation" of him. There were, of course, millions of men with toothbrush moustaches, but the choice by a performer or politician to keep or discard a symbolic appurtenance is never accidental. Chaplin chose to use the moustache because, as Peter Sellers[15] once said of the little moustache he placed on *his* petty-bourgeois hero, Inspector Clouseau, it is the natural armour of the insecure social classes. The twitch of the moustache is the focal point

---

12 *"yellow peril"* Racist metaphor used to describe the Western fear of being overwhelmed and outsmarted by Asian peoples.

13 *Francophobia* Anti-French prejudice; hatred towards France.

14 *Charlie Chaplin* English actor and filmmaker (1889–1977) known for his physical comedy and rectangular moustache; *fearful symmetries* See William Blake's "The Tyger," lines 21–24: "Tyger tyger burning bright / In the forests of the night / What immortal hand or eye / Dare frame thy fearful symmetry?"

15 *Peter Sellers* English actor, comedian, and singer who famously portrays Inspector Clouseau, a bumbling detective with a distinctive moustache, in *The Pink Panther* (1964) and other comedy films.

of the Tramp's[16] social nervousness, as much as his flat, awkward feet are the focal point of his ingenuousness. Chaplin's insecurity-armour is gallant and Hitler's aggrieved, but both wear the moustache to claim more social dignity than the wearer suspects society wants to give him. (Hitler seems to have been forced during the Great War to trim an earlier, more luxuriant moustache—the point is that he kept and cultivated the abbreviation.)

Mein Kampf is a miserable book, but should it be banned? I could certainly sympathize with any German who would like to see it kept illegitimate; some speech should, in fact, be off-limits. But is it a *dangerous* book? Does it circulate sinister ideas best kept silent? Putting aside the book's singularly creepy tone, it contains little argumentation that wasn't already commonplace in other, still-circulating anti-Semitic and extreme-right literature. Hitler's character remains bewildering, in the obvious mismatch between the extent of his miserableness and the capacity of his will to power, although perhaps it should not be—many other personal stories suggest that miserable people have the will to power in the greatest intensity. But his themes are part of the inheritance of modernity, ones that he merely adapted with a peculiar, self-pitying edge and then took to their nightmarish conclusion: the glory of war over peace; disgust with the messy bargaining and limited successes of reformist, parliamentary democracy and, with that disgust, contempt for the political class as permanently compromised; the certainty that all military setbacks are the results of civilian sabotage and a lack of will; the faith in a strong man; the love of the exceptional character of one nation above all others; the selection of a helpless group to be hated, who can be blamed for feelings of national humiliation. He didn't invent these arguments. He adapted them, and then later showed where in the real world they led, if taken to their logical outcome by someone possessed, for a time, of absolute power. Resisting those arguments is still our struggle, and so they are, however unsettling, still worth reading, even in their creepiest form.

(2016)

16 *the Tramp* Charlie Chaplin's screen persona.

Questions

1. How is buying *Mein Kampf* a "symbolic act"?
2. Why would some argue that *Mein Kampf* should be banned? Do you agree?
3. Why, according to Gopnik, is the "creepiness" of Hitler's text noteworthy? How does he link this "creepiness" to the appeal the text held for the millions of Germans who read it during the 1920s and 30s?
4. How are the themes and arguments of *Mein Kampf* still "our modern inheritance"? Is there evidence in Europe and North America of similar arguments surfacing in political discourse?
5. German intellectual Nils Minkmar recently warned in the newspaper *Der Spiegel* that "haughtiness towards poorly educated classes" has been leading to "the alienation of the lower classes from liberal society," and that this in turn is causing a resurgence of right-wing nationalism in Germany. How could the publication of, and re-engagement with, *Mein Kampf* make this problem worse? How could it make it better?

JUSTICE WILLIAM B. HORKINS

from THE GHOMESHI VERDICT

On 24 March 2016, Ontario Court Justice William B. Horkins acquitted Jian Ghomeshi on four charges of sexual assault and one charge of overcoming resistance by choking. Ghomeshi, the celebrity host of the popular CBC radio program* Q, *had been fired from the CBC in 2014 as a scandal emerged regarding allegations that he had committed non-consensually violent sex acts. It is difficult to know exactly how many people contributed to these allegations, because several were made anonymously to reporters and not all of the cases brought to police were pursued in court, but at least nine people publicly accused him. The scandal surrounding Ghomeshi drew a great deal of media attention to sexual assault and rape culture, and his acquittal from all charges angered supporters of his accusers. Questions also arose concerning how sexual assault cases are handled in the Canadian criminal justice system (for example, please see Katie Toth's article "After Not Guilty" in this anthology). The following excerpts from Judge Horkins's decision give context for the charges, his examination of the testimony of one of the complainants, and his conclusions and verdict.*

FROM INTRODUCTION

At the time of the events in question, 2002 to 2003, Mr. Ghomeshi was the host of a CBC television show called "PLAY." Subsequently, and for several years prior to when these complainants came forward in 2014, he was the host of a CBC radio show called *Q*. *Q* is a show which features interviews with prominent cultural and entertainment figures. With Mr. Ghomeshi as the host, *Q* enjoyed a large and dedicated following.

It is fair to say that in 2014 Mr. Ghomeshi had achieved celebrity status and was a prominent and well-known personality in the arts and entertainment community in Canada. Then, suddenly, in 2014 the CBC publicly terminated him in the midst of several allegations of disreputable behaviour towards a number of women.

The publicity surrounding what I will call the "Ghomeshi Scandal" in 2014 is the context in which the complainants in this case came forward with reports of sexual assaults that they say occurred in 2002 and 2003.

Each charge presented against Mr. Ghomeshi is based entirely on the evidence of the complainant. Given the nature of the allegations this is not unusual or surprising; however it is significant because, as a result, the judgment of this Court depends entirely on an assessment of the credibility and the reliability of each complainant as a witness.

THE COMPLAINT OF L.R.

5 The first two counts of the Information[1] are allegations that the accused sexually assaulted the complainant L.R. on two different occasions. The first occasion is identified as having occurred on a date between December 1st and 31st, 2002. The second allegation is identified as having occurred on the 2nd of January 2003.

L.R. first met Mr. Ghomeshi while working as a server at the 2002 CBC Christmas party. She felt that they made a connection. They flirted with each other and she found Mr. Ghomeshi to be charming and charismatic. When speaking of this first meeting, she reported: "He was smitten with me." He seemed very enthusiastic. Mr. Ghomeshi invited L.R. to attend a future taping of his show "PLAY" and gave her a note with the time and the place of the taping.

L.R.'s evidence was that on the evening she went to the show Mr. Ghomeshi's eyes lit up when he saw her arrive and he exclaimed, excitedly, "You came!"

The show was taped in a restaurant bar. L.R. sat at the bar where she was close to Mr. Ghomeshi during the show. After the show he asked her to accompany him and some other CBC personalities to a nearby pub for a drink. L.R. remembers that Mr. Ghomeshi was sweet and humble. She recalled certain small details of the evening, for instance, he ordered a Heineken and she had a ginger ale. She thought he was funny, intelligent, charming and a nice person.

After about half an hour Mr. Ghomeshi and L.R. left the pub. He drove her to her car that was parked a short distance away. L.R. had a clear and very specific recollection of his car being a bright yellow Volkswagen Beetle. It struck her as being a "Disney car," a "Love Bug." She said she was impressed that he was not driving a Hummer or some such vehicle. The "Love Bug" car was significant to her because it contributed to her impression of his softness, his kindness and generally, that it was safe to be with him.

---

1 *Information* Document drafted by the prosecutor containing the formal criminal charge(s).

When they arrived at the parking lot where L.R.'s car was parked they sat in his car and talked. Mr. Ghomeshi was flirtatious and it was playful. He asked her to undo some of the buttons of her blouse and she said no. She was flirting with him. They were kissing, when suddenly he grabbed hold of her long hair and yanked it "really, really hard." She said her thoughts at the time were: "What have I gotten into here?"

L.R. described the yank to her hair as painful. Mr. Ghomeshi asked her if she liked it like that, or words to that effect. They sat and talked for a while longer. Mr. Ghomeshi had reverted back to being very nice. It was confusing and L.R. was unsure what to think. She wondered if maybe he did not know his own strength. They kissed goodbye. L.R. got out of the car and drove home. She continued to ask herself whether he had really intended to hurt her.

L.R. was obviously very much taken with Mr. Ghomeshi. She was separated from her husband at the time and agreed that she was considering Mr. Ghomeshi as someone she would potentially be interested in going out with. She decided to attend another taping of Mr. Ghomeshi's show. He met her there and was very nice to her. It was, to use her expression, "uneventful."

During the first week of January 2003, L.R. attended another taping of Mr. Ghomeshi's show. On this occasion she went with a girlfriend. L.R. recounts that Mr. Ghomeshi was happy to see them. They interacted and after the show they all went to the pub. They were at the pub for less than an hour. L.R. said that she flirted with Mr. Ghomeshi. He invited both women back to his home. L.R.'s friend declined. After they dropped off her friend at the subway, L.R. and Mr. Ghomeshi drove to his home.

While at Mr. Ghomeshi's home the music was playing. They had a drink, and they sat on the couch and talked. At one point L.R. was standing up near the couch, looking at various things in the room and thinking what a charming person he was. Then, suddenly, "out of the blue," he came up behind her, grabbed her hair and pulled it. He then punched her in the head several times and pulled her to her knees. The force of the blow was significant. She said it felt like walking into a pole or hitting her head on the pavement. L.R. thought she might pass out.

Then, suddenly again, the rage was gone and Mr. Ghomeshi said, "You should go now; I'll call you a cab." L.R. waited for the cab then left. She said, "He threw me out like the trash."

L.R.'s evidence was that at the time of these events in 2003, she never thought of calling the police. She did not think anyone would listen to her. L.R. said she never saw Mr. Ghomeshi again after this incident.

Over a decade later, Mr. Ghomeshi was fired from the CBC and the "Ghomeshi Scandal" broke in the media. L.R. came forward publicly with her complaint in response to the publicity and specifically, in response to then Chief

Blair of the Toronto Police Service publicly encouraging those with complaints about Jian Ghomeshi to come forward.

Several areas of concern in L.R.'s evidence were identified in cross-examination.

AN EVOLVING SET OF FACTS

Prior to speaking with police, L.R. gave three media interviews about her allegations against Mr. Ghomeshi. In these interviews, she described the first assault as happening "out of the blue," as opposed to having happened in the midst of a kissing session. Her police statement was initially similar to her media interviews. It was only near the end of her police statement that L.R. had the hair pulling and kissing "intertwined." Then at trial, the account of the event had developed to the point of the hair pulling clearly occurring at the same time as "sensuous" kissing. The event had evolved from a "common" assault into a sexual assault.

When pressed about the shifting facts in her version of the events, L.R. explained that while she was giving the media interviews, she was unsure of the sequencing of events and "therefore … didn't put it in."

THE HAIR EXTENSIONS

The day following her police interview, L.R. sent a follow up email to the police to explain that she remembered very clearly that she was wearing clip-on hair extensions during the hair pulling incident in the car. In cross-examination, L.R. testified that at some point she reversed this "clear" memory and is now adamant that she was not wearing clip-on hair extensions during the incident.

L.R. frequently communicated with police by email and phone. She met and spoke with Crown counsel. She did nothing to correct the misinformation she provided to the police about the hair extensions. Equally as concerning as the reversals on this point, was her claim that she had, in fact, disclosed this reversed memory to the Crown. When pressed in cross-examination, she conceded that this was not true.

THE CAR WINDOW HEAD SMASH

The day after her police interview, L.R. emailed the police to explain that she was then beginning to remember that during the car incident, Mr. Ghomeshi smashed her head into the window. In her previous four accounts of the incident, provided to police and the media, she had never claimed that her head had been smashed into the car window. Under cross-examination, she reverted to the version of the car incident with no head smash. She then added that her head had been resting against the window; something she had never mentioned previously, at any time.

When pressed to explain these variations, L.R. said that at her police interview she was simply "throwing thoughts" at the investigators.

When cross-examined about her new allegation of having her head smashed into the window, L.R. denied demonstrating in her sworn police video statement that her hair was pulled back towards the seat of the car, not towards or into the window. She persisted in her denial of this, even when the police video was played, clearly showing her demonstrating to the detectives how her hair was pulled back. Her explanation for this shifting in her evidence was that during the police interview she was "high on nerves."

L.R.'s memory about the assault at the house also shifted and changed significantly. She told the *Toronto Star* and CBC TV that she was pulled down to the floor prior to being assaulted at the house. She told CBC Radio that she was thrown down to the ground. Then she told the police that the events were "blurry" and did not know how she got to the ground. When trying to reconcile all of these inconsistencies she said that, to her, being "thrown" and being "pulled" to the ground are the same thing.

In her police interview, L.R. did not initially describe kissing as part of the alleged assault and was unable to describe a clear sequence of events. At trial, for the first time, she had kissing clearly intertwined with the alleged assault. She remembered kissing on the couch and kissing standing up. L.R. could not describe the conversation or what they were each doing prior to the assault. In her evidence in-chief,[2] there was no mention of doing a yoga pose just prior to the assault. In cross-examination, L.R. was reminded of the yoga moves and her earlier statement that Mr. Ghomeshi was bothered by them.

THE "LOVE BUG"

One of L.R.'s clear memories was simply, and demonstrably, wrong. She testified at length about Mr. Ghomeshi's bright yellow Volkswagen "Love Bug" or "Disney car." This was a significant factor in her impression that Mr. Ghomeshi was a "charming" and nice person. However, I find as a fact that Mr. Ghomeshi did not acquire the Volkswagen Beetle that she described until seven months after the event she was remembering.

In a case which turns entirely on the reliability of the evidence of the complainant, this otherwise, perhaps, innocuous error takes on greater significance. This was a central feature of her assessment of Mr. Ghomeshi as a "nice guy" and a safe date. Her description of his car was an important feature of her recollection of the first date. And yet we know that this memory is simply

2 *evidence-in-chief* Evidence given during the questioning of one's own witnesses (in this case, the questioning of L.R. by her own lawyer).

wrong. The impossibility of this memory makes one seriously question, what else might be honestly remembered by her and yet actually be equally wrong? This demonstrably false memory weighs in the balance against the general reliability of L.R.'s evidence as a whole.

THE FLIRTATIOUS EMAILS

30 L.R. was firm in her evidence that following the second incident she chose never to have any further contact with Mr. Ghomeshi. She testified that every time she heard Mr. Ghomeshi on TV or radio, she had to turn it off. The sound of Mr. Ghomeshi's voice and the sight of his face made her relive the trauma of the assault. L.R. could not even listen to the new host of *Q* because of the traumatizing association with Mr. Ghomeshi.

L.R.'s evidence in this regard is irreconcilable with subsequently proven facts. She sent a flirtatious email to Mr. Ghomeshi a year later. In her email, L.R. calls Mr. Ghomeshi "Play-boy"; a reference to his show. She refers, oddly, to him ploughing snow, naked. She says it was "good to see you again." She is either watching him, or watching his show. "Your show is still great," she writes. She invites him to review a video she made and provides a hot link embedded into the body of the message. L.R. provides him with her email address and phone number so he can reply. Despite her invitation, she received no response. This is not an email that L.R. could have simply forgotten about and it reveals conduct that is completely inconsistent with her assertion that the mere thought of Jian Ghomeshi traumatized her.

Six months later, L.R. sent another email to Mr. Ghomeshi. In it she said, "Hi Jian, I've been watching you …" (here expressly referencing another TV show), "hope all is well." She attached to this email a picture entitled "beach1.jpg," which is a picture of her, reclined on a sandy beach, wearing a red string bikini. This is not an email that she could have simply forgotten about. It reveals conduct completely inconsistent with her assertion that the mere thought of Mr. Ghomeshi traumatized her.

The negative impact that this after-the-fact conduct has on L.R.'s credibility is surpassed by the fact that she never disclosed any of this to the police or to the Crown.

It was only after she was confronted in cross-examination with the actual emails and attachment that L.R. suddenly remembered not just attempting to contact Mr. Ghomeshi but also that it was part of a plan. She said that her emails were sent as "bait" to try to draw out Mr. Ghomeshi to contact her directly so that she could confront him with what he had done to her.

35 I suppose this explanation could be true, except that this spontaneous explanation of a plan to bait Mr. Ghomeshi is completely inconsistent with her earlier stance that she wanted nothing to do with him, and that she was

traumatized by the mere thought of him. I am unable to satisfactorily reconcile her evidence on these points.

The expectation of how a victim of abuse will, or should, be expected to behave must not be assessed on the basis of stereotypical models. Having said that, I have no hesitation in saying that the behaviour of this complainant is, at the very least, odd. The factual inconsistencies in her evidence cause me to approach her evidence with great scepticism.

L.R.'s evidence in-chief seemed rational and balanced. Under cross-examination, the value of her evidence suffered irreparable damage. Defence counsel's questioning revealed inconsistencies, and incongruous and deceptive conduct. L.R. has been exposed as a witness willing to withhold relevant information from the police, from the Crown and from the Court. It is clear that she deliberately breached her oath to tell the truth. Her value as a reliable witness is diminished accordingly....

FROM CONCLUSIONS

... There is no legal bar to convicting on the uncorroborated evidence of a single witness. However, one of the challenges for the prosecution in this case is that the allegations against Mr. Ghomeshi are supported by nothing in addition to the complainant's word. There is no other evidence to look to to determine the truth. There is no tangible evidence. There is no DNA. There is no "smoking gun."* There is only the sworn evidence of each complainant, standing on its own, to be measured against a very exacting standard of proof.[3] This highlights the importance of the assessment of the credibility and the reliability and the overall quality, of that evidence.

At trial, each complainant recounted their experience with Mr. Ghomeshi and was then subjected to extensive and revealing cross-examination. The cross-examination dramatically demonstrated that each complainant was less than full, frank and forthcoming in the information they provided to the media, to the police, to Crown counsel and to this Court.

Ultimately my assessment of each of the counts against the accused turns entirely on the assessment of the reliability and credibility of the complainant, when measured against the Crown's burden of proof. With respect to each charge, the only necessary determination is simply this: Does the evidence have sufficient quality and force to establish the accused's guilt beyond a reasonable doubt? ...

---

3 *standard of proof* Legal term for the level of proof (amount and kind of evidence) required to win a given case. In criminal cases such as this one, the standard of proof is "beyond a reasonable doubt," the highest standard of proof in a Canadian court.

As I have stated more than once, the courts must be very cautious in assessing the evidence of complainants in sexual assault and abuse cases. Courts must guard against applying false stereotypes concerning the expected conduct of complainants. I have a firm understanding that the reasonableness of reactive human behaviour in the dynamics of a relationship can be variable and unpredictable. However, the twists and turns of the complainants' evidence in this trial, illustrate the need to be vigilant in avoiding the equally dangerous false assumption that sexual assault complainants are always truthful. Each individual and each unique factual scenario must be assessed according to their own particular circumstances.

Each complainant in this case engaged in conduct regarding Mr. Ghomeshi, after the fact, which seems out of harmony with the assaultive behaviour ascribed to him. In many instances, their conduct and comments were even inconsistent with the level of animus[4] exhibited by each of them, both at the time and then years later. In a case that is entirely dependent on the reliability of their evidence standing alone, these are factors that cause me considerable difficulty when asked to accept their evidence at full value.

Each complainant was confronted with a volume of evidence that was contrary to their prior sworn statements and their evidence in-chief. Each complainant demonstrated, to some degree, a willingness to ignore their oath to tell the truth on more than one occasion. It is this aspect of their evidence that is most troubling to the Court.

The success of this prosecution depended entirely on the Court being able to accept each complainant as a sincere, honest and accurate witness. Each complainant was revealed at trial to be lacking in these important attributes. The evidence of each complainant suffered not just from inconsistencies and questionable behaviour, but was tainted by outright deception.

45 The harsh reality is that once a witness has been shown to be deceptive and manipulative in giving their evidence, that witness can no longer expect the Court to consider them to be a trusted source of the truth. I am forced to conclude that it is impossible for the Court to have sufficient faith in the reliability or sincerity of these complainants. Put simply, the volume of serious deficiencies in the evidence leaves the Court with a reasonable doubt.

My conclusion that the evidence in this case raises a reasonable doubt is not the same as deciding in any positive way that these events never happened. At the end of this trial, a reasonable doubt exists because it is impossible to determine, with any acceptable degree of certainty or comfort, what is true and what is false. The standard of proof in a criminal case requires sufficient clarity in the evidence to allow a confident acceptance of the essential facts. In

4 *animus* Motivating feelings, particularly hostile feelings.

these proceedings the bedrock foundation of the Crown's case is tainted and incapable of supporting any clear determination of the truth.

I have no hesitation in concluding that the quality of the evidence in this case is incapable of displacing the presumption of innocence. The evidence fails to prove the allegations beyond a reasonable doubt.

I find Mr. Ghomeshi not guilty on all of these charges and they will be noted as dismissed.

Released: March 24, 2016
Signed: "Justice William B. Horkins"

(2016)

Questions

1. What is the burden of proof for criminal cases tried in Canada? Why can this level of proof be particularly difficult to establish in cases of sexual assault?
2. Judge Horkins draws a distinction between acquitting Ghomeshi and believing in his innocence: "My conclusion that the evidence in this case raises a reasonable doubt is not the same as deciding in any positive way that these events never happened." Consider, in light of this statement, Katie Toth's article "After Not Guilty." In your opinion, should the judicial process for sexual assault trials change in Canada? Why or why not?
3. Keira Smith-Tague, a front-line worker with Vancouver Rape Relief & Women's Shelter, was quoted in a CTV news article after the verdict, addressing the "inconsistent" behaviour of assault victims after their traumas: "It's not black and white when it comes to how we feel about the men who've attacked us. Men who we love become our abusers often … and it doesn't mean you stop loving them right away or that you change your behaviour right away, because it's confusing and it's also hard to accept that somebody you care about would do that to you." In your opinion, was Judge Horkins right to consider the complainant's behaviour after the alleged attack as part of his reason for finding Ghomeshi not guilty? Why or why not?
4. At the time of his decision, many commentators considered Judge Horkins's comment regarding the "dangerous false assumption that sexual assault complainants are always truthful" to be evidence of misogynist attitudes underlying his decision. Do you agree with this assessment? Why or why not?

5. In this verdict, the judge considers each crime separately (and therefore considers separately the testimony of each of the alleged victims). Why does he do this? Do you think this is the best approach for the Canadian justice system to take in cases like these?
6. In his analysis of the complainant's testimony, Judge Horkins identifies a series of "factual inconsistencies" in L.R.'s testimony. To what extent do you agree with his assessment that these inconsistencies render her testimony not credible?

KATIE TOTH

AFTER NOT GUILTY: ON SEXUAL ASSAULT AND THE CARCERAL[1] STATE

In October 2014, celebrity radio host Jian Ghomeshi was fired from the CBC. As sexual assault and sexual harassment allegations surfaced in the following weeks, the scandal brought sexual assault to the forefront of public discourse in Canada. At the end of November 2014, Ghomeshi was accused of four counts of sexual assault and one count of overcoming resistance by choking. In March 2016, Ghomeshi was cleared of all charges; the judge found the key testimonies to be internally inconsistent and therefore unreliable. (A portion of the court decision is also included in this anthology.) The following article discusses sexual assault in the context of the criminal justice system, questioning whether there might be a better way to pursue justice for victims and rehabilitation for offenders. It was posted by* GUTS Magazine *the day after the Ghomeshi trial verdict.*

"I find Mr. Ghomeshi not guilty on all these charges," a judge[2] said yesterday morning in an Ontario court. Just over a month earlier, Jian Ghomeshi—the former radio host who had been a feminist hero to those of us who only knew him by his interviews with the likes of Toni Morrison and Joni Mitchell[3]—had been at the centre of a trial for allegations of multiple counts of sexual assault and choking.

Before Ghomeshi was acquitted, there was already a general sense from the disastrous proceedings that he was not going to be found guilty of any crime. For presiding Judge Horkins, a stream of new evidence on the stand that witnesses hadn't remembered or discussed with lawyers first called their credibility into question. Reporters, including me, wondered why the Crown*

1 *Carceral* Relating to prisons.

2 *judge* The Honourable William B. Horkins, judge in the Ontario Court of Justice.

3 *Toni Morrison* American writer, best known for her Pulitzer prize-winning novel *Beloved* (1987); *Joni Mitchell* Esteemed Canadian singer and songwriter (b. 1943).

hadn't asked the witnesses more questions or investigated more thoroughly before bringing a case forward—if not for themselves, then for the witnesses' sake. At the very least, why had they not prepared better to prevent wasting the time of a busy court system?

In response to the low rates of conviction in Canadian sexual assault cases, some legal commentators have suggested changing the standard of proof for these crimes from a beyond-a-reasonable-doubt standard to a balance of probability,[4] with reduced penalties. Another suggestion has been to increase limits on the ability of defense lawyers to do their job, which is, by definition, poking holes in the trustworthiness of any accusations levelled against their client and keeping them out of prison. Other experts have dug in their heels,* pointing out that conviction and acquittal rates for sexual assault are similar to other violent crimes, describing the courts' adversarial approach to fact-finding and burden of proof as "one of the very institutions that makes civil society possible."

Meanwhile, I have been wondering: Is this it? Are these our only choices?

5 Ardath Whynacht, a professor of sociology at Mount Allison University specializing in criminal justice, is asking herself the same questions.

Whynacht says a guilty verdict of a high-profile figure accused of assault would have felt "like a 'win' for victims" of sexual assault around the country who don't see their experiences taken seriously. "And I don't want to minimize how important that is," she says, in an email. "But at the same time, I think we need to question whether or not a guilty verdict is 'justice' for sexual assault."

"Does it help us heal? Does it help the offender come to recognize how and why they learned that this behaviour was acceptable? Does it empower both the victim and offender to transform their communities?"

There are other options. Lauren Chief Elk, an Assiniboine[5] feminist who co-founded the hashtag #GiveYourMoneyToWomen, says she'd like to see more "monetary justice"—compensation to victims of sexual assault, directly from the people who perpetrated violence. (That's something that some Canadian lawyers have explored, too; they've suggested letting the Crown

---

4 *standard of proof* Legal term for the level of proof (amount and kind of evidence) required to win a given case; *beyond-a-reasonable-doubt standard* The highest standard of proof, required in criminal cases in Canada; the prosecutor, to win the case, must leave the jurors with no reasonable doubts concerning an offender's guilt; *balance of probability* The standard of proof for civil, rather than criminal, cases. This is a less exacting standard of proof: to win a civil case, a plaintiff must advance a case that is more likely to be valid than the defendant's (rather than a case that is valid beyond any reasonable doubt).

5 *Assiniboine* The Assiniboine are an Aboriginal people originally from the northern Great Plains of North America; today they are located primarily in Saskatchewan.

pursue civil cases against sex offenders and sue for monetary compensation on behalf of victims in court.)

"People don't see the actual financial cost to being raped," she says. Therapy for PTSD* is expensive. You can lose your job or your scholarship when you're falling down the rabbit hole of trauma. If you were close to your attacker and need to get away from them for your safety, restarting your life can mean a plane ticket, a damage deposit, two months' rent up front. "This is an actual tangible material means of justice. Money can fix the wrongs that have been done more than a prison sentence can."

10 Elk also wants to see people respond to sexual assault by "building support networks and systems of friends and family" who will focus their efforts on helping the victims they know, instead of convicting perpetrators. "Literally, just asking victims, what would you like to do?"

In some communities, survivor support networks are set up so that people can try to find support or protection outside of the courts. In Philadelphia, members of the Philly Survivor Support Collective work with people who've been sexually assaulted to help them figure out what they want, like safety or money for therapy, and how the community can rally to help make that happen.

Then there's the task of rehabilitating perpetrators of violence. It's difficult and emotionally draining, but it works.

Canada, for example, has a world-renowned program called Circles of Support and Accountability (CoSA), which provides group counselling for sex offenders and keeps an eye on the offenders in the community, to make sure they don't reoffend. The program has been emulated in countries around the world, like South Korea and the United Kingdom, but funding for the program was severely cut under the Harper government.[6] Existing research shows that offenders in CoSA are 80 percent less likely to reoffend than those outside the program.

Work like this is often referred to as "restorative justice": a system that works to repair the harm done and prevent it from reoccuring, rather than just punishing the people who caused it. There's an idea that this kind of approach is soft on crime—letting perpetrators get away with something heinous.

15 Whynacht says that's a myth.

"I have worked with men and women in prison who have spent years on suicide watch after coming to terms with how they have harmed their victims. After they accepted and acknowledged the harm they have done, they were in tremendous pain," she writes. "Putting someone on a 'time out'* in a cell for three years is letting them get away with it. It doesn't hold them accountable to the actual harm."

---

6 *Harper government* Stephen Harper was Prime Minister of Canada from 2006 to 2015.

And it doesn't protect future victims: "If we want to repair the damage done, we must fund programs that help [offenders] heal and address their own wounds. We must resource programs for men that teach different forms of masculinity so that they can be accountable for their actions.... Sexual assault is pathological."

Ghomeshi's acquittal leaves the lingering question of whether carceral feminism itself—the move to achieve gender equality, security, or fairness for sexual assault survivors through courts and prison lockdowns—must now go to trial. Because a lot of times it looks like that movement hurts more than it helps. It hurts survivors, left deciding whether or not to subject themselves to public scrutiny. It hurts perpetrators of violence, who continue their lives without the kind of real accountability that makes a person become whole. And it hurts the rest of us. Because while for the witnesses, Ghomeshi and their respective families, this trial was deeply personal, for spectators this was a public show—state-sponsored theatre giving many people the impression that if they are sexually assaulted, it won't be taken seriously.

Perhaps, then, it's time for us to consider something entirely different.

(2016)

Questions

1. Toth mentions several alternatives to the Canadian legal system's current treatment of sexual assault. What are these alternatives? In your opinion, do any of these ideas seem like improvements to the current system?
2. Why does Professor Whynacht question whether a guilty verdict means "justice" in sexual assault cases? Do you agree with her? Why or why not?
3. What is "restorative justice"? Why does Whynacht think it is a good alternative to punitive justice?
4. What does Toth suggest is the message the Ghomeshi trial sent to women? Do you agree with her? Why or why not?

Anonymous [The Economist]

from Pocket World in Figures 2016

Since 1991, The Economist, *a widely respected news magazine, has released an annual* Pocket World in Figures, *a compendium of statistics profiling countries and ranking them according to various demographic, social, economic, and other measures. In the following selection from the introduction to the volume's twenty-fifth edition, the creators reflect upon how the world has changed since the first edition was published.*

Twenty-Five Years On

In the past 25 years the planet's population has surged and its distribution has been far from equal. Developing countries have experienced booms while developed economies have stagnated. India added 418m people to its population between 1988 (the base year for data in the first edition of the *Pocket World in Figures*, published in 1991) and 2013 (the base year for this edition). Germany and Japan, meanwhile, mustered fewer than 9m between them.

Alongside this, the world has seen dramatic urbanisation, most pronounced in China and India. In 1988, Seoul, South Korea's capital, was one of the world's biggest cities with a population of 10m. Today, it does not even make the top 30. The world's biggest city is still Tokyo, with a population now almost four times that of Seoul. In 2015, six cities in China and five in India were larger than Seoul.[1]

As poorer countries have developed, birth rates and fertility rates have fallen steadily. In Kenya, for example, the average number of children born to each woman has dropped from 8.1 in the late 1980s to 4.3 in 2013. In many rich world countries, however, they are beginning to rise.

As health care, diet and nutrition have improved, so has life expectancy. In 1988 Japan topped the table with an average of 78 years. In the 25 years since, Mexico, Lebanon, Cuba, the Czech Republic and dozens more have improved

1 *larger than Seoul* Page references to the full *Pocket World in Figures* are omitted here and throughout the selection.

on this. Monaco now ranks highest with a remarkable 89 years. At the other end of the spectrum, Sierra Leoneans are now expected to live to 47, six years more than in 1988. As a result of such gains, the percentage of people aged over 65 has surged. In the 1980s, not a single country had to cope with 20% of its population being over 65. Now Japan, Germany and Italy all face this. African countries, however, continue to have the world's youngest populations. In the late 1980s, 40–50% of people were under 15 years old across much of the continent. In 2013, this remained the case.

5 Despite the health improvements, an AIDS pandemic has gripped Africa throughout this period. Twenty-five years ago, Congo–Brazzaville reported 66 cases per 100,000 people, by far the highest rate on the continent. Now 22 African countries report more than 100 deaths per 100,000. Even this rate is substantially down from the mid-2000s.

The causes of death have changed as people's lifestyles have become increasingly comfortable. In many developed countries, the average person has some 3,000 calories per day available for consumption. As a result, diabetes and obesity, not recorded in the *Pocket World in Figures* until 2005 and 2006 respectively, are now endemic. On a more positive note, smoking has fallen steeply in the rich world. The Greeks, previously serial puffers, have halved their cigarette intake to an average of four-and-a-half a day per person.

In the rich world the marriage rate has fallen, with a third fewer unions in the United States than 25 years ago. Divorce rates have also fallen, down by two-fifths in the United States. Globally, more young women than young men graduate from university every year. And this increased focus on careers has pushed back the average age of marriage. In the United Kingdom the average age of a bride is now 32, up from 24 in 1987.

WORLD'S BIGGEST CITIES

Population in Urban Agglomeration, m

1988		2015	
1 Tokyo, Japan	31.6	1 Tokyo, Japan	38.0
2 Osaka, Japan	18.1	2 Delhi, India	25.7
3 New York, US	16.0	3 Shanghai, China	23.7
4 Mexico City, Mexico	15.1	4 São Paulo, Brazil	21.1
5 São Paulo, Brazil	14.2	5 Mumbai, India	21.0
6 Mumbai, India	11.6	6 Mexico City, Mexico	21.0
7 Los Angeles, US	10.6	7 Beijing, China	20.4
8 Kolkata, India	10.5	8 Osaka, Japan	20.2
9 Buenos Aires, Argentina	10.3	9 Cairo, Egypt	18.8
10 Seoul, South Korea	10.0	10 New York, US	18.6

Perhaps the most startling backward step in the past 25 years has taken place in the Americas. In 1986, only two countries in the world had murder rates above 20 per 100,000 people: Philippines at 38.7, and Lesotho, at 36.4. Now, 13 countries in the Americas alone exceed this.

MURDERS

Homicides per 100,000 population

1985		2012 or latest	
1 Philippines	38.7	1 Honduras	91.0
2 Lesotho	36.4	2 Venezuela	53.6
3 Sri Lanka	18.9	3 Virgin Islands (US)	52.6
4 Jamaica	18.0	4 El Salvador	41.5
5 Guyana	15.6	5 Jamaica	39.1
6 Lebanon	13.2	6 Lesotho	38.0
7 Zimbabwe	12.6	7 Guatemala	34.6
8 Thailand	12.4	8 Colombia	30.7
9 Bahamas	12.2	9 South Africa	30.7
10 Botswana	11.0	10 Bahamas	29.7

The economic scene over the past quarter-century has been dominated by the rise of China. With an average annual growth rate of 9.7%, it is now the world's second largest economy. (Only one country has exceeded 10% annual growth across the entire period—Equatorial Guinea, with 18%.)

BIGGEST ECONOMIES

$bn, 2013 prices

1988		2013	
1 United States	9,612	1 United States	16,768
2 Japan	5,630	2 China	9,240
3 West Germany	2,379	3 Japan	4,920
4 France	1,869	4 Germany	3,730
5 Italy	1,631	5 France	2,806
6 United Kingdom	1,627	6 United Kingdom	2,678
7 USSR	1,148	7 Brazil	2,246
8 Canada	961	8 Italy	2,149
9 Brazil	697	9 Russia	2,097
10 Spain	666	10 India	1,875

China's GDP[2] per person has risen eightfold to $6,807. It may not compete with Monaco's $173,000 per person, but in these years it has pulled roughly 600m of its population above the poverty line ($1.25 a day in 2005 prices). It has also become by far the largest consumer of the world's resources.

China's industrial output, which was a seventh of the United States' in 1988, overtook it in 2010. As a result, China's share of world exports has risen from 1.4% to 10.4%, behind only the United States in the euro area.

Thanks to the rapid evolution of consumer goods, the items ranked in 1988 for the first edition have almost all been replaced. No longer does the *Pocket World in Figures* compile statistics on the share of households with video cassette recorders, microwaves and dishwashers. It now ranks mobile phone ownership, computer sales and the number of broadband subscribers.

In many ways, the world we documented in 1988 seems a simpler, more innocent time. Hans Christian Andersen and Enid Blyton[3] were among the most translated authors in the world and there were no rankings for teenage pregnancies, gambling, prisoners, robberies and refugees. In part that is because there are more, and better, data available today. And for all that's changed, for better or worse, there is one constant truth: France still draws the most tourists in the world.

(2016)

Questions

1. Do any of the statistics quoted in this introduction surprise you? Why or why not? To what extent do you consider this passage to be objective? Can you detect any bias in the selection of the statistics the authors report?
2. Given the statistics above, does the world overall seem to be improving, getting worse, or staying the same? Does what the statistics suggest match your experience? Does it match what you see reported in the news?

---

2 *GDP* Gross domestic product, a number indicating the combined value of all the goods and services produced by a country over a given period (here, over the course of a year). It is considered an important measure of economic success.

3 *Hans Christian Andersen* Danish writer best known for his classic fairy tales (1805–75); *Enid Blyton* Best-selling English author of works for children (1897–1968).

MARY ROGAN

from GROWING UP TRANS: WHEN DO CHILDREN KNOW THEIR TRUE GENDER?

In December 2015, the Child Youth and Family Gender Identity Clinic at Toronto's Centre for Addiction and Mental Health (CAMH) was shut down in response to protest by trans activists. Activists objected to the clinic's approach to young children with gender dysphoria.[1] *The clinic believed that parents and doctors should wait until the child is older before affirming the identified gender of the child, in the expectation that the majority of children who express gender dysphoria will grow out of it. Many activists objected to this approach, believing instead that early affirmation is crucial to a child's self-esteem and mental health. The closing of the CAMH clinic brought debate about transgender children to the forefront of discussion about trans issues in Canada. The following article by Mary Rogan was published in* The Walrus *magazine in September 2016.*

One day, not long after I turned five, I heard my brothers howling like wild dogs. They were taking turns hurling themselves off the top bunk bed. Their faces were on fire, and their hair was soaked with sweat. I stared longer than I wanted, but they didn't notice me.

Over the next few years, I muscled my way in. Bloodying touch football, chicken fights,* barefooted knife-throwing contests, one concussion. I pinned a poster of Walt Frazier[2] to my bedroom wall, because I was going to be point guard for the New York Knicks. Then my brother Owen told me that could never happen, because I wasn't a boy.

---

1 *gender dysphoria* Distress caused by a mismatch between one's gender identity and the gender one appears to have biologically. Formerly known as Gender Identity Disorder.

2 *Walt Frazier* Former basketball player (b. 1945) who led the New York Knicks to NBA (National Basketball Association) championships in 1970 and 1973.

I didn't believe him.

I butchered my long hair with my father's toenail clippers and wore boy's shorts under my Catholic-school uniform until I was caught out during recess by one of the nuns. I begged my mother to buy me the same clothes as my brothers, but she insisted I wear dresses she made herself. She'd wake me in the middle of the night and have me stand on a kitchen chair. Then, turning me this way and that, she would make adjustments with sewing pins pressed between her lips like bullets.

I didn't get my period until I was fifteen, and by then, I had become convinced it wouldn't happen. Couldn't happen. I was furious and helpless. I hung my head out the window and smoked a cigarette. Then I stared at myself in the mirror for a long time. I didn't tell my mother I was menstruating. Every period I got for the next thirty-five years felt as if it had nothing to do with me.

I left my family home in Connecticut for university when I was seventeen. I came out as a lesbian at twenty, the same year I moved to Toronto, and became a mother at twenty-nine. By then, I had scrambled to higher ground, away from those early years, and found a livable compromise in feeling genderless. Eyes closed, I would try to imagine myself as male or female and was reassured every time I came up empty. Yet I couldn't avoid misunderstandings. At my son's elementary school, I was mistaken for his big brother more than once. I stayed away from public washrooms because it was painful when women stared, and I felt ashamed when I had to reassure people that I was in the right place.

As I got older, shame gave way to anger every time I was taken for a man. I told myself that other people lacked imagination and nuance. They were hostage to binary notions of gender and rigid expectations of what a woman should look like. But in this narrative, I never acknowledged my own relationship with my gender. Instead, I fought for as long as I could to stay on that higher ground.

In the mid '90s, anxiety and depression almost pulled me underwater. I was hospitalized at Mount Sinai's[3] psychiatric unit. One day, I walked off and headed over to Kensington Market[4] and into a Vietnamese barbershop and got my hair buzzed. In the twenty years since, I've never grown it back. I didn't know it at the time, but that act was my lodestar. It gave people a way to see me, to acknowledge their insistent confusion, without my having to see myself.

From Caitlyn Jenner's[5] glamorous come-hither magazine photos to newly created summer camps for "gender variant" kids, the debate over what it means

---

3 *Mount Sinai* Hospital in Toronto, Ontario.

4 *Kensington Market* Neighbourhood market in Toronto.

5 *Caitlyn Jenner* Olympic gold medallist, football player, and television personality Caitlyn Jenner (b. 1949) came out as a transgender woman in a July 2015 *Vanity Fair* cover story. From 2015–16 she starred in a reality television show called *I Am Cait.*

to be transgender has become part of our zeitgeist. At one end of the conversation are indefensibly regressive ideas that associate transgender people with deviance. Those in the business of sowing moral panic offer lurid descriptions of men in dresses lying in wait in public washrooms to molest little girls.

At the other end is the sympathetic reflex to affirm and celebrate—to insist, publicly at least, that we don't need to understand why someone is transgender. Intuitively, each of us understands how vital it is to be accepted, and in turn, we want to show transgender people that we see them as they want to be seen.

Gender isn't something most people think about critically. We don't have to explain to each other what it feels like to be settled in this "male" or "female" experience of ourselves. We've already silently agreed on what those terms mean. A transgender person makes us reexamine this agreement. We're thrown off balance when something as elemental as gender is questioned. Transgender people have the same abiding sense of self as every other human being, but when they put their essential selves into words and say, "I am transgender," they are also saying, "This thing we agreed upon—it's not the same for me." Some are frightened by what they might hear in response.

We have tangled before, and will again, with equally fractious issues: race, class, religion, sexual orientation. But unlike gender, these others leave room for us to look away—we can't or won't see ourselves in that skin, in that neighbourhood, that bed. Gender is an unavoidable flashpoint, because many count on it as the basis for perceiving each other. Even in that kippah,[6] that brown skin, that same-sex relationship, you have a gender, and I see it.

Too often, we hanker after simplicity: the public conversation many of us are having about gender is facile and oppressively careful. Some of this is in response to an earlier narrative that caused transgender people so much suffering. Until recently, psychiatrists rejected a biological basis for what was called gender-identity disorder—the distress associated with feeling out of sync with the sex one was assigned at birth. Instead, they offered treatments aimed at "curing" people by rooting out the psychological forces behind their presumed confusion. According to this approach, a surgical solution was reserved for only the most drastic cases.

The Diagnostic and Statistical Manual of Mental Disorders (DSM) is a comprehensive list of psychiatric illnesses that helps clinicians make diagnoses. It was introduced in 1952 and has gone through four major revisions. In 2013, the DSM-5 replaced "gender identity disorder" with "gender dysphoria." This new definition represents a sea change* in how psychiatry understands transgender people. It shifts the focus away from seeing gender misalignment

---

6 *kippah* Brimless cloth hat worn by Orthodox male Jews at all times and by male Jews more generally at prayer or at religious gatherings.

solely as a subjective problem and opens the door for a biological explanation. This has profound treatment implications. For someone who believes they have been born into the wrong gender, transitioning to their stated gender becomes a remedy, not a palliative treatment.

15 Where does gender identity come from? Current biological research focuses on fetal development. Normally, every fertilized egg has twenty-three pairs of chromosomes. If a fetus has an XY pair, it will become male—if it has an XX pair, female. Around six weeks into gestation, these chromosomes assert themselves, releasing hormones that lead to genital development and play a role in the differences between female and male brains.

That's the typical scenario. Scientists, however, learn from exceptions and want to know whether atypical early fetal development might disrupt our relationship with gender. In addition to studying chromosomal variations, researchers are examining the myriad ways in which hormones, maternal biology, and the external environment affect fetal development.

As yet, there are no concrete answers as to why someone is transgender. What does feel concretized is an increasing social consensus, among progressives at least, that the science—the why of this—doesn't matter. Or, more accurately, shouldn't matter. For trans activists, any debate about gender dysphoria is suspect, even hateful.

A gender-questioning child is ground zero in any investigation of transgender issues. Gender variance in a young person is not like other challenges a parent might face. When a young boy tells his parents he likes boys, or a pubescent teen tells her parents that she's a lesbian, nobody has to do anything. But as soon as a child identifies with a gender different from their natal sex, decisions need to be made. Hormone blockers? Social transition? Cross-sex hormones to prepare for transition? It's a fast-paced game of double dutch,* except it involves several ropes turning at once like an eggbeater. The parent of a gender-questioning child has to jump in, weigh differing opinions and shifting social forces, and do something.

Some in the scientific community advocate against affirming a young child's stated gender if they exhibit dysphoria. But many front-line physicians treat transgender kids with hormones and surgery because they believe that not affirming contributes to increased rates of suicide, addiction, self-harm, and homelessness. One survey of 3,700 Canadian teenagers revealed that 74 percent of trans students had experienced verbal harassment at school. Another survey, which looked at 433 trans youth in Ontario, found that 20 percent had been physically or sexually assaulted for being transgender—and that almost half had attempted suicide.

20 The DSM-5 defines gender dysphoria in children as "a marked incongruence between one's experienced/expressed gender and assigned gender, of at

least 6 months' duration." There are eight symptoms listed. To qualify for the diagnosis, a child needs to exhibit six of the eight symptoms, and the first is mandatory: "a strong desire to be of the other gender or an insistence that one is the other gender."

The DSM didn't have a category for gender misalignment in children until 1980. As a child in the late '60s and early '70s, I had seven out of the eight symptoms—including the first. Even without the language to name it, my mother was exquisitely attuned to my dysphoria, and it enraged her. We clashed bitterly, and often, about clothing, hair, how I walked, talked, played, and ate my food.

What would happen to someone like me today? How would a doctor, a different family, or the world see me?

How would I see myself?

It's now assumed that being transgender is not something people choose, in much the same way most agree that homosexual people are "born this way." This tagline helped gays and lesbians secure basic human rights such as job protection, access to spousal benefits, adoption, and marriage. It effectively stopped people from viewing gays and lesbians solely through a sexually voyeuristic lens—and we're now seeing a similar destigmatization of transgender people.

One of the facilities in Canada that resisted a strictly biological explanation 25
for gender dysphoria was the Child Youth and Family Gender Identity Clinic at Toronto's Centre for Addiction and Mental Health (CAMH). Ken Zucker, a psychologist, ran the clinic and also chaired the committee on gender dysphoria for the DSM-5. Over its four-decade-long history, the clinic assessed more than a thousand young people between the ages of three and eighteen—in recent years, the waiting list for its services was a year long.

While Zucker and his staff always offered parents a range of options to explain and address their gender-questioning child's symptoms, in many cases parents were counselled to encourage their child to accept their natal sex—meaning parents should not agree to pronoun changes or cross-dressing, or they should dissuade their child from playing with toys that didn't match their natal sex. The clinic's reluctance to immediately affirm a child's stated gender was based on decades of clinical experience—backed up by the results of small sample studies from the Netherlands—that suggested that many younger children moved past their dysphoria without transitioning. When it came to older children, the developmental model used by the clinic was such that the majority were put on hormone blockers.

When a PhD student at the clinic did a follow-up study with 139 of Zucker's former patients a few years ago, she found that 88 percent of them were now happy with their natal sex. Eighty-eight percent is a stunning statistic—one that challenges the increasing trend toward affirming a child's stated gender.

For years, trans activists had been vocal about their concerns that Zucker's clinic was practising "conversion therapy"—a discredited pseudo-therapy that attempts to change a person's sexual orientation through psychoanalysis, aversion therapy, and, in more extreme cases, electric shock, lobotomies, or chemical castration. The DSM removed homosexuality from its list of ailments in 1973, but the term "conversion therapy" still packs an emotional wallop in the LGBT community.

Trans activists went to Rainbow Health Ontario (RHO) with their fears. An influential government-funded organization, RHO educates health-care providers about LGBT issues and advises ministries on policy development. Zucker was shown the door in December 2015, the clinic was shut down, and trans activists celebrated.

30 It's not clear what happened to the families on the clinic's waiting list. Many gender-dysphoria resources for children in Canada are grounded in philosophies diametrically opposed to those of Zucker. Some parents presumably sought out Zucker's clinic in the hope that their gender-questioning child might be one of the many who end up resolving their dysphoria without transitioning.

As parents, we often say we want our kids to be happy. Or, if we're trying to be more realistic, we hope for a balance of happiness and adversity: just enough to generate grit—not enough to break them down. But we can't titrate[7] the perfect dose, and transgender children will face levels of adversity well beyond what any parent can control. Does affirming a child's stated gender ameliorate the inevitable adversity? The simple answer is yes. Studies show that youth who receive support from their parents are significantly less likely to attempt suicide.

But gender affirmation isn't a panacea. For many transgender youth, their journey begins at a doctor's office, and the relationships they form with medical professionals will last throughout their lifetime. There will be medications with known short-term side effects and unknown long-term side effects. Some transgender people choose surgery. Given the sobering statistics about dysfunction, despair, and victimization, it's naive to think that parental affirmation alone can guarantee immunity from the anguish they reveal. Is it so unthinkable that a parent might hope their gender-questioning child will be part of the large majority of kids who resolve their gender dysphoria without transitioning?

"Let's say it were possible to take a ten-year-old kid and make them either a well-adjusted lesbian or turn them into a female-to-male transsexual. I don't see anything wrong with saying it's better to make this kid into a lesbian, because being a lesbian doesn't require breast amputation, the construction of a not-very-convincing false penis, and a lifetime of testosterone shots."

---

7 *titrate* In medicine, the term means to measure and adjust the balance of a solution (a drug dosage, for example).

So says Ray Blanchard, an adjunct professor of psychiatry at the University of Toronto and a colleague and friend of Zucker. He worked at the Gender Identity Clinic at the Clarke Institute of Psychiatry in Toronto for fifteen years and then at CAMH from 1995 until 2010. He was part of the DSM-IV committee that set the diagnostic criteria for gender-identity disorder (before the name was changed to gender dysphoria). Unlike Zucker, Blanchard has never worked directly with children, but he is keenly interested in the transgender debate unfolding today.

Blanchard views some young trans males as butch lesbians who have 35
capitulated to social pressures stemming from the media's sensationalizing focus on transgender issues. According to him, the narrative of their transgender experience is a fiction fuelled by an emphasis on hormonal and surgical treatments.

He divides trans females into two categories: extremely feminine homosexual men, and very masculine men who are sexually aroused by making themselves look and feel like women. In this formulation, both categories can manifest through gender dysphoria. Blanchard believes men in the first category are simply not masculine enough to succeed as men and will be more successful as women. He describes the second category as the result of an unusual sexual proclivity.

When Blanchard received a prestigious committee appointment to develop criteria for the DSM-5, the United States's National LGBTQ Task Force sent a letter to the American Psychiatric Association protesting his involvement. For many in the LGBT community, he is the incarnation of the darkest beliefs that people have about trans people. Not surprisingly, the vitriol directed against him online is ferocious. In one post, he is accused of being a tortured Catholic, a closet homosexual, and a narcissist with an unwholesome attachment to his widowed mother.…

Devita Singh, a former student of Zucker's, is a clinical child psychologist based in London, Ontario. She authored the study detailing the 88 percent of Zucker's patients who, in the language of the literature, have "desisted" in their gender dysphoria without transitioning.

Singh is frustrated that, despite the findings of her study and others like it, there's now more pressure than ever for doctors and families to affirm a young child's stated gender. She doesn't recommend immediate affirmation and instead suggests an approach that involves neither affirming nor denying, but starting with an exploration of how very young children are feeling. Affirmation, she argues, should be a last resort. Singh concedes that in cases involving older children approaching puberty, clinicians might need to move more quickly before the development of permanent secondary sex characteristics—broad shoulders, for example, or breasts—significantly increases the child's distress. However, even with an older child, there is room for discussion if a slower approach is needed.

40 For her crucial study, described earlier, Singh approached 145 former patients between 2009 and 2010—all of whom had entered the clinic as boys who identified as girls—and asked whether they wanted to participate in her follow-up study: 139 agreed. When they'd originally consulted with Zucker at the Gender Identity Clinic, the youngest patient had been three and the oldest, twelve. By the time Singh reached out to them to answer questions about their present-day lives, most of them were in their late teens to early twenties.

Of the 139 former patients in Singh's study, 122—or 88 percent—had desisted in their gender dysphoria. They were now happy with their natal gender and living as males, with no desire to transition to female. The remaining seventeen patients had, in medical parlance, "persisted" in their gender dysphoria. Some were living as males but wanted to transition; some had begun to transition socially through informal name changes or more feminine clothing and hairstyles; and a few had legally changed their names to match their stated gender. Not one of the seventeen had pursued surgery.

After the survey, some of the participants who had desisted became intensely curious about what they had said to Zucker all those years ago. Singh went through their charts with them.

"Some sort of remembered that they really liked dolls or they wanted to play only with girls. Some didn't remember that they liked those things or said that they wanted to be a girl. There were boys in there who had said, 'I'm going to be a girl. I don't want my penis.' When I read them the extent of what they said at the time, they were quite surprised."

Singh asked some follow-up questions, including "Do you think your parents should have brought you to someone like Dr. Zucker?" "A fair amount of them said to me, 'I can see why my parents did it, because they wouldn't have known what else to do, but somehow in my mind, I knew this was something that was going to go away eventually.'"

45 Singh dismisses the claim made by many trans activists that asking questions about a child's stated gender is transphobic or regressive. "A professional can't be scared to ask important questions," she says. "How could you presume to know how someone feels about themselves without asking them how they feel about themselves? The folks who are doing the activism work are not the desisters—they're the persisters. Is there a way to appreciate that someone else with gender-identity confusion in childhood could have a different experience from yours? You're seeing that child's experience through the lens of an adult who has gone through various experiences for decades. And when you do that, you're going to miss things that the child may be trying to communicate to you."

I'm waiting for Andrew outside a coffee shop, and he's late. Andrew is twenty-three, so that's not unexpected. We've never met, but I spot him when he's still half a block away. He's wearing a navy peacoat over a pair of tight-fitting jeans that accentuate his curves. Later, he tells me he heard some nasty comments when he first came out as transgender, because he's "pretty effeminate and very queer." A couple of young trans males had mockingly accused him of "not even trying to look like a boy."

There is something instantly likeable about Andrew. He's a nimble thinker and hyper-articulate, but almost every sentence is followed by a short laugh. I can't tell whether it's a nervous tic or a form of punctuation, but it feels disconnected from the content of what he's saying.

Andrew tells me that the dysphoria he felt before beginning his transition still lingers, but that it no longer dominates the way it did before. Early in his transition, he had bad days when he was frightened to go out in public because his voice wasn't deep enough yet or he hadn't bound his breasts.

Still, he can't imagine himself as anything but transgender. And he sees his own experience of dysphoria as having played a crucial role in his development. "I would say it's inextricably linked. Not that I can't exist without dysphoria. Fingers crossed, I can exist without it eventually." Andrew laughs. "But my politics have been so shaped by my trans experience. If I were a cisgender woman, I would not have had the exposure to all the things that define me as a person."

Andrew left his family home in Orangeville, Ontario, the day after his last 50
high-school exam. He headed out West, connected with a small trans community in Nanaimo, British Columbia, and started his transgender journey.

"I said I think maybe I'm bisexual, and my mom was like, 'Okay.' And then it was, maybe because I'm so afraid of getting pregnant, I'll just be a lesbian. It was an actual terror, almost to the point of being a phobia."

It takes me a second to grasp what he's trying to convey: that this paralyzing fear of getting pregnant is what made Andrew consider he might be transgender. At nineteen, he began his social transition, but he didn't tell his mother and father right away. He told his friends his gender identity and his new name. Then he came home to Ontario for a summer job.

"I was out to everybody except my parents, because I wasn't sure how that was going to fly. I got outed by accident when one of my employers called my house and asked, 'Is Andrew there?' And my mom was like, 'What?' She wasn't upset, exactly; she just wasn't sure how to respond. She's the kind of person who says, 'My baby, you're already perfect—why do you want to change?'"

Andrew navigated his transition, including the medical decisions, without his parents' input. Back in BC, he found doctors who were sympathetic to his needs and who wouldn't second-guess his decision to transition. He began receiving testosterone injections once every two weeks. Almost immediately, his voice got deeper, and he felt energized and hungry all the time. Andrew calls the initial effects of testosterone "tuberty," because his moods were all over the map. He split the dose of testosterone in half and now injects himself with it once a week to smooth out the emotional highs and lows. He'll do that for the rest of his life.

55 Last year, Andrew decided to have his uterus and ovaries removed, because his fear of getting pregnant had never completely gone away. And knowing that he still had female reproductive organs contributed to the sense of dysphoria.

He found a surgeon in BC who was well-known in the trans community.

"My surgeon was awesome, this really nice guy who had done hysterectomies for pretty much all of the trans dudes in the area. We had the good fortune of having a doc who jumps through hoops for a living, so he was like, 'Okay, to get this covered by insurance, we'll say abnormal bleeding. If you're a guy bleeding out of your junk, that's abnormal bleeding.' That was his workaround, and that worked really well for a lot of people."

In the absence of a clear medical consensus, clinicians have to make their own decisions about how best to support a person with gender dysphoria. Andrew's surgeon made a decision, as did Singh.

Joey Bonifacio is equally confident in the approach he pursues with young transgender patients. At thirty-seven, Bonifacio has a wheelbarrow full of diplomas including an undergraduate degree in linguistics, an MA in anthropology, and a medical degree from UBC. He's currently working on his master's in theology. Over the course of a ninety-minute-long conversation before his evening clinic shift begins, he offers a wide-angle view of society's evolving relationship with transgender people.

60 Bonifacio works at the Adolescent Medicine Clinic at St. Michael's Hospital in Toronto and leads the Transgender Youth Clinic at Sick Kids Hospital. He also sees patients at two centres for street-involved youth. He wears many hats and deals with some of the worst-case scenarios involving transgender kids.

From his perspective, it's impossible to believe that a wait-and-see approach to gender dysphoria reflects a neutral stance. Not doing anything is still doing something. "I think the risk in taking the wait-and-see approach is low self-esteem and self-worth. Kids are really savvy, and they know what's going on. They know what their parents are thinking about them. They're not being validated, and that can have major effects on mental health. Then I see them for depression or anxiety or self-harm."

In his relatively short career, Bonifacio has seen how language shifts have changed the conversation. The shift from "trans-sexual" to "transgender" made it possible for us to stop thinking primarily about vaginas and penises and start embracing a fuller appreciation of transgender people. It also opened the door for the word "cisgender," which can be applied to the vast majority of people who are aligned with their natal sex.

Bonifacio believes that as our language evolves, so, too, should clinicians. Most family doctors now ask their teenage patients about their sexual orientation as a matter of course while taking down their histories. Bonifacio says doctors should also include questions about a patient's gender identity. More critically, as the social consensus shifts toward affirming a person's stated gender, doctors should as well.

But what does affirming involve? At conferences and media events about transgender youth, most of the questions Bonifacio is asked are about medications and surgeries. Despite all the postmodern deconstructing of language, he's concerned that we're putting everything back together through the same old binary lens. If the first question a transgender person is asked when they come out is about hormones or surgery, we're limiting the choices kids feel they can make. What about the more ordinary questions we would ask other young people?

"You're boxing this community into persons that need medications and 65
need surgery," Bonifacio says. "And you're not taking into account the lived narratives of a diverse group." There's no shortage of Internet videos showing trans kids taking their first testosterone shots. What happens if children absorb the message that there is only one way to be transgender? Only one way to be seen?

"They know the script. They're supposed to say, 'It started when I was three or four years old and got worse and worse. Then in my teenage years, that's when I definitely knew.' And my concern is if I don't hear the real narrative, I get one that's edited in order to meet the criteria to access care." …

When Singh revisited those 139 former patients from Zucker's Gender Identity Clinic, she discovered that 122 of them had desisted in their gender dysphoria without transitioning. We don't know why or how this occurred, but some believe the clinic's non-affirming approach for young kids with gender dysphoria might have been a contributing factor.

What would have happened to those 122 if they had been affirmed at Bonifacio's clinic instead? We can't know. But implicit in our fascination with the question itself is the assumption that one outcome would be "better" than the other.

The seventeen other participants persisted in their gender dysphoria and today identify as transgender. We don't know how or why this happened either, but we know they were not affirmed in their stated identities. It's hard to imagine what that felt like.

But I know what it felt like. As a child, I met the full criteria for gender 70
dysphoria and lived with a mother who was determined to extinguish this part

of me. As a young adult, I met the DSM-5 criteria for gender dysphoria in adolescents and adults—I still do today.

We are driven inexorably to reveal ourselves. To be seen. It's what we do, often imperfectly and against powerful forces. Despite my mother's best efforts and, later, my own, I came to see what my mother had suspected fifty years ago.

In the writing of this essay, I now see me, and I identify as male.

Would my life have unfolded differently in another family or another era? Likely, yes. Would I have chosen hormone blockers during the worst of my pubescent years? Yes. Would I have transitioned? I can't say. And I don't need to know the answer to that. I am deeply attached to my rich and complex lived experience.

Here I am, today.

Where are those seventeen others?

(2016)

Questions

1. What is gender dysphoria? How is it defined?
2. What are the possible dangers faced by children experiencing gender dysphoria as they grow up? Which psychiatric and medical approaches seem to offer the best results in terms of the child's happiness?
3. Why did trans activists oppose Ray Blanchard's appointment to the committee deciding the criteria for the DSM–5? In your view, were they right to do so?
4. What approach did Ken Zucker and his staff take toward young children with gender dysphoria? Toward older children? What, by contrast, is Joey Bonifacio's approach? What is your opinion of these differing approaches?
5. When considering whether the children who "desisted in their gender dysphoria without transitioning" might have chosen to transition had their gender identities been affirmed, Rogan writes that "implicit in our fascination with the question itself is the assumption that one outcome would be 'better' than the other." What is the root of this assumption? To what extent is it justified?
6. This article concludes with a personal statement about the author's own gender identity. How (if at all) does this conclusion affect your response as a reader to the article as a whole?

Jacqueline Rose

from Who Do You Think You Are?

Transgender narratives—personal stories of trans experience, especially those focusing on transition from one gender to another—have become increasingly visible in the mainstream media. This has led to growing public consciousness regarding the trans struggle for social justice. In the following essay, Jacqueline Rose discusses the possibilities for social change presented by trans experience; she also discusses the prejudice and violence that trans people continue to face. Her article, published in The London Review of Books *in 2016, uses primarily British and American examples and statistics, but the picture in Canada is similar. For some examples of Canadian trans narratives, please see Mary Rogan's piece in this anthology, "Growing Up Trans."*

… Transsexual people are brilliant at telling their stories. That has been a central part of their increasingly successful struggle for acceptance. But it is one of the ironies of their situation that attention sought and gained is not always in their best interest, since the most engaged, enthusiastic audience may have a prurient, or brutal, agenda of its own. Being seen is, however, key. Whatever stage of the trans journey or form of transition, the crucial question is whether you will be recognized as the other sex, the sex which, contrary to your birth assignment, you wish and believe yourself to be. Even if, as can also be the case, transition does not so much mean crossing from one side to the other as hovering in the space in between, something has to be acknowledged by the watching world (out of an estimated 700,000 trans women and men in the United States, only about a quarter of the trans women have had genital surgery). Despite much progress, transsexuality—"transsexualism" is the preferred term[1]—is still treated today as an anomaly or exception. However

1 *transsexualism ... term* The terminology used in this British article does not fully align with the usage recommended by most trans organizations in North America. "Transsexual" is used primarily in reference to people who use surgery and/or hormones to physically transition to their identified gender. Many trans people do not take this approach, and not everyone who does identifies as transsexual. Under most circumstances,

normalized, it unsettles the way most people prefer to think of themselves and pretty much everyone else. In fact, no human can survive without recognition. To survive, we all have to be seen. A transsexual person merely brings that fact to the surface, exposing the latent violence lurking behind the banal truth of our dependency on other people. After all, if I can't exist without you, then you have, among other things, the power to kill me.

The rate of physical assault and murder of trans people is a great deal higher than it is for the general population. A 1992 London survey reported 52 per cent MTF and 43 per cent FTM[2] transsexuals physically assaulted that year. A 1997 survey by GenderPAC[3] found that 60 per cent of transgender-identified people had experienced some kind of harassment or physical abuse. The violence would seem to be on the rise. In the first seven weeks of 2015, seven trans women were killed in the US (compared with 13 over the whole of the previous year). In July 2015, two trans women were reported killed in one week, one in California, one in Florida. In the US just 19 states have laws to protect transgender workers (only in 2014 did the Justice Department start taking the position that discrimination on the basis of gender identity, including transgender, constitutes discrimination under the Civil Rights Act). The House of Commons report *Transgender Equality* notes the serious consequences of the high levels of prejudice (including in the provision of public services) experienced by trans people on a daily basis. Half of young trans people and a third of adult trans people attempt suicide. The report singles out the recent deaths in custody of two trans women, Vicky Thompson and Joanne Latham, and the case of Tara Hudson, a trans woman who was placed in a men's prison, as "particularly stark illustrations" (after public pressure, Hudson was moved to a women's jail). "I saw," Jacques[4] writes in *Trans*, "that for many people around the world, expressing themselves as they wished meant risking death."

In 2007, Kellie Telesford, a trans woman from Trinidad, was murdered on Thornton Heath.[5] Telesford's 18-year-old killer was acquitted on the grounds that Telesford may have died from a consensual sex game that went wrong or may have inflicted the fatal injuries herself (since she was strangled with a scarf, how she would have managed this is unclear). As Jacques points out in *Trans*, the *Sun* headline, "Trannie killed in sex mix up," anticipates the "transsexual

---

"transgender person" and "being transgender" are less controversial and more inclusive than "transsexual" and "transsexualism."

2 *MTF* Male to female; *FTM* Female to male.

3 [Rose's note] GenderPAC is a lobbying group founded in 1996 by trans activist Riki Anne Wilchins with the aim of promoting "gender, affectional and racial equality."

4 *Jacques* Juliet Jacques (b. 1981); *Trans* is her memoir, published in 2015.

5 *Thornton Heath* Suburb of London.

panic"[6] defence which argues that if a trans person fails to disclose before the sexual encounter, she is accountable for whatever happens next. Murder, this suggests, is the logical response to an unexpected transsexual revelation. "Those points," Jacques writes, "where men are attracted to us when we 'pass'[7] and then repulsed when we don't are the most terrifying ... all bets are off." ... In fact, whatever may have been said in court, we have no way of knowing whether Telesford's killer was aware that she was trans, whether her identity was in some way ambiguous, whether ... this may indeed have been the lure. Either way, "transsexual panic" suggests that confrontation with a trans woman is something that the average man on the street can't be expected to survive. Damage to him outweighs, nullifies, her death. Not to speak of the unspoken assumption that thwarting an aroused man whatever the reason is a mortal offence.

That Telesford was a woman of colour is also crucial. If the number of trans people who are murdered is disproportionate, trans people of colour constitute by far the largest subset—the seven trans women murdered in the US in the first seven weeks of 2015 were all women of colour. Today, those fighting for trans freedom are increasingly keen to address this racial factor (like the feminists before them who also ignored it at first)—in the name of social justice and equality, but also because placing trans in the wider picture can help challenge the assumption that transsexuality is an isolated phenomenon, beyond human endurance in and of itself. It is a paradox of the transsexual bid for emancipation that the more visible trans people become, the more they seem to excite, as well as greater acceptance, a peculiarly murderous hatred. "I know people have to learn about other people's lives in order to become more tolerant," Jayne County writes in *Man Enough to Be a Woman* (one of Jacques's main inspirations), but "sometimes that makes bigotry worse. The more straight people know about us, the more they have to hate." ...

Trans is not one thing. In the public mind crossing over—the Caitlyn 5
Jenner[8] option—is the most familiar version, but there are as many trans people who do not choose this path. In addition to "transition" ("A to B") and

6 *Trannie* Derogatory term for a transgender person; *transsexual panic* Legal defense in which the perpetrators of violent crime claim to have committed the crime out of revulsion or panic after discovering they were engaged in sexual activity with a trans person.

7 *'pass'* In this context, for transgender people to "pass" means for them to look like their identified gender to the extent that nobody suspects they are trans.

8 *Caitlyn Jenner* Olympic gold medallist, football player, and television personality (b. 1949) who came out as a transgender woman in a July 2015 *Vanity Fair* cover story. From 2015–16 she starred in a reality television show called *I Am Cait*. She underwent plastic surgery to conform to conventional standards of female beauty.

"transitional" ("between A and B"), trans can also mean "A as well as B" or "neither A nor B"—that's to say, "transcending," as in "above," or "in a different realm from," both. Thus Jan Morris in *Conundrum* in 1974: "There is neither man nor woman … I shall transcend both." … In 2011 the New York-based journal *Psychoanalytic Dialogues* brought out a special issue on transgender subjectivities. "In these pages," the psychoanalyst Virginia Goldner wrote in her editor's note, "you will meet persons who could be characterized, and could recognize themselves, as one—or some—of the following: a girl and a boy, a girl in a boy, a boy who is a girl, a girl who is a boy dressed as a girl, a girl who has to be a boy to be a girl." We are dealing, Stryker explains, with "a heteroglossic[9] outpouring of gender positions from which to speak."…

In her current TV series *I Am Cait*, Jenner is keen to extend a hand to transsexual women and men who don't enjoy her material privileges. She has made a point of giving space to minority transsexuals such as Zeam Porter who face double discrimination as both black and trans, although it is Laverne Cox in *Orange Is the New Black*[10] who has truly taken on the mantle of presenting to the world what it means to be a black, incarcerated, transsexual woman. Cox also insists that, even now she has the money, she won't undergo surgery to feminize her face. Jenner's facial surgery lasted ten hours and led to her one panic attack: "What did I just do? What did I just do to myself?" But, despite her greater inclusivity, faced with Kate Bornstein[11] exhorting her to "accept the freakdom," Jenner seemed nonplussed (as one commentator pointed out, Bornstein used the word "freak" six times in a three-minute interview). This was not a meeting of true minds, even though in the second series of *I Am Cait* Bornstein is given a more prominent role. Like Stryker, Bornstein believes it is the strangeness of being trans, the threat it poses to those who are looking on whether with or without sympathy, that's the point. Compare the impeccable, Hollywood moodboarded images of Jenner broadcast across the world—"moodboarded," the word used by the stylist on the shoot, refers to a collage of images used in production to get the right feel or flow—with the image of Stryker in 1994 welcoming monstrosity via an analogy between

---

9 *Stryker* Susan O'Neill Stryker is an American professor and theorist. She is the director of the Institute for LGBT Studies at the University of Arizona, as well as the founder of the Transgender Studies Initiative; *heteroglossic* Incorporating many varieties of language and/or perspective.

10 *Laverne Cox* American actor who plays Sophia Burset, a trans character, in *Orange Is the New Black*. Cox is the first openly transgender person to be nominated for an Emmy Award in the acting category; *Orange Is the New Black* Hit television series (2013–) set in a women's prison.

11 *Kate Bornstein* American performance artist and writer (b. 1948). Bornstein identifies as gender non-conforming and has played a significant role in the trans movement.

herself and Frankenstein: "The transsexual body is an unnatural body. It is the product of medical science. It is a technological construction. It is flesh torn apart and sewn together again in a shape other than that in which it was born." Stryker stood at the podium wearing what she calls "genderfuck drag":

> combat boots, threadbare Levi 501s over a black lace bodysuit, a shredded Transgender Nation T-shirt with the neck and sleeves cut out, a pink triangle, quartz crystal pendant, grunge metal jewellery, and a six inch long marlin hook dangling around my neck on a length of heavy stainless steel chain. I decorated the set by draping my black leather biker jacket over my chair at the panellists' table. The jacket had handcuffs on the left shoulder, rainbow freedom rings on the right side lacings, and Queer Nation-style stickers reading SEX CHANGE, DYKE and FUCK YOUR TRANSPHOBIA plastered on the back.

She was—is—wholly serious. It is the myth of the natural, for all of us, which she has in her sights. This is her justly renowned, exhortatory moment, unsurpassed in anything else I have read:

> Hearken unto me, fellow creatures. I who have dwelt in a form unmatched with my desire, I whose flesh has become an assemblage of incongruous anatomical parts, I who achieve the similitude of a natural body only through an unnatural process, I offer you this warning: the Nature you bedevil me with is a lie. Do not trust it to protect you from what I represent, for it is a fabrication that cloaks the groundlessness of the privilege you seek to maintain for yourself at my expense. You are as constructed as me; the same anarchic Womb has birthed us both. I call upon you to investigate your nature as I have been compelled to confront mine. I challenge you to risk abjection and flourish as well as have I. Heed my words, and you may well discover the seams and sutures in yourself.

For many post-operative transsexual people, the charge of bodily mutilation is a slur arising from pure prejudice. It's true that without medical technology none of this would have been possible. It's also the case that the need for, extent and pain of medical intervention puts a strain on the argument that the transsexual woman or man is simply returning to her or his naturally ordained place—with the surgeon as nature's agent who restores what nature intended to be there in the first place. Kaveney's[12] medical transition, for example, lasted

12 *Kaveney* Roz Kaveney (b.1949) is a British writer. Her novel *Tiny Pieces of Skull* (2015) is widely praised as an important contribution to literature exploring transgender identity.

two years, involving 25 general anaesthetics, a ten-stone[13] weight gain, thromboses, more than one major haemorrhage, fistula and infections. She barely survived, though none of this has stopped her from going on to lead one of the most effective campaigning lives as a transsexual woman. In 1931, Lili Elbe died after a third and failed operation to create an artificial womb (the film *The Danish Girl* sentimentally changes this to the prior operation to create a vagina so that she dies having fulfilled her dream). When I met April Ashley in Oxford in the early 1970s—she was in the midst of the legal hearing[14] and Oxford was a kind of retreat—she expressed her sorrow that she would never be a mother. On this, female-to-male transsexuals have gone further. In 2007, Thomas Beatie, having retained his female reproductive organs on transition, gave birth to triplets through artificial insemination. They died, but he has since given birth to three children.

But for Stryker, mutilation is at once a badge of honour and a counter to the myth of nature in a pure state. There is no body without debilitation and pain. We are all made up of endlessly permuting bits and pieces which sometimes do, mostly do not, align with each other. We are all always adjusting, manipulating, perfecting, sometimes damaging (sometimes perfecting and damaging) ourselves. Today non-trans women, at the mercy of the cosmetic industry, increasingly submit to surgical intervention as a way of conforming to an image; failure makes them feel worthless (since nature is equated with youth, this also turns the natural process of ageing into some kind of aberration). "I've seen women mutilate themselves to try to meet that norm," says Melissa, mother of Skylar, who had top surgery with his parents' permission at the age of 16. Shakespeare described man as a thing of "shreds and patches," Freud as a "prosthetic God," Donna Haraway as a cyborg.[15] Rebarbative as it may at first seem, Stryker's vision is the most inclusive. Enter my world: "I challenge you to risk abjection[16] and flourish as well as have I." What you would most violently repudiate is an inherent and potentially creative part of the self.…

13 *ten-stone* 140 pounds; the stone is an English unit of mass.

14 *April Ashley* British model and writer (b. 1935). She was one of the first British people to have sexual reassignment surgery; *legal hearing* Ashley's high-profile divorce case. Her husband (who had known her gender history when they married) petitioned to end the marriage on the grounds that Ashley was male; the judge granted this petition, setting a precedent suggesting that trans people could not alter their legal gender.

15 *Donna Haraway ... cyborg* See Haraway's *A Cyborg Manifesto* (1991), a feminist essay in which she argues that we should take "*pleasure* in the confusion of boundaries," including gender boundaries.

16 *abjection* Here, rejection from society for not conforming to social norms.

Today trans is everywhere. Not just the most photogenic instances such as Bruce [Caitlyn] Jenner and Laverne Cox, or *The Danish Girl* at a cinema near you, or the special August 2015 issue of *Vanity Fair* on 'Trans America' (co-edited by *GQ*, the *New Yorker*, *Vogue* and *Glamour*...; but also, for instance, the somewhat unlikely, sympathetic front-page spread of the *Sun* in January 2015 on the British Army's only transgender officer ('an officer and a gentlewoman'), plus the *Netflix* series *Transparent*, Bethany Black, *Doctor Who*'s first trans actress, *EastEnders*'s Riley Carter Millington, the first trans actor in a mainstream UK soap opera, and Rebecca Root of *Boy Meets Girl*, the first trans star of a British TV show; or again reports of the first trans adopters and foster carers, or the 100 per cent surge in children seeking gender change, as shown in figures released by the Tavistock Clinic[17] in November 2015. From 2009 to 2014, the number of cases referred to the Portman NHS Trust's Gender Identity Service rose from 97 to 697.

Transgender children in the UK today have the option of delaying puberty by taking hormone blockers; they can take cross-sex hormones from 16 and opt for sex reassignment surgery from the age of 18. Cassie Wilson's daughter Melanie announced he was Tom at the age of two and a half (now five, he has annual appointments at the Tavistock); Callum King decided she was Julia as soon as she could talk. In 2014, the mental health charity Pace surveyed 2000 young people who were questioning their gender: 48 per cent had attempted suicide and 58 per cent self-harmed. "They kill themselves," Julia's mother commented: "I want a happy daughter, not a dead son." Julia gives herself more room for manoeuvre and defines herself as "both." She likes to ask her girlfriends at school if they would like to be a boy for a day just to see what it would feel like and, whatever they answer, she retorts: "I don't have to because I'm both."

It would seem, then, that in some, but by no means all cases, the desire for transition comes as much from the parents and adults as from the child. One mother in San Francisco was told by the school principal that her son should choose one gender or the other because he was being harassed at school. He could either jettison his pink Crocs* and cut his long blond hair, or socially transition and come to school as a girl—he'd abandoned the dresses he used to like wearing and had never had any trouble calling himself a boy. She was wary: "It can be difficult for people to accept a child who is in a place of ambiguity." At a conference in Philadelphia attended by Margaret Talbot, the journalist

---

17 *The Danish Girl* 2015 film directed by Tom Hooper, about the Danish painter Lili Elbe, one of the first recipients of sex reassignment therapy; *Doctor Who* BBC television series that began in 1963. Bethany Black, a trans stand up comedian, was a guest actor in Series 9 of the revival begun in 2005; *Tavistock Clinic* The Tavistock and Portman NHS Foundation Trust, a specialist mental health clinic located in London.

who wrote about Skylar, one woman admitted that she was the one who needed to know: "We want to know—are you trans or not?" "Very little information in the public domain talks about the normality of gender questioning and gender role exploration," Walter Meyer, a child psychologist and endocrinologist in Texas, remarks. "It may be hard to live with the ambiguity, but just watch and wait." "How," Polly Carmichael of the Tavistock asks, "do we keep in mind a diversity of outcomes?" What desire is being laid on a child who is expected to resolve the question of transition? On whose behalf? Better transition over and done with, it seems, than adults having to acknowledge, remember, relive, the sexual uncertainty of who we all are.

The increase in the number of trans children may be a striking, and for some shocking, new development. But transgenderism is not new. Far from being a modern-day invention, it may be more like a return of the repressed, as humans slowly make their way back, after a long and cruel detour, to where they were meant to be. One of my friends, when she heard I was writing on the topic, said we should all hang on in there, as the ageing body leads everyone to transition in the end anyway. (I told her she had somewhat missed the point.) The Talmud,[18] for example, lists six genders (though Deuteronomy 22.5 thunders against cross-dressing). "Strange country this," Leslie Feinberg quotes a white man arriving in the New World in 1850, "where males assume the dress and duties of females, while women turn men and mate with their own sex." Colonialists referred to these men and women as *berdache*, and set wild dogs on them, in many cases torturing and burning them. In pre-capitalist societies, before conquest and exploitation, Feinberg argues, transgender people were honoured and revered. Feinberg's essay, "Transgender Liberation: A Movement Whose Time Has Come," first published in 1992, called for a pangender umbrella to cover all sexual minorities. It was the beginning of a movement. The first *Transgender Studies Reader* stretches back into the medical archive then forward into the 1990s: the activism of that decade was the ground and precondition of the engagement, the defiance, the manifestos which, in the face of a blind and/or hostile world, the *Reader* offered. These volumes are vast, they contain multitudes, as if to state: "Look how many we are and how much we have to say." We need to remember that these bold and unprecedented interventions predated by more than two or even three decades, the phenomenon known as "trans" in popular culture today.

At the end of his foreword to the first *Transgender Studies Reader*, Stephen Whittle lists as one of the new possibilities for trans people opened up by critical thought the right to claim a "unique position of suffering." But, as with all political movements, and especially any grounded in identity politics, there

18 *Talmud* Central text of Rabbinic Judaism and the basis of Jewish law.

is always a danger that suffering will become competitive, a prize possession and goal in itself. The example of the *berdache*, or of Brandon Teena[19] caught in a cycle of deprivation, shows, however, that trans can never be—without travestying itself and the world—its own sole reference point. However distinct a form of being and belonging, it has affiliations that stretch back in time and across the globe. I have mainly focused on stories from the US and UK, but transgender is as much an issue in Tehran, where trans people have had to fight against being co-opted into an anti-Islam argument that makes sexual progressivism an exclusive property of the West (in fact sex reassignment was legalized following a personal diktat from the Ayatollah Khomeini[20])....

In 1998, the Remembering Our Dead project was founded in the US in response to the killing of Rita Hester, an African American trans woman who was found murdered in her Massachusetts apartment. By 2007, 378 murders had been registered, and the number continues to climb today. Commemoration is crucial but also risky. There is a danger, Sarah Lamble writes in the second *Transgender Studies Reader*, that "the very existence of transgender people is verified by their death": that trans people come to define themselves as objects of violence over and above everything else (the violence that afflicts them usurping the identity they seek). "In this model," Lamble continues, "justice claims rest on proof that one group is not only most oppressed but also most innocent," which implies that trans people can never be implicated in the oppression of others. Apparently, the list of victims in the archives gives no information about age, race, class or circumstances, although the activists are mostly white and the victims almost invariably people of colour, so that when the images are juxtaposed, they reproduce one of the worst tropes of colonialism: whites as redeemers of the black dead. At the core of the remembrance ceremony, individuals step forward to speak in the name of the dead. What is going on here? What fetishization—Lamble's word—of death? What is left of these complex lives which, in failing fully to be told, fail fully to be honoured? ...

I would tentatively suggest that we are witnessing the first signs that the 15
category of the transsexual might one day, as the ultimate act of emancipation, abolish itself. In "Women's Time" (1981), Julia Kristeva argued that feminists, and indeed the whole world, would enter a third stage in relation to sexual difference: after the demand for equal rights and then the celebration of femininity as other than the norm, a time will come when the distinction between woman and man will finally disappear, a metaphysical relic of a bygone age....

---

19 *Brendon Teena* Brandon Teena, an American trans man (1972–93) who was raped and then murdered. The hate crime received a great deal of media attention and became a rallying point for trans activism.

20 *Ayatollah Khomeini* Supreme Leader of Iran from 1979 to 1989.

"Critical trans resistance to unjust state power," Bassichis, Lee and Spade argue, "must tackle such problems as poverty, racism and incarceration if it is to do more than consolidate the legitimate citizenship status of the most privileged segments of trans populations." As soon as you talk about privilege, everything starts to look different. Bassichis, Lee and Spade call for trans and queer activists to become part of a movement, no longer geared only to sexual minorities but embracing the wider, and now seen as more radical, aim of abolishing prisons in the US. "We can no longer," they state, "allow our deaths to be the justification of so many other people's deaths through policing, imprisonment and detention." Trans people can't afford to be co-opted by discriminatory and death-dealing state power. The regular and casual police killings of black men on the streets of America comes immediately to mind as part of this larger frame in which, they are insisting, all progressive politics should be set.

Death must not be an excuse for more death. Obviously it is not for me to make this call on behalf of trans people. I have written this essay from the position of a so-called "cis" woman,[21] a category which I believe, as I hope is by this point clear, to be vulnerable to exposure and undoing. Today, trans people—men, women, neither, both—are taking the public stage more than ever before. In the words of a *Time* magazine cover story in June last year, trans is "America's next civil rights frontier." Perhaps, even though it doesn't always look this way on the ground, trans activists will also—just—be in a position to advance what so often seems impossible: a political movement that tells it how it uniquely is, without separating one struggle for equality and human dignity from all the rest.

(2016)

Among the texts consulted for this article:[22]

The First Lady by April Ashley and Douglas Thompson (Blake, 2006, out of print)

Transgender Equality: First Report of Session 2015-16 by the House of Commons Women and Equalities Committee (January)

A Queer and Pleasant Danger: The True Story of a Nice Jewish Boy Who Joins the Church of Scientology and Leaves Twelve Years Later to Become the Lovely Lady She Is Today by Kate Bornstein (Beacon, 258 pp., £11.30, July 2013, 978 0 8070 0183 7)

Trans: A Memoir by Juliet Jacques (Verso, 330 pp., £16.99, September 2015, 978 1 7847 8164 4)

The Transgender Studies Reader, edited by Susan Stryker and Stephen Whittle (Routledge, 752 pp., £41.99, 2006, 978 0 415 94709 1)

---

21 *"cis" woman* A cis woman is a woman who identifies with the gender she was assumed to be at birth—that is, a woman who is not transgender. Cisgender is the opposite of transgender.

22 This list includes titles and authors mentioned in the selections printed in this anthology. The full list and complete article can be found in the *LRB* archives.

The Transgender Studies Reader 2, edited by Susan Stryker and Aren Aizura (Routledge, 693 pp., £46.99, March 2013, 978 0 415 51773 7)

Tiny Pieces of Skull or A Lesson in Manners by Roz Kaveney (Team Angelica, 190 pp., £9.99, April 2015, 978 0 9569719 7 5)

Man Enough to Be a Woman by Jayne County and Rupert Smith (Serpent's Tail, 1996, out of print)

Conundrum by Jan Morris (Faber, 160 pp., £8.99, 2002, 978 0 571 20946 7)

Psychoanalytic Dialogues, Vol. 21, Issue 2 (2011), Special Issue: "Transgender Subjectivities: Theories and Practices"

Man into Woman: The First Sex Change, a Portrait of Lili Elbe edited by Niels Hoyer (Blue Boat, 2004, out of print)

Vanity Fair Special Edition: Trans America (August 2015)

Questions

1. Why, according to Rose, is "being seen" important for trans people? What are some of the dangers that attend being seen?
2. How, according to this article, is the experience of trans people affected by race?
3. How do trans activists place themselves in the larger struggle against inequality and state power?
4. What is Susan Stryker's response to accusations that surgery and hormone therapy constitute self-mutilation? How does her response challenge, conflict with, or reinforce your own views?
5. How do gender categories make it more difficult to parent a trans child? What does this suggest about these categories more generally?
6. Rose quotes many statements by trans theorists in this article. Do any of those statements affect the way you perceive your own gender? Why or why not?
7. What does Rose suggest might happen to our gender categorizations? Do you agree with this prediction?

Denise Balkissoon

Migrant Farm Workers Deserve Better from Canada

In 1966, in response to farm labour shortages, the Canadian government introduced the Seasonal Agricultural Worker Program. Initially, the program was an agreement between Canada and Jamaica, allowing Canadian farmers to hire Jamaican workers for the growing season. The program has since expanded to include workers from Mexico and the Caribbean. These workers are highly skilled and contribute a great deal to the success of Canadian farms. In this September 2016 opinion piece, Globe and Mail *columnist Denise Balkissoon discusses workers' rights within the SAWP program.*

It's harvest season and our stores and farmers' markets are bursting with the Earth's bounty. It's the best time to crunch into local apples and slice ripe tomatoes—and to reflect on the people who grew them. Especially because 2016 marks the 50th anniversary of Canada's Seasonal Agricultural Worker Program, which brings 30,000 labourers annually from Mexico, Jamaica and other Caribbean countries to reap and sow our crops.

SAWP, as it's known, is a cornerstone of Canadian food. The *Greenhouse Canada* website last spring quoted an Ontario greenhouse owner, Anthony Cervini, as saying that SAWP is "the lifeblood of our industry." A recent item on a Dutch farming website, Hortibiz, agreed, noting: "Migrant workers have proven to be a vital part of every growing season in Ontario, as they commit months of their time each year to help farmers around the clock."

Yes, around the clock. Farm labourers in Ontario, including SAWP migrants, are exempt from labour laws that govern minimum wage, overtime and rest periods.

That's not the only troubling thing about SAWP, which brings in workers on eight-month contracts and allows them to return to Canada annually, but does not permit family members to accompany them. Other farm workers come via the agricultural stream of the Temporary Foreign Worker program, which allows migrants to stay in Canada for up to four years, then requires them to leave for at least two years, meaning they have to abandon their housing and social ties.

Both programs require workers to stay with one employer. Neither gives 5
workers immigrant status, or a path to Canadian citizenship.

"For 50 years, the SAWP has been framed as being used to meet acute labour shortage in periods we need more workers, but it's actually meeting a long-term labour demand," Jenna Hennebry, director of the International Migrant Research Centre at Wilfrid Laurier University, told me.

In its first year, SAWP brought in 63 migrants from Jamaica. Now, about 17,000 farm labourers come annually to Ontario alone, and Dr. Hennebry said the average SAWP migrant now comes here for 10 years in a row.

"These workers live in conditions most Canadians would not accept, often with no access to phone or transportation," she added. In July, 32 workers lost all of their possessions when the Brant County barn in which they lived burned down. This summer, a reporter for *The Globe* saw a farm workers' dorm where 150 people slept in one open-air barracks.*

Although SAWP workers are entitled to provincial health insurance when they arrive, those who are injured are often "medically repatriated" to their home country. In 2014, the Canadian Medical Association Journal reported that 787 migrant farm workers were medically repatriated between 2001 and 2011. These workers also pay employment insurance and pension-plan premiums, as well as income tax.

On Sept. 1, the activist group Justicia for Migrant Workers kicked off 10
"Harvesting Freedom," a farm labourers' march through Southern Ontario that is to end in Ottawa on Oct. 3. Its demand is that migrant workers be given landed immigrant status as soon as they arrive.

"Permanent residency on arrival has challenges, but there's no reason there can't be an avenue," said Dr. Hennebry, who is to speak at a Sept. 19 Harvesting Freedom event in Waterloo. She has previously shared her views with the House of Commons and the Senate, and recently addressed a UN forum in Geneva on migration and development.

She believes that the lack of a path to citizenship for migrant workers is tarnishing Canada's image. Similar programs elsewhere let workers apply for residency after a given time period. This includes Britain and Spain, which also lets migrants bring their families along during work periods.

In the *Greenhouse Canada* article, Mr. Cervini called SAWP a "win-win" because agricultural companies get workers, and migrants earn money to send home. Dr. Hennebry estimates that amounts, on average, to about $9,900 a worker each year.

Mr. Cervini went on to say that he enjoyed getting to know the migrants, especially one worker who had been returning to one of his greenhouses for 27 years. For nearly three decades, then, a person who laboured to produce Canadian food had spent two-thirds of the year away from home, in a situation that affords no possibility of citizenship, no pension and no guarantee of health care here after an injury.

In this season of abundance, Canada should do better than that.

(2016)

Questions

1. Balkissoon quotes Anthony Cervini's description of SAWP as a "'win-win.'" How does he justify this description? What objections can be raised against this description? Is it an accurate way to describe SAWP?
2. How (if at all) do Canadians benefit from SAWP? Would there be any benefits for Canadians if the program were replaced or improved?
3. Balkissoon notes that all of Ontario's farm workers (including SAWP workers) "are exempt from labour laws that govern minimum wage, overtime and rest periods." Why do you think this is? Should it be the case?
4. Research SAWP and the alternatives that activists have proposed. Which seems to you to be the most just approach? Is that approach realistic?

Barack Obama

from Farewell Address

Obama's farewell speech—in which he addressed his supporters, his staff, and the people of Chicago, as well as the nation as a whole—was delivered in Chicago at McCormick Place, a large convention hall, on 10 January 2017. As he often did with major speeches, Obama dictated a first draft of the speech, and then worked on various drafts over the course of several weeks with Cody Keenan (who in 2013 had succeeded Jon Favreau as Obama's Director of Speechwriting). This was Obama's last major speech as President of the United States; Donald Trump was inaugurated as President on 20 January 2017.

… I first came to Chicago when I was in my early twenties, and I was still trying to figure out who I was; still searching for a purpose to my life. And it was a neighbourhood not far from here where I began working with church groups in the shadows of closed steel mills.

It was on these streets where I witnessed the power of faith, and the quiet dignity of working people in the face of struggle and loss.

[Crowd chanting "Four More Years"]

I can't do that.

Now this is where I learned that change only happens when ordinary people get involved, and they get engaged, and they come together to demand it.… That's what we mean when we say America is exceptional. Not that our nation has been flawless from the start, but that we have shown the capacity to change, and make life better for those who follow.

Yes, our progress has been uneven. The work of democracy has always 5
been hard. It has been contentious. Sometimes it has been bloody. For every two steps forward, it often feels we take one step back. But the long sweep of America has been defined by forward motion, a constant widening of our founding creed to embrace all, and not just some.

If I had told you eight years ago that America would reverse a great recession, reboot our auto industry, and unleash the longest stretch of job creation in our history; if I had told you that we would open up a new chapter with the

Cuban people, shut down Iran's nuclear weapons program without firing a shot, take out the mastermind of 9-11;[1] if I had told you that we would win marriage equality and secure the right to health insurance for another 20 million of our fellow citizens[2]—if I had told you all that, you might have said our sights were set a little too high.

But that's what we did. That's what you did. You were the change. The answer to people's hopes and, because of you, by almost every measure, America is a better, stronger place than it was when we started.

In ten days the world will witness a hallmark of our democracy—the….

[Scattered boos and groans]

No, no, no, no, no. The peaceful transfer of power from one freely-elected President to the next. I committed to President-elect Trump that my administration would ensure the smoothest possible transition, just as President Bush did for me. Because it's up to all of us to make sure our government can help us meet the many challenges we still face. We have what we need to do so. We have everything we need to meet those challenges. After all, we remain the wealthiest, most powerful, and most respected nation on earth. Our youth, our drive, our diversity and openness, our boundless capacity for risk and reinvention means that the future should be ours.

10 But that potential will only be realized if our democracy works…. And that's what I want to focus on tonight, the state of our democracy. Understand: democracy does not require uniformity. Our founders argued, they quarrelled, and eventually they compromised. They expected us to do the same. But they knew that democracy does require a basic sense of solidarity. The idea that, for all our outward differences, we're all in this together, that we rise or fall as one.

There have been moments throughout our history that threatened that solidarity. And the beginning of this century has been one of those times. A

---

1 *open up ... Cuban people* After 54 years without an embassy in Cuba, the United States resumed diplomatic relations with the country in 2015; *Iran's nuclear weapons* In 2015 the threat of continued economic sanctions pressured Iran into signing an agreement to significantly reduce its nuclear program. During his campaign, Trump stated an intention to "dismantle" the agreement; *take out ... 9-11* In 2011, the United States military killed Osama bin Laden, leader of al-Qaeda, the terrorist organization responsible for the attacks on the World Trade Center and other American targets on 11 September 2001.

2 *marriage equality* In 2015, marriage between people of the same sex became legal across the United States when the Supreme Court ruled that laws against it were unconstitutional; *right to ... citizens* The Affordable Care Act (2010), often called "Obamacare," extended health insurance coverage to at least 20 million more Americans than had previously had insurance. Repealing the Act was one of Trump's major campaign promises.

shrinking world, growing inequality, demographic change, and the spectre of terrorism. These forces haven't just tested our security and our prosperity, but are testing our democracy as well. And how we meet these challenges to our democracy will determine our ability to educate our kids and create good jobs and protect our homeland.

In other words, it will determine our future. To begin with, our democracy won't work without a sense that everyone has economic opportunity. And the good news is that today the economy is growing again. Wages, incomes, home values and retirement accounts are all rising again. Poverty is falling again. The wealthy are paying a fair share of taxes. Even as the stock market shatters records, the unemployment rate is near a 10-year low. The uninsured rate[3] has never, ever been lower. Health care costs are rising at the slowest rate in 50 years—and, as I've said, and I mean it, if anyone can put together a plan that is demonstrably better than the improvements we've made to our health care system, that covers as many people at less cost, I will publicly support it.

Because that, after all, is why we serve. Not to score points or take credit. But to make people's lives better.

But, for all the real progress that we've made, we know it's not enough. Our economy doesn't work as well or grow as fast when a few prosper at the expense of a growing middle class, and ladders for folks who want to get into the middle class. That's the economic argument. But stark inequality is also corrosive to our democratic idea. While the top 1 percent has amassed a bigger share of wealth and income, too many of our families in inner cities and in rural counties have been left behind. The laid off factory worker, the waitress or health care worker who's just barely getting by and struggling to pay the bills. Convinced that the game is fixed against them. That their government only serves the interest of the powerful. That's a recipe for more cynicism and polarization in our politics.

There are no quick fixes to this long-term trend. I agree, our trade should 15
be fair and not just free. But the next wave of economic dislocations won't come from overseas. It will come from the relentless pace of automation that makes a lot of good middle class jobs obsolete.

And so we're going to have to forge a new social compact to guarantee all our kids the education they need. To give workers the power to unionize for better wages. To update the social safety net to reflect the way we live now. And make more reforms to the tax code so corporations and the individuals who reap the most from this new economy don't avoid their obligations to the country that's made their very success possible.

---

3 *uninsured rate* Proportion of people who do not have health insurance.

We can argue about how to best achieve these goals. But we can't be complacent about the goals themselves. For if we don't create opportunity for all people, the disaffection and division that has stalled our progress will only sharpen in years to come.

There's a second threat to our democracy. And this one is as old as our nation itself.

After my election there was talk of a post-racial America. And such a vision, however well intended, was never realistic. Race remains a potent and often divisive force in our society.

20 Now I've lived long enough to know that race relations are better than they were 10 or 20 or 30 years ago, no matter what some folks say. You can see it not just in statistics. You see it in the attitudes of young Americans across the political spectrum. But we're not where we need to be. And all of us have more work to do.

If every economic issue is framed as a struggle between a hardworking white middle class and an undeserving minority, then workers of all shades are going to be left fighting for scraps while the wealthy withdraw further into their private enclaves. If we're unwilling to invest in the children of immigrants, just because they don't look like us, we will diminish the prospects of our own children—because those brown kids will represent a larger and larger share of America's workforce.... So if we're going to be serious about race going forward, we need to uphold laws against discrimination—in hiring, and in housing, and in education, and in the criminal justice system.

That is what our Constitution and highest ideals require.

But laws alone won't be enough. Hearts must change. It won't change overnight. Social attitudes oftentimes take generations to change. But if our democracy is to work the way it should in this increasingly diverse nation, then each one of us needs to try to heed the advice of a great character in American fiction, Atticus Finch,[4] who said "You never really understand a person until you consider things from his point of view, until you climb into his skin and walk around in it."

For blacks and other minority groups, that means tying our own very real struggles for justice to the challenges that a lot of people in this country face. Not only the refugee or the immigrant or the rural poor or the transgender American, but also the middle-aged white guy who from the outside may seem like he's got all the advantages, but has seen his world upended by economic, and cultural, and technological change.

25 We have to pay attention and listen.

---

4 *Atticus Finch* Morally upstanding white lawyer who defends an innocent black man from a false accusation in Harper Lee's classic novel *To Kill a Mockingbird* (1960).

For white Americans, it means acknowledging that the effects of slavery and Jim Crow* didn't suddenly vanish in the '60s; that when minority groups voice discontent, they're not just engaging in reverse racism or practising political correctness; when they wage peaceful protest, they're not demanding special treatment, but the equal treatment that our founders promised.

For native-born Americans, it means reminding ourselves that the stereotypes about immigrants today were said, almost word for word, about the Irish, and Italians, and Poles, who it was said were going to destroy the fundamental character of America. And as it turned out, America wasn't weakened by the presence of these newcomers; these newcomers embraced this nation's creed, and this nation was strengthened.

So regardless of the station we occupy; we all have to try harder; we all have to start with the premise that each of our fellow citizens loves this country just as much as we do; that they value hard work and family just like we do; that their children are just as curious and hopeful and worthy of love as our own. And that's not easy to do. For too many of us it's become safer to retreat into our own bubbles, whether in our neighbourhoods, or on college campuses, or places of worship, or especially our social media feeds, surrounded by people who look like us and share the same political outlook and never challenge our assumptions. In the rise of naked partisanship and increasing economic and regional stratification, the splintering of our media into a channel for every taste, all this makes this great sorting seem natural, even inevitable. And increasingly we become so secure in our bubbles that we start accepting only information, whether it's true or not, that fits our opinions, instead of basing our opinions on the evidence that is out there.

And this trend represents a third threat to our democracy. Look, politics is a battle of ideas. That's how our democracy was designed. In the course of a healthy debate, we prioritize different goals, and the different means of reaching them. But without some common baseline of facts, without a willingness to admit new information and concede that your opponent might be making a fair point, and that science and reason matter, then we're going to keep talking past each other....

[P]rotecting our way of life is not just the job of our military. Democracy 30
can buckle when it gives in to fear. So just as we as citizens must remain vigilant against external aggression, we must guard against a weakening of the values that make us who we are.... That's why I reject discrimination against Muslim Americans—who are just as patriotic as we are.

That's why we cannot withdraw from big global fights to expand democracy and human rights and women's rights and LGBT rights.

No matter how imperfect our efforts, no matter how expedient ignoring such values may seem, that's part of defending America. For the fight against extremism and intolerance and sectarianism and chauvinism are of a piece with the fight against authoritarianism and nationalist aggression. If the scope of freedom and respect for the rule of law shrinks around the world, the likelihood of war within and between nations increases, and our own freedoms will eventually be threatened.

So let's be vigilant, but not afraid. ISIL[5] will try to kill innocent people. But they cannot defeat America unless we betray our Constitution and our principles in the fight. Rivals like Russia or China cannot match our influence around the world—unless we give up what we stand for, and turn ourselves into just another big country that bullies smaller neighbours.

Which brings me to my final point: our democracy is threatened whenever we take it for granted.

All of us, regardless of party, should be throwing ourselves into the task of rebuilding our democratic institutions. When voting rates in America are some of the lowest among advanced democracies, we should be making it easier, not harder, to vote. When trust in our institutions is low, we should reduce the corrosive influence of money in our politics, and insist on the principles of transparency and ethics in public service. When Congress is dysfunctional, we should draw our districts to encourage politicians to cater to common sense and not rigid extremes.

But remember, none of this happens on its own. All of this depends on our participation; on each of us accepting the responsibility of citizenship, regardless of which way the pendulum of power happens to be swinging. Our Constitution is a remarkable, beautiful gift. But it's really just a piece of parchment. It has no power on its own. We, the people,[6] give it power. We, the people, give it meaning—with our participation, and with the choices that we make and the alliances that we forge.

Whether or not we stand up for our freedoms, whether or not we respect and enforce the rule of law—that's up to us. America is no fragile thing. But the gains of our long journey to freedom are not assured. In his own farewell address, George Washington wrote … that we should reject "the first dawning of every attempt to alienate any portion of our country from the rest or to enfeeble the sacred ties" that make us one. America, we weaken those ties when we allow our political dialogue to become so corrosive that people of good character aren't even willing to enter into public service. So coarse with

---

5 *ISIL* The Islamic State of Iraq and the Levant, also known as ISIS (Islamic State of Iraq and Syria). This militarized extremist group has been designated a terrorist organization by the United Nations.

6 *We, the people* The first words of the American constitution are "We, the people of the United States."

rancour that Americans with whom we disagree are seen, not just as misguided, but as malevolent. We weaken those ties when we define some of us as more American than others. When we write off the whole system as inevitably corrupt. And when we sit back and blame the leaders we elect without examining our own role in electing them.

It falls to each of us to be … guardians of our democracy—to embrace the joyous task we have been given to continually try to improve this great nation of ours because, for all our outward differences, we in fact all share the same proud type, the most important office in a democracy: citizen.

Citizen. So, you see, that's what our democracy demands. It needs you. Not just when there's an election, not just when your own narrow interest is at stake, but over the full span of a lifetime. If you're tired of arguing with strangers on the Internet, try talking with one of them in real life. If something needs fixing, then lace up your shoes and do some organizing. If you're disappointed by your elected officials, grab a clip board, get some signatures, and run for office yourself.

Show up, dive in, stay at it. Sometimes you'll win, sometimes you'll lose. 40
Presuming a reservoir of goodness in others—that can be a risk. And there will be times when the process will disappoint you. But … let me tell you, it can [also] energize and inspire.… [T]hat faith that I placed all those years ago, not far from here, in the power of ordinary Americans to bring about change, that faith has been rewarded in ways I could not have possibly imagined.…

[To] Michelle, Michelle LaVaughn Robinson of the South Side…, Malia and Sasha…, to Joe Biden, the scrappy kid from Scranton…, to my remarkable staff…, and to all of you out there—every organizer who moved to an unfamiliar town, every kind family who welcomed them in, every volunteer who knocked on doors, every young person who cast a ballot for the first time, every American who lived and breathed the hard work of change—you are the best supporters and organizers anybody could ever hope for, and I will forever be grateful. Because you did change the world. You did. And that's why I leave this stage tonight even more optimistic about this country than when we started. Because I know our work has not only helped so many Americans; it has inspired so many Americans—especially so many young people out there—to believe that you can make a difference.…

Let me tell you, this generation coming up—unselfish, altruistic, creative, patriotic—I've seen you in every corner of the country. You believe in a fair, and just, and inclusive America; you know that constant change has been America's hallmark, and that it's not something to fear but something to embrace. You are willing to carry this hard work of democracy forward. You'll soon outnumber any of us, and I believe as a result the future is in good hands.

My fellow Americans, it has been the honour of my life to serve you. I won't stop; in fact, I will be right there with you, as a citizen, for all my remaining days….

(2017)

Questions

1. Obama's speech had carried on for several minutes before he announced that what he wanted "to focus on tonight" was "the state of our democracy." Those writing essays are generally advised to make clear right from the start what their main subject is—and what their main argument concerning that subject is. Do you think the guidelines for speeches should be different? Why, or why not?
2. Obama's final point is that democracy is threatened when we take it for granted—and that "all of us, regardless of party"—should be "throwing ourselves into the task of rebuilding our democratic institutions." How relevant do you think his call to become more involved is for Canadians? Should we too feel an obligation to become more active participants in our democracy?
3. Obama is highly trained as a writer and speaker, and well aware of the rules of formal English grammar. Yet he makes frequent use of sentence fragments. Identify three parts of this speech in which several incomplete sentences are used in succession, and discuss the rhetorical effectiveness of this strategy.
4. How educated do you think an audience member would have to be to appreciate Obama's speech? Should Obama have tried harder to make the speech accessible to people with less education? Why or why not?

CATHAL KELLY

TIM RAINES IS A POSTER BOY FOR SPORTS INJUSTICE, BUT HIS SNUB DOESN'T DESERVE OUR OBSESSION

On 23 November 2016, Canadian MP Chris Bittle made a statement in Parliament that addressed an unusual subject for discussion in the House of Commons. He argued that Tim Raines, an American baseball player who had spent a significant portion of his career with the former Canadian team the Montreal Expos, should be selected for the Baseball Hall of Fame. (Raines was indeed elected to the Hall of Fame the following January.) This short editorial by sports columnist Cathal Kelly was published in The Globe and Mail *on 24 November, the day after Bittle's speech.*

This week, Chris Bittle, Liberal MP for St. Catharines,[1] addressed an issue of importance to all Canadians.

"I rise today to speak of an upcoming ballot," Bittle told the House of Commons. "This is not a matter for the Minister of Democratic Institutions. I am, Mr. Speaker, speaking about the baseball hall of fame[2] ballot."

Sounding a bit like a Reddit* sub-thread brought to life, Bittle launched into an appeal on behalf of former Montreal Expo Tim Raines.

He reminded us that Raines "had an impressive on-base percentage. On par with Tony Gwynn."[3] He won a batting title. "For five years, he was measured as one of the most valuable players in the National League."

---

1 *St. Catharines* City in southern Ontario.

2 *baseball hall of fame* Players are elected into the Baseball Hall of Fame, based in Cooperstown, New York, by the Baseball Writers' Association of America. A player is considered eligible for ten years upon five years of retirement; 2017 marked the final year of Raines' eligibility for induction.

3 *Tony Gwynn* American baseball player and member of the Baseball Hall of Fame (1960–2014).

5 In all, it was a stats-dork fever dream made real. The geeks have won. They're in control.

As he speaks, Bittle's colleagues can be seen in the background giving him a "What's happening here?" look. Maybe they've been too busy wrestling with the machinery of power to give close attention to Tim Raines's astounding walks-per-season ratio.

Should Raines be in the Hall of Fame? Probably. If you drill down in the numbers, the case is there. He was a remarkably efficient player on a series of posthumously fetishized Expos teams. If Raines had enjoyed his best years as a New York Yankee,* he'd have been in ages ago. But he made the terrible mistake of carpetbagging* his way onto a team Americans—and, more importantly, voters from the Baseball Writers' Association of America—did not pay any attention to. Now, all he has to show for his toil is millions and millions of dollars.

Should any of the rest of us care? Absolutely not. I'm going to do you the favour of assuming you have real problems. If Tim Raines's hall-of-fame tragedy ranks near the top of that list, then congratulations. Your life is blessed beyond measure.

Should our elected representatives be raising the issue in Parliament? Well, you don't need to be reminded that this is how government works. People stand up and talk all sorts of meaningless nonsense in the hopes someone will notice. It's rather like life in that sense. This one worked a charm.* Everyone's talking about it.

10 "Sometimes, it's the items that cut through the seriousness that get the attention," Bittle said Thursday. "And maybe that's unfortunate."

Although clearly meant light-heartedly, Bittle's YouTube moment speaks to a growing infantilism at the core of our public life. It's called sports.

Somewhere along the line, we have managed to convince ourselves that sports *matter*. Not the emotions they evoke or the friendly tribalism they promote—things that actually do matter. But the results.

We kid ourselves that life should be this simple—winners and losers. It's all down there on a sheet of paper, expressed in the comfort of numbers. The meritocracy[4] is no longer just evident to the eye on the ice or the field. It's computable. If you apply enough rigour to the investigation, every outcome seems inevitable in hindsight.

Raines has become one of the *ne plus ultras*[5] of this trend—a very good, if not especially remarkable player during his career; turned hero after the fact

---

4 *meritocracy* Society or organization in which members are rewarded and valued based on their individual skill or talent.

5 *ne plus ultras* Latin: best or most perfect instances.

because the thing he did best—get on base—wasn't particularly rated at the time.

From the modern perspective, that his skill is not recognized isn't just unfortunate. It's unjust. It's worth getting worked up over. The list of things like that is growing exponentially.

The passion with which grown-ups can argue this or a thousand other small points of order when it comes to the games men play continues to boggle my mind.

Most people can't articulate strong feelings about Syria[6] beyond a "Yes, that's terrible." But they will work themselves purple arguing whether Jose Bautista[7] should be paid and how much and for how long.

Because Syria is complicated. And Jose Bautista (who should not be paid and I will fight you if you think different) is easy.

As the world gets more complicated and the background noise gets louder, we retreat into easy things. What should be a pleasant distraction becomes a central focus.

Since sport has become the last cultural niche everyone recognizes, serious people who should have better things to worry about worry about that instead. A corrosive feedback loop is created whereby everyone feels compelled to give over all their free time to caring deeply about the Jays' playoff push.

Eventually, unconscionable swaths of time are given over to cogitating Wins Against Replacement[8] and what it all really means. For Tim Raines.

This obsession with the arcane* minutiae* of games is one of the things that typifies childhood. I think this every time I see a grown man wearing a Josh Donaldson[9] jersey out in public. Like an 8-year-old. A few of them—and this is the lowest of the low—bring baseball gloves to the game.

If your great-grandfather could see you now—and I don't care where he's from or what he was like—he'd punch you in the face, and he'd be right to do so.

At their best, sports are a connector of disparate people and a harmless escape. However, they were never meant to be taken with seriousness—as in

---

6 *Syria* Site of an extremely violent civil war that began in 2011. The war involves multiple factions and the participation of multiple foreign powers, and as of February 2017 had produced 5 million refugees.

7 *Jose Bautista* Dominican Major League Baseball player (b. 1980) who in 2016 controversially demanded US $150 million for re-signing with the Toronto Blue Jays in 2016. The Blue Jays refused.

8 *Wins Against Replacement* Baseball statistic intended to measure the value of a player's role on their team, contrasting the number of wins that team has enjoyed against the estimated number of wins were that player to be replaced by a player of average skill.

9 *Josh Donaldson* American Major League Baseball player for the Toronto Blue Jays.

the eerie way Canadians now talk about hockey, as if it were some patrimony brought down from Mt. Sinai.[10] A list of the places where people care so much about sports that they're willing to beat each other up over them[11] is a pretty good list of places you wouldn't want to live.

I expect sports to become even more central to our public discourse, especially given recent events to the south.[12] When there isn't enough bread for everyone, the people in charge like to go heavy on circuses.[13] They are unique in appealing to all the classes.

What's dispiriting is how complicit smart people are in their own dumbing down. Play sports, watch sports, talk sports, care about sports. That's all great. But not if you begin to think that sports and how they turn out explains something vital about your culture. They only do that if you choose not to pay attention to anything else.

(2016)

Questions

1. Watch Chris Bittle's "YouTube moment" yourself. How does your impression of the event—of Bittle's tone, of his audience's reaction—compare to Kelly's interpretation?
2. Do you think Bittle's speech in Parliament was inappropriate? Why or why not?
3. What place do you think sports deserve in our society?
4. How would you describe the tone of Kelly's article? Is it effective?

---

10 *patrimony brought ... Mt. Sinai* Allusion to the Book of Exodus, in which Moses brings the Ten Commandments from God down to his people from Mount Sinai—a fundamental episode in the shaping of Jewish and Christian religion; *patrimony* Inheritance.

11 *willing to ... over them* Allusion to the phenomenon of violent sports riots. Several riots surrounding hockey have transpired in Canada, such as the 2011 riots in Vancouver following the Boston Bruins' win over the Vancouver Canucks in the Stanley Cup finals.

12 *recent events to the south* Probable allusion to the controversial election of businessman and television personality Donald Trump to the US Presidency, which occurred earlier in November 2016. Many commentators predicted that the presidency would be disastrous for the country and the world.

13 *When there isn't ... circuses* Reference to the ancient Roman satirist Juvenal's complaint that the people of Rome were no longer engaged in politics but were interested only in "bread and circuses"—food and entertaining spectacles (a circus was a type of arena).

José Luis Pardo Veiras

A Decade of Failure in the War on Drugs[1]

Eight days after taking office in 2006, Mexican president Felipe Calderón launched his war on drugs. This war is waged by the state against drug producers and traders; the state attempts to destroy the drugs themselves, to pass anti-drug legislation, and to use military and police intervention to stop the movement of drugs within Mexico and across borders. In Mexico, where drug cartels wield considerable military power and territorial influence, this assault is met with armed resistance, causing a devastating cycle of violence, not only for those involved in the drug trade, but also for civilians. In order to bolster the appearance of "winning" the war, corrupt security forces funded by the state use torture to obtain confessions and arrests, contributing to an atmosphere of fear and mistrust.

The United States has contributed billions to this war through the Mérida Initiative, a cooperative security agreement between the US and Mexico. While the war has achieved some high-profile arrests and drug seizures, there has been no progress in curtailing drug production or trade: sales to the US continue to increase yearly. "A Decade of Failure in the War on Drugs" analyzes the effects of Mexico's war. It was published in The New York Times *in October 2016.*

In 2006, Felipe Calderón, then the incoming president of Mexico, vowed that change was coming to fix the problem of drug trafficking and drug-related violence. To fulfill this promise he sent the army into the streets and embarked on a full-on war against drug trafficking.

Things did indeed change.

1 *A Decade of Failure in the War on Drugs* Translated from the Spanish by Jacinto Fombona.

The year before he took over, Mexico's homicide rate was 9.5 per 100,000 inhabitants. The rate soon doubled, prompting the government to deny there were any civilian victims: those dead in the war against drugs were either evildoers (drug traffickers) or heroes (the policemen and soldiers who fought them). A decade later, too many unknown victims have fallen in this war. The estimates are close to 150,000 dead and 28,000 missing. Mr. Calderón's promise was epic; his strategy, simplistic.

The war of drug traffickers against the government and among themselves has expanded. In places like Tamaulipas, along the border with the United States, to speak out is often a death sentence. In what's known as the Golden Triangle (Chihuahua, Durango, Sinaloa), controlled by the Sinaloa drug cartel, threats by "sicarios" (the cartel's hit men) force the inhabitants to flee their communities. Tourist resorts are no longer sanctuaries. Acapulco is now the country's most violent city, and one of the world's most violent.

5 Even if Mexicans believed Mr. Calderón's promise, the question to ask was and still is: Why would thousands of people work in drug trafficking?

Drugs and drug trafficking are a social, cultural, economic and health-related phenomenon; social violence and insecurity is just one of its many facets. Travelling through Mexico's depressed areas makes anyone understand that organized crime is, in many of them, the only constant presence, the start and the end of everyday life. There, where the state does not reach, or does only to fight crime, illicit means are often the [only] source of employment.

For thousands of Mexicans, drug trafficking is a way to survive. The weakest links in the chain, like the growers or the drug mules,[2] do not ponder whether it is right or wrong. They work only to subsist.

The war on drugs turned out to be a complete failure. Drugs continue to stream north to the United States, the great user, and firearms enter Mexico in return, where they kill thousands. The systematic hunting of drug traffickers has yielded a large number of detainees, even some big names like Joaquín Guzmán Loera, known as El Chapo.[3] Jails are overflowing. But 41 percent of those jailed for drug crimes were arrested for possession of controlled substances worth less than 500 pesos (under $30).

Meanwhile, there are steady flows of cocaine, human trafficking and natural resources, and extortion and poppy growing are rampant. According to United States Drug Enforcement Administration data, Mexican heroin is the

---

2 *drug mules* People who smuggle drugs across borders.

3 *Joaquín Guzmán Loera ... El Chapo* Loera (b.1954 or 1957), whose nickname, "El Chapo," means "Shorty," was one of the most powerful drug lords in the world. Roughly half of the US supply of heroin, methamphetamines, cocaine, and marijuana were shipped through his cartel, the Sinaloa Cartel. He was captured by Mexican authorities and extradited to the US in 2016.

most commonly used type in America, surpassing the Colombian supply. In the state of Guerrero, the top producer of Mexican heroin, 50 criminal groups vie for control of the territory.

10 If Mr. Calderón was the father of this drug policy, his successor as president, Enrique Peña Nieto, seems to be playing the role of the teenager who, in trying to rebel, repeats what he saw his father do.

This past August and July [2016] were the most violent months of Mr. Peña Nieto's presidency, with nearly 4,000 dead—similar to the record numbers of 2011, the bloodiest year of the Calderón administration.

Ten years is enough to get a clearer view and try different approaches. Decriminalizing possession of all drugs for personal use would be a sound first step: It would ease the burden on the collapsed judiciary system, reduce the incentives for the police to make arrests and focus their efforts on violence-prone traffickers who terrify citizens, and not on users.

The great shift in Mr. Peña Nieto's policy was his backing of medicinal use of marijuana, a needed action, but not enough, particularly when it is compared with other similar efforts throughout the region.

In recent years, Colombia has stopped destroying the coca plantations and has sponsored a nationwide crop substitution program, while the country's president, Juan Manuel Santos, issued a law allowing the medical use of marijuana. Costa Rica, a country without an army, has begun a drug-treatment program. In Jamaica, laws for the traditional and medicinal use of cannabis have been approved. In 2009, Argentina's Supreme Court declared punishment for drug possession for personal consumption unconstitutional, and Uruguay has legalized the production, distribution and use of marijuana.

15 Mexico tabulates the amounts of a drug anyone can possess before being considered a trafficker. But this tabulation does not fit the reality of users. For example, it allows for only five grams or less than 0.18 ounces, of marijuana. While drug policies must address each country's characteristics, decriminalizing drug use should be a shared premise.

More than 15 years ago, Portugal decriminalized drug possession for personal use and created a system for drug treatment and social reintegration; cannabis use has levelled, the number of heroin addicts is down 70 percent, and deaths by overdoses have also been reduced. In the Netherlands, a cafeteria-style system has created a legal work force around cannabis and, in part because users are not prosecuted, that country's jails are virtually empty. Recently, a lack of business has led to the closing of a few Dutch prisons. Drug use—of all drugs—is a health issue, not a criminal one. And it should be dealt with as such.

In Mexico the war on drugs turned out to be a worse evil than the one it set out to fight. Ten years locked in a state of emergency and with an army insulated from any criminal investigation of its behaviour have proven to be another failure.

For things to really change, the government should gradually return antidrug programs to the civil authorities. After this decade of mourning, of killings with impunity, of government corruption, Mexico needs to devise a comprehensive drug policy that understands drug trafficking beyond a clash between heroes and villains.

Caught between these extremes, society has been forced to adapt to a state of permanent violence. Decriminalizing drug use will not fix a deeply rooted problem in this country, but it will allow Mexicans to differentiate between drugs and the war on drugs, between drug users and drug traffickers. This is the first step in acknowledging that a different approach is possible.

(2016)

Questions

1. Veiras argues that drug use is a health issue, not a criminal one. Do you agree? Why or why not?
2. Veiras claims that Mexico's drug policy is based on an understanding of drug trafficking as "a clash between heroes and villains."
    a. How does the narrative of "heroes vs. villains" play out in the Mexican government's approach to the drug trade? Is this a useful narrative in shaping policy? Why or why not?
    b. To what extent do you see a "heroes vs. villains" narrative playing out in the Canadian approach to drug policy?
3. According to Veiras, what should Mexico do to begin moving away from the current cycle of violence? Does this strike you as the right approach?
4. Veiras cites the approaches some other countries are taking to address drugs in their communities. What are some of these examples? In your view, should any of these policies be implemented in Mexico, the US, Canada? Why or why not?

Travis Lupick

Our Fentanyl Crisis

According to a recent United Nations report, Canada consumes more opioids[1] *per capita than anywhere else in the world.*[2] *Fentanyl, a synthetic opioid that is 50 to 100 times more powerful than morphine, began to surface in the country's drug supply around 2012. Fentanyl is easily ordered online from Chinese suppliers; it is disguised in packages and shipped through the mail to anyone who places an order. An amount of fentanyl equivalent to two grains of salt can kill an adult; the potency of the drug, and the impossibility of monitoring its concentration in illegally made and distributed forms, have led to an unprecedented number of deaths from overdose. "Our Fentanyl Crisis," published in* The Walrus *magazine in December 2016, focuses on the impact of fentanyl in Vancouver's Downtown Eastside, a neighbourhood with high rates of addiction, mental illness, and homelessness that have made it particularly susceptible to the devastating effects of fentanyl.*

It was the middle of the night on November 25 when Barbara Carter was jolted awake by a fast knocking on her door. A small woman in her late forties, Carter lives on the eighth floor of the Regent Hotel on East Hastings Street. Even by the poor standards of Vancouver's Downtown Eastside, it's a decrepit building that can feel like there are more homeless people taking shelter in the hallways than there are tenants living in its small rooms. Carter's unit is terribly cluttered. There's barely room for her to lie down, with clothing and every sort of knickknack covering the floor, the walls, and even hanging on strings from the ceiling.

She called through the door to ask who was there. "Somebody was overdosing on the fourth floor," she recounts during an interview in her room.

---

1 *opioids* Drugs that act on opioid receptors in the brain; they are effective painkillers. Opium, morphine, heroin, cocaine, and prescription painkillers such as OxyContin are all opioids.

2 See Howlett, Karen et al. "A Killer High," *Globe and Mail*, 5 January 2017.

"There was a young girl at the door, who said, 'I don't know what to do. You have to come do it.'" Children aren't allowed in the Regent Hotel and Carter was startled by the girl who stood in her doorway. "She looked like she was like twelve or something," Carter says.

As a long-time drug user herself, she has learned to manage her own addictions relatively safely. In her room, Carter keeps naloxone, the so-called overdose antidote that's used to reverse the effects of opioids like heroin and fentanyl. Upon entering the blood stream, naloxone seeks out opioid receptors in the brain and pushes drugs away from those connections, temporarily blocking their effects.

Carter grabbed a kit—a small pouch resembling a sunglasses case that holds three vials of naloxone, three needles, rubber gloves, and a face guard for mouth-to-mouth resuscitation—and followed the girl down four flights of stairs. In a room, Carter found a First Nations woman, no older than twenty, lying naked in a bathtub filled with cold water. "She was turning blue and I wasn't sure if it was from the water or from her drugs," Carter says. She took a syringe from her overdose-response kit, snapped the top off a vial of naloxone, filled the needle, and injected the girl in the muscle of her shoulder. A minute passed and nothing happened. Carter pulled the plug from the drain, jumped into the water, and began performing CPR. She loaded another needle with a second dose of naloxone and again injected the girl in her shoulder. Again, nothing. Another round of CPR and a third shot. Still there was no response.

5 "I had to get another kit," Carter says. She ran back up four flights of stairs to her room, grabbed a second naloxone kit, and sprinted back to the fourth floor. "It took six times," she says. Six injections. "It was very scary."

Finally, the girl returned to life. "She said 'Thank you,'" Carter says. To this day, she doesn't know the woman's name. "I don't ask," she explains. That was the sixth tenant at the Regent Hotel whose life Carter saved with naloxone. After the first one, in early November, she put a sign up on her door that reads, *Hey you can get Narcan here*, in reference to naloxone's brand name. Almost immediately tenants began showing up when someone had overdosed. "I was hearing people running through the hallways looking for Narcan kits," Carter says. "So I thought, if they have somewhere to go, maybe we could save somebody's life."

Carter is part of a shadow health-care system that has slowly developed in Vancouver since an overdose epidemic swept into British Columbia in 2011. There are others like her in many of the Downtown Eastside's hotels acting as de facto* paramedics. Out on the streets, two unsanctioned supervised-injection tents operate outside the legal health care system, offering addicts a safer place to use intravenous drugs under the watchful care of volunteers trained in overdose response. Drug users have formed foot patrols and bike teams that monitor the Downtown Eastside's alleys, distributing naloxone and using it themselves when they find somebody in trouble.

It's a community response to the arrival of fentanyl, a synthetic opioid significantly more toxic than heroin. From 2000 to 2010, the number of illicit drug-overdose deaths in BC remained relatively stable, at an average of 207 per year. Then, in 2011, the annual death toll jumped to 292. It dipped slightly the following year, to 273, but then in 2013 rose again, to 330. In 2014: 370 people; and 510 in 2015. In 2016, it is projected that more than 800 people will die from illegal drugs in the province with more than 60 percent of those linked to fentanyl.

Through October and November [2016], frontline staff who work for nonprofits in the Downtown Eastside and paramedics warned that something had changed—that even after years with fentanyl existing in Vancouver, the situation was rapidly deteriorating. On December 16, Vancouver mayor Gregor Robertson convened a press conference to warn that the epidemic appears to have entered a more deadly stage. The night before, eight people had died of suspected overdoses in the Downtown Eastside alone plus one more elsewhere in Vancouver. Across all of BC, there were 13 fatal overdoses that day. "It's desperate times in Vancouver and it's hard to see any silver lining right now when we don't seem to have hit rock bottom with the number of people dying on any given day from an overdose," Robertson said. "We're not able to tread water anymore. We're losing way too many people."

Over the weekend that followed, there were another seven deaths that Van- 10
couver police classified as suspected overdoses. In four days, sixteen people had died of drugs in Vancouver, the majority of them in the ten square blocks that constitutes the Downtown Eastside.

Something in Vancouver's drug supply has changed to cause overdose deaths to spike above where the fentanyl crisis had already taken them. Toxicology tests won't confirm an answer for two-to-three months, but officials suspect another synthetic opioid has arrived to Vancouver. Called carfentanil,[3] it's believed to be roughly a hundred times more toxic than fentanyl. Having lived through a similar epidemic in the 1990s, residents of the Downtown Eastside have taken matters into their own hands and are rallying to care for each other in the absence of government.

There isn't much to the supervised-injection site that Sarah Blyth established in September: a white canvas tarp draped over a steel frame. Underneath, there's a semi-circle of tables and chairs. Near the entrance, there's a stack of supplies for intravenous drug use: clean needles, a water cooler, and little

---

3 *carfentanil* In the months following the publication of this article, urine tests confirmed the presence of carfentanil in metro Vancouver's drug supply.

dishes used to cook heroin, cocaine, or, increasingly, fentanyl. Watching over it all is a volunteer trained in overdose response and equipped with naloxone.

Blyth explains that her decision to launch an operation outside the law was one of necessity. "There were people on the street overdosing in the alley right in front of us," she says. "So we thought we would do something about it."

Three months on, authorities have reluctantly given the operation tacit approval to continue. Vancouver police say they consider the tents a health-care matter and therefore won't intervene. And while the BC Ministry of Health officially states it does not condone the tents, the minister paid a quiet visit on December 12 and thanked volunteers for their work.

Blyth guesses the government's tolerance for the tents is rooted in an acknowledgment that without them more people would die. When she started in September, there were one or two overdoses a day. "And then, all of the sudden, it was back-to-back overdoses. Or two overdoses at a time and situations that were completely chaotic," she says.

Fatal overdose statistics for BC are only specific to cities. But 911 call data for the Downtown Eastside supports the picture Blyth paints. For the one block that runs west from the intersection of Main and East Hastings, it shows that from January to August of this year, there was a relatively consistent monthly average of thirty-two overdose calls. Then, in September, that number jumped to seventy-four. In October, there were ninety-three, and then, in November, 155.

At Blyth's second tent, located in an alley off that block of East Hastings, a retired nurse named Sue Ouelette begins to explain why she chooses to donate her time, but a First Nations man using heroin drops from his chair. It's raining, and the upper half of his body has fallen in a puddle outside the tent. Oulette rushes to him and injects naloxone into the muscle of his thigh. The overdose is caught early, and there's no need to begin mouth-to-mouth resuscitation. Two minutes later, he slowly sits up.

"Hey, you've OD'd* now three times," Ouelette tells him. "Fourth, you won't be lucky." Later that night, still working a long shift at the tent despite having responded to several overdoses that day, she resumes trying to explain why she's there. Ouelette recounts a week in October when a batch of heroin likely spiked with fentanyl caused fourteen overdoses in the building where she lives. She met a man named Corey Fry who was volunteering in homeless shelters, helping respond to overdoses. When his neighbours started to fall, he made sure everybody in his building knew he had naloxone in his room and was available to help. "He rescued at least seven of them himself," Ouelette says. Just when they thought the bad batch had worked its way through their building, Fry was found in his room, dead of an overdose. "It was an emotional shut down for everyone—because he was the heart of the building," Ouelette recalls, crying. “For several days, people were trying not to use drugs. But they were getting too sick from withdrawal. For me, that was when it became really apparent that we have a huge problem.” She has been volunteering since. “Everybody that volunteers here has lost somebody. Everybody.”

In the same alley is the Washington Needle Depot, a window that functions as what is likely the busiest needle distribution program anywhere in North America. It is operated by the Portland Hotel Society (PHS), a non-profit organization that the province contracts to run Vancouver’s sanctioned supervised-injection facility, Insite, plus sixteen supportive-housing buildings in the Downtown Eastside. At the depot, Coco Culbertson, a senior program manager, emphasizes how the overdose epidemic has turned front desk staff into first responders. In the first ten months of this year, PHS reversed more than 1,000 overdoses in those sixteen hotels alone—more overdoses than occurred during the same period at Insite. “It’s not just folks on the street that we’re out trying to help,” Culbertson says. “It’s our residence as well.”

At one of those buildings, the Stanley Hotel, PHS staff speak openly about how they’re affected by the crisis. “I don’t shake anymore, but it’s still traumatic,” Peter Radomski says. He has dealt with so many overdoses that the experience has become nearly routine. “But I often have dreams about the OD after,” he says. “That’s happened multiple times.” Radomski estimates he’s intervened in more than twenty overdoses since he began work at the Stanley ten months ago. His colleague, Tegan Dempsey, has been there for two-and-a-half years. “I would say in the fifties,” she says. “But I’ve lost count.”

The next morning, back at the Washington Needle Depot, a pair of PHS peers—the organization’s term for past and present drug users it employs in frontline positions—sets off on bicycles. When overdoses spiked in November, Culbertson equipped teams with naloxone and fluorescent safety vests, and sent them out to patrol the neighbourhood. The program is called Spikes on Bikes. “They hand out harm-reduction supplies for folks who need them, and they also train people in the alleys on how to use intramuscular naloxone and how to respond to an overdose.” Culbertson says the initiative remains in a trial phase but is recording five or six overdose interventions every day.

While PHS operates with a degree of separation from government the majority of its funding comes from the province, and Culbertson is reluctant to disparage its response to the crisis. Many frontline staff in the Downtown Eastside are in the same position, which has softened criticism of authorities. But Ann Livingston doesn’t hesitate. A long-time activist who took a lead role in the community’s response to Vancouver’s first overdose epidemic of the 1990s, Livingston emphasizes how many people in BC died of drug overdoses since 2011: more than 2,400 people in six years, she notes. (The annual average number of people who die in traffic accidents in BC is 300, for a total of approximately 1,800 for the same period.)

"The government really needs to step up," Livingston says. "Meanwhile, you stack the bodies. It's a lot of dead people. Yet there is no sense of urgency for them."

On December 8, the response finally came. BC health minister Terry Lake enacted a ministerial order under the Health Emergency Services Act to immediately open three new supervised-injection sites in the Downtown Eastside. The unprecedented move sidestepped federal drug laws that for years prevented Canadian cities from establishing injection facilities like Insite. "We don't want to break the law, obviously, but at the same time, our major concern is saving lives," Lake said during the announcement. He also announced the government would deploy a mobile medical unit to the Downtown Eastside, establishing a field-style emergency room in a vacant lot. "With the September numbers, a lot of us were cautiously optimistic that we had turned a corner," Lake says while standing outside that facility a few days later. "When we saw sixty deaths in October, we still thought maybe we're still plateauing here," he says. "I understand the November numbers will be higher. We don't feel like we've turned a corner yet."

On December 19 the BC Coroner's Service released the November numbers, which showed an increase in fatal overdoses had indeed continued. Forty-nine across BC in August. Fifty-seven in September. Sixty-three in October.

In November: one hundred and twenty-eight.

(2016)

Questions

1. Many criticize the Canadian government's slow response to the fentanyl crisis. In your opinion, what measures should the government be taking, in the short term and the long term? Why do you think the government has not done more already?
2. Some people consider the crisis with fentanyl as parallel to that which occurred during Prohibition, when people died from tainted illegal alcohol. This argument suggests that, just as the decriminalization and regulation of alcohol went a long way to remedy the problem of deaths from tainted alcohol, similar policies could also help end the fentanyl crisis. Do you think this is an appropriate comparison? Why or why not?

3. In 2001, Portugal decriminalized all drugs; the result has been a reduction in drug use, lower rates of HIV infection, and very low rates of death by overdose. Research Portugal's policy and its effects. In your opinion, should Canada consider adopting a similar policy? Why or why not?
4. Fentanyl is shipped to Canada in various ways, among them disguised in small packages (in those little packets of silica included in packaging for freshness, for example). Police chiefs across Canada are arguing for a change to the Canada Post Act, which forbids the searching of mail sent through Canada Post unless there is specific reason to be suspicious of a package. Would you agree with changes to the Canada Post Act that would give the police more flexibility to intercept packages of fentanyl? Why or why not?
5. This article incorporates statistics regarding overdose and death rates. What strategies does the author use to increase the persuasive impact of these statistics? How effective are these strategies?

TIMOTHY D. SNYDER

TWENTY LESSONS FROM THE TWENTIETH CENTURY

The scholarly reputation of Yale University Professor Timothy D. Snyder rests in particular on two groundbreaking studies of tyranny: Bloodlands: Europe Between Hitler and Stalin *(2010), which explores the ways in which the regimes of Adolf Hitler and Joseph Stalin acquired and then exerted tyrannical control over central and Eastern Europe in the 1930s and 1940s; and* Black Earth: The Holocaust as History and Warning, *which argues that racial animus (rather than nationalism) was at the heart of Hitler's tyrannical project. In the wake of the 8 November 2016 American election, Snyder was moved to try to distill his knowledge of the history of tyranny into an op-ed piece that would provide advice to Americans. He first submitted the piece to* The New York Times, *but that newspaper declined to publish it; Snyder then decided to publish it as a post on Facebook. He did so on 15 November, posting it with no title; it has come to be referred to by the title we have given it here—after a phrase Snyder uses in his opening paragraph. The post had soon been shared over 15,000 times (including by several news outlets).*

Following on the explosive reaction to the post, Snyder wrote a 128-page book in which he expanded on each of the twenty points; On Tyranny: Twenty Lessons from the Twentieth Century *was published 28 February 2017.*

Americans are no wiser than the Europeans who saw democracy yield to fascism, Nazism, or communism. Our one advantage is that we might learn from their experience. Now is a good time to do so. Here are twenty lessons from the twentieth century, adapted to the circumstances of today.

1. Do not obey in advance. Much of the power of authoritarianism* is freely given. In times like these, individuals think ahead about what a more repressive government will want, and then start to do it without being asked.

You've already done this, haven't you? Stop. Anticipatory obedience teaches authorities what is possible and accelerates unfreedom.

2. Defend an institution. Follow the courts or the media, or a court or a newspaper. Do not speak of "our institutions" unless you are making them yours by acting on their behalf. Institutions don't protect themselves. They go down like dominoes unless each is defended from the beginning.

3. Recall professional ethics. When the leaders of state set a negative example, professional commitments to just practice become much more important. It is hard to break a rule-of-law state without lawyers, and it is hard to have show trials without judges.

4. When listening to politicians, distinguish certain words. Look out for the expansive use of "terrorism" and "extremism." Be alive to the fatal notions of "exception" and "emergency." Be angry about the treacherous use of patriotic vocabulary.

5. Be calm when the unthinkable arrives. When the terrorist attack comes, remember that all authoritarians at all times either await or plan such events in order to consolidate power. Think of the Reichstag fire.[1] The sudden disaster that requires the end of the balance of power, the end of opposition parties, and so on, is the oldest trick in the Hitlerian book. Don't fall for it.

6. Be kind to our language. Avoid pronouncing the phrases everyone else does. Think up your own way of speaking, even if only to convey that thing you think everyone is saying. (Don't use the internet before bed. Charge your gadgets away from your bedroom, and read.) What to read? Perhaps "The Power of the Powerless" by Václav Havel, *1984* by George Orwell, *The Captive Mind* by Czesław Milosz, *The Rebel* by Albert Camus, *The Origins of Totalitarianism* by Hannah Arendt, or *Nothing Is True and Everything Is Possible* by Peter Pomerantsev.

7. Stand out. Someone has to. It is easy, in words and deeds, to follow along. It can feel strange to do or say something different. But without that unease, there is no freedom. And the moment you set an example, the spell of the status quo is broken, and others will follow.

8. Believe in truth. To abandon facts is to abandon freedom. If nothing is true, then no one can criticize power, because there is no basis upon which to do so. If nothing is true, then all is spectacle. The biggest wallet pays for the most blinding lights.

---

1 *Reichstag fire* Hitler used a 27 February 1933 arson attack on the German parliament (known as the Reichstag) as an excuse to expel from parliament members of the opposition Communist Party (whom he claimed, with no evidence, had conspired with the arsonist), and then to suspend a broad range of civil liberties, including freedom of speech, freedom of association, and freedom of the press.

10 9. Investigate. Figure things out for yourself. Spend more time with long articles. Subsidize investigative journalism by subscribing to print media. Realize that some of what is on your screen is there to harm you. Learn about sites that investigate foreign propaganda pushes.

10. Practice corporeal* politics. Power wants your body softening in your chair and your emotions dissipating on the screen. Get outside. Put your body in unfamiliar places with unfamiliar people. Make new friends and march with them.

11. Make eye contact and small talk. This is not just polite. It is a way to stay in touch with your surroundings, break down unnecessary social barriers, and come to understand whom you should and should not trust. If we enter a culture of denunciation, you will want to know the psychological landscape of your daily life.

12. Take responsibility for the face of the world. Notice the swastikas* and the other signs of hate. Do not look away and do not get used to them. Remove them yourself and set an example for others to do so.

13. Hinder the one-party state. The parties that took over states were once something else. They exploited a historical moment to make political life impossible for their rivals. Vote in local and state elections while you can.

15 14. Give regularly to good causes, if you can. Pick a charity and set up autopay. Then you will know that you have made a free choice that is supporting civil society helping others doing something good.

15. Establish a private life. Nastier rulers will use what they know about you to push you around. Scrub your computer of malware. Remember that email is skywriting. Consider using alternative forms of the internet, or simply using it less. Have personal exchanges in person. For the same reason, resolve any legal trouble. Authoritarianism works as a blackmail state, looking for the hook on which to hang you. Try not to have too many hooks.

16. Learn from others in other countries. Keep up your friendships abroad, or make new friends abroad. The present difficulties here are an element of a general trend. And no country is going to find a solution by itself. Make sure you and your family have passports.

17. Watch out for the paramilitaries.* When the men with guns who have always claimed to be against the system start wearing uniforms and marching around with torches and pictures of a Leader, the end is nigh. When the pro-Leader paramilitary and the official police and military intermingle, the game is over.

18. Be reflective if you must be armed. If you carry a weapon in public service, God bless you and keep you. But know that evils of the past involved policemen and soldiers finding themselves, one day, doing irregular things. Be

ready to say no. (If you do not know what this means, contact the United States Holocaust Memorial Museum and ask about training in professional ethics.)

19. Be as courageous as you can. If none of us is prepared to die for free- 20
dom, then all of us will die in unfreedom.

20. Be a patriot. The incoming president is not. Set a good example of what America means for the generations to come. They will need it.

(2016)

Questions

1. Snyder alludes in his first paragraph to the tradition known as American exceptionalism when he asserts that Americans are "no wiser than Europeans." The best-known fictionalized treatment of a dictatorship arising in America (Sinclair Lewis's 1935 novel *It Can't Happen Here*) also alludes to the assumption on the part of many Americans that America is exceptional—a nation blessed with such sound safeguards in its democratic institutions and such good sense amongst its citizenry that a tyrannical regime could never come to power. What do you think? Is America exceptional in this way? Is Canada? Could tyranny take root in any nation, given a particular conjunction of circumstances?
2. Snyder refers to a different sort of exception in #4:

   > Look out for the expansive use of "terrorism" and "extremism." Be alive to the fatal notions of "exception" and "emergency." Be angry about the treacherous use of patriotic vocabulary.

   Explain in your own words what he is saying here.
3. Though Snyder's post has met with a very positive response in many quarters, he has also been accused by some of alarmism and of exaggerating the threat posed by the Trump presidency. Snyder himself has said that he would be delighted to be proved wrong as to the risk of authoritarianism taking root, but stoutly defends his decision to issue a warning in the terms that he did. In defending his response to the election he has asked: "If your choices in life are alarmism and authoritarianism, which one would you choose?"

   What do you think? Are Snyder's fears turning out to be exaggerated? More generally, is it an appropriate strategy to make a danger seem as large as possible in order to try to improve the chances of the feared scenario *not* becoming a reality?

4. As mentioned in the headnote, Snyder first submitted this piece to *The New York Times*. Is the style and substance of the piece more suited to a Facebook post than an op-ed column in a major newspaper? If so, why?
5. To what extent do you think Snyder's "Twenty Lessons" represent good advice even when no threat of tyranny exists?

DAVID FRUM

from HOW TO BUILD AN AUTOCRACY[1]

David Frum, a senior editor at the influential news and literature magazine The Atlantic, *has long identified as a conservative Republican and worked as a speechwriter for George W. Bush in 2001 and 2002. Despite his ties to the Republican party, he strongly opposed the election of Trump. In the following article—* The Atlantic*'s cover story less than two months after Trump's inauguration—he offers a vision of how the new president's administration could undermine freedom in the United States.*

It's 2021, and President Donald Trump will shortly be sworn in for his second term. The 45th president has visibly aged over the past four years. He rests heavily on his daughter Ivanka's arm during his infrequent public appearances.

Fortunately for him, he did not need to campaign hard for reelection. His has been a popular presidency: Big tax cuts, big spending, and big deficits have worked their familiar expansive magic. Wages have grown strongly in the Trump years, especially for men without a college degree, even if rising inflation is beginning to bite into the gains. The president's supporters credit his restrictive immigration policies and his TrumpWorks infrastructure program.

The president's critics, meanwhile, have found little hearing for their protests and complaints. A Senate investigation of Russian hacking during the 2016 presidential campaign[2] sputtered into inconclusive partisan wrangling. Concerns about Trump's purported conflicts of interest excited debate in Washington but never drew much attention from the wider American public.

Allegations of fraud and self-dealing in the TrumpWorks program, and elsewhere, have likewise been shrugged off. The president regularly tweets out news of factory openings and big hiring announcements: "I'm bringing back

---

1 *Autocracy* Political system in which one person holds unrestrained power.

2 *Russian ... campaign* The Russian government ordered a campaign of interference in the 2016 American election, including the spreading of fake news and the hacking and subsequent publication of Democrats' emails, to promote Trump's victory. At the time this article was published, it was still unclear whether Trump knew about or encouraged this interference.

your jobs," he has said over and over. Voters seem to have believed him—and are grateful.

5 Most Americans intuit that their president and his relatives have become vastly wealthier over the past four years. But rumours of graft* are easy to dismiss. Because Trump has never released his tax returns, no one really knows.

Anyway, doesn't everybody do it? On the eve of the 2018 congressional elections, WikiLeaks released years of investment statements by prominent congressional Democrats indicating that they had long earned above-market returns. As the air filled with allegations of insider trading and crony capitalism, the public subsided into weary cynicism. The Republicans held both houses of Congress that November, and Trump loyalists shouldered aside the pre-Trump leadership.

The business community learned its lesson early. "You work for me, you don't criticize me," the president was reported to have told one major federal contractor, after knocking billions off his company's stock-market valuation with an angry tweet. Wise business leaders take care to credit Trump's personal leadership for any good news, and to avoid saying anything that might displease the president or his family.

The media have grown noticeably more friendly to Trump as well. The proposed merger of AT&T and Time Warner was delayed for more than a year, during which Time Warner's CNN[3] unit worked ever harder to meet Trump's definition of fairness. Under the agreement that settled the Department of Justice's antitrust complaint against Amazon,[4] the company's founder, Jeff Bezos, has divested himself of *The Washington Post*. The paper's new owner—an investor group based in Slovakia—has closed the printed edition and refocused the paper on municipal politics and lifestyle coverage.

Meanwhile, social media circulate ever-wilder rumours. Some people believe them; others don't. It's hard work to ascertain what is true.

10 Nobody's repealed the First Amendment,* of course, and Americans remain as free to speak their minds as ever—provided they can stomach seeing their timelines fill up with obscene abuse and angry threats from the pro-Trump troll armies that police Facebook and Twitter. Rather than deal with digital

---

3 *AT&T and Time Warner* During his campaign, Trump repeatedly stated that he would not allow a merger between AT&T (a large telecommunications company that provides phone and television) and Time Warner Inc. (a large mass media company that produces film and television content); *CNN* News network owned by Time Warner. Though CNN is generally viewed as a centrist network, Trump has condemned it as biased, calling it "fake news."

4 *Amazon* During his campaign, Trump repeatedly stated that Amazon had "a huge antitrust problem." Amazon's founder and CEO, Jeff Bezos, owns *The Washington Post*, a major newspaper that Trump has condemned.

thugs, young people increasingly drift to less political media like Snapchat and Instagram.

Trump-critical media do continue to find elite audiences. Their investigations still win Pulitzer Prizes; their reporters accept invitations to anxious conferences about corruption, digital-journalism standards, the end of NATO, and the rise of populist authoritarianism.* Yet somehow all of this earnest effort feels less and less relevant to American politics. President Trump communicates with the people directly via his Twitter account, ushering his supporters toward favourable information at Fox News or Breitbart.[5]

Despite the hand-wringing, the country has in many ways changed much less than some feared or hoped four years ago. Ambitious Republican plans notwithstanding, the American social-welfare system, as most people encounter it, has remained largely intact during Trump's first term. The predicted wave of mass deportations of illegal immigrants never materialized. A large illegal workforce remains in the country, with the tacit understanding that so long as these immigrants avoid politics, keeping their heads down and their mouths shut, nobody will look very hard for them.

African Americans, young people, and the recently naturalized encounter increasing difficulties casting a vote in most states. But for all the talk of the rollback of rights, corporate America still seeks diversity in employment. Same-sex marriage remains the law of the land. Americans are no more and no less likely to say "Merry Christmas" than they were before Trump took office.

People crack jokes about Trump's National Security Agency listening in on them. They cannot deeply mean it; after all, there's no less sexting in America today than four years ago. Still, with all the hacks and leaks happening these days—particularly to the politically outspoken—it's just common sense to be careful what you say in an email or on the phone. When has politics not been a dirty business? When have the rich and powerful not mostly gotten their way? The smart thing to do is tune out the political yammer, mind your own business, enjoy a relatively prosperous time, and leave the questions to the troublemakers.

In an 1888 lecture, James Russell Lowell, a founder of this magazine, chal- 15
lenged the happy assumption that the Constitution was a "machine that would go of itself." Lowell was right. *Checks and balances** is a metaphor, not a mechanism.

---

5 *Fox News* American News network that has been widely censured for pro-Republican bias; *Breitbart* American news and political commentary website associated with right-wing extremism.

Everything imagined above—and everything described below—is possible only if many people other than Donald Trump agree to permit it. It can all be stopped, if individual citizens and public officials make the right choices. The story told here, like that told by Charles Dickens's Ghost of Christmas Yet to Come,[6] is a story not of things that will be, but of things that may be. Other paths remain open. It is up to Americans to decide which one the country will follow.

No society, not even one as rich and fortunate as the United States has been, is guaranteed a successful future. When early Americans wrote things like "Eternal vigilance is the price of liberty,"[7] they did not do so to provide bromides for future bumper stickers. They lived in a world in which authoritarian rule was the norm, in which rulers habitually claimed the powers and assets of the state as their own personal property.

The exercise of political power is different today than it was then—but perhaps not so different as we might imagine. Larry Diamond, a sociologist at Stanford, has described the past decade as a period of "democratic recession." Worldwide, the number of democratic states has diminished. Within many of the remaining democracies, the quality of governance has deteriorated.

What has happened in Hungary since 2010 offers an example—and a blueprint for would-be strongmen. Hungary is a member state of the European Union and a signatory of the European Convention on Human Rights. It has elections and uncensored internet. Yet Hungary is ceasing to be a free country.

The transition has been nonviolent, often not even very dramatic. Opponents of the regime are not murdered or imprisoned, although many are harassed with building inspections and tax audits. If they work for the government, or for a company susceptible to government pressure, they risk their jobs by speaking out. Nonetheless, they are free to emigrate anytime they like. Those with money can even take it with them. Day in and day out, the regime works more through inducements than through intimidation. The courts are packed, and forgiving of the regime's allies. Friends of the government win state contracts at high prices and borrow on easy terms from the central bank. Those on the inside grow rich by favouritism; those on the outside suffer from the general deterioration of the economy. As one shrewd observer told me on a recent visit, "The benefit of controlling a modern state is less the power to persecute the innocent, more the power to protect the guilty."

---

6 *Charles ... to Come* In *A Christmas Carol* (1843), Ebenezer Scrooge, an unkind miser, is visited by three ghosts. The last, the "Ghost of Christmas Yet to Come," shows him the terrible future that will occur if he fails to change his ways.

7 *Eternal ... liberty* Statement sometimes attributed to Thomas Jefferson, though it was used by many early American political figures.

Prime Minister Viktor Orbán's rule over Hungary does depend on elections. These remain open and more or less free—at least in the sense that ballots are counted accurately. Yet they are not quite fair. Electoral rules favour incumbent power-holders in ways both obvious and subtle. Independent media lose advertising under government pressure; government allies own more and more media outlets each year. The government sustains support even in the face of bad news by artfully generating an endless sequence of controversies that leave culturally conservative Hungarians feeling misunderstood and victimized by liberals, foreigners, and Jews.

You could tell a similar story of the slide away from democracy in South Africa under Nelson Mandela's successors, in Venezuela under the thug-thief Hugo Chávez, or in the Philippines under the murderous Rodrigo Duterte.[8] A comparable transformation has recently begun in Poland, and could come to France should Marine Le Pen, the National Front's candidate, win the presidency.[9]

Outside the Islamic world, the 21st century is not an era of ideology. The grand utopian visions of the 19th century have passed out of fashion. The nightmare totalitarian projects of the 20th have been overthrown or have disintegrated, leaving behind only outdated remnants: North Korea, Cuba. What is spreading today is repressive kleptocracy,[10] led by rulers motivated by greed rather than by the deranged idealism of Hitler or Stalin or Mao. Such rulers rely less on terror and more on rule-twisting, the manipulation of information, and the co-optation of elites.

The United States is of course a very robust democracy. Yet no human contrivance is tamper-proof, a constitutional democracy least of all. Some features of the American system hugely inhibit the abuse of office: the separation of powers within the federal government; the division of responsibilities between

---

8 *Nelson Mandela's successors* Nelson Mandela's first successor, Thabo Mbeki, resigned in 2008 after being charged with interfering in the trial of a fellow party member, Jacob Zuma, who had been accused of corruption. Zuma himself became president in 2009; *Hugo Chávez* President of Venezuela from 1999 until his death in 2013. Chávez's policies reduced poverty and improved access to education and health care—but he also made undemocratic changes to the country's government in order to expand his own power, and corruption and violent crime increased during his time in office; *Rodrigo Duterte* Duterte became president of the Philippines in 2016. As mayor of Davao City, he fought crime by means of vigilante "death squads," and campaigned with the promise to impose a similar policy on the whole nation.

9 *should Marine ... presidency* Le Pen was defeated by a liberal, Emmanuel Macron, in the April-May 2017 election.

10 *kleptocracy* Corrupt government in which rulers use their positions to enhance their own wealth and power. The word combines the ancient Greek terms "klepto," meaning "theft," and "kratos," meaning "rule."

the federal government and the states. Federal agencies pride themselves on their independence; the court system is huge, complex, and resistant to improper influence.

Yet the American system is also perforated by vulnerabilities no less dangerous for being so familiar. Supreme among those vulnerabilities is reliance on the personal qualities of the man or woman who wields the awesome powers of the presidency. A British prime minister can lose power in minutes if he or she forfeits the confidence of the majority in Parliament. The president of the United States, on the other hand, is restrained first and foremost by his own ethics and public spirit. What happens if somebody comes to the high office lacking those qualities?

Over the past generation, we have seen ominous indicators of a breakdown of the American political system: the willingness of congressional Republicans to push the United States to the brink of a default on its national obligations in 2013 in order to score a point in budget negotiations; Barack Obama's assertion of a unilateral executive power to confer legal status upon millions of people illegally present in the United States—despite his own prior acknowledgment that no such power existed.

Donald Trump, however, represents something much more radical. A president who plausibly owes his office at least in part to a clandestine intervention by a hostile foreign intelligence service? Who uses the bully pulpit to target individual critics? Who creates blind trusts that are not blind, invites his children to commingle private and public business, and somehow gets the unhappy members of his own political party either to endorse his choices or shrug them off? If this were happening in Honduras, we'd know what to call it. It's happening here instead, and so we are baffled.

"Ambition must be made to counteract ambition."[11] With those words, written more than 200 years ago, the authors of the Federalist Papers explained the most important safeguard of the American constitutional system. They then added this promise: "In republican government, the legislative authority necessarily predominates." Congress enacts laws, appropriates funds, confirms the president's appointees. Congress can subpoena records, question officials, and even impeach them. Congress can protect the American system from an overbearing president.

---

11 *Ambition ... ambition* Statement made in *The Federalist No. 51* (1788), one of a series of papers, written primarily by Alexander Hamilton and James Madison, intended to encourage the adoption of the US Constitution. Paper 51, titled "The Structure of the Government Must Furnish the Proper Checks and Balances between the Different Departments," discussed the constitution's means of preventing any one branch of government from overpowering the others.

But will it?

As politics has become polarized, Congress has increasingly become a 30
check only on presidents of the opposite party. Recent presidents enjoying a same-party majority in Congress—Barack Obama in 2009 and 2010, George W. Bush from 2003 through 2006—usually got their way. And congressional oversight might well be performed even less diligently during the Trump administration.

The first reason to fear weak diligence is the oddly inverse relationship between President Trump and the congressional Republicans. In the ordinary course of events, it's the incoming president who burns with eager policy ideas. Consequently, it's the president who must adapt to—and often overlook—the petty human weaknesses and vices of members of Congress in order to advance his agenda. This time, it will be Paul Ryan, the speaker of the House, doing the advancing—and consequently the overlooking.

Trump has scant interest in congressional Republicans' ideas, does not share their ideology, and cares little for their fate. He can—and would—break faith with them in an instant to further his own interests. Yet here they are, on the verge of achieving everything they have hoped to achieve for years, if not decades. They owe this chance solely to Trump's ability to deliver a crucial margin of votes in a handful of states—Wisconsin, Michigan, and Pennsylvania—which has provided a party that cannot win the national popular vote a fleeting opportunity to act as a decisive national majority. The greatest risk to all their projects and plans is the very same X factor* that gave them their opportunity: Donald Trump, and his famously erratic personality. What excites Trump is his approval rating, his wealth, his power. The day could come when those ends would be better served by jettisoning the institutional Republican Party in favour of an ad hoc populist coalition, joining nationalism to generous social spending—a mix that's worked well for authoritarians in places like Poland. Who doubts Trump would do it? Not Paul Ryan. Not Mitch McConnell, the Senate majority leader. For the first time since the administration of John Tyler in the 1840s, a majority in Congress must worry about their president defecting from *them* rather than the other way around.

A scandal involving the president could likewise wreck everything that Republican congressional leaders have waited years to accomplish. However deftly they manage everything else, they cannot prevent such a scandal. But there is one thing they can do: their utmost not to find out about it....

Donald Trump will not set out to build an authoritarian state. His immediate priority seems likely to be to use the presidency to enrich himself. But as he does so, he will need to protect himself from legal risk. Being Trump, he will also inevitably wish to inflict payback on his critics. Construction of an apparatus of impunity and revenge will begin haphazardly and opportunistically. But it will accelerate. It will have to.

35 If Congress is quiescent, what can Trump do? A better question, perhaps, is what can't he do?

Newt Gingrich, the former speaker of the House, who often articulates Trumpist ideas more candidly than Trump himself might think prudent, offered a sharp lesson in how difficult it will be to enforce laws against an uncooperative president. During a radio roundtable in December, on the topic of whether it would violate anti-nepotism laws to bring Trump's daughter and son-in-law onto the White House staff, Gingrich said: The president "has, frankly, the power of the pardon. It is a totally open power, and he could simply say, 'Look, I want them to be my advisers. I pardon them if anybody finds them to have behaved against the rules. Period.' And technically, under the Constitution, he has that level of authority."

That statement is true, and it points to a deeper truth: The United States may be a nation of laws, but the proper functioning of the law depends upon the competence and integrity of those charged with executing it. A president determined to thwart the law in order to protect himself and those in his circle has many means to do so.

The power of the pardon, deployed to defend not only family but also those who would protect the president's interests, dealings, and indiscretions, is one such means. The powers of appointment and removal are another. The president appoints and can remove the commissioner of the IRS. He appoints and can remove the inspectors general who oversee the internal workings of the Cabinet departments and major agencies. He appoints and can remove the 93 U.S. attorneys, who have the power to initiate and to end federal prosecutions. He appoints and can remove the attorney general, the deputy attorney general, and the head of the criminal division at the Department of Justice.

There are hedges on these powers, both customary and constitutional, including the Senate's power to confirm (or not) presidential appointees. Yet the hedges may not hold in the future as robustly as they have in the past....

40 The traditions of independence and professionalism that prevail within the federal law-enforcement apparatus, and within the civil service more generally, will tend to restrain a president's power. Yet in the years ahead, these restraints may also prove less robust than they look. Republicans in Congress have long advocated reforms to expedite the firing of underperforming civil servants. In the abstract, there's much to recommend this idea. If reform is dramatic and happens in the next two years, however, the balance of power between the political and the professional elements of the federal government will shift, decisively, at precisely the moment when the political elements are most aggressive. The intelligence agencies in particular would likely find themselves

exposed to retribution from a president enraged at them for reporting on Russia's aid to his election campaign. "As you know from his other career, Donald likes to fire people." So New Jersey Governor Chris Christie joked to a roomful of Republican donors at the party's national convention in July. It would be a mighty power—and highly useful.

The courts, though they might slowly be packed with judges inclined to hear the president's arguments sympathetically, are also a check, of course. But it's already difficult to hold a president to account for financial improprieties. As Donald Trump correctly told reporters and editors from *The New York Times* on November 22, presidents are not bound by the conflict-of-interest rules that govern everyone else in the executive branch....

Trump is poised to mingle business and government with an audacity and on a scale more reminiscent of a leader in a post-Soviet republic than anything ever before seen in the United States. Glimpses of his family's wealth-seeking activities will likely emerge during his presidency, as they did during the transition. Trump's Indian business partners dropped by Trump Tower and posted pictures with the then-president-elect on Facebook, alerting folks back home that they were now powers to be reckoned with. The Argentine media reported that Trump had discussed the progress of a Trump-branded building in Buenos Aires during a congratulatory phone call from the country's president. (A spokesman for the Argentine president denied that the two men had discussed the building on their call.) Trump's daughter Ivanka sat in on a meeting with the Japanese prime minister—a useful meeting for her, since a government-owned bank has a large ownership stake in the Japanese company with which she was negotiating a licensing deal....

It is essential to recognize that Trump will use his position not only to enrich himself; he will enrich plenty of other people too, both the powerful and—sometimes, for public consumption—the relatively powerless. Venezuela, a stable democracy from the late 1950s through the 1990s, was corrupted by a politics of personal favouritism, as Hugo Chávez used state resources to bestow gifts on supporters. Venezuelan state TV even aired a regular program to showcase weeping recipients of new houses and free appliances. Americans recently got a preview of their own version of that show as grateful Carrier employees thanked then-President-elect Trump for keeping their jobs in Indiana.

"I just couldn't believe that this guy … he's not even president yet and he worked on this deal with the company," T.J. Bray, a 32-year-old Carrier employee, told *Fortune*. "I'm just in shock. A lot of the workers are in shock. We can't believe something good finally happened to us. It felt like a victory for the little people."

Trump will try hard during his presidency to create an atmosphere of per- 45
sonal munificence, in which graft does not matter, because rules and institutions

do not matter. He will want to associate economic benefit with personal favour. He will create personal constituencies, and implicate other people in his corruption. That, over time, is what truly subverts the institutions of democracy and the rule of law. If the public cannot be induced to care, the power of the investigators serving at Trump's pleasure will be diminished all the more....

... In true police states, surveillance and repression sustain the power of the authorities. But that's not how power is gained and sustained in backsliding democracies. Polarization, not persecution, enables the modern illiberal regime.

By guile or by instinct, Trump understands this.

Whenever Trump stumbles into some kind of trouble, he reacts by picking a divisive fight. The morning after *The Wall Street Journal* published a story about the extraordinary conflicts of interest surrounding Trump's son-in-law, Jared Kushner, Trump tweeted that flag burners should be imprisoned or stripped of their citizenship. That evening, as if on cue, a little posse of oddballs obligingly burned flags for the cameras in front of the Trump International Hotel in New York. Guess which story dominated that day's news cycle? ...

Calculated outrage is an old political trick, but nobody in the history of American politics has deployed it as aggressively, as repeatedly, or with such success as Donald Trump. If there is harsh law enforcement by the Trump administration, it will benefit the president not to the extent that it quashes unrest, but to the extent that it enflames more of it, ratifying the apocalyptic vision that haunted his speech at the convention.

50 At a rally in Grand Rapids, Michigan, in December, Trump got to talking about Vladimir Putin.[12] "And then they said, 'You know he's killed reporters,'" Trump told the audience. "And I don't like that. I'm totally against that. By the way, I hate some of these people, but I'd never kill them. I hate them. No, I think, no—these people, honestly—I'll be honest. I'll be honest. I would never kill them. I would never do that. Ah, let's see—nah, no, I wouldn't. I would never kill them. But I do hate them."

In the early days of the Trump transition, Nic Dawes, a journalist who has worked in South Africa, delivered an ominous warning to the American media about what to expect. "Get used to being stigmatized as 'opposition,'" he wrote. "The basic idea is simple: to delegitimize accountability journalism by framing it as partisan."

---

12 *Vladimir Putin* Putin, who wields unconstrained power over the Russian Federation, became president of the nation for the second time in 2012. He was Prime Minister from 1999 to 2000, President from 2000 to 2008, and Prime Minister from 2008 to 2012.

The rulers of backsliding democracies resent an independent press, but cannot extinguish it. They may curb the media's appetite for critical coverage by intimidating unfriendly journalists, as President Jacob Zuma and members of his party have done in South Africa. Mostly, however, modern strongmen seek merely to discredit journalism as an institution, by denying that such a thing as independent judgment can exist. All reporting serves an agenda. There is no truth, only competing attempts to grab power.

By filling the media space with bizarre inventions and brazen denials, purveyors of fake news hope to mobilize potential supporters with righteous wrath—and to demoralize potential opponents by nurturing the idea that everybody lies and nothing matters. A would-be kleptocrat is actually better served by spreading cynicism than by deceiving followers with false beliefs: Believers can be disillusioned; people who expect to hear only lies can hardly complain when a lie is exposed. The inculcation of cynicism breaks down the distinction between those forms of media that try their imperfect best to report the truth, and those that purvey falsehoods for reasons of profit or ideology. *The New York Times* becomes the equivalent of Russia's RT; *The Washington Post* of Breitbart; NPR of Infowars.[13]

One story, still supremely disturbing, exemplifies the falsifying method. During November and December, the slow-moving California vote count gradually pushed Hillary Clinton's lead over Donald Trump in the national popular vote further and further: past 1 million, past 1.5 million, past 2 million, past 2.5 million. Trump's share of the vote would ultimately clock in below Richard Nixon's in 1960, Al Gore's in 2000, John Kerry's in 2004, Gerald Ford's in 1976, and Mitt Romney's in 2012—and barely ahead of Michael Dukakis's in 1988.[14]

This outcome evidently gnawed at the president-elect. On November 27, Trump tweeted that he had in fact "won the popular vote if you deduct the millions of people who voted illegally." He followed up that astonishing, and unsubstantiated, statement with an escalating series of tweets and retweets.

It's hard to do justice to the breathtaking audacity of such a claim. If true, it would be so serious as to demand a criminal investigation at a minimum, presumably spanning many states. But of course the claim was not true. Trump had not a smidgen of evidence beyond his own bruised feelings and internet flotsam from flagrantly unreliable sources. Yet once the president-elect lent

---

13 *The New York ... Infowars* NPR, *The New York Times*, and *The Washington Post* are all credible news sources. RT is a Russian news network that spreads propaganda favouring the Russian government; Infowars is a right-wing extremist site known for propagating fake news.

14 *Richard ... 1988* This list is of presidential candidates who lost in the years indicated.

his prestige to the crazy claim, it became fact for many people. A survey by YouGov found that by December 1, 43 percent of Republicans accepted the claim that millions of people had voted illegally in 2016.

A clear untruth had suddenly become a contested possibility. When CNN's Jeff Zeleny correctly reported on November 28 that Trump's tweet was baseless, Fox's Sean Hannity accused Zeleny of media bias—and then proceeded to urge the incoming Trump administration to take a new tack with the White House press corps, and to punish reporters like Zeleny. "I think it's time to reevaluate the press and maybe change the traditional relationship with the press and the White House," Hannity said. "My message tonight to the press is simple: You guys are done. You've been exposed as fake, as having an agenda, as colluding. You're a fake news organization." ...

In an online article for *The New York Review of Books*, the Russian-born journalist Masha Gessen brilliantly noted a commonality between Donald Trump and the man Trump admires so much, Vladimir Putin. "*Lying is the message*," she wrote. "It's not just that both Putin and Trump lie, it is that they lie in the same way and for the same purpose: blatantly, to assert power over truth itself."

The lurid mass movements of the 20th century—communist, fascist, and other—have bequeathed to our imaginations an outdated image of what 21st-century authoritarianism might look like.

Whatever else happens, Americans are not going to assemble in parade-ground formations, any more than they will crank a gramophone or dance the turkey trot. In a society where few people walk to work, why mobilize young men in matching shirts to command the streets? If you're seeking to domineer and bully, you want your storm troopers to go online, where the more important traffic is. Demagogues need no longer stand erect for hours orating into a radio microphone. Tweet lies from a smartphone instead.

"Populist-fuelled democratic backsliding is difficult to counter," wrote the political scientists Andrea Kendall-Taylor and Erica Frantz late last year. "Because it is subtle and incremental, there is no single moment that triggers widespread resistance or creates a focal point around which an opposition can coalesce.... Piecemeal democratic erosion, therefore, typically provokes only fragmented resistance." Their observation was rooted in the experiences of countries ranging from the Philippines to Hungary. It could apply here too.

If people retreat into private life, if critics grow quieter, if cynicism becomes endemic, the corruption will slowly become more brazen, the intimidation of opponents stronger. Laws intended to ensure accountability or prevent graft or protect civil liberties will be weakened.

If the president uses his office to grab billions for himself and his family, his supporters will feel empowered to take millions. If he successfully exerts power to punish enemies, his successors will emulate his methods.

If citizens learn that success in business or in public service depends on the favour of the president and his ruling clique, then it's not only American politics that will change. The economy will be corrupted too, and with it the larger culture. A culture that has accepted that graft is the norm, that rules don't matter as much as relationships with those in power, and that people can be punished for speech and acts that remain theoretically legal—such a culture is not easily reoriented back to constitutionalism, freedom, and public integrity.

The oft-debated question "Is Donald Trump a fascist?" is not easy to 65
answer. There are certainly fascistic elements to him: the subdivision of society into categories of friend and foe; the boastful virility and the delight in violence; the vision of life as a struggle for dominance that only some can win, and that others must lose.

Yet there's also something incongruous and even absurd about applying the sinister label of fascist to Donald Trump. He is so pathetically needy, so shamelessly self-interested, so fitful and distracted. Fascism fetishizes hardihood, sacrifice, and struggle—concepts not often associated with Trump.

Perhaps this is the wrong question. Perhaps the better question about Trump is not "What is he?" but "What will he do to us?"

By all early indications, the Trump presidency will corrode public integrity and the rule of law—and also do untold damage to American global leadership, the Western alliance, and democratic norms around the world. The damage has already begun, and it will not be soon or easily undone. Yet exactly how much damage is allowed to be done is an open question—the most important near-term question in American politics. It is also an intensely personal one, for its answer will be determined by the answer to another question: What will you do? And you? And you?

Of course we want to believe that everything will turn out all right. In this instance, however, that lovely and customary American assumption itself qualifies as one of the most serious impediments to everything turning out all right. If the story ends without too much harm to the republic, it won't be because the dangers were imagined, but because citizens resisted.

The duty to resist should weigh most heavily upon those of us who—be- 70
cause of ideology or partisan affiliation or some other reason—are most predisposed to favour President Trump and his agenda. The years ahead will be years of temptation as well as danger: temptation to seize a rare political opportunity to cram through an agenda that the American majority would normally reject. Who knows when that chance will recur?

A constitutional regime is founded upon the shared belief that the most fundamental commitment of the political system is to the rules. The rules matter more than the outcomes. It's because the rules matter most that Hillary Clinton conceded the presidency to Trump despite winning millions more votes. It's because the rules matter most that the giant state of California will accept the supremacy of a federal government that its people rejected by an almost two-to-one margin.

Perhaps the words of a founding father of modern conservatism, Barry Goldwater, offer guidance. "If I should later be attacked for neglecting my constituents' 'interests,'" Goldwater wrote in *The Conscience of a Conservative*, "I shall reply that I was informed their main interest is liberty and that in that cause I am doing the very best I can." These words should be kept in mind by those conservatives who think a tax cut or health-care reform a sufficient reward for enabling the slow rot of constitutional government....

Those citizens who fantasize about defying tyranny from within fortified compounds have never understood how liberty is actually threatened in a modern bureaucratic state: not by diktat and violence, but by the slow, demoralizing process of corruption and deceit. And the way that liberty must be defended is not with amateur firearms, but with an unwearying insistence upon the honesty, integrity, and professionalism of American institutions and those who lead them. We are living through the most dangerous challenge to the free government of the United States that anyone alive has encountered. What happens next is up to you and me. Don't be afraid. This moment of danger can also be your finest hour as a citizen and an American.

(2017)

Questions

1. This article was published in March 2017. Consider political events that have occurred since then. Does the possible future Frum describes seem any more or less likely now than it did in the first months of Trump's presidency?
2. Compare this article with Timothy D. Snyder's "Twenty Lessons from the Twentieth Century," another article published in response to Trump's rise to power. What is similar—and what is different—about the political developments each article seems to forecast? What is similar—and what is different—about the forms of resistance each suggests?

3. Frum is a self-described conservative. To what extent does this article reflect conservative ideology? Give examples in support of your assessment.
4. Frum writes that "[t]he lurid mass movements of the 20th century—communist, fascist, and other—have bequeathed to our imaginations an outdated image of what 21st-century authoritarianism might look like" (paragraph 59). How and why, according to Frum, would a 21st-century American autocracy look different from a 20th-century totalitarian state? Do you agree with this claim?
5. The call to action at the end of this essay is addressed to Americans. What, if anything, should Canadians do in response to the "democratic recession"?
6. Explain the meaning of Frum's claim that "[a] constitutional regime is founded upon the shared belief that the most fundamental commitment of the political system is to the rules" (paragraph 71). Do you agree? Are there any circumstances under which following the rules of democratic political systems should *not* be prioritized?

Sue Donaldson and Will Kymlicka

Born Allies: Child and Animal Citizens

The backstory to the writing of this piece is highly unusual. Donaldson and Kymlicka, authors well-known for their 2011 book Zoopolis: A Political Theory of Animal Rights *(as well as for Kymlicka's earlier work on multiculturalism), published on 5 May 2016 a* Globe and Mail *op-ed piece on zoos, arguing that these institutions teach children not to love and respect non-human animals but rather to denigrate them. In subsequent correspondence between the authors and one of the editors of this anthology, they shared with him the draft of a 7,000-word academic paper that was to be published in a forthcoming volume of philosophical scholarship,* The Routledge Handbook of the Philosophy of Childhood and Children *(now scheduled for publication in 2018). The editors of this anthology then requested that selections from that long scholarly piece be included in the third edition of* The Broadview Anthology of Expository Prose. *The publishers of the* Routledge Handbook, *however, did not wish to allow excerpts from a forthcoming volume to be reprinted elsewhere in advance of publication, and refused permission. Broadview's editors then asked if Donaldson and Kymlicka might be willing to write a shorter piece on the same theme, with the student readers of this anthology (rather than scholars) as the intended audience. The essay included here emerged out of those discussions.*

Throughout history, children and animals have been linked as paradigmatic* examples of groups deemed unable to exercise the rights and responsibilities of citizenship, and therefore unable to participate in collective self-government. Simplican (2015) calls this the "capacity contract"—the idea that individuals who fall below a certain threshold of cognitive or linguistic capacity are naturally governed by others, not equal citizens. She notes that this hierarchy between those who are self-governing and those who are "naturally governed" runs very deep in the Western philosophical tradition.

Indeed, the exclusion of children and animals is a constitutive feature of modern citizenship. As Rollo (2016) notes, the concepts of childhood and democratic politics emerged together but as "mutually exclusive," so that democratic politics has been conceptualized precisely as the outcome of a progression of "the feral child" out of childhood and animality into full human agency.[1] This account of democratic citizenship envisages that children can eventually become citizens, once mature, but only by distancing themselves from animals, who remain perpetually excluded. Indeed, throughout history, access to citizenship for individuals, groups (e.g., women) or indeed entire societies (e.g., colonized peoples) has depended on demonstrating their progression from childhood/animality into a "fully human" state of the mature use of reason and language.

While this capacity contract runs deep, it fits uneasily with another core democratic principle, which is that all who are governed by shared rules should have a say in shaping those rules. Children are members of society, and as such are expected to comply with social rules, including duties of civility and self-restraint, responsibilities to care (for other family members or companion animals), and to contribute (to work at home and at school). Children are profoundly affected by the way these social rules distribute benefits and burdens, and so have a strong interest in, and often strong preferences about, the shaping of these rules. It seems unfair, and undemocratic, to deny them a right to a say.

And indeed we see a growing call to extend citizenship to children on the basis of social membership. As Roche puts it, "the demand that children be included in citizenship is simply a request that children be seen as members of society too, with a legitimate and valuable voice and perspective" (Roche 1999: 479). Children are involved in dense webs of trust, communication and cooperation with others, and as such have rights of participation to help shape social norms, as well as responsibilities to comply with those social norms. These rights and responsibilities may be differentially enacted, given the spectrum of cognitive and linguistic capacities in society, but democracy requires that all members of society be seen as co-citizens. This membership-based view of citizenship is slowly challenging, and displacing, the inherited capacity-contract view of citizenship.[2]

We view this as an important advance in children's rights and in democratizing society, but we would take it one step further. If citizenship should track

1 *democratic politics ... full human agency* I.e., we conceive of the process of becoming an active adult participant in the democratic process as necessarily entailing in large part a giving up of the wild and animal natures that are so much a part of childhood.

2 [Donaldson and Kymlicka's note] The capacity contract is also being challenged by advocates of citizenship for people with cognitive disability.

social membership, then we need also to rethink the status of domesticated animals (e.g., companion animals, labouring animals, farmed animals and others who have been brought into our society and selectively bred to live and work alongside us). They too are members of society, capable of physically proximate, communicative, trusting and cooperative relations with humans (and vice versa), and as such are expected to exercise self-restraint and to comply with social norms. Indeed, domestication is only possible with animals that are capable of this sort of interspecies sociability with humans. Of course, domesticated animals were originally incorporated into society as a caste group, to serve us, and so existing social rules systematically ignore or sacrifice animals' interests to serve human interests. But having brought domesticated animals into our society, we must now acknowledge that they are members of a shared society which belongs as much to them as it does to us. And as long as they are members of society, they too have a right to a say regarding the rules that govern our shared life (Donaldson and Kymlicka 2011).

We believe that this extension of citizenship to domesticated animals is the logical progression of a shift from the capacity contract to the membership view. This has not been recognized by children's rights advocates, who have tended to uncritically reproduce the assumption in the broader human rights literature that there is a zero-sum relationship* between human rights and animal rights, and that respect for humanity requires drawing a sharp species hierarchy between humans and animals. Even as children's rights advocates dispute that democracy should be defined in opposition to childhood, they continue to assume that democracy should be defined in opposition to animality.

We believe this is a mistake. Children and animals are natural allies, and their fates are intertwined. The political ideologies and legal mechanisms used to subordinate animals also operate to diminish children's standing. Children and animals share powerful interests in relation to adult/human society, interests which have been obscured and suppressed. Attempting to enhance children's rights, without simultaneously rethinking our relations to animals, is a lost opportunity to build a better world for everyone.

We begin by exploring the intense social bonds between children and animals—and how these are too often ruptured—and then consider common interests that children and animals share which adult human citizens have failed to act upon. We hope to offer a compelling glimpse into the sort of society that *could* emerge if the voices and concerns of children and animals were empowered to shape political decision-making.

A Shared Social World

Gail Melson's 2001 book, *Why the Wild Things Are*, was the first major work of psychology devoted to the exploration of children's relationships with animals. The field of developmental psychology, from its origins, has been profoundly humanocentric, "assuming that only human relationships—with parents, siblings, relatives, friends, teachers, other children—are consequential for development," without ever bothering to consider interspecies relationships (Melson 2001). The results of Melson's research are astounding. Children live and breathe animals. Their earliest dreams are of animals, and their first words, apart from mama and daddy, are names of animals. For children aged 2–10, 50% of inkblot interpretations involve animals. Children between 7 and 10 years use the same vocabulary to describe both pets and siblings as playmates. When asked to identify their most important relationships (after parents), half of Scottish 9–12 year olds said a pet, higher than the number who said grandfather, friend, aunt, teacher, or neighbour. And elementary school children say that relations with their pets are more likely to last "no matter what" than are relations with friends and family. Subsequent research has confirmed not only the vital role companion animals play as attachment figures for humans, but also the vital role humans play as attachment figures for companion animals. These bi-directional attachment bonds can be documented using the same standard measures (proximity seeking, safe haven, secure base, separation distress) (Amiot & Bastian 2015). In short, "the emotions and personalities of animals, real and symbolic, are immediate to children in the same way that the emotions and personalities of people are"; it is only later that the "categorically human self" emerges, with its "strict division between human attributes and often negatively valued animal characteristics" (Melson 2001: 20).

In parallel with Melson's work, sociologists, social workers, and health 10
practitioners have explored the more-than-human nature of families and neighbourhoods, societies and cultures. Criminologists have long recognized that animal abuse predicts and co-occurs with abuse of humans, especially domestic violence. A vast industry of animal therapy is dedicated to the healing power of relationships with animals for children with ADD and ASD, as well as people suffering from depression, PTSD,[3] loneliness, and anxiety. Evolutionary psychologists claim that we co-evolved with other animals, specifically dogs. Sociologists have come to recognize that animals are responsive agents in interspecies social relationships—at home, on the street, at the park, at school, at work. Indeed, no human society is known to have existed without close human-animal relationships of companionship and cooperation.

Given this overwhelming evidence for the reality that children inhabit an interspecies social world, the puzzle becomes how this interspecies

---

3 *ADD* Attention deficit disorder; *ASD* Autism spectrum disorder; *PTSD* Post-traumatic stress disorder.

fellowship becomes broken. In Melson's words, how can we "pinpoint the process by which children shift from engaging animals as coequal other beings to straddling the barrier of a radical species divide" (Melson 2001: 190)? The rupture is accomplished through multiple processes. Louv (2005) examines how modern urbanization, technology and development separate children from the natural world, and the relationships to be formed there. Stewart and Cole (2014) analyze the vast ideological enterprise operating in homes, schools and the media for transforming animals from the equal fellow beings of childhood into objects for instrumental use. The violent processes of animal industry are hidden away; children's sociality with nonhumans is transferred onto fuzzy sentimental toys and images (and pets); children are habituated into eating (and developing pleasure from) meat before they understand what it is; and children are gradually indoctrinated with ideologies of human superiority.

The rupture for rural and farm children is often particularly brutal, as captured in Matt Stensland's photo of Tyler Boyer (a 4-H member, aged 11) sobbing into the neck of his steer, Leonard, whom Tyler has raised since infancy and is now sending off to slaughter.

The internet is full of YouTube videos of children being "socialized," "cajoled," or "shamed" into killing farmed and wild animals.

Humans have killed and consumed animals in most times and places, and for most traditional societies killing animals was necessary for survival. But this was usually seen as a regrettable necessity, and cultural practices of apology, gratitude and expiation helped to assuage the psychological trauma of killing (Serpell 1996). In modern societies, the practice is largely hidden, and practices of regret and gratitude have given way to ideologies of self-righteous entitlement—ideologies that require rupturing the interspecies fellowship of children and animals.

This process is so normalized that we have barely asked—let alone measured—the possible costs to children of this rupture. Social psychologists have long studied the harmful effects on children of participating in "abnormal" acts of animal cruelty—that is, acts of cruelty that flow from deviant individual personality—but have only recently begun to investigate the harmful effects on children of being indoctrinated into "normal" acts of animal exploitation.

We do however have growing evidence that this ideological indoctrination has negative spillover effects on human rights. Defenders of a steep species hierarchy often argue that, by dignifying or sacralising "the human" and instrumentalizing "the animal," we provide a clear and secure foundation for protecting the rights of all humans, including vulnerable groups. In reality, however, the evidence shows that inculcating attitudes of human superiority over other animals worsens negative attitudes towards minorities, immigrants and other outgroups. This body of evidence (known as the "interspecies model of prejudice") suggests we "need to face an inconvenient truth: The premium placed on humans over animals—overvaluing humans as an unchallenged truism—fuels some forms of human dehumanization" (Hodson, MacInnis & Costello 2014: 106). Conversely, humane education regarding animals (emphasizing interspecies affinities and solidarities) encourages greater empathy towards other humans (Thompson & Gullone 2003).

In short, rupturing children's sense of interspecies solidarity and inculcating them into ideologies of human supremacism is one of the most consequential—and, we would argue, damaging—features of contemporary practices of childhood socialization and education. It is traumatic for many children, it exacerbates inter-group prejudice,* and it is catastrophic for animals. Both groups are being sacrificed to uphold the animal-exploiting interests of certain sectors of adult human society.

REIMAGINING THE FUTURE

What would happen if society empowered children and domesticated animals to act upon their interests, many of them shared? We believe it could have a transformative effect on democratic politics. While many adults might be puzzled by the idea of recognizing animals as co-citizens, we suspect that countless children would happily accept the principle that domesticated animals should have a right to a say in how their families, homes, workplaces, and neighbourhoods are governed, and how the terms of their participation in society are determined.[4]

Protecting the Environment: It is widely noted that adults and children may have diverging interests regarding environmental protection. Many adults benefit from existing growth-based extractive economies,[5] whereas children are likely to bear the costs down the road (Zakaras 2016). And not just down the road—children and domesticated animals are already paying the environmental costs. As beings who like to spend time outdoors, playing in parks and fields, swimming in lakes and rivers, exploring woods, tidal pools, vacant lots, back streets and alleys, rail and dockyards, abandoned industrial sites, and ground-level mud, detritus and cubby holes, they share powerful interests in these places being safe and uncontaminated. Human adults spend less time in the muck, and can tolerate much higher levels of environmental pollutants (due to their larger bodies). Indeed the five major illnesses affecting children in industrialized societies are all environmentally related (Trasande 2006). Domesticated animals, too, are increasingly affected by neurodevelopmental disorders, cancers, and poisoning. Both groups are also facing increased obesity and diabetes as individuals are increasingly kept inside, away from an outdoors that has become unsafe and inaccessible. Thus children and domesticated animals share a profound interest in restoring the outdoor environment to ecological health rather than treating it as a dumping ground for the externalized costs[6] of adult wealth creation.

Accessing Public Space: Public spaces are overwhelmingly designed by and for human adults; spaces to conduct business, to enjoy a quiet drink or meal, to relax and read, to consume culture, to shop, to park, and to drive, moving as efficiently as possible from A to B. Children and animals are often perceived as not belonging in such public spaces, except for the occasional dog park or "child-friendly" space. Societies which don't restrict children and animals

---

4 [Donaldson and Kymlicka's note] For discussion of the mechanisms that could be created to give children and animals a voice in collective self-government, see Meijer 2013; Donaldson & Kymlicka 2017.

5 *extractive economies* Economies based on the extraction of resources from the planet—and their gradual depletion.

6 *externalized costs* The economic concept of *externalities* refers to costs that are not captured in a primary economic transaction. If, for example, a company pollutes the air and the water in the process of manufacturing the product it sells, and does not include in the price of the product the cost of cleaning up that pollution, then the pollution is external to the primary economic transaction involved in the sale of the product; either the company or someone else will have to pay for it later, in other ways.

in this way—think of the unsupervised children, dogs, donkeys, cows, and other animals sharing public space in countries like India, for example—are often dismissed as backward, disorganized, and/or inattentive to child/animal welfare. The amount of unsupervised free time that (Western) children spend outside, and their range of movement, has plummeted in the past 50 years—due in large part to parental perceptions of increased risks (real and illusory). Fifty years ago, breaking a bone was a childhood rite of passage. Now it is a rarity. Children are moving closer to the situation of domesticated animals, whose movement is highly restricted by human adults.

If we ask children and youth themselves, they are clear that they do not want to be restricted and monitored in these ways (Alderson 2008). If cars are dangerous, they say, restrict the cars, not us. If the outdoors is polluted, clean it up—don't restrict our right to explore. If you're worried that crowds of urban youth will vandalize adult-oriented public spaces, then invest in spaces which respond to, and respect, our interests—don't impose curfews. A common political agenda for children and domesticated animals would not just halt the century-long ascendancy of car culture and lessen its impact on urban design. It would also re-prioritize design of public space around creatures who like to walk, run, bike, skate-board, hop on and off public transportation, play, hang out, disrupt, and explore. It would reimagine public space, and the outdoors, as places where they feel at home and can take ownership—rather than feeling like barely tolerated interlopers.

Social Integration: Even with healthy natural environments and redesigned public spaces, children and domesticated animals, especially in their younger years, will still be dependent on adult humans to protect and provide for them. This, naturally, sets limits on their independence and free movement. Currently, they are assigned to specific spaces (homes, schools, farms, recreational sites), within which a few designated adults (parents, teachers, farmers) exercise enormous power over them, often in spaces that are hidden from public view, and which they cannot escape. Even adults with the best intentions have only so much energy to attend and respond to children and animals in their care. Children and animals are structurally vulnerable to caregivers, and caregiving is subject to inevitable failures (Gheaus 2011). However, it is not inevitable that children or domesticated animals be dependent on such a limited circle of adults. We can distribute care and interaction across multiple relationships and sites.

Imagine, then, a more socially distributed approach to caring and interdependent relationships. Under such an approach, the social and geographic segregation of adults from children, seniors, people with sicknesses and disabilities, and domesticated animals would be replaced with a more integrated social life. Crèches* and schools would be integrated with workplaces, seniors' residences, therapeutic settings, farmed animal sanctuaries, companion animal daycares, green spaces, community gardens, and community kitchens. Large, linked, car-free spaces would be created for safe movement within multi-purpose, socially integrated mini-communities. By multiplying the number of adults with eyes on individual children and animals, there would be less likelihood of abuse, neglect, or isolation. Animals in family homes or farms wouldn't pine alone (or in small groups) all day, lonely and dependent on a handful of others for all of their social interaction, but would have an enlarged sphere of social contacts—senior volunteers, school visitors, and numerous domesticated animals of multiple species. Children and animals wouldn't be completely dependent on parents, teachers, or peers for attention, support and stimulation but would be able to build complex social networks and cooperative activities with a variety of others. Mutual interaction, care, and support could emerge across diverse social groupings. In such circumstances, greater freedom and mobility for children and animals would not pose increased risks, but rather would increase their safety by reducing social isolation and their vulnerability to pecking orders, or the vagaries of any one individual's will.

Work: Finally, consider how such a society might think about work. Work is widely seen as the most important source of self-respect and social recognition. Yet at the moment, the rhetoric of western societies is that we don't want or expect children to work. Childhood is defined as a time for play and education, insulated from adult responsibilities. This perspective obscures the fact that children do in fact work, in all societies, sharing in the burdens as well as the benefits of social cooperation. And while it is crucial to protect time for play and education, children are adamant that this shouldn't preclude opportunities for appropriate and safe employment. Studies show that children do not want to be banned from work, which they, too, see as a source of self-esteem, personal development, and social recognition. They want access to safe and properly-compensated jobs that are compatible with their interests in furthering their education and other activities, and they want their contributions to be valued and recognized (Gasson & Linsell 2011). However, because our prevailing ideology privileges[7] paid adult work, children's work tends to be unrecognized, inadequately compensated, and out of children's control. For example, education is typically framed as a privilege or benefit, rather than a compulsory job. Similarly, children's work in the domestic sphere (caring for younger siblings, for sick family members, for domesticated animals, doing household tasks) is often unrecognized or undervalued—they are said to "help out" rather than

7 *privileges* Places an unjustified importance on.

"to work"—and is unprotected by labour legislation. In short, even as society in fact depends heavily on the contribution of children, it denies them social recognition, compensation, or labour rights.

Domesticated animals face a more extreme version of this hypocrisy. Millions of domesticated animals fulfil contributing roles in society (transportation, haulage, plowing, vegetation control, therapy, assistance, rescue, detection, protection, companionship). Yet, like children, their forms of contribution are not recognized as "work," and they are accorded no recognition or rights as workers (Coulter 2016). It may serve adult society's narrowly-defined self-interest to define work in ways that render invisible the work of children and domesticated animals, and to paint them instead as recipients of adult care or welfare protection, not contributing citizens entitled to rights. But it is not in the interest of society as a whole. A common agenda for children and domesticated animals would recognize the diverse forms of work that social members engage in, and ensure that they are safe, non-exploitative and fairly compensated.

In short, if we take seriously the shared interests of children and animals, new horizons emerge for thinking about the natural environment, the built environment, the structure of social relationships, and the nature of work. Is the world we have begun to sketch out in these pages the kind of world that children and domesticated animals might create if they had power in shaping society? We don't know. But what is clear is that philosophical theories that conceptualize children and animals as adversaries and incompetents are a reflection of adult ideologies and interests, not of the capacities, hopes, dreams, or identities of children or animals themselves.

(2017)

References

Alderson, Priscilla (2008) *Young Children's Rights* (London: Jessica Kingsley).

Amiot, Catherine and Brock Bastian (2015) "Toward a Psychology of Human-Animal Relations", *Psychological Bulletin* 141/1: 22–23.

Coulter, Kendra (2016) *Animals, Work, and the Promise of Interspecies Solidarity* (Palgrave).

Donaldson, Sue and Will Kymlicka (2011) *Zoopolis* (Oxford University Press).

Donaldson, Sue and Will Kymlicka (2017) "Rethinking Membership and Participation in an Inclusive Democracy: Cognitive Disability, Children, Animals" in Barbara Arneil and Nancy Hirschmann (eds) *Disability and Political Theory* (Cambridge University Press), 233–62.

Gasson, Ruth and Chris Linsell (2011) "Young Workers: A New Zealand Perspective", *International Journal of Children's Rights* 19: 641–59.

Gheaus, Anca (2011) "Arguments for Nonparental Care for Children", *Social Theory and Practice* 37/3: 483–509.

Hodson, Gordon, Cara MacInnis and Kimberly Costello (2014) "(Over)Valuing 'Humanness' as an Aggravator of Intergroup Prejudices and Discrimination" in Paul Bain et al. (eds) *Humanness and Dehumanization* (Routledge).

Joy, Melanie (2011) *Why We Love Dogs, Wear Cows and Eat Pigs* (Newbury Port: Conari).
Louv, Richard (2005) *Last Child in the Woods* (Chapel Hill; Algonquin).
Meijer, Eva (2013) "Political Communication with Animals", *Humanimalia* 5/1.
Melson, Gail (2001) *Why the Wild Things Are: Animals in the Lives of Children* (Harvard University Press).
Roche, Jeremy (1999) "Children: Rights, Participation and Citizenship", *Childhood* 6/4.
Rollo, Toby (2016) "Feral Children: Settler Colonialism, Progress, and the Figure of the Child", *Settler Colonial Studies* 6.
Serpell, James (1996) *In the Company of Animals* (Cambridge University Press).
Simplican, Stacy (2015) *The Capacity Contract: Intellectual Disability and the Question of Citizenship* (University of Minnesota Press).
Stewart, Kate and Matthew Cole (2014) *Our Children and Other Animals* (Ashgate).
Thompson, Kelly and Eleonora Gullone (2003) "Promotion of Empathy and Prosocial Behaviour in Children through Humane Education", *Australian Psychologist* 38: 175–82.
Trasande, Leonardo et al. (2006) "The Environment in Pediatric Practice", *Journal of Urban Health* 83/4: 760–72.
Zakaras, Alex (2016) "Democracy, Children, and the Environment", *Critical Review of International Social and Political Philosophy* 19/2: 141–62.

Questions

1. In a paragraph of between 100 and 150 words, summarize the argument made by Donaldson and Kymlicka in the section of their paper entitled "A Shared Social World."
2. The authors have written this piece for an undergraduate audience, but they nevertheless write as academics, often citing scholarly studies and employing academic language. Choose one paragraph from their essay that includes a good deal of such material, and rewrite it for an entirely non-academic audience, using simpler, non-scholarly language.
3. Using pets, meat-eating, zoos, and illustrated children's books as reference points, discuss your own education (by parents and other family members, teachers, and society at large) as to the relationship between humans and other animals.
4. Donaldson and Kymlicka do not get into the specifics of how children and non-human animals might be represented in legislative bodies. How would representatives be chosen to speak (and vote) on their behalf? On what basis should seats be allotted to children and non-human animals? Write a short essay putting forward your own proposal for how this might best be done.

Biographical Notes

Afshar, Kaveh (unknown)
An economist with Health Canada, Kaveh Afshar was also President and Co-Founder of The Ottawa International Centre for Learning.

Ai Weiwei (1957–)
A leading Chinese artist and activist, Ai Weiwei has received worldwide acclaim for his video art, installations, and photographs. Within China, however, Ai, who has strongly criticized the government over a variety of issues, has been subjected to government censorship measures including arrest, the shutdown of his popular blog, the demolition of his studio, and restrictions on his ability to travel. In 2008, Ai received a lifetime achievement award from the Chinese Contemporary Art Awards; in 2012, he was awarded the Václav Havel Prize for Creative Dissent.

Alexie, Sherman (1966–)
Sherman Alexie is an American writer. A member of the Spokane and Coeur d'Alene tribes, he confronts in his writing the systemic poverty that marked his childhood experience of rural reservation life. His works, which often hover on the border between fiction and non-fiction, include *Reservation Blues* (1996), *The Lone Ranger and Tonto Fistfight in Heaven* (1993), *The Absolutely True Diary of a Part-Time Indian* (2007), and *Ten Little Indians* (2009).

Arendt, Hannah (1906–75)
Arendt was a German-Jewish political theorist best known for her writings on power, democracy, totalitarianism, and human nature. She fled Nazi Germany in 1933, eventually emigrating to the US in 1941; there, she wrote and taught at various universities. Among her works are *The Origins of Totalitarianism* (1951), *The Human Condition* (1958), and *Eichmann in Jerusalem: A Report on the Banality of Evil* (1963).

Armstrong, Jeannette C. (1948–)
Armstrong is an Okanagan author, artist, and activist. She is the executive director of the En'owkin Centre, where she also teaches creative writing. She is best known for her poetry and for her first novel, *Slash* (1985). She is a campaigner for Aboriginal rights and speaks frequently about Aboriginal education and literature.

Atwood, Margaret (1939–)
Atwood's collection of poetry *The Circle Game* won the 1966 Governor General's Award, and her critical book *Survival: A Thematic Guide to Canadian Literature* (1972) led to the entrenchment of Canadian Literature as a legitimate field of study in Canadian universities. Despite these lofty achievements, Atwood is perhaps best known for her novels, including *The Edible Woman* (1969), *The Handmaid's Tale* (1985) *The Blind Assassin* (winner of the 2000 Booker Prize), and the MaddAddam trilogy (2003–13).

Bachan, Nadine (unknown)
A graduate of UBC's MFA program in creative writing, Nadine Bachan's work has been published in *Maisonneuve* and *Hazlitt* magazine, and anthologized in *Best Canadian Essays 2015*. Born in Trinidad, Bachan was raised in Toronto and now resides in Vancouver.

Balkissoon, Denise (unknown)
National Magazine award-winner Denise Balkissoon is an editor and columnist for *The Globe and Mail*. She is also editor-in-chief of a blog about race and ethnicity in Toronto, *The Ethnic Aisle*, and in 2016 co-hosted "Colour Code," an eleven-part podcast series on race in Canada, for the *Globe and Mail*.

Barthes, Roland (1915–80)
Roland Barthes was a French social and literary critic known for his influential writings on semiotics and structuralism. His written works include *Mythologies* (1957), *Elements of Semiology* (1967), *The Empire of Signs* (1970), and *The Luminous Room* (1980).

Benedetti, Fabrizio (1956–)
Fabrizio Benedetti is a Professor of Clinical and Applied Psychology at the University of Turin Medical School. A consultant for the Placebo Project at the US National Institute of Health and a member of Harvard University's Placebo Study Group, he focuses his research on the functioning of the placebo effect.

Berger, John (1926–2017)
An English social commentator, visual arts critic, and writer, John Berger was the author of novels, plays, screenplays, volumes of poems, and over 30 non-fiction works. He received the Booker Prize for his novel *G.* (1972), but is perhaps best-known for his introduction to the study of artistic images, *Ways of Seeing* (1972).

Biss, Eula, (?1977–)
An award-winning American essayist, Eula Biss has published her work in *Harper's* and *The New York Times Magazine*, among many others. Her books

include a collection of prose poems, *The Balloonists* (2002); *Notes from No Man's Land* (2009), a collection of essays; and an examination of the anti-vaccination movement, *On Immunity: An Inoculation* (2014).

Boudway, Ira (unknown)
Ira Boudway is a Bloomberg Businessweek reporter who focuses on the NBA.

Bozikovic, Alex (unknown)
Alex Bozikovic is a journalist who covers urbanism and architecture for *The Globe and Mail*. He has also written for *Azure*, *Dwell*, *Wallpaper*, *Architect*, *The Walrus*, and *The Literary Review of Canada*.

Bozkurt, Eda (unknown)
A Research Assistant with the Education Policy Research Initiative, Eda Bozkurt holds a Doctorate in Economics from the University of Western Ontario.

Card, David (1956–)
Canadian-born economist David Card is a Professor at the University of California, Berkeley as well as Director of Labor Studies at the National Bureau of Economic Research. The author of close to 100 journal articles and book chapters, Card is the recipient of many honours in the discipline of Economics.

Carson, Anne (1950–)
Carson's many books include *Autobiography of Red: A Novel in Verse* (1998) and its sequel, *Red Doc>* (2013); *Men in the Off Hours* (2001), winner of the Griffin Poetry Prize; and *Eros the Bittersweet* (1986), her first book, which was listed by The Modern Library as one of the 100 best non-fiction books of all time. Poet-in-residence at New York University, Carson was for many years a professor of Classics; she is also renowned for her translations from ancient Greek, which include *Grief Lessons: Four Plays by Euripides* (2006) and *An Oresteia* (2009).

Cavendish, Margaret (Duchess of Newcastle) (1623–73)
The first English woman to write mainly for publication, Cavendish was both widely criticized and celebrated for her public disregard of social and literary conventions, particularly with regard to her views on the education of women. Works include *Poems and Fancies* (1653), *Philosophical and Physical Opinions* (1656), *Observations upon Experimental Philosophy* (1666), and a work of science fiction entitled *The Description of a New World, called The Blazing World* (1668).

Coates, Ta-Nehisi (1975–)
An American born writer and journalist, Ta-Nehisi Coates is a national correspondent for *The Atlantic* magazine. He is also journalist-in-residence at the City

University of New York, and previously was Martin Luther King visiting professor at the Massachusetts Institute of Technology. His *Between the World and Me* (2015), about black life in the United States, received the National Book Award and was a finalist for the Pulitzer Prize.

Cole, Desmond (unavailable)
Canadian activist and freelance journalist Desmond Cole lives in Toronto, where he is a staff writer for *The Torontoist*. His work has also appeared in such publications as the *Toronto Star*, *Toronto Life*, *VICE*, and *The Walrus*.

Colloca, Luana (1977–)
Luana Colloca is an Associate Professor at the University of Maryland School of Nursing. Her research focuses on pain and on conceptual and empirical aspects of placebo phenomena.

Coyne, Andrew (1960–)
Ontario-born journalist and editor Andrew Coyne is a long-time columnist for the Canadian newspaper *The National Post*, and has also worked for *Maclean's* and *The Globe and Mail*. Coyne has studied at the University of Manitoba, Trinity College in Toronto, and the London School of Economics. He is also a voice on the At Issue panel on the CBC's popular television news program *The National*.

Darwin, Charles (1809–82)
The son of an English doctor, Darwin attended medical school at the University of Edinburgh from 1825–27. During his later service as a naturalist aboard *HMS Beagle*, 1831–36, he observed similarities and differences among various species, and began to formulate his theory regarding evolution by means of natural selection. Darwin delayed publishing his theory for more than twenty years; *On the Origin of Species* was eventually published in 1859.

de Leeuw, Sarah (unknown)
A Canadian writer and human geographer, de Leeuw is a prize-winning writer of poetry and creative non-fiction. She is associate professor in the Northern Medical Program at UNBC and the Faculty of Medicine at UBC, where she works in the areas of medical humanities and health inequalities. She publishes her literary and academic work widely in journals and magazines.

de Montaigne, Michel Eyquem (1533–92)
French thinker Michel Eyquem de Montaigne arguably did more than any other individual to establish the essay form—including giving it a name. His *Essais* were published in three volumes between 1580 and 1588. Montaigne also published a translation of Spanish theologian Raymond of Sebond's *Theologia Naturalis* (1569).

Donaldson, Sue (1962–)

A Canadian writer and scholar, Sue Donaldson is a research fellow at Queen's University. She is the author of a vegan cookbook, a children's novel, and a body of scholarly work on animal ethics. Her book *Zoopolis: A Political Theory of Animal Rights* (2011), co-authored with her husband, Will Kymlicka, was awarded the Canadian Philosophical Association Biennial Book Prize in 2013.

Douglas, Thomas (1904–86)

Born in Scotland and raised in Saskatchewan, Tommy Douglas spent his career as a social democratic politician with the federal Co-operative Commonwealth Federation's provincial and federal parties, and went on to lead the federal New Democratic Party upon its formation. He is best known for his leading role in the establishment of the universal single-payer health care system in Canada. Douglas was also responsible for the implementation of programs such as unionization of the public service and public automobile insurance.

Douglass, Frederick (1818–95)

Frederick Douglass, an escaped slave who became America's leading abolitionist, developed a reputation for inspiring oratory and powerful writing. He wrote several versions of his autobiography; *Narrative of the Life of Frederick Douglass, an American Slave* (1845) has become a classic American text.

Du Bois, W.E.B. (1868–1963)

W.E.B. Du Bois was an African American educator and historian, a founder of the Niagara Movement and of the National Association for the Advancement of Colored People, and the editor of the NAACP journal *Crisis* from 1910 to 1934. His books include *The Philadelphia Negro* (1899) and *The Souls of Black Folk* (1903); the latter has long been recognized as a classic of American non-fiction.

Finnie, Ross (unknown)

Ross Finnie is Director of the Education Policy Research Initiative and a professor at the University of Ottawa in the Graduate School of Public and International Affairs; he holds degrees from the University of Wisconsin-Madison and Queen's University.

Flanner, Janet (1892–1978)

Although an American, Janet Flanner lived in Paris for most of her life. As a journalist, she provided reports and commentary on European culture and political affairs for five decades. Some of her most famous work includes her "Letter from Paris" column for *The New Yorker* and her important articles on Hitler's rise to power.

Foer, Jonathan Safran (1977–)
American writer Jonathan Safran Foer is a distinguished writer-in-residence at New York University. His best-selling debut novel *Everything Is Illuminated* (2002) was named Book of the Year by *The Los Angeles Times* and his second novel, *Extremely Loud and Incredibly Close* (2005) was also widely acclaimed. Since the publication of *Eating Animals* (2009), Foer has continued to campaign for change in the way humans treat other animals.

Foucault, Michel (1926–84)
French philosopher and historian Michel Foucault was a leading figure in late twentieth-century poststructuralist thought. His histories of medical and social sciences—notable among them *L'Histoire de la sexualité* (*The History of Sexuality*, first English translation 1978–86) and *Surveiller et punir: Naissance de la prison* (*Discipline and Punish: The Birth of the Prison*, first English translation 1977)—study the relationship between power and knowledge, and explore how societies use power to "objectivize subjects."

Franklin, Ursula M. (1921–)
Ursula Franklin, an experimental physicist and University Professor Emerita at the University of Toronto, is the author of many scholarly articles and several books, including *The Real World of Technology* (1989). The recipient of more than twelve honorary degrees, she was inducted into the Canadian Science and Engineering Hall of Fame in 2012.

Frum, David (1960–)
A Canadian-American journalist, David Frum became a senior editor of *The Atlantic* in 2014. A self-identified "conservative Republican," Frum was a speechwriter for President George W. Bush in 2001 and 2002, and has authored numerous books on American right-wing politics, including *Dead Right* (1994) and *Comeback: Conservatism that Can Win Again* (2007).

Galloway, Gloria (unknown)
Gloria Galloway has been a reporter for the Canadian newspaper *The Globe and Mail* since 2001.

Gay, Roxane (1974–)
Roxane Gay is Associate Professor of English at Purdue University, an editor, and a writer of essays, reviews, and short fiction. Her books include *Ayiti* (2011), the bestselling *Bad Feminist* (2014), and *Hunger* (2016), a memoir. She has also contributed to numerous newspapers and both online and print magazines, among them *McSweeney's*, *The New York Times*, *xoJane*, *Jezebel*, *The Nation*, and *Salon*.

Gilchrist, Kristen (unknown)
Kristen Gilchrist is working on a PhD in Sociology and Anthropology at Carleton University. Her research explores government, media, and community responses to missing/murdered Aboriginal women in Canada; Gilchrist is an activist and non-Indigenous ally; she is co-founder of Families of Sisters in Spirit, an organization dedicated to providing support for the families of missing/murdered Aboriginal women.

Gladwell, Malcolm (1963–)
Malcolm Gladwell was born in England and raised in Canada; since 1996 he has been a staff writer for *The New Yorker* magazine. He is the bestselling author of *The Tipping Point* (2000), *Blink* (2005), *Outliers* (2008), and *What the Dog Saw* (2009). In 2013 he released *David and Goliath: Underdogs, Misfits, and the Art of Battling Giants*, a collection of journalism.

Gopnik, Adam (1956–)
A contributor to *The New Yorker* since 1986, Adam Gopnik has received the National Magazine Award for Essay and Criticism as well as the George Polk Award for Magazine Reporting. He is also a regular broadcaster for the Canadian Broadcasting Corporation, and is the author of *Paris to the Moon* (2000) and *The Table Comes First: Family, France, and the Meaning of Food* (2012).

Gourevitch, Philip (1961–)
As a staff writer for *The New Yorker*, Philip Gourevitch was sent by that magazine to Rwanda in 1995 to study the aftermath of the 1994 genocide of the Tutsi minority. He stayed nine months in Rwanda and in neighbouring Congo; out of his experiences there came one of the most important non-fiction books of the 1990s, *We Wish to Inform You That Tomorrow We Will Be Killed with Our Families* (1998). Gourevitch's other works include *A Cold Case* (2001) and *The Ballad of Abu Ghraib* (2008).

Halton, Carissa (unknown)
A freelance writer based in Edmonton, Alberta, Carissa Halton is also Director of Correspondence in the Office of the Alberta Premier. Her creative non-fiction writing has covered such topics as contemporary urban culture and revitalization, politics, and arts and design, and has been published in newspapers and journals such as *Eighteen Bridges*, *The Globe and Mail*, and *Alberta Views*.

Hannah-Jones, Nikole (1976–)
Nikole Hannah-Jones is an American investigative journalist whose work has focused largely on racial injustice. Her work has appeared in *The Atlantic*, *The Huffington Post*, *Essence Magazine*, *Grist*, and *Politico*. She became a staff writer for *The New York Times Magazine* in 2015.

Harris, Marvin (1927–2001)
Marvin Harris was an American anthropologist and theoretician known for his research in cultural materialism. His works include *The Rise of Anthropological Theory* (1968), *Cannibals and Kings: The Origins of Cultures* (1977) and *Cultural Anthropology* (1983).

Harris, Michael (1948–)
Michael Harris is the author of *Solitude* (2017) and *The End of Absence* (2014), which won the Governor General's Literary Award. He writes about media, civil liberties, and the arts, for dozens of publications, including *The Washington Post*, *Wired*, *Salon*, *The Huffington Post*, and *The Globe & Mail*. His work has been a finalist for the RBC Taylor Prize, the BC National Award for Canadian Non-Fiction, the Chautauqua Prize, the CBC Bookie Awards, and several National Magazine Awards. He lives in Vancouver with his partner, the artist Kenny Park.

Heller, Nathan (unknown)
An American journalist and film critic, Heller is a staff writer at *The New Yorker*. He is also a regular contributor, both as writer and editor, to *Vogue*. His essays span a range of subjects, including language, technology, and politics. While working at *Slate* magazine, Heller was a finalist for a National Magazine Award for essays and criticism.

hooks, bell (1952–)
An award-winning author and social activist, Gloria Jean Watkins—writing under the name bell hooks—has written over 30 books of feminist and critical theory, social commentary, and poetry. Her 1981 book *Ain't I a Woman?: Black Women and Feminism* has become an important touchstone in feminist thought. hooks, who became a professor of English in 1976, has also been active in media and film theory; her *Reel to Real* was published in 1996.

Hope, Jessamyn (unknown)
Canadian writer Jessamyn Hope's work in fiction and memoir has appeared in *PRISM International*, *Colorado Review*, *Five Points*, and *Ploughshares*. Her debut novel, *Safekeeping*, was published in 2015 to critical acclaim.

Horkins, William B. (unknown)
The Honourable William B. Horkins is a judge in the Ontario Court of Justice; he was appointed to the Court in 1998. Previous to this appointment, he worked for 18 years as an attorney, both as a defence lawyer and as a prosecutor.

Hurston, Zora Neale (1891–1960)
African American novelist, playwright, and folklorist Zora Neale Hurston was a significant figure in the Harlem Renaissance of the 1920s. Her novel *Their Eyes Were Watching God* (1937) has come to be considered a twentieth-century classic—though it had been largely forgotten by 1975, when Alice Walker published her essay "In Search of Zora Neale Hurston"; Walker argued that Hurston deserved recognition as "the intellectual and spiritual foremother of a generation of black women writers." Hurston's other books include the novels *Jonah's Gourd Vine* (1934) and *Dust Tracks on a Road* (1942), and an anthropological study, *Mules and Men* (1935). She died in a welfare home in Florida and was buried in an unmarked grave.

Iyer, Pico (1957–)
Born in England to Indian parents and partly raised in California, Pico Iyer attended Oxford and Harvard universities. Best known for travel writing and essays on cross-cultural themes, Iyer is a regular columnist for *TIME* magazine. His books include *Video Night in Kathmandu* (1988), *Falling Off the Map: Some Lonely Places of the World* (1994), and *The Art of Stillness: Adventures in Going Nowhere* (2014).

Jalal, Malik (unknown)
Malik Jalal is a tribal elder in North Waziristan, Pakistan.

Johnson, Nathanael (unknown)
An award-winning journalist and Food writer for *Grist*, Nathanael Johnson has contributed to *Harper's*, *Outside*, *San Francisco*, and *New York* magazine. His books include *All Natural* (2013) and *Unseen City* (2016).

Johnson, Samuel (1709–84)
An English writer and lexicographer, Samuel Johnson published the periodicals *The Rambler* (1750–52) and *The Idler* (1758–60). A prolific writer, Johnson made several significant contributions to eighteenth-century literature, including his *Dictionary of the English Language* (1755) and *The Lives of the English Poets* (1781). Johnson is the subject of one of English literature's most significant biographies, James Boswell's *Life of Samuel Johnson* (1791).

Justice, Daniel Heath (1975–)
Born and raised in the small gold mining town of Victor, Colorado, Daniel Heath Justice (Cherokee Nation) now calls Canada home, having arrived in 2002 and become a Canadian citizen in 2009. A fantasy novelist as well as a literary scholar and editor, he is a professor of First Nations and Indigenous Studies at the University of British Columbia.

Kay, Jonathan (1968–)

Jonathan Kay is a two-time recipient of Canada's National Newspaper Award and a former editor and columnist for the *National Post*, as well as a former editor-in-chief of *The Walrus*. He is a regular contributor to the *New York Post* and *Commentary* magazine and has also appeared in *Newsweek*, *The New York Times*, *The New Yorker*, *Harper's Magazine*, and the *Literary Review of Canada*. He is also an author of non-fiction books, including *Among the Truthers: A Journey Through America's Growing Conspiracist Underground* (2011).

Keegan, Marina (1989–2012)

Marina Keegan graduated from Yale University magna cum laude in the spring of 2012, and was killed in a car crash less than a week afterwards. Her short story "Cold Pastoral" was published later that year by *The New Yorker*, where she had been about to start work as an editorial assistant when she died. A selection of her writing was published in the posthumous collection *The Opposite of Loneliness* (2014).

Kelly, Cathal (unknown)

Previously a sports columnist for the *Toronto Star*, Cathal Kelly became a sports columnist for *The Globe and Mail* in 2014.

Kincaid, Jamaica (1949–)

Jamaica Kincaid is an Antiguan-born American novelist and Professor of Literature at Claremont McKenna College. Her writings, which often explore issues of colonialism, include the novels *Annie John* (1985), *Lucy* (1990), and *See Now Then* (2013), and the essay collection *A Small Place* (1988).

King, Martin Luther, Jr. (1929–68)

A Baptist minister and the leading figure of the American civil-rights movement in the 1950s and 1960s, Martin Luther King Jr. received the 1964 Nobel Peace Prize in recognition of his work promoting both civil rights and nonviolence. King was a charismatic speaker and bestselling author; his books include *Stride Toward Freedom* (1958), *Why We Can't Wait* (1964), and *Where Do We Go from Here: Chaos or Community?* (1967). He was assassinated in Memphis, Tennessee.

Klein, Naomi (1970–)

A Canadian journalist, scholar, and social activist, Klein is known for her environmentalism and criticism of corporate capitalism. Her work has appeared in such publications as *Harper's Magazine*, *Rolling Stone*, *The Nation*, and *The Guardian*. Her book *No Logo: Taking Aim at the Brand Bullies* (2000) has been translated into more than 28 languages, and her bestselling *Shock Doctrine: The Rise of Disaster Capitalism* (2007) was awarded the Warwick Prize for Writing. She is also a co-author of *The Leap Manifesto*, a call to Canadians to pass legislation limiting fossil fuel consumption and to fully implement the United Nations Declaration on the Rights of Indigenous Peoples.

Kolbert, Elizabeth (1961–)
An American journalist and staff writer for *The New Yorker*, Elizabeth Kolbert is best known for her writings on environmental issues. She is the author of *Field Notes from a Catastrophe: Man, Nature, and Climate Change* (2006) and was awarded the 2015 Pulitzer Prize for General Non-Fiction for *The Sixth Extinction: An Unnatural History* (2014).

Kristof, Nicholas (1959–)
Seven times a finalist for the Pulitzer Prize, American-born journalist Nicholas Kristof has won that award twice (once together with this wife, Sheryl WuDunn). Kristof is best-known as a writer for *The New York Times* (where he has worked since 1984); he and WuDunn have also co-authored four best-selling books together, among them *Half the Sky: Turning Oppression into Opportunity for Women Worldwide* (2009).

Kross, Ethan (unknown)
Associate Professor of Social Psychology at the University of Michigan-Ann Arbor and Director of the University of Michigan Self-Control and Emotion Laboratory, Ethan Kross has been teaching and conducting research since 2005. His article on the psychological effects of Facebook use, co-authored with several of his students, was covered extensively in mainstream broadcast and print media.

Krueger, Alan B. (1960–)
A former chair of the Council of Economic Advisers and a former Chief Economist at the US Treasury, Alan B. Krueger teaches Economics and Public Affairs at Princeton University. He has been the recipient of numerous awards since he and David Card broke new ground in contemporary economic theory with the article excerpted in this anthology and the book that followed, *Myth and Measurement: The New Economics of the Minimum Wage* (1995).

Kurchak, Sarah (unknown)
Sarah Kurchak is a writer and autistic self-advocate from Toronto, Canada. Her writing has focused on music, film, mixed martial arts, and autistic issues; she has been a contributor to *Vice*, *The Huffington Post*, *The National Post*, and *Consequence of Sound*.

Kymlicka, Will (1962–)
Will Kymlicka, the Canada Research Chair in Political Philosophy at Queen's University, has authored more than 200 articles on subjects such as multiculturalism

and animal ethics. His books include *Contemporary Political Philosophy* (1990, 2002), *Multicultural Citizenship* (1995), and *Multicultural Odysseys: Navigating the New International Politics of Diversity* (2007). In 2011, he published *Zoopolis: A Political Theory of Animal Rights* with his wife, Sue Donaldson.

Lai, Larissa (1967–)
Larissa Lai is a writer, cultural organizer, and academic. She is the author of the novels *When Fox Is a Thousand* (1995) and *Salt Fish Girl* (2002), as well as works of poetry and criticism. She has been shortlisted for such awards as the Books in Canada First Novel Award and the Dorothy Livesay Prize.

Lalami, Laila (1968–)
A Moroccan-American writer, Laila Lalami is best known for her novel *The Moor's Account* (2014), which was a finalist for the Pulitzer Prize and was long-listed for the Man Booker Prize. Lalami, who moved from Morocco to America in 1992 and began to publish her work shortly thereafter, is known for her literary and social criticism as well as her several works of fiction.

Laurier, Sir Wilfrid (1841–1919)
As leader of the Liberal party, Sir Wilfrid Laurier served as Prime Minister of Canada for four consecutive terms, from 1896 to 1911. The era of his leadership was a period of rapid change, including increased industrialization and the incorporation of two provinces (Alberta and Saskatchewan).

Lorde, Audre (1934–92)
Poet, non-fiction writer, novelist, and educator, Audre Lorde was part of the Black Arts Movement, dedicated to exploring the cultural and political foundations of African American experience. She is known for her sensitive depictions of lesbian sexuality, as well as for her powerful attacks on racism, sexism, and other forms of social injustice. Her books include *The First Cities* (1968), *Cables to Rage* (1970), *From a Land Where Other People Live* (1973), *Coal* (1976), *The Cancer Journals* (1980), and *Sister Outsider* (1984).

Lupick, Travis (unknown)
Travis Lupick is a staff writer at *The Georgia Straight*, a Vancouver arts magazine; he has also contributed to the *Toronto Star* and *The Walrus*. An award-winning journalist, Lupick has in recent years focused his reporting on addiction and the social issues surrounding addiction, particularly mental health and drug policy.

Macdonald, Sir John A. (1815–91)
Sir John A. Macdonald was an instrumental figure in the negotiations that lead to the confederation of Canada in 1867. He served as the country's first prime minister from 1867 to 1873.

MacLeish, Kenneth T. (1979–)

Assistant Professor of Medicine, Health, and Society and Anthropology at Vanderbilt College, Kenneth MacLeish studies the effects of war on those in military service and their families. His book, *Making War at Fort Hood: Life and Uncertainty in a Military Community*, was published in 2013.

MacMillan, Margaret (1943–)

Margaret MacMillan is Warden of St. Antony's College and a Professor of International History at the University of Oxford, and a former Provost of Trinity College and professor of history at the University of Toronto. In 2003 she was awarded the Governor General's Literary Award and the Samuel Johnson Prize for *Paris 1919: Six Months That Changed the World* (2001). Her other books include *The War that Ended Peace: The Road to 1914* (2013) and *The Uses and Abuses of History* (2008). In 2006 MacMillan was invested as an Officer of the Order of Canada, and in 2015 she was appointed a Companion of the Order of Canada.

Mandela, Nelson (1918–2013)

Nelson Mandela was a South African activist and politician. Initially committed to purely non-violent protest against apartheid, he eventually participated in the sabotage campaign that had been launched in reaction to the violent actions of the white minority government. He was arrested in 1962 and served 27 years in prison, never faltering in his dedication to democracy, equality, and education. Together with F.W. de Klerk (with whom he negotiated the ground rules for a transition to majority rule), he was awarded the Nobel Peace Prize in 1993. Mandela served as the first democratically elected President of South Africa from 1994 to 1999.

Martin, Emily (1944–)

A socio-cultural anthropology professor at New York University, Emily Martin studies the effects of race, gender, and class on science and medicine in culture. Her books include *The Cult of the Dead in a Chinese Village* (1973), *The Anthropology of Taiwanese Society* (1981), and *Bipolar Expeditions: Mania and Depression in American Culture* (2007).

Martineau, Harriet (1802–76)

Harriet Martineau was one of the Victorian era's foremost writers on social and political issues. A professional writer at a time when that was a rare profession for women, Martineau became famous for her *Illustrations of Political Economy* (1834), a collection of narrative vignettes designed to educate readers on the principles of economic society. Her other works include *Society in America* (1837) and *A Retrospect of Western Travel* (1838), both of which combine travel writing with incisive social commentary; the novel *Life in the Sickroom* (1844); and her acclaimed *Autobiography* (1877).

McDonald-Gibson, Charlotte (unknown)
A journalist based in Brussels, McDonald-Gibson reports on Europe for the international media, including the *Independent*, *Time*, and *The Guardian*. From 2011–13 she was deputy foreign editor for the *Independent*. She is the author of *Cast Away: Stories of Survival from Europe's Refugee Crisis* (2016).

McKenna, Barrie (unknown)
Born in Montreal, Barrie McKenna is a National Business Correspondent and columnist for the newspaper *The Globe and Mail*. McKenna holds degrees in History and Journalism from McGill and Carleton, respectively.

McLeod, Neal (1970–)
Poet, painter, filmmaker, and Indigenous scholar from James Smith Cree First Nation, Saskatchewan. His poetry publications include *Songs to Kill a Whitlow* (2006 winner of the National Aboriginal Poetry Award) and *Gabriel's Beach* (2008), and he is the author of *Cree Narrative Memory: From Treaties to Contemporary Times* (2007). He is a professor of Indigenous Studies at Trent University and the leader of the comedy troupe the Bionic Bannock Boys.

Metzl, Jonathan M. (unknown)
Jonathan Metzl is Associate Professor of Psychiatry and Women's Studies at the University of Michigan, where he also practises psychiatry. He is the author of *Prozac on the Couch: Prescribing Gender in the Era of Wonder Drugs* (2003) and *The Protest Psychosis: How Schizophrenia Became a Black Disease* (2010).

Milgram, Stanley (1933–84)
Stanley Milgram's human obedience experiments at Yale University (1961–62) established him as one of the most famous—and most controversial—psychologists of the twentieth century. He is also noted for the small-world method, which became the inspiration for John Guare's *Six Degrees of Separation*, and for an experiment on the effects of televised antisocial behaviour. His books include *Obedience to Authority: An Experimental View* (1983).

Miyairi, Masashi (unknown)
Masashi Miyairi, a Research Associate with the Education Policy Research Initiative, holds a PhD in Economics from the University of Western Ontario.

Moran, Rachel (unknown)
The author of *Paid For* (2013), a memoir of her years as a prostituted woman in Dublin, Rachel Moran has been deeply involved in the fight against human trafficking since she freed herself from the sex trade in 1998. She is a co-founder of SPACE (Survivors of Prostitution-Abuse Calling for Enlightenment), an

international foundation dedicated "to raising the public's consciousness of the harm of prostitution and to lobbying governments to do something about it." Moran has a degree in Journalism from the Dublin City University.

Ngũgĩ wa Thiong'o (1938–)
Ngũgĩ wa Thiong'o, East Africa's leading novelist, social critic, and essayist, writes both in English and in Gĩkũyũ. His novels include *Weep Not, Child* (1964), *The River Between* (1965), and *Devil on the Cross* (1980). His non-fiction works include *Detained* (1982), *Decolonising the Mind: The Politics of Language in African Literature* (1986), *Dreams in a Time of War: A Childhood Memoir* (2010), and *In the House of the Interpreter: A Memoir* (2012). A collection of his essays, *Secure the Base: Making Africa Visible in the Globe*, was published in 2015.

Nicholson, Ian (unknown)
A clinical psychologist, Ian Nicholson is the director of the University of Waterloo's Centre for Mental Health Research, a professor of psychology at Western University, and a member of the College of Psychologists of Ontario Jurisprudence and Ethics Committee. He received an Excellence in Hospital and Healthcare Psychology Award in 2013.

Nussbaum, Emily (1966–)
Emily Nussbaum, the 2016 winner of the Pulitzer Prize for Criticism, has been the television critic for *The New Yorker* since 2011. She has also worked as a writer and editor for *New York* magazine and as Editor-in-Chief of *Nerve* (one of the first digital-only magazines). In 2014 her columns "Shark Week," "Difficult Women," and "Private Practice" together won her the National Magazine Award for columns and commentary.

Obama, Barack (1961–)
The first African American President of the United States, Barack Obama was inaugurated in 2009, and led America out of the 2008–09 recession; his signature legislative achievement was the passage of the 2009 Affordable Care Act. Obama is also known for his writing—notably his memoir *Dreams from My Father* (1995).

Orwell, George (1903–50)
Born Eric Blair to English parents in Motihari, India, and educated largely at English boarding schools, Blair published his writing under the pseudonym George Orwell. He served with the Indian Imperial Police in Burma, 1922–27, and fought with the Republicans in the Spanish Civil War (an experience he described in his 1938 *Homage to Catalonia*). During World War II he established a reputation as one of Britain's leading journalists—but he remains best-known for two novels, *Animal Farm* (1945) and *Nineteen Eighty-Four* (1949).

Pardo Veiras, José Luis (unknown)
José Luis Pardo Veiras is a freelance Mexican journalist. He has published in *El Pais*, *El Universal*, *Etiqueta Negra*, *Vice*, *Soho*, *Esquire*, *Animal Politico*, and *The New York Times*. He is also the cofounder of *Dromómanos*, a "creative laboratory" producing journalistic projects "that cross borders." He has been the recipient of many journalism awards, in Mexico and internationally.

Pavlic, Dejan (unknown)
Dejan Pavlic, Senior Research Associate with the Education Policy Research Initiative, holds degrees in Planning, Political Science, and Anthropology from the University of Waterloo.

Pepperberg, Irene (1949–)
A scientist known for her groundbreaking research in animal cognition, Irene Pepperberg spent thirty years working intensively with Alex, a remarkably intelligent African Grey Parrot. She is the author of *Animal Cognition in Nature: The Convergence of Psychology and Biology in Lab and Field* (1998) and *The Alex Studies: Cognitive and Communicative Abilities of Grey Parrots* (2000), as well as the personal memoir *Alex & Me* (2008). She is a professor of psychology at Brandeis University and a lecturer at Harvard University.

Pfeiff, Margo (unknown)
Margo Pfeiff is a contributing editor for *Up Here* magazine. An award-winning Canadian freelance writer and photographer, her work has appeared in *enRoute*, *Canadian Geographic*, *The Walrus*, the *National Post*, and *The Globe and Mail*, as well as in *Lonely Planet* guidebooks. Pfeiff's work focuses on the Canadian Arctic and life in the North.

Pollan, Michael (1955–)
An award-winning essayist and bestselling author, Michael Pollan is a professor at UC Berkeley's Graduate School of Journalism, and the director of the Knight Program in Science and Environmental Journalism; he has also been a contributing writer for *The New York Times Magazine* since 1987. He has written several bestselling books, among them *The Omnivore's Dilemma: A Natural History of Four Meals* (2006); *In Defense of Food: An Eater's Manifesto* (2008); *Food Rules: An Eater's Manual* (2010); and *Cooked: A Natural History of Transformation* (2013).

Pollo, Antonella (1961–)
Antonella Pollo is an Italian neuroscientist at the University of Turin. Her research focuses on the placebo effect on pain, neurological disorders, and muscular performance in athletes.

Proulx, Lawrence. G. (unknown)
Lawrence Proulx is a copyeditor at the *International New York Times* in France.

Rankine, Claudia (1963–)
Claudia Rankine was born in Kingston, Jamaica, and earned degrees from Williams College and Columbia University. Her published work, which straddles the boundary between poetry and non-fiction prose, includes *Nothing in Nature Is Private* (1995), *Don't Let Me Be Lonely: An American Lyric* (2004), and *Citizen: An American Lyric* (2014), which received a National Book Critics Circle Award.

Rich, Adrienne (1929–2012)
Adrienne Rich was a major poet, feminist critic, and activist. Over her long career, she published more than sixteen volumes of poetry and five volumes of critical prose. She was the 2006 recipient of the National Book Foundation's Medal for Distinguished Contribution to American Letters. Her poetry and essays have been widely translated and published internationally.

Robinson, Eden (1968–)
A graduate of the UBC MFA program in creative writing, Eden Robinson is the daughter of a Haisla father and Heiltsuk mother. Robinson's novel *Monkey Beach* (2000) is set in the Kitamaat territory on BC's central coast where she was raised. In 1997 her debut short story collection, *Traplines* (1996), won Britain's Royal Society of Literature's 1997 Winifred Holtby Prize for the best regional work by a Commonwealth writer. Robinson's other books include *Blood Sports* (2006), *The Sasquatch at Home: Traditional Protocols and Modern Storytelling* (2011), and *Son of a Trickster* (2017).

Rodriguez, Richard (1944–)
Eloquent and at times controversial, Richard Rodriguez has received critical acclaim since the publication of his first book, *Hunger of Memory: The Education of Richard Rodriguez* (1982). Notable among his other works is *Days of Obligation: An Argument with My Mexican Father* (1992), in which Rodriguez revealed that he was gay; the book was a finalist for the Pulitzer Prize.

Rogan, Mary (unknown)
A Toronto-based freelance journalist, Rogan contributes to publications including *GQ*, *Esquire*, *Toronto Life*, *The Walrus*, and *The New York Times Magazine*.

Rose, Jacqueline (1949–)
Rose is a British academic whose work focuses on psychoanalysis, feminism, and literature; she is best known for her 1991 book *The Haunting of Sylvia Plath*. She is Professor of Humanities at the Birkbeck Institute for the Humanities.

Roubini, Nouriel (1958–)
Nouriel Roubini is an American economist. He has been an advisor at the International Monetary Fund, the Federal Reserve, the World Bank, and the Bank of Israel. He was a senior economist under the Bill Clinton administration and worked as an advisor in the United States Treasury Department. Roubini is the founder of Roubini Global Economics, a consultancy firm, and he is a professor of Economics at the Stern School of Business, New York University.

Saunders, Doug (1967–)
Canadian-British journalist and author Doug Saunders is the international-affairs columnist for *The Globe and Mail* and a five-time recipient of Canada's National Newspaper Award. Saunders's books include *Arrival City: The Final Migration and Our Next World* (2011) and *The Myth of the Muslim Tide* (2012).

Schalet, Amy (unknown)
American-born, Dutch-raised Professor of Sociology Amy Schalet was educated at Berkeley, Harvard, and the University of Rotterdam; she has been a professor at the University of Massachusetts, Amherst since 2006. *Not Under My Roof: Parents, Teens and the Culture of Sex* (2011) was the recipient of both an American Sociological Association Distinguished Scholarly Research Award and a Goode Book Award from the American Sociological Association.

Shadd, Mary Ann (Cary) (1823–93)
Born in Delaware to free black parents who were prominent abolitionists, Mary Ann Shadd was a political writer; an abolitionist; a newspaper editor; a campaigner for women's suffrage; and a teacher who focused her efforts on the education of black children. Her important writings include "Hints to the Coloured People of the North" (1849), *A Plea for Emigration; or Notes of Canada West* (1852), and her work on *The Provincial Freeman* (1853–57), an abolitionist newspaper which she founded and edited. Shadd spent several years in Canada, where she fled following the passage of the Fugitive Slave Act (1850), but returned to the United States during the Civil War.

Showalter, Elaine (1941–)
A professor in the English department of Princeton University, Elaine Showalter is one of the founders of contemporary feminist criticism. Her works include *A Literature of Their Own* (1977), *The Female Malady: Women, Madness, and English Culture 1830–1980* (1985), *Hystories: Historical Epidemics and Modern Culture* (1997), *Inventing Herself: Claiming a Feminist Intellectual Heritage* (2001), and *A Jury of Her Peers: American Women Writers from Anne Bradstreet to Annie Proulx* (2009).

Singer, Peter (1946–)
Peter Singer, often described as the world's most influential philosopher, is a professor both at Princeton University and at the University of Melbourne in his native Australia. In addition to his groundbreaking writings on human and non-human animals, he is known for taking a utilitarian approach to the ethical issues involved in genetic engineering, abortion, euthanasia, and embryo experimentation. Singer's books include *Animal Liberation* (1975), *Practical Ethics* (1979), *The Life You Can Save* (2009), and *The Most Good You Can Do: How Effective Altruism Is Changing Ideas about Living Ethically* (2016).

Smith, Zadie (1975–)
The daughter of a black Jamaican mother and a white English father, Zadie Smith was raised in North London, and began her writing career while a student at Cambridge University. The great success of her first book, *White Teeth* (2000), established her reputation as an important writer of fiction; her subsequent novels include *On Beauty* (2005), *NW* (2012), and *Swing Time* (2016). In 2010 Smith became a professor of Creative Writing at New York University.

Snyder, Timothy D. (1969–)
A prominent scholar of twentieth-century Eastern European history, Timothy Snyder is a professor at Yale University and a fellow at Vienna's Institute for Human Sciences. His critically acclaimed works include *Bloodlands: Europe Between Hitler and Stalin* (2010) and *Black Earth: The Holocaust as History and Warning* (2015).

Solnit, Rebecca (1961–)
An award-winning American writer and contributing editor at *Harper's* magazine, Rebecca Solnit has written on many topics, among them the arts, politics, and the environment. Her books include *Wanderlust: A History of Walking* (2001), *Hope in the Dark: Untold Histories, Wild Possibilities* (2004), *A Field Guide to Getting Lost* (2006), *The Faraway Nearby* (2014), and *Men Explain Things to Me* (2015).

Sontag, Susan (1933–2004)
Susan Sontag was for several decades a central figure in American intellectual life. Among her most important works of non-fiction are *Against Interpretation* (1966), *On Photography* (1977), and *Regarding the Pain of Others* (2003). She was also known for her several volumes of fiction and for her outspoken political views.

Srigley, Ron (unknown)
A professor of religious studies at Prince Edward Island University, Ron Srigley pursues diverse research interests within the humanities, including political philosophy, religion, literature, technology, and globalization. His books include *Albert Camus' Critique of Modernity* (2011) and co-author of *A Perfect World? The Promises and Perils of Globalization* (2011).

Stanton, Elizabeth Cady (1815–1902)
An anti-slavery activist, Elizabeth Cady Stanton was also a leader of the early American women's rights movement. As well as campaigning for women's suffrage, she addressed issues such as employment and income rights, parental and custody rights, birth control, and property rights for women.

Surowiecki, James (1967–)
James Surowiecki has written on a wide range of topics for magazines including *Fortune*, *Slate*, *Talk*, and *Wired*, as well as contributing to *The Washington Post* and *The Wall Street Journal*. His most influential book, *The Wisdom of Crowds: Why the Many Are Smarter than the Few and How Collective Wisdom Shapes Business, Economies, Societies, and Nations*, was published in 2004. Surowiecki has been a staff writer at *The New Yorker* since 2000.

Swaim, Barton (unknown)
Swaim is an American journalist. His well-received book *The Speechwriter: A Brief Education in Politics* (2015) chronicles his experience working as a speechwriter for the Republican politician Mark Sanford, when Sanford was governor of South Carolina (2007–10). Swaim regularly contributes articles to major newspapers, including *The Washington Post* and *The Wall Street Journal*.

Swift, Jonathan (1667–1745)
Jonathan Swift was an Irish poet, fiction writer, essayist, and political pamphleteer, best known for works of satire aimed at political hypocrisy, literary pretension, and the folly of human society. Among his best-known works are *Tale of a Tub* (1704) and *Gulliver's Travels* (1726).

Taylor, Drew Hayden (1962–)
Drew Hayden Taylor, a member of Ontario's Curve Lake First Nation, writes documentaries for film and television, short stories, journalism, essays, and scripts for the screen and stage. His award-winning plays include *Toronto at Dreamer's Rock* (1998), *The Bootlegger Blues* (1990), *Only Drunks and Children Tell the Truth* (1995), and *The Baby Blues* (1996). He has also worked extensively in documentary films. His other works include the novels *The Night Wanderer* (2007) and *Motorcycles and Sweetgrass* (2010), as well as *Take Us to Your Chief* (2016), a collection of science-fiction short stories.

Toews, Miriam (1964–)
Miriam Toews's work is heavily influenced by her upbringing in Manitoba, Canada; her award-winning 2000 memoir, *Swing Low: A Life*, details her experiences growing up in a Mennonite town. Her bestselling novel *A Complicated Kindness* (2004), which won the Governor General's Award, is also set in a Manitoba

Mennonite community. Her other novels include *The Flying Troutmans* (2008) and *All My Puny Sorrows* (2014).

Toth, Katie (unknown)
Katie Toth is a Canadian writer, freelance reporter, and radio producer. Much of her work is focused on Canadian politics, American politics, and feminist issues.

Wainaina, Binyavanga (1971–)
A Kenyan satirist and short story writer, Wainaina Binyavanga won the Caine Prize for African Writing in 2002. He is the founding editor of the literary magazine *Kwani?*, and his work has appeared in *The New York Times*, *Granta*, *The Guardian*, and *National Geographic*. He is also an expert on African cuisines, and has collected more than 13,000 traditional and modern African recipes. His memoir about his youth in Kenya, *One Day I Will Write about This Place* (2011), was named a *New York Times* notable book.

Wallace, David Foster (1962–2008)
David Foster Wallace, an American writer of short stories, novels, and essays, is perhaps best-known for his ambitious novel *Infinite Jest* (1996). His essays, several of which have been widely anthologized, have become touchstones in discussions of alternative styles of contemporary essay writing. Wallace's unfinished draft of a novel, *The Pale King* (2011), was published after his death; it was a finalist for the 2012 Pulitzer Prize in fiction.

wallace, j (unknown)
j wallace is a writer and activist focused on LGBTQ issues in education, support, and policy direction.

Wann, Marilyn (1966–)
As a vocal member of the fat acceptance movement and speaker on weight diversity, American author Marilyn Wann began her writing career in the 1990s with the zine *FAT!SO?* (1994–96), which was followed by a book of the same name in 1998. She has since published many articles for newspapers such as *The Guardian* and *The New York Times*, and contributed to volumes such as *The Fat Studies Reader* (2009) and the *Health at Every Size* journal. Wann holds degrees in linguistics and literature from Stanford University.

Whetter, Darryl (unknown)
A Canadian writer of fiction, poetry, and essays, Darryl Whetter teaches English literature and creative writing at Université Sainte-Anne in Pointe-de-l'Église, Nova Scotia. His short-story collection *A Sharp Tooth in the Fur* was one of *The Globe and Mail's* Top 100 Books of 2003; his novel *The Push & the Pull* was

published in 2008, followed by a book of poems, *Origins*, in 2012. He regularly writes reviews and essays for major Canadian newspapers and literary magazines.

Wilde, Oscar (1854–1900)
Born and raised in Ireland, Oscar Wilde attended Oxford University and then settled in London. His works include the novel *The Picture of Dorian Gray* (1890) and the plays *Lady Windermere's Fan*, *A Woman of No Importance*, *An Ideal Husband*, and *The Importance of Being Earnest* (all 1892–95). In 1895 he was tried, convicted, and imprisoned for having sexual relationships with men. After serving two years of hard labour, he left England for France, where he died a few years later.

Williams, Raymond (1921–88)
A prodigious Welsh author and pioneer in the field of cultural studies, Williams originated the concept of "cultural materialism." His written works include *Culture and Society* (1958), *The Long Revolution* (1961), and *Marxism and Literature* (1977).

Wilson, Carl (unknown)
Carl Wilson is a Canadian writer and music critic at *Slate Magazine*, and his work has appeared in *The Globe and Mail*, *The New York Times*, and many other publications. His 2007 book about Céline Dion, *Let's Talk About Love: Journey to the End of Taste*, developed a cult following and was reissued in an expanded edition by Bloomsbury in 2014. He has taught at the University of Victoria Creative Writing program, as well as at the Flying Books School of Reading and Writing in Toronto.

Wollstonecraft, Mary (1759–97)
Mary Wollstonecraft, an English writer and political activist, was a trailblazing advocate of women's rights; she is best known for *A Vindication of the Rights of Woman* (1792), which has become a classic of political philosophy. Her other works include political writings such as *A Vindication of the Rights of Men* (1790), novels such as *Maria: or, the Wrongs of Woman* (posthumously published in 1798), and the travel narrative *Letters Written during a Short Residence in Sweden, Norway, and Denmark* (1796).

Wong, Jan (1952–)
Award-winning Canadian writer Jan Wong is a contributor to *Chatelaine*, *Toronto Life*, and Halifax's *The Chronicle-Herald*, and a former journalist with *The Globe and Mail*. Her books include *Red China Blues: My Long March from Mao to Now* (1997); *Jan Wong's China: Reports from a Not-So-Foreign Correspondent* (1999); *Beijing Confidential: A Tale of Comrades Lost and Found* (2007); and the memoir *Out of the Blue: A Memoir of Workplace Depression, Recovery, Redemption and, Yes, Happiness* (2012).

Woolf, Virginia (1882–1941)
Virginia Woolf was among the most innovative and influential English writers of the twentieth century. Her novels include *Mrs. Dalloway* (1925), *To the Lighthouse* (1927), and *The Waves* (1931). She was also an important literary critic and a strong voice for feminism, most notably in her books *A Room of One's Own* (1929) and *Three Guineas* (1938).

York, Geoffrey (1960–)
Geoffrey York became a journalist for *The Globe and Mail* in 1981 and a foreign correspondent for the paper in 1994. York has received National Magazine and National Newspaper Awards, and is the author of non-fiction books including *The High Price of Health: A Patient's Guide to the Hazards of Medical Politics* (1987), *People of the Pines: The Warriors and the Legacy of Oka* (1989), and *The Dispossessed: Life and Death in Native Canada* (1992).

Permissions Acknowledgments

Ai, Weiwei. "Heartless," and "Let Us Forget," pages 201–203 from *Ai Weiwei's Blog: Writings, Interviews, and Digital Rants, 2006–2009*, edited and translated by Lee Ambrozy. Copyright © 2011 Massachusetts Institute of Technology. Reprinted with the permission of The MIT Press.

Alexie, Sherman. "Indian Education," from *The Lone Ranger and Tonto Fistfight in Heaven*. Copyright © 1993, 2005 by Sherman Alexie. Used by permission of Grove/Atlantic, Inc. Any third party use of this material, outside of this publication, is prohibited.

Arendt, Hannah. Excerpts from *The Origins of Totalitarianism*. Copyright © 1948, 1976 by Hannah Arendt. Reprinted by permission of Georges Borchardt, Inc., on behalf of the Hannah Arendt Bluecher Literary Trust.

Armstrong, Jeannette C. "En'owkin: What It Means to a Sustainable Community," as seen at https://www.ecoliteracy.org/article/enowkin-what-it-means-sustainable-community. Copyright © 2009, Center for Eco Literacy. Excerpted from Armstrong, Jeannette C. "Let Us Begin with Courage," in *Ecoliteracy: Mapping the Terrain*. Berkeley, CA: Learning in the Real World, 2000: 8–11.

Atwood, Margaret. "First Job," copyright © 2001 by O.W. Toad Ltd. Originally published in *The New Yorker*, April 2001. Reprinted with the permission of Curtis Brown Group Ltd., on behalf of O.W. Toad Ltd.

Bachan, Nadine. "Ol' Talk," from *Maisonneuve* 52 (Summer 2014) and online (23 October 2014). Reprinted with the permission of Nadine Bachan.

Balkissoon, Denise. "Migrant Farm Workers Deserve Better from Canada," from *The Globe and Mail*, 19 September 2016. Reprinted with the permission of Denise Balkissoon.

Barthes, Roland. "Soap-Powders and Detergents" and "Toys," from *Mythologies*, translated by Annette Lavers. Translation copyright © 1972 by Jonathan Cape Ltd. Reprinted with the permission of Hill and Wang, a division of Farrar, Straus and Giroux LLC.

Benedetti, Fabrizio, et al. "Opioid-Mediated Placebo Responses Boost Pain Endurance and Physical Performance: Is It Doping in Sport Competitions?" from *The Journal of Neuroscience* 27 (44), 31 October 2007: 11934–39. Republished with permission of the Society for Neuroscience via Copyright Clearance Center, Inc.

Berger, John. "Photographs of Agony," from *About Looking*. Copyright © 1980 by John Berger. Used by permission of Pantheon Books, an imprint of the Knopf Doubleday Publishing Group, a division of Penguin Random House LLC. All rights reserved. Any third party use of this material, outside of this publication, is prohibited. Interested parties must apply directly to Penguin Random House LLC for permission.

Biss, Eula. "Time and Distance Overcome," from *Notes from No Man's Land: American Essays*. Copyright © 2009 by Eula Biss. Reprinted with the permission of The Permissions Company on behalf of Graywolf Press: www.graywolfpress.org.

Boudway, Ira. "NBA Refs Learned They Were Racist, and That Made Them Less Racist," from Bloomberg.com, February 7, 2014. Reprinted with the permission of The YGS Group.

Bozikovic, Alex. "Remaking Space to Remake a Culture," from *The Globe and Mail*, April 4, 2016. Copyright © The Globe and Mail Inc. All rights reserved.

Card, David, and Alan B. Krueger. Excerpts from "Minimum Wages and Employment: A Case Study of the Fast-Food Industry in New Jersey and Pennsylvania," from *American Economic Review* 84 (4), September 1994: 772–793. Reprinted with the permission of the authors and the American Economic Association.

Carson, Anne. "Introduction [Short Talks]"; "On Parmenides"; "On Sleep Stones"; "On Walking Backwards"; "On the Total Collection"; and "On Sunday Dinner with Father," from *Plainwater: Essays and Poetry*. Copyright © 1995 by Anne Carson. Used by permission of Alfred A. Knopf, an imprint of the Knopf Doubleday Publishing Group, a division of Penguin Random House LLC. All rights reserved. Any third party use of this material, outside of this publication, is prohibited. Interested parties must apply directly to Penguin Random House LLC for permission.

Coates, Ta-Nehisi. "The Case for Reparations," from *The Atlantic*, June 2014. Copyright © 2014 The Atlantic Media Co., as first published in The Atlantic Magazine. All rights reserved. Distributed by Tribune Content Agency.

Cole, Desmond. "The Skin I'm In," from *Toronto Life*, April 21, 2015. Copyright © 2015 Desmond Cole. Reprinted with the permission of the author.

Coyne, Andrew. "Guarantee a Minimum Income, Not a Minimum Wage," from *The National Post*, 10 June 2015.

de Leeuw, Sarah. "Soft Shouldered," from *Where It Hurts*, NeWest Press, 2017. Previously published in *Prism* 52 (1), Fall 2013. Reprinted with the permission of Sarah de Leeuw.

Donaldson, Sue, and Will Kymlicka. "Born Allies: Child and Animal Citizens." Copyright © Sue Donaldson and Will Kymlicka.

The Economist. Excerpt from "Twenty-Five Years On," Introduction to *Pocket World in Figures 2016*. Economist Books, 2016. Reprinted with the permission of Profile Books Ltd., London.

Finnie, Ross, Kaveh Afshar, Eda Bozkurt, Masashi Miyairi, and Dejan Pavlic. Excerpt from the Executive Summary of "Barista or Better? New Evidence on the Earnings of Post-Secondary Education Graduates: A Tax Linkage Approach." Education Policy Research Initiative, University of Ottawa, July 26, 2016. As seen at https://goo.gl/EuHRi7. Reprinted with the permission of the Education Policy Research Initiative.

Flanner, Janet. "Mme. Marie Curie (1866–1934)," originally published in *The New Yorker*, August 4, 1934. Reprinted with the permission of Sanford Schwartz.

Foer, Jonathan Safran. Excerpts from "The Last Thanksgiving of My Childhood," in *Eating Animals*. Copyright © 2009 by Jonathan Safran Foer. Used by permission of Little, Brown and Company.

Foucault, Michel. Excerpt from "The Perverse Implantation," in *The History of Sexuality* Vol. 1: An Introduction, translated by Robert Hurley. Originally published in French as *La Volonté du Savoir*. Copyright © 1976 by Editions Gallimard. Reprinted by permission of Georges Borchardt, Inc., for Editions Gallimard.

Franklin, Ursula. "Silence and the Notion of the Commons," originally presented as a lecture at the First International Conference on Acoustic Ecology, Banff, Alberta, 1993. Originally published in *Musicworks* 59, Summer 1994: 38–42. Reprinted with the permission of Monica Franklin, literary executor to Ursula Franklin.

Frum, David. "How to Build an Autocracy," from *The Atlantic*, copyright © March 2017. Republished with permission of The Atlantic Monthly Group via Copyright Clearance Center, Inc.

Galloway, Gloria. "Dr. Bjorn Lomborg Argues the Climate Change Fight Isn't Worth the Cost," from *The Globe and Mail*, June 12, 2015. Copyright © The Globe and Mail Inc. All rights reserved.

Gay, Roxane. "Bad Feminist: Take One," from *Bad Feminist*. Copyright © 2014 by Roxane Gay. Reprinted with the permission of HarperCollins Publishers.

Gilchrist, Kristen. "'Newsworthy' Victims? Exploring Differences in Canadian Local Press Coverage of Missing/Murdered Aboriginal and White Women," from *Feminist Media Studies* 10 (4): 373–385. Reprinted with the permission of Taylor & Francis Ltd., http://www.tandfonline.com.

Gladwell, Malcolm. "None of the Above: What I.Q. Doesn't Tell You about Race," from *The New Yorker*, 17 December 2007. Reprinted with the permission of Malcolm Gladwell.

Gopnik, Adam. "Does *Mein Kampf* Remain a Dangerous Book?" from *The New Yorker*, January 12, 2016.

Gourevitch, Philip. Excerpt from *We Wish to Inform You That Tomorrow We Will Be Killed with Our Families*. Copyright © 1998 by Philip Gourevitch. Reprinted with the permission of Farrar, Straus & Giroux LLC.

Halton, Carissa. "A New Kind of Simakanis," excerpted from *Eighteen Bridges*, June 12, 2015. http://eighteenbridges.com/story/a-new-kind-of-simakanis-aboriginal-edmonton-police-force/. Reprinted with the permission of Carissa Halton.

Hannah-Jones, Nikole. "How School Segregation Divides Ferguson—and the United States," from *The New York Times*, December 19, 2014. Excerpted and adapted from "School Segregation: The Continuing Tragedy of Ferguson," *ProPublica*, December 19, 2014. https://www.propublica.org/article/ferguson-school-segregation. Reprinted with the permission of ProPublica, https://www.propublica.org/.

Harris, Marvin. Excerpt from "Pig Lovers and Pig Haters," in *Cows, Pigs, Wars, and Witches: The Riddles of Culture*. Copyright © 1974 by Marvin Harris. Used by permission of Random House, an imprint and division of Penguin Random House LLC. All rights reserved. Any third party use of this material, outside of this publication, is prohibited. Interested parties must apply directly to Penguin Random House LLC for permission.

Harris, Michael. "The Unrepentant Whore: How Jamie Lee Hamilton Changed the Way We Look at Canada's Underclass," from *The Walrus*, June 2010. Reprinted with the permission of Michael Harris.

Heller, Nathan. "The Failure of Facebook Democracy," from *The New Yorker*, November 18, 2016.

hooks, bell. "Coming to Class Consciousness," Chapter 2 of *Where We Stand: Class Matters*. Routledge, 2000. Copyright © 2000 by bell hooks. Reproduced by permission of Taylor and Francis Group, LLC, a division of Informa plc, via Copyright Clearance Center, Inc.

Hope, Jessamyn. "The Reverse," from *Prism* 52 (4), Summer 2014; subsequently published in *Best Canadian Essays*, 2015. Copyright © 2014 by Jessamyn Hope. Reprinted with the permission of Jessamyn Hope.

Iyer, Pico. "The Terminal Check," first published in *Granta 116: Ten Years Later*, Summer 2011. Copyright © 2011 by Pico Iyer. Reprinted with the permission of the author.

Jalal, Malik. "I'm on the Kill List. This Is What It Feels Like to Be Hunted by Drones," from *The Independent*, April 12, 2016. Reprinted with the permission of Independent Print Limited.

Johnson, Nathanael. "Is There a Moral Case for Eating Meat?" *Grist* 50, July 20, 2015. Reprinted with the permission of Grist Magazine.

Justice, Daniel Heath. "Fear of a Changeling Moon," from *Me Sexy: An Exploration of Native Sex and Sexuality*, edited by Drew Hayden Taylor. Copyright © 2008 by Douglas and McIntyre, an imprint of D&M Publishers Inc. Reprinted with the permission of Daniel Heath Justice.

Keegan, Marina. "Why We Care about Whales," from *The Opposite of Loneliness: Essays and Stories*. Copyright © 2014 by Tracy and Kevin Keegan. Originally published in *Yale Daily News*, Sept 11, 2009. Reprinted with the permission of Scribner, a division of Simon & Schuster, Inc. All rights reserved.

Kelly, Cathal. "Tim Raines Is a Poster Boy for Sports Injustice, but His Snub Doesn't Deserve Our Obsession," from *The Globe and Mail*, November 24, 2016. Copyright © The Globe and Mail Inc. All rights reserved.

Kincaid, Jamaica. "On Seeing England for the First Time," originally published in *Harper's Magazine*, August 1991. Copyright © 1991 by Jamaica Kincaid. Used by permission of The Wylie Agency LLC.

King, Martin Luther Jr. "Letter from Birmingham Jail," copyright © 1963 Dr. Martin Luther King Jr. Copyright renewed 1991 Coretta Scott King. Reprinted by arrangement with The Heirs to the Estate of Martin Luther King Jr., c/o Writers House as agent for the proprietor New York, NY.

Klein, Naomi. Excerpt from "Let Them Drown," *London Review of Books* 38 (11), 2 June 2016.

Kolbert, Elizabeth. "The Sixth Extinction?" from *The New Yorker*, May 25, 2009. Reprinted with the permission of Elizabeth Kolbert.

Kristof, Nicholas. "When Whites Just Don't Get It," from *The New York Times*, August 30, 2014. Copyright © 2014 The New York Times. "When Whites Just Don't Get It, Part 6," from *The New York Times*, April 2, 2016. Copyright © 2016 The New York Times. All rights reserved. Used by permission and protected by the Copyright Laws of the United States. The printing, copying, redistribution, or retransmission of the Content without express written permission is prohibited.

Kross E., Verduyn P., Demiralp E., Park J., Lee D.S., Lin N., et al. Excerpt from "Facebook Use Predicts Declines in Subjective Well-Being in Young Adults." Copyright © Kross et al. *PLoS ONE* 8(8): e69841. doi:10.1371/journal.pone.0069841.

Kurchak, Sarah. "Autistic People Are Not Tragedies," from *The Guardian*, April 20, 2015. Copyright © Guardian News & Media Ltd., 2017.

Lai, Larissa. "Political Animals and the Body of History," from *Canadian Literature* 163 (Winter 1999): 145–54. Reprinted with the permission of Canadian Literature.

Lalami, Laila. "My Life as a Muslim in the West's 'Gray Zone,'" from *The New York Times Magazine*, November 20, 2015. Copyright © 2015 The New York Times. All rights reserved. Used by permission and protected by the Copyright Laws of the United States. The printing, copying, redistribution, or retransmission of the Content without express written permission is prohibited.

London, Scott. Excerpt from "Crossing Borders," an interview with Richard Rodriguez. *The Sun Magazine* 260, August 1997. Reprinted with the permission of Scott London.

Lorde, Audre. "Poetry Is Not a Luxury," and "The Uses of Anger," from *Sister Outsider: Essays and Speeches*, published by Crossing Press. Copyright © 1984, 2007 by Audre Lorde. Reprinted with the permission of the Charlotte Sheedy Literary Agency.

Lupick, Travis. "Our Fentanyl Crisis," from *The Walrus*, December 19, 2016. Reprinted with the permission of Travis Lupick.

MacMillan, Margaret. Excerpt (Victor Klemperer) from "Observers," in *History's People: Personalities and the Past*. Copyright © 2015 by Margaret MacMillan. Reprinted by permission of House of Anansi Press Inc., Toronto. www.houseofanansi.com.

Mandela, Nelson. "An Ideal for Which I Am Prepared to Die," excerpted from the Speech from the Dock, April 20, 1964. Reprinted with permission.

Martin, Emily. "The Egg and the Sperm: How Science Has Constructed a Romance Based on Stereotypical Male-Female Roles," from *Signs: Journal of Women in Culture and Society* 16 (3), 1991: 485–501. Copyright © 1991 by The University of Chicago. Reprinted with the permission of The University of Chicago Press.

McDonald-Gibson, Charlotte. Excerpts from *Cast Away: Stories of Survival from Europe's Refugee Crisis*. Copyright © 2016 by Charlotte McDonald-Gibson. Reprinted with the permission of The New Press, www.thenewpress.com.

McKenna, Barrie. "It's Time to Retire the Myth of the Educated Barista," from *The Globe and Mail*, 31 July 2016. Reprinted with the permission of Globe and Mail Inc.

McLeod, Neal. "Cree Poetic Discourse," from *Across Cultures/Across Borders*, edited by Paul DePasquale, Renate Eigenbrod, and Emma LaRocque. Broadview Press, 2010. Reprinted with the permission of Neal McLeod.

Metzl, Jonathan M., and Kenneth T. MacLeish. Excerpt from "Mental Illness, Mass Shootings, and the Politics of American Firearms," from *American Journal of Public Health* 105 (2), Feburary 2015: 240–249. Reprinted with the permission of The Sheridan Press on behalf of The American Public Health Association.

Milgram, Stanley. "Behavioral Study of Obedience," from *Journal of Abnormal and Social Psychology* 67 (4), October 1963. Reprinted with the permission of Alexandra Milgram.

Montaigne, Michel de. Excerpt from *On Cannibals*. This translation, prepared for Broadview Press by Professor Emeritus Ian Johnston of Vancouver Island University, is based upon the final (1595) version of the essay.

Moran, Rachel. "Buying Sex Should Not Be Legal," from *The New York Times*, 28 August 2015. Copyright © 2015 The New York Times. All rights reserved. Used by permission and protected by the Copyright Laws of the United States. The printing, copying, redistribution, or retransmission of the Content without express written permission is prohibited.

Nicholson, Ian. "'Torture at Yale': Experimental Subjects, Laboratory Torment and the 'Rehabilitation' of Milgram's 'Obedience to Authority,'" from *Theory & Psychology* 21 (6), December 2011: 737–761. Copyright © 2011, Sage Publications. Reprinted with the permission of Sage Publications, Ltd.

Ngũgĩ wa Thiong'o. "Decolonizing the Mind," from *Decolonizing the Mind: the Politics of Language in African Literature*. Copyright © 1981, 1982, 1984, and 1986 by Ngũgĩ wa Thiong'o. Reprinted with the permission of Ngũgĩ wa Thiong'o and the Watkins/Loomis Agency.

Nussbaum, Emily. "The Price Is Right," from *The New Yorker*, October 12, 2015. Copyright © 2015, Condé Nast Publications.

Obama, Barack. Excerpts from "Farewell Address," January 10, 2017.

Ontario Court of Justice. R. v. Ghomeshi, 2016 ONCJ 155 (CanLII), <http://canlii.ca/t/gnzpj>, retrieved on 2017-01-25; as seen at http://www.canlii.org/en/on/oncj/doc/2016/2016oncj155/2016oncj155.html.

Pardo Veiras, José Luis. "A Decade of Failure in the War on Drugs," from *The New York Times*, October 9, 2016. Copyright © 2016 The New York Times. All rights reserved. Used by permission and protected by the Copyright Laws of the United States. The printing, copying, redistribution, or retransmission of the Content without express written permission is prohibited.

Pepperberg, Irene. Excerpt from *Alex & Me: How a Scientist and a Parrot Uncovered a Hidden World of Animal Intelligence—and Formed a Deep Bond in the Process*. Copyright © 2008 by Irene Pepperberg. Reprinted with the permission of HarperCollins Publishers.

Pfeiff, Margo. "When the Vikings Were in Nunavut," from *Up Here*, July/August 2013. Reprinted with the permission of Margo Pfeiff.

Pollan, Michael. "Why 'Natural' Doesn't Mean Anything Anymore," from *The New York Times Magazine*, April 28, 2015. Used by permission. All rights reserved.

Proulx, Lawrence. "A Group You Can Safely Attack," from *The Providence Journal*, September 2, 2015. Reprinted with the permission of Lawrence Proulx.

Rankine, Claudia. Excerpt (Part II) from *Citizen: An American Lyric*, pp 23–36. Copyright © 2014 by Claudia Rankine. Reprinted with the permission of The Permissions Company, Inc., on behalf of Graywolf Press: www.graywolfpress.org.

Rich, Adrienne. Excerpts from "Compulsory Heterosexuality and Lesbian Existence," from *Blood, Bread, and Poetry: Selected Prose 1979–1985*. Copyright © 1986 by Adrienne Rich.

Robinson, Eden. Excerpt from *The Sasquatch at Home: Traditional Protocols and Storytelling*. Edmonton: The University of Alberta Press. Copyright © 2011 Eden Robinson. Reprinted with the permission of Eden Robinson.

Rogan, Mary. Excerpt from "Growing Up Trans: When Do Children Know Their True Gender?" from *The Walrus*, September 2016. Reprinted with the permission of Mary Rogan.

Rose, Jacqueline. Excerpt from "Who Do You Think You Are?" from *The London Review of Books* 38 (9), May 5, 2016: 3–13. Reprinted with the permission of *The London Review of Books*, www.lrb.co.uk.

Roubini, Nouriel. "Economic Insecurity and the Rise of Nationalism," from *The Guardian*, June 2, 2014. Reprinted with permission.

Saunders, Doug. "Don't Blame Dark Voting Trends on Online Thought Bubbles," from *The Globe and Mail*, October 1, 2016. Copyright © The Globe and Mail Inc. All rights reserved.

Schalet, Amy. Excerpt from "Raging Hormones, Regulated Love," Chapter 1 of *Not Under My Roof: Parents, Teens, and the Culture of Sex*. Copyright © 2011 by The University of Chicago. Reprinted with permission.

Showalter, Elaine. "Representing Ophelia: Women, Madness, and the Responsibilities of Feminist Criticism," from *Shakespeare and the Question of Theory*, edited by Patricia Parker and Geoffrey Hartman. Copyright © 1985, Methuen & Co. Reprinted with the permission of Taylor & Francis Books UK.

Singer, Peter. Excerpts from *Animal Liberation*. Ecco, an imprint of HarperCollins Publishers, 2009. Reprinted with the permission of Peter Singer.

Smith, Zadie. "Generation Why?" from *The New York Review of Books*, November 25, 2010. Copyright © Zadie Smith. Reprinted with the permission of the author, c/o Rogers, Coleridge & White Ltd., 20 Powis Mews, London W11 1JN.

Snyder, Timothy. "Twenty Lessons from the Twentieth Century," posted November 15, 2016 at https://m.facebook.com/timothy.david.snyder/posts/1206636702716110. Reprinted with the permission of Timothy Snyder.

Solnit, Rebecca. "The Mother of All Questions," copyright © 2015 *Harper's Magazine*. All rights reserved. Reprinted from the October issue by special permission. "Climate Change Is Violence," from *The Encyclopedia of Trouble and Spaciousness*. Trinity University Press, 2015. Copyright © 2014 by Rebecca Solnit. Reprinted with the permission of the publisher via Copyright Clearance Center, Inc.

Sontag, Susan. Excerpt from *Regarding the Pain of Others*, copyright © 2003 by Susan Sontag. Reprinted with the permission of Farrar, Straus and Giroux LLC.

Srigley, Ron. Excerpts from "Pass, Fail," in *The Walrus*, April 2016. Reprinted with the permission of Ron Srigley.

The Toronto Star. "'Basic Income' Is Tempting—But It Could Backfire," from *The Toronto Star*, February 12, 2016.

Surowiecki, James. "A Fair Day's Wage," from *The New Yorker*, February 9, 2015. Copyright © 2015, Condé Nast Publications.

Swaim, Barton. "How Trump's Language Works for Him," from *The Washington Post*, September 15, 2015. Copyright © 2015 The Washington Post. All rights reserved. Used by permission and protected by the Copyright Laws of the United States. The printing, copying, redistribution, or retransmission of this Content without express written permission is prohibited.

Taylor, Drew Hayden. "Pretty Like a White Boy," Introduction to *Funny, You Don't Look Like One: Observations of A Blue-Eyed Ojibway* (revised edition). Theytus Books, 1998. Copyright © Drew Hayden Taylor. Reprinted with permission.

Toews, Miriam. "A Father's Faith," first published in *Saturday Night Magazine*. Copyright © 1999 by Miriam Toews. Used by permission of The Wylie Agency LLC.

Toth, Katie. "After Not Guilty: On Sexual Assault and the Carceral State," from *GUTS Magazine*, 25 March 2016; http://gutsmagazine.ca/after-not-guilty/. Reprinted with the permission of Katie Toth.

Truth and Reconciliation Commission of Canada. Excerpt from the Introduction of *Honouring the Truth, Reconciling for the Future: Summary of the Final Report of the Truth and Reconciliation Commission of Canada,* 2015. www.trc.ca.

Wainaina, Binyavanga. "How to Write about Africa," first published in *Granta 92: The View from Africa*. Copyright © 2006 by Binyavanga Wainaina. Used by permission of The Wylie Agency LLC.

Wallace, David Foster. "Consider the Lobster," copyright © 2005, David Foster Wallace. Reprinted with the permission of the David Foster Wallace Literary Trust.

wallace, j. "The Manly Art of Pregnancy," from *Gender Outlaws: The Next Generation*, edited by Kate Bornstein and S. Bear Bergman, copyright © 2010. Reprinted by permission of Seal Press, an imprint of Perseus Books LLC, a subsidiary of Hachette Book Group, Inc.

Wann, Marilyn. Excerpt from Foreword to *The Fat Studies Reader*, edited by Esther Rothblum and Sondra Solovay. Copyright © 2009 by New York University. Reprinted with the permission of New York University Press.

Whetter, Darryl. "The Kids Are Alright," from *The Walrus*, March 2016; as seen at https://thewalrus.ca/the-kids-are-alright/. Reprinted with the permission of Darryl Whetter.

Williams, Raymond. Excerpt from "The Growth of 'Standard English,'" in *The Long Revolution*. Parthian Books, UK. Copyright © 1961, 2001 by The Estate of Raymond Williams. Reprinted with permission.

Wilson, Carl. "I Knew about Jian Ghomeshi," from *Slate*, November 3, 2014. Copyright © 2014, The Slate Group. All rights reserved. Used by permission and protected by the Copyright Laws of the United States. The printing, copying, redistribution, or retransmission of this Content without express written permission is prohibited.

Wong, Jan. Excerpt from "Coming Clean," in *The Globe and Mail*, April 1, 2006. Copyright © The Globe and Mail Inc. All rights reserved.

York, Geoffrey. "Can 'Harvesting' Its Horns Save the Rhino?" from *The Globe and Mail*, September 30, 2016. Copyright © The Globe and Mail Inc. All rights reserved.

Image:

Stensland, Matt. "Tyler Boyer, 11, of Hayden, says goodbye to his steer Leonard after it was sold during Saturday's Junior Livestock Sale at the Routt County Fairgrounds." *Steamboat Today*, Saturday, August 20, 2011. Copyright © 2017 Steamboat Pilot & Today. All rights reserved.

INDEX